5 REASONS
to buy your textbooks and course materials at
CENGAGEbrain.com

1 SAVINGS:
Prices up to 75% off, daily coupons, and free shipping on orders over $25

2 CHOICE:
Multiple format options including textbook, eBook and eChapter rentals

3 CONVENIENCE:
Anytime, anywhere access of eBooks or eChapters via mobile devices

4 SERVICE:
Free eBook access while your text ships, and instant access to online homework products

5 STUDY TOOLS:
Study tools* for your text, plus writing, research, career and job search resources
*availability varies

Find your course materials and start saving at:
www.cengagebrain.com

Source Code: 14M-AA0107

Engaged with you.
www.cengage.com

MindTap
QUICK START GUIDE

1. **To get started, navigate to www.cengagebrain.com and select "Register a Product."**

A new screen will appear prompting you to add a Course Key. A Course Key is a code given to you by your instructor — this is the first of two codes you will need to access MindTap. Every student in your course section should have the same Course Key.

2. **Enter the Course Key and click "Register."**

If you are accessing MindTap through your school's Learning Management System, such as BlackBoard or Desire2Learn, you may be redirected to use your Course Key/Access Code there. Follow the prompts you are given and feel free to contact support if you need assistance.

3. **Confirm your course information above and proceed to the log in portion below.**

If you have a CengageBrain username and password, enter it under "Returning Students" and click "Login." If this is your first time, register under "New Students" and click "Create a New Account."

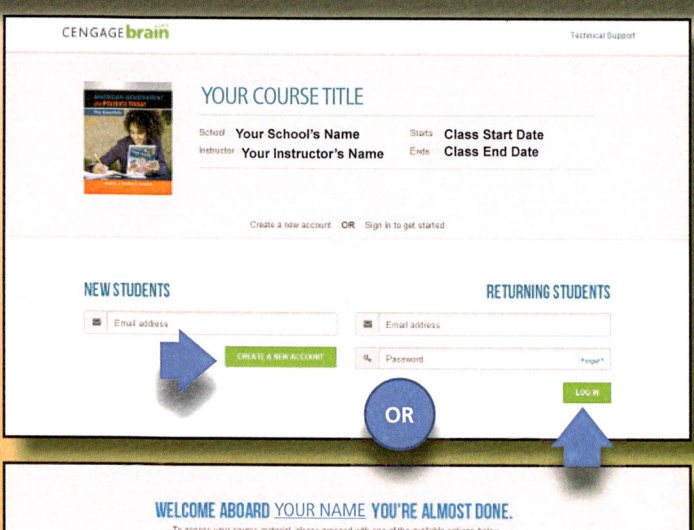

4. **Now that you are logged in, you can access the course for free by selecting "Start Free Trial" for 20 days or enter in your Access Code.**

Your Access Code is unique to you and acts as payment for MindTap. You may have received it with your book or purchased separately in the bookstore or at www.cengagebrain.com. Enter it and click "Register."

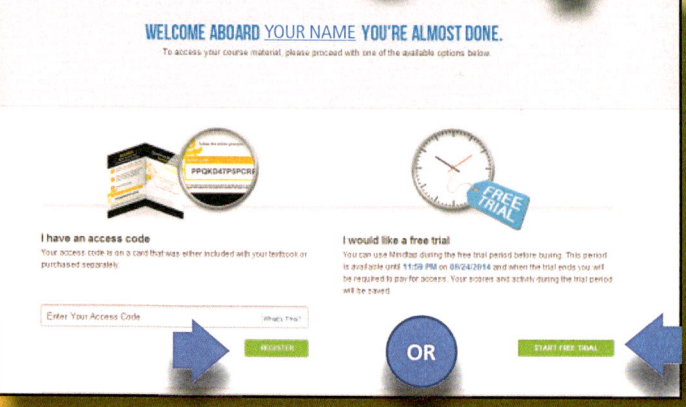

NEED HELP?

For CengageBrain Support: Login to **Support.Cengage.com**. Call **866-994-2427** or access our **24/7 Student Chat!** Or access the **First Day of School PowerPoint Presentation** found at **www.cengagebrain.com**.

The Brief
AMERICAN PAGEANT

The Brief

AMERICAN PAGEANT

A HISTORY OF THE REPUBLIC

NINTH EDITION

David M. Kennedy
Stanford University

Lizabeth Cohen
Harvard University

Mel Piehl
Valparaiso University

Australia • Brazil • Mexico • Singapore • United Kingdom • United States

The Brief American Pageant: A History of the Republic Ninth Edition

David M. Kennedy / Lizabeth Cohen / Mel Piehl

Product Director: Paul R. Banks

Product Manager: Clint Attebery

Senior Content Developer: Margaret McAndrew Beasley

Content Developer: Kate MacLean

Product Assistant: Andrew Newton

Marketing Development Manager: Kyle Zimmerman

Senior Content Project Manager: Carol Newman

Senior Art Director: Cate Rickard Barr

Manufacturing Planner: Fola Orekoya

IP Analyst: Alexandra Ricciardo

Production Service and Compositor: Cenveo® Publisher Services

Text Designer: Lisa Devenish, Devenish Design

Cover Designer: Diana Graham

Cover Image: *Liberty and Washington*, c. 1805. Oil painting by an anonymous painter. The Granger Collection

© 2017, 2012, 2008 Cengage Learning

WCN: 01-100-101

ALL RIGHTS RESERVED. No po part of this work covered by the copyright herein may be reproduced, transmitted, stored, or used in any form or by any means graphic, electronic, or mechanical, including but not limited to photocopying, recording, scanning, digitizing, taping, web distribution, information networks, or information storage and retrieval systems, except as permitted under Section 107 or 108 of the 1976 United States Copyright Act, without the prior written permission of the publisher.

For product information and technology assistance, contact us at
Cengage Learning Customer & Sales Support, 1-800-354-9706
For permission to use material from this text or product, submit all requests online at **www.cengage.com/permissions**.
Further permissions questions can be emailed to **permissionrequest@cengage.com**.

Library of Congress Control Number: 2015946508

Student Edition:
ISBN: 978-1-285-19329-8

Cengage Learning
20 Channel Center Street
Boston MA 02210
USA

Cengage Learning is a leading provider of customized learning solutions with employees residing in nearly 40 different countries and sales in more than 125 countries around the world. Find your local representative at **www.cengage.com**.

Cengage Learning products are represented in Canada by Nelson Education, Ltd.

To learn more about Cengage Learning Solutions, visit **www.cengage.com**.

Purchase any of our products at your local college store or at our preferred online store **www.cengagebrain.com**.

Printed at CLDPC, USA, 08-20

BRIEF CONTENTS

Part One

FOUNDING THE NEW NATION

ca. 33,000 B.C.E.–1783 C.E.

2

1	New World Beginnings 33,000 B.C.E.–1769 C.E.	4
2	The Planting of English America 1500–1733	21
3	Settling the Northern Colonies 1619–1700	34
4	American Life in the Seventeenth Century 1607–1692	49
5	Colonial Society on the Eve of Revolution 1700–1775	60
6	The Duel for North America 1608–1763	76
7	The Road to Revolution 1763–1775	87
8	America Secedes from the Empire 1775–1783	101

Part Two

BUILDING THE NEW NATION

1776–1860

118

9	The Confederation and the Constitution 1776–1790	120
10	Launching the New Ship of State 1789–1800	139

ix

11 The Triumphs and Travails of the Jeffersonian Republic 1800-1812 — 156

12 The Second War for Independence and the Upsurge of Nationalism 1812-1824 — 171

13 The Rise of a Mass Democracy 1824-1840 — 189

14 Forging the National Economy 1790-1860 — 211

15 The Ferment of Reform and Culture 1790-1860 — 232

Part Three

TESTING THE NEW NATION
1820-1877
252

16 The South and the Slavery Controversy 1793-1860 — 254

17 Manifest Destiny and Its Legacy 1841-1848 — 269

18 Renewing the Sectional Struggle 1848-1854 — 282

19 Drifting toward Disunion 1854-1861 — 296

20 Girding for War: The North and the South 1861-1865 — 312

21 The Furnace of Civil War 1861-1865 — 326

22 The Ordeal of Reconstruction 1865-1877 — 347

Part Four

FORGING AN INDUSTRIAL SOCIETY
1865–1909
364

23 Political Paralysis in the Gilded Age 1869–1896 — 366

24 Industry Comes of Age 1865–1900 — 385

25 America Moves to the City 1865–1900 — 404

26 The Great West and the Agricultural Revolution 1865–1896 — 427

27 Empire and Expansion 1890–1909 — 451

Part Five

STRUGGLING FOR JUSTICE AT HOME AND ABROAD
1901–1945
474

28 Progressivism and the Republican Roosevelt 1901–1912 — 476

29 Wilsonian Progressivism in Peace and War 1913–1920 — 495

30 American Life in the "Roaring Twenties" 1920–1929 — 518

31 The Politics of Boom and Bust 1920–1932 — 535

BRIEF CONTENTS

32 The Great Depression and the New Deal 1933–1939 — 550

33 Franklin D. Roosevelt and the Shadow of War 1933–1941 — 570

34 America in World War II 1941–1945 — 584

Part Six

MAKING MODERN AMERICA
1945 To The Present
604

35 The Cold War Begins 1945–1952 — 606

36 American Zenith 1952–1963 — 627

37 The Stormy Sixties 1963–1973 — 650

38 Challenges to the Postwar Order 1973–1980 — 670

39 The Resurgence of Conservatism 1980–1992 — 686

40 America Confronts the Post–Cold War Era 1992–2000 — 703

41 The American People Face a New Century 2001–2015 — 719

APPENDIX
Declaration of Independence A1
Constitution of the United States of America A4

INDEX A21

CONTENTS

Preface xxix

Part One

FOUNDING THE NEW NATION
ca. 33,000 B.C.E.–1783 C.E.
2

1 New World Beginnings 33,000 B.C.E.–1769 C.E. 4

The Geology of the New World • Native Americans Before Columbus • Europeans and Africans • The Ecological Consequences of Columbus's Discovery • Spain Builds a New World Empire
- ★ EXAMINING THE EVIDENCE   Making Sense of the New World   9
- ★ MAKERS OF AMERICA   The Spanish *Conquistadores*   16

2 The Planting of English America 1500–1733 21

England in the Age of Expansion • The Planting of Jamestown, 1607 • The Growth of Virginia and Maryland • England in the Caribbean • Settling the Carolinas and Georgia
- ★ MAKERS OF AMERICA   The Iroquois   30

3 Settling the Northern Colonies 1619–1700 34

The Puritan Faith • Plymouth Colony, 1620 • The Puritan Commonwealth of Massachusetts Bay Colony, 1630 • The Expansion of New England • New Netherland Becomes New York • Pennsylvania and the Middle Colonies
- ★ EXAMINING THE EVIDENCE   A Seventeenth-Century Valuables Cabinet   46
- ★ VARYING VIEWPOINTS   Europeanizing America or Americanizing Europe?   47

4 American Life in the Seventeenth Century 1607–1692 49

Life and Labor in the Chesapeake Region • Indentured Servants and Bacon's Rebellion in Virginia, 1676 • Slavery Families in New England • The Salem Witchcraft Trials, 1692 • The Changing New England Way of Life
- ★ EXAMINING THE EVIDENCE   An Indentured Servant's Contract, 1746   52
- ★ THINKING GLOBALLY   The Atlantic Slave Trade, 1500–1860   54

xiii

5 Colonial Society on the Eve of Revolution 1700–1775 — 60

Population Growth and Ethnic Diversity • Enslaved African Americans • Colonial Society and Economy • The Atlantic Economy • The Great Awakening • Education and Culture • Political Patterns
- ★ MAKERS OF AMERICA   From African to African American   64
- ★ VARYING VIEWPOINTS   Colonial America: Communities of Conflict or Consensus?   75

6 The Duel for North America 1608–1763 — 76

New France • Anglo-French Colonial Rivalries • The French and Indian War, 1754–1763 • The Ousting of France from North America, 1763 • The Consequences of War

7 The Road to Revolution 1763–1775 — 87

The Merits and Menace of Mercantilism • The Stamp Act Crisis, 1765 • The Townshend Acts, 1767 • The Boston Tea Party, 1773 • The Intolerable Acts and the Continental Congress, 1774 • Lexington, Concord, and the Gathering Clouds of War, 1775

8 America Secedes from the Empire 1775–1783 — 101

Early Skirmishes, 1775 • American "Republicanism" • The Declaration of Independence, 1776 • Patriots and Loyalists • The Fighting Fronts • The French Alliance, 1778 • Yorktown, 1781 • The Peace of Paris, 1783
- ★ MAKERS OF AMERICA   The Loyalists   107
- ★ EXAMINING THE EVIDENCE   A Revolution for Women? Abigail Adams Chides Her Husband, 1776   111
- ★ VARYING VIEWPOINTS   Whose Revolution?   116

Part Two

BUILDING THE NEW NATION
1776–1860
118

9 The Confederation and the Constitution 1776–1790 — 120

Post-Revolutionary Politics and Economics • The Articles of Confederation, 1781–1788 • The Northwest Ordinance, 1787 • Shays's Rebellion, 1786 • The Constitutional Convention, 1787 • Ratifying the Constitution, 1787–1790 • Steps Toward Social Equality

★ EXAMINING THE EVIDENCE   Copley Family Portrait, ca. 1776–1777   **123**

★ VARYING VIEWPOINTS   The Constitution: Revolutionary or Counterrevolutionary?   **137**

10 Launching the New Ship of State 1789–1800 — 139

Problems of the Young Republic • The First Presidency, 1789–1793 • The Bill of Rights, 1791 • Hamilton's Economic Policies • The Emergence of Political Parties • The Impact of the French Revolution • Jay's Treaty, 1794 • President Adams Keeps the Peace • The Alien and Sedition Acts, 1798 • The Virginia and Kentucky Resolutions, 1798–1799 • Federalists versus Democratic-Republicans

★ THINKING GLOBALLY   Two Revolutions   **146**

11 The Triumphs and Travails of the Jeffersonian Republic 1800–1812 — 156

The "Revolution of 1800" • The Jefferson Presidency • John Marshall and the Supreme Court • The Louisiana Purchase, 1803 • The Embargo, 1807–1809 • Napoleon Manipulates Madison • Battle with the Shawnees • A Declaration of War

★ EXAMINING THE EVIDENCE   Thomas Jefferson–Sally Hemings Controversy   **159**

12 The Second War for Independence and the Upsurge of Nationalism 1812–1824 — 171

Invasion of Canada, 1812 • The War on Land and Sea • The Treaty of Ghent, 1814 • The Hartford Convention, 1814–1815 • A New National Identity • "The American System" • James Monroe and the Era of Good Feelings • Westward Expansion • The Missouri Compromise, 1820 • The Supreme Court under John Marshall • Canada and Florida • The Monroe Doctrine, 1823

★ MAKERS OF AMERICA   Settlers of the Old Northwest   **182**

13 The Rise of a Mass Democracy 1824–1840 — 189

The "Corrupt Bargain" of 1824 • President John Quincy Adams, 1825–1829 • The Triumph of Andrew Jackson, 1828 • The "Tariff of Abominations," 1828 • The Spoils System • The South Carolina Nullification Crisis, 1832–1833 • Indian Removal • Jackson's War on the Bank of the United States • The Emergence of the Whig Party, 1836 • Martin Van Buren and the Depression of 1837 • The Texas Revolution • William Henry Harrison's "Log Cabin" Campaign, 1840 • The Establishment of the Two-Party System

★ THINKING GLOBALLY   Alexis de Tocqueville on Democracy in America and Europe   196
★ EXAMINING THE EVIDENCE   Satiric Bank Note, 1837   204
★ VARYING VIEWPOINTS   What Was Jacksonian Democracy?   209

14 Forging the National Economy 1790–1860 — 211

The Westward Movement • Irish and German Immigrants • Nativism and Assimilation • The Coming of the Factory System • Women and the Economy • The Ripening of Commercial Agriculture • The Transportation Revolution • Overseas Trade and Communication

★ MAKERS OF AMERICA   The Irish   217
★ MAKERS OF AMERICA   The Germans   220
★ EXAMINING THE EVIDENCE   The Invention of the Sewing Machine   223

15 The Ferment of Reform and Culture 1790–1860 — 232

Religious Revivals • The Mormons • Educational Advances • The Roots of Reform • Women's Roles and Women's Rights • Utopian Experiments • A National Literature

★ EXAMINING THE EVIDENCE   Dress as Reform   242
★ MAKERS OF AMERICA   The Oneida Community   244
★ VARYING VIEWPOINTS   Reform: Who? What? How? and Why?   250

Part Three

TESTING THE NEW NATION
1820–1877
252

16 The South and the Slavery Controversy 1793–1860 — 254

The Economy of the Cotton Kingdom • Poor Whites and Free Blacks • The Plantation System • The Human Face of the "Peculiar Institution" • The Abolitionist Crusade • Southern and Northern Responses to Abolitionism

★ EXAMINING THE EVIDENCE Bellegrove Plantation, Donaldsville, Louisiana, Built 1857 264

★ VARYING VIEWPOINTS What Was the True Nature of Slavery? 267

17 Manifest Destiny and Its Legacy 1841–1848 — 269

"Tyler Too" Becomes President, 1841 • The Annexation of Texas, 1845 • Oregon and California • James K. Polk, The "Dark Horse" of 1844 • War with Mexico, 1846–1848

★ MAKERS OF AMERICA The Californios 279

18 Renewing the Sectional Struggle 1848–1854 — 282

"Popular Sovereignty" • Growing Sectional Tensions • The Compromise of 1850 • The Inflammatory Fugitive Slave Law • The Death of the Whig Party • President Pierce and Proslavery Expansionist Ventures, 1853–1857 • Senator Douglas and the Kansas-Nebraska Act, 1854

19 Drifting toward Disunion 1854–1861 — 296

Uncle Tom's Cabin and the Spread of Abolitionist Sentiment in the North • The Bloody Contest for Kansas • The Election of James Buchanan, 1856 • The *Dred Scott* Case, 1857 • The Lincoln-Douglas Debates, 1858 • John Brown's Raid on Harpers Ferry, 1859 • Lincoln and the Republican Victory, 1860 • Secession

★ EXAMINING THE EVIDENCE Harriet Beecher Stowe, *Uncle Tom's Cabin* 299

★ VARYING VIEWPOINTS The Civil War: Repressible or Irrepressible? 310

20 Girding for War: The North and the South 1861–1865 — 312

The Attack on Fort Sumter, April 1861 • The Crucial Border States • The Balance of Forces • Diplomacy and the Threat of European Intervention • Lincoln and Civil Liberties • Men in Uniform • Wartime Finance and Economy • Women and the War • The Fate of the South

★ MAKERS OF AMERICA Billy Yank and Johnny Reb 323

21 The Furnace of Civil War 1861–1865 326

Bull Run Ends the "Ninety-Day War" • The Peninsula Campaign • The Union Wages Total War • The Battle of Antietam • The Emancipation Proclamation, 1863 • Black Soldiers • Confederate High Tide at Gettysburg • Politics in Wartime • Appomattox, 1865 • The Assassination of Lincoln, April 1865 • The Legacy of War

★ **Examining the Evidence**   Abraham Lincoln's Gettysburg Address   335
★ **Thinking Globally**   The Era of Nationalism   344
★ **Varying Viewpoints**   What Were the Consequences of the Civil War?   345

22 The Ordeal of Reconstruction 1865–1877 347

The Defeated South • The Freed Slaves • President Andrew Johnson's Reconstruction Policies • Moderate and Radical Republicans • Congressional Reconstruction Policies • Military Reconstruction, 1867–1877 • Freed People Enter Politics • "Black Reconstruction" and the Ku Klux Klan • The Impeachment of Andrew Johnson • The Legacy of Reconstruction

★ **Examining the Evidence**   Letter from a Freedman to His Old Master, 1865   352
★ **Varying Viewpoints**   How Radical Was Reconstruction?   362

Part Four

FORGING AN INDUSTRIAL SOCIETY
1865–1909
364

23 Political Paralysis in the Gilded Age 1869–1896 — 366

Ulysses S. Grant, Soldier-President • Corruption and Reform in the Post–Civil War Era • The Depression of the 1870s • Political Parties and Partisans • The Compromise of 1877 and the End of Reconstruction • Class Conflict and Ethnic Clashes • Civil Service Reform • Grover Cleveland and the Tariff • President Harrison and the "Billion-Dollar" Congress • Populists • Cleveland and the Depression of the 1890s

★ MAKERS OF AMERICA   The Chinese   375
★ VARYING VIEWPOINTS   The Populists: Radicals or Reactionaries?   383

24 Industry Comes of Age 1865–1900 — 385

The Railroad Boom • Speculators and Financiers • Early Efforts at Government Regulation • Lords of Industry • Industry in the South • Workers and Unions

★ EXAMINING THE EVIDENCE   The Photography of Lewis W. Hine   399
★ VARYING VIEWPOINTS   Industrialization: Boon or Blight?   402

25 America Moves to the City 1865–1900 — 404

The Rise of the City • Skyscrapers, Tenements, and Suburbs • The "New Immigrants" • New Jobs for Women • Nativists and Immigration Restriction • Churches in the City • Black Leaders: Booker T. Washington and W. E. B. Du Bois • Literary Achievements • The "New Woman" and the New Morality • Art and Entertainment in Urban America

★ MAKERS OF AMERICA   The Italians   409
★ EXAMINING THE EVIDENCE   Manuscript Census Data, 1900   411

26 The Great West and the Agricultural Revolution 1865–1896 — 427

The Conquest of the Indians • The Mining and Cattle Frontiers • The Industrialization of Agriculture • Farmers Protest • Challenge from the People's Party • Panic and Depression • Bryan versus McKinley, 1896

★ MAKERS OF AMERICA   The Plains Indians   433
★ EXAMINING THE EVIDENCE   Robert Louis Stevenson's Transcontinental Journey, 1879   438
★ THINKING GLOBALLY   The Great Frontier   442
★ VARYING VIEWPOINTS   Was the West Really "Won"?   449

27 Empire and Expansion 1890–1909 — 451

The Sources of American Expansionism • Cleveland and the Venezuelan Boundary Dispute, 1895–1896 • The Hawaii Question • The Explosion of the Maine, February 15, 1898 • The Spanish-American War, 1898 • The Invasion of Cuba • Acquiring Puerto Rico (1898) and the Philippines (1899) • Crushing the Filipino Insurrection • The Open Door Notes, 1899 and 1900 • TR Becomes President, 1901 • The Panama Canal • The Roosevelt Corollary to the Monroe Doctrine, 1904 • Roosevelt and East Asia

★ Makers of America The Puerto Ricans 460
★ Makers of America The Filipinos 464
★ Thinking Globally The Age of Empire 470
★ Varying Viewpoints Why Did America Become a World Power? 472

Part Five

STRUGGLING FOR JUSTICE AT HOME AND ABROAD

1901–1945

474

28 Progressivism and the Republican Roosevelt 1901–1912 — 476

The Origins of Progressivism • Progressive Political Reforms • Progressive Women at the Forefront • Roosevelt, Labor, and the Trusts • Consumer Protection and Conservation • The Roosevelt Legacy • The Troubled Presidency of William Howard Taft • Roosevelt's Progressive Revolt • Roosevelt's New Nationalism vs. Wilson's New Freedom, 1912

★ EXAMINING THE EVIDENCE   *Muller* v. *Oregon*, 1908   484
★ MAKERS OF AMERICA   The Environmentalists   486

29 Wilsonian Progressivism in Peace and War 1913–1920 — 495

Wilsonian Progressivism: Reforming the Tariff, the Banks, and the Trusts • Wilson's Diplomacy in Mexico and Latin America • War in Europe and American Neutrality • The Reelection of Wilson, 1916 • German Submarines Push America into War, 1917 • Wilsonian Idealism and the Fourteen Points • Wartime Propaganda and the Stifling of Dissent • Workers, Blacks, and Women on the Home Front • The American Doughboys • The American Forces Fight in France • Wilsonian Peacemaking in Paris • The Senate Rejects the Versailles Treaty

★ EXAMINING THE EVIDENCE   "Mademoiselle from Armentières"   510
★ VARYING VIEWPOINTS   Woodrow Wilson: Realist or Idealist?   516

30 American Life in the "Roaring Twenties" 1920–1929 — 518

The Red Scare and the Ku Klux Klan • Immigration Restriction, 1921–1924 • Prohibition and Gangsterism • Cultural Conflict and the Scopes Trial • The Mass-Consumption Economy and the Automobile Age • Radio, Film, and Music in the Jazz Age • Changes in Sexuality and Race • The Economic Boom

★ MAKERS OF AMERICA   The Poles   523
★ EXAMINING THE EVIDENCE   *The Jazz Singer*, 1927   529

31 The Politics of Boom and Bust 1920–1932 — 535

Conservative Republicans Take Power • Disarmament and Isolation • The Harding Scandals • Calvin Coolidge and the Election of 1924 • Foreign Policy and the International Debt Tangle • Herbert Hoover's Competing Ideologies • The Great Crash, 1929 • Hoover and the Great Depression

★ EXAMINING THE EVIDENCE   Lampooning Hoover, 1932   547

32 The Great Depression and the New Deal 1933-1939 — 550

Franklin D. Roosevelt as President • The Hundred Days Congress, 1933 • The National Recovery Administration, 1933-1935 • The Agricultural Adjustment Administration, 1933-1936 • The Tennessee Valley Authority • The Social Security Act, 1935 • Gains for Organized Labor • The Election of 1936 and the "Roosevelt Coalition" • The Supreme Court Fight, 1937 • The New Deal Assessed

★ **Varying Viewpoints** How Radical Was the New Deal? 568

33 Franklin D. Roosevelt and the Shadow of War 1933-1941 — 570

Roosevelt's Early Foreign Policies • The Rise of Fascism and American Isolationism • War in Europe and the Debate over American Neutrality • Roosevelt's Third-Term Victory and Lend-Lease Aid to Britain • Refugees from Hitler's Holocaust • The Japanese Attack on Pearl Harbor, December 7, 1941

★ **Examining the Evidence** Public Opinion Polling in the 1930s 577

34 America in World War II 1941-1945 — 584

The Grand American Strategy for War • Mobilizing for War • Women in Wartime • Changes for African Americans, Native Americans, and Mexican Americans • The Social and Economic Impact of War • Turning the Japanese Tide in the Pacific • Campaigns in North Africa (1942) and Italy (1943) • D-Day and the German Surrender • The Atomic Bomb Ends the War with Japan

★ **Makers of America** The Japanese 587
★ **Examining the Evidence** Franklin Roosevelt at Tehran, 1943 597
★ **Thinking Globally** America and the World in Depression and War: A Study in Contrasts 600
★ **Varying Viewpoints** The Atomic Bombs: Were They Justified? 602

Part Six

MAKING MODERN AMERICA
1945 To The Present
604

35 The Cold War Begins 1945–1952 — 606

Harry S. Truman as President • The Yalta Conference, February 1945 • Origins of the Cold War • The Cold War in East Asia • The Korean War, 1950–1953 • Anticommunism at Home • Truman Defeats Dewey, 1948 • Postwar Prosperity • The Rise of the "Sunbelt" and the Suburbs • The Postwar Baby Boom

★ MAKERS OF AMERICA   The Suburbanites   623
★ VARYING VIEWPOINTS   Who Was to Blame for the Cold War?   625

36 American Zenith 1952–1963 — 627

Affluence and Consumer Culture • Eisenhower Republicanism • Martin Luther King, Jr., and the Early Civil Rights Movement • Eisenhower's Domestic and Foreign Policies • The Fluctuating Cold War • John F. Kennedy Defeats Richard Nixon, 1960 • Postwar Literature and Culture • The Kennedy Promise • Ventures in Vietnam and Cuba • Civil Rights Rising

★ MAKERS OF AMERICA   The Great African American Migration   633
★ EXAMINING THE EVIDENCE   The Shopping Mall as New Town Square, 1960   641

37 The Stormy Sixties 1963–1973 — 650

Lyndon Baines Johnson and the "Great Society" • From Civil Rights to Black Power • The Vietnam Disaster • The Election of Richard Nixon • The Cultural Upheavals of the 1960s • Nixon and the Vietnam War • New Policies toward China and the Soviet Union • Nixon's Domestic Policies • Nixon's Re-election and Watergate • Israelis, Arabs, and Oil

★ THINKING GLOBALLY   The Global 1960s   661
★ VARYING VIEWPOINTS   The Sixties: Constructive or Destructive?   668

38 Challenges to the Postwar Order 1973–1980 — 670

Watergate • Economic Stagnation • Nixon's Resignation and the Ford Presidency • Feminism and Race in the 1970s • Carter's Troubled Presidency • The Energy Crisis and Inflation • The Iranian Hostage Humiliation

★ EXAMINING THE EVIDENCE   The "Smoking Gun" Tape, June 23, 1972, 10:04–11:39 A.M.   672
★ THINKING GLOBALLY   The Era of Globalization   674
★ MAKERS OF AMERICA   The Vietnamese   677
★ MAKERS OF AMERICA   The Feminists   678

39 The Resurgence of Conservatism 1980–1992 — 686

Ronald Reagan and the New Right • "Reaganomics" and Its Consequences • Reagan Renews the Cold War • The Iran-Contra Scandal • Reagan's Economic Legacy • The Religious Right and Conflict over Abortion • George H. W. Bush • The End of the Cold War • The Persian Gulf War, 1991 • Bush's Battles at Home

★ **Varying Viewpoints** Where Did Modern Conservatism Come From? 701

40 America Confronts the Post-Cold War Era 1992–2000 — 703

Bill Clinton in the White House • Congressional Republicans Battle Clinton • Clinton and the Prosperous '90s Economy • Racial Gains and Tensions • Globalization and U.S. Foreign Policy • Clinton's Impeachment and Acquittal • The Controversial 2000 Election • Postmodern American Culture

★ **Makers of America** The Latinos 709

41 The American People Face a New Century 2001–2015 — 719

George W. Bush and September 11, 2001 • The Iraq War • George W. Bush's Troubled Second Term • Barack Obama and the "Great Recession" • Obama's Foreign and Domestic Policies • The Politics of Inequality • Obama's Reelection and Second-Term Stalemate • Immigration and Civil Rights • The American Prospect

APPENDIX

Declaration of Independence A1
Constitution of the United States of America A4

INDEX   A21

MAPS

Territorial Growth of the United States ii
The World Today iv
1.1 The First Discoverers of America 7
1.2 North American Indian Peoples at the Time of First Contact with Europeans 10
1.3 The World Known to Europe and Major Trade Routes with Asia, 1492 12
1.4 Principal Voyages of Discovery 15
2.1 Early Maryland and Virginia 25
2.2 Iroquois Lands and European Trade Centers, ca. 1590–1650 30
3.1 Seventeenth-Century New England Settlements 40
3.2 Early Settlements in the Middle Colonies, with Founding Dates 43
4.1 Main Sources of African Slaves, ca. 1500 to ca. 1860 55
5.1 Immigrant Groups in 1775 62
5.2 Colonial Trade Patterns, ca. 1770 67
6.1 The French and Indian War in North America, 1754–1760 80
6.2a North America Before 1754 85
6.2b North America After 1763 (after French losses) 85
7.1 Quebec Before and After 1774 96
8.1 Revolution in the North, 1775–1776 104
8.2 War in the South, 1780–1781 113
9.1 Western Land Cessions to the United States, 1782–1802 124
9.2 Surveying the Old Northwest 126
9.3 The Struggle over Ratification 132
10.1 American Posts Held by the British and British-American Clashes after 1783 148
11.1 Presidential Election of 1800 (with electoral vote by state) 158
11.2 Exploring the Louisiana Purchase and the West 165
12.1 Battles in the War of 1812 174
12.2 The Missouri Compromise and Slavery, 1820–1821 181
12.3 U.S.-British Boundary Settlement, 1818 184
13.1 Presidential Election of 1828 (with electoral vote by state) 193
13.2 Indian Removals, 1830–1846 200
13.3 The Texas Revolution, 1836 206
14.1 Westward Movement of the Center of Population, 1790–2000 213
14.2 The Railroad Revolution 228
15.1 The Mormon World 237
16.1 Southern Distribution of Slaves, 1820 and 1860 258
17.1 The Oregon Controversy, 1846 275
17.2 Major Campaigns of the Mexican War 277
18.1 Slavery after the Compromise of 1850 287
18.2 The Gadsden Purchase, 1853 292
18.3 Kansas and Nebraska, 1854 293
19.1 Bleeding Kansas, 1854–1860 298
19.2 Presidential Election of 1860: Electoral Vote by State (top) and Popular Vote by County (bottom) 307
19.3 Southern Opposition to Secession, 1860–1861 (showing vote by county) 308
20.1 Seceding States (with dates and order of secession) 315
21.1 Main Thrusts, 1861–1865 330
21.2 The Battle of Gettysburg, 1863 334
21.3 The Mississippi River and Tennessee, 1862–1863 336
21.4 Sherman's March, 1864–1865 338
21.5 Presidential Election of 1864 (showing popular vote by county) 341
22.1 Military Reconstruction, 1867 (five districts and commanding generals) 356
23.1 Hayes-Tilden Disputed Election of 1876 (with electoral vote by state) 373
23.2 Presidential Election of 1892 (showing vote by county) 380
24.1 Federal Land Grants to Railroads 387
26.1 Indian Wars, 1860–1890 431
26.2 Presidential Election of 1896 (with electoral vote by state) 448
27.1 United States Expansion, 1857–1917 455
27.2 Big Stick in the Caribbean in 1901 466
29.1 The United States in the Caribbean, 1898–1941 499
29.2 Presidential Election of 1916 (with electoral vote by state)
29.3 Major U.S. Operations in France, 1918 509
31.1 Presidential Election of 1924 (showing popular vote by county) 541
32.1 The Extent of Erosion in the 1930s 560
33.1 Main Flow of Lend-Lease Aid (width of arrows indicates relative amount) 579
34.1 Internal Migration in the United States during World War II 590

xxv

34.2 United States Thrusts in the Pacific, 1942–1945 592
34.3 World War II in Europe and North Africa, 1939–1945 596
35.1 Postwar Partition of Germany 611
35.2 The Shifting Front in Korea 615
35.3 Distribution of Population Increase, 1950–2013 622
36.1 Presidential Election of 1960 (with electoral vote by state) 639
36.2 Vietnam and Southeast Asia, 1954–1975 645
37.1 Presidential Election of 1968 (with electoral vote by state) 659
39.1 The Middle East 691
39.2 Central America and the Caribbean 692
39.3 The End of the Cold War Changed the Map of Europe 699
40.1 Presidential Election of 2000 (with electoral vote by state) 715
41.1 Presidential Election of 2008 726

CHARTS AND TABLES

Figure 16.1 Slave-Owning Families, 1850   257
Figure 25.1 The Shift to the American City   406
Figure 30.1 Annual Immigration and the Quota Laws   522
Figure 31.1 Aspects of the Financial Merry-Go-Round, 1921–1933   542
Figure 31.2 Index of Common Stock Prices (1926 = 100)   544

Table 5.1 Estimated Religious Census, 1775   69
Table 9.1 Strengthening the Central Government   130
Table 10.1 Evolution of the Cabinet   141
Table 13.1 Election of 1824   191
Table 14.1 Irish and German Immigration by Decade, 1830–1900   215
Table 18.1 Compromise of 1850   288
Table 20.1 Immigration to United States, 1860–1866   317
Table 25.1 Educational Levels, 1870–2011   417
Table 32.1 Principal New Deal Acts During Hundred Days Congress, 1933 (items in parentheses indicate secondary purposes)   553
Table 32.2 Later Major New Deal Measures, 1933–1939 (items in parentheses indicate secondary purposes)   556
Table 34.1 The Comparative Costs of World War II   601

PREFACE

This new edition of *The Brief American Pageant*, a concise version of *The American Pageant*, sixteenth edition, includes significant innovations. As always, this Brief Edition presents the core content of *The American Pageant* in an efficient and engaging fashion. It preserves the central distinguishing features of *The American Pageant*—its strong narrative and consistent focus on the great themes of American history: liberty, democracy, the struggle for justice in a modern industrial economy, and America's place in the world.

A new feature of this edition is Contending Voices, which presents paired quotes from the past to encourage critical thinking about controversial issues. The Thinking Globally features highlight the global context of key moments in American history. More highlighted quotes throughout the text help students hear the language of real people who experienced historical events.

In addition, the Examining the Evidence features enable students to deepen their understanding of the historical craft by conveying how historians develop interpretations of the past through research in many different kinds of primary sources. Here students learn to probe a wide range of historical documents and artifacts: correspondence between Abigail and John Adams in 1776, and what it reveals about women's place in the American Revolution; the Gettysburg Address and the light it sheds not only on President Lincoln's brilliant oratory but also on his vision of the American nation; a letter from a black freedman to his former master in 1865 that illuminates his family's experience in slavery as well as their hopes for a new life; the manuscript census of 1900 and what it teaches us about immigrant households on the Lower East Side of New York at the dawn of the twentieth century; and a new kind of architectural structure—the shopping mall—and how it changed both consumers' behavior and politicians' campaign tactics after World War II.

The text incorporates these features while preserving the liveliness and readability that have long been *The American Pageant*'s hallmark. We are often told that the *Pageant* is the sole American history text that has a distinctive personality—defined by clarity, concreteness, a consistent chronological narrative, strong emphasis on major themes, avoidance of clutter, access to a variety of interpretive perspectives, and a colorful writing style leavened, as appropriate, with wit. That personality, we strongly believe, is what has made *The Brief American Pageant* both appealing and useful to countless students for several decades.

The Brief American Pageant's goal is not to teach the art of prophecy but the much subtler and more difficult arts of seeing things in context, of understanding the roots and direction and pace of change, and of distinguishing what is truly new under the sun from what is not. The study of history, it has been rightly said, does not make one smart for the next time, but wise forever. We hope that *The Brief American Pageant* will help to develop this art of critical thinking in its readers, and that those who use the book will take from it both a fresh appreciation of what has gone before and a seasoned perspective on what is to come.

New to the Ninth Edition

Like *The American Pageant*, *The Brief American Pageant* provides students with a firm foundation in American history. *The Brief American Pageant* has also followed the lead of its parent text in terms of revisions for this most recent edition. For this edition we have consolidated and combined two chapters (eighth edition Chapters 29 and 30) into a single chapter (ninth edition Chapter 29; now titled Wilsonian Progressivism in Peace and War), resulting in renumbering of subsequent chapters for a total of 41 chapters in the ninth edition. Other changes include the following:

- **Part Six on the post-1945 era** has been substantially revised, reorganized, and updated to impart greater thematic coherence on the most recent past. Reflecting an emerging scholarly consensus, our new framework roughly divides the period into two eras, which can be summarized as follows: a midcentury era defined by sustained economic growth, broadly shared prosperity, and the international context of Cold War confrontation with the Soviet Union, followed by a new historical phase, originating in the pivotal decade of the 1970s, that has seen more fitful growth alongside both decreasing economic equality and increasing social inclusiveness, as well as a struggle to define America's international role after the collapse of the Soviet Union in 1991.

- **Contending Voices** features, all new to the ninth edition, offer paired quotes from original historical sources, accompanied by questions prompting students to assess conflicting perspectives on often hotly debated subjects. This feature is designed to nurture students' historical thinking skills by exposing them to the contested nature of history as well as historical interpretation.

- The **marginal glossary** has been substantively revised for the ninth edition to focus on the key terms—events, movements, organizations, laws, and so on—that are essential to the student's ability to understand larger historical developments. In contrast to previous editions, the glossary no longer includes general vocabulary definitions, which can be easily accessed in online or print dictionaries.

- A **strong global context** once again deepens the *Pageant*'s treatment of American history. Within each chapter, both text and graphics help students compare American developments to developments around the world. Boxed quotes bring more international voices to the events chronicled in the narrative. In addition, the expanded "Thinking Globally" essays present a different context for the American experience within world history.

- The text includes **updated coverage throughout** with updated scholarship and new documentary photos, political cartoons, graphs, and tables.

Notes on Content Revisions

Chapter 1: New images and revised treatment of the Indian civilizations of Mexico, South America, and North America; new Contending Voices: "Europeans and Indians" (Juan Ginés de Sepulveda, Bartolomé de Las Casas)

Chapter 2: Enhanced treatment of changing early Indian cultures and of the links between the West Indies and North American slavery; new Contending Voices: "Old World Dreams and New World Realities" (Richard Hakluyt, George Percy)

Chapter 3: New Contending Voices: "Anne Hutchinson Accused and Defended" (John Winthrop, Anne Hutchinson)

Chapter 4: New Contending Voices: "Berkeley Versus Bacon" (Nathaniel Bacon, William Berkeley)

Chapter 5: Substantially revised treatment of lives of enslaved African Americans; new Contending Voices: "Race and Slavery" (Samuel Sewall, Virginia slave code of 1705)

Chapter 6: New map of French and Indian War; new Contending Voices: "The Proclamation of 1763" (Royal Proclamation of 1763, George Washington)

Chapter 7: New Contending Voices: "Reconciliation or Independence?" (John Dickinson, Thomas Paine)

Chapter 8: Expanded discussion of international context of the American Revolution; new Contending Voices: "Two Revolutions: French and American" (Friedrich von Gentz, John Quincy Adams)

Chapter 9: New material on the debate over the Constitution; a revised and expanded discussion of the impact of *both* the Revolution and the Constitution on ideas of equality, religious freedom, and civic virtue; new Contending Voices: "Debating the New Constitution" (Jonathan Smith, Patrick Henry)

Chapter 10: Focused discussion of Hamiltonian Federalists vs. Jeffersonian Republicans; new Contending Voices: "Human Nature and the Nature of Government" (Alexander Hamilton, Thomas Jefferson)

Chapter 11: New boxed quotes and information on Marshall and the federal judiciary; new Contending Voices: "The Divisive Embargo" (Federalist pamphlet, W. B. Giles)

Chapter 12: New Contending Voices: "Sizing Up the Monroe Doctrine" (Klemens von Metternich, Colombian newspaper)

Chapter 13: New attention to spreading American democracy in global context; new Thinking Globally feature: "Alexis de Tocqueville on Democracy in America and Europe"; revised Varying Viewpoints essay on Jacksonian Democracy; new Contending Voices: "Taking the Measure of Andrew Jackson" (Maryland supporter, Thomas Jefferson)

Chapter 14: Revised treatment of anti-immigrant sentiment; new Contending Voices: "Immigration, Pro and Con" (Know-Nothing party platform, Orestes Brownson)

Chapter 15: Revised Examining the Evidence feature on "Dress as Reform"; revised material on later fate of the Oneida Community; revised Varying Viewpoints essay on "Reform: Who? What? How? and Why?"; new Contending Voices: "The Role of Women" (differing newspaper commentaries on Seneca Falls)

Chapter 16: Expanded coverage of international context of antislavery, including religiously motivated abolitionism; revised Varying Viewpoints essay on the true nature of slavery; new Contending Voices: "Perspectives on Race and Slavery" (William A. Smith, American Anti-Slavery Society)

Chapter 17: New Contending Voices: "Warring over the Mexican War" (*New York Evening Post*, Henry Clay)

Chapter 18: New Contending Voices: "The Compromise of 1850" (John C. Calhoun, Daniel Webster)

Chapter 19: New material on John Brown and Harper's Ferry; new Contending Voices: "Judging John Brown" (Harriet Tubman, Abraham Lincoln); revised Varying Viewpoints essay includes attention to international context of southern secession

Chapter 20: New Contending Voices: "War Aims: Emancipation or Union?" (Horace Greeley, Abraham Lincoln)

Chapter 21: Revised Thinking Globally feature: "The Era of Nationalism" compares Lincoln's American nationalism with that of contemporaries in Germany and Italy; new Contending Voices: "The Controversy over Emancipation" (*Cincinnati Enquirer*, Abraham Lincoln)

Chapter 22: New material on radical Reconstruction, including blacks' roles in the Reconstruction regime; new

Contending Voices: "Radical Republicans and Southern Democrats" (Thaddeus Stevens, James Lawrence Orr)

Chapter 23: New Contending Voices: "The Spoils System" (George Washington Plunkitt, Theodore Roosevelt); revised Varying Viewpoints essay on "The Populists: Radicals or Reactionaries?"

Chapter 24: New material on subsidies for railroad-building, and their advantages and disadvantages for the public; new Contending Voices: "Class and the Gilded Age" (Populist platform, William Graham Sumner); revised Varying Viewpoints essay on "Industrialization: Boon or Blight?"

Chapter 25: This chapter now includes revised discussion of religious conservatism as well as social reform, and expanded treatment of women as urban social reformers. Also revised and expanded are the discussions of moral controversies, women and family life in the cities, and the revived but altered suffrage movement. The new discussion of literature and the arts is now organized around the distinct but related cultural movements of realism, naturalism, and regionalism—all of which reflected in different ways the emerging national urban civilization. New Contending Voices: "The New Immigration" (Henry Cabot Lodge, Grover Cleveland)

Chapter 26: More quotes from both the Plains Indians and the soldiers who fought against them; new Contending Voices: "The Ghost Dance and the Wounded Knee Massacre" (James McLaughlin, Black Elk)

Chapter 27: New material on the debate over imperialism and race; new Contending Voices: "Debating Imperialism" (Albert Beveridge, George Hoar); revised Varying Viewpoints essay on "Why Did America Become a World Power?"

Chapter 28: New material on Roosevelt's conservation policies, including debates over "mixed use" versus "preservation"; expanded treatment of Roosevelt's break with Taft, and the Roosevelt ("New Nationalism") versus Wilson ("New Freedom") versus Taft (Republican Old Guard) ideological campaign of 1912; new Contending Voices: "Debating the Muckrakers" (Theodore Roosevelt, Ida Tarbell); revised Varying Viewpoints essay highlights female and international role in Progressive reform, with differing American and European emphases.

Chapter 29: Completely revised and reorganized treatment of "Wilsonian Progressivism at Home and Abroad" highlights the links between Wilson's domestic reform program and his eventual leadership of the idealistic American crusade in World War I; new Contending Voices: "Battle of the Ballot" (Carrie Chapman Catt, Mrs. Barclay Hazard)

NOTE: Due to the consolidation of two chapters (eighth edition Chapters 29 and 30) into a single chapter (ninth edition Chapter 29), subsequent chapters have been renumbered for a total of 41 chapters in the ninth edition.

Chapter 30: Substantially revised treatment of American literature and culture in the 1920s, with emphasis on the intersection of American developments with the wider international movement of modernism in the arts; new Contending Voices: "All that Jazz" (Henry van Dyke, Duke Ellington)

Chapter 31: Expanded coverage of American isolationism, including economic isolation; new Contending Voices: "Depression and Protection" (Willis Hawley, economists' petition)

Chapter 32: Revised discussion of the Social Security Act and the Fair Labor Standards Act points out their initial exclusion of several categories of workers, for example, farm laborers and domestic workers; new Contending Voices: "The New Deal at High Tide" (Franklin Roosevelt, Herbert Hoover); revised Varying Viewpoints essay describes various radical critiques of the New Deal, as well as historians of the constraints school who stress the limits on FDR's ability to change American society.

Chapter 33: Substantially revised section on the Atlantic Charter as an attempt to revive liberal hopes for a new democratic world order; fresh emphasis on the isolationist-internationalist debate; new Contending Voices: "To Intervene or Not to Intervene" (Sterling Morton, Franklin Roosevelt)

Chapter 34: New Thinking Globally feature: "America and the World in Depression and War: A Study in Contrasts"; increased attention to the impact of race during the war; new Contending Voices: "War and the Color Line" (Franklin Roosevelt, African American soldier)

Chapter 35: Revised and reorganized treatment of the origins of the Cold War, as well as expanded discussion of the long economic boom in the decades after World War II and its impact on American politics and society; new Contending Voices: "Debating the Cold War" (George Kennan, Henry Wallace)

Chapter 36: The chapter presents a fresh treatment of the Eisenhower and Kennedy administrations under the new title "American Zenith," emphasizing the pervasive affluence and confidence of the immediate postwar era; includes a new treatment of the beat writers as critics of a conformist society; new Contending Voices: "The 'Kitchen Debate'" (Richard Nixon, Nikita Khrushchev)

Chapter 37: New Thinking Globally feature, "The Global 1960s," locates American cultural upheavals of the time in relation to similar youth-led upheavals around the globe; new Contending Voices: "Differing Visions of Black Freedom" (Martin Luther King, Jr., Malcolm X)

Chapter 38: The revised and compressed chapter treats the 1970s in the context of "Challenges to the Postwar

Order," highlighting the economic troubles, international conflicts, and increasing loss of faith in American government and other institutions in the wake of Vietnam and Watergate; new Contending Voices: "The Political Mobilization of Business" (Lewis Powell, Douglas Fraser)

Chapter 39: Revised Varying Viewpoints essay on "Where Did Modern Conservatism Come From?"; new Contending Voices: "Who Ended the Cold War?" (Margaret Thatcher, Mikhail Gorbachev)

Chapter 40: Extensively revised treatment of the 1990s and the Clinton administration as an attempt to adjust to a post-Cold War world as well as growing conflict over the role of government; fresh discussions of cultural pluralism, the postmodern mind, and the increasing fragmentation of American culture into narrow niches; new Contending Voices: "Welfare Reform Divides the Democrats" (Joseph Lieberman, Marian Wright Edelman)

Chapter 41: Almost entirely new chapter on America in the post-9/11 era, includes discussion of the global war on terror in Iraq and Afghanistan, and the growing political polarization and gridlock between the two parties, especially after the elections of George W. Bush and Barack Obama; new Contending Voices: "Populist Politics in a Polarized Age" (Tea Party activist, Occupy Wall Street activist)

Pedagogical Features

The special pedagogical features of *The Brief American Pageant* are many and varied, and may be used in different ways by students and instructors.

- **"What if...?"** questions at the end of each part-opening essay prompt students to consider how history might have changed if certain events turned out differently, reinforcing the contingent nature of history. This element is unique to the Brief Edition.

- **Chapter Outlines** begin each chapter to provide a roadmap for the student. This element is unique to the Brief Edition.

- **Focus Questions** come at the beginning of each chapter, pointing to the key issues and ideas in the account that follows, and guiding the student's reading and understanding. This element is unique to the Brief Edition.

- **Chronologies** have been updated to include even more political occurrences and historical events.

- **Marginal Glossary** highlights and defines in a concise, accessible way the key terms—events, movements, organizations, laws, and so on—that are essential to the student's ability to understand larger historical developments. In contrast to previous editions, the glossary no longer includes general vocabulary definitions.

- **Key Terms** are listed at the end of the chapter, with page numbers included, for ease of reference.

- **People to Know** are listed at the end of each chapter, providing students with a useful study tool as they learn about some of the most important individuals in American history.

- **Examining the Evidence** features enable students to deepen their understanding of the historical craft by conveying how historians develop interpretations of the past through research in many different kinds of primary sources.

- **Contending Voices** features offer students two different perspectives on a single event or issue, and include a question to help develop critical thinking skills.

- **Chapter Summaries** provide a handy review that highlights the chapter's main points. This element is unique to the Brief Edition.

Teaching and Learning Aids

Instructor Resources

MindTap™ for *The Brief American Pageant*, 9e is a personalized, online digital learning platform providing students with an immersive learning experience that builds critical thinking skills. Through a carefully designed chapter-based learning path, MindTap allows students to easily identify the chapter's learning objectives, improve writing skills by completing unit-level essay assignments, read short, manageable sections from the e-book, and test their content knowledge with a chapter test that employs Aplia™ questions (see Chapter Test description below).

- *Setting the Scene:* Each chapter within MindTap begins with a brief video that introduces the chapter's major themes in a compelling, visual way that encourages students to think critically about the subject matter.

- *Review Activities:* Each chapter within MindTap includes reading comprehension assignments designed to cover the content of each major heading within the chapter.

- *Chapter Test*: Each chapter within MindTap ends with a summative chapter test. It covers each chapter's learning objectives and is built using Aplia critical thinking questions. All chapter tests include at least one map-based activity. Aplia provides automatically graded critical thinking assignments with detailed, immediate explanations on every question. Students can also choose to see another set of related questions if they did not earn all available points in their first attempt and want more practice.

- *Reflection Activity:* Every chapter ends with an assignable, gradable reflection activity, intended as a brief writing assignment through which students can apply a theme or idea they've just studied. Reflection activities are based upon primary source features within the book.

- *Unit Activities:* Chapters in MindTap are organized into multi-chapter units. Each unit includes a brief set of higher-level activities for instructors to assign, designed to assess students on their writing and critical thinking skills, and their ability to engage larger themes, concepts, and material across multiple chapters.

- *Classroom Activities*: MindTap includes a brief list of class activity ideas for instructors. These are designed to increase student collaboration, engagement, and understanding of selected topics or themes. These activities, including class debate scenarios and primary source discussion guides, can enrich an online or in-class experience for both instructors and students.

MindTap also includes a variety of other tools that support history teaching and learning:

- The Instructor Resource Center provides additional 4,000+ primary source documents that professors can search within and add to any chapter in MindTap.

- Questia allows professors to search a database of thousands of peer-reviewed journals, newspapers, magazines, and full-length books—all assets can be added to any relevant chapter in MindTap.

- Kaltura allows instructors to create and insert inline video and audio into the MindTap platform.

- ReadSpeaker reads the text out loud to students in a voice they can customize.

- Note taking and highlighting are organized in a central location that can be synced with EverNote on any mobile device accessible to students.

- ConnectYard allows instructors to create digital "yards" and communicate with students based upon their preferred social media sites—without "friending" students.

MindTap for *The Brief American Pageant* goes well beyond an eBook and a homework solution. It is truly a *personal learning experience* that allows instructors to synchronize the reading with engaging assignments. To learn more, ask your Cengage Learning sales representative to demo it for you—or go to www.Cengage.com/MindTap.

Instructor Companion Website

This website is an additional resource for class preparation, presentation, and testing for instructors. Accessible through Cengage.com/login with your faculty account, you will find an Instructor's Manual, PowerPoint presentations (descriptions below), and testbank files (please see Cognero description).

- *Instructor's Manual:* For each chapter, this manual contains: focus questions, chapter themes, a chapter summary, suggested lecture topics, and discussion questions.

- *PowerPoint® Lecture Tools:* These presentations are ready-to-use, visual outlines of each chapter. They are easily customized for your lectures. There are presentations of only lecture or only images, as well as combined lecture and image presentations. Also available is a per-chapter JPEG library of images and maps.

- *Cengage Learning Testing, powered by Cognero®:* A test bank that contains multiple-choice and essay questions for each chapter. Cognero® is a flexible, online system that allows you to author, edit, and manage test bank content. Create multiple test versions instantly and deliver through your LMS with no special installs or downloads required. The following test bank format types are available for download from the Instructor Companion Site: Blackboard, Angel, Moodle, Canvas, and Desire2Learn. You can import these files directly into your LMS to edit, manage questions, and create tests.

Cengagebrain.com

Save your students time and money. Direct them to www.cengagebrain.com for choice in formats and savings and a better chance to succeed in your class. Cengagebrain.com, Cengage Learning's online store, is a single destination for more than 10,000 new textbooks, eTextbooks, eChapters, study tools, and audio supplements. Students have the freedom to purchase a-la-carte exactly what they need when they need it. Students can save 50 percent on the electronic textbook and can pay as little as $1.99 for an individual eChapter.

Custom Options

Nobody knows your students like you, so why not give them a text that is tailored to their needs? Cengage Learning offers custom solutions for your course—whether it's modifying *The Brief American Pageant* to match your syllabus or combining multiple sources to create something truly unique. You can pick and choose chapters and include your own material, to create a text that fits the way you teach. Ensure that your students get the most out of their textbook dollar by giving them exactly what they need. Contact your Cengage Learning representative to explore custom solutions for your course.

Reader Program

Cengage Learning publishes a number of readers, some containing exclusively primary sources, others a combination of primary and secondary sources, and some designed to guide students through the process of historical inquiry. Visit Cengage.com/history for a complete list of readers.

Student Resources

MindTap™ for *The Brief American Pageant*, 9e incorporates a set of resources designed to help students develop historical thinking skills, and identify the relevance of those skills beyond the history classroom. These resources include interactive tutorials for map skills, essay writing, and critical thinking, as well as other opportunities to read and write about history. With MindTap, students can access the entire e-book, plus many more valuable study tools.

***Writing for College History*, 1e [ISBN: 9780618306039]** Prepared by Robert M. Frakes, Clarion University. This brief handbook for survey courses in American history, Western civilization/European history, and world civilization guides students through the various types of writing assignments they encounter in a history class. Providing examples of student writing and candid assessments of student work, this text focuses on the rules and conventions of writing for the college history course.

***The History Handbook*, 2e [ISBN: 9780495906766]** Prepared by Carol Berkin of Baruch College, City University of New York and Betty Anderson of Boston University. This book teaches students both basic and history-specific study skills such as how to read primary sources, research historical topics, and correctly cite sources. Substantially less expensive than comparable skill-building texts, *The History Handbook* also offers tips for Internet research and evaluating online sources.

***Doing History: Research and Writing in the Digital Age*, 2e [ISBN: 9781133587880]** Prepared by Michael J. Galgano, J. Chris Arndt, and Raymond M. Hyser of James Madison University. Whether you're starting down the path as a history major, or simply looking for a straightforward and systematic guide to writing a successful paper, you'll find this text to be an indispensable handbook to historical research. This text's "soup to nuts" approach to researching and writing about history addresses every step of the process, from locating your sources and gathering information, to writing clearly and making proper use of various citation styles to avoid plagiarism. You'll also learn how to make the most of every tool available to you—especially the technology that helps you conduct the process efficiently and effectively.

***The Modern Researcher*, 6e [ISBN: 9780495318705]** Prepared by Jacques Barzun and Henry F. Graff of Columbia University. This classic introduction to the techniques of research and the art of expression is used widely in history courses, but is also appropriate for writing and research methods courses in other departments. Barzun and Graff thoroughly cover every aspect of research, from the selection of a topic through the gathering, analysis, writing, revision, and publication of findings, presenting the process not as a set of rules but through actual cases that put the subtleties of research in a useful context. Part One covers the principles and methods of research; Part Two covers writing, speaking, and getting one's work published.

***Rand McNally Historical Atlas of the World*, 2e [ISBN: 9780618841912]** This valuable resource features more than 70 maps that portray the rich panoply of the world's history from preliterate times to the present. They show how cultures and civilization were linked and how they interacted. The maps make it clear that history is not static. Rather, it is about change and movement across time. The maps show change by presenting the dynamics of expansion, cooperation, and conflict. This atlas includes maps that display the world from the beginning of civilization; the political development of all major areas of the world; expanded coverage of Africa, Latin America, and the Middle East; the current Islamic World; and the world population change in 1900 and 2000.

Acknowledgments

Many people contributed to *The Brief American Pageant*. Foremost among them are the countless students and teachers who have written unsolicited letters of comment or inquiry. We also offer thanks to the following colleagues for their particular contributions to improving the text:

- Sheryl Ballard-Smith, Houston Community College
- William Barnhart, Caldwell University
- Edward Bond, Alabama A&M University
- Thomas Born, Blinn College
- Shearer Bowman, University of Kentucky
- Steven Boyd, University of Texas at San Antonio
- Tracy Campbell, University of Kentucky
- Coreen Derifield, East Central College
- Thomas Devine, California State University, Northridge
- Mike Downs, Tarrant County College, Southeast Campus
- Vance Kincade, Arcadia University
- Jennifer Lawrence, Tarrant County College
- Nancy Maurer, University of Central Florida
- Bob McConaughy, Austin Community College, Rio Grande Campus
- Lindsey McNellis, University of Central Florida
- Manuel Medrano, University of Texas at Brownsville
- Russell Mitchell, Tarrant County College, Southeast Campus
- Jaime Olivares, Houston Community College
- Kathleen Riley, Ohio Dominican University
- John Sacher, University of Central Florida
- Manfred Silva, El Paso Community College
- Sandra Slater, College of Charleston
- Bianka Stumpf, Central Carolina Community College
- Gary Topping, Salt Lake Community College
- Amanda Wallace-Wittnebel, University of Texas at San Antonio
- Chad Wooley, Tarrant County College

D.M.K.
L.C.
M.P.

Sail, sail thy best, ship of Democracy,

Of value is thy freight, 'tis not the Present only,

The Past is also stored in thee,

Thou holdest not the venture of thyself alone, not of the Western continent alone,

Earth's résumé entire floats on thy keel, O ship, is steadied by thy spars,

With thee Time voyages in trust, the antecedent nations sink or swim with thee,

With all their ancient struggles, martyrs, heroes, epics, wars, thou bear'st the other continents,

Theirs, theirs as much as thine, the destination-port triumphant . . .

WALT WHITMAN
THOU MOTHER WITH THY EQUAL BROOD, 1872

The Brief
AMERICAN PAGEANT

Part **1**

FOUNDING THE NEW NATION

ca. 33,000 B.C.E.–1783 C.E.

The European explorers who followed Christopher Columbus to North America in the sixteenth century had no notion of founding a new nation. Neither did the first European settlers who peopled the thirteen English colonies on the eastern shores of the continent in the seventeenth and eighteenth centuries. These original colonists may have fled poverty or religious persecution in the Old World, but they continued to view themselves as Europeans, and as subjects of the English king. They regarded America as but the western rim of a transatlantic European world.

Yet life in the New World made the colonists different from their European cousins, and eventually, during the American Revolution, the Americans came to embrace a vision of their country as an independent nation. How did this epochal transformation come about? How did the colonists overcome the conflicts that divided them, unite against Britain, and declare themselves at great cost to be an "American" people?

They had much in common to begin with. Most were English-speaking. Most came determined to create an agricultural society modeled on English customs. Conditions in the New World deepened their common bonds. Most colonists strove to live lives unfettered by the tyrannies of royal authority, official religion, and social hierarchies that they had left behind. They grew to cherish ideals that became synonymous with American life—individual liberty, self-government, religious tolerance, and economic opportunity. They also commonly displayed a willingness to subjugate outsiders—first Indians, who were nearly annihilated through war and disease, and then Africans, who were brought in chains to serve as enslaved workers, especially on the tobacco, rice, and indigo plantations of the southern colonies.

But if the settlement experience gave people a common stock of values, both good and bad, it also divided them. The thirteen colonies were quite different from one another. Puritans carved tight, pious, and relatively democratic communities of small family farms out of rocky-soiled New England. Theirs was a homogeneous world in comparison with most of the southern colonies, where large landholders, mostly Anglicans, built plantations along the coast from which they lorded over a labor force of enslaved blacks and looked down upon the poor white farmers who settled the backcountry. Different still were the middle colonies stretching from New York to Delaware. There diversity reigned. Well-to-do merchants put their stamp on New York City, as Quakers did on Philadelphia, while out in the countryside sprawling estates were interspersed with modest homesteads. Within individual colonies, conflicts festered over economic interests, ethnic rivalries, and religious practices. All those clashes made it difficult for colonists to imagine that they were a single people with a common destiny, much less that they ought to break free from Britain.

The American colonists in fact had little reason to complain about Britain. Each of the thirteen colonies enjoyed a good deal of self-rule. Many colonists profited from trade within the British Empire. But by the 1760s this stable arrangement began to crumble, a victim of the imperial rivalry between France and Britain. Their struggle

The Town of Secota, Engraving, by Theodore de Bry, 1590, after John White Painting. John White was an English watercolorist who accompanied the first English expedition to Roanoke Island (later part of Virginia) in 1585. His paintings faithfully recorded the Indian way of life that was now imperiled by the arrival of the Europeans.

for supremacy in North America began in the late seventeenth century and finally dragged in the colonists during the French and Indian War from 1756 to 1763. That war in one sense strengthened ties with Britain, since colonial militias fought triumphantly alongside the British army against their mutual French and Indian enemies. But once the French were driven from the North American continent, the colonists no longer needed Britain for protection. More importantly, after 1763 a financially overstretched British government made the fateful choice of imposing taxes on colonies that had been accustomed to answering mainly to their own colonial assemblies. By the 1770s issues of taxation, self-rule, and trade restrictions brought the crisis of imperial authority to a head. Although as late as 1775 most people in the colonies clung to the hope of some kind of accommodation short of outright independence, royal intransigence soon thrust the colonists into a war of independence that neither antagonist could have anticipated just a few years before.

Eight years of revolutionary war did more than anything in the colonial past to bring Americans together as a nation. Comradeship in arms and the struggle to shape a national government forced Americans to subdue their differences as best they could. But the spirit of national unity was hardly universal. One in five colonists sided with the British as "Loyalists," and a generation would pass before the wounds of this first American "civil war" fully healed. Yet in the end, Americans won the Revolution, with no small measure of help from the French, because in every colony people shared a firm belief that they were fighting for the "unalienable rights" of "life, liberty, and the pursuit of happiness," in the words of Thomas Jefferson's magnificent Declaration of Independence. Almost two hundred years of living a new life had prepared Americans to found a new nation.

What if...?

- What if France had won the French and Indian War and maintained its colonial power in Canada and the land west of the Appalachians?

- Would Britain's American colonies still have protested taxes and declared their independence?

Chapter 1

New World Beginnings

33,000 B.C.E.–1769 C.E.

I have come to believe that this is a mighty continent which was hitherto unknown.... Your Highnesses have an Other World here.

CHRISTOPHER COLUMBUS, 1498

Chapter Outline

- The Geology of the New World
- Native Americans Before Columbus
- Europeans and Africans
- The Ecological Consequences of Columbus's Discovery
- Spain Builds a New World Empire
- *Examining the Evidence: Making Sense of the New World*
- *Makers of America: The Spanish Conquistadores*

About six thousand years ago—only a minute in geological time—recorded history began among certain peoples of the ancient Middle East who developed a written culture. Just five hundred years ago—only a few seconds figuratively speaking—European explorers stumbled on the Americas. This dramatic accident forever altered the future of both the Old World and the New, and of Africa and Asia as well.

FOCUS QUESTIONS

1. What geological, geographical, and climatic conditions set the stage for human history in America?
2. What were the primary features of the diverse Indian cultures of the Americas, and how did those features change over time?
3. What developments in European and global history paved the way for Columbus's voyage and the subsequent collision of "two worlds"?
4. How did the mutual interaction of Indians, Europeans, and Africans shape a genuinely new biological, cultural, and economic world in the Americas?
5. How did Spain's conquest of the great Indian civilizations of Mexico and South America shape the essential features of its vast New World empire?

CHRONOLOGY

ca. 33,000–8000 B.C.E.	First humans cross over to the Americas from Asia
ca. 5000 B.C.E.	Corn is developed as a staple crop in highland Mexico
ca. 4000 B.C.E.	First civilized societies develop in the Middle East
ca. 2000 B.C.E.	Corn planting reaches present-day American Southwest
ca. 1000 C.E.	Norse voyagers discover and briefly settle in northeastern North America
	Corn cultivation reaches Midwest and southeastern Atlantic seaboard
ca. 1100 C.E.	Height of Mississippian settlement at Cahokia
ca. 1100–1300 C.E.	Christian crusades arouse European interest in the East
1295	Marco Polo returns to Europe
late 1400s	Spain becomes united
1488	Días rounds southern tip of Africa
1492	Columbus lands in the Bahamas
1494	Treaty of Tordesillas between Spain and Portugal
1498	Da Gama reaches India
	Cabot explores northeastern coast of North America for England
1513	Balboa claims all lands touched by the Pacific Ocean for Spain
1513, 1521	Ponce de León explores Florida
1519–1521	Cortés conquers Mexico for Spain
1524	Verrazano explores eastern seaboard of North America for France
1532	Pizarro crushes Incas
1534	Cartier journeys up the St. Lawrence River
1539–1542	De Soto explores the Southeast and discovers the Mississippi River
1540–1542	Coronado explores present-day Southwest
1542	Cabrillo explores California coast for Spain
1565	Spanish build fortress at St. Augustine
late 1500s	Iroquois Confederacy founded, according to Iroquois legend
ca. 1598–1609	Spanish under Oñate conquer Pueblo peoples of Rio Grande Valley
1609	Spanish found New Mexico
1680	Popé's Rebellion in New Mexico
1680s	French expedition down Mississippi River under La Salle
1769	Serra founds first California mission, at San Diego

★ The Shaping of North America

Planet Earth took on its present form slowly. Some 225 million years ago, a single supercontinent contained all of the world's dry land. Then enormous chunks of terrain began to drift away from this colossal continent, opening the Atlantic and Indian Oceans, narrowing the Pacific Ocean, and forming the great landmasses of Eurasia, Africa, Australia, Antarctica, and the Americas.

Continued shifting and folding of the earth's crust thrust up mountain ranges. The Appalachians were probably formed even before continental separation, perhaps 350 million years ago. The majestic ranges of western North America—the Rockies, the Sierra Nevada, the Cascades, and the Coast Ranges—arose much more recently, geologically speaking, some 135 million to 25 million years ago.

By about 10 million years ago, nature had sculpted the basic geological shape of North America. The continent was anchored in its northeastern corner by the massive **Canadian Shield**—a zone undergirded by ancient rock, probably the first part of what became the North American landmass to have emerged above sea level. A narrow eastern coastal plain, or "tidewater" region, creased by many valleys, sloped gently upward to the

Canadian Shield *First part of the North American landmass to emerge above sea level.*

timeworn ridges of the Appalachians. Those ancient mountains slanted away on their western side into the huge midcontinental basin that rolled downward to the Mississippi Valley bottom and then rose relentlessly to the towering peaks of the Rockies. From the Rocky Mountain crest—the "roof of America"—the land fell off jaggedly into the intermountain Great Basin, bounded by the Rockies on the east and the Sierra and Cascade ranges on the west. The valleys of the Sacramento and San Joaquin rivers and the Willamette–Puget Sound trough seamed the interiors of present-day California, Oregon, and Washington. The land at last met the foaming Pacific, where the Coast Ranges rose steeply from the sea.

Beginning about 2 million years ago, two-mile-thick ice sheets crept across much of northern Europe, Asia, and the Americas. In North America, the glaciers spread as far southward as a line stretching from Pennsylvania through the Ohio country and the Dakotas to the Pacific Northwest.

When the glaciers finally retreated about ten thousand years ago, they left the North American landscape transformed and much as we know it today. The grinding and flushing action of the moving and melting ice pitted the rocky surface of the Canadian Shield with thousands of shallow depressions, into which the melting glaciers flowed to form lakes. The same glacial action scooped out and filled the Great Lakes. The Great Lakes eventually found an outlet to the Atlantic Ocean through the St. Lawrence River. The rest of the enormous midcontinental basin between the Appalachians and the Rockies was left to be drained by the Missouri–Mississippi–Ohio river system that emptied into the Gulf of Mexico.

Similarly, in the West, water from the melting glaciers filled sprawling Lake Bonneville, covering much of present-day Utah, Nevada, and Idaho. Eventually deprived of both inflow and drainage as the glaciers retreated, the giant lake became a shrinking inland sea. The lake grew increasingly saline, slowly evaporated, and left an arid, mineral-rich desert, with only the Great Salt Lake as a relic of its former vastness. Today Lake Bonneville's ancient beaches are visible on mountainsides up to one thousand feet above the dry floor of the Great Basin.

★ Peopling the Americas

The Great Ice Age shaped more than the geological history of North America. It also contributed to the origins of the continent's human history. Some thirty-five thousand years ago, the Ice Age congealed much of the world's oceans into massive ice-pack glaciers, lowering the level of the sea. As the sea level dropped, it exposed a land bridge connecting Eurasia with North America. Across that bridge, spanning the present-day Bering Sea between Siberia and Alaska, ventured small bands of nomadic Asian hunters—the "immigrant" ancestors of the Native Americans. They continued to trek across the Bering isthmus for some 250 centuries, slowly peopling the American continents (see Map 1.1).

As the Ice Age ended and the glaciers melted, the sea level rose again, inundating the land bridge about ten thousand years ago. Nature thus barred the door to further immigration for many thousands of years, leaving this part of the human family to develop its separate existence on the American continents.

Time did not stand still for these original Americans. Roaming slowly through this awesome wilderness, they eventually reached the far tip of South America, some fifteen thousand miles from Siberia. By the time the Europeans arrived in America in 1492, perhaps 54 million people inhabited the two American continents. Over the centuries, they split into countless tribes, evolved more than two thousand separate languages, and developed many diverse religions, cultures, and ways of life.

Incas in Peru, Mayans in Central America, and **Aztecs** in Mexico shaped stunningly sophisticated civilizations. Their advanced agricultural practices, based primarily on the cultivation of maize (Indian corn), fed large populations, perhaps as many as 20 million in Mexico alone. Though lacking technologies such as the wheel, these peoples built elaborate cities and carried on far-flung commerce. Talented mathematicians, they made strikingly accurate astronomical observations. The Aztecs also sought the favor of their gods by offering human sacrifices, cutting the hearts out of the chests of living victims who were often captives conquered in battle.

Incas *Highly advanced South American civilization that occupied present-day Peru until it was conquered by Spanish forces under Francisco Pizarro in 1532. The Incas developed sophisticated agricultural techniques, such as terrace farming, in order to sustain large, complex societies in the unforgiving Andes Mountains.*

Aztecs *Native American empire that controlled present-day Mexico until 1521, when they were conquered by Spanish Hernán Cortés. The Aztecs maintained control over their vast empire through a system of trade and tribute. They came to be known for their advances in mathematics and writing and their use of human sacrifices in religious ceremonies.*

Map 1.1 The First Discoverers of America The origins of the first Americans remain something of a mystery. According to the most plausible theory of how the Americas were populated, for some twenty-five thousand years, people crossed the Bering Strait land bridge from Eurasia to North America. Gradually, the first Americans dispersed southward down ice-free valleys, populating both of the American continents.

⭐ The Earliest Americans

Agriculture, especially corn growing, accounted for the size and sophistication of the Native American civilizations in Mexico and South America. About 5000 B.C.E. hunter-gatherers in highland Mexico developed a wild grass into the staple of corn, which became the foundation of the complex, large-scale, centralized Aztec and Incan civilizations. As cultivation of corn spread across the Americas from the Mexican heartland, it transformed some nomadic hunting bands into settled agricultural villagers.

Corn planting reached the present-day American Southwest as early as 2000 B.C.E. and powerfully molded Pueblo culture. The Pueblo peoples in the Rio Grande Valley constructed intricate irrigation systems to water their cornfields, and they built villages of terraced, multistory buildings. Corn cultivation reached other parts of North America considerably later, and the timing of its arrival explains much about the relative rates of development of different Native American peoples (see Map 1.2). North and east of the Pueblos, elaborately developed "societies," in the modern sense of the word, scarcely existed. The lack of dense concentrations of population or complex **nation-states** comparable to the Aztec empire was one reason for the relative ease with which the European colonizers subdued the native North Americans.

The Mound Builders of the Ohio River valley, the Mississippian culture of the lower Midwest, and the desert-dwelling Anasazi peoples of the Southwest did sustain some large settlements after the incorporation of corn planting into their way of life during the first millennium C.E. The Mississippian settlement at **Cahokia**, near present-day East St. Louis, Illinois, was at one time home to as many as twenty-thousand people. The Anasazis built an elaborate pueblo of more than six hundred interconnected rooms in Chaco Canyon in modern-day New Mexico. But mysteriously, perhaps due to prolonged drought, all those ancient cultures fell into decline by about 1300 C.E.

nation-states *The form of political society that traditionally combines centralized government with a high degree of ethnic and cultural unity.*

Cahokia (ca. 1100 C.E.) *Mississippian settlement near present-day East St. Louis, home to as many as twenty-five thousand Native Americans.*

Cahokia Houses and mounds dot the landscape in an artist's rendering of ancient Cahokia circa 1150, when its population of twenty thousand exceeded London's.

Examining the Evidence

Making Sense of the New World

This map from 1546 by Sebastian Münster represents one of the earliest efforts to make geographic sense out of the New World (*Nouus Orbis* and *Die Nüw Welt* on the map). The very phrase New World suggests just how staggering a blow to the European imagination was the discovery of the Americas. Europeans reached instinctively for the most expansive of all possible terms—*world*, not simply *places*, or even *continents*—to comprehend Columbus's startling report that lands and peoples previously unimagined lay beyond the horizon of Europe's western sea.

Gradually, the immense implications of the New World's existence began to impress themselves on Europe, with consequences for literature, art, politics, the economy, and, of course, cartography. Maps can only be *representations* of reality and are therefore necessarily distortions. This map bears a recognizable resemblance to modern mapmakers' renderings of the American continents, but it also contains gross geographic inaccuracies (note the location of Japan—*Zipangri*—relative to the North American west coast) as well as telling commentaries on what sixteenth-century Europeans found remarkable (note the Land of Giants—*Regio Gigantum*—and the indication of cannibals—*Canibali*—in present-day Argentina and Brazil, respectively).

1. What further clues to the European mentality of the time does the map offer? In what ways might misconceptions about the geography of the Americas have influenced further exploration and settlement patterns?

2. Which portions of "New World" geography were somewhat accurately mapped by European cartographers in 1546? Which were almost completely distorted? Why?

3. Notice the closeness of *Zipangri* (Japan) and India to the North American west coast on the map. What does this tell you about why Europeans vigorously continued to seek a "western route to the Indies" half a century after Columbus stumbled upon the Americas?

4. Look closely at the very small illustration of *Canibali* (cannibals) located on the map in today's South America. What does it reveal about Europeans' views of Native Americans?

Map 1.2 North American Indian Peoples at the Time of First Contact with Europeans Because this map depicts the location of various Native American peoples *at the time of their first contact with Europeans*, and because initial contacts ranged from the sixteenth to the nineteenth centuries, it is necessarily subject to considerable chronological skewing and is only a crude approximation of the "original" territory of any given group. The map also cannot capture the fluidity and dynamism of Native American life even before Columbus's "discovery." For example, the Navajo and Apache peoples had migrated from present-day northern Canada only shortly before the Spanish first encountered them in the present-day American Southwest in the 1500s. The map also places the Sioux on the Great Plains, where Europeans met up with them in the early nineteenth century—but the Sioux had spilled onto the Plains not long before then from the forests surrounding the Great Lakes. The indigenous populations of the southeastern and mid-Atlantic regions are especially difficult to represent accurately in a map like this because pre-Columbian intertribal conflicts had so scrambled the native inhabitants that it is virtually impossible to determine which groups were originally where.

Maize cultivation, as well as the cultivation of high-yielding strains of beans and squash, reached the southeastern Atlantic seaboard region of North America about 1000 C.E. The rich diet provided by these three crops produced some of the highest population densities on the continent, among them the Creek, Choctaw, and Cherokee peoples. In the northeastern woodlands, the Iroquois, inspired by their legendary leader Hiawatha, created in the sixteenth century perhaps the closest North American approximation to the great nation-states of Mexico and Peru. The Iroquois Confederacy developed the political and organizational skills to sustain a robust military alliance that menaced its neighbors, Native American and European alike, for well over a century (see "Makers of America: The Iroquois," p. 30).

But for the most part, the native peoples of North America were living in scattered and impermanent settlements on the eve of the Europeans' arrival. In more settled agricultural groups, women tended the crops while men hunted, fished, gathered fuel, and cleared fields for planting. This pattern of life frequently conferred substantial authority on women, and many North American native peoples, including the Iroquois, developed matrilinear cultures, in which power and possessions passed down the female side of the family line.

Unlike the Europeans, who would soon arrive with the presumption that humans had dominion over the earth and with the technologies to alter the very face of the land, Native Americans had neither the desire nor the means to manipulate nature aggressively. They revered the physical world and endowed nature with spiritual properties. Yet they did sometimes ignite massive forest fires, deliberately torching trees to create better hunting habitats, especially for deer. This practice accounted for the open, parklike appearance of the eastern woodlands, which so amazed early European explorers.

But in a broad sense, Native Americans did not lay a heavy hand upon the land, partly because they were so few in number. In the fateful year 1492, probably no more than 4 million Native Americans padded through the whispering, primeval forests and paddled across the sparkling, virgin waters of North America. The Native Americans were blissfully unaware that the historic isolation of the Americas was about to end forever, as both the land and the native peoples alike felt the full shock of the European "discovery."

★ Indirect Discoverers of the New World

Europeans were equally unaware of the existence of the Americas. Blond-bearded Norse seafarers from Scandinavia chanced upon northeastern North America about 1000 C.E., and briefly settled in a place they called Vinland, near L'Anse aux Meadows in present-day Newfoundland. But no strong nation-state, yearning to expand, supported these venturesome voyagers. Their flimsy settlements consequently were soon abandoned, and their discovery was forgotten, except in Scandinavian saga and song.

For several centuries thereafter, other restless Europeans, with the growing power of ambitious governments behind them, sought contact with a wider world, whether for conquest or trade. They thus set in motion the chain of events that led to a drive toward Asia, the exploitation of Africa, and the completely accidental discovery of the New World.

Christian crusaders of the eleventh to the fourteenth centuries rank high among America's indirect discoverers. Though ultimately foiled in their attempts to wrest the Holy Land from Muslim control, the crusaders nevertheless acquired a taste for the exotic delights of Asia—silk for clothing, drugs for aching flesh, perfumes for unbathed bodies, colorful draperies for gloomy castles, and sugar and spices for preserving and flavoring food. The Italian adventurer Marco Polo further whetted European appetites for Asian luxury goods when he returned from China in 1295 telling tales of its golden pagodas and rose-tinted pearls.

But the distance and difficulties of transportation, for which Muslim and Italian **middlemen** charged dearly, made European consumers and distributors eager to find a less expensive route to the riches of Asia (see Map 1.3). Their hopes for an ocean route to Asia were long frustrated. Before the mid-fifteenth century, European sailors refused to sail southward along the coast of West Africa because they could not beat their way home again against the prevailing northerly winds and south-flowing currents.

middlemen In trading systems, those dealers who operate between the original producers of goods and the retail merchants who sell to consumers.

12 CHAPTER 1

Map 1.3 **The World Known to Europe and Major Trade Routes with Asia, 1492** Goods on the early routes passed through so many hands along the way that their ultimate sources remained mysterious to Europeans.

★ Europeans Enter Africa

caravel *Small, regular vessel with a high deck and three triangular sails. Caravels could sail more closely into the wind, allowing European sailors to explore the Western shores of Africa, previously made inaccessible due to prevailing winds on the homeward journey.*

About 1450, Portuguese mariners overcame these obstacles by developing the **caravel**, a ship that could sail more closely into the wind. They also learned that they could return to Europe by sailing northwesterly from the African coast toward the Azores islands, where the prevailing westward breezes would carry them home.

The new world of sub-Saharan Africa, previously remote and mysterious to Europeans, now came within their questing grasp. African gold, perhaps two-thirds of Europe's supply, crossed the Sahara on camelback, and tales may have reached Europe about the flourishing West African kingdom of Mali in the Niger River valley, with its impressive Islamic university at Timbuktu. But Europeans had no direct access to sub-Saharan Africa until Portuguese navigators began to creep down the West African coast in the mid-fifteenth century.

The Portuguese promptly set up trading posts along the African shore for the purchase of gold—and slaves. Arab and African merchants had traded slaves for centuries before the Europeans arrived. African slave traders routinely charged higher prices for captives from distant sources, because the newly enslaved could not easily flee to their native villages. Slave brokers also deliberately separated people from the same tribes to frustrate organized resistance.

plantation(s) *Large-scale agricultural enterprise growing commercial crops, historically often employing coerced or slave labor. European settlers established plantations in Africa, South America, the Caribbean, and the American South.*

The Portuguese adopted these Arab and African practices on the sugar **plantations** that they, and later the Spanish, established on the African coastal islands of Madeira, the Canaries, São Tomé, and Principe. The Portuguese appetite for slaves was enormous, and slave trading became big business. Some forty thousand Africans were carried away to the Atlantic sugar islands in the last half of the fifteenth century. Millions more were to be wrenched from their home continent after the discovery of the Americas. In these fifteenth-century Portuguese adventures in Africa were to be found the origins of the modern plantation system, based on large-scale commercial agriculture and the wholesale exploitation of slave labor. This kind of plantation economy would shape the destiny of much of the New World.

After years of cautious exploration down the African coast, the Portuguese mariner Bartholomeu Días rounded the southernmost tip of Africa in 1488. Ten years later Vasco da Gama reached India and returned home with a small but tantalizing cargo of jewels and spices.

Meanwhile, the kingdom of Spain became united in the late fifteenth century as a result of the marriage of two sovereigns, Ferdinand of Aragon and Isabella of Castile. After the brutal expulsion of the Muslim Moors from Spain, the new Spanish nation was eager to outstrip its Portuguese rivals in the race to tap the wealth of the Indies. Because Portugal controlled the round-Africa water route to India, Spain of necessity looked westward.

★ Columbus Comes upon a New World

The stage was now set for a cataclysmic shift in the course of history—the history not only of Europe but of all the world. Europeans clamored for more and cheaper products from the lands beyond the Mediterranean. Africa had been established as a source of abundant slave labor for plantation agriculture. The Portuguese voyages had demonstrated the feasibility of long-range ocean navigation. In Spain a modern national state was taking shape, with the unity, wealth, and power to shoulder the formidable tasks of discovery, conquest, and colonization. The dawn of the Renaissance in the fourteenth century nurtured an ambitious spirit of optimism and adventure. Printing presses, introduced about 1450, facilitated the spread of scientific knowledge. The mariner's compass, possibly borrowed from the Arabs, eliminated some of the uncertainties of sea travel.

Onto this stage stepped Christopher Columbus. This skilled Italian seafarer persuaded the Spanish monarchs to outfit him with three tiny but seaworthy ships. Columbus sailed westward into the oceanic unknown, and after six weeks at sea his fearful sailors grew increasingly mutinous. But on October 12, 1492, the crew sighted an island in the Bahamas. This was Europeans' first glimpse of a vast new world, previously unknown to them.

But only gradually did Europeans realize that Columbus had in fact bumped into enormous new continents. For decades explorers tried to get through or around the "islands" that they assumed blocked the ocean pathway to East Asia. Columbus himself was at first so certain that he had skirted the rim of the "Indies" that he called the native peoples "Indians," a gross geographical misnomer that somehow stuck.

Columbus's discovery would eventually convulse four continents—Europe, Africa, and the two Americas. Thanks to his epochal voyage, an interdependent global economic system emerged on a scale undreamed of before he set sail. The system's workings touched every shore washed by the Atlantic Ocean. Europe provided the markets, the capital, and the technology; Africa furnished the labor; and the New World offered its raw materials, especially its precious metals and its soil for the cultivation of sugar cane. For Europeans as well as for Africans and Native Americans, the world after 1492 would never be the same, for better or worse.

★ When Worlds Collide

Two ecosystems—the fragile, naturally evolved networks of relations among organisms in a stable environment—commingled and clashed when Columbus waded ashore. The reverberations from that historic encounter—often called the **Columbian exchange**—echoed for centuries after 1492. The flora and fauna of the Old and New Worlds had been separated for thousands of years. European explorers marveled at the strange sights that greeted them, including exotic beasts such as iguanas and "snakes with castanets" (rattlesnakes). Native, New World plants such as tobacco, maize, beans, tomatoes, and especially the lowly potato eventually revolutionized the international economy and fed the rapid population growth of

Columbian exchange *The transfer of goods, crops, and diseases between New and Old World societies after 1492.*

Contending Voices

Europeans and Indians

In 1550–1551, two renowned scholars in Valladolid, Spain, formally debated whether the native peoples of the New World were "true men," capable of governing themselves and becoming Christians. Juan Ginés de Sepulveda (1489–1573), who had never seen the New World, believed that:

"The Spanish have a perfect right to rule these barbarians of the New World and the adjacent islands, who in prudence, skill, virtues, and humanity are as inferior to the Spanish as children to adults, or women to men, for there exists between the two as great a difference as between . . . apes and men."

The Dominican friar Bartolomé de Las Casas (1484–1566), who had long labored among the Indians, replied:

"I call the Spaniards who plunder that unhappy people torturers. . . . The Indians are our brothers, and Christ has given his life for them. Why, then, do we persecute them with such inhuman savagery when they do not deserve such treatment?"

> To what extent did attitudes like those persist over the next several centuries?

---

the Old World. These foodstuffs were among the most important Indian gifts to the Europeans and the rest of the world. Ironically, the introduction into Africa of New World foodstuffs such as maize, manioc, and sweet potatoes may have fed an African population boom that numerically, though not morally, more than offset the losses inflicted by the slave trade.

In exchange the Europeans introduced Old World crops and animals, such as cattle and horses, to the Americas. Horses reached the North American mainland through Mexico. North American tribes such as the Apaches, Sioux, and Blackfoot swiftly adopted the horse, transforming their cultures into highly mobile, wide-ranging hunter societies that pursued the shaggy buffalo across the grassy Great Plains. Columbus also brought sugar cane to the Americas. Thriving in the warm Caribbean climate, this crop prompted a "sugar revolution" in the European diet that fueled the forced migration of millions of Africans to work the cane fields and sugar mills of the New World.

Unwittingly, the Europeans also brought in their bodies the germs that caused smallpox, yellow fever, and malaria—diseases that quickly devastated the Native Americans. During the Indians' millennia of separate existence in the Americas, most of the Old World's killer maladies had disappeared from among them. But generations of freedom from those illnesses had also wiped out protective antibodies. Devoid of natural resistance to Old World sicknesses, Indians died in droves. Within fifty years of the Spanish arrival, the population of the Taino natives on the Caribbean island of Hispaniola (present-day Haiti and the Dominican Republic) dwindled from some 1 million people to about 200. The lethal germs spread among New World peoples with the speed and force of a hurricane, swiftly sweeping far ahead of the human invaders; most of those afflicted never laid eyes on a European. In the centuries after Columbus's landfall, as many as 90 percent of Native Americans perished, a demographic catastrophe without parallel in human history. Depopulation was so severe that entire cultures and ancient ways of life were extinguished forever. Perhaps it was poetic justice that the Indians unintentionally infected the early explorers with syphilis, injecting that lethal, sexually transmitted disease for the first time into Europe.

★ The Spanish Conquistadores

Gradually, Europeans realized that the American continents held rich prizes, especially the gold and silver of the advanced civilizations in Mexico and Peru. Spain secured its claim to Columbus's discoveries in the **Treaty of Tordesillas** (1494), dividing with Portugal the "heathen lands" of the New World (see Map 1.4).

Spain became the dominant exploring and colonizing power of the 1500s. Seeking both the glitter of gold and the glory of God, Spanish *conquistadores* (conquerors) fanned out across the Caribbean and eventually onto the mainland of the American continents (see "Makers of America: The Spanish *Conquistadores*, p. 16"). Some early explorers, among them Ponce de León, Coronado, and de Soto, ventured into territory that eventually became part of the United States. But the permanent Spanish conquests of Peru and Mexico were by far the most consequential achievements of the *conquistadores*.

Treaty of Tordesillas (1494) Signed by Spain and Portugal, dividing the territories of the New World. Spain received the bulk of territory in the Americas, compensating Portugal with titles to lands in Africa and Asia.

conquistadores Sixteenth-century Spanish military adventurers who fanned out across the Americas, from Colorado to Argentina, and eventually conquered the Aztec and Incan empires.

Map 1.4 Principal Voyages of Discovery Spain, Portugal, France, and England reaped the greatest advantages from the New World, but much of the earliest exploration was done by Italians, notably Christopher Columbus of Genoa. John Cabot, another native of Genoa (his original name was Giovanni Caboto), sailed for England's King Henry VII. Giovanni da Verrazano was a Florentine employed by France.

In South America, the ironfisted conqueror Francisco Pizarro crushed the Incas of Peru in 1532 and added a huge horde of booty, especially silver, to Spanish coffers. This flood of precious metal touched off a price revolution in Europe that increased consumer costs by as much as 500 percent in the hundred years after the mid-sixteenth century. Some scholars see in this ballooning European money supply the fuel that fed the growth of the economic system known as **capitalism**.

The islands of the Caribbean Sea—the West Indies—served as offshore bases where supplies could be stored and men and horses rested for the Spanish invasion of the mainland Americas. The vulnerable native communities of the West Indies also provided laboratories for testing the techniques that would eventually subdue Mexico and Peru. Most important was the institution of the *encomienda*, which allowed the government to "commend," or give, Indians to certain colonists in return for the promise to try to Christianize them. It was slavery in all but name, and the Spanish missionary Bartolome de Las Casas called it "a moral pestilence invented by Satan."

★ The Conquest of Mexico

The conquest of Mexico was engineered by Hernán Cortés, who set sail from Cuba in 1519 with sixteen horses and several hundred men. From an island near the coast of Mexico, he picked up a female Indian slave named Malinche, who knew both Mayan and Nahuatl,

capitalism Economic system characterized by private property, generally free trade, and open and accessible markets. European colonization of the Americas, and in particular, the discovery of vast bullion deposits, helped bring about Europe's transition to capitalism.

encomienda Spanish government's policy to "commend," or give, Indians to certain colonists in return for the promise to Christianize them. Part of a broader Spanish effort to subdue Indian tribes in the West Indies and on the North American mainland.

Makers of America

The Spanish Conquistadores

In 1492, the same year that Columbus sighted America, the great Moorish city of Grenada fell after a ten-year siege. For five centuries, the Christian kingdoms of Spain had tried to drive the North African Muslim Moors off the Iberian peninsula, and with the fall of Grenada this "Reconquista" succeeded. Centuries of religious war nurtured an obsession with status and honor, bred religious zealotry and intolerance, and created a large class of men who regarded manual labor and commerce contemptuously. With the *Reconquista* ended, some of these men turned their restless gaze to Spain's New World frontier.

Between 1519 and 1540, Spanish *conquistadores* swept across the Americas in two wide arcs of conquest—one driving from Cuba through Mexico into what is now the southwestern United States, the other pushing south into Peru from Panama, previously conquered by Vasco Balboa, who had also claimed all the lands touched by the Pacific Ocean for Spain. The military conquest of this vast region of the Americas was achieved by just ten thousand men, organized in a series of private expeditions. Hernán Cortés, Francisco Pizarro, and other aspiring conquerors signed contracts with the Spanish monarch, raised money from investors, and then proceeded to recruit private armies. Only a minority of the *conquistadores* were nobles. About half were professional soldiers or sailors; the rest comprised peasants, artisans, and members of the middle classes. Most were in their twenties and early thirties.

Some of these motley adventurers hoped to win royal titles or favors. Others sought to ensure God's favor by spreading Christianity to the pagans. Some men aspired to escape dubious pasts, while others sought the kind of historical adventure experienced by heroes of classical antiquity. Nearly all shared a lust for gold.

But most of these adventurers never achieved their dreams of glory or riches. Even when an expedition captured exceptionally rich booty, the spoils were unevenly divided: men from the commander's home region often received more, and men on horseback generally got two shares to the infantryman's one. The *conquistadores* lost still more power as the crown tightened its control in the New World. By the 1550s, the day of the *conquistador* had ended.

Nevertheless, the *conquistadores* achieved a kind of immortality. Because of a scarcity of Spanish women in the early days of the conquest, many *conquistadores* married Native American women. Their offspring, the *mestizos*, formed a cultural and biological bridge between Latin America's European and Indian peoples.

An Aztec View of the Conquest, 1531 Produced just a dozen years after Cortés's arrival in 1519, this drawing by an Aztec artist pictures his people rendering tribute to their conquerors. The inclusion of the banner showing Madonna and child also illustrates the early incorporation of Christian beliefs by the Native Americans.

the language of the powerful Aztecs. From Malinche, who learned Spanish and took the Spanish name of Doña Marina, Cortés learned of the unrest among subordinate peoples within the Aztec empire and of the gold and other wealth in its capital of Tenochtitlán. "We Spanish suffer from a strange disease of the heart," Cortés allegedly informed emissaries of the Aztec ruler Moctezuma, "for which the only known remedy is gold." The ambassadors reported this comment to Moctezuma, along with the astonishing fact that the newcomers rode on the backs of "deer" (horses). Believing that Cortés was the god Quetzalcoatl, whose return from the eastern sea was predicted in Aztec legends, Moctezuma allowed the *conquistadores* to approach his capital unopposed.

Bartolomé de Las Casas (1474–1566), a reform-minded Dominican friar, wrote The Destruction of the Indies *in 1542 to chronicle the awful fate of the Native Americans and to protest Spanish policies in the New World. He was especially horrified at the catastrophic effects of disease on the native peoples:*

"Who of those in future centuries will believe this? I myself who am writing this and saw it and know the most about it can hardly believe that such was possible."

The Spaniards were amazed by the beauty and wealth of Tenochtitlán, with its 300,000 inhabitants and marvelous temples, aqueducts, and floating gardens. Moctezuma treated Cortés hospitably at first, but soon the Spanish were unable to contain their lust for gold. After warfare broke out on the **noche triste** (sad night) of June 30, 1520, Cortés laid siege to the city, which capitulated on August 13, 1521.

The Aztec empire thus gave way to three centuries of Spanish rule. Its people suffered not only from the armed conquest but from smallpox and other epidemics that burned through the Valley of Mexico. The temples of Tenochtitlán were destroyed to make way for the Christian cathedrals of Mexico City, built on the site of the ruined Aztec capital. The native population of Mexico shrank from some 20 million to 2 million people in less than a century.

Yet despite the destruction, the invader brought more than conquest and death. He brought his language, laws, customs, and religion, all of which proved adaptable to the peoples of Mexico. He intermarried with the surviving Indians, creating a distinctive culture of **mestizos**, people of mixed Indian and European heritage. To this day Mexican

noche triste (June 30, 1520) *"Sad night," when the Aztecs attacked Hernán Cortés and his forces in the Aztec capital, Tenochtitlán, killing hundreds. Cortés laid siege to the city the following year, precipitating the fall of the Aztec empire and inaugurating three centuries of Spanish rule.*

mestizos *People of mixed Indian and European heritage, notably in Mexico.*

Arrival of Cortés, with Doña Marina, at Tenochtitlán in 1519 This painting by a Mexican artist depicts Cortés in the dress of a Spanish gentleman. His translator Malinche, whose Christian name was Marina, is given an honorable place at the front of the procession. She eventually married one of Cortés's soldiers, with whom she traveled to Spain and was received by the Spanish court.

Conquistadores, ca. 1534 This illustration for a book called the *Köhler Codes of Nuremberg* may be the earliest depiction of the *conquistadores* in the Americas. It portrays men and horses alike as steadfast and self-assured in their work of conquest.

civilization remains a unique blend of the Old World and the New, producing both ambivalence and pride among people of Mexican heritage. Cortés's translator Malinche, for example, has given her name to the Mexican language in the word *malinchista*, or "traitor." But Mexicans also celebrate Columbus Day as the *Dia de la Raza*—the birthday of a wholly new race of people.

★ The Spread of Spanish America

Spain's colonial empire grew swiftly and impressively. Within about half a century of Columbus's landfall, hundreds of Spanish-controlled cities and towns flourished in the Americas. Majestic cathedrals dotted the land, printing presses turned out books, and scholars studied at distinguished universities, including those at Mexico City and Lima, Peru, both founded in 1551, eighty-five years before Harvard, the first college established in the English colonies.

But how secure were these imperial possessions? Other powers were already sniffing around the edges of the Spanish domain, eager to bite off their share of the promised wealth of the new lands. The upstart English sent Giovanni Caboto (known in English as John Cabot) to explore the northeastern coast of North America in 1497 and 1498. The French king dispatched Giovanni da Verrazano to probe the eastern seaboard in 1524 and Jacques Cartier to explore the St. Lawrence River in 1534. To protect sea lanes and secure their northern borderlands against such encroachments, the Spanish erected a fortress at St. Augustine, Florida, in 1565, thus founding the oldest continually inhabited European settlement in the future United States.

The tales of Francisco Coronado's expedition of the 1540s beckoned *conquistadores* northward from Mexico into the Rio Grande and Colorado River regions. A Spanish expedition led by Don Juan de Oñate entered the Rio Grande Valley in 1598 and cruelly abused the Pueblo peoples they encountered. In the **Battle of Acoma** in 1599, the Spanish severed

Battle of Acoma (1599) *Fought between Spaniards under Don Juan de Oñate and the Pueblo Indians in present-day New Mexico. Spaniards brutally crushed the Pueblo peoples and established the territory as New Mexico in 1609.*

one foot of each survivor. They proclaimed the area to be the province of New Mexico in 1609 and founded its capital at Santa Fe the following year. The Spanish settlers found precious little gold, but Catholic missionaries did discover a wealth of souls to be harvested for their faith. The efforts of the Spanish settlers to suppress Pueblo religious customs provoked an Indian uprising called **Popé's Rebellion** in 1680. The Pueblo rebels destroyed every Catholic church in the province and killed a score of priests and hundreds of Spanish settlers. It took nearly half a century for the Spanish to reclaim New Mexico from the insurrectionary Indians.

Popé's Rebellion (1680) *Pueblo Indian rebellion that drove Spanish settlers from New Mexico.*

Meanwhile, as a further hedge against the ever-threatening French, who had sent an expedition under Robert La Salle down the Mississippi River in the 1680s, the Spanish began around 1716 to establish a few settlements and missions in Texas, including the one at San Antonio later known as the Alamo. To the west, in California, no serious foreign threat loomed, and Spain directed its attention there only belatedly. Juan Rodriguez Cabrillo had explored the California coast in 1542, but for some two centuries thereafter California slumbered undisturbed by European intruders.

Then in 1769, Spanish missionaries led by Father Junipero Serra founded in San Diego the first of a chain of twenty-one missions that wound up the coast as far as Sonoma, north of San Francisco Bay. Father Serra's brown-robed Franciscan friars toiled with zealous devotion to Christianize the 300,000 native Californians and teach them horticulture and crafts. These "mission Indians" did adopt Christianity, but they lost their native cultures and often lost their lives as well, because the white man's diseases doomed many of these biologically vulnerable peoples.

The misdeeds of the Spanish in the New World obscured their substantial achievements and helped give birth to the "**Black Legend**." This false concept held that the conquerors did nothing but torture and butcher the Native Americans, steal their gold, and infect them with deadly smallpox, leaving only misery behind. The Spanish invaders did indeed kill, enslave, and infect countless natives, but they also grafted their culture, laws, religion, and language onto a wide array of native societies, laying the foundations for a score of Spanish-speaking nations.

Black Legend *False notion that Spanish conquerors did little but butcher the Indians and steal their gold in the name of Christ.*

Clearly, the Spanish, who had more than a century's head start over the English, were genuine empire builders and cultural innovators in the New World. Compared with their Anglo-Saxon rivals, their colonial establishment was larger and richer, and it was destined to endure more than a quarter of a century longer. And in the last analysis, the Spanish paid the Native Americans the high compliment of fusing with them through marriage and incorporating indigenous culture into their own, rather than shunning and eventually isolating the Indians as their English adversaries would do.

CHAPTER SUMMARY ★ ★ ★ ★ ★ ★ ★ ★ ★ ★ ★ ★ ★ ★

Millions of years ago, the two American continents became geologically separated from the Eastern Hemisphere landmasses where humanity originated. The first people to enter these continents came across a temporary land bridge from Siberia about 35,000 years ago. Spreading across the two continents, these first people developed a great variety of societies based largely on hunting and corn agriculture. In North America, some ancient peoples such as the Pueblos, the Anasazi, and the Mississippian culture centered in Cahokia developed elaborate settlements. But on the whole, North American Native American societies were less numerous and urbanized than those in Central and South America, though they were equally diverse in culture and social organization.

The impetus for European exploration came from the desire for new trade routes to Asia, the spirit and technological discoveries of the Renaissance, and the power of the new European national monarchies. The European encounters with America and Africa, beginning with the Portuguese and Spanish explorers, convulsed the entire world. Biological change, disease, population loss, conquest, African slavery, cultural change, and economic expansion were just some of the consequences of the commingling of two ecosystems.

After they conquered and then intermarried with Indians of the great civilizations of South America and Mexico, the Spanish *conquistadores* expanded northward into the northern border territories of Florida, New Mexico, Texas, and California that later became part of the United States. There they established small but permanent settlements in competition with the French and English explorers who also were venturing into North America.

KEY TERMS

- Canadian Shield (05)
- Incas (06)
- Aztecs (06)
- nation-states (08)
- Cahokia (08)
- middlemen (11)
- caravel (12)
- plantation (12)
- Columbian exchange (13)
- Treaty of Tordesillas (14)
- conquistadores (14)
- capitalism (15)
- encomienda (15)
- noche triste (17)
- mestizos (17)
- Battle of Acoma (18)
- Popé's Rebellion (19)
- Black Legend (19)

PEOPLE TO KNOW

- Ferdinand of Aragon
- Isabella of Castile
- Christopher Columbus
- Francisco Pizarro
- Bartolome de Las Casas
- Hernán Cortés
- Malinche (Doña Marina)
- Moctezuma
- Giovanni Caboto (John Cabot)
- Francisco Coronado
- Robert La Salle
- Father Junipero Serra

MindTap is a fully online, highly personalized learning experience built upon Cengage Learning content. MindTap combines student learning tools—readings, multimedia, activities, and assessments—into a singular Learning Path that guides students through the course.

Chapter 2

The Planting of English America
1500–1733

. . . For I shall yet live to see it [Virginia] an Inglishe nation.

Sir Walter Raleigh, 1602

Chapter Outline

- England in the Age of Expansion
- The Planting of Jamestown, 1607
- The Growth of Virginia and Maryland
- England in the Caribbean
- Settling the Carolinas and Georgia
- *Makers of America: The Iroquois*

As the seventeenth century dawned, scarcely a hundred years after Columbus's momentous landfall, the face of much of the New World had already been profoundly transformed. European crops and livestock had begun to alter the very landscape, touching off an ecological revolution that would reverberate for centuries to come. From Tierra del Fuego in the south to Hudson's Bay in the north, disease and armed conquest had cruelly winnowed and disrupted the native peoples. Several hundred thousand enslaved Africans toiled on Caribbean and Brazilian sugar plantations. From Florida and New Mexico southward, most of the New World lay firmly in the grip of imperial Spain.

But north of Mexico, North America in 1600 remained largely unexplored and effectively unclaimed by Europeans. Then, as if to herald the coming century of colonization and conflict in the northern continent, three European powers planted primitive outposts in three distant corners of the continent within three years of one another: the Spanish in Santa Fe in 1610, the French at Quebec in 1608, and, most consequentially for the future United States, the English at Jamestown, Virginia, in 1607.

FOCUS QUESTIONS

1. Why did England lag so far behind Spain in its colonization efforts, and what factors finally enabled the English to establish successful colonies?
2. How did the Jamestown colony evolve from its disastrous beginnings into the successful colony of Virginia?
3. What was the relationship between early Virginia settlers and the Powhatan Indians, and how did Indian policies in the southern colonies eventually establish the basis for forced removal and reservations?
4. What was the basis for the economic and labor systems of Virginia and the other southern colonies?
5. What were the fundamental similarities and lesser differences among the five southern colonies of Virginia, Maryland, North Carolina, South Carolina, and Georgia?

CHRONOLOGY

1558	Elizabeth I becomes queen of England
ca. 1565–1590	English crush Irish uprising
1577	Drake circumnavigates the globe
1585	Raleigh founds "lost colony" at Roanoke Island
1588	England defeats Spanish Armada
1603	James I becomes king of England
1607	Virginia colony founded at Jamestown
1612	Rolfe perfects tobacco culture in Virginia
1614	First Anglo-Powhatan War ends
1619	First Africans arrive in Jamestown; Virginia House of Burgesses is established
1624	Virginia becomes royal colony
1634	Maryland colony founded
1640s	Large-scale, slave-labor system established in English West Indies
1644	Second Anglo-Powhatan War
1649	Act of Toleration in Maryland; Charles I beheaded; Cromwell rules England
1660	Charles II restored to English throne
1661	Barbados slave code adopted
1670	Carolina colony created
1711–1713	Tuscarora War in North Carolina
1712	North Carolina formally separates from South Carolina
1715–1716	Yamasee War in South Carolina
1733	Georgia colony founded

★ England's Imperial Stirrings

Feeble indeed were England's efforts in the 1500s to compete with the sprawling Spanish Empire. In the early years of the century, England, then allied with Spain, took little interest in establishing its own overseas colonies. But in the 1530s, King Henry VIII broke with the Roman Catholic Church, launching the English **Protestant Reformation**. After Henry's daughter, the Protestant Elizabeth I, ascended to the English throne in 1558, Protestantism became dominant in England, and rivalry with Catholic Spain intensified.

An early scene of that rivalry was Ireland, where the Catholic Irish sought help from Catholic Spain to throw off the yoke of the new Protestant English queen. In crushing the Irish uprising of the 1570s and 1580s with terrible ferocity, many English soldiers developed a sneering contempt for the "savage" natives, an attitude the English brought with them to the New World.

Encouraged by the ambitious Queen Elizabeth I, hardy English buccaneers now swarmed out upon the shipping lanes to plunder Spanish treasure ships and raid Spanish settlements. The most famous of these semipiratical "sea dogs" was the courtly Francis Drake, who swashbuckled and looted his way around the planet and returned in 1580 laden with Spanish gold.

The first English attempt at colonization, on the bleak coast of Newfoundland, collapsed when its promoter, Sir Humphrey Gilbert, lost his life at sea in 1583. Inspired by Gilbert's ill-starred dream, his gallant half-brother, Sir Walter Raleigh, organized another group of settlers, who landed in 1585 on North Carolina's **Roanoke Island**. But the hapless Roanoke colony mysteriously vanished, swallowed up by the wilderness.

These pathetic English failures at colonization contrasted embarrassingly with the glories of the Spanish Empire, whose profits were fabulously enriching Spain. Philip II of Spain, self-anointed foe of the Protestant Reformation, used part of his imperial gains to amass an "Invincible Armada" of ships for an invasion of England in 1588. But the skillful English sea dogs inflicted heavy damage on the armada, and a devastating storm (the "Protestant wind") scattered the crippled Spanish fleet.

Protestant Reformation *Movement to reform the Catholic Church launched in Germany by Martin Luther. Reformers questioned the authority of the Pope, sought to eliminate the selling of indulgences, and encouraged the translation of the Bible from Latin, which few at the time could read. The Reformation was launched in England in the 1530s when King Henry VIII broke with the Roman Catholic Church.*

Roanoke Island (1585) *Sir Walter Raleigh's failed colonial settlement off the coast of North Carolina.*

The rout of the **Spanish Armada** marked the beginning of the end of Spanish imperial dreams, though Spain's New World empire would not fully collapse for three more centuries. England's victory also started that country on its way to becoming master of the world oceans—a fact of enormous importance to the American people. Indeed, England now possessed many of the characteristics that Spain displayed on the eve of its colonizing adventure a century earlier: a strong, unified nation-state under a popular monarch; a measure of religious unity after a protracted struggle between Protestants and Catholics; and a vibrant sense of nationalism and national destiny.

This new sense of national pride and patriotism blossomed in the Elizabethan golden age of culture and politics. William Shakespeare, who made occasional poetic references to England's American colonies, was only one of many contemporary poets and writers who expressed boundless faith in the future of the English nation.

But England's scepter'd isle, as Shakespeare called it, also throbbed with social and economic tensions as the seventeenth century opened. England's population was mushrooming, from some 3 million people in 1550 to about 4 million in 1600. In the evergreen English countryside, landlords were "enclosing" croplands for sheep grazing, forcing many small farmers into precarious tenancy or off the land altogether. It was no accident that the woolen districts of eastern and western England—where Puritanism had taken strong root—supplied many of the earliest immigrants to America. When economic depression hit the woolen trade in the late 1500s, thousands of unemployed farmers took to the roads, often ending up as beggars and paupers in cities such as Bristol and London.

At the same time, laws of **primogeniture** decreed that only eldest sons were eligible to inherit landed estates. Landholders' ambitious younger sons, among them Gilbert, Raleigh, and Drake, were forced to seek their fortunes elsewhere. Bad luck plagued their early, lone-wolf enterprises. But by the early 1600s, when the **joint-stock company**, forerunner of the modern corporation, was perfected, a considerable number of investors were able to pool their capital.

Spanish Armada *Spanish fleet defeated in the English Channel in 1588. The defeat of the Armada marked the beginning of the decline of the Spanish Empire.*

primogeniture *Legal principle that the oldest son inherits all family property or land. Landowner's younger sons, forced to seek their fortunes elsewhere, pioneered early exploration and settlement of the Americas.*

joint-stock company *Short-term partnership between multiple investors to fund a commercial enterprise; such arrangements were used to fund England's early colonial ventures.*

Elizabeth I (1533–1603), by George Gower, ca. 1588 In this "Armada Portrait" of Queen Elizabeth I, the artist proclaims her the Empress of the World. She was accused of being vain, fickle, prejudiced, and miserly, but Elizabeth proved to be an unusually successful ruler. She never married (hence, the "Virgin Queen"), although many romances were rumored and royal matches schemed.

Contending Voices

Old World Dreams and New World Realities

In the years immediately following the defeat of the Spanish Armada, the English writer Richard Hakluyt (1552?–1616)—a tireless promoter who never set foot in the Americas—extravagantly exhorted his countrymen to cast off their "sluggish security" and undertake the colonization of the New World:

"There is under our noses the great and ample country of Virginia; the inland whereof is found of late to be so sweet and wholesome a climate, so rich and abundant in silver mines, a better and richer country than Mexico itself. If it shall please the Almighty to stir up Her Majesty's heart to continue with transporting one or two thousand of her people, she shall by God's assistance, in short space, increase her dominions, enrich her coffers, and reduce many pagans to the faith of Christ."

A few years later, George Percy (1580–1631) saw Virginia firsthand. He accompanied Captain John Smith on his expedition to Virginia in 1606–1607 and served as deputy governor of the colony in 1609–1610. He returned to England in 1612, where he wrote A Discourse of the Plantation of Virginia *about his experiences:*

"Our men were destroyed with cruel diseases as swellings, burning fevers, and by wars, and some departed suddenly, but for the most part they died of mere famine. There were never Englishmen left in a foreign country in such misery as we were in this new discovered Virginia."

How does one account for the difference in these views—or were both accurate?

Virginia Company English joint-stock company that received a charter from King James I allowing it to found the Virginia colony.

Peace with a chastened Spain provided the opportunity for English colonization. Population growth provided the workers. Unemployment, as well as a thirst for adventure, for markets, and for religious freedom, provided the motives. Joint-stock companies provided the financial means. The stage was set for a historic effort to establish an English beachhead in the still uncharted North American wilderness.

★ England Plants the Jamestown Seedling

In 1606, two years after peace with Spain, the hand of destiny beckoned toward Virginia. A joint-stock company, the **Virginia Company** of London, received a **charter** from King James I for a settlement in the New World. The main attractions were the promise of gold and the desire to find a passage through America to the Indies. Like most joint-stock companies of the day, the Virginia Company was intended to endure for only a few years, after which its stockholders hoped to liquidate it for a profit. This arrangement put severe pressure on the luckless colonists, who were threatened with abandonment in the wilderness if they did not quickly strike it rich on the company's behalf. Few of the investors thought in terms of long-term colonization. Apparently no one even faintly suspected that the seeds of a mighty nation were being planted.

The charter of the Virginia Company is a significant document in American history. It guaranteed to the overseas settlers the same rights of Englishmen that they would have enjoyed if they had stayed at home. This precious boon was gradually extended to the other English colonies, helping to reinforce the colonists' sense that even on the far shore of the Atlantic they remained comfortably within the embrace of traditional English institutions. But ironically, a century and a half later, the colonists' insistence on the "rights of Englishmen" fed their hot resentment against an increasingly meddlesome mother country and nourished their appetite for independence.

Setting sail in late 1606, the Virginia Company's tiny band of colonists eventually landed at a site on the wooded and malarial banks of the James River. There, on May 24, 1607, about a hundred English settlers, all men, disembarked. They called the place **Jamestown** (see Map 2.1).

The early years of Jamestown proved to be a nightmare for all concerned—except the buzzards. Once ashore, the settlers died by the dozens from disease, malnutrition, and starvation. The woods rustled with game, and the rivers flopped with fish, but the greenhorn settlers, many of them self-styled "gentlemen" unaccustomed to fending for themselves, wasted valuable time grubbing for nonexistent gold when they should have been gathering provisions.

Virginia was saved from utter collapse at the start largely by the leadership and resourcefulness of an intrepid young adventurer, Captain John Smith. Taking over in 1608, he whipped the gold-hungry colonists into line with the rule, "He who shall not work shall not eat." He had been kidnapped in December 1607 and subjected to a mock execution by the Indian chieftain Powhatan, whose daughter Pocahontas "saved" Smith by dramatically interposing her head between his and the war clubs of his captors. Pocahontas became an intermediary between the Indians and the settlers, helping to preserve a shaky peace and provide needed food.

Still, the colonists died in droves, and living skeletons were driven to desperate acts. They were reduced to eating "dogges, Catts, Ratts, and Myce" and even to digging up corpses for food. One hungry man killed, salted, and ate his wife, for which misbehavior he was executed. Of the four hundred settlers who managed to make it to Virginia by 1609, only sixty survived the "starving time" winter of 1609–1610. Diseased and despairing, the remaining colonists had boarded ships to return to England in the spring of 1610 when a relief party suddenly arrived, headed by a new governor, Lord De La Warr.

De La Warr ordered the settlers back to Jamestown, imposed a harsh military regime on the colony, and soon undertook aggressive military action against the Indians. But disease continued to reap a gruesome harvest among the Virginians. By 1625 Virginia contained only some twelve hundred hard-bitten survivors of the nearly eight thousand adventurers who had tried to start life anew in the ill-fated colony.

★ Cultural Clash in the Chesapeake

When the English landed in 1607, the chieftain Powhatan dominated the native peoples in the James River area. Powhatan at first may have considered the English potential allies in his struggle to extend his power over his Indian rivals, and he tried to be conciliatory. But relations between the Indians and the English remained tense, especially as the starving colonists took to raiding Indian food supplies.

Map 2.1 Early Maryland and Virginia

The atmosphere grew even more strained after Lord De La Warr arrived in 1610. He carried orders from the Virginia Company that amounted to a declaration of war against the Indians in the Jamestown region. A veteran of the vicious campaigns against the Irish, De La Warr introduced "Irish tactics" against the Indians. His troops raided Indian villages, burned houses, confiscated provisions, and torched cornfields. A peace settlement ended this **First Anglo-Powhatan War** in 1614, sealed by the marriage of Pocahontas to the colonist John Rolfe—the first known interracial union in Virginia.

A fragile peace prevailed for eight years. But the Indians, pressed by the land-hungry whites and ravaged by European diseases, struck back in 1622. A series of Indian attacks left 347 settlers dead, including John Rolfe. Pushed westward by retaliatory settler raids, the Indians made one last effort to dislodge the Virginians in the **Second Anglo-Powhatan War** in 1644. They were again defeated. The peace treaty of 1646 repudiated any thought of assimilating the native peoples into Virginian society or of peacefully coexisting with them. Instead, the treaty effectively banished the Chesapeake Indians from their ancestral lands and formally separated Indian from white areas of settlement—the origins of the later reservation system. By 1669 an official census revealed that only about two thousand Indians remained in Virginia, perhaps 10 percent of the population the original English settlers had encountered in 1607. By 1685 the English considered the Powhatan peoples extinct.

It had been the Powhatans' calamitous misfortune to fall victim to three Ds: disease, disorganization, and disposability. Like native peoples throughout the New World, they were extremely susceptible to European-borne epidemics of smallpox and measles. They also lacked the unity to effectively oppose the relatively well-organized and militarily disciplined whites. Finally, the Powhatans served no economic function for the Virginia

charter *Legal document granted by a government to some group or agency to implement a stated purpose, and spelling out the attending rights and obligations. British colonial charters guaranteed inhabitants all the rights of Englishmen, which helped solidify colonists' ties to Britain during the early years of settlement.*

Jamestown (1607) *First permanent English settlement in North America founded by the Virginia Company.*

First Anglo-Powhatan War (1610-1614) *Series of clashes between the Powhatan Confederacy and English settlers in Virginia. English colonists torched and pillaged Indian villages, applying tactics used in England's campaigns against the Irish.*

Second Anglo-Powhatan War (1644-1646) *Last-ditch effort by the Indians to dislodge Virginia settlements. The resulting peace treaty formally separated white and Indian areas of settlement.*

Pocahontas (ca. 1595–1617) Taken to England by her husband, Pocahontas was received as a princess. She died when preparing to return to Virginia. Her infant son ultimately reached Virginia, where hundreds of his descendants have lived, including the second Mrs. Woodrow Wilson.

colonists, providing no labor and having no gold or valuable commodities to offer in commerce. Indeed, the Indian presence frustrated the colonists' desire for a local commodity the Europeans desperately wanted: land.

★ The Indians' New World

The fate of the Powhatans foreshadowed the destinies of indigenous peoples throughout the continent as the process of European settlement went forward. Native Americans, of course, were no strangers to change, adaptation, and even catastrophe throughout their history, well before Columbus's arrival. But the shock of large-scale European colonization disrupted Native American life on a vast scale, inducing unprecedented demographic and cultural transformations.

Some changes were fairly benign. Horses acquired from the Spanish catalyzed a substantial migration of previously sedentary forest-dwelling peoples such as the Lakotas (Sioux) onto the Great Plains in the eighteenth century. There they thrived impressively, adopting an entirely new way of life as mounted nomadic hunters. But the effects of contact with Europeans proved less salutary for most other native peoples.

Disease was by far the biggest disrupter, as Old World pathogens licked lethally through biologically defenseless Indian populations. Disease took more than human life; it extinguished entire cultures and occasionally helped to

> *The authorities meted out harsh discipline in the young Virginia colony. One Jamestown settler who publicly criticized the governor was sentenced to:*
>
> "be disarmed [and] have his arms broken and his tongue bored through with an awl [and] shall pass through a guard of forty men and shall be butted [with muskets] by every one of them and at the head of the troop kicked down and footed out of the fort."

shape new ones. Epidemics often robbed native peoples of the elders who preserved their oral traditions and forced the survivors to literally reinvent themselves without benefit of accumulated wisdom or kin networks. The decimation and forced migration of native peoples sometimes scrambled them together in wholly new ways. The Catawba nation of the southern Piedmont region, for example, was formed from the splintered remnants of several different groups uprooted by the Europeans.

Trade also transformed Indian life, as traditional barter-and-exchange networks gave way to the temptations of European commerce. The drive to acquire European firearms in exchange for fur pelts intensified competition among the tribes for prime hunting grounds and led to an escalating cycle of Indian-on-Indian violence.

Indians along the Atlantic seaboard felt the most ferocious effects of European contact. Farther inland, native peoples had the advantages of time, space, and numbers as they sought to adapt to the European incursion. The Algonquins in the Great Lakes area, for instance, became a substantial regional power, able to deal from a position of strength with the few Europeans who managed to penetrate the interior. As a result, a British or French trader wanting to do business with the inland tribes had little choice but to conform to Indian ways, often taking an Indian wife. Thus was created a middle ground, a zone where both Europeans and Native Americans were compelled to accommodate one another—at least until the Europeans arrived in large numbers.

★ Virginia: Child of Tobacco

John Rolfe, the husband of Pocahontas, became the father of the tobacco industry and an economic savior of the Virginia colony. By 1612 he had perfected methods of raising and curing the pungent weed. A tobacco rush swept over Virginia, as crops were planted in the streets of Jamestown and even between the numerous graves. Colonists who had once hungered for food now hungered for ever more land on which to plant ever more tobacco. Relentlessly, they pressed the frontier of settlement up the river valleys to the west, abrasively edging against the Indians.

The wife of a Virginia governor wrote to her sister in England in 1623 of her voyage:

"For our Shippe was so pestered with people and goods that we were so full of infection that after a while we saw little but throwing folkes over board: It pleased god to send me my helth till I came to shoare and 3 dayes after I fell sick but I thank god I am well recovered. Few else are left alive that came in that Shippe."

Benjamin Franklin (1706–1790) in a 1753 letter to Peter Collinson commented on the attractiveness of Indian life to Europeans:

"When an Indian child has been brought up among us, taught our language and habituated to our customs, yet if he goes to see his relations and make one Indian ramble with them, there is no persuading him ever to return. [But] when white persons of either sex have been taken prisoners by the Indians, and lived awhile among them, though ransomed by their friends, and treated with all imaginable tenderness to prevail with them to stay among the English, yet in a short time they become disgusted with our manner of life, and the care and pains that are necessary to support it, and take the first good opportunity of escaping again into the woods, from whence there is no reclaiming them."

Virginia's prosperity was finally built on tobacco smoke. This "bewitching weed" played a vital role in putting the colony on firm economic foundations. But tobacco—King Nicotine—was something of a tyrant. It was ruinous to the soil when greedily planted in successive years, and it chained Virginia's fortunes to the fluctuating price of a single crop. Tobacco also promoted the immense-acreage plantation system and with it a brisk demand for slave labor.

In 1619, the year before the Plymouth Pilgrims landed in New England, what was described as a Dutch warship appeared off Jamestown and sold some twenty Africans. The scanty record does not reveal whether the Africans were purchased as lifelong slaves or as servants committed to limited years of servitude. This commercial transaction planted the seeds of the North American slave system. Yet blacks were too costly for most of the hard-pinched white colonists to acquire, and for decades few were brought to Virginia. In 1650 Virginia counted but three hundred blacks, although by the end of the century blacks, most of them enslaved, made up approximately 14 percent of the colony's population.

House of Burgesses *Representative parliamentary assembly created to govern Virginia, establishing a precedent for government in the English colonies.*

Representative self-government was also born in primitive Virginia, in the same cradle with slavery and in the same year—1619. The Virginia Company authorized the settlers to summon an assembly, known as the **House of Burgesses**. A momentous precedent was thus feebly established, for this assemblage was the first of many miniature parliaments to flourish on the soil of America.

As time passed, James I grew increasingly hostile to Virginia. He detested tobacco, and he distrusted the representative House of Burgesses, which he branded a "seminary of sedition." In 1624 he revoked the charter of the bankrupt Virginia Company, thus making Virginia a royal colony directly under his control.

★ Maryland: Catholic Haven

Maryland—the second plantation colony but the fourth English colony to be planted—was founded in 1634 by Lord Baltimore, of a prominent English Catholic family. He embarked on the venture partly to reap financial profits and partly to create a refuge for his fellow Catholics, who were harshly persecuted in Protestant England.

Absentee proprietor Lord Baltimore hoped that the two hundred settlers who founded Maryland at St. Marys, on Chesapeake Bay, would be the vanguard of a vast new feudal domain. Huge estates were to be awarded to his largely Catholic relatives, and gracious manor houses, modeled on those of England's aristocracy, were intended to arise amidst the fertile forests. As in Virginia, colonists proved willing to come only if offered the opportunity to acquire land of their own. Soon they were dispersed around the Chesapeake region on modest farms, and the haughty land barons, mostly Catholic, were surrounded by resentful backcountry planters, mostly Protestant. Resentment flared into open rebellion near the end of the century, and the Baltimore family, for a time, lost its proprietary rights.

Despite these tensions, Maryland prospered. Like Virginia, it blossomed forth in acres of tobacco. Also like Virginia, it depended for labor in its early years mainly on white indentured servants—penniless persons who bound themselves to work for a number of years to pay their passage. In both colonies, it was only in the later years of the seventeenth century that black slaves began to be imported in large numbers.

Act of Toleration (1649) *Passed in Maryland, it guaranteed toleration to all Christians but decreed the death penalty for those, like Jews and atheists, who denied the divinity of Jesus Christ. Ensured that Maryland would continue to attract a high proportion of Catholic migrants throughout the colonial period.*

Lord Baltimore at first permitted unusual freedom of worship for Protestant settlers in Maryland. But when the heavy tide of Protestants threatened to submerge the Catholics and place severe restrictions on them, as in England, the Maryland Catholics threw their support behind the famed **Act of Toleration**, passed in 1649 by the local representative assembly. Maryland's religious statute guaranteed toleration to all Christians, but it decreed the death penalty for anyone who denied the divinity of Jesus. While falling far short of later standards of religious liberty, Maryland's law did extend a temporary cloak of protection to the uneasy Catholic minority.

African slaves destined for the West Indian sugar plantations were bound and branded on West African beaches and ferried out in canoes to the waiting slave ships. An English sailor described the scene:

"The Negroes are so wilful and loth to leave their own country, that have often leap'd out of the canoes, boat and ship, into the sea, and kept under water till they were drowned, to avoid being taken up and saved by our boats, which pursued them; they having a more dreadful apprehension of Barbadoes than we can have of hell."

★ The West Indies: Way Station to Mainland America

While the English were planting the first frail colonial shoots in the Chesapeake, they were also busily colonizing the West Indies. By the mid-seventeenth century, England had secured its claim to several West Indian islands, including the large prize of Jamaica in 1655.

Sugar formed the foundation of the West Indian economy. What tobacco was to the Chesapeake, sugarcane was to the Caribbean—with one crucial difference. Tobacco was a poor man's crop that could be planted and processed easily. Sugarcane, by contrast, was a rich man's crop, requiring extensive planting and an elaborate process of refining in a sugar mill. The need for land, and for the labor to clear the land and to run the mills, made sugar cultivation a capital-intensive business. Only wealthy growers with abundant resources to invest could succeed in sugar.

The sugar lords extended their dominion over the West Indies in the seventeenth century. To work their sprawling plantations, they imported enormous numbers of African slaves—more than a quarter of a million in the five decades after 1640. By about 1700, black slaves outnumbered white settlers in the English West Indies by nearly four to one, and the region's population has remained predominantly black ever since. West Indians thus take their place among the numerous children of the African diaspora—the vast scattering of African peoples throughout the New World in the three and a half centuries following Columbus's discovery.

To control this large and potentially restive population of slaves, English authorities devised formal "codes" that defined the slaves' legal status and their masters' prerogatives. The notorious Barbados slave code of 1661 denied even the most fundamental rights to slaves and gave masters virtually complete control over their laborers.

A group of English settlers from Barbados arrived in Carolina in 1670, bringing with them a few enslaved Africans, as well as the model of the Barbados slave code. In 1696 Carolina officially adopted a version of the code, which eventually inspired statutes governing slavery throughout the mainland colonies. The Caribbean islands thus served as a staging area for the slave system that would take root elsewhere in British North America.

> *The Barbados slave code (1661) declared:*
>
> "If any Negro or slave whatsoever shall offer any violence to any Christian by striking or the like, such Negro or slave shall for his or her first offence be severely whipped by the Constable. For his second offence of that nature he shall be severely whipped, his nose slit, and be burned in some part of his face with a hot iron. And being brutish slaves, [they] deserve not, for the baseness of their condition, to be tried by the legal trial of twelve men of their peers, as the subjects of England are. And it is further enacted and ordained that if any Negro or other slave under punishment by his master unfortunately shall suffer in life or member, which seldom happens, no person whatsoever shall be liable to any fine therefore."

Barbados slave code (1661) *First formal statute governing the treatment of slaves, which provided for harsh punishments against offending slaves but lacked penalties for the mistreatment of slaves by masters. Similar statutes were adopted by southern plantation societies on the North American mainland in the seventeenth and eighteenth centuries.*

★ Colonizing the Carolinas

Civil war convulsed England in the 1640s. King Charles I had dismissed Parliament in 1629, and when he eventually recalled it in 1640, the members were mutinous. Finding their great champion in the Puritan soldier Oliver Cromwell, they ultimately beheaded Charles in 1649, and Cromwell ruled England for nearly a decade. Finally, Charles II, son of the decapitated king, was restored to the throne in 1660.

Colonization had been interrupted during this period of bloody unrest. Now, in the so-called Restoration period, empire building resumed with even greater intensity—and royal involvement. Carolina was formally created in 1670, after King Charles II granted to eight of his court favorites, the Lords Proprietors, an expanse of wilderness that ribboned across the continent to the Pacific. These aristocratic founders hoped to grow foodstuffs to provision the sugar plantations in Barbados and to export non-English products such as wine, silk, and olive oil.

Carolina prospered by developing close economic ties with the flourishing sugar islands of the English West Indies. Among the colonists' ventures was the capture and sale of Indians, which the colonists turned into a thriving export business. As many as ten thousand Indians were dispatched to lifelong labor in the West Indies, and others were sold as slaves to New England. A war with the Savannah Indians that began in 1707 virtually annihilated the Indians of coastal Carolina by 1710.

After much experimentation, rice emerged as the principal export crop in Carolina. Because rice was grown in Africa, the Carolinians were soon paying premium prices for West African slaves experienced in rice cultivation. The Africans' agricultural skills and their relative immunities to malaria made them ideal laborers on the hot and swampy rice plantations. By 1710 they constituted a majority of Carolinians.

Moss-festooned Charles Town—named for King Charles II—rapidly became the busiest seaport in the South. Many high-spirited sons of English landed families, deprived of an inheritance, came to the Charleston area and gave it a rich aristocratic flavor. The village became a colorfully diverse community, to which French Protestant refugees, Jews, and others were attracted by religious toleration.

Makers of America

The Iroquois

Well before the crowned heads of Europe turned their eyes and their dreams of empires toward North America, a great military power had emerged in the Mohawk Valley of what is now New York State. The **Iroquois Confederacy**, dubbed by whites the "League of the Iroquois," bound together five Indian nations—the Mohawks, the Oneidas, the Onondagas, the Cayugas, and the Senecas (see Map 2.2). According to Iroquois legend, the alliance was founded in the late 1500s by two leaders, Deganawidah and Hiawatha. This proud and potent league vied with neighboring Indians for territorial supremacy, then with invading Europeans for control of the fur trade. Ultimately, decimated by the white man's diseases, whiskey, and muskets, the Iroquois struggled for their very survival as a people.

The building block of Iroquois society was the longhouse. Twenty-five feet wide and up to two hundred feet long, these wooden structures sheltered several closely related nuclear families, their connections of blood running exclusively through the maternal line. The oldest woman in a clan was the honored matriarch. Men dominated the society, but they owed their positions of prominence to their mothers' families.

As if sharing one great longhouse, the five nations joined in the Iroquois Confederacy but kept their own separate fires. Although they celebrated together and shared a common policy toward outsiders, they remained essentially independent of one another. On the eastern flank, the Mohawks, known as the Keepers of the Eastern Fire, specialized as middlemen with European traders, whereas the outlying Senecas, the Keepers of the Western Fire, became fur suppliers. In the early 1700s, the Tuscaroras from the Carolina region gained affiliation with the Iroquois Confederacy.

Throughout the seventeenth and eighteenth centuries the Iroquois allied alternately with the British against the French and vice versa, for a time successfully working this perpetual rivalry to their advantage. But the confederacy divided during the American Revolution, with most tribes siding with the British. The British defeat in the Revolution

Map 2.2 Iroquois Lands and European Trade Centers, ca. 1590–1650.

Iroquois Confederacy Bound together five tribes—the Mohawks, the Oneidas, the Onondagas, the Cayugas, and the Senecas—in the Mohawk Valley of what is now New York State.

Nearby, in Florida, the Catholic Spaniards abhorred the intrusion of these Protestant heretics. Carolina's frontier was often aflame. Armor-clad Spanish soldiers, aided by their Indian allies, frequently attacked English settlements during the successive Anglo-Spanish wars. But by 1700, Carolina was too strong to be wiped out.

The wild northern expanse of the huge Carolina grant bordered on Virginia. From the older colony drifted down a ragtag group of poverty-stricken outcasts and religious dissenters, many of them repelled by the wealthy plantation gentry of Virginia, who belonged to

The Longhouse (reconstruction) This photo shows a modern-day reconstruction of an Iroquois Indian longhouse typical of the kind built by many tribes in the northeastern United States and parts of Canada. Bent saplings and sheets of elm bark made for sturdy, weather-tight shelters. Longhouses were typically furnished with deerskin-covered bunks and shelves for storing baskets, pots, fur pelts, and corn.

left the Iroquois Confederacy in tatters. Most Iroquois moved to British Canada or were relegated to reservations in western New York.

Reservation life proved unbearable to the proud Iroquois, who fell into feuding and alcoholism. But in 1799 an Iroquois prophet named Handsome Lake arose, warning his people to mend their ways, affirm family values, and revive their old Iroquois customs. Handsome Lake died in 1813, but his teachings, in the form of the Longhouse religion, survive to this day.

the established Church of England. These small farmers, who frequently were "**squatters**" without legal right to the soil, raised their tobacco and other crops with little need for slaves. Regarded as riffraff by their snobbish neighbors, the North Carolinians earned a reputation for being resistant to authority, irreligious, and hospitable to pirates. Their location between aristocratic Virginia and aristocratic South Carolina caused the area to be dubbed "a vale of humility between two mountains of conceit." North Carolina was officially separated from South Carolina in 1712, and subsequently each segment became a royal colony.

squatters *Frontier farmers who illegally occupied land owned by others or not yet officially opened for settlement. Many of North Carolina's early settlers were squatters, who contributed to the colony's reputation as being more independent minded and "democratic" than its neighbors.*

31

Tuscarora War (1711–1713) *Began with an Indian attack on New Bern, North Carolina. After the Tuscaroras were defeated, remaining Indian survivors migrated northward, eventually joining the Iroquois Confederacy as its sixth nation.*

Yamasee Indians *Defeated by the South Carolinians in the war of 1715–1716. The Yamasee defeat devastated the last of the coastal Indian tribes in the southern colonies.*

North Carolina, unlike its sister colony, did not at first import large numbers of African slaves. But both Carolinas shared in the ongoing tragedy of bloody relations between Indians and Europeans. After Tuscarora Indians fell upon the fledgling settlement of New Bern in 1711, North and South Carolinians retaliated by crushing the Indians in the **Tuscarora War** and selling hundreds of them into slavery. In another ferocious encounter four years later, the South Carolinians defeated and scattered the **Yamasee Indians**, thereby utterly devastating the last of the coastal Indian tribes in the southern colonies. Yet, in the interior Appalachian Mountains, the powerful Cherokees, Creeks, and Iroquois remained (see "Makers of America: The Iroquois," p. 30). Stronger and more numerous than their coastal cousins, they managed for half a century more to contain British settlement on the coastal plain east of the mountains.

★ Late-Coming Georgia: The Buffer Colony

Pine-forested Georgia, with the harbor of Savannah nourishing its chief settlement, was formally founded in 1733. It proved to be the last of the thirteen colonies to be planted—126 years after the first, Virginia, and 52 years after the twelfth, Pennsylvania.

buffer *In politics, a territory between two antagonistic powers, intended to minimize the possibility of conflict between them. In British North America, Georgia was established as a buffer colony between British and Spanish territory.*

The British crown intended Georgia to serve chiefly as a **buffer**. It would protect the more valuable Carolinas against vengeful Spaniards from Florida and hostile French from Louisiana. Georgia indeed suffered much buffeting, especially when wars broke out between Spain and Britain in the European arena.

Named in honor of Britain's King George II, Georgia was launched by a high-minded group of philanthropists. In addition to protecting their neighboring northern colonies and producing silk and wine, they were determined to carve out a haven for wretched souls imprisoned for debt. They were also determined, at least at first, to keep slavery out of Georgia. The ablest of the founders was the dynamic soldier-statesman James Oglethorpe, who became keenly interested in prison reform after one of his friends died in a debtors' jail. As a competent military leader, Oglethorpe repelled Spanish attacks. As an imperialist and a philanthropist, he saved "the Charity Colony" by his energetic leadership and by heavily mortgaging his own personal fortunes.

The hamlet of Savannah, like Charleston, was a melting-pot community that included German Lutherans and kilted Scottish Highlanders, among others. All Christian worshipers except Catholics enjoyed religious toleration. Many Bible-carrying missionaries arrived to work among debtors and Indians. Prominent among them was young John Wesley, who later returned to Britain and founded the Methodist church.

Georgia grew with painful slowness and at the end of the colonial era was perhaps the least populous of the colonies. The development of a plantation economy was thwarted by an unhealthful climate, by early restrictions on black slavery, and by demoralizing Spanish attacks.

★ The Plantation Colonies

Certain distinctive features were shared by all of Britain's southern mainland colonies: Maryland, Virginia, North Carolina, South Carolina, and Georgia. With expansive, fertile acreage, these outposts of empire were all, to some degree, devoted to exporting commercial agricultural crops such as tobacco, rice, and indigo. Slavery was found in all the plantation colonies, though only after 1750 in reform-minded Georgia. Immense acreage in the hands of a favored few fostered a strong aristocratic atmosphere, except in North Carolina and to some extent in debtor-tinged Georgia. The wide scattering of plantations and farms, often along stately rivers, retarded the growth of cities and made the establishment of churches and schools both difficult and expensive.

The tax-supported Church of England was the dominant faith of the southern colonies, but all the colonies permitted some religious toleration. The plantation colonies were all, to some degree, expansionist. "Soil butchery" by excessive tobacco growing drove settlers westward, and the long, lazy rivers invited penetration of the continent—and continuing confrontation with Native Americans.

CHAPTER SUMMARY ★ ★ ★ ★ ★ ★ ★ ★ ★ ★ ★ ★ ★ ★

The defeat of the Spanish Armada and the exuberant spirit of Elizabethan nationalism finally drew England into the colonial race. After some early failures, the first permanent English colony was established at Jamestown, Virginia. Harsh conditions, gentlemanly aversion to work, and Indian hostility nearly caused the colony to fail, but John Smith's stern leadership and tobacco cultivation finally brought prosperity and population growth.

The early encounters of English settlers with the Powhatan Indians in Virginia established many of the patterns that characterized later Indian-white relations in North America, including disease, warfare, and removal. Indian societies underwent their own substantial changes as a result of warfare, disease, and trade. For a time after the Atlantic coastal tribes were nearly wiped out, the larger tribes of Indian peoples of the Appalachian area formed a formidable barrier to white expansion.

Maryland and South Carolina were founded by aristocratic proprietors. Maryland was originally a Catholic refuge but later attracted a Protestant majority. South Carolina flourished by establishing close ties with the British sugar colonies in the West Indies and brought the West Indian pattern of harsh slave codes and large-plantation agriculture to North America. North Carolina was a less hierarchical settlement of largely poor white colonists who owned small farms and disdained authority. Latecomer Georgia developed slowly, serving initially as a buffer against the Spanish and a haven for debtors.

Despite some differences, all the southern colonies depended on staple plantation agriculture for their survival and on the institutions of indentured servitude and African slavery for their labor. With widely scattered rural settlements, the southern colonies had relatively weak religious and social institutions and tended to develop hierarchical economic and social orders.

KEY TERMS

- Protestant Reformation (22)
- Roanoke Island (22)
- Spanish Armada (23)
- primogeniture (23)
- joint-stock company (23)
- Virginia Company (24)
- charter (25)
- Jamestown (25)
- First Anglo-Powhatan War (25)
- Second Anglo-Powhatan War (25)
- House of Burgesses (28)
- Act of Toleration (28)
- Barbados slave code (29)
- Iroquois Confederacy (30)
- squatter (31)
- Tuscarora War (32)
- Yamasee Indians (32)
- buffer (32)

PEOPLE TO KNOW

- Henry VIII
- Elizabeth I
- Sir Francis Drake
- Sir Walter Raleigh
- James I
- Captain John Smith
- Powhatan
- Pocahontas
- Lord De La Warr
- John Rolfe
- Lord Baltimore
- Oliver Cromwell
- Hiawatha
- James Oglethorpe

MindTap is a fully online, highly personalized learning experience built upon Cengage Learning content. MindTap combines student learning tools—readings, multimedia, activities, and assessments—into a singular Learning Path that guides students through the course.

Chapter 3

Settling the Northern Colonies
1619–1700

• • •

*God hath sifted a Nation that
he might send Choice Grain
into this Wilderness.*

WILLIAM STOUGHTON [OF MASSACHUSETTS BAY], 1669

Chapter Outline

- The Puritan Faith
- Plymouth Colony, 1620
- The Puritan Commonwealth of Massachusetts Bay Colony, 1630
- The Expansion of New England
- New Netherland Becomes New York
- Pennsylvania and the Middle Colonies
- *Examining the Evidence:* A Seventeenth-Century Valuables Cabinet
- *Varying Viewpoints:* Europeanizing America or Americanizing Europe?

Although colonists both north and south were bound together by a common language and a common allegiance to Mother England, they established different patterns of settlements, different economies, different political systems, and even different sets of values—defining distinctive regional characteristics that would persist for generations. The promise of riches—especially from golden-leaved tobacco—drew the first settlers to the southern colonies. But to the north, in the fertile valleys of the middle Atlantic region and especially along the rocky shores of New England, it was not worldly wealth but religious devotion that principally shaped the earliest settlements.

FOCUS QUESTIONS

1. What motivated English Pilgrims and Puritans to emigrate to the New World, and how did their religious beliefs affect the character and organization of the Plymouth and Massachusetts Bay Colonies?

2. How did religious dissent, economic circumstances, and Indian relations shape the founding and development of all the New England colonies?

3. What attempts were made to promote intercolonial unity in New England, and why did those efforts fail?

4. What were the original motives for the founding of New York and Pennsylvania? In what ways were the two colonies different, and in what ways were they similar?

5. What were the central features of the four middle colonies, and how did they differ from the New England colonies?

CHRONOLOGY

1517	Martin Luther begins Protestant Reformation	1639	Connecticut's Fundamental Orders drafted
1536	John Calvin of Geneva publishes *Institutes of the Christian Religion*	1642–1651	English Civil War
		1643	New England Confederation formed
1620	Pilgrims sail on the *Mayflower* to Plymouth Bay	1650	William Bradford completes *Of Plymouth Plantation*
1624	Dutch found New Netherland	1655	New Netherland conquers New Sweden
1629	Charles I dismisses Parliament and persecutes Puritans	1664	England seizes New Netherland from Dutch
1630	Puritans found Massachusetts Bay Colony		East and West Jersey colonies founded
1635–1636	Roger Williams convicted of heresy and founds Rhode Island colony	1675–1676	King Philip's War
1635–1638	Connecticut and New Haven colonies founded	1681	William Penn founds Pennsylvania colony
1636–1638	Pequot War	1686	Royal authority creates Dominion of New England
1638	Anne Hutchinson banished from Massachusetts colony	1688–1689	Glorious Revolution overthrows Stuarts and Dominion of New England

⭐ The Protestant Reformation Produces Puritanism

Little did the German monk Martin Luther suspect, when he nailed his protests against Catholic doctrines to the door of Wittenberg's castle church in 1517, that he was shaping the destiny of a yet unknown nation. Denouncing the authority of priests and popes, Luther declared that the Bible alone was the source of God's word. He ignited a fire of religious reform (the "Protestant Reformation") that licked its way across Europe for more than a century, dividing people, toppling sovereigns, and kindling the spiritual fervor of millions of men and women—some of whom helped to found America.

The reforming flame burned especially brightly in the bosom of John Calvin of Geneva. This somber and severe religious leader elaborated Martin Luther's ideas in ways that profoundly affected the thought and character of generations of Americans yet unborn. **Calvinism** became the dominant theological credo not only of the New England **Puritans** but of other American settlers as well, including Scottish Presbyterians, French Huguenots, and Dutch Reformed.

Calvin argued in the *Institutes of the Christian Religion* (1536) that God was all-powerful and all-good. Humans, because of the corrupting effect of original sin, were weak and wicked. God was also all-knowing, and since the first moment of creation God had destined some souls—the elect—for eternal bliss and others for eternal torment. Good works could not save those whom **predestination** had marked for the infernal fires.

But neither could the elect count on their predetermined salvation and lead lives of wild, immoral abandon. For one thing, no one could be certain of his or her status in the heavenly ledger. Gnawing doubts about their eternal fates caused Calvinists constantly to seek signs of **conversion**, or the receipt of God's free gift of saving grace, in themselves and others. Those who had the intense and identifiable personal experience of conversion were expected to lead "sanctified" lives, demonstrating by their holy behavior that they were among the "visible saints."

Calvinism *Dominant theological credo of the New England Puritans based on the teachings of John Calvin. Calvinists believed in predestination—that only "the elect" were destined for salvation.*

Puritans *English Protestant reformers who sought to purify the Church of England of Catholic rituals and creeds. Some of the most devout Puritans believed that only "visible saints" should be admitted to church membership.*

predestination *Calvinist doctrine that God has foreordained some people to be saved and some to be damned. Though their fate was irreversible, Calvinists, particularly those who believed they were destined for salvation, sought to lead sanctified lives in order to demonstrate to others that they were in fact members of the "elect."*

conversion *Intense religious experience that confirmed an individual's place among the "elect," or the "visible saints." Calvinists who experienced conversion were then expected to lead sanctified lives to demonstrate their salvation.*

These doctrines swept into England just as King Henry VIII was breaking his ties with the Roman Catholic Church in the 1530s, making himself the head of the Church of England. Henry would have been content to retain Catholic rituals and creeds, but some English religious reformers sought a total purification of English Christianity. As they grew increasingly unhappy with the snail-like progress of the Protestant Reformation in England, these "Puritans" burned with pious zeal to see the Church of England wholly de-Catholicized.

The most devout Puritans, including those who eventually settled New England, believed that only "visible saints" (that is, persons who felt the stirrings of grace in their souls and could demonstrate its presence to their fellow Puritans) should be admitted to church membership. But the Church of England enrolled all the king's subjects, which meant that the "saints" had to share pews and communion rails with the "damned." Appalled by this unholy fraternizing, a tiny group of dedicated Puritans, known as **Separatists**, vowed to break away entirely from the Church of England. King James I, who was head of both the church and the state in England from 1603 to 1625, threatened to harass the more bothersome Separatists out of the land.

⭐ The Pilgrims End Their Pilgrimage at Plymouth

The most famous congregation of Separatists, fleeing royal wrath, departed for Holland in 1608. During the ensuing twelve years of toil and poverty, they were increasingly distressed by the "Dutchification" of their children. They longed to find a haven where they could live and die as English men and women—and as purified Protestants. America was the logical refuge.

A group of the Separatists in Holland, after negotiating with the Virginia Company at length, secured rights to settle under that Company's jurisdiction. But their crowded *Mayflower*, sixty-five days at sea, missed its destination and arrived off the rocky coast of New England in 1620, with a total of 102 persons. Because their settlement at inhospitable Plymouth Bay was outside the domain of the Virginia Company, the Pilgrims became squatters without legal right to the land or specific authority to establish a government.

Before disembarking, the Pilgrim leaders drew up and signed the brief **Mayflower Compact**. Although setting an invaluable precedent for later written constitutions, this document was not a constitution at all. It was a simple agreement to form a crude

> **Separatists** *Small group of Puritans who sought to break away entirely from the Church of England; after initially settling in Holland, a number of English Separatists made their way to Plymouth Bay, Massachusetts, in 1620.*

> **Mayflower Compact (1620)** *Agreement to form a majoritarian government in Plymouth, signed aboard the Mayflower. Created a foundation for self-government in the colony.*

Plymouth Plantation Carefully restored, the modest village at Plymouth looks today much as it did nearly four hundred years ago.

government and to submit to the will of the majority under the regulations agreed upon. The compact was signed by forty-one adult males, eleven of them with the exalted rank of "mister," though not by the servants and two seamen. The pact was a promising step toward genuine self-government, for soon the adult male settlers were assembling to make their own laws in open-discussion town meetings—a great laboratory of liberty.

The Pilgrims' first winter of 1620–1621 took a grisly toll. Only 44 out of the 102 survived. Yet when the *Mayflower* sailed back to England in the spring, not a single one of the courageous band of Separatists left. As one of them wrote, "It is not with us as with other men, whom small things can discourage."

> *William Bradford (1590–1657) wrote in* Of Plymouth Plantation:
>
> "Thus out of small beginnings greater things have been produced by His hand that made all things of nothing, and gives being to all things that are; and, as one small candle may light a thousand, so the light here kindled hath shone unto many, yea in some sort to our whole nation."

God made his children prosperous, so the Pilgrims believed. The next autumn, that of 1621, brought bountiful harvests and with them the first Thanksgiving Day in New England. In time the frail colony found sound economic legs in fur, fish, and lumber. The beaver and the Bible were the early mainstays: the one for the sustenance of the body, the other for the sustenance of the soul. The Pilgrims were also extremely fortunate in their leaders, especially William Bradford, a self-taught scholar who read Hebrew, Greek, Latin, French, and Dutch and was elected governor thirty times.

Quiet and quaint, the little colony of Plymouth was never important economically or numerically. Its population numbered only seven thousand by 1691, when, still charterless, it merged with its giant neighbor, the **Massachusetts Bay Colony**. But the tiny settlement of Pilgrims was big both morally and spiritually.

Massachusetts Bay Colony (founded in 1630) *Established by non-separating Puritans, it soon grew to be the largest and most influential of the New England colonies.*

★ The Bay Colony Bible Commonwealth

The Separatist Pilgrims were dedicated extremists—the purest Puritans. More moderate Puritans sought to reform the Church of England from within. But they faced catastrophe when Charles I dismissed Parliament in 1629 and sanctioned the anti-Puritan persecutions of the reactionary Archbishop William Laud.

In 1629 an energetic group of non-Separatist Puritans, fearing for their faith and for England's future, secured a royal charter to form the Massachusetts Bay Company. Stealing a march on both king and church, the newcomers brought their charter with them when they emigrated to Massachusetts. For many years they used it as a kind of constitution, out of easy reach of royal authority.

The Massachusetts Bay Colony was singularly blessed. The well-equipped expedition of 1630, with eleven vessels carrying nearly a thousand immigrants, started the colony off on a larger scale than any of the other English settlements. Continuing turmoil in England tossed up additional enriching waves of Puritans on the shores of Massachusetts in the following decade. During the **Great English Migration** of the 1630s, about seventy thousand refugees left England. But not all of them were Puritans, and only about twenty thousand came to Massachusetts. Many were attracted to the warm and fertile West Indies, especially sugar-rich Barbados.

Great English Migration (1630–1642) *Migration of seventy thousand refugees from England to the North American colonies, primarily New England and the Caribbean. The twenty thousand migrants who came to Massachusetts largely shared a common sense of purpose—to establish a model Christian settlement in the New World.*

Many fairly prosperous, educated persons emigrated to the Bay Colony, including John Winthrop, a well-to-do pillar of English society. A successful attorney and manor lord in England, Winthrop eagerly accepted the offer to become the first governor of the Massachusetts Bay Colony, believing that he had a "calling" from God to lead the new religious experiment. He served as governor or deputy governor for nineteen years. The resources and skills of talented settlers like Winthrop helped Massachusetts prosper, and the Bay Colony rapidly shot to the fore as the biggest and the most influential of the New England outposts.

Massachusetts also benefited from a shared sense of purpose among most of the first settlers. "We shall be as a city upon a hill," a beacon to humanity, declared Governor Winthrop. The Puritan bay colonists believed that they had a covenant with God, an agreement to build a holy society that would be a model for humankind.

★ Building the Bay Colony

These common convictions deeply shaped the infant colony's life. Soon after arrival the settlers extended the franchise to all "freemen"—adult males who belonged to the Puritan congregations, which in time came to be called collectively the Congregational Church. On this basis about two-fifths of adult males enjoyed the franchise in provincial affairs, a far larger proportion than in contemporary England. Town governments, which conducted much important business, were even more inclusive. There all male property holders, and in some cases other residents as well, discussed and voted on local issues.

Yet the provincial government, liberal by the standards of the time, was not a democracy. "If the people be governors," asked one Puritan clergyman, "who shall be the governed?" True, the freemen annually elected the governor and his assistants, as well as a representative assembly called the General Court. But only Puritans—the "visible saints" who alone were eligible for church membership—could be freemen. And according to the doctrine of the covenant, the whole purpose of government was to enforce God's laws—which applied to believers and nonbelievers alike. Moreover, nonbelievers as well as believers paid taxes for the government-supported church.

Religious leaders thus wielded enormous influence in the Massachusetts "Bible commonwealth." They powerfully influenced admission to church membership, by conducting public interrogations of persons claiming to have experienced conversions. But the power of preachers, such as the eminent and learned John Cotton, was not absolute. Because Puritans had suffered so much at the hands of a "political" Anglican clergy, they barred clergymen from holding formal political office. In a limited way, the bay colonists thus endorsed the idea of the separation of church and state.

The Puritans were a worldly lot, despite—or even because of—their spiritual intensity. Like John Winthrop, they believed in the doctrine of a "calling" to do God's work on this earth. They shared in what was later called the "Protestant ethic," which involved serious commitment to work and to engagement in worldly pursuits. Legend to the contrary, they also enjoyed simple pleasures; they ate plentifully, drank heartily, sang songs occasionally, and made love mostly monogamously.

Yet, to the Puritans, life was serious business, and hellfire was real—a hell where sinners shriveled and shrieked in vain and forever for divine mercy. Puritan clergyman Michael Wigglesworth's popular poem "Day of Doom" (1662) described the horrifying fate of the damned:

Anne Hutchinson, Dissenter Mistress Hutchinson (1591–1643) held unorthodox views that challenged the authority of the clergy and the very integrity of the Puritan experiment in the Massachusetts Bay Colony. (Picture Research Consultants & Archives)

> *They cry, they roar for anguish sore,*
> *and gnaw their tongues for horrour,*
> *But get away without delay,*
> *Christ pitties not your cry:*
> *Depart to hell, there may you yell,*
> *and roar Eternally.*

★ Trouble in the Bible Commonwealth

The Bay Colony enjoyed a high degree of social harmony, stemming from common beliefs, in its early years. But even in this tightly knit community, dissension soon appeared. **Quakers**, who flouted the authority of the Puritan clergy, were persecuted with fines, floggings, and banishment. In one extreme case, four Quakers were hanged on Boston Common.

A sharp challenge to Puritan orthodoxy came from Anne Hutchinson. An exceptionally intelligent, strong-willed, and talkative woman, she claimed that the truly saved need not bother to obey the law of either God or man. This assertion, known as *antinomianism* (from the Greek, "against the law"), was high heresy. Brought to trial in 1638, the quick-witted Hutchinson bamboozled her clerical inquisitors for days, until she eventually boasted that she had come by her beliefs through a direct revelation from God. This was

Quakers *Religious group known for their tolerance, emphasis on peace, and idealistic Indian policy, who settled heavily in Pennsylvania in the seventeenth and eighteenth centuries.*

antinomianism Belief that the elect need not obey the law of either God or man; most notably espoused in the colonies by Anne Hutchinson.

even higher heresy. After the Puritan magistrates banished her, she traveled on foot to Rhode Island and finally moved to New York, where she and all but one of her household were killed by Indians.

More threatening to the Puritan leaders was a personable and popular Salem minister, Roger Williams. An extreme Separatist with an unrestrained tongue, Williams demanded a clean break with the corrupt Church of England and challenged the legality of the Bay Colony's charter, which he condemned for expropriating land from the Indians without compensation. As if all this were not enough, he went on to deny the authority of civil government to regulate religious behavior—a seditious blow at the Puritan idea of government's very purpose. Their patience exhausted by 1635, the Bay Colony authorities found Williams guilty of disseminating "newe & dangerous opinions" and ordered him banished.

★ New England Spreads Out

Aided by friendly Indians, Roger Williams fled to the Rhode Island area in 1636, where he built in Providence a Baptist church, probably the first in America. He established complete freedom of religion, even for Jews and Catholics, a degree of toleration far ahead of the other English settlements in the New World. He demanded no oaths regarding religious beliefs, no compulsory attendance at worship, no taxes to support a state church. He even sheltered the abused Quakers, although disagreeing sharply with their views.

Those outcasts who clustered about Roger Williams also enjoyed additional blessings. They exercised simple manhood suffrage from the start, though this broad-minded practice was later narrowed by a property qualification. Opposed to special privilege of any sort, the malcontents and exiles who largely populated "Rogues' Island" had little in common with Roger Williams—except being unwelcome anywhere else. The Puritan clergy back in Boston sneered at Rhode Island as a "sewer" where the "Lord's debris" collected and rotted. Stubbornly individualistic, the squatters in "Little Rhody" finally acquired legal rights to the soil when they secured a charter from Parliament in 1644. A huge bronze statue of the "Independent Man" appropriately stands today on the dome of the statehouse in Providence.

The fertile valley of the Connecticut River had meanwhile attracted different types of Dutch and English settlers. Hartford was founded in 1635 (see Map 3.1), and the next year an energetic group of Boston Puritans, led by the Reverend Thomas Hooker, swarmed into the area. In 1639 the settlers of the new Connecticut River colony drafted a trailblazing document known as the **Fundamental Orders**, which established a regime controlled by the "substantial" citizens.

Another flourishing Connecticut settlement began to spring up at New Haven in 1638. It was a prosperous community, founded by Puritans who contrived to set up an even closer church-government alliance than in Massachusetts. These colonists dreamed of making New Haven a bustling seaport, but they fell into disfavor with King Charles II because they sheltered two of the judges who had condemned his father, Charles I, to death. In 1662 the crown granted a charter that merged New Haven with the more democratic settlements in the Connecticut Valley.

Two smaller settlements grew up to the north of Massachusetts Bay. The fishermen and fur traders who had been active along the coast of Maine even before the founding of Plymouth were absorbed by Massachusetts Bay in 1677. The Maine territory remained

---

Contending Voices

Anne Hutchinson Accused and Defended

In his opening remarks at the examination of Anne Hutchinson in 1637, Governor John Winthrop (1587–1649) declared:

"... you have spoken diverse things ... very prejudicial to the honour of the churches ... and you have maintained a meeting and an assembly in your house that hath been condemned by the general assembly as a thing not tolerable ... nor fitting for your sex...."

Hutchinson (1591–1643) defended herself as follows:

"Will it please you to answer me this and to give me a rule for then I will willingly submit to any truth. If any come to my house to be instructed in the ways of God what rule have I to put them away?"

In what ways did the accusations against Anne Hutchinson go beyond doctrinal heresy?

Fundamental Orders (1639) *Drafted by settlers in the Connecticut River valley, this document was the first "modern constitution" establishing a democratically controlled government. Key features of the document were borrowed for Connecticut's colonial charter and, later, its state constitution.*

Map 3.1 Seventeenth-Century New England Settlements The Massachusetts Bay Colony was the hub of New England. All earlier colonies grew into it; all later colonies grew out of it.

Pequot War (1636–1638) Series of clashes between English settlers and Pequot Indians in the Connecticut River valley. Ended in the slaughter of the Pequots by the Puritans and their Narragansett Indian allies.

King Philip's War (1675–1676) Series of assaults by Metacom, King Philip, on English settlements in New England. The attacks slowed the westward migration of New England settlers for several decades.

English Civil War (1642–1651) Armed conflict between royalists and parliamentarians, resulting in the victory of pro-Parliament forces and the execution of Charles I.

New England Confederation (1643) Weak union of the colonies in Massachusetts and Connecticut led by Puritans for the purposes of defense and organization; an early attempt at self-government during the benign neglect of the English Civil War.

part of Massachusetts for nearly a century and a half before becoming a separate state. In 1641 the Bay Colony also annexed its immediate northern neighbor, New Hampshire, under a strained interpretation of the Massachusetts charter. The king, annoyed by this display of greed, separated New Hampshire from Massachusetts in 1679 and made it a royal colony.

★ Puritans Versus Indians

The spread of English settlements inevitably led to clashes with the Indians, who were particularly weak in New England. Shortly before the Pilgrims arrived at Plymouth in 1620, an epidemic, probably triggered by contact with English fishermen, had swept through the coastal tribes and killed more than three-fourths of the native people. The deserted fields and scattered skulls and bones that greeted the Plymouth settlers provided grim evidence of the impact of the disease.

In no position to resist the English incursion, the local Wampanoag Indians at first befriended the settlers. Cultural accommodation was facilitated by Squanto, a Wampanoag who had learned English from a ship's captain who had kidnapped him some years earlier. The Wampanoag chieftain Massasoit signed a treaty with the Plymouth Pilgrims in 1621 and helped them celebrate the first Thanksgiving after the autumn harvests that same year.

As more English settlers arrived and pushed inland into the Connecticut River valley, confrontations between Indians and whites ruptured these peaceful relations. Hostilities exploded in 1637 between the settlers and the powerful Pequot tribe. In the brutal **Pequot War** the English militiamen and their Narragansett Indian allies virtually annihilated the Pequots.

During the ensuing four decades of tense peace, the Puritans made some feeble efforts to convert the remaining Indians to Christianity. But their missionary zeal never equaled that of the Spanish and French Catholics, and a mere handful of Indians were gathered into Puritan "praying towns."

The Indians' only hope for resisting English encroachment lay in intertribal unity—a pan-Indian alliance against the swiftly spreading settlements. In 1675 Massasoit's son Metacom, called King Philip by the English, forged such an alliance and mounted a series of coordinated assaults on English villages throughout New England. When the war ended in 1676, fifty-two Puritan towns had been attacked and twelve destroyed entirely. Hundreds of colonists and many more Indians lay dead. Metacom was captured, beheaded, and drawn and quartered. His head was carried on a pike back to Plymouth, where it was on grisly display for years.

King Philip's War slowed the westward march of English settlement in New England for several decades. But the war inflicted a lasting defeat on New England's Indians. Drastically reduced in numbers, dispirited, and disbanded, they thereafter posed only sporadic threats to the New England colonists.

★ Seeds of Colonial Unity and Revolt

In the 1640s the **English Civil War** between King Charles I and the Puritan parliament distracted old England. Left largely on their own, four colonies banded together to form the path-breaking **New England Confederation**. The confederation's purpose was to provide defense against foes such as the Indians, French, and Dutch, as well as to solve intercolonial problems such as runaway servants and criminals. Each member colony, regardless of size, wielded two votes.

Weak though it was, the confederation was the first notable milestone on the long and rocky road toward colonial unity. The delegates took tottering but long-overdue steps toward acting together on matters of intercolonial importance.

English monarchs had paid little attention to the American colonies from the early years of settlement through the Civil War and political turmoil of the 1640s and 1650s. This era of benign neglect allowed the colonies, in effect, to become semiautonomous commonwealths. But with the Puritans finally defeated and King Charles II restored to the throne in 1660, the royalists and their Church of England allies determined to take an aggressive hand in the management of the colonies. The king's agents took particular aim at proud and stubborn Massachusetts by giving rival Connecticut a sea-to-sea charter in 1662 and granting a charter to the outcasts in Rhode Island in 1663. A final and crushing blow fell on the stiff-necked Bay Colony in 1684, when its precious charter was revoked by royal authorities.

Massachusetts suffered further humiliation in 1686, when the royal government created the **Dominion of New England**, which was expanded two years later to include New York and East and West Jersey. Unlike the homegrown New England Confederation, the Dominion was imposed from London and designed primarily to stitch England's overseas possessions more tightly to the motherland by throttling American trade with countries not ruled by the British crown.

The new Dominion's governor was autocratic Sir Edmund Andros, an able but tactless English military man who established his headquarters in puritan Boston and promptly outraged the colonists with his profane soldiers and iron-fisted tactics. Andros ruthlessly curbed the cherished town meetings, restricted the courts, and taxed the people without the consent of their duly elected representatives in the assemblies.

On the verge of revolt, the New Englanders were beaten to the punch by the people of old England. In the **Glorious Revolution** of 1688–1689 they overthrew the despotic Catholic King James II and then invited the Dutch Protestant rulers William III and his English wife Mary II, daughter of James II, to assume the English throne. When news of the Glorious Revolution reached America, a Boston mob rose against the existing regime, and the ramshackle Dominion of New England collapsed like a house of cards. Sir Edmund Andros reportedly attempted to flee in women's clothing but was betrayed by boots protruding beneath his dress. He was hastily shipped off to England. Though rid of the despotic Andros, Massachusetts did not gain as much from the upheaval as it had hoped. In 1691 Massachusetts was arbitrarily made a royal colony, and the proud Puritans were forced to yield the privilege of voting, once a monopoly of church members, to all qualified male property holders.

The new English monarchs relaxed the royal grip on colonial trade, inaugurating a period of "**salutary neglect**" in which the much-resented **Navigation Laws** were only weakly enforced. Yet residues remained of Charles II's effort to assert tighter administrative control over his empire. More English officials—judges, clerks, customs officials—staffed the courts and strolled the wharves of English America. Many were incompetent, corrupt hacks who knew little and cared less about American affairs. Aggrieved Americans viewed the English officials with mounting contempt and resentment as the eighteenth century wore on.

Dominion of New England (1686–1689)
Administrative union created by royal authority, incorporating all of New England, New York, and East and West Jersey. Placed under the rule of Sir Edmund Andros, who curbed popular assemblies, taxed residents without their consent, and strictly enforced Navigation Laws. Its collapse after the Glorious Revolution in England demonstrated colonial opposition to strict royal control.

Glorious Revolution (1688–1689)
Relatively peaceful overthrow of the unpopular Catholic monarch, James II, who was replaced with Dutch-born William III and Mary II, daughter of James II. William and Mary accepted increased parliamentary oversight and new limits on monarchical authority.

salutary neglect (1688–1763)
Unofficial policy of relaxed royal control over colonial trade and only weak enforcement of Navigation Laws. Lasted from the Glorious Revolution to the end of the French and Indian War in 1763.

Navigation Laws *Series of laws passed, beginning in 1651, to regulate colonial shipping; the acts provided that only English ships would be allowed to trade in English and colonial ports and that all goods destined for the colonies would first pass through England.*

★ New Netherland Becomes New York

Late in the sixteenth century, the oppressed people of the Netherlands unfurled the standard of rebellion against Catholic Spain. After bloody and protracted fighting, they finally succeeded in winning their independence. This vigorous little lowland nation quickly emerged as a major commercial and naval power that challenged the naval supremacy of England.

New Amsterdam, 1664 The future metropolis, already a bustling port, is shown here as it was in the year that the English took over New Netherland and renamed it New York.

The Dutch Republic also became a leading colonial power through the activities of the enterprising Dutch East India Company (see Map 3.2). The company's vast riches came mostly from the East Indies (present-day Indonesia), where it maintained an enormous and profitable empire for over three hundred years. Seeking greater riches, in 1609 it employed an English explorer, Henry Hudson, who ventured into Delaware Bay and New York Bay and then ascended the Hudson River, hoping that he had at last chanced upon the coveted shortcut through the continent. But there was no transcontinental waterway, so Hudson merely filed a Dutch claim to the magnificently watered and wooded area.

New Netherland was permanently planted in 1623–1624 by the Dutch West India Company, the less wealthy counterpart of the East India Company. Never more than a secondary interest of the founders, who operated mostly in the West Indies and Brazil, the colony was exploited for its quick-profit fur trade. The company's most brilliant stroke was to buy Manhattan Island from the Indians (who did not actually "own" it) for trinkets—twenty-two thousand acres of what is now perhaps the most valuable real estate in the world for pennies per acre.

New Amsterdam—later New York City—was a company town. It was run by and for the Dutch company, in the interests of the stockholders. The investors had no enthusiasm for religious toleration, free speech, or democratic practices; and the governors appointed by the company were usually harsh and despotic. Religious dissenters, such as the Quakers, who opposed the official Dutch Reformed Church were savagely abused.

The picturesque Dutch colony of New Netherland took on a strongly aristocratic tinge and retained it for generations. Vast feudal estates fronting the Hudson River, known as **patroonships**, were granted to promoters who agreed to settle fifty people on them. One patroonship in the Albany area was larger than the later state of Rhode Island.

A threat to New Netherland soon came from the Swedes, who trespassed on Dutch preserves by planting the colony of New Sweden on the Delaware River in 1638. Resenting the Swedish intrusion, the Dutch dispatched a small military expedition in 1655, led by the able but despotic director-general Peter Stuyvesant. The main fort fell after a bloodless siege, and Swedish rule came to an abrupt end, leaving behind in later Delaware only

---

patroonships *Vast tracts of land along the Hudson River in New Netherland granted to wealthy promoters in exchange for bringing fifty settlers to the property.*

a sprinkling of Swedish place-names and Swedish log cabins (the first in America), as well as an admixture of Swedish blood.

Just as New Netherland absorbed New Sweden, it was soon the turn of the Dutch to be swallowed up by the English. In 1664, after the imperially ambitious King Charles II granted the area to his brother, the Duke of York, a strong English squadron appeared off the decrepit defenses of New Amsterdam. A fuming Peter Stuyvesant, short of all munitions except courage, was forced to surrender without firing a shot. New Amsterdam was thereupon renamed New York, in honor of the Duke of York. England won a splendid harbor, strategically located in the middle of the mainland colonies, with the stately Hudson River penetrating the interior. With the removal of this foreign wedge, the English banner waved triumphantly over a solid stretch of territory from Maine to the Carolinas.

The conquered Dutch province tenaciously retained many of the illiberal features of earlier days. An autocratic spirit survived, and the aristocratic element gained strength when certain corrupt English governors granted immense acreage to their favorites. Influential landowning families—such as the Livingstons and the De Lanceys—wielded disproportionate power in the affairs of colonial New York. These monopolistic land policies, combined with the lordly atmosphere, discouraged many European immigrants from coming. The physical growth of New York was correspondingly retarded.

Map 3.2 Early Settlements in the Middle Colonies, with Founding Dates

★ Penn's Holy Experiment in Pennsylvania

A remarkable group of dissenters, commonly known as Quakers, arose in England during the mid-1600s. Their name derived from the report that they "quaked" when touched by deep religious emotion. Their official name was the Religious Society of Friends.

Quakers were especially offensive to the authorities, both religious and civil. They refused to support the established Church of England with taxes. They built simple meetinghouses, congregated without a paid clergy, and "spoke up" themselves in meetings when moved. Believing that all were equal children in the sight of God, Quakers kept their broad-brimmed hats on in the presence of their "betters" and addressed others with a simple "thee" or "thou," rather than with conventional titles. They would take no oaths because Jesus had commanded, "Swear not at all." This peculiarity often embroiled them with government officials, for "test oaths" were still required to establish the fact that a person was not a Roman Catholic.

The Quakers, beyond a doubt, were a people of deep conviction. They abhorred strife and warfare and refused military service. As advocates of passive resistance, they would turn the other cheek and rebuild their meetinghouse on the sites where their enemies had torn it down. Their

> *In a Boston lecture in 1869, Ralph Waldo Emerson (1803–1882) declared:*
>
> **"The sect of the Quakers in their best representatives appear to me to have come nearer to the sublime history and genius of Christ than any other of the sects."**

courage and devotion to principle finally triumphed. Although at times they seemed stubborn and unreasonable, they were a simple, devoted, democratic people, contending in their own way for religious and civic freedom.

William Penn, a wellborn and athletic young Englishman, was attracted to the Quaker faith in 1660, when only sixteen years old. His father, disapproving, administered a sound flogging. After various adventures in the army (the best portrait of the peaceful Quaker has him in armor), the youth firmly embraced the despised faith and suffered much persecution.

Penn felt keenly the plight of his fellow Quakers, thousands of whom were executed, flogged, or cast into dank prisons. Penn's thoughts naturally turned to the New World, where a sprinkling of Quakers had already fled, notably to Rhode Island, North Carolina, and New Jersey. Eager to establish an asylum for his people, he also hoped to experiment with liberal ideas in government and at the same time make a profit. Finally, in 1681, he managed to secure from the king an immense grant of fertile land, in consideration of a monetary debt that the crown owed to his deceased father. The king called the area Pennsylvania ("Penn's Woodland") in honor of the father.

Pennsylvania was by far the best advertised of all the colonies. Its founder sent out paid agents and distributed countless pamphlets printed in English, Dutch, French, and German. Unlike the lures of many American real estate promoters, then and later, Penn's inducements were generally truthful. He especially welcomed substantial citizens, including industrious carpenters, masons, and shoemakers. His liberal land policy, which encouraged substantial holdings, was instrumental in attracting a heavy inflow of immigrants.

Penn formally launched his colony in 1681. He farsightedly bought land along the Delaware River from the Indians for his town of Philadelphia ("brotherly love" in Greek). His treatment of the native people was so fair that the Quaker "broad brims" went among them unarmed and even employed them as babysitters. For a brief period, Pennsylvania seemed the promised land of amicable Indian-white relations. Some southern tribes even migrated there, seeking the Quaker haven. But ironically, Quaker tolerance proved the undoing of Quaker Indian policy. As non-Quaker European immigrants flooded into the welcoming province, they undermined the Quakers' own benevolent policy toward the Indians. The feisty Scots-Irish were particularly unpersuaded by Quaker idealism.

Penn's new proprietary regime was unusually liberal and included a representative assembly elected by the landowners. Freedom of worship was guaranteed to all residents, although Penn was forced by London to deny Catholics and Jews the privilege of voting or holding office. The peace-loving Quakers of Pennsylvania made no provision for military defense. No restrictions were placed on immigration, and naturalization was made easy. The humane Quakers early developed a strong dislike of black slavery, and in the genial glow of Pennsylvania some progress was made toward social reform.

With its many liberal features, Pennsylvania attracted a rich mix of ethnic groups. They included numerous religious misfits who were repelled by the harsh practices of neighboring colonies. This Quaker refuge boasted a surprisingly modern atmosphere in an unmodern age, and to an unusual degree it afforded economic opportunity, civil liberty, and religious freedom. Even so, "**blue laws**" prohibited "ungodly revelers," stage plays, playing cards, dice, games, and excessive hilarity.

Under such generally happy auspices, Penn's brainchild grew lustily. The Quakers were shrewd businesspeople, and in a short time the settlers were exporting grain and other foodstuffs. Within two years Philadelphia claimed three hundred houses and twenty-five hundred people. Within nineteen years—by 1700—the colony was surpassed in population and wealth only by long-established Virginia and Massachusetts.

William Penn spent only about four years in the colony and eventually died full of sorrows back in England. But Pennsylvania, his enduring monument, was not only a noble experiment in government but also a new commonwealth. Based on civil and religious liberty and dedicated to freedom of conscience and worship, Pennsylvania held aloft a hopeful torch in a world of semidarkness.

---

blue laws *Also known as sumptuary laws, they are designed to restrict personal behavior in accord with a strict code of morality. Blue laws were passed across the colonies, particularly in Puritan New England and Quaker Pennsylvania.*

Small Quaker settlements flourished next door to Pennsylvania. New Jersey was started in 1664, when two noble proprietors received the area from the Duke of York. One of the proprietors sold West New Jersey in 1674 to a group of Quakers, and Quakers also acquired East New Jersey a few years later. In 1702, the crown clipped the Quakers' wings and combined the two Jerseys in a royal colony.

Swedish-tinged Delaware consisted of only three counties—two at high tide, the witticism goes—and was named after Lord De La Warr, the harsh military governor who had arrived in Virginia in 1610. Harboring some Quakers, and closely associated with Penn's flourishing colony, Delaware was granted its own assembly in 1703. But until the American Revolution it remained under the governor of Pennsylvania.

★ The Middle Way in the Middle Colonies

The middle colonies—New York, New Jersey, Delaware, and Pennsylvania—enjoyed certain features in common. In general, the soil was deep and fertile, unlike rocky New England. Pennsylvania, New York, and New Jersey came to be known as the "bread colonies" because of their heavy exports of grain.

Rivers also played a vital role. Broad, languid streams—notably the Susquehanna, the Delaware, and the Hudson—tapped the fur trade of the interior and beckoned adventuresome spirits into the backcountry. The rivers, unlike New England's, had few cascading waterfalls and hence presented little inducement to manufacturing with water-wheel power.

A surprising amount of industry nonetheless hummed in the middle colonies. Virginal forests abounded for lumbering and shipbuilding. The presence of deep river estuaries and landlocked harbors stimulated both commerce and the growth of seaports, such as New York and Philadelphia. Even Albany, more than a hundred miles up the Hudson, was a port of some consequence in colonial days.

The middle colonies stood midway between New England and the southern plantation group in many respects besides geography. Except in aristocratic New York, the landholdings were generally intermediate in size—smaller than in the plantation South but larger than in small-farm New England. Local government lay somewhere between the personalized town meeting of New England and the diffused county government of the South. There were fewer industries in the middle colonies than in New England, but more than in the South.

Yet the middle colonies could claim certain distinctions in their own right. Generally speaking, the population was more ethnically mixed than that of other settlements. The people were blessed with an unusual degree of religious toleration and democratic control. Earnest and devout Quakers, in particular, made a contribution to human freedom out of all proportion to their numbers. Desirable land was more easily acquired in the middle colonies than in New England or in the tidewater South. One result was that a considerable amount of economic and social democracy prevailed, though again less so in aristocratic New York.

Modern-minded Benjamin Franklin, often regarded as the most representative American personality of this era, was a child of the middle colonies. Although it is true that Franklin was born a Yankee in puritanical Boston, he entered Philadelphia as a seventeen-year-old in 1720 with a loaf of bread under each arm and immediately found a congenial home in the urbane, open atmosphere of what was then North America's biggest city. One Pennsylvanian later boasted that Franklin "came to life, at seventeen, in Philadelphia."

By the time Franklin arrived in the City of Brotherly Love, the American colonies themselves were "coming to life." Population was growing robustly. Transportation and communication were improving. The British, for the most part, left the colonists to fashion their own local governments, run their own churches, and develop networks of intercolonial trade. As people and products crisscrossed the colonies with increasing frequency and increasing volume, Americans began to realize that—far removed from Mother England—they were not merely surviving, but truly thriving.

Examining the Evidence
A Seventeenth-Century Valuables Cabinet

In 1999 a boatyard worker on Cape Cod and his sister, a New Hampshire teacher, inherited a small (20-pound, 16-1/2 inch-high) chest that had always stood on their grandmother's hall table, known in the family as the "Franklin chest." Eager to learn more about it, they set out to discover the original owner, tracing their family genealogy and consulting with furniture experts. In January 2000 this rare seventeenth-century cabinet, its full provenance now known, appeared on the auction block and sold for a record $2.4 million to the Peabody Essex Museum in Salem, Massachusetts. No less extraordinary than the price was the history of its creator and its owners embodied in the piece. Salem cabinetmaker James Symonds (1636–1726) had made the chest for his relatives Joseph Pope (1650–1712) and Bathsheba Folger (1652–1726) to commemorate their 1679 marriage. Symonds carved the Popes' initials and the date on the door of the cabinet. He also put elaborate S curves on the sides remarkably similar to the Mannerist carved oak paneling produced in Norfolk, England, from where his own cabinetmaker father had emigrated. Behind the chest's door are ten drawers where the Popes would have kept jewelry, money, deeds, and writing materials. Surely they prized the chest as a sign of refinement to be shown off in their best room, a sentiment passed down through the next thirteen generations even as the Popes' identities were lost. The chest may have become known as the "Franklin chest" because Bathsheba was Benjamin Franklin's aunt, but also because that identification appealed more to descendants ashamed that the Quaker Popes, whose own parents had been persecuted for their faith, were virulent accusers during the Salem witch trials of 1692.

1. Which significant features of this seventeenth-century chest could be determined simply by careful examination of the material object itself, and which could be learned only by historical research?
2. Which elements of the chest's construction and carving might provide significant clues about what historical inquiries to pursue?
3. What does the nature of the chest and its original function as a storage place for valuables tell you about the economic status of the original owners, Joseph and Bathsheba Pope? Why might this chest have been handed down through their descendants for over three hundred years, when most other material artifacts disappeared?

Christie's Images/The Bridgeman Art Library

Varying Viewpoints

Europeanizing America or Americanizing Europe?

The history of discovery and the earliest colonization raises perhaps the single most fundamental question about all American history. Should it be understood as the extension of European civilization into the New World or as the gradual development of a uniquely "American" culture? One school of thought tended to emphasize the Europeanization of America. Historians of that persuasion paid close attention to the situation in Europe, particularly in England and Spain, in the fifteenth and sixteenth centuries. They also focused on the various means by which the values and institutions of the mother continent were exported to the new lands in the western sea. Some European writers varied this general question by asking what transforming effect the discovery of America had on Europe itself. Both of these approaches are Eurocentric. More recently, historians have concentrated on the distinctiveness of America. The concern with European origins has evolved into a comparative treatment of English, Spanish, Dutch, and French settlements in the New World. The newest trend to emerge is a transatlantic history that views European empires and their American colonies as players in a process of cultural cross-fertilization affecting not only the colonies but Europe and Africa as well.

This less Eurocentric approach has changed the way historians explain the colonial development of America. Historians increasingly view the colonial period as one of "contact" and "adaptation" between European, African, and Native American ways of life. Scholars including Richard White, Alfred W. Crosby, William Cronon, Karen Kupperman, and Timothy Silver have enhanced understanding of the cultural as well as physical transformations that resulted from contact.

The variety of American societies that emerged out of the interaction of Europeans, Africans, and Native Americans has also become better appreciated. Studies such as Richard S. Dunn's *Sugar and Slaves* (1972) emphasize the importance of the Caribbean in early English colonization efforts. Similarly, Edmund S. Morgan's *American Slavery, American Freedom* (1975) stresses the role of economic ambition in explaining the English peopling of the Chesapeake and the eventual importation of African slaves to that region. Studies by Bernard Bailyn and David Hackett Fischer demonstrate that there was scarcely a "typical" English migrant to the New World. English colonists migrated both singly and in families, and for economic, social, political, and religious reasons.

The picture of colonial America that is emerging from all this new scholarship is of a society unique—and diverse—from its inception. No longer simply Europe transplanted, American colonial society by 1700 is now viewed as an outgrowth of many intertwining roots—of different European and African heritages, of varied encounters with native peoples, and of complicated mixtures of settler populations, each with its own distinctive set of ambitions.

CHAPTER SUMMARY ★ ★ ★ ★ ★ ★ ★ ★ ★ ★ ★ ★ ★ ★ ★

The New England colonies were founded primarily by English Calvinist religious dissenters called Puritans. While most Puritans sought to "purify" the Church of England from within, and not to break away from it, a small group of Separatists—the Pilgrims—founded the first small, pious Plymouth Colony in New England. More important was the larger group of nonseparating Puritans, led by John Winthrop, who founded the Massachusetts Bay Colony as part of a "great migration" of Puritans fleeing persecution in England in the 1630s.

A strong sense of common religious and moral purpose shaped the Massachusetts Bay Colony. Because of the close alignment of religion and politics in the colony, those who challenged religious orthodoxy, among them Anne Hutchinson and Roger Williams, were considered guilty of sedition as well and driven out of Massachusetts. The banished Williams founded Rhode Island, by far the most religiously and politically tolerant of the colonies. Other New England settlements, all originating in Massachusetts Bay, were established in Connecticut, Maine, and New Hampshire. Although they shared a common way of life, and occasionally engaged in common action (for instance, against the Indians), each of the New England colonies developed a substantial degree of independence.

The middle colonies took shape quite differently. New York, founded as New Netherland by the Dutch and later conquered by England, was economically and ethnically diverse, socially hierarchical, and politically quarrelsome. Pennsylvania, founded as a Quaker haven by William Penn, attracted an economically ambitious and religiously tolerant but politically troublesome population of diverse ethnic groups.

With their economic variety, ethnic and religious diversity, and political factionalism, the middle colonies were the most typically "American" of England's thirteen Atlantic seaboard colonies.

KEY TERMS

- Calvinism (35)
- Puritans (35)
- predestination (35)
- conversion (35)
- Separatists (36)
- Mayflower Compact (36)
- Massachusetts Bay Colony (37)
- Great English Migration (37)
- Quakers (38)
- *antinomianism* (38)
- Fundamental Orders (39)
- Pequot War (40)
- King Philip's War (40)
- English Civil War (40)
- New England Confederation (40)
- Dominion of New England (41)
- Glorious Revolution (41)
- salutary neglect (41)
- Navigation Laws (41)
- patroonships (42)
- blue laws (44)

PEOPLE TO KNOW

- Martin Luther
- John Calvin
- William Bradford
- John Winthrop
- Anne Hutchinson
- Roger Williams
- Massasoit
- Metacom (King Philip)
- Charles II
- Sir Edmund Andros
- William III
- Mary II
- Henry Hudson
- Peter Stuyvesant
- Duke of York
- William Penn

MindTap is a fully online, highly personalized learning experience built upon Cengage Learning content. MindTap combines student learning tools—readings, multimedia, activities, and assessments—into a singular Learning Path that guides students through the course.

Chapter 4

American Life in the Seventeenth Century
1607–1692

Being thus passed the vast ocean, and a sea of troubles before in their preparation..., they had now no friends to wellcome them, nor inns to entertaine or refresh their weatherbeaten bodys, no houses or much less towns to repaire too, to seeke for succore.

WILLIAM BRADFORD, *OF PLYMOUTH PLANTATION*, CA. 1630

As the seventeenth century unfolded, the crude encampments of the first colonists slowly gave way to permanent settlements. Durable and distinctive ways of life emerged, as Europeans and Africans adapted to the New World and as Native Americans adapted to the newcomers. Even the rigid doctrines of Puritanism softened somewhat in response to the circumstances of life in America. And though all the colonies remained tied to England and stitched tightly into the fabric of an Atlantic economy, regional differences continued to crystallize, notably the increasing importance of slavery to the southern way of life.

Chapter Outline

- Life and Labor in the Chesapeake Region
- Indentured Servants and Bacon's Rebellion in Virginia, 1676
- Slavery Families in New England
- The Salem Witchcraft Trials, 1692
- The Changing New England Way of Life
- *Examining the Evidence: An Indentured Servant's Contract, 1746*
- *Thinking Globally: The Atlantic Slave Trade, 1500-1860*

FOCUS QUESTIONS

1. What were the major features of the economy, population, and social structure of England's North American colonies in the seventeenth century?
2. How did the social order and ways of life differ between the southern and northern colonies?
3. How did the labor system of white indentured servitude work in the early seventeenth century, and why did plantation owners eventually replace this labor system with African slavery?
4. How did the African slave trade develop, and what enabled diverse enslaved Africans to develop their own culture and practices in America?
5. What were the major features of the "New England way of life," and how did religion, family life, and women's roles change in the later seventeenth century?

49

CHRONOLOGY

1619	First Africans arrive in Virginia	1680s	Mass expansion of slavery in colonies
1625	Population of English colonies in America about two thousand	1689–1691	Leisler's Rebellion in New York
1636	Harvard College founded	1692	Salem witch trials in Massachusetts
1662	Half-Way Covenant for Congregational Church membership established	1693	College of William and Mary founded
1670	Virginia assembly disfranchises landless freemen	1698	Royal African Company slave trade monopoly ended
1676	Bacon's Rebellion in Virginia	1700	Population of English colonies in America about 250,000

★ The Unhealthy Chesapeake

Life in the American wilderness was nasty, brutish, and short for the earliest Chesapeake settlers. Malaria, dysentery, and typhoid took a cruel toll, cutting ten years off the life expectancy of newcomers from England. Half the people born in early Virginia and Maryland did not survive to celebrate their twentieth birthdays. Few of the remaining half lived to see their fiftieth—or even their fortieth, if they were women.

The disease-ravaged settlements of the Chesapeake grew only slowly in the seventeenth century, mostly through fresh immigration from England. The great majority of immigrants were single men in their late teens and early twenties, and most perished soon after arrival. Surviving males competed for the affections of the extremely scarce women, whom they outnumbered nearly six to one in 1650 and still outnumbered by three to two at the end of the century. Eligible women did not remain single for long.

Families were few and fragile in this ferocious environment. Most men could not find mates. Most marriages were destroyed by the death of a partner within seven years. Scarcely any children reached adulthood under the care of two parents, and almost no one knew a grandparent. Weak family ties were reflected in the many pregnancies among unmarried young girls. In one Maryland county, more than a third of all brides were already pregnant when they wed.

Yet, despite these hardships, the Chesapeake colonies struggled on. The native-born inhabitants eventually acquired immunity to the killer diseases that had ravaged the original immigrants. The presence of more women allowed more families to form, and by the end of the seventeenth century the white population of the Chesapeake was growing on the basis of its own birthrate. As the eighteenth century opened, Virginia, with some fifty-nine thousand people, was the most populous colony. Maryland, with about thirty thousand, was the third largest (after Massachusetts).

An agent for the Virginia Company in London submitted the following description of the Virginia colony in 1622:

"I found the plantations generally seated upon mere salt marshes full of infectious bogs and muddy creeks and lakes, and thereby subjected to all those inconveniences and diseases which are so commonly found in the most unsound and most unhealthy parts of England."

★ The Tobacco Economy

Although unhealthy for human life, the Chesapeake was immensely hospitable to tobacco cultivation. Profit-hungry settlers often planted tobacco to sell before they planted corn to eat. But intense tobacco cultivation quickly exhausted the soil, creating a nearly insatiable demand for new land. Relentlessly seeking fresh fields to plant in tobacco, commercial growers plunged ever farther up the river valleys, provoking ever more Indian attacks.

Leaf-laden ships annually hauled some 1.5 million pounds of tobacco out of Chesapeake Bay by the 1630s and almost 40 million pounds by the end of the century. This enormous production depressed prices, but colonial Chesapeake tobacco growers responded to falling prices by planting still more acres in tobacco and bringing still more product to market.

More tobacco meant more labor, but where was it to come from? Families procreated too slowly to provide it by natural population increase. Indians died too quickly on contact with whites, and African slaves cost too much money. But England still had a "surplus" of displaced farmers desperate for employment. Many of them boarded ship for America as **indentured servants**, voluntarily mortgaging the sweat of their bodies for several years (usually four to seven) to Chesapeake masters. In exchange they received transatlantic passage and eventual "freedom dues," including an axe, a few barrels of corn, a suit of clothes, and perhaps a small parcel of land.

Both Virginia and Maryland employed the **headright system** to encourage the importation of servant workers. Under its terms, whoever paid the passage of a laborer received the right to acquire fifty acres of land. Taking advantage of this system, some masters soon parlayed their investments in servants into vast holdings in real estate. They became the great merchant-planters who came to dominate the agriculture and commerce of the southern colonies. Chesapeake planters had brought some 100,000 indentured servants to the region by 1700. These "white slaves" represented more than three-quarters of all European immigrants to Virginia and Maryland in the seventeenth century.

Indentured servants led a hard but hopeful life in the early days of the Chesapeake settlements. They looked forward to becoming free and acquiring land of their own after completing their term of servitude. But as prime land became scarcer toward the end of the seventeenth century, masters became increasingly resistant to including land grants in "freedom dues." Even after formal freedom was granted, penniless freed workers often had little choice but to hire themselves out for pitifully low wages to their former masters.

indentured servants *Migrants who, in exchange for transatlantic passage, bound themselves to a colonial employer for a term of service, typically between four and seven years. Their migration addressed the chronic labor shortage in the colonies and facilitated settlement.*

headright system *Employed in the tobacco colonies to encourage the importation of indentured servants. It allowed an individual to acquire fifty acres of land if he paid for a laborer's passage to the colony.*

⭐ Frustrated Freemen and Bacon's Rebellion

An accumulating mass of footloose, impoverished freemen was drifting discontentedly about the Chesapeake region by the late seventeenth century. Mostly single young men, they were frustrated by their broken hopes of acquiring land as well as by their gnawing failure to find single women to marry.

The swelling number of these wretched bachelors rattled the established planters. Encouraged by Governor William Berkeley, the Virginia assembly in 1670 disfranchised most of the landless knockabouts. About a thousand poverty-stricken Virginians then broke out of control in 1676, led by a twenty-nine-year-old planter, Nathaniel Bacon. Angered by Berkeley's mild Indian policies as well as economic grievances, Bacon and his followers first mercilessly attacked Indians on the frontier. They then chased Berkeley from Jamestown and put the torch to the capital. Chaos swept the raw colony as frustrated freemen and resentful servants—described as "a rabble of the basest sort of people"—went on a rampage of plundering and pilfering.

As this civil war in Virginia ground on, Bacon suddenly died of disease. Berkeley thereupon crushed the uprising with brutal cruelty, hanging more than twenty rebels. Back in England, King Charles II complained, "That old fool has put to death more people in that naked country than I did here for the murder of my father."

Contending Voices

Berkeley Versus Bacon

Nathaniel Bacon (ca. 1647–1676) assailed Virginia's Governor William Berkeley (1606–1677) in 1676

"for having protected, favored, and emboldened the Indians against His Majesty's loyal subjects, never contriving, requiring, or appointing any due or proper means of satisfaction for their many invasions, robberies, and murders committed upon us."

For his part, Governor William Berkeley (1605–1677) declared,

"I have lived thirty-four years amongst you [Virginians], as uncorrupt and diligent as ever [a] Governor was, [while] Bacon is a man of two years amongst you, his person and qualities unknown to most of you, and to all men else, by any virtuous act that ever I heard of. . . . I will take counsel of wiser men than myself, but Mr. Bacon has none about him but the lowest of the people."

What do these accusations reveal about the two men's views of the relation between rulers and the ruled?

Examining the Evidence

An Indentured Servant's Contract, 1746

Legal documents, such as this contract signed in Virginia in 1746, not only provide evidence about the ever-changing rules by which societies have regulated their affairs, but also furnish rich information about the conditions of life and the terms of human relationships in the past. This agreement between Thomas Clayton and James Griffin provides a reminder that not all indentured servants in early America came from abroad. Indentured servitude could be equivalent to an apprenticeship, in which a young person traded several years of service to a master in exchange for instruction in the master's craft. Here Clayton pledges himself to five years in Griffin's employ in return for a promise to initiate the young man into the "Mystery" of the master's craft.

1. Why might the master's trade be described as a "mystery"?

2. From the evidence of this contract, what are the principal objectives of each of the parties to the contract?

3. What problems does the contract suggest that the master and the servant/apprentice each anticipate? What obligations does each assume?

4. What does the required consent of Clayton's mother to the contract suggest about the young man's status and situation?

5. The first sentence of the contract says that Clayton "doth voluntarily and of his own free will and accord, and with the consent and approbation of his mother, put himself apprentice to James Griffin. ..." Why was it legally important that Clayton affirm that he had *voluntarily* made himself an unpaid, bound servant/laborer for a term of five years?

6. The contract also declares that Griffin may not, among other things, "commit fornication," marry, or play cards or dice during his term of servitude. What does this provision reveal about the relationship of master to servant? Should this document be considered an "employment contract" or something else?

The distant English king could scarcely imagine the depths of passion and fear that **Bacon's Rebellion** excited in Virginia. Bacon had ignited the smoldering unhappiness of landless former servants, and he had pitted the hardscrabble backcountry frontiersmen against the haughty gentry of the tidewater plantations. The rebellion was suppressed, but these tensions remained. Lordly planters, surrounded by a still-seething sea of malcontents, anxiously looked about for less troublesome laborers to toil in their restless tobacco kingdom. Their eyes soon lit on Africa.

Bacon's Rebellion (1676) *Uprising of Virginia backcountry farmers and indentured servants led by planter Nathaniel Bacon; initially a response to Governor William Berkeley's refusal to protect backcountry settlers from Indian attacks, the rebellion eventually grew into a broader conflict between impoverished settlers and the planter elite.*

★ Colonial Slavery

More than 7 million Africans were carried in chains to the New World in the three centuries or so following Columbus's landing (see "Thinking Globally: The Atlantic Slave Trade, 1500–1860," p. 54). Only about 400,000 of them ended up in North America. Most were hauled to Spanish and Portuguese South America or to the sugar-rich West Indies. Africans had been brought to Jamestown as early as 1619, but as late as 1670 they numbered only about 7 percent of the 50,000 people in the southern plantation colonies as a whole. For hard-pinched colonists, white servants were far less costly than high-priced slaves, who might die soon after arrival.

Drastic change came in the 1680s. Rising wages in England shrank the pool of potential indentured servants, while large planters were growing increasingly fearful of the potentially mutinous former servants in their midst. By the mid-1680s, for the first time, black slaves outnumbered white servants among the plantation colonies' new arrivals. In 1698 the **Royal African Company**, first chartered in 1672, lost its crown-granted monopoly on carrying slaves to the colonies. Enterprising Americans, especially Rhode Islanders, rushed to cash in on the lucrative slave trade, and the supply of slaves rose steeply. By 1750 blacks accounted for nearly half the population of Virginia, and in South Carolina they outnumbered whites two to one.

Royal African Company *English joint-stock company that enjoyed a state-granted monopoly on the colonial slave trade from 1672 until 1698. The supply of slaves to the North American colonies rose sharply once the company lost its monopoly privileges.*

Most of the slaves who reached North America came from the west coast of Africa, especially the area stretching from present-day Senegal to Angola. They were originally captured by African coastal tribes, who traded them in crude markets on the shimmering tropical beaches to itinerant European—and American—flesh merchants. Usually branded and bound, the captives were herded aboard sweltering ships for the gruesome **middle passage**, on which death rates ran as high as 20 percent. Terrified survivors were eventually shoved onto auction blocks in New World ports such as Newport, Rhode Island, or Charleston, South Carolina, where a giant slave market traded in human misery for more than a century.

middle passage *Transatlantic voyage that slaves endured between Africa and the colonies. Mortality rates were notoriously high.*

slave codes *Set of laws beginning in 1662 defining racial slavery. They established the hereditary nature of slavery and limited the rights and education of slaves.*

A few of the earliest African immigrants gained their freedom, and some even became slaveowners themselves. But as the number of Africans in their midst increased dramatically toward the end of the seventeenth century, white colonists reacted remorselessly to this supposed racial threat. Beginning in Virginia in 1662, the iron conditions of bondage were spelled out in **slave codes** that made blacks *and their children* the property (or "chattels") for life of their white masters. Not even conversion to Christianity could qualify a slave for freedom. Slavery might have begun in America for economic reasons, but by the end of the seventeenth century, it was clear that racial discrimination also powerfully molded the American slave system.

The Mennonites of Germantown, Pennsylvania, recorded the earliest known protest against slavery in America in 1688:

"There is a saying, that we should do to all men like as we will be done ourselves.... But to bring men hither, or to rob and sell them against their will, we stand against.... Pray, what thing in the world can be done worse towards us, than if men should rob or steal us away, and sell us for slaves to strange countries, separating husbands from their wives and children?"

★ Southern Society

As slavery spread, the gaps in the South's social structure widened. The rough equality of poverty and disease of the early days was giving way to a defined hierarchy of wealth and status. At the top of this southern social ladder perched

Thinking Globally

The Atlantic Slave Trade, 1500–1860

In the three and a half centuries following Columbus's discovery, slave merchants crammed over 11 million African men, women, and children into the holds of ships and carried them like common cargo to the New World. Roughly 2 million souls perished mid-voyage before confronting the agonies and indignities of slavery in the Americas. Nearly half a million enslaved Africans came ashore in North America, while the overwhelming majority were destined for Latin America and the Caribbean (see Map 4.1).

European trading companies and New England merchants reaped enormous profits from this human trafficking, and the slavers were not the only ones to benefit. Slave trading fed off the insatiable appetite for sugar, tobacco, cotton, and other New World products that Europeans and Americans craved. It thrived, too, on the willingness of Africans themselves to sell their fellow Africans to European and American slavers. Marketing human beings on such a vast scale required the complicity of African warlords, slave-ship captains and crew, stevedores, planters, tea drinkers, tailors, bakers, smokers, bankers, and a host of middlemen on four continents.

Only in the nineteenth century did nations in Europe and the Americas begin to outlaw the international slave trade, beginning with Britain in 1807. After Congress banned further slave importations to the United States in 1808, a flourishing internal market developed. Masters in the Upper South bred slaves for sale on the rapidly expanding cotton frontier in the old Southwest. Europeans as well as Americans in the "free states" lent indirect support to that domestic slave trade as they continued to consume slave-produced goods.

The "Middle Passage" Human cargo in the hold of a slave ship.

a small but powerful covey of great planters. Owning gangs of slaves and vast domains of land, the planters ruled the region's economy and virtually monopolized political power. Yet, legend to the contrary, these great seventeenth-century merchant-planters were not silk-swathed cavaliers gallantly imitating the ways of English country gentlemen. For the most part they were a hard-working, businesslike lot, laboring long hours over the problems of plantation management. Far beneath the planters in wealth, prestige, and political power were the small farmers, the largest social group. They might or might not own one or two slaves, but in either case they lived a ragged, hand-to-mouth existence on their modest plots. Still lower on the social scale were landless whites and, below them, indentured servants still serving out their terms. The oppressed black slaves, of course, remained enchained in society's basement.

Few cities sprouted in the colonial South, and consequently an urban professional class, including lawyers and financiers, was slow to emerge. Southern life revolved around the great plantations, distantly isolated from one another. Waterways, rather than the wretched roads, provided the principal means of transportation from one plantation to another.

Map 4.1 Main Sources of African Slaves, ca. 1500 to ca. 1860 More than three centuries of the "African Diaspora" scattered blacks throughout the New World. Britain's North American colonies (the future United States) constituted the extreme northern periphery of this system, receiving about 400,000 of the nearly 10 million arrivals, the great majority of whom ended up in the West Indies and Brazil.

★ The New England Family

Nature smiled more benignly on pioneer New Englanders than on their disease-plagued fellow colonists to the south. Clean water and cool temperatures, which retarded the spread of microbes, created healthier living conditions that enabled settlers in seventeenth-century New England to *add* ten years to their life spans by migrating from the Old World, in stark contrast to the fate of Chesapeake immigrants. The first generations of Puritan colonists enjoyed, on the average, about seventy years on this earth—not very different from the life expectancy of present-day Americans.

In further contrast with the Chesapeake, New Englanders tended to migrate not as single individuals but as families, and the family remained at the center of New England life. Early marriage and prolific childbearing enabled New England's population to grow from natural reproductive increase almost from the outset. Women typically wed by their early twenties and produced babies about every two years thereafter until menopause. A married woman could expect to experience up to ten pregnancies and rear as many as eight surviving children. A New England woman might well have dependent

55

Mrs. Elizabeth Freake and Baby Mary This portrait of a Boston mother and child in about 1674 suggests the strong family ties that characterized early New England society

children living in her household from the earliest days of her marriage until the day of her death, and child raising became, in essence, her full-time occupation.

The longevity of the New Englanders contributed to family stability. Children received nurturing love and guidance not only from their parents but from their grandparents as well. Family stability was reflected in low premarital pregnancy rates (again in contrast with the Chesapeake) and in the generally strong, tranquil social structure characteristic of colonial New England.

Oddly enough, the strength of New England families actually weakened the economic independence of women in that region compared with women in the South. Because southern men frequently died young, leaving widows with small children to support, the southern colonies allowed married women to retain separate titles to their property and gave widows the right to inherit their husbands' estates. But in New England, Puritan lawmakers worried that recognizing women's separate property rights would undercut the unity of husband and wife. New England women, therefore, usually gave up their property rights when they married.

"A true wife accounts subjection her honor," one Massachusetts Puritan leader declared, expressing a sentiment then common in Europe as well as America. But in the New World, a rudimentary conception of women's rights as individuals was beginning to appear in the seventeenth century. Women still could not vote, and the popular attitude persisted that they were morally weaker than men. But a husband's power over his wife was not absolute. The New England authorities could and did intervene to restrain abusive spouses, and women had some spheres of autonomy. Midwifery—assisting with childbirths—was a virtual female monopoly, and midwives often fostered networks of women bonded by the common travails of motherhood.

Above all, the laws of Puritan New England sought to defend the integrity of marriage. Divorce was exceedingly rare: outright abandonment was among the few permissible grounds for divorce. Adultery was another. Convicted adulterers—especially if they were women—were whipped in public and forced forever after to wear the capital letter "A" cut out in cloth and sewn on their outer garments—the basis for Nathaniel Hawthorne's famous 1850 tale *The Scarlet Letter*.

★ Life in the New England Towns

Sturdy New Englanders evolved a tightly knit society, the basis of which was small villages and farms. Puritanism especially made for unity of purpose—and for concern about the moral health of the whole community.

Even territorial expansion occurred in orderly, communal fashion, in contrast to the Chesapeake's normal mode of expansion by lone-wolf planters on their own initiative. New towns were legally chartered by the colonial authorities, and the distribution of land was entrusted to the steady hands of sober-minded town fathers, or "proprietors." After receiving a grant of land from the colonial legislature, the proprietors usually laid out their town around a meetinghouse, which served as both the place of worship and the town hall. Also marked out was a village green, where the militia could drill. Each family received several parcels of land.

Towns of more than fifty families were required to provide elementary education, and roughly half of the adults knew how to read and write. As early as 1636, just six years after the colony's founding, the Massachusetts Puritans established Harvard College to train local boys for the ministry. Only in 1693, eighty-six years after the founding of Jamestown, did the Virginians establish their first college, William and Mary.

Puritans ran their own churches, and democracy in **Congregational Church** government led logically to democracy in political government. The town meeting, in which the adult males met together and each man voted, was a showcase and a classroom for democracy. The New England town meeting, observed Thomas Jefferson, was "the best school of political liberty the world ever saw."

Congregational Church *Self-governing Puritan congregations without the hierarchical establishment of the Anglican Church.*

★ The Changing New England Way of Life

Yet, worries plagued the God-fearing pioneers of these tidy New England settlements. The pressure of a growing population was gradually dispersing the Puritans onto outlying farms, far from the control of church and neighbors. And although the core of Puritan belief still burned brightly, the passage of time was dampening the first generation's religious zeal. About the middle of the seventeenth century, earnest preachers began scolding parishioners for their waning piety in a new form of sermon—the **jeremiad**.

jeremiad *Often-fiery sermons lamenting the waning piety of parishioners first delivered in New England in the mid-seventeenth century; named after the doom-saying Old Testament prophet Jeremiah.*

In response to the apparent decline in conversions, troubled ministers in 1662 announced a new formula for church membership, the **Half-Way Covenant**. This new arrangement admitted the unconverted children of existing members to baptism, but not to "full communion." By conferring partial membership rights in the once-exclusive Puritan congregations, the Half-Way Covenant weakened the distinction between the "elect" and other members of society. In effect, strict religious purity was sacrificed somewhat to the cause of wider religious participation. Interestingly, from about this time onward, women were in the majority in the Puritan congregations.

Half-Way Covenant (1662) *Agreement allowing unconverted offspring of church members to baptize their children. It signified a waning of religious zeal among second- and third-generation Puritans.*

Women also played a prominent role in one of New England's most frightening religious episodes. A group of adolescent girls in Salem, Massachusetts claimed to have been bewitched by certain older women. A hysterical "witch hunt" ensued, leading to the execution in 1692 of twenty individuals.

The reign of horror in Salem grew not only from the superstitions and prejudices of the age but also from the unsettled social and religious conditions of the rapidly evolving Massachusetts village. Most of the accused witches came from families associated with Salem's burgeoning market economy; their accusers came largely from the ranks of subsistence farming families in Salem's hinterland. The **Salem Witch Trials** thus reflected the widening social stratification of New England, as well as the fear of many religious traditionalists that the Puritan heritage was being eclipsed by Yankee commercialism. The Salem witchcraft delusion marked an all-time high in the American experience of popular passions run wild.

Salem Witch Trials (1692–1693) *Series of witchcraft trials launched after a group of adolescent girls in Salem, Massachusetts claimed to have been bewitched by certain older women of the town. Twenty individuals were put to death before the trials were put to an end by the governor of Massachusetts.*

New England soil, like New England religion, was hard and unyielding. Scratching a living from the rock-strewn land put a premium on industry and penny-pinching frugality, for which New Englanders became famous. The grudging land also left colonial New England less ethnically mixed than its southern neighbors. European immigrants were not attracted in great numbers to a site where the soil was so stony—and the sermons so sulfurous.

Yet, the harsh climate and unproductive soil of New England eventually encouraged a diversified agriculture and industry. Staple products such as tobacco did not flourish, as in the South. Black slavery, although attempted, could not exist profitably on small farms. Turning away from the land, New Englanders more and more looked to the sea for a living. Hacking timber from their dense forests, they became experts in shipbuilding and commerce. They also ceaselessly exploited the self-perpetuating codfish lode off the coast of Newfoundland—the fishy "gold mines of New England." As a reminder of the importance of fishing, a handsome replica of the "sacred cod" is proudly displayed to this day in the Massachusetts State House in Boston.

The Massachusetts School Law of 1647 stated:

"It being one chief project of the old deluder, Satan, to keep men from the knowledge of the Scriptures, as in former times by keeping them in an unknown tongue, it is therefore ordered that every township in this jurisdiction, after the Lord has increased them [in] number to fifty householders, shall then forthwith appoint one within their town to teach all such children as shall resort to him to write and read, whose wages shall be paid either by the parents or masters of such children, or by the inhabitants in general."

> *New England early acquired a reputation as a healthy environment. Urging his fellow Englishmen to emigrate to Massachusetts Bay Colony in 1630, the Reverend John White described New England (somewhat fancifully) as follows:*
>
> "No country yields a more propitious air for our temper than New England.... Many of our people that have found themselves always weak and sickly at home, have become strong and healthy there: perhaps by the dryness of the air and constant temper[ature] of it, which seldom varies from cold to heat, as it does with us.... Neither are the natives at any time troubled with pain of teeth, soreness of eyes, or ache in their limbs."

Just as the land shaped New Englanders, so they shaped the land. Native Americans of the region had left an early imprint on the earth, beating trails through the woods and periodically burning woodlands to restore leafy first-growth forests. But in contrast with Native Americans, who *used* the land but recognized no right to *own* it, the English settlers felt a virtual duty to "improve" the land by clearing woodlands for pasturage and tillage, building roads and fences, and laying out permanent settlements. The introduction of livestock also led colonists to clear ever more forests for pastureland, while the animals' voracious appetites and heavy hooves compacted the soil, speeding erosion and flooding.

The combination of Calvinism, soil, and climate in New England made for energy, purposefulness, sternness, stubbornness, self-reliance, and resourcefulness. Righteous New Englanders prided themselves on being God's chosen people. They long boasted that Boston was "the hub of the universe"—at least in spirit. A famous jingle of later days ran:

> *I come from the city of Boston*
> *The home of the bean and the cod*
> *Where the Cabots speak only to Lowells*
> *And the Lowells speak only to God.*

New England has had an incalculable impact on the rest of the nation. Ousted by their sterile soil, thousands of New Englanders scattered from Ohio to Oregon and even Hawaii. The democratic town meeting, the tidy schoolhouse, and "Yankee ingenuity," all originally fostered by the flinty fields and comfortless climate of New England, came to be claimed by all Americans as a proud national heritage. And the fabled "New England conscience," born of the steadfast Puritan faith, left a legacy of high idealism in the national character and inspired many later reformers.

★ The Early Settlers' Days and Ways

The cycles of the seasons and the sun set the schedules of all the earliest American colonists, men as well as women, blacks as well as whites. The overwhelming majority of colonists were farmers. They planted in the spring, tended their crops in the summer, harvested in the fall, and prepared in the winter to begin the cycle anew. They usually rose at dawn and went to bed at dusk. Chores might be performed after nightfall only if they were "worth the candle," a phrase that has persisted in American speech.

Women, enslaved or free, on southern plantations or northern farms, cooked, cleaned, and cared for children. Men worked the land, cut firewood, and butchered livestock as needed. Children helped with all these tasks, while picking up such schooling as they could.

Life was humble but comfortable by the standards of the time. Compared to most seventeenth-century Europeans, Americans lived in affluent abundance. Land was relatively cheap, though somewhat less available in the planter-dominated South than elsewhere. Wages for workmen were roughly three times those of their English counterparts.

"Dukes don't emigrate," the saying goes, for if people enjoy wealth and security, they are not likely to risk exposing their lives in the wilderness. Similarly, the very poorest members of a society may not possess even the modest means needed to pull up stakes and seek a fresh start in life. Accordingly, most white migrants to early colonial America came neither from the aristocracy nor from the dregs of European society—with the partial exception of the impoverished indentured servants.

Seventeenth-century society in all the colonies had a certain simple sameness to it, especially in the more egalitarian New England and middle colonies. Yet, many settlers who considered themselves to be of the "better sort" tried to re-create on a modified scale the social structure they had known in the Old World. Resentment against such upper-class pretensions helped to spark outbursts such as Bacon's Rebellion in Virginia in 1676, the uprising of Maryland's Protestants toward the end of the seventeenth century, and **Leisler's Rebellion**, an ill-starred and bloody insurgence that rocked New York City from 1689 to 1691.

For their part, would-be American blue bloods resented the pretensions of the "meaner sort" and passed laws to try to keep them in their place. Massachusetts in 1651 prohibited poorer folk from "wearing gold or silver lace," and in eighteenth-century Virginia a tailor was fined and jailed for arranging to race his horse—"a sport only for gentlemen." But these efforts to reproduce the finely stratified societies of Europe proved feeble in the early American wilderness, where equality and democracy found fertile soil—at least for white people.

Leisler's Rebellion (1689–1691)
Armed conflict between aspiring merchants led by Jacob Leisler and the ruling elite of New York. One of many uprisings that erupted across the colonies when wealthy colonists attempted to re-create European social structures in the New World.

CHAPTER SUMMARY ★ ─★─★─★─★─★─★─★─★─★─★─★─★─★─

Life was hard in the seventeenth-century southern colonies. Disease drastically shortened life spans in the Chesapeake region, even for the young single men who made up the majority of settlers. Families were few and fragile, with men greatly outnumbering women, who were much in demand and seldom remained single for long.

The tobacco economy first thrived using the labor of white indentured servants, who hoped to work their way up to become landowners and perhaps even become wealthy. But by the late seventeenth century, this hope was increasingly frustrated, and the discontents of the largely single, poor white males exploded in Bacon's Rebellion in Virginia.

With white labor increasingly troublesome, slaves (earlier a small fraction of the work force) began to be imported from West Africa by the tens of thousands in the 1680s and soon became essential to the colonial economy. As the percentage of slaves in the population increased, white colonists responded by sharpening the distinction between indentured servitude and slavery. New laws made slaves and their descendants lifelong chattels, and tightened the link between blackness and slavery.

By contrast with the South, New England's clean water and cool air contributed to a healthy way of life, which actually *added* ten years to the average English life span. The New England way of life centered on strong families and tightly knit towns and churches, which were relatively democratic and equal by seventeenth-century standards. By the late seventeenth century, however, social and religious tensions developed in these narrow communities, as the Salem witch hysteria dramatically illustrates.

Rocky soil forced many New Englanders to turn to fishing and merchant shipping for their livelihoods. Their difficult lives and stern religion made New Englanders tough, idealistic, purposeful, and resourceful. In later years they spread these same values across much of American society.

All of seventeenth-century American society was relatively simple and almost entirely agrarian. Would-be aristocrats who tried to re-create the strict social hierarchies of Europe were generally frustrated.

KEY TERMS

- indentured servants (51)
- headright system (51)
- Bacon's Rebellion (53)
- Royal African Company (53)
- middle passage (53)
- slave codes (53)
- Congregational Church (57)
- jeremiad (57)
- Half-Way Covenant (57)
- Salem Witch Trials (57)
- Leisler's Rebellion (59)

PEOPLE TO KNOW

- William Berkeley
- Nathaniel Bacon

MindTap is a fully online, highly personalized learning experience built upon Cengage Learning content. MindTap combines student learning tools—readings, multimedia, activities, and assessments—into a singular Learning Path that guides students through the course.

Chapter 5

Colonial Society on the Eve of Revolution

1700–1775

• • •

Driven from every other corner of the earth, freedom of thought and the right of private judgment in matters of conscience direct their course to this happy country as their last asylum.

Samuel Adams, 1776

Chapter Outline

- Population Growth and Ethnic Diversity
- Enslaved African Americans
- Colonial Society and Economy
- The Atlantic Economy
- The Great Awakening
- Education and Culture
- Political Patterns
- *Makers of America: From African to African American*
- *Varying Viewpoints: Colonial America—Communities of Conflict or Consensus?*

The common term *thirteen original colonies* is misleading. Britain ruled thirty-two colonies in North America by 1775, including Canada, the Floridas, and various Caribbean islands. But only thirteen of the colonies unfurled the standard of rebellion. A few of the nonrebels, such as Canada and Jamaica, were larger, wealthier, or more populous than some of the rebellious thirteen. Why, then, did some British colonies eventually strike for their independence, while others did not? Part of the answer is to be found in the distinctive social, economic, and political structures of the thirteen Atlantic seaboard colonies—and in the halting, gradual appearance of a recognizably *American* way of life.

FOCUS QUESTIONS

1. What were the major demographic and social conditions that characterized Britain's eighteenth-century colonies, and why were there greater class divisions compared to the early seventeenth-century settlements?

2. How did enslaved Africans from diverse cultures create a distinctive African American culture in the colonies, and what conditions enabled many slaves in North America to establish family life?

3. What were the causes of the first religious "Great Awakening" in American history, and how did the Great Awakening affect colonial identity, education, and politics?

4. What were the major features of education, culture, and daily life in the eighteenth century?

5. What issues and conflicts dominated colonial politics, and how did both formal institutions (legislatures and governors) and informal practices of public opinion affect those issues?

CHRONOLOGY

1693	College of William and Mary founded	1738	George Whitefield spreads Great Awakening
1701	Yale College founded	1739	South Carolina slave revolt
1712	New York slave revolt	1746	Princeton College founded
1721	Smallpox inoculation introduced	1760	Britain vetoes South Carolina anti-slave trade measures
1732	First edition of Franklin's *Poor Richard's Almanack*	1764	Brown College founded
1734	Jonathan Edwards begins Great Awakening	1766	Rutgers College founded
1734–1735	Zenger free-press trial in New York	1769	Dartmouth College founded

★ Conquest by the Cradle

Among the distinguishing characteristics that the eventually rebellious settlements shared was lusty population growth. In 1700 they contained fewer than 300,000 souls, about 20,000 of whom were black. By 1775, 2.5 million people inhabited the thirteen colonies, of whom about half a million were black. White immigrants made up nearly 400,000 of the increased number, and black "forced immigrants" accounted for almost as many again. But most of the growth spurt stemmed from the remarkable natural fertility of all Americans, white and black. The youthful Americans, whose average age in 1775 was about sixteen, were doubling their numbers every twenty-five years. Unfriendly Dr. Samuel Johnson, back in Britain, growled that the Americans were multiplying like their own rattlesnakes.

This population boom had political consequences. In 1700 there were twenty Britons for each American colonist. By 1775 the British advantage in numbers had fallen to three to one—setting the stage for a momentous shift in the balance of power between the colonies and Britain.

The bulk of the population was cooped up east of the Alleghenies. The most populous colonies in 1775 were Virginia, Massachusetts, Pennsylvania, North Carolina, and Maryland—in that order. Only four communities could properly be called cities: Philadelphia, including suburbs, was first with about 34,000 residents, trailed by New York, Boston, and Charleston. About 90 percent of the people lived in rural areas.

★ A Potpourri of Peoples

Colonial America was a melting pot and had been from the outset. The population, although basically English in stock and language, was picturesquely mottled with numerous foreign groups (see Map 5.1).

Germans constituted about 6 percent of the total population, or 150,000, by 1775. Fleeing religious persecution, economic oppression, and the ravages of war, they had flocked to America in the early 1700s and had settled chiefly in Pennsylvania. They belonged to several different Protestant groups—primarily Lutheran—and thus further enhanced the religious diversity of the colony. Known popularly but erroneously as the Pennsylvania Dutch

---

The young Frenchman Michel-Guillaume Jean de Crèvecoeur (1735–1813) wrote of the diverse population in about 1770:

"They are a mixture of English, Scotch, Irish, French, Dutch, Germans, and Swedes. From this promiscuous breed, that race now called Americans have arisen.... I could point out to you a family whose grandfather was an Englishman, whose wife was Dutch, whose son married a French woman, and whose present four sons have now four wives of different nations."

(a corruption of the German word *Deutsch*, for "German"), they totaled about one-third of the colony's population. In parts of Philadelphia, street signs were painted in both German and English. In the Pennsylvania backcountry, where many of them moved, German immigrants clung tenaciously to their language and customs.

The Scots-Irish, who in 1775 numbered about 175,000, or 7 percent of the population, were an important non-English group, although they spoke English. They were not Irish at all but turbulent Scots Lowlanders who had been transplanted over many decades to Northern Ireland, where they had not prospered. The Irish Catholics already there, hating Scottish Presbyterianism, resented the intruders and still do. Early in the 1700s tens of thousands of these embittered Scots-Irish finally abandoned Ireland and came to America, chiefly to tolerant and deep-soiled Pennsylvania.

Finding the best acres already taken by Quakers and Germans, the Scots-Irish pushed out onto the Appalachian frontier, often drifting southward into the backcountry of Virginia, Maryland, and the western Carolinas. There many of them illegally but defiantly squatted on the unoccupied lands and quarreled with both Indian and white owners. Pugnacious, lawless, and individualistic, the Scots-Irish brought with them the Scottish secrets of whiskey distilling and dotted the Appalachian hills and hollows with their stills. They cherished no love for the British government that had uprooted them, and many of them—including the young Andrew Jackson—eventually joined the embattled American revolutionists.

Approximately 5 percent of the colonial population consisted of other European groups, including French Huguenots, Welsh, Dutch, Swedes, Jews, Irish, Swiss, and Scots Highlanders. Except for the Scots Highlanders, these ethnic groups felt little loyalty to the British crown. By far, the largest single non-English group was African, accounting for nearly 20 percent of the colonial population in 1775 and heavily concentrated in the South.

The population of the thirteen colonies, though mainly Anglo-Saxon, was among the most mixed to be found anywhere in the world. The South, holding about 90 percent of the slaves, already displayed its historic black-and-white racial composition. New England, mostly staked out by the original Puritan migrants, showed the least ethnic diversity. The middle colonies, especially Pennsylvania, received the bulk of later white immigrants and boasted an astonishing variety of peoples. Outside of New England, about half of the population was non-English in 1775.

As these various immigrant groups mingled and intermarried, they laid the foundations for a new multicultural American national identity unlike anything known in Europe. Nor were white colonists alone in creating new societies out of diverse ethnic groups. In the New England "praying towns" where Indians were gathered to be Christianized, and in Great Lakes villages such as Detroit, home to dozens of different displaced indigenous peoples, polyglot Native American communities emerged, blurring the boundaries of individual tribal identities. Similarly, the African slave trade long had mixed peoples from many different tribal backgrounds, giving birth to an African *American* community far more variegated in its cultural origins than anything to be found in Africa itself.

Map 5.1 Immigrant Groups in 1775 America was already a nation of diverse ethnic groups in the colonial period. This map shows the great variety of immigrant groups, especially in Pennsylvania and New York. It also illustrates the tendency of later arrivals, particularly the Scots-Irish, to push into the backcountry.

New York slave revolt (1712) *Uprising of approximately two dozen enslaved Africans that resulted in the deaths of nine whites and the brutal execution of twenty-one participating blacks.*

⭐ Africans in America

Slavery exploded in the North American colonies during the eighteenth century. Life for slaves was terrible, though not everywhere was the same. In the deep South, slave life was especially severe. The climate was hostile to health, and the labor was life-draining. The widely scattered South Carolina rice and indigo plantations were lonely hells on earth where gangs of mostly male Africans toiled and perished. Only fresh imports could sustain the slave population under these loathsome conditions.

Blacks in the tobacco-growing Chesapeake region of Maryland and Virginia experienced somewhat less brutal treatment. Tobacco was a less physically demanding crop than those of the deep South, and tobacco plantations were smaller and closer to one another than rice plantations. The size and proximity of these tobacco farms permitted the slaves more frequent contact with friends and relatives. By about 1720 the proportion of females in the Chesapeake slave population had begun to rise, making family life possible. The captive black population of the Chesapeake region soon began to grow through its own fertility—making it one of the few slave societies in history to perpetuate itself by its own natural reproduction. From this point forward, slave imports to the Chesapeake from the West Indies and Africa dropped significantly, while South Carolina and Georgia remained heavily dependent on the continuing transatlantic slave trade.

Slavery existed in all the northern colonies as well, but on a much smaller scale. Some slaves in New York and New Jersey worked in large agricultural gangs. But many of the approximately 48,000 northern slaves worked in cities and smaller towns for individual artisans or small businesses.

As the ratio of native-born blacks to imported Africans grew during the 1700s, a distinctive African American culture began to flourish throughout the colonies that was a mixture of African and American elements of speech, religion, and folkways (see "Makers of America: From African to African American," pp. 64–65). On the sea islands off South Carolina's coast, blacks evolved a unique language, *Gullah*, that blended English with several African languages, including Yoruba, Igbo, and Hausa. The ringshout, a West African religious dance performed by shuffling in a circle while answering a preacher's shouts, was brought to colonial America by Africans and eventually contributed to the development of jazz as well as African American religion.

Enslaved Africans also helped mightily to build the country with their labor. A few became skilled artisans— carpenters, bricklayers, and tanners. But chiefly they performed the sweaty toil of clearing swamps, grubbing out trees, and other menial agricultural tasks. Condemned to life under the lash, slaves naturally pined for freedom. The New York slave revolt that erupted in 1712 cost the lives of nine whites and caused the execution of twenty-one blacks. In the South Carolina slave revolt of 1739 about fifty blacks, who attempted to escape to Spanish Florida, were captured by local militia. But in the end, enslaved Africans in the South were more tightly controlled than the white indentured servants they gradually replaced, and there were no successful large-scale slave rebellions.

Contending Voices

Race and Slavery

Samuel Sewall (1652–1730), a Massachusetts judge and one of the magistrates at the Salem witch trials, was among the earliest critics of slavery in the colonies. In 1700 he advised:

"And seeing GOD hath said, He that stealeth a man and selleth him . . . he shall surely be put to death. . . . What louder cry can there be made of the celebrated warning, Caveat Emptor! . . . It would conduce more to the welfare of the province, to have white servants for a term of years, than to have slaves for life. Few can endure to hear of a Negro's being made free; and . . . there is such a disparity in their conditions, color & hair, that they can never embody with us . . . and grow up into orderly families, to the peopling of the land."

Meanwhile, colonial legislatures were beginning to define the legal status of slavery. The Virginia slave code of 1705 declared that

"if any [runaway] slave resist his master . . . and shall happen to be killed [during his punishment] . . . the master . . . shall be free and acquit [ted] of all punishment . . . as if such accident had never happened . . . baptism of slaves doth not exempt them from bondage . . . whatsoever English, or other white man or woman, being free, shall intermarry with a negro or mulatto man or woman, bond or free, shall, by judgment of the county court, be committed to prison."

> What attitudes about race were shared by pro- and antislavery advocates alike?

South Carolina slave revolt (Stono River) (1739) *Uprising, also known as the Stono Rebellion, of more than fifty South Carolina blacks along the Stono River. They attempted to reach Spanish Florida but were stopped by the South Carolina militia.*

Makers of America

From African to African American

Dragged in chains from West African shores, the first African Americans struggled to preserve their diverse heritages from the ravages of slavery. Their children, the first generation of American-born slaves, melded these various traditions—Guinean, Ibo, Yoruba, Angolan—into a distinctive African American culture. Their achievement sustained them during the cruelties of enslavement and has endured to this day to enrich American life.

Yarrow Mamout, by Charles Willson Peale, 1819 When Peale painted this portrait, Mamout was over 100 years old. A devout Muslim brought to Maryland as a slave, he eventually bought his freedom and settled in Georgetown.

With the arrival of the first Africans in the seventeenth century, a cornucopia of African traditions poured into the New World: handicrafts and skills in numerous trades; a plethora of languages, music, and cuisines; even rice-planting techniques that conquered the inhospitable soil of South Carolina. It was North America's rice paddies, tilled by experienced West Africans, that introduced the staple rice into the English diet.

These first American slaves were mostly males who lived and worked on small, isolated farms. But by the beginning of the eighteenth century, a settled slave society was emerging in the southern colonies. Laws tightened; slave traders stepped up their deliveries of human cargo; large plantations formed. Most significantly, a new generation of American-born slaves joined their forebears at labor in the fields. By 1740 large groups of slaves lived together on sprawling plantations, the American-born outnumbered the African-born, and the importation of African slaves slowed.

Plantation life was an endless cycle of miserable toil for the slaves. After a day's backbreaking work, women were expected to sit up for hours spinning, weaving, or sewing clothes for themselves and their families. Enslaved women also lived in constant fear of sexual exploitation by conscienceless masters.

Slave religion illustrates how new ideas were combined with a traditional heritage. Most slaves became Christians but fused elements of African and Western traditions and drew their own conclusions from Scripture. White Christians might encourage slaves to "stay in their place," but black Christians emphasized God's role in freeing the Hebrews from slavery and saw Jesus as the Messiah who would deliver them from bondage.

At their Sunday and evening prayer meetings, slaves also patched African remnants onto conventional Christian ritual. Black Methodists, for example, evaded the traditional

★ The Structure of Colonial Society

In comparison to contemporary Europe, eighteenth-century America seemed like a shining land of equality and opportunity—with the notorious exception of slavery. No titled nobility dominated society from on high, and no pauperized underclass threatened it from below. Most white Americans, and even a handful of free blacks, were small farmers. The cities contained a small class of skilled artisans, as well as shopkeepers, tradespeople, and some unskilled day laborers. The most remarkable feature of the social ladder was its openness. An ambitious colonist, even a former indentured servant, could rise from a lower rung to a higher one, a rare step in Britain.

Yet, in contrast with seventeenth-century America, colonial society on the eve of the Revolution was beginning to show signs of stratification and barriers to mobility that

The Emergence of an African American Culture In this scene from the mid-nineteenth century, African Americans play musical instruments of European derivation, like the fiddle, as well as instruments of African origin, like the bones and banjo—a vivid illustration of the blending of the two cultures in the crucible of the New World.

Methodist ban on dancing by practicing the "ringshout." Some worshipers clapped their hands and beat time in a circle while others walked around the ring, singing in unison. Christian slaves also often used outwardly religious songs as encoded messages about escape or rebellion. The hymn "Wade in the Water," for instance, taught fleeing slaves one way of covering their trails. The "Negro spirituals" that took shape as a distinctive form of American music thus had their origins in both Christianity and slavery. Indeed, much American music was born in the slave quarters from African importations. But this rich cultural harvest came at the cost of generations of human agony.

raised worries about the "Europeanization" of America. A new class of merchant princes in New England and the middle colonies, many of whom had made their fortunes as military suppliers in the colonial wars, roosted regally atop the social ladder. They sported imported clothing and dined at tables laid with English china and gleaming silverware. Prominent individuals came to be seated in churches and schools according to their social rank.

The plague of war also created a class of widows and orphans, who became dependent for their survival on charity. Both Philadelphia and New York built almshouses in the 1730s to care for the destitute. Yet the numbers of poor people remained tiny compared with the numbers in England, where about a third of the population lived in squalor.

In the New England countryside, the descendants of the original settlers faced more limited prospects than had their pioneering forebears. As families grew and existing landholdings were repeatedly divided, the average size of farms shrank drastically. Younger sons as well as daughters were forced to hire out as wage laborers. By 1750, Boston contained a large number of homeless poor, who were supported by public charity and forced to wear a large red "P" on their clothing.

In the South the power of the great planters continued to be bolstered by their disproportionate ownership of slaves. Wealth was concentrated in the hands of the largest slave owners, widening the gap between the prosperous gentry and the "poor whites," who were more and more likely to become tenant farmers. In all the colonies, the ranks of the lower classes were further swelled by the continuing stream of indentured servants.

Far less fortunate than the voluntary indentured servants were the paupers and convicts involuntarily shipped to America. Altogether, about fifty thousand "jayle birds"—including robbers, rapists, and murderers—were dumped on the colonies by the London authorities. But many of the convicts were the unfortunate victims of a viciously unfair British penal code, and some eventually became highly respectable citizens.

Least fortunate of all, of course, were the black slaves. Oppressed and downtrodden, the slaves were America's closest approximation to Europe's volatile lower classes, and fears of black rebellion plagued the white colonists. Some colonial legislatures, notably South Carolina's in 1760, attempted to restrict or halt the importation of slaves, but British authorities repeatedly vetoed all such efforts. Thomas Jefferson, himself a slaveholder, assailed the British vetoes in an early draft of the Declaration of Independence but was forced to withdraw the proposed clause by a torrent of protest from southern slaveholders.

★ Clergy, Physicians, and Jurists

The most honored of the professions was the Christian ministry. In 1775 the clergy wielded less influence than in the early days of Massachusetts, when piety had burned more warmly. But they still occupied a position of high prestige.

Most physicians, on the other hand, were poorly trained and not highly esteemed. Not until 1765 was the first medical school established, although European centers attracted some students. Aspiring young doctors served for a while as apprentices to older practitioners and were then turned loose on their "victims." Bleeding was a favorite and frequently fatal remedy; when the physician was not available, a barber was often summoned.

Epidemics were a constant nightmare. Especially dreaded was smallpox, which afflicted one out of five persons, including the heavily pockmarked George Washington. A crude form of inoculation was introduced in 1721, despite the objections of many physicians and some of the clergy, who opposed tampering with the will of God. Powdered dried toad was a favorite prescription for smallpox. Diphtheria was also a deadly killer, especially of young people. One epidemic in the 1730s took the lives of thousands.

At first, the law profession was not favorably regarded. In this pioneering society of farmers and manual laborers, the parties to a dispute often presented their own cases in court. Lawyers were commonly regarded as noisy windbags or troublemaking rogues; an early Connecticut law classed them with drunkards and brothel keepers.

Cotton Mather (1663–1728), Puritan clergyman and avid scientist, became frustrated with Boston residents' opposition to inoculation during the Boston smallpox epidemic of 1721. He wrote to a doctor friend,

"Never till now was that rule contested, of two evils, choose the least. ... I would ask them whether it be not a most criminal ingratitude unto the God of Health, when He has acquainted us with a most invaluable method of the saving of our lives from so great a death, to treat with neglect and contempt, and multiply abuses on them who thankfully and in a spirit of obedience to Him, embrace His blessings?"

★ Workaday America

Agriculture was the leading industry, involving about 90 percent of the people. Tobacco continued to be the staple crop in Maryland and Virginia, though wheat cultivation also spread in the Chesapeake, often on lands depleted by the overgrowth of tobacco. The fertile middle ("bread") colonies produced large quantities of grain, and by 1759 New York alone was exporting eighty thousand barrels of flour a year. Seemingly the farmer had only to tickle the soil with a hoe and it would laugh with a harvest. Overall, Americans probably enjoyed a higher average standard of living than the masses of any country in history up to that time.

Fishing (including whaling), though ranking in scale far below agriculture, was rewarding. Pursued in all the American colonies, this harvesting of the sea was a major industry in New England, which exported smelly shiploads of dried cod to the Catholic countries of Europe. The fishing fleet also stimulated shipbuilding and served as a nursery for the seamen who manned the navy and merchant marine.

Yankee seamen were famous in many climes not only as skilled mariners but as tightfisted traders. They provisioned the Caribbean sugar islands with food and forest products. They hauled Spanish and Portuguese gold, wine, and oranges to London, to be exchanged for industrial goods, which were then sold for a juicy profit in America.

The so-called **triangular trade** was infamously profitable, though small in relation to total colonial commerce (see Map 5.2). A skipper would leave a New England port with a cargo of rum and sail to the Gold Coast of Africa. Bartering the fiery liquor with African chiefs for captured African slaves, the skipper would proceed to the West Indies with his suffocating cargo sardined below deck. There he would exchange the slaves for molasses, which he would then carry to New England, where the molasses would be distilled into rum. He would then repeat the trip, making a handsome profit on each leg of the triangle.

triangular trade Exchange of rum, slaves, and molasses between the North American colonies, Africa, and the West Indies. A small but immensely profitable subset of the Atlantic trade.

Map 5.2 Colonial Trade Patterns, ca. 1770 Future president John Adams noted about this time that "the commerce of the West Indies is a part of the American system of commerce. They can neither do without us, nor we without them. The Creator has placed us upon the globe in such a situation that we have occasion for each other."

Manufacturing in the colonies was of only secondary importance, although there was a surprising variety of small enterprises. Huge quantities of "kill devil" rum were distilled in Rhode Island and Massachusetts, and even some of the "elect of the Lord" developed an overfondness for it. Beaver hats, iron, and clothing, spun and woven by women in the household, constituted other colonial manufactures. As in all pioneering countries, strong-backed laborers and skilled craftspeople were scarce and highly prized.

Lumbering was perhaps the most important single manufacturing activity. Countless cartloads of virgin timber were consumed by shipbuilders, who by 1770 were sending four hundred new vessels splashing into the sea each year. Colonial naval stores—such as tar, pitch, rosin, and turpentine—were highly valued. Towering trees, ideal as masts for His Majesty's navy, were marked with the king's broad arrow for future use. The luckless colonist who was caught cutting down this reserved timber was subject to a fine.

Americans held an important flank of a thriving, many-sided Atlantic economy by the dawn of the eighteenth century. Yet strains appeared in this complex network as early as the 1730s. Fast-breeding Americans demanded more and more British products—yet the slow-growing British population early reached the saturation point for absorbing imports from America. How, then, could the colonists sell the goods to make the money to buy what they wanted in Britain? The answer was obvious: by seeking foreign (non-British) markets.

By the eve of the Revolution, the bulk of Chesapeake tobacco was filling pipes in France and other European countries, though it passed through the hands of British re-exporters, who took a slice of the profits for themselves. More important was the trade with the West Indies, especially the French islands. West Indian purchases of North American timber and foodstuffs provided the crucial cash for the colonists to continue to make their own purchases in Britain. But in 1733, bowing to pressure from influential *British* West Indian planters, Parliament passed the **Molasses Act**, aimed at squelching North American trade with the *French* West Indies. If successful, this scheme would have struck a crippling blow to American international trade and to the colonists' standard of living. American merchants responded by bribing and smuggling their way around the law. Thus was foreshadowed the impending imperial crisis, when headstrong Americans would revolt rather than submit to the dictates of a far-off Parliament apparently bent on destroying their very livelihood.

Molasses Act (1733) *Tax on imported molasses passed by Parliament in an effort to squelch the North American trade with the French West Indies. It proved largely ineffective due to widespread smuggling.*

⭐ Horsepower and Sailpower

As a sprawling and sparsely populated pioneer community, America was cursed with oppressive problems of transportation. Not until the 1700s did roads connect even the major cities. The few dirt thoroughfares that did exist were treacherously deficient, throwing up clouds of dust in summer and turning into quagmires of mud in winter. Stagecoach travelers braved additional dangers such as tree-strewn roads, rickety bridges, carriage overturns, and runaway horses. Travel was so slow that it actually took twenty-nine days after the Fourth of July in 1776 for the news of the Declaration of Independence to reach Charleston from Philadelphia.

Where man-made roads were wretched, heavy reliance was placed on God-grooved waterways. Population tended to cluster along the banks of navigable rivers. There was also much coastwise traffic, which was cheap and pleasant but slow and undependable.

Taverns sprang up along the main routes of travel as well as in the cities. Along with such attractions as bowling alleys, pool tables, and gambling equipment, taverns were clearinghouses of information, misinformation, and rumor—frequently stimulated by alcoholic refreshment and impassioned political talk. Before a cheerful, roaring log fire all social classes would mingle, including the village loafers and drunks. Taverns were important in crystallizing public opinion, and alehouses such as Boston's Green Dragon proved to be hotbeds of agitation as the revolutionary movement gathered momentum.

Table 5.1 Estimated Religious Census, 1775

Name	Name Number	Chief Locale
Congregationalists	575,000	New England
Anglicans	500,000	N.Y., South
Presbyterians	410,000	Frontier
German churches (incl. Lutheran)	200,000	Pa.
Dutch Reformed	75,000	N.Y., N.J.
Quakers	40,000	Pa., N.J., Del.
Baptists	25,000	R.I., Pa., N.J., Del.
Roman Catholics	25,000	Md., Pa.
Methodists	5,000	Scattered
Jews	2,000	N.Y., R.I.
EST. TOTAL MEMBERSHIP	1,857,000	
EST. TOTAL POPULATION	2,493,000	
PERCENTAGE CHURCH MEMBERS	74%	

★ Dominant Denominations

Two "established," or tax-supported, churches were conspicuous in 1775: the Church of England and the Congregational Church. The Church of England, or Anglican Church, was the official faith in Georgia, North and South Carolina, Virginia, Maryland, and part of New York. British officials made vigorous attempts to impose it on additional colonies but ran into a stone wall of opposition. On the eve of the American Revolution, there was serious talk of creating a resident Anglican bishop in North America, but this scheme was also violently opposed by non-Anglicans, who feared a tightening of the royal reins. This controversy poured holy oil on the smoldering fires of rebellion.

Secure, self-satisfied, and often worldly, the Church of England itself fell distressingly short of its promise. So dismal was the reputation of the Anglican clergy in seventeenth-century Virginia that the College of William and Mary was founded in 1693 to train a better class of clerics.

The influential Congregational Church, the successor of the Puritans, was formally established in all the New England colonies except independent-minded Rhode Island. Presbyterianism, though closely associated with Congregationalism, was never the official church of any colony. Sometimes turning from the Bible to worldly politics, many Congregationalist and Presbyterian ministers of the gospel joined in stirring up opposition to the British crown in the 1760s and 1770s. Presbyterianism, Congregationalism, and rebellion became a neo-trinity. But most Anglican clergymen, aware of which side their tax-provided bread was buttered on, naturally supported their king.

Despite the presence of established churches, religious toleration had made enormous strides in America. Roman Catholics were still generally discriminated against, as in Britain, though the anti-papist laws were less severe and less strictly enforced. In general, people could worship—or not worship—as they pleased.

★ The Great Awakening

In all the colonial churches, religion was less fervid in the early eighteenth century than it had been a century earlier, when the colonies were first planted. The Puritan churches in particular sagged under the weight of two burdens: their elaborate theological doctrines and their compromising efforts to liberalize membership requirements. Churchgoers increasingly complained about the "dead dogs" who droned out tedious sermons from the pulpit. Some ministers, on the other hand, worried that their parishioners had gone soft and no longer embraced orthodox Calvinism. These twin trends toward clerical rigidity and lay indifference were sapping the spiritual vitality of many denominations.

Great Awakening (1730s and 1740s) *Religious revival that swept the colonies. Participating ministers, most notably Jonathan Edwards and George Whitefield, placed an emphasis on direct, emotive spirituality. A Second Great Awakening arose in the nineteenth century.*

new lights *Ministers who took part in the revivalist, emotive religious tradition pioneered by George Whitefield during the Great Awakening.*

old lights *Orthodox clergymen who rejected the emotionalism of the Great Awakening in favor of a more rational spirituality.*

The stage was thus set for a rousing religious revival. Known as the **Great Awakening**, it exploded in the 1730s and 1740s and swept through the colonies like a fire through prairie grass. The Awakening was first ignited in Northampton, Massachusetts, by a tall, delicate, and intellectual pastor, Jonathan Edwards. Perhaps the deepest theological mind ever nurtured in America, Edwards proclaimed with burning righteousness the need for complete dependence on God's grace. His preaching style was learned and closely reasoned, but his stark doctrines sparked a warmly sympathetic reaction among his parishioners in 1734.

Four years later, the itinerant English parson George Whitefield loosed a different style of evangelical preaching on America and touched off a conflagration of religious ardor that revolutionized the spiritual life of the colonies. A former alehouse attendant, Whitefield was a magnificent orator whose voice boomed sonorously over thousands of enthralled listeners in the open fields where he preached. Triumphantly touring the colonies, Whitefield displayed an eloquence that reduced Jonathan Edwards to tears and even caused the skeptical and thrifty Benjamin Franklin to empty his pockets into the collection plate. During Whitefield's roaring revival meetings, countless sinners professed conversion, and hundreds of the "saved" groaned, shrieked, or rolled in the snow from religious excitation. Soon, American imitators took up Whitefield's electrifying new style of preaching and shook enormous audiences with emotional appeals. These advocates of emotional preaching and fervent religious experience came to be known as **new lights**.

Orthodox clergymen, known as **old lights**, were deeply skeptical of the emotionalism and the theatrical antics of the revivalists. New light ministers, on the other hand, defended the Awakening for its role in revitalizing American religion. The Awakening left

George Whitefield Preaching Americans of both genders and all races and regions were spellbound by Whitefield's fervent oratory.

many lasting effects. Its emphasis on direct, emotive spirituality seriously undermined the older clergy, whose authority had derived from their education and erudition. The schisms that the Awakening set off in many denominations increased the numbers and competitiveness of American churches. The Awakening also encouraged a fresh wave of missionary work among the Indians and even among black slaves, many of whom attended open-air revivals. It also led to the founding of "new light" centers of higher learning such as Princeton, Dartmouth, Brown, and Rutgers. Perhaps most significant, the Great Awakening was the first spontaneous mass movement of the American people. By breaking down sectional boundaries and denominational lines, it contributed to the growing sense Americans had of themselves as a single people united by a common history and shared experience.

> *John Adams (c. 1736–1826) the future second president, wrote to his wife:*
>
> **"The education of our children is never out of my mind. . . . I must study politics and war that my sons may have the liberty to study mathematics and philosophy. My sons ought to study mathematics and philosophy, geography, natural history, naval architecture, navigation, commerce, and agriculture, in order to give their children a right to study painting, poetry, music, architecture, statuary, tapestry, and porcelain."**

★ Schools and Colleges

Only slowly and painfully did American colonists break away from the English idea that education should be reserved for the aristocratic few. In Puritan New England, education was dominated by the Congregational Church, which stressed the need for Bible reading to make good Christians. Education, principally for boys, thus flourished almost from the outset in New England, which boasted an impressive number of graduates from the British universities, especially Cambridge. New Englanders, at a relatively early date, established primary and secondary schools, which varied widely in the quality of instruction and in the length of time their doors remained open each year.

The College of New Jersey at Princeton, 1764 Later known as Princeton University, the college was chartered in 1746 by the Presbyterian Synod, though open to students of all religious persuasions. The fourth college to be founded in British North America, it met in Elizabeth and Newark, New Jersey, until a gift of ten acres of land precipitated a move to Princeton in 1756. All classes were held in the large building, Nassau Hall. Here the Continental Congress met for three months during the summer of 1783, making Princeton for a short time the capital of the nation. This copper engraving, based on a drawing by one of Princeton's earliest students, was part of a series of college views that reflected colonial Americans' growing pride in institutions of higher learning.

Fairly adequate elementary schools were also hammering knowledge into the heads of reluctant "scholars" in the middle colonies and in the South. Some of these institutions were tax supported; others were privately operated. The South, with its white and black populations diffused over wide areas, was severely handicapped in attempting to establish an effective school system. Wealthy families leaned heavily on private tutors.

The general atmosphere in the colonial schools and colleges continued grim and gloomy. Most of the emphasis was on religion and the classical languages, Latin and Greek. Instruction was poor, independent thinking was discouraged, and severe discipline was often administered with a switch cut from a birch tree. But by 1750 a distinct trend had emerged toward teaching "live" languages and other modern subjects in the nine small colonial colleges. A significant contribution was made by Benjamin Franklin, who played a major role in launching what became the University of Pennsylvania, the first American college free from denominational control.

⭐ A Provincial Culture

When it came to art and culture, colonial Americans were still in thrall to European tastes, especially British. The simplicity of pioneering life had not yet bred many homespun patrons of the arts, nor artists either. One aspiring painter, John Trumbull of Connecticut (1756–1843), was discouraged in his youth by his father's chilling remark, "Connecticut is not Athens." Trumbull, as well as his talented artistic contemporaries Charles Willson Peale (1741–1827), Benjamin West (1738–1820), and John Singleton Copley (1738–1815) all eventually succeeded in their ambition to become famous painters. But they had to go to Britain to complete their training and find patrons to support them.

Colonial architecture, too, was largely imported from the Old World. The red-bricked Georgian style, so common in the pre-Revolutionary decades, was introduced about 1720 and is best exemplified by the beauty of now-restored Williamsburg, Virginia.

Colonial literature, like art, was generally undistinguished, but a few outstanding individuals produced original and enduring work. Precocious black poet Phillis Wheatley (ca. 1753–1784) was an uneducated slave girl who was brought to Boston at age eight and then taken to London when she was twenty. She overcame her disadvantages and produced polished poems that revealed the influence of Alexander Pope.

Poor Richard's Almanack (1732–1758) *Widely read annual pamphlet edited by Benjamin Franklin. Best known for its proverbs and aphorisms emphasizing thrift, industry, morality, and common sense.*

Versatile Benjamin Franklin, often called "the first civilized American," also shone as a literary light. His now-classic autobiography was his greatest literary achievement, but he was best known to his contemporaries for *Poor Richard's Almanack*, which he edited from 1732 to 1758. Emphasizing the homespun virtues of thrift, industry, and common sense, "Poor Richard" was most famous for his pithy sayings: "Honesty is the best policy"; "Plough deep while sluggards sleep"; "Fish and visitors stink in three days." *Poor Richard's* was well known in Europe and was more widely read in America than anything except the Bible. Dispensing witty advice to old and young alike, Franklin had an incalculable influence in shaping the American character.

Franklin's scientific efforts, including his spectacular kite-flying experiments with electricity, made him the colonies' only first-rate scientist and won him numerous honors in Europe. Among the inventions produced by his practical mind were bifocal spectacles, the Franklin stove, and the lightning rod.

> *Benjamin Franklin's (1706–1790)* Poor Richard's Almanack *contained thoughts on religion such as these:*
>
> "A good example is the best sermon."
>
> "Many have quarreled about religion that never practiced it."
>
> "Serving God is doing good to man, but praying is thought an easier service, and therefore more generally chosen."
>
> "How many observe Christ's birthday; how few his precepts! O! 'tis easier to keep holidays than commandments."

⭐ Pioneer Presses

Stump-grubbing Americans were generally too poor to buy quantities of books and too busy to read them. A few fine private libraries, however, such as that of the Byrd family in Virginia, could be found. Bustling Benjamin Franklin established in Philadelphia the first privately supported circulating library, and by 1776 there were about fifty public libraries and collections supported by subscription.

On the eve of the Revolution there were about forty colonial newspapers, chiefly weeklies that consisted of a single large sheet folded once. The "news," especially from overseas, often lagged many weeks behind the event, and the papers devoted much column space to somber essays. Nevertheless, newspapers proved to be a powerful agency for airing colonial grievances and rallying opposition to British control.

A celebrated legal case in 1734–1735 involved John Peter Zenger, a newspaper printer. Significantly, the Zenger trial arose in New York, reflecting the tumultuous give-and-take of politics in the middle colonies, where so many different ethnic groups jostled against one another. Zenger's newspaper had assailed the corrupt royal governor. Charged with seditious libel, the accused was hauled into court, where he was defended by a former indentured servant, now a distinguished Philadelphia lawyer, Andrew Hamilton. Zenger argued that he had printed the truth, but the royal chief justice ruled that the mere fact of printing, regardless of the truth, was enough to convict. But the jury, swayed by Hamilton's eloquence, defied the bewigged judge and daringly returned a verdict of not guilty. Cheers burst from the spectators.

The Zenger decision was a banner achievement for freedom of the press. It pointed the way to the kind of open public discussion required by the diverse society that colonial New York already was and that all America was to become. Although contrary to existing law and not immediately accepted by other judges and juries, in time the ruling helped establish the doctrine that true statements about public officials could not be prosecuted as libel. Newspapers were thus eventually free to print responsible criticisms of powerful officials, though full freedom of the press was unknown during the pre-Revolutionary era.

> *Andrew Hamilton (ca. 1676–1741) concluded his eloquent plea in the Zenger case with these words:*
>
> "The question before the court and you, gentlemen of the jury, is not of small nor private concern. It is not the cause of a poor printer, nor of New York alone, which you are now trying. No! It may, in its consequence, affect every freeman that lives under a British government on the main [land] of America. It is the best cause. It is the cause of liberty."

Zenger trial (1734–1735) *New York libel case against John Peter Zenger. Established the principle that truthful statements about public officials could not be prosecuted as libel.*

★ The Great Game of Politics

American colonists may have been backward in natural or physical science, but they were making noteworthy contributions to political science.

The thirteen colonial governments took a variety of forms. By 1775 eight of the colonies had royal governors appointed by the king. Three—Maryland, Pennsylvania, and Delaware—were under proprietors who themselves chose the governors. And two—Connecticut and Rhode Island—elected their own governors under self-governing charters.

Practically every colony utilized a two-house legislative body. The upper house, or council, was normally appointed by the crown in the royal colonies and by the proprietor in the proprietary colonies. The council was chosen by the voters in the self-governing colonies. The lower house, as the popular branch, was elected by the people—or rather by those who owned enough property to qualify as voters. In several of the colonies, the backcountry settlers were seriously underrepresented, and they hated the ruling colonial clique perhaps more than they did kingly authority. Legislatures, in which the people enjoyed direct representation, voted such taxes as they deemed necessary for the expenses of colonial government. Self-taxation through representation was a precious privilege that Americans had come to cherish above most others.

Governors appointed by the king were generally able men. Some, unfortunately, were incompetent or corrupt—broken-down politicians badly in need of jobs. The worst of the group was probably impoverished Lord Cornbury, first cousin of Queen Anne, who was made governor of New York and New Jersey in 1702. He proved to be a drunkard, a spendthrift, a grafter, an embezzler, a religious bigot, and a vain fool. He was also accused (probably inaccurately) of dressing like a woman. Even the best appointees had trouble with the colonial legislatures, basically because every royal governor embodied a bothersome transatlantic authority some three thousand miles away.

The colonial assemblies found various ways to assert their authority and independence. Some of them employed the trick of withholding the governor's salary unless he

royal colonies *Colonies where governors were appointed directly by the king. Though often competent administrators, the governors frequently ran into trouble with colonial legislatures, which resented the imposition of control from across the Atlantic.*

proprietary colonies *Colonies—Maryland, Pennsylvania, and Delaware—under the control of local proprietors, who appointed colonial governors.*

yielded to their wishes. Because the governor was normally in need of money, the power of the purse usually forced him to terms.

Administration at the local level was also varied. County government remained the rule in the plantation South; town-meeting government predominated in New England; and a modification of the two developed in the middle colonies. In the town meeting, with its open discussion and open voting, direct democracy functioned at its best. In this unrivaled cradle of self-government, Americans learned to cherish their privileges and exercise their duties as citizens of the New World commonwealths.

Yet the ballot was by no means a birthright. Religious or property qualifications for voting, with even stiffer qualifications for office holding, existed in all the colonies in 1775. The privileged upper classes, fearful of democratic excesses, were unwilling to grant the ballot to every "biped of the forest." Perhaps half of the adult white males were thus disenfranchised. But because of the ease of acquiring land and thus satisfying property requirements, the right to vote was not beyond the reach of most industrious and enterprising colonists.

By 1775 America was not yet a true democracy—socially, economically, or politically. But it was far more democratic than Britain and the European continent. Colonial institutions were giving freer rein to the democratic ideals of tolerance, education, equality of economic opportunity, freedom of speech, freedom of the press, freedom of assembly, and representative government. And these democratic seeds, planted in rich soil, were to bring forth a lush harvest in later years.

★ Colonial Folkways

Everyday life in the colonies may now seem glamorous, especially as reflected in antique shops. But judged by modern standards, it was drab and tedious. For most people, the labor was heavy and constant—from "can see" to "can't see."

Basic comforts now taken for granted were lacking. Food was plentiful, though the diet could be coarse and monotonous. Churches were unheated except for charcoal foot warmers that the women carried. During the frigid New England winters, the preaching of hellfire may not have seemed altogether unattractive. There was no running water in the houses, no plumbing, and probably not a single bathtub in all colonial America. Candles and whale-oil lamps provided faint and flickering illumination. Garbage disposal was primitive. Long-snouted hogs customarily ranged the streets to consume refuse, while buzzards, protected by law, flapped greedily over tidbits of waste.

Amusement was eagerly pursued where time and custom permitted. Militia "musters," house-raisings, quilting bees, funerals, and weddings everywhere afforded opportunities for social gatherings, which customarily involved the swilling of much strong liquor. Winter sports were common in the North, whereas in the South dancing, theater, card playing, horse racing, fox hunting, and cockfighting were favored pastimes. The agile George Washington, not surprisingly, was equally skilled at riding and dancing.

Lotteries were universally approved, even by the clergy, and were used to raise money for churches and colleges, including Harvard. Holidays were celebrated everywhere, but Christmas was frowned upon in New England as an offensive reminder of "Popery." Thanksgiving Day came to be a truly American festival, for it combined giving thanks to God with an opportunity for jollification, gorging, and guzzling.

By the mid-eighteenth century, Britain's North American colonies, despite their differences, revealed some striking similarities. All were basically English in language and customs and Protestant in religion, while the widespread presence of other peoples and faiths compelled every colony to cede at least some degree of ethnic and religious toleration. Compared with contemporary Europe, the colonies all afforded unusual opportunities for social mobility. They all possessed some measure of self-government, though by no means complete democracy. British North America by 1775 looked like a patchwork quilt—each section slightly different but stitched together by common origins, common ways of life, and common beliefs in toleration, economic development, and, above all, self-rule. Fatefully, all the colonies were also separated from the seat of imperial authority by a vast ocean moat some three thousand miles wide. These simple facts of shared history, culture, and geography set the stage for the colonists' struggle to unite as an independent people.

Varying Viewpoints

Colonial America: Communities of Conflict or Consensus?

The earliest historians of colonial society portrayed close-knit, homogeneous, and hierarchical communities. Richard Bushman in *From Puritan to Yankee* (1967) challenged that traditional view. He described colonial New England as an expanding, open society in which the colonists gradually lost the religious discipline and social structure of the founding generations. Rhys Isaac viewed the Great Awakening in the South as similar evidence of erosion in the social constraints and deference that once held colonial society together.

Some scholars dispute that a loss of common faith and morals undermined colonial communities. Christine Heyrmann in particular argued in *Commerce and Culture* (1984) that the decline of traditional mores was overstated and that religious beliefs and commercial activities coexisted throughout the late seventeenth and early eighteenth centuries. Similarly, colonial historian Jack Greene has suggested that the obsession with the decline of deference obscures the fact that colonies outside New England, such as Virginia and Maryland, actually experienced a consolidation of religious and social authority throughout the seventeenth and eighteenth centuries, becoming more hierarchical and paternalistic, not less.

Since the 1970s, some historians have also attacked the traditional idea that New England was the home of American freedom and that the South spawned hierarchical, aristocratic communities. They argue that not only did the South produce many of the founders—Washington, Jefferson, and Madison—but that republican principles were actually strongest in Virginia. Some scholars, notably Edmund S. Morgan in *American Slavery, American Freedom* (1975), consider the willingness of wealthy planters to concede the equality and freedom of all white males a device to ensure racial solidarity and to mute class conflict.

Few historians still argue that the colonies offered boundless opportunities for inhabitants, white or black. Whether one accepts Morgan's arguments that "Americans bought their independence with slave labor" or those interpretations that point to the rising social conflict between whites as the salient characteristic of colonial society on the eve of the Revolution, the once-common assumption that America was a world of equality and consensus no longer reigns undisputed. Yet, because one's life chances were still unquestionably better in America than in Europe, immigrants who viewed America as a land of opportunity continued to pour in.

CHAPTER SUMMARY ★ ★ ★ ★ ★ ★ ★ ★ ★ ★ ★ ★ ★ ★ ★

By 1775 there were thirty-two British colonies in the Americas, but only thirteen eventually revolted to form the United States of America. These latter territories were inhabited by a rapidly expanding, youthful population of about 2 million whites and half a million blacks. The white population was a melting pot of diverse ethnic groups, with Germans and Scots-Irish the largest non-English contingent.

Compared with Europe, America was a land of equality and opportunity (for whites); but relative to the seventeenth-century colonies, there was a rising economic hierarchy and increasing social complexity. Ninety percent of Americans worked in agriculture. But a growing class of wealthy planters and merchants appeared at the top of the social pyramid, in contrast with slaves and "jayle birds" forcibly shipped from Britain, who formed a visible lower class. The large "middle class" of whites consisted mostly of small farmers, along with artisans and tradespeople in the few small cities.

By the early eighteenth century, the established New England Congregational church was losing religious fervor. The Great Awakening, sparked by fiery preachers such as Jonathan Edwards and George Whitefield, spread a new style of emotional worship that revived religious zeal. While the Awakening led to greater religious diversity, it also created a greater sense of a shared "American" identity across the colonies. Colonial education and culture were generally undistinguished, although science and journalism displayed some vigor. Politics was everywhere an important activity, as representative colonial assemblies battled with politically appointed governors from Britain. Despite their differences, the thirteen colonies already shared something of a common "American way of life."

KEY TERMS

- New York slave revolt (62)
- South Carolina slave revolt (63)
- triangular trade (67)
- Molasses Act (68)
- Great Awakening (70)
- new lights (70)
- old lights (70)
- *Poor Richard's Almanack* (72)
- Zenger trial (73)
- royal colonies (73)
- proprietary colonies (73)

PEOPLE TO KNOW

- Jonathan Edwards
- George Whitefield
- John Trumbull
- John Singleton Copley
- Phillis Wheatley
- John Peter Zenger

MindTap is a fully online, highly personalized learning experience built upon Cengage Learning content. MindTap combines student learning tools—readings, multimedia, activities, and assessments—into a singular Learning Path that guides students through the course.

The Duel for North America
1608–1763

• • •

*A torch lighted in the forests of America
set all Europe in conflagration.*

VOLTAIRE, CA. 1756

Chapter Outline

- New France
- Anglo-French Colonial Rivalries
- The French and Indian War, 1754–1763
- The Ousting of France from North America, 1763
- The Consequences of War

As the seventeenth century neared its sunset, a titanic struggle was shaping up for mastery of the North American continent. The contest involved three Old World nations—Britain (England),* France, and Spain—and it unavoidably swept up Native American peoples as well. From 1688 to 1763, four bitter wars convulsed Europe. All four of those conflicts were world wars. Fought on the waters and on the soil of two hemispheres, they amounted to a death struggle for domination in Europe as well as in the New World. Counting these first four clashes, nine world wars have been waged since 1688. The American people, whether as British subjects or as American citizens, proved unable to stay out of a single one of them. And one of those wars—known as the Seven Years' War in Europe and the French and Indian War in America—set the stage for America's independence.

FOCUS QUESTIONS

1. What were the fundamental causes of the imperial conflict between France and Britain for control of North America?
2. What was the social and political character of New France, and how did it differ from Britain's North American colonies?
3. How was the North American imperial conflict between Britain and France shaped by rivalries on the larger European stage?
4. Why did Britain finally win the French and Indian War, and what role did the American colonists play in the victory?
5. How did the British victory in the Seven Years' War ironically become one of the precipitating causes of the American Revolution?

---

*After the political union of England and Scotland in 1707, the nation's official name became "Great Britain."

CHRONOLOGY

1598	Edict of Nantes (repealed in 1685)	1744–1748	King George's War (War of Austrian Succession)
1608	Champlain colonizes Québec for France	1754	Washington battles French on frontier; Albany Congress
1643	Louis XIV becomes king of France		
1682	La Salle explores Mississippi River to the Gulf of Mexico	1755	Braddock's defeat
		1756–1763	Seven Years' War (French and Indian War)
1689–1697	King William's War (War of the League of Augsburg)	1757	Pitt emerges as leader of British government
1702–1713	Queen Anne's War (War of Spanish Succession)	1759	Battle of Québec
1718	French found New Orleans	1763	Peace of Paris; Pontiac's uprising; Proclamation of 1763
1739	War of Jenkins's Ear		

★ France Finds a Foothold in Canada

Like England and Holland, France was a latecomer in the scramble for New World real estate, and for basically the same reasons. France was convulsed during the 1500s by foreign wars and domestic religious strife, including the bloody massacre of more than ten thousand French Protestant **Huguenots** on St. Bartholomew's Day, 1572.

A new era dawned in 1598 when the **Edict of Nantes**, issued by the crown, granted limited toleration to the French Huguenots. Religious wars ceased, and in the new century France blossomed into the mightiest and most feared nation in Europe.

After rocky beginnings, success finally rewarded the exertions of France in the New World. In 1608, the year after the founding of Jamestown, the permanent beginnings of a vast empire were established at Québec, a granite sentinel commanding the St. Lawrence River. The leading figure was Samuel de Champlain, an intrepid soldier and explorer whose energy and leadership fairly earned him the title "Father of New France."

Champlain entered into friendly relations—a fateful friendship—with the nearby Huron Indian tribes. At their request, he joined them in battle against their foes, the federated Iroquois tribes of the upper New York area. Two volleys from the "lightning sticks" of the whites routed the Iroquois, who left behind three dead and one wounded. France, to its sorrow, thus earned the lasting enmity of the Iroquois tribes, who thereafter hampered French penetration of the Ohio Valley, sometimes ravaging French settlements and frequently serving as allies of the British in the prolonged struggle for supremacy on the continent.

The government of New France (Canada) finally fell under the direct control of the king after various commercial companies had faltered or failed. This royal regime was almost completely autocratic. The people elected no representative assemblies, nor did they enjoy the right of trial by jury as English colonists did.

The population of Catholic New France grew at a listless pace. As late as 1750 only sixty thousand or so whites inhabited New France. Landowning French peasants, unlike the dispossessed English tenant farmers who embarked for the British colonies, had little economic motive to move. Protestant Huguenots, who might have had a religious motive to migrate, were denied a refuge in this raw colony. The French government, in any case, favored its Caribbean island colonies, rich in sugar and rum, over the snow-cloaked wilderness of Canada.

Huguenots French Protestant dissenters, the Huguenots were granted limited toleration under the Edict of Nantes. After King Louis XIV outlawed Protestantism in 1685, many Huguenots fled elsewhere, including to British North America.

Edict of Nantes (1598) Decree issued by the French crown granting limited toleration to French Protestants. Ended religious wars in France and inaugurated a period of French preeminence in Europe and across the Atlantic. Its repeal in 1685 prompted a fresh migration of Protestant Huguenots to North America.

★ New France Fans Out

New France did contain one valuable resource: the beaver. To adorn the heads of fashionable Europeans, French fur trappers ranged over the woods and waterways of North America in pursuit of the thick-furred beavers. These colorful *coureurs de bois* (runners of the woods) were also runners of risks—two-fisted drinkers, free spenders, free livers and lovers. They littered the land with scores of place names, including Baton Rouge (red stick), Terre Haute (high land), Des Moines (some monks), and Grand Teton (big breast).

Singing, paddle-swinging French *voyageurs* also recruited Indians into the fur business. But the Indians were decimated by the white man's diseases and debauched by his alcohol. Slaughtering beaver by the boatload also violated many Indian religious beliefs and sadly demonstrated the shattering effect that contact with Europeans wreaked on traditional Indian ways of life.

Pursuing the sharp-toothed beaver ever deeper into the heart of the continent, French trappers and their Indian partners covered amazing distances. They trekked in a huge arc across the Great Lakes, into present-day Saskatchewan and Manitoba, along the valleys of the Platte, the Arkansas, and the Missouri, west to the Rockies, and south to the border of Spanish Texas. In the process, they all but extinguished the beaver population in many areas, inflicting incalculable ecological damage.

French Catholic missionaries, notably the Jesuits, labored zealously to save the Indians for Christ and from the fur trappers. Some of the Jesuit missionaries, their efforts scorned, suffered unspeakable tortures at the hands of the Indians. But though they made few permanent converts, the Jesuits played a vital role as explorers and geographers.

coureurs de bois French-Canadian fur trappers; literally, "runners of the woods."

voyageurs French-Canadian explorers, adventurers, and traders.

Chief of the Taensa Indians Receiving La Salle, March 20, 1682, by George Catlin, 1847–1848 Driven by the dream of a vast North American empire for France, La Salle spent years exploring the Great Lakes region and the valleys of the Illinois and Mississippi Rivers. This scene of his encounter with an Indian chieftain was imaginatively re-created by the nineteenth-century artist George Catlin.

Other explorers sought neither souls nor fur, but empire. To thwart the English in the Ohio Valley, Antoine Cadillac founded Detroit in 1701. To check Spanish penetration into the region around the Gulf of Mexico, ambitious Robert La Salle floated down the Mississippi in 1682 to the point where the river mingles with the Gulf. Three years later he tried to return to the territory he had named "Louisiana," but he failed to find the Mississippi delta. He landed instead in Spanish Texas and in 1687 was murdered by his mutinous men.

Persistent French officials planted several fortified posts in what is now Mississippi and Louisiana, the most important of which was New Orleans (1718). Commanding the mouth of the Mississippi River, this strategic semitropical outpost controlled the trade of the huge interior valley, especially the fertile Illinois country. There the French also established forts and trading posts at Vincennes, Cahokia, and Kaskaskia.

★ The Clash of Empires

The earliest contests among the European powers for control of North America, the War of the League of Augsburg and the War of Spanish Succession, known to the British colonists respectively as **King William's War** (1689–1697) and **Queen Anne's War** (1702–1713), mostly pitted British colonists against the French *coureurs de bois*, with both sides recruiting whatever Indian allies they could. Neither France nor Britain considered America worth the commitment of large detachments of regular troops, so the combatants in these conflicts waged a kind of guerrilla warfare. France's Indian allies ravaged with torch and tomahawk the British colonial frontiers from New York to Massachusetts. Spain, eventually allied with France, probed from its Florida base at outlying South Carolina settlements. For their part, the British colonists failed miserably in sallies against Québec and Montreal but did temporarily seize the stronghold of Port Royal in Acadia (present-day Nova Scotia).

In the Peace of Utrecht (1713), victorious Britain acquired French-populated Acadia and the wintry wastes of Newfoundland and Hudson Bay. These immense tracts pinched the St. Lawrence settlements of France. The British also won limited trading rights in Spanish America, but these later created much friction over smuggling. Ill feeling between Britain and Spain led to war in 1739, when the British Captain Robert Jenkins, whose ear had been sliced off by a Spanish sword, returned to London with a tale of woe on his tongue and a shriveled ear in his hand. The **War of Jenkins's Ear** was confined to the Caribbean Sea and to the much-buffeted buffer colony of Georgia.

This small-scale scuffle with Spain in America soon merged with the large-scale War of the Austrian Succession in Europe (called **King George's War** in America). Once again, France allied itself with Spain. And once again a rustic force of New Englanders, with the help of the British fleet, captured the reputedly impregnable French fortress of Louisbourg on Cape Breton Island, which commanded the approaches to the St. Lawrence River. When the peace treaty of 1748 handed Louisbourg back to their French foe, the victorious New Englanders were outraged. The glory of their arms seemed tarnished by the wiles of Old World diplomats. Worse, Louisbourg remained a cocked pistol pointed at the heart of the American continent. France, powerful and unappeased, still clung to its vast holdings in North America.

King William's War (1689–1697) *War fought largely between French trappers, British settlers, and their respective Indian allies. The colonial theater of the larger War of the League of Augsburg in Europe.*

Queen Anne's War (1702–1713) *Second in a series of conflicts between the European powers for control of North America, fought between the English and French colonists in the North, and the English and Spanish in Florida. Under the peace treaty, the French ceded Acadia (Nova Scotia), Newfoundland, and Hudson Bay to Britain.*

War of Jenkins's Ear (began in 1739) *Small-scale clash between Britain and Spain in the Caribbean and in the buffer colony, Georgia. It merged with the much larger War of Austrian Succession in 1742.*

King George's War (1744–1748) *North American theater of Europe's War of Austrian Succession that once again pitted British colonists against their French counterparts in the North. The peace settlement did not involve any territorial realignment, leading to conflict between New England settlers and the British government.*

★ George Washington Inaugurates War with France

As the dogfight intensified in the New World, the Ohio Valley became the chief bone of contention between the French and British. The Ohio Country was the critical area into which the westward-pushing British would inevitably penetrate. It was the key to the continent that the French had to retain, particularly if they were going to link their Canadian holdings with those of the lower Mississippi Valley. By the mid-1700s the British colonists, painfully aware of these basic truths, were no longer so reluctant to bear the burdens of empire. Alarmed by French land-grabbing and cutthroat fur-trade competition in the Ohio Valley, they were determined to fight for their economic security and for the supremacy of their way of life in North America.

Rivalry for the lush lands of the upper Ohio Valley brought tensions to the snapping point. In 1749 a group of British colonial speculators, chiefly influential Virginians, including the Washington family, had secured shaky legal "rights" to some 500,000 acres in this region. In the same disputed wilderness, the French were in the process of erecting a chain of forts commanding the Ohio River, including Fort Duquesne on the strategic site where the Monongahela and Allegheny Rivers join to form the Ohio—the later site of Pittsburgh.

In 1754 the governor of Virginia ushered George Washington, a twenty-one-year-old surveyor and fellow Virginian, onto the stage of history. Washington was sent to the Ohio Country as a lieutenant colonel in command of about 150 Virginia militiamen. Encountering a small detachment of French troops in the forest about forty miles from Fort Duquesne (see Map 6.1), the Virginians fired the first shots of the globe-girdling new war. The French leader was killed, and his men retreated. An exultant Washington wrote: "I heard the bullets whistle, and believe me, there is something charming in the sound." It soon lost its charm.

The French promptly returned with reinforcements, who surrounded Washington's hastily constructed bastion, Fort Necessity. After a ten-hour siege, Washington was forced to surrender his entire command in July 1754—ironically on the fourth of July.

Map 6.1 The French and Indian War in North America, 1754–1760

★ Global War and Colonial Disunity

The first three Anglo-French colonial wars had all started in Europe, but the tables were now reversed. The fourth struggle, known as the **French and Indian War**, began in America. Touched off by George Washington in the wilds of the Ohio Valley in 1754, it rocked along on an undeclared basis for two years and then widened into the most far-flung conflict the world had yet seen—the Seven Years' War. It was fought not only in America but in Europe, the West Indies, the Philippines, Africa, and on the ocean. The Seven Years' War was a seven-seas war.

In Europe, Britain liberally subsidized Frederick the Great of Prussia to fight against his traditional enemy, France. The French wasted so much strength in this European bloodbath that they were unable to throw an adequate force into the New World. "America was conquered in Germany," declared British statesman William Pitt.

Famous Cartoon by Benjamin Franklin Delaware and Georgia were omitted.

In previous colonial clashes, the Americans had revealed an astonishing lack of unity. Colonists who were nearest the shooting had responded much more generously with volunteers and money than those enjoying the safety of remoteness. Now, with musketballs already splitting the air in the Ohio Country, the crisis demanded concerted action.

In 1754 the British government summoned an intercolonial congress to Albany, New York, near the Iroquois country. Travel-weary delegates from only seven of the thirteen colonies showed up. The immediate purpose was to keep the Iroquois chiefs loyal to the British in the spreading war.

The longer-range purpose at Albany was to achieve greater colonial unity and thus bolster the common defense against France. Leading this effort was wise and witty Benjamin Franklin. Before the **Albany Congress** assembled, Franklin published the famous cartoon showing the separate colonies as parts of a disjointed snake above the slogan, "Join, or Die." Franklin gained the Albany Congress's unanimous approval for his well-devised but premature scheme for colonial home rule, but the individual colonies and the London regime both spurned it. To the colonists it did not seem to give enough independence; to the British officials, it seemed to give too much.

French and Indian War (1754–1763) *Nine-year war between the British and the French in North America. It helped spark the Seven Years' War in Europe, and resulted in the expulsion of the French from the North American mainland.*

Albany Congress (1754) *Intercolonial congress summoned by the British government to foster greater colonial unity and assure Iroquois support in the escalating war against the French.*

★ Braddock's Blundering and Its Aftermath

Led by haughty and bullheaded General Edward Braddock, the British stumbled badly in their opening clashes with the French and Indians. Braddock set out from Virginia in 1755 with a mixed force of two thousand British **regulars** and ill-disciplined colonial militiamen to capture Fort Duquesne. Experienced in European warfare, "Bulldog" Braddock displayed professional contempt for the colonial "buckskins" and their behind-the-trees method of fighting Indians.

Dragging heavy artillery through the dense forest, Braddock's expedition came within a few miles of Fort Duquesne. There it encountered a much smaller French and Indian army. At first the enemy force was repulsed, but it quickly melted into the thickets and poured a murderous fire into the ranks of the redcoats. Braddock's energetic and fearless aide, George Washington, had two horses shot from under him and four bullets pierced his coat. Braddock himself was mortally wounded, and the entire British force was routed with appalling losses.

Inflamed by this easy victory, the Indians took to a wider warpath. The whole frontier from Pennsylvania to North Carolina, left virtually naked by Braddock's bloody defeat, felt their fury. Scalping forays occurred within eighty miles of Philadelphia, and in desperation the local authorities offered bounties for Indian scalps: $50 for a woman's and $130 for a warrior's.

regulars *Trained professional soldiers, as distinct from militia or conscripts.*

View of the Taking of Québec, 1759 On the night of September 13, British forces scaled the rocky cliffs of Québec and defeated the French army defending the city. The following year, Montreal, France's last bastion in North America, surrendered. Fighting continued in the Caribbean, Europe, and the Philippines for two more years, until the Treaty of Paris was signed in 1763, eliminating France as a colonial power in North America.

The British launched a full-scale invasion of Canada in 1756, now that the undeclared war in America had at last merged into a world conflict. But they unwisely tried to attack a number of exposed wilderness posts simultaneously, instead of throwing all their strength at the key strongholds of Québec and Montreal. By ignoring such sound strategy, the British armies experienced defeat after defeat, both in America and in Europe.

★ Pitt's Palms of Victory

In the hour of crisis, Britain brought forth, as it repeatedly would, a superlative leader—William Pitt. A tall and imposing figure, whose flashing eyes were set in a hawklike face, Pitt was popularly known as the "Great Commoner." He drew much of his strength from the common people, who admired him so greatly that on occasion they kissed his horses.

In 1757 Pitt became the foremost leader in the London government. He wisely decided to concentrate the war effort on the vitals of Canada—the Québec-Montreal area. Pitt first dispatched a powerful expedition in 1758 against Louisbourg. The frowning fortress, though greatly strengthened by the French, fell after a blistering siege. Wild rejoicing swept Britain, for this was the first significant British victory of the entire war.

Québec was next on Pitt's list. For this crucial expedition he chose thirty-two-year-old James Wolfe. Though slight and sickly, Wolfe combined dash with painstaking attention to detail. In a daring night move, he sent a detachment up a poorly guarded part of the rocky eminence protecting Québec. This vanguard scaled the cliff, pulling itself upward by the bushes and showing the way for the others. In the morning the two armies faced each other on the Plains of Abraham on the outskirts of Québec, the British under Wolfe and the French under the Marquis de Montcalm. Both commanders fell fatally wounded, but the French were defeated, and the city surrendered.

The **Battle of Québec** in 1759 ranks as one of the most significant engagements in British and American history. When Montreal fell in 1760, the French flag had fluttered in Canada for the last time. By the peace settlement at Paris (1763), French power was thrown completely off the continent of North America, leaving behind a fertile French population that is to this day a strong minority in Canada. Britain thus emerged as the dominant power in North America, while taking its place as the leading naval power of the world.

Québec, Battle of (1759) Historic British victory over French forces on the outskirts of Québec. The surrender of Québec marked the beginning of the end of French rule in North America.

★ Restless Colonists

Britain's colonists, baptized by fire, emerged with increased confidence in their military strength. They had borne the brunt of battle at first; they had fought bravely alongside the crack British regulars; and both officers and men had gained valuable experience. In the closing days of the conflict some twenty thousand American recruits were under arms.

The French and Indian War, while bolstering colonial self-esteem, simultaneously shattered the myth of British invincibility. On Braddock's bloody field the "buckskin" militia had seen the demoralized regulars huddling helplessly together or fleeing their unseen enemy.

Ominously, friction had developed during the war between arrogant British officers and the raw colonial "boors." Displaying the professional soldier's contempt for amateurs, the British refused to recognize any American militia commission above the rank of captain—a demotion humiliating to "Colonel" George Washington. The British also showed the usual condescension of snobs from the civilized Old Country toward the "scum" who had confessed failure by fleeing to the "outhouses of civilization." Energetic and hard-working American settlers, by contrast, believed themselves to be on the cutting edge of British civilization. They felt that they deserved credit rather than contempt for risking their lives to erect a New World empire.

British officials were further distressed by the reluctance of the colonists to support the common cause wholeheartedly. American shippers developed a treasonable but lucrative trade with the Spanish and French West Indies at the very time the British navy was trying to subdue them. Other self-centered colonists refused to provide troops and money for the conflict until Pitt reimbursed the colonies for their mounting expenditures.

The curse of intercolonial disunity, present from early days, had continued throughout the recent hostilities. It had been caused mainly by enormous distances and geographical barriers; by religious differences spanning everyone from Catholic to Quaker; by various nationalities, from German to Irish; by differing types of colonial governments; by many boundary disputes; and by the resentment that the crude backcountry settlers felt against the aristocratic bigwigs.

Yet unity received some encouragement during the French and Indian War. When soldiers and statesmen from widely separated colonies met around common campfires and council tables, they were often agreeably surprised to discover that they were all fellow Americans who generally spoke the same language and shared common ideals. Barriers of disunity began to melt, although a long and rugged road lay ahead before a coherent nation would emerge.

The Reverend Andrew Burnaby, an observant Church of England clergyman who visited the colonies in the closing months of the Seven Years' War, scoffed at any possibility of unification (1760):

"... for fire and water are not more heterogeneous than the different colonies in North America. Nothing can exceed the jealousy and emulation which they possess in regard to each other.... In short ... were they left to themselves there would soon be a civil war from one end of the continent to the other, while the Indians and Negros would ... impatiently watch the opportunity of exterminating them all together."

★ Americans: A People of Destiny

The removal of the French menace in Canada profoundly affected American attitudes. While the French hawk had been hovering in the North and West, the colonial chicks

Contending Voices

The Proclamation of 1763

The Royal Proclamation of 1763 explicitly forbade the acquisition of western lands by individual colonists:

"We do, with the advice of our Privy Council strictly enjoin and require, that no private person do presume to make any purchase from the said Indians of any lands reserved to the said Indians... but that, if at any time any of the said Indians should be inclined to dispose of the said lands, the same shall be purchased only for us [the British Crown], in our name...."

In 1767, George Washington (1732–1799) wrote in confidence to a friend:

"I can never look upon that Proclamation in any other light (but this I say between ourselves) than as a temporary expedient to quiet the minds of the Indians.... Any person therefore who neglects the present opportunity of hunting out good lands and in some measure marking and distinguishing them for their own (in order to keep others from settling them) will never regain it...."

> Were the colonists justified in their resentment of the Proclamation?

---

had been forced to cling close to the wings of their British mother hen. Now that the hawk was killed, they could range far afield with a new spirit of independence.

The French, humiliated by the British and saddened by the fate of Canada, consoled themselves with one wishful thought. Perhaps the loss of their American empire would one day result in Britain's loss of its American empire. In a sense, the history of the United States began with the fall of Québec and Montreal; the infant Republic was conceived on the Plains of Abraham.

The Spanish and Indian menaces were also substantially reduced. Spain was (temporarily) eliminated from Florida, although entrenched in Louisiana and New Orleans. As for the Indians, the Treaty of Paris dealt a harsh blow to the Iroquois, Creeks, and other interior tribes. Sensing the newly precarious position of the Indian peoples, the Ottawa chief Pontiac in 1763 led several tribes in a violent campaign to drive the British out of the Ohio Country. Pontiac's warriors laid siege to Detroit in the spring of 1763 and eventually overran all but three British outposts west of the Appalachians.

The British retaliated swiftly and cruelly. Waging a primitive version of biological warfare, one British commander ordered blankets infected with smallpox to be distributed among the Indians. Such tactics crushed the uprising, and Pontiac's death in 1769 brought an uneasy truce to the frontier. The bloody episode convinced the British of the need to stabilize relations with the western Indians and to station regular troops along the restless frontier, a measure for which they soon asked the colonists to foot the bill.

With the defeat of the French, land-hungry American colonists thought they were now free to burst over the dam of the Appalachian Mountains and flood out over the verdant western lands. A tiny rivulet of pioneers, such as Daniel Boone, had already trickled into Tennessee and Kentucky. Other courageous pioneers made their preparations for the long, dangerous trek over the mountains.

Then, out of a clear sky, the London government issued its **Proclamation of 1763**, which flatly prohibited settlement in the area beyond the Appalachians, pending further adjustments (see Map 6.2). The truth is that this hastily drawn document was not designed to oppress the colonists at all, but to work out the Indian problem fairly and prevent another bloody eruption like **Pontiac's uprising**.

But countless Americans, especially land speculators, were dismayed and angered. Was not the land beyond the mountains their birthright? Had they not, in addition, bought it with their blood in the recent war? In complete defiance of the proclamation, they clogged the westward trails. In 1765 an estimated one thousand wagons rolled through the town of Salisbury, North Carolina, on their way "up west." This wholesale flouting of royal authority boded ill for the longevity of British rule in America.

The Seven Years' War also caused the colonists to develop a new vision of their destiny. With the path cleared for the conquest of a continent, with their birthrate high and their energy boundless, they sensed that they were a potent people on the march. Lordly Britons, whose suddenly swollen empire had tended to produce swollen heads, were in no mood for back talk. Puffed up over their recent victories, they were already annoyed with their unruly colonial subjects. The stage was thus set for a violent family quarrel.

Proclamation of 1763 Decree issued by Parliament in the wake of Pontiac's uprising, prohibiting settlement beyond the Appalachians. Contributed to rising resentment of British rule in the American colonies.

Pontiac's uprising (1763) Bloody campaign waged by Ottawa chief Pontiac to drive the British out of Ohio Country. It was brutally crushed by British troops, who resorted to distributing blankets infected with smallpox as a means to put down the rebellion.

Map 6.2a North America Before 1754

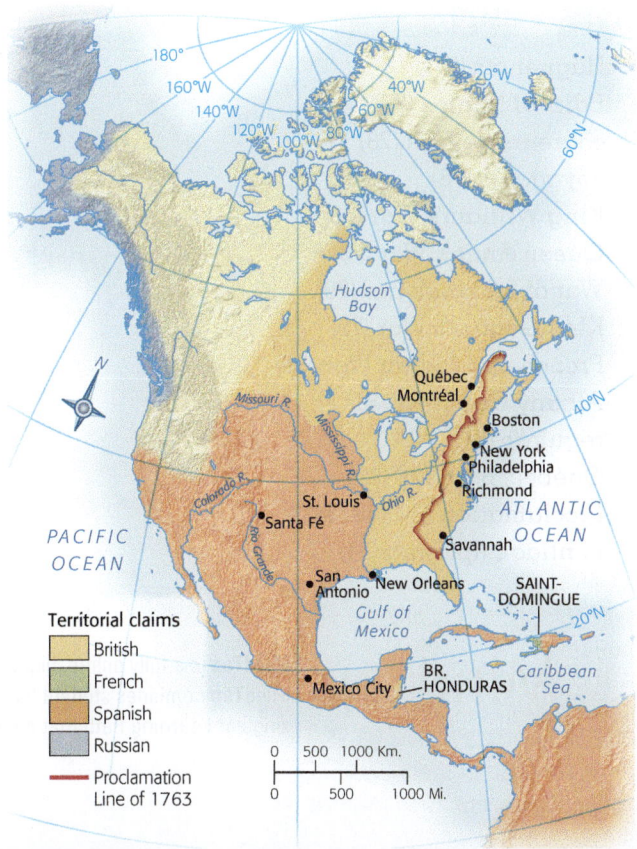

Map 6.2b North America After 1763 (after French losses)

CHAPTER SUMMARY ★ ★ ★ ★ ★ ★ ★ ★ ★ ★ ★ ★ ★ ★ ★

Like Britain, France entered late into the American colonial scramble, eventually developing an extensive though thinly settled empire in the St. Lawrence and Mississippi River valleys based primarily on the fur trade. During much of the eighteenth century, Britain and France engaged in a bitter power struggle that frequently erupted into worldwide wars. In North America these wars constituted an extended military duel for imperial control of the continent.

The culminating phase of this struggle was inaugurated by young George Washington's venture into the sharply contested Ohio Country. After early reversals in this French and Indian War (called the Seven Years' War in Europe), the British under William Pitt revived their fortunes and won a decisive victory at Québec, finally forcing the French from North America.

The American colonists had played a subordinate role in Britain's earlier imperial wars with France. But during the French and Indian War, the colonists emerged with increased confidence in their own abilities, and developed a growing resentment of the British treatment of them as provincial inferiors. The removal of the French threat to British control of North America also decreased the colonists' reliance on Britain for their defense. The Ottawa chief Pontiac's unsuccessful uprising in 1763 convinced the British of the need to continue stationing troops in America. But the colonists no longer felt the need for British protection, and increasingly chafed at Britain's authority over them.

KEY TERMS

Huguenots (77)
Edict of Nantes (77)
coureurs de bois (78)
voyageurs (78)
King William's War (79)
Queen Anne's War (79)
War of Jenkins's Ear (79)
King George's War (79)
French and Indian War (81)
Albany Congress (81)
regulars (81)
Québec, Battle of (83)
Proclamation of 1763 (84)
Pontiac's uprising (84)

PEOPLE TO KNOW

Louis XIV
Samuel de Champlain
Edward Braddock
William Pitt
James Wolfe
Pontiac

 MindTap is a fully online, highly personalized learning experience built upon Cengage Learning content. MindTap combines student learning tools—readings, multimedia, activities, and assessments—into a singular Learning Path that guides students through the course.

Chapter 7

The Road to Revolution
1763–1775

*The Revolution was effected before the war commenced.
The Revolution was in the minds and hearts of the people.*

John Adams, 1818

Chapter Outline

- The Merits and Menace of Mercantilism
- The Stamp Act Crisis, 1765
- The Townshend Acts, 1767
- The Boston Tea Party, 1773
- The Intolerable Acts and the Continental Congress, 1774
- Lexington, Concord, and the Gathering Clouds of War, 1775

Victory in the Seven Years' War made Britain the master of a vastly enlarged imperial domain in North America. But victory—including the subsequent need to garrison ten thousand troops along the sprawling American frontier—was painfully costly. The London government therefore struggled after 1763 to compel the American colonists to shoulder some of the financial costs of empire. This change in British colonial policy reinforced an emerging sense of American political identity and helped to precipitate the American Revolution.

The eventual conflict was by no means inevitable. Indeed, given the tightening commercial, military, and cultural bonds between the colonies and mother country since the first crude settlements a century and a half earlier, it might be considered remarkable that the Revolution happened at all. The truth is that Americans were reluctant revolutionaries. Until late in the day, they sought only to claim the "rights of Englishmen," not to separate from the mother country. But what began as a squabble about economic policies soon exposed irreconcilable differences between Americans and Britons over cherished political principles. The ensuing clash gave birth to a new nation.

FOCUS QUESTIONS

1. What long-term historical factors moved America toward independence from Britain?
2. Why did Britain seek tighter control and heavier taxation of its North American colonies after 1763, and why did these policies produce such a strong reaction from the colonists?
3. What were the major events that shaped colonial resistance to taxation? What methods of protests did the colonists use? How did Britain respond to these protests?
4. Why did the British respond to the Boston Tea Party with the harsh and repressive Intolerable Acts, when all the earlier conflicts had died down or been settled through compromise?
5. What advantages and disadvantages did the American Patriots and Britain each possess as the two sides entered upon armed conflict?

CHRONOLOGY

1650	First Navigation Laws to control colonial commerce	1770	Boston Massacre All Townshend Acts except tea tax repealed
1763	Seven Years' War (French and Indian War) ends	1772	Committees of correspondence formed
1764	Sugar Act	1773	British East India Company granted tea monopoly Governor Hutchinson's actions provoke Boston Tea Party
1765	Quartering Act Stamp Act Stamp Act Congress		
1766	Declaratory Act	1774	"Intolerable Acts" Quebec Act First Continental Congress The Association boycotts British goods
1767	Townshend Acts New York legislature suspended by Parliament		
1768	British troops occupy Boston	1775	Battles of Lexington and Concord

⭐ The Deep Roots of Revolution

In a broad sense, America was a revolutionary force from the day of its discovery. The New World nurtured new ideas about the nature of society, citizenship, and government. In the Old World many humble folk had long lived in the shadow of graveyards that contained the bones of their ancestors for a thousand years past. Few people born into such changeless surroundings dared to question their social status. But in the American wilderness ordinary people encountered a world that was theirs to make afresh.

Two ideas in particular had taken root in the minds of the American colonists by the mid-eighteenth century: One idea was what historians call **republicanism**. Looking to the models of the ancient Greek and Roman republics, exponents of republicanism defined a just society as one in which all citizens willingly subordinated their private, selfish interests to the common good. Both the stability of society and the authority of government thus depended on the virtue of the citizenry, especially its appetite for civic involvement.

A second idea that fundamentally shaped American political thought derived from a group of British political commentators known as **radical Whigs**. Widely read by the colonists, the Whigs feared the threat to liberty posed by the arbitrary power of the monarch and his ministers, especially the "corruption" revealed by patronage and bribes. Whigs warned citizens to be eternally vigilant against corruption and possible conspiracies to denude them of their hard-won liberties. Together, republican and Whig ideas predisposed the American colonists to be on hair-trigger alert against any threat to their rights.

The circumstances of colonial life had done much to bolster those attitudes. Dukes and princes and barons and bishops were unknown in the colonies, while property ownership and political participation were relatively widespread. The Americans had also grown accustomed to running their own affairs, largely unmolested by remote officials in London. Distance weakens authority; great distance weakens authority greatly. So it came as an especially jolting shock when Britain, after 1763, tried to enclose its American colonists more snugly in its grip.

⭐ Mercantilism and Colonial Grievances

Britain's empire was acquired in a "fit of absentmindedness," an old saying goes, and there is much truth in the jest. Not one of the original thirteen colonies except Georgia was formally planted by the British government. All the others were haphazardly founded by trading companies, religious groups, or land speculators.

---

republicanism *Political theory of representative government, based on the principle of popular sovereignty, with a strong emphasis on liberty and civic virtue. Influential in eighteenth-century American political thought, it stood as an alternative to monarchical rule.*

radical Whigs *Eighteenth-century British political commentators who agitated against political corruption and emphasized the threat to liberty posed by arbitrary power. Their writings shaped American political thought and made colonists especially alert to encroachments on their rights.*

The British authorities nevertheless embraced a theory, called "mercantilism," that justified their control of the colonies. Mercantilists believed that wealth was power and that a country's economic wealth could be measured by the amount of gold or silver in its treasury. To amass gold or silver, a country needed to export more than it imported. Possessing colonies thus conferred distinct advantages, because the colonies could both supply raw materials to the mother country (thereby reducing the need for foreign imports) and provide a guaranteed market for exports.

The London government therefore looked on the American colonists more or less as tenants. The colonists were expected to furnish raw products needed in the mother country; refrain from making finished products, such as cloth or beaver hats for export; buy imported manufactured goods exclusively from Britain; and not indulge in dangerous dreams of economic independence or, worse, self-government.

From time to time, Parliament passed laws to regulate the mercantile system. The first of these, the Navigation Law of 1650, required that all commerce flowing to and from the colonies must be transported only in British (including colonial) vessels. Subsequent laws stipulated that European goods destined for America first had to be landed in Britain, where tariff duties could be collected and British middlemen would take a slice of the profits. American merchants also had to ship certain "enumerated" products, notably tobacco, exclusively to Britain, even though prices might be better elsewhere.

British policy also inflicted a currency shortage on the colonies. Because the colonists bought more from Britain than they sold there, the difference had to be made up in hard cash. Every year, gold and silver coins, mostly earned in illicit trade with the Spanish and French West Indies, drained out of the colonies, creating an acute money shortage. To facilitate everyday purchases, the colonists resorted to using butter, nails, pitch, and feathers for purposes of exchange.

Currency issues came to a boil when dire financial need finally forced many of the colonies to issue paper money, which swiftly depreciated. British merchants and creditors squawked so loudly that Parliament prohibited the colonial legislatures from printing paper currency and from passing indulgent bankruptcy laws—practices that might harm British merchants.

The British crown also reserved the right to nullify any colonial legislation that might work mischief with the mercantile system. This royal veto was used rather sparingly—just 469 times in connection with 8,563 laws. But the colonists nevertheless fiercely resented its very existence—another example of how principle could weigh more heavily than practice in fueling colonial grievances.

mercantilism *Economic theory that closely linked a nation's political and military power to its bullion reserves. Mercantilists generally favored protectionism and colonial acquisition as means to increase exports.*

★ The Merits and Menace of Mercantilism

In theory, the British mercantile system seemed thoroughly selfish and deliberately oppressive. But the truth is that, until 1763, the various Navigation Laws imposed no intolerable burden, mainly because they were loosely enforced. Enterprising colonial merchants learned early to disregard or evade troublesome restrictions. Some of the first American fortunes, such as that of John Hancock, were amassed by wholesale smuggling.

Americans also reaped direct benefits from the mercantile system. If the colonies existed for the benefit of the mother country, it was hardly less true that Britain existed for the benefit of the colonies. London paid liberal bounties to colonial producers of ships' parts, over the protests of British competitors. Virginia tobacco planters enjoyed a monopoly in the British market. The colonists also benefited from the protection of the world's mightiest navy and a strong, seasoned army of redcoats—all without a penny of cost.

But even when painted in its rosiest colors, the mercantile system burdened the colonists with annoying liabilities. Mercantilism stifled economic initiative and imposed a rankling dependency on British agents and creditors. Most grievously, many Americans simply found the mercantilist system debasing. They felt used, kept in a state of perpetual economic adolescence, and never allowed to come of age. As Benjamin Franklin wrote in 1775:

We have an old mother that peevish is grown;
She snubs us like children that scarce walk alone;
She forgets we're grown up and have sense of our own.

Paul Revere, by John Singleton Copley, ca. 1768 This painting of the famed silversmith-horseman challenged convention—and reflected the new democratic spirit of the age—by portraying an artisan in working clothes. Notice how Copley has depicted the serene confidence of the master craftsman and Revere's quiet pride in his work.

"Revolution broke out," as Theodore Roosevelt later remarked, "because Britain failed to recognize an emerging nation when it saw one."

⭐ The Stamp Tax Uproar

Victory-flushed Britain emerged from the Seven Years' War holding one of the biggest empires in the world—and also, less happily, the biggest debt, some £140 million, about half of which had been incurred defending the American colonies. To justify and service that debt, British officials now moved to redefine their relationship with their North American colonies.

Prime Minister George Grenville first aroused the resentment of the colonists in 1763 by ordering the British navy to enforce the Navigation Laws. He also secured from Parliament the **Sugar Act** of 1764, the first law ever passed by that body for raising tax revenue in the colonies for the crown. Among various provisions, the Sugar Act increased the duty on foreign sugar imported from the West Indies. After bitter protests from the colonists, the duties were lowered substantially, and the agitation died down. But resentment was kept burning by the **Quartering Act** of 1765, which required certain colonies to provide food and quarters for British troops.

Then in the same year, 1765, Grenville proposed the most odious measure of all: a **stamp tax**, to raise revenues to support the new military force. The Stamp Act mandated the use of stamped paper or the affixing of stamps certifying payment of tax. Stamps were required on bills of sale for about fifty trade items as well as on certain types of commercial and legal documents, including playing cards, pamphlets, newspapers, diplomas, and marriage licenses.

Sugar Act (1764) *Duty on imported sugar from the West Indies. It was the first tax levied on the colonists by the crown and was lowered substantially in response to widespread protests.*

Quartering Act (1765) *Required colonies to provide food and quarters for British troops. Many colonists resented the act, which they perceived as an encroachment on their rights.*

stamp tax (1765) *Widely unpopular tax on an array of paper goods, repealed in 1766 after mass protests erupted across the colonies. Colonists developed the principle of "no taxation without representation" that questioned Parliament's authority over the colonies and laid the foundation for future revolutionary claims.*

admiralty courts *In British law, special administrative courts designed to try maritime cases without a jury.*

Grenville regarded all these measures as reasonable and just. He was simply asking the Americans to pay their fair share of the costs for their own defense, through taxes that were already familiar in Britain. In fact, the British people for two generations had endured a stamp tax far heavier than that passed for the colonies.

Yet the Americans were angrily aroused at what they regarded as Grenville's fiscal aggression. The new laws did not merely pinch their pocketbooks. Far more ominously, Grenville seemed also to be striking at the local liberties they had come to assume as a matter of right. Thus, some colonial assemblies defiantly refused to comply with the Quartering Act, or voted for only a fraction of the supplies that it called for.

Worst of all, Grenville's noxious legislation seemed to jeopardize the basic rights of the colonists as Englishmen. Both the Sugar Act and the Stamp Act provided for trying offenders in the hated **admiralty courts**, where juries were not allowed. The burden of proof was on the defendants, who were assumed to be guilty unless they could prove themselves innocent. Trial by jury and the precept of "innocent until proved guilty" were ancient privileges that British people everywhere, including the American colonists, held most dear.

And why was a British army needed at all in the colonies, now that the French were expelled from the continent and Pontiac's warriors crushed? Could its real purpose be to whip rebellious colonists themselves into line? Many Americans, weaned on the radical Whigs' suspicion of all authority, began to sniff the strong scent of a conspiracy to strip them of their historic liberties. They lashed back violently, and the Stamp Act became the target that drew their most ferocious fire.

Angry throats raised the cry, "No taxation without representation." There was some irony in the slogan, because the seaports and tidewater towns that were most wrathful against the Stamp Act had long denied full representation to their own backcountry pioneers. But now the aggravated colonists took the high ground of principle.

The Americans made a distinction between "legislation" and "taxation." They conceded the right of Parliament to legislate about matters that affected the entire empire, including the regulation of trade. But they steadfastly denied the right of Parliament, in which no Americans were seated, to impose taxes on Americans. Only their own elected colonial legislatures, the Americans insisted, could legally tax them.

Grenville dismissed these American protests as hairsplitting absurdities. The power of Parliament was supreme and undivided, he asserted, and in any case the Americans were represented in Parliament. Elaborating the theory of "virtual representation," Grenville claimed that every member of Parliament represented all British subjects, even those Americans in Boston or Charleston who had never voted for a member of the London Parliament. The Americans scoffed at this notion of virtual representation. Some British and American moderates proposed a compromise whereby the colonies would elect representatives to the British Parliament. But truthfully most Americans did not want direct representation in Parliament, where they could be easily outvoted.

Thus, the principle of no taxation without representation was supremely important, and the colonists clung to it with tenacious consistency. When the British replied that the sovereign power of government could not be divided between "legislative" authority in London and "taxing" authority in the colonies, they forced the Americans to deny the authority of Parliament altogether and to begin to consider their own political independence. This chain of logic eventually led to revolutionary consequences.

★ Parliament Forced to Repeal the Stamp Act

Among colonial outcries against the hated stamp tax, the most conspicuous was the **Stamp Act Congress**, held in New York City in 1765. Twenty-seven distinguished delegates from nine colonies petitioned the king and Parliament to repeal the repugnant legislation. The Stamp Act Congress made little splash in America at the time, but it was one more significant (if halting) step toward intercolonial unity.

More effective than the Congress was the widespread adoption of **nonimportation agreements** against British goods. Homespun woolen garments became fashionable, and the eating of lamb chops was discouraged so that the wool-bearing sheep would be allowed to mature. Nonimportation agreements were, in fact, a promising stride toward union; the agreements spontaneously united the American people for the first time in common action.

Mobilizing in support of nonimportation gave ordinary men and women new opportunities to participate in colonial protests by signing petitions or refusing to purchase British goods. Organizing consumer boycotts, groups of women assembled in public to hold spinning bees and make homespun cloth as a replacement for shunned British textiles. Such public defiance helped spread angry resistance throughout American colonial society.

Contending Voices

Reconciliation or Independence?

John Dickinson (1732–1808), a lawyer and popular essayist, advocated a middle-of-the-road response to the new British revenue acts of the 1760s that appealed to most colonists at the time:

"The constitutional modes of obtaining relief are those which I wish to see pursued on the present occasion.... We have an excellent prince, in whose good disposition we may confide.... Let us behave like dutiful children who have received unmerited blows from a beloved parent. Let us complain to our parent; but let our complaint speak at the same time the language of affliction and veneration."

Thomas Paine (1737–1809), a radical English propagandist who emigrated to America in 1774 with the help of Benjamin Franklin, argued in his famous tract of 1776, Common Sense, *that separation from England was the only logical course for the rebellious colonists:*

"Everything that is right or reasonable pleads for separation. The blood of the slain, the weeping face of nature, cries, 'tis time to part.... [T]here is something absurd in supposing a continent to be perpetually governed by an island. In no instance hath nature made the satellite larger than its primary planet; and as England and America, with respect to each other, reverse the common order of nature, it is evident that they belong to different systems. England to Europe: America to itself...."

Why did Paine's advice prevail over Dickinson's?

Stamp Act Congress (1765) *Assembly of delegates from nine colonies who met in New York City to draft a petition for the repeal of the Stamp Act. Helped ease sectional suspicions and promote intercolonial unity.*

nonimportation agreements *Pledges to boycott, or decline to purchase, certain goods from abroad.*

Sons of Liberty *Patriotic groups that played a central role in agitating against the Stamp Act and enforcing nonimportation agreements.*

Daughters of Liberty *Patriotic groups that played a central role in agitating against the Stamp Act and enforcing nonimportation agreements.*

Sometimes violence accompanied colonial protests. Crying, "Liberty, Property, and No Stamps," ardent **Sons of Liberty** and **Daughters of Liberty** enforced the nonimportation agreements against violators, often with a generous coat of tar and feathers. Patriotic mobs ransacked the houses of unpopular officials and hanged effigies of stamp agents on liberty poles.

Shaken by colonial commotion, the machinery for collecting the stamp tax broke down. On that dismal day in 1765 when the new act was to go into effect, the stamp agents had all been forced to resign, and there was no one to sell the stamps. While flags flapped at half-mast, the law was openly and flagrantly defied—or rather, nullified.

Britain was hard hit. Merchants, manufacturers, and shippers suffered from the colonial nonimportation agreements, and hundreds of laborers were thrown out of work. Loud demands converged on Parliament for repeal of the Stamp Act. But many of the members could not understand why 7.5 million Britons had to pay heavy taxes to protect the colonies, whereas some 2 million colonists refused to pay for only one-third of the cost of their own defense.

Declaratory Act (1766) *Passed alongside the repeal of the Stamp Act, it reaffirmed Parliament's unqualified sovereignty over the North American colonies.*

After a stormy debate, Parliament, in 1766, grudgingly repealed the Stamp Act. But in virtually the same breath, it provocatively passed the **Declaratory Act**, reaffirming Parliament's right "to bind" the colonies "in all cases whatsoever." The British government thereby drew its line in the sand. It defined the constitutional principle it would not yield: absolute and unqualified sovereignty over its North American colonies. The colonists had already drawn their own battle line by making it clear that they wanted a measure of sovereignty of their own and they would undertake drastic action to secure it. The stage was set for a continuing confrontation.

★ The Townshend Tea Tax and the Boston "Massacre"

Control of the British ministry was now seized by the gifted but erratic Charles ("Champagne Charley") Townshend, a man who could deliver brilliant speeches in Parliament even while drunk. Rashly promising to pluck feathers from the colonial goose with a minimum of squawking, he persuaded Parliament in 1767 to pass the **Townshend Acts**. The most important of these new regulations was a light import duty on glass, white lead, paper, paint, and tea. Townshend made this tax, unlike the Stamp Act, an indirect customs duty payable at American ports.

Townshend Acts (1767) *External, or indirect, levies on glass, white lead, paper, paint, and tea, the proceeds of which were used to pay colonial governors, who had previously been paid directly by colonial assemblies. Sparked another round of protests in the colonies.*

Flushed with their recent victory over the stamp tax, the colonists were in a rebellious mood. The impost on tea was especially irksome, for an estimated 1 million people drank the refreshing brew twice a day.

The new Townshend revenues, worse yet, would be used to pay the salaries of the royal governors and judges in America. The ultrasuspicious Americans, who had beaten the royal governors into line by controlling the purse, regarded Townshend's tax as another attempt to enchain them. Their worst fears took on a greater reality when the London government, after passing the Townshend taxes, suspended the New York legislature in 1767 for failure to comply with the Quartering Act.

Giving new meaning to the proverbial tempest in a teapot, a group of 126 Boston women signed an agreement, or "subscription list," which announced:

"We the Daughters of those Patriots who have and now do appear for the public interest ... do with Pleasure engage with them in denying ourselves the drinking of Foreign Tea, in hopes to frustrate a Plan that tends to deprive the whole Community of ... all that is valuable in Life."

Nonimportation agreements, previously potent, were quickly revived against the Townshend Acts. But the agreements proved less effective than those devised against the Stamp Act. The colonists, again enjoying prosperity, took the new tax less seriously than might have been expected, largely because it was light and indirect. They found, moreover, that they could secure smuggled tea at a cheap price, and consequently smugglers increased their activities, especially in Massachusetts.

British officials, faced with a breakdown of law and order, landed two regiments of troops in Boston in 1768. With liberty-loving colonists mercilessly taunting the often profane and drunken redcoats, a clash between citizens and the "bloody backs" was inevitable. On the

Two Views of the Boston Massacre, 1770 and 1856 Both of these prints of the Boston Massacre were art as well as propaganda. Paul Revere's engraving (left) began circulating within three weeks of the event in March 1770, depicting not a clash of brawlers but armed soldiers taking aim at peaceful citizens. Absent also was any evidence of the mulatto ringleader, Crispus Attucks. Revere wanted his print to convince viewers of the indisputable justice of the colonists' cause. By the mid-1850s, when the chromolithograph (right) circulated, it served a new political purpose. In the era of the abolitionist movement, freedman Crispus Attucks held center place in the scene, which portrayed his death as an American martyr in the revolutionary struggle for freedom.

evening of March 5, 1770, a crowd of some sixty townspeople, angry over the earlier death of an eleven-year old boy, began taunting and throwing snowballs at a squad of ten redcoats. Acting apparently without orders but nervous and provoked by the jeering crowd, the troops opened fire and killed or wounded eleven citizens—an event that became known as the **Boston Massacre**. One of the first to die was Crispus Attucks, described by contemporaries as a "mulatto" and a leader of the mob. Both sides were in some degree to blame, and in the subsequent trial (in which future president John Adams served as defense attorney for the soldiers) only two redcoats were found guilty of manslaughter.

Boston Massacre (1770) *Clash between unruly Bostonian protestors and locally stationed British redcoats, who fired on the jeering crowd, killing or wounding eleven citizens.*

★ The Seditious Committees of Correspondence

By 1770 King George III was strenuously attempting to assert the power of the British monarchy. Earnest, industrious, stubborn, and lustful for power, he surrounded himself with cooperative "yes men," notably his corpulent Tory prime minister, Lord North.

The ill-timed Townshend Acts had failed to produce revenue, though they did produce near-rebellion. Net proceeds from the tax in one year were a paltry £295, while in the same year Britain's military costs in the colonies had mounted to £170,000. Nonimportation agreements, though feebly enforced, were pinching British manufacturers. The government of Lord North, bowing to various pressures, finally persuaded Parliament to repeal the Townshend revenue duties. But the three-pence tax on tea was retained to keep alive the principle of Parliament's right to tax the colonies.

Flames of discontent in America, fanned by periodic incidents involving British officials, were further kindled by a master propagandist and engineer of rebellion, Samuel Adams. This cousin of John Adams was so unimpressive in appearance that his friends had to buy him a presentable suit of clothes when he left Massachusetts on intercolonial business. Zealous, tenacious, and courageous, Samuel Adams cherished a deep faith in the common people.

committees of correspondence (1772 and after) *Local committees established across Massachusetts, and later in each of the thirteen colonies, to maintain colonial opposition to British policies through the exchange of letters and pamphlets.*

Samuel Adams's signal contribution was to organize in Massachusetts the local **committees of correspondence**. After he had formed the first committee in Boston, during 1772 some eighty towns in the colony speedily set up similar organizations. The chief function of the committees was to spread the spirit of resistance by exchanging letters and thus keep alive opposition to British policy.

Intercolonial committees of correspondence were the next logical step. Virginia led the way in 1773 by creating such a body as a standing committee of the House of Burgesses. Within a short time, every colony had established a central committee through which it could exchange ideas and information with other colonies. These intercolonial groups were supremely significant in stimulating and disseminating sentiment in favor of united action. They evolved directly into the first American congresses.

★ Tea Parties at Boston and Elsewhere

Thus far—that is, by 1773—nothing had happened to make rebellion inevitable. Nonimportation was weakening. Increasing numbers of colonists were reluctantly paying the tea tax because the legal tea was cheaper than the smuggled tea.

A new ogre entered the picture in 1773. The powerful British East India Company, overburdened with 17 million pounds of unsold tea, was facing bankruptcy. If it collapsed, the London government would lose heavily in tax revenue. The ministry therefore decided to assist the company by awarding it a complete monopoly of the American tea business. The giant corporation would now be able to sell the coveted leaves more cheaply than ever before, even with the three-pence tax tacked on. But many American tea drinkers saw this as a shabby attempt to trick them into swallowing the hated tax. To the determined Americans, principle remained far more important than price.

Fatefully, the British officials decided to enforce the letter of the law. Once more, the colonists rose up in wrath to defy it. Not a single one of the several thousand chests of tea shipped by the East India Company ever reached the hands of the consignees. In Philadelphia and New York, mass demonstrations forced the tea-bearing ships to return to Britain. At Annapolis, Marylanders burned both cargo and vessel, while proclaiming "Liberty and Independence or death in pursuit of it."

Only in Boston did a British official stubbornly refuse to be cowed. Massachusetts governor Thomas Hutchinson agreed that the tea tax was unjust, but he believed even more strongly that the colonists had no right to flout the law. Hutchinson further inflamed the situation when he declared that "an abridgement of what are called English liberties" was necessary for the preservation of law and order in the colonies—apparently confirming the darkest conspiracy theories of the American radicals. On December 16, 1773, roughly a hundred Bostonians, disguised as Indians, boarded the docked ships, smashed open 342 chests of tea, and dumped their contents into the Atlantic. A crowd watched approvingly from the shore as Boston harbor became a vast teapot.

Reactions varied. All up and down the eastern seaboard, sympathetic colonists applauded destruction of the tea as "the hated badge of slavery." But conservatives complained that the destruction of private property violated the law and threatened anarchy. Hutchinson, disgusted with the colonies, retreated to Britain. The British authorities saw little alternative to whipping the upstart colonists into shape. Granting the Americans some measure of home rule at this stage might still have prevented rebellion, but few British politicians were willing to take the high road. The perilous path they chose instead led only to reprisals, bitterness, and escalating conflict.

Ann Hulton (d. 1779?), a Loyalist, described colonial political divisions and her hopes and fears for her own future in a letter she sent to a friend in England in 1774:

"Those who are well disposed towards Government are termed Tories. They daily increase & have made some efforts to take the power out of the hands of the Patriots, but they are intimidated & overpowered by Numbers. . . . However I don't despair of seeing Peace & tranquility in America, tho' they talk very high & furious at present. They are all preparing their Arms & Ammunition & say if any of the Leaders are seized, they will make reprisals on the friends of Government."

The Boston Tea Party, December 16, 1773 Crying "Boston harbor a tea-pot this night," Sons of Liberty disguised as Indians hurled chests of tea into the sea to protest the tax on tea and to make sure that the tea's cheap price did not prove an "invincible temptation" to the people.

★ Parliament Passes the "Intolerable Acts"

An irate Parliament responded speedily to the **Boston Tea Party** with measures that brewed a revolution. By huge majorities, in 1774, Parliament passed a series of acts designed to chastise Boston in particular and Massachusetts in general.

Most drastic of all was the Boston Port Act, which closed the tea-stained harbor until damages were paid and order could be ensured. In the other **"Intolerable Acts"**—as they were called in America—many of the chartered rights of colonial Massachusetts were swept away. Restrictions were likewise placed on the precious town meetings. Contrary to previous practice, enforcing officials who killed colonists in the line of duty could now be sent to Britain for trial. Particularly intolerable to Bostonians was a new Quartering Act that gave local authorities the power to lodge British soldiers in private homes.

By a fateful coincidence, the "Intolerable Acts" were accompanied in 1774 by the Quebec Act. Passed at the same time, the **Quebec Act** was erroneously regarded in English-speaking America as part of the British reaction to the turbulence in Boston. Actually, the Quebec Act was a good law in bad company. For many years the British government had debated how it should administer the sixty thousand or so conquered French subjects in Canada, and it had finally framed this farsighted and statesmanlike measure. The French Canadians were guaranteed their Catholic religion. They were also permitted to retain many of their old customs and institutions, which did not include a representative assembly or trial by jury in civil cases. In addition, the old boundaries of the Province of Quebec were extended southward all the way to the Ohio River.

The Quebec Act, from the viewpoint of the French Canadians, was a shrewd and conciliatory measure. If Britain had only shown as much foresight in dealing with its English-speaking colonies, it might not have lost them.

But from the viewpoint of the American colonists, the Quebec Act was especially noxious. All the other "Intolerable Acts" slapped directly at Massachusetts, but this one had a much wider range. By endorsing unrepresentative assemblies and denials of jury trials, it seemed to set a dangerous precedent in America. The Quebec Act also alarmed land speculators, who were distressed to see the huge trans-Appalachian region snatched from their grasp (see Map 7.1). And it aroused anti-Catholics, who were shocked by the extension of Roman Catholic jurisdiction southward into a huge region once earmarked for Protestantism.

Boston Tea Party (1773) *Rowdy protest against the British East India Company's newly acquired monopoly on the tea trade. Colonists, disguised as Indians, dumped 342 chests of tea into Boston harbor, prompting harsh sanctions from the British Parliament.*

"Intolerable Acts" (1774) *Series of punitive measures passed in retaliation for the Boston Tea Party, closing the Port of Boston, revoking a number of rights in the Massachusetts colonial charter, and expanding the Quartering Act to allow for the lodging of soldiers in private homes. In response, colonists convened the First Continental Congress and called for a complete boycott of British goods.*

Quebec Act (1774) *Allowed the French residents of Québec to retain their traditional political and religious institutions, and extended the boundaries of the province southward to the Ohio River. Mistakenly perceived by the colonists to be part of Parliament's response to the Boston Tea Party.*

Map 7.1 Quebec Before and After 1774 Young Alexander Hamilton voiced the fears of many colonists when he warned that the Quebec Act of 1774 would introduce "priestly tyranny" into Canada, making that country another Spain or Portugal. "Does not your blood run cold," he asked, "to think that an English Parliament should pass an act for the establishment of arbitrary power and Popery in such a country?"

★ The Continental Congress and Bloodshed

Chafing over the Quebec Act and the other "Intolerable Acts," American dissenters responded to the plight of Massachusetts with acts of sympathy and solidarity. Their most memorable step was the summoning of the **First Continental Congress** in the fall of 1774. All of the thirteen colonies except Georgia sent well-respected delegates—including Samuel Adams, George Washington, and Patrick Henry—who met in Philadelphia from September 5 to October 26, 1774. A stellar role in the First Continental Congress was played by John Adams. Eloquently swaying his colleagues to a revolutionary course, he helped defeat by the narrowest of margins a proposal by moderates for a species of American home rule under British direction.

The most significant action of the Congress was the creation of **The Association**. Unlike previous nonimportation agreements, The Association called for a complete boycott of all British goods: nonimportation, nonexportation, and nonconsumption. Yet it is important to note that the delegates were not yet calling for independence. They sought merely to repeal the offensive legislation and return to the happy days before parliamentary taxation. Resistance had not yet ripened into open rebellion.

But the fatal drift toward war continued. Parliament rejected the First Continental Congress's petitions. In America, chickens squawked and tar kettles bubbled as violators of The Association were tarred and feathered. Muskets were gathered, men began to drill openly, and a clash seemed imminent.

First Continental Congress (1774)
Convention of delegates from twelve of the thirteen colonies that convened in Philadelphia to craft a response to the Intolerable Acts. Delegates established The Association, which called for a complete boycott of British goods.

The Association (1774)
Nonimportation agreement crafted during the First Continental Congress calling for the complete boycott of British goods.

In April 1775, the British commander in Boston sent a detachment of troops to nearby **Lexington and Concord**. They intended to seize stores of colonial gunpowder and also to bag the "rebel" ringleaders, Samuel Adams and John Hancock. At Lexington the colonial "Minute Men" refused to disperse rapidly enough, and shots were fired that killed eight Americans and wounded several more. The redcoats then pushed on to Concord, from which they were soon forced to retreat by the rough-and-ready Americans, whom Emerson immortalized:

Lexington and Concord, Battles of (April 1775) *First battles of the Revolutionary War, fought outside of Boston. The colonial militia successfully defended their stores of munitions, forcing the British to retreat to Boston.*

> *By the rude bridge that arched the flood,*
> *Their flag to April's breeze unfurled,*
> *Here once the embattled farmers stood,*
> *And fired the shot heard round the world.**

The bewildered British, fighting off murderous fire from militiamen crouched behind thick stone walls, finally regained the sanctuary of Boston. Licking their wounds, the British could count about three hundred casualties, including some seventy killed. Britain now had a war on its hands.

★ Imperial and Colonial Strengths and Weaknesses

Aroused Americans had brashly rebelled against a mighty empire. The population odds were about three to one against the rebels—some 7.5 million Britons to 2.5 million American colonists. The odds in monetary wealth and naval power overwhelmingly favored the mother country.

Britain then boasted a professional army of some fifty thousand men, as compared with the numerous but wretchedly trained American militia. King George III, in addition, hired some thirty thousand German soldiers—so-called Hessians—to bolster his army. The British also enlisted the services of about fifty thousand American Loyalists and many Indians in their cause.

Yet Britain was weaker than it seemed at first glance. British troops had to be detached to watch the smoking volcano of oppressed Ireland. Recently defeated France was bitterly awaiting an opportunity to stab Britain in the back. The London government, under stubborn King George III and his pliant Tory prime minister, Lord North, was confused and inept.

Many earnest and God-fearing Britons had no desire to kill their American cousins. Many British Whigs believed that the battle for their own liberties was actually being fought in America. If George III triumphed there, they believed, his rule at home might become more tyrannical. This outspoken sympathy in Britain, though plainly a minority voice, greatly encouraged the Americans. If they continued their resistance long enough, the Whigs might come to power and deal generously with them.

Britain's army in America had to operate under endless difficulties. The generals were second rate; the soldiers, though on the whole capable, were brutally treated. Provisions were often scarce, rancid, and wormy.

Other handicaps loomed. The redcoats had to completely conquer the Americans. But for the colonists, simply restoring the pre-1763 status quo would be a victory. Britain was operating some three thousand miles from its home base, and distance often delayed military orders from London for months, so the received orders no longer fit the changing situation.

The great conservative political theorist and champion of the American cause, Edmund Burke, made a stirring speech in Britain's House of Commons in 1775, pleading in vain for reconciliation with the colonies:

"As long as you have the wisdom to keep the sovereign authority of this country as the sanctuary of liberty . . . they will turn their faces towards you. . . . Slavery they can have anywhere; freedom they can have from none but you. This is the commodity of price, of which you have the monopoly. This is the true Act of Navigation, which binds to you the commerce of the colonies, and through them secures to you the wealth of the world. Deny them this participation of freedom, and you break that sole bond which originally made, and must still preserve, the unity of the empire."

---

*Ralph Waldo Emerson, Concord Hymn.

America's geographical expanse was enormous: roughly one thousand by six hundred miles. The united colonies had no urban nerve center like France's Paris, whose capture would cripple the country as a whole. During the war British armies captured every city of any size, yet like a boxer punching a feather pillow, they made little more than a dent in the entire country. The Americans wisely traded space for time.

The revolutionaries were also blessed with outstanding leadership. George Washington was a giant among men. Master diplomat Benjamin Franklin eventually secured open foreign aid from France. In a class by himself was the Marquis de Lafayette, a wealthy young French nobleman who loved both liberty and glory. Lafayette was appointed a major general in the Continental army at age nineteen, and the services of the teenage "French gamecock" helped secure further aid from France.

Other conditions aided the Americans. They were fighting defensively on their own terrain. In agriculture, the colonies were mainly self-sustaining, like a kind of Robinson Crusoe's island. The Americans also enjoyed the moral advantage that came from belief in a just cause.

Yet the American rebels were badly organized for war. Almost fatally lacking in unity, the new nation lurched forward uncertainly like an uncoordinated centipede. Even the Continental Congress, which directed the conflict, was hardly more than a debating society, and it grew feebler as the struggle dragged on. The disorganized colonists fought almost the entire war before adopting a written constitution—the Articles of Confederation—in 1781.

Economic difficulties were nearly insuperable. With metallic money drained away and taxation an explosive issue, the Continental Congress was forced to print "Continental" paper money in great amounts. As this currency poured from the presses, it depreciated until the expression "not worth a Continental" became current. Inflation of the currency inevitably skyrocketed prices, hitting the families of soldiers at the front especially hard. Debtors easily acquired handfuls of the quasi-worthless money and gleefully paid their debts "without mercy."

★ A Thin Line of Heroes

Basic military supplies, especially firearms, were dangerously scanty in the colonies. While many families and towns did own firearms, the colonists had long relied heavily on Britain for troops, armaments, and military subsidies. When the supply of British funds and war materiel evaporated, sufficient stores of gunpowder, cannons, and ships could not be found.

Other shortages bedeviled the rebels. Manufactured goods were generally in short supply in agricultural America, and clothing and shoes were appallingly scarce. The path of the Patriot fighting men was often marked by bloody snow. At frigid **Valley Forge** during the cruel winter of 1777-1778, twenty-eight hundred soldiers went barefoot and nearly naked.

American militiamen were numerous but highly unreliable. Able-bodied American males—perhaps several hundred thousand of them—had received rudimentary training, and many of these recruits served for short terms in the rebel armies. But poorly trained plowboys could not stand up in the open field against professional British troops advancing with bare bayonets. Many of these undisciplined warriors would, in the words of Washington, "fly from their own shadows."

A few thousand regulars—perhaps seven or eight thousand at the war's end—were finally whipped into shape by stern drillmasters. Notable among them was an organizational genius, the salty German Baron von Steuben. He spoke no English when he arrived in America, but he soon taught his men that bayonets were not for broiling beefsteaks over open fires. As they gained experience, these soldiers of the Continental Army more than held their own in battle against crack British troops.

Blacks also fought and died for the American cause. Although many states initially barred them from militia service, by war's end more than five thousand blacks, most from

Valley Forge (1777-1778)
Encampment where George Washington's poorly equipped army spent a wretched, freezing winter. Hundreds of men died and more than a thousand deserted. The plight of the starving, shivering soldiers reflected the main weakness of the American army—a lack of stable supplies and munitions.

the northern states, had enlisted in the American armed forces. Blacks fought at Trenton, Brandywine, Saratoga, and other important battles.

African Americans also served on the British side. In November 1775 Lord Dunmore, royal governor of Virginia, issued a proclamation offering freedom to any enslaved black in Virginia who joined the British army. In time, thousands of blacks fled plantations in response to British promises of emancipation. At war's end the British kept their word, to some at least, evacuating as many as fourteen thousand "Black Loyalists" to Nova Scotia, Jamaica, and Britain.

Morale in the Revolutionary army was badly undermined by American profiteers. Putting profits before patriotism, these speculators sold supplies to the British and made profits of 50–200 percent on army garb while the American army was freezing at Valley Forge. The failures of revolutionary zeal meant that Washington never had as many as twenty thousand effective troops in one place at one time.

The brutal truth is that only a select minority of colonists attached themselves to the cause of independence with a spirit of selfless devotion. These were the dedicated souls who bore the burden of battle and the risks of defeat. Seldom have so few done so much for so many.

> *Enslaved blacks hoped that the Revolutionary crisis would make it possible for them to secure their own liberty. On the eve of the war in South Carolina, merchant Josiah Smith, Jr., noted such a rumor among the slaves:*
>
> "[Freedom] is their common Talk throughout the Province, and has occasioned impertinent behavior in many of them, insomuch that our Provincial Congress now sitting hath voted the immediate raising of Two Thousand Men Horse and food, to keep those mistaken creatures in awe."
>
> *Despite such repressive measures, slave uprisings continued to plague the southern colonies through 1775 and 1776.*

CHAPTER SUMMARY ★ ★ ★ ★ ★ ★ ★ ★ ★ ★ ★ ★ ★

The American War of Independence was a military conflict fought from 1775 to 1783, but the American Revolution was a deeper transformation of thought and loyalty that began when the first settlers arrived in America and finally led to the colonies' political separation from Britain.

One source of long-term conflict was the tension between the considerable freedom and self-government the colonists enjoyed in the American wilderness and their participation in the British Empire's mercantile system. While British mercantilism actually provided economic benefits to the colonies along with certain liabilities, its limits on freedom and its patronizing goal of keeping America in a state of perpetual economic adolescence stirred growing resentment.

The short-term movement toward the War of Independence began with British attempts to impose higher taxes and tighter imperial controls after the French and Indian War. To the British these were reasonable measures, requiring the colonists simply to bear their fair share of the costs of the empire. To the colonists, however, the measures constituted attacks on fundamental rights.

Through well-orchestrated agitation and boycotts, the colonists forced repeal of the Stamp Act of 1765 as well as the Townshend Acts that replaced it, except for a symbolic tax on tea. A temporary lull in conflict between 1770 and 1773 ended with the Boston Tea Party in December 1773. This radical action was instigated by a network of Boston agitators who refused to bow to the stubborn Massachusetts governor's attempt to enforce a law that benefited primarily the British East India Company monopoly.

In response to the Tea Party, the British imposed the harsh Intolerable Acts, and coincidentally passed the Quebec Act, which roused deep fears of religious as well as political tyranny. These twin actions stirred ferocious American resistance throughout the colonies and led directly to the calling of the First Continental Congress in September 1774, followed by the clash of arms at Lexington and Concord in April 1775.

As the two sides headed into war, the British enjoyed the advantages of a larger population, a professionally trained army, and much greater economic strength. American rebels had advantages of an expansive territory and talented leadership, but their greatest asset was the fervent commitment of that minority of Patriots who were ready to sacrifice everything for their rights.

KEY TERMS

- republicanism (88)
- radical Whigs (88)
- mercantilism (89)
- Sugar Act (90)
- Quartering Act (90)
- stamp tax (90)
- admiralty courts (90)
- Stamp Act Congress (91)
- nonimportation agreements (91)
- Sons of Liberty (92)
- Daughters of Liberty (92)
- Declaratory Act (92)
- Townshend Acts (92)
- Boston Massacre (93)
- committees of correspondence (94)
- Boston Tea Party (95)
- "Intolerable Acts" (95)
- Quebec Act (95)
- First Continental Congress (96)
- The Association (96)
- Lexington and Concord (97)
- Valley Forge (98)

PEOPLE TO KNOW

- John Hancock
- George Grenville
- Charles ("Champagne Charley") Townshend
- Crispus Attucks
- George III
- Lord North
- Samuel Adams
- Thomas Hutchinson
- Marquis de Lafayette
- Baron von Steuben
- Lord Dunmore

 MindTap is a fully online, highly personalized learning experience built upon Cengage Learning content. MindTap combines student learning tools—readings, multimedia, activities, and assessments—into a singular Learning Path that guides students through the course.

Chapter 8

America Secedes from the Empire
1775–1783

* * *

These are the times that try men's souls. The summer soldier and the sunshine patriot will, in this crisis, shrink from the service of their country; but he that stands it now, deserves the love and thanks of man and woman.

Thomas Paine, December 1776

Chapter Outline

- Early Skirmishes, 1775
- American "Republicanism"
- The Declaration of Independence, 1776
- Patriots and Loyalists
- The Fighting Fronts
- The French Alliance, 1778
- Yorktown, 1781
- The Peace of Paris, 1783
- Makers of America: The Loyalists
- Examining the Evidence: A Revolution for Women? Abigail Adams Chides Her Husband, 1776
- Varying Viewpoints: Whose Revolution?

Second Continental Congress (1775–1781) *Representative body of delegates from all thirteen colonies. Drafted the Declaration of Independence and managed the colonial war effort.*

Bloodshed at Lexington and Concord in April 1775 was a clarion call to arms. About twenty thousand musket-bearing "Minute Men" swarmed around Boston, there to entrap the outnumbered British.

The **Second Continental Congress** met in Philadelphia the next month, on May 10, 1775; and this time the full slate of thirteen colonies was represented. The conservative element in the Congress was still strong, despite the shooting in Massachusetts. There was still no well-defined sentiment for independence—merely a desire to continue fighting in the hope that king and Parliament would consent to a redress of grievances. Congress hopefully drafted new appeals to the British people and king—appeals that were spurned. Anticipating a possible rebuff, the delegates also adopted measures to raise money and to create an army and a navy. The British and the Americans now teetered on the brink of all-out warfare.

FOCUS QUESTIONS

1. How and why did Americans move in 1775–1776 from fighting only for "the rights of Englishmen" *within* the British Empire to declaring their independence?
2. What specific arguments and general political principles did Thomas Paine's *Common Sense* and Thomas Jefferson's Declaration of Independence use to promote and justify American independence?
3. Is it correct to call the American Revolution a "civil war" between American Patriots and American Loyalists, as well as a war for independence against Britain?
4. How and why did the initial British grand strategy to swiftly crush the rebellion fail? What strategies did Washington and his generals use after 1778 to prolong the war and gain French assistance?
5. Why were Americans able to win not only the war but a stunning diplomatic victory in the peace settlement of 1783?

CHRONOLOGY

1775	■ Battles of Lexington and Concord ■ Second Continental Congress ■ Americans capture British garrisons at Ticonderoga and Crown Point ■ Battle of Bunker Hill ■ King George III formally proclaims colonies in rebellion ■ Failed invasion of Canada	1778	■ Formation of French-American alliance ■ Battle of Monmouth
		1778–1779	■ Clark's victories in the West
		1781	■ Battle of King's Mountain ■ Battle of Cowpens ■ Greene leads Carolina campaign ■ French and Americans force Cornwallis to surrender at Yorktown
1776	■ Paine's *Common Sense* ■ Declaration of Independence ■ Battle of Trenton	1782	■ North's ministry collapses in Britain
1777	■ Battle of Brandywine ■ Battle of Germantown ■ Battle of Saratoga	1783	■ Treaty of Paris

★ Congress Drafts George Washington

Perhaps the most important single action of the Congress was to select George Washington, one of its members already in officer's uniform, to head the hastily improvised army besieging Boston. This choice was made with considerable misgivings. The tall, powerfully built, dignified Virginia planter, then forty-three, had never risen above the rank of colonel in the militia. His largest command had numbered only twelve hundred men, and that had been some twenty years earlier. Falling short of true military genius, Washington would actually lose more pitched battles than he won.

But the distinguished Virginian was gifted with outstanding powers of leadership and immense strength of character. He radiated patience, courage, self-discipline, and a sense of justice. He was a great moral force rather than a great military mind—a symbol and a rallying point. People instinctively trusted him; they sensed that when he put himself at the head of a cause, he was prepared, if necessary, to go down with the ship. He insisted on serving without pay, though he would keep a careful wartime expense account amounting to more than $100,000.

The Continental Congress initially selected Washington more for political reasons than for his leadership qualities. Americans in other colonies distrusted the large New England army gathering around Boston, and prudence suggested a commander from Virginia.

★ Bunker Hill and Hessian Hirelings

The clash of arms continued on a strangely contradictory basis. On the one hand, the Americans were emphatically affirming their loyalty to the king and earnestly voicing their desire to patch up difficulties. On the other hand, they were raising armies and shooting down His Majesty's soldiers. This curious war of inconsistency was fought for fourteen long months—from April 1775 to July 1776—before the fateful plunge into independence was taken.

Gradually the tempo of warfare increased. In May 1775 a tiny American force under Ethan Allen and Benedict Arnold surprised and captured the British garrisons at Ticonderoga and Crown Point, on the scenic lakes of upper New York. A priceless store of gunpowder and artillery for the siege of Boston was thus secured.

In June 1775 the colonists seized a hill, now known as **Bunker Hill** (actually Breed's Hill), from which they menaced the enemy in Boston. The British blundered bloodily when they launched a frontal attack with three thousand men. Sharpshooting

Battle of Bunker Hill (June 1775)
Fought on the outskirts of Boston, on Breed's Hill, the battle ended in the colonial militia's retreat, though at a heavy cost to the British.

Americans, numbering fifteen hundred and strongly entrenched, mowed down the advancing redcoats with frightful slaughter. But the colonists' scanty store of gunpowder finally gave out, and they were forced to abandon the hill in disorder. With two more such victories, remarked the French foreign minister, the British would have no army left in America.

Following Bunker Hill, King George III slammed the door on all hope of reconciliation. In August 1775 he formally proclaimed the colonies in rebellion. The skirmishes were now out-and-out treason, a hanging crime. The next month he widened the chasm by hiring thousands of troops from the German principality of Hesse, shocking colonists who feared the **Hessians'** exaggerated reputation for butchery. But the Hessian hirelings turned out to be more interested in booty than in duty. Hundreds of them eventually deserted and remained in America as respected citizens.

★ The Failed Attempt to Conquer Canada

The unsheathed sword continued to take its toll. In October 1775 the British burned Falmouth (Portland), Maine. That same autumn the rebels daringly undertook a two-pronged invasion of Canada. American leaders believed, erroneously, that the conquered French were explosively restive under the British yoke. A successful assault on Canada would add a fourteenth colony, while depriving Britain of a valuable base for striking at the colonies in revolt. But this large-scale attack, involving some two thousand American troops, contradicted the claim of the colonists that they were merely fighting defensively for a redress of grievances. Invasion northward was undisguised offensive warfare.

This bold stroke for Canada narrowly missed success (see Map 8.1). One invading column under the Irish-born General Richard Montgomery pushed up the Lake Champlain route and captured Montreal. He was joined at Quebec by the bedraggled army of General Benedict Arnold, whose men had been reduced to eating dogs and shoe leather during their grueling march through the Maine woods. An assault on Quebec, launched on the last day of 1775, was beaten off. The able Montgomery was killed; the dashing Arnold was wounded in one leg. Scattered remnants under Arnold's command retreated up the St. Lawrence River. But French Canadian leaders, who had been generously treated by the British in the Quebec Act of 1774, showed no real desire to welcome the plundering anti-Catholic invaders.

Bitter fighting persisted in the colonies, though the Americans still continued to disclaim a desire for independence. In January 1776 the British set fire to the Virginia town of Norfolk. In March they were finally forced to evacuate Boston, taking with them the leading friends of the king. In the South the rebellious colonists won two victories in 1776: one in February against some fifteen hundred **Loyalists** at Moore's Creek Bridge in North Carolina, and the other in June against an invading British fleet in Charleston harbor.

Washington at Verplanck's Point, New York, 1782, Reviewing the French Troops After the Victory at Yorktown, by John Trumbull, 1790 This noted American artist accentuated Washington's height (six feet, two inches) by showing him towering over his horse. Washington so appreciated this portrait of himself that he hung it in his dining room at his home at Mount Vernon, Virginia.

Hessians *German troops hired from their princes by George III to aid in putting down the colonial insurrection. This hardened the resolve of American colonists, who resented the use of paid foreign fighters.*

Loyalists *American colonists who opposed the Revolution and maintained their loyalty to the king; sometimes referred to as "Tories."*

Map 8.1 Revolution in the North, 1775–1776 Benedict Arnold's troops were described as "pretty young men" when they sailed from Massachusetts. They were considerably less pretty on their arrival in Quebec, after eight weeks of struggling through wet and frigid forests, often without food. "No one can imagine," one of them wrote, "the sweetness of a roasted shot-pouch [ammunition bag] to the famished appetite."

★ Thomas Paine Preaches Common Sense

Why did Americans continue to deny any intention of independence? Loyalty to the empire was deeply ingrained; many Americans continued to consider themselves part of a transatlantic community in which the mother country of Britain played a leading role; colonial unity was poor; and open rebellion was dangerous, especially against a formidable Britain. Irish rebels of that day were customarily hanged, drawn, and quartered. American rebels might have fared no better. As late as January 1776—five months before independence was declared—the king's health was being toasted by the officers of Washington's mess near Boston.

Gradually the Americans were shocked into recognizing the necessity of separating from the crown. Their eyes were jolted open by harsh British acts such as the burning of Falmouth and Norfolk and especially by the hiring of the Hessians. Then in 1776 came the publication of *Common Sense*, one of the most influential pamphlets ever written. Its author was the radical Thomas Paine, once an impoverished corset-maker's apprentice, who had come over from Britain a year earlier. His incendiary tract became a whirlwind best seller and within a few months reached the astonishing total of 120,000 copies sold.

Paine flatly branded the shilly-shallying of the colonists as contrary to "common sense." Nowhere in the physical universe did the smaller heavenly body control the larger one. So why should the tiny island of Britain control the vast continent of America? As for the king, whom the Americans professed to revere, he was nothing but "the Royal Brute of Great Britain."

Paine's passionate protest was as compelling as it was eloquent and radical—even doubly radical. It called not simply for independence but for the creation of a new kind of political society, a *republic*, where power flowed from the people themselves, not from a corrupt and despotic monarch. In language laced with biblical imagery familiar to common folk, Paine argued that all government officials—governors, senators, and judges, not just representatives in a house of commons—should derive their authority from popular consent.

The colonists' experience with governance had prepared them well for Paine's summons to create a republic. Many settlers, particularly New Englanders, had practiced a kind of republicanism in their democratic town meetings and annual elections, while the popularly elected committees of correspondence during 1774 and 1775 had demonstrated the feasibility of republican government. The absence of a hereditary aristocracy and the relative equality of condition enjoyed by landowning farmers meshed well with the republican repudiation of a fixed hierarchy of power.

Most Americans considered citizen "virtue" fundamental to any successful republican government. Because political power no longer rested with the king, individuals in a republic needed to sacrifice their personal self-interest to the public good. The collective good of "the people" mattered more than the private rights and interests of individuals. Paine inspired his contemporaries to view America as fertile ground for the cultivation of such civic virtue.

Yet not all **Patriots** agreed with Paine's ultrademocratic approach to republicanism. Some favored a republic ruled by a "natural aristocracy" of talent. Republicanism for them meant an end to hereditary aristocracy but not an end to all social hierarchy. These more conservative republicans feared that the fervor for liberty would overwhelm the stability of the social order. They watched with trepidation as the "lower orders" of society—poorer farmers, tenants, and laboring classes in towns and cities—seemed to embrace a kind of runaway republicanism that amounted to radical "leveling." The contest to define the nature of American republicanism would noisily continue for the next hundred years.

Common Sense (1776) *Thomas Paine's pamphlet urging the colonies to declare independence and establish a republican government. The widely read pamphlet helped convince colonists to support the Revolution.*

Patriots *Colonists who supported the American Revolution; they were also known as "Whigs."*

In Common Sense *Thomas Paine (1737–1809) argued for the superiority of a republic over a monarchy:*

"The nearer any government approaches to a republic the less business there is for a king. It is somewhat difficult to find a proper name for the government of England. Sir William Meredith calls it a republic; but in its present state it is unworthy of the name, because the corrupt influence of the crown, by having all the places in its disposal, hath so effectively swallowed up the power, and eaten out the virtue of the house of commons (the republican part of the constitution) that the government of England is nearly as monarchical as that of France or Spain."

★ Jefferson's "Explanation" of Independence

Members of the Philadelphia Congress, instructed by their respective colonies, gradually edged toward a clean break. On June 7, 1776, fiery Richard Henry Lee of Virginia moved that "These United Colonies are, and of right ought to be, free and independent states. . . ." After considerable debate, the motion was adopted nearly a month later, on July 2, 1776.

> The American signers of the Declaration of Independence had reason to fear for their necks. In 1802, twenty-six years later, George III (1738–1820) approved this death sentence for seven Irish rebels:
>
> "... [You] are to be hanged by the neck, but not until you are dead; for while you are still living your bodies are to be taken down, your bowels torn out and burned before your faces, your heads then cut off, and your bodies divided each into four quarters, and your heads and quarters to be then at the King's disposal; and may the Almighty God have mercy on your souls."

Declaration of Independence (July 4, 1776) *Formal pronouncement of independence drafted by Thomas Jefferson and approved by Congress. The Declaration allowed Americans to appeal for foreign aid and served as an inspiration for later revolutionary movements worldwide.*

The passing of Lee's resolution was the formal "declaration" of independence by the American colonies, and technically this was all that was needed to cut the British tie. John Adams wrote confidently that ever thereafter July 2 would be celebrated annually with fireworks. But something more was required. An epochal rupture of this kind called for some formal explanation to "a candid world." An inspirational appeal was also needed to enlist other British colonies in the Americas, to invite assistance from foreign nations, and to rally resistance at home.

Shortly after Lee made his memorable motion on June 7, Congress appointed a committee to prepare a more formal statement of separation. The task of drafting it fell to Thomas Jefferson, a tall, freckled, sandy-haired Virginia lawyer of thirty-three. Despite his youth, he was already recognized as a brilliant writer, and he measured up splendidly to the awesome assignment. After some debate and amendment, the **Declaration of Independence** was formally approved by the Congress on July 4, 1776.

Jefferson's pronouncement, couched in a lofty style, was magnificent. He gave his appeal universality by invoking the "natural rights" of humankind—not just British rights. He argued persuasively that, because the king had flouted these rights, the colonists were justified in cutting their connection. He then set forth a long list of the presumably tyrannous misdeeds of George III. The overdrawn bill of indictment included imposing taxes without consent, dispensing with trial by jury, abolishing valued laws, establishing a military dictatorship, maintaining standing armies in peacetime, cutting off trade, burning towns, hiring mercenaries, and inciting hostility among the Indians (for an annotated text of the Declaration of Independence, see Appendix).

The formal Declaration of Independence cleared the air as a thundershower does on a muggy day. Foreign assistance could be solicited with greater hope of success. Those Patriots who defied the king were now rebels, not loving subjects shooting their way into reconciliation. They must all hang together, Franklin is said to have grimly remarked, or they would all hang separately. Or, in the eloquent language of the great Declaration, "We mutually pledge to each other our lives, our fortunes and our sacred honor."

★ Patriots and Loyalists

The War of Independence, strictly speaking, was a civil war between two factions of Americans as well as a war between Americans and the British. Besides battling the British redcoats, the American rebels, called Patriots or "Whigs," fought Americans loyal to the king, called Loyalists or "Tories" (see "Makers of America: The Loyalists," p. 107).

Like many revolutions, the American Revolution was a minority movement. Many colonists were apathetic or neutral, including the Byrds of Virginia, who sat on the fence. The opposing forces contended not only against each other but also for the allegiance and support of the civilian population. In this struggle for the hearts and minds of the people, the Patriot militia proved far more successful than the inept British. The British military proved able to control only those areas where it could maintain a massive military presence. Elsewhere, as soon as the redcoats had marched on, the rebel militiamen appeared and took up the task of "political education"—sometimes by coercive means. Often lacking bayonets but always loaded with political zeal, the ragtag militia units convinced many colonists, even those indifferent to independence, that the British army was an unreliable friend and that they had better throw in their lot with the Patriot cause.

Loyalists, numbering perhaps 15 percent of the American people, remained true to their king. Some fifty thousand Loyalist volunteers at one time or another bore arms for

Makers of America

The Loyalists

In late 1776 Catherine Van Cortlandt wrote to her husband, a New Jersey merchant fighting in a Loyalist brigade, about the Patriot troops who had quartered themselves in her house. "They were the most disorderly of species," she complained, "and their officers were from the dregs of the people."

Like the Van Cortlandts, many Loyalists thought of themselves as "the better sort of people." Conservative, wealthy, and well-educated, Loyalists of this breed thought a break with Britain would invite anarchy. But Loyalism was hardly confined to the well-to-do. It also appealed to many people of modest means who identified strongly with Britain or who had reason to fear a Patriot victory. Loyalists included British veterans of the Seven Years' War who had received land grants from the crown and recent immigrants from Scotland and Ireland who had settled the backcountry of Georgia or the Carolinas. Resenting the plantation elites who ran these colonies, they filled the ranks of Tory brigades organized by the British army.

Other ethnic minorities found their own reasons to support the British. Some Dutch, German, and French religious sects believed that religious tolerance would be greater under the British than under the Americans. Encouraged by British officials, thousands of African Americans joined the Loyalist ranks in hopes that their service might bring an escape from bondage. Many of them joined black regiments that specialized in making small sorties against Patriot militia.

As the war drew to an end in 1783, the fate of black Loyalists varied enormously. Many thousands who came to Loyalism as fugitive slaves managed to find a way to freedom, especially in Nova Scotia. Other African American Loyalists suffered betrayal. British general Lord Cornwallis abandoned over four thousand former slaves in Virginia, and others found themselves sold back into slavery in the West Indies.

White Loyalists faced no threat of enslavement, but they did often suffer arrest, exile, confiscation of property, and loss of legal rights. Faced with such retribution, some eighty thousand Loyalists fled abroad, mostly to Britain or Canada. Some settled contentedly as exiles, but many, especially in Britain, had difficulty becoming accepted and lived lonely and diminished lives.

Most Loyalists, though, remained in America, despite the daunting burden of reestablishing themselves in a society that viewed them as traitors. Some succeeded remarkably, such as Hugh Gaine, a New York City printer who reopened his business and even won printing contracts from the new government. Gaine reintegrated himself into public life by siding with the Federalist call for a strong central government and a powerful executive. When New York ratified the Constitution in 1788, Gaine rode the float at the head of the city's celebration parade. He had, like many other former Loyalists, become an American.

Tough Times for Loyalists Under the shadow of the tar bucket and bag of feathers shown in the upper right background, these Virginia Loyalists were roughly handled by a club-wielding crowd of Patriots.

the British. They also helped the king's cause by serving as spies, by inciting the Indians, and by keeping Patriot soldiers at home to protect their families.

Many people of education and wealth, of culture and caution, remained loyal. Loyalists were more numerous among the older generation, for young people make revolutions. Loyalists also included the king's officers and other beneficiaries of the crown—people who knew which side their daily bread came from. Loyalists were most numerous where the Anglican Church was strongest, except in Virginia, where debt-burdened Anglican aristocrats flocked into the rebel camp. The king's followers were well entrenched in aristocratic New York City and Charleston and also in Quaker Pennsylvania and New Jersey, where General Washington felt that he was fighting in "the enemy's country." Loyalists were least numerous in New England, where Presbyterianism and Congregationalism flourished, producing strong support for rebellion.

Before the Declaration of Independence in 1776, persecution of the Loyalists was relatively mild. But once independence was declared, Loyalists were treated more harshly. Hundreds of Loyalists were imprisoned and a few were hanged. About eighty thousand loyal supporters of King George III were driven out or fled the country, and their estates were confiscated and sold to finance the war. But there was no wholesale reign of terror comparable to that of the later blood-drenched French and Russian revolutions. Confiscation often worked great economic hardship, but most Loyalists did not regret their stand. Ardent Loyalists had their hearts in their cause, and a major blunder of the haughty British was not to make full use of them in the fighting.

★ General Washington at Bay

After evacuating Boston in March 1776, the British made New York City their central base of operations. Here was a splendid seaport, centrally located, where the king could count on cooperation from the numerous Loyalists. An awe-inspiring British fleet appeared off New York in July 1776. It consisted of some five hundred ships and thirty-five thousand men—the largest armed force to be seen in America until the Civil War. General Washington, dangerously outnumbered, could muster only eighteen thousand ill-trained troops with which to meet the crack army of the invader.

Battle of Long Island (August 1776)
Battle for the control of New York. British troops overwhelmed the colonial militias and retained control of the city for most of the war.

Disaster befell the Americans in the summer and fall of 1776. Outgeneraled and outmaneuvered, they were routed at the **Battle of Long Island**, where panic seized the raw recruits. By the narrowest of margins, and thanks to a favoring wind and fog, Washington escaped to Manhattan Island. Retreating northward, he crossed the Hudson River to New Jersey and finally reached the Delaware River with the British close at his heels. Tauntingly, enemy buglers sounded the fox-hunting call so familiar to Virginians of Washington's day. The Patriot cause was at low ebb when the rebel remnants fled across the river after collecting all available boats to forestall pursuit.

Battle of Trenton (December 1776)
George Washington surprised and captured a garrison of sleeping German Hessians, raising the morale of his crestfallen army and setting the stage for his victory at Princeton a week later.

The wonder is that Washington's adversary, General William Howe, did not speedily crush the demoralized American forces. But Howe was no military genius, and he well remembered the horrible slaughter at Bunker Hill, where he had commanded. The country was rough, supplies were slow in coming, and Howe did not relish the rigors of winter campaigning. Washington, who was now almost counted out, stealthily recrossed the ice-clogged Delaware River. At the **Battle of Trenton**, on December 26, 1776, he surprised and captured a thousand Hessians who were sleeping off the effects of their Christmas celebration. A week later, leaving his campfires burning as a ruse, he slipped away and inflicted another sharp defeat on the British army at Princeton. This brilliant New Jersey campaign, crowned by these two lifesaving victories, revealed "Old Fox" Washington at his military best.

★ Burgoyne's Blundering Invasion

In 1777 London officials adopted an intricate scheme for capturing the vital Hudson River Valley. If successful, the British would sever New England from the rest of the states and paralyze the American cause. The main invading force, under the soldier-actor-playwright

General John ("Gentleman Johnny") Burgoyne, would push down the Lake Champlain route from Canada. General Howe's troops in New York would advance up the Hudson River to meet Burgoyne near Albany. A third British force under Colonel Barry St. Leger would come in from the west by way of Lake Ontario and the Mohawk Valley.

British planners did not reckon with General Benedict Arnold. Retreating slowly from Quebec after being repulsed there in 1775, Arnold had by heroic efforts kept his army in the field and assembled a small fleet on Lake Champlain. The British finally constructed a sizable fleet that defeated Arnold's tiny flotilla. But by then winter was descending, and the British were forced to retire back to Canada. This delay was critical to the American cause.

Compelled to start over in the spring of 1777, General Burgoyne began his fateful invasion with seven thousand regular troops who were encumbered by a heavy baggage train and many accompanying officers' wives. Progress was painfully slow, for sweaty axmen had to chop a path through the forest, while American militiamen began to swarm like hornets on Burgoyne's flanks.

Meanwhile, astonished eyebrows rose as General Howe marched the main British army toward the rebel capital of Philadelphia at a time when it seemed obvious he should be starting up the Hudson River from New York to meet the advancing Burgoyne. As scholars now know, Howe wanted to engage and destroy Washington's army, apparently assuming he had ample time to assist Burgoyne directly should he be needed.

General Washington, keeping a wary eye on the British in New York, hastily transferred his army to the vicinity of Philadelphia. There, late in 1777, he was defeated in two pitched battles at Brandywine Creek and Germantown. Pleasure-loving General Howe then settled down comfortably in the lively capital, leaving Burgoyne to flounder through the wilds of upstate New York. Benjamin Franklin, recently sent to Paris as an envoy, truthfully jested that Howe had not captured Philadelphia but that Philadelphia had captured Howe. Washington finally retired to winter quarters at Valley Forge, a strong hilly position some twenty miles northwest of Philadelphia. There his frostbitten and hungry men were short of about everything except misery. This rabble was nevertheless whipped into a professional army by the recently arrived Prussian drillmaster, the profane but patient Baron von Steuben.

Burgoyne meanwhile had begun to bog down north of Albany, while a host of American militiamen, scenting the kill, hounded him on all sides. After a series of sharp engagements, the British army was trapped. Meanwhile, the Americans had driven back St. Leger's force at Oriskany, New York. Unable to advance or retreat, Burgoyne was forced to surrender his entire command at the **Battle of Saratoga**, on October 17, 1777, to the American General Horatio Gates.

Saratoga ranks high among the decisive battles of both American and world history. The victory immensely revived the faltering colonial cause. Even more important, it made possible the urgently needed foreign aid from France, which in turn helped ensure American independence.

Battle of Saratoga (October 1777)
Decisive colonial victory in upstate New York, which helped secure French support for the Revolutionary cause.

★ Revolutionary America and the World

France, thirsting for revenge against Britain, was eager to inflame the quarrel that had broken out in America and cripple British imperial power. For their part, the American revolutionaries badly needed help to throw off the British yoke. The stage seemed set for the embattled new nation to make its diplomatic debut by sealing an alliance with France against the common foe.

Yet just as they stood for revolutionary political ideals at home, the rebellious Americans also harbored revolutionary ideas about international affairs. They wanted to end colonialism and mercantilism, promote free trade and freedom of the seas, and substitute the rule of law for the ancient reliance on raw power to arbitrate the affairs of nations. The Continental Congress accordingly instructed its emissaries to France to seek no political or military alliance, but only a commercial connection. These remarkably self-denying restrictions reflected a belief among enlightened American

Benjamin Franklin (1706–1790), by Charles Willson Peale, 1789 He left school at age ten and became a wealthy businessman, a journalist, an inventor, a scientist, a legislator, and preeminently a statesman-diplomat. He was sent to France in 1776 as the American envoy at age seventy, and he remained there until 1785, negotiating the alliance with the French and helping to negotiate the treaty of peace. His fame had preceded him, and when he discarded his wig for the fur cap of a simple "American agriculturist," he took French society by storm. French aristocratic women, with whom he was a great favorite, honored him by adopting the high coiffure à la Franklin in imitation of his cap. (RMN-Grand Palais/Art Resource, NY)

and European thinkers of the time that history had reached a momentous turning point when military conflict would be abandoned in favor of commerce and peaceful relations between nations. Many critics considered this dream hopelessly naïve and utopian, yet it infused an element of idealism into American attitudes toward international affairs that has proved stubbornly persistent.

When wily old Benjamin Franklin arrived in Paris to negotiate the treaty with France, he was determined that his very appearance should herald the diplomatic revolution the Americans hoped to achieve. Forsaking the ermined robes and fancy wigs expected in the royal court, he sported homespun garments and a simple fur cap. Pompous French diplomats were shocked, but ordinary Parisians adored him as a specimen of a new democratic social order, devoid of pretense and ornament. Franklin's personal popularity was a valuable card in the diplomatic game.

Franklin also played skillfully on French fears of reconciliation between Britain and America. After the humiliation of Saratoga in 1777, the British had belatedly offered the Americans a species of home rule within the empire. To counter this, France offered Franklin a treaty of alliance that bound both parties to wage war until the United States had fully secured its freedom and until both agreed to terms with the common enemy. In an early example of practical self-interest trumping abstract idealism in the conduct of foreign affairs, the young Republic concluded its first entangling military alliance. The treaty with France, signed in February 1778, constituted an official recognition of America's independence and lent powerful military heft to the Patriot cause.

With France now supporting the Americans' cause, the shot fired at Lexington rapidly widened into a global conflagration. Spain entered the fray against Britain in 1779, as did Holland. Combined Spanish and French fleets outnumbered those of Britain,

Examining the Evidence

A Revolution For Women? Abigail Adams Chides Her Husband, 1776

In the midst of the revolutionary fervor of 1776, at least one woman—Abigail Adams, wife of noted Massachusetts Patriot (and future president) John Adams—raised her voice on behalf of women. Yet she apparently raised it only in private—in this personal letter to her husband. Private documents such as the correspondence and diaries of individuals both prominent and ordinary offer invaluable sources for the historian seeking to discover sentiments, opinions, and perspectives that are often difficult to discern in the official public record.

1. What does it suggest about the historical circumstances of the 1770s that Abigail Adams confined her claim for women's equality to this confidential exchange with her spouse?
2. What ideas and events inspired the arguments Adams employed?
3. Despite her privileged position and persuasive power and despite her threat to "foment a rebellion," Abigail Adams's plea went largely unheeded in the Revolutionary era—as did comparable pleadings to extend the revolutionary principle of equality to blacks. What accounts for this limited application of the ideas of liberty and equality in the midst of a supposedly democratic revolution?

Massachusetts Historical Society

111

and on two occasions the British Isles seemed to be at the mercy of hostile warships. In 1780 Catherine the Great of Russia lined up almost all the remaining European neutrals into the "Armed Neutrality," which assumed an attitude of passive hostility toward Britain.

To Britain, now struggling for its very life, the scuffle in the New World soon became secondary. The Americans deserve credit for having kept the war going until 1778. But they did not achieve their independence until the conflict erupted into a world war that was too big for Britain to handle. From 1778 to 1783, France provided the rebels with guns, money, immense amounts of equipment, about one-half of America's regular armed forces, and practically all of the new nation's naval strength.

France's entrance into the conflict forced the British to change their basic strategy in America. With powerful French fleets in American waters, Britain could no longer blockade the colonial coast and command the seas. To shorten their lines of supply, the British evacuated Philadelphia and escaped to New York City after the indecisive Battle of Monmouth in June 1778. Washington followed them to the New York area, where he hemmed them in.

Blow and Counterblow

In the summer of 1780 a powerful French army of six thousand regular troops, commanded by the Comte de Rochambeau, arrived in Newport, Rhode Island. Preparations began for a Franco-American attack on New York.

Improving American morale was staggered later in 1780 when General Benedict Arnold turned traitor. A leader of undoubted dash and brilliance, he was ambitious, greedy, and unscrupulous, and he suffered from a well-grounded but petulant feeling that his valuable services were not fully appreciated. He plotted with the British to sell out the key stronghold of West Point, which commanded the Hudson River, for £6,300 and an officer's commission. By the sheerest accident the plot was detected in the nick of time, and Arnold fled to the British. "Whom can we trust now?" cried General Washington in anguish.

The British meanwhile had devised a new plan to roll up the colonies, beginning with the South, where the Loyalists were numerous (see Map 8.2). Georgia was ruthlessly overrun in 1778–1779. Charleston, South Carolina, fell in 1780. The surrender of that city to the British involved the capture of five thousand men and four hundred cannon and was a heavier loss to the Americans, in relation to existing strength, than Burgoyne's was to the British.

Warfare now intensified in the Carolinas, where Patriots bitterly fought their Loyalist neighbors. It was not uncommon for prisoners on both sides to be butchered in cold blood after they had thrown down their arms. The tide turned later in 1780 and early in 1781, when American riflemen wiped out a British detachment at King's Mountain and then defeated a smaller force at Cowpens. In the Carolina campaign of 1781, General Nathanael Greene, a Quaker-reared tactician, distinguished himself by his strategy of delay. Standing and then retreating, he exhausted his foe, General Cornwallis, in vain pursuit. By losing battles but winning campaigns, the "Fighting Quaker" finally succeeded in clearing most of Georgia and South Carolina of British troops.

The Land Frontier and the Sea Frontier

The West was ablaze during much of the war. Indian allies of King George III, hoping to protect their land, were busy attacking and burning frontier settlements. They were egged on by British agents, who allegedly paid bounties for American scalps. Although two nations of the Iroquois Confederacy, the Oneidas and the Tuscaroras, sided with the Americans, the Senecas, Mohawks, Cayugas, and Onondagas joined the British. They were led by Mohawk chief Joseph Brant, a convert to Anglicanism who believed that a victorious Britain would restrain American expansion into the West. Brant and the

America Secedes from the Empire   113

Map 8.2 War in the South, 1780–1781

British ravaged large areas of backcountry Pennsylvania and New York until checked by an American force in 1779.

In the wild Illinois country, the British were especially vulnerable to attack, for they held only scattered posts that they had captured from the French. An audacious frontiersman, George Rogers Clark, conceived the idea of seizing these forts by surprise. In 1778–1779 he floated down the Ohio River with about 175 men and captured in quick succession the forts at Kaskaskia, Cahokia, and Vincennes.

America's infant navy, commanded by daring officers such as the hard-fighting young Scotsman John Paul Jones, was more successful in destroying British merchant shipping than in engaging Britain's powerful fleets. More numerous and damaging than ships of the regular American navy were swift **privateers**. Authorized by Congress, over a thousand of these privately owned armed ships preyed on enemy shipping and

privateers *Privately owned armed ships authorized by Congress to prey on enemy shipping during the Revolutionary War. More numerous than the tiny American navy, privateers inflicted heavy damages on British shippers.*

> *Baron von Steuben (1730–1794), a Prussian general who helped train the Continental Army, found the Americans to be very different from other soldiers he had known. As von Steuben explained to a fellow European:*
>
> "The genius of this nation is not in the least to be compared with that of the Prussians, Austrians, or French. You say to your soldier, 'Do this' and he doeth it; but I am obliged to say, 'This is the reason why you ought to do that,' and then he does it."

Battle of Yorktown (October 1781)
George Washington, with the aid of the French army, besieged Cornwallis at Yorktown, while the French naval fleet prevented British reinforcements from coming ashore. Cornwallis surrendered, dealing a heavy blow to the British war effort and paving the way for an eventual peace.

captured some six hundred British prizes. Although they diverted manpower from the main war effort and involved Americans in speculation and graft, privateers brought in urgently needed gold, harassed the enemy, and raised American morale. Unhappy British shippers and manufacturers brought increasing pressure on Parliament to end the war on honorable terms.

★ Yorktown and the Final Curtain

One of the darkest periods of the war was 1780–1781, just before the last decisive victory. Inflation of the currency continued at full gallop, and the government was virtually bankrupt. Despair prevailed; the sense of unity withered; and mutinous sentiments infected the army.

Meanwhile, the British General Cornwallis was blundering into a trap. After futile operations in Virginia, he had fallen back to Chesapeake Bay at Yorktown to await seaborne supplies and reinforcements. He assumed Britain would continue to control the sea. But these few fateful weeks just happened to be one of the brief periods during the war when British naval superiority slipped away.

The French were now prepared to cooperate energetically in a brilliant stroke. Admiral de Grasse, operating with a powerful fleet in the West Indies, sent word to the Americans that he was free to join with them in an assault on Cornwallis, to be known to history as the **Battle of Yorktown**. Quick to seize this opportunity, General Washington made a swift march of more than three hundred miles to the Chesapeake from the New York area. Accompanied by Rochambeau's French army, Washington beset the British by land, while de Grasse blockaded them by sea after beating off the British fleet. Completely cornered, Cornwallis surrendered his entire force of seven thousand men on October 19, 1781, as his band appropriately played "The World Turn'd Upside Down." Stunned by news of the disaster, Prime Minister Lord North cried, "Oh God! It's all over! It's all over!" But it was not. King George III stubbornly planned to continue the struggle, for Britain still had fifty-four thousand troops in North America, including thirty-two thousand in the United States. Washington returned with his army to New York, where he kept a vigilant eye on a British force of ten thousand men there.

Fighting actually continued for more than a year after Yorktown, with Patriot-Loyalist warfare in the South especially savage. "No quarter for Tories" was the common battle cry. One of Washington's most valuable contributions was to keep the cause alive, the army in the field, and the states together during these critical months. Otherwise, a satisfactory peace treaty might never have been signed.

★ Peace at Paris

After Yorktown, many Britons were weary of war and increasingly ready to come to terms. They had suffered heavy reverses in India and in the West Indies. Lord North's Tory ministry collapsed in March 1782 and was replaced by a Whig ministry rather favorable to the Americans.

Three American peace negotiators had meanwhile gathered at Paris: the aging but astute Benjamin Franklin; the flinty John Adams, vigilant for New England interests; and the impulsive John Jay of New York, deeply suspicious of Old World intrigue. The three envoys had explicit instructions from Congress to make no separate peace and to consult with their French allies at all stages of the negotiations. But the American representatives chafed under this directive. They well knew that it had been written by a subservient Congress, with the French Foreign Office indirectly guiding the pen.

France was in a painful position. France had induced Spain to enter the war on its side, and the Spanish coveted the immense trans-Appalachian area for themselves. Wanting an America that would be independent but feeble, the French therefore joined the scheme to keep the new Republic cooped up east of the Appalachian Mountains.

But John Jay was unwilling to play France's game. Suspiciously alert, he perceived that the French could not satisfy the conflicting ambitions of both Americans and Spaniards. He saw signs—or thought he did—indicating that the Paris Foreign Office was about to betray America's trans-Appalachian interests to satisfy those of Spain. He therefore secretly made separate overtures to London, contrary to his instructions from Congress. The hard-pressed British, eager to entice one of their enemies from the alliance, speedily came to terms with the Americans. The final **Treaty of Paris** concluding the war was signed in 1783.

By terms of the treaty, the British formally recognized the independence of the United States. In addition, they granted generous boundaries, stretching majestically to the Mississippi on the west, to the Great Lakes on the north, and to Spanish Florida on the south. (Spain had recently captured Florida from Britain.)

The Americans, on their part, had to yield important concessions. Loyalists were not to be further persecuted, and Congress was to *recommend* to the state legislatures that confiscated Loyalist property be restored. As for the debts long owed to British creditors, the states vowed to put no lawful obstacles in the way of their collection. Unhappily for future harmony, the assurances regarding both Loyalists and debts were not carried out in the manner hoped for by London.

★ A New Nation Legitimized

Britain's terms were liberal almost beyond belief. The enormous trans-Appalachian area was thrown in as a virtual gift, for George Rogers Clark had captured only a small segment of it. Why the generosity? Had the United States beaten Britain to its knees?

The key to the riddle may be found in the Old World. At the time the peace terms were drafted, Britain was trying to seduce America from its French alliance, so Britain made the terms as alluring as possible. The shaky Whig ministry, hanging on by its fingernails for only a few months, was more friendly to the Americans than were the Tories. It was determined, by a policy of liberality, to salve recent wounds, reopen old trade channels, and prevent future wars over the coveted trans-Appalachian region. This farsighted policy was regrettably not followed by the successors of the Whigs.

In spirit, the Americans made a separate peace—contrary to the French alliance. In fact, they did not. The Paris Foreign Office formally approved the terms of peace, though disturbed by the lone-wolf course of its American ally. France was immensely relieved by the prospect of bringing the costly conflict to an end and of freeing itself from its embarrassing promises to the Spanish crown.

America alone gained from the world-girdling war. The British, though soon to stage a comeback, were battered and beaten. The French savored sweet revenge but plunged headlong down the slippery slope to bankruptcy and revolution. The Americans fared much better. Snatching their independence from the furnace of world conflict, they began their national career with a splendid territorial birthright and a priceless heritage of freedom. Seldom, if ever, have any people been so favored.

Contending Voices

Two Revolutions: French and American

The French Revolution broke out in the decade following America's own revolution, which partly inspired it. Yet the French upheaval swiftly descended into mob violence and soon led to Napoleon Bonaparte's wars, which convulsed Europe for a decade before the French monarchy was restored in 1814. Then and later, scholars have tried to understand the relation between the two revolutions. In 1800 the Prussian statesman Friedrich von Gentz (1764–1832) published an essay titled "Origins and Principles of the American Revolution, Compared with the French." In it he argued that

"the Americans escaped the most dangerous of all the rocks, which in our times threatens the founders of any revolution: the deadly passion for making political experiments with abstract theories and untried systems."

Future American Secretary of State and President John Quincy Adams (1767–1848) translated von Gentz's work into English, because, he said,

"it rescues [the American] revolution from the disgraceful imputation of having proceeded from the same principles as the French."

> According to von Gentz and Adams, what elements in the American experience before 1776 accounted for the major differences between the revolutions in France and America?

Treaty of Paris (1783) *Peace treaty signed by Britain and the United States ending the Revolutionary War. The British formally recognized American independence and ceded territory east of the Mississippi while the Americans, in turn, promised to restore Loyalist property and repay debts to British creditors.*

Varying Viewpoints

Whose Revolution?

Historians once assumed that the American Revolution was just another chapter in the unfolding story of human liberty—an important way station on a divinely ordained pathway toward moral perfection in human affairs. This approach, often labeled the "Whig view of history," was best expressed in George Bancroft's ten-volume *History of the United States*, published between the 1830s and the 1870s.

In the nineteenth century, an "imperial school" of historians such as Charles Andrews and Lawrence Gipson argued that the Revolution was primarily a constitutional conflict within the British Empire. By the early twentieth century, both the Whig and imperial-school interpretations were sharply challenged by so-called progressive historians, who argued that neither divine destiny nor constitutional squabbles had much to do with the Revolution. Rather, progressives such as Carl Becker and J. Franklin Jameson claimed the Revolution stemmed from deep-seated class tensions within American society that, once released by revolt, produced a truly transformed social order. The Revolution, therefore, was not only about "home rule" within the British Empire but about "who should rule at home" in America.

In the 1950s, historians such as Robert Brown and Edmund Morgan downplayed the role of class conflict in the Revolutionary era and emphasized that colonists of all ranks shared a commitment to certain fundamental political principles of self-government. The unifying power of ideas was now back in fashion almost a hundred years after Bancroft.

Since the 1950s, two broad interpretations have contended with each other and perpetuated the controversy over whether political ideals or economic and social realities were most responsible for the Revolution. The first, articulated most prominently by Bernard Bailyn, has emphasized inherent ideological and psychological factors. Bailyn argued that the colonists, incited by their reading of earlier English theorists, grew extraordinarily suspicious of any attempts to tighten the imperial reins. When confronted with new taxes and imperial regulations, the colonists screamed "conspiracy against liberty" and took up armed insurrection in defense of their intellectual commitment to liberty.

A second school of historians, inspired by the social movements of the turbulent 1960s and 1970s, revived the progressive interpretation of the Revolution. Gary Nash in *An Urban Crucible* (1979) and Edward Countryman in *A People in Revolution* (1981) pointed to attacks by laborers on political elites and expressions of resentment toward wealth as evidence of a society breeding revolution from within, quite aside from British provocations. Woody Holton, in *Forced Founders* (1999), argued that pressures exerted by the presence of Indians, enslaved Africans, and poor whites forced the Virginia elite onto the road toward independence. These neoprogressives claimed that the varying material circumstances of American participants gave the Revolution a less unified and more complex ideological underpinning than the idealistic historians had previously suggested.

Other scholars have taken a more transatlantic view of the Revolution's origins, asking when and how colonists shifted from identifying as "British" to viewing themselves as "American." Fred Anderson argued that the Seven Years' War helped create a sense of American identity apart from Britain, and T. H. Breen said that American nationalism emerged because the British failed to see Americans as equal imperial citizens, entitled to the same rights as Englishmen. Taking a broader global view, David Armitage has argued that the American Declaration of Independence had an impact far beyond the British Atlantic world, shaping the rhetoric of countries claiming their independence into the following century and beyond.

CHAPTER SUMMARY ★ ★ ★ ★ ★ ★ ★ ★ ★ ★ ★ ★ ★ ★

Even after the shooting began at Lexington and Concord in April 1775, the Second Continental Congress did not at first pursue independence. Instead, it continued to appeal to the king to respect "the rights of Englishmen." The Congress's most important action was selecting George Washington as military commander.

After further armed clashes, King George III formally proclaimed the colonists in rebellion. In early 1776, Thomas Paine's *Common Sense* finally persuaded Americans to fight for independence as well as liberty. Paine and other radical leaders promoted the Revolution as an opportunity to create equality and self-government by ordinary people, though more conservative republicans disliked revolutionary egalitarianism and hoped to retain a strong political hierarchy without monarchy. Jefferson's Declaration of Independence deepened the meaning of the American Revolution by proclaiming it a fight for self-evident and universal human rights applicable to all peoples everywhere.

The committed revolutionary Patriots, only a minority of the American population, had to fight a civil war with Loyalist Americans as well as the professionally trained and better-armed British army and navy. Loyalists were strongest among conservatives, city dwellers, and Anglicans (except in Virginia). Patriots were strongest in New England and among Presbyterians and Congregationalists.

In the first phase of the war, Washington was barely able to hold off the British, who botched their grand plan to isolate New England and quash the rebellion quickly. Victory in the Battle of Saratoga brought Americans new respect and international assistance from France and Holland. Partially compromising their idealistic revolutionary beliefs that traditional military alliances were wrong, Franklin and other U.S. emissaries joined an alliance with France. With active French involvement, the Revolutionary War became a world war.

American fortunes were at their lowest ebb in 1780–1781, as political and economic troubles and military stalemate again nearly led to defeat. But General Nathanael Greene's Continental Army in the South held on until Cornwallis stumbled into a French-American trap at Yorktown. Lord North's ministry collapsed in Britain, and American negotiators achieved an extremely generous settlement from the new Whig government in London.

KEY TERMS

- Second Continental Congress (101)
- Battle of Bunker Hill (102)
- Hessians (103)
- Loyalists (103)
- *Common Sense* (105)
- Patriots (105)
- Declaration of Independence (106)
- Battle of Long Island (108)
- Battle of Trenton (108)
- Battle of Saratoga (109)
- privateers (113)
- Battle of Yorktown (114)
- Treaty of Paris (115)

PEOPLE TO KNOW

- Ethan Allen
- Benedict Arnold
- Richard Montgomery
- Thomas Paine
- Abigail Adams
- Richard Henry Lee
- Lord Charles Cornwallis
- William Howe
- John ("Gentleman Johnny") Burgoyne
- Benjamin Franklin
- Comte de Rochambeau
- Nathanael Greene
- Joseph Brant
- George Rogers Clark
- Admiral de Grasse

MindTap is a fully online, highly personalized learning experience built upon Cengage Learning content. MindTap combines student learning tools—readings, multimedia, activities, and assessments—into a singular Learning Path that guides students through the course.

Part 2

BUILDING THE NEW NATION

1776–1860

By 1783 Americans had won their freedom. Now they had to build their country. To be sure, they were blessed with a vast and fertile land, and they inherited from their colonial experience a proud legacy of self-rule. But history provided scant precedent for erecting a democracy on a national scale. No law of nature guaranteed that the thirteen rebellious colonies would stay glued together as a single nation or that they would preserve, not to mention expand, their democratic way of life. New institutions had to be created, new habits of thought cultivated. Who could predict whether the American experiment in government by the people would succeed?

The ramshackle national government cobbled together under the Articles of Confederation during the Revolutionary War soon proved woefully inadequate to the task of nation building. Less than ten years after the war's conclusion, the Articles were replaced by a new constitution, but even its adoption did not end the debate over what form American democracy should take. Would the president, or the congress, or the courts be the dominant branch of government? What should be the proper division of authority between the federal government and the states? How could the rights of individuals be protected against a potentially powerful government? What economic policies would best serve the infant Republic? How should the nation defend itself against foreign foes? What principles should guide foreign policy? Was America a nation at all, or was it merely a geographic expression, destined to splinter into several bitterly quarreling sections, as had happened to so many other would-be countries?

After a shaky start under George Washington and John Adams in the 1790s, buffeted by foreign troubles and domestic crises, the new Republic passed a major test when power was peacefully transferred from the conservative Federalists to the more liberal Jeffersonians in the election of 1800. A confident President Jefferson proceeded boldly to expand the national territory with the landmark Louisiana Purchase in 1803. But before long, Jefferson and then his successor, James Madison, were embroiled in what eventually proved to be a fruitless effort to spare the United States from the ravages of the war then raging in Europe.

America was dangerously divided during the War of 1812 and suffered a humiliating defeat. But a new sense of national unity and purpose was unleashed in the land thereafter. President Monroe, presiding over this "Era of Good Feelings," proclaimed in the Monroe Doctrine of 1823 that both of the American continents were off-limits to further European intervention. The foundations of a continental-scale economy were laid, as a "transportation revolution" stitched the country together with canals and railroads and turnpikes. Settlers flooded over those new arteries into the burgeoning West, often brusquely shouldering aside the native peoples. Immigrants, especially from Ireland and Germany, flocked to American shores. The combination of new lands and new labor fed the growth of a market economy, including the commercialization of agriculture and the beginnings of the factory system of production. Old ways of life withered as the market economy drew women as well as men, children as well as adults, blacks as well as whites, into its embrace.

The Verdict of the People (detail) This election-day crowd exudes the exuberant spirit of the era of Andrew Jackson, when the advent of universal white male suffrage made the United States the modern world's first mass participatory democracy. Yet the black man with the wheelbarrow, literally pushing his way into the painting, is a pointed reminder that the curse of slavery still blighted this happy scene.

Ominously, the slave system grew robustly as cotton production, mostly for sale on European markets, exploded into the booming Southwest.

Meanwhile, the United States, in the era of Andrew Jackson, gave the world an impressive lesson in political science. Between roughly 1820 and 1840 Americans virtually invented mass democracy, creating huge political parties and enormously expanding political participation by enfranchising nearly all adult white males. Nor was the spirit of innovation confined to the political realm. A wave of reform and cultural vitality swept through many sectors of American society. Utopian experiments proliferated. Religious revivals and even new religions, such as Mormonism, flourished. A national literature blossomed. Crusades were launched for temperance, prison reform, women's rights, and the abolition of slavery.

By the second quarter of the nineteenth century, the outlines of a distinctive American national character had begun to emerge. Americans were a diverse, restless people, tramping steadily westward, eagerly forging their own nascent industrial revolution, proudly exercising their democratic political rights, impatient with the old, in love with the new, testily asserting their superiority over all other peoples—and increasingly divided, in heart, in conscience, and in politics, over the single greatest blight on their record of nation making and democracy building: slavery.

What if...?

■ What if the American people had failed to ratify the Constitution in 1788 and the United States had persisted as a loosely tied group of states under the Articles of Confederation? What would have been the consequences for the development of political democracy, the character of the economy, the nature of foreign policy—and the fate of slavery?

Chapter 9

The Confederation and the Constitution

1776–1790

This example of changing the constitution by assembling the wise men of the state, instead of assembling armies, will be worth as much to the world as the former examples we have given it.

THOMAS JEFFERSON, 1789

Chapter Outline

- Post-Revolutionary Politics and Economics
- The Articles of Confederation, 1781–1788
- The Northwest Ordinance, 1787
- Shays's Rebellion, 1786
- The Constitutional Convention, 1787
- Ratifying the Constitution, 1787–1790
- Steps Toward Social Equality
- *Examining the Evidence: Copley Family Portrait, ca. 1776–1777*
- *Varying Viewpoints: The Constitution: Revolutionary or Counterrevolutionary?*

The American Revolution was not a revolution in the sense of a radical or total change. It did not suddenly and violently overturn an entire political and social framework, as later occurred in the French and Russian revolutions. What happened was accelerated evolution rather than outright revolution.

During the conflict itself, people went on working and praying, marrying and playing. Many of them were not seriously disturbed by the actual fighting, and the most isolated communities scarcely knew that a war was on. But at war's end, all Americans faced a great question: what would be done with the independence that had been so dearly won?

FOCUS QUESTIONS

1. What were the political and social consequences of the American Revolution?
2. What were the primary accomplishments and deficiencies of the United States government under the Articles of Confederation?
3. What caused the movement to scrap the Articles of Confederation and create an entirely new federal government, and how did the Constitution written in Philadelphia reflect the Founders' central intentions?
4. What were the fundamental disagreements between the federalists and antifederalists, and why were the federalists successful in achieving ratification of the Constitution?
5. In what ways did the Constitution represent in part a "conservative" reaction to the American Revolution? How did it at the same time preserve and protect the essential "radical" principles of the Revolution?

CHRONOLOGY

1774	First Continental Congress calls for abolition of slave trade	1783	Military officers form Society of the Cincinnati
1775	Philadelphia Quakers found world's first antislavery society	1785	Land Ordinance of 1785
1776	New Jersey constitution temporarily gives women the vote	1786	Virginia Statute for Religious Freedom Shays's Rebellion Meeting of five states to discuss revision of the Articles of Confederation
1777	Articles of Confederation adopted by Second Continental Congress	1787	Northwest Ordinance Constitutional Convention in Philadelphia
1780	Massachusetts adopts first constitution drafted in convention and ratified by popular vote	1788	Ratification by nine states guarantees a new government under the Constitution
1781	Articles of Confederation put into effect		

★ A Shaky Start toward Union

Prospects for erecting a lasting regime were far from bright. It is always difficult to set up a new government and doubly difficult to set up a new type of government. The picture was further clouded in America by leaders preaching "natural rights" and looking suspiciously at all persons clothed with authority. America was more a name than a nation, and unity ran little deeper than the color on the map.

Disruptive forces stalked the land. The departure of the conservative Loyalists left the political system inclined toward experimentation and innovation. Patriots had fought the war with a high degree of disunity, but they at least had concurred on allegiance to a common cause. Now even that was gone. It would have been almost a miracle if any government fashioned in all this confusion had long endured.

Hard times, the bane of all regimes, set in shortly after the war and hit bottom in 1786. As if other troubles were not enough, British manufacturers, with dammed-up surpluses, began flooding the American market with cut-rate goods. War-baby American industries, in particular, suffered industrial colic from such ruthless competition.

Yet hopeful signs could be discerned. The thirteen sovereign states were basically alike in governmental structure and functioned under similar constitutions. Americans enjoyed a rich political inheritance, derived partly from Britain and partly from their own homegrown devices for self-government. Finally, Americans were blessed with political leaders of a high order in men such as George Washington, James Madison, John Adams, Thomas Jefferson, and Alexander Hamilton.

★ Constitution Making in the States

The Continental Congress in 1776 called on the colonies to draft new constitutions. In effect, Congress was actually asking the colonies to summon themselves into being as new states, whose sovereignty, according to the theory of republicanism, would rest on the authority of the people. In most of the states, writers of new constitutions worked tirelessly to capture on black-inked parchment the republican spirit of the age.

Massachusetts contributed one especially noteworthy innovation when it called a special convention to draft its constitution and then submitted the final draft directly to the people for ratification. Once adopted in 1780, the Massachusetts constitution could be changed only by another special convention. This procedure was later imitated in the drafting and ratification of the federal Constitution.

The newly penned state constitutions enjoyed many features in common. As *written* documents, they were intended to represent a *fundamental* law, superior to the transient whims of ordinary legislation. Most of these documents included bills of rights, specifically guaranteeing long-prized liberties against later legislative encroachment. All of the new state constitutions deliberately created weak executive and judicial branches. A generation of quarreling with His Majesty's officials had implanted a deep distrust of despotic governors and arbitrary judges. The legislatures, presumably the most democratic branch of government, were given sweeping powers.

The democratic character of the new state legislatures was vividly reflected in the presence of many members from the recently enfranchised poorer western districts. The influence of the western districts was powerfully felt in their several successful movements to relocate state capitals from the haughty eastern seaports into the less pretentious interior. These geographical shifts portended political shifts that deeply discomfited many more-conservative Americans.

★ Economic Crosscurrents

Economic changes begotten by the war were likewise noteworthy but not overwhelming. States seized control of former crown lands, and although rich speculators had their day, many of the large Loyalist holdings were confiscated and eventually cut up into small farms. Roger Morris's huge estate in New York, for example, was sliced into 250 parcels—thus accelerating the spread of economic democracy. The frightful excesses of the French Revolution were avoided, partly because cheap land was easily available. It is highly significant that, in the United States, economic democracy, broadly speaking, preceded political democracy.

A sharp stimulus was given to manufacturing by the prewar nonimportation agreements and later by the war itself. Goods that formerly had been imported from Britain were mostly cut off, and the ingenious Yankees were forced to make their own. Ten years after the Revolution, busy Brandywine Creek, south of Philadelphia, was turning the water wheels of numerous mills along an eight-mile stretch. Yet America remained overwhelmingly a nation of soil tillers.

Economically speaking, independence had drawbacks. Much of the coveted commerce of Britain was still reserved for the loyal parts of the empire. American ships were now barred from British and British West Indian harbors. But new commercial outlets, fortunately, partially compensated for the loss of old ones. Americans could now trade freely with foreign nations, subject to local restrictions—a boon they had not enjoyed in the days of mercantilism. Enterprising Yankee shippers ventured boldly—and profitably—into the Baltic and China Seas.

Yet the general economic picture was far from rosy. War had spawned demoralizing extravagance, speculation, and profiteering, with profits for some as indecently high as 300 percent. Runaway inflation had been ruinous to many citizens, and Congress had failed in its feeble attempts to curb economic laws. While a newly rich class of profiteers was noisily conspicuous, the average citizen was probably worse off financially at the end of the shooting than before.

★ Creating a Confederation

The Second Continental Congress of Revolutionary days was little more than a conference of ambassadors from the thirteen states. In nearly all respects, the thirteen states were sovereign, for they coined money, raised armies and navies, and erected tariff barriers.

Examining the Evidence

Copley Family Portrait, ca. 1776–1777

A portrait painting such as this one by John Singleton Copley (1738–1815) documents physical likenesses, clothing styles, and other material possessions typical of an era. But it can do more than that. In the execution of the painting itself, the preeminent portrait painter of colonial America revealed important values of his time. Copley's composition and use of light emphasized the importance of the mother in the family. Mrs. Copley is the visual center of the painting; the light falls predominantly on her, and she provides the focus of activity for the family group. Although Copley had moved to England in 1774 to avoid the disruptions of war, he had made radical friends in his hometown of Boston and surely had imbibed the sentiment of the age about "republican motherhood"—a sentiment that revered women as homemakers and mothers, the cultivators of good republican values in young citizens.

1. What prevalent eighteenth-century attitudes about gender and age might this painting reveal?
2. How does the scene visible through the opening in the rear suggest that this family is intended to be representative of an American future?
3. What attitudes toward children are revealed in the painting? What does it suggest about proper relationships among mothers, fathers, and children?

John Singleton Copley, The Copley Family, Andrew W. Mellon Fund, image courtesy of the Board of Trustees, National Gallery of Art, Washington, D.C.

Articles of Confederation (1781) *First American constitution that established the United States as a loose confederation of states under a weak national Congress, which was not granted the power to regulate commerce or collect taxes. The Articles were replaced by a more efficient Constitution in 1789.*

Northwest Ordinance (1787) *Created a policy for administering the Northwest Territories. It included a path to statehood and forbade the expansion of slavery into the territories.*

Shortly before declaring independence in 1776, Congress appointed a committee to draft a written constitution for the new nation. The finished product was the **Articles of Confederation**. Adopted by Congress in 1777, this document was translated into French after the Battle of Saratoga so as to convince France that America had a genuine government in the making. The Articles were not ratified by all thirteen states until 1781, less than eight months before the victory at Yorktown.

The chief apple of discord was western lands. Six of the jealous states, including Pennsylvania and Maryland, had no holdings beyond the Appalachian Mountains. Seven states, notably New York and Virginia, were favored with enormous acreage on the basis of earlier charter grants. The six land-hungry states argued that the more fortunate states would not have retained possession of this splendid prize if all the other states had not fought for it also. Why not turn the whole western area over to the central government?

Unanimous approval of the Articles of Confederation by the thirteen states was required, and land-starved Maryland stubbornly held out until March 1, 1781. Maryland at length gave in when New York surrendered its western claims and Virginia seemed about to do so. To sweeten the pill, Congress pledged itself to dispose of these vast areas for the "common benefit." Congress further agreed to carve from the new public domain not colonies but a number of "republican" states, which in time would be admitted to the Union on terms of complete equality with all the others. This extraordinary commitment faithfully reflected the anticolonial spirit of the Revolution, and the pledge was later fully redeemed in the famed **Northwest Ordinance** of 1787 (see Map 9.1).

Fertile public lands thus transferred to the central government proved to be an invaluable bond of union. The states that had thrown their heritage into the common

Map 9.1 Western Land Cessions to the United States, 1782–1802

pot had to remain in the Union if they were to reap their share of the advantages from the land sales. An army of westward-moving pioneers purchased their farms from the federal government, directly or indirectly, and they learned to look to the national capital, rather than to the state capitals—with a consequent weakening of local influence. Finally, a uniform national land policy was made possible.

★ The Articles of Confederation: America's First Constitution

The Articles of Confederation provided for a loose confederation or "firm league of friendship." Thirteen independent states were thus linked together for joint action in dealing with common problems, such as foreign affairs. A clumsy Congress was to be the chief agency of government. There was no executive branch—King George III had left a bad taste—and the vital judicial arm was left almost exclusively to the states.

Congress, though dominant, was severely hobbled. Each state had a single vote. All bills dealing with subjects of importance required the support of nine states; any amendment of the Articles themselves required unanimous ratification. Purposely designed to be weak, Congress was crippled by its lack of power to regulate commerce, which left the states free to establish conflicting laws regarding tariffs and navigation. Lacking any power to enforce its tax-collection program, Congress set a tax quota for each of the states and then asked them please to contribute their share on a voluntary basis. This "government by supplication" was lucky if in any year it received one-fourth of its requests.

In spite of their defects, the anemic Articles of Confederation were a significant steppingstone toward the present Constitution. The Articles clearly outlined the general powers that were to be exercised by the central government, such as making treaties and establishing a postal service. As the first written constitution of the Republic, the Articles kept alive the flickering ideal of union and held the states together—until such time as they were ripe for the establishment of a strong constitution by peaceful, evolutionary methods. Without this intermediary jump, the states probably would never have consented to the breathtaking leap from the old boycott Association of 1774 to the Constitution of the United States.

★ Landmarks in Land Laws

Handcuffed though the Congress of the Confederation was, it succeeded in passing supremely farsighted pieces of legislation. The legislation related to an immense part of the public domain recently acquired from the states and commonly known as the Old Northwest. This area of land lay north of the Ohio River, east of the Mississippi River, and south of the Great Lakes.

The first of these red-letter laws was the **Land Ordinance of 1785** (see Map 9.2), which provided that the acreage of the **Old Northwest** should be sold and that the proceeds should be used to help pay off the national debt. The vast area was to be surveyed before sale and settlement, thus forestalling endless confusion and lawsuits. The land was to be divided into townships six miles square, each of which in turn was to be split into thirty-six sections of one square mile each. The sixteenth section of each township was set aside to be sold for the benefit of the public schools—a priceless gift to education in the Old Northwest.

Even more noteworthy was the Northwest Ordinance of 1787, which related to the governing of the Old Northwest. This law came to grips with the problem of how a nation should deal with its colonies—the same problem that had bedeviled the king and Parliament in London. The solution provided by the Northwest Ordinance was a judicious compromise: temporary tutelage, then permanent equality. First, there would be two evolutionary territorial stages, during which the area would be subordinate to the federal government. Then, when a territory could boast sixty thousand inhabitants, it might be admitted by Congress as a state, with all the privileges of the thirteen charter members. The ordinance also forbade slavery in the Old Northwest—a path-breaking step, though it exempted slaves already present.

Land Ordinance of 1785 *Provided for the sale of land in the Old Northwest and earmarked the proceeds toward repaying the national debt.*

Old Northwest *Territories acquired by the federal government from the states, encompassing land northwest of the Ohio River, east of the Mississippi River, and south of the Great Lakes. The well-organized management and sale of the land in the territories under the land ordinances of 1785 and 1787 established a precedent for handling future land acquisitions.*

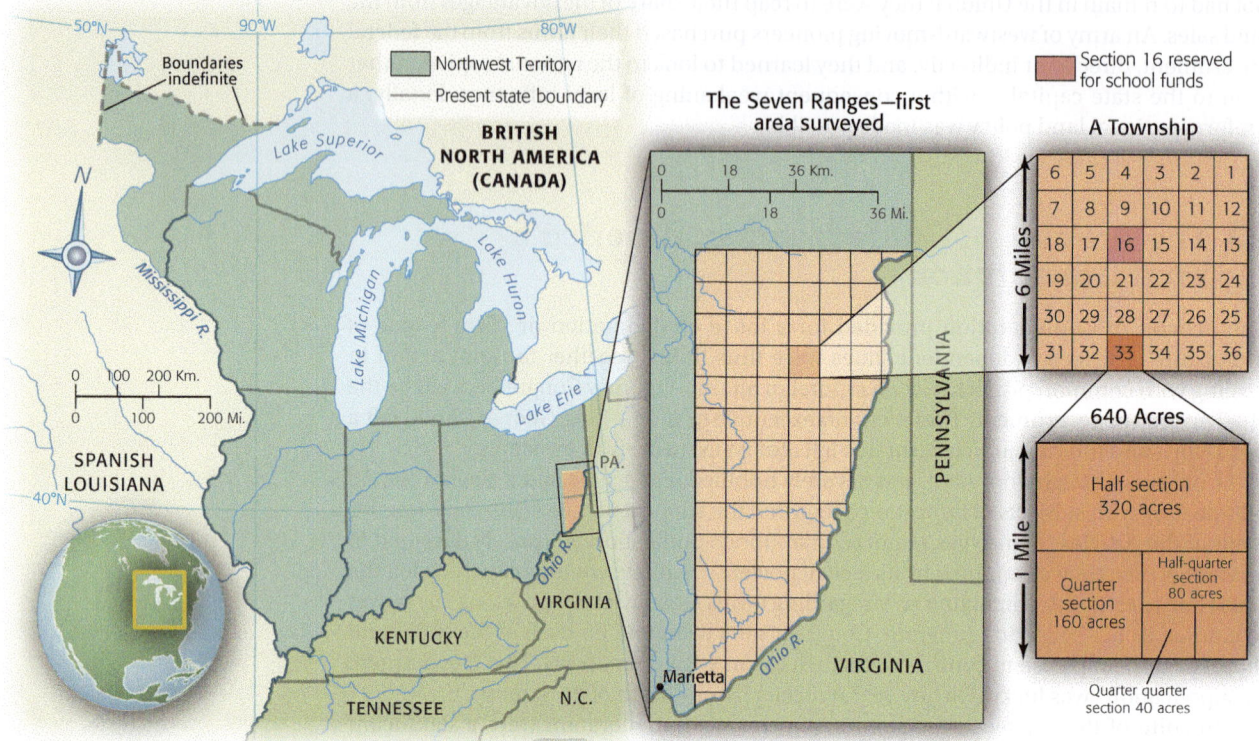

Map 9.2 Surveying the Old Northwest Sections of a township under the Land Ordinance of 1785

The wisdom of Congress in handling this explosive problem deserves warm praise. If Congress had attempted to chain the new territories in permanent subordination, a second American Revolution almost certainly would have erupted in later years, fought this time by the West against the East. Congress thus neatly solved the seemingly insoluble problem of empire. The scheme worked so well that the basic principles were ultimately carried over from the Old Northwest to other frontier areas.

★ The World's Ugly Duckling

Foreign relations, especially with London, continued to be troubled during these anxious years of the Confederation. Britain flatly declined to send a minister to America, to make a commercial treaty, or to repeal its ancient Navigation Laws. The British Lord Sheffield argued that Britain would win back America's trade anyhow, because commerce would naturally return to old channels. The British also officially closed their profitable West Indian trade to the United States, though the Yankees still engaged in illegal smuggling.

In Vermont, adjacent to Canada, scheming British agents intrigued with the disgruntled Allen brothers and sought to annex that rebellious area to Britain. Along the far-flung northern frontier, Redcoats continued to hold a chain of trading posts on U.S. soil, maintaining their fur trade and bolstering the Indians as a barrier against future American attacks on Canada.

Maddened by these grievances, some patriotic Americans demanded that the United States force the British into line by imposing restrictions on their imports to America. But Congress could not control commerce, and the states refused to adopt a uniform tariff policy.

Spain, though recently an enemy of Britain, was openly unfriendly to the new Republic. Spain controlled the mouth of the all-important Mississippi, down which the pioneers of Tennessee and Kentucky were forced to float their produce. In 1784 Spain closed the river to American commerce, threatening the West with strangulation. Spain likewise claimed a large area north of the Gulf of Mexico, including a part of West Florida granted to the United States by the British in 1783. From its important fort at Natchez, Spain schemed with neighboring Indians to hem in the Americans east of the Appalachians. Spain and Britain together, radiating their influence out among the powerful Indian tribes, prevented America from exercising effective control over about half of its total territory.

Even France, America's comrade-in-arms, demanded the repayment of money loaned during the war and restricted trade with its bustling West Indies ports. North African pirates, including the arrogant Dey of Algiers, were ravaging America's Mediterranean commerce and enslaving Yankee sailors. The British purchased protection for their subjects, but as an independent nation the United States was too weak to fight and too poor to bribe. John Jay, secretary for foreign affairs, hoped that these insults would at least humiliate the American people into framing a new government at home that would be strong enough to command respect abroad.

★ The Horrid Specter of Anarchy

Economic storm clouds continued to loom in the mid-1780s. Interest on the public debt was piling up at home, and the nation's credit was evaporating abroad. Quarreling states were levying duties on goods from their neighbors: New York, for example, taxed firewood from Connecticut and cabbages from New Jersey.

An alarming uprising, known as **Shays's Rebellion**, flared up in western Massachusetts in 1786 and set off widespread fear of further insurrection. Impoverished backcountry farmers, many of them Revolutionary War veterans, were losing their farms through mortgage foreclosures and tax delinquencies. Led by Captain Daniel Shays, a veteran of the Revolution, these desperate debtors demanded cheap paper money, lighter taxes, and a suspension of mortgage foreclosures. Hundreds of angry agitators, again seizing their muskets, attempted to enforce their demands.

Massachusetts authorities responded with drastic action. Supported partly by contributions from wealthy citizens, they raised a small army. After a few skirmishes near Springfield, the revolt collapsed. Daniel Shays, who believed that he was fighting anew against tyranny, was condemned to death but later pardoned.

Shays's followers were crushed—but the nightmarish memory lingered on. The outbursts of Shays and other distressed debtors struck fear in the hearts of the propertied class, who began to suspect that the Revolution had created a monster of "mobocracy." Unbridled republicanism, it seemed to many of the elite, had fed an insatiable appetite for liberty that was fast becoming license. Civic virtue was no longer sufficient to rein in self-interest and greed. It had become "undeniably evident," one skeptic sorrowfully lamented, "that some malignant disorder has seized upon our body politic." If republicanism was too shaky a ground on which to construct a new nation, a stronger central government would provide the needed foundation.

How critical were conditions under the Confederation? Conservatives, anxious to safeguard their wealth and position, naturally exaggerated the seriousness of the nation's plight. They were eager to persuade their fellow citizens to amend the Articles of Confederation in favor of a muscular central government. But the poorer states' rights people pooh-poohed the talk of anarchy. Many were debtors who feared that a powerful federal government would force them to pay their creditors.

Yet friends and critics of the Confederation agreed that it needed strengthening. Popular toasts were "Cement to the Union" and "A hoop to the barrel." The chief differences arose over how this goal should be attained and how a maximum degree of states' rights could be reconciled with a strong central government.

Shays's Rebellion (1786) Armed uprising of western Massachusetts debtors seeking lower taxes and an end to property foreclosures. Though quickly put down, the insurrection inspired fears of "mob rule" among leading Revolutionaries.

Social tensions reached a fever pitch during Shays's Rebellion in 1787. In an interview with a local Massachusetts paper, instigator Daniel Shays (1747–1825) explained how the debt-ridden farmers hoped to free themselves from the demands of a merchant-dominated government. The rebels would seize arms and:

"march directly to Boston, plunder it, and then . . . destroy the nest of devils, who by their influence, make the Court enact what they please, burn it and lay the town of Boston in ashes."

Independence Hall, Philadelphia, 1776 Originally built in the 1730s as a meeting place for the Pennsylvania colonial assembly, this building witnessed much history: here Washington was given command of the Continental Army, the Declaration of Independence was signed, and the Constitution was hammered out. The building began to be called "Independence Hall" in the late 1820s and is today a major tourist destination in Philadelphia.

A Convention of "Demigods"

Control of commerce, more than any other problem, touched off the chain reaction that led to a constitutional convention. Interstate squabbling over this issue had become so alarming by 1786 that Virginia issued a call for a convention at Annapolis, Maryland. When delegates from only five states showed up, nothing could be done about the ticklish question of commerce. But a charismatic New Yorker, thirty-one-year-old Alexander Hamilton, brilliantly saved the convention from complete failure by engineering a call for another convention to meet in Philadelphia the next year to bolster the entire fabric of the Articles of Confederation.

Congress was reluctant to take a step that might lead to signing its own death warrant. But after six states appointed delegates anyhow, Congress belatedly issued the call for a convention "*for the sole and express purpose of revising*" the Articles of Confederation.

Every state chose representatives, except for independent-minded Rhode Island, a stronghold of paper-moneyites. These leaders were all appointed by the state legislatures, whose members had been elected by voters who could qualify as property holders. This double distillation inevitably brought together a select group of propertied men.

A quorum of the fifty-five emissaries from twelve states finally convened at Philadelphia on May 25, 1787, in the imposing red-brick statehouse. The smallness of the assemblage facilitated intimate acquaintance and hence compromise. Sessions were held in complete secrecy, with armed sentinels posted at the doors. Delegates knew that they would generate heated differences, and they did not want to advertise their own dissensions or put the ammunition of harmful arguments into the mouths of the opposition.

The caliber of the participants was extraordinarily high—"demigods," Jefferson called them. The urgency of the crisis induced the ablest men to drop their personal pursuits and come to the aid of their country. Most of the members were lawyers, and most of them fortunately were old hands at constitution making in their own states.

George Washington, towering austere and aloof among the "demigods," was unanimously elected chairman. His enormous prestige as "the Sword of the Revolution" served to quiet overheated tempers. Benjamin Franklin, then eighty-one, added the urbanity of an elder statesman, though he was inclined to be indiscreetly talkative in his declining years. Concerned for the secrecy of their deliberations, the convention assigned chaperones to accompany Franklin to dinner parties and make sure he held his tongue. James Madison, then thirty-six and a profound student of government, made contributions so notable that he has been dubbed "the Father of the Constitution." Alexander Hamilton, then only thirty-two, was present as the eloquent advocate of a super-powerful central government.

Most of the fiery Revolutionary leaders of 1776 were absent. Thomas Jefferson, John Adams, and Thomas Paine were in Europe; Samuel Adams and John Hancock were not elected by Massachusetts. Patrick Henry, ardent champion of states' rights, was chosen as a delegate from Virginia but declined to serve, declaring that he "smelled a rat." It was perhaps well that these architects of revolution were absent. The time had come to yield the stage to leaders interested in fashioning solid political systems.

★ Patriots in Philadelphia

The fifty-five delegates were a conservative, well-to-do body: lawyers, merchants, shippers, land speculators, and moneylenders. Not a single spokesperson was present from the poorer debtor groups. Nineteen of the fifty-five owned slaves. They were young (the average age was about forty-two) but experienced statesmen. Above all, they were nationalists, more interested in preserving and strengthening the young Republic than in further stirring the roiling cauldron of popular democracy.

The delegates hoped to crystallize the evaporating pools of revolutionary idealism into a stable political structure that would endure. They strongly desired a firm, dignified, and respected government. They believed in republicanism but sought to protect the American experiment from its weaknesses abroad and excesses at home. They aimed to clothe the central authority with genuine power, especially in controlling tariffs, so that the United States could wrest satisfactory commercial treaties from foreign nations.

Other motives hovered in the Philadelphia hall. Delegates were determined to preserve the Union, forestall anarchy, and ensure security of life and property against dangerous uprisings by the "mobocracy." Above all, they sought to curb the unrestrained democracy rampant in the various states. The specter of the recent outburst in Massachusetts was especially alarming, and in this sense, Daniel Shays was another Founding Father. Grinding necessity extorted the Constitution from a reluctant nation. Fear occupied the fifty-sixth chair.

Virginia Plan *"Large state" proposal for the new constitution, calling for proportional representation in both houses of a bicameral Congress. The plan favored larger states and thus prompted smaller states to come back with their own plan for apportioning representation.*

New Jersey Plan (1787) *"Small-state plan" put forth at the Philadelphia convention, proposing equal representation by state, regardless of population, in a unicameral legislature. Small states feared that the more populous states would dominate the agenda under a proportional system.*

★ Hammering Out a Bundle of Compromises

Some of the travel-stained delegates, when they first reached Philadelphia, decided on a daring step. They would completely *scrap* the old Articles of Confederation, despite explicit instructions from Congress to *revise*. Technically, these bolder spirits were determined to overthrow the existing government of the United States by peaceful means.

A scheme proposed by populous Virginia, known as "the large-state plan," was first pushed forward as the framework of the Constitution. The essence of the **Virginia Plan** was that representation in both houses of a bicameral Congress should be based on population—an arrangement that would naturally give the larger states an advantage. Tiny New Jersey, suspicious of brawny Virginia, countered with "the small-state plan." The **New Jersey Plan** provided for equal representation in a unicameral Congress by states, regardless of size and population.

Thomas Jefferson (1743–1826), despite his high regard for the leaders at the Philadelphia convention, still was not unduly concerned about Shaysite rebellions. He wrote in November 1787:

"What country before ever existed a century and a half without a rebellion? . . . The tree of liberty must be refreshed from time to time with the blood of patriots and tyrants. It is its natural manure."

> One of the Philadelphia delegates recorded in his journal a brief episode involving Benjamin Franklin, who was asked by a woman when the convention ended:
>
> "Well, Doctor, what have we got, a republic or a monarchy?"
>
> The elder statesman answered,
>
> "A republic, if you can keep it."

Great Compromise (1787) *Popular term for the measure that reconciled the New Jersey and Virginia Plans at the Constitutional Convention, giving states proportional representation in the House and equal representation in the Senate. The compromise broke the stalemate at the convention and paved the way for subsequent compromises over slavery and the Electoral College.*

three-fifths compromise (1787) *Determined that each slave would be counted as three-fifths of a person for the purpose of apportioning taxes and representation. The compromise granted disproportionate political power to southern slave states.*

After bitter and prolonged debate, the "**Great Compromise**" of the convention was hammered out and agreed upon. The larger states were conceded representation by population in the House of Representatives (Art. I, Sec. II, para. 3; see the Appendix), and the smaller states were appeased by equal representation in the Senate (see Art. I, Sec. III, para. 1). Each state, no matter how poor or small, would have two senators. The big states obviously yielded more. As a sop to them, the delegates agreed that every tax bill or revenue measure must originate in the House, where population counted more heavily (see Art. I, Sec. VII, para. 1). This critical compromise broke the logjam, and from then on success seemed within reach.

In a significant reversal of the arrangement most state constitutions had embodied, the new Constitution provided for a robust—though still legally restrained—executive in the presidency. The president was to have broad authority to appoint officials and judges, veto legislation, and wage war as commander in chief of the military. But Congress retained the crucial right to *declare* war—a division of responsibilities that has been an invitation to conflict between president and Congress ever since.

The Constitution as drafted was a bundle of compromises; they stand out in every section. A key compromise was the method of electing the president indirectly by the Electoral College, rather than by direct means (see Art. II, Sec. I, para. 2). While the large states would have the advantage in the first round of popular voting, the small states would gain a larger voice if no candidate got a majority of electoral votes and the election was thrown to the House of Representatives, where each state would have, for this purpose, just one vote (see Art. II, Sec. I, para. 2). Although the framers of the Constitution expected election by the House to occur frequently, it has happened just twice, in 1800 and 1824.

Sectional jealousy also intruded. Should the voteless slave of the southern states count as a person in apportioning direct taxes and representation in the House of Representatives? The South, not wishing to be deprived of influence, answered "yes." The North replied "no," arguing that slaves were not citizens. As a compromise between total representation and none at all, it was decided that a slave might count as three-fifths of a person. Hence the memorable, if arbitrary, "**three-fifths compromise**" (see Art. I, Sec. II, para. 3).

Table 9.1 Strengthening the Central Government

Under Articles of Confederation	Under Federal Constitution
A loose confederation of states	A firm union of people
One vote in Congress for each state	Two votes in Senate for each state; representation by population in House (see Art. I, Secs. II, III)
Vote of nine states in Congress for all important measures	Simple majority vote in Congress, subject to presidential veto (see Art. I, Sec. VII, para. 2)
Laws administered loosely by committees of Congress	Laws executed by powerful president (see Art. II, Secs. II, III)
No congressional power over commerce	Congress to regulate both foreign and interstate commerce (see Art. I, Sec. VIII, para. 3)
No congressional power to levy taxes	Extensive power in Congress to levy taxes (see Art. I, Sec. VIII, para. 1)
Limited federal courts	Federal courts, capped by Supreme Court (see Art. III)
Unanimity of states for amendment	Amendment less difficult (see Art. V)
No authority to act directly upon individuals and no power to coerce states	Ample power to enforce laws by coercion of individuals and to some extent of states

Most of the states wanted to shut off the African slave trade. But slaveholding South Carolina and Georgia, demanding fresh slave labor for their rice fields, raised vehement protests. In another compromise the convention stipulated that the slave trade might continue until the end of 1807, at which time Congress could stop the trade (see Art. I, Sec. IX, para. 1). Congress did so as soon as the prescribed interval had elapsed.

★ Safeguards for Conservatism

Heated clashes among the delegates have been overplayed. The area of agreement was actually large; otherwise the convention would have speedily disbanded. Economically, the members of the Constitutional Convention generally saw eye to eye; they demanded sound money and the protection of private property. Politically, they were in basic agreement; they favored a stronger government, with three branches and with checks and balances among them—what critics branded a "triple-headed monster." Finally, the convention was virtually unanimous in believing that manhood-suffrage democracy—government by "democratick babblers"—was something to be feared and fought.

Daniel Shays, the prime bogeyman, still frightened the conservative-minded delegates. They deliberately erected safeguards against the excesses of the "mob," and they made these barriers as strong as they dared. The awesome federal judges were to be appointed for life. The powerful president was to be elected *indirectly* by the Electoral College; the lordly senators were to be chosen *indirectly* by state legislatures (see Art. I, Sec. III, para. 1). Only in the case of one-half of one of the three great branches—the House of Representatives—were qualified (propertied) citizens permitted to choose their officials by *direct* vote (see Art. I, Sec. II, para. 1).

Yet the new charter also contained democratic elements. Above all, it stood foursquare on the two great principles of republicanism: that the only legitimate government was one based on the consent of the governed, and that the powers of the government should be limited by a written constitution. The virtue of the people, not the authority of the state, was to be the ultimate guarantor of liberty, justice, and order. "We the people," the preamble began, in a ringing affirmation of these republican doctrines.

At the end of seventeen muggy weeks—May 25 to September 17, 1787—only forty-two of the original fifty-five members remained to sign the Constitution. Three of the forty-two, refusing to do so, returned to their states to resist ratification. The remainder, adjourning to the City Tavern, celebrated the toastworthy occasion.

★ The Clash of Federalists and Antifederalists

The Framing Fathers early foresaw that nationwide acceptance of the Constitution would not be easy to obtain. A formidable barrier was unanimous ratification by all thirteen states, as required for amendment by the still-standing Articles of Confederation. But because absent Rhode Island was certain to veto the Constitution, the delegates boldly adopted a different scheme. They stipulated that, when nine states had registered their approval through specially elected conventions, the Constitution would become the supreme law of the land in those states ratifying (see Art. VII).

This was extraordinary, even revolutionary. It was in effect an appeal over the heads of the Congress that had called the convention, and over the heads of the legislatures that had chosen its members, to the people—or those of the people who could vote. In this way the framers could claim greater popular sanction for their handiwork. A divided Congress submitted the document to the states on this basis, without recommendation of any kind.

The American people were somewhat astonished, so well had the secrets of the convention been kept. The public had expected the old Articles of Confederation to be patched up; now it was handed a startling new document in which, many thought, the precious jewel of state sovereignty was swallowed up. One of the hottest debates of American history forthwith erupted. The **antifederalists**, who opposed the stronger federal government, were arrayed against the **federalists**, who obviously favored it.

antifederalists *Opponents of the 1787 Constitution, they cast the document as antidemocratic, objected to the subordination of the states to the central government, and feared encroachment on individuals' liberties in the absence of a bill of rights.*

federalists *Proponents of the 1787 Constitution, they favored a strong national government, arguing that the checks and balances in the new Constitution would safeguard the people's liberties.*

Map 9.3 The Struggle over Ratification The mottled map shows that federalist support tended to cluster around the coastal areas, which had enjoyed profitable commerce with the outside world, including the export of grain and tobacco. Impoverished frontiersmen, suspicious of a powerful new central government under the Constitution, were generally antifederalists.

A motley crowd gathered in the antifederalist camp. Its leaders included prominent revolutionaries such as Samuel Adams, Patrick Henry, and Richard Henry Lee. Their followers consisted primarily, though not exclusively, of states' rights devotees, backcountry dwellers, and one-horse farmers—in general, the poorest classes (see Map 9.3). They were joined by paper-moneyites and debtors. Many antifederalists saw in the Constitution a plot by the upper crust to steal power back from the common folk.

Silver-buckled federalists had power and influence on their side. They enjoyed the support of such commanding figures as George Washington and Benjamin Franklin. Most of them lived along the seaboard. Overall, they were wealthier than the antifederalists, more educated, and better organized. They also controlled the press. About a hundred newspapers were published in America in the 1780s; only a dozen supported the antifederalist cause.

Antifederalists voiced vehement objections to the "gilded trap" known as the Constitution. They cried with much truth that it had been drawn up by the aristocratic elements and hence was antidemocratic. They likewise charged that the sovereignty of the states was being submerged and that the freedoms of the individual were jeopardized by the absence of a bill of rights. They decried the dropping of annual elections for congressional representatives, the erecting of a federal stronghold ten miles square (later the District of Columbia), the creation of a standing army, the omission of any reference to God, and the highly questionable procedure of ratifying with only two-thirds of the states.

★ The Great Debate in the States

Special elections, some apathetic but others hotly contested, were held in the various states for members of the ratifying conventions. The candidates—federalist or antifederalist—were elected on the basis of their pledges for or against the Constitution.

With the ink barely dry on the parchment, four small states quickly accepted the Constitution, for they had come off much better than they expected. Pennsylvania, number two on the list of ratifiers, was the first large state to act, but not until high-handed irregularities had been employed by the federalist legislature in calling a convention. These questionable tactics included the forcible seating of two antifederalist members, their clothes torn and their faces red with rage, in order to complete a quorum.

Massachusetts, the second most populous state, provided an acid test. If the Constitution had failed in Massachusetts, the entire movement might easily have bogged down. The Boston ratifying convention at first contained an antifederalist majority, including grudging Shaysites and the aging Samuel Adams, as suspicious of government power in 1787 as he had been in 1776. The absence of a bill of rights especially alarmed the antifederalists. But the federalists gave them solemn assurances that the first Congress would add such a safeguard by amendment, and Massachusetts then ratified by the narrow margin of 187 to 168.

Three more states—Maryland, South Carolina, and New Hampshire—fell into line, though the struggle in New Hampshire was fierce. Nine states—all but Virginia, New York, North Carolina, and Rhode Island—had now taken shelter under the "new federal roof," and the document was officially adopted on June 21, 1788. But federalist rejoicing was premature so long as the four dissenters, including conspicuously powerful New York and Virginia, dug in their heels.

Signing of the Constitution of the United States, 1787 George Washington presided from the dais as the Constitutional Convention's president. At a table in the front row sat James Madison, later called the Father of the Constitution, who recorded the proceedings in shorthand. Daily from 10 A.M. to 3 P.M., from late May through mid-September 1787, the fifty-five delegates wrangled over ideas for a new federal government.

Contending Voices

Debating the New Constitution

The Constitution drafted at Philadelphia in 1787 was hotly contested at the time and has been both warmly revered and sharply criticized ever since. Jonathan Smith, a Massachusetts farmer unsympathetic to Shays's Rebellion of 1787, wrote approvingly of the new federal constitution:

"I am a plain man, and I get my living by the plow. I have lived in a part of the country where I have known the worth of good government by the want of it. The black cloud of Shays rebellion rose last winter in my area. It brought on a state of anarchy that led to tyranny.... When I saw this Constitution I found that it was a cure for these disorders. I got a copy of it and read it over and over.... I don't think the worse of the Constitution because lawyers, and men of learning, and moneyed men are fond of it. [They] are all embarked in the same cause with us, and we must all swim or sink together."

Yet prominent Virginia Patriot Patrick Henry (1736–1799) countered in 1788 that the proposed constitution endangered everything the Revolution had sought to protect:

"This constitution is said to have beautiful features; but when I come to examine these features, Sir, they appear to me horridly frightful: Among other deformities, it has an awful squinting; it squints towards monarchy: And does not this raise indignation in the breast of every American? Your President may easily become King: Your Senate is so imperfectly constructed that your dearest rights may be sacrificed by what may be a small minority;... Where are your checks in this Government?"

> In what ways did the positions of Smith and Henry foreshadow debates about the Constitution over the next two centuries?

★ The Four Laggard States

Proud Virginia, the biggest and most populous state, provided fierce antifederalist opposition. There the college-bred federalist orators, for once, encountered worthy antagonists, including the fiery Patrick Henry. He professed to see in the fearsome document the death warrant of liberty. George Washington, James Madison, and John Marshall, on the federalist side, lent influential support. The new Union was going to be formed anyhow, and Virginia could not very well continue comfortably as an independent state. After exciting debate in the state convention, ratification carried, 89 to 79.

New York also experienced an uphill struggle, burdened as it was with its own heavily antifederalist state convention. Alexander Hamilton at heart favored a much stronger central government than that under debate, but he contributed his sparkling personality and persuasive eloquence to whipping up support for federalism as framed. He also joined John Jay and James Madison in penning a masterly series of articles for the New York newspapers. Though designed as propaganda, these essays remain the most penetrating commentary ever written on the Constitution and are still widely sold in book form as *The Federalist*. Probably the most famous of these is Madison's *Federalist No. 10*, which brilliantly refuted the conventional wisdom that a republic could not extend over a large territory.

New York finally yielded. Realizing that the state could not prosper apart from the Union, the convention ratified the document by the close count of 30 to 27.

Last-ditch dissent developed in only two states. A hostile convention met in North Carolina and adjourned without taking a vote. Rhode Island did not even summon a ratifying convention, rejecting the Constitution by popular referendum. The two most ruggedly individualist centers of the colonial era—homes of the "otherwise minded"—thus ran true to form. They were to change their course, albeit unwillingly, only after the new government had been in operation for some months.

The race for ratification was close and quite bitter in some localities. No lives were lost, but riotous disturbances broke out in New York and Pennsylvania, involving bruises and bloodshed. There was much behind-the-scenes pressure on delegates who had promised their constituents to vote against the Constitution. The last four states ratified not because they wanted to but because they had to. They realized they could not safely exist outside the fold.

★ A Conservative Triumph

A minority had triumphed—twice. A militant minority of American radicals had engineered the military Revolution that cast off the unwritten British constitution. A militant minority of conservatives—now embracing many of the earlier radicals—had engineered the peaceful revolution that overthrew the inadequate Articles of Confederation. Eleven states, in effect, had seceded from the Confederation, leaving the last two still out in the cold.

A majority had not spoken. Only about one-fourth of the adult white males in the country, chiefly the propertied people, had voted for delegates to the ratifying conventions. Careful estimates indicate that, if the new Constitution had been submitted to a manhood-suffrage vote, as in New York, it would have encountered much more opposition, probably defeat.

Conservatism was victorious. Safeguards had been erected against mob-rule excesses, while the republican gains of the Revolution were conserved. Radicals such as Patrick Henry, who had ousted British rule, saw themselves in turn upended by American conservatives. The federalists were convinced that, by setting the drifting ship of state on a steady course, they could restore economic and political stability.

Yet if the architects of the Constitution were conservative, it is worth emphasizing that they conserved the principle of republican government through a redefinition of popular sovereignty. Unlike the antifederalists, who believed that the sovereignty of the people resided in a single branch of government—the legislature—the federalists contended that every branch—executive, judiciary, and legislature—effectively represented the people. By ingeniously embedding the doctrine of self-rule in a self-limiting system of checks and balances among those branches, the Constitution reconciled the potentially conflicting principles of liberty and order. It elevated the ideals of the Revolution even while setting boundaries to them. One of the distinctive—and enduring—paradoxes of American history was thus revealed: in the United States, conservatives and radicals alike have championed the heritage of republican revolution.

★ The Pursuit of Equality

"All men are created equal," the Declaration of Independence had proclaimed, and equality was everywhere the watchword. Most states reduced (but usually did not eliminate altogether) property-holding requirements for voting. Ordinary men and women demanded to be addressed as "Mr." and "Mrs."—titles once reserved for the wealthy and highborn. Most Americans ridiculed the elitist pretensions of Continental Army officers who formed an exclusive hereditary order, the **Society of the Cincinnati**. Social democracy was further stimulated by the growth of trade organizations for artisans and laborers.

A protracted fight for separation of church and state resulted in notable gains. The well-entrenched Congregational Church continued to be legally established in some New England states, but the Anglican Church, tainted by association with the British crown, was humbled. De-anglicized, it was renamed as the Protestant Episcopal Church and was everywhere **disestablished**. The struggle for divorce between religion and government proved fiercest in Virginia. It was prolonged to 1786, when freethinking Thomas Jefferson and his co-reformers, including the Baptists, won a complete victory with the passage of the **Virginia Statute for Religious Freedom**.

The egalitarian sentiments unleashed by the war likewise provoked the first challenges to the institution of slavery. Philadelphia Quakers in 1775 founded the world's first antislavery society. The Continental Congress in 1774 called for the complete abolition of the slave trade, a summons to which most of the states responded positively. Several northern states went further and either abolished slavery outright or provided for the gradual emancipation of blacks. In Maryland and Virginia, especially, a few idealistic masters, inspired by Revolutionary principles, freed their own slaves.

But this revolution of sentiments was sadly incomplete. No states south of Pennsylvania abolished slavery, and in both North and South, the law discriminated harshly against freed blacks and enslaved blacks alike. Emancipated African Americans in the North could still be barred from purchasing property, holding certain jobs, and educating their children. Laws against interracial marriage also sprang up at this time.

Why, in this dawning democratic age, did abolition not go further and cleanly blot the evil of slavery from the fresh face of the new nation? The sorry truth is that the fledgling idealism of the Founding Fathers was sacrificed to political expediency. A fight over slavery would have fractured

Society of the Cincinnati (established 1783) *Exclusive, hereditary organization of former officers in the Continental Army. Many resented the pretentiousness of the order, viewing it as a vestige of pre-Revolutionary traditions.*

disestablished *To separate an official state church from its connection with the government. Following the Revolution, all states disestablished the Anglican Church, though some New England states maintained established Congregational Churches well into the nineteenth century.*

Virginia Statute for Religious Freedom (1786) *Measure enacted by the Virginia legislature prohibiting state support for religious institutions and recognizing freedom of worship. Served as a model for the religion clause of the First Amendment to the Constitution.*

> *The impact of the American Revolution was worldwide. About 1783 a British ship stopped at some islands off the East African coast, where the natives were revolting against their Arab masters. When asked why they were fighting, they replied,*
>
> **"America is free. Could not we be?"**

> The Revolution enhanced the expectations and power of women as wives and mothers. As one "matrimonial republican" wrote in 1792,
>
> "I object to the word 'obey' in the marriage-service because it is a general word, without limitations or definition.... The obedience between man and wife, I conceive, is, or ought to be mutual.... Marriage ought never to be considered a contract between a superior and an inferior, but a reciprocal union of interest, an implied partnership of interests, where all differences are accommodated by conference; and where the decision admits of no retrospect."

civic virtue Willingness on the part of citizens to sacrifice personal self-interest for the public good. Deemed a necessary component of a successful republic.

republican motherhood Ideal of family organization and female behavior after the American Revolution that stressed the role of women in guiding family members toward republican virtue.

the fragile national unity that was so desperately needed. "Great as the evil [of slavery] is," the young Virginian James Madison wrote in 1787, "a dismemberment of the union would be worse."

Likewise incomplete was the extension of the doctrine of equality to women. Some women did serve (disguised as men) in the military, and New Jersey's new constitution in 1776 even, for a time, enabled women to vote. But though Abigail Adams teased her husband, John, in 1776 that "the Ladies" were determined "to foment a rebellion" of their own if they were not given political rights, the civil status of women did not change meaningfully.

Yet women did not go untouched by Revolutionary ideals. Central to republican ideology was the concept of **civic virtue**—the notion that democracy depended on the unselfish commitment of each citizen to the public good. And who could better cultivate the habits of a virtuous citizenry than mothers, to whom society entrusted the moral education of the young? Indeed the selfless devotion of a mother to her family was often cited as the very model of proper republican behavior. The idea of "**republican motherhood**" thus took root, elevating women to a newly prestigious role as the special keepers of the nation's conscience. Educational opportunities for women expanded, in the expectation that educated wives and mothers could better cultivate the virtues demanded by the Republic in their husbands, daughters, and sons. Republican women now bore crucial responsibility for the survival of the nation.

Elizabeth "Mumbet" Freeman (ca. 1744–1829), by Susan Anne Livingston Ridley Sedgwick, 1811 In 1781, having overheard Revolutionary-era talk about the "rights of man," Mumbet sued her Massachusetts master for her freedom from slavery. She won her suit and lived the rest of her life as a paid domestic servant in the home of the lawyer who had pleaded her case.

Varying Viewpoints

The Constitution: Revolutionary or Counterrevolutionary?

Although the Constitution has endured for two centuries as the basis of American government, historians have differed sharply over how to interpret its origins and meaning. Early historians of the Nationalist School, such as John Fiske, viewed the Constitution as the logical culmination of the Revolution and a crucial step in the God-given progress of Anglo-Saxon peoples.

By the early twentieth century, however, the progressive historians had turned a more critical eye to the Constitution. For historians such as Carl Becker and Charles Beard, the Constitution was part of a revolutionary struggle between the lower classes (small farmers, debtors, and laborers) and the upper classes (merchants, financiers, and manufacturers). Beard's *An Economic Interpretation of the Constitution of the United States* (1913) argued that the Articles of Confederation had protected debtors and displeased wealthy elites heavily invested in trade, the public debt, and manufacturing. Reviewing the economic holdings of the Framers, Beard argued that the Constitution represented a successful attempt by conservative elites to buttress their own economic supremacy at the expense of less fortunate Americans.

Beard's economic interpretation of the Constitution held sway through the 1940s. In the 1950s, however, this analysis fell victim to "consensus" historians such as Robert Brown and Forrest McDonald, who convincingly disputed Beard's evidence and argued that the Constitution derived from an emerging consensus that the country needed a stronger central government.

Scholars since the 1950s have searched for new ways to understand the origins of the Constitution. The most influential work has been Gordon Wood's *The Creation of the American Republic* (1969). Wood reinterpreted the ratification controversy as a struggle to define the true essence of republicanism. While antifederalists feared human corruption and consequently a strong central government, federalists believed that a strong, balanced government would rein in selfish human instincts and channel them toward pursuit of the common good. James Madison in particular (especially in *Federalist* No. 10) developed the novel idea of an "extensive republic," a polity that would achieve stability by virtue of its great size and diversity. In this sense, Wood argued, the Constitution represented a bold experiment—fulfillment, rather than the repudiation, of the most advanced ideas of the Revolutionary era—even though it emanated from traditional elites determined to curtail dangerous disruptions to the social order.

CHAPTER SUMMARY ★ ★ ★ ★ ★ ★ ★ ★ ★ ★ ★ ★ ★

The American Revolution did not overturn the social order, but it did produce substantial changes in social customs, political institutions, and ideas about society and government.

The first weak national government, the Articles of Confederation, was unable to exercise real authority, although it did successfully deal with the western lands issue. The Confederation's weaknesses in handling foreign policy, commerce, and Shays's Rebellion spurred the movement to alter the Articles.

Instead of revising the Articles, the young, nationalistic, and well-off delegates to the Constitutional Convention created a permanent charter for a whole new government. In a series of compromises, the convention produced a plan that provided for a vigorous central government, a strong executive, and protection for property, while still upholding republican principles and states' rights. The pro-Constitution federalists, generally representing wealthier and more commercial forces, were opposed by less sophisticated and less educated portions of the population who feared that a strong federal government would undermine their rights and their interests.

The federalists met their strongest opposition from antifederalists in Virginia and New York, but they triumphed through the use of more effective organization and argument, as well as through promises to incorporate a bill of rights into the document. By establishing the new national government, the federalists checked the Revolutionary momentum toward equality and decentralization of authority. But their "conservative" regime actually embraced the central Revolutionary values of popular republican government and liberty, making the Constitution the permanent bedrock of American political values.

Neither the Revolution nor the Constitution created complete democracy, but they did foster a definite movement toward greater equality. Among the changes were the separation of church and state in most states, the push to end the international slave trade, and the gradual end of slavery in the North (where it was weakest). Although stopping far short of democratic equality for women, the Revolutionary era did advance the idea of "republican motherhood," giving women a crucial responsibility for upholding the nation's civic virtue.

KEY TERMS

Articles of Confederation (124)
Northwest Ordinance (124)
Land Ordinance of 1785 (125)
Old Northwest (125)
Shays's Rebellion (127)
Virginia Plan (129)
New Jersey Plan (129)
Great Compromise (130)
three-fifths compromise (130)
antifederalists (131)
federalists (131)
Society of the Cincinnati (135)
disestablish (135)
Virginia Statute for Religious Freedom (135)
civic virtue (136)
republican motherhood (136)

PEOPLE TO KNOW

Lord Sheffield
Daniel Shays
Patrick Henry

 MindTap is a fully online, highly personalized learning experience built upon Cengage Learning content. MindTap combines student learning tools—readings, multimedia, activities, and assessments—into a singular Learning Path that guides students through the course.

Chapter 10

Launching the New Ship of State
1789–1800

I shall only say that I hold with Montesquieu, that a government must be fitted to a nation, as much as a coat to the individual; and, consequently, that what may be good at Philadelphia may be bad at Paris, and ridiculous at Petersburg [Russia].

ALEXANDER HAMILTON, 1799

Chapter Outline

- Problems of the Young Republic
- The First Presidency, 1789–1793
- The Bill of Rights, 1791
- Hamilton's Economic Policies
- The Emergence of Political Parties
- The Impact of the French Revolution
- Jay's Treaty, 1794
- President Adams Keeps the Peace
- The Alien and Sedition Acts, 1798
- The Virginia and Kentucky Resolutions, 1798–1799
- Federalists versus Democratic-Republicans
- *Thinking Globally: Two Revolutions*

America's new ship of state did not spread its sails to the most favorable breezes. Within twelve troubled years, the American people had risen up and thrown overboard both the British yoke and the Articles of Confederation. A decade of lawbreaking and constitution smashing was not the best training for government making. Americans had come to regard central authority, replacing that of George III, as a necessary evil—something to be distrusted, watched, and curbed.

The finances of the infant government were likewise precarious. The revenue had declined to a trickle, whereas the public debt, with interest heavily in arrears, was mountainous. Worthless paper money, both state and national, was as plentiful as metallic money was scarce. America's precarious national security was also threatened by the wars that rocked Europe in the wake of the French Revolution of 1789—an event that also roiled domestic politics in the fledgling United States. In the face of these difficulties, the Americans were brashly trying to erect a republic on an immense scale, something that no other people had attempted and that traditional political theory deemed impossible. The eyes of a skeptical world were on the upstart United States.

FOCUS QUESTIONS

1. How did George Washington's personal prestige and Alexander Hamilton's financial policies get the new federal government off to a strong beginning?
2. What were the policy differences between Alexander Hamilton and Thomas Jefferson within Washington's cabinet, and how did their disagreements lead to the formation of the first American political parties, the Federalists and Democratic-Republicans?
3. How did the French Revolution create conflict and polarization between Federalists and Democratic-Republicans over American foreign policy, and how did President Washington maintain American neutrality?
4. How did the Alien and Sedition Acts reflect popular anti-French hysteria as well as Federalist political interests?
5. What were the underlying philosophical and political differences between Hamiltonian Federalists and Jeffersonian Democratic-Republicans?

CHRONOLOGY

1789	- Constitution formally put into effect - Judiciary Act of 1789 - Washington elected president - French Revolution begins - Declaration of the Rights of Man (French)	1794	- Whiskey Rebellion - Battle of Fallen Timbers - Jay's Treaty with Britain
1790	- First official census	1795	- Treaty of Greenville: Indians cede Ohio - Pinckney's Treaty with Spain
1791	- Bill of Rights adopted - Vermont becomes fourteenth state - Bank of the United States created - Excise tax passed	1796	- Washington's Farewell Address
		1797	- Adams becomes president - XYZ Affair
1792	- Washington reelected president	1798	- Alien and Sedition Acts
1792–1793	- Federalist and Democratic-Republican parties formed	1798–1799	- Virginia and Kentucky resolutions
1793	- Louis XVI beheaded; radical phase of French Revolution - Washington's Neutrality Proclamation - Citizen Genêt affair	1798–1800	- Undeclared war with France
		1800	- Convention of 1800: peace with France

⭐ Growing Pains

When the Constitution was launched in 1789, the Republic was continuing to grow at an amazing rate. Population was doubling about every twenty-five years, and the first official census of 1790 recorded almost 4 million people. Cities had blossomed proportionately: Philadelphia numbered 42,000; New York, 33,000; Boston, 18,000; Charleston, 16,000; and Baltimore, 13,000.

America's population was still about 90 percent rural, despite the flourishing cities. All but 5 percent of the people lived east of the Appalachian Mountains. The trans-Appalachian overflow was concentrated chiefly in Kentucky, Tennessee, and Ohio, all of which were welcomed as states within fourteen years. (Vermont had preceded them, becoming the fourteenth state in 1791.) Foreign visitors to the new Republic looked down their noses at the roughness and crudity resulting from ax-and-rifle pioneering life.

⭐ Washington for President

General Washington, the esteemed war hero, was unanimously drafted as president by the Electoral College in 1789—the only presidential nominee ever to be honored by unanimity.

His presence was imposing: 6 feet, 2 inches, 175 pounds, broad and sloping shoulders, strongly pointed chin, and pockmarks (from smallpox) on nose and cheeks. Much preferring the quiet of Mount Vernon to the turmoil of politics, he was perhaps the only president who did not in some way angle for this exalted office. Balanced rather than brilliant, he commanded his followers by strength of character rather than by the arts of the politician.

Washington's long journey from Mount Vernon to New York City, the temporary capital, was a triumphal procession. He was greeted by roaring cannons, pealing bells, flower-carpeted roads, and singing and shouting citizens. With appropriate ceremony, he solemnly and somewhat nervously took the oath of office on April 30, 1789, on a crowded balcony overlooking Wall Street.

Washington soon put his stamp on the new government by establishing the cabinet. The Constitution does not mention a cabinet; it merely provides that the president "may require" written opinions of the heads of the executive branch departments (see Art. II, Sec. II, para. 1). But this system proved so cumbersome that cabinet meetings gradually evolved in the Washington administration. At first only three department heads served under the president: Secretary of State Thomas Jefferson, Secretary of the Treasury Alexander Hamilton, and Secretary of War Henry Knox.

★ The Bill of Rights

The new nation faced some unfinished business. Many antifederalists had sharply criticized the Constitution drafted at Philadelphia for its failure to provide guarantees of individual rights such as freedom of religion and trial by jury. Many states had ratified the federal Constitution with the understanding that it would soon be amended to include such guarantees. Drawing up a bill of rights headed the list of imperatives facing the new government.

The proposed amendments were drafted and submitted to Congress by James Madison, whose intellectual and political skills were quickly making him the leading figure in the new body. Adopted by the necessary number of states in 1791, the first ten amendments to the Constitution, popularly known as the **Bill of Rights**, safeguard some of the most precious American principles. Among these are protections for freedom of religion, speech, and the press; the right to bear arms and to be tried by a jury; and the right to assemble and petition the government for redress of grievances. The Bill of Rights also prohibits cruel and unusual punishments and arbitrary government seizure of private property.

Bill of Rights (1791) *Popular term for the first ten amendments to the U.S. Constitution. The amendments secure key rights for individuals and reserve to the states all powers not explicitly delegated or prohibited by the Constitution.*

Table 10.1 Evolution of the Cabinet

Position	Date Established	Comments
Secretary of state	1789	
Secretary of treasury	1789	
Secretary of war	1789	Loses cabinet status, 1947
Attorney general	1789	Not head of Justice Dept. until 1870
Secretary of navy	1798	Loses cabinet status, 1947
Postmaster general	1829	Loses cabinet status, 1970
Secretary of interior	1849	
Secretary of agriculture	1889	
Secretary of commerce and labor	1903	Office divided in 1913
Secretary of commerce	1913	
Secretary of labor	1913	
Secretary of defense	1947	Subordinate to this secretary, without cabinet rank, are secretaries of army, navy, and air force
Secretary of health, education, and welfare	1953	Office divided in 1979
Secretary of housing and urban development	1965	
Secretary of transportation	1966	
Secretary of energy	1977	
Secretary of health and human services	1979	
Secretary of education	1979	
Secretary of veterans affairs	1989	
Secretary of homeland security	2002	

To guard against the danger that enumerating such rights might lead to the conclusion that they were the only ones protected, Madison inserted the crucial Ninth Amendment. It declares that specifying certain rights "shall not be construed to deny or disparage others retained by the people." To reassure states' righters, he included the equally significant Tenth Amendment, which reserves all rights not explicitly delegated or prohibited by the federal Constitution "to the States respectively, or to the people." By preserving a strong central government while specifying protections for minority and individual liberties, Madison's amendments partially swung the federalist pendulum back in an antifederalist direction. (See Amendments I–X, in the Appendix.)

The first Congress also nailed other newly sawed governmental planks into place. It created effective federal courts under the **Judiciary Act of 1789**. The act organized the Supreme Court, with a chief justice and five associates, as well as federal district and circuit courts, and established the office of attorney general. New Yorker John Jay, Madison's collaborator on *The Federalist*, became the first chief justice of the United States.

Judiciary Act of 1789 *Organized the federal legal system, establishing the Supreme Court, federal district and circuit courts, and the office of the attorney general.*

★ Hamilton Revives the Corpse of Public Credit

The key figure in the new government was the still youthful Treasury Secretary Alexander Hamilton, a native of the British West Indies. Hamilton's genius was unquestioned, but critics claimed he loved his adopted country more than he loved his countrymen. Doubt about his character and his loyalty to the republican experiment always swirled about his head. Hamilton regarded himself as a kind of prime minister in Washington's cabinet, and on occasion he thrust his hands into the affairs of other departments, including that of his archrival, Secretary of State Thomas Jefferson.

A financial wizard, Hamilton set out immediately to correct the economic vexations that had crippled the Articles of Confederation. His plan was to shape the fiscal policies of the administration in such a way as to favor the wealthier groups, who in turn would gratefully lend the government monetary and political support. The new federal regime would thrive, the propertied classes would fatten, and prosperity would trickle down to the masses.

The energetic financier's first objective was to bolster the national credit. Without public confidence in the government, Hamilton could not secure the funds with which to float his risky schemes. He therefore boldly urged Congress to "fund" the entire national debt "at par" and to assume completely the debts incurred by the states during the recent war.

funding at par *Payment of debts, such as government bonds, at face value. In 1790, Alexander Hamilton proposed that the federal government pay its Revolutionary war debts in full in order to bolster the nation's credit.*

"**Funding at par**" meant that the federal government would pay off its debts at face value, plus accumulated interest—a then-enormous total of more than $54 million. So many people believed the infant Treasury incapable of meeting those obligations that government bonds had depreciated to ten or fifteen cents on the dollar. Yet speculators held fistfuls of them, and when Congress passed Hamilton's measure in 1790, they grabbed for more. Some of them galloped into rural areas ahead of the news, buying for a song the depreciated paper holdings of farmers, war veterans, and widows.

assumption *Transfer of debt from one party to another. In order to strengthen the union, the federal government assumed states' Revolutionary War debts in 1790, thereby tying the interests of wealthy lenders with those of the national government.*

Hamilton was willing, even eager, to have the new government shoulder additional obligations. While pushing the funding scheme, he urged Congress to assume the debts of the states, totaling some $21.5 million. The secretary made a convincing case for **assumption**. The state debts could be regarded as a proper national obligation, for they had been incurred in the war for independence. But, foremost in Hamilton's thinking was the belief that assumption would chain the states more tightly to the "federal chariot." Thus the secretary's maneuver would shift the attachment of wealthy creditors from the states to the federal government. The support of the rich for the national administration was a crucial link in Hamilton's political strategy of strengthening the central government.

States burdened with heavy debts, such as Massachusetts, were delighted by Hamilton's proposal. States with small debts, such as Virginia, were less charmed.

> *One of the most eloquent tributes to Hamilton's apparent miracle working came from Daniel Webster (1782–1852) in the Senate (1831):*
>
> "He smote the rock of the national resources, and abundant streams of revenue gushed forth. He touched the dead corpse of public credit, and it sprung upon its feet."

The stage was set for some old-fashioned horse trading. Virginia did not want the state debts assumed, but it did want the forthcoming federal district*—now the District of Columbia—to be located on the Potomac River. Hamilton persuaded a reluctant Jefferson to line up enough votes in Congress for assumption. In return, Virginia would get the federal district in its backyard. The bargain was carried through in 1790.

★ Customs Duties and Excise Taxes

The new ship of state thus set sail dangerously overloaded. The national debt had swelled to $75 million owing to Hamilton's insistence on honoring the outstanding federal and state obligations alike. But Hamilton, "Father of the National Debt," was not greatly worried. His objectives were as much political as economic. He believed that, within limits, a national debt was a "national blessing"—a kind of adhesive of the Union. The more creditors to whom the government owed money, the more people there would be with a personal stake in the success of his ambitious enterprise.

Where was the money to come from to pay interest on this huge debt and to run the government? Hamilton's first answer was customs duties, derived from a **tariff**. Tariff revenues, in turn, depended on a vigorous foreign trade, another crucial link in Hamilton's overall economic strategy for the new Republic.

The first tariff law, which imposed a low tariff of about 8 percent on dutiable imports, was speedily passed by the first Congress in 1789. Revenue was by far the main goal, but the measure was also designed to erect a low protective wall around infant industries, which bawled noisily for more shelter than they received. Hamilton had the vision to see that the Industrial Revolution would soon reach America, and he argued strongly in favor of more protection for the well-to-do manufacturing groups—another vital element in his economic program. But Congress was still dominated by agricultural and commercial interests, and it voted only two slight increases in the tariff during Washington's presidency.

Hamilton, with characteristic vigor, sought additional internal revenue and in 1791 secured from Congress an **excise tax** on a few domestic items, notably whiskey. The new levy of seven cents a gallon was borne chiefly by the distillers who lived in the mountains and backcountry. Whiskey flowed so freely on the frontier that it was used for money.

tariff *Tax levied on imports. Traditionally, manufacturers support tariffs as protective and revenue-raising measures, while agricultural interests, dependent on world markets, oppose high tariffs.*

excise tax *Tax on goods produced domestically. Excise taxes, particularly the 1791 tax on whiskey, were a highly controversial component of Alexander Hamilton's financial program.*

★ Hamilton Battles Jefferson for a Bank

As the capstone for his financial system, Hamilton proposed a **Bank of the United States**. With the Bank of England as his model, he envisioned a private institution with the government as its major stockholder. The bank would provide a convenient strongbox for surplus federal funds, stimulate business by keeping money in circulation, and print an urgently needed and sound paper currency.

Jefferson, whose written opinion on this question Washington requested, argued vehemently against the bank. The Constitution, he insisted, provided no specific authorization for such a financial octopus. He was convinced that all powers not specifically granted to the central government were reserved to the states, as provided in the about-to-be-ratified Bill of Rights (see Amendment X). He therefore concluded that only the states, not Congress, had the power to charter banks. Believing that the Constitution should be interpreted "literally" or "strictly," Jefferson and his states' rights disciples zealously embraced the theory of "strict construction."

Hamilton, also at Washington's request, prepared a brilliantly reasoned reply to Jefferson's arguments. He boldly invoked the clause of the Constitution that stipulates that Congress may pass any laws "necessary and proper" to carry out the powers vested in the various government agencies (see Art. I, Sec. VIII, para. 18). The government was explicitly empowered to collect taxes and regulate trade. In carrying out these basic functions,

Bank of the United States (1791) *Chartered by Congress as part of Alexander Hamilton's financial program, the bank printed paper money and served as a depository for Treasury funds. It drew opposition from Jeffersonian Republicans, who argued that the bank was unconstitutional.*

---

*Authorized by the Constitution, Art. I., Sec. VIII, para. 17.

Contending Voices

Human Nature and the Nature of Government

Alexander Hamilton and Thomas Jefferson were adversaries in the realms of politics and ideas alike. Underlying their differences about the role of government were radically different assessments of human nature.

Hamilton:

"Your people, sir, is a great beast.... The people are turbulent and changing; they seldom judge or determine the right."

Jefferson:

"I have great confidence in the common sense of mankind in general."

> How did Hamilton's and Jefferson's differing perspectives on human psychology affect their political views?

Whiskey Rebellion (1794) *Popular uprising of whiskey distillers in southwestern Pennsylvania in opposition to an excise tax on whiskey. In a show of strength and resolve by the new central government, Washington put down the rebellion with militia drawn from several states.*

Hamilton argued, a national bank would be not only "proper" but "necessary." By inference or by implication—that is, by virtue of "implied powers"—Congress would be fully justified in establishing the Bank of the United States. In short, Hamilton contended for a "loose" or "broad" interpretation of the Constitution. He and his federalist followers thus evolved the theory of "loose construction" by invoking the "elastic clause" of the Constitution—a precedent for enormous federal powers.

Hamilton's financial views prevailed. Washington accepted his eloquent and realistic arguments and signed the bank measure into law. This explosive issue had been debated with much heat in Congress, where the old North-South cleavage still lurked ominously. The most enthusiastic support for the bank naturally came from the commercial and financial centers of the North, whereas the strongest opposition arose from the agricultural South.

The Bank of the United States, as created by Congress in 1791, was chartered for twenty years. Located in Philadelphia, it was to have capital of $10 million, one-fifth of it owned by the federal government, the rest by private investors.

★ Mutinous Moonshiners in Pennsylvania

The **Whiskey Rebellion**, which flared up in southwestern Pennsylvania in 1794, sharply challenged the new national government. Hamilton's high excise tax bore harshly on these homespun pioneer folk. They regarded it not as a tax on a luxury, but as a burden on an economic necessity and a medium of exchange. Even preachers of the gospel were paid in "Old Monongahela rye." Defiant distillers finally erected whiskey poles, similar to the liberty poles of anti–stamp tax days in 1765, and raised the cry "Liberty and No Excise." Boldly tarring and feathering revenue officers, they brought collections to a halt.

President Washington, once a revolutionary, was alarmed by what he called these "self-created societies." With the hearty encouragement of Hamilton, he summoned the militia of several states. The resulting army of about thirteen thousand men, in two widely separated columns, marched briskly forth in a gorgeous, leaf-tinted Indian summer. But when the troops reached the hills of western Pennsylvania, the insurrection melted away. The "Whiskey Boys" were overawed, dispersed, or captured. Only three rebels were killed.

The Whiskey Rebellion was minuscule, but its consequences were mighty. George Washington's government, now substantially strengthened, commanded a new respect. Yet the foes of the administration condemned its brutal display of force—for having used a sledgehammer to crush a gnat.

★ The Emergence of Political Parties

Almost overnight, Hamilton's fiscal feats had established the government's sound credit rating. The Treasury could now borrow needed funds in the Netherlands on favorable terms.

But Hamilton's financial successes—funding, assumption, the excise, the bank, suppression of the Whiskey Rebellion—created some political liabilities. All these schemes encroached sharply on states' rights. Many Americans, dubious about the new Constitution in the first place, might never have approved it if they had foreseen how the states were going to be overshadowed by the federal colossus. Now, out of resentment against Hamilton's revenue-raising and centralizing policies, an organized opposition began to build. What once was a personal feud between Hamilton and Jefferson developed into a full-blown and frequently bitter political rivalry.

National political parties, in the modern sense, were unknown to America when George Washington took the inaugural oath. There had been Whigs and Tories, federalists and antifederalists, but these groups were factions rather than parties. They had sprung into existence over hotly contested special issues; they had faded away when their cause had triumphed or fizzled.

The Founders at Philadelphia had not envisioned the existence of permanent political parties. Organized opposition to the government seemed tainted by disloyalty, an affront to the spirit of national unity that the glorious cause of the Revolution had inspired.

The notion of a formal party apparatus was thus a novelty in the 1790s, and when Jefferson and Madison first organized their opposition to the Hamiltonian program, they did not anticipate creating a long-lived and popular party. But as their antagonism to Hamilton stiffened, and as the amazingly boisterous and widely read newspapers of the day spread their political message, and Hamilton's, among the people, primitive semblances of political parties began to emerge.

The two-party system has existed in the United States since that time. Ironically, in light of the early suspicions about the very legitimacy of parties, their competition for power has actually proved to be among the indispensable ingredients of a sound democracy. The party out of power—"the loyal opposition"—traditionally plays the invaluable role of the balance wheel on the machinery of government, ensuring that politics never drifts too far out of kilter with the wishes of the people.

Alexander Hamilton (1755–1804), by John Trumbull, 1792
He was one of the youngest and most brilliant of the Founding Fathers, who might have been president but for his ultraconservatism, a scandalous adultery, and a duelist's bullet. Hamilton favored a strong central government with a weak legislature to unify the infant nation and encourage industry. His chief rival, Thomas Jefferson, who extolled states' rights as a bulwark of liberty and thought the United States should remain an agricultural society, regarded Hamilton as a monarchist plotter and never forgave him for insisting that "the British Govt. was the best in the world: and that he doubted much whether any thing short of it would do in America."

★ The Impact of the French Revolution

When Washington's first administration ended in early 1793, Hamilton's domestic policies had already fostered two political camps—Hamiltonian Federalists and Jeffersonian Democratic-Republicans. As Washington's second term began, foreign-policy issues brought the differences between them to a fever pitch.

Only a few weeks after Washington's inauguration in 1789, the curtain had risen on the first act of the French Revolution (see "Thinking Globally: Two Revolutions," pp. 146–147). Twenty-six years were to pass before the seething continent of Europe collapsed into a peace of exhaustion. Few non-American events have left a deeper scar on American political and social life. In a sense the French Revolution was misnamed: it was a revolution that sent tremors through much of the Western world and beyond.

Most Americans, loving liberty and deploring despotism, cheered the early, peaceful stages of the French Revolution, involving as it did a successful attempt to impose constitutional shackles on King Louis XVI. The Revolution entered a more ominous phase in 1792, when France declared war on hostile Austria. Late that year the electrifying news reached America that French citizen armies had hurled back the invading foreigners and that France had proclaimed itself a republic. Americans enthusiastically sang the rousing revolutionary anthem "The Marseillaise" and renamed roads Liberty Street and Equality Lane.

But centuries of pent-up poison could not be purged without baleful results. The guillotine was set up, the king was beheaded in 1793, the Roman Catholic Church was

Thinking Globally

Two Revolutions

On July 14, 1789, a howling mob stormed the Bastille—a dank Parisian prison described by the Marquis de Lafayette as France's "fortress of despotism"—killed half a dozen soldiers, and paraded the severed heads of its commanding officer and the mayor of Paris throughout the city. The French Revolution was thus bloodily launched. Bastille Day is still celebrated as France's national birthday, just as Americans celebrate the Fourth of July.

The roots of the two revolutions were thickly intertwined. To defray the cost of the war that had ousted France from North America in 1763, Britain had levied new taxes on its colonists, provoking them to revolt in 1776. In turn, aiding the rebellious Americans forced the French government to seek new revenues, lighting the fuse that led to the political explosion in Paris in 1789.

Even more notable was the intellectual commonality between the two upheavals. The ideas that inspired the American and French revolutionaries grew from the common heritage of radical eighteenth-century Enlightenment thinking about equality, freedom, and the sovereignty of the people. The French Declaration of the Rights of Man (1789) deliberately echoed Thomas Jefferson's Declaration of Independence (1776) when it said that "men are born and remain free and equal in rights," among which were "liberty, property, security, and resistance to oppression." Many French thinkers openly credited the American Revolution as the inspiration for their own. As the American revolutionary Thomas Paine remarked to George Washington, "The principles of America opened the Bastille." Indeed, in many ways the French were even more radical than the Americans; their Revolution abolished slavery (temporarily), something the Americans failed to do for almost one hundred years more.

And yet the two revolutions unfolded in dramatically different ways and left vastly different legacies. The American revolutionaries largely disarmed after winning their independence; allowed some eighty thousand hard-core Loyalists to depart without suffering grievous retribution; peacefully resumed their habits of worship, toil, and governance; and proceeded to draft the U.S. Constitution, under which they have lived with amendments, for more than two centuries. The American revolutionaries, in short, secured the fruits of their Revolution fairly easily, while the French

Storming the Bastille, 1789 This event signaled the outbreak of the French Revolution.

struggled through ghastly bloodshed to ultimate failure—an outcome that haunted European politics for at least a century thereafter.

Revolutionaries in France had to grapple with the constant threats of counterrevolution at home and armed intervention from abroad. As a result, they soon descended into grisly violence, including the execution of some forty thousand Frenchmen in the notorious Reign of Terror of 1793–1794, the guillotining of the king and queen, and pre-emptive attacks on neighboring countries. They stripped the Catholic Church of its property and privileges, briefly experimented with a new state religion called the Cult of Reason, and eventually conceded supreme power to a brash young general, Napoleon Bonaparte, who convulsed all of Europe in the name of "liberty, equality, and fraternity." Napoleon was finally defeated at the Battle of Waterloo in 1815, after which the Bourbon monarchy was restored to the throne.

Why did these two great eruptions, sprung from a shared chain of events and espousing almost identical political philosophies, fare so differently? Many scholars have found the answer in the two countries' markedly different pre-Revolutionary histories. France's revolutions confronted implacably entrenched adversaries in the landed nobility and the clergy. Those two "estates," as they were called, clung tenaciously to their ancient privileges, as did the princes and potentates who ruled in all the countries on France's borders.

To succeed, the French Revolution had to concentrate power in the hands of a state powerful enough to extinguish its internal enemies and to forestall foreign intervention as well. Those stark necessities help account for the fact that down to the present day, central governments are stronger in almost all European societies than in the United States.

The Americans faced no such obstacles. They had no aristocracy worthy of the name, no church with the kind of influence that the Catholic Church commanded in France, and no menacing neighbors to fear. They had the luxury of being able to focus on limiting the power of the state, not enlarging it. Theirs was largely a *colonial* conflict, whereas France had to endure a *class* conflict. Not until Reconstruction following the Civil War would America confront a comparable task of mustering sufficient power to uproot and permanently extinguish an entire social order.

It has been said that to mount a revolution is "to murder and create." What was exceptional about the American revolutionaries was that they were spared the necessity to murder. The American Revolution grew not from abstract ideas, but from the preceding two centuries of American experience. It was less a revolution in the usual sense than a consolidation of already well-established norms, values, and behaviors. Alexander Hamilton understood that crucial point when he wrote to the Marquis de Lafayette in 1789, "I dread the reveries of your *philosophic* politicians."

---

attacked, and the head-rolling **Reign of Terror** was begun. Back in America, God-fearing Federalist aristocrats nervously fingered their tender white necks and eyed the Jeffersonian masses apprehensively. Lukewarm Federalist approval of the early French Revolution turned, almost overnight, to heated talk of "blood-drinking cannibals."

Sober-minded Jeffersonians regretted the bloodshed. But they felt, with Jefferson, that one could not expect to be carried from "despotism to liberty in a feather bed," and that a few thousand aristocratic heads were a cheap price to pay for human freedom.

Such approbation was shortsighted, for dire peril loomed ahead. The earlier battles of the French Revolution had not hurt America directly, but now Britain was sucked into the contagious conflict. The conflagration speedily spread to the New World, where it vividly affected the expanding young American republic.

Reign of Terror (1793–1794) *Ten-month period of brutal repression when some forty thousand individuals were executed as enemies of the French Revolution. While many Jeffersonians maintained their faith in the French Republic, Federalists withdrew their already lukewarm support once the Reign of Terror commenced.*

★ Washington's Neutrality Proclamation

Ominously, the Franco-American alliance of 1778 was still on the books, and many Jeffersonian Democratic-Republicans favored honoring the pact. Aflame with the liberal ideals of the French Revolution, red-blooded Jeffersonians were eager to enter the conflict against Britain, the recent foe, at the side of France, the recent friend.

But levelheaded President Washington was not swayed by the clamor of the crowd. Backed by Hamilton, he believed that war had to be avoided at all costs.

Neutrality Proclamation (1793)
Issued by George Washington, it proclaimed America's formal neutrality in the escalating conflict between England and France, a statement that enraged pro-French Jeffersonians.

Accordingly, Washington boldly issued his **Neutrality Proclamation** in 1793, shortly after the outbreak of war between Britain and France. This epochal document not only proclaimed the government's official neutrality in the widening conflict but sternly warned American citizens to be impartial toward both armed camps. As America's first formal declaration of aloofness from Old World quarrels, Washington's Neutrality Proclamation proved to be a major prop of the spreading isolationist tradition.

The pro-French Jeffersonians were enraged by the Neutrality Proclamation; the pro-British Federalists were heartened. Debate intensified when an impetuous, thirty-year-old representative of the French Republic, Citizen Edmond Genêt, landed at Charleston, South Carolina. With unrestrained zeal he undertook to fit out privateers and otherwise take advantage of the existing Franco-American alliance. Swept away by his enthusiastic reception by the Jeffersonian Democratic-Republicans, Genêt foolishly came to believe that the Neutrality Proclamation did not reflect the true wishes of the American people. He consequently embarked on an outrageous campaign to appeal over the head of "Old Washington" to the sovereign voters, and to recruit armies to invade Spanish Florida and British Canada. The president quickly demanded Genêt's withdrawal, and the Frenchman was replaced by a less impulsive emissary.

★ Embroilments with Britain

President Washington's far-visioned policy of neutrality was sorely tried by the British. For ten years they had been retaining the chain of northern frontier posts on U.S. soil, all in defiance of the peace treaty of 1783 (see Map 10.1). British agents openly sold firearms and firewater to the Miami Indians, who attacked Americans invading their lands northwest

Map 10.1 American Posts Held by the British and British-American Clashes after 1783

of the Ohio River. In 1790 and 1791, the Miami chief Little Turtle's braves defeated armies led by Generals Josiah Harmer and Arthur St. Clair, killing hundreds of American soldiers and handing the United States what remains one of its worst military defeats in the history of the frontier.

But in 1794 General "Mad Anthony" Wayne's army routed the Miamis at the **Battle of Fallen Timbers**. In the **Treaty of Greenville**, signed in August 1795, the confederacy gave up most of the present-day states of Ohio and Indiana. In exchange the Indians received monetary compensation, the right to hunt on the lands they had ceded, and what they hoped was recognition of their sovereign status.

On the sea frontier, the British were eager to starve out the French West Indies and naturally expected the United States to defend these French colonies under the Franco-American alliance. Hard-boiled commanders of the Royal Navy, ignoring America's neutral rights, struck savagely. They seized about three hundred American merchant ships in the West Indies, impressed scores of seamen into service on British vessels, and threw hundreds of others into foul dungeons. A mighty outcry arose, chiefly from Jeffersonians, that America should once again fight George III in defense of its liberties.

President Washington, in a last desperate gamble to avert war, sent Chief Justice John Jay to London in 1794. The Jeffersonians were acutely unhappy over the choice, partly because they feared that so notorious a Federalist and Anglophile would sell out his country.

Unhappily, Jay entered the negotiations with weak cards and could win only a few concessions. The British did promise to evacuate the chain of posts on U.S. soil—a pledge that inspired little confidence, because it had been made before in Paris (to the same John Jay!) in 1783. In addition, Britain consented to pay damages for the recent seizures of American ships. But the British stopped short of pledging anything about *future* maritime seizures and impressments or about supplying arms to Indians.

When the Jeffersonians learned of Jay's concessions, their rage was fearful to behold. The treaty seemed like an abject surrender to Britain, as well as a betrayal of the Jeffersonian South. Jeffersonian mobs hanged, burned, and guillotined in effigy that "damn'd archtraitor, Sir John Jay." Jay's unpopular pact, more than any other issue, vitalized the newborn Democratic-Republican party of Thomas Jefferson.

Jay's Treaty had other unforeseen consequences. Fearing that the treaty foreshadowed an Anglo-American alliance, Spain moved hastily to strike a deal with the United States. **Pinckney's Treaty** of 1795 with Spain granted the Americans virtually everything they demanded, including free navigation of the Mississippi and the large disputed territory of western Florida.

Exhausted after the diplomatic and partisan battles of his second term, President Washington decided to retire. His choice contributed powerfully to establishing a two-term tradition for American presidents.* In his **Farewell Address** to the nation in 1796, Washington strongly advised the avoidance of "permanent alliances" such as the still-vexatious Franco-American treaty of 1778. Contrary to general misunderstanding, Washington did not oppose all alliances, but favored only "temporary alliances" for "extraordinary emergencies."

Washington's contributions as president were enormous, even though the sparkling Hamilton at times seemed to outshine him. The central government, its fiscal feet now under it, was solidly established. The West was expanding. The merchant marine was plowing the seas. Above all, Washington had kept the nation out of both overseas entanglements and foreign wars. The experimental stage had passed, and the presidential chair could now be turned over to a less impressive figure.

★ John Adams Becomes President

Who should succeed the exalted "Father of His Country"? Alexander Hamilton was the best-known Federalist leader now that Washington had bowed out. But his financial policies, some of which had fattened speculators, had made him so unpopular that he could

---

Fallen Timbers, Battle of (1794) *Decisive battle between the Miami Confederacy and the U.S. Army. British forces refused to shelter the routed Indians, forcing the latter to attain a peace settlement with the United States.*

Greenville, Treaty of (1795) *Under the terms of the treaty, the Miami Confederacy agreed to cede territory in the Old Northwest to the United States in exchange for cash payment, hunting rights, and formal recognition of their sovereign status.*

Jay's Treaty (1794) *Negotiated by Chief Justice John Jay in an effort to avoid war with Britain, the treaty included a British promise to evacuate outposts on U.S. soil and pay damages for seized American vessels, in exchange for which Jay bound the United States to repay pre-Revolutionary war debts and to abide by Britain's restrictive trading policies toward France.*

Pinckney's Treaty (1795) *Signed with Spain, which, fearing an Anglo-American alliance, granted Americans free navigation of the Mississippi and the disputed territory of western Florida.*

Farewell Address (1796) *George Washington's address at the end of his presidency, warning against "permanent alliances" with other nations. Washington did not oppose all alliances, but believed that the young, fledgling nation should forge alliances only on a temporary basis, in extraordinary circumstances.*

---

*This tradition, not broken until 1940 by Franklin D. Roosevelt, was made part of the Constitution in 1951 by the Twenty-second Amendment. (See text in the Appendix.)

not hope to be elected president. The Federalists were forced to turn to Washington's experienced but ungracious vice president John Adams, a rugged chip off old Plymouth Rock. The Democratic-Republicans naturally rallied behind their master organizer and leader, Thomas Jefferson.

Political passions ran feverishly high in the presidential campaign of 1796. The lofty presence of Washington had hitherto imposed some restraints on partisan attacks; now the lid was off. Cultured Federalists referred to the Jeffersonians as "fire-eating salamanders, poison-sucking toads." Federalists and Democratic-Republicans even drank their ale in separate taverns. The Jeffersonians again assailed the too-forceful crushing of the Whiskey Rebellion and, above all, the negotiation of Jay's hated treaty.

John Adams, with most of his support in New England, squeezed through by the narrow margin of 71 votes to 68 in the Electoral College. Jefferson, as runner-up, became vice president.* One of the ablest statesmen of his day, Adams at sixty-two was bald, short, and thickset ("His Rotundity"). He impressed observers as a man of stern principles who did his duty with stubborn devotion. Although learned and upright, he was a tactless and prickly intellectual aristocrat with no appeal to the masses and no desire to cultivate any. Many citizens regarded him with "respectful irritation."

The crusty New Englander suffered from other handicaps. He had stepped into Washington's shoes, which no successor could hope to fill. In addition, Adams was hated by Hamilton, who now headed the pro-war faction of the Federalist party, known as "High Federalists." The famed financier even secretly plotted with certain members of the cabinet against the new president, who soon had a conspiracy rather than a cabinet on his hands. Most ominous of all, Adams inherited a violent quarrel with France—a quarrel whose gunpowder lacked only a spark.

> *Although Thomas Jefferson (1743–1826) and John Adams hardly saw eye to eye, Jefferson displayed grudging respect for Adams in a piece of private correspondence in 1787:*
>
> "He is vain, irritable, and a bad calculator of the force and probable effect of the motives which govern men. This is all the ill which can possibly be said of him. He is as disinterested as the Being who made him."

★ Unofficial Fighting with France

The French were infuriated by Jay's Treaty. They condemned it as the initial step toward an American alliance with Britain, their perpetual foe. French warships, in retaliation, seized about three hundred defenseless American merchant vessels by mid-1797.

President Adams kept his head, temporarily, even though the nation was mightily aroused. Trying to reach an agreement with the French, he appointed a diplomatic commission of three men, including John Marshall, the future chief justice. When Adams's envoys reached Paris in 1797, they were secretly approached by three French go-betweens, later referred to as X, Y, and Z in the published dispatches. The French spokesmen demanded an unneutral loan of 32 million florins, plus what amounted to a bribe of $250,000, for the privilege of merely talking with Charles Maurice de Talleyrand, the crafty French foreign minister.

These terms were intolerable. The American trio knew that bribes were standard diplomatic devices in Europe, but they gagged at paying a quarter of a million dollars for mere talk, without any assurances of a settlement. Negotiations quickly broke down.

The **XYZ Affair** sent a wave of war hysteria through the United States, catching up even President Adams. The slogan of the hour became "Millions for defense, but not one cent for tribute." Despite considerable Jeffersonian opposition in Congress, war preparations were pushed along at a feverish pace. The Navy Department was created, the three-ship navy expanded, and the United States Marine Corps re-established (it had been created in 1775 but disbanded at the end of the Revolutionary War).

Bloodshed was confined to the sea, principally in the West Indies. In two and a half years of undeclared hostilities (1798–1800), American privateers and men of war of the

XYZ Affair (1797) *Diplomatic conflict between France and the United States when American envoys to France were asked to pay a hefty bribe for the privilege of meeting with the French foreign minister. Many in the United States called for war against France, while American sailors and privateers waged an undeclared war against French merchants in the Caribbean.*

---

*The possibility of such an inharmonious two-party combination in the future was removed by the Twelfth Amendment to the Constitution in 1804. (See text in the Appendix.)

new navy captured over eighty armed vessels flying the French colors, though several hundred Yankee merchant ships were lost to the enemy. Only a slight push, it seemed, might plunge both nations into a full-dress war.

⭐ Adams Puts Patriotism Above Party

Embattled France, its hands full in Europe, wanted no war. An outwitted Talleyrand realized that to fight the United States would add one more foe to his enemy roster. He therefore let it be known, through roundabout channels, that if the Americans would send a new minister, he would be received with proper respect.

Adams might have enjoyed unexpected popular acclaim—and perhaps election to a second term—by leading the nation into a full-fledged war. But like the other Founding Fathers, he realized full well that war must be avoided because the nation was so relatively weak. Adams therefore exploded a bombshell in early 1799 by sending to the Senate the name of a new minister to France. Hamilton and his war-hawk faction were enraged. But public opinion—Jeffersonian and reasonable Federalist alike—was favorable to one last try for peace.

America's envoys (now three) found the political skies brightening when they reached Paris early in 1800. The ambitious "Little Corporal," the Corsican Napoleon Bonaparte, had recently seized dictatorial power. He was eager to free his hands of the American squabble so that he might continue to redraw the map of Europe and perhaps create a New World empire in Louisiana. The afflictions and ambitions of the Old World were again working to America's advantage.

After a great deal of haggling, a memorable treaty known as the **Convention of 1800** was signed in Paris. France agreed to annul the twenty-two-year-old marriage of (in)convenience, but as a kind of alimony the United States agreed to pay the damage claims of American shippers. So ended the nation's only peacetime military alliance for a century and a half. Its troubled history does much to explain the traditional antipathy of the American people to foreign entanglements.

Convention of 1800 *Agreement to formally dissolve the United States' treaty with France, originally signed during the Revolutionary War. The difficulties posed by America's peacetime alliance with France contributed to Americans' long-standing opposition to entangling alliances with foreign powers.*

Preparation for War to Defend Commerce: The Building of the Frigate *Philadelphia* In 1803 this frigate ran onto the rocks near Tripoli harbor, and about three hundred officers and men were imprisoned by the Tripolitans. The ship was refloated for service against the Americans, but Stephen Decatur led a party of men that set it afire.

John Adams, flinty to the end, deserves immense credit for his belated push for peace, even though he was moved in part by jealousy of Hamilton. Adams not only avoided the hazards of war but also unwittingly smoothed the path for the peaceful purchase of Louisiana three years later. If America had drifted into a full-blown war with France in 1800, Napoleon would not have sold Louisiana to Jefferson on any terms in 1803.

President Adams, the bubble of his popularity pricked by peace, was aware of his signal contribution to the nation. He later suggested as the epitaph for his tombstone (not used), "Here lies John Adams, who took upon himself the responsibility of peace with France in the year 1800."

★ The Federalist Witch Hunt

Exulting Federalists had meanwhile capitalized on the anti-French frenzy to drive through Congress in 1798 a sheaf of laws designed to muffle or minimize their Jeffersonian foes.

The first of these oppressive laws was aimed at supposedly pro-Jeffersonian "aliens." The Federalist Congress, hoping to discourage the "dregs" of Europe, erected a disheartening barrier. They raised the residence requirements for aliens who desired to become citizens from a tolerable five years to an intolerable fourteen. This drastic new law violated the traditional American policy of open-door hospitality and speedy assimilation.

Alien Laws (1798) *Acts passed by a Federalist Congress raising the residency requirement for citizenship to fourteen years and granting the president the power to deport dangerous foreigners in times of peace.*

Two additional **Alien Laws** struck heavily at undesirable immigrants. The president was empowered to deport dangerous foreigners in time of peace and to deport or imprison them in time of hostilities. This was an arbitrary grant of executive power, contrary to American tradition and to the spirit of the Constitution, even though the stringent Alien Laws were never enforced.

Sedition Act (1798) *Enacted by the Federalist Congress in an effort to clamp down on Jeffersonian opposition, the law made anyone convicted of defaming government officials or interfering with government policies liable to imprisonment and a heavy fine. The act drew heavy criticism from Republicans, who let the act expire in 1801.*

The "lockjaw" **Sedition Act**, the last measure of the harsh Federalist clampdown, was a direct slap at two priceless freedoms guaranteed in the Constitution by the Bill of Rights in the First Amendment—freedom of speech and freedom of the press. This law provided that anyone who impeded the policies of the government or falsely defamed its officials, including the president, would be liable to a heavy fine and imprisonment.

Many outspoken Jeffersonian editors were indicted under the Sedition Act. Ten were brought to trial and convicted by packed juries swayed by prejudiced Federalist judges. Among them was Vermont congressman Matthew Lyon (the "Spitting Lion"), who had earlier gained fame by spitting in the face of a Federalist and fighting on the floor of Congress.

The Sedition Act seemed to be in direct conflict with the Constitution. But the Supreme Court, dominated by Federalists, was of no mind to declare this Federalist law unconstitutional. (The law expired in March 1801.) This attempt by the Federalists to crush free speech and silence the opposition party undoubtedly made many converts for the Jeffersonians.

Yet the Alien and Sedition Acts, despite pained outcries from the Jeffersonians they muzzled, commanded widespread popular support. Anti-French hysteria played directly into the hands of witch-hunting conservatives. In the congressional elections of 1798–1799, the Federalists, riding a wave of popularity, scored the most sweeping victory of their entire history.

In 1800 James Callender (1758–1803) published a pamphlet that assailed the president in strong language. For blasts such as the following tirade, Callender was prosecuted under the Sedition Act, fined $250, and sentenced to prison for nine months:

"The reign of Mr. Adams has, hitherto, been one continued tempest of *malignant* passions. As president, he has never opened his lips, or lifted his pen, without threatening and scolding. The grand object of his administration has been to exasperate the rage of contending parties, to calumniate and destroy every man who differs from his opinions. . . . Every person holding an office must either quit it, or think and vote exactly with Mr. Adams."

★ The Virginia (Madison) and Kentucky (Jefferson) Resolutions

Resentful Jeffersonians naturally refused to take the Alien and Sedition Acts lying down. Jefferson himself feared that if the Federalists managed to choke free speech and free press, they would then wipe out other precious constitutional guarantees. His own fledgling political party might even be stamped out of existence.

Fearing prosecution for sedition, Jefferson secretly penned a series of resolutions, which the Kentucky legislature approved in 1798 and 1799. His friend and fellow Virginian James Madison drafted a similar but less extreme statement, which was adopted by the Virginia legislature in 1798.

Both Jefferson and Madison stressed the compact theory—a theory popular among English political philosophers in the seventeenth and eighteenth centuries. As applied to America by the Jeffersonians, this concept meant that the thirteen sovereign states, in creating the federal government, had entered into a "compact," or contract, regarding its jurisdiction. The national government was consequently the agent or creation of the states. Because water can rise no higher than its source, the individual states were the final judges of whether their agent had broken the "compact" by overstepping the authority originally granted. Invoking this logic, Jefferson's Kentucky resolutions concluded that the federal regime *had* exceeded its constitutional powers and that, with regard to the Alien and Sedition Acts, "nullification"—a refusal to accept them—was the "rightful remedy."

The **Virginia and Kentucky resolutions** were a brilliant formulation of the extreme states' rights view regarding the Union—indeed more sweeping in their implications than their authors had intended. They were later used by southerners to support nullification—and ultimately secession. Yet neither Jefferson nor Madison, as Founding Fathers of the Union, had any intention of breaking it up: They were groping for ways to preserve it. Their resolutions were basically campaign documents designed to crystallize opposition to the Federalist party and to unseat it in the upcoming presidential election of 1800. The only real nullification that Jefferson had in view was the nullification of Federalist abuses.

Virginia and Kentucky resolutions (1798–1799) *Statements secretly drafted by Jefferson and Madison for the legislatures of Kentucky and Virginia. Argued that states were the final arbiters of whether the federal government overstepped its boundaries and could therefore nullify, or refuse to accept, national legislation the deemed unconstitutional.*

★ Federalists versus Democratic-Republicans

As the presidential contest of 1800 approached, the differences between Federalists and Democratic-Republicans were sharply etched. As might be expected, most federalists of the pre-Constitutional period (1787–1789) became Federalists in the 1790s. Largely welded by Hamilton into an effective group by 1793, they openly advocated rule by the "best people." "Those who own the country," remarked Federalist John Jay, "ought to govern it." With their intellectual arrogance and Tory tastes, Hamiltonians distrusted full-blown democracy as the fountain of all mischiefs and feared the "swayability" of the untutored common folk.

Hamiltonian Federalists also advocated a strong central government with the power to crush democratic excesses such as Shays's Rebellion, protect the lives and estates of the wealthy, and subordinate the sovereignty-loving states. They believed the national government should support private enterprise but not interfere with it. This attitude came naturally to the Atlantic seaboard merchants, manufacturers, and shippers who made up the majority of Federalist support. Farther inland, few Hamiltonians dwelled.

Leading the anti-Federalists, who eventually came to be known as Democratic-Republicans or sometimes simply Republicans, was Thomas Jefferson. Lanky and relaxed in appearance, lacking personal aggressiveness, and unable to deliver a rabble-rousing speech, he became a master political organizer through his ability to lead people rather than drive them. His strongest appeal was to the middle class

Thomas Jefferson at Natural Bridge, by Caleb Boyle, ca. 1801 A great statesman, Jefferson wrote his own epitaph: "Here was buried Thomas Jefferson, Author of the Declaration of Independence, of the Statute of Virginia for Religious Freedom, and Father of the University of Virginia."

and to the underprivileged—the "dirt" farmers, the laborers, the artisans, and the small shopkeepers.

Liberal-thinking Jefferson, with his aristocratic head set on a farmer's frame, was a bundle of inconsistencies. By one set of tests he should have been a Federalist, for he was a Virginia aristocrat and slave-owner who lived in an imposing hilltop mansion at Monticello. A so-called traitor to his own upper class, Jefferson cherished uncommon sympathy for the common people, especially the downtrodden, the oppressed, and the persecuted. As he wrote in 1800, "I have sworn upon the altar of God eternal hostility against every form of tyranny over the mind of man."

Jeffersonian Republicans demanded a weak central regime. They believed that the best government was one that governed least, and that the bulk of power should be retained by the states. There the people could keep a more vigilant eye on their public servants. The national debt should be paid off, and government should provide no special privileges for special classes, especially manufacturers. Agriculture, to Jefferson, was the favored branch of the economy and formed the foundation of his political thought. "Those who labor in the earth are the chosen people of God," he said. Most of his followers naturally came from the agricultural South and Southwest.

Above all, Jefferson advocated the rule of the people. But he did not propose thrusting the ballot into the hands of *every* adult white male. He favored government *for* the people but not by *all* the people. Because in his view the ignorant were incapable of self-government, only white men literate enough to inform themselves about citizenship should have the ballot. Universal education would have to precede universal suffrage. Jefferson had a profound faith in the reasonableness and teachableness of the masses and in their collective wisdom when taught.

Landlessness among American citizens threatened popular democracy as much as illiteracy, in Jefferson's eyes. He feared that propertyless dependents would be political pawns in the hands of their landowning superiors. How could the emergence of a landless class of voters be avoided? The answer, in part, was by slavery. A system of black slave labor ensured that white yeoman farmers would remain independent landowners and not be forced to labor for low wages in others' tobacco and rice fields. Jefferson thus tortuously reconciled slaveholding—his own included—with his more democratic impulses.

Yet for his time, Jefferson's confidence that white, free men could become responsible and knowledgeable citizens was open-minded. He championed freedom of speech, for without free speech and a free press, the misdeeds of tyranny could not be exposed. Although Jefferson suffered much foul abuse from editorial pens, he said that he would choose "newspapers without a government" rather than "a government without newspapers."

Differences over foreign policy defined another sharp distinction between Hamilton and Jefferson. Hamilton looked outward and eastward across the Atlantic. He sought to build a strong national state that would assert America's commercial interests and expand foreign trade, especially with Britain. Jeffersonian Republicans, unlike the Federalist "British boot-lickers," were basically pro-French. They earnestly believed that it was to America's advantage to support the liberal ideals of the French Revolution rather than reactionary British Tories. Jefferson, in effect, faced inward and westward. His priorities were to strengthen democracy at home, especially in the frontier regions beyond the Appalachians, rather than to flex America's muscles abroad.

So as the young Republic's first full decade of nationhood came to a close, the Founders' hopes seemed already imperiled. Conflicts over domestic politics and foreign policy undermined the unity of the Revolutionary era and called into question the very viability of the American experiment in democracy. As the presidential election of 1800 approached, the danger loomed that the fragile and battered American ship of state would founder on the rocks of controversy. The shores of history are littered with the wreckage of nascent nations torn asunder before they could grow to stable maturity. Why should the United States expect to enjoy a happier fate?

Thomas Jefferson's vision of a republican America was peopled with virtuous farmers, not factory hands. As early as 1784, he wrote:

"While we have land to labor then, let us never wish to see our citizens occupied at a workbench, or twirling a distaff.... For the general operations of manufacture, let our workshops remain in Europe.... The mobs of great cities add just so much to the support of pure government, as sores do to the strength of the human body."

CHAPTER SUMMARY ★ ★ ★ ★ ★ ★ ★ ★ ★ ★ ★ ★ ★

The fledgling federal government under the new Constitution faced severe difficulties and deep skepticism about its durability, especially because traditional political theory held that large-scale republics were bound to fail. But President Washington brought credibility to the new government, while his cabinet, led by Alexander Hamilton, strengthened its political and economic foundations.

The government's first achievements were the Bill of Rights and Hamilton's financial system. Through effective leadership, Hamilton carried out his program of funding the national debt, assuming state debts, imposing customs and excise taxes, and establishing a Bank of the United States.

The bank was the most controversial part of Hamilton's program because it raised basic constitutional issues. Opposition to the bank from Jefferson and his followers reflected more fundamental political disagreements about republicanism, economics, federal power, and foreign policy. As the French Revolution evolved from moderation to radicalism, it intensified the ideological divisions between the pro-French Jeffersonians and the pro-British Hamiltonians. Their disagreements solidified into the first American political parties, the Republicans and the Federalists—a development not anticipated in the Constitution.

Washington's Neutrality Proclamation angered Republicans, who wanted America to aid revolutionary France. Washington's policy was sorely tested by the British, who routinely violated American neutrality. In order to avoid war, Washington endorsed the conciliatory Jay's Treaty, further outraging the Jeffersonian Republicans in the United States as well as revolutionary France.

After the humiliating XYZ affair, the United States began to fight a "quasi-war" with France, but President John Adams sacrificed his political popularity and divided his party by choosing to negotiate peace.

These foreign-policy disagreements deeply embittered domestic politics: Federalists passed the repressive Alien and Sedition Acts, to which Jefferson and Madison responded with the Virginia and Kentucky resolutions, which challenged federal authority. These political conflicts of the 1790s soon hardened into a deeper philosophical disagreement between Hamiltonian Federalists, who favored a powerful federal government controlled by commercial elites, and Jeffersonian Republicans, who advocated a weak central authority and greater equality for ordinary citizens and yeoman farmers.

KEY TERMS

Bill of Rights (141)
Judiciary Act of 1789 (142)
funding at par (142)
assumption (142)
tariff (143)
excise tax (143)
Bank of the United States (143)
Whiskey Rebellion (144)
Reign of Terror (147)
Neutrality Proclamation (148)
Fallen Timbers, Battle of (149)
Greenville, Treaty of (149)
Jay's Treaty (149)
Pinckney's Treaty (149)
Farewell Address (149)
XYZ Affair (150)
Convention of 1800 (151)
Alien Laws (152)
Sedition Act (152)
Virginia and Kentucky resolutions (153)

PEOPLE TO KNOW

Alexander Hamilton
George Washington
Louis XVI
Edmond Genêt
Little Turtle
"Mad Anthony" Wayne
John Jay
John Adams
Charles Maurice de Talleyrand

 MindTap is a fully online, highly personalized learning experience built upon Cengage Learning content. MindTap combines student learning tools—readings, multimedia, activities, and assessments—into a singular Learning Path that guides students through the course.

Chapter 11

The Triumphs and Travails of the Jeffersonian Republic
1800–1812

Timid men . . . prefer the calm of despotism to the boisterous sea of liberty.

THOMAS JEFFERSON, 1796

Chapter Outline

- The "Revolution of 1800"
- The Jefferson Presidency
- John Marshall and the Supreme Court
- The Louisiana Purchase, 1803
- The Embargo, 1807–1809
- Napoleon Manipulates Madison
- Battle with the Shawnees
- A Declaration of War
- *Examining the Evidence: The Thomas Jefferson–Sally Hemings Controversy*

In the critical presidential election of 1800, the first in which Federalists and Democratic-Republicans functioned as two national political parties, John Adams and Thomas Jefferson again squared off against each other. The choice seemed clear and dramatic. Adams's Federalists waged a defensive struggle for a strong central government and public order. Their Jeffersonian opponents presented themselves as the guardians of agrarian purity, liberty, and states' rights.

The next dozen years, however, would turn what seemed like a clear-cut choice in 1800 into a messier reality, as the Jeffersonians in power were confronted with a series of opportunities and crises requiring the assertion of federal authority. As the first challengers successfully to rout a reigning party, the Republicans were also the first to learn that it is far easier to condemn from the stump than to govern consistently.

FOCUS QUESTIONS

1. How did Jefferson adapt his intellectual ideals to practical realities as he carried out the "Revolution of 1800"?
2. Why did Republicans and Federalists clash so sharply over the judiciary, and how did John Marshall successfully perpetuate Federalist principles on the Supreme Court?
3. What were Jefferson's basic foreign policy goals, and how successful was he in achieving them?
4. What were the causes and effects of the Louisiana Purchase?
5. How did America become embroiled in the turbulent crisis of the Napoleonic Wars, and why did President Madison see a new war with Britain as essential to maintaining America's republican experiment?

CHRONOLOGY

1791	Toussaint L'Ouverture launches Haitian Revolution	1805	Peace treaty with Tripoli Battle of Trafalgar Battle of Austerlitz
1800	Jefferson defeats Adams for presidency	1805–1807	Pike's explorations
1801	Judiciary Act of 1801	1806	Burr treason trial
1801–1805	Naval war with Tripoli	1807	*Chesapeake* affair Embargo Act
1802	Revised naturalization law Judiciary Act of 1801 repealed	1808	Madison elected president
		1809	Non-Intercourse Act replaces Embargo Act
1803	*Marbury* v. *Madison* Louisiana Purchase	1810	Macon's Bill No. 2 Napoleon announces (falsely) repeal of blockade decrees Madison reestablishes nonimportation against Britain
1804	Haiti emerges as first independent black republic Jefferson reelected president Impeachment of Justice Chase	1811	Battle of Tippecanoe
1804–1806	Lewis and Clark expedition	1812	United States declares war on Britain

★ Federalist and Republican Mudslingers

In fighting for survival, the Federalists labored under heavy handicaps. Their Alien and Sedition Acts had aroused a host of enemies, although most of these critics were dyed-in-the-wool Jeffersonians anyhow. The Hamiltonian wing of the Federalist party, robbed of its glorious war with France, split openly with President Adams, and Hamilton himself attacked the president.

The most damaging blow to the Federalists, however, was the refusal of Adams to give them a rousing fight with France. Their feverish war preparations had swelled the public debt and had required disagreeable new taxes, including a stamp tax. After all these unpopular measures, the war scare had petered out, and the country was left with an all-dressed-up-but-no-place-to-go feeling.

Thrown on the defensive, the Federalists concentrated their fire on Jefferson himself, who became the victim of one of America's earliest "whispering campaigns." He was accused of having robbed a widow and her children of a trust fund and of having fathered numerous mulatto children by his own slave women. (Jefferson's long-rumored intimacy with his slave Sally Hemings has recently been confirmed by DNA testing; see "Examining the Evidence," p. 159.) As a liberal in religion, Jefferson had earlier incurred the wrath of the orthodox clergy, largely through his successful struggle to separate church and state in Virginia. From the New England stronghold of Federalism and Congregationalism, preachers thundered against his alleged atheism. Old ladies of Federalist families, fearing Jefferson's election, even buried their Bibles or hung them in wells.

★ The Jeffersonian "Revolution of 1800"

Jefferson won by a majority of seventy-three electoral votes to sixty-five (see Map 11.1). In defeat, the colorless and presumably unpopular Adams polled more electoral strength than he had gained four years earlier—except for New York. The Empire State fell into the

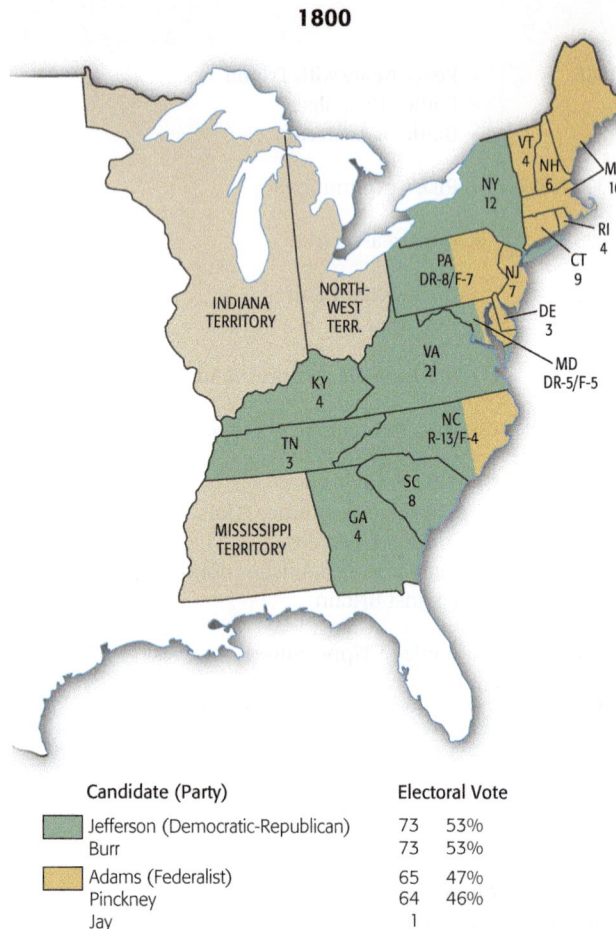

Map 11.1 Presidential Election of 1800 (with electoral vote by state) New York was the key state in this election, and Aaron Burr helped to swing it away from the Federalists with tactics that anticipated the political "machines" of a later day. Federalists complained that Burr "travels every night from one meeting of Republicans to another, haranguing . . . them to the most zealous exertions. [He] can stoop so low as to visit every low tavern that may happen to be crowded with his dear fellow citizens." But Burr proved that the price was worth it. "We have beat you," Burr told kid-gloved Federalists after the election, "by superior Management."

Revolution of 1800 Electoral victory of Democratic Republicans over the Federalists, who lost their congressional majority and the presidency. The peaceful transfer of power between rival parties solidified faith in America's political system.

Jeffersonian basket, and with it the election, largely because Aaron Burr, a master wire-puller, turned New York to Jefferson by the narrowest of margins. The Virginian polled the bulk of his strength in the South and West.

Decisive in Jefferson's victory was the three-fifths clause of the Constitution. By counting three-fifths of the slave population for the purposes of congressional and Electoral College representations, the Constitution gave white southern voters a bonus that helped Jefferson win the White House. Northern critics fumed that Jefferson was a "Negro President" and an illegitimate embodiment of the "slave power" that southern states wielded in the Union.

Jeffersonian joy was dampened by an unexpected deadlock. Through a technicality Jefferson, the presidential candidate, and Burr, his vice-presidential running mate, received the same number of electoral votes for the presidency. Under the Constitution the tie could be broken only by the House of Representatives (see Art. II, Sec. I, para. 2). This body was controlled for several more months by the lame duck Federalists, who preferred Burr to the hated Jefferson.*

Voting in the House moved slowly to a climax. The agonizing deadlock was broken at last when a few Federalists, despairing of electing Burr and hoping for moderation from Jefferson, refrained from voting. The election then went to the rightful candidate. John Adams proved to be the last Federalist president of the United States, and his party sank slowly into political oblivion and ultimately disappeared.

Jefferson later claimed that the election of 1800 was a "revolution" comparable to that of 1776, and historians sometimes refer to the **Revolution of 1800**. But the election was no revolution in the sense of a massive popular upheaval or an upending of the political system, for Jefferson had narrowly squeaked through to victory. Jefferson meant that his election represented a return to what he considered the original spirit of the Revolution. In his eyes, Hamilton and Adams had betrayed the ideals of 1776 and 1787. Jefferson's mission, as he saw it, was to restore the republican experiment, to check the growth of government power, and to halt the decay of virtue that had set in under Federalist rule.

No less "revolutionary" was the peaceful and orderly transfer of power on the basis of an election whose results all parties accepted. This was a remarkable achievement for a raw young nation, especially after all the partisan bitterness that had agitated the country during Adams's presidency. After a decade of division and doubt, Americans could take justifiable pride in the vigor of their experiment in democracy.

★ Responsibility Breeds Moderation

"Long Tom" Jefferson was inaugurated president on March 4, 1801, in the swampy village of Washington, the crude new national capital. Tall (six feet, two and a half inches), with large hands and feet, red hair ("the Red Fox"), and prominent cheekbones and chin, he was an arresting figure. Fluent in French and a sophisticated, cosmopolitan "citizen of

---

*A "lame duck" has been humorously defined as a politician whose goose has been cooked at the recent elections. The possibility of another such tie was removed by the Twelfth Amendment in 1804 (for text, see the Appendix). Before then, each elector had two votes, and the second-place finisher became the vice president.

Examining the Evidence

Thomas Jefferson–Sally Hemings Controversy

In the aftermath of the rumor-fueled election of 1800, the firebrand journalist and political *provocateur* James Callender asserted in print that Thomas Jefferson had engaged in sexual relations with his Monticello slave, Sally Hemings. Promptly and gleefully, Federalist newspapers broadcast this ripe gossip across the country. This print, titled "A Philosophic Cock," attacked Jefferson by depicting him as a rooster and Hemings as a hen. The rooster, or cock, was also a symbol of Revolutionary France. Jefferson's enemies sought to discredit him for personal indiscretions as well as radical sympathies. Although he resolutely denied having an affair with Hemings, the charge that at first seemed to be only a politically motivated defamation refused to go away. In the 1870s two new oral sources of evidence came to light. Madison Hemings, Sally's next-to-last child, claimed that his mother had identified Jefferson as the father of all five of her children. Soon thereafter James Parton's biography of Jefferson revealed that among Jefferson's white descendants, it was said that his nephew had fathered all or most of Sally's children. In the 1950s several large publishing projects on Jefferson's life and writings uncovered new evidence and inspired renewed debate. Most convincing was Dumas Malone's calculation that Jefferson had been present at Monticello nine months prior to the birth of each of Sally's children.

Speculation continued throughout the rest of the century, with little new evidence, until scientific advances made possible DNA testing of the remains of Jefferson's white and possible black descendants to determine paternity. Two centuries after Callender first cast aspersions on Jefferson's morality, cutting-edge science helped establish the high probability that Jefferson had fathered Sally's youngest son and the likelihood that he was the father of all of her children.

1. Are there ways that historians can use unproven rumors and charges made during political campaigns—such as those leveled against Thomas Jefferson regarding Sally Hemings—to better understand a person or event, even if the accusations themselves are false or unproven? Or should such material be totally disregarded?

2. Which piece of "unscientific" historical information that existed in the nineteenth and early twentieth centuries regarding Jefferson's affair with Sally Hemings was most persuasive: the oral traditions of a liaison within the Hemings family, the Jefferson family's denial, or the recorded evidence that Jefferson had been at Monticello nine months before the birth of each of Hemings's five children? How should historians treat such material?

3. How does the scientific DNA proof that Jefferson did father Hemings's children alter historians' perceptions of Jefferson, his political opponents, and the larger issues of race relations?

Courtesy, American Antiquarian Society

> The toleration of Thomas Jefferson (1743-1826) was reflected in his inaugural address:
>
> "If there be any among us who would wish to dissolve this Union or to change its republican form, let them stand undisturbed as monuments of the safety with which error of opinion may be tolerated where reason is left free to combat it."

the world," Jefferson never lost the common touch. Believing that the customary pomp did not befit his democratic ideals, he spurned a horse-drawn coach and strode to the Capitol from his boardinghouse.

Jefferson's inaugural address, beautifully phrased, was a classic statement of democratic principles. Seeking to allay Federalist fears of a bull-in-the-china-shop overturn, Jefferson ingratiatingly intoned, "We are all Republicans, we are all Federalists." As for foreign affairs, he pledged "honest friendship with all nations, entangling alliances with none."

With its rustic setting, Washington lent itself admirably to the simplicity and frugality of the Jeffersonian Republicans. In this respect, Washington contrasted sharply with the elegant atmosphere of Federalist Philadelphia, the former temporary capital.

As president, Jefferson could be shockingly unconventional. He would receive callers in sloppy attire—once in a dressing gown and slippers. He started the precedent, unbroken until Woodrow Wilson's presidency 112 years later, of sending messages to Congress to be read by a clerk. Personal appearances, in the Federalist manner, suggested too strongly a monarchical speech from the throne.

As if compelled by an evil twin, Jefferson was forced to reverse many of the political principles he had so vigorously championed. There were in fact two Thomas Jeffersons. One was the scholarly private citizen who philosophized in his study. The other was the harassed public official who made the disturbing discovery that bookish theories worked out differently in the noisy arena of practical politics. The open-minded Virginian was therefore consistently inconsistent; it is easy to quote one Jefferson to refute the other.

Jefferson quickly proved an able politician. He was especially effective in the informal atmosphere of a dinner party, where he wooed congressional representatives while personally pouring imported wines and serving tasty dishes prepared by his French chef. In part Jefferson had to rely on his charm because his party was so weak jointed. Jefferson's refusal to practice widespread patronage made it difficult for Democratic-Republicans to build a loyal political following. Opposition to the Federalists was the chief glue holding them together, and as the Federalists faded, so did Democratic-Republican unity. The era of well-developed, well-disciplined political parties still lay in the future. At the outset, Jefferson was determined to undo the Federalist abuses begotten by the anti-French hysteria. The hated Alien and Sedition Acts had already expired. The incoming president speedily pardoned the "martyrs" serving sentences under the Sedition Act. Shortly after Congress met, the Jeffersonians enacted the new naturalization law of 1802, which reduced the requirement of fourteen years of residence to a more reasonable five years.

Jefferson actually kicked away only one substantial prop of the Hamiltonian economic system. He hated the excise tax, which bred bureaucrats and bore heavily on his farmer following, and he early persuaded Congress to repeal it. But except for excising the excise tax, Jefferson and his talented treasury secretary, Swiss-born Albert Gallatin, left the Hamiltonian framework essentially intact. They launched no attack on the Bank of the United States, nor did they repeal the mildly protective Federalist tariff.

Paradoxically, Jefferson's moderation thus further cemented the gains of the "Revolution of 1800." By shrewdly absorbing the major Federalist programs, Jefferson showed that a change of regime need not be disastrous for the defeated group. His restraint pointed the way toward the two-party system that was later to become a characteristic feature of American politics.

Judiciary Act of 1801 Passed by the departing Federalist Congress, it created sixteen new federal judgeships, ensuring a Federalist hold on the judiciary.

midnight judges (1801) Federal justices appointed by John Adams during the last days of his presidency. Their positions were revoked when the newly elected Republican Congress repealed the Judiciary Act.

★ The "Dead Clutch" of the Judiciary

The "deathbed" **Judiciary Act of 1801** was one of the last important laws passed by the expiring Federalist Congress. The Judiciary Act created sixteen new federal judgeships and other judicial offices. President Adams remained at his desk until nine o'clock in the evening on his last day in office, supposedly signing the commissions of the Federalist "**midnight judges**."

This Federalist-sponsored Judiciary Act, though a long-overdue reform, aroused bitter resentment. "Packing" of these lifetime posts with anti-Jeffersonian partisans was, in Republican eyes, a brazen attempt by the ousted party to entrench itself in one of the three powerful branches of government. Jeffersonians condemned the last-minute appointees in violent language.

The newly elected Republican Congress moved swiftly to repeal the Judiciary Act of 1801 in the year after its passage. Jeffersonians thus swept sixteen benches from under the recently seated "midnight judges."

Jeffersonians likewise had their knives sharpened for the scalp of Chief Justice John Marshall, whom Adams had appointed to the Supreme Court in the dying days of his term. The strong-willed Marshall, with his rasping voice and steel-trap mind, was Thomas Jefferson's cousin. As a lifelong Federalist and fervent advocate of a powerful central government, Marshall was vigorously condemned by the states' rights Jeffersonians. But with his powerful intellect and commanding personality, Marshall pushed ahead on his inflexible Federalist course. The Federalist party died out, but Marshall lived on, handing down Federalist decisions for thirty-four years under Democratic-Republican administrations. For more than three decades, the ghost of Alexander Hamilton spoke through the lanky, black-robed judge.

One of the "midnight judges" of 1801 presented John Marshall with a historic opportunity. When obscure William Marbury, whom President Adams had named a justice of the peace for the District of Columbia, learned that his commission was being shelved by the new Secretary of State James Madison, he sued for its delivery. Chief Justice Marshall knew that his Jeffersonian rivals, entrenched in the executive branch, would hardly spring forward to enforce a writ to deliver the commission to his fellow Federalist Marbury. Marshall therefore dismissed Marbury's suit, avoiding a direct political showdown. But the wily Marshall snatched victory from the jaws of this judicial defeat. In explaining his ruling, Marshall said that the part of the Judiciary Act of 1789 on which Marbury tried to base his appeal was unconstitutional. The act had attempted to assign to the Supreme Court powers that the Constitution had not foreseen.

In this self-denying opinion, Marshall greatly magnified the authority of the Court—and slapped at the Jeffersonians. Until the case of ***Marbury v. Madison*** (1803), controversy had clouded the question of who had the final authority to determine the meaning of the Constitution. Jefferson in the Kentucky resolutions (1798) had tried to assign that right to the individual states. But now his cousin on the Court had cleverly promoted the contrary principle of "judicial review"—the idea that the Supreme Court alone had the last word on the question of constitutionality. In this landmark case, Marshall inserted the keystone into the arch that supports the tremendous power of the Supreme Court in American life.*

> *In his decision in* Marbury v. Madison, *Chief Justice John Marshall (1755–1835) vigorously asserted his view that the Constitution embodied a "higher" law than ordinary legislation and that the Court must interpret the Constitution:*
>
> **"The Constitution is either a superior paramount law, unchangeable by ordinary means, or it is on a level with ordinary legislative acts, and like other acts, is alterable when the legislature shall please to alter it.**
>
> **"If the former part of the alternative be true, then a legislative act contrary to the constitution is not law; if the latter part be true, then written constitutions are absurd attempts, on the part of the people, to limit a power in its own nature illimitable....**
>
> **"It is emphatically the province and duty of the judicial department to say what the law is....**
>
> **"If, then, the courts are to regard the Constitution, and the Constitution is superior to any ordinary act of the legislature, the Constitution, and not such ordinary act, must govern the case to which they are both applicable."**

Marbury v. Madison **(1803)** *Supreme Court case that established the principle of "judicial review"—the idea that the Supreme Court had the final authority to determine constitutionality.*

★ Jefferson: A Reluctant Warrior

One of Jefferson's first actions as president was to reduce the military establishment to a mere twenty-five hundred officers and men. Jefferson's reluctance to invest in soldiers and ships was less about money than about republican ideals. He fondly hoped that America would transcend Europe's bloody wars and set an example for the world by

---

*The next invalidation of a federal law by the Supreme Court came fifty-four years later with the explosive *Dred Scott* decision (see pp. 302–303).

winning friends through "peaceful coercion" rather than military force. The Republicans strongly distrusted standing armies as standing invitations to dictatorships. A large navy, the Jeffersonians also feared, might embroil the Republic in costly and corrupting wars far from America's shores.

But harsh realities forced Jefferson's principles to bend. Pirates of the North African Barbary States had long made a national industry of blackmailing and plundering merchant ships that ventured into the Mediterranean. Preceding Federalist administrations had been forced to buy protection. At the time of the French crisis of 1798, when Americans were shouting, "Millions for defense, but not one cent for tribute," twenty-six barrels of blackmail dollars were being shipped to Algiers.

War across the Atlantic was not part of the Jeffersonian vision—but neither was paying tribute to a pack of pirate states. The showdown came in 1801. The pasha of Tripoli, dissatisfied with his share of protection money, informally declared war on the United States by cutting down the flagstaff of the American consulate. A gauntlet was thus thrown squarely into the face of Jefferson—the noninterventionist, the critic of a big-ship navy, and the political foe of Federalist shippers. He reluctantly rose to the challenge by dispatching the infant navy to "the shores of Tripoli," as related in the song of the U.S. Marine Corps. After four years of intermittent fighting, Jefferson succeeded in obtaining a peace treaty with Tripoli in 1805.

★ The Louisiana Godsend

A secret pact, fraught with peril for America, was signed in 1800. Napoleon Bonaparte induced the king of Spain to cede to France, for attractive considerations, the immense trans-Mississippi region of Louisiana, which included the New Orleans area. Then, in 1802, the right of deposit at New Orleans, guaranteed America by Pinckney's Treaty of 1795, was withdrawn. Deposit (warehouse) privileges were vital to frontier farmers who floated their produce down the Mississippi to its mouth, there to await oceangoing vessels. A roar of anger rolled up the mighty river and into its tributary valleys. American pioneers talked wildly of descending on New Orleans, rifles in hand.

Thomas Jefferson was again on the griddle. Louisiana in the senile grip of Spain posed no real threat, but Louisiana in the iron fist of Napoleon, the preeminent military genius of his age, foreshadowed a dark and blood-drenched future. Hoping to quiet the clamor of the West, Jefferson moved decisively. Early in 1803 he sent James Monroe to Paris to join the regular minister there, Robert R. Livingston. The two envoys were instructed to buy New Orleans and as much land to the east as they could get for a maximum of $10 million.

At this critical juncture, Napoleon suddenly abandoned his dream of a New World empire and decided to sell all of Louisiana. Two developments prompted his change of mind. First, he had failed to reconquer the sugar-rich island of Santo Domingo (Haiti), for which Louisiana was to serve as a source of foodstuffs. Rebellious slaves, inspired by the French Revolution's promise of equality and ably led by the gifted Toussaint L'Ouverture, had struck for their freedom in 1791. Santo Domingo could not be reconquered by the French armies, except perhaps at a staggering cost. Second, Napoleon was about to end the twenty-month lull in his deadly conflict with Britain. Because the British controlled the seas, he feared that he might be forced to make them a gift of Louisiana. Rather than drive America into the arms of Britain by attempting to hold the area, he decided to sell the huge wilderness to the Americans and pocket the money for his schemes nearer home.

Events now unrolled dizzily. Suddenly, out of a clear sky, the French foreign minister asked the American minister Robert Livingston how much he would give for all Louisiana. Scarcely able to believe his ears (he was partially deaf anyhow), Livingston nervously entered upon the negotiations. After about a week of haggling, the treaties were signed on April 30, 1803, ceding Louisiana to the United States for about $15 million.

When news of the bargain reached America, Jefferson was startled. He had authorized his envoys to offer not more than $10 million for New Orleans, and as much to the east in the Floridas as they could get. Instead, they had signed three treaties that pledged $15 million for New Orleans and a vast tract entirely to the west—an area that would more than double the size of the United States. They had bought a wilderness to get a city.

Once again two Jeffersons wrestled with each other: the theorist and strict constructionist versus the democratic visionary. Where in his beloved Constitution was the president authorized to negotiate treaties incorporating a huge new expanse into the Union—an expanse containing tens of thousands of Indian, white, and black inhabitants? There was no such clause. Yet Jefferson also perceived that the vast domain now within his reach could form a sprawling "empire of liberty" that would ensure the health and life of America's experiment in democracy. So Jefferson shamefacedly submitted the treaties to the Senate while privately admitting that the purchase was unconstitutional.

The senators were less finicky than Jefferson. Reflecting enthusiastic public support, they registered their prompt approval of the transaction. Land-hungry Americans were not disposed to split constitutional hairs when confronted with perhaps the most magnificent real-estate bargain in history—828,000 square miles at about three cents an acre.

Jefferson's bargain with Napoleon was epochal. With the **Louisiana Purchase**, America secured at one bloodless stroke the western half of the richest river valley in the world and further laid the foundations of a future major power. The ideal of a great agrarian republic, as envisioned by Jefferson, could now be realized in the vast "Valley of Democracy." At the same time, the transfer established a precedent for acquiring foreign territories and peoples by purchasing and incorporating them into the Union as full equals.

The purchase also contributed to making operational the isolationist principles of Washington's Farewell Address. By removing the last significant European power from the North American continent, the United States was now free to disengage from the ancient system of European power politics and rivalries.

The enormous extent of the huge new area was more fully unveiled by a series of explorations under Jefferson's direction. In the spring of 1804, Jefferson sent Meriwether Lewis and William Clark to explore the northern part of the Louisiana Purchase. Departing from St. Louis, Lewis and Clark's **Corps of Discovery** ascended the Missouri River (the "Great Muddy"), crossed the Rockies, and descended the Columbia River to the Pacific coast. Aided by the Shoshone woman guide Sacajawea, Lewis and Clark's two-and-one-half-year expedition yielded a rich harvest of scientific observations, demonstrated the viability of an overland trail to the Pacific, and bolstered American claims to Oregon. Other explorers also pushed into the uncharted West. Zebulon M. Pike explored the headwaters of the Mississippi River in 1805–1806 and the southern portion of the Louisiana territory in 1807.

★ The Aaron Burr Conspiracies

In the long run, the Louisiana Purchase greatly expanded the fortunes of the United States and the power of the federal government. In the short term, the vast expanse of territory and the feeble reach of the government obliged to control it raised fears of secession and foreign intrigue (see Map 11.2).

Aaron Burr, Jefferson's first-term vice president, played no small part in provoking—and justifying—such fears. Dropped as vice president for Jefferson's second term, Burr joined a group of Federalist extremists to plot the secession of New England and New York. Alexander Hamilton, though no friend of Jefferson, exposed and foiled this conspiracy. Incensed, Burr challenged his foe to a duel, and

Louisiana Purchase (1803) *Acquisition of Louisiana Territory from France. The purchase more than doubled the territory of the United States, opening vast tracts for settlement.*

Corps of Discovery (1804–1806) *Team of adventurers, led by Meriwether Lewis and William Clark, sent by Thomas Jefferson to explore Louisiana Territory and find a water route to the Pacific. Louis and Clark brought back detailed accounts of the West's flora, fauna, and native populations, and their voyage demonstrated the viability of overland travel to the West.*

Meriwether Lewis Lewis is portrayed as he looked on his return from the great expedition through the Louisiana Purchase and the West.

Hamilton reluctantly accepted. Burr killed Hamilton with one shot. Burr's pistol blew the brightest brain out of the Federalist party and destroyed its one remaining hope of effective leadership.

His political career as dead as Hamilton's, Burr now turned his disunionist plottings to the trans-Mississippi West, where he struck up an alliance with General James Wilkinson, the unscrupulous military governor of Louisiana. Burr's schemes are still shrouded in mystery, but he and Wilkinson apparently planned to break the western territories away from the United States and then expand their new confederacy by invading Spanish Mexico and Florida. In the fall of 1806 Burr and his followers floated down the Mississippi to meet Wilkinson's army at Natchez, but Wilkinson betrayed Burr and fled to New Orleans. The former vice president was arrested and tried for treason but was finally acquitted. Chief Justice Marshall ruled that there was insufficient proof that Burr had committed overt acts of treason according to the Constitution (see Art. III, Sec. III). Burr then fled to Europe. His insurrectionary brashness demonstrated that purchasing a large expanse of western territory was far easier than controlling it.

★ A Precarious Neutrality

Jefferson was triumphantly reelected in 1804, with 162 electoral votes to only 14 votes for his Federalist opponent. But the laurels of Jefferson's first administration soon withered under the blasts of the new storm that broke in Europe. After unloading Louisiana in 1803, Napoleon deliberately provoked a new war with Britain, an awesome conflict that raged for eleven long years. After the Battle of Trafalgar in 1805, Britain's navy controlled the seas, while Napoleon's victory in the Battle of Austerlitz in Austria made him master of the whole European continent. Like the tiger and the shark, France and Britain each reigned supreme in their chosen elements.

Unable to hurt each other directly, the two antagonists were forced to strike indirect blows. Britain ruled the waves and waived the rules. The London government, beginning in 1806, issued a series of **Orders in Council** that closed all ports under French control to foreign shipping, including American, unless the vessels first stopped at a British port. Napoleon struck back, ordering the seizure of all merchant ships, including American, that entered British ports. There was thus no way to trade with either nation without facing the other's guns. American vessels were, quite literally, caught between the devil and the deep blue sea.

Even more galling to American pride than the seizure of wooden ships was the seizure of flesh-and-blood American seamen. **Impressment**—the forcible enlistment of sailors—was a crude form of conscription that the British, among others, had employed for more than four centuries. Clubs and stretchers (for men knocked unconscious) were standard equipment of press gangs from His Majesty's crew-hungry ships. Some six thousand U.S. citizens were impressed by the "piratical man stealers" of Britain from 1808 to 1811 alone.

Britain's determination was spectacularly highlighted in 1807 in what came to be known as the *Chesapeake* affair. A British warship, seeking deserters, fired on a U.S. frigate, the *Chesapeake*, killing three Americans and wounding eighteen. Britain was clearly in the wrong, as the London foreign office admitted. But London's contrition availed little; a roar of national wrath went up from infuriated Americans. Jefferson, the peace lover, could easily have had war if he had wanted it.

★ The Hated Embargo

National honor would not permit a slavish submission to British and French mistreatment. Yet a large-scale foreign war was contrary to the settled policy of the new Republic—and in addition a war would be futile. The navy was weak, and the army was even weaker. A disastrous defeat would not improve America's plight.

Orders in Council (1806–1807) *Edicts issued by the British crown closing French-owned European ports to foreign shipping. The French responded by ordering the seizure of all vessels entering British ports, thereby cutting off American merchants from trade with both parties.*

impressment *Act of forcibly drafting an individual into military service, employed by the British navy against American seamen in times of war against France, 1793–1815. Impressment was a continual source of conflict between Britain and the United States in the early national period.*

***Chesapeake* affair (1807)** *Conflict between Britain and the United States that precipitated the 1807 embargo. The conflict developed when a British ship, in search of deserters, fired on the American* Chesapeake *off the coast of Virginia.*

Map 11.2 Exploring the Louisiana Purchase and the West Seeking to avert friction with France by purchasing all of Louisiana, Jefferson bought trouble because of the vagueness of the boundaries. Among the disputants were Spain in the Floridas, Spain and Mexico in the Southwest, and Great Britain in Canada.

The warring nations of Europe depended heavily on the United States for raw materials and foodstuffs. In his eager search for an alternative to war, Jefferson seized on this essential fact. He reasoned that, if America voluntarily cut off its exports, the offending powers would be forced to respect U.S. rights. Responding to the presidential lash, Congress hastily passed the **Embargo Act** late in 1807. This rigorous law forbade the export of all goods from the United States, whether in American or in foreign ships. More than just a compromise between submission and shooting, the embargo embodied Jefferson's idea of "peaceful coercion." If it worked, the embargo would vindicate the rights of neutral nations and point to a new way of conducting foreign affairs.

The American economy staggered under the effect of the embargo long before Britain or France began to bend. Forests of dead masts gradually filled once-bustling harbors; docks that had once rumbled were deserted (except for illegal trade); and soup kitchens cared for some of the hungry unemployed. Jeffersonian Republicans probably hurt the commerce of New England, which they avowedly were trying to protect, far more than Britain and France together were doing.

Farmers of the South and West, the strongholds of Jefferson, suffered no less disastrously than New England. They were alarmed by the mounting piles of exportable cotton, grain, and tobacco. Jefferson seemed to be waging war on his fellow citizens rather than on the offending foreign powers.

An enormous illicit trade mushroomed in 1808, especially along the Canadian border, where bands of armed Americans on loaded rafts overpowered federal agents. Irate citizens cynically transposed the letters of "Embargo" to read "O Grab Me," "Go Bar 'Em," and "Mobrage," while heartily cursing the "Dambargo."

Jefferson nonetheless induced Congress to pass iron-toothed enforcing legislation. These laws were so inquisitorial and tyrannical as to cause some Americans to think more kindly of George III, whom Jefferson had berated in the Declaration of Independence.

Embargo Act (1807) *Enacted in response to British and French mistreatment of American merchants, the act banned the export of all goods from the United States to any foreign port. The embargo placed great strains on the American economy, while only marginally affecting its European targets, and was therefore repealed in 1809.*

Contending Voices

The Divisive Embargo

The Embargo Act of 1807 provoked bitter divisions—divisions that foreshadowed the sectional conflict that would one day erupt into civil war. A Federalist circular in Massachusetts against the embargo cried out:

"Let every man who holds the name of America dear to him, stretch forth his hands and put this accursed thing, this Embargo from him. Be resolute, act like sons of liberty, of God, and your country; nerve your arm with vengeance against the Despot [Jefferson] who would wrest the inestimable germ of your Independence from you—and you shall be *Conquerors!!!*"

Virginia Senator W. B. Giles (1762–1830) offered this defense of Jefferson's embargo:

"The first effect of the embargo upon the aggressing belligerents was to lessen their inducements to war, by keeping out of their way the rich spoils of our commerce, which had invited their cupidity, and which was saved by those laws.... The second effect which the embargo laws have had on the aggressing belligerents is to enhance the prices of all American produce."

[Why might Massachusetts and Virginia have had different perspectives on the embargo?

One indignant New Hampshirite denounced the president with this ditty:

> *Our ships all in motion,*
> *Once whiten'd the ocean;*
>   *They sail'd and return'd with a cargo;*
> *Now doom'd to decay*
> *They are fallen a prey,*
>   *To Jefferson, worms, and EMBARGO.*

The embargo even had the effect of reviving the moribund Federalist party. Gaining new converts, its leaders hurled their nullification of the embargo into the teeth of the "Virginia lordlings" in Washington. In 1804 the discredited Federalists had polled only 14 electoral votes out of 176; in 1808, the embargo year, the figure rose to 47 out of 175. New England seethed with talk of secession, and Jefferson later admitted that he felt the foundations of government tremble under his feet.

An alarmed Congress, yielding to the storm of public anger, finally repealed the embargo on March 1, 1809, three days before Jefferson's retirement. A half-loaf substitute was provided by the **Non-Intercourse Act**. This measure formally reopened trade with all the nations of the world, except the two most important, Britain and France. Though thus watered down, economic coercion continued to be the policy of the Jeffersonians from 1809 to 1812, when the nation finally plunged into war.

Why did the embargo, Jefferson's most daring act of statesmanship, collapse after fifteen dismal months? First, the president overestimated the dependence of both belligerents on America's trade. Bumper grain crops blessed the British Isles during these years, and the revolutionary Latin American republics unexpectedly threw open their ports for compensating commerce. With most of Europe under his control, Napoleon simply tightened his belt and went without American trade even as he mocked the United States by seizing American ships and cargo with the claim that he was simply helping them enforce the embargo.

More critically, perhaps, Jefferson miscalculated the unpopularity of such a self-crucifying weapon and the difficulty of enforcing it. The hated embargo was not continued long enough or tightly enough to achieve the desired results—and a leaky embargo was perhaps more costly than none at all.

Curiously enough, New England plucked a new prosperity from the ugly jaws of the embargo. With shipping tied up and imported goods scarce, the resourceful Yankees reopened old factories and erected new ones. The real foundations of modern America's industrial might were laid behind the protective wall of the embargo, followed by non-intercourse and the War of 1812. Jefferson, the avowed critic of factories, may have unwittingly done more for American manufacturing than Alexander Hamilton, industry's outspoken friend.

★ Madison's Gamble

Following Washington's precedent, Jefferson left the presidency after two terms, happy to escape what he called the "splendid misery" of the highest office in the land. As his successor, Jefferson strongly favored the nomination and election of his friend and fellow Virginian, the quiet, intellectual, and unassuming James Madison.

Madison took the presidential oath on March 4, 1809, as the awesome conflict in Europe was roaring to its climax. The scholarly Madison was short, thin, bald, and weak

---

Non-Intercourse Act (1809) *Passed alongside the repeal of the Embargo Act, it reopened trade with all but the two belligerent nations, Britain and France. The act continued Jefferson's policy of economic coercion, still with little effect.*

of voice. Despite a distinguished career as a legislator, he was crippled as president by factions within his party and his cabinet. Unable to dominate Congress as Jefferson had done, Madison often found himself holding the bag for risky foreign policies not of his own making.

The Non-Intercourse Act of 1809—a diluted embargo aimed solely at Britain and France—was due to expire in 1810. To Madison's dismay, Congress dismantled the embargo completely with a bargaining measure known as **Macon's Bill No. 2**. While reopening American trade with all the world, Macon's Bill dangled what Congress hoped was an attractive lure. If either Britain or France repealed its commercial restrictions, America would restore its embargo against the nonrepealing nation. To Madison the bill was a shameful capitulation that emphasized America's economic weakness and left the determination of who would be America's trading partner to the potentates of London and Paris.

The crafty Napoleon saw his chance. Without actually promising to do so, he signaled in August 1810 that France might repeal its trade restrictions if Britain also lifted its Orders in Council. Madison knew better than to trust Napoleon, but he chose to accept the French offer as evidence of repeal, gambling that the threat of seeing the United States trade exclusively with France would lead the British to repeal their restrictions. But they did not. In firm control of the seas, London saw little need to bargain. Madison's gamble failed. The president saw no choice but to reestablish the embargo against Britain alone—a decision that he knew meant the end of American neutrality and that he feared was the last step toward war.

> *Rivals for the presidency, and for the soul of the young Republic, Thomas Jefferson and John Adams died on the same day—the Fourth of July, 1826—fifty years to the day after both men had signed the Declaration of Independence. Adams's last words were:*
>
> **"Thomas Jefferson still survives."**
>
> *But he was wrong, for three hours earlier, Jefferson had drawn his last breath.*

★ Tecumseh and the Prophet

Not all of Madison's party was reluctant to fight. The complexion of the Twelfth Congress, which met late in 1811, differed markedly from that of its predecessor. Recent elections had swept away many of the older "submission men" and replaced them with young hotheads, many from the South and West. Dubbed **war hawks** by their Federalist opponents, the newcomers were indeed on fire for a new war with the old enemy. The war hawks detested the British for their manhandling of American sailors and their Orders in Council that dammed the flow of American farm products headed for Europe. The western war hawks also yearned to wipe out a renewed Indian threat to the flood of pioneer settlers who were streaming into the trans-Appalachian wilderness.

Two remarkable Shawnee brothers, Tecumseh and Tenskwatawa, known to non-Indians as "the Prophet," concluded that the time had come to stop this onrushing tide. They began to weld together a far-flung confederacy of all the tribes east of the Mississippi, inspiring a vibrant movement of Indian unity and cultural renewal. Their followers gave up textile clothing for traditional buckskin garments and foreswore alcohol, the better to fight a last-ditch battle with the white invaders. Rejecting whites' concept of "ownership," Tecumseh urged his supporters never to cede land to whites unless all Indians agreed.

Meanwhile, frontiersmen and their war-hawk spokesmen in Congress became convinced that British "scalp buyers" in Canada were nourishing the Indians' growing strength. In the fall of 1811 General William Henry Harrison, governor of Indiana Territory, gathered an army and advanced on Tecumseh's headquarters at the junction of the Wabash and Tippecanoe Rivers in present-day Indiana. Tecumseh was absent, recruiting supporters in the South, but the Prophet attacked Harrison's army—foolishly, in Tecumseh's eyes—with a small force of Shawnees. The Shawnees were routed and their settlement burned.

The **Battle of Tippecanoe** made Harrison a national hero. It also discredited the Prophet and drove Tecumseh

Macon's Bill No. 2 (1810) *Aimed at resuming peaceful trade with Britain and France, the act stipulated that if either Britain or France repealed its trade restrictions, the United States would reinstate the embargo against the nonrepealing nation. When Napoleon offered to lift his restrictions on British ports, the United States was forced to declare an embargo on Britain, thereby pushing the two nations closer toward war.*

war hawks (1811–1812) *Democratic-Republican congressmen who pressed James Madison to declare war on Britain. Largely drawn from the South and West, the war hawks resented British constraints on American trade and accused the British of supporting Indian attacks against American settlements on the frontier.*

Battle of Tippecanoe (1811) *Resulted in the defeat of Shawnee chief Tenskwatawa, "the Prophet," at the hands of William Henry Harrison in the Indiana wilderness. After the battle, the Prophet's brother, Tecumseh, forged an alliance with the British against the United States.*

> *In a speech at Vincennes, Indiana Territory, Tecumseh (1768?–1813) said:*
>
> **"Sell a country! Why not sell the air, the clouds, and the great sea, as well as the earth? Did not the Great Spirit make them all for the use of his children?"**

The Battle of the Thames, 1813 Here the Shawnee leader Tecumseh stood his ground against the superior American force and died. A gifted organizer and military chieftain, he had denounced the tribal custom of torturing prisoners and opposed the practice of allowing any one tribe to sell land that, he believed, belonged to all Indians.

into an alliance with the British. When America's war with Britain came, Tecumseh fought fiercely for the redcoats until his death in 1813 at the Battle of the Thames. With him perished the dream of an Indian confederacy.

★ Mr. Madison's War

By the spring of 1812, Madison believed war with Britain to be inevitable. The British arming of hostile Indians pushed him toward this decision, as did the whoops of the war hawks in his own party who believed the only way to remove the menace of the Indians was to wipe out their Canadian base. "On to Canada, on to Canada" was the war hawks' chant. Southern expansionists, less vocal, cast a covetous eye on Florida, then held by Britain's ally Spain.

Above all, Madison turned to war to restore confidence in the republican experiment. For five years the Republicans had tried to steer a noble course between submission and battle with the warring European powers. But their policies had brought them only international derision and internal strife. Madison and the Republicans came to believe that only a vigorous assertion of American rights could demonstrate the viability of American nationhood—and of democracy as a form of government. If America could not fight to protect itself, its experiment in republicanism would be discredited in the eyes of a scoffing world.

> *William Henry Harrison (1773–1841), Indian fighter and later president, called Tecumseh:*
>
> "one of those uncommon geniuses who spring up occasionally to produce revolutions and overturn the established order of things. If it were not for the vicinity of the United States, he would perhaps be founder of an Empire that would rival in glory that of Mexico or Peru."

Madison asked Congress to declare war on June 1, 1812. Congress obliged him two weeks later. The vote in the House was 79 to 49 for war, in the Senate 19 to 13. The close tally revealed deep divisions over the wisdom of fighting. The split was both sectional and partisan. Support for war came from the South and West, but also from Republicans in the populous middle states such as Pennsylvania and Virginia. Federalists in both North and South damned the conflict, but their stronghold was New England, which greeted the declaration of war with muffled bells, flags at half-mast, and public fasting.

Why should seafaring New England oppose the war for a free sea? The answer is that Federalists in the Northeast sympathized with Britain and resented the Republicans' sympathy with Napoleon, whom they regarded as the "Corsican butcher" and the "anti-Christ of the age." The Federalists also opposed the acquisition of Canada, which would merely add more agrarian states and increase Jeffersonian Republican voting strength. The bitterness of New England Federalists against "Mr. Madison's War" led them to treason or near-treason. They were determined, charged one Republican versifier,

To rule the nation if they could,
But see it damned if others should.

New England gold holders probably lent more dollars to the British Exchequer than to the federal Treasury. Federalist farmers sent huge quantities of supplies and foodstuffs to Canada, enabling British armies to invade New York. New England governors stubbornly refused to permit their militias to serve outside their own states. In a sense America had to fight two enemies simultaneously: old England and New England.

Thus perilously divided, the barely United States plunged into armed conflict against Britain, then the world's most powerful empire. No sober American could have much reasonable hope of victory, but by 1812 the Jeffersonian Republicans saw no other choice.

CHAPTER SUMMARY

The ideological conflicts of the early Republic culminated in the bitter election of 1800 between Adams and Jefferson. Despite the fierce rhetoric of the campaign, Jefferson's defeat of an incumbent president in the "Revolution of 1800" demonstrated that the infant Republic could peacefully transfer power from one party to another. The election of 1800 also signaled the decline of the conservative Federalist Party, which proved unable to adjust to the democratic future of American politics.

Jefferson, as a renowned political philosopher and idealist, came to Washington determined to restore what he saw as the original American revolutionary doctrines and to implement his Republican principles of limited and frugal government, strict construction, and an antimilitarist foreign policy. But Jefferson the practical politician had to compromise many of these goals, thereby moderating the Republican-Federalist ideological conflict.

The sharpest political conflicts occurred over the judiciary, where John Marshall worked effectively to enshrine the principles of judicial review and a strong federal government. Against his original intentions, Jefferson himself also enhanced federal power by waging war against the Barbary pirates and especially by his dramatic purchase of Louisiana from Napoleon. The Louisiana Purchase was Jefferson's greatest success, increasing national unity and pointing to America's long-term future in the West. But in the short term the vast geographical expansion fostered problems, such as Aaron Burr's secessionist scheme to break the West away from the United States.

Nevertheless, Jefferson became increasingly entangled in the horrific European wars between Napoleonic France and Britain, as both great powers obstructed American trade and violated freedom of the seas. Jefferson attempted to avoid war through his embargo policy, which damaged the American economy and stirred bitter opposition in New England.

Jefferson's successor, James Madison, faced more British assaults on American neutrality, as well as cries from western "war hawks" in his own party who wanted to defeat the Indians and seize Canada. Fearing for the very future of American republicanism, Madison reluctantly called for war in order to regain American national confidence. The nation went to war totally unprepared, bitterly divided, and devoid of any coherent strategy.

KEY TERMS

Revolution of 1800 (158)
Judiciary Act of 1801 (160)
midnight judges (160)
Marbury v. Madison (161)
Louisiana Purchase (163)
Corps of Discovery (163)
Orders in Council (164)
impressment (164)
Chesapeake affair (164)
Embargo Act (165)
Non-Intercourse Act (166)
Macon's Bill No. 2 (167)
war hawks (167)
Battle of Tippecanoe (167)

PEOPLE TO KNOW

Thomas Jefferson
Sally Hemings
Albert Gallatin
John Marshall
Napoleon Bonaparte
Robert R. Livingston
Toussaint L'Ouverture
Meriwether Lewis
William Clark
Sacajawea
Aaron Burr
James Madison
Tecumseh
Tenskwatawa ("the Prophet")

MindTap

MindTap is a fully online, highly personalized learning experience built upon Cengage Learning content. MindTap combines student learning tools—readings, multimedia, activities, and assessments—into a singular Learning Path that guides students through the course.

Chapter 12

The Second War for Independence and the Upsurge of Nationalism

1812–1824

The American continents . . . are henceforth not to be considered as subjects for future colonization by any European powers.

JAMES MONROE, DECEMBER 2, 1823

Chapter Outline

- Invasion of Canada, 1812
- The War on Land and Sea
- The Treaty of Ghent, 1814
- The Hartford Convention, 1814–1815
- A New National Identity
- "The American System"
- James Monroe and the Era of Good Feelings
- Westward Expansion
- The Missouri Compromise, 1820
- The Supreme Court under John Marshall
- Canada and Florida
- The Monroe Doctrine, 1823
- *Makers of America: Settlers of the Old Northwest*

The War of 1812 was an especially divisive and ill-fought war. There was no burning national anger, as there had been in 1807 following the *Chesapeake* outrage. The supreme lesson of the conflict was the folly of leading a divided and apathetic people into war. And yet, despite the unimpressive military outcome and the even less decisive negotiated peace, Americans came out of the war with a renewed sense of nationhood. For the next dozen years an awakened spirit of nationalism would inspire activities ranging from protecting manufacturing to building roads to defending the authority of the federal government over the states.

FOCUS QUESTIONS

1. Why was the War of 1812 so politically divisive and poorly fought by the United States, and how did the course of the war reflect these problems?
2. Why did the War of 1812, despite its stalemated outcome, lead to an outburst of proud postwar nationalism and an "era of good feelings" in the United States?
3. Why did a serious conflict over slavery suddenly burst on the American scene in 1819, and how did the Missouri Compromise resolve it (at least temporarily)?
4. How did John Marshall's Supreme Court promote the spirit of nationalism and counter growing sectionalism through its rulings in favor of federal power?
5. What were the origins and essential principles of the Monroe Doctrine, and what were its short- and long-term effects in Latin America and elsewhere?

CHRONOLOGY

1810	*Fletcher* v. *Peck* ruling asserts right of Supreme Court to invalidate state laws deemed unconstitutional	1817	Rush-Bagot agreement limits naval armament on Great Lakes
1812	Madison reelected president United States declares war on Britain	1818	Jackson invades Florida Anglo-American Convention
1812–1813	American invasions of Canada fail	1819	Panic of 1819 Spain cedes Florida to United States in Adams-Onís treaty *McCulloch* v. *Maryland* *Dartmouth College* v. *Woodward*
1813	Battle of the Thames Battle of Lake Erie		
1814	Battle of Horseshoe Bend Napoleon exiled to Elba British burn Washington, D.C. Battle of Plattsburgh Treaty of Ghent signed ending War of 1812	1820	Missouri Compromise Missouri and Maine admitted to Union Land Act of 1820 Monroe reelected
1814–1815	Hartford Convention Congress of Vienna	1823	Secretary Adams proposes Monroe Doctrine
1815	Battle of New Orleans Napoleon's army defeated at Waterloo	1824	*Gibbons* v. *Ogden*
1816	Second Bank of the United States founded Protectionist Tariff of 1816 Monroe elected president	1825	Erie Canal completed

⭐ On to Canada over Land and Lakes

War of 1812 (1812–1815) *Fought between Britain and the United States largely over the issues of trade and impressment. Though the war ended in a relative draw, it demonstrated America's willingness to defend its interests militarily, earning the young nation newfound respect from European powers.*

On the eve of the **War of 1812**, the regular army was ill trained, ill disciplined, and widely scattered. The army had to be supplemented by the even more poorly trained militia, who were sometimes distinguished by their speed of foot in leaving the battlefield. Some of the ranking generals were semi-senile heirlooms from the Revolutionary War, rusting on their laurels and lacking in vigor and vision.

The Americans' opening offensive strategy against the British in Canada was especially poorly conceived (see Map 12.1). Had the United States captured Montreal, the center of population and transportation, everything to the west might have died, just as the leaves of a tree wither when the trunk is girdled. But instead of laying ax to the trunk, the Americans frittered away their strength in the three-pronged invasion of 1812. The trio of invading forces that set out from Detroit, Niagara, and Lake Champlain were all beaten back shortly after they crossed the Canadian border.

By contrast, the British and Canadians displayed energy from the outset. Early in the war they captured the American fort of Michilimackinac, which commanded the upper Great Lakes and the Indian-inhabited area to the south and west. Their brilliant defensive operations were led by the inspired British General Isaac Brock, assisted (in the American camp) by "General Mud" and "General Confusion."

When several American land invasions of Canada were again hurled back in 1813, Americans looked for success on the water. Man for man and ship for ship, the American navy did much better than the army. In comparison to British ships, American craft on the whole were more skillfully handled, had better gunners, and were manned by non--press-gang crews who were burning to avenge numerous indignities. Similarly, the American frigates, notably the *Constitution* ("Old Ironsides"), had thicker sides, heavier firepower, and larger crews, of which one sailor in six was a free black.

Control of the Great Lakes was vital, and an energetic American naval officer, Oliver Hazard Perry, managed to build a fleet of green-timbered ships on the shores of Lake Erie,

***Constitution* and *Guerrière*, 1812** The *Guerrière* was heavily outweighed and outgunned, yet its British captain eagerly—and foolishly—sought combat. His ship was totally destroyed. Historian Henry Adams later concluded that this duel "raised the United States in one half hour to the rank of a first-class Power in the world." Today, the *U.S.S. Constitution*, berthed in Boston harbor, remains the oldest actively commissioned ship in the U.S. Navy.

manned by even greener seamen. When Perry captured a British fleet in a furious engagement on Lake Erie, he reported to his superior, "We have met the enemy and they are ours." Perry's victory and his slogan infused new life into the drooping American cause. Forced to withdraw from Detroit and Fort Malden, the retreating redcoats were overtaken by General William Henry Harrison's army and beaten at the Battle of the Thames in October 1813.

Despite these successes, the Americans by 1814, far from invading Canada, were grimly defending their own soil against the invading British. In Europe the diversionary power of Napoleon's European adversaries had vanquished him—temporarily as it turned out—by mid-1814, and had exiled the dangerous despot to the Mediterranean isle of Elba. The United States, which had so brashly provoked war behind the protective skirts of Napoleon, was now left to face the music alone. Thousands of victorious veteran redcoats began to pour into Canada from Europe.

Assembling some ten thousand crack troops, the British prepared in 1814 for a crushing blow into New York along the familiar lake-river route. In the absence of roads, the invader was forced to bring supplies over the Lake Champlain waterway. A weaker American fleet, commanded by the thirty-year-old Thomas Macdonough, challenged the British. The ensuing battle was desperately fought near Plattsburgh on September 11, 1814, on floating slaughterhouses. The American flagship at one point was in grave trouble. But Macdonough, unexpectedly turning his ship about with cables, confronted the enemy with a fresh broadside and snatched victory from the fangs of defeat.

The results of this heroic naval battle were momentous. The invading British army was forced to retreat. Macdonough thus saved at least upstate New York from conquest, New England from further disaffection, and the Union from possible dissolution. He also profoundly affected the concurrent negotiations of the Anglo-American peace treaty in Europe.

Despite its success on the Great Lakes, the American navy could not match the powerful British fleet in the Atlantic. Its wrath aroused, the Royal Navy finally retaliated by throwing a ruinous naval blockade along America's coast and by landing raiding parties

Map 12.1 Battles in the War of 1812

almost at will. American economic life, including fishing, was crippled. Customs revenues were choked off, and as the war continued the bankrupt Treasury was unable to meet its obligations.

★ Washington Burned and New Orleans Defended

A second formidable British force, numbering about four thousand, landed in the Chesapeake Bay area in August 1814. This British army advanced rapidly on Washington and easily dispersed some six thousand panicky American militia at Bladensburg, Maryland ("the Bladensburg races"). The invaders then entered the capital and set fire to most of the public buildings, including the Capitol and the White House. But while Washington burned, the Americans at Baltimore held firm. The British fleet hammered Fort McHenry with their cannons but could not capture the city. Francis Scott Key, a detained American anxiously watching the bombardment from a British ship, was inspired by the doughty defenders to write the words of "The Star-Spangled Banner." Set to the tune of a saucy English tavern refrain, the song quickly attained popularity.

A third British blow of 1814, aimed at New Orleans, menaced the entire Mississippi Valley. Gaunt and hawk-faced Andrew Jackson, fresh from crushing the southwest

Indians at the Battle of Horseshoe Bend, was placed in command. His hodgepodge force consisted of seven thousand sailors, regular army, pirates, and Frenchmen, as well as militiamen from Louisiana, Kentucky, and Tennessee. Among the defenders were two Louisiana regiments of free black volunteers, numbering about four hundred men. The Americans threw up their entrenchment, and in the words of a popular song:

> *Behind it stood our little force—*
> *None wished it to be greater;*
> *For ev'ry man was half a horse,*
> *And half an alligator.*

The overconfident British, numbering some eight thousand battle-seasoned veterans, blundered badly. They made the mistake of launching a frontal assault, on January 8, 1815, on the entrenched American riflemen and cannoneers. The attackers suffered the most devastating defeat of the entire war, losing over two thousand killed and wounded in half an hour, compared with only seventy for the Americans. It was an astonishing victory for Jackson and his men.

News of the American victory in the **Battle of New Orleans** struck the country "like a clap of thunder," according to one contemporary. Andrew Jackson became a national hero, as poets and politicians lined up to sing the praises of the defenders of New Orleans. It hardly mattered when word arrived that a peace treaty had been signed at Ghent, Belgium, ending the war two weeks before the battle. The United States had fought for honor as much as material gain. The Battle of New Orleans restored that honor, at least in American eyes, and unleashed a wave of nationalism and self-confidence.

Battle of New Orleans (January 1815) *Resounding victory of American forces against the British, restoring American confidence and fueling an outpouring of nationalism. Final battle of the War of 1812.*

★ The Treaty of Ghent

Tsar Alexander I of Russia, hard-pressed by Napoleon's army and not wanting his British ally to fritter away its strength in America, had proposed mediation between the clashing Anglo-Saxon cousins as early as 1812. The tsar's feeler eventually set in motion the machinery that brought five American peacemakers to the quaint Belgian city of Ghent in 1814. The bickering group was headed by early rising, puritanical John Quincy Adams, son of John Adams, who deplored the late-hour card playing of his high-living colleague Henry Clay.

Confident after their military successes, Britain's envoys made sweeping demands for a neutralized Indian buffer state in the Great Lakes region, control of the Great Lakes, and a substantial part of conquered Maine. The Americans flatly rejected these terms, and the talks appeared stalemated. But news of British reverses in upstate New York and Baltimore and increasing war-weariness in Britain itself made London more willing to compromise. Preoccupied with the **Congress of Vienna** (1814–1815) that concluded the Napoleonic wars and eyeing still-dangerous France, the British lion resigned itself to licking its wounds.

The **Treaty of Ghent**, signed on Christmas Eve, 1814, was essentially an armistice. Both sides simply agreed to stop fighting and to restore conquered territory. No mention was made of those grievances for which America had ostensibly fought: the Indian menace, search and seizure, Orders in Council, impressment, and confiscations. With neither side able to impose its will, the treaty negotiations—like the war itself—ended as a virtual draw. Relieved Americans boasted, "Not One Inch of Territory Ceded or Lost"— a watchword that contrasted strangely with the "On to Canada" rallying cry at the war's outset.

Congress of Vienna (1814–1815) *Convention of major European powers to redraw the boundaries of continental Europe after the defeat of Napoleonic France.*

Treaty of Ghent (1814) *Ended the War of 1812 in a virtual draw, restoring prewar borders but failing to address any of the grievances that first brought America into the war.*

In a letter to her friend Mercy Otis Warren, Abigail Adams (1744-1818) fretted that the British were taking advantage of Americans' disagreement over the War of 1812:

"We have our firesides, our comfortable habitations, our cities, our churches and our country to defend, our rights, privileges and independence to preserve. And for these are we not justly contending? Thus it appears to me. Yet I hear from our pulpits, and read from our presses, that it is an unjust, a wicked, a ruinous, and unnecessary war. . . . A house divided upon itself—and upon that foundation do our enemies build their hopes of subduing us."

★ Federalist Grievances and the Hartford Convention

Defiant New England remained a problem. It prospered during the conflict, owing largely to illicit trade with the enemy in Canada and to the absence of a British blockade until 1814. But the embittered opposition of the Federalists to the war continued unabated.

As the war dragged on, New England extremists became more vocal. The most spectacular manifestation of Federalist discontent was the ill-omened **Hartford Convention**. Late in 1814, when the British capture of New Orleans seemed imminent, Massachusetts issued a call for a convention at Hartford, Connecticut. Twenty-six prominent delegates from all of the New England states met in complete secrecy for about three weeks—December 15, 1814, to January 5, 1815—to discuss their grievances and to seek redress for their wrongs. The convention's final report was actually quite moderate. It demanded financial compensation to New England for lost trade, abolition of the "three-fifths" clause of the Constitution that gave the South added representation, and a single-term limit for the presidency—the last aimed at the much-resented "Virginia dynasty" of presidents. These and other proposed measures reflected Federalist fears that a once-proud New England was falling subservient to an agrarian South and West.

Three special envoys from Massachusetts brought these demands to the burned-out capital of Washington in early January 1815. The trio arrived just in time to be overwhelmed by the glorious news from New Orleans, followed by that from Ghent. As the rest of the nation congratulated itself on a glorious victory, New England's wartime complaints seemed petty at best and treasonous at worst. Pursued by the sneers and jeers of the press, the envoys slinked away in disgrace and sank into obscurity.

The Hartford resolutions, as it turned out, were the death dirge of the Federalist party. The Federalists were never again to mount a successful presidential campaign, and the party disappeared altogether in the 1820s.

Federalist doctrines of disunity, which long survived the party, blazed a portentous trail. Until 1815 there was far more talk of nullification and secession in New England than in any other section, including the South. The outright flouting of the Jeffersonian embargo and the later crippling of the war effort were the two most damaging acts of nullification in America prior to the events leading to the Civil War.

Hartford Convention (1814–1815) *Convention of Federalists from five New England states who opposed the War of 1812 and resented the strength of southern and western interests in Congress and in the White House.*

★ The Second War for American Independence

The War of 1812 was a small war, involving about six thousand Americans killed or wounded. It was but a footnote to the mighty European conflagration that had been ignited by the French Revolution and Napoleon's imperial ambitions. In 1812, when Napoleon invaded Russia with about 500,000 men, Madison tried to invade Canada with about 5,000 men. But if the American conflict was globally unimportant, it had huge consequences for the United States.

The Republic had shown that it would take sword in hand to resist what it regarded as grievous wrongs. Other nations developed a new respect for America's fighting prowess. America's emissaries abroad were henceforth treated with less scorn. In a diplomatic sense, if not in a military sense, the conflict could be called the Second War for American Independence.

A new nation, moreover, was welded in the fiery furnace of armed conflict. Sectionalism, now identified with discredited New England Federalists, was given a black eye. The painful events of the war glaringly revealed, as perhaps nothing else could have done, the folly of sectional disunity. In a sense, the most conspicuous casualty of the war was the Federalist party.

War heroes emerged, especially the two Indian-fighters, Andrew Jackson and William Henry Harrison. Both of them were to become president. Left in the lurch by their British friends at Ghent, the Indians were forced to make such terms as they could. They reluctantly consented, in a series of treaties, to relinquish vast areas of forested land north of the Ohio River.

Manufacturing prospered behind the wooden wall of the British blockade. In both an economic and a diplomatic sense, the War of 1812 bred greater American independence. The industries stimulated by the fighting rendered America less dependent on Europe's workshops.

Canadian patriotism and nationalism also received a powerful stimulus from the clash. Many Canadians felt betrayed by the Treaty of Ghent. They were especially aggrieved by the failure to secure an Indian buffer state or even mastery of the Great Lakes. Canadians fully expected the frustrated Yankees to return, and for a time the Americans and British engaged in a naval arms race on the Great Lakes. But in 1817 the **Rush-Bagot agreement** between Britain and the United States severely limited naval armament on the lakes. Better relations brought the last border fortifications down in the 1870s, with the happy result that the United States and Canada came to share the world's longest unfortified boundary—stretching 5,527 miles long.

After Napoleon's final defeat at Waterloo in 1815, Europe slumped into a peace of exhaustion. Deposed monarchs returned to battered thrones, as the Old World took the rutted road back to conservatism, illiberalism, and reaction. But the American people were largely unaffected by these European developments. Turning their backs on the Old World, they faced resolutely toward the untamed West—and toward the task of building their democracy.

Rush-Bagot agreement (1817) Signed by Britain and the United States, it established strict limits on naval armaments in the Great Lakes, a first step in the full demilitarization of the U.S.-Canadian border, completed in the 1870s.

★ Nascent Nationalism

The most impressive by-product of the War of 1812 was heightened nationalism—the spirit of nation-consciousness or national oneness. America may not have fought the war as one nation, but it emerged as one nation. The changed mood even manifested itself in the birth of a distinctively national literature. Washington Irving and James Fenimore

The White House and Capitol, by Anthony St. John Baker, 1826 This watercolor painting reveals the rustic conditions of the early days in the nation's capital. The President's House (now called the White House), on the left, was designed by Irish-born James Hoban and built between 1792 and 1800 in the neoclassical style. It has been the residence of every president since John Adams. When Thomas Jefferson moved into the house in 1801, he worked with architect Benjamin Henry Latrobe to expand it, creating two colonnades that were meant to conceal stables and storage. In 1814, during the War of 1812, the British army set the President's House ablaze, destroying the interior and charring much of the exterior. Reconstruction began almost immediately, and President James Monroe moved into a partially finished house in 1817. The Capital dome is visible in the background on the right. It, too, burned in 1814. Its rebuilding, not completed until 1830, was overseen by Boston's Charles Bulfinch.

Cooper attained international recognition in the 1820s as the nation's first writers of importance to use American scenes and themes. School textbooks, often British in an earlier era, were now being written by Americans for Americans. In the world of magazines, the highly intellectual *North American Review* began publication in 1815—the year of the triumph at New Orleans. Even American painters increasingly celebrated their native landscapes on their canvases.

A fresh nationalistic spirit could be recognized in many other areas as well. The revived Bank of the United States established by Congress in 1816 reflected nationalism in finance. A more handsome national capital began to rise from the ashes of Washington. The army was expanded to ten thousand men. The navy further covered itself with glory in 1815 when it administered a thorough beating to the piratical plunderers of North Africa. Stephen Decatur, naval hero of the War of 1812 and of the Barbary Coast expeditions, pungently captured the country's nationalist mood in a famous toast made on his return from the Mediterranean campaigns: "Our country! In her intercourse with foreign nations may she always be in the right; but our country, right or wrong!"

★ The American System

Nationalism likewise manifested itself in manufacturing. Patriotic Americans took pride in the factories that had recently mushroomed, largely as a result of the self-imposed embargoes and the war. When hostilities ended in 1815, British competitors tried to strangle the American war-baby factories in the cradle by cutting prices below cost and dumping goods on U.S. markets. In response, the infant industries bawled lustily for protection.

A nationalist Congress, out-Federalizing the old Federalists, responded by passing the path-breaking **Tariff of 1816**—the first tariff in American history instituted primarily for protection, not revenue. Its rates—roughly 20–25 percent on the value of dutiable imports—were not high enough to provide completely adequate safeguards, but the law was a bold beginning. A strongly protective trend was started that stimulated the appetites of the protected for more protection.

Nationalism was further highlighted by Henry Clay's grandiose plan for developing a profitable home market. Still radiating the nationalism of war-hawk days, Clay threw himself behind an elaborate scheme known by 1824 as the **American System**. This system had three main parts. The first was a strong banking system to provide easy and abundant credit. Then a high protective tariff would enable eastern manufacturing to flourish. Revenues gushing from the tariff would provide funds for the third component of the American System—a network of roads and canals, especially in the burgeoning Ohio Valley. Through these new arteries of transportation would flow foodstuffs and raw materials from the South and West to the North and East. In exchange, a stream of manufactured goods would flow in the return direction, knitting the country together economically and politically.

Persistent and eloquent demands by Henry Clay and others for internal improvements struck a responsive chord with the public. An outcry for better transportation, rising most noisily in the road-poor West, was one of the most striking aspects of the nationalism inspired by the War of 1812.

But attempts to secure federal funding for roads and canals stumbled on Republican constitutional scruples. Congress voted in 1817 to distribute $1.5 million to the states for internal improvements. But President Madison sternly vetoed the measure because he believed it to be unconstitutional, thereby forcing the individual states to undertake transportation construction programs on their own. The most important of these was the Erie Canal, triumphantly completed by New York in 1825. Jeffersonian Republicans, who had gulped down Hamiltonian **loose construction** on other important problems, choked on the idea of direct federal support for intrastate internal improvements. New England also strongly opposed federally constructed roads and canals because such outlets would further drain away population and create competing states beyond the mountains.

Tariff of 1816 *First protective tariff in American history, created primarily to shield New England manufacturers from the inflow of British goods after the War of 1812.*

American System (1820s) *Henry Clay's three-pronged system to promote American industry. Clay advocated a strong banking system, a protective tariff, and a federally funded transportation network.*

loose construction *Legal doctrine that the federal government can use powers not specifically granted or prohibited in the Constitution to carry out its constitutionally mandated responsibilities.*

The So-Called Era of Good Feelings

James Monroe—six feet tall, somewhat stooped, courtly, and mild mannered—was nominated for the presidency in 1816 by the Republicans. They thus undertook to continue the so-called Virginia dynasty of Washington, Jefferson, and Madison. The fading Federalists ran a candidate for the last time in their checkered history, and he was crushed by 183 electoral votes to 34. The vanquished Federalist party was gasping its dying breaths, leaving the field to the triumphant Republicans and one-party rule.

In James Monroe, the man and the times auspiciously met. As the last president to wear an old-style cocked hat, he straddled two generations: the bygone age of the Founding Fathers and the emergent age of nationalism. The serene Virginian with gray-blue eyes was in intellect and personal force the least distinguished of the first eight presidents. But Monroe was an experienced, level-headed executive, in tune with the public in a time that required sober administration, not heroics.

> Boston's Columbian Centinel *was not the only newspaper to regard President Monroe's early months as the Era of Good Feelings.* Washington's National Intelligencer *observed in July 1817:*
>
> "Never before, perhaps, since the institution of civil government, did the same harmony, the same absence of party spirit, the same national feeling, pervade a community. The result is too consoling to dispute too nicely about the cause."

President Monroe further cemented America's emerging nationalism with a goodwill tour in early 1817 that took him deep into Federalist New England and then westward as far as Detroit. The heartwarming welcome he received even in "the enemy's country" of New England ushered in what one Boston newspaper hailed as the "**Era of Good Feelings**," as the Monroe administrations have commonly been called ever since.

The Era of Good Feelings, unfortunately, was something of a misnomer. Considerable tranquility and prosperity did in fact smile on the early years of Monroe, but the period was a troubled one. The acute issues of the tariff, the bank, internal improvements, and the sale of public lands were hotly contested. Sectionalism was crystallizing, and the conflict over slavery was beginning to raise its hideous head.

Era of Good Feelings (1816–1824)
Popular name for the period of one-party, Republican, rule during James Monroe's presidency. The term obscures bitter conflicts over internal improvements, slavery, and the national bank.

The Panic of 1819 and the Curse of Hard Times

Much of the goodness went out of the good feelings in 1819, when a paralyzing economic panic descended on the country. This sudden financial collapse brought deflation, depression, bankruptcies, bank failures, unemployment, and the overcrowded pesthouses known as debtors' prisons.

This was the first national financial panic since President Washington took office. Many factors contributed to the catastrophe of 1819, but looming large was overspeculation in frontier lands. The Bank of the United States, through its western branches, had become deeply involved in this popular type of outdoor gambling.

Financial paralysis from the panic, which lasted for several years, dealt a rude setback to the nationalistic ardor. The West was especially hard hit. When the pinch came, the Bank of the United States forced the speculative ("wildcat") western banks to the wall and foreclosed mortgages on countless farms. All this was technically legal but politically unwise. In the eyes of western debtors, the nationalist Bank of the United States soon became a kind of financial devil.

The **panic of 1819** also created backwashes in the political and social world. The poorer classes—the one-suspender men and their families—were severely strapped, and in their troubles was sown the seed of Jacksonian democracy. Hard times also directed attention to the inhumanity of imprisoning debtors. Mounting agitation against that often-cruel practice bore fruit in remedial legislation in an increasing number of states.

panic of 1819 *Severe financial crisis brought on primarily by the efforts of the Bank of the United States to curb overspeculation on western lands. It disproportionately affected the poorer classes, especially in the West, sowing the seeds of Jacksonian democracy.*

⭐ Growing Pains of the West

The onward march to the West continued: Nine frontier states had joined the original thirteen between 1791 and 1819. With an eye to preserving the North–South sectional balance, most of these commonwealths had been admitted alternately, free or slave. (See Admission of States in the Appendix.)

Why this explosive expansion? In part, it was simply a continuation of the generations-old westward movement, which had been going on since early colonial days. In addition, the siren song of cheap land—"the Ohio fever"—had a special appeal to European immigrants. With the return of peace in Europe and America, eager newcomers from abroad were beginning to stream down the gangplanks in impressive numbers. Land exhaustion in the older southern tobacco states, where the soil was "mined" rather than cultivated, likewise drove people westward. Glib speculators accepted small down payments, making it easier to buy new holdings.

The western boom was stimulated by additional developments. Acute economic distress during the embargo years turned many pinched faces toward the setting sun. The crushing of the Indians in the Northwest and South by Generals Harrison and Jackson pacified the frontier and opened up vast virgin tracts of land. The building of highways improved the land routes to the Ohio Valley. Noteworthy was the Cumberland Road, begun in 1811, which ultimately ran from western Maryland to Illinois. The arrival of the first steamboat on western waters, also in 1811, heralded a new era of upstream navigation.

But the West, despite the inflow of settlers, was still weak in population and influence. It could only make its voice heard when it formed alliances with other sections. Western pioneers' principal demands were for cheap federal land, cheap transportation, and cheap money issued by its own "wildcat" banks rather than the restrictive Bank of the United States. With the passage of the **Land Act of 1820**, which authorized a buyer to purchase eighty acres at a minimum price of $1.25 an acre, the West began to make headway in achieving these goals (see "Makers of America: Settlers of the Old Northwest," p. 182).

Land Act of 1820 *Fueled the settlement of the Northwest and Missouri Territories by lowering the price of public land. Also prohibited the purchase of federal acreage on credit, thereby eliminating one of the causes of the panic of 1819.*

⭐ Slavery and Sectional Balance

Sectional tensions were stunningly revealed in 1819, when the territory of Missouri knocked on the doors of Congress seeking admission as a slave state. This fertile area contained sufficient population to warrant statehood. But the House of Representatives stymied the plans of the Missourians by passing the incendiary **Tallmadge amendment**, which stipulated that no more slaves should be brought into Missouri and also provided for the gradual emancipation of children born to slave parents already there. A roar of anger burst from slaveholding southerners.

Tallmadge amendment (1819) *Failed proposal to prohibit the importation of slaves into Missouri Territory and pave the way for gradual emancipation. Southerners vehemently opposed the amendment, which they perceived as a threat to the sectional balance between North and South.*

Southerners saw in the Tallmadge amendment, which they eventually managed to defeat in the Senate, an ominous threat to the sectional balance. When the Constitution was adopted in 1788, the North and South were running neck and neck in wealth and population. But with every passing decade, the North was becoming wealthier and also more thickly settled—an advantage reflected in an increasing northern majority in the House of Representatives. Yet in the Senate, with eleven free states and eleven slave states, the southerners had maintained equality. They were therefore in a good position to thwart any northern effort to interfere with the expansion of slavery, and they did not want to lose this equal balance in the Senate.

The future of the slave system caused southerners profound concern. Missouri was the first state entirely west of the Mississippi River to be carved out of the Louisiana Purchase, and the Missouri emancipation amendment might set a damaging precedent for all the rest of the area. Even more disquieting was another possibility. If Congress could abolish the **peculiar institution** in Missouri, might it not attempt to do likewise in the older states of the South? The wounds of the Constitutional Convention of 1787 were once more ripped open.

peculiar institution *Widely used term for the institution of American slavery in the South. Its use in the first half of the nineteenth century reflected a growing division between the North, where slavery was gradually abolished, and the South, where slavery became increasingly entrenched.*

Map 12.2 The Missouri Compromise and Slavery, 1820–1821 Note the 36° 30' line. In the 1780s Thomas Jefferson had written of slavery in America: "Indeed I tremble for my country when I reflect that God is just; that his justice cannot sleep forever; that . . . the Almighty has no attribute which can take side with us in such a contest." Now, at the time of the Missouri Compromise, Jefferson feared that his worst forebodings were coming to pass. "I considered it at once," he said of the Missouri question, "as the knell of the Union."

Burning moral questions also protruded, even though the main issue was political and economic balance. A small but growing group of antislavery agitators in the North seized the occasion to raise an outcry against the evils of slavery. They were determined that the plague of human bondage should not spread farther into the untainted territories.

★ The Uneasy Missouri Compromise

Deadlock in Washington was at length broken in 1820 by the time-honored American solution of compromise. Courtly Henry Clay of Kentucky played a leading role as a conciliator. Congress first agreed to admit Missouri as a slave state. But at the same time, free-soil Maine, which until then had been part of Massachusetts, was admitted as a separate free state. The balance between North and South was thus kept at twelve states each and remained there for the next fifteen years. Although Missouri was permitted to retain slaves, all future bondage was prohibited in the remainder of the Louisiana Purchase north of the line of 36° 30'—the southern boundary of Missouri (see Map 12.2).

Neither North nor South was completely happy with this horse-trading adjustment, though they had each gained something as well as yielded something. Fortunately, the Missouri Compromise lasted thirty-four years—a vital formative period in the life of the young Republic—and during that time it preserved the shaky compact of the states. Yet the embittered dispute over slavery heralded the future breakup of the Union. Ever after, the morality of the South's "peculiar institution" was an issue that could not be swept under the rug. The Missouri Compromise only ducked the question—it did not resolve it. Sooner or later, Thomas Jefferson predicted, it will "burst on us as a tornado."

Missouri Compromise (1820)
Allowed Missouri to enter as a slave state but preserved the balance between North and South by carving free-soil Maine out of Massachusetts and prohibiting slavery from territories acquired in the Louisiana Purchase, north of the line of 36°30'.

Makers of America

Settlers of the Old Northwest

The Old Northwest beckoned to settlers after the War of 1812. The withdrawal of the British protector weakened the Indians' grip on the territory. Then the canal and highway boom of the 1820s opened broad arteries along which the westward movement flowed.

The first wave of newcomers came mainly from Kentucky, Tennessee, and the upland regions of Virginia and the Carolinas. Most migrants were rough-hewn white farmers who had been pushed from good land to bad by an expanding plantation economy. Some settlers acquired land for the first time. John Palmer, whose family left Kentucky for Illinois in 1831, recalled his father telling him "of land so cheap that we could all be landholders, where men were *equal*." Migrants from the South settled mainly in the southern portions of Ohio, Indiana, and Illinois.

Having escaped from a lowly social position in a slaveholding society, many of these new immigrants sought to prevent the spread of slavery by enacting Black Codes in their new territories that prevented blacks from following them. They wanted their own democratic communities, free of rich planters and African Americans alike.

If southern "Butternuts," as these settlers were called, dominated settlement in the 1820s, the next decade brought equally land-starved Yankees from the Northeast. Yankee settlers came especially to the northern parts of Ohio, Indiana, and Illinois. Unlike the Butternuts who wanted to quit forever the imposing framework of southern society, northerners hoped to re-create the world they had left behind.

Conflict soon emerged between Yankees and southerners. As self-sufficient farmers who did not produce for the market, southerners viewed the northern newcomers as inhospitable, greedy, and excessively ambitious. Northerners, in turn, viewed the southerners as uncivilized, a "coon dog and butcher knife tribe" with no interest in education, self-improvement, or agricultural innovation. While Yankees advocated taxes to establish public schools and fund roads and canals, southerners opposed such efforts, especially public schooling. Religion also divided settlers. Northerners typically embraced denominations such as Congregationalism and Presbyterianism that supported a learned ministry. Southerners embraced the more revivalist Methodists and Baptists and preferred humble, uneducated preacher-farmers who would, in their eyes, stay closer to the Lord and his people.

As the population swelled and the region acquired its own character, the stark contrasts between northerners and southerners started to fade. Some residents such as Abraham Lincoln, with roots in Kentucky, came to adopt views more akin to those of the Yankees than the southerners. Railroads and Great Lakes shipping tied the region economically ever more tightly to the Northeast. Yankees and southerners sometimes allied as new kinds of economic, ethnic, and religious cleavages emerged.

Still, echoes of the clash between Yankees and Butternuts persisted. During the Civil War, the southern counties of Ohio, Indiana, and Illinois, where southerners had first settled, harbored sympathizers with the South and served as a key area for Confederate military infiltration into the North. Decades later these same counties became a stronghold of the Ku Klux Klan. The Old Northwest may have become firmly anchored to the economy of the Northeast, but vestiges of its early dual personality persisted.

The Missouri Compromise and the concurrent panic of 1819 should have dimmed the political star of President Monroe. Certainly both unhappy events had a dampening effect on the Era of Good Feelings. But smooth-spoken James Monroe was so popular, and the Federalist opposition so weak, that he received every electoral vote in the election of 1820 except one. Unanimity was an honor reserved for George Washington.

★ John Marshall and Judicial Nationalism

McCulloch v. Maryland (1819)
Supreme Court case that strengthened federal authority and upheld the constitutionality of the Bank of the United States by establishing that the State of Maryland did not have power to tax the bank.

The upsurging nationalism of the post-Ghent years, despite the ominous setbacks concerning slavery, was further reflected and reinforced by the Supreme Court. The high tribunal continued to be dominated by the tall, thin, and aggressive Chief Justice John Marshall. And many of Marshall's most famous decisions bolstered the power of the federal government at the expense of the states.

A notable case in this category was *McCulloch v. Maryland* (1819). The suit involved an attempt by the state of Maryland to destroy a branch of the Bank of the United States by imposing a tax on its notes. John Marshall, speaking for the Court, declared the bank constitutional by invoking the Hamiltonian doctrine of implied powers (see pp. 143–144). At the same time, he strengthened federal authority and slapped at state infringements when he denied the right of Maryland to tax the bank, with the ringing declaration that "the power to tax is the power to destroy."

Marshall's ruling in this case gave the doctrine of loose construction its most famous formulation. The Constitution, he said, was "intended to endure for ages to come and, consequently, to be adapted to the various crises of human affairs." Finally, he declared, "Let the end be legitimate, let it be within the scope of the Constitution, and all means which are appropriate, which are plainly adapted to that end, which are not prohibited, but consist with the letter and spirit of the Constitution, are constitutional." Five years later, in the "steamboat case" of *Gibbons v. Ogden* (1824), Marshall again upheld federal supremacy by striking down New York's awarding of a monopoly on waterborne commerce between New Jersey and New York to a private company.

Another set of Marshall's decisions bolstered judicial barriers against democratic or demagogic attacks on property rights. The notorious case of *Fletcher v. Peck* (1810) arose when the Georgia legislature, swayed by bribery, granted 35 million acres in the Yazoo River country (present-day Mississippi) to private speculators. The next legislature, yielding to an angry public outcry, canceled the crooked transaction. But the Supreme Court, with Marshall presiding, decreed that the legislative grant was a contract (even though fraudulently secured) and that the Constitution forbids state laws "impairing" contracts (see Art. I, Sec. X, para. 1). The decision is perhaps most noteworthy for further protecting property rights against popular pressures. It was one of the earliest clear assertions of the right of the Court to invalidate state laws conflicting with the federal Constitution.

A similar principle was upheld in the case of *Dartmouth College v. Woodward* (1819), perhaps the best-remembered of Marshall's decisions. The college had been granted a charter by King George III in 1769, but the democratic New Hampshire state legislature had seen fit to change it. Dartmouth appealed the case, employing as counsel its most distinguished alumnus, Daniel Webster, himself an ardent nationalist. The "Godlike Daniel" pulled out all the stops of his tear-inducing eloquence when he declaimed, "It is, sir, as I have said, a small college. And yet there are those who love it." Marshall put the states firmly in their place when he ruled in Dartmouth's favor that the original charter must stand. It was a contract, and the Constitution protected contracts against state encroachments. The *Dartmouth* decision had the fortunate effect of safeguarding business enterprise from domination by state governments. But it had the unfortunate effect of creating a precedent that enabled chartered corporations, in later years, to escape the handcuffs of needed public control.

Marshall's decisions are felt even today. In this sense his nationalism was the most tenaciously enduring of the era. He buttressed the federal Union and helped to create a stable, nationally uniform environment for business. In an age when America was veering toward stronger popular control, Marshall almost single-handedly shaped the Constitution along conservative, centralizing lines that ran somewhat counter to the dominant spirit of the new country. Through him the conservative Hamiltonians partly triumphed from the tomb.

> *While the debate over Missouri was raging, Thomas Jefferson (1743–1826) wrote to a correspondent:*
>
> "The Missouri question . . . is the most portentous one which ever yet threatened our Union. In the gloomiest moment of the revolutionary war I never had any apprehensions equal to what I feel from this source. . . . [The] question, like a firebell in the night, awakened and filled me with terror. . . . [With slavery] we have a wolf by the ears, and we can neither hold him nor safely let him go."
>
> *John Quincy Adams confided to his diary:*
>
> "I take it for granted that the present question is a mere preamble—a title-page to a great, tragic volume."

Gibbons v. Ogden (1824) Suit over whether New York State could grant a monopoly to a ferry operating on interstate waters. The ruling reasserted that Congress had the sole power to regulate interstate commerce.

Fletcher v. Peck (1810) Established firmer protection for private property and asserted the right of the Supreme Court to invalidate state laws in conflict with the federal Constitution.

Dartmouth College v. Woodward (1819) Supreme Court case that sustained Dartmouth University's original charter against changes proposed by the New Hampshire state legislature, thereby protecting corporations from domination by state governments.

★ Sharing Oregon and Acquiring Florida

The robust nationalism of the years after the War of 1812 was likewise reflected in foreign policy. To this end, the nationalistic President Monroe teamed with his nationalistic secretary of state, John Quincy Adams, the cold and scholarly son of the frosty ex-president.

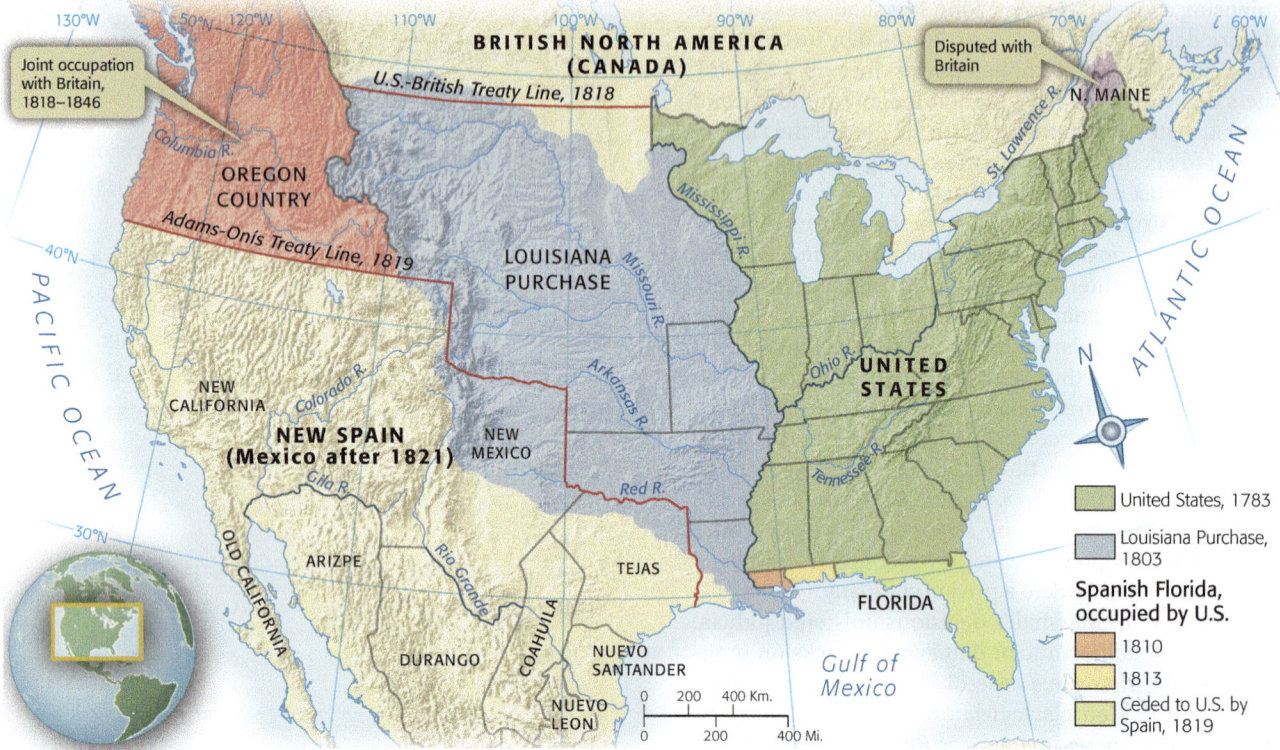

Map 12.3 U.S.-British Boundary Settlement, 1818 Note that the United States gained considerable territory by securing a treaty boundary rather than the natural boundary of the Missouri River watershed. The line of 49° was extended westward to the Pacific Ocean under the Treaty of 1846 with Britain.

The younger Adams, a statesman of the first rank, happily rose above the ingrown Federalist sectionalism of his native New England and proved to be one of the great secretaries of state.

To its credit, the Monroe administration negotiated the much-underrated **Anglo-American Convention** of 1818 with Britain. This pact fixed the vague northern limits of Louisiana along the forty-ninth parallel from the Lake of the Woods (in present-day Minnesota) to the Rocky Mountains (see Map 12.3). The treaty also provided for a ten-year joint occupation of the untamed Oregon country, without a surrender of the rights or claims of either America or Britain.

To the south lay semitropical Spanish Florida, which many Americans believed geography and providence had destined to become part of the United States. Americans already claimed West Florida, where uninvited American settlers had torn down the hated Spanish flag in 1810. Congress ratified this grab in 1812, and during the War of 1812 a small American army seized the Mobile region. But the bulk of Florida remained under Spanish rule.

When an epidemic of revolutions in South America, beginning in 1816, led to the birth of several new republics there, Spain was forced to denude Florida of troops in a vain attempt to squelch the rebels. General Andrew Jackson, idol of the West and scourge of the Indians, saw opportunity in the undefended swamplands. On the pretext that hostile Seminole Indians and fugitive slaves were using Florida as a refuge, Jackson secured a commission to enter Spanish territory, punish the Indians, and recapture the runaways. But the Monroe administration ordered him to respect all posts under the Spanish flag.

Early in 1818 Jackson swept across the Florida border with all the fury of an avenging angel. He hanged two Indian chiefs and executed two British subjects for assisting the Indians. He also seized the two most important Spanish forts in the area, St. Marks and Pensacola, where he deposed the Spanish governor.

Anglo-American Convention (1818) *Signed by Britain and the United States, the pact allowed New England fishermen access to Newfoundland fisheries, established the northern border of Louisiana Territory, and provided for the joint occupation of the Oregon Country for ten years.*

Jackson had clearly exceeded his instructions from Washington. Alarmed, President Monroe consulted his cabinet. Its members were for disavowing or disciplining the overzealous Jackson—all except the lone wolf John Quincy Adams, who refused to howl with the pack. An ardent patriot and nationalist, the flinty New Englander took the offensive and demanded huge concessions from Spain.

In the mislabeled **Florida Purchase Treaty** of 1819, Spain ceded Florida as well as shadowy Spanish claims to Oregon, in exchange for America's abandonment of equally murky claims to Texas, soon to become part of independent Mexico. The hitherto vague western boundary of Louisiana was made to zigzag northwesterly toward the Rockies to the forty-second parallel and then to turn due west to the Pacific, dividing Oregon from Spanish holdings.

Florida Purchase Treaty (Adams-Onís Treaty) (1819) *Under the agreement, Spain ceded Florida to the United States, and the two nations agreed on the southwestern boundary of the Louisiana Purchase. Spain retained the territory from Texas to California while abandoning its claims to the Oregon country.*

★ The Menace of Monarchy in America

After the Napoleonic nightmare, the rethroned autocrats of Europe banded together in a kind of monarchical protective association. Determined to restore the good old days, they undertook to stamp out the democratic tendencies that had sprouted from soil they considered richly manured by the ideals of the French Revolution. The world must be made safe *from* democracy.

The crowned despots acted promptly. With complete ruthlessness, they smothered the embers of rebellions in Italy (1821) and in Spain (1823). According to the European rumor factory, they were also gazing across the Atlantic. Russia, Austria, Prussia, and France, acting in partnership, would presumably send powerful fleets and armies to the revolted colonies of Spanish America and there restore the autocratic Spanish king to his ancestral domains.

Many Americans were alarmed. Sympathetic to democratic revolutions everywhere, they had cheered when the Latin American republics rose from the ruins of monarchy. Americans feared that if the European powers intervened in the New World, the cause of republicanism would suffer irreparable harm. The physical security of the United States—the mother lode of democracy—would be endangered by the proximity of powerful and unfriendly forces.

The southward push of the Russian bear from the chilly region now known as Alaska had already publicized the menace of monarchy to North America. In 1821 the tsar of Russia issued a decree extending Russian jurisdiction over one hundred miles to a line that embraced most of the coast of present-day British Columbia. The Russians had already established trading posts almost as far south as San Francisco Bay. The fear prevailed in the United States that the Russians were planning to cut the Republic off from California, its prospective window to the Pacific.

Britain, still Ruler of the Seas, recoiled from joining the continental European powers in crushing the newly won liberties of the Latin Americans. These revolutionaries had thrown open their monopoly-bound ports to outside trade, and British shippers, as well as Americans, had found the profits sweet. Accordingly, in August 1823, George Canning, the haughty British foreign secretary, approached the American minister in London to ask if the United States would join Britain in warning the European despots to keep their harsh hands off the Latin American republics. The American minister, lacking instructions, referred this fateful scheme to his superiors in Washington.

★ Monroe and His Doctrine

The tenacious nationalist, Secretary Adams, was hardheaded enough to be wary of Britons bearing gifts. Why should the lordly British, with the mightiest navy afloat, need America as an ally—an America that had neither naval nor military strength? Such a union, argued Adams, was undignified—like a tiny American "cockboat" sailing "in the wake of the British man-of-war."

President Monroe Thinking Globally Surrounded by his cabinet, the president is depicted explaining the Monroe Doctrine. Secretary of State John Quincy Adams is the first on the left; Secretary of War John C. Calhoun is the third from the right.

Monroe Doctrine (1823) *Statement delivered by President James Monroe, warning European powers to refrain from seeking any new territories in the Americas. The United States largely lacked the power to back up the pronouncement, which was actually enforced by the British, who sought unfettered access to Latin American markets.*

Adams, ever alert, thought that he detected a joker in the Canning proposal. If Canning could seduce the United States into guaranteeing existing territorial arrangements in the New World, America's hands would be morally tied against its own expansion. Adams suspected—correctly—that European powers had no definite plans for invading the Americas. In any event the British navy would prevent hostile fleets from interfering with South American markets, so Adams decided it was safe for Uncle Sam to blow a defiant nationalistic blast at all Europe.

The **Monroe Doctrine** was born in 1823, when the nationalistic Adams won the nationalistic Monroe over to his way of thinking. The president, in his regular annual message to Congress on December 2, 1823, incorporated a stern warning to the European powers. The two basic features of Monroe's message were (1) noncolonization and (2) nonintervention.

Monroe first directed his verbal volley primarily at the Russian bear in the Northwest. He proclaimed, in effect, that the era of colonization in the Americas had ended and that henceforth the hunting season was permanently closed. What the great powers had they might keep, but neither they nor any other Old World governments could seize or otherwise acquire more.

At the same time Monroe trumpeted a warning blast against foreign intervention. He was clearly concerned with regions to the south, where the fledgling Latin American republics were extremely vulnerable. Monroe bluntly directed the crowned heads of Europe to keep their hated monarchical systems out of the Western Hemisphere. For its part the United States would not intervene in the war that the Greeks were then fighting against the Turks for their independence.

⭐ Monroe's Doctrine Appraised

The ermined monarchs of Europe were angered at Monroe's doctrine. Having resented the incendiary American experiment from the beginning, they were deeply offended by Monroe's high-flown declaration—all the more so because of the gulf between America's pretentious pronouncements and its puny military strength. But though offended by the upstart Yankees, the European powers found their hands tied, and their frustration increased their annoyance. Even if they had worked out plans for invading the Americas, they would have been helpless before the booming broadsides of the British navy.

Monroe's solemn warning made little splash in the newborn republics to the south. Anyone could see that Uncle Sam was only secondarily concerned about his neighbors, because he was primarily concerned about defending himself against future invasion. Only a relatively few educated Latin Americans knew of the message, and they generally recognized that the British navy—not the paper pronouncement of James Monroe—stood between them and a hostile Europe.

In truth, Monroe's message did not have very much contemporary significance. Americans applauded it and then forgot it. Not until 1845 did President James Polk revive it, and not until midcentury did it become an important national dogma.

The Monroe Doctrine might more accurately have been called the Self-Defense Doctrine. President Monroe was concerned basically with the security of his own country—not of Latin America. The United States has never willingly permitted a powerful foreign nation to secure a foothold near its strategic Caribbean vitals. Yet in the absence of the British navy or other allies, the strength of the Monroe Doctrine has never been greater than America's power to eject the trespasser.

The Monroe Doctrine has had a long career of ups and downs. It was never law—domestic or international. It was not, technically speaking, even a pledge or an agreement. It was merely a simple statement of the policy of President Monroe. What one president says, another may unsay. And Monroe's presidential successors have ignored, revived, distorted, or expanded the original version, chiefly by adding interpretations. In 1823 the Monroe Doctrine was largely an expression of post-1812 American nationalism directed at a specific menace, and hence a kind of period piece. But the doctrine proved to be the most famous and long-lived offspring of that nationalism. While giving vent to a spirit of patriotism, it simultaneously deepened the American illusion of isolationism. Many Americans falsely concluded, then and later, that the Republic was in fact insulated from European dangers simply because it wanted to be.

Contending Voices

Sizing Up the Monroe Doctrine

Prince Klemens von Metternich (1773–1859), the fabled foreign minister of the Austrian empire from 1809 to 1848, greeted the Monroe Doctrine with scathing contempt in a letter in 1824:

"The United States of America . . . have astonished Europe with a new act of revolt. . . . They have distinctly and clearly announced their intention to set not only power against power, but, to express it more exactly, altar against altar. . . . If this flood of evil doctrines should extend over the whole of America, what would become of our religious and political institutions, and of the moral force of our governments?"

A newspaper in the Latin American nation of Colombia, meanwhile, breathed defiance at Europe and lauded Monroe's proclamation:

"The United States has now begun to play among the civilized nations of the world that powerful and majestic role which befits the oldest and most powerful nation of our hemisphere. . . . [T]he American continent is now so free and independent that henceforth it cannot be made the theater of colonization by any European power. Indeed the Americans of the North and of the South of this continent shall not again behold in their lands those hordes of foreigners, who, with the cross in one hand and a dagger in the other, would disturb the happiness and the peace which they today enjoy."

Why did the European and American perspectives on the Monroe Doctrine diverge so radically?

CHAPTER SUMMARY

Americans began the War of 1812 with high hopes of conquering Canada and delivering a severe blow to their British tormentors. But their strategy and efforts were badly flawed, and before long British and Canadian forces had thrown the United States on the defensive. The Americans fared somewhat better in naval warfare on the Great Lakes, but by 1814 the British had burned Washington and were threatening elsewhere. The Treaty of Ghent in 1814 ended the war in a stalemate that solved none of the original issues. But largely because of Andrew Jackson's "postwar" victory in the Battle of New Orleans in 1815, Americans counted the war a success and increasingly turned away from European affairs and toward isolationism.

Despite some secessionist talk by New Englanders at the Hartford Convention, the ironic outcome of the divisive and near-disastrous war was a strong surge of American nationalism and unity. Partisan political conflict disappeared during the "Era of Good Feelings" under President Madison. A fervent new nationalism appeared in diverse areas of culture, economics, and foreign policy.

But the Era of Good Feelings was soon threatened by the economic panic of 1819, caused largely by excessive land speculation and unstable banks. An even more serious threat to national unity came from the first major sectional dispute over slavery, which was postponed but not really resolved by the Missouri Compromise of 1820.

Under Chief Justice John Marshall, the Supreme Court further enhanced its role as the major force upholding a powerful national government and conservative defense of property rights. Marshall's rulings partially checked the general movement toward states' rights and popular democracy.

Nationalism also led to a more assertive American foreign policy. Andrew Jackson's military adventures in Spanish Florida resulted in the forced purchase of that territory by the United States. American fears of European intervention in Latin America encouraged President Monroe and Secretary of State J. Q. Adams to declare the Monroe Doctrine. The announcement had little immediate practical effect, but it carried large consequences for the future of United States foreign policy in the Americas.

KEY TERMS

War of 1812 (172)
Battle of New Orleans (174)
Congress of Vienna (174)
Treaty of Ghent (174)
Hartford Convention (176)
Rush-Bagot agreement (177)
Tariff of 1816 (178)
American System (178)
loose construction (178)
Era of Good Feelings (179)
panic of 1819 (179)
Land Act of 1820 (180)
Tallmadge amendment (180)
peculiar institution (180)
Missouri Compromise (181)
McCulloch v. Maryland (182)
Gibbons v. Ogden (183)
Fletcher v. Peck (183)
Dartmouth College v. Woodward (183)
Anglo-American Convention (184)
Florida Purchase Treaty (Adams-Onís Treaty) (185)
Monroe Doctrine (186)

PEOPLE TO KNOW

Isaac Brock
Oliver Hazard Perry
Thomas Macdonough
Francis Scott Key
James Monroe
George Canning

 MindTap is a fully online, highly personalized learning experience built upon Cengage Learning content. MindTap combines student learning tools—readings, multimedia, activities, and assessments—into a singular Learning Path that guides students through the course.

Chapter 13

The Rise of a Mass Democracy
1824–1840

In the full enjoyment of the gifts of Heaven and the fruits of superior industry, economy, and virtue, every man is equally entitled to protection by law; but when the laws undertake to add to those natural and just advantages artificial distinctions . . . and exclusive privileges . . . the humble members of society—the farmers, mechanics, and laborers . . . have a right to complain of the injustice of their government.

ANDREW JACKSON, 1832

Chapter Outline

- The "Corrupt Bargain" of 1824
- President John Quincy Adams, 1825–1829
- The Triumph of Andrew Jackson, 1828
- The "Tariff of Abominations," 1828
- The Spoils System
- The South Carolina Nullification Crisis, 1832–1833
- Indian Removal
- Jackson's War on the Bank of the United States
- The Emergence of the Whig Party, 1836
- Martin Van Buren and the Depression of 1837
- The Texas Revolution
- William Henry Harrison's "Log Cabin" Campaign, 1840
- The Establishment of the Two-Party System
- Thinking Globally: Alexis de Tocqueville on Democracy in America and Europe
- Examining the Evidence: Satiric Bank Note, 1837
- Varying Viewpoints: What Was Jacksonian Democracy?

The so-called Era of Good Feelings was never entirely tranquil, but even the illusion of national consensus was shattered by the panic of 1819 and the Missouri Compromise of 1820. Economic distress and the slavery issue raised the political stakes in the 1820s and 1830s. Vigorous political conflict, once feared, came to be celebrated as necessary for the health of democracy. New political parties emerged. A new chapter opened in the history of American—and world—politics, as many European societies began haltingly to expand their electorates and broaden democratic practices. The American political landscape of 1824 was similar, in its broad outlines, to that of 1796. By 1840 those eighteenth-century politics would be almost unrecognizable.

The deference, apathy, and virtually nonexistent party organizations of the Era of Good Feelings yielded to the boisterous democracy, frenzied vitality, and strong political parties of the Jacksonian era. The old suspicion of political parties as illegitimate disrupters of society's natural harmony gave way to an acceptance, even a celebration, of the sometimes wild contentiousness of political life.

In 1828 an energetic new party, the Democrats, captured the White House. By the 1830s the Democrats faced an equally vigorous opposition party in the form of the Whigs. This two-party system institutionalized divisions that had vexed the Revolutionary generation and came to constitute an important part of the nation's checks and balances on political power.

New forms of politicking emerged in this era, as candidates used banners, badges, parades, barbecues, free drinks, and baby kissing to get out the vote. Voter turnout rose dramatically; only about one-quarter of eligible voters cast a ballot in the presidential election of 1824, but that proportion doubled in 1828, and in the election of 1840 it reached 78 percent. Everywhere people flexed their political muscles.

FOCUS QUESTIONS

1. How did John Quincy Adams's victory through an alleged "corrupt bargain" in the election of 1824 set the stage for Andrew Jackson's election as the popular hero of the Democratic party in 1828 and the emergence of a new democratic politics?

CHRONOLOGY

1822	Vesey slave rebellion conspiracy in Charleston, South Carolina	1832–1833	South Carolina Nullification Crisis
1823	Mexico opens Texas to American settlers	1836	Bank of the United States expires Specie Circular issued Bureau of Indian Affairs established Battle of the Alamo Battle of San Jacinto Texas wins independence from Mexico Van Buren elected president
1824	Lack of electoral majority for presidency throws election into the House of Representatives		
1825	House elects John Quincy Adams president		
1828	Tariff of 1828 ("Tariff of Abominations") Jackson elected president *The South Carolina Exposition* published		
		1837	Seminole Indians defeated and most eventually removed from Florida Panic of 1837 United States recognizes republic of Texas but refuses annexation
1830	Indian Removal Act		
1831–1832	Alexis de Tocqueville tours United States		
1832	"Bank War"—Jackson vetoes bill to recharter Bank of the United States Reform Bill in Britain expands electorate Tariff of 1832 Jackson defeats Clay for presidency Black Hawk War	1838–1839	Cherokee Indians removed on "Trail of Tears"
		1840	Independent Treasury established Harrison defeats Van Buren for presidency

2. How did Jackson's policies of westward expansion and Indian removal lead to the "Trail of Tears" to Oklahoma and the Seminole Wars in Florida?
3. How did Andrew Jackson's "war" against the Second Bank of the United States fuel popular democracy as well as lead to the formation of the anti-Jackson Whig party?
4. What were the causes of the Texas revolution and independence, and why did efforts to bring Texas into the Union stir such sharp controversy?

★ The "Corrupt Bargain" of 1824

corrupt bargain *Alleged deal between presidential candidates John Quincy Adams and Henry Clay to throw the election, to be decided by the House of Representatives, in Adams's favor. Though never proven, the accusation became the rallying cry for supporters of Andrew Jackson, who had actually garnered a plurality of the popular vote in 1824.*

The last of the old-style elections was marked by the controversial "**corrupt bargain**" of 1824. The woods were full of presidential timber as James Monroe, last of the Virginia dynasty, completed his second term. Four candidates towered above the others: John Quincy Adams of Massachusetts, highly intelligent, experienced, and aloof; Henry Clay of Kentucky, the gamy and gallant "Harry of the West"; William H. Crawford of Georgia, an able though ailing giant of a man; and Andrew Jackson of Tennessee, the gaunt and gutsy hero of New Orleans.

All four rivals professed to be "Republicans." Well-organized parties had not yet emerged; their identities were so fuzzy, in fact, that South Carolina's John C. Calhoun appeared as the vice presidential candidate on both the Adams and the Jackson tickets.

The results of the noisy campaign were interesting but confusing. Jackson, the war hero, clearly had the strongest personal appeal, especially in the West, where his campaign against the forces of corruption and privilege in government resonated deeply. He polled almost as many popular votes as his next two rivals combined, but he failed to win a majority of the electoral vote (see Table 13.1). In such a deadlock the House of Representatives, as directed by the Twelfth Amendment (see Appendix), must choose among the top three candidates. Clay was thus eliminated, yet as Speaker of the House he presided over the very chamber that had to pick the winner.

Table 13.1 Election of 1824

Candidates	Electoral Vote	Popular Vote	Popular Percentage
Jackson	99	153,544	42.16%
Adams	84	108,740	31.89%
Crawford	41	46,618	12.95%
Clay	37	47,136	12.99%

The influential Clay was in a position to throw the election to the candidate of his choice. He reached the decision by the process of elimination. Crawford, recently felled by a paralytic stroke, was out of the picture. Clay hated the "military chieftain" Jackson, who in turn bitterly resented Clay's public denunciation of his Florida foray in 1818. The only candidate left was the puritanical Adams, with whom Clay—a free-living gambler and duelist—had never established cordial personal relations. But the two men had much in common politically: Both were fervid nationalists and advocates of the American System. Shortly before the final ballot in the House, Clay met privately with Adams and assured him of his support.

Decision day came early in 1825. The House of Representatives met amid tense excitement, with sick members being carried in on stretchers. On the first ballot, thanks largely to Clay's behind-the-scenes influence, Adams was elected president. A few days later, the victor announced that Henry Clay would be the new secretary of state.

Masses of angered Jacksonians, most of them common folk, roared in protest against this "corrupt bargain." Jackson condemned Clay as the "Judas of the West," and John Randolph of Virginia declared that Clay "shines and stinks like . . . a rotten mackerel by moonlight." No positive evidence has ever been unearthed to prove that Adams and Clay entered into a formal bargain. Clay was a natural choice for secretary of state, and Adams

First State Election in Detroit, Michigan, by Thomas Mickell Burnham This painting shows the "new politics" of the Jacksonian era. Politicians now had to take their message to the common man.

was scrupulously honest and not given to patronage. Even if a bargain had been struck, it was not necessarily corrupt. Deals of this nature have long been the stock-in-trade of politicians. But the outcry over Adams's election showed that change was in the wind. What had once been common practice was now condemned as furtive, elitist, and subversive of democracy. The next president would not be chosen behind closed doors.

★ A Yankee Misfit in the White House

John Quincy Adams was an ice chip off the old family glacier. Short, thickset, and billiard-bald, he was even more frigidly austere than his presidential father, John Adams. Shunning people, he often went for early morning swims, sometimes stark naked, in the then-pure Potomac River. Essentially a closeted thinker rather than a politician, he was irritable, sarcastic, and tactless. Yet few individuals have ever come to the presidency with a more brilliant record in statecraft, especially in foreign affairs. He ranks as one of the most successful secretaries of state, yet one of the least successful presidents.

A man of scrupulous honor, Adams entered upon his four-year "sentence" in the White House smarting under charges of "bargain," "corruption," and "usurpation." Fewer than one-third of the voters had voted for him. As the first "minority president," he would have found it difficult to win popular support even under the most favorable conditions. But Adams possessed almost none of the arts of the politician and scorned those who did. He refused to engage in the growing practice of patronage, appointing almost none of his political supporters to office. In the dawning age of back-slapping and baby-kissing democracy, the cold fish John Quincy Adams could hardly hope for success at the polls.

Adams's nationalistic views contributed to his woes in the White House. Much of the nation was turning away from post-Ghent nationalism toward states' rights and sectionalism. But Adams swam against the tide. Confirmed nationalist that he was, the new president urged Congress in his first annual message to construct a national network of roads and canals. He also renewed George Washington's proposal for a national university and went so far as to advocate federal support for an astronomical observatory.

The public reaction to these proposals was prompt and unfavorable. To many workaday Americans grubbing out stumps, astronomical observatories seemed like a scandalous waste of public funds. The South in particular bristled. If the federal government could meddle in local concerns such as education and roads, it might some day try to lay its hand on the "peculiar institution" of black slavery.

★ Going "Whole Hog" for Jackson in 1828

Andrew Jackson's next presidential campaign started early—on February 9, 1825, the day of John Quincy Adams's controversial election by the House—and it continued noisily for nearly four years.

Even before the election of 1828, the temporarily united Republicans of the Era of Good Feelings had split into two camps. One was the National Republicans, with Adams as their standard-bearer. The other was the Democratic-Republicans, with the fiery Jackson heading their ticket. Chanting "All hail, Old Hickory" and planting hickory poles for their hickory-tough hero, Jackson's zealots argued that the will of the people had been thwarted in 1825 by the backstairs "corrupt bargain" between Adams and Clay. The only way to right the wrong was to seat Jackson, who would then bring about "reform" by sweeping out the "dishonest" Adams gang.

Mudslinging reached new lows in 1828, and the electorate developed a taste for bare-knuckle politics. Adams would not stoop to gutter tactics, but many of his backers were less squeamish. They described Jackson's mother as a prostitute and his wife as an adulteress, and they recounted "Old Hickory's" numerous duels and brawls and his hanging of six militiamen.

Jackson's men also hit below the belt. A billiard table that President Adams had purchased with his own money became, in the mouths of rabid Jacksonites, "gambling tables" in the "presidential palace." Jackson campaigners mocked Adams's large federal salaries and even accused him of having served as a pimp for the Russian tsar during his time as minister to St. Petersburg.

On voting day the electorate split on largely sectional lines. Jackson's strongest support came from the West and South (see Map 13.1). The middle Atlantic states and the Old Northwest were divided, while Adams won the backing of his own New England as well as the propertied "better elements" of the Northeast. But when the popular vote was converted to electoral votes, General Jackson's triumph could not be denied. Old Hickory had trounced Adams by an electoral count of 178 to 83. Although a considerable part of Jackson's support was lined up by machine politicians in eastern cities, particularly in New York and Pennsylvania, the political center of gravity clearly had shifted away from the conservative eastern seaboard toward the emerging states across the mountains.

★ The Advent of Old Hickory Jackson

The new president cut a striking figure—tall, lean, with bushy iron-gray hair brushed high above a prominent forehead, craggy eyebrows, and blue eyes. His irritability and emaciated condition resulted in part from long-term bouts with dysentery, malaria, tuberculosis, and lead poisoning from two bullets that he carried in his body from near-fatal duels. Jackson's autobiography was written in his lined face.

Jackson's upbringing had its shortcomings. Born in the Carolinas and early orphaned, "Mischievous Andy" grew up without parental restraints. As a youth, he displayed much more interest in brawling and cockfighting than in his scanty opportunities for reading and spelling. Although he eventually learned to express himself in writing with vigor and clarity, Jackson's grammar was always rough-hewn and his spelling original. He sometimes misspelled a word two different ways in the same letter.

The youthful Carolinian shrewdly moved "up West" to Tennessee, where fighting was prized above writing. There—through native intelligence, force of personality, and powers of leadership—he became a judge and a member of Congress. Afflicted with a violent temper, Jackson early became involved in numerous duels, stabbings, and bloody frays. His passions were so profound that on occasion he would choke into silence when he tried to speak.

The first president from the West, the first nominated in a formal party convention (in 1832), and only the second without a college education (Washington was the first), Jackson was unique. His university was adversity. He had risen from the masses but was not one of them, except insofar as he shared many of their prejudices. Essentially a frontier aristocrat, he owned many slaves, cultivated broad acres, and lived in one of the finest mansions in America—the Hermitage, near Nashville, Tennessee.

Jackson's inauguration symbolized the ascendancy of the masses. "Hickoryites" poured into Washington from far away, sleeping on hotel floors and in hallways. They were eager to see their hero take office and perhaps to pick up a well-paying office for themselves. Nobodies mingled with notables as the White House, for the first time, was thrown open to the multitude. A milling crowd of rubbernecking clerks and shopkeepers, hobnailed artisans, and grimy laborers surged in, allegedly wrecking the china and furniture and threatening the "people's champion" with cracked ribs. Jackson was hastily spirited through a side door, and the White House miraculously emptied itself when the word was passed that huge bowls of well-spiked punch had been placed on the lawns. Such was the "inaugural brawl."

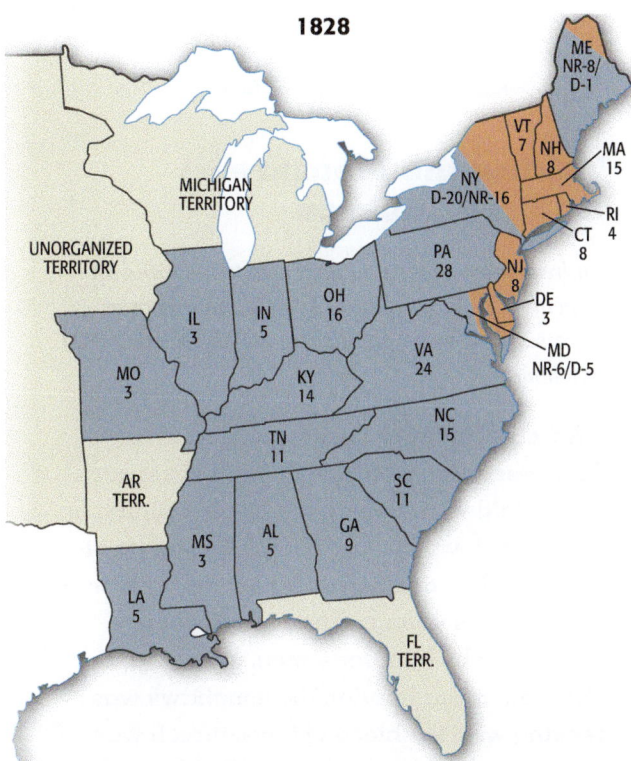

Map 13.1 Presidential Election of 1828 (with electoral vote by state) Jackson swept the South and West, while Adams retained the old Federalist stronghold of the Northeast. Yet Jackson's inroads in the Northeast were decisive. He won twenty of New York's electoral votes and all twenty-eight of Pennsylvania's. If those votes had gone the other way, Adams would have been victorious—by a margin of one vote.

Contending Voices

Taking the Measure of Andrew Jackson

Andrew Jackson was a military hero to some and an impetuous ruffian to others. A Maryland supporter endorsed Jackson for president in the campaign of 1824 as follows:

"[As] chief judge of the supreme court of Tennessee, [Jackson] acted until his services in the field were demanded by his country; he then laid down his law books, the sweets of domestic life, and seized his sword to revenge his country's wrongs. The savages were murdering by hundreds, men, women, and children, of our frontier; the tomahawk was reeking with the blood of innocence. It was then, my countrymen, that JACKSON led the van; it was then this noble soldier made his pillow of snow, and had for his roof the canopy of heaven. Yea, countrymen, I might extend my hand-bill to a volume, and I could not then give you a correct idea of the magnanimous and generous soul, of this unparalleled hero."

In the same year Thomas Jefferson (1743-1826) wrote of Jackson:

"When I was President of the Senate he was a Senator; and he could never speak on account of the rashness of his feelings. I have seen him attempt it repeatedly, and as often choke with rage. His passions are no doubt cooler now . . . but he is a dangerous man."

> Do these two observations agree on any aspects of Jackson's character, or do they seem to be describing two different people? Why might Jefferson, himself a revolutionary, regard Jackson as "dangerous"?

To conservatives, this orgy seemed like the end of the world. "King Mob" reigned triumphant as Jacksonian vulgarity replaced Jeffersonian simplicity. Faint-hearted traditionalists shuddered, drew their blinds, and recalled with trepidation the opening scenes of the French Revolution.

★ Jackson Nationalizes the Spoils System

Once in power, the Democrats, famously suspicious of the federal government, demonstrated they were not above striking some bargains of their own. Under Jackson the **spoils system**—that is, rewarding political supporters with public office—was introduced into the federal government on a large scale. Its name came from Senator William Marcy's classic remark in 1832, "To the victors belong the spoils of the enemy." The system had already secured a firm hold in New York and Pennsylvania, where well-greased machines ladled out the "gravy" of office.

Jackson defended the spoils system on democratic grounds. "Every man is as good as his neighbor," he declared—perhaps "equally better." As this was believed to be so, and as the routine of office was thought to be simple enough for any upstanding American to learn quickly, why encourage the development of an aristocratic, bureaucratic, officeholding class? Better to bring in new blood, Jackson argued. But the spoils system was less about qualifications than about rewarding old cronies. The questions Democrats asked each appointee were not "What can he do for the country?" but "What has he done for the party?" and "Is he loyal to Jackson?"

Scandal inevitably accompanied the new system. Men who had openly bought their posts by campaign contributions were appointed to high office. Illiterates, incompetents, and plain crooks were given positions of public trust; men on the make lusted for the spoils—rather than the toils—of office. Samuel Swartwout, despite ample warnings of his untrustworthiness, was awarded the lucrative post of collector of customs for the port of New York. Nearly nine years later he "Swartwouted out" for Britain, leaving his accounts more than a million dollars short—the first person to steal a million from the Washington government.

But despite its undeniable abuses, the spoils system was an important element of the emerging two-party order, cementing as it did loyalty to party over competing claims from economic class or geographic region. The promise of patronage provided a compelling reason for Americans to pick a party and stick with it through thick and thin.

★ The Tricky "Tariff of Abominations"

The touchy tariff issue had been one of John Quincy Adams's biggest headaches. Now Andrew Jackson felt his predecessor's pain. In 1824 Congress had increased the general tariff significantly, but wool manufacturers bleated for still-higher barriers. Ardent

---

spoils system Policy of rewarding political supporters with public office, first widely employed at the federal level by Andrew Jackson. The practice was widely abused by unscrupulous office seekers, but it also helped cement party loyalty in the emerging two-party system.

Jacksonites played a cynical political game. They promoted a high-tariff bill, expecting it to be defeated, which would give a black eye to then-President Adams. To their surprise the tariff passed in 1828, and Andrew Jackson inherited the political hot potato.

Southerners, as heavy consumers of manufactured goods with little manufacturing of their own, were hostile to tariffs, particularly to this high Tariff of 1828. Hotheads branded it the "Black Tariff" and the "Tariff of Abominations." Several southern states adopted formal protests, and in South Carolina flags were lowered to half-mast.

Why did the South react so angrily to the tariff? Southerners believed, not illogically, that the "Yankee tariff" discriminated against them. Southerners who sold their cotton in an unprotected world market were forced to buy expensive manufactured goods from Yankee and middle state producers heavily protected by tariffs, and the tariff provided a convenient and plausible scapegoat for the hard times befalling the Old South.

But much deeper issues underlay the southern outcry—in particular, a growing anxiety about possible federal interference with the institution of slavery. The congressional debate on the Missouri Compromise had kindled those anxieties, and they were further fanned by an abortive slave rebellion in Charleston in 1822, led by a free black named Denmark Vesey. South Carolinians, still closely tied to the British West Indies, knew full well that slaveholding West Indians were feeling the mounting pressures of British abolitionism on the London government. American abolitionists might similarly use the power of the Washington government to suppress slavery. If so, now was the time, and the tariff was the issue, for making a strong stand against all federal encroachments on states' rights.

South Carolinians took the lead in protesting the "Tariff of Abominations." Vice President John C. Calhoun, a topflight political theorist, secretly authored a pamphlet known as the "South Carolina Exposition" that the state legislature published in 1828. (As vice president he was forced to conceal his authorship.) Going a stride beyond the Kentucky and Virginia resolutions of 1798, the pamphlet bluntly and explicitly proposed that the states should nullify the tariff—that is, they should declare it null and void within their borders.

★ "Nullies" in South Carolina

The stage was set for a showdown. Through Jackson's first term the South Carolina nullifiers—"nullies" they were called—tried strenuously to muster the necessary two-thirds vote in the legislature, but they were blocked by a determined minority of Unionists. Congress pared away the worst "abominations" by passing the new, somewhat lower Tariff of 1832, but it was still frankly protectionist and fell far short of satisfying southern demands. The **Nullification Crisis** deepened.

South Carolina was now nerved for drastic action. After the "nullies" won a commanding majority in the state election of 1832, the legislature called a special convention. Meeting in Columbia, the delegates solemnly declared the existing tariff null and void in South Carolina and threatened to take their state out of the Union if Washington attempted to collect the customs duties by force.

Such tactics might have intimidated John Quincy Adams, but Andrew Jackson was the wrong president to stare down. The cantankerous general would never permit defiance or disunion. Privately threatening to invade the state and hang the nullifiers, he publicly dispatched naval and military forces to the Palmetto State and issued a ringing proclamation against nullification. Governor Robert Hayne responded with a counterproclamation, and the lines were drawn. If civil war was to be avoided, one side would have to surrender, or both would have to compromise.

Conciliatory Senator Henry Clay of Kentucky stepped forward. Although himself a supporter of tariffs, he had no desire to see his old enemy Andrew Jackson win laurels by crushing the Carolinians and returning with the scalp of John C. Calhoun. The gallant Kentuckian therefore pushed through Congress a compromise bill that would gradually reduce the Tariff of 1832 by about 10 percent over eight years, to the mildly protective level of 1816.

South Carolinians welcomed this opportunity to extricate themselves from a dangerously tight corner without loss of face. To the consternation of the Calhounites, no other southern states had sprung to their support, and an appreciable Unionist minority within South Carolina was gathering guns and nailing the Stars and Stripes to flagpoles. Faced

Nullification Crisis (1832–1833)
Showdown between President Andrew Jackson and the South Carolina legislature, which declared the 1832 tariff null and void in the state and threatened secession if the federal government tried to collect duties. It was resolved by a compromise negotiated by Henry Clay in 1833.

Thinking Globally

Alexis de Tocqueville on Democracy in America and Europe

On May 11, 1831, a twenty-six-year-old Frenchman, Alexis de Tocqueville, stepped ashore in New York City and began his fateful acquaintance with Andrew Jackson's America. For nine months he visited the cities of the Atlantic seaboard from Boston to Washington, trekked west to Detroit, and floated down the Ohio and Mississippi Rivers to New Orleans, keenly observing the American scene. Four years later he published the first volume of his monumental work *Democracy in America*. It remains to this day probably the most insightful analysis of American society ever written and provides an indispensable starting point for understanding both the nature of modern democracy and the American national character.

Tocqueville was born in the French Revolutionary era. He personally witnessed the so-called July Revolution in France in 1830, which widened the French electorate. He was a close observer of other emerging democratic movements across Europe and Latin America, including Britain's landmark Reform Bill of 1832 and the successful revolt against Spain of the newly independent republics of Venezuela (1811), Argentina (1816), Chile (1818), Mexico (1821), and Peru (1821). Those events convinced Tocqueville that democracy was the irresistible wave of the future, but he was far less certain about what that democratic future might mean for human happiness, political stability, and social justice. Thus he studied America to understand Europe's—indeed the world's—fate. "In America I saw more than America," he wrote. "I sought there the image of democracy itself . . . in order to learn what we have to fear or to hope from its progress."

Tocqueville announced his central insight in his book's first sentence: "Among the novel objects that attracted my attention during my stay in the United States, nothing struck me more forcibly than the general equality of condition among the people." (He acknowledged the gross inequality of slavery, but he considered slavery to be something that was "peculiar to America, not to democracy.") The "primary fact" of equality, he argued, exercised a "prodigious influence on the whole course of society."

It is easy to understand why the scale and pervasiveness of American equality made such an impression on Tocqueville. Mass democratic participation was already a well-established fact when he arrived. Almost 1.2 million voters—nearly 50 percent of the adult white male population—had cast their ballots in the election that brought Jackson to the White House in 1828. In contrast, France's July Revolution had enfranchised fewer than 200,000 propertied males, less than 1 percent of the total population, in 1830. And Britain's Reform Bill of 1832 would extend voting rights only to some 800,000 male property holders—in a country with 50 percent more people than the United States.

Tocqueville repeatedly remarked on the seething, restless energy that American equality unleashed. But he warned of two great potential dangers for the future of the great American democratic experiment. Tocqueville first worried that the doctrine of equality might breed a suffocating conformity that would eventually invoke the power of the state to enforce a stern and repressive consensus—the kind of "tyranny of the majority" that had worried Founders like James

Alexis de Tocqueville (1805–1859) (The Granger Collection, NYC)

with civil war within and invasion from without, the Columbia convention met again and repealed the ordinance of nullification.

Neither Jackson nor the "nullies" won a clear-cut victory in 1833. Clay was the true hero of the hour, hailed in Charleston and Boston alike for saving the country. Armed conflict had been avoided, but the fundamental issues had not been resolved. When next the "nullies" and the Union clashed, compromise would prove more elusive.

Election Day in Philadelphia, by John Lewis Krimmel, 1815 The German immigrant Krimmel recorded as early as 1815 the growing popular interest in elections that would culminate in Jacksonian democracy a decade later. Although politics was serious business, it also provided the occasion for much socializing and merriment. Even disfranchised free blacks, women, and children turned out for the festivities on election day.

Madison. Tocqueville thought he saw signs that such a future was already emerging. "I know of no country in which there is so little independence of mind and real freedom of discussion as in America," he wrote.

Second, he speculated that equality might foster radical *individualism*, a word that Tocqueville coined to capture the unique psychology he encountered everywhere in America. "As social conditions become more equal," he wrote, people "acquire the habit of always considering themselves as standing alone, and they are apt to imagine that their whole destiny is in their own hands." In this case, gnawing individual loneliness and even social anarchy might define America's future. "Democracy makes every man forget his ancestors," Tocqueville wrote. "It throws him back forever upon himself alone and threatens in the end to confine him entirely within the solitude of his own heart."

Tocqueville noted several factors that mitigated both of those grim prospects and held American democracy in a healthy balance: the absence of hostile countries on its borders; a vigorously free press; robust voluntary associations (especially churches and political parties); and, crucially, "habits of the heart," which sustained a sense of civic belonging and responsibility. But Tocqueville raised troubling questions about whether those factors would prove durable. If not, what would the ultimate fate of democracy be?

Ironically, today the United States has markedly *lower* rates of political participation than many other countries, especially those in Europe. Can it be that America—the pioneering mass democracy that served as Tocqueville's laboratory and his window on the future—has proved to be less fertile soil for the development of democracy than the Old World societies with which he compared it in the 1830s?

★ The Trail of Tears

Jackson's Democrats were committed to western expansion, but such expansion necessarily meant confrontation with the current inhabitants of the land. More than 125,000 Native Americans lived in the forests and prairies east of the Mississippi in the 1820s. Federal policy toward them varied. Beginning in the 1790s, the Washington government

197

The "Trail of Tears" In the fall and winter of 1838–1839, the U.S. Army forcibly removed about 15,000 Cherokees, some of them in manacles, from their ancestral homelands in the southeastern United States and marched them to Indian Territory (present-day Oklahoma). Freezing weather and inadequate food supplies led to unspeakable suffering. The escorting troops refused to slow the forced march so that the ill could recover, and some 4,000 Cherokees died on the 116-day journey.

ostensibly recognized the tribes as separate nations and agreed to acquire land from them only through formal treaties. The Indians were shrewd and determined negotiators, but this availed them little when Americans routinely violated their own covenants as white settlement pushed west.

Many white Americans felt respect and admiration for the Indians and believed that the Native Americans could be assimilated into white society. Much energy was therefore devoted to Christianizing and "civilizing" the Indians. Many denominations sent missionaries into Indian villages, and in 1793 Congress appropriated $20,000 for Indian literacy programs and agricultural instruction.

Although many tribes violently resisted white encroachment, others followed the path of accommodation. The Cherokees of Georgia made especially remarkable efforts to learn white ways. They composed a written legal code and constitution, adopted a system of settled agriculture, and vigorously promoted education, using a Cherokee alphabet devised by the Indian Sequoyah. Some Cherokees became prosperous cotton planters and even turned to slaveholding. Nearly thirteen hundred black slaves toiled for their Native American masters in the Cherokee nation in the 1820s. For these efforts, the Cherokees—along with the Creeks, Choctaws, Chickasaws, and Seminoles—were numbered by the whites among the "Five Civilized Tribes."

All this embrace of "civilization" apparently was not good enough for whites. In 1828 the Georgia legislature declared the Cherokee tribal council illegal and asserted its own jurisdiction over Indian affairs and Indian lands. The Cherokees appealed this move to the Supreme Court, which thrice upheld the rights of the Indians. But President Jackson, who clearly wanted to open Indian lands to white settlement, refused to recognize the Court's decisions. In a callous jibe at the Indians' defender,

Indian Removal Act (1830) *Ordered the removal of Indian tribes still residing east of the Mississippi to newly established Indian Territory west of Arkansas and Missouri. Tribes resisting eviction were forcibly removed by American forces, often after prolonged legal or military battles.*

Jackson reportedly snapped, "John Marshall has made his decision; now let him enforce it."*

Feeling some obligation to "this much injured race," Jackson proposed a bodily removal of the "Five Civilized Tribes" of the Southeast beyond the Mississippi. Emigration was supposed to be voluntary because it would be "cruel and unjust to compel the aborigines to abandon the graves of their fathers," Jackson declared.

Jackson's policy, passed by Congress as the **Indian Removal Act** of 1830, led to the forced uprooting of more than 100,000 Indians (see Map 13.2). In the ensuing decade, countless Indians—especially the Cherokees—died on the notorious **Trail of Tears** to the newly established Indian Territory (present-day Oklahoma) where they were to be "permanently" free of white encroachments. The Bureau of Indian Affairs was established in 1836 to administer relations with America's original inhabitants. But as the land-hungry "palefaces" pushed rapidly west, the government's guarantees of a "permanent" Indian homeland went up in smoke.

Suspicious of white intentions from the start, the Sauk and Fox tribes of Illinois and Wisconsin, ably led by Black Hawk, resisted eviction. They were bloodily crushed in the **Black Hawk War** of 1832 by regular troops, including Lieutenant Jefferson Davis of Mississippi, and by militia volunteers, including Captain Abraham Lincoln of Illinois. In Florida the Seminoles, under the leadership of Osceola, retreated into the swampy Everglades and for seven years (1835–1842) waged a bitter guerrilla war that took the lives of some fifteen hundred soldiers. The American commander's treacherous seizure of Osceola under a flag of truce finally led to the Seminoles' defeat. Some Seminoles fled deeper into the Everglades, where their descendants now live, but about four-fifths of them were moved to Oklahoma, where several thousand of the tribe survived.

★ The Bank War

President Jackson did not hate all banks and all businesses, but he distrusted monopolistic banking and overbig business, as did his followers. A man of virulent dislikes, he came to share the prejudices of his own West against the "moneyed monster" known as the Bank of the United States.

What made the bank a monster in Jackson's eyes? The national government minted gold and silver coins in the mid-nineteenth century but did not issue paper money. Paper notes issued by private banks in effect functioned as money, giving private bankers considerable power over the nation's economy.

No bank in America had more power than the Bank of the United States. In many ways the bank acted like a branch of government. It was the principal depository for the funds of the Washington government and controlled much of the nation's gold and silver.

Black Hawk and His Son Whirling Thunder, by John Wesley Jarvis, 1833 Chief Black Hawk and his son are depicted here in captivity. After their surrender in the Black Hawk War of 1832, they were put on public display throughout the United States.

One survivor of the Indians' forced march in 1838–1839 on the "Trail of Tears" to Indian Territory, farther west, remembered:

"One each day, and all are gone. Looks like maybe all dead before we get to new Indian country, but always we keep marching on. Women cry and make sad wails. Children cry, and many men cry, and all look sad when friends die, but they say nothing and just put heads down and keep on toward west.... She [his mother] speak no more; we bury her and go on."

Trail of Tears (1838–1839) *Forced march of fifteen thousand Cherokee Indians from their Georgia and Alabama homes to Indian Territory. Some four thousand Cherokees died on the arduous journey.*

Black Hawk War (1832) *Series of clashes in Illinois and Wisconsin between American forces and Indian chief Black Hawk of the Sauk and Fox tribes, who unsuccessfully tried to reclaim territory lost under the 1830 Indian Removal Act.*

---

*One hundred sixty years later, in 1992, the state of Georgia formally pardoned the two white missionaries, Samuel Austin Worcester and Elihu Butler, who had figured prominently in the decision Jackson condemned. They had been convicted of living on Cherokee lands without a license from the state of Georgia. They served sixteen months at hard labor on a chain gang and later accompanied the Cherokees on the "Trail of Tears" to Oklahoma.

A source of credit and stability, the bank was an important and useful part of the nation's expanding economy.

But the Bank of the United States was a private institution, accountable not to the people but only to its elite circle of moneyed investors. Its president, the brilliant but arrogant Nicholas Biddle—dubbed "Czar Nicholas I" by his enemies—held immense power over the nation's financial affairs.

To some, the bank's very existence seemed to sin against the egalitarian credo of American democracy. That conviction formed the deepest source of Jackson's opposition. The bank also won no friends by foreclosing on many western farms and draining "tribute" into eastern coffers. Profit, not public service, was its first priority.

The **Bank War** erupted in 1832, when Daniel Webster and Henry Clay presented Congress with a bill to renew the Bank of the United States' charter. The charter was not set to expire until 1836, but Clay pushed for renewal four years early to make it an election issue in 1832. As Jackson's leading rival for the presidency, Clay, with fateful blindness, believed he had set a perfect trap for Jackson. If Jackson signed the bill he would alienate his worshipful followers, but if he vetoed it he would lose the presidency to Clay.

Clay's recharter bill slid through Congress on greased skids but was killed by a scorching veto from Jackson. The "Old Hero" declared the monopolistic bank to be unconstitutional, ignoring the Supreme Court's earlier decision upholding its constitutionality in *McCulloch* v. *Maryland* (1819). The old general growled privately, "The Bank...is trying to kill me, but I will kill it." Jackson's veto message not only squashed the bank bill but vastly amplified the powers of the presidency. If the legislative and executive branches were partners in government, Jackson implied, the president was unmistakably the senior partner.

Bank War (1832) *Battle between President Andrew Jackson and congressional supporters of the Bank of the United States over the bank's renewal. Jackson vetoed the bank bill, arguing that the bank favored moneyed interests at the expense of western farmers.*

Map 13.2 Indian Removals, 1830–1846

Henry Clay's political instincts continued to fail him. Delighted with the veto message's financial fallacies, but blind to its political appeal to the common people, Clay arranged to have thousands of copies printed as a campaign document. The bank issue was now thrown into the noisy arena of the presidential contest of 1832.

★ "Old Hickory" Wallops Clay in 1832

Clay and Jackson were the chief gladiators in the fierce electoral combat of 1832. The grizzled old general's supporters again raised hickory poles and shouted "Jackson Forever: Go the Whole Hog!" Clay's admirers called for "Freedom and Clay," while his detractors harped on his dueling, gambling, cockfighting, and fast living.

Novel features made the campaign of 1832 especially memorable. For the first time, a third party entered the field—the newborn **Anti-Masonic party**, which opposed the influence and fearsome secrecy of the Masonic order. Energized by the mysterious disappearance and probable murder in 1826 of a New Yorker who was threatening to expose the Masons' secret rituals, the Anti-Masonic party quickly became a potent political force throughout the middle Atlantic and New England states. The Anti-Masons appealed to Americans' democratic suspicions of secret societies, but because Jackson was a proud Mason, the anti-Masonic party was also an anti-Jackson party. The Anti-Masonic party also attracted support from many evangelical Protestants seeking to use political power to effect moral and religious reforms, such as prohibiting mail deliveries on Sunday.

A further novelty of the presidential contest in 1832 was the calling of national nominating conventions (three of them) to name candidates. The Anti-Masons and National Republicans added still another innovation when they adopted formal platforms, articulating and publicizing their positions on the issues.

Henry Clay and his overconfident National Republicans sailed into the campaign with a lush $50,000 campaign chest, much of it from the Bank of the United States, and strong newspaper backing, some of it "bought" with Biddle's bank loans. Yet Jackson, idol of the masses, easily defeated the big-money Kentuckian. A Jacksonian wave again swept over the West and South, surged into Pennsylvania and New York, and even washed into rock-ribbed New England. The popular vote stood at 687,502 to 530,189 for Jackson; the electoral count was a lopsided 219 to 49.

Anti-Masonic party (established ca. 1826) *First founded in New York, it gained considerable influence in New England and the mid-Atlantic during the 1832 election, campaigning against the politically influential Masonic order, a secret society. Anti-Masons opposed Andrew Jackson, a Mason, and drew much of their support from evangelical Protestants.*

★ Burying Biddle's Bank

Its charter denied, the Bank of the United States was due to expire in 1836. But Jackson was not one to let the financial octopus die in peace. He was convinced that he now had a mandate from the voters for its extermination, and he feared that the slippery Biddle might try to manipulate the bank (as he did) so as to force its recharter. Jackson therefore proposed to bury the bank for good by removing all federal deposits from its vaults, thereby bleeding the bank dry and ensuring its demise.

Even the president's closest advisers opposed this vindictive and possibly unconstitutional policy. Jackson, his dander up, was forced to reshuffle his cabinet twice before he could find a secretary of the treasury who would bend to his iron will. Hoping to demonstrate the bank's importance, the desperate Biddle called in its loans in order to produce a minor financial crisis—"Biddle's Panic." But Jackson's resolution was firm. If anything, the vengeful conduct of the dying "monster" seemed to justify the earlier accusations of its adversaries.

But the death of the Bank of the United States left a financial vacuum in the American economy and kicked off a lurching cycle of booms and busts. Surplus federal funds were placed in several dozen pro-Jackson state banks, the so-called "**pet banks**." Without a sober central bank in control, the pet banks and smaller "wildcat" banks—fly-by-night operations that often consisted of little more than a few chairs and a suitcase full of printed notes—flooded the country with unsound paper money.

pet banks *Popular term for pro-Jackson state banks that received the bulk of federal deposits when Andrew Jackson moved to dismantle the Bank of the United States in 1833.*

Specie Circular (1836) *U.S. Treasury decree requiring that all public lands be purchased with "hard," or metallic, currency. Issued after small state banks flooded the market with unreliable paper currency, fueling land speculation in the West.*

Jackson tried to rein in the runaway economy in 1836, the year Biddle's bank breathed its last. "Wildcat" currency had become so unreliable, especially in the West, that Jackson authorized the Treasury to issue a **Specie Circular**—a decree that required all public lands to be purchased with "hard," or metallic, money. This drastic step slammed the brakes on the speculative boom, a neck-snapping change of direction that contributed to a financial crash in 1837.

But by then Jackson had retired to his Nashville home, hailed as the hero of his age. His successor would have to deal with the damage.

The Birth of the Whigs

New political parties were gelling as the 1830s lengthened. As early as 1828, the Democratic-Republicans of Jackson had unashamedly adopted the once-tainted name of "Democrats." Jackson's opponents condemned him as "King Andrew I" and began to coalesce as the Whigs—a name deliberately chosen to recollect eighteenth-century British and Revolutionary American opposition to the monarchy.

The Whig party contained so many diverse elements that it was mocked at first as "an organized incompatibility." Hatred of Jackson and his "executive usurpation" was its only apparent cement in its formative days. The Whigs first emerged as an identifiable group in the Senate, where Clay, Webster, and Calhoun joined forces in 1834 in opposition to Jackson's bank policies. Thereafter, the Whigs rapidly evolved into a potent national political force by attracting other groups alienated by Jackson: supporters of Clay's American System, southern states' righters offended by Jackson's stand on nullification, the larger northern industrialists and merchants, and eventually many of the evangelical Protestants associated with the Anti-Masonic party.

Whigs thought of themselves as conservatives, yet they were progressive in their support of active government programs and reforms. Instead of boundless territorial acquisition, they called for internal improvements such as canals, railroads, and telegraph lines, and they supported institutions such as prisons, asylums, and public schools. The Whigs welcomed the market economy, drawing support from manufacturers in the North, planters in the South, and merchants and bankers in all sections. But they were not simply a party of wealthy fat cats, however dearly the Democrats wanted to paint them as such. By absorbing the egalitarian Anti-Masonic party, the Whigs blunted much of the Democratic appeal to the common man. Turning Jacksonian rhetoric on its head, the Whigs portrayed Jackson and his successor, Martin Van Buren, as imperious aristocrats, and the Democrats as the party of cronyism and corruption.

The Election of 1836

The smooth-tongued and keen-witted vice president, Martin Van Buren of New York, was Jackson's choice as his successor in 1836. Leaving nothing to chance, Jackson carefully rigged the nominating convention and rammed his favorite down the throats of the delegates. Van Buren was supported by the Jacksonites without wild enthusiasm, even though he had promised "to tread generally" in the military-booted footsteps of his predecessor.

As the election neared, the still-ramshackle organization of the Whigs showed in their inability to nominate a single presidential candidate. Their long-shot strategy was instead to run several prominent "favorite sons" from different regions, hoping thereby to scatter the vote and throw the election into the House of Representatives. With Henry Clay elbowed aside, the leading Whig "favorite son" was heavy-jawed General William Henry Harrison, hero of the Battle of Tippecanoe (see p. 167). The fine-spun schemes of the Whigs availed nothing, however. Van Buren, the dapper "Little Magician," squirmed into office by the close popular vote of 765,483 to 735,795 but by the comfortable margin of 170 to 124 votes (for all the Whigs combined) in the Electoral College.

Big Woes for the "Little Magician"

Martin Van Buren was the first president to be born under the American flag. Short and slender, bland and bald, the adroit little New Yorker has been described as "a first-class second-rate man." An accomplished strategist and spoilsman—"the wizard of Albany"— he was also a statesman of wide experience in both legislative and administrative life. Unfortunately, he fell victim to a series of misfortunes over which he had little control.

From the outset, the new president labored under severe handicaps. As a machine-made candidate, he incurred the resentment of many Democrats. Jackson, the master showman, had been the dynamic type of chief executive whose administration had resounded with furious quarrels and cracked heads. Mild-mannered Martin Van Buren seemed to rattle about in the military boots of his bull-in-the-china-shop predecessor. The people felt let down. Inheriting Jackson's mantle without his popularity, Van Buren also inherited the ex-president's numerous and vengeful enemies.

Van Buren's four years overflowed with toil and trouble. In 1837 a rebellion in Canada—mostly over political reforms but aggravated by unregulated immigration from the United States—led to ugly border incidents that threatened to trigger war with Britain. Anti-slavery agitators in the North were in full cry, condemning among other things the prospective annexation of Texas.

Worst of all, Jackson bequeathed to Van Buren the makings of a searing depression. Much of Van Buren's energy had to be devoted to the purely negative task of battling the panic, and there were not enough rabbits in the "Little Magician's" tall silk hat. Hard times ordinarily blight the reputation of a president, and Van Buren was no exception.

Depression Doldrums and the Independent Treasury

The **panic of 1837** was a symptom of the financial sickness of the times. Its basic cause was rampant speculation prompted by a mania of get-rich-quick-ism. Gamblers in western lands were doing a "land-office business" on borrowed capital, much of it in the shaky currency of "wildcat" banks. The speculative craze spread to canals, roads, railroads, and slaves.

But speculation alone did not cause the crash. Jacksonian finance, including the Bank War and the Specie Circular, gave an additional jolt to an already teetering structure. The collapse of two British banks late in 1836 caused investors to call in loans in the United States. Failures of wheat crops deepened the distress. Grain prices were forced so high that three weeks before Van Buren took the oath of office mobs in New York City stormed warehouses and broke open flour barrels.

Soon the depression's full fury burst about Van Buren's bewildered head. Hardship was acute and widespread. American banks collapsed by the hundreds, including some of the "pet banks," which carried down with them several million in government funds. Commodity prices drooped, sales of public lands fell off, and customs revenues dried to a rivulet. Factories closed their doors, and unemployed workers milled about in the streets.

The Whigs came forward with proposals for active government remedies for the economy's ills. They called for the expansion of bank credit, higher tariffs, and subsidies for internal improvements. But Van Buren, shackled by the Jacksonian philosophy of keeping the government's paws off the economy, spurned all such ideas.

The beleaguered Van Buren tried to apply vintage Jacksonian medicine to the ailing economy through his controversial "Divorce Bill." Convinced that some of the financial fever was fed by the injection of federal funds into private banks, he championed the principle of "divorcing" the government from banking altogether. By establishing a so-called independent treasury, the government could lock its surplus money in vaults. Government funds would thus be safe, but they would also be denied to the banking system as reserves, thereby shriveling available credit resources.

Van Buren's "divorce" scheme was never highly popular. His fellow Democrats, many of whom longed for the risky but lush days of the "pet banks," supported it only lukewarmly. The Whigs condemned it because it shriveled their hopes for a revived Bank of

panic of 1837 *Economic crisis triggered by bank failures, elevated grain prices, and Andrew Jackson's efforts to curb overspeculation on western lands and transportation improvements. In response, President Martin Van Buren proposed the "Divorce Bill," which pulled treasury funds out of the banking system altogether, contracting the credit supply.*

Examining the Evidence

Satiric Bank Note, 1837

*P*olitical humor can take more forms than the commonly seen caustic cartoon. Occasionally historians stumble upon other examples, such as this fake bank note. A jibe at Andrew Jackson's money policies, the note appeared in New York in 1837 after Jackson's insistence on shutting down the Bank of the United States resulted in the suspension of specie payments. The clever creator of this satiric bank note for six cents left little doubt about the worthlessness of the note or Jackson's responsibility for it. The six cents payable by the "Humbug Glory Bank"—whose symbols were a donkey and a "Hickory Leaf" (for Old Hickory)—were redeemable "in mint drops or Glory at cost." The bank's cashier was "Cunning Reuben," possibly an anti-Semitic allusion to usurious Jewish bankers. Can you identify other ways in which this document takes aim at Jackson's banking policies? What symbols did the note's creator assume the public would comprehend?

1. Identify at least three *visual* images or symbols that serve to link this satirical currency with Andrew Jackson's "pet banks."
2. Point to at least three *verbal* terms or phrases that highlight the supposed fraudulency of Jacksonian banking practices.
3. What historical conclusions about the bitterness of the "Bank War" might you draw from the printing of this kind of fake "money" by Jackson's opponents? Exactly what political purpose does this form of satire serve that more straightforward argument would not?

Collection of the New York Historical Society

the United States. After a prolonged struggle, the Independent Treasury Bill passed Congress in 1840. Repealed the next year by the victorious Whigs, the scheme was reenacted by the triumphant Democrats in 1846 and then continued until merged with the Federal Reserve System in the next century.

★ Gone to Texas

Americans, greedy for land, continued to covet the vast expanse of Texas, which the United States had abandoned to Spain when acquiring Florida in 1819. The Spanish authorities wanted to populate this virtually unpeopled area, but before they could carry through their contemplated plans, the Mexicans won their independence. A new regime in Mexico City thereupon concluded arrangements in 1823 for granting a huge tract of land to Stephen Austin, with the understanding that he would bring into Texas three hundred American families. Immigrants were to be of the established Roman Catholic faith and upon settlement were to become properly Mexicanized.

Those two stipulations were largely ignored. Hardy Texan pioneers remained Americans at heart, resenting the trammels imposed by a "foreign" government. They were especially annoyed by the presence of Mexican soldiers, many of whom were ragged ex-convicts.

Energetic and prolific, Texan Americans numbered about thirty thousand by 1835. Most of them were law-abiding, God-fearing pioneers, but some of them had left the "states" only one or two jumps ahead of the sheriff. Among the adventurers were Davy Crockett, the famous rifleman and former Congressman, and James Bowie, the presumed inventor of the murderous knife that bears his name. A distinguished latecomer and leader was an ex-governor of Tennessee, Sam Houston. Houston's life had been temporarily shattered in 1829 when his bride of a few weeks left him and he took up temporary residence with the Arkansas Indians, who dubbed him "Big Drunk."

> *Philip Hone (1780–1851), a New York businessman, described in his diary (May 10, 1837) a phase of the financial crisis:*
>
> "The savings-bank also sustained a most grievous run yesterday. They paid 375 depositors $81,000. The press was awful; the hour for closing the bank is six o'clock, but they did not get through the paying of those who were in at that time till nine o'clock. I was there with the other trustees and witnessed the madness of the people—women nearly pressed to death, and the stoutest men could scarcely sustain themselves; but they held on as with a death's grip upon the evidences of their claims, and, exhausted as they were with the pressure, they had strength to cry 'Pay! Pay!'"

The pioneer individualists who came to Texas were not easy to push around. Friction rapidly increased between Mexicans and Texans over such issues as slavery, immigration, and local rights. Slavery was a particularly touchy topic. Mexico emancipated its slaves in 1830 and prohibited their further importation into Texas, as well as further colonization by troublesome Americans. The Texans refused to honor this decree. They kept their slaves in bondage, and new American settlers kept bringing more slaves into Texas. The explosion finally came in 1835, when Mexican dictator Santa Anna wiped out all local rights and started to raise an army to suppress the upstart Texans.

★ The Lone Star Rebellion

Early in 1836 the Texans unfurled their Lone Star flag and declared their independence, naming Sam Houston as Commander in Chief. Santa Anna, at the head of about six thousand men, stormed ferociously into Texas. Trapping a band of nearly two hundred pugnacious Texans at the **Alamo** in San Antonio, he wiped them out to a man after a thirteen-day siege. A short time later a band of about four hundred surrounded and defeated American volunteers, having thrown down their arms at **Goliad**, were butchered as "pirates."

Slain heroes such as Jim Bowie and Davy Crockett, well known in life, became legendary in death. Texan war cries—"Remember the Alamo!" "Remember Goliad!" and "Death to Santa Anna!"—swept up into the United States. Scores of vengeful Americans seized their rifles and rushed to the aid of relatives, friends, and compatriots.

General Sam Houston's small army retreated to the east, luring Santa Anna near the site of present-day Houston, Texas. The Mexicans numbered about thirteen hundred men, the Texans about nine hundred. Suddenly, on April 21, 1836, Houston turned, wiping out the pursuing force in the **Battle of San Jacinto** (see Map 13.3). The captured Santa Anna was forced to sign two treaties in which he agreed to withdraw Mexican troops and to recognize the Rio Grande as the extreme southwestern boundary of Texas. When released, he repudiated the whole agreement as illegal because it was extorted under duress.

These events put the U.S. government in a sticky situation. As the Mexicans bitterly complained, the Washington government's weak enforcement of neutrality laws

Alamo *Fortress in Texas where two hundred American volunteers were slain by Santa Anna in 1836. "Remember the Alamo" became a battle cry in support of Texan independence.*

Goliad *Texas outpost where American volunteers, having laid down their arms and surrendered, were massacred by Mexican forces in 1836. The incident, along with the slaughter at the Alamo, fueled American support for Texan independence.*

Battle of San Jacinto (1836) *Resulted in the capture of Mexican dictator Santa Anna, who was forced to withdraw his troops from Texas and recognize the Rio Grande as Texas's southwestern border.*

Map 13.3 The Texas Revolution, 1836 General Houston's strategy was to retreat and use defense in depth. His line of supply from the United States was shortened as Santa Anna's lengthened. The Mexicans were forced to bring up supplies by land because the Texas navy controlled the sea. This force consisted of only four small ships, but it was big enough to do the job.

had permitted American men and supplies to leak across the border and aid the Texans. But American public opinion, overwhelmingly favorable to the Texans, left the federal authorities powerless to act. On the day before he left office in 1837, President Jackson extended the right hand of recognition to the Lone Star Republic led by his old comrade-in-arms against the Indians, Sam Houston.

Many Texans wanted not just recognition of their independence but outright union with the United States. The radiant Texan bride, officially petitioning for annexation in 1837, presented herself for marriage. But the expectant groom, Uncle Sam, was jerked back by the strong arm of the slavery issue. Anti-slavery crusaders in the North were opposing annexation with increasing vehemence; they contended that the whole scheme was merely a conspiracy cooked up by the southern "slavocracy" to bring new slave pens into the Union.

At first glance, the "slavery plot" charge seemed plausible. Most of the early settlers in Texas, as well as American volunteers during the revolution, had come from slaveholding states of the South and Southwest. But scholars have concluded that the settlement of Texas was merely the normal and inexorable march of the westward movement. The explanation was proximity rather than conspiracy. Yet the fact remained that many Texans were slaveholders, and admitting Texas to the Union inescapably meant enlarging American slavery.

★ Log Cabins and Hard Cider of 1840

Martin Van Buren was renominated by the Democrats in 1840, albeit without terrific enthusiasm. The party had no acceptable alternative to the man the Whigs called "Martin Van Ruin."

The Whigs, hungering for the spoils of office, scented victory in the breeze. Pangs of the panic were still being felt, and voters blamed their woes on the party in power. Learning from their mistake in 1836, the Whigs united behind one candidate, Ohio's William Henry Harrison. He was not their ablest statesman—that would have been Webster or Clay—but he was believed to be their ablest vote getter.

The aging hero, nearly sixty-eight when the campaign ended, was known for his successes against Indians and the British at the Battles of Tippecanoe (1811) and the Thames (1813). Harrison's views on current issues were only vaguely known. "Old Tippecanoe" was nominated primarily because he was issueless and enemyless—a tested recipe for electoral success that still appeals today. John Tyler of Virginia, an afterthought, was selected as his vice presidential running mate.

The Whigs, eager to avoid offense, published no official platform, hoping to sweep their hero into office with a frothy huzza-for-Harrison campaign reminiscent of Jackson's triumph in 1828. A dull-witted Democratic editor played directly into Whig hands. Stupidly insulting the West, he lampooned Harrison as an impoverished old farmer who should be content with a pension, a log cabin, and a barrel of hard cider—the poor westerner's champagne. Whigs gleefully adopted honest hard cider and the sturdy log cabin as symbols of their campaign. Harrisonites portrayed their hero as the poor "Farmer of North Bend" who had been called from his cabin and his plow to drive corrupt Jackson spoilsmen from the "presidential palace." They denounced Van Buren as a supercilious

The Battle of the Alamo, 1836 Long celebrated in song and story, the battle was a military defeat but a spiritual victory for the Texas rebels, whose annihilation to a man inspired others and led eventually to independence from Mexico.

aristocrat, a simpering dandy who wore corsets and ate French food from golden plates. As a jeering Whig campaign song proclaimed,

> Old Tip, he wears a homespun shirt,
> He has no ruffled shirt, wirt, wirt.
> But Matt, he has the golden plate,
> And he's a little squirt, wirt, wirt.

The Whig campaign was a masterpiece of hoopla. Log cabins were dished up in every conceivable form. Howling Whigs, stimulated by fortified cider, rolled huge balls from village to village and state to state, representing the snowballing majority for "Tippecanoe and Tyler too." In truth, Harrison was not lowborn but from one of the FFVs ("First Families of Virginia"). He was not a poverty-stricken dweller in a one-room log cabin but rather lived in a sixteen-room mansion on a three-thousand-acre estate. He did not swill down gallons of hard cider (he evidently preferred whiskey). And he did not plow his fields with his own "huge paws." But such details had not mattered when General Jackson rode to victory, and they did not matter now.

The Democrats who hurrahed Jackson into the White House in 1828 now discovered to their chagrin that whooping it up for a backwoods westerner was a game two could play. Harrison won by the surprisingly close margin of 1,275,016 popular votes to 1,129,102 but by an overwhelming electoral margin of 234 to 60. With hardly a real issue debated, though with hard times blighting the incumbent's fortunes, Van Buren was washed out of Washington in a wave of apple juice.

Although campaigners in 1840 did their best to bury substantive issues beneath the ballyhoo, voters actually faced a stark choice between economic visions of how to cope with the nation's first major depression. Whigs sought to expand and stimulate the economy, while Democrats favored retrenchment and an end to high-flying banks and aggressive corporations.

★ Politics for the People

The election of 1840 conclusively demonstrated two major changes in American politics since the Era of Good Feelings. The first was the triumph of a populist democratic style. Democracy had been something of a taint in the days of the lordly Federalists. But by the 1840s, aristocracy was the taint, and democracy was respectable. Politicians were forced to unbend and curry favor with the voting masses. Lucky indeed was the aspiring office seeker who could boast of birth in a log cabin. The semiliterate frontiersman Davy Crockett of Tennessee had been elected to Congress mainly on the basis of his bear-hunting prowess. Hopelessly handicapped was the candidate who appeared too well dressed, too grammatical, too high-browishly intellectual. In truth, most high political offices continued to be filled by "leading citizens," but now these wealthy and prominent men had to forsake all social pretensions and cultivate the common touch if they hoped to win elections.

Snobbish bigwigs sneered at the "coonskin Congressmen" elected by newly enfranchised "bipeds of the forest." But these critics protested in vain. The common man—the sturdy American who donned plain trousers rather than breeches, who sported a plain haircut and a coonskin cap rather than a silk top hat—was moving to the center of the national political stage. Instead of the old divine right of kings, America was now bowing to the divine right of the people.

★ The Two-Party System

The second dramatic change resulting from the 1840 election was the formation of a vigorous and durable two-party system. The Jeffersonians of an earlier day had been so successful in absorbing the programs of their Federalist opponents that a full-blown two-party system had never truly emerged in the subsequent Era of Good Feelings. The idea had prevailed that parties of any sort smacked of conspiracy and "faction" and were injurious to the health of the body politic in a virtuous republic. By 1840 political parties had fully come of age, a lasting legacy of Andrew Jackson's tenaciousness.

Both national parties, the Democrats and the Whigs, grew out of the rich soil of Jeffersonian republicanism, and each laid claim to different aspects of the republican inheritance. Jacksonian Democrats glorified the liberty of the individual and were fiercely on guard against the inroads of "privilege" into government. Whigs trumpeted the natural harmony of society and the value of community and were willing to use government to realize their objectives. Whigs also berated those leaders—and they considered Jackson to be one—whose appeals to self-interest fostered conflict among individuals, classes, or sections.

Democrats clung to states' rights and federal restraint in social and economic affairs as their basic doctrines. Whigs tended to favor a renewed national bank; protective tariffs; internal improvements; public schools; and, increasingly, moral reforms such as the prohibition of liquor and eventually the abolition of slavery.

The two parties were thus separated by real differences of philosophy and policy. But they also had much in common. Both were mass-based "catchall" parties that tried deliberately to mobilize as many voters as possible for their causes. Although it is true that Democrats tended to be more humble folk and Whigs more prosperous, both parties nevertheless commanded the loyalties of all kinds of Americans, from all social classes, and in all sections. The social diversity of the two parties fostered horse-trading compromises *within* each party that prevented either from assuming extreme or radical positions. By the same token, the geographical diversity of the two parties retarded the emergence of purely sectional political parties—temporarily suppressing, through compromise, the ultimately uncompromisable issue of slavery. When the two-party system began to creak in the 1850s, the Union was mortally imperiled.

President Andrew Jackson advised a supporter in 1835 on how to tell the difference between Democrats and "Whigs, nullies, and blue-light federalists." In doing so, he neatly summarized the Jacksonian philosophy:

"The people ought to inquire [of political candidates]—are you opposed to a national bank; are you in favor of a strict construction of the Federal and State Constitutions; are you in favor of rotation in office; do you subscribe to the republican rule that the people are the sovereign power, the officers their agents, and that upon all national or general subjects, as well as local, they have a right to instruct their agents and representatives, and they are bound to obey or resign; in short, are they true Republicans agreeable to the true Jeffersonian creed?"

Varying Viewpoints

What Was Jacksonian Democracy?

Aristocratic, eastern-born historians of the nineteenth century damned Jackson as a backwoods barbarian and Jacksonianism as democracy run riot. In the late nineteenth and early twentieth centuries, however, another generation of historians, many of whom had grown up in the Midwest, rejected the elitist views of their predecessors. Frederick Jackson Turner and his disciples saw the western frontier as the fount of democratic virtue, and they hailed Jackson as a true popular hero sprung from the forests of the West to protect the people against the moneyed interests.

When Arthur M. Schlesinger, Jr., published *The Age of Jackson* in 1945, however, the debate on Jacksonianism shifted dramatically. Schlesinger cast the Jacksonian era not as a sectional conflict but as a class conflict between poor farmers, laborers, and noncapitalists on the one hand and the business community on the other.

Soon after Schlesinger's book appeared, the discussion again shifted ground and entirely new interpretations of Jacksonianism emerged. Richard Hofstadter argued in *The American Political Tradition and the Men Who Made It* (1948) that Jacksonian democracy was not a rejection of capitalism, as Schlesinger insisted, but rather the effort of aspiring entrepreneurs to serve their own interests against their entrenched, monopolistic, eastern competitors. Lee Benson contended in *The Concept of Jacksonian Democracy* (1961) that the political conflicts of the Jacksonian era were rooted not in class or region but in religious and ethnic splits within American society that led to local conflicts over cultural issues.

In the 1980s Sean Wilentz and other scholars began to resurrect some of Schlesinger's arguments about the importance of class to Jacksonianism. In *Chants Democratic* (1984), Wilentz maintained that Jacksonian politics could not be understood without reference to the changing national economy. Artisans and small producers, Wilentz argued, believed that impersonal institutions and large-scale employers threatened the very existence of a republic founded on virtuous self-sufficiency. Jackson's attack on the Bank of the United States symbolized the antagonism these individuals felt toward the emerging capitalist economy.

The scholarly cycle came full circle in Charles Sellers's *The Market Revolution: Jacksonian America, 1815–1846* (1991). In many ways this ambitious synthesis offered an updated version of Schlesinger's argument about class conflict. American democracy and free-market capitalism, Sellers suggested, were not natural twins but rather adversaries, with Jacksonians inventing mass democracy in order to hold capitalist expansion in check. Like Schlesinger's thesis, Sellers's interpretation provoked a storm of controversy. To critics, Sellers suffered from a hopelessly romantic view of preindustrial society and a pronounced ideological bias. In an era of tightly contested elections, they argued, no party could expect to prevail by appealing exclusively to rich or poor along class lines.

Published a decade and a half later, *What Hath God Wrought: The Transformation of America, 1815–1848* (2007), Daniel Walker Howe's equally sweeping synthesis of the period, took a different view of the relationship between commercialization and democracy. Howe argued that mass political participation did not emerge as an antidote to the crushing yoke of industrialization; rather, it evolved out of the same forces that drove market expansion—the "twin revolutions" in transportation and communications. Advances in printing and the proliferation of newspapers were prerequisites for mass political parties, which depended on the largely partisan press to publicize their platforms and rally support. The turnpikes, canals, and railroads that delivered local goods to increasingly distant markets also carried ministers to far-off parishes, setting off a religious revival that helped transform the political landscape. New churches, representing a multitude of faiths, created venues for debates on issues ranging from abolition to women's rights, issues that were intentionally kept out of the halls of Congress. Howe argued that Jackson's supporters did not object to new commercial opportunities. According to Howe, Jacksonians welcomed commerce, but they disagreed with Whigs over the *direction* of development, favoring a more agrarian, atomized economy.

CHAPTER SUMMARY

Beginning in the 1820s, a powerful movement celebrating the common person and promoting the "New Democracy" transformed the earlier elitist character of American politics. The controversial election of the Yankee sophisticate John Quincy Adams in 1824 angered the followers of Andrew Jackson, who had received more popular votes.

Jackson's sweeping presidential victory in 1828 represented the political triumph of the New Democracy, including the spoils-rich political machines that thrived in the new environment. Jackson's simple, popular ideas and rough-hewn style reinforced the patronage system's growing belief that any ordinary person could hold public office. The "Tariff of Abominations" and the Nullification Crisis with South Carolina revealed a growing sectionalism and anxiety about slavery that challenged Jackson's fierce nationalism.

Jackson vigorously wielded the powers of the presidency against his opponents, particularly Calhoun and Clay. He made the Bank of the United States a symbol of evil financial power and killed it after a bitter political fight. Destroying the bank reinforced Jacksonians' hostility to all forms of concentrated political or financial power in the hands of elites but also left the United States without any effective financial system. In opposition to Jackson's aggressive assertion of power and his numerous controversial policies, a new Whig party emerged to compete with the Jacksonian Democrats.

Jackson's presidency also focused on issues of westward expansion. Pressured to adopt paths of "civilization," Native Americans of the Southeast engaged in extensive agricultural and educational development. But white settlers and state governments still encroached upon the Cherokees and other tribes, and Jackson ordered the forced removal of all southeastern Indians to Oklahoma along the "Trail of Tears."

Jackson's ill-considered economic policies came home to roost under the unlucky Martin Van Buren, his handpicked successor. As the country plunged into a serious depression following the panic of 1837, Van Buren continued futile Jacksonian policies by forcing the removal of all federal funds from private banks.

In Texas, American settlers successfully rebelled against Mexico and declared their independence. Jackson recognized the Texas Republic, but because of the slavery controversy, he refused its application for annexation to the United States.

The Whigs saw these economic and political troubles as a path to the White House. But rather than campaign on issues, they used the political hoopla of the new mass democratic process to turn a western aristocrat and military hero, William Henry Harrison, into a democratic symbol of the "log cabin and hard cider." The Whig victory signaled the emergence of a new two-party system, in which the two parties' genuine philosophical differences and somewhat different constituencies proved less important than their widespread popularity and shared roots in the new American democratic spirit.

KEY TERMS

- corrupt bargain (190)
- spoils system (194)
- Nullification Crisis (195)
- Indian Removal Act (198)
- Trail of Tears (199)
- Black Hawk War (199)
- Bank War (200)
- Anti-Masonic party (201)
- pet banks (201)
- Specie Circular (202)
- panic of 1837 (203)
- Alamo (205)
- Goliad (205)
- Battle of San Jacinto (205)

PEOPLE TO KNOW

- John Quincy Adams
- Henry Clay
- Andrew Jackson
- John C. Calhoun
- Denmark Vesey
- Black Hawk
- Nicholas Biddle
- Daniel Webster
- Martin Van Buren
- Stephen Austin
- Sam Houston
- Santa Anna
- William Henry Harrison

MindTap is a fully online, highly personalized learning experience built upon Cengage Learning content. MindTap combines student learning tools—readings, multimedia, activities, and assessments—into a singular Learning Path that guides students through the course.

Chapter 14

Forging the National Economy
1790–1860

The progress of invention is really a threat [to monarchy]. Whenever I see a railroad I look for a republic.

RALPH WALDO EMERSON, 1866

Chapter Outline

- The Westward Movement
- Irish and German Immigrants
- Nativism and Assimilation
- The Coming of the Factory System
- Women and the Economy
- The Ripening of Commercial Agriculture
- The Transportation Revolution
- Overseas Trade and Communication
- *Makers of America: The Irish*
- *Makers of America: The Germans*
- *Examining the Evidence: The Invention of the Sewing Machine*

The new nation bounded into the nineteenth century in a burst of movement. New England Yankees, Pennsylvania farmers, southern yeomen, cotton lords and their enslaved workers, all pushed west in search of land and opportunity, soon to be joined by vast numbers of immigrants from Europe. But not only people were in motion. Newly invented machinery boomed the cultivating of crops and the manufacturing of goods, while workers labored longer, harder, and faster. Better roads, faster steamboats, farther-reaching canals, and ribboning railroad lines all moved people, foodstuffs, raw materials, and manufactured goods from coast to hinterland and Gulf to Great Lakes, and from American shores to the wider world. Burgeoning American capitalism gave rise to an economy that was remarkably dynamic, market driven, and internationally consequential.

FOCUS QUESTIONS

1. How did westward migration and German and Irish immigration alter the geographical distribution and composition of the American population in the early nineteenth century?
2. Why was America relatively slow to embrace urbanization, industrialization, and the factory system of production?
3. How did new technologies and advances in transportation and communications lay the foundations for the first wave of American industrialization?
4. How did early industrialization affect workers and alter the role of women both inside and outside the home?
5. What were the large-scale effects of the emerging national American market economy, including its impact on regional economic specialization and social class relationships?

CHRONOLOGY

ca. 1750	Industrial Revolution begins in Britain
1791	Samuel Slater builds first U.S. textile factory
1793	Eli Whitney invents cotton gin
1798	Whitney develops interchangeable parts for muskets
1807	Robert Fulton's first steamboat Embargo spurs American manufacturing
1811	Cumberland Road construction begins
1817	Erie Canal construction begins
1825	Erie Canal completed
1828	First railroad in United States
1830s	Cyrus McCormick invents mechanical mower-reaper
1834	Anti-Catholic riot in Boston
1837	John Deere develops steel plow
1840	President Van Buren establishes ten-hour day for federal employees
1842	Massachusetts declares labor unions legal in *Commonwealth* v. *Hunt*
ca. 1843–1868	Era of clipper ships
1844	Samuel Morse invents telegraph Anti-Catholic riot in Philadelphia
1845–1849	Potato famine in Ireland
1846	Elias Howe invents sewing machine
1848	First general incorporation laws in New York Democratic revolutions collapse in Germany
1849	American, or Know-Nothing, party formed
1851	London World's Fair
1852	Cumberland Road completed
1858	Cyrus Field lays first transatlantic cable
1860	Pony Express established
1861	First transcontinental telegraph
1866	Permanent transatlantic cable established

⭐ The Westward Movement

The rise of Andrew Jackson, the first president from beyond the Appalachian Mountains, exemplified the inexorable westward march of the American people. The West, with its raw frontier, was the most typically American part of the nation. As Ralph Waldo Emerson wrote in 1844, "Europe stretches to the Alleghenies; America lies beyond."

The Republic was young, and so were the people—as late as 1850, half of Americans were under the age of thirty. They were also restless and energetic, seemingly always on the move, and always westward. By 1840 the "demographic center" of the American population had crossed the Alleghenies (see Map 14.1). By the eve of the Civil War, it had marched beyond the Ohio River.

Legend portrays an army of muscular axmen triumphantly carving civilization out of the western woods. But in reality life was downright grim for most pioneer families. Poorly fed, ill-clad, housed in hastily erected shanties, they were perpetual victims of disease, depression, and premature death. Above all, unbearable loneliness haunted them, especially the women, who were often cut off from human contact, even their neighbors, for days or even weeks, while confined to the cramped orbit of a dark cabin erected in a secluded clearing. Breakdowns and even madness were all too frequently the "opportunities" that the frontier offered to pioneer women.

Frontier life could be tough and crude for men as well. No-holds-barred wrestling, which permitted such niceties as the biting off of noses and the gouging out of eyes, was a popular entertainment. Pioneering Americans, marooned by geography, were often ill-informed, superstitious, provincial, and fiercely individualistic. Emerson's popular

Map 14.1 Westward Movement of the Center of Population, 1790–2000 The triangles indicate the points at which a map of the United States weighted for the population of the country in a given year would balance. Note the remarkable equilibrium of the north–south pull from 1790 to about 1940, and the strong spurt west and south thereafter. The 1980 census revealed that the nation's center of population had at last moved west of the Mississippi River. The map also shows the slowing of the westward movement between 1890 and 1940—the period of heaviest immigration from Europe, which ended up mainly in East Coast cities.

lecture-essay "Self-Reliance" struck a deeply responsive chord. Popular literature of the period abounded with portraits of heroically unique, isolated figures such as James Fenimore Cooper's courageous Natty Bumppo and Herman Melville's restless Captain Ahab—just as Jacksonian politics aimed to emancipate the lone-wolf, enterprising businessperson. Yet even in this heyday of "rugged individualism," there were important exceptions. Pioneers, in tasks clearly beyond their own individual resources, would call upon neighbors for logrolling and barn raising and upon their governments for help in building internal improvements.

"**Self-Reliance**" **(1841)** *Ralph Waldo Emerson's popular lecture-essay that reflected the spirit of individualism pervasive in American popular culture during the 1830s and 1840s.*

★ Shaping the Western Landscape

The westward movement also molded the physical environment. Pioneers in a hurry often exhausted the land and then pushed on, leaving behind barren and rain-gutted fields. In the Kentucky bottomlands, settlers discovered that they could burn off the native cane and plant "Kentucky bluegrass," which made ideal pasture for livestock.

The American West felt the pressure of civilization in additional ways. By the 1820s American fur trappers were setting their trap lines all over the vast Rocky Mountain region. Each summer, trappers came down from the mountains and swapped their beaver pelts for manufactured goods from the East. This trade thrived for some two decades, until the hapless beavers had all but disappeared from the region. Trade in buffalo robes also flourished. On the California coast, other traders pursued sea-otter pelts, driving the once-bountiful otters nearly to extinction. Some historians have called this aggressive and often heedless exploitation of the West's natural bounty "**ecological imperialism**."

Yet Americans in this period also revered nature and admired its beauty. Indeed the spirit of nationalism fed a growing belief in the uniqueness of the American wilderness. Searching for the United States' distinctive characteristics in this nation-conscious age, many observers found the wild, unspoiled land of the West to be among the young nation's defining attributes. Devotion to the pristine natural beauty of the American

ecological imperialism *Historians' term for the spoliation of western natural resources through excessive hunting, logging, mining, and grazing.*

Mouth of the Platte River, 900 Miles Above St. Louis, by George Catlin, 1832 Catlin's West unfolded as a vast panorama of flat, open space peopled only by the Indians shown in the foreground. Catlin believed that capturing the unending prairie on canvas required a new aesthetic, the sublime horizontal, and an acceptance of a landscape bereft of man-built features, without "anything rising above the horizon, which was a perfect straight line around us, like that of the blue and boundless ocean."

wilderness became in time a national mystique, inspiring literature and painting and eventually kindling a powerful conservation movement.

George Catlin, a painter and student of Native American life, was among the first Americans to advocate the preservation of nature as a deliberate national policy. Appalled at the reckless slaughter of Indians and buffalo alike, Catlin proposed the creation of a national park to preserve nature and wildlife. His idea later bore fruit with the creation of the world's first national park system, beginning with Yellowstone Park in 1872.

★ The March of the Millions

As the American people moved west, they also multiplied at an amazing rate. By midcentury the population was still doubling approximately every twenty-five years, as in fertile colonial days. By 1860 the original thirteen states had more than doubled in number: thirty-three stars graced the American flag. The United States was the fourth most populous nation in the western world, exceeded only by three European countries—Russia, France, and Austria.

Urban growth continued explosively. In 1790 only two American cities could boast populations of twenty thousand or more: Philadelphia and New York. By 1860 there were forty-three, and about three hundred other places claimed over five thousand inhabitants apiece. New York was the metropolis; New Orleans, the "Queen of the South"; and Chicago, the swaggering lord of the Midwest, destined to be "hog butcher for the world."

Such overrapid urbanization unfortunately brought undesirable by-products. It intensified the problems of smelly slums, feeble street lighting, impure water, foul sewage, ravenous rats, and improper garbage disposal. Hogs poked their scavenging snouts about many city streets as late as the 1840s. Boston in 1823 pioneered with a sewage system, and

Table 14.1 Irish and German Immigration by Decade, 1830–1900

Years	Irish	Germans
1831–1840	207,381	152,454
1841–1850	780,719	434,626
1851–1860	914,119	951,667
1861–1870	435,778	787,468
1871–1880	436,871	718,182
1881–1890	655,482	1,452,970
1891–1900	388,416	505,152
TOTAL	3,818,766	5,000,519

New York in 1842 abandoned wells and cisterns for a piped-in water supply. The city thus unknowingly eliminated many of the breeding places of disease-carrying mosquitoes.

A continuing high birthrate accounted for most of the increase in population, but by the 1840s the tides of immigration were adding hundreds of thousands more. Before this decade, immigrants had been flowing in at the rate of about sixty thousand a year, but suddenly the influx tripled in the 1840s and then quadrupled in the 1850s. During these two feverish decades, over a million and a half Irish, and nearly as many Germans, swarmed down the gangplanks. Why did they come?

The immigrants came partly because Europe seemed to be running out of room. The population of the Old World more than doubled in the nineteenth century, and Europe began to generate a seething pool of apparently "surplus" people. They were displaced and footloose in their homelands before they felt the tug of the American magnet. Indeed, at least as many people moved about *within* Europe as crossed the Atlantic.

Yet America still beckoned most strongly to the struggling masses of Europe. About 35 million of the nearly 60 million emigrants who abandoned Europe in the century after 1840 headed for "the land of freedom and opportunity," where no aristocratic caste or state church oppressed the individual. Much-read letters sent home by immigrants—"America letters"—often described in glowing terms the richer life: low taxes, no compulsory military service, and "three meat meals a day." The introduction of transoceanic steamships also meant that the immigrants could come speedily and cheaply. The journey to the United States on a steamship now took ten or twelve days instead of ten or twelve weeks on a sailing vessel and was much less expensive than a voyage to more distant immigrant destinations such as Australia or Argentina. The United States also received a far more diverse array of immigrants than did other countries. Argentina, for example, had a higher proportion of immigrants relative to its population than did the United States, but they came mostly from Spain and Italy—while the United States beckoned to migrants from dozens of different nations. On board steamships, immigrants were still jammed into unsanitary quarters, thus suffering an appalling death rate from infectious diseases, but the nightmare was more endurable because it was shorter.

★ The Emerald Isle Moves West

Ireland, already groaning under the heavy hand of British overlords, was prostrated in the mid-1840s. A terrible rot attacked the potato crop, on which the people had become dangerously dependent, and about one-fourth of them were swept away by disease and hunger. Dead bodies were found by the roadsides with grass in their mouths. All told, about 2 million perished.

Tens of thousands of destitute souls, fleeing the Land of Famine for the Land of Plenty, flocked to America in the "Black Forties." Ireland's great export has been population, and the Irish take their place beside the Africans and the Jews as a dispersed people (see "Makers of America: The Irish," p. 217). These uprooted newcomers swarmed into the larger seaboard cities, such as Boston and New York, which rapidly became the largest Irish city in the world. Before many decades, more people of Irish descent lived in America than on the "ould sod" of Erin's isle.

Margaret McCarthy, a recent arrival in America, captured much of the complexity of the immigrant experience in a letter she wrote from New York to her family in Ireland in 1850:

"This is a good place and a good country, but there is one thing that's ruining this place. The emigrants have not money enough to take them to the interior of the country, which obliges them to remain here in New York and the like places, which causes the less demand for labor and also the great reduction in wages. For this reason I would advise no one to come to America that would not have some money after landing here that would enable them to go west in case they would get no work to do here."

Ancient Order of Hibernians (mid-nineteenth century) *Irish semisecret society that served as a benevolent organization for downtrodden Irish immigrants in the United States.*

Molly Maguires (1860s–1870s) *Secret organization of Irish miners who campaigned, at times violently, against poor working conditions in the Pennsylvania mines.*

Tammany Hall (established 1789) *Powerful New York political machine that primarily drew support from the city's immigrants, who depended on Tammany Hall patronage, particularly social services.*

The luckless Irish immigrants received no red-carpet treatment. They were scorned by the older American stock, especially "proper" Protestant Bostonians, who regarded the scruffy Catholic arrivals as a social menace. Barely literate "Biddies" (Bridgets) took jobs as kitchen maids. Broad-shouldered "Paddies" (Patricks) were pushed into pick-and-shovel drudgery on canals and railroads, where thousands left their bones as victims of disease and accidental explosions. It was said that an Irishman lay buried under every railroad tie. As wage-depressing competitors for jobs, the Irish were hated by native workers. "No Irish Need Apply" was a sign commonly posted at factory gates. The Irish, for similar reasons, fiercely resented the blacks, with whom they shared society's basement. Race riots between black and Irish dockworkers flared up in several port cities, and the Irish were generally cool to the abolitionist cause.

The friendless "famine Irish" were forced to fend for themselves. The **Ancient Order of Hibernians**, a semisecret society founded in Ireland to fight rapacious landlords, served in America as a benevolent society, aiding the downtrodden. It also helped to spawn the "**Molly Maguires**," a shadowy Irish miners' union that rocked the Pennsylvania coal districts in the 1860s and 1870s.

The Irish tended to remain in low-skill occupations but gradually improved their lot, usually by acquiring modest amounts of property. The education of children was cut short as families struggled to save money to purchase a home. But for humble Irish peasants, cruelly cast out of their homeland, property ownership counted as a grand "success."

Politics quickly attracted these gregarious Gaelic newcomers. They soon began to gain control of powerful city machines, notably New York's **Tammany Hall**, and reaped the patronage rewards. Before long, brogued Irishmen dominated police departments in many big cities, where they drove the "Paddy wagons" that had once carted their forebears to jail.

★ The German Forty-Eighters

The influx of refugees from Germany between 1830 and 1860 was hardly less spectacular than that from Ireland. During these troubled years, over a million and a half Germans stepped onto American soil (see "Makers of America: The Germans," p. 220). Most were uprooted farmers, displaced by crop failures and by other hardships, but a strong sprinkling were liberal political refugees. Saddened by the collapse of the democratic revolutions of 1848, they had decided to leave the autocratic fatherland and flee to America—the brightest hope of democracy. Germany's loss was America's gain. Zealous German liberals such as the public-spirited and anti-slavery Carl Schurz contributed richly to the elevation of American political life.

Unlike the Irish, many of the German newcomers possessed a modest amount of material goods. Most of them pushed out to the lush lands of the Midwest, notably Wisconsin, where they settled and established model farms.

The hand of Germans in shaping American life was widely felt in other ways. Like the Irish, they formed an influential body of voters. Having fled German militarism and European wars, they came to be a bulwark of isolationist sentiment in the upper Mississippi Valley. Better educated on the whole than the stump-grubbing Americans, they warmly supported public schools, including their *Kindergarten* ("children's garden"). They likewise did much to stimulate art and music. As outspoken champions of freedom, they became relentless enemies of slavery during the fevered years before the Civil War.

Makers of America

The Irish

During the wars that ravaged Europe from 1793 to 1815, Irish tenant farmers temporarily prospered by planting every available acre with wheat and potatoes to feed ravenous armies. But when peace came, wheat prices plummeted, and hard-pressed landlords, aided by British police, forced their tenants off the unprofitable land. Many displaced Irish farmers sought work in England; some went to America. Then in 1845 a blight that ravaged the potato crop sounded the final knell for the Irish peasantry. The resultant famine spread desolation throughout the island. In five years, more than a million people died. Another million sailed for America.

Most of the emigrants were under thirty-five years old. Families typically pooled money to send strong young sons to the New World, where they would earn wages to pay the fares for those who waited at home. These "famine Irish" mostly remained in the port cities of the Northeast, abandoning the farmer's life for the dingy congestion of the urban metropolis.

The disembarking Irish were poorly prepared for urban life. They found progress up the economic ladder painfully slow. Their work as domestic servants or construction laborers was dull and arduous, and mortality rates were astoundingly high. Escape from the potato famine hardly guaranteed a long life to an Irish-American; a gray-bearded Irishman was a rare sight in nineteenth-century America. For Irish-born women, opportunities were even scarcer; they worked mainly as domestic servants.

But it was their Roman Catholicism, even more than their penury or their perceived fondness for alcohol, that earned the Irish the distrust and resentment of their native-born Protestant American neighbors. The cornerstone of social and religious life for Irish immigrants was the Catholic parish. Worries about safeguarding their children's faith inspired the construction of parish schools, financed by the pennies of struggling working-class Irish parents.

If Ireland's green fields scarcely equipped her sons and daughters for the scrap and scramble of economic life in America's cities, life in the Old Country had instilled in them an aptitude for politics. Irish Catholic resistance against centuries of English-Anglican domination had instructed many Old Country Irish in the ways of mass politics. That political experience readied them for the boss system of the political "machines" in America's northeastern cities. Irish voters soon became a bulwark of the Democratic party, reliably supporting the party of Jefferson and Jackson in cities such as New York and Boston. As Irish-Americans such as New York's "Honest John" Kelly themselves became bosses, white-collar jobs in government service opened up to the Irish. They became building inspectors, aldermen, and even policemen—an astonishing irony for a people driven from their homeland by the nightsticks and bayonets of the British police.

Outward Bound, The Quay at Dublin, 1854 Thousands fled famine in Ireland by coming to America in the 1840s and 1850s.

Yet the Germans—often dubbed "damned Dutchmen"—were occasionally regarded with suspicion by their old-stock American neighbors. Seeking to preserve their language and culture, they sometimes settled in compact "colonies" and kept aloof from the surrounding community. Accustomed to the "Continental Sunday" and uncurbed by Puritan tradition, they made merry on the Sabbath and drank huge quantities of their favorite amber beverage, *Bier* (beer). Their Old World drinking habits, like those of the Irish newcomers, spurred advocates of temperance in the use of alcohol to redouble their reform efforts.

Contending Voices

Immigration, Pro and Con

Strong antiforeignism was reflected in the platform of the American (Know-Nothing) party in 1856:

"Americans must rule America; and to this end, native-born citizens should be selected for all state, federal, or municipal offices of government employment, in preference to naturalized citizens."

Yet the Boston transcendentalist and eventual convert to Roman Catholicism Orestes Brownson (1803–1876) wrote of Boston's Irish immigrant ghetto in 1852:

"Out from these . . . dirty streets will come forth some of the noblest sons of our country, whom we shall delight to own and honor."

[How have these kinds of attitudes toward immigrants affected American society over the last two centuries?]

Know-Nothing party (1850s) Nativist political party, also known as the American party, that emerged in response to an influx of immigrants, particularly Irish Catholics.

Awful Disclosures (1836) Maria Monk's sensational exposé of alleged horrors in Catholic convents. Its popularity reflected nativist fears of Catholic influence.

Crooked Voting A bitter "nativist" cartoon charging Irish and German immigrants with "stealing" elections.

★ Flare-Ups of Antiforeignism

The invasion by this so-called immigrant "rabble" in the 1840s and 1850s inflamed the prejudices of American "nativists." Not only did the newcomers take jobs from "native" Americans, but most of the displaced Irishmen were Roman Catholics, as were a substantial minority of the Germans. The Church of Rome was still widely regarded by many old-line Americans as a "foreign" and "popish" church.

Roman Catholics were now on the move. Seeking to protect their children from Protestant indoctrination in the public schools, they began in the 1840s to construct an entirely separate Catholic educational system—an enormously expensive undertaking for a poor immigrant community, but one that revealed the strength of its religious commitment. A negligible minority during colonial days, Catholics became a powerful religious group with the enormous influx of the Irish and Germans in the 1840s and 1850s. In 1840 they had ranked fifth, behind the Baptists, Methodists, Presbyterians, and Congregationalists. By 1850, with some 1.8 million communicants, they had bounded into first place—a position they have never lost.

Older-stock Americans were alarmed by these mounting figures. They professed to believe that in due time the "alien riffraff" would "establish" the Catholic Church at the expense of Protestantism and introduce "popish idols." The noisier American "nativists" rallied for political action. In 1849 they formed the Order of the Star-Spangled Banner, which soon developed into the formidable American, or **Know-Nothing party**—a name derived from its secretiveness. "Nativists" agitated for rigid restrictions on immigration and naturalization, and for laws authorizing the deportation of alien paupers. They also promoted a lurid literature of exposure, most of it pure fiction. The authors, sometimes posing as "escaped nuns," described shocking sins they imagined the cloisters concealed, including the secret burial of babies. One of these sensational books—Maria Monk's *Awful Disclosures* (1836)—sold over 300,000 copies.

Even uglier was occasional mass violence. As early as 1834 a Catholic convent near Boston was burned by a howling mob, and in ensuing years a few scattered attacks fell upon Catholic schools and churches. The most frightful flare-up occurred during 1844 in Philadelphia, where the Irish Catholics fought back against the threats of the "nativists." The City of Brotherly Love did not quiet down until two Catholic churches had been burned and some thirteen citizens had been killed and fifty wounded in several days of fighting. These outbursts of intolerance, though infrequent and generally localized, remain an unfortunate blot on the record of America's treatment of minority groups.

Immigrants were undeniably making America a more pluralistic society—one of the most ethnically and racially varied in the history of the world. Why, in fact, were such episodes of intolerance not even more frequent and more violent? Part of the answer lies in the robust American economy. The vigorous growth of the economy in these years ensured that immigrants could claim their share of American wealth without jeopardizing the wealth of others. Their hands and brains, in fact, helped fuel economic expansion. Immigrants and the American economy, in short, needed one another.

Without the newcomers, a preponderantly agricultural United States might have been condemned to watch in envy as the **Industrial Revolution** swept through nineteenth-century Europe.

Industrial Revolution *Shift toward mass production and mechanization that included the creation of the modern factory system.*

★ Creeping Mechanization

A group of gifted British inventors, beginning about 1750, perfected a series of machines for the mass production of textiles. This enslavement of steam multiplied the power of human muscles some ten-thousandfold and ushered in the modern factory system—and with it the so-called Industrial Revolution.

The factory system gradually spread from Britain to other lands. It took a generation or so to reach Western Europe, and even more time to take hold in the United States. Why was the youthful American Republic, eventually to become an industrial giant, so slow to embrace the machine?

Money for capital investment was not plentiful in pioneering America, whose industrial revolution, like that of many a developing country in later centuries, awaited an influx of foreign capital—which in turn awaited assurance of secure property rights, sufficient infrastructure, an adequate work force, and political stability. With the Republic lacking capital, raw materials lay undeveloped, undiscovered, or unsuspected. The Republic was one day to become the world's leading coal producer, but much of the coal burned in colonial times was imported from Britain.

The young country also had difficulty producing goods of high enough quality and cheap enough cost to compete with mass-produced European products. Long-established British factories provided especially cutthroat competition. Their superiority was attested by the fact that a few unscrupulous Yankee manufacturers, out to make a dishonest dollar, stamped their own products with faked English trademarks.

The British also enjoyed a monopoly of the textile machinery, whose secrets they were anxious to hide from foreign competitors. Parliament enacted laws forbidding the export of the machines or the emigration of mechanics able to reproduce them.

Although a number of small manufacturing enterprises existed in the early Republic, the future industrial colossus was still snoring. Not until well past the middle of the nineteenth century did the value of the output of factories exceed that of farms.

★ Whitney Ends the Fiber Famine

Samuel Slater has been acclaimed the "Father of the Factory System" in America, and seldom can the paternity of a movement more properly be ascribed to one person. A skilled British mechanic of twenty-one, he was attracted by bounties being offered to British workers familiar with the textile machines. After memorizing the plans for the machinery, he escaped in disguise to America, where he won the backing of Moses Brown, a Quaker capitalist in Rhode Island. Laboriously reconstructing the essential apparatus with the aid of a blacksmith and a carpenter, he put into operation in 1791 the first efficient American machinery for spinning cotton thread.

The ravenous mechanism was now ready, but where was the cotton fiber? Handpicking one pound of lint from three pounds of seed was a full day's work for one slave, and this process was so expensive that American-made cotton cloth was relatively rare.

Another mechanical genius, Massachusetts-born Eli Whitney, now made his mark. After graduating from Yale, he journeyed to Georgia to serve as a private tutor while preparing for the law. There he was told that the poverty of the South would be relieved if someone could only invent a workable device for separating the seed from the short-staple cotton fiber. Within ten days, in 1793, he built a crude machine called the **cotton gin** (short for engine), which was fifty times more effective than the handpicking process.

cotton gin (1793) *Eli Whitney's invention that sped up the process of harvesting cotton. The gin made cotton cultivation more profitable, revitalizing the southern economy and increasing the importance of slavery in the South.*

Few machines have ever wrought so wondrous a change. Almost overnight the raising of cotton became highly profitable, and the South was tied hand and foot to the throne of King Cotton. Human bondage had been dying out, but the insatiable demand for cotton reriveted the chains on the limbs of the downtrodden southern blacks.

Makers of America

The Germans

Between 1820 and 1920, a sea of Germans lapped at America's shores and seeped into its very heartland. Their numbers surpassed those of any other immigrant group, even the prolific and often detested Irish. Yet this Germanic flood, unlike its Gaelic equivalent, stirred little panic in the hearts of native-born Americans because the Germans largely stayed to themselves, far from the madding crowds and nativist fears of northeastern cities.

These "Germans" actually hailed from many different lands, because there was no unified nation of Germany until 1871, when the ruthless and crafty Prussian Otto von Bismarck assembled the German state out of a mosaic of independent principalities, kingdoms, and duchies. Until that time, "Germans" came to America as Prussians, Bavarians, Hessians, Rhinelanders, Pomeranians, and Westphalians. They arrived at different times and for many different reasons. Some, particularly the so-called Forty-Eighters—refugees from the abortive democratic revolution of 1848—hungered for the democracy they had failed to win in Germany. Others, particularly Jews, Catholics, Pietists, and Anabaptist groups such as the Amish and the Mennonites, coveted religious freedom.

Typical German immigrants arrived with fatter purses than their Irish counterparts. Small landowners or independent artisans in their native countries, they did not have to settle for bottom-rung industrial employment in the grimy factories of the Northeast and instead could afford to push on to the open spaces of the West.

In Wisconsin these immigrants found a home away from home, a place with a climate, soil, and geography much like central Europe's. Milwaukee, a crude frontier town before their arrival, became the "German Athens." It boasted a German theater, German beer gardens, a German volunteer fire company, and a German-English academy. In distant Texas, German settlements such as New Braunfels and Friedrichsburg flourished. These German colonies in the frontier Southwest mixed high European elegance with Texas ruggedness. When landscape architect and writer Frederick Law Olmsted toured these frontier outposts, he came across a German household where the settlers sat on "barrels for seats, to hear a Beethoven symphony on the grand piano."

These German colonizers of America's heartland also formed religious communities, none more distinctive or durable than the Amish settlements of Pennsylvania, Indiana, and Ohio. The Amish took their name from their founder and leader, the Swiss Anabaptist Jacob Amman. Like other Anabaptist groups, they shunned extravagance and reserved baptism for adults, repudiating the tradition of infant baptism. For this they were persecuted, even imprisoned, in Europe. Seeking escape from their oppression, some five hundred Amish ventured to Pennsylvania in the 1700s, followed by three thousand in the years from 1815 to 1865.

In America they formed enduring religious communities—isolated enclaves where they could shield themselves from the corruption and the conveniences of the modern world. To this day the German-speaking Amish travel in horse-drawn carriages and farm without heavy machinery. No ringing telephones punctuate the reverent tranquility of their mealtime prayer; no ornaments relieve the simplicity of their black garments. The Amish remain a stalwart, traditional religious community in a rootless, turbulent society.

"Little Germany" Cincinnati's "Over-the-Rhine" district in 1887.

South and North both prospered. Slave-driving planters cleared more acres for cotton, pushing the Cotton Kingdom westward off the depleted tidewater plains, over the Piedmont, and onto the black loam bottomlands of Alabama and Mississippi. Humming gins poured out avalanches of snowy fiber for the spindles of the Yankee machines. The American phase of the Industrial Revolution, which first blossomed in cotton textiles, was well on its way.

Factories at first flourished most actively in New England. Its stony soil made farming difficult and manufacturing attractive, and the rapid rivers provided abundant water power to turn the cogs of the machines. By 1860 more than 400 million pounds of southern cotton poured annually into the gaping maws of over a thousand mills. Factories eventually branched out into the populous areas of New York, New Jersey, and Pennsylvania. But the South, increasingly wedded to the production of cotton, developed little manufacturing because most of its capital was bound up in slaves.

★ Marvels in Manufacturing

America's factories spread slowly until about 1807, when there began the fateful sequence of the embargo, non-intercourse, and the War of 1812. The stoppage of European commerce drove both capital and labor from the waves onto the factory floor. Generous bounties were offered by local authorities for homegrown goods. "Buy American" and "Wear American" became popular slogans, and patriotism prompted the wearing of baggy homespun garments. President Madison donned some at his inauguration, where he was said to have been a walking argument for the better processing of native wool.

But the manufacturing boomlet broke abruptly with the peace of Ghent in 1815, as British competitors unloaded their dammed-up surpluses at ruinously low prices. Responding to pained outcries, Congress provided some relief when it passed the mildly protective Tariff of 1816—among the earliest political contests to control the shape of the economy.

As the factory system flourished, it embraced numerous other industries in addition to textiles. Prominent among them was the manufacturing of firearms, and here the wizardly Eli Whitney again appeared with an extraordinary contribution. Frustrated in his earlier efforts to monopolize the cotton gin, he turned to the mass production of muskets for the U.S. Army. Up to this time each part of a firearm had been hand-tooled, and if the trigger of one broke, the trigger of another might or might not fit. About 1798 Whitney seized upon the idea of having machines make each part, so that all the triggers, for example, would be as much alike as the successive imprints of a copperplate engraving. Journeying to Washington, he reportedly dismantled ten of his new muskets in the presence of skeptical officials, scrambled the parts together, and then quickly reassembled ten different muskets.

The principle of interchangeable parts was widely adopted by 1850. It gave rise to a host of other innovations, including Samuel Colt's fabled revolver, and it ultimately became the basis of modern mass-production, assembly-line methods. Ironically, the Yankee Eli Whitney, by perfecting the cotton gin, gave slavery a renewed lease on life, and thus perhaps made inevitable the Civil War. At the same time, by popularizing the principle of interchangeable parts, Whitney helped factories to flourish in the North, giving the Union a decided advantage when that showdown came.

The sewing machine, invented by Elias Howe in 1846 and perfected by Isaac Singer, gave another strong boost to industrialization. The sewing machine became the foundation of the ready-made clothing industry, which took root about the time of the Civil War. It drove many a seamstress from the shelter of the private home to the factory where, like a human robot, she tended the clattering mechanisms.

Each momentous new invention seemed to stimulate still more imaginative inventions. For the decade ending in 1800 only 306 patents were registered in Washington; but the decade ending in 1860 saw the amazing total of 28,000. Yet in 1838 the clerk of the **Patent Office** resigned in despair, complaining that all worthwhile inventions had been discovered.

Patent Office *Federal government bureau that reviews patent applications. A patent is a legal recognition of a new invention, granting exclusive rights to the inventor for a period of years.*

limited liability *Legal principle that facilitates capital investment by offering protection for individual investors, who, in cases of legal claims or bankruptcy, cannot be held responsible for more than the value of their individual shares.*

Technical advances spurred equally important changes in the form and legal status of business organizations. The principle of **limited liability** aided the concentration of capital by permitting the individual investor, in cases of legal claims or bankruptcy, to risk no more than his or her own share of the corporation's stock. Laws of "free incorporation," first passed in New York in 1848, meant that businessmen could create corporations without applying for individual charters from the legislature.

Samuel F. B. Morse's telegraph was among the inventions that tightened the sinews of an increasingly complex business world. A distinguished but poverty-stricken portrait painter, Morse finally secured from Congress, to the accompaniment of the usual jeers, an appropriation of $30,000 to support his experiment with "talking wires." In 1844 Morse strung a wire forty miles from Washington to Baltimore and tapped out the historic message, "What hath God wrought?" The invention brought fame and fortune to Morse, as he put distant people into almost instant communication with one another. By the eve of the Civil War, a web of singing wires spanned the continent, revolutionizing news gathering, diplomacy, and finance.

By the time of the fabled London World's Fair in 1851, American products were prominent among the world's commercial wonders. Fairgoers crowded into the dazzling "Crystal Palace" to see McCormick's reaper, Morse's telegraph, Colt's firearms, and Charles Goodyear's vulcanized rubber goods.

★ Workers and "Wage Slaves"

One ugly outgrowth of the factory system was an increasingly acute labor problem. Hitherto manufacturing had been done in the home, or in the small shop, where the master craftsman and his apprentice, rubbing elbows at the same bench, could maintain an intimate and friendly relationship. The Industrial Revolution submerged this personal association in the impersonal ownership of stuffy factories in "spindle cities." Around these, like tumors, the slumlike hovels of the "wage slaves" tended to cluster.

Clearly the early factory system did not shower its benefits evenly on all. While many owners grew plump, working people often wasted away at their workbenches. Hours were long, wages were low, and meals were skimpy and hastily gulped. Workers were forced to toil in unsanitary buildings that were poorly ventilated, lighted, and heated. They were forbidden by law to form labor unions to raise wages, for such cooperative activity was regarded as a criminal conspiracy. Not surprisingly, only twenty-four recorded strikes occurred before 1835.

Especially vulnerable to exploitation were child workers. In 1820 half the nation's industrial toilers were children under ten years of age. Victims of factory labor, many children were mentally blighted, emotionally starved, physically stunted, and even brutally whipped in special "whipping rooms." In Samuel Slater's mill of 1791, the first machine tenders were seven boys and two girls, all under twelve years of age.

By contrast, the lot of most adult wage workers improved markedly in the 1820s and 1830s. In the full flush of Jacksonian democracy, many of the states granted the laboring man the vote. Brandishing the ballot and strongly backing Andrew Jackson, workers pushed for the ten-hour workday, better wages and working conditions, public education for their children, and an end to the inhuman practice of imprisonment for debt.

Employers, abhorring the rise of the "rabble" in politics, fought the ten-hour day to the last ditch. But labor registered a red-letter gain in 1840 when President Van Buren established the ten-hour day for federal employees on public works. In ensuing years a number of states gradually fell into line by reducing the hours of working people.

> *A woman worker in the Lowell mills wrote a friend in 1844:*
>
> "You wish to know minutely of our hours of labor. We go in [to the mill] at five o'clock; at seven we come out to breakfast; at half-past seven we return to our work, and stay until half-past twelve. At one, or quarter-past one four months in the year, we return to our work, and stay until seven at night. Then the evening is all our own, which is more than some laboring girls can say, who think nothing is more tedious than a factory life."

Examining the Evidence

The Invention of the Sewing Machine

Historians of technology examine not only the documentary evidence of plans and patents left behind by inventors, but surviving machines themselves. In 1845 Elias Howe, a twenty-six-year-old apprentice to a Boston watchmaker, invented a sewing machine that could make 250 stitches a minute, five times what the swiftest hand-sewer could do. A year later Howe received a patent for his invention, but because the hand-cranked machine could only stitch straight seams for a short distance before requiring resetting, it had limited commercial appeal. Howe took his sewing machine abroad, where he worked with British manufacturers to improve it, and then returned to America and combined his patent with those of other inventors, including Isaac M. Singer. Hundreds of thousands of sewing machines were produced beginning in the 1850s for commercial manufacturing of clothing, books, shoes, and many other products and also for home use. The sewing machine became the first widely advertised consumer product. Due to its high cost, the Singer company introduced an installment buying plan, which helped place sewing machines in most middle-class households. Why was the sewing machine able to find eager customers in commercial workshops and home sewing rooms alike? How might the sewing machine have changed other aspects of American life, such as work patterns, clothing styles, and retail selling? What other advances in technology might have been necessary for the invention of the sewing machine?

1. Examine the photo of this sewing machine, built only one year after Elias Howe invented the first such machine in 1845. What are the key components that Howe had to combine in order improve on hand sewing? In what ways was this machine more limited than hand sewing—even if it was more efficient?

2. What functional and economic differences were there between Howe-Singer machines aimed at sewing within the home and those that came to be built for factory production of the ready-made clothing industry?

3. What made the sewing machine the rare invention that was *both* a capital-intensive industrial product *and* the "first widely advertised consumer product" sold "on the installment plan"?

National Museum of American History, Smithsonian Institution, Behring Center

Day laborers at last learned that their strongest weapon was to lay down their tools, even at the risk of prosecution under the law. Dozens of strikes erupted in the 1830s and 1840s, most of them for higher wages, some for the ten-hour day. The workers usually lost more strikes than they won, for the employer could resort to such tactics as importing strikebreakers—often derisively called "scabs" or "rats," and often fresh off the boat from the Old World. Labor long raised its voice against the unrestricted inpouring of wage-depressing and union-busting immigrant workers.

Labor's early and painful efforts at organization had netted some 300,000 trade unionists by 1830. But such encouraging gains were dashed on the rock of hard times following the severe depression of 1837. Yet toilers won a promising legal victory in 1842 when the Massachusetts Supreme Court ruled in *Commonwealth v. Hunt* that labor unions were not illegal conspiracies, provided that their methods were "honorable and peaceful." This enlightened decision did not legalize the strike overnight throughout the country, but it was a significant signpost of the times. Trade unions still had nearly a century to go before they could meet management on relatively even terms.

Commonwealth v. Hunt (1842) *Massachusetts Supreme Court decision that strengthened the labor movement by upholding the legality of unions.*

⭐ Women and the Economy

Women were also sucked into the clanging mechanism of factory production. Farm women and daughters had an important place in the pre-industrial economy, spinning yarn, weaving cloth, and making candles, soap, butter, and cheese. New factories undermined these activities, cranking out manufactured goods faster than they could be made by hand at home. Yet these same factories offered employment to the very young women whose work they were displacing. Factory jobs promised greater economic independence for women, as well as the means to buy the manufactured products of the new market economy.

"**Factory girls**" typically toiled six days a week, earning a pittance for dreary, ear-splitting stints of twelve or thirteen hours—"from dark to dark." The Boston Associates' textile mills at Lowell, Massachusetts, employed New England farm girls, carefully supervised on and off the job by watchful matrons who escorted them to church from their company boardinghouses.

factory girls *Young women employed in the growing factories of the early nineteenth century, who labored long hours in difficult conditions, living in socially new conditions away from farms and families.*

But factory jobs of any kind were still unusual for women. Opportunities for women to be economically self-supporting were scarce and consisted mainly of nursing, domestic service, and especially teaching. The dedicated Catharine Beecher, daughter of a famous preacher and sister of Harriet Beecher Stowe, tirelessly urged women to enter the teaching profession. She eventually succeeded beyond her dreams, as men left teaching for other lines of work and school teaching became a thoroughly "feminized" occupation. By 1850 about 10 percent of white women were working for pay outside their own homes, and about 20 percent of all women had been employed at some time prior to marriage.

The vast majority of working women were single. Upon marriage, they left their paying jobs and took up their new work (without wages) as wives and mothers. In the home they were enshrined in a **cult of domesticity**, a widespread cultural creed that glorified the traditional functions of the homemaker. From their pedestals, married women commanded immense moral power, and they increasingly made decisions that altered the character of the family itself.

cult of domesticity *Pervasive nineteenth-century cultural creed that venerated the domestic role of women. It gave married women greater authority to shape home life but limited opportunities outside the domestic sphere.*

Women's changing roles and the spreading Industrial Revolution brought some important changes in the life of the nineteenth-century home—the traditional "women's sphere." Love, not parental "arrangement," more and more frequently determined the choice of a spouse—yet parents often retained the power of veto. Families thus became more closely knit and affectionate, providing the emotional refuge that made the threatening impersonality of big-city industrialism tolerable to many people.

Most striking, families grew smaller. The average household had nearly six members at the end of the eighteenth century but fewer than five members a century later. The "fertility rate," or number of births among women age fourteen to forty-five, dropped sharply among white women in the years after the Revolution and, in the course of the nineteenth century as a whole, fell by half. Birth control was still a taboo topic for polite conversation,

The Sewing Floor of Thompson's Skirt Factory, 1859 The burgeoning textile industry provided employment for thousands of women in antebellum America—and also produced the clothes that women wore. This view of a New York City shop in 1859 illustrates the transition from hand-sewing (on the right) to machine-stitching (on the left). It also vividly illustrates the contrast between the kinds of "sewing circles" in which women had traditionally sought companionship to the impersonal mass-production line of the modern manufacturing plant. Note especially the stark exhortation on the wall: "Strive to Excel."

and contraceptive technology was primitive, but clearly some form of family limitation was being practiced quietly and effectively in countless families, rural and urban alike. Women undoubtedly played a large part—perhaps the leading part—in decisions to have fewer children. This newly assertive role for women has been called "domestic feminism" because it signified the growing power and independence of women, even while they remained trapped in the "cult of domesticity."

Smaller families, in turn, meant child-centered families, because where children are fewer, parents can lavish more care on them individually. European visitors to the United States in the nineteenth century often complained about the unruly behavior of American "brats." But though American parents may have increasingly spared the rod, they did not spoil their children. What Europeans saw as permissiveness was in reality the consequence of an emerging new idea of child-rearing, in which the child's will was not to be simply broken, but shaped.

In the little republic of the family, as in the Republic at large, good citizens were raised not to be meekly obedient to authority, but to be independent individuals who could make their own decisions on the basis of internalized moral standards. Thus, the outlines of the "modern" family were clear by midcentury: It was small, affectionate, and child-centered, and it provided a special arena for the talents of women. Feminists of a later day might decry the stifling atmosphere of the nineteenth-century home, but to many women of the time it seemed a big step upward from the conditions of grinding toil—often alongside men in the fields—in which their mothers had lived.

★ Western Farmers Reap a Revolution in the Fields

As smoke-belching factories altered the eastern skyline, flourishing farms were changing the face of the West. The trans-Allegheny region—especially the Ohio-Indiana-Illinois tier—was fast becoming the nation's breadbasket. Before long, it would become a granary to the world.

Pioneer farmers first hacked a clearing out of the forest and then planted their painfully furrowed fields in corn. The yellow grain was amazingly versatile. It could be fed to hogs ("corn on the hoof") or distilled into liquor ("corn in the bottle"). Both these products could be transported more easily than the bulky grain itself, and they became the early western farmer's staple market items. So many corn-fed hogs were butchered, traded, or shipped at Cincinnati that the city was known as the "Porkopolis" of the West.

Most western produce was at first floated down the Ohio-Mississippi river system to feed the booming Cotton Kingdom. Spurred on by the easy availability of the seemingly boundless acres, farmers continuously sought ways to bring more and more acres into cultivation. They were often frustrated by the thickly matted soil of the West that snagged and snapped fragile wooden plows. John Deere of Illinois in 1837 finally produced a light, steel plow that broke the stubborn soil.

In the 1830s Virginia-born Cyrus McCormick contributed the most wondrous contraption of all: a mechanical mower-reaper. The clattering cogs of McCormick's horse-drawn machine were to the western farmers what the cotton gin was to the southern planters. Seated on his red-chariot reaper, a single harvester could do the work of five men with sickles and scythes.

No other American invention cut so wide a swath as **McCormick's reaper**. It made ambitious capitalists out of humble plowmen, who now scrambled for more acres on which to plant more fields of billowing wheat. Subsistence farming gave way to food production for both domestic and foreign markets, as large-scale ("extensive"), specialized, cash-crop agriculture came to dominate the trans-Appalachian West. With commercial agriculture came mounting indebtedness, as farmers bought more land and more machinery to work it. With hustling Midwestern farmers producing more than the South could devour, they began to dream of markets in the mushrooming eastern factory towns, or across the faraway Atlantic. But they were still largely landlocked. Commerce moved north and south on the river systems. Before it could begin to move east-west in bulk, a transportation revolution would have to occur.

McCormick's reaper (1831) *Mechanized the harvest of grains, such as wheat, allowing farmers to cultivate larger plots. The introduction of the reaper in the 1830s fueled the establishment of large-scale commercial agriculture in the Midwest.*

★ Highways and Steamboats

In 1789, when the Constitution was launched, primitive methods of travel were still in use. Waterborne commerce, whether along the coast or on the rivers, was slow, uncertain, and often dangerous. Stagecoaches and wagons lurched over bone-shaking roads. Passengers would be rousted out to lay nearby fence rails across muddy stretches, and occasionally horses would drown in muddy pits while wagons sank slowly out of sight.

Cheap and efficient carriers were imperative if raw materials were to be transported to the factories, and if the finished product was to be delivered to consumers. A promising improvement came in the 1790s, when a private company completed the Lancaster **turnpike**, a broad, hard-surfaced highway that ran sixty-two miles from Philadelphia to Lancaster, Pennsylvania. The highly successful Lancaster turnpike returned dividends as high as 15 percent annually to its stockholders, attracted a rich trade to Philadelphia, and touched off the westward migration of the canvas-covered Conestoga wagons.

Western road building, always expensive, encountered many obstacles. One pesky roadblock was the noisy states' righters, who opposed federal aid to local projects. Eastern states also protested against being bled of their populations by the westward-reaching arteries.

Westerners scored a notable triumph in 1811 when the federal government started construction on the elongated National Road, also known as the Cumberland Road in

turnpike *Privately funded, toll-based public road constructed in the early years of the Republic to facilitate commerce.*

honor of its starting point in Cumberland, Maryland. Though construction was interrupted by the War of 1812 and by states' righters' complaints, the road finally reached Vandalia, Illinois, in 1839.

The steamboat craze, which overlapped the turnpike craze, was touched off by an ambitious painter-engineer named Robert Fulton. In 1807 he installed a powerful steam engine in the *Clermont*, dubbed "Fulton's Folly" by a dubious public. Belching sparks from its single smokestack, the quaint little ship steadily churned up the Hudson River from New York City to Albany, making the run of 150 miles in 32 hours.

The success of the steamboat was sensational. People could now in large degree defy wind, wave, tide, and downstream current. Within a few years Fulton had changed all of America's navigable streams into two-way arteries, thereby doubling their carrying capacity. Hitherto keelboats had been pushed up the Mississippi, with quivering poles and raucous profanity, at less than one mile an hour—a process that was prohibitively expensive. Now the steamboats could churn rapidly against the current, ultimately attaining speeds in excess of ten miles an hour. The mighty Mississippi had finally met its master. By 1820 there were some sixty steamboats on the Mississippi and its tributaries; by 1860 about a thousand steamboats, including some luxurious river palaces, were plying the inland waters.

★ Canals and the Iron Horse

A canal-cutting craze paralleled the boom in turnpikes and steamboats. Blessed with the driving leadership of Governor DeWitt Clinton, New York State started the trend when it dug the **Erie Canal** linking the Hudson River to the Great Lakes.

Begun in 1817, the canal eventually ribboned 363 miles. On its completion in 1825, a garland-bedecked canal boat glided from Buffalo, on Lake Erie, to the Hudson River and on to New York harbor. There, with colorful ceremony, Governor Clinton emptied a cask of water from the lake to symbolize "the marriage of the waters."

The water from Clinton's keg baptized the Empire State. Mule-drawn passengers and bulky freight could now be handled with thrift and dispatch, at the dizzy speed of five miles an hour. The cost of shipping a ton of grain from Buffalo to New York City fell from $100 to $5, and the time of transit from about twenty days to six.

Ever-widening economic ripples followed the completion of the Erie Canal. The value of land along the route skyrocketed, and new cities—such as Rochester and Syracuse—blossomed. Industry in the state boomed. The new profitability of farming in the Old Northwest—notably in Ohio, Michigan, Indiana, and Illinois—attracted thousands of European immigrants to the unaxed and untaxed lands now available. Flotillas of steamships soon traversed the Great Lakes, connecting with waiting canal barges at Buffalo. Interior waterside villages such as Cleveland, Detroit, and Chicago exploded into mighty cities.

Other profound economic and political changes followed the canal's completion. Many dispirited New England farmers, no longer able to face the ruinous competition from more productive midwestern farms, abandoned their rocky holdings and became industrial millhands or moved westward themselves. Still others shifted to more specialized fruit, vegetable, and dairy farming. The transformations in the Northeast showed how long-established local market structures could be swamped by the emerging behemoth of a continental economy. And as American products began to flow into international markets, even far-off Europeans began to feel the effects of America's economic vitality. Before long, Italian and Polish peasants displaced from their marginal farms by the arrival of cheap American grains would themselves come to America to build new lives.

The greatest single contribution to the developing continental economy initiated by the canals proved to be the railroad. It was fast, reliable, cheaper than canals to construct, and not frozen over in winter. Able to go almost anywhere, even through the Appalachian barrier, it defied terrain and weather. The first railroad appeared in the United States in 1828, and new lines spread with amazing swiftness. Andrew Jackson rode to his first

Erie Canal (completed 1825) *New York State canal that linked Lake Erie to the Hudson River. It dramatically lowered shipping costs, fueling an economic boom in upstate New York and increasing the profitability of farming in the Old Northwest.*

Map 14.2 The Railroad Revolution Note the explosion of new railroad construction in the 1850s and its heavy concentration in the North.

clipper ships (1840s–1850s) Small, swift vessels that gave American shippers an advantage in the carrying trade. Clipper ships were made largely obsolete by the advent of sturdier, roomier iron steamers on the eve of the Civil War.

Pony Express (1860–1861) Short-lived, speedy mail service between Missouri and California that relied on lightweight riders galloping between closely placed outposts.

presidential inauguration in 1829 in a horse-drawn carriage. At the end of his second term, eight years later, he departed from Washington in a railway car. By 1860, on the eve of the Civil War, only thirty-two years later, the United States boasted thirty thousand miles of railroad track, three-fourths of it in the rapidly industrializing North (see Map 14.2).

At first the railroad faced strong opposition from vested interests, especially canal backers. Anxious to protect its investment in the Erie Canal, the New York legislature in 1833 prohibited the railroads from carrying freight—at least temporarily. Early railroads were also considered a dangerous public menace, for flying sparks could set fire to haystacks and houses, and appalling railway accidents could turn the wooden "miniature hells" into flaming funeral pyres for their riders.

Railroad pioneers had to overcome other obstacles as well. Arrivals and departures were conjectural, and numerous differences in gauge (the distance between the rails) meant frequent changes of trains for passengers. In 1840 there were seven transfers between Philadelphia and Charleston. But gauges gradually became standardized, safety devices were adopted, and the Pullman "sleeping palace" was introduced in 1859. America at long last was being bound together with braces of iron, later to be made of steel.

★ Cables, Clippers, and Pony Riders

Other forms of transportation and communication were binding together the United States and the world. A crucial step came in 1858 when Cyrus Field, called "the greatest wire puller in history," stretched a telegraph cable under the deep North Atlantic waters from Newfoundland to Ireland. Although this initial cable went dead after three weeks of public rejoicing, a heavier cable laid in 1866 permanently linked the American and European continents.

American commercial shipping fell behind in the early nineteenth century, and American naval designers made few contributions to maritime progress. A pioneer American steamer, the *Savannah*, crept across the Atlantic in 1819, but it used sail most of the time and was pursued for a day by a British captain who thought it afire.

In the 1840s and 1850s, a golden age dawned for American shipping. Yankee naval yards, notably Donald McKay's at Boston, began to send down the ways sleek new crafts called **clipper ships**. Long, narrow, and majestic, they glided across the sea under towering masts and clouds of canvas. In a fair breeze they could outrun any steamer. The stately clippers sacrificed cargo space for speed, and their captains made killings by hauling high-value cargoes across the oceans in record times.

But the hour of glory for the clipper was relatively brief. On the eve of the Civil War, the British had clearly won the world race for maritime ascendancy with their iron tramp steamers ("teakettles"). Although slower and less romantic than the clipper, these vessels were steadier, roomier, more reliable, and hence more profitable.

No story of rapid American communication would be complete without including the Far West. By 1858 horse-drawn overland stage coaches, immortalized in Mark Twain's *Roughing It*, were a familiar sight. Their dusty tracks stretched from the banks of the muddy Missouri River clear to California.

Even more dramatic was the **Pony Express**, established in 1860 to carry mail speedily the two thousand lonely miles from St. Joseph, Missouri, to Sacramento, California. Daring, lightweight riders, leaping onto wiry ponies saddled at stations approximately ten miles apart, could make the trip in an amazing ten days. These unarmed horsemen galloped on, summer or winter, day or night, through dust or snow, past Indians and bandits. The speeding postmen missed only one trip, though the whole enterprise lost money and folded after only eighteen legend-leaving months.

Just as the clippers had succumbed to steam, the Pony Express riders were unhorsed by Samuel Morse's clacking telegraph keys, which began tapping messages to California in 1861. The swift ships and fleet ponies ushered out a dying technology of wind and muscle. In the future, machines would be in the saddle.

★ The Transport Web Binds the Union

More than anything else, the desire of the East to tap the West stimulated the **transportation revolution**. Until about 1830, the produce of the western region drained southward to the cotton belt or to the heaped-up wharves of New Orleans. The steamboat vastly aided the reverse flow of finished goods up the watery western arteries and helped bind the West and South together. But the truly revolutionary changes in commerce and communication came in the three decades before the Civil War, as canals and railroad tracks radiated out from the East, across the Appalachians, and into the blossoming heartland. The ditch-diggers and tie-layers were attempting nothing less than a conquest of nature itself. They would offset the "natural" flow of trade on the interior rivers by laying down an impressive grid of "internal improvements."

The builders succeeded beyond their wildest dreams. The Mississippi was increasingly robbed of its traffic, as goods moved eastward on chugging trains, puffing lake boats, and mule-tugged canal barges. By the 1840s Buffalo was handling more western produce than New Orleans. Between 1836 and 1860, grain shipments through Buffalo increased a staggering sixtyfold. New York City became the seaboard queen of the nation, a gigantic port through which a vast hinterland poured its wealth and to which it daily paid economic tribute.

By the eve of the Civil War, a truly continental economy had emerged. The principle of division of labor, which spelled productivity and profits in the factory, applied on a national scale as well. Each region now specialized in a particular type of economic activity. The South raised cotton for export to New England and Britain; the West grew grain and livestock to feed factory workers in the East and in Europe; the East made machines and textiles for the South and West.

The economic pattern thus woven had fateful political and military implications. Many southerners regarded the Mississippi as a silver chain that naturally linked together the upper valley states and the Cotton Kingdom. They would become convinced, as secession approached, that some or all of these states would have to secede with them or be strangled. But they overlooked the man-made links that now bound the upper Mississippi Valley to the East in intimate commercial union. Southern rebels would have to fight not only Northern armies but the tight bonds of an interdependent continental economy. Economically, the two northerly sections were conjoined twins.

transportation revolution *Term referring to a series of nineteenth-century transportation innovations—turnpikes, steamboats, canals, and railroads—that linked local and regional markets, creating a national economy.*

★ The Market Revolution

No less revolutionary than the political upheavals of the antebellum era was the **market revolution** that transformed a subsistence economy of scattered farms and tiny workshops into a national network of industry and commerce. As more and more Americans linked their economic fates to the burgeoning market economy, the self-sufficient households of colonial days were transformed. Most families had once raised all their own food, spun their own wool, and bartered with their neighbors for the few necessities they could not make themselves. In growing numbers, they now scattered to work for wages in the mills, or they planted just a few crops for sale at market and used the money to buy goods made by strangers in far-off factories.

market revolution *Eighteenth- and nineteenth century transformation from a disaggregated, subsistence economy to a national commercial and industrial network.*

As store-bought fabrics, candles, and soap replaced homemade products, a quiet revolution occurred in the household division of labor and status. Traditional women's work was rendered superfluous and devalued. The home itself, once a center of economic production in which all family members cooperated, grew into a place of refuge from the world of work, a refuge that became increasingly the special and separate sphere of women.

Revolutionary advances in manufacturing and transportation brought increased prosperity to all Americans, but they also widened the gulf between the rich and the poor. Millionaires had been rare in the early days of the Republic, but by the eve of the Civil War, several specimens of colossal financial success were strutting across the national stage. Spectacular was the case of fur-trader and real estate speculator John Jacob Astor, who left an estate of $30 million on his death in 1848.

Cities bred the greatest extremes of economic inequality. Unskilled workers, then as always, fared worst. Many of them came to make up a floating mass of "drifters," buffeted from town to town by the shifting prospects for menial jobs. These wandering workers accounted at various times for up to half the population of the brawling industrial centers. Although their numbers were large, they left little behind them but the homely fruits of their transient labor. Largely unstoried and unsung, they are among the forgotten men and women of American history.

Many myths about "social mobility" grew up over the buried memories of these unfortunate day laborers. Mobility did exist in industrializing America—but not in the proportions that legend often portrays. Rags-to-riches success stories were relatively few.

Yet America, with its dynamic society and its wide open spaces, undoubtedly provided more "opportunity" than did the contemporary countries of the Old World—which is why millions of immigrants packed their bags and headed for New World shores. Moreover, a rising tide lifts all boats, and the improvement in overall standards of living was real. Wages for unskilled workers in labor-hungry America rose about 1 percent a year from 1820 to 1860. This general prosperity helped to defuse the potential class conflict that otherwise might have exploded—and that did explode in many European countries.

CHAPTER SUMMARY

The youthful American republic expanded dramatically on the frontier in the early nineteenth century. Frontier life was often crude and hard on the pioneers, especially women.

Westward-moving pioneers often ruthlessly exploited the environment, exhausting the soil and exterminating wildlife. Yet the wild beauty of the West was also valued as a symbol of American national identity, and eventually environmentalists would create a national park system to preserve pieces of the wilderness.

Other changes altered the character of American society and its work force. Old cities expanded, and new cities sprang up in the wilderness. Irish and German immigrants poured into the country in the 1830s and 1840s, and the Irish in particular aroused nativist hostility because of their Roman Catholic faith.

Inventions and business innovations such as free incorporation laws spurred economic growth. Women and children were the most exploited early factory laborers. Male wage workers made some genuine gains in wages and hours but generally failed in unionization attempts.

The economic changes brought new roles not only for those women who worked in factories (usually only in their early years) but within the traditional sphere of the home. Families became smaller as well as more close-knit and affectionate, and women gained a larger share of authority within the home, exerting a kind of "domestic feminism." Families also became more child-centered, as child-rearing practices changed from authority to nurture.

The most far-reaching economic advances before the Civil War occurred in agriculture and transportation. The early railroads, despite many obstacles, gradually spread their tentacles across the country. Foreign trade remained only a small part of the American economy, but changing technology gradually created growing economic links to Europe. By the early 1860s the telegraph, railroad, and steamship had gone far toward replacing older means of travel and communication such as the canals, clipper ships, stagecoach, and pony express.

The new means of transportation and distribution laid the foundations for a continental market economy. The new national economy created a pattern of sectional specialization and altered the traditional economic functions of the family. There was growing concern over the class differences spawned by industrialization, especially in the cities. But the general growth of opportunities and the increased standard of living made America a magnetic "land of opportunity" to many people at home and abroad.

KEY TERMS

"Self-Reliance" (213)
ecological imperialism (213)
Ancient Order of Hibernians (216)
Molly Maguires (216)
Tammany Hall (216)
Know-Nothing party (218)
Awful Disclosures (218)
Industrial Revolution (219)
cotton gin (219)
Patent Office (221)
limited liability (222)
Commonwealth v. Hunt (224)
factory girls (224)
cult of domesticity (224)
McCormick's reaper (226)
turnpike (226)
Erie Canal (227)
clipper ships (228)
Pony Express (228)
transportation revolution (229)
market revolution (229)

PEOPLE TO KNOW

Samuel Slater
Eli Whitney
Elias Howe
Isaac Singer
Samuel F. B. Morse
John Deere
Cyrus McCormick
Robert Fulton
DeWitt Clinton
Cyrus Field
John Jacob Astor

MindTap is a fully online, highly personalized learning experience built upon Cengage Learning content. MindTap combines student learning tools—readings, multimedia, activities, and assessments—into a singular Learning Path that guides students through the course.

Chapter 15

The Ferment of Reform and Culture
1790–1860

• • •

*We [Americans] will walk on our own feet; we will work
with our own hands; we will speak our own minds.*

RALPH WALDO EMERSON, "THE AMERICAN SCHOLAR," 1837

Chapter Outline

- Religious Revivals
- The Mormons
- Educational Advances
- The Roots of Reform
- Women's Roles and Women's Rights
- Utopian Experiments
- A National Literature
- *Examining the Evidence: Dress as Reform*
- *Makers of America: The Oneida Community*
- *Varying Viewpoints: Reform: Who? What? How? and Why?*

A third revolution accompanied the reformation of American politics and the transformation of the American economy in the mid-nineteenth century. The revolution consisted of a diffuse yet deeply felt commitment to improve the character of ordinary Americans, to make them more upstanding, God fearing, and literate. Some high-minded souls were disillusioned by the rough-and-tumble realities of democratic politics. Others, notably women, were excluded from the political game altogether. As the young Republic grew, increasing numbers of Americans poured their considerable energies into an astonishing variety of religious revivals and reform movements.

Reform campaigns of all types flourished in sometimes bewildering abundance. There was not "a reading man" who was without some scheme for a new utopia in his "waistcoat pocket," claimed Ralph Waldo Emerson. Reformers promoted better public schools and rights for women, as well as polygamy, celibacy, rule by prophets, and guidance by spirits. Societies were formed against alcohol, tobacco, profanity, and the transit of mail on the Sabbath. Eventually overshadowing all other reforms was the great crusade against slavery (see pp. 262–265). Many reformers drew their crusading zeal from religion. Beginning in the late 1790s and boiling over into the early nineteenth century, the Second Great Awakening swept through America's Protestant churches, transforming the place of religion in American life and sending a generation of believers out on their mission to perfect the world.

FOCUS QUESTIONS

1. What were the most important changes in American religion in the early nineteenth century, and how did they foster movements for social reform?
2. What were the most important social and educational reform movements of the period, and how successful were they?
3. Why did the early women's movement sharply criticize the widespread "cult of domesticitiy" and "separate spheres" gender ideologies, and what successes and failures did female reformers experience?
4. How did the early utopian experiments and ideologies reflect the general religious, social, and intellectual ferment of early American democracy?
5. How did American intellectual and literary life generally reflect the spirit of American democracy? Which notable writers dissented from the idealistic spirit of transcendentalism and other optimistic beliefs?

CHRONOLOGY

1747	Shaker movement founded in Manchester, England	1837	Emerson delivers "The American Scholar" address Mary Lyon establishes Mount Holyoke Seminary Oberlin College admits female students
1770s	First Shaker communities established in New York		
1790s	Second Great Awakening begins	1840	London antislavery convention refuses to recognize female delegates
1794	Thomas Paine publishes *The Age of Reason*	1841	Brook Farm commune established
1795	University of North Carolina founded	1843	Dorothea Dix petitions Massachusetts legislature on behalf of the insane
1819	Jefferson founds University of Virginia	1845	Poe publishes "The Raven"
1825	New Harmony commune established	1846–1847	Mormon migration to Utah
1826	American Temperance Society founded Cooper publishes *The Last of the Mohicans*	1848	Seneca Falls Woman's Rights Convention held Oneida community established
1828	American Peace Society founded Noah Webster publishes dictionary	1850	Hawthorne publishes *The Scarlet Letter*
1830	Joseph Smith founds Mormon church *Godey's Lady's Book* first published	1851	Melville publishes *Moby Dick* Maine passes first law prohibiting liquor
1830–1831	Finney conducts revivals in eastern cities	1854	Thoreau publishes *Walden*
1835	Lyceum movement flourishes	1855	Whitman publishes *Leaves of Grass*

★ Reviving Religion

Church attendance was still a regular ritual for about three-fourths of the 23 million Americans in 1850. Alexis de Tocqueville declared that there was "no country in the world where the Christian religion retains a greater influence over the souls of men than in America." Yet the austere Calvinist rigor had long been seeping out of the nation's churches.

The rationalist ideas of the French Revolutionary era had done much to soften the older orthodoxy. Thomas Paine's widely circulated book *The Age of Reason* (1794) shockingly declared that all churches were set up "to terrorize and enslave mankind." American anticlericalism was seldom that vehement, but many of the Founders, including Jefferson and Franklin, embraced the liberal doctrines of **Deism**. Deists relied on reason rather than revelation, rejected the concept of original sin, and denied Christ's divinity. Yet they believed in a Supreme Being who had endowed human beings with a capacity for moral behavior.

Deism helped to inspire an important spinoff from Puritanism—the Unitarian faith, which began to gather momentum in New England at the end of the eighteenth century. Unitarians held that God existed in only *one* person (hence *uni*tarian) and not in the orthodox Trinity (God the Father, God the Son, and God the Holy Spirit). Although denying the deity of Jesus, Unitarians stressed the essential goodness of human nature, the possibility of salvation through good works, and God as a loving Father rather than a stern Creator. Embraced by many leading thinkers (including Ralph Waldo Emerson), the Unitarian movement appealed mostly to intellectuals whose rationalism and optimism contrasted sharply with the Calvinist doctrines of predestination and human depravity.

The Age of Reason (1794) Thomas Paine's anticlerical treatise that accused churches of seeking to acquire "power and profit" and to "enslave mankind."

Deism Eighteenth-century religious doctrine that emphasized reasoned moral behavior and the scientific pursuit of knowledge. Most Deists rejected biblical inerrancy and the divinity of Christ, but they did believe that a Supreme Being created the universe.

Second Great Awakening (early nineteenth century) *Religious revival characterized by emotional mass "camp meetings" and widespread conversion. Brought about a democratization of religion as a multiplicity of denominations vied for members.*

A boiling reaction against the growing liberalism in religion set in about 1800. A fresh wave of roaring revivals, beginning on the southern frontier but soon rolling even into the cities of the Northeast, sent the Second Great Awakening surging across the land. Sweeping up more people than the First Great Awakening almost a century earlier (see pp. 69–71), the Second Awakening was one of the most momentous episodes in the history of American religion. This tidal wave of spiritual fervor left in its wake countless converted souls, shattered and reorganized churches, and numerous new sects.

The Second Great Awakening was spread to the masses on the frontier by huge "camp meetings" where as many as twenty-five thousand people would gather for an encampment of several days. Thousands of spiritually starved souls "got religion" at these gatherings, which boosted church membership and stimulated a variety of humanitarian reforms. Responsive easterners were moved to engage in missionary work among the Indians, in Hawaii, and in Asia. Everywhere the Second Awakening encouraged an effervescent evangelicalism that bubbled up into innumerable areas of American life—including prison reform, the temperance cause, the women's movement, and the crusade to abolish slavery.

Methodists and Baptists reaped the most abundant harvest of souls from the fields fertilized by revivalism. Both sects stressed personal conversion (contrary to predestination), a relatively democratic control of church affairs, and a rousing emotionalism. As a frontier jingle ran,

The devil hates the Methodists
Because they sing and shout the best.

Powerful Peter Cartwright (1785–1872) was the best known of the Methodist "circuit riders," or traveling frontier preachers. This sinewy servant of the Lord ranged for a half-century from Tennessee to Illinois, calling upon sinners to repent. Bell-voiced Charles Grandison Finney, the greatest of the revival preachers, abandoned his career as a lawyer

Camp Meeting, by Alexander Rider (ca. 1829) At huge, daylong encampments, repentant sinners dedicated themselves to lives of personal rectitude and social reform. Fire-and-brimstone preachers like the one depicted here inspired convulsions, speaking in tongues, and ecstatic singing and dancing among the converted. Out of this religious upheaval grew many of the movements for social improvement in the pre-Civil War decades, including the abolitionist crusade.

to become an evangelist after a deeply moving conversion experience as a young man. Tall and athletically built, Finney held huge crowds spellbound with the power of his oratory. He led massive revivals in Rochester and New York City in 1830 and 1831. Holding out the promise of a perfect Christian kingdom on earth, Finney denounced both alcohol and slavery. He eventually served as president of Oberlin College in Ohio, which he helped to make a hotbed of revivalist activity and abolitionism.

A key feature of the Second Great Awakening was the feminization of religion, in terms of both church membership and theology. Middle-class women were the first and most fervent enthusiasts of religious revivalism, and they were the most likely to stay within the fold when the tents were packed up and the traveling evangelist left town. Perhaps women's greater ambivalence than men about the changes wrought by the expanding market economy made them such eager converts to piety. It helped as well that evangelicals preached a gospel of female spiritual worth and offered women an active role in bringing their husbands and families back to God. That accomplished, many women turned to saving the rest of society. They formed a host of benevolent and charitable organizations and spearheaded crusades for most, if not all, of the era's ambitious reforms.

> *In his lecture "Hindrances to Revivals," delivered in the 1830s, Charles Grandison Finney (1792–1875) proposed the excommunication of drinkers and slaveholders:*
>
> "Let the churches of all denominations speak out on the subject of temperance, let them close their doors against all who have anything to do with the death-dealing abomination, and the cause of temperance is triumphant. A few years would annihilate the traffic. Just so with slavery.... It is a great national sin. It is a sin of the church. The churches by their silence, and by permitting slaveholders to belong to their communion, have been consenting to it.... The church cannot turn away from this question. It is a question for the church and for the nation to decide, and God will push it to a decision."

★ Denominational Diversity

Revivals also furthered the fragmentation of religious faiths. Western New York, where many descendants of New England Puritans had settled, was so blistered by sermonizers preaching "hellfire and damnation" that it came to be known as the **Burned-Over District**. Millerites, or Adventists, who mustered several hundred thousand adherents, rose from the superheated soil of the Burned-Over District in the 1830s. The failed prophecy of their eloquent leader, William Miller, that Christ would return to Earth on October 22, 1844, dampened but did not destroy the movement.

Like the First Great Awakening, the Second Great Awakening tended to widen the gaps between classes and regions. The more prosperous and conservative denominations in the East were little touched by revivalism, and Episcopalians, Presbyterians, Congregationalists, and Unitarians continued to rise mostly from the wealthier, better-educated levels of society. Methodists, Baptists, and members of the new denominations spawned by the swelling evangelistic fervor tended to come from less prosperous, less "learned" communities in the rural South and West.

Religious diversity further reflected social cleavages when the churches faced up to the slavery issue. By 1844–1845 both the southern Baptists and the southern Methodists had split with their northern brethren over human bondage. In 1857 the Presbyterians, North and South, parted company. The secession of the southern churches foreshadowed the secession of the southern states. First the churches split, then the political parties split, and then the Union split.

Burned-Over District *Popular name for western New York, a region particularly swept up in the religious fervor of the Second Great Awakening.*

★ A Desert Zion in Utah

The smoldering spiritual embers of the Burned-Over District kindled one especially ardent flame in 1830. In that year Joseph Smith—a rugged visionary, proud of his prowess at wrestling—reported that he had received some golden plates from an angel. When deciphered, they constituted the Book of Mormon, and the Church of Jesus Christ of Latter-Day Saints (**Mormons**) was launched. It was a native American product, a new religion, destined to spread its influence worldwide.

Mormons *Religious followers of Joseph Smith, who founded a communal, oligarchic religious order in the 1830s, officially known as the Church of Jesus Christ of Latter-Day Saints. Mormons, facing deep hostility from their non-Mormon neighbors, eventually migrated west and established a flourishing settlement in the Utah desert.*

After establishing a religious oligarchy, Smith ran into serious opposition from his non-Mormon neighbors, first in Ohio and then in Missouri and Illinois. His cooperative sect antagonized rank-and-file Americans, who were individualistic and dedicated to free enterprise. The Mormons aroused further antagonism by voting as a unit and by openly but understandably drilling their militia for defensive purposes. Accusations of polygamy likewise arose and increased in intensity, for Joseph Smith was reputed to have several wives.

Continuing hostility finally drove the Mormons to desperate measures. In 1844 Joseph Smith and his brother were murdered and mangled by a mob in Carthage, Illinois, and the movement seemed near collapse. The falling torch was seized by a remarkable Mormon Moses named Brigham Young. Stern and austere, in contrast to Smith's charm and affability, the barrel-chested Young quickly proved to be an aggressive leader, eloquent preacher, and gifted administrator. Determined to escape further persecution, Young in 1846–1847 led his oppressed Latter-Day Saints over vast rolling plains to Utah as they sang "Come, Come, Ye Saints."

Overcoming pioneer hardships, the Mormons soon made the desert bloom like a new Eden by means of ingenious and cooperative methods of irrigation. The crops of 1848, threatened by hordes of crickets, were saved when flocks of gulls appeared, as if by a miracle, to gulp down the invaders.

Semiarid Utah grew remarkably. By the end of 1848 some five thousand settlers had arrived, and other large bands were to follow them (see Map 15.1). Many dedicated Mormons in the 1850s actually made the 1,300-mile trek across the plains pulling two-wheeled carts.

Under the rigidly disciplined management of Brigham Young, the community became a prosperous frontier theocracy and cooperative commonwealth. Young married as many as twenty-seven women and begot fifty-six children.

A crisis developed when the Washington government seemed unable to control the hierarchy of Brigham Young, who had been made territorial governor in 1850. A federal army marched in 1857 against the Mormons, who harassed its lines of supply and rallied to die in their last dusty ditch. Fortunately, the quarrel was finally adjusted without serious bloodshed. The Mormons later ran afoul of the anti-polygamy laws passed by Congress in 1862 and 1882, and their unique marital customs delayed statehood for Utah until 1896.

★ Free Schools for a Free People

Tax-supported primary schools were scarce in the early years of the Republic. They had the odor of pauperism about them, because they existed chiefly to educate the children of the poor—the so-called ragged schools. Advocates of "free" public education met stiff opposition.

Between 1825 and 1850, the spread of democratic ideals and manhood suffrage for whites gradually won acceptance for the public schools, except in the slavery-cursed South. A free vote cried aloud for free education. A civilized nation that was both ignorant and free, declared Thomas Jefferson, "never was and never will be."

But most of the one-room, one-teacher "little red schoolhouses" of the time were imperfect shrines of democracy. Early free schools stayed open only a few months of the year. Schoolteachers, most of them men in this era, were often ill trained, ill tempered, and ill paid. These knights of the blackboard often "boarded around" in the community, and some knew scarcely more than their older pupils. They usually taught only the "three Rs—readin,' 'ritin,' and 'rithmetic."

Reform was urgently needed. Into the breach stepped Horace Mann (1796–1859), a brilliant and idealistic graduate of Brown University. As secretary of the Massachusetts Board of Education, he campaigned effectively for more and better schoolhouses, longer school terms, higher pay for teachers, and an expanded curriculum. His influence radiated out to other states, and impressive improvements were chalked up. Yet education remained

Map 15.1 The Mormon World After Joseph Smith's murder at Carthage, Illinois, in 1844, the Mormons abandoned their thriving settlement at Nauvoo, Illinois (which had about twenty thousand inhabitants in 1845) and set out for the valley of the Great Salt Lake, then still part of Mexico. When the Treaty of Guadalupe Hidalgo in 1848 brought the vast Utah Territory into the United States, the Mormons rapidly expanded their desert colony, which they called Deseret, especially along the "Mormon Corridor" that stretched from Salt Lake to southern California.

an expensive luxury for many communities. As late as 1860 the nation counted only about a hundred public secondary schools—and nearly a million white adult illiterates. Black slaves in the South were legally forbidden to receive instruction in reading or writing, and even free blacks, in the North as well as the South, were usually excluded from the schools.

Educational advances were aided by improved textbooks, notably those of Noah Webster (1758–1843), a Yale-educated Connecticut Yankee who was known as the "Schoolmaster of the Republic." His "reading lessons," used by millions of children in the nineteenth century, were partly designed to promote patriotism. Webster devoted twenty years to his famous dictionary, published in 1828, which helped to standardize the American language.

Equally influential was Ohioan William H. McGuffey (1800–1873), a teacher-preacher of rare power. His grade-school readers, first published in the 1830s, sold 122 million copies in the following decades. *McGuffey's Readers* hammered home lasting lessons in morality, patriotism, and idealism.

★ Higher Goals for Higher Learning

Higher education was likewise stirring. The religious zeal of the Second Great Awakening led to the planting of many small, denominational, liberal arts colleges, chiefly in the South and West. The first state-supported universities sprang up in the South, beginning with North Carolina in 1795. Conspicuous among the early group was the University of

The Country School, by Winslow Homer, 1871 Stark and simple by latter-day standards, the one-room schoolhouse nevertheless contributed richly to the development of the young Republic.

Virginia, founded in 1819 by Thomas Jefferson, who also designed its beautiful architecture. He dedicated the university to freedom from religious or political shackles, and modern languages and the sciences received unusual emphasis.

Women's higher education was frowned upon in the early decades of the nineteenth century. A woman's place was believed to be in the home, and training in needlecraft seemed more important than training in algebra. Prejudices prevailed that too much learning injured the feminine brain, undermined health, and rendered a young lady unfit for marriage. The teachers of Susan B. Anthony, the future feminist, refused to instruct her in long division.

Women's schools at the secondary level began to attain some respectability in the 1820s, thanks in part to the dedicated work of Emma Willard (1787–1870). In 1821 she established the Troy (New York) Female Seminary. Oberlin College in Ohio shocked traditionalists in 1837 when it opened its doors to women as well as men. (Oberlin had already created shock waves by admitting black students.) In the same year, Mary Lyon established an outstanding women's school, Mount Holyoke Seminary (later College), in South Hadley, Massachusetts.

Adults who craved more learning satisfied their thirst for knowledge at private subscription libraries or, increasingly, at tax-supported libraries. House-to-house peddlers also did a lush business in feeding the public appetite for culture. Traveling lecturers helped to carry learning to the masses through the **lyceum** lecture associations, which numbered about three thousand by 1835. The lyceums provided platforms for speakers in such areas as science, literature, and moral philosophy. Talented talkers such as Ralph Waldo Emerson journeyed thousands of miles on the lyceum circuits, casting their pearls of civilization before appreciative audiences.

Magazines flourished in the pre-Civil War years. The *North American Review*, founded in 1815, was the long-lived leader of the intellectuals. *Godey's Lady's Book*, founded in 1830, survived until 1898 and attained an enormous circulation (for those days) of 150,000. It was devoured devotedly by millions of women, many of whom read the dog-eared copies of their relatives and friends.

lyceum *(From the Greek name for the ancient Athenian school where Aristotle taught.) Public lecture hall that hosted speakers on topics ranging from science to moral philosophy. Part of a broader flourishing of higher education in the mid-nineteenth century.*

The Women Graduates of the Oberlin College Class of 1855 Oberlin was the first coeducational institution of higher education in the United States, accepting women in 1837, two years after it had welcomed African Americans. Feminists continued to press for coeducation and by 1872, ninety-seven American universities accepted women. At some of these institutions, however, such as Radcliffe College of Harvard University and Barnard College at Columbia University, women were educated in associated schools, not alongside male students.

★ An Age of Reform

As the young Republic grew, reform campaigns of all types flourished in sometimes bewildering abundance. Some of the reformers, usually touched by the fire of evangelical religion, were simply cranks, but most were intelligent, inspired idealists. The optimistic fervor of the Second Great Awakening stirred countless souls to do battle against earthly evils. These modern idealists dreamed anew the old Puritan vision of a perfected society free from cruelty, war, intoxicating drink, discrimination, and—ultimately—slavery. Women were particularly prominent in these reform crusades, especially in their own struggle for suffrage. For many middle-class women, the campaigns provided a unique opportunity to escape the confines of the home and enter the arena of public affairs.

In part the practical, activist Christianity of these reformers resulted from their desire to reaffirm traditional values as they plunged ever further into a world disrupted and transformed by the turbulent forces of a market economy. Often blissfully unaware that they were witnessing the dawn of the industrial era, they either ignored the factory workers or blamed their problems on bad habits. Reformers sometimes applied conventional virtue to refurbishing an older order—while events hurtled them headlong into the new.

Imprisonment for debt continued to be a nightmare. As late as 1830 hundreds of penniless people were languishing in filthy holes. The poorer working classes were especially hard hit by this merciless practice. But as the embattled laborer won the ballot and asserted himself, state legislators gradually abolished the debtors' prisons and softened the criminal codes. The number of capital offenses was reduced, and brutal punishments, such as whipping and branding, were slowly eliminated. A refreshing idea began taking hold that prisons should reform as well as punish—hence, "reformatories," "houses of correction," and "penitentiaries" (for penance).

Sufferers from so-called insanity were still being treated with incredible cruelty. The mentally deranged were considered willfully perverse and depraved—to be treated only as beasts. A formidable New England teacher-author, Dorothea Dix (1802–1887) spent eight years observing these conditions at first hand and then presented her classic petition to the Massachusetts legislature in 1843. Her description of cells so foul that visitors were driven back by the stench turned legislative stomachs and hearts. Her persistent prodding resulted in improved conditions and in a gain for the concept that the demented were not willfully perverse but mentally ill.

Agitation for peace also gained momentum in the pre–Civil War years. In 1828 the American Peace Society was formed, with a ringing declaration of war on war. The American peace crusade, linked with a European counterpart, was making promising progress by midcentury, but the crusade was set back by the bloodshed of the Crimean War in Europe and the Civil War in America.

★ Demon Rum: The "Old Deluder"

The ever-present drink problem also attracted dedicated reformers. Excessive drinking of hard liquor was common even among women, clergymen, and members of Congress. Weddings and funerals all too often became disgraceful brawls, and occasionally a drunken mourner would fall into the open grave with the corpse. Drunkenness also fouled the sanctity of the family, threatening the spiritual welfare—and physical safety—of women and children.

American Temperance Society *Founded in Boston in 1826 as part of a growing effort of nineteenth-century reformers to limit alcohol consumption.*

After earlier and feebler efforts, the **American Temperance Society** was formed at Boston in 1826. Within a few years about a thousand local groups sprang into existence. They implored drinkers to sign the temperance pledge and organized children's clubs, known as the "Cold Water Army."

The most popular anti-alcohol tract of the era was T. S. Arthur's melodramatic novel, *Ten Nights in a Barroom and What I Saw There* (1854). It described in shocking detail how a once-happy village was ruined by Sam Slade's tavern. The book was second only to Harriet Beecher Stowe's *Uncle Tom's Cabin* as a best seller in the 1850s, and it enjoyed a highly successful run on the stage.

Maine Law of 1851 *Prohibited the manufacture and sale of alcohol. A dozen other states followed Maine's lead, though most statutes proved ineffective and were repealed within a decade.*

Early foes of Demon Drink adopted two major lines of attack. One was to stiffen the individual's will to resist the wiles of the little brown jug. The moderate reformers thus stressed temperance rather than the total elimination of intoxicants. But less patient zealots came to believe that temptation should be removed by legislation. Prominent among this group was Neal S. Dow of Maine, a blue-nosed reformer who, as mayor of Portland and an employer of labor, had often witnessed the debauching effect of alcohol.

Dow—the "Father of Prohibition"—sponsored the so-called **Maine Law of 1851**. This drastic new statute, hailed as "the law of Heaven Americanized," prohibited the manufacture and sale of intoxicating liquor. Other states in the North followed Maine's example, and by 1857 about a dozen had passed various prohibitory laws.

On the eve of the Civil War the prohibitionists had registered inspiring gains. There was much less drinking among women than earlier in the century and probably much less per capita consumption of hard liquor.

> *In presenting her case to the Massachusetts legislature for more humane treatment for the mentally ill, Dorothea Dix (1802–1887) quoted from the notebook she carried with her as she traveled around the state:*
>
> *"Lincoln. A woman in a cage. Medford. One idiotic subject chained, and one in a close stall for seventeen years. Pepperell. One often doubly chained, hand and foot; another violent; several peaceable now.... Dedham. The insane disadvantageously placed in the jail. In the almshouse, two females in stalls ...; lie in wooden bunks filled with straw; always shut up. One of these subjects is supposed curable. The overseers of the poor have declined giving her a trial at the hospital, as I was informed, on account of expense."*

★ Women in Revolt

When the nineteenth century opened, it was still a man's world, both in America and in Europe. A wife was supposed to immerse herself in her home and subordinate herself to her husband. Like black slaves, she could not vote; like black slaves, she could be legally beaten by her overlord "with a reasonable instrument." When she married, she could not retain title to her property; it passed to her husband. Women in America were still the "submerged sex" in the early part of the century, though their position was somewhat better than that of their European cousins. French visitor Alexis de Tocqueville noted that in his native France rape was punished only lightly, whereas in America it was one of the few crimes punishable by death.

But as the decades unfolded, American women increasingly surfaced to breathe the air of freedom and self-determination. In contrast to women in colonial times, many women now avoided marriage altogether—about 10 percent of adult women remained "spinsters" at the time of the Civil War.

Gender differences were strongly emphasized in nineteenth-century America—largely because the burgeoning market economy was increasingly separating women and men into sharply distinct economic roles. Women were thought to be physically and emotionally weak but also artistic and refined. Endowed with finely tuned moral sensibilities, women were the keepers of society's conscience, with special responsibility to teach the young how to be good citizens of the Republic. Men were considered strong but crude, always in danger of slipping into some savage or beastly way of life if not guided by the gentle hands of their loving ladies.

The home was a woman's special sphere, the centerpiece of the "cult of domesticity." Even reformers such as Catharine Beecher, who urged her sisters to seek employment as teachers, endlessly celebrated the role of the good homemaker. But some women increasingly felt that the glorified sanctuary of the home was in fact a gilded cage. They yearned to tear down the bars that separated the private world of women from the public world of men.

Clamorous female reformers—most of them white and well-to-do—began to gather strength as the century neared its halfway point. Most were broad-gauge battlers; while demanding rights for women, they joined in the general reform movement of the age, fighting for temperance and the abolition of slavery. Like men, they had been touched by the evangelical spirit that offered the promise of earthly reward for human endeavor. Neither foul eggs nor foul words, when hurled by disapproving men, could halt women heartened by these doctrines.

The women's rights movement was mothered by some arresting characters. Prominent among them was Lucretia Mott, a sprightly Quaker whose ire had been aroused when she and her fellow female delegates to the London anti-slavery convention of 1840 were not recognized. Elizabeth Cady Stanton, a mother of seven who had insisted on leaving "obey" out of her marriage ceremony, shocked fellow feminists by going so far as to advocate suffrage for women. Quaker-reared Susan B. Anthony, a militant lecturer for women's rights, fearlessly exposed herself to rotten garbage and vulgar epithets.

Other feminists challenged the man's world. Dr. Elizabeth Blackwell, a pioneer in a previously forbidden profession for women, was the first female graduate of a medical college. Precocious Margaret Fuller edited a transcendentalist journal, *The Dial*, and took part in the struggle to bring unity and republican government to Italy.

Contending Voices

The Role of Women

The emerging movement for women's social and political rights was often dismissed with sarcasm and contempt. With the title "Women out of their Latitude," a writer in an Albany, New York, newspaper in 1848 mocked the Seneca Falls Convention:

"We are sorry to see that the women, in several parts of this State, are holding what they call 'Woman's Rights Conventions,' and setting forth a formidable list of those Rights, in a parody upon the Declaration of American Independence. . . . The women who attend these meetings, no doubt at the expense of their more appropriate duties . . . are holding conventions and making an agitatory movement, with the object of revolutionizing public opinion. . . . Now it requires no argument to prove that this is all wrong."

A reform-minded newspaper replied:

"This is disposing of the matter very easily. *No argument can be given*, and so he says none is required. Then he presumes to dictate the place of women—the 'latitude,' as his heading has it. He talks of the awful change in society—the breaking away from the custom of *six thousand years ago*, as if women, or any institution among men remained now as they were in the darkness of ignorance and vice when women did the chief physical labor of the world."

Why did feelings run so high on this issue?

Examining the Evidence

Dress as Reform

Among the many social movements that swept nineteenth-century America, dress reform emerged in the 1840s as a critique of materialism and the constraints that fashion imposed on women. Medical professionals, social reformers, and transcendentalist intellectuals all argued that corsets constricting vital organs and voluminous skirts dragging along garbage-strewn streets unfairly restricted women's mobility, prevented women from bearing healthy children, and even induced serious sickness and death. The "Bloomer costume" depicted in this illustration from 1853 included Turkish-style trousers, a jacket, and a short overskirt. Named after reformer Amelia Bloomer (1818–1894), who publicized the new style in her magazine, *The Lily*, the bloomer dress was first adopted by utopian communities such as the Owenites in New Harmony, Indiana, and the Oneidans in New York. Radical social critic Henry David Thoreau also advocated rational dress as a way of rejecting the artificial desires created by industrialization. But while applauded by reformers, new-style dress was viciously ridiculed by mainstream society. Critics claimed that women blurred gender distinctions by adopting "male" attire, endangering the family and even American civilization. After only a decade, practitioners gave up wearing bloomers in public, adopting plain and simplified clothing instead. But Owenites, some Mormons, women's rights advocates, farmers, and travelers on the overland trail continued to wear bloomers in private. How did dress reform intersect with other religious and social movements of the era? Why did bloomers upset so many antebellum Americans? Have there been other historical eras when new styles of dress came to symbolize broader social change?

1. In this illustration of the "Bloomer costume," what is the apparent attitude of the illustrator toward the experimental dress? Enthusiastic? Hostile? Amused? What details might convey this perspective? How does the bloomer outfit itself contrast with the more traditional female dress of the nineteenth century? Does it seem to accomplish the goal of "liberating" women from both physical and social constraints?

2. How do the various female wearers of the "bloomers" seem to be adopting different stances toward stereotypical "femininity" and "masculinity"? Which woman or pair of women seem to be most vigorously challenging conventional gender roles, e.g., by adopting supposedly "male" dress or behaviors?

BLOOMER COSTUMES OR WOMAN'S EMANCIPATION.

Harry T. Peters "America on Stone" Collection, National Museum of American History, Smithsonian Institution.

The talented Grimké sisters, Sarah and Angelina, championed antislavery. Lucy Stone retained her maiden name after marriage—hence, the latter-day "Lucy Stoners," who follow her example. Amelia Bloomer revolted against the current "street-sweeping" female attire by donning a short skirt with Turkish trousers—"bloomers," they were called—amid much bawdy ridicule about "Bloomerism" and "loose habits." A jeering male rhyme of the times jabbed:

> *Gibbey, gibbey gab*
> *The women had a confab*
> *And demanded the rights*
> *To wear the tights*
> *Gibbey, gibbey gab.*

Unflinching feminists met in 1848 in a memorable **Woman's Rights Convention at Seneca Falls**, New York. The defiant Stanton read a "Declaration of Sentiments," which in the spirit of the Declaration of Independence declared that "all men and women are created equal." One resolution formally demanded the ballot for females. Amid scorn and denunciation from press and pulpit, the Seneca Falls meeting launched the modern women's rights movement.

The crusade for women's rights was eclipsed by the campaign against slavery in the decade before the Civil War. Still, any white male over twenty-one could vote, while no woman could. Yet women were being gradually admitted to colleges, and some states, beginning with Mississippi in 1839, were even permitting wives to own property after marriage.

> *When early feminist Lucy Stone (1818–1893) married fellow abolitionist Henry B. Blackwell (1825–1909) in West Brookfield, Massachusetts, in 1855, they added the following vow to their nuptial ceremony:*
>
> "While acknowledging our mutual affection by publicly assuming the relation of husband and wife, yet in justice to ourselves and a great principle, we deem it a duty to declare that this act on our part implies no ... promise of voluntary obedience to such of the present laws of marriage, as refuse to recognize the wife as an independent, rational being, while they confer upon the husband an injurious and unnatural superiority."

★ Wilderness Utopias

Bolstered by the utopian spirit of the age, various reformers, ranging from the high-minded to the "lunatic fringe," set up more than forty communities of a cooperative, communistic, or "communitarian" nature. Seeking human betterment, a wealthy and idealistic Scottish textile manufacturer, Robert Owen, founded in 1825 a communal society of about a thousand people at **New Harmony**, Indiana. Little harmony prevailed in the colony, which, in addition to hardworking visionaries, attracted a sprinkling of radicals, work-shy theorists, and outright scoundrels. The colony sank in a morass of contradiction and confusion.

Brook Farm in Massachusetts, comprising two hundred acres of grudging soil, was started in 1841 by about twenty intellectuals committed to the philosophy of **transcendentalism**. They prospered reasonably well until 1846, when they lost by fire a large new communal building shortly before its completion. The whole venture in "plain living and high thinking" then collapsed in debt. The Brook Farm experiment inspired Nathaniel Hawthorne's classic novel *The Blithedale Romance* (1852) in which the main character was modeled on the feminist writer Margaret Fuller.

A more radical experiment was the Oneida Colony, founded in New York in 1848. It practiced free love ("complex marriage"), birth control (through "male continence," or *coitus reservatus*), and the eugenic selection of parents to produce superior offspring. This curious enterprise flourished for more than thirty years, largely because its artisans made superior steel traps and **Oneida Community** (silver) Plate. In 1879–1880 the group embraced monogamy and abandoned communism (see "Makers of America: The Oneida Community," p. 244).

Woman's Rights Convention at Seneca Falls (1848) *Gathering of feminist activists in Seneca Falls, New York, where Elizabeth Cady Stanton read her "Declaration of Sentiments," stating that "all men and women are created equal."*

New Harmony (1825–1827) *Communal society of around one thousand members, established in New Harmony, Indiana, by Robert Owen. The community attracted a hodgepodge of individuals, from scholars to crooks, and fell apart due to infighting and confusion after just two years.*

Brook Farm (1841–1846) *Transcendentalist commune founded by a group of intellectuals, who emphasized living plainly while pursuing the life of the mind. The community fell into debt and dissolved when their communal home burned to the ground in 1846.*

transcendentalism (mid-nineteenth century) *Literary and intellectual movement that emphasized individualism and self-reliance, predicated upon a belief that each person possesses an "inner light" that can point the way to truth and direct contact with God.*

Oneida Community *One of the more radical utopian communities established in the nineteenth century, it advocated "free love," birth control, and eugenics. Utopian communities reflected the reformist spirit of the age.*

Makers of America

The Oneida Community

John Humphrey Noyes (1811–1886), the founder of the Oneida Community, repudiated the old Puritan doctrines that God was vengeful and that sinful mankind was doomed to dwell in a vale of tears. Noyes believed in a benign deity, in the sweetness of human nature, and in the possibility of a perfect Christian community on earth. "The more we get acquainted with God," he declared, "the more we shall find it our special duty to be happy."

That sunny thought was shared by many early-nineteenth-century American utopians (a word derived from Greek that slyly combines the meanings of "a good place" and "no such place"). But Noyes added some wrinkles of his own. The key to happiness, he taught, was the suppression of selfishness. True Christians should possess no private property—nor should they indulge in exclusive emotional relationships, which bred jealousy, quarreling, and covetousness. Material things and sexual partners alike, Noyes preached, should be shared. Marriage should not be monogamous. Instead all members of the community should be free to love one another in "complex marriage." Noyes called his system "Bible Communism."

Tall and slender, with piercing blue eyes and reddish hair, the charismatic Noyes began voicing these ideas in his hometown of Putney, Vermont, in the 1830s. He soon attracted a group of followers who called themselves the Putney Association, a kind of extended family whose members farmed five hundred acres by day and sang and prayed together in the evenings.

The Putney Association also indulged in sexual practices that outraged the surrounding community's sense of moral propriety. Indicted for adultery in 1847, Noyes led his followers to Oneida, in the supposedly more tolerant region of New York's Burned-Over District, the following year.

The Oneidans struggled in New York until the manufacture of steel animal traps and other goods put the Community on a sound financial footing. By the 1860s Oneida was a flourishing commonwealth of some three hundred people. Men and women shared equally in all the community's tasks, from field to factory to kitchen. Children at the age of three were removed from direct parental care and raised communally until the age of thirteen or fourteen, when they took up jobs in the community's industries. They imbibed their religious doctrines with their school lessons:

> I-spirit
> With me never shall stay,
> We-spirit
> Makes us happy and gay.

Oneida's apparent success fed the utopian dreams of others, and for a time it became a great tourist attraction. Visitors from as far away as Europe came to picnic on the shady lawns, speculating on the sexual secrets that the Community guarded, while their hosts fed them strawberries and cream and entertained them with music.

But eventually the same problems that had driven Noyes and his band from Vermont began to shadow their lives at Oneida. Their New York neighbors grew increasingly horrified at the Oneidans' licentious sexual practices, including the selective breeding program by which the community matched mates and gave permission—or orders—to procreate, without regard to the niceties of matrimony.

Yielding to their neighbors' criticisms, the Oneidans gave up complex marriage in 1879. Soon other "communistic" practices withered away as well. In 1880 the Oneidans abandoned communism altogether and became a joint-stock company specializing in the manufacture of silver tableware. Led by Noyes's son Pierrepont, Oneida Community, Ltd., grew into the world's leading manufacturer of stainless steel knives, forks, and spoons, until forced into bankruptcy in 2006. Ironically, what grew from Noyes's religious vision was not utopia but a mighty capitalist corporation.

The Founding Father John Humphrey Noyes (1811–1886) (The Granger Collection, NYC)

Among the longest-lived sects were the **Shakers**, founded in England by Mother Ann Lee. She moved her tiny band of followers to upstate New York in the 1770s—the first of a score or so of American Shaker communities. The Shakers attained a membership of about six thousand in 1840, but because their monastic customs prohibited both marriage and sexual relations, they were virtually extinct by 1940.

Shakers (established ca. 1770s) *Called "Shakers" for their lively dance worship, they emphasized simple, communal living and were all expected to practice celibacy. First transplanted to America from England by Mother Ann Lee, the Shakers counted six thousand members by 1840, though by the 1940s the movement had largely died out.*

★ Artistic Achievements

The arts in practical, pioneering, early America were slow to gain momentum and even slower to achieve real distinction. Architecturally, America contributed little of note in the first half of the century. The rustic Republic, still under pressure to erect shelters in haste, was continuing to imitate European models. Public buildings and other important structures followed Greek and Roman lines, which seemed curiously out of place in a wilderness setting. A remarkable **Greek Revival** came between 1820 and 1850. About midcentury strong interest developed in a revival of Gothic forms, with their emphasis on pointed arches and large windows.

Greek Revival *Inspired by the contemporary Greek independence movement, this building style, popular between 1820 and 1850, imitated ancient Greek structural forms in search of a democratic architectural vernacular.*

Talented Thomas Jefferson, architect of revolution, was probably the ablest American architect of his generation. He brought a classical design to his Virginia hilltop home, Monticello—perhaps the most stately mansion in the nation. The quadrangle of the University of Virginia at Charlottesville, another of Jefferson's creations, remains one of the finest examples of classical architecture in America.

Painting, like the theater, suffered from the Puritan prejudice that art was a sinful waste of time—and often obscene. When Edward Everett, the eminent Boston scholar and orator, placed a statue of Apollo in his home, he had its naked limbs draped.

Competent painters nevertheless emerged. Gilbert Stuart (1775–1828), a Rhode Islander and one of the most gifted of the early group, wielded his brush in Britain in competition with the best artists. He produced several portraits of Washington, all of them somewhat idealized and dehumanized. Charles Willson Peale (1741–1827), a Marylander, painted some sixty portraits of Washington, who patiently sat for about fourteen of them. John Trumbull (1756–1843), who had fought in the Revolutionary War, recaptured its scenes and spirit on scores of striking canvases.

During the nationalistic upsurge after the War of 1812, American painters turned increasingly from human subjects to romantic landscapes. The **Hudson River school** excelled in this type of art. At the same time, portrait painters gradually encountered some unwelcome competition from the invention of a crude photograph known as the daguerreotype, perfected about 1839 by a Frenchman, Louis Daguerre.

Hudson River school (mid-nineteenth century) *American artistic movement that produced romantic renditions of local landscapes.*

Music was slowly shaking off the restraints of colonial days, when the prim Puritans had frowned upon nonreligious singing. Rhythmic and nostalgic "darky" tunes were becoming immense hits by midcentury. Special favorites were the uniquely American **minstrel shows**, featuring white actors with darkened faces. The most famous black songs, ironically, came from a white Pennsylvanian, Stephen C. Foster (1826–1864). Foster made a valuable contribution to American folk music by capturing the plaintive spirit of the slaves in songs such as "Old Folks at Home." An odd and pathetic figure, he finally lost both his art and his popularity and died in a charity ward after drowning his sorrows in drink.

minstrel shows *Variety shows performed by white actors in blackface. First popularized in the mid-nineteenth century.*

★ The Blossoming of a National Literature

"Who reads an American book?" sneered a British critic in 1820. The painful truth was that the nation's rough-hewn, pioneering civilization gave little encouragement to "polite" literature. America produced praiseworthy political essays such as *The Federalist*, political orations such as the masterpieces of Daniel Webster, and classics such as Benjamin Franklin's *Autobiography* (1818). But most reading matter before 1820 was imported or plagiarized from Britain.

A genuinely American literature received a strong boost from the wave of nationalism that followed the Revolutionary War and especially the War of 1812. By 1820 the older seaboard areas were sufficiently removed from the survival mentality of tree chopping so that literature could be supported as a profession. The Knickerbocker Group in New York blazed brilliantly across the literary heavens, enabling America for the first time to boast of a literature to match its magnificent landscapes.

Washington Irving (1783–1859), born in New York City, was the first American to win international recognition as a literary figure. Steeped in the traditions of New Netherland, he published in 1809 his *Knickerbocker's History of New York*, with its amusing caricatures of the Dutch. Irving won fame at home and abroad with his *Sketch Book* (1819–1820), which included such immortal Dutch-American tales as "Rip Van Winkle" and "The Legend of Sleepy Hollow." Europe was amazed to find at last an American with a feather in his hand, not in his hair.

James Fenimore Cooper (1789–1851) was the first American novelist, as Washington Irving was the first general writer, to gain world fame and make New World themes respectable. After an initial failure, Cooper launched his illustrious career in 1821 with his second novel *The Spy*—an absorbing tale of the American Revolution. His fame rests most enduringly on the *Leatherstocking Tales*. A deadeye rifleman named Natty Bumppo, one of nature's noblemen, meets with Indians in stirring adventures such as *The Last of the Mohicans*. Some Europeans who read Cooper's novels came to think of all Americans as born with a tomahawk in hand. Actually Cooper was exploring the viability and destiny of America's republican experiment by contrasting the values of "natural men" of the wilderness with the artificiality of modern civilization.

A third member of the Knickerbocker Group in New York was the belatedly Puritan William Cullen Bryant (1794–1878). At age sixteen he wrote the meditative and melancholy "Thanatopsis" (published in 1817), one of the first high-quality poems produced in the United States. Critics could hardly believe that it had been written on "this side of the water."

★ Trumpeters of Transcendentalism

A golden age in American literature dawned in the second quarter of the nineteenth century, when an amazing outburst shook New England. One of the mainsprings of this literary flowering was transcendentalism, especially around Boston, which preened itself as "the Athens of America."

The transcendentalist movement of the 1830s resulted in part from a liberalizing of the straitjacket Puritan theology. It also owed much to foreign influences, including the German romantic philosophers and the religions of Asia. The transcendentalists rejected the prevailing theory, derived from John Locke, that all knowledge comes to the mind through the senses. Truth, rather, "transcends" the senses: it cannot be found by observation alone. Every person possesses an inner light that can illuminate the highest truth and put him or her in direct touch with God, or the "Oversoul."

These mystical doctrines of transcendentalism defied precise definition, but they underlay concrete beliefs. Foremost was a stiff-backed individualism in matters religious as well as social. Closely associated was a commitment to self-reliance, self-culture, and self-discipline. These traits naturally bred hostility to authority and to formal institutions of any kind, as well as to all conventional wisdom. Finally came exaltation of the dignity of the individual, whether black or white—the mainspring of a whole array of humanitarian reforms.

Best known of the transcendentalists was Boston-born Ralph Waldo Emerson (1803–1882). Tall, slender, and intensely blue-eyed, he mirrored serenity in his noble features. Trained as a Unitarian minister, he early forsook his pulpit and ultimately reached a wider audience by pen

---

In 1849 Henry David Thoreau (1817–1862) published "Resistance to Civil Government," (later renamed "Civil Disobedience"), asserting:

"All men recognize the right of revolution; the right to refuse allegiance to and to resist the government, when its tyranny or its inefficiency are great and endurable. But almost all say that such is not the case now.... I say, when a sixth of the population of a nation which has undertaken to be the refuge of liberty are slaves, and a whole country is unjustly overrun and conquered by a foreign army, and subjected to military law, I think that it is not too soon for honest men to rebel and revolutionize. What makes this duty more urgent is the fact, that the country so overrun is not our own, but ours is the invading army."

and platform. He was a never-failing favorite as a lyceum lecturer and for twenty years took a western tour every winter. Perhaps his most thrilling public effort was a Phi Beta Kappa address, **"The American Scholar,"** delivered at Harvard College in 1837. This brilliant appeal was an intellectual Declaration of Independence, for it urged American writers to throw off European traditions and delve into the riches of their own backyards.

"The American Scholar" (1837)
Ralph Waldo Emerson's address at Harvard College, in which he declared an intellectual independence from Europe, urging American scholars to develop their own traditions.

Hailed as both a poet and a philosopher, Emerson was not of the highest rank as either. He was more influential as a practical philosopher and through his fresh and vibrant essays enriched thousands of humdrum lives. Catching the individualistic mood of the Republic, he stressed self-reliance, self-improvement, optimism, and freedom. The secret of Emerson's popularity lay largely in the fact that his ideals reflected those of an expanding America. By the 1850s he was an outspoken critic of slavery, and he ardently supported the Union cause in the Civil War.

Henry David Thoreau (1817–1862) was Emerson's close associate—a poet, a mystic, a transcendentalist, and a nonconformist. Condemning a government that supported slavery, Thoreau refused to pay his Massachusetts poll tax and was jailed for a night.* A gifted prose writer, he is well known for *Walden: Or Life in the Woods* (1854). The book is a record of Thoreau's two years of simple existence in a hut that he built on the edge of Walden Pond, near Concord, Massachusetts. A stiff-necked individualist, he believed that he should reduce his bodily wants so as to gain time for a pursuit of truth through study and meditation. Thoreau's *Walden* and his essay *On the Duty of Civil Disobedience* exercised a strong influence in furthering idealistic thought, both in America and abroad. His writings later encouraged Mohandas Gandhi to resist British rule in India and, still later, inspired the development of American civil rights leader Martin Luther King, Jr.'s thinking about nonviolence.

Bold, brassy, and swaggering was the open-collared figure of Brooklyn's Walt Whitman (1819–1892). In his famous collection of poems, *Leaves of Grass* (1855), he gave free rein to his gushing genius with what he called a "barbaric yawp." Highly romantic, emotional, and unconventional, Whitman dispensed with titles, stanzas, rhymes, and at times even regular meter. He handled sex with shocking frankness, and his book was banned in Boston.

Whitman's *Leaves of Grass* was at first a financial failure. The only three enthusiastic reviews that it received were written by the author himself—anonymously. But in time the once-withered *Leaves of Grass*, revived and honored, won for Whitman an enormous following in both America and Europe.

Leaves of Grass gained for Whitman the informal title "Poet Laureate of Democracy." Singing with transcendental abandon of his love for the masses, he caught the exuberant enthusiasm of an expanding America that had turned its back on the Old World:

All the Past we leave behind;
We debouch upon a newer, mightier world, varied world;
Fresh and strong the world we seize—world of labor and the march—
Pioneers! O Pioneers!

Here at last was the native art for which critics had been crying.

Two women writers whose work remains enormously popular today also sprouted from this New England literary world. Louisa May Alcott (1832–1888) grew up in Concord, Massachusetts, in the bosom of transcendentalism, alongside neighbors Emerson, Thoreau, and Fuller. Her philosopher father Bronson Alcott occupied himself more with ideas than with earning a living, leaving his daughter to write *Little Women* (1868) and other books to support her mother and sisters. Not far away, in Amherst, Massachusetts, poet Emily Dickinson (1830–1886) lived as a recluse but created her own original world through precious gems of poetry. In deceptively spare language and simple rhyme schemes, she explored universal themes of nature, love, death, and immortality. Although

---

*The story (probably apocryphal) is that Emerson visited Thoreau at the jail and asked, "Why are you here?" The reply came, "Why are you not here?"

Dickinson hesitated during her lifetime to publish more than a dozen of her poems, when she died, nearly two thousand of them were found among her papers and eventually made their way into print.

⭐ Literary Individualists and Dissenters

Not all writers in these years believed so keenly in human goodness and social progress as Whitman and the New England transcendentalists. Edgar Allan Poe (1809-1849), who spent much of his youth in Virginia, was an eccentric genius. Orphaned at an early age, cursed with ill health, and married to a child-wife of thirteen who fell fatally ill of tuberculosis, he suffered hunger, cold, poverty, and debt. Poe was a gifted lyric poet, as the mesmerizing rhythms of "The Raven" attest. If he did not invent the modern detective novel, he at least set new high standards for it in tales like "The Murders in the Rue Morgue (1841)." A master stylist, he also excelled in the short story, especially of the horror genre, in which he shared his nightmares with fascinated readers.

Poe was fascinated by the ghostly and ghastly, as in "The Fall of the House of Usher" and other stories; Poe reflected a dark sensibility distinctly at odds with the usually optimistic tone of American culture. Partly for this reason, Poe has perhaps been even more prized by Europeans than by Americans. His brilliant career was cut short when he was found drunk in a Baltimore gutter and shortly thereafter died.

Two other writers reflected the continuing Calvinist obsession with original sin and with the never-ending struggle between good and evil. In somber Salem, Massachusetts, Nathaniel Hawthorne (1804-1864) grew up in an atmosphere heavy with the memories of his Puritan forebears and the tragedy of his father's premature death on an ocean voyage. His masterpiece was *The Scarlet Letter* (1850), which describes the Puritan practice of forcing an adulteress to wear a scarlet "A" on her clothing. In *The Marble Faun* (1860), Hawthorne dealt with a group of young American artists who witness a mysterious murder in Rome. The book explores the concepts of the omnipresence of evil and the dead hand of the past weighing upon the present.

Herman Melville (1819-1891), an orphaned and ill-educated New Yorker, went to sea as a youth and served eighteen adventuresome months on a whaler. "A whale ship was my Yale College and my Harvard," he wrote. Jumping ship in the South Pacific, he lived among cannibals, from whom he providentially escaped uneaten. His fresh and charming adventure tales were immediately popular, but his masterpiece, *Moby Dick* (1851), was not. The epic novel is a complex allegory of good and evil, told by its narrator Ishmael in terms of the conflict between a whaling captain, Ahab, and a giant white whale, Moby Dick. Captain Ahab, having lost a leg to the marine monster, lives only for revenge. His pursuit finally ends when Moby Dick rams and sinks his ship, leaving only one survivor. The whale's exact identity and Ahab's motives remain obscure. In the end, the sea, like the terrifyingly impersonal and unknowable universe of Melville's imagination, simply rolls on.

Moby Dick was widely ignored at the time of its publication; people were accustomed to more straightforward and upbeat prose. A disheartened Melville continued to write unprofitably for some years, part of the time eking out a living as a customs inspector in New York City, and then died in relative obscurity and poverty. Ironically, his brooding masterpiece about the mysterious white whale had to wait until the more jaded twentieth century for readers and for proper recognition.

⭐ Portrayers of the Past

A distinguished group of American historians was emerging at the same time that other writers were winning distinction. Energetic George Bancroft (1800-1891), who as secretary of the navy helped found the Naval Academy at Annapolis in 1845, has deservedly

Capturing a Sperm Whale, painted by William Page from a sketch by C. B. Hulsart, 1835 This painting and Melville's *Moby Dick* vividly portray the hazards of whaling. Despite the dangers, it proved to be an important industry from colonial times to the end of the nineteenth century.

received the title "Father of American History." He published a spirited, superpatriotic history of the United States to 1789 in six volumes (1834–1876), a work that grew out of his vast research in dusty archives in Europe and America.

Two other historians are read with greater pleasure and profit today. William H. Prescott (1796–1859) published classic accounts of the conquest of Mexico (1843) and Peru (1847). Francis Parkman (1823–1893) penned a brilliant series of volumes beginning in 1851. In epic style he chronicled the struggle between France and Britain in colonial times for the mastery of North America.

Early American historians of prominence were almost without exception New Englanders, largely because the Boston area provided well-stocked libraries and a stimulating literary tradition. These writers numbered abolitionists among their relatives and friends and hence were disposed to view the South unsympathetically. This "made in New England" interpretation dominated the writing of American history until the close of the nineteenth century.

Varying Viewpoints

Reform: Who? What? How? and Why?

Early chronicles of the antebellum period universally lauded the era's reformers, portraying them as idealistic, altruistic crusaders intent on improving American society. After World War II, however, some historians began to detect selfish and even conservative motives underlying the apparent benevolence of the reformers. They described reforms such as temperance, asylums, prison, and mandatory public education as efforts by anxious upper-class men and women to assert social control over the ferment of antebellum life. In this vein, one historian described a reform movement as "the anguished protest of an aggrieved class against a world they never made."

The wave of reform activity in the 1960s prompted a reevaluation of the reputations of the antebellum reformers. These more recent interpretations found much to admire in the authentic religious commitments of reformers and especially in the participation of women, who sought various social improvements as an extension of their function as protectors of the home and family.

Abolitionism, for example, which had once been blamed by some historians for the Civil War, received new favorable treatment as the racial climate began to change during the 1960s. Historians such as Benjamin Quarles and James Brewer Stewart once again showed sympathy for the abolitionist struggle. By the end of the twentieth century abolitionist men and women were revered as ideologically committed individuals dedicated not just to freeing the enslaved but to saving the soul of America.

Scholars animated by the modern feminist movement have also inspired a reconsideration of women's reform activity. Historians such as Nancy Cott, Kathryn Sklar, and Mary Ryan began to look more closely at what Cott called "the bonds of womanhood" and uncover the links between women's domestic lives and their public benevolent behavior. When men behaved in immoral or illegal ways, women reformers claimed that they had the right and duty to leave the confines of their homes and actively purify society.

More recently, historians Nancy Hewitt and Lori Ginzburg have challenged the idea of a single female reform identity, pointing to class-based tensions within female ranks and detecting a shift from an early focus on moral uplift to a more class-based appeal for social control. Historians of the suffrage movement have emphasized another kind of exclusivity among women reformers—the boundaries of race. Ellen DuBois has shown that, after a brief alliance with the abolitionist movement, many female suffrage reformers abandoned the cause of black liberation in order to achieve their own goal. Whatever historians may conclude about the liberating or leashing character of early reform, it is clear that they now have to contend with the ways in which class, gender, and race divided reformers, making the plural—*reform movements*—the more accurate depiction of the impulse to "improve" that pervaded American society in the early nineteenth century.

More recently, historians of all kinds of reform have highlighted the transatlantic dimensions of these movements. American reformers adopted ideas from their European counterparts, participating in waves of reform that extended well beyond the shores of the United States.

CHAPTER SUMMARY ★ ★ ★ ★ ★ ★ ★ ★ ★ ★ ★ ★ ★ ★

In early nineteenth-century America, movements of moral and religious reform accompanied the democratization of politics and the creation of a national market economy. After a period of growing rationalism in religion, a new wave of revivals beginning about 1800 swept out of the West. This "Second Great Awakening" not only transformed religious life but inspired energetic movements to reform other areas of society. Existing religious groups were further fragmented, and new groups such as the Mormons emerged. Women were especially prominent in these developments, becoming a major presence in the churches and discovering in reform movements an outlet for energies that were often stifled in masculinized political and economic life.

Among the first areas to benefit from the reform impulse was education. The public elementary school movement gained strength, while a few women made their way into still tradition-bound colleges. Women were also prominent in movements for improved treatment of the mentally ill, peace, temperance, and other causes. By the 1840s some women also began to agitate for their own rights, including suffrage. The movement for women's rights, closely linked to the antislavery crusade, gained adherents even while it met strong obstacles and vehement opposition.

While many reformers worked to improve society as a whole, others created utopian experiments to model their religious and social ideals. Some of these groups promoted radical sexual and economic doctrines, while others appealed to high-minded intellectuals and artists.

American culture was still quite weak in theoretical sciences and the fine arts, but a vigorous national literature blossomed after the War of 1812. In New England the literary renaissance was closely linked to the philosophy of transcendentalism promoted by Emerson and others. Many of the great American writers such as Walt Whitman reflected the national spirit of utopian optimism, but a few dissenters such as Hawthorne and Melville explored the darker side of life and of their own society.

KEY TERMS

- *The Age of Reason* (233)
- Deism (233)
- Second Great Awakening (234)
- Burned-Over District (235)
- Mormons (235)
- lyceum (238)
- American Temperance Society (240)
- Maine Law of 1851 (240)
- Woman's Rights Convention at Seneca Falls (243)
- New Harmony (243)
- Brook Farm (243)
- transcendentalism (243)
- Oneida Community (243)
- Shakers (245)
- Greek Revival (245)
- Hudson River school (245)
- minstrel shows (245)
- "The American Scholar" (247)

PEOPLE TO KNOW

- Peter Cartwright
- Charles Grandison Finney
- Joseph Smith
- Brigham Young
- Horace Mann
- Dorothea Dix
- Neal S. Dow
- Lucretia Mott
- Elizabeth Cady Stanton
- Susan B. Anthony
- Lucy Stone
- Amelia Bloomer
- Robert Owen
- Stephen C. Foster
- James Fenimore Cooper
- Ralph Waldo Emerson
- Henry David Thoreau
- Walt Whitman
- Louisa May Alcott
- Emily Dickinson
- Edgar Allan Poe
- Nathaniel Hawthorne
- Herman Melville
- Francis Parkman

MindTap is a fully online, highly personalized learning experience built upon Cengage Learning content. MindTap combines student learning tools—readings, multimedia, activities, and assessments—into a singular Learning Path that guides students through the course.

Part 3

TESTING THE NEW NATION
1820–1877

The Civil War of 1861 to 1865 was the awesome trial by fire of American nationhood and of the American soul. All Americans knew, said Abraham Lincoln, that slavery "was somehow the cause of this war." The war tested, in Lincoln's ringing phrase at Gettysburg, whether any nation "dedicated to the proposition that all men are created equal . . . can long endure." How did this great and bloody conflict come about? And what were its results?

American slavery was by any measure a "peculiar institution." It was rooted in both racism and economic exploitation and depended for its survival on brutal repression. Yet the American slave population was the only enslaved population in history that grew by means of its own biological reproduction—a fact that suggests to many historians that conditions under slavery in the United States were somehow less punitive than in other slave societies. Indeed, a distinctive and durable African American culture managed to flourish under slavery, further suggesting that the slave regime provided some "space" for African American cultural development. But however benignly it might be painted, slavery remained a cancer in the heart of American democracy, a moral outrage that mocked the nation's claim to be a model of social and political enlightenment. As time went on, more and more voices called more and more stridently for its abolition.

The nation lived uneasily with slavery from the outset. Thomas Jefferson was only one among many in the founding generation who felt acutely the conflict between the high principle of equality and the ugly reality of slavery. The federal government in the early Republic took several steps to check the growth of slavery. It banned slavery in the Old Northwest in 1787, prohibited the further importation of slaves after 1808, and declared in the Missouri Compromise of 1820 that the vast western territories secured in the Louisiana Purchase were forever closed to slavery north of the state of Missouri. Antislavery sentiment even abounded in the South in the immediate post-Revolutionary years. But as time progressed, and especially after Eli Whitney's invention of the cotton gin in the 1790s, the southern planter class became increasingly dependent on slave labor to wring profits from the sprawling plantations that carpeted the South. As cotton cultivation spread westward, the South's stake in slavery grew deeper, and the abolitionist outcry grew louder.

The controversy over slavery significantly intensified following the war with Mexico in the 1840s. "Mexico will poison us," predicted the philosopher Ralph Waldo Emerson, and he proved distressingly prophetic. The lands acquired from Mexico—most of the present-day American Southwest, from Texas to California—reopened the question of extending slavery into the western territories. The decade and a half following the Mexican War—from 1846 to 1861—witnessed a series of ultimately ineffective efforts to come to grips with that question, including the ill-starred Compromise of 1850, the conflict-breeding Kansas-Nebraska Act of 1854, and the Supreme Court's inflammatory decision in the *Dred Scott* case of 1857. Ultimately, the slavery question was settled by force of arms, in the Civil War itself.

The 1st Virginia Regiment These Virginia militiamen were photographed in 1859 while attending the trial of the abolitionist John Brown for treason against the state of Virginia. Two years later their regiment formed part of the Confederate army that struck for southern independence.

The Civil War, as Lincoln observed, was assuredly about slavery. But as Lincoln also repeatedly insisted, the war was about the viability of the Union as well and about the strength of democracy itself. Could a democratic government, built on the principle of popular consent, rightfully deny some of its citizens the same right to independence that the American revolutionaries had exercised in seceding from the British Empire in 1776? Southern rebels, calling the conflict "The War for Southern Independence," asked that question forcefully, but ultimately it, too, was answered not in the law courts or in the legislative halls but on the battlefield.

The war unarguably established the supremacy of the Union, and it ended slavery as well. But as the victorious Union set about the task of "reconstruction" after the war's end in 1865, a combination of weak northern will and residual southern power frustrated the goal of making the emancipated blacks full-fledged American citizens. The Civil War in the end brought nothing but freedom—but over time, freedom proved a powerful tool indeed.

What if ...?

- What if some sort of compromise between the North and South had prevented the Civil War?
- What might such a compromise have looked like?
- Would slavery have come to a peaceable end, and if so how?
- Was *any* such compromise politically possible—or morally defensible?

Chapter 16

The South and the Slavery Controversy

1793–1860

Those who deny freedom to others deserve it not for themselves, and, under a just God, cannot long retain it.

ABRAHAM LINCOLN, 1859

Chapter Outline

- The Economy of the Cotton Kingdom
- Poor Whites and Free Blacks
- The Plantation System
- The Human Face of the "Peculiar Institution"
- The Abolitionist Crusade
- Southern and Northern Responses to Abolitionism
- *Examining the Evidence: Bellegrove Plantation, Donaldsville, Louisiana, Built 1857*
- *Varying Viewpoints: What Was the True Nature of Slavery?*

At the dawn of the Republic, slavery faced an uncertain future. Touched by Revolutionary idealism, some southern leaders, including Thomas Jefferson, were talking openly of freeing the slaves. Others predicted that the iron logic of economics would eventually expose slavery's unprofitability, speeding its demise.

But the introduction of Eli Whitney's cotton gin in 1793 scrambled all those predictions. Whitney's invention made possible the wide-scale cultivation of short-staple cotton. The white fiber rapidly became the dominant southern crop, eclipsing tobacco, rice, and sugar. The explosion of cotton cultivation created an insatiable demand for labor, chaining the slave to the gin and the planter to the slave. As the nineteenth century opened, the reinvigoration of southern slavery carried fateful implications for blacks and whites alike—and threatened the survival of the nation itself.

FOCUS QUESTIONS

1. How did a small, elite planter aristocracy come to dominate the "Cotton Kingdom" of the South, and what were the strengths and weaknesses of the region's plantation-controlled economic and social system?
2. Why did the majority of nonslaveholding whites in the South support slavery, and what was their relationship with both the slaveholding planters and the black slaves?
3. What were the central features of slavery, and what was life like for African Americans under slavery (as well as for the small number of free blacks)?
4. What were the effects of the "peculiar institution" on blacks, whites, and the nation as a whole?
5. How and why did abolitionism gradually gain strength, despite the strong initial hostility of most northerners, and why did southerners respond so fiercely to the movement's very existence?

CHRONOLOGY

1793	Whitney's cotton gin transforms southern economy	1831–1832	Virginia legislature debates slavery and emancipation
1800	Gabriel slave rebellion in Virginia	1833	British abolish slavery in West Indies American Anti-Slavery Society founded
1807	Britain abolishes slave trade	1834	Abolitionist students expelled from Lane Theological Seminary
1808	Congress outlaws slave trade Royal Navy forms West African Squadron	1835	U.S. Post Office orders destruction of abolitionist mail "Broadcloth Mob" attacks Garrison
1817	American Colonization Society formed	1836	House of Representatives passes "Gag Resolution"
1820	Missouri Compromise		
1822	Republic of Liberia established in Africa Vesey slave rebellion in Charleston, South Carolina	1837	Mob kills abolitionist Lovejoy in Alton, Illinois
		1839	Weld publishes *American Slavery As It Is* Slave revolt aboard *Amistad*
1829	Walker publishes *Appeal to the Colored Citizens of the World*	1845	Douglass publishes *Narrative of the Life of Frederick Douglass*
1831	Garrison begins publishing the *The Liberator* Nat Turner slave rebellion in Virginia	1848	Free Soil party organized

⭐ "Cotton Is King!"

As time passed, the Cotton Kingdom developed into a huge agricultural factory, pouring out avalanches of the fluffy fiber. Quick profits drew planters to the virgin bottomlands of the Gulf states. As long as the soil was still vigorous, the yield was bountiful, and the rewards were high. Caught up in an economic spiral, the planters bought more slaves and land to grow more cotton, so as to buy still more slaves and land.

To a large degree, the prosperity of both North and South—and of Britain, too—rested on the bent backs of enslaved bondsmen. So did the young nation's growing wealth. Cotton accounted for half the value of all American exports after 1840, and export earnings provided much of the capital that stoked the Republic's economic growth.

Cotton even held foreign nations in partial bondage. Britain's most important single manufacture in the 1850s was cotton cloth, from which about one-fifth of its population, directly or indirectly, drew their livelihood. About 75 percent of this precious supply of fiber came from the white-carpeted acres of the South.

Southern leaders were fully aware that Britain was tied to them by cotton threads, and this dependence gave them a heady sense of power. In their eyes "Cotton Was King," the gin was his throne, and the black slaves were his henchmen. If war should ever break out between North and South, northern warships would presumably cut off the outflow of cotton. Fiber-famished British factories would then close their gates, starving mobs would force the London government to break the blockade, and the South would triumph. Cotton appeared to be a powerful monarch indeed.

⭐ Slaves of the Slave System

Before the Civil War the South was in some respects not so much a democracy as an oligarchy—or a government by the few, in this case a planter aristocracy. In 1850 only 1,733 families owned more than 100 slaves each, and this select group provided the cream

> Basil Hall (1788–1844), an Englishman, visited part of the cotton belt on a river steamer (1827–1828). Noting the preoccupation with cotton, he wrote:
>
> "All day and almost all night long, the captain, pilot, crew, and passengers were talking of nothing else; and sometimes our ears were so wearied with the sound of cotton! cotton! cotton! that we gladly hailed a fresh inundation of company in hopes of some change—but alas! ... 'What's cotton at?' was the first eager inquiry. 'Ten cents [a pound].' 'Oh, that will never do!'"

of the political and social leadership of the section and nation. Here was the mint-julep South of the tall-columned and white-painted plantation mansion—the "big house," where dwelt the "cottonocracy."

The planter aristocrats, with their blooded horses and Chippendale chairs, enjoyed the lion's share of southern wealth. They could educate their children in the finest schools, often in the North or abroad. Their money provided the leisure for study, reflection, and statecraft, as was notably true of men like John C. Calhoun (a Yale graduate) and Jefferson Davis (a West Point graduate).

The plantation system also shaped the lives of southern women. The mistress of a great plantation commanded a sizable household staff of mostly female slaves. She gave daily orders to cooks, maids, seamstresses, laundresses, and personal servants. Some mistresses showed tender regard for their bondswomen, while others treated their slaves atrociously. But virtually no slaveholding women believed in abolition, and relatively few protested when the husbands and children of their slaves were sold.

Despite the occasional benevolent relations between owners and slaves, the moonlight-and-magnolia tradition concealed much that was worrisome, distasteful, and sordid. The domination of southern society by a slaveholding aristocracy was fundamentally undemocratic, widening the gap between rich and poor and hampering public education. Plantation agriculture was wasteful, largely because King Cotton and his money-hungry subjects despoiled the good earth. Quick profits led to excessive cultivation or "land butchery," which in turn caused a heavy leakage of population to the West and Northwest.

The economic structure of the South became increasingly monopolistic. As the land wore thin, many small farmers sold their holdings to more prosperous neighbors. The big got bigger and the small got smaller. When the Civil War finally erupted, a large percentage of southern farms had passed from the hands of the families that had originally cleared them.

Another cancer in the bosom of the South was the financial instability of the plantation system. The temptation to overspeculate in land and slaves caused many planters, including Andrew Jackson in his later years, to plunge in beyond their depth. The slaves represented a heavy investment of capital, perhaps $1,200 each in the case of "prime field hands," and they might deliberately injure themselves or run away.

Dominance by King Cotton likewise led to a dangerous dependence on a one-crop economy, whose price level was at the mercy of world conditions. The whole system discouraged a healthy diversification of agriculture and particularly of manufacturing.

Southern planters resented watching the North grow fat at their expense. They were pained by the heavy outward flow of commissions and interest to northern middlemen, bankers, agents, and shippers. Staunch sons and daughters of the South, especially by the 1850s, deplored the fact that when they were born they were wrapped in Yankee-made swaddling clothes, spent their lives in servitude to Yankee manufacturing, and when they died were buried in graves dug with Yankee shovels. The South furnished the corpse and the hole in the ground.

The Cotton Kingdom also repelled large-scale European immigration, which added so richly to the manpower and wealth of the North. In 1860 only 4.4 percent of the southern population was foreign born, compared with 18.7 percent for the North. The diverting of non-British immigration to the North caused the white South to become the most Anglo-Saxon section of the nation.

★ The White Majority

Only a handful of southern whites lived in pillared mansions. Below those 1,733 families in 1850 who owned one hundred or more slaves were some 345,000 less wealthy, slave-owning families, representing about 1,725,000 white persons (see Figure 16.1).

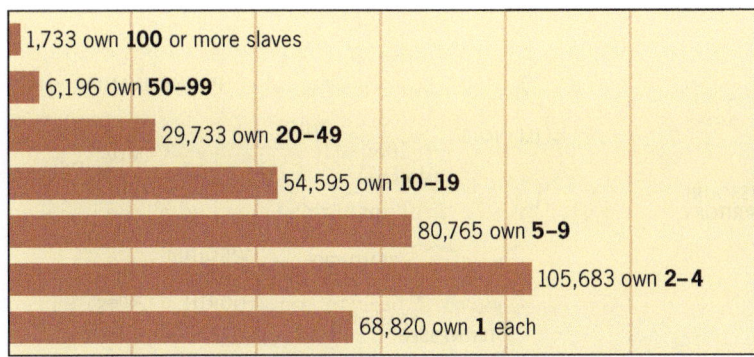

Figure 16.1 Slave-Owning Families, 1850 More than half of all slaveholding families owned fewer than four slaves. In contrast, 2 percent of slave owners owned more than fifty slaves each. A tiny, slaveholding elite held a majority of slave property in the South. The great majority of white southerners owned no slaves at all.

Over two-thirds of these families—255,268 in all—owned fewer than ten slaves each. All told, only about one-fourth of white southerners owned any slaves or belonged to a slave-owning family.

The smaller slave owners did not own a majority of the slaves, but they made up a majority of the masters. With the striking exception that their households contained a slave or two, or perhaps an entire slave family, the small slave owners' lifestyles resembled that of small farmers in the North more than it did that of the southern planter aristocracy. They lived in modest farmhouses and sweated beside their bondsmen in the cotton fields, laboring callus for callus just as hard as their slaves.

Beneath the slave owners in the population pyramid was the great body of whites who owned no slaves at all. By 1860 their numbers had swelled to 6,120,825—three-quarters of all southern whites. Shouldered off the richest bottomlands by the mighty planters, they scratched a simple living from the thinner soils of the backcountry and the mountain valleys (see Map 16.1). These red-necked farmers participated in the market economy scarcely at all. As subsistence farmers, they raised corn and hogs, not cotton, and often lived isolated lives, punctuated by extended socializing and sermonizing at religious revival meetings. Some of the least prosperous nonslaveholding whites were scorned even by slaves as "poor white trash," "hillbillies," or "crackers."

All these whites without slaves had no direct economic stake in the preservation of slavery, yet they were among the stoutest defenders of the system. Why? The answer is not far to seek.

The carrot on the stick ever dangling before their eyes was the hope of buying a slave or two and of parlaying their holdings into riches—all in accord with the "American dream" of upward social mobility. They also took fierce pride in their presumed racial superiority, which would be watered down if the enslaved blacks were freed. Many of the poorer whites were hardly better off economically than the slaves, but even the most wretched whites could take perverse comfort from the knowledge that they outranked someone in status: the still more wretched African American slave. Thus, did the logic of economics join with the illogic of racism in buttressing the slave system.

In a special category among white southerners were the mountain whites, more or less isolated in the valleys of the Appalachian range that stretched from western Virginia to northern Georgia and Alabama. As independent small farmers, hundreds of miles distant from the heart of the Cotton Kingdom and rarely if ever in sight of a slave, these mountain whites had little in common with the whites of the flatlands. Many of them, including future president Andrew Johnson of Tennessee, hated both the haughty planters and their gangs of blacks. When the Civil War came, the tough-fibered mountain whites constituted a vitally important peninsula of Unionism jutting down into the

Map 16.1 Southern Distribution of Slaves, 1820 and 1860 The philosopher Ralph Waldo Emerson, a New Englander, declared in 1856, "I do not see how a barbarous community and a civilized community can constitute a state. I think we must get rid of slavery or we must get rid of freedom."

secessionist southern sea. They ultimately played a significant role in crippling the Confederacy. And for generations after the Civil War, the mountain white areas formed the only source of concentrated Republican strength in the South.

Free Blacks: Slaves Without Masters

Precarious in the extreme was the standing of the South's free blacks, who numbered about 250,000 by 1860. In the upper South, the free black population traced its origins to a wavelet of emancipation inspired by the idealism of Revolutionary days. In the deep South, many free blacks were mulattoes, usually the emancipated children of a white planter and his black mistress. Throughout the South were some free blacks who had purchased their freedom with earnings from labor after hours.

These free blacks in the South constituted a kind of "third race." Prohibited from certain occupations and from testifying against whites in court, they were always vulnerable to being hijacked back into slavery by unscrupulous slave traders. As free men and women, they were walking examples of what might be achieved by emancipation and hence were detested by defenders of the slave system.

Free blacks were also unpopular in the North, where about another 250,000 of them lived. Several states forbade their entrance, most denied them the right to vote, and some barred blacks from public schools. Much of the agitation in the North against the spread of slavery into the new territories in the 1840s and 1850s grew out of race prejudice, not humanitarian idealism.

Anti-black feeling was in fact frequently stronger in the North than in the South. It was sometimes observed that white southerners, who were often suckled and reared by black nurses, liked black people as individuals but despised the race. The white northerner, on the other hand, often professed to like the race but disliked individual blacks.

Plantation Slavery

In society's basement in the South of 1860 were nearly 4 million black human chattels. Their numbers had quadrupled since the dawn of the century, as the booming cotton economy created a seemingly unquenchable demand for slave labor. Legal importation of African slaves into the United States ended in 1808, when Congress outlawed slave imports. Britain had abolished the slave trade (but not slavery itself) in 1807, a milestone in the continuing struggle to establish human rights as a principle of international law. In the decades thereafter the Royal Navy's **West Africa Squadron** seized hundreds of slave ships and freed thousands of captives. Yet, despite that effort, as many as 3 million enslaved Africans were shipped to Brazil and the West Indies in the several decades after 1807. In the United States, the price of "black ivory" was so high in the years before the Civil War that thousands of slaves were smuggled into the South, despite the death penalty for international slave traders.

Ironically, the suppression of the international slave trade fostered the growth of a vigorous *internal* slave trade, as upper South states like Virginia became major sources of supply for the booming cotton economy of the deep South. Most of the increase in the slave population in the United States came not from imports but instead from natural reproduction—a fact that distinguished slavery in America from that in other New World societies and implied much about the tenor of the slave regime and the conditions of family life under slavery in the United States.

Above all, the planters regarded the slaves as investments, into which they had sunk nearly $2 billion by 1860. Slaves were the primary form of wealth in the South, and as such they were cared for as any asset is cared for by a prudent capitalist. Masters sometimes hired cheap Irish wage laborers to perform dangerous work such as tunnel blasting or swamp draining, rather than risk the life of a valuable slave, worth $1,800 by 1860 (a price that had quintupled since 1800).

West Africa Squadron (established 1808) *British Royal Navy force formed to enforce the abolition of the slave trade in 1807. It intercepted hundreds of slave ships and freed thousands of Africans.*

A Slave Auction Abraham Lincoln said in 1865, "Whenever I hear anyone arguing for slavery, I feel a strong impulse to see it tried on him personally."

In 1852 Maria Perkins, a woman enslaved in Virginia, wrote plaintively to her husband about the disruption that the commercial traffic in slaves was visiting upon their family:

"I write you a letter to let you know of my distress my master has sold albert to a trader on Monday court day and myself and other child is for sale also and I want you to let hear from you very soon before next cort if you can I dont know when I dont want you to wait till Christmas I want you to tell Dr Hamelton and your master if either will buy me they can attend to it know and then I can go after-wards I dont want a trader to get me they asked me if I had got any person to buy me and I told them no they took me to the court houste too they never put me up a man buy the name of brady bought albert and is gone I dont know whare they say he lives in Scottesville my things is in several places some is in staunton and if I should be sold I dont know what will become of them I dont expect to meet with the luck to get that way till I am quite heart sick nothing more I am and ever will be your kind wife Maria Perkins."

Slavery was profitable for the great planters, though it hobbled the economic development of the region as a whole. The profits from the cotton boom sucked ever more slaves from the upper to the lower South. Thousands of blacks from the soil-exhausted states of the Old South, especially Virginia, were "sold down the river" to the cotton frontier of the lower Mississippi Valley. By 1860 the deep South states of South Carolina, Georgia, Florida, Mississippi, Alabama, and Louisiana each had a majority or near-majority of blacks and accounted for about half of all slaves in the South.

The forced "breeding" of slaves was not openly encouraged. But white masters all too frequently forced their attention on female slaves, fathering a sizable mulatto population, most of which remained enchained.

Slave auctions were brutal sights. The open selling of human flesh under the hammer was among the most revolting aspects of slavery. On the auction block, families were separated with distressing frequency, usually for economic reasons such as bankruptcy or the division of "property" among heirs. The sundering of families in this fashion was perhaps slavery's greatest psychological horror. Abolitionists decried the practice, and Harriet Beecher Stowe seized on the emotional power of this theme by putting it at the heart of the plot of her acclaimed 1852 novel *Uncle Tom's Cabin*.

★ Life Under the Lash

White southerners often romanticized about the happy life of their singing, dancing, banjo-strumming "darkies." But how did the slaves actually live? There is no simple answer to this question. Conditions varied greatly from region to region, from large plantation to small farm, and from master to master. Everywhere, of course, slavery meant hard work, ignorance, and oppression. The slaves—both men and women—usually toiled from dawn to dusk in the fields, under the watchful eyes and ready whip-hand of a white overseer or black "driver." They had no civil or political rights, and even minimal protection from murder or unusually cruel punishment was difficult to enforce. Slaves were forbidden to testify in court, and their marriages were not legally recognized.

Floggings were common, for the whip was the substitute for the wage-incentive system and the most visible symbol of the planter's mastery. Strong-willed slaves were sometimes sent to "**breakers**," whose technique consisted mostly in lavish laying on of the lash. As an abolitionist song of the 1850s lamented,

Tonight the bond man, Lord
Is bleeding in his chains;
And loud the falling lash is heard
On Carolina's plains!

breakers *Slave drivers who employed the lash to brutally "break" the souls of strong-willed slaves.*

But savage beatings made sullen laborers, and lash marks hurt resale values. There are, to be sure, sadistic monsters in any population, and the planter class contained its share. But the typical planter had too much of his own prosperity riding on the backs of his slaves to beat them bloody on a regular basis.

By 1860 most slaves were concentrated in the "**black belt**" of the Deep South that stretched from South Carolina and Georgia into the new southwest states of Alabama, Mississippi, and Louisiana. A majority of blacks lived on larger plantations that harbored communities of twenty or more slaves. In some counties of the Deep South, especially along the lower Mississippi River, blacks accounted for more than 75 percent of the population. There the family life of slaves tended to be relatively stable, and a distinctive African American culture developed. Forced separations of spouses, parents, and children were evidently more common on smaller plantations and in the upper South. Slave marriage vows sometimes proclaimed, "Until death or *distance* do you part."

black belt *Region of the Deep South with the highest concentration of slaves. The "black belt" emerged in the nineteenth century as cotton production became more profitable and slavery expanded south and west.*

responsorial *Call and response style of preaching that melded Christian and African traditions. Practiced by African slaves in the South.*

With impressive resilience, blacks managed to sustain family life in slavery, and most slaves were raised in stable two-parent households. Continuity of family identity across generations was evidenced in the widespread practice of naming children for grandparents or adopting the surname not of a current master but of a forebear's master. African Americans also displayed their African cultural roots when they avoided marriage between first cousins, in contrast to the frequent intermarriage of close relatives among the ingrown planter aristocracy.

African roots were also visible in the slaves' religious practices. Though heavily Christianized by itinerant evangelists of the Second Great Awakening, blacks in slavery molded their own distinctive religious forms from a mixture of Christian and African elements. They emphasized those aspects of the Christian heritage that seemed most pertinent to their own situation—especially the captivity of the Israelites in Egypt. One of the most haunting spirituals implored,

Tell old Pharaoh,
"Let my people go."

And another lamented,

Nobody knows de trouble I've had
Nobody knows but Jesus.

African practices also persisted in the **responsorial** style of preaching, in which the congregation frequently punctuated the minister's remarks with assents and amens—an adaptation of the give-and-take between caller and dancers in the African ring-shout dance.

Slave Nurse and Young White Master Southern whites would not allow slaves to own property or exercise civil rights, but, paradoxically, they often entrusted them with the raising of their own precious children. Many a slave "mammy" served as a surrogate mother for the offspring of the planter class.

Contending Voices

Perspectives on Race and Slavery

American slavery was inextricably bound up with American attitudes about race. William A. Smith (1802–1870), a southern clergyman and college president, defended slavery on explicitly racial grounds in 1856:

"[Africans] are a distinct race of people, separated by strongly marked lines of moral and physical condition from those amongst whom they reside. This difference is so strongly marked that there can be no spontaneous amalgamation by intermarriage, and consequently no reciprocity of social rights and privileges between the races.... They must therefore continue to exist as a separate race."

At its founding meeting in 1833, the American Anti-Slavery Society declared

"that all persons of color who possess the qualifications which are demanded of others ought to be admitted forthwith to the enjoyment of the same privileges, and the exercise of the same prerogatives, as others; and that the paths of preferment, of wealth, and of intelligence should be opened as widely to them as to persons of a white complexion."

What common ground, if any, lay between those two positions?

Nat Turner's rebellion (1831) Virginia slave revolt that resulted in the deaths of sixty whites and raised fears among white southerners of further uprisings.

Amistad (1839) Spanish slave ship dramatically seized off the coast of Cuba by the enslaved Africans aboard. The ship was driven ashore on Long Island and the slaves were put on trial. Former president John Quincy Adams argued their case before the Supreme Court, securing their eventual release.

The Burdens of Bondage

Slavery was intolerably degrading to the victims. They were deprived of the dignity and sense of responsibility that come from independence and the right to make choices. Slaves were denied an education, because reading brought ideas, and ideas brought discontent. Many states passed laws forbidding their instruction, and perhaps nine-tenths of adult slaves at the beginning of the Civil War were illiterate. For all slaves—indeed for virtually all blacks, slave or free—the "American dream" of bettering one's lot through study and hard work was a cruel and empty mockery.

Not surprisingly, victims of the "peculiar institution" devised countless ways to throw sand in its gears. Slaves often slowed the pace of their labor to the barest minimum that would spare them the lash, thus fostering the myth of black "laziness" in the minds of whites. They filched food from the "big house" and pilfered other goods that had been produced by their labor. They sometimes sabotaged expensive equipment and occasionally even poisoned their masters' food.

The slaves also universally pined for freedom. Many ran away, frequently in search of a separated family member. A black girl, asked if her mother was dead, replied, "Yessir, master, she is dead, but she's free." Others rebelled, though never successfully. In 1800 an armed insurrection led by a slave named Gabriel in Richmond, Virginia, was foiled by informers, and its leaders were hanged. Denmark Vesey, a free black, led another ill-fated rebellion in Charleston, South Carolina, in 1822. Also betrayed by informers, Vesey and more than thirty followers were publicly strung from the gallows. In 1831 Nat Turner, a visionary black preacher, led an uprising that slaughtered about sixty Virginians, mostly women and children. Reprisals were swift and bloody, and **Nat Turner's rebellion** was soon extinguished.

An especially dramatic episode involved enslaved Africans who rebelled aboard the Spanish slave ship **Amistad** in 1839. They seized command of the vessel off the coast of Cuba and attempted to sail back to Africa, but were driven ashore on Long Island. After two years of imprisonment and several trials, former president John Quincy Adams finally secured their freedom in a brilliant, moving argument before the United States Supreme Court in 1841, and the Africans returned to the British colony of Sierra Leone in West Africa.

The dark taint of slavery also left its mark on whites. It fostered the brutality of the whip, the bloodhound, and the branding iron. White southerners increasingly lived in a state of imagined siege, surrounded by potentially rebellious blacks inflamed by abolitionist propaganda from the North. Their fears bolstered an intoxicating theory of biological racial superiority and turned the South into a reactionary backwater in an era of progress—one of the last bastions of slavery in the Western world. The defenders of slavery were forced to degrade themselves, along with their victims. As Booker T. Washington, a distinguished black leader and former slave, later observed, whites could not hold blacks in a ditch without getting down there with them.

Early Abolitionism

The inhumanity of the "peculiar institution" gradually caused antislavery societies to sprout forth. Abolitionist sentiment first stirred at the time of the Revolution, especially among Quakers. Because of the widespread loathing of blacks, some of the earliest abolitionist efforts focused on transporting blacks back to Africa. The **American Colonization Society** was founded for this purpose in 1817, and in 1822 the Republic of **Liberia** was established for former slaves on the West African coast. Some fifteen thousand freed blacks were transported there over the next four decades. But most native-born African Americans had no wish to be transplanted into a strange civilization. Yet the colonization idea appealed to some antislaveryites, including Abraham Lincoln, until the time of the Civil War.

In the 1830s the abolitionist movement took on new energy and momentum, mounting to the proportions of a crusade. American abolitionists took heart in 1833 when their British counterparts, inspired by the redoubtable William Wilberforce, a member of Parliament and an evangelical Christian reformer whose family had been touched by the preaching of George Whitefield (see Chapter 5), unchained the slaves in the West Indies. (Wilberforce University in Ohio, a historically African American college that later sent many missionaries to Africa, is named for him.)

As with Wilberforce, the religious spirit of the Second Great Awakening now inflamed the hearts of many American abolitionists against the sin of slavery. Prominent among them was lanky, tousle-haired Theodore Dwight Weld, who had been evangelized by Charles Grandison Finney in the 1820s. Spiritually inspired by Finney, Weld was aided by two wealthy and devout New York merchants, the brothers Arthur and Lewis Tappan. In 1832 Weld enrolled at Lane Theological Seminary in Cincinnati, whose president was the formidable Lyman Beecher, father of novelist Harriet Beecher Stowe, reformer Catharine Beecher, and preacher-abolitionist Henry Ward Beecher. Expelled along with several other students in 1834 for organizing an eighteen-day debate on slavery, Weld and his fellow "Lane Rebels"—full of the energy and idealism of youth—fanned out across the Old Northwest preaching the antislavery gospel. Weld also assembled a potent propaganda tract, *American Slavery As It Is* (1839), which greatly influenced Harriet Beecher Stowe's *Uncle Tom's Cabin*.

Sojourner Truth Also known simply as "Isabella," she held audiences spellbound with her deep, resonant voice and the religious passion with which she condemned the sin of slavery. This photo was taken about 1870.

★ Radical Abolitionism

On New Year's Day, 1831, a shattering abolitionist blast came from the bugle of William Lloyd Garrison, a mild-looking reformer of twenty-six. A spiritual child of the Second Great Awakening, Garrison published in Boston the first issue of his militantly antislavery newspaper *The Liberator*. With this mighty paper broadside, Garrison triggered a thirty-year war of words and in a sense fired one of the opening barrages of the Civil War.

Stern and uncompromising, Garrison proclaimed in strident tones that under no circumstances would he tolerate the poisonous weed of slavery:

> *I will be as harsh as truth and as uncompromising as justice. . . . I am in earnest—I will not equivocate—I will not excuse—I will not retreat a single inch—and I WILL BE HEARD!*

Other dedicated abolitionists rallied to Garrison's standard, and in 1833 they founded the **American Anti-Slavery Society**. Prominent among them was eloquent Wendell Phillips, a Boston patrician known as "abolition's golden trumpet."

Black abolitionists distinguished themselves as living monuments to the cause of African American freedom. Their ranks included David Walker, whose incendiary *Appeal to the Colored Citizens of the World* advocated a bloody end to white supremacy. Also noteworthy were Sojourner Truth, a freed black woman who fought tirelessly for black emancipation and women's rights, and Martin Delany, one of the few black leaders to take seriously the notion of black recolonization in Africa.

American Colonization Society *Reflecting the focus of early abolitionists on transporting freed blacks back to Africa, the organization established Liberia, a West African settlement intended as a haven for emancipated slaves.*

Liberia *West African nation founded in 1822 as a haven for freed blacks, fifteen thousand of whom made their way back across the Atlantic by the 1860s.*

The Liberator **(1831–1865)** *Antislavery newspaper published by William Lloyd Garrison, who called for the immediate emancipation of all slaves.*

American Anti-Slavery Society (1833–1870) *Abolitionist society founded by William Lloyd Garrison, who advocated the immediate abolition of slavery. By 1838, the organization had more than 250,000 members across 1,350 chapters.*

Appeal to the Colored Citizens of the World **(1829)** *Incendiary abolitionist tract advocating the violent overthrow of slavery. Published by David Walker, a southern-born free black.*

Examining the Evidence

Bellegrove Plantation, Donaldsville, Louisiana, Built 1857

The sugar-growing Bellegrove Plantation—on the banks of the Mississippi River ninety-five miles north of New Orleans—was laid out on a grander scale than many southern plantations. In this rendering from an advertisement for Bellegrove's sale in 1867, the planter John Orr's home was identified as a "mansion," and quarters for his field hands proved extensive: twenty double cabins built for slaves (now for "Negroes") and a dormitory, described in the ad but not pictured here, housing 150 laborers. Because of the unhealthy work involved in cultivating sugar cane, such as constant digging of drainage canals to keep the cane from rotting in standing water, many planters hired immigrant (usually Irish) labor to keep their valuable slaves out of physical danger. The presence of a hospital between the slave cabins and the mansion indicates the very real threat to health. The layout of Bellegrove reflects the organization of production as well as the social relations on a sugar plantation. The storehouse where preserved sugar awaited shipping stood closest to the Mississippi River, the principal transportation route, whereas the sugar house, the most important building on the plantation, with its mill, boilers, and cooking vats for converting syrup into sugar, dominated the cane fields. Although the "big house" and slave quarters stood in close proximity, hedges surrounding the planter's home shut out views of both sugar production and labor. Within the slave quarters, the overseer's larger house signified his superior status, while the arrangement of cabins ensured his supervision of domestic as well as work life.

1. What does the physical layout of the plantation reveal about settlement patterns, sugar cultivation, and social relationships along the Mississippi?
2. Besides living quarters and facilities for the production and shipping of sugar, what other major buildings were required on a large plantation such as Bellegrove? What functions did these ancillary structures serve?
3. In rough terms, what proportion of the total acreage of Bellegrove Plantation was given over to a) growing sugar cane, b) residential dwellings, c) sugar refining facilities, and d) woodlands?

264

The greatest of the black abolitionists was Frederick Douglass. Escaping from bondage in 1838 at the age of twenty-one, Douglass was "discovered" by the abolitionists in 1841 when he gave a stunning impromptu speech at an antislavery meeting in Massachusetts. Thereafter Douglass lectured widely for the cause, despite frequent beatings and threats against his life. In 1845 he published his classic autobiography, *Narrative of the Life of Frederick Douglass*, which depicted his remarkable origins as the son of an enslaved black woman and a white father, his struggle to learn to read and write, and his eventual escape to the North.

Douglass was as flexibly practical as Garrison was stubbornly principled. Garrison often appeared to be more interested in his own righteousness than in the substance of the slavery evil itself. He repeatedly demanded that the "virtuous" North secede from the "wicked" South. Renouncing politics, on the Fourth of July, 1854, he publicly burned a copy of the Constitution as "a covenant with death and an agreement with hell." Douglass, on the other hand, along with other abolitionists, increasingly looked to politics to end the blight of slavery. These political abolitionists backed the antislavery Liberty party in 1840, the Free Soil party in 1848, and eventually the Republican party in the 1850s. In the end, most abolitionists, including even the pacifist Garrison himself, followed the logic of their beliefs and supported a frightfully costly fratricidal war as the price of emancipation.

High-minded and courageous, the abolitionists were men and women of goodwill and various colors who faced the cruel choice that people of conscience in many ages have had thrust upon them: when is evil so enormous that it must be denounced, even at the risk of precipitating bloodshed and butchery?

> *After hearing Frederick Douglass speak in Bristol, England, in 1846, Mary A. Estlin wrote to an American abolitionist:*
>
> "[T]here is but one opinion of him. Wherever he goes he arouses sympathy in your cause and love for himself... Our expectations were highly roused by his narrative, his printed speeches, and the eulogisms of the friends with whom he has been staying: but he far exceeds the picture we had formed both in outward graces, intellectual power and culture, and eloquence."*
>
> *From Clare Taylor, ed., *British and American Abolitionists, An Episode in Transatlantic Understanding* (Edinburgh University Press, 1974), p. 282.

Narrative of the Life of Frederick Douglass (1845) Vivid autobiography of the escaped slave and renowned abolitionist Frederick Douglass.

★ The South Lashes Back

Antislavery sentiment was not unknown in the South up to the 1820s, but after about 1830 the voice of white southern abolitionism was silenced. The Virginia legislature actually debated and eventually defeated various emancipation proposals in 1831–1832. Nat Turner's rebellion in 1831 sent a wave of hysteria sweeping over the snowy cotton fields, and planters in growing numbers, recollecting the massive slave revolt that had erupted in Haiti in the 1790s, slept with pistols by their pillows. Although Garrison had no connection with the Turner conspiracy, his *Liberator* appeared at about the same time, and he was bitterly condemned as a terrorist and an inciter of murder.

The Nullification Crisis of 1832 further implanted haunting fears in white southern minds, conjuring up nightmares of black incendiaries and abolitionist devils. Jailings, whippings, and lynchings now greeted rational efforts to discuss the slavery problem in the South.

Proslavery whites responded to the abolitionist groundswell by launching a massive defense of slavery as a positive good. In doing so they forgot their own section's previous doubts about the morality of the "peculiar institution." Slavery, they claimed, was supported by the authority of the Bible and the wisdom of Aristotle. It was good for the Africans, who were lifted from the "barbarism of the jungle" and clothed with the blessings of Christian civilization.

Slavemasters strongly encouraged religion in the slave quarters, emphasizing those teachings that encouraged obedience. White apologists also claimed that master-slave relationships really resembled those of a family. Southern whites were quick to contrast the "happy" lot of their "servants" with that of the overworked northern wage slaves, including exploited women and stunted children. The blacks mostly toiled in the fresh air and sunlight, not in dark and stuffy factories. They did not have to worry about slack times or unemployment, as did the "hired hands" of the North. Provided with a jail-like form of Social Security, slaves were cared for in sickness and old age, unlike the northern workers, who were set adrift when they outlived their usefulness.

These curious proslavery arguments only widened the chasm between a backward-looking South and a forward-looking North—and indeed much of the rest of the Western world. The southerners reacted defensively to the pressure of their own fears and the merciless nagging of the northern abolitionists. Increasingly the white South turned in upon itself and grew hotly intolerant of any embarrassing questions about the status of slavery.

Regrettably, also, the controversy over free people endangered free speech in the entire country. Piles of petitions poured into Congress from the antislavery reformers, and in 1836 sensitive southerners drove through the House the so-called **Gag Resolution**. It required all such antislavery appeals to be tabled without debate. This attack on the right of petition aroused the aged ex-president, Representative John Quincy Adams, who waged a successful eight-year fight for its repeal.

Southern whites likewise resented the flooding of their mails with incendiary abolitionist literature. In 1835 a mob in Charleston, South Carolina looted the local post office and burned a pile of abolitionist propaganda. Capitulating to southern pressures, the Washington government in 1835 ordered southern postmasters to destroy abolitionist material and called on southern state officials to arrest federal postmasters who did not comply. Such was "freedom of the press" as guaranteed by the Constitution.

Gag Resolution *Prohibited debate or action on antislavery appeals. Driven through the House by proslavery southerners, the Gag Resolution passed every year for eight years and was eventually overturned with the help of John Quincy Adams.*

★ The Abolitionist Impact in the North

Abolitionists—especially the extreme Garrisonians—were for a long time unpopular in many parts of the North. Northerners had been brought up to revere the Constitution and to regard the clauses on slavery as a lasting bargain. The ideal of Union, hammered home by the thundering eloquence of Daniel Webster and others, had taken deep root; and Garrison's wild talk of secession grated harshly on northern ears.

The North also had a heavy economic stake in Dixieland. By the late 1850s, southern planters owed northern bankers and other creditors about $300 million, and much of this immense sum would be lost—as, in fact, it later was—should the Union dissolve. New England textile mills were fed with cotton raised by the slaves, and a disrupted labor system might cut off this vital supply and bring unemployment. The Union during these critical years was partly bound together with cotton threads, tied by lords of the loom in collaboration with the so-called lords of the lash. It was not surprising that strong hostility developed in the North against the boat-rocking tactics of the radical antislaveryites.

Repeated tongue-lashings by the extreme abolitionists provoked many mob outbursts in the North, some led by respectable gentlemen. A gang of young toughs broke into abolitionist Lewis Tappan's New York house in 1834 and demolished its interior, while a crowd in the street cheered. In 1835 Garrison, with a rope tied around him, was dragged through the streets of Boston by the so-called Broadcloth Mob but escaped almost miraculously. Reverend Elijah P. Lovejoy, of Alton, Illinois, had his printing press destroyed four times. In 1837 he was killed in a ferocious gun battle with an anti-abolitionist mob and became "the martyr abolitionist." So unpopular were the antislavery zealots that ambitious politicians, such as Abraham Lincoln, usually avoided the taint of Garrisonian abolition like the plague.

Yet by the 1850s the abolitionist outcry had made a deep dent in the northern mind. Many citizens had come to see the South as the land of the unfree and the home of a hateful institution. Few northerners were prepared to abolish slavery outright, but a growing number, including Lincoln, opposed extending it to the western territories. People of this stamp, commonly called "free-soilers," swelled their ranks as the Civil War approached.

Varying Viewpoints

What Was the True Nature of Slavery?

By the early twentieth century, the predictable accounts of slavery written by partisans of the North or South had receded in favor of a romantic vision of the Old South. A scholarly version of that vision was Ulrich Bonnell Phillips's landmark study, *American Negro Slavery* (1918), which portrayed slavery as a dying, unprofitable economic institution in which benevolent masters treated their slaves with kindly paternalism and racially inferior blacks submissively accepted the system that enslaved them.

Later in the twentieth century historians challenged many of these views. Sophisticated economic analysis has decisively refuted Phillips's claim that slavery was unprofitable by showing that it was a viable, profitable, expanding system. But no such definitive conclusion has been reached in the disputes over slave treatment. Frank Tannenbaum's classic comparative study, *Slave and Citizen* (1947), argued that slavery was more humane in Latin America than in the United States, leaving a legacy of less sharply defined racial castes there. Beginning in the late 1950s, historians increasingly emphasized the harshness of the slave system. One study, Stanley Elkins's *Slavery* (1959), went so far as to compare the "peculiar institution" to the Nazi concentration camps of World War II.

Still later, scholars such as Eugene Genovese conceded that slavery did embrace a strange form of paternalism, one reflecting not slaveholders' benevolence but their need to control and coax work out of their reluctant and often recalcitrant "investments." Furthermore, within this paternalistic system, black slaves were able to make reciprocal demands of their white owners and to protect a "cultural space" of their own in which family and religion particularly could flourish.

The revised conceptions of the master–slave relationship also spilled over into the debate about slave personality. Kenneth Stampp rejected Stanley Elkins's view that slaves were "infantilized" like concentration camp inmates and stressed the frequency and variety of slave resistance, both mild and militant. A third view, imaginatively documented by Lawrence Levine in *Black Culture and Black Consciousness* (1977), argued that the Sambo character was an act, an image that slaves used to confound their masters without incurring punishment. More recently, historians have attempted to avoid the polarity of repression versus autonomy. The challenge before historians today is to capture the vibrancy of slave culture and its legacy for African American society after emancipation, without diminishing the brutality of life under the southern slave regime. For example, Walter Johnson's *Soul by Soul* (1999) details the horrors of the slave market but explains the multitude of ways that enslaved people could influence their own sale and position.

Women's history has also expanded the horizons of slavery studies. Historians such as Elizabeth Fox-Genovese, Jacqueline Jones, and Jennifer Morgan have focused on the ways in which slavery differed for men and women, both slaves and slaveholders. Enslaved black women, for example, had the unique task of negotiating an identity out of their multiple responsibilities as plantation laborers, caretakers of white women and children, and anchors of their families. By tracing the interconnectedness of race and gender in the American South, these historians have also shown how slavery shaped conceptions of masculinity and femininity within southern society, further distinguishing its culture from that of the North.

Scholarship on slavery continues to grow. Work by Philip D. Morgan and Ira Berlin has drawn attention to how both the institution of slavery and the experience of the enslaved changed over time. Slavery adapted to particular geographic and environmental factors and also changed from one generation to the next. As southern slaveholders responded to new social and economic conditions, they gradually altered the legal status of slaves, outlawing manumission in many places and rendering freedom for the enslaved increasingly difficult to attain. A work of overarching synthesis on Atlantic slavery, David Brion Davis's *Inhuman Bondage* (2008), stresses the dehumanization inherent to slavery, especially in harsh New World systems.

CHAPTER SUMMARY

Whitney's cotton gin made cotton production enormously profitable, and created an ever-increasing demand for slave labor. The South's dependence on cotton production tied the South economically to the plantation system and racially to white supremacy. The elite culture and political sophistication of the relatively small plantation aristocracy concealed slavery's great social and economic costs for whites as well as blacks.

Most slaves were held in large groups of twenty or more by a few large and wealthy planters. But most slave owners had just a few slaves, and three-fourths of southern whites had no slaves at all. Nevertheless, except for a few mountain whites, the majority of southern whites strongly supported slavery and racial supremacy because they cherished the hope of becoming slave owners themselves and because white racial identity gave them a sense of superiority to the blacks.

The treatment of the economically valuable slaves varied considerably. Within the bounds of the cruel system, slaves yearned for freedom and struggled to maintain their humanity, including family life.

The older black colonization movement was largely replaced in the 1830s by a radical Garrisonian abolitionism demanding an immediate end to slavery. Abolitionism and the Nat Turner rebellion caused a strong backlash in the South. Earlier southern criticism of slavery disappeared, and proslavery whites increasingly defended slavery as a positive good that actually benefited the slaves. In defending slavery, the South turned its back not only on many of the liberal political and social ideas gaining strength in the North, but on most of progressive Western civilization.

Most northerners were hostile to radical abolitionism as a threat to the cherished Union, and respected the Constitution's evident protection of slavery where it existed. But many also gradually came to see the South as a land of oppression, and came to believe that any attempt to extend slavery was a threat to free society.

KEY TERMS

West Africa Squadron (259)
breakers (261)
black belt (261)
responsorial (261)
Nat Turner's rebellion (262)
Amistad (262)
American Colonization Society (263)
Liberia (263)
The Liberator (263)
American Anti-Slavery Society (263)
Appeal to the Colored Citizens of the World (263)
Narrative of the Life of Frederick Douglass (265)
Gag Resolution (266)

PEOPLE TO KNOW

Nat Turner
William Wilberforce
Theodore Dwight Weld
William Lloyd Garrison
David Walker
Sojourner Truth
Martin Delany
Frederick Douglass

MindTap is a fully online, highly personalized learning experience built upon Cengage Learning content. MindTap combines student learning tools—readings, multimedia, activities, and assessments—into a singular Learning Path that guides students through the course.

Chapter 17

Manifest Destiny and Its Legacy
1841–1848

Our manifest destiny [is] to overspread the continent allotted by Providence for the free development of our yearly multiplying millions.

JOHN L. O'SULLIVAN, 1845*

Chapter Outline

- "Tyler Too" Becomes President, 1841
- The Annexation of Texas, 1845
- Oregon and California
- James K. Polk, The "Dark Horse" of 1844
- War with Mexico, 1846–1848
- *Makers of America: The Californios*

Territorial expansion dominated American diplomacy and politics in the 1840s. Settlers swarming into the still-disputed Oregon country aggravated relations with Britain, which had staked its own claims in the Pacific Northwest. The clamor to annex Texas to the Union provoked bitter tension with Mexico, which continued to regard Texas as a Mexican province in revolt. And when Americans began casting covetous eyes on Mexico's northernmost province, the great prize of California, open warfare erupted between the United States and its southern neighbor. Victory over Mexico added vast new domains to the United States, but it also raised thorny questions about the status of slavery in the newly acquired territories—questions that would be answered in blood in the Civil War of the 1860s.

FOCUS QUESTIONS

1. What was "Manifest Destiny," and why did it inspire a burst of American expansionism in the 1840s?
2. What were the fundamental causes of the growing conflict between America and Britain over Oregon and between the North and the South over the annexation of Texas?
3. How did the issues of Oregon and Texas become central to the election of 1844, and why was Polk's victory generally perceived as a public "mandate" for him to pursue a policy of Manifest Destiny?
4. What were the fundamental causes of the Mexican War? Was the charge, by Congressman Abraham Lincoln and others, that Polk provoked a "war of aggression" a fair one? Why or why not?
5. How did the Mexican War reignite the slavery question?

---

*This is the earliest known use of the term *Manifest Destiny*.

269

CHRONOLOGY

1837	Canadian rebellion and *Caroline* incident	1846	Walker Tariff Independent treasury restored United States settles Oregon dispute with Britain United States and Mexico clash over Texas boundary Kearny takes Santa Fe Frémont conquers California Wilmot Proviso passes House of Representatives
1839	"Aroostook War" breaks out over Maine boundary		
1840	Antislavery Liberty party organized		
1841	Harrison dies after four weeks in office Tyler assumes presidency		
1842	Webster-Ashburton Treaty	1846–1848	Mexican War
1844	Polk defeats Clay in "Manifest Destiny" election	1847	Battle of Buena Vista Scott takes Mexico City
1845	United States annexes Texas	1848	Treaty of Guadalupe Hidalgo

★ The Accession of "Tyler Too"

A horde of office-hungry hard-ciderites descended on Washington in 1841, bewildering newly elected President William Henry Harrison. The real leaders of the Whig party regarded "Old Tippecanoe" as little more than an impressive figurehead. Daniel Webster, as Secretary of State, and Henry Clay, the uncrowned king of the Whigs and their ablest spokesman in the Senate, would grasp the helm.

Unluckily for Clay and Webster, their schemes soon hit a fatal snag. Before the new term had fairly started, Harrison contracted pneumonia and died after only four weeks in the White House—by far the shortest administration in American history.

The "Tyler too" part of the Whig ticket, hitherto only a rhyme, now claimed the spotlight. With blue eyes, classical features, and a high forehead, John Tyler was a Virginia gentleman of the old school—gracious and kindly, yet stubbornly attached to principle. He had earlier resigned from the Senate, quite unnecessarily, rather than accept distasteful instructions from the Virginia legislature. Still a lone wolf, he had forsaken the Jacksonian Democratic fold for that of the Whigs, largely because he could not stomach the dictatorial tactics of Jackson.

Tyler's enemies accused him of being a Democrat in Whig clothing. But the Whig party, like the Democratic party, was something of a catchall, and the accidental president simply belonged to the minority wing, which embraced a number of Jeffersonian states' righters. Tyler had in fact been put on the ticket partly to attract the vote of this fringe group, many of whom were influential southern gentry.

It was true, however, that on virtually every major issue the obstinate Virginian was at odds with the majority of his Whig party, which was pro–bank, pro–protective tariff, and pro–internal improvements. "Tyler too" rhymed with "Tippecanoe," but there the harmony ended. As events turned out, President Harrison, the Whig, served for only four weeks, whereas Tyler, the ex-Democrat who was still largely a Democrat at heart, served for 204 weeks.

★ John Tyler: A President Without a Party

After their hard-won, hard-cider victory, the Whigs brought their not-so-secret platform out of Clay's waistcoat pocket. To the surprise of no one, it outlined a strongly nationalistic program.

Financial reform came first. The Whig Congress hastened to pass a law ending the independent treasury system, and President Tyler, disarmingly agreeable, signed it. Clay next drove through Congress a bill to establish a new Bank of the United States.

Tyler's hostility to a centralized bank was notorious, and Clay—the "Great Compromiser"—would have done well to conciliate him. But the Kentuckian, robbed repeatedly of the presidency by lesser men, was in an imperious mood and riding for a fall. When the bank bill reached the presidential desk, Tyler flatly vetoed it on both practical and constitutional grounds. A drunken mob gathered late at night near the White House and shouted insultingly, "Huzza for Clay!" "A Bank! A Bank!" "Down with the Veto!"

Whig extremists, seething with indignation, condemned Tyler as "His Accidency" and as an "Executive Ass." To the delight of Democrats, the stiff-necked Virginian was formally expelled from his party by a caucus of Whig congressmen, and a serious attempt to impeach him was broached in the House of Representatives. His entire cabinet resigned in a body, except Secretary of State Webster, who was in the midst of delicate negotiations with Britain.

The proposed Whig tariff also felt the prick of the president's well-inked pen. Tyler vetoed a tariff bill that included a scheme for distributing to the states revenues from the sale of public land. But he reluctantly signed the revised Clay-sponsored **Tariff of 1842**, which pushed rates back down to the moderately protective level of 1832, about 32 percent.

Tariff of 1842 *Protective measure passed by Congressional Whigs, raising tariffs to pre-compromise Tariff of 1833 rates.*

★ Tensions with Britain

Hatred of Britain during the nineteenth century periodically came to a head and had to be lanced by treaty settlement or by war. The poison festered ominously in the late 1830s, especially because of private American involvement in an unsuccessful Canadian rebellion in 1837. When an American steamer, the *Caroline*, attempted to deliver supplies to Canadian insurgents, British troops sank the ship in the Niagara River, killing one American.

Anglo-American controversy then exploded in the early 1840s over the disputed Maine boundary. Hoping to bypass the icebound St. Lawrence River, the British planned to build a road westward from the seaport of Halifax to Quebec. But the proposed route ran through territory claimed by Maine under the treaty of 1783. Tough-knuckled lumberjacks from both Maine and Canada commenced fighting in the disputed no-man's-land of the tall-timbered Aroostook River valley. When both sides summoned the local militias, the small-scale lumberjack clash, dubbed the "**Aroostook War**," threatened to widen into a full-dress shooting war.

As the crisis deepened in 1842, the London Foreign Office sent to Washington a conciliatory diplomat, Lord Ashburton, who had married a wealthy American woman. He speedily established cordial relations with Secretary of State Webster. After protracted and nerve-wracking negotiations in the heat of a Washington summer, the two statesmen finally agreed to compromise on the Maine boundary. On the basis of a rough, split-the-difference arrangement, the Americans retained some 7,000 square miles of the 12,000 square miles of wilderness in dispute. The British got less land but won the desired Halifax-Quebec route.

An overlooked bonus sneaked by in small print of the same treaty: the British, in adjusting the U.S.-Canadian boundary farther west, surrendered 6,500 square miles. The area was later found to contain the priceless Mesabi iron range of Minnesota.

Caroline **(1837)** *Diplomatic row between the United States and Britain. Developed after British troops set fire to an American steamer carrying supplies across the Niagara River to Canadian insurgents, during Canada's shortlived insurrection.*

Aroostook War (began 1839) *Series of clashes between American and Canadian lumberjacks in the disputed territory of northern Maine, resolved when a permanent boundary was agreed upon in 1842.*

★ Old Glory Adds the Lone Star of Texas

During the uncertain eight years since winning its independence in 1836, Texas had led a precarious existence. Mexico regarded the Lone Star Republic not as an independent nation but as a province in revolt, to be reconquered in the future. Mexican officials loudly threatened war if the American eagle should ever gather the fledgling republic under its protective wings.

Confronted with such perils, Texas was driven to open negotiations with Britain and France in the hope of securing a degree of protection. In 1839 and 1840 the Texans concluded treaties with France, Holland, and Belgium.

Britain was intensely interested in maintaining an independent Texas. Such a republic would check the southward surge of the American colossus, whose bulging biceps posed a constant threat to nearby British possessions in the New World. Clashes between a puppet Texas and the Yankees would create a smoke-screen diversion behind which foreign powers could move into the Americas and challenge the insolent Monroe Doctrine. French schemers likewise hoped that an independent Texas would result in the fragmentation and militarization of America.

British abolitionists were also busily intriguing in Texas, hoping that gaining freedom for blacks there would inflame the nearby slaves of the South. In addition, British merchants regarded Texas as a potentially important free-trade area—an offset to the tariff-walled United States. British textile manufacturers believed that an independent Texas, with its vast cotton-producing plains, would relieve British looms of their dependence on American fiber—a supply that might be cut off by embargo or war.

Partly because of the fears aroused by these British and French schemers, Texas became a leading issue in the presidential campaign of 1844. The pro-expansion Democrats under James K. Polk finally triumphed over the Whigs under Henry Clay, the hardy perennial candidate. Lame duck President Tyler thereupon promptly interpreted the narrow Democratic victory as a "mandate" to acquire Texas.

Eager to crown his troubled administration with this splendid prize, Tyler quickly shepherded Texas into the fold. Many "**Conscience Whigs**" feared that Texas in the Union would be red meat to nourish the lusty "slave power." Aware of their opposition, Tyler despaired of securing the needed two-thirds vote for a treaty in the Senate. He therefore arranged for annexation by a joint resolution. This solution required only a simple majority in both houses of Congress. After a spirited debate, the resolution passed early in 1845, and Texas was formally invited to become the twenty-eighth star on the American flag.

Mexico angrily charged that the Americans had despoiled it of Texas. Yet realistic observers could see that the Mexicans would not be able to reconquer their lost province. By 1845 the Lone Star Republic had become a danger spot, inviting foreign intrigue that menaced the American people. The continued existence of Texas as an independent nation threatened to involve the United States in a series of ruinous wars, both in America and in Europe.

What other power would have spurned the imperial domain of Texas? The bride was so near, so rich, so fair, so willing. Whatever the peculiar circumstances of the Texas Revolution, the United States can hardly be accused of unseemly haste in achieving annexation. Nine long years were surely a decent wait between the beginning of the courtship and the consummation of the marriage.

Conscience Whigs (1840s and 1850s)
Northern Whigs who opposed slavery on moral grounds. Conscience Whigs sought to prevent the annexation of Texas as a slave state, fearing that the new slave territory would only serve to buttress the southern "slave power."

★ Oregon Fever Populates Oregon

The Oregon Country was an enormous wilderness. It sprawled magnificently west of the Rockies to the Pacific Ocean, and north of California to the line of 54° 40'—the present southern tip of the Alaska panhandle. All or substantial parts of this immense area were claimed at one time or another by four nations: Spain, Russia, Britain, and the United States.

Two claimants dropped out of the scramble. Spain, though the first to raise its banner in Oregon, bartered away its claims to the United States in the Florida Treaty of 1819. Russia retreated to the line of 54° 40' by the treaties of 1824 and 1825 with America and Britain. These two remaining rivals now had the field to themselves.

British claims to Oregon were strong—at least to that portion north of the Columbia River. They were based squarely on prior discovery and exploration, on treaty rights, and on actual occupation. The most important colonizing agency was the far-flung Hudson's Bay Company, which was trading profitably with the Indians of the Pacific Northwest for furs.

In winning Oregon, the Americans had great faith in their procreative powers. Boasted one congressman in 1846:

"Our people are spreading out with the aid of the American multiplication table. Go to the West and see a young man with his mate of eighteen; after the lapse of thirty years, visit him again, and instead of two, you will find twenty-two. That is what I call the American multiplication table."

Americans, for their part, could also point to exploration and occupation. Captain Robert Gray in 1792 had stumbled upon the majestic Columbia River, which he named after his ship; and the famed Lewis and Clark expedition of 1804–1806 had ranged overland through the Oregon Country to the Pacific. This shaky American toehold was ultimately strengthened by the presence of missionaries and other settlers, a sprinkling of whom reached the grassy Willamette River valley, south of the Columbia, in the 1830s. These men and women of God, bent on saving the souls of the Indians, were also instrumental in saving the soil of Oregon for the United States. They stimulated interest in a faraway domain that Americans had earlier assumed would not be settled for centuries.

The scattered American and British pioneers in Oregon continued to live peacefully side by side. At the time of negotiating the Anglo-American Convention of 1818 (see pp. 184–185), the United States had sought to divide the vast domain at the forty-ninth parallel. But the British, who regarded the Columbia River as the St. Lawrence of the West, were unwilling to yield this vital artery. A scheme for peaceful "joint occupation" was thereupon adopted, pending future settlement.

The handful of Americans in the Willamette Valley was suddenly multiplied in the early 1840s, when "Oregon fever" seized hundreds of restless pioneers. In increasing numbers, their creaking covered wagons jolted over the two-thousand-mile Oregon Trail as the human rivulet widened into a stream. By 1846 about five thousand Americans, some of them tough ruffians, had settled south of the Columbia River.

The British, in the face of this rising torrent of humanity, could muster only seven hundred or so subjects north of the Columbia. Losing out lopsidedly in the population race, they were beginning to see the wisdom of arriving at a peaceful settlement before being engulfed by their neighbors.

A curious fact is that only a relatively small segment of the Oregon Country was in actual controversy by 1845. The area in dispute consisted of the rough quadrangle between the Columbia River on the south and east, the forty-ninth parallel on the north, and the Pacific Ocean on the west—most of the present state of Washington. Britain had repeatedly offered the line of the Columbia; America had repeatedly offered the forty-ninth parallel. The whole fateful issue was now tossed into the presidential election of 1844, where it was largely overshadowed by the question of annexing Texas.

★ A Mandate for Manifest Destiny

The two major parties nominated their presidential standard-bearers in May 1844. Ambitious but often-frustrated Henry Clay, easily the most popular man in the country, was enthusiastically chosen by the Whigs at Baltimore. The Democrats, meeting later in the same city, spurned former President Martin Van Buren and nominated James K. Polk of Tennessee, America's first "dark horse," or "surprise," presidential candidate.

Polk may have been a dark horse, but he was hardly an unknown or decrepit nag. Speaker of the House of Representatives for four years and governor of Tennessee for two terms, Polk was a determined, industrious, ruthless, and intelligent public servant. Whigs attempted to jeer him into oblivion with the taunt, "Who is James K. Polk?" They soon found out.

The campaign of 1844 was in part an expression of the mighty emotional upsurge known as **Manifest Destiny**. Countless citizens in the 1840s and 1850s, feeling a sense of mission, believed that Almighty God had "manifestly" destined the American people for a hemispheric career. They would irresistibly spread their uplifting and ennobling democratic institutions over at least the entire North American continent, and possibly over South America as well. Land greed and ideals—"empire" and "liberty"—were thus conveniently conjoined.

Expansionist Democrats were strongly swayed by the intoxicating spell of Manifest Destiny. They came out flat footedly in their platform for the "Reannexation of Texas" and the "Reoccupation of Oregon," all the way to 54° 40′. The Whigs countered with such slogans as "Polk, Slavery, and Texas, or Clay, Union, and Liberty."

Manifest Destiny (1840s and 1850s) *Belief that the United States was destined by God to spread its "empire of liberty" across North America. Served as a justification for mid-nineteenth-century expansionism.*

Westward the Course of Empire Takes Its Way This romantic tribute to the spirit of Manifest Destiny was commissioned by Congress in 1860 and may still be seen in the Capitol.

On the crucial issue of Texas, the acrobatic Clay tried to ride two horses at once. The "Great Compromiser" compromised away the presidency when he wrote confusing letters saying that, while he personally favored annexing slave-holding Texas (an appeal to the South), he also favored postponement (an appeal to the North). By straddling the issue this way, Clay alienated ardent antislaveryites.

In the stretch drive, "Dark Horse" Polk nipped Henry Clay at the wire, 170 to 105 votes in the Electoral College and 1,338,464 to 1,300,097 in the popular column. Clay would have won if he had not lost New York by a scant 5,000 votes. There the tiny antislavery **Liberty party** absorbed nearly 16,000 votes, many of which would otherwise have gone to the unlucky Kentuckian. Ironically, the anti-Texas Liberty party, by helping to elect the pro-Texas Polk, hastened the annexation of Texas. The victorious Democrats proclaimed that they had received a mandate from the voters to take Texas, and three days before leaving office President Tyler signed the joint resolution of annexation.

★ Polk the Purposeful

"Young Hickory" Polk, unlike "Old Hickory" Jackson, was not an impressive figure. Lean, white-haired, gray-eyed, and stern-faced, he took life seriously and drove himself mercilessly into a premature grave. His burdens were increased by an unwillingness to delegate authority. Methodical and hardworking but not brilliant, Polk was shrewd, narrow-minded, and persistent. "What he went for he fetched," wrote a contemporary. Purposeful in the highest degree, he developed a positive four-point program and with remarkable success achieved it completely in less than four years.

Polk's first goal was a lowered tariff. His Secretary of the Treasury, Robert J. Walker, pushed through Congress a tariff bill that reduced the average rates of the Tariff of 1842 from about 32 percent to 25 percent. The **Walker Tariff** of 1846 proved to be an excellent revenue producer.

Liberty party (1840–1848) *Antislavery party that ran candidates in the 1840 and 1844 elections before merging with the Free Soil party. Supporters of the Liberty party sought the eventual abolition of slavery, but in the short term hoped to halt the expansion of slavery into the territories and abolish the domestic slave trade.*

Walker Tariff (1846) *Revenue-enhancing measure that lowered tariffs from 1842 levels, thereby fueling trade and increasing Treasury receipts.*

A second objective of Polk was restoration of the independent treasury, unceremoniously dropped by the Whigs in 1841. Pro-bank Whigs in Congress raised a storm of opposition, but victory at last rewarded the president's efforts in 1846.

The third and fourth points on Polk's "must list" were the settlement of the Oregon dispute (see Map 17.1) and the acquisition of California.

"Reoccupation" of the "whole" of Oregon had been promised by northern Democrats in the campaign of 1844. But southern Democrats, once they had annexed Texas, rapidly cooled off. Polk, himself a southerner, had no intention of insisting on the 54° 40′ pledge of his own platform. He again proposed the compromise line of 49°, but the British minister in Washington brusquely spurned this olive branch.

Fortunately for peace, British anti-expansionists ("Little Englanders") were now persuaded that the Columbia River after all was not the St. Lawrence of the West. Early in 1846 the British came around, and they themselves proposed the line of 49°. The senators speedily accepted the offer and approved the subsequent treaty, despite angry shouts of **"Fifty-four forty or fight!"**

Satisfaction with the Oregon settlement among Americans was not unanimous. The northwestern states, hotbeds of Manifest Destiny and "fifty-four fortyism," joined the antislavery forces in condemning what they regarded as a base betrayal by the South. Why *all* of Texas and not *all* of Oregon? Because, retorted the expansionist Senator Thomas Hart Benton of Missouri, "Great Britain is powerful and Mexico is weak."

So Polk, despite all the campaign bluster, got neither "fifty-four forty" nor a fight. But he did get something that in the long run was better: a reasonable compromise without a rifle being raised.

Map 17.1 The Oregon Controversy, 1846

"Fifty-four forty or fight!" (1846)
Slogan adopted by mid-nineteenth-century expansionists who advocated the occupation of Oregon Territory, jointly held by Britain and the United States. Though President Polk had pledged to seize all of Oregon, to 54° 40′, he settled on the forty-ninth parallel as a compromise with the British.

★ Misunderstandings with Mexico

Faraway California was Polk's final objective. He and other disciples of Manifest Destiny had long coveted its verdant valleys, and especially the spacious bay of San Francisco. This splendid harbor was widely regarded as America's future gateway to the Pacific Ocean.

The population of California in 1845 was curiously mixed. It consisted of perhaps thirteen thousand sun-blessed Spanish Mexicans and as many as seventy-five thousand dispirited Indians. There were fewer than a thousand "foreigners," mostly Americans, some of whom had "left their consciences" behind them as they rounded Cape Horn. Given time, these transplanted Yankees might bring California into the Union by "playing the Texas game."

Polk was eager to buy California from Mexico, but relations with Mexico City were dangerously embittered. One point of friction was some $3 million in claims against Mexico for damages to American citizens and their property. The most serious bone of contention was Texas. After threatening war if the United States acquired the Lone Star Republic, the Mexican government completely severed diplomatic relations following annexation.

Deadlock with Mexico over Texas was further tightened by a question of boundaries. During the long era of Spanish occupation of Mexico, the southwestern boundary of Texas had been the Nueces River. But the expansive Texans, on rather far-fetched grounds, were claiming the more southerly Rio Grande River as the boundary instead. Polk, for his part, felt a strong obligation to defend Texas in its claim, once it was annexed.

The Mexicans were far less concerned about this boundary quibble than the United States. In their eyes all of Texas was still theirs, although temporarily in revolt, and a dispute over the two rivers seemed pointless. Yet Polk was careful to keep American troops out of virtually all of the explosive no-man's-land between the Nueces and the Rio Grande, as long as there was any real prospect of peaceful adjustment.

The golden prize of California continued to cause Polk much anxiety. Disquieting rumors (now known to have been ill-founded) were circulating that Britain was about to buy or seize California—a grab that Americans could not tolerate under the Monroe Doctrine. In a last desperate throw of the dice, Polk dispatched John Slidell to Mexico City as minister late in 1845. The new envoy, among other alternatives, was instructed to offer a maximum of $25 million for California and territory to the east. But the proud Mexican people would not even permit Slidell to present his "insulting" proposition.

American Blood on American Soil

A frustrated Polk was now prepared to force a showdown. On January 13, 1846, he ordered four thousand men, under General Zachary Taylor, to march from the Nueces River to the Rio Grande, provocatively near Mexican forces. Polk's presidential diary reveals that he expected at any moment to hear of a clash. When none occurred after an anxious wait, he informed his cabinet on May 9, 1846, that he proposed to ask Congress to declare war on the basis of (1) unpaid claims and (2) Slidell's rejection. These, at best, were rather flimsy pretexts. Two cabinet members spoke up and said that they would feel better satisfied if Mexican troops should fire first.

That very evening news of bloodshed arrived. On April 25, 1846, Mexican troops had crossed the Rio Grande and attacked General Taylor's command, with a loss of sixteen Americans killed or wounded.

Polk, further aroused, sent a vigorous war message to Congress. He declared that despite "all our efforts" to avoid a clash, hostilities had been forced upon the country by the shedding of "American blood upon the American soil." A patriotic Congress overwhelmingly voted for war, and enthusiastic volunteers cried, "Ho for the Halls of the Montezumas!" and "Mexico or Death!" Inflamed by the war fever, even antislavery Whig bastions joined with the rest of the nation, though they later condemned "Jimmy Polk's war." As James Russell Lowell of Massachusetts lamented,

Massachusetts, God forgive her,
She's akneelin' with the rest.

In his message to Congress, Polk was making history—not writing it. If he had been a historian, he would have explained that American blood had been shed on soil that the Mexicans had good reason to regard as their own. A gangling, rough-featured Whig congressman from Illinois, one Abraham Lincoln, introduced certain resolutions that requested information as to the precise "spot" on American soil where American blood had been shed. He pushed his "spot" resolutions with such persistence that he came to be known as the "spotty Lincoln" who could die of "spotted fever." More extreme antislavery agitators branded the president a liar—"Polk the Mendacious."

Did Polk provoke war? California was an imperative point in his program, and Mexico would not sell it at any price. The only way to get it was to use force or wait for an internal American revolt. But in 1846, patience had ceased to be a virtue as far as Polk was concerned. Bent on grasping California by fair means or foul, he pushed the quarrel to a bloody showdown.

Both sides, in fact, were spoiling for a fight. Feisty Americans, especially southwestern expansionists, were eager to teach the Mexicans a lesson. The Mexicans, in turn, were burning to humiliate the "Bullies of the North." Possessing a considerable standing army, they boasted of invading the United States, freeing the black slaves, and lassoing whole regiments of Americans. They were hoping that the quarrel with Britain over Oregon would blossom into a full-dress war, as it came near doing, and further pin down the hated *yanquis*. Fired by indignation, Mexicans and Americans each believed the other was the aggressor.

Manifest Destiny and Its Legacy   277

⭐ The Mastering of Mexico

Polk wanted California—not war. But when war came, he hoped to fight it on a limited scale and then pull out when he had captured the prize. The conflict would not be so simple. The dethroned and devious Mexican dictator Santa Anna, temporarily exiled in Cuba, returned to Mexico and proceeded to rally his countrymen to a desperate defense of their soil.

American operations in the Southwest and in California were completely successful (see Map 17.2). In 1846 General Stephen W. Kearny led a detachment of seventeen hundred troops over the famous Santa Fe Trail from Fort Leavenworth to Santa Fe. This sunbaked outpost, with its drowsy plazas, was easily captured. But before Kearny could reach California, the fertile province was won. When war broke out, Captain John C. Frémont, the dashing explorer, just "happened" to be there with several dozen well-armed men. In helping to overthrow Mexican rule in 1846, he collaborated with American naval officers and with the local Americans, who had hoisted the banner of the short-lived California Bear Flag Republic.

General Zachary Taylor meanwhile had been spearheading the main thrust. Known as "Old Rough and Ready" because of his iron constitution and unsoldierly dress, he fought his way across the Rio Grande into Mexico. After several gratifying victories, he reached **Buena Vista**. There, on February 22–23, 1847, his weakened force of five thousand

Battle of Buena Vista (1847) *Key American victory against Mexican forces in the Mexican War. Elevated General Zachary Taylor to national prominence and helped secure his success in the 1848 presidential election.*

Map 17.2 Major Campaigns of the Mexican War

men was attacked by some twenty thousand march-weary troops under Santa Anna. The Mexicans were finally repulsed with extreme difficulty, and overnight Zachary Taylor became the "Hero of Buena Vista."

Sound American strategy now called for a crushing blow at the enemy's vitals—Mexico City. Though a good leader, General Taylor could not decisively win the war in the semideserts of northern Mexico. The command of the main expedition, which pushed inland from the coastal city of Veracruz early in 1847, was entrusted to General Winfield Scott. A handsome giant of a man, Scott had emerged as a hero from the War of 1812 and later earned the nickname "Old Fuss and Feathers" because of his resplendent uniforms and strict discipline. Scott succeeded in battling a more numerous enemy through mountainous terrain up to Mexico City by September 1847 in one of the most brilliant campaigns in American military annals. He proved to be the most distinguished general produced by his country between the Revolution and the Civil War.

⭐ Fighting Mexico for Peace

Polk was anxious to end the shooting as soon as he could secure his territorial goals. Accordingly, he sent along with Scott's invading army a State Department official, Nicholas P. Trist. Grasping a fleeting opportunity to negotiate with the Mexicans, Trist signed the **Treaty of Guadalupe Hidalgo** on February 2, 1848, and forwarded it to Washington.

The terms of the treaty were breathtaking. They confirmed the American title to Texas and yielded the enormous area stretching northward to Oregon and west to the ocean, embracing coveted California. This total expanse, including Texas, was about one-half of Mexico. The United States agreed to pay $15 million for the land and to assume the claims of its citizens against Mexico in the amount of $3,250,000 (see "Makers of America: The Californios").

Polk quickly submitted the treaty to the Senate. Speed was imperative. The antislavery Conscience Whigs in Congress were denouncing this "damnable war" with increasing heat. Having secured control of the House in 1847, they were even threatening to vote down supplies for the armies in the field. If they had done so, Scott probably would have been forced to retreat, and the fruits of victory might have been tossed away.

Another peril impended. A swelling group of expansionists, intoxicated by Manifest Destiny, was clamoring for the United States to take all of Mexico. If America had seized it, the nation would have been saddled with a vexatious problem. Farseeing southerners like Calhoun, alarmed by the mounting anger of antislavery agitators, realized that the South would do well not to be too greedy. The treaty was finally approved by the Senate, 38 to 14. Oddly enough, it was condemned both by those opponents who wanted all of Mexico and by opponents who wanted none of it.

Treaty of Guadalupe Hidalgo (1848) *Ended the war with Mexico. Mexico agreed to cede territory reaching northwest from Texas to Oregon in exchange for $18.25 million in cash and assumed debts.*

War News from Mexico, by Richard Caton Woodville The newfangled telegraph kept the nation closely informed of events in far-off Mexico.

Makers of America

The Californios

When the United States acquired the Mexican Cession in 1848, it took in a vast land that stretched from the arid desert Southwest to the fruited valleys and port cities of California. There, at the conclusion of the Mexican War, dwelled some thirteen thousand Californios—descendants of the Spanish and Mexican conquerors who had once ruled California.

The Spanish had first arrived in California in 1769, extending their New World empire and outracing Russian traders to bountiful San Francisco Bay. Father Junipero Serra, an enterprising Franciscan friar, soon established twenty-one missions along the coast. Indians in the iron grip of the missions were encouraged to adopt Christianity and often forced to toil endlessly as farmers and herders, in the process suffering disease and degradation. These frequently maltreated mission Indians occupied the lowest rungs on the ladder of Spanish colonial society.

Upon the loftiest rungs perched the Californios. Pioneers from the Mexican heartland of New Spain, they had trailed Serra to California, claiming land and civil offices in their new home. Yet even the proud Californios had deferred to the all-powerful Franciscan missionaries until Mexico threw off the Spanish colonial yoke in 1821 and transferred power from the missions to secular (that is, governmental) authorities.

This "secularization" program eroded the immense power of the Franciscans, who had confidently commanded their rich fiefdoms and resisted even minor efforts to reform their harsh treatment of the Indians. But during the 1830s much of the missions' land and assets were confiscated by the Californios. Vast *ranchos* (ranches) formed, and from those citadels the Californios ruled until the Mexican War.

The Californios' glory faded in the wake of the American victory. Overwhelmed by the inrush of Anglo gold-diggers—some eighty-seven thousand after the discovery at Sutter's Fort in 1848—the Californios saw their recently acquired lands and political power slip through their fingers. When the Civil War broke out in 1861, so harshly did the word *Yankee* ring in their ears that many Californios supported the South.

By 1870 the Californios' brief ascendancy had utterly vanished—a short and sad tale of riches to rags in the face of the Anglo onslaught. Half a century later, beginning in 1910, hundreds of thousands of young Mexicans would flock into California and the Southwest. They would enter a region liberally endowed with Spanish architecture and artifacts, bearing the names of Spanish missions and Californio ranchos. But they would find it a land dominated by Anglos, a place far different from that which their Californio ancestors had settled so hopefully in earlier days.

Dance of Native Californians at San Francisco de Assis Mission, 1816, by Ludwig Choris In the sixty years that they operated, the twenty-one California missions employed 142 priests and baptized 87,787 Indians. Missions became a combination of churches, towns, schools, farms, factories, and prisons.

Contending Voices

Warring over the Mexican War

The war against Mexico was both warmly applauded and hotly condemned. The prowar New York Evening Post *trumpeted in 1848:*

"Now we ask, whether any man can coolly contemplate the idea of recalling our troops from the [Mexican] territory we at present occupy . . . and . . . resign this beautiful country to the custody of the ignorant cowards and profligate ruffians who have ruled it for the last twenty-five years? Why, humanity cries out against it. Civilization and Christianity protest against this reflux of the tide of barbarism and anarchy."

The eminent Kentuckian and founder of the Whig party, Henry Clay (1777–1852), though a "war hawk" in the War of 1812, strongly opposed the expansionism of the 1840s, which contributed to his defeat by Democrat James K. Polk in the presidential election of 1844. His son Henry died fighting in the battle of Buena Vista in February 1847. Nine months later, Clay made a passionate antiwar speech in Lexington, Kentucky. In the audience was newly elected Illinois congressman Abraham Lincoln, who later called the Mexican War "unnecessary." Clay said:

"Of all the dangers and misfortunes which could befall this nation, I should regard that of its becoming a warlike and conquering power, the most direful and fatal.... This is no war of defense, but one unnecessary and of offensive aggression. It is Mexico that is defending her fire-sides, her castles and her altars, not we."

[Was the war against Mexico wise or unwise, just or unjust?

★ Profit and Loss in Mexico

As wars go, the Mexican War was a small one. It cost some thirteen thousand American lives, most of them taken by disease. But the fruits of the fighting were enormous.

America's total expanse, already vast, was increased by about one-third (counting Texas)—an addition even greater than that of the Louisiana Purchase. A sharp stimulus was given to the spirit of Manifest Destiny for, as the proverb has it, the appetite comes with eating.

The Mexican War proved to be the blood-spattered schoolroom of the Civil War. The campaigns provided priceless field experience for most of the officers destined to become leading generals in the forthcoming conflict, including Captain Robert E. Lee and Lieutenant Ulysses S. Grant. The Military Academy at West Point, founded in 1802, fully justified its existence through the well-trained officers. Useful also was the navy, which did valuable work in throwing a crippling blockade around Mexican ports. Navy Secretary and historian George Bancroft had established the Naval Academy at Annapolis, Maryland, in 1846. The Marine Corps, in existence since 1798, won new laurels and to this day sings, in its stirring hymn, about the "Halls of Montezuma."

The army waged war without defeat and without a major blunder, despite formidable obstacles and a half-dozen or so achingly long marches. Chagrined British critics, as well as other foreign skeptics, reluctantly revised upward their estimate of Yankee military prowess. The opposing armies, moreover, emerged with increased respect for each other. The Mexicans, though poorly led, fought heroically. At Chapultepec, near Mexico City, the teenage lads of the military academy there (*los niños*) perished to a boy.

Long-memoried Mexicans have never forgotten that their northern enemy tore away about half of their country. The argument that they were lucky not to lose all of it, and that they had been paid something for their land, has scarcely lessened their bitterness. The war also marked an ugly turning point in the relations between the United States and Latin America as a whole. Hitherto, Uncle Sam had been regarded with some friendliness. Henceforth, he was increasingly feared as the "Colossus of the North." Suspicious neighbors to the south condemned him as a greedy and untrustworthy bully, who might next despoil them of their soil.

Most ominous of all, the war rearoused the snarling dog of the slavery issue, and the beast did not stop yelping until drowned in the blood of the Civil War. Abolitionists assailed the Mexican conflict as one provoked by the southern "slavocracy" for its own evil purposes.

Quarreling over slavery extension also erupted on the floors of Congress. In 1846, shortly after the shooting started, Polk requested an appropriation of $2 million with which to buy a peace. Representative David Wilmot of Pennsylvania, fearful of the southern "slavocracy," introduced a fateful amendment, which stipulated that slavery should never exist in any of the territory wrested from Mexico.

The disruptive Wilmot amendment twice passed the House but not the Senate. Southern members, unwilling to be robbed of prospective slave states, fought the restriction tooth and nail. Antislavery men, in Congress and out, battled no less bitterly for the exclusion of slaves. The "Wilmot Proviso" never became law, but it soon came to symbolize the burning issue of slavery in the territories.

Seen in historical perspective, the opening shots of the Mexican War were the opening shots of the Civil War. President Polk left the nation the splendid physical heritage of California and the Southwest but also the ugly moral heritage of an embittered slavery dispute. "Mexico will poison us," said the philosopher Ralph Waldo Emerson. Mexicans could later take some satisfaction in knowing that the territory wrenched from them had proved to be a venomous apple of discord that could well be called Santa Anna's revenge.

Wilmot Proviso (1846) *Amendment that sought to prohibit slavery from territories acquired from Mexico. Introduced by Pennsylvania congressman David Wilmot, the failed amendment ratcheted up tensions between North and South over the issue of slavery.*

CHAPTER SUMMARY ★ ★ ★ ★ ★ ★ ★ ★ ★ ★ ★ ★ ★

As Tyler assumed the presidency after Harrison's early death, the United States became engaged in a series of sharp disputes with Britain. A conflict over the Maine boundary was resolved, but British involvement in Texas revived the movement to annex the Lone Star Republic to the United States.

The Texas and Oregon questions became embroiled in the hotly contested 1844 campaign, as the Democrats nominated and elected the militantly expansionist Polk. After Texas was added to the Union, Polk pursued an aggressive policy of expansion. He successfully acquired part of the disputed Oregon country from Britain. Unable to obtain Mexican California peaceably, Polk led the nation into war with an equally belligerent Mexico in 1846.

American forces quickly conquered California and New Mexico. Winfield Scott's and Zachary Taylor's invasion of Mexico was also successful, and the United States obtained large new territories in the peace treaty.

Besides adding California, New Mexico, and Utah to American territory, the Mexican War trained a new generation of military leaders and aroused long-term Latin American resentment of the United States. But the war's most important consequence was to force the slavery controversy to the center of national politics, as first indicated by the Wilmot Proviso proposing to ban slavery from the newly acquired territories.

KEY TERMS

Tariff of 1842 (271)
Caroline (271)
"Aroostook War" (271)
Conscience Whigs (272)
Manifest Destiny (273)
Liberty party (274)
Walker Tariff (274)
"Fifty-four forty or fight" (275)
Battle of Buena Vista (277)
Treaty of Guadalupe Hidalgo (278)
Wilmot Proviso (281)

PEOPLE TO KNOW

John Tyler
James K. Polk
Stephen W. Kearny
John C. Frémont
Winfield Scott
Nicholas P. Trist
David Wilmot

MindTap is a fully online, highly personalized learning experience built upon Cengage Learning content. MindTap combines student learning tools—readings, multimedia, activities, and assessments—into a singular Learning Path that guides students through the course.

Chapter 18

Renewing the Sectional Struggle
1848–1854

• • •

*Secession! Peaceable secession! Sir, your eyes and mine
are never destined to see that miracle.*

Daniel Webster, 1850

Chapter Outline

- "Popular Sovereignty"
- Growing Sectional Tensions
- The Compromise of 1850
- The Inflammatory Fugitive Slave Law
- The Death of the Whig Party
- President Pierce and Proslavery Expansionist Ventures, 1853–1857
- Senator Douglas and the Kansas–Nebraska Act, 1854

The year 1848, highlighted by a rash of revolutions in Europe, was filled with unrest in America. The Treaty of Guadalupe Hidalgo had officially ended the war with Mexico but initiated a new and perilous round of political warfare in the United States. The vanquished Mexicans had been forced to relinquish an enormous tract of real estate, including Texas, California, and all the area between. The acquisition of this huge domain raised anew the burning issue of extending slavery into the territories. Northern antislaveryites had rallied behind the Wilmot Proviso, which flatly prohibited slavery in any territory acquired in the Mexican War. Southern senators had blocked the passage of the proviso, but the issue did not die. Ominously, debate over slavery in the area of the Mexican Cession threatened to disrupt the ranks of both Whigs and Democrats and to split national politics along North–South sectional lines.

FOCUS QUESTIONS

1. What were the major terms of the Compromise of 1850, and how did these agreements attempt to defuse the furious controversies over the territories acquired from Mexico in 1848?
2. How successful was the Compromise of 1850?
3. Why did the Whig party disintegrate and then disappear?
4. Why did the Democratic Pierce administration, as well as private American adventurers, pursue aggressive overseas schemes designed to expand slavery?
5. What was the "popular sovereignty" doctrine, and why did Senator Stephen Douglas push it forward in the Kansas–Nebraska Act? Why did the Kansas–Nebraska Act set off the fiercest round of sectional antagonism?

CHRONOLOGY

1844	Caleb Cushing signs Treaty of Wanghia with China	1852	Pierce defeats Scott for presidency
1848	British seize port of San Juan del Norte in Nicaragua Treaty of Guadalupe Hidalgo ends Mexican War Taylor defeats Cass and Van Buren for presidency	1853	Gadsden Purchase from Mexico
		1854	Commodore Perry opens Japan Ostend Manifesto proposes seizure of Cuba Kansas-Nebraska Act repeals Missouri Compromise of 1820 Republican party organized
1849	California gold rush		
1850	Fillmore assumes presidency after Taylor's death Compromise of 1850, including Fugitive Slave Law Clayton-Bulwer Treaty with Britain	1856	William Walker becomes president of Nicaragua and legalizes slavery

★ The Popular Sovereignty Panacea

Each of the two great political parties was a vital bond of national unity, for each enjoyed powerful support in both North and South. If they should be replaced by two purely sectional groupings, the Union would be in peril. To politicians, the wisest strategy seemed to be to sit on the lid of the slavery issue and ignore the boiling beneath. Even so, the cover bobbed up and down ominously in response to the agitation of zealous northern abolitionists and impassioned southern "fire-eaters."

President Polk, broken in health, did not seek a second term. The Democratic National Convention in Baltimore turned to aging General Lewis Cass, an experienced but pompous senator whose enemies dubbed him "General Gass." The Democratic platform, in line with the lid-sitting strategy, was silent on the burning issue of slavery in the territories. But Cass himself was well known as the reputed father of "**popular sovereignty**," the doctrine that the people of a territory, under the principles of the Constitution, should themselves determine the status of slavery.

Popular sovereignty had a persuasive appeal. The public liked it because it accorded with the democratic tradition of self-determination. Politicians liked it because it seemed a comfortable compromise between the abolitionist bid for a ban on slavery in the territories and southern demands that Congress protect slavery in the territories. Popular sovereignty tossed the slavery problem into the laps of the people in the various territories. Advocates of the principle thus hoped to dissolve the most stubborn national issue of the day into a series of local issues. Yet popular sovereignty had one fatal defect: it might serve to spread the blight of slavery.

Meeting in Philadelphia, the Whigs turned away from the controversial Henry Clay and nominated blunt-talking General Zachary Taylor, the "Hero of Buena Vista," who had never held civil office or even voted for president. As usual, the Whigs pussyfooted in their platform. Eager to win at any cost, they dodged all troublesome issues and extolled the homespun virtues of their candidate. Taylor had not committed himself on the issue of slavery extension, but as a wealthy Louisiana sugar planter he owned scores of slaves.

Aroused by the conspiracy of silence in the Democratic and Whig platforms, ardent antislavery northerners organized the **Free Soil party**. They came out foursquare for the Wilmot Proviso and against slavery in the territories. The new party nominated former President Martin Van Buren as its candidate and went into the campaign shouting "Free soil, free speech, free labor, and free men."

These freedoms provided the bedrock of its principles, but the new party assembled a strange assortment of new fellows in the same political bed. It contained a large element

---

popular sovereignty *Notion advanced before the Civil War that the sovereign people of a given territory should decide whether to allow slavery. Seemingly a compromise, it was largely opposed by northern abolitionists, who feared it would promote the spread of slavery to the territories.*

Free Soil party (1848–1854) *Antislavery party in the 1848 and 1852 elections that opposed the extension of slavery into the territories, arguing that the presence of slavery would limit opportunities for free laborers.*

> *Ralph Waldo Emerson, the philosopher and moderate abolitionist, was outraged by Webster's support of concessions to the South in the Fugitive Slave Act. In February 1851 he wrote in his* Journal:
>
> "I opened a paper to-day in which he [Webster] pounds on the old strings [of liberty] in a letter to the Washington Birthday feasters at New York. 'Liberty! liberty!' Pho! Let Mr. Webster, for decency's sake, shut his lips once and forever on this word. The word *liberty* in the mouth of Mr. Webster sounds like the word *love* in the mouth of a courtesan."

Seventh of March speech (1850)
Daniel Webster's impassioned address urging the North to support the Compromise of 1850. Webster argued that topography and climate would keep slavery from becoming entrenched in Mexican Cession territory and urged northerners to make all reasonable concessions to prevent disunion.

his fateful words predicting that if the antislavery agitation were not ended disunion would follow. Rejecting Clay's proposed concessions, Calhoun's impassioned plea was to leave slavery alone, return runaway slaves, give the South its rights as a minority, and restore the political balance. Calhoun died in 1850, before the debate was over, murmuring the sad words, "The South! The South! God knows what will become of her!"

Daniel Webster, sixty-eight years old and also ailing, next took the Senate spotlight to uphold Clay's compromise measures in his own last great speech. Webster urged all reasonable concessions to the South, including a new fugitive slave law with teeth. Because climate and topography would prevent the spread of cotton production to the Mexican Cession territory, Webster argued, it was unnecessary to legislate on slavery there.* Webster's famed **Seventh of March speech** was his finest effort. It visibly strengthened Union sentiment and especially pleased northern banking and commercial centers, which stood to lose millions of dollars by secession. But the Free-Soilers and abolitionists, who had assumed Webster was one of them, upbraided him as a traitor.

The stormy congressional debate of 1850 was not finished, for the Young Guard from the North were yet to have their say. Led by wiry freshman Senator William Seward of New York, this new generation of antislavery leaders was more interested in purifying the Union than in patching and preserving it. Seward unequivocally opposed further concessions to the South. Seward argued earnestly that Christian legislators must obey God's moral law as well as man's mundane law and therefore appealed to a "higher law" than the Constitution to exclude slavery from the territories.

As the great debate in Congress ran its heated course, deadlock seemed certain. Blunt old President Taylor seemed bent on vetoing any compromise passed by Congress. In response to threats of Texas to seize Santa Fe, the crusty soldier-president seemed ready to lead the U.S. army into Texas in person and hang all the "damned traitors." If troops had marched, the South probably would have rallied to the defense of Texas, and the Civil War might have erupted in 1850.

★ Breaking the Congressional Logjam

But at the very height of the 1850 controversy, President Taylor unknowingly helped the cause of concession by suddenly dying. The portly and colorless Vice President Millard Fillmore then took the reins. As presiding officer of the Senate, he had been impressed with the arguments for conciliation, and he gladly signed the series of compromise measures that passed Congress after seven long months of stormy debate.

The struggle to get these measures accepted by the country was hardly less heated than in Congress. In the northern states, "Union savers" such as Senators Clay, Webster, and Douglas orated on behalf of the compromise. The ailing Clay himself delivered more than seventy speeches, as a powerful sentiment for acceptance gradually crystallized in the North. It was strengthened by a growing feeling of goodwill and an upsurge of prosperity enriched by California gold.

But the southern "fire-eaters" were still violently opposed to concessions. In June 1850 an assembly of southern extremists met in Nashville, Tennessee, to condemn the impending compromise. Meeting again in November after the bills had passed, the convention proved to be a dud. By that time southern opinion had reluctantly accepted the verdict of Congress.

---

*Webster was wrong here; within one hundred years California had become one of the great cotton-producing states of the Union.

heavens with their protests against the man-stealing statute. A meeting presided over by William Lloyd Garrison in 1851 declared, "We execrate it, we spit upon it, we trample it under our feet."

Beyond question, the Fugitive Slave Law was an appalling blunder on the part of the South. No single irritant of the 1850s was more persistently galling to both sides, and none did more to awaken in the North a spirit of antagonism against the South. The southerners in turn were embittered because the northerners would not in good faith execute the law—the one real and immediate southern "gain" from the Great Compromise. Slave-catchers, with some success, redoubled their efforts.

Should the shooting showdown have come in 1850? From the standpoint of the secessionists, yes; from the standpoint of the Unionists, no. Time was fighting for the North. With every passing decade, this huge section was forging further ahead in population and wealth—in crops, factories, foundries, ships, and railroads.

Delay also added immensely to the moral strength of the North—to its will to fight for the Union. In 1850 thousands of northern moderates were unwilling to pin the South to the rest of the nation with bayonets. But the inflammatory events of the 1850s did much to bolster the Yankee will to resist secession, whatever the cost. This one feverish decade gave the North time to accumulate the material and moral strength that provided the margin of victory. Thus, the Compromise of 1850, from one point of view, won the Civil War for the Union.

> ## Contending Voices
>
> ### The Compromise of 1850
>
> *Two senatorial giants hotly debated the nature—and future—of the Union as they tried to hammer out the Compromise of 1850:*
>
> *John C. Calhoun (1782-1850), South Carolina:*
>
> "If you, who represent the stronger portion, cannot agree to settle . . . [then] let the states we both represent agree to separate and part in peace. If you are unwilling we should part in peace, tell us so; and we shall know what to do, when you reduce the question to submission or resistance."
>
> *Daniel Webster (1782-1852) of Massachusetts replied:*
>
> "There can be no such thing as a peaceable secession. Peaceable secession is an utter impossibility. . . . I see that disruption must produce such a war as I will not describe."
>
> Who proved the more accurate prophet?

★ Defeat and Doom for the Whigs

Meeting in Baltimore, the deadlocked Democratic convention of 1852 startled the nation by stampeding to the second "dark horse" candidate in American history, Franklin Pierce, an unrenowned New Hampshire lawyer-politician. Weak and indecisive, Pierce was called the "Fainting General" by his opponents because a painful groin injury had caused him to fall off a horse during the Mexican War. As a prosouthern northerner, Pierce was acceptable to the slavery wing of the Democratic party. His platform emphatically endorsed the Compromise of 1850, Fugitive Slave Law and all.

The Whigs, also convening in Baltimore, might logically have nominated figures associated with the Compromise of 1850, such as President Fillmore or Senator Webster. But having won in the past only with military heroes, they turned to another, "Old Fuss and Feathers," Winfield Scott. Although Scott was the ablest American general of his generation as well as an impressive statesman, his haughty personality repelled the masses. Democrats ridiculed Scott's pomposity and cried exultantly, "We Polked 'em in '44; we'll Pierce 'em in '52."

Luckily for the Democrats, the Whig party was hopelessly split. Antislavery Whigs of the North swallowed Scott as their nominee but deplored his platform, which endorsed the hated Fugitive Slave Law. Southern Whigs, who doubted Scott's loyalty to the Compromise of 1850 and especially to the Fugitive Slave Law, accepted the platform but spat on the candidate. In the end the politically inexperienced Scott was stabbed in the back by his fellow Whigs, notably in the South. The Free-Soil candidate, New Hampshire Senator John P. Hale, also siphoned off northern Whig votes that might have gone to Scott. The pliant Pierce won in a landslide, 254 electoral votes to 42, although the popular vote was closer, 1,601,117 to 1,385,453.

The election of 1852 was fraught with frightening significance, though it seemed tame at the time. It marked the effective end of the disorganized Whig party and, within a few years, its complete death. The Whigs' demise augured the eclipse of *national* parties and the worrisome rise of purely *sectional* political alignments. The Whigs were governed at times by the crassest opportunism, and they won only two presidential elections in their colorful career (1840, 1848), both with war heroes. They finally choked to death trying to swallow the distasteful Fugitive Slave Law. But their one great contribution was to uphold the ideal of Union through their electoral strength in the South and through the eloquence of leaders such as Henry Clay and Daniel Webster. Both of these statesmen, by unhappy coincidence, died during the 1852 campaign. But the good they had done lived after them and contributed powerfully to the eventual preservation of a *united* United States.

★ The Expansionist Legacy of the Mexican War

The intoxicating victory in the Mexican War reinvigorated the spirit of Manifest Destiny and a lust for new slave territory among "slavocrats." Many Americans were also looking for transportation routes across the narrow isthmus of Central America, through either Panama or Nicaragua, to California's new gold fields. Whoever controlled that route would hold imperial sway over all maritime nations, including the United States. A full-blown confrontation between the United States and Britain, which had been encroaching on Nicaragua's "Mosquito Coast," was avoided by the **Clayton-Bulwer Treaty** of 1850. It stipulated that neither America nor Britain would fortify or seek exclusive control over any future isthmian waterway (later rescinded by the Hay-Pauncefote Treaty of 1901).

Southerner "slavocrats" cast especially covetous eyes southward in the 1850s. They lusted for new slave territory after the Compromise of 1850 seemingly closed most of the Mexican Cession to the "peculiar institution." In 1856 a Texan proposed a toast "to the Southern republic bounded on the north by the Mason and Dixon line and on the South by the Isthmus of Tehuantepec [southern Mexico], including Cuba and all the lands on our Southern shore."

Nicaragua beckoned beguilingly. A brazen American adventurer, William Walker, tried repeatedly to grab control of this Central American country in the 1850s. Backed by an armed force recruited largely in the South, he installed himself as president in July 1856 and promptly legalized slavery. One southern newspaper proclaimed to the planter aristocracy that Walker—the "gray-eyed man of destiny"—"now offers Nicaragua to you and your slaves." But a coalition of Central American nations formed an alliance to overthrow him. President Pierce withdrew diplomatic recognition, and the gray-eyed man's destiny was to crumple before a Honduran firing squad in 1860.

Sugar-rich Cuba, lying just off the nation's southern doorstep, was also an enticing prospect for annexation. This remnant of Spain's once-mighty New World empire, with its large population of enslaved blacks, might be carved into several states, restoring the political balance in the Senate. President Polk had considered offering Spain $100 million for Cuba, but the proud Spaniards replied that they would sooner see the island sunk into the sea than in the hands of the hated Yankees.

Some southern adventurers now undertook to shake the tree of Manifest Destiny on their own. During 1850–1851, two "filibustering" expeditions, each numbering several hundred armed men, descended on Cuba. Both feeble efforts were repelled, and fifty of the invaders were summarily shot or strangled.

When Spanish officials in Cuba rashly seized an American steamer in 1854, southern-dominated President Pierce decided that now was the time to provoke a war with Spain and seize Cuba. An incredible cloak-and-dagger episode followed. Pierce's secretary of state instructed the American ministers to Spain, Britain, and France to meet in Ostend, Belgium, and draw up a plan to acquire Cuba. Their top-secret dispatch, known as the "**Ostend Manifesto**," urged the administration to offer $120 million for Cuba. If Spain refused to sell, the United States would "be justified in wresting" the island from the Spanish.

When the secret Ostend Manifesto leaked out, Northern free-soilers rose up in wrath against the "manifesto of brigands." The red-faced Pierce administration hurriedly dropped its reckless schemes for Cuba. The slavery issue thus checked territorial expansion in the 1850s.

Clayton-Bulwer Treaty (1850) *Signed by Great Britain and the United States, it provided that the two nations would jointly protect the neutrality of Central America and that neither power would seek to fortify or exclusively control any future isthmian waterway. Later revoked by the Hay-Pauncefote Treaty of 1901, which gave the United States control of the Panama Canal.*

Ostend Manifesto (1854) *Secret Franklin Pierce administration proposal to purchase or, that failing, to wrest militarily Cuba from Spain. Once leaked, it was quickly abandoned due to vehement opposition from the North.*

Besides Latin America, another arena of American international assertiveness in the 1850s was in the Pacific and East Asia. The acquisition of California and Oregon had made the United States a Pacific power—or would-be power. In 1842 Britain gained free access to so-called treaty ports in China as well as outright control of the island of Hong Kong. To secure comparable concessions for the United States, President Tyler in 1844 dispatched dashing Massachusetts diplomat Caleb Cushing, along with four warships, to the southern Chinese port of Macao. In July 1844 Cushing signed the **Treaty of Wanghia** with China. The treaty secured the United States equal trading rights with other nations and the principle of "extraterritoriality" that provided for trying accused Americans in American, not Chinese, courts. American trade with China flourished, and thousands of American missionaries soon arrived through the treaty ports to convert the "heathen Chinese."

Success in China inspired a still more consequential mission to pry open the bamboo gates of Japan, which had been closed to outsiders for centuries. In 1852 President Millard Fillmore dispatched to Edo (later Tokyo) Bay, Japan, a fleet of four awesome, smoke-belching warships, commanded by Commodore Matthew C. Perry. Perry returned in February 1854 with an even larger fleet and, with a combination of bluster and bravado, persuaded the Japanese to sign the landmark **Treaty of Kanagawa** on March 31, 1854. It provided for proper treatment of shipwrecked sailors, American coaling rights in Japan, and the establishment of consular relations. This commercial toe in the door cracked Japan's two-century shell of isolation open and began to propel the Land of the Rising Sun headlong into the modern world.

Treaty of Wanghia (1844) *Signed by the United States and China, it assured the United States the same trading concessions granted to other powers, greatly expanding America's trade with the Chinese.*

Treaty of Kanagawa (1854) *Ended Japan's two-hundred-year period of economic isolation, establishing an American consulate in Japan and securing American coaling rights in Japanese ports.*

★ Pacific Railroad Promoters and the Gadsden Purchase

Acute transportation problems were another legacy of the Mexican War. The newly acquired prizes of California and Oregon might just as well have been islands some eight thousand miles west of the nation's capital. The sea routes to and from the Isthmus of Panama, to say nothing of those around South America, were too long. Covered-wagon travel past bleaching animal bones was possible but slow and dangerous. A popular song recalled the formidable trek.

> *They swam the wide rivers and crossed the tall peaks,*
> *And camped on the prairie for weeks upon weeks.*
> *Starvation and cholera and hard work and slaughter,*
> *They reached California spite of hell and high water.*

Feasible land transportation was imperative—or the newly won possessions on the Pacific Coast might break away. Camels were even imported from the Middle East as an attempted answer, but mule-driving Americans did not adjust to them. A transcontinental railroad was clearly the only real solution to the problem.

Should its terminus be in the North or in the South? The favored section would reap rich rewards in wealth, population, and influence. The South, losing the economic race with the North, was eager to extend a railroad through adjacent southwestern territory all the way to California.

Another chunk of Mexico now seemed desirable, because the best railway route across the Southwest ran slightly south of the Mexican border. Secretary of War Jefferson Davis therefore appointed a South Carolina railroad man, James Gadsden, as minister to Mexico. He negotiated a treaty in 1853 that ceded to the United States the **Gadsden Purchase** area for $10 million (see Map 18.2). The transaction aroused northern criticism, but the Senate approved the pact.

Southerners now argued that, because their proposed rail line ran through the state of Texas and the already organized New Mexico Territory, the southern route should be

Gadsden Purchase (1853) *Acquired additional land from Mexico for $10 million to facilitate the construction of a southern transcontinental railroad.*

> *The first platform of the newly born (antislavery) Republican party in 1856 lashed out at the Ostend Manifesto, with its transparent suggestion that Cuba be seized. The plank read:*
>
> **"Resolved, That the highwayman's plea, that 'might makes right,' embodied in the Ostend Circular, was in every respect unworthy of American diplomacy, and would bring shame and dishonor upon any Government or people that gave it their sanction."**

Map 18.2 The Gadsden Purchase, 1853

built first. Northern railroad boosters quickly replied that, if organized territory was the test, then Nebraska, site of the proposed northern route, should also be organized. But southerners in Congress greeted all schemes for organizing Nebraska with apathy or hostility. Why should the South help create new free-soil states and thus cut its own throat by facilitating a northern railroad?

★ Douglas's Kansas–Nebraska Scheme

At this point in 1854, Senator Stephen A. Douglas of Illinois delivered a counterstroke to offset the Gadsden thrust for southern expansion westward. A squat, bull-necked, and heavy-chested figure, the "Little Giant" radiated the energy and breezy optimism of the self-made man. An ardent booster for the West, he longed to break the North–South deadlock over westward expansion and stretch a line of settlements across the continent. He also had invested heavily in Chicago real estate and in railway stock and was eager to have the Windy City become the eastern terminus of the proposed Pacific railroad. He would thus endear himself to the voters of Illinois, benefit his section, and enrich his own purse.

A veritable "steam engine in breeches," Douglas threw himself behind a legislative scheme that would enlist the support of a reluctant South. The proposed Territory of Nebraska would be carved into two territories, Kansas and Nebraska (see Map 18.3). Their status regarding slavery would be settled by popular sovereignty—a democratic concept to which Douglas and his western constituents were deeply attached. Kansas, which lay due west of slaveholding Missouri, would presumably choose to become a slave state. But Nebraska, lying west of free-soil Iowa, would presumably become a free state.

Douglas's Kansas–Nebraska scheme flatly contradicted the Missouri Compromise of 1820, which had forbidden slavery in the proposed Nebraska Territory north of the sacred 36° 30' line. The only way to open the region to popular sovereignty was to repeal the ancient compact outright. This bold step Douglas was prepared to take, even at the risk of shattering the uneasy truce patched together by the Compromise of 1850.

Many southerners, who had not conceived of Kansas as slave soil, rose to the bait. Here was a chance to gain one more slave state. The pliable President Pierce, under the thumb of southern advisers, threw his full weight behind the Kansas–Nebraska Bill.

But the Missouri Compromise, now thirty-four years old, could not be brushed aside lightly. Whatever Congress passes, it can repeal, but by this time the North had

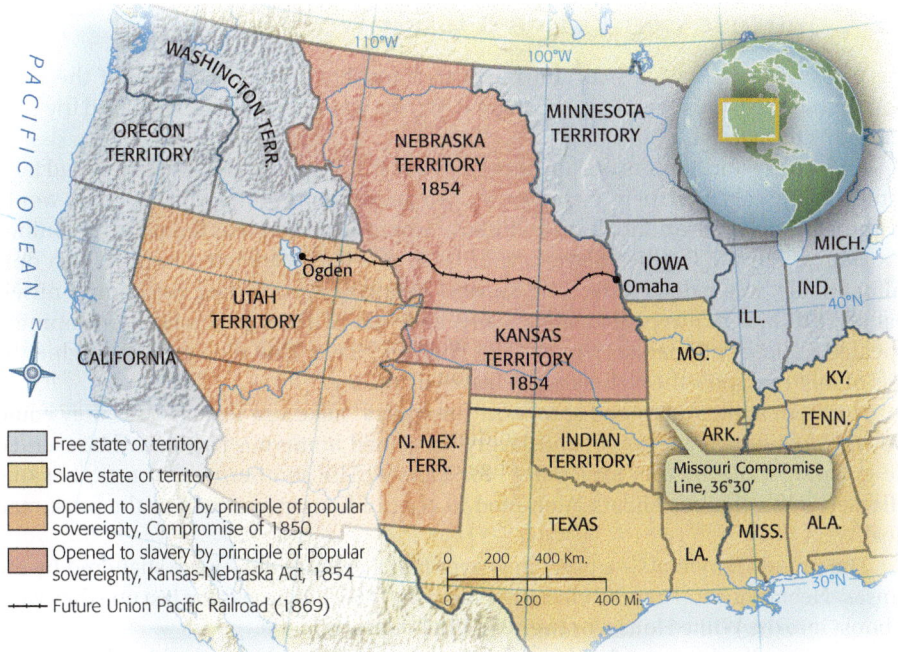

Map 18.3 Kansas and Nebraska, 1854 The route of the future Union Pacific Railroad (completed in 1869) is shown. Notice the Missouri Compromise line of 36° 30' (1820).

come to regard the sectional pact as almost as sacred as the Constitution itself. Free-soil members of Congress struck back with a vengeance. They met their match in the violently gesticulating Douglas, who was the ablest rough-and-tumble debater of his generation. Employing twisted logic and oratorical fireworks, he rammed the bill through Congress with strong support from many southerners. So heated were political passions that bloodshed was barely averted. Some members carried a concealed revolver or a bowie knife—or both.

Douglas's motives in prodding anew the snarling dog of slavery have long puzzled historians. His personal interests have already been mentioned. In addition, his foes accused him of angling for the presidency in 1856. Yet his admirers have argued in his defense that if he had not championed the ill-omened bill, someone else would have.

The truth seems to be that Douglas acted somewhat impulsively and recklessly. His heart did not bleed over the issue of slavery, and he declared repeatedly that he did not care whether it was voted up or down in the territories. What he failed to perceive was that hundreds of thousands of his fellow citizens in the North *did* feel deeply on this moral issue. They regarded the repeal of the Missouri Compromise as an intolerable breach of faith, and they would henceforth resist to the last trench all future southern demands for slave territory.

Genuine leaders, like skillful chess players, must foresee the possible effects of their moves. Douglas predicted a "hell of a storm," but he grossly underestimated its proportions. His critics in the North, branding him a "Judas" and a "traitor," greeted his name with frenzied boos, hisses, and "three groans for Doug." But he still enjoyed a high degree of popularity among his following in the Democratic party, especially in Illinois, a stronghold of popular sovereignty.

Massachusetts senator Charles Sumner (1811–1874) described the Kansas-Nebraska Bill as "at once the worst and the best Bill on which Congress ever acted." It was the worst because it represented a victory for the slave power in the short run. But it was the best, he said prophetically, because it:

"Annuls all past compromises with slavery, and makes all future compromises impossible. Thus it puts freedom and slavery face to face, and bids them grapple. Who can doubt the result?"

Kansas-Nebraska Act (1854)
Proposed that the issue of slavery be decided by popular sovereignty in the Kansas and Nebraska Territories, thus revoking the 1820 Missouri Compromise. Introduced by Stephen Douglas in an effort to bring Nebraska into the Union and pave the way for a northern transcontinental railroad.

★ Congress Legislates a Civil War

The Kansas-Nebraska Act—curtain raiser to a terrible drama—was one of the most momentous measures ever to pass Congress. By one way of reckoning, it greased the slippery slope to civil war.

Antislavery northerners were angered by what they condemned as an act of bad faith by the "Nebrascals" and their "Nebrascality." All future compromise with the South would be immeasurably more difficult, and without compromise there was bound to be conflict.

Henceforth the Fugitive Slave Law of 1850, previously enforced in the North only halfheartedly, was a dead letter. The Kansas–Nebraska Act wrecked two compromises: that of 1820, which it repealed specifically, and that of 1850, which northern opinion repealed indirectly. Emerson wrote, "The Fugitive [Slave] Law did much to unglue the eyes of men, and now the Nebraska Bill leaves us staring."

Northern abolitionists and southern "fire-eaters" alike saw less and less they could live with. The growing legion of antislaveryites gained numerous recruits, who resented the grasping move by the "slavocracy" for Kansas. The southerners, in turn, became inflamed when the free-soilers attempted to control Kansas, contrary to the presumed "deal."

The proud Democrats—a party now over half a century old—were shattered by the Kansas–Nebraska Act. They did elect a president in 1856, but he was the last one they were to boost into the White House for twenty-eight long years.

Undoubtedly the most durable offspring of the Kansas–Nebraska blunder was the new Republican party. It sprang up spontaneously in the Midwest, notably in Wisconsin and Michigan, as a mighty moral protest against the gains of slavery. Gathering together dissatisfied elements, it soon included disgruntled Whigs (among them Abraham Lincoln), Democrats, Free-Soilers, Know-Nothings, and other foes of the Kansas–Nebraska Act. The hodgepodge party spread eastward with the swiftness of a prairie fire and with the zeal of a religious crusade. Unheard of and unheralded at the beginning of 1854, it elected a Republican Speaker of the House of Representatives within two years. Never really a third-party movement, it erupted with such force as to become almost overnight the second major political party—and a purely sectional one at that.

At long last the dreaded sectional rift had appeared. The new Republican party would not be allowed south of the Mason-Dixon line. Countless southerners subscribed wholeheartedly to the sentiment that it was "a nigger stealing, stinking, putrid, abolition party." The Union was in dire peril.

CHAPTER SUMMARY ★ ★ ★ ★ ★ ★ ★ ★ ★ ★ ★ ★ ★ ★

The acquisition of territory from Mexico created acute new dilemmas concerning the expansion of slavery, especially for the two major political parties, which had long tried to avoid the issue. The antislavery Free Soil party pushed the issue into the election of 1848. The application of gold-rich California for admission to the Union forced the controversy into the Senate, which engaged in stormy debates over slavery and the Union.

After the timely death of President Taylor, who had blocked a settlement, Congress resolved the crisis by passing the delicate Compromise of 1850. The compromise eased sectional tension for the moment, although the Fugitive Slave Law aroused opposition in the North.

As the sectionally divided Whig party died, the Democratic Pierce administration became the tool of proslavery expansionists. Attempts at further expansion into Nicaragua, Cuba, and the Gadsden Purchase showed the increasing assertiveness of proslavery expansionists, who stirred strong resistance in the North.

For complex and somewhat mysterious reasons that included the desire for a northern railroad route, Senator Stephen Douglas rammed the Kansas–Nebraska Act through Congress in 1854. By repealing the Missouri Compromise and making new territory subject to "popular sovereignty" on slavery, this law aroused the fury of the North, sparked the rise of the new Republican party, and set the stage for the Civil War.

KEY TERMS

- popular sovereignty (283)
- Free Soil party (283)
- California gold rush (284)
- Underground Railroad (284)
- Seventh of March speech (286)
- Compromise of 1850 (287)
- Fugitive Slave Law (287)
- Clayton-Bulwer Treaty (290)
- Ostend Manifesto (290)
- Treaty of Wanghia (291)
- Treaty of Kanagawa (291)
- Gadsden Purchase (291)
- Kansas-Nebraska Act (294)

PEOPLE TO KNOW

- Lewis Cass
- Zachary Taylor
- Harriet Tubman
- Millard Fillmore
- Franklin Pierce
- William Walker
- Caleb Cushing
- Matthew C. Perry

MindTap is a fully online, highly personalized learning experience built upon Cengage Learning content. MindTap combines student learning tools—readings, multimedia, activities, and assessments—into a singular Learning Path that guides students through the course.

Chapter 19

Drifting toward Disunion
1854–1861

*A house divided against itself cannot stand.
I believe this government cannot endure
permanently half slave and half free.*

ABRAHAM LINCOLN, 1858

Chapter Outline

- *Uncle Tom's Cabin* and the Spread of Abolitionist Sentiment in the North
- The Bloody Contest for Kansas
- The Election of James Buchanan, 1856
- The *Dred Scott* Case, 1857
- The Lincoln–Douglas Debates, 1858
- John Brown's Raid on Harpers Ferry, 1859
- Lincoln and the Republican Victory, 1860
- Secession
- Examining the Evidence: Harriet Beecher Stowe, Uncle Tom's Cabin
- Varying Viewpoints: The Civil War: Repressible or Irrepressible?

The slavery question continued to churn the cauldron of controversy throughout the 1850s. As moral temperatures rose, prospects for a peaceful political solution to the slavery issue simply evaporated. Kansas Territory erupted in violence between proslavery and antislavery factions in 1855. Two years later the Supreme Court's *Dred Scott* decision invalidated the Missouri Compromise of 1820, which had imposed a shaky lid on the slavery problem for more than a generation. Attitudes on both sides progressively hardened. When in 1860 the newly formed Republican party nominated for president Abraham Lincoln, an outspoken opponent of the further expansion of slavery, the stage was set for all-out civil war.

FOCUS QUESTIONS

1. What were the major crises in the 1850s that led from the Kansas–Nebraska Act to secession? How did each work to further alienate North and South from one another and create the climate for the Civil War?

2. How and why did "bleeding Kansas" become a small-scale dress rehearsal for the Civil War?

3. What personal qualities and political circumstances enabled Abraham Lincoln to emerge from obscurity to become the new Republican party's most effective leader and presidential nominee in 1860?

4. What were the central issues in the campaign of 1860? What other issues besides antislavery expansion did Republicans use to appeal to ordinary Northern voters?

5. Why did the lower South secede immediately after Lincoln's victory despite his promises not to interfere with slavery where it existed? Why did last-ditch efforts such as the Crittenden Compromise fail to prevent civil war, as previous compromises had done?

CHRONOLOGY

1852	▪ Harriet Beecher Stowe publishes *Uncle Tom's Cabin*		▪ Panic of 1857 ▪ Tariff of 1857 ▪ Hinton R. Helper publishes *The Impending Crisis of the South*
1854	▪ Kansas–Nebraska Act ▪ Republican party forms		
		1858	▪ Lincoln–Douglas debates
1856	▪ Buchanan defeats Frémont and Fillmore for presidency ▪ Sumner beaten by Brooks in Senate chamber ▪ Brown's Pottawatomie Massacre	1859	▪ Brown raids Harpers Ferry
		1860	▪ Lincoln wins four-way race for presidency ▪ South Carolina secedes from the Union ▪ Crittenden Compromise fails
1856–1861	▪ Civil war in "bleeding Kansas"		
1857	▪ *Dred Scott* decision ▪ Lecompton Constitution rejected	1861	▪ Seven seceding states form Confederate States of America

★ Stowe and Helper: Literary Incendiaries

Sectional tensions were further strained in 1852 and later by an inky phenomenon: Harriet Beecher Stowe, a wisp of a woman and the mother of a half-dozen children, published her heart-rending novel *Uncle Tom's Cabin*. Dismayed by the passage of the Fugitive Slave Law, she was determined to awaken the North to the wickedness of slavery by laying bare its terrible inhumanity, especially the cruel splitting of families. Her wildly popular book relied on powerful imagery and touching pathos. "God wrote it," she explained in later years—a reminder that the deeper sources of her antislavery sentiments lay in the evangelical religious crusades of the Second Great Awakening.

The success of the novel at home and abroad was sensational. Several hundred thousand copies were published in the first year, and the totals soon ran into the millions as the tale was translated into more than a score of languages. The story was also put on the stage in "Tom shows" for lengthy runs. No other novel in American history—perhaps in all history—can be compared with it as a political force. To millions of people the novel made slavery appear almost as evil as it really was.

When Mrs. Stowe was introduced to President Lincoln in 1862, he reportedly remarked, "So you're the little woman who wrote the book that made this great war." The truth is that *Uncle Tom's Cabin* did help start the Civil War—and win it.

Uncle Tom, endearing and enduring, left a profound impression on the North. Thousands of readers swore that henceforth they would have nothing to do with the enforcement of the Fugitive Slave Law. The tale was devoured by millions of impressionable youths in the 1850s—some of whom later became the Boys in Blue who volunteered to fight the Civil War through to its grim finale. The memory of a beaten and dying Uncle Tom helped sustain them in their determination to wipe out the plague of slavery.

Another trouble-brewing book appeared in 1857, five years after the debut of *Uncle Tom*. Titled *The Impending Crisis of the South*, the book was written by Hinton R. Helper, a nonaristocratic white from North Carolina. Hating both slavery and blacks, he attempted to prove by an array of statistics that indirectly nonslaveholding whites were the ones who suffered most from the millstone of slavery. Helper's book, with its "dirty allusions," was banned in the South and fed to the flames at book-burning parties. But in the North thousands of copies, many in condensed form, were distributed as campaign literature by the Republicans.

Uncle Tom's Cabin **(1852)** *Harriet Beecher Stowe's widely read novel that dramatized the horrors of slavery. It heightened northern support for abolition and escalated the sectional conflict.*

The Impending Crisis of the South **(1857)** *Antislavery tract, written by white southerner Hinton R. Helper, arguing that nonslaveholding whites actually suffered most in a slave economy.*

"**The Book that Made This Great War**" Lincoln's celebrated remark to author Harriet Beecher Stowe reflected the enormous emotional impact of her impassioned novel.

New England Emigrant Aid Company (founded 1854) *Organization created to facilitate the migration of free laborers to Kansas in order to prevent the establishment of slavery in the territory.*

★ The North–South Contest for Kansas

The rolling plains of Kansas had meanwhile been providing an example of the worst possible workings of popular sovereignty. Newcomers who ventured into Kansas were a motley lot. Most of the northerners were just ordinary westward-moving pioneers. But a small part of the inflow was financed by groups of northern abolitionists or free-soilers, especially the **New England Emigrant Aid Company**, which sent about two thousand people to the troubled area to forestall the South. Shouting "Ho for Kansas!" many of them carried the deadly new breech-loading Sharps rifles, nicknamed "Beecher's Bibles" after the Reverend Henry Ward Beecher (Harriet Beecher Stowe's brother), who had helped raise money for their purchase. Many of the Kansas-bound pioneers sang Whittier's marching song (1854):

> *We cross the prairie as of old*
> *The pilgrims crossed the sea,*
> *To make the West, as they the East,*
> *The homestead of the free!*

Southern spokesmen, now more than ordinarily touchy, raised furious cries of betrayal. They had supported the Kansas–Nebraska scheme of Stephen A. Douglas with the unspoken understanding that Kansas would become slave and Nebraska free. The northern "Nebrascals" were now apparently out to "abolitionize" *both* Kansas and Nebraska.

A few southern hotheads, quick to respond in kind, attempted to "assist" small groups of well-armed slave owners to Kansas. But despite such efforts, slavery never took hold in Kansas. The census of 1860 found only 2 slaves among 107,000 souls in all Kansas Territory, and only 15 in Nebraska. Nevertheless, crisis conditions in Kansas rapidly worsened (see Map 19.1). When the day came in 1855 to elect members of the first territorial legislature, proslavery "border ruffians" poured in from Missouri to vote early and often. The slavery supporters triumphed and then set up their own puppet government at Shawnee Mission. The free-soilers, unable to stomach

Map 19.1 Bleeding Kansas, 1854–1860 "Enter every election district in Kansas . . . and vote at the point of a bowie knife or revolver," one proslavery agitator exhorted a Missouri crowd. Proslavery Missouri senator David Atchison declared that "there are 1,100 men coming over from Platte County to vote, and if that ain't enough we can send 5,000—enough to kill every Goddamned abolitionist in the Territory."

Examining the Evidence

Harriet Beecher Stowe, Uncle Tom's Cabin

As works of fiction, novels pose tricky problems to historians, whose principal objective is to get the factual record straight. Works of the imagination are notoriously unreliable as descriptions of reality, and only rarely is it known with any degree of certainty what a reader might have felt when confronting a particular fictional passage or theme. Yet a novel such as Harriet Beecher Stowe's *Uncle Tom's Cabin* had such an unarguably large impact on the American (and worldwide) debate over slavery that historians have inevitably looked to it for evidence of the mid-nineteenth-century ideas and attitudes to which Stowe appealed. The passage quoted here is especially rich in such evidence—and even offers an explanation for the logic of the novel's title. Stowe cleverly aimed to mobilize not simply her readers' sense of injustice, but also their sentiments, on behalf of the antislavery cause.

1. What sentimental values does the *cabin* represent, and why is it so central to Stowe's novel?
2. What is the nature of the threat to those values?
3. How does Stowe convey the importance of both religion and family for her slave characters, and why might these elements particularly appeal to the novel's middle-class readers?

THE February morning looked gray and drizzling through the window of Uncle Tom's cabin. It looked on downcast faces, the images of mournful hearts. The little table stood out before the fire, covered with an ironing-cloth; a coarse but clean shirt or two, fresh from the iron, hung on the back of a chair by the fire, and Aunt Chloe had another spread out before her on the table. Carefully she rubbed and ironed every fold and every hem, with the most scrupulous exactness, every now and then raising her hand to her face to wipe off the tears that were coursing down her cheeks.

Tom sat by, with his Testament open on his knee, and his head leaning upon his hand;—but neither spoke. It was yet early, and the children lay all asleep together in their little rude trundle-bed.

Tom, who had, to the full, the gentle, domestic heart, which, woe for them! has been a peculiar characteristic of his unhappy race, got up and walked silently to look at his children.

"It's the last time," he said.

University of Virginia Library

> *In the closing scenes of Harriet Beecher Stowe's novel, Uncle Tom's brutal master, Simon Legree, orders the $1,200 slave savagely beaten (to death) by two fellow slaves. Through tears and blood, Tom exclaims:*
>
> *"No! no! no! my soul an't yours, Mas'r! You haven't bought it,—ye can't buy it! It's been bought and paid for, by one that is able to keep it,—no matter, no matter, you can't harm me!" "I can't," said Legree, with a sneer; "we'll see,—we'll see! Here, Sambo, Quimbo, give this dog such a breakin' in as he won't get over, this month!"*

this fraudulent conspiracy, established an extralegal regime of their own in Topeka. The confused Kansans thus had their choice between two governments—one based on fraud, the other on illegality. Tensions reached the breaking point in 1856 when a gang of proslavery raiders shot up and burned a part of the free-soil town of Lawrence. This outrage was but the prelude to a bloodier tragedy.

★ Kansas in Convulsion

The fanatical figure of John Brown now stalked upon the Kansas battlefield. Spare, gray-bearded, and iron-willed, he was obsessively dedicated to the abolitionist cause. The power of his glittering gray eyes was such, so he claimed, that his stare could force a dog or cat to slink out of a room. Brooding over the recent attack on Lawrence, "Old Brown" of Osawatomie led a band of his followers to Pottawatomie Creek, in May 1856. There they literally hacked to pieces five surprised men, presumed to be proslaveryites. This terrorist butchery brought vicious retaliation from proslavery forces. Civil war in Kansas thus flared forth in 1856 and continued intermittently until it merged with the large-scale Civil War of 1861–1865.

The proslavery forces intensified the conflict in 1857 when they attempted to bring Kansas into the Union under a tricky document known as the **Lecompton Constitution**. Although the majority of Kansans were free-soilers, the vote on the proposed constitution was arranged so that it was impossible to prohibit all black bondage and still obtain statehood. With infuriated free-soilers boycotting the election, the proslaveryites approved the constitution with slavery late in 1857.

The new president, James Buchanan, was just as much under southern influence as President Pierce had been, and he threw the weight of his administration behind the notorious Lecompton Constitution. But Senator Douglas, who had championed true popular sovereignty, would have none of this semipopular fraudulency. Deliberately tossing away his strong support in the South for the presidency, he fought courageously to submit the entire Lecompton Constitution to a fair popular vote. The free-soil voters thereupon snowed it under at the polls. Kansas remained a territory until 1861, when the southern secessionists left Congress.

President Buchanan, by antagonizing the numerous Douglas Democrats in the North, hopelessly divided the once-powerful Democratic party. Until then, it had been the only remaining national party, for the Whigs were dead and the Republicans were sectional. With the disruption of the Democrats came the snapping of one of the last important strands in the rope that was barely binding the Union together.

★ "Bully" Brooks and His Bludgeon

Bleeding Kansas also spattered blood on the floor of the Senate in 1856. The abolitionist Senator Charles Sumner of Massachusetts, a tall and imposing figure, delivered a blistering speech titled "The Crime Against Kansas," in which he viciously condemned proslavery men as "hirelings picked from the drunken spew and vomit of an uneasy civilization." The speech also insulted white-haired Senator Andrew Butler of South Carolina.

Hot-tempered South Carolina Congressman Preston S. Brooks, Butler's distant cousin, took vengeance into his own hands. On May 22, 1856, he approached Sumner, then sitting at his Senate desk, and pounded the orator with an eleven-ounce cane until it broke. The victim fell bleeding and unconscious to the floor, suffering serious injuries to his head and nervous system.

Bleeding Sumner thus joined bleeding Kansas as a hotly divisive political issue. South Carolina triumphantly reelected Brooks to Congress, and Massachusetts defiantly

---

Lecompton Constitution (1857) *Proposed Kansas constitution, whose ratification was unfairly rigged so as to guarantee slavery in the territory. Initially ratified by proslavery forces, it was later voted down when Congress required that the entire constitution be put up for a vote.*

Bleeding Kansas (1856–1861) *Civil war in Kansas over the issue of slavery in the territory, fought intermittently until 1861, when it merged with the wider national Civil War.*

Preston Brooks Caning Charles Sumner, 1856 Cartoonist John Magee of Philadelphia depicted Brooks's beating of Sumner in the Senate as a display of southern ruthlessness in defending slavery, ironically captioned "southern chivalry."

did the same for Sumner, even though the battered abolitionist was unable to take his seat for over three years. Meanwhile, Sumner's abusive speech sold by the thousands in the North, while southern admirers deluged Brooks with canes to replace the one he had broken over Sumner's head.

The Sumner-Brooks clash and the ensuing reactions revealed how dangerously inflamed passions were becoming, North and South. It was ominous that the cultured Sumner should have used the language of a barroom bully and that the gentlemanly Brooks should have employed the tactics and tools of a thug. Emotion was displacing thought. The blows rained on Sumner's head were, broadly speaking, among the first blows of the Civil War.

★ "Old Buck" Versus "The Pathfinder"

With bullets whining in Kansas, the Democrats met in Cincinnati to nominate their presidential standard-bearer of 1856. Both weak-kneed President Pierce and dynamic Senator Douglas were too indelibly tainted by the Kansas–Nebraska Act, so the delegates finally turned to a well-to-do Pennsylvania lawyer and diplomat, James Buchanan, who had been serving as minister to London during the recent Kansas–Nebraska uproar. Although his "Kansasless" neutrality made him acceptable to the party, "Old Buck" Buchanan was mediocre, irresolute, and confused.

The fast-growing Republican party, in their enthusiastic convention in Philadelphia, passed over "Higher Law" Senator William Seward, their most conspicuous leader, and instead chose John C. Frémont, a dashing but erratic explorer-soldier-surveyor. Republicans hoped that the so-called "Pathfinder of the West" would blaze them a path to the White House. Vigorously condemning the extension of slavery into the territories, Republicans sang,

> *Arise, arise ye brave!*
>   *And let our war-cry be*
> *Free speech, free press, free soil, free men,*
>   *Fré-mont and victory!*

An ugly dose of antiforeignism was injected into the campaign, even though slavery extension loomed largest. The recent influx of immigrants from Ireland and Germany had alarmed the old-stock Protestant nativists who had organized the American, or Know-Nothing, party. Antiforeign and anti-Catholic, these super-patriots nominated former President Millard Fillmore as their candidate and campaigned under the slogan, "Americans Must Rule America." With remnants of the dying Whig party also endorsing Fillmore, the Know-Nothings threatened to cut into Republican strength.

The bland Buchanan, although polling less than a majority of the popular vote, won handily. His tally in the Electoral College was 174, to 114 for Frémont, with Fillmore garnering eight. The popular vote was 1,832,955 for Buchanan to 1,339,932 for Frémont, with 871,731 for Fillmore.

Democrats had carried the hapless "Old Buck" into office, but the Republicans could rightfully claim a "victorious defeat" in 1856. The new party—a mere two-year-old toddler—had made an astonishing showing against the well-oiled Democratic machine. John Greenleaf Whittier exulted:

Then sound again the bugles,
  Call the muster-roll anew;
If months have well-nigh won the field,
  What may not four years do?

That question cast a long shadow forward, as politicians, North and South, peered anxiously toward 1860.

★ The Dred Scott Bombshell

Dred Scott v. Stanford (1857)
Supreme Court decision that extended federal protection to slavery by ruling that Congress did not have the power to prohibit slavery in any territory. Also declared that slaves, as property, were not citizens of the United States.

The *Dred Scott v. Stanford* decision, handed down by the Supreme Court on March 6, 1857, abruptly ended the two-day presidential honeymoon of the unlucky bachelor, James Buchanan. Basically, the case was simple. Dred Scott, a black slave, had lived with his master for five years in free-state Illinois and Wisconsin Territory. Backed by interested abolitionists, he sued for freedom on the basis of his long residence on free soil.

The Supreme Court proceeded to turn a simple legal case into a complex political issue. The Court ruled, not surprisingly, that Dred Scott was a black slave and not a citizen and hence could not sue in federal courts.* The tribunal could then have thrown out the case on these technical grounds alone. But a majority decided to go further, under the leadership of emaciated Chief Justice Roger B. Taney from the slave state of Maryland.

Taney's sweeping judgment on the larger question of slavery rocked the free-soilers back on their heels. Speaking for a majority of the Court, Taney decreed that because a slave was private property, he or she could be taken into *any* territory and legally held there in slavery. The reasoning was that the Fifth Amendment clearly forbade Congress to deprive people of their property without due process of law. The Court, to be consistent, went further. The Missouri Compromise of 1820, banning slavery north of 36° 30', had been repealed three years earlier by the Kansas–Nebraska Act. But its spirit was still venerated in the North. Now the Court ruled that the Missouri Compromise had been unconstitutional all along: Congress had no power to ban slavery from the territories, regardless even of what the territorial legislatures might want.

Southerners were delighted with this unexpected victory. Champions of popular sovereignty, including Senator Douglas and most northern Democrats, were aghast. Another lethal wedge was thus driven between the northern and southern wings of the once-united Democratic party.

Foes of slavery extension, especially the Republicans, were infuriated by the *Dred Scott* setback. Because a majority of the Supreme Court justices were southerners, Republicans insisted that the ruling was merely an opinion, not a decision, and no more binding than the views of a "southern debating society." Southerners in turn wondered how much longer they could remain joined to a section that refused to honor the Supreme Court, to say nothing of the constitutional compact that had established it.

---

*This part of the ruling, denying blacks their citizenship, seriously menaced the precarious position of the South's quarter-million free blacks.

⭐ The Financial Crash of 1857

Bitterness caused by the *Dred Scott* decision was deepened by hard times, which dampened a period of feverish prosperity. Then the **panic of 1857** burst about Buchanan's harassed head. The storm was not so bad economically as the panic of 1837, but psychologically it was probably the worst of the nineteenth century.

The North, including its grain growers, was hardest hit by the sharp economic downturn. The South, enjoying favorable cotton prices abroad, rode out the storm with flying colors. Panic conditions seemed further proof that cotton was king, and that its economic kingdom was stronger than that of the North. This fatal delusion helped drive the overconfident southerners closer to a shooting showdown.

Financial distress in the North, especially in agriculture, gave a new vigor to the demand for free farms of 160 acres from the public domain. Overcoming the objections of both eastern industrialists and southern slaveholders, Congress in 1860 finally passed a homestead act that made public lands available at the nominal sum of twenty-five cents an acre. But it was stabbed to death by the veto pen of Buchanan, near whose elbow sat leading southern sympathizers.

The panic of 1857 also created a clamor for higher tariff rates. The **Tariff of 1857** had lowered duties to about 20 percent, but hardly had the revised rates been placed on the books when financial misery descended like a black pall. Northern manufacturers noisily blamed their misfortunes on the low tariff and clamored for increased protection. Thus, the panic of 1857 gave the Republicans two surefire economic issues for 1860: protection for the unprotected and farms for the farmless.

> *Spiritual overtones developed in the Frémont campaign, especially over slavery.* The Independent, *a prominent religious journal, saw in Frémont's nomination "the good hand of God." As election day neared, it declared:*
>
> "Fellow-Christians! Remember it is for Christ, for the nation, and for the world that you vote at this election! Vote as you pray! Pray as you vote!"

panic of 1857 *Financial crash brought on by gold-fueled inflation, overspeculation, and excess grain production. Raised calls in the North for higher tariffs and for free homesteads on western public lands.*

Tariff of 1857 *Lowered duties on imports in response to a high Treasury surplus and pressure from southern farmers.*

⭐ An Illinois Rail-Splitter Emerges

The Illinois senatorial election of 1858 now claimed the national spotlight. Senator Stephen Douglas's term was about to expire, and the Republicans decided to run against him a rustic Springfield lawyer, one Abraham Lincoln. The Republican candidate—6 feet 4 inches in height and 180 pounds in weight—presented an awkward but arresting figure. Lincoln's legs, arms, and neck were grotesquely long; his head was crowned by coarse, black, and unruly hair; and his face was sad, sunken, and weather-beaten.

Lincoln was no silver-spoon child of the elite. Born in 1809 in a Kentucky log cabin to impoverished parents, he attended a frontier school for not more than a year; being an avid reader, he was mainly self-educated. All his life he said "git," "thar," and "heered." Although narrow-chested and somewhat stoop-shouldered, Lincoln shone in his frontier community as a wrestler and weight lifter and spent some time, among other pioneering pursuits, as a splitter of logs for fence rails. A superb teller of earthy and amusing stories, he would sometimes plunge into protracted periods of melancholy.

Lincoln's private and professional lives had not been especially noteworthy. He married "above himself" socially, into the influential Todd family of Kentucky. After reading a little law, he gradually emerged as one of the dozen or so better-known trial lawyers in Illinois, although still accustomed to carrying important papers in his stovepipe hat. He was widely referred to as "Honest Abe," partly because he would refuse cases that he had to suspend his conscience to defend.

> *Lincoln expressed his views on the relation of the black and white races in 1858, in his first debate with Stephen A. Douglas:*
>
> "I, as well as Judge Douglas, am in favor of the race to which I belong, having the superior position. I have never said anything to the contrary, but I hold that notwithstanding all this, there is no reason in the world why the negro is not entitled to all the natural rights enumerated in the Declaration of Independence, the right to life, liberty, and the pursuit of happiness. I hold that he is as much entitled to those rights as the white man. I agree with Judge Douglas he is not my equal in many respects—certainly not in color, perhaps not in moral or intellectual endowment. But in the right to eat the bread, without leave of anybody else, which his own hand earns, he is my equal and the equal of Judge Douglas, and the equal of every living man."

Contending Voices

Judging John Brown

Upon hearing of John Brown's execution, escaped slave and abolitionist Harriet Tubman (ca. 1820-1913) paid him the highest tribute for his self-sacrifice:

"I've been studying, and studying upon it, and its clar to me, it wasn't John Brown that died on that gallows. When I think how he gave up his life for our people, and how he never flinched, but was so brave to the end; its clar to me it wasn't mortal man, it was God in him."

Not all opponents of slavery, however, shared Tubman's reverence for Brown. Republican presidential candidate Abraham Lincoln dismissed Brown as deluded:

"[The Brown] affair, in its philosophy, corresponds with the many attempts, related in history, at the assassination of kings and emperors. An enthusiast broods over the oppression of a people till he fancies himself commissioned by Heaven to liberate them. He ventures the attempt, which ends in little else than his own execution."

[Did John Brown help or harm the antislavery cause?

Lincoln–Douglas debates (1858) *Series of debates between Abraham Lincoln and Stephen Douglas during the U.S. Senate race in Illinois. Douglas won the election, but Lincoln gained national prominence and emerged as the leading candidate for the 1860 Republican nomination.*

Freeport question (1858) *Raised during one of the Lincoln-Douglas debates by Abraham Lincoln, who asked whether the Court or the people should decide the future of slavery in the territories.*

The rise of Lincoln as a political figure was less than rocketlike. After making his mark in the Illinois legislature as a Whig politician of the logrolling variety, he served one undistinguished term in Congress, 1847–1849. Until 1854, when he was forty-five years of age, he had done nothing to establish a claim to statesmanship. But the passage of the Kansas-Nebraska Act in that year lighted within him unexpected fires. After mounting the Republican bandwagon, he emerged as one of the foremost politicians and orators of the Northwest. At the Philadelphia convention of 1856, where Frémont was nominated, Lincoln actually received 110 votes for the vice-presidential nomination.

★ The Great Debate: Lincoln Versus Douglas

Lincoln, as Republican nominee for the Senate seat, boldly challenged Douglas to a series of joint debates. This was a rash act, because the stumpy senator was probably the nation's most devastating debater. Douglas promptly accepted Lincoln's challenge, and seven meetings—the famed **Lincoln–Douglas debates**—were arranged from August to October 1858.

The most famous debate came at Freeport, Illinois, where Lincoln nearly impaled his opponent on the horns of a dilemma by posing what came to be called the **Freeport question**. Suppose, he queried, the people of a territory should vote slavery down? The Supreme Court in the *Dred Scott* decision had decreed that they could not do so. Who would prevail, the Court or the people?

Douglas's reply, which came to be known as the "**Freeport Doctrine**," was that no matter how the Supreme Court ruled, slavery would stay down if the people voted it down. Laws to protect slavery would have to be passed by the territorial legislatures. These would not be forthcoming in the absence of popular approval, and black bondage would soon disappear.

The upshot was that Douglas defeated Lincoln for the Senate seat. The "Little Giant's" loyalty to popular sovereignty, which still had a powerful appeal in Illinois, probably was decisive. But Douglas, in winning Illinois, hurt his chances of winning the presidency, while further splitting his splintering Democratic party. After his opposition to the Lecompton Constitution for Kansas and his further defiance of the Supreme Court at Freeport, southern Democrats were determined to break up the party (and the Union) rather than accept him. For his part, Lincoln lost the election but shambled into the national limelight as a leading northern spokesman and potential Republican nominee for president. The Lincoln–Douglas debate platform thus proved to be one of the preliminary battlefields of the Civil War.

★ John Brown: Murderer or Martyr?

The gaunt, grim figure of John Brown of bleeding Kansas infamy now once again took the stage. After studying the tactics of the black rebels Nat Turner and Toussaint L'Ouverture, he hatched a daring scheme to invade the South secretly with a handful of followers, call upon the slaves to rise, furnish them with arms, and establish a kind of black free state as a sanctuary. Brown secured several thousand dollars for firearms from northern abolitionists and finally arrived in hilly western Virginia with some twenty men. He seized the federal arsenal at scenic **Harpers Ferry** in October 1859, incidentally killing seven innocent people, including a free black, and injuring ten or so more. But the slaves failed to rise, and the wounded Brown and the remnants of his tiny band were quickly captured by U.S. Marines under the command of Lieutenant Colonel Robert E. Lee. "Old Brown" was convicted of murder and treason after a hasty but legal trial.

But Brown—"God's angry man"—was given every opportunity to pose and to enjoy martyrdom. He was clever enough to see that he was worth much more to the abolitionist cause dangling from a rope than in any other way. His demeanor during the trial was dignified and courageous, and he marched up the scaffold steps without flinching. So the hangman's trap was sprung, and Brown plunged not into oblivion but into world fame. A memorable marching song of the impending Civil War ran,

> *John Brown's body lies a-mould'ring in the grave, His soul is marching on.*

The effects of Harpers Ferry were inflammatory. In the eyes of the South, already embittered, "Osawatomie Brown" was a wholesale murderer and an apostle of treason. Many southerners asked how they could possibly remain in the Union while a "murderous gang of abolitionists" were financing armed bands to "Brown" them. Moderate northerners, including Republican leaders, openly deplored this mad exploit. But the South naturally concluded that the violent abolitionist view was shared by the entire North, dominated by "Brown-loving" Republicans.

Abolitionists and other ardent free-soilers were infuriated by Brown's execution. On the day of his hanging, free-soil centers in the North tolled bells, fired guns, lowered flags, and held rallies. Some spoke of "Saint John" Brown, and Ralph Waldo Emerson compared the new martyr-hero with Jesus. The gallows became a cross. E. C. Steman wrote,

> *And Old Brown,*
>   *Osawatomie Brown,*
> *May trouble you more than ever when you've nailed his coffin down!*

The ghost of the martyred Brown would not be laid to rest.

Last Moments of John Brown, by Thomas Hovenden Sentenced to be hanged, John Brown wrote to his brother, "I am quite cheerful in view of my approaching end, being fully persuaded that I am worth inconceivably more to hang than for any other purpose.... I count it all joy. 'I have fought the good fight,' and have, as I trust, 'finished my course.'" This painting of Brown going to his execution may have been inspired by the journalist Horace Greeley, who was not present but wrote that "a black woman with a little child stood by the door. He stopped for a moment, and stooping, kissed the child." That scene never took place, as Brown was escorted from the jail only by a detachment of soldiers. But this painting has become famous as a kind of allegorical expression of the pathos of Brown's martyrdom for the abolitionist cause.

★ Democrats Divide and Republicans Rise

Beyond question the presidential election of 1860 was the most fateful in American history. Deeply divided, the Democrats met in Charleston, South Carolina. Northern Democrats looked to Douglas as the leading candidate of their party, but southern "fire-eaters" regarded him as a traitor. After a bitter platform fight, delegates from most of the cotton states walked out of the convention. When the remainder could not scrape together the necessary two-thirds vote for Douglas, the entire body dissolved. The southerners' departure from the Democratic convention was the first tragic act of secession. Departure became habit forming.

The Democrats tried again in Baltimore. With northern Douglas Democrats firmly in the saddle, the cotton-state delegates again took a walk, and the rest of the convention enthusiastically nominated their hero. Angered southern Democrats promptly organized a rival convention in Baltimore and selected as their nominee the stern-jawed vice president, John C. Breckinridge, from the border state of Kentucky. The platform favored the extension of slavery into the territories and the annexation of slave-populated Cuba.

Freeport Doctrine (1858) *Declared that since slavery could not exist without laws to protect it, territorial legislatures, not the Supreme Court, would have the final say on the slavery question. First argued by Stephen Douglas in 1858 in response to Abraham Lincoln's "Freeport question."*

Harpers Ferry *Federal arsenal in Virginia seized by abolitionist John Brown in 1859. Though Brown was later captured and executed, his raid alarmed southerners, who believed that northerners shared in Brown's extremism.*

Constitutional Union party (1860) *Formed by moderate Whigs and Know-Nothings in an effort to elect a compromise candidate and avert a sectional crisis.*

A middle-of-the-road group, fearing for the Union, hastily organized the **Constitutional Union party**, which consisted mainly of former Whigs and Know-Nothings. This "gathering of graybeards" met in Baltimore and nominated John Bell of Tennessee for the presidency on a platform of "the Union, the Constitution, and the enforcement of the law."

Elated Republicans, scenting victory in the breeze as their opponents split hopelessly, gathered in Chicago in a huge boxlike wooden structure called the Wigwam. William H. Seward was by far the best known of the contenders, but Seward's radical utterances, including his "irrepressible conflict" speech at Rochester in 1858,* had ruined his prospects. Lincoln, the favorite son of Illinois, was a stronger candidate because he had made fewer enemies than Seward. Overtaking Seward on the third ballot, he was nominated amid scenes of the wildest excitement.

The Republican platform had a seductive appeal for almost every important nonsouthern group: for the free-soilers, the nonextension of slavery; for northern manufacturers, a protective tariff; for immigrants, no abridgement of rights; and for farmers, free homesteads from the public domain.

Southern secessionists promptly served notice that the election of the "baboon" Lincoln would split the Union. In fact, "Honest Abe," though hating slavery, was no outright abolitionist. He campaigned quietly and issued no new statements in response to these threats. The most active opposition to southern extremism came from the "Little Giant" Douglas, who waged a vigorous speaking campaign, even in the South, and threatened to put the rope with his own hands around the neck of the first secessionist.

The returns, breathlessly awaited, proclaimed a sweeping victory for Lincoln (see the table and map, p. 307).

★ The Electoral Upheaval of 1860

Awkward "Abe" Lincoln had run a curious race. To a greater degree than any other holder of the nation's highest office (except John Quincy Adams), he was a minority president. 60 percent of the voters preferred some other candidate. He was also a sectional president, for in ten southern states, where he was not allowed on the ballot, he polled no popular votes. The election of 1860 was virtually two elections: one between Lincoln and Douglas in the North, the other between Bell and Breckinridge in the South (see Map 19.2). South Carolinians rejoiced over Lincoln's victory; they now had their excuse to secede. In winning the North, the "rail-splitter" had split off the South.

Douglas, though scraping together only twelve electoral votes, made an impressive showing. He drew important strength from all sections and ranked a fairly close second in the popular-vote column. In fact, the Douglas Democrats and the Breckinridge Democrats together amassed 366,484 more popular votes than did Lincoln. But contrary to myth, Lincoln's electoral vote victory did not occur because his opponents were divided. Even if all the Democrats and Constitutional Unionists had united behind Douglas, Lincoln would have carried the populous northern states and therefore would still have won the electoral vote 169 to 134 instead of 180 to 123.

Significantly, the verdict of the ballot box did not indicate a strong sentiment for secession (see Map 19.3). Breckinridge, while favoring the extension of slavery, was no disunionist. Although the candidate of the "fire-eaters," he polled fewer votes in the slave states than Douglas and Bell combined. Despite its electoral defeat, the South was not badly off. Southerners still controlled the Supreme Court, both houses of Congress, and more than enough states to block any attempt to end slavery by constitutional amendment.

★ The Secessionist Exodus

But a tragic chain reaction of secession now began to erupt. South Carolina had threatened to leave the United States if the "Illinois baboon" were elected, and in December 1860 a special convention called by the legislature carried out the threat by voting

---

*Seward had referred to an "irrepressible conflict" between slavery and freedom, though not necessarily a bloody one.

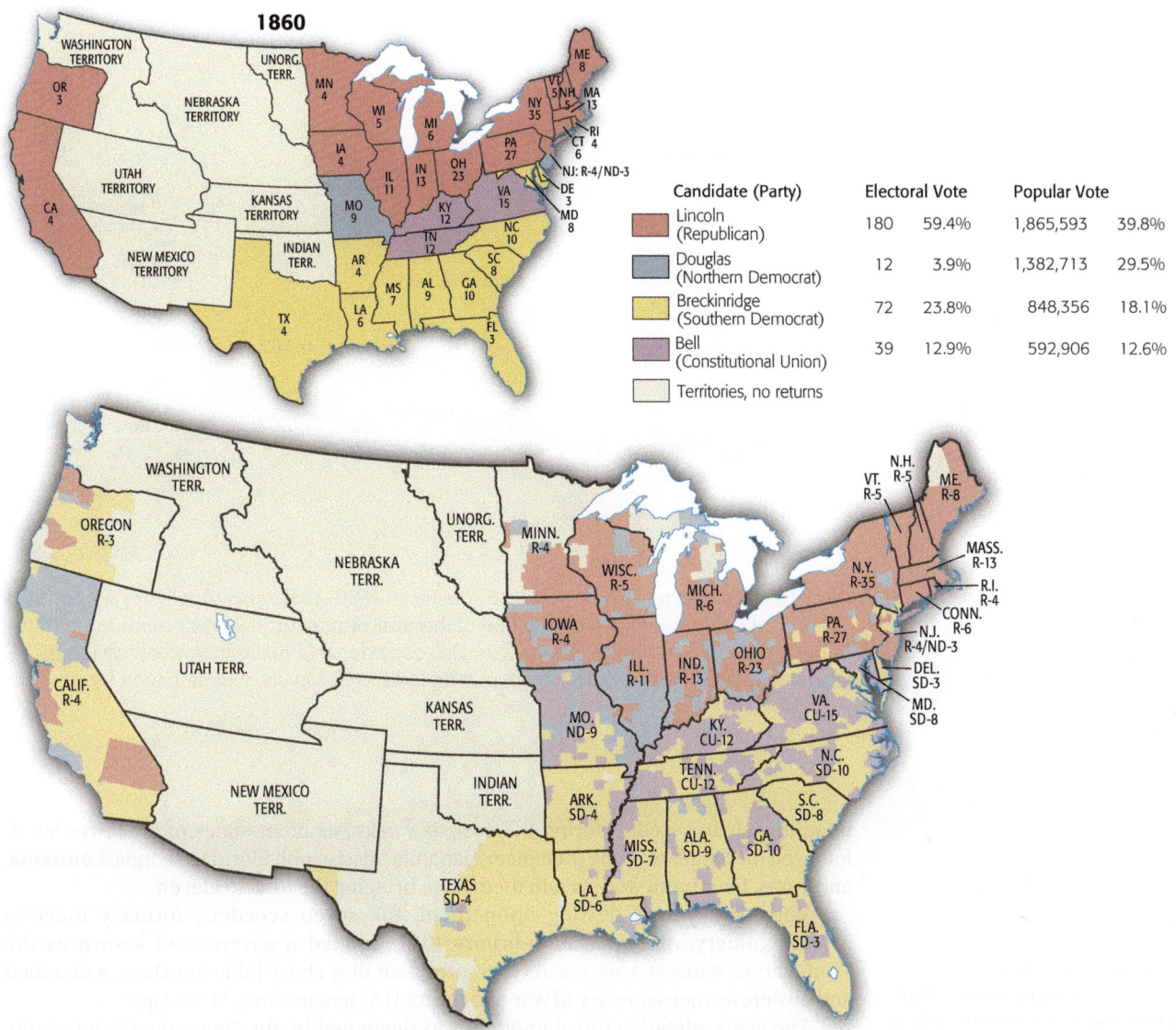

Map 19.2 Presidential Election of 1860: Electoral Vote by State (top) and Popular Vote by County (bottom) It is a surprising fact that Lincoln, often rated among the greatest presidents, ranks near the bottom in percentage of popular votes. In all the eleven states that seceded, he received only a scattering of one state's votes—about 1.5 percent in Virginia. The vote by county for Lincoln was virtually all cast in the North. The northern Democrat, Douglas, was also nearly shut out in the South, which divided its votes between Breckinridge and Bell. (Note that only citizens of states could vote; inhabitants of territories could not.)

Candidate	Popular Vote	Percentage of Popular Vote	Electoral Vote
Lincoln	1,865,593	39.79	180 (every vote of the free states except for 3 of New Jersey's 7 votes)
Douglas	1,382,713	29.40	12 (only Missouri and 3 of New Jersey's 7 votes)
Breckinridge	848,356	18.20	72 (all the cotton states)
Bell	592,906	12.61	39 (Virginia, Kentucky, Tennessee)

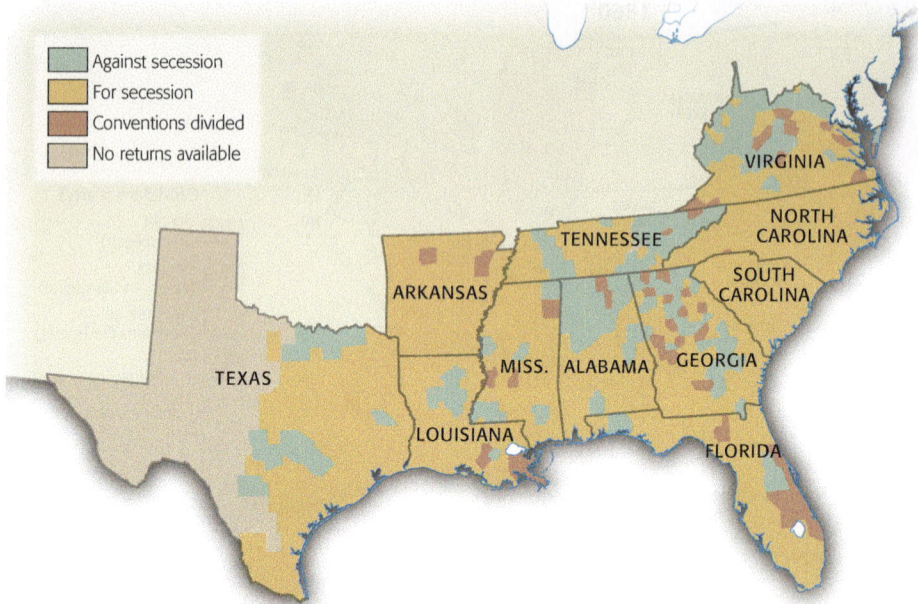

Map 19.3 Southern Opposition to Secession, 1860–1861 (showing vote by county) This county vote shows the opposition of the anti-planter, antislavery mountain whites in the Appalachian region. There was also considerable resistance to secession in Texas, where Governor Sam Houston, who led the Unionists, was deposed by secessionists.

unanimously to secede. During the next six weeks, six other states of the lower South followed the leader over the precipice: Alabama, Mississippi, Florida, Georgia, Louisiana, and Texas. Four more were to join them later, bringing the total to eleven.

With the eyes of destiny upon them, the seven seceders, formally meeting in Montgomery, Alabama, in February 1861, created a government known as the **Confederate States of America**. As their president they chose Jefferson Davis, a dignified and austere former secretary of war and recent U.S. senator from Mississippi.

The crisis, already critical enough, was deepened by the "lame duck"* interlude. Lincoln, although elected president in November 1860, could not take office until four months later, March 4, 1861. During this period of protracted uncertainty, when Lincoln was still a private citizen in Illinois, seven of the eleven deserting states pulled out of the Union.

Meanwhile, the aging incumbent President Buchanan chose to wring his hands rather than secessionist necks. Surrounded by prosouthern advisers, Buchanan found constitutional and practical justifications for inaction. One important reason why he did not resort to force was that the tiny standing army of fifteen thousand men was widely scattered, fighting Indians in the West. Public opinion in the North, at that time, was far from willing to unsheathe the sword. Fighting would shatter all prospects of adjustment, and until the guns began to boom, there was still a flickering hope of reconciliation rather than a contested divorce. The weakness lay not so much in Buchanan as in the Constitution and in the Union itself. Ironically, when Lincoln became president in March, he essentially continued Buchanan's wait-and-see policy.

Confederate States of America (1861–1865) *Government established after seven southern states seceded from the Union. Later joined by four more states from the upper South.*

---

*The lame-duck period was shortened to ten weeks in 1933 by the Twentieth Amendment (see the Appendix).

★ A Failed Compromise and Secession

Impending bloodshed spurred final and frantic attempts at compromise, most notably by Senator John Jordan Crittenden of Kentucky. His proposed **Crittenden amendments** to the constitution were essentially designed to appease the South. Slavery in the territories was to be prohibited north of 36° 30', but south of that line it was to be given federal protection in all territories existing or "hereafter to be acquired" (such as Cuba). Future states, north or south of 36° 30', could come into the Union with or without slavery, as they should choose. In short, the slavery supporters were to be guaranteed full rights in the southern territories, as long as they were territories, regardless of the wishes of the majority under popular sovereignty. Federal protection in a territory south of 36° 30' might conceivably, though improbably, turn the entire area permanently to slavery.

Lincoln flatly rejected the Crittenden scheme, which offered some slight prospect of success, and all hope of compromise evaporated. Lincoln had been elected on a platform that opposed the extension of slavery, and he felt that as a matter of principle he could not afford to yield, even though gains for slavery in the territories might be only temporary. Larger gains for slavery, he feared, might come later in Cuba and Latin America. Crittenden's proposal, said Lincoln, "would amount to a perpetual covenant of war against every people, tribe, and state owning a foot of land between here and Tierra del Fuego."

Secessionists who parted company with their sister states left for a number of avowed reasons, mostly relating in some way to slavery. They were alarmed by the inexorable tipping of the political balance against them—"the despotic majority of numbers." The "crime" of the North, observed James Russell Lowell, was the census returns. Southerners were also dismayed by the triumph of the new sectional Republican party, which seemed to threaten their rights as a slaveholding minority. They were weary of free-soil criticism, abolitionist nagging, and northern interference, ranging from the Underground Railroad to John Brown's raid. "All we ask is to be let alone," declared Confederate President Jefferson Davis in an early message to his congress.

Many southerners supported secession because they felt sure that their departure would be unopposed, despite "Yankee yawp" to the contrary. They were confident that the clodhopping and cod fishing Yankee would not or could not fight. They also believed that northern manufacturers and bankers, so heavily dependent on southern cotton and markets, would not dare to cut their own economic throats with their own unionist swords.

Southern leaders regarded secession as a golden opportunity to cast aside their generations of "vassalage" to the North. An independent Dixieland could develop its own banking and shipping, trade directly with Europe, and forever rid itself of the threat of high tariffs. For decades this fundamental friction had pitted the manufacturing North against the agricultural South.

Worldwide principles of nationalism—then stirring in Italy, Germany, Poland, and elsewhere—were also fermenting in the South. This huge area, with its distinctive culture and institutions, was not so much a section as a subnation. It looked to avoid the possibility of being lorded over, then or later, by what it regarded as a different and hostile nation of northerners.

The principles of self-determination—of the Declaration of Independence—seemed to many southerners to apply perfectly to them. Few, if any, of the seceders felt that they were doing anything wrong or immoral. The thirteen original states had voluntarily entered the Union, and now seven—ultimately eleven—southern states were voluntarily withdrawing from it.

Historical parallels ran even deeper. In 1776 thirteen American colonies, led by the rebel George Washington, had seceded from the British Empire by throwing off the yoke of King George III. In 1860–1861 eleven American states, led by the rebel Jefferson Davis, were seceding from the Union by throwing off the yoke of "King" Abraham Lincoln. With that burden gone, the South was confident that it could work out its own peculiar destiny more quietly, happily, and prosperously.

Crittenden amendments (1860)
Failed constitutional amendments that would have given federal protection for slavery in all territories south of 36°30' where slavery was supported by popular sovereignty. Proposed in an attempt to appease the South.

Varying Viewpoints

The Civil War: Repressible or Irrepressible?

Few topics have generated as much controversy among American historians as the causes of the Civil War. Interpretations of the great conflict have naturally differed according to section and have been charged with both emotional and moral fervor. Yet despite long and keen interest in the origins of the conflict, the causes of the Civil War remain as passionately debated today as they were a century ago.

The so-called Nationalist School of the late nineteenth century, typified by James Ford Rhodes, claimed that slavery caused the Civil War and credited the conflict with ending "the peculiar institution" and preserving the Union. But in the early twentieth century, progressive historians such as Charles and Mary Beard argued that the war was not fought over slavery per se, but rather was a deeply rooted economic struggle between an industrial North and an agricultural South. Anointing the Civil War "the Second American Revolution," the Beards claimed that the war transferred the dominant class power in America from the southern plantation aristocracy to the rising class of northern industrialists.

Shaken by the disappointing results of World War I, a new wave of historians argued that the Civil War, too, had actually been a big mistake. James G. Randall and Avery Craven asserted that the war had been a "repressible conflict," and they attributed the bloody confrontation to overzealous reformers and blundering political leaders.

Following the Second World War, however, a neonationalist view, echoing the earlier views of Rhodes, began depicting the Civil War as an unavoidable conflict between two societies, one slave and one free. For Allan Nevins and David M. Potter, irreconcilable differences in morality, politics, culture, social values, and economic systems increasingly eroded the ties between the sections and inexorably set the United States on the road to Civil War.

Eric Foner and Eugene Genovese have emphasized each section's nearly paranoid fear that the survival of its way of life was threatened by the expansion of the other section. In *Free Soil, Free Labor, Free Men* (1970), Foner emphasized that most northerners detested slavery not because it enslaved blacks but because its rapid extension threatened the position of free white laborers. Genovese has argued that the South, convinced that its labor system was superior to the northern factory system, saw northern designs to destroy their way of life lurking at every turn.

Historians of the "Ethnocultural School," especially Michael Holt, have offered a different analysis of how the collapse of the two established political parties caused the Civil War. They noted that the two great political parties had earlier muted sectional differences over slavery by focusing on issues such as the tariff, banking, and internal improvements. According to this argument, it was the temporary *consensus* on almost all national issues *other than* slavery that enabled the slavery issue to rise to the fore. Slavery fueled the rise of purely regional parties that identified their political opponents not simply as competitors for power but as threats to their way of life, even to the life of the Republic itself.

CHAPTER SUMMARY ★ ★ ★ ★ ★ ★ ★ ★ ★ ★ ★ ★ ★

The 1850s were punctuated by a series of increasingly violent incidents and confrontations that deepened sectional hostility, until it broke out in the Civil War.

Harriet Beecher Stowe's *Uncle Tom's Cabin* fanned northern antislavery feeling. In Kansas, Douglas's "popular sovereignty" scheme proved a disaster, as proslavery and antislavery forces fought a bloody little preview of the Civil War. Prosouthern President Buchanan's support of the proslavery Lecompton Constitution alienated moderate northern Democrats such as Douglas. Congressman Brooks's beating of Senator Sumner aroused passions in both sections.

The 1856 election signaled the rise of the sectionally based Republican party. The Supreme Court's proslavery decision in the *Dred Scott* v. *Stanford* case delighted the South, while northern Republicans pledged defiance. The Lincoln–Douglas debates of 1858 made Lincoln a national Republican leader and deepened the controversy over slavery. The fanatical abolitionist John Brown's raid on Harpers Ferry made him a heroic martyr in the North but caused outraged southerners to fear a slave uprising.

In the campaign of 1860, the Democratic party split along sectional lines. Lincoln won the resulting four-way election with support only from the North. Seven southern states quickly seceded and organized the Confederate States of America.

As southerners enthusiastically cast off their ties to the hated North, lame-duck President Buchanan proved unable to act. The last-minute Crittenden Compromise effort failed because of Lincoln's conviction that it would allow slavery to expand into Latin America.

KEY TERMS

- *Uncle Tom's Cabin* (297)
- *The Impending Crisis of the South* (297)
- New England Emigrant Aid Company (298)
- Lecompton Constitution (300)
- Bleeding Kansas (300)
- *Dred Scott v. Stanford* (302)
- panic of 1857 (303)
- Tariff of 1857 (303)
- Lincoln-Douglas debates (304)
- Freeport question (304)
- Freeport Doctrine (305)
- Harpers Ferry (305)
- Constitutional Union party (306)
- Confederate States of America (308)
- Crittenden amendments (309)

PEOPLE TO KNOW

- Harriet Beecher Stowe
- Henry Ward Beecher
- James Buchanan
- Charles Sumner
- Preston S. Brooks
- Dred Scott
- Roger B. Taney
- Stephen A. Douglas
- Abraham Lincoln
- John Brown
- John C. Breckinridge
- John Jordan Crittenden

MindTap is a fully online, highly personalized learning experience built upon Cengage Learning content. MindTap combines student learning tools—readings, multimedia, activities, and assessments—into a singular Learning Path that guides students through the course.

Chapter 20

Girding for War: The North and the South

1861–1865

I consider the central idea pervading this struggle is the necessity that is upon us, of proving that popular government is not an absurdity. We must settle this question now, whether in a free government the minority have the right to break up the government whenever they choose. If we fail it will go far to prove the incapability of the people to govern themselves.

Abraham Lincoln, May 7, 1861

Chapter Outline

- The Attack on Fort Sumter, April 1861
- The Crucial Border States
- The Balance of Forces
- Diplomacy and the Threat of European Intervention
- Lincoln and Civil Liberties
- Men in Uniform
- Wartime Finance and Economy
- Women and the War
- The Fate of the South
- *Makers of America: Billy Yank and Johnny Reb*

Abraham Lincoln solemnly took the presidential oath of office on March 4, 1861, after having slipped into Washington at night, partially disguised to thwart assassins. He thus became president not of the *United* States of America, but of the *dis-United* States of America. Seven had already departed; eight more teetered on the edge. The girders of the unfinished Capitol dome loomed nakedly in the background, as if to symbolize the imperfect state of the Union. Before the nation was restored—and the slaves freed at last—the American people would endure four years of anguish and bloodshed, and Lincoln would face tortuous trials of leadership such as have been visited upon few presidents.

FOCUS QUESTIONS

1. Why did the South fire the first shots of the Civil War? How did that assault and Lincoln's call for troops galvanize both sides for war and lead to the secession of four more Southern states?
2. What were the strengths and weaknesses of both sides as they went to war, and why were the Border States so critical to the balance of forces?
3. Why was the issue of British or French recognition of the Confederacy so central to the diplomacy of both sides?
4. How did Lincoln and Davis each mobilize their nation's forces and shape the moral and political character of the struggle?
5. What were the economic and social consequences of the war for both sides, including its effects on the roles of women?

CHRONOLOGY

1861	■ Confederate government formed ■ Lincoln takes office (March 4) ■ Fort Sumter fired upon (April 12) ■ Four upper South states secede (April–June) ■ Morrill Tariff Act passed ■ *Trent* affair ■ Lincoln suspends writ of habeas corpus	1862–1864	■ *Alabama* raids Northern shipping
		1863	■ Union enacts conscription ■ New York City draft riots ■ National Banking System established
		1863–1864	■ Napoleon III installs Archduke Maximilian as emperor of Mexico
1862	■ Confederacy enacts conscription ■ Homestead Act	1864	■ *Alabama* sunk by Union warship

★ The Menace of Secession

Lincoln's inaugural address was firm yet conciliatory: there would be no conflict unless the South provoked it. Secession, the president declared, was wholly impractical because, "physically speaking, we cannot separate."

Here Lincoln put his finger on a profound geographical truth. The North and South were bound inseparably together. If they had been divided by the Pyrenees Mountains or the Danube River, a sectional divorce might have been more feasible. But the Appalachian Mountains and the mighty Mississippi River both ran the wrong way.

Uncontested secession would create new controversies. What share of the national debt should the South be forced to take with it? What portion of the jointly held federal territories, if any, should the Confederate states be allotted—areas so largely won with Southern blood? How would the fugitive-slave issue be resolved? The Underground Railroad would certainly redouble its activity, and it would have to transport its passengers only across the Ohio River, not all the way to Canada. Was it conceivable that all such problems could have been solved without ugly armed clashes?

A *united United* States had hitherto been the paramount republic in the Western Hemisphere. If this powerful democracy broke into two hostile nations, the European nations would be delighted. They could gleefully transplant to America their ancient concept of the balance of power. Playing the no-less-ancient game of divide and conquer, they could incite one snarling fragment of the *dis-United* States against the other. The colonies of the European powers in the New World, notably those of Britain, would thus be made safer against the rapacious Yankees. And European imperialists, with no unified republic to stand across their path, could more easily defy the Monroe Doctrine and seize territory in the Americas.

★ South Carolina Assails Fort Sumter

The issue of the divided Union came to a head over the matter of federal forts in the South. As the seceding states left, they seized the United States' arsenals, mints, and other public property within their borders. When Lincoln took office, only two significant forts in the South still flew the Stars and Stripes. The more important of the pair was square-walled **Fort Sumter**, in Charleston harbor, with fewer than a hundred men.

Ominously, the choices presented to Lincoln by Fort Sumter were all bad. This stronghold had provisions that would last only a few weeks—until the middle of April 1861. If no supplies were forthcoming, the fort's commander would have to surrender without firing a shot. Lincoln, quite understandably, did not feel that such a weak-kneed course squared with his obligation to protect federal property. But if he sent reinforcements, the South Carolinians would undoubtedly fight back; they could not tolerate a federal fort blocking the mouth of their most important Atlantic seaport.

Fort Sumter *South Carolina location where Confederate forces fired the first shots of the Civil War in April of 1861, after Union forces attempted to provision the fort.*

> Secretary of State William H. Seward (1801–1872) entertained the dangerous idea that, if the North picked a fight with one or more European nations, the South would once more rally around the flag. On April Fools' Day, 1861, he submitted to Lincoln a memorandum:
>
> "I would demand explanations from Spain and France, categorically, at once. I would seek explanations from Great Britain and Russia.... And, if satisfactory explanations are not received from Spain and France ... would convene Congress and declare war against them."
>
> Lincoln quietly but firmly quashed Seward's scheme.

After agonizing indecision, Lincoln adopted a middle-of-the-road solution. He notified the South Carolinians that an expedition would be sent to *provision* the garrison, though not to *reinforce* it. But to Southern eyes "provision" still spelled "reinforcement."

A Union naval force started on its way to Fort Sumter—a move that the South regarded as an act of aggression. On April 12, 1861, the cannons of the Carolinians opened fire on the fort, while crowds in Charleston applauded and waved handkerchiefs. After a thirty-four-hour bombardment, the dazed garrison surrendered.

The shelling of the fort electrified the North, which at once responded with cries of "Remember Fort Sumter!" and "Save the Union!" Hitherto, countless Northerners had been saying that if the Southern states wanted to go, they should not be pinned to the rest of the nation with bayonets. "Wayward sisters, depart in peace" was a common sentiment. But the assault on Fort Sumter provoked the North to a fighting pitch: the fort was lost, but the Union was saved.

Lincoln had turned a tactical defeat into a strategic victory. Southerners had wantonly fired upon the glorious Stars and Stripes, and honor demanded an armed response. Lincoln promptly (April 15) issued a call to the states for seventy-five thousand militiamen, and volunteers sprang to the colors in such enthusiastic numbers that many were turned away. On April 19 and 27, the president proclaimed a leaky blockade of Southern seaports.

The call for troops, in turn, aroused the South much as the attack on Fort Sumter had aroused the North. Lincoln was now waging war—from the Southern view an aggressive war—on the Confederacy. Virginia, Arkansas, and Tennessee, all of which had earlier voted down secession, reluctantly joined their embattled sister states, as did North Carolina (see Map 20.1). Thus, the seven states became eleven as the "submissionists" and "Union shriekers" were overcome. Richmond, Virginia, replaced Montgomery, Alabama, as the Confederate capital—too near Washington for strategic comfort on either side.

★ Brothers' Blood and Border Blood

Border States *Five slave states—Missouri, Kentucky, Maryland, Delaware, and West Virginia—that did not secede during the Civil War. To keep the states in the Union, Abraham Lincoln insisted that the war was not about abolishing slavery but rather protecting the Union.*

West Virginia (admitted to the Union 1863) *Mountainous region that broke away from Virginia in 1861 to form its own state after Virginia seceded from the Union. Most of the residents of West Virginia were independent farmers and miners who did not own slaves and thus opposed the Confederate cause.*

The only slave states left were the crucial **Border States**. This group consisted of Missouri, Kentucky, Maryland, Delaware, and later **West Virginia**—the "mountain white" area that somewhat illegally uprooted itself from Virginia in mid-1861. If the North had fired the first shot, some or all of these doubtful states probably would have seceded, and the South might well have succeeded. The border group actually contained a white population more than half that of the entire Confederacy. Lincoln reportedly said that he *hoped* to have God on his side but he *had* to have Kentucky.

In dealing with the Border States, President Lincoln did not rely solely on moral suasion but successfully used methods of dubious legality. In Maryland he declared martial law where needed and sent in troops because this state threatened to cut off Washington from the North. Lincoln also deployed Union soldiers in western Virginia and notably in Missouri, where they fought beside Unionists in a local civil war within the larger Civil War.

Any official statement of the North's war aims was profoundly influenced by the teetering Border States. At the very outset, Lincoln was obliged to declare publicly that he was not fighting to free the blacks. An antislavery declaration would no doubt have driven the Border States into the welcoming arms of the South. An anti-slavery war was also extremely unpopular in the so-called Butternut region of southern Ohio, Indiana, and Illinois, originally settled largely by racially prejudiced Southerners (see "Makers of America: Settlers of the Old Northwest," p. 182). Lincoln insisted repeatedly—even though undercutting his high moral ground—that his paramount purpose was to save the Union

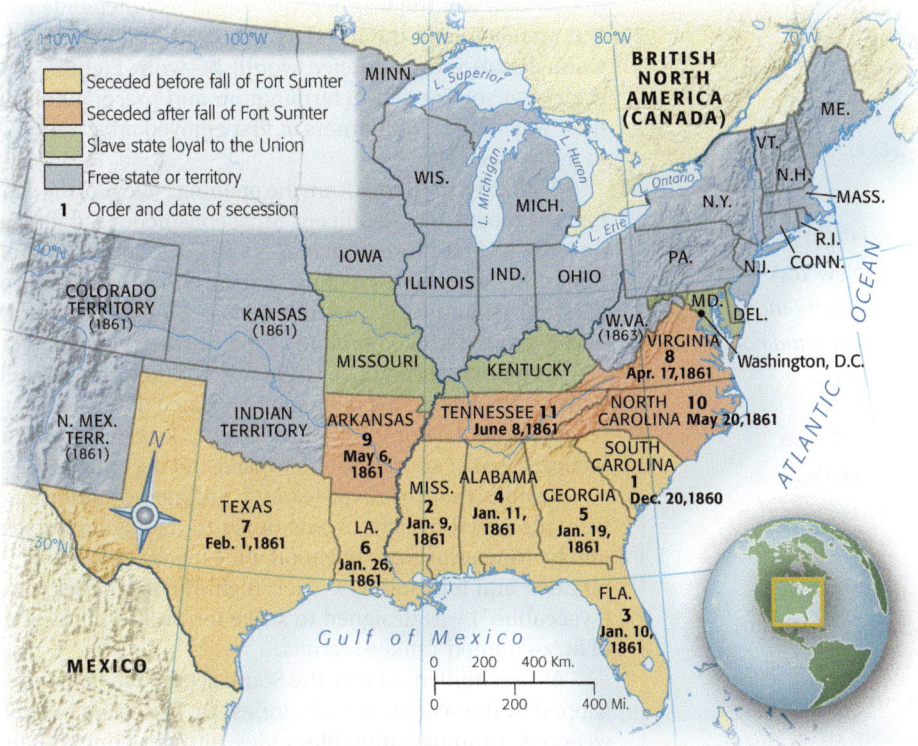

Map 20.1 Seceding States (with dates and order of secession) Note the long interval—nearly six months—between the secession of South Carolina, the first state to go, and that of Tennessee, the last state to leave the Union. These six months were a time of terrible trial for moderate Southerners. When a Georgia statesman pleaded for restraint and negotiations with Washington, he was rebuffed with the cry, "Throw the bloody spear into this den of incendiaries!"

at all costs. Thus, the war began not as one between slave soil and free soil, but one for the Union—with slaveholders on both sides and many proslavery sympathizers in the North.

Slavery also colored the character of the war in the West. In Indian Territory (present-day Oklahoma), most of the Five Civilized Tribes—the Cherokees, Creeks, Choctaws, Chickasaws, and Seminoles—sided with the Confederacy. Some of these Indians, notably the Cherokees, owned slaves and thus felt themselves to be making common cause with the slave-owning South. The Confederate government invited the Native Americans to send delegates to the Confederate congress, and they in return supplied troops to the Confederate army. A rival faction of Cherokees and most of the Plains Indians, however, sided with the Union.

Unhappily, the conflict between "Billy Yank" and "Johnny Reb" was a brothers' war (see "Makers of America: Billy Yank and Johnny Reb," p. 323). There were many Northern volunteers from the Southern states and many Southern volunteers from the Northern states. The "mountain whites" of the South sent north some 50,000 men, and the loyal slave states contributed some 300,000 soldiers to the Union. In many a family of the Border States, one brother rode north to fight with the Blue, another south to fight with the Gray. Senator Crittenden of Kentucky, who had fathered the abortive Crittenden Compromise, also had fathered two sons: one became a general in the Union army, the other a general in the Confederate army.

★ The Balance of Forces

When war broke out, the South seemed to have great advantages. The Confederacy could fight defensively behind interior lines. The North had to invade the vast territory of the Confederacy, conquer it, and drag it bodily back into the Union. In fact, the South did

Contending Voices

War Aims: Emancipation or Union?

On August 19, 1862, Horace Greeley (1811–1872), a passionate abolitionist and editor of the New York Tribune, *published an open letter to President Lincoln expressing disappointment that the president had not embraced full and unqualified emancipation.*

"Had you, Sir, in your Inaugural Address... proclaimed that Rebellion would strike the shackles from the slaves of every traitor, the wealthy and the cautious would have been supplied with a powerful inducement to remain loyal. As it was, every coward in the South soon became a traitor from fear; for Loyalty was perilous, while Treason seemed comparatively safe.... The Rebels from the first have been eager to confiscate, imprison, scourge and kill: we have fought wolves with the devices of sheep."

Lincoln replied on August 22, even as he was about to announce the Emancipation Proclamation:

"If I could save the Union without freeing any slave, I would do it; and if I could save it by freeing all the slaves, I would do it; and if I could do it by freeing some and leaving others alone, I would also do that."

> Why did Lincoln not champion emancipation earlier in the war?

not have to win the war in order to win its independence. If it merely fought the invaders to a draw and stood firm, Confederate independence would be won. Fighting on their own soil for self-determination and preservation of their way of life, Southerners at first enjoyed an advantage in morale as well.

Militarily, the South from the opening volleys of the war had the most talented officers. Most conspicuous among a dozen or so first-rate commanders was gray-haired General Robert E. Lee, whose knightly bearing and chivalric sense of honor embodied the Southern ideal. Lincoln had unofficially offered him command of the Northern armies, but when Virginia seceded Lee felt honor-bound to go with his native state. Lee's chief lieutenant for much of the war was black-bearded Thomas J. ("Stonewall") Jackson, a gifted tactical theorist and a master of speed and deception.

Besides their brilliant leaders, ordinary Southerners were also bred to fight. Accustomed to managing horses and bearing arms from boyhood, they made excellent cavalrymen and foot soldiers. Their high-pitched "rebel yell" ("yeeeahhh") was designed to strike terror into the hearts of fuzz-chinned Yankee recruits.

As one immense farm, the South seemed to be handicapped by the scarcity of its factories. Yet by seizing federal weapons, running Union blockades, and developing their own ironworks, Southerners managed to obtain sufficient weaponry. "Yankee ingenuity" was not confined to Yankees.

Nevertheless, as the war dragged on, grave shortages of shoes, uniforms, and blankets afflicted the South. Even with immense stores of food on Southern farms, civilians and soldiers often went hungry because of supply problems. "Forward, men! They have cheese in their haversacks," cried one Southern officer as he attacked the Yankees. Much of the hunger was caused by a breakdown of the South's rickety transportation system, especially where the railroad tracks were cut or destroyed by the Yankee invaders.

The economy was the greatest Southern weakness; it was the North's greatest strength. The North was not only a huge farm but a sprawling factory as well. Yankees boasted about three-fourths of the nation's wealth, including three-fourths of the thirty thousand miles of the railroads.

The North also controlled the sea. With its vastly superior navy, it established a blockade that, though a sieve at first, soon choked off Southern supplies and eventually shattered Southern morale. Its sea power also enabled the North to exchange huge quantities of grain for munitions and supplies from Europe, thus adding the output from the factories of Europe to its own.

The Union also enjoyed a much larger reserve of manpower. The loyal states had a population of some 22 million; the seceding states had 9 million people, including about 3.5 million slaves. Adding to the North's overwhelming supply of soldiery were immigrants from Europe, who continued to pour into the North even during the war (see Table 20.1). More than 800,000 newcomers arrived between 1861 and 1865, most of them British, Irish, and German. Large numbers of them were induced to enlist in the Union armies. Altogether about one-fifth of the Union forces were foreign born, and in some units military commands were given in four different languages.

Whether immigrant or native, ordinary Northern boys were much less prepared than their Southern counterparts for military life. Yet the Northern "clodhoppers" and "shopkeepers" eventually adjusted themselves to soldiering and became known for their discipline and determination.

Table 20.1 Immigration to United States, 1860–1866

Year	Total	Britain	Ireland	Germany	All Others
1860	153,640	29,737	48,637	54,491	20,775
1861	91,918	19,675	23,797	31,661	16,785
1862	91,985	24,639	23,351	27,529	16,466
1863	176,282	66,882	55,916	33,162	20,322
1864	193,418	53,428	63,523	57,276	19,191
1865*	248,120	82,465	29,772	83,424	52,459
1866	318,568	94,924	36,690	115,892	71,062

*Only the first three months of 1865 were war months.

The North was much less fortunate in its higher commanders. Lincoln was forced to use a costly trial-and-error method to sort out effective leaders from the many incompetent political officers, until he finally uncovered a general, Ulysses Simpson Grant, who was determined to slog his way to victory at whatever cost to life and limb.

In the long run, as the Northern strengths were brought to bear, they outweighed those of the South. But when the war began, the chances for Southern independence were unusually favorable—certainly better than the prospects for success of the thirteen colonies in 1776. The turn of a few events could easily have produced a different outcome.

The might-have-beens are fascinating. *If* the Border States had seceded, or *if* the uncertain states of the upper Mississippi Valley had turned against the Union, or *if* a wave of Northern defeatism had demanded an armistice, or *if* Britain and/or France had broken the naval blockade, the South might well have won. All of these possibilities almost became realities, but none of them actually occurred, and lacking their impetus, the South could not win.

★ Dethroning King Cotton

Successful revolutions, including the American Revolution of 1776, have generally succeeded because of foreign intervention. The South counted on it, did not get it, and lost. Of all the Confederacy's potential assets, none counted more weightily than the prospect of foreign intervention. Europe's ruling classes, which had long abhorred the incendiary example of American democracy, were openly sympathetic to the semifeudal, aristocratic South and the Confederate cause.

In contrast, the masses of working people in Britain, and to some extent in France, were pulling and praying for the North. Many of them had read *Uncle Tom's Cabin*, and they sensed that the war—though at the outset officially fought only over the question of union—might extinguish slavery if the North emerged victorious. The hostility of British common folk to any official intervention on behalf of the South had a sobering effect on the British government. Yet the fact remained that British textile mills depended on the American South for 75 percent of their cotton supplies. Humanitarian sympathies aside, Southerners counted on hard economic need to bring Britain to their aid. Why did King Cotton fail them?

He failed in part because he had been so lavishly productive in the immediate prewar years of 1857–1860. When the shooting started in 1861, British manufacturers had on hand enormous surpluses of cotton piled up in their warehouses. The real pinch did not come until about a year and a half later, when thousands of hungry operatives were thrown out of work. But by this time Lincoln had announced his slave-emancipation policy, and the "wage slaves" of Britain were not going to demand a war to defend the slave owners of the South.

The direst effects of the "cotton famine" in Britain were relieved in several ways. As Union armies penetrated the South, they captured or bought considerable supplies of cotton and shipped them to Britain; the Confederates also ran a limited quantity through the blockade. In addition, the cotton growers of Egypt and India, responding to high prices, increased their output, and captured a share of the world cotton market that they held onto well after the war's conclusion. Finally, booming war industries in England, which supplied both the North and the South, relieved unemployment.

King Wheat and King Corn—the monarchs of Northern agriculture—proved to be more potent potentates than King Cotton. Blessed with ideal weather and the efficient harvesting of McCormick's mechanical reaper, the North produced bountiful crops during the war years. The grain was purchased by Britain, which suffered a series of bad harvests in the same period. If the British had broken the blockade to gain cotton, they would have provoked the North to war and would have lost this precious granary.

★ Foreign Flare-Ups

America's diplomatic front has seldom been so critical as during the Civil War. The South never wholly abandoned its dream of foreign intervention, and Europe's rulers schemed to take advantage of America's distress.

The first major crisis with Britain came over the *Trent* **affair**, late in 1861. A Union warship cruising on the high seas north of Cuba stopped a British mail steamer, the *Trent*, and forcibly removed two Confederate diplomats bound for Europe.

Britons were outraged: upstart Yankees could not so boldly offend the Mistress of the Seas. War preparations buzzed, and red-coated troops embarked for Canada with bands blaring "I Wish I Was in Dixie." The London Foreign Office prepared an ultimatum demanding surrender of the prisoners and an apology. But luckily, slow communications gave passions on both sides a chance to cool. Lincoln came to see the *Trent* prisoners as "white elephants" and reluctantly released them.

Another major crisis in Anglo-American relations arose over the unneutral building in Britain of Confederate commerce-raiders, notably the *Alabama*. These vessels were not warships within the meaning of loopholed British law because they left their shipyards unarmed and picked up their guns elsewhere. The *Alabama* escaped in 1862 to the Portuguese Azores and there took on weapons and a crew from two British ships that followed it.

The *Alabama* lighted the skies from Europe to East Asia with the burning hulks of Yankee merchantmen. All told, this "British pirate" captured more than sixty vessels. Competing British shippers were delighted, while an angered North had to divert naval strength from its blockade for wild-goose chases. The *Alabama* was finally sunk by a Union cruiser off the coast of France in 1864.

A final Anglo-American crisis was touched off in 1863 by the **Laird rams**—two Confederate warships being constructed in Great Britain. Designed to destroy the wooden ships of the Union navy with their iron rams and large-caliber guns, they were far more dangerous than the swift and lightly armed *Alabama*. If delivered to the South, they probably would have sunk the blockading squadrons and then brought Northern cities under their fire. In retaliation, the North doubtless would have invaded Canada, and a full-dress war with Britain would have erupted. But America's minister to Britain, Charles Francis Adams, took a hard line, warning that "this is war" if the rams were released. At the last minute the London government relented and bought the two ships for the Royal Navy. Everyone seemed satisfied—except the disappointed Confederates.

Emperor Napoleon III of France, taking advantage of America's preoccupation with its own internal problems, dispatched a French army to occupy Mexico City in 1863. The following year he installed on the ruins of the crushed republic his puppet, the Austrian Archduke Maximilian, as emperor of Mexico. Sending the army and enthroning Maximilian were both flagrant violations of the Monroe Doctrine. Napoleon was gambling that the Union would collapse and thus America would be too weak to enforce its hands-off policy in the Western Hemisphere.

The North, as long as it was convulsed by war, pursued a walk-on-eggs policy toward France. The Washington government did provide aid to the resistance movement headed by Mexico's beloved national hero (and the first full-blooded Indian president of Mexico), Benito Juarez. But when the shooting stopped in 1865, Secretary of State Seward, speaking

---

Trent **affair (1861)** *Diplomatic row that threatened to bring the British into the Civil War on the side of the Confederacy, after a Union warship stopped a British steamer and arrested two Confederate diplomats on board.*

Alabama **(1862–1864)** *British-built and manned Confederate warship that raided Union shipping during the Civil War. One of many built by the British for the Confederacy, despite Union protests.*

Laird rams (1863) *Two well-armed ironclad warships constructed for the Confederacy by a British firm. Seeking to avoid war with the United States, the British government purchased the two ships for its Royal Navy instead.*

with the authority of nearly a million war-tempered bayonets, prepared to march south. Napoleon realized that his costly gamble was doomed. He reluctantly took "French leave" of his ill-starred puppet in 1867, and Maximilian soon crumpled ingloriously before a Mexican firing squad.

★ President Davis Versus President Lincoln

The Confederate government, like King Cotton, harbored fatal weaknesses. Its constitution, borrowing liberally from that of the Union, contained one deadly defect. Created by secession, it could not logically deny future secession to its constituent states. Jefferson Davis, while making his bow to states' rights, had in view a well-knit central government. But determined states' rights supporters fought him bitterly to the end. The Richmond regime encountered difficulty even in persuading certain state troops to serve outside their own borders.

Sharp-featured President Jefferson Davis—tense, humorless, legalistic, and stubborn—was repeatedly in hot water. Although an eloquent orator and an able administrator, he at no time enjoyed real personal popularity and was often at loggerheads with his congress. At times there was serious talk of impeachment. Unlike Lincoln, Davis was somewhat imperious and inclined to defy rather than lead public opinion. Suffering acutely from neuralgia and other nervous disorders (including a tic), he overworked himself with the details of both civil government and military operations. No one could doubt his courage, sincerity, integrity, and devotion to the South, but the task proved beyond his powers.

Lincoln also had his troubles, but on the whole they were less prostrating. The North enjoyed the prestige of a long-established government, financially stable and fully recognized both at home and abroad. Lincoln, the inexperienced prairie politician, proved superior to the more experienced but less flexible Davis. Able to relax with droll stories at critical times, "Old Abe" grew as the war dragged on. Tactful, quiet, patient, yet firm, he developed a genius for interpreting and leading a fickle public opinion. Holding aloft the banner of Union with inspiring utterances, he revealed charitableness toward the South and forbearance toward backbiting colleagues. "Did [Secretary of War Edwin] Stanton say I was a damned fool?" he reportedly replied to a talebearer. "Then I dare say I must be one, for Stanton is generally right and he always says what he means."

One of "Honest Abe" Lincoln's greatest challenges was to preserve the Union while upholding America's *constitutionally* protected freedoms in wartime. But driven by necessity, he reluctantly concluded that if he did not abridge some civil liberties in order to quell the rebellion, there might not be a Constitution of a *united United* States to mend.

Congress was not in session when war broke out, so Lincoln proclaimed a blockade and increased the size of the federal army—something that only Congress can do under the Constitution (see Art. I, Sec. VIII, para. 12). He also advanced federal funds to private citizens without appropriation and suspended the precious **writ of habeas corpus** so that anti-Unionists might be summarily arrested. These questionable acts led critics to call him a "Simple Susan Tyrant." But Lincoln believed that his ironhanded authority would be lifted once the Union was preserved. He pointedly remarked in 1863 that a man suffering from a "temporary illness" would not persist in taking bitter medicines for "the remainder of his healthful life."

writ of habeas corpus *Petition requiring law enforcement officers to present detained individuals before the court to examine the legality of the arrest. Protects individuals from arbitrary state action. Suspended by Lincoln during the Civil War.*

★ Volunteers and Draftees: North and South

Ravenous, the gods of war demanded men—lots of men. Northern armies were at first manned solely by volunteers, with each state assigned a quota based on population. But in 1863, after volunteering had slackened off, Congress passed a federal conscription law for the first time on a nationwide scale in the United States. The provisions were grossly unfair to the poor. Rich boys, including young John D. Rockefeller, could hire substitutes to go in their places or purchase exemption outright by paying $300.

Amputation on the Battlefields of Virginia A surgeon wearing a hat and a sword amputates the leg of a wounded soldier, while an anesthetist (facing the camera) holds a sponge dipped in chloroform over the patient's nose. A surgical assistant ties a tourniquet to stem the flow of blood. Other soldiers, dressed in Zouave uniforms modeled on North African designs, which were popular among some Northern and Southern regiments, watch closely, likely aware of the dangers accompanying such crude surgery. An estimated 30 percent of amputees died from postoperative complications, most often infections.

New York draft riots (1863) *Uprising, mostly of working-class Irish Americans, in protest of the draft. Rioters were particularly incensed by the ability of the rich to hire substitutes or purchase exemptions.*

Morrill Tariff Act (1861) *Increased duties back up to 1846 levels to raise revenue for the Civil War.*

Greenbacks *Paper currency issued by the Union Treasury during the Civil War. Inadequately supported by gold, greenbacks fluctuated in value throughout the war, reaching a low of 39 cents on the dollar.*

The draft was especially damned in the Democratic strongholds of the North, notably in New York City. A frightful riot broke out in 1863, touched off largely by underprivileged and antiblack Irish Americans who shouted "Down with Lincoln!" and "Down with the draft!" For several days the **New York draft riots** put the city at the mercy of a rampaging, pillaging mob. Scores of lives were lost, and the victims included many lynched blacks. Elsewhere in the North, conscription met with resentment and an occasional minor riot.

More than 90 percent of the Union troops were volunteers, because social and patriotic pressures to enlist were strong. As able-bodied men became scarcer, generous bounties for enlistment were offered by federal, state, and local authorities. With money flowing so freely, an unsavory crew of "bounty brokers" and "substitute brokers" sprang up at home and abroad. They combed the poorhouses of the British Isles and western Europe, and many an Irishman or German was befuddled with whiskey and induced to enlist.

Like the North, the South at first relied mainly on volunteers. But because the Confederacy was much less populous, it scraped the bottom of its manpower barrel much more quickly. The Richmond regime, robbing both "cradle and grave" (ages seventeen to fifty), was forced to resort to conscription as early as April 1862, nearly a year earlier than the Union.

Confederate draft regulations also worked serious injustices. As in the North, a rich man could hire a substitute or purchase exemption. Slaveowners or overseers with twenty slaves might also claim exemption. These special privileges, later modified, made for bad feelings among the less prosperous, many of whom complained that this was "a rich man's war and a poor man's fight." No large-scale draft riots broke out in the South, as in New York City. But Confederate conscription agents often found it prudent to avoid areas inhabited by sharpshooting mountain whites, who were branded "traitors," and "Yankee lovers."

★ The Dollar Goes to War

Blessed with the lion's share of the wealth, the North rode through the financial breakers much more smoothly than the South. Excise taxes on tobacco and alcohol were substantially increased by Congress. An income tax was levied for the first time in the nation's experience.

Customs receipts likewise proved to be important revenue raisers. Early in 1861, after enough antiprotection Southern members had seceded, Congress passed the **Morrill Tariff Act**. It increased the existing duties some 5 to 10 percent, but these modest rates were soon pushed sharply upward by the necessities of war. The increases were designed partly to raise additional revenue and partly to provide more protection for the prosperous manufacturers who were being plucked by the new internal taxes. A protective tariff thus became identified with the Republican party, as American industrialists, mostly Republicans, waxed fat on these welcome benefits.

The Washington Treasury also issued greenback paper money totaling nearly $450 million at face value. This printing-press currency was inadequately supported by gold, and hence its value was determined by the nation's credit. **Greenbacks** thus fluctuated with the fortunes of Union arms and at one low point were worth only 39 cents on the gold dollar.

Borrowing far outstripped both greenbacks and taxes as a money raiser. The federal Treasury netted $2,621,916,786 through the sale of bonds, which bore interest and were payable at a later date. A financial landmark of the war was the **National Banking System**, authorized by Congress in 1863. Launched partly as a stimulant to the sale of government bonds, it was also designed to establish a standard banknote currency. (The country was then flooded with depreciated "rag money" issued by unreliable bankers.) Banks that joined the National Banking System could buy government bonds and issue sound paper money backed by them. The war-born National Banking Act thus turned out to be the first significant step taken toward a unified banking network since 1836, when the "monster" Bank of the United States was killed by Andrew Jackson. Spawned by the war, this new system continued to function for fifty years, until replaced by the Federal Reserve System in 1913.

The impoverished South was beset by different financial woes. Customs duties were choked off as the coils of the Union blockade tightened. Large issues of Confederate bonds were sold at home and abroad, amounting to nearly $400 million. The Richmond regime also increased taxes sharply and imposed a 10 percent levy on farm produce. But, in general, the states' rights Southerners were immovably opposed to heavy direct taxation by the central authority: only about 1 percent of the total income was raised this way.

As revenue began to dry up, the Confederate government was forced to print blue-backed paper money with complete abandon. "Runaway inflation" occurred as Southern presses continued to grind out the poorly backed treasury notes, totaling in all more than $1 billion. The Confederate paper dollar finally sank to the point where it was worth only 1.6 cents when Lee surrendered. Overall, the war inflicted a 9,000 percent inflation rate on the Confederacy, contrasted with 80 percent for the Union.

> *A contemporary (October 22, 1863) Richmond diary portrays the ruinous effects of inflation:*
>
> "A poor woman yesterday applied to a merchant in Carey Street to purchase a barrel of flour. The price he demanded was $70. 'My God!' exclaimed she, 'how can I pay such prices? I have seven children; what shall I do?' 'I don't know, madam,' said he coolly, 'unless you eat your children.'"

National Banking System (1863) *Network of member banks that could issue currency against purchased government bonds. Created during the Civil War to establish a stable national currency and stimulate the sale of war bonds.*

★ The North's Economic Boom

Wartime prosperity in the North was little short of miraculous. New factories, sheltered by the friendly umbrella of the new protective tariffs, mushroomed forth. Soaring prices, resulting from inflation, unfortunately pinched the laborers and white-collar workers to some extent, but manufacturers and businesspeople raked in "the fortunes of war." The Civil War bred a millionaire class for the first time in American history.

Yankee "sharpness" appeared at its worst during the war. Dishonest agents, putting profits above patriotism, palmed off aged and blind horses on government purchasers. Unscrupulous Northern manufacturers supplied shoes with cardboard soles and fast-disintegrating uniforms of reprocessed or "shoddy" wool rather than virgin wool. Hence, the reproachful term "shoddy millionaires" was doubly fair.

Newly invented laborsaving machinery enabled the North to expand economically, even though the cream of its manpower was being drained off to the fighting front. The sewing machine wrought wonders in fabricating uniforms and military footwear. Clattering mechanical reapers, which numbered about 250,000 by 1865, proved hardly less potent than thundering guns. They not only released tens of thousands of farm boys for the army but fed them their field rations.

Other industries were humming. The discovery of petroleum gushers in 1859 had led to a rush of "Fifty-Niners" to Pennsylvania. The result was the birth of a new industry, with its "petroleum plutocracy" and "coal oil Johnnies." Pioneers continued to push westward during the war, altogether an estimated 300,000 people. Major magnets were free gold nuggets and free lands under the **Homestead Act** of 1862.

Homestead Act (1862) *A federal law that sold settlers 160 acres of land for about $30 if they lived on it for five years and improved it by, for instance, building a house on it. The act helped make land accessible to hundreds of thousands of westward-moving settlers, but many people also found disappointment when their land was infertile or they saw speculators grabbing up the best land.*

Booth at the Sanitary Fair in Chicago, 1863
The Chicago Sanitary Fair was the first of many such fairs throughout the nation to raise funds for soldier relief efforts. Mainly organized by women, the fair sold captured Confederate flags, battle relics, handicrafts such as these potholders (right), and donated items, including President Lincoln's original draft of the Emancipation Proclamation (which garnered $3,000 in auction). When the fair closed, the Chicago headquarters of the U.S. Sanitary Commission had raised $100,000, and its female managers had gained organizational experience that many would put to work in the postwar movement for women's rights. (Left: Image and inset: Chicago History Museum)

U.S. Sanitary Commission (established 1861) *Government agency founded with the help of Elizabeth Blackwell that trained nurses, collected medical supplies, and equipped hospitals in an effort to help the Union army. The commission helped professionalize nursing and gave many women the confidence and organizational skills to propel the women's movement in the postwar years.*

The Civil War was a woman's war, too. The protracted conflict opened new opportunities for women. When men departed in uniform, women often took their jobs. In Washington, D.C., five hundred women clerks ("government girls") became government workers, with more than one hundred in the Treasury Department alone. The booming military demand for shoes and clothing, combined with technological marvels such as the sewing machine, likewise drew countless women into industrial employment. Before the war, one industrial worker in four had been female; during the war, the ratio rose to one in three.

Other women on both sides stepped up to the fighting front—or close behind it. More than four hundred women accompanied husbands and sweethearts into battle by posing as male soldiers. Other women took on dangerous spy missions. One woman was executed for smuggling gold to the Confederacy. Dr. Elizabeth Blackwell, America's first female physician, helped organize the **U.S. Sanitary Commission** to assist Union armies in the field. The commission trained nurses, collected medical supplies, and equipped hospitals. Commission work helped many women to acquire the organizational skills and the self-confidence that would propel the women's movement forward after the war. Heroically energetic Clara Barton and dedicated Dorothea Dix, superintendent of nurses for the Union army, helped transform nursing from a lowly service into a respected profession—and in the process opened up another major sphere of employment for women in the postwar era. Equally renowned in the South was Sally Tompkins, who ran a Richmond infirmary for wounded Confederate soldiers and was awarded the rank of captain by Confederate president Jefferson Davis. Still other women, North as well as South, organized bazaars and fairs that raised millions of dollars for the relief of widows, orphans, and disabled soldiers.

Makers of America

Billy Yank and Johnny Reb

The Prussian general Helmuth von Moltke (1800–1891) allegedly remarked that the American Civil War was merely a contest waged by "armed mobs." Whether he meant it or not, the Prussian's famous insult actually contains an important insight. Unlike the professional standing armies of nineteenth-century Europe, Civil War armies were overwhelmingly amateur and volunteer. Taken from all walks of life, citizen-soldiers gave the Civil War drama its uniquely plebeian cast.

With 2 million men in Union blue and 1 million men in Confederate gray, Civil War soldiers represented a vast cross section of American society. (At nearly 10 percent of the 1860 population, the same rate of mobilization would amount to more than 27 million troops today.) Most soldiers had been farmers or farm laborers. Poor, unskilled workers, despite vehement anti-draft rhetoric to the contrary, were actually underrepresented. Most troops were native born, but immigrants did serve in rough proportion to their presence in the general population. Black fighting men accounted for about 10 percent of Union enlistments by war's end (see "Blacks Battle Bondage," pp. 333–334). Perhaps one-third of the soldiers were married. Nearly 40 percent were under twenty-two years of age at the time of enlistment.

Inheritors of the values of Jacksonian mass democracy and Victorian sentiments, Civil War citizen-soldiers brought strong ideological commitments to the struggle. Neither army regulars nor reluctant conscripts, these men fought in the name of country, duty, honor, manhood, and righteousness. Though enemies, Union and Confederate soldiers shared a common commitment to the patriotic "spirit of '76" and the cause of liberty, independence, and republican government. A man's moral obligation to defend his country and preserve his personal reputation provided added motivation. Many interpreted the war as a religious crusade. In short, convictions, not coercion, created Civil War armies.

Despite their similarities, "Billy Yank" (the ordinary Union soldier) and "Johnny Reb" (the typical Confederate) were not necessarily cut from the same cloth. Both armies reflected the societies from which they came. Billy Yank tended to be more literate, intellectual, practical, and efficient, while Johnny Reb was often more jocular, emotional, religious, and personally concerned about the war. Defense of home and hearth meant more to Confederate troops, for the simple reason that most of the fighting occurred on Southern soil. Above all else, the men in gray maintained a distinctive rural individualism and homegrown disrespect for authority. Their counterparts in blue, often familiar with the strict regimen of Northern cities and factories, adapted more quickly to army discipline.

One aspect of soldiering Johnny Reb and Billy Yank shared was the dull routine of camp life. For all its promises of adventure, the life of a Civil War soldier could be downright boring and unpleasant. Men spent fifty days in camp for everyone in battle. Reveille, roll call, and drill were daily chores. A soldier's first concern was usually his stomach, even when pork ("sowbelly"), beef ("salt horse"), coffee, and bread (or its unwelcome substitute, "hardtack") were in abundance. Food shortages plagued both armies, especially the Confederates as the war progressed. Uniforms deteriorated from "finery" to "tatters," as did moral standards. Gambling, drinking, stealing, swearing, and Sabbath breaking proliferated; even widespread religious revivals could not keep up.

The gravest hardship of all, however, was disease. Germs—especially camp and campaign maladies such as dysentery, diarrhea, typhoid, and malaria—took twice as many lives as bullets. By modern standards, the mortality rates of wounded soldiers were appallingly high. (World War II marked the first time in American warfare when more soldiers died from combat wounds than from sickness and disease.) Without proper medical understanding of sterilization or sanitation, the risk of sepsis (bacterial infection) accompanied every wound. Head, chest, and stomach wounds were usually considered fatal; arm and leg injuries often resulted in amputation. Only the presence of nurses made life in field hospitals tolerable. Overcoming the vocal hostility of male army doctors and the filth, stench, and agony of these hospitals, some twenty thousand women volunteered as nurses during the war. Working with the maimed and the dying was never pleasant, but female nurses earned the respect of countless wounded soldiers for their dedicated service.

Yet for all its brutality, not even the field hospital could match the traumatic experience of combat. Tension mounted in the final moments before battle, as officers strove to maintain close-order ranks in the face of harrowing enemy gunfire. Artillery shells blanketed the battlefield with a smoky haze. Bullets zinged through the air like a driving rain. Once soldiers joined the action, a rush of adrenaline could transform frightened civilians into frenzied and ferocious fighters. First-timers likened the experience to "seeing the elephant" (an antebellum expression of awe). One sight of mangled limbs or one whiff of decaying flesh was often enough to push men over the edge. "Even when I sleep," a Massachusetts soldier moaned, "I hear the whistling of the shells and the shouts and groans, and to sum it up in two [sic] words it is *horrible*." Given the extraordinary stress of battle, many men avoided combat as much as they could.

Shell-shocked and weary, most soldiers returned home from the war utterly transformed. For nearly a decade and a half, silence reigned, as veterans and civilians entered into a tacit agreement to put the ordeal behind them. By 1880 interest revived in the war, and a new battle over its proper meaning commenced. Ignoring the conflict's original significance as a moral victory for slave emancipation, many Americans embraced a new reconciliationist and white supremacist script. In the interest of sectional harmony and national prosperity, Northerners abandoned earlier commitments to black rights. A reunion of sections spelled a division of races. Casting aside their original ideological convictions, many Americans came to regard the conflict as a tragic brothers' war meaningful only for its show of martial valor. Principles that had compelled 3 million men to enlist and caused 620,000 to die were largely forgotten. Instead, a sentimental, sanitized, and whitened version of the Civil War became commonplace by the late nineteenth century. Von Moltke's "armed mobs" came to be remembered as the noblest of knights.

⭐ A Crushed Cotton Kingdom

The South fought to the point of exhaustion. The suffocation caused by the blockade, together with the destruction wrought by invaders, took a terrible toll. Possessing 30 percent of the national wealth in 1860, the South claimed only 12 percent in 1870. Transportation collapsed. The South was even driven to the economic cannibalism of pulling up rails from the less-used lines to repair the main lines. Window weights were melted down into bullets; gourds replaced dishes; pins became so scarce that they were loaned with reluctance.

To the brutal end, the South mustered remarkable resourcefulness and spirit. Women buoyed up their menfolk, many of whom had seen enough of war at first hand to be heartily sick of it. A number of women proposed that they cut off their long hair and sell it abroad to support the cause. Self-sacrificing Southern women took pride in denying themselves the silks and satins of their Northern sisters.

The chorus of a song, "The Southern Girl," touched a cheerful note:

So hurrah! hurrah! For Southern Rights,
  Hurrah!
Hurrah! for the homespun dress the Southern
  ladies wear.

At war's end, the Northern Captains of Industry had conquered the Southern Lords of the Manor. A crippled South left the capitalistic North free to work its own way, with high tariffs and other benefits. The manufacturing moguls of the North, ushering in the full-fledged Industrial Revolution, were headed for increased dominance over American economic and political life. Hitherto the agrarian "slavocracy" of the South had partially checked the rising plutocracy of the North. Now cotton capitalism had lost out to industrial capitalism. The South of 1865 was to be rich in little but amputees, war heroes, ruins, and memories.

CHAPTER SUMMARY

South Carolina's firing on Fort Sumter aroused the North for war. Lincoln's call for troops to suppress the rebellion drove four upper South states into the Confederacy. Lincoln used an effective combination of political persuasion and force to keep the deeply divided Border States in the Union.

The Confederacy enjoyed initial advantages of upper-class European support, military leadership, and a defensive position on its own soil. The North enjoyed the advantages of lower-class European support, industrial and population resources, and political leadership.

The British upper classes sympathized with the South and abetted Confederate naval efforts, while France's Emperor Napoleon III took advantage of the war to intervene in Mexico. But effective diplomacy and Union military success prevented foreign recognition and further assistance for the Confederacy.

Lincoln's political leadership proved effective in mobilizing the North for war, despite political opposition and resistance to his infringement on civil liberties. The North eventually mobilized its larger troop resources for war and ultimately turned to an unpopular and unfair draft system.

Northern economic and financial strengths enabled it to gain an advantage over the less-industrialized South. The changes in society opened new opportunities for women, who had contributed significantly to the war effort in both the North and South. Because most of the war was waged on Southern soil, the South was left devastated by the war.

KEY TERMS

Fort Sumter (313)
Border States (314)
West Virginia (314)
Trent affair (318)
Alabama (318)
Laird rams (318)
writ of habeas corpus (319)
New York draft riots (320)
Morrill Tariff Act (320)
greenbacks (320)
National Banking System (321)
Homestead Act (321)
U.S. Sanitary Commission (322)

PEOPLE TO KNOW

Charles Francis Adams
Napoleon III
Maximilian
Jefferson Davis
Elizabeth Blackwell
Clara Barton
Sally Tompkins

MindTap is a fully online, highly personalized learning experience built upon Cengage Learning content. MindTap combines student learning tools—readings, multimedia, activities, and assessments—into a singular Learning Path that guides students through the course.

Chapter 21

The Furnace of Civil War
1861–1865

My paramount object in this struggle is to save the Union, and is not either to save or to destroy slavery.

Abraham Lincoln, 1862

Chapter Outline

- Bull Run Ends the "Ninety-Day War"
- The Peninsula Campaign
- The Union Wages Total War
- The Battle of Antietam
- The Emancipation Proclamation, 1863
- Black Soldiers
- Confederate High Tide at Gettysburg
- Politics in Wartime
- Appomattox, 1865
- The Assassination of Lincoln, April 1865
- The Legacy of War
- *Examining the Evidence: Abraham Lincoln's Gettysburg Address*
- *Thinking Globally: The Era of Nationalism*
- *Varying Viewpoints: What Were the Consequences of the Civil War?*

When President Lincoln issued his call to the states for seventy-five thousand militiamen on April 15, 1861, he envisioned them serving for only ninety days. Reaffirming his limited war aims, he declared that he had "no purpose, directly or indirectly, to interfere with slavery in the States where it exists." With a swift flourish of federal force, he hoped to show the folly of secession and rapidly return the rebellious states to the Union. But the war was to be neither brief nor limited. When the guns fell silent four years later, hundreds of thousands of soldiers on both sides lay dead, slavery was ended forever, and the nation faced the challenge of reintegrating the defeated but still recalcitrant South into the Union.

FOCUS QUESTIONS

1. How did the Northern defeats in the First Battle of Bull Run and the Peninsula Campaign actually serve to transform the Civil War from a limited struggle to preserve the Union to a total war against slavery?
2. What was the significance of the Battles of Antietam, Vicksburg, and Gettysburg as key turning points of the Civil War?
3. How did the politics of emancipation change during the Civil War? What did the Emancipation Proclamation actually accomplish?
4. How did the Copperheads and Peace Democrats threaten Lincoln's wartime policies, and how did he successfully outmaneuver them to win reelection in 1864?
5. How did Sherman's "March to the Sea" and Grant's 1864–1865 campaign in Virginia finally complete the Union's grand military strategy and force Lee's surrender?

CHRONOLOGY

1861	- First Battle of Bull Run		- Battle of Gettysburg
			- Fall of Vicksburg
1862	- Grant takes Fort Henry and Fort Donelson		- Fall of Port Hudson
	- Battle of Shiloh		
	- McClellan's Peninsula Campaign	1864	- Sherman's march through Georgia
	- Seven Days' Battles		- Grant's Wilderness Campaign
	- Second Battle of Bull Run		- Battle of Cold Harbor
	- Naval battle of the *Merrimack* (the *Virginia*) and the *Monitor*		- Lincoln defeats McClellan for presidency
	- Battle of Antietam	1865	- Hampton Roads Conference
	- Preliminary Emancipation Proclamation		- Lee surrenders to Grant at Appomattox
	- Battle of Fredericksburg		- Lincoln assassinated
	- Northern army seizes New Orleans		- Thirteenth Amendment ratified
1863	- Final Emancipation Proclamation		
	- Battle of Chancellorsville		

⭐ Bull Run Ends the "Ninety-Day War"

Northern newspapers, at first sharing Lincoln's expectation of quick victory, raised the cry "On to Richmond!" In this yeasty atmosphere, a Union army of some thirty thousand men drilled near Washington in the summer of 1861. The army was ill prepared for battle, but the press and the public clamored for action. Lincoln eventually concluded that an attack on a smaller Confederate force at **Bull Run (Manassas Junction)**, some thirty miles southwest of Washington, might be worth a try. If successful, it would demonstrate the superiority of Union arms. It might even lead to the capture of the Confederate capital at Richmond, one hundred miles to the south. If Richmond fell, secession would be thoroughly discredited, and the Union could be restored without damage to the economic and social systems of the South.

Raw Yankee recruits swaggered out of Washington toward Bull Run on July 21, 1861, as if they were headed for a sporting event. Congressmen and spectators trailed along with their lunch baskets to witness the fun. At first the battle went well for the Yankees. But "Stonewall" Jackson's gray-clad warriors stood like a stone wall (here he won his nickname), and Confederate reinforcements arrived unexpectedly. Panic seized the green Union troops, many of whom fled in shameful confusion. The Confederates, themselves too exhausted or disorganized to pursue, feasted on captured lunches.

The "military picnic" at Bull Run, though not decisive militarily, had significant psychological and political consequences. Victory was worse than defeat for the South because it inflated an already dangerous overconfidence. Many of the Southern soldiers promptly deserted, feeling that the war was now surely over. Southern enlistments fell off sharply, and preparations for a protracted conflict slackened. Defeat was better than victory for the Union, because it dispelled all illusions of a one-punch war and caused the Northerners to buckle down to the staggering task at hand. It also set the stage for a war that would be waged not merely for the cause of Union but also, eventually, for the abolitionist ideal of emancipation.

Battle of Bull Run (Manassas Junction) (July 1861) *First major battle of the Civil War and a victory for the South, it dispelled Northern illusions of swift victory.*

⭐ "Tardy George" McClellan and the Peninsula Campaign

Northern hopes brightened later in 1861, when General George B. McClellan was given command of the Army of the Potomac, as the major Union force near Washington was now called. Red-haired and red-mustached, strong and stocky, McClellan ("Young

Napoleon") was a brilliant, thirty-four-year-old West Pointer who had seen plenty of fighting in the Mexican War.

Cocky George McClellan embodied a curious mixture of virtues and defects. He was a superb organizer and drillmaster, and he injected splendid morale into the Army of the Potomac. Hating to sacrifice his troops, he was idolized by his men, who affectionately called him "Little Mac." But he was a perfectionist who seems not to have realized that an army is never ready to the last button and that wars cannot be won without running some risks. He consistently but erroneously believed that the enemy outnumbered him, partly because his intelligence reports from the head of Pinkerton's Detective Agency were unreliable. McClellan was overcautious—Lincoln once accused him of having "the slows"—and he addressed the president in an arrogant tone that a less forgiving person than Lincoln would never have tolerated. Privately the general referred to his chief as a "baboon."

After threatening to "borrow" the army if it was not going to be used, Lincoln finally issued McClellan firm orders to advance. The reluctant general at last decided on the roundabout strategy of a waterborne approach to Richmond. Moving up the narrow peninsula formed by the James and York Rivers, McClellan warily inched toward the Confederate capital in the spring of 1862 with about 100,000 men in what was called the **Peninsula Campaign**. After taking a month to capture historic Yorktown, which bristled with imitation wooden cannons, he finally came within sight of the spires of Richmond. Aided by "Jeb" Stuart's Confederate cavalry, General Robert E. Lee suddenly launched a devastating counterattack—the Seven Days' Battles—June 26–July 2, 1862. The Confederates slowly drove McClellan back to the sea. The Union forces abandoned the Peninsula Campaign as a costly failure, and Lincoln temporarily removed McClellan as commander of the Army of the Potomac.

Lee had achieved a brilliant, if bloody, triumph. Yet the ironies of his accomplishment are striking. If McClellan had succeeded in taking Richmond and ending the war in mid-1862, the Union probably would have been restored with minimal disruption, and slavery would have survived, at least for a time. By his successful defense of Richmond and defeat of McClellan, Lee had in effect ensured that the war would endure until slavery was uprooted and the Old South thoroughly destroyed. Lincoln himself now declared that the rebels "cannot experiment for ten years trying to destroy the government and if they fail still come back into the Union unhurt." He began to draft an emancipation proclamation.

Union strategy now turned toward total war (see Map 21.1). As finally developed, the Northern military plan had six components: first, slowly suffocate the South by blockading its coasts; second, liberate the slaves and hence undermine the economic foundations of the Old South; third, cut the Confederacy in half by seizing control of its Mississippi River backbone; fourth, chop the Confederacy to pieces by sending troops from Tennessee through Georgia and then the Carolinas; fifth, decapitate it by capturing its capital at Richmond; and sixth (this was Ulysses Grant's idea, especially), try everywhere to engage the enemy's main strength and grind it into submission.

Peninsula Campaign (1862) *Union general George B. McClellan's failed effort to seize Richmond, the Confederate capital. Had McClellan taken Richmond and toppled the Confederacy, slavery would have most likely survived in the South for some time.*

Abraham Lincoln (1809–1865) treated the demands of George McClellan for reinforcements and his excuses for inaction with infinite patience. One exception came when the general complained that his horses were tired. On October 24, 1862, Lincoln wrote:

"I have just read your dispatch about sore-tongued and fatigued horses. Will you pardon me for asking what the horses of your army have done since the battle of Antietam that fatigues anything?"

★ The War at Sea

The blockade started leakily; it was not clamped down all at once but extended by degrees. Blockading was simplified by concentrating on the principal ports and inlets, where dock facilities were available for loading bulky bales of cotton. The blockade was further strengthened when Britain recognized it as binding and warned its shippers that they ignored it at their peril.

Blockade-running was risky but profitable, as the growing scarcity of Southern goods drove prices skyward. A leading rendezvous for successful blockade runners was the West Indies port of Nassau, in the British Bahamas, where at one time thirty-five of the speedy ships rode at anchor.

Preparing for Battle These troops of the 69th New York State Militia, a largely Irish regiment, were photographed attending Sunday morning Mass in May 1861, just weeks before the Battle of Bull Run. Because the regiment was camped near Washington, D.C., women were able to visit.

But the lush days of blockade running finally passed as Union squadrons gradually pinched off the leading Southern ports from New Orleans to Charleston.

The most alarming Confederate threat to the blockade came in 1862. Resourceful Southerners raised and reconditioned a former wooden United States warship, the *Merrimack*, and plated its sides with old iron railroad rails. Renamed the *Virginia*, this clumsy but powerful monster easily destroyed two wooden ships of the Union navy in the Virginia waters of Chesapeake Bay; it also threatened catastrophe to the entire Yankee blockading fleet. A tiny Union ironclad, the *Monitor*, built in about one hundred days, arrived on the scene in the nick of time. For four hours, on March 9, 1862, the little "Yankee cheesebox on a raft" fought the wheezy *Merrimack* to a standstill. Britain and France had already built several powerful ironclads, but the first battle test of these new craft heralded the doom of wooden warships.

Merrimack and Monitor (1862) *Confederate and Union ironclads, respectively, whose successes against wooden ships signaled an end to wooden warships. They fought a historic though inconsequential battle in 1862.*

★ The Pivotal Point: Antietam

Robert E. Lee, having broken the back of McClellan's assault on Richmond, next moved northward. Emboldened by a victory at the **Second Battle of Bull Run** (August 29–30, 1862), Lee daringly thrust into Maryland. He hoped to strike a blow that would not only

Second Battle of Bull Run (August 1862) *Civil War battle that ended in a decisive victory for Confederate general Robert E. Lee, who was emboldened to push further into the North.*

330 CHAPTER 21

Map 21.1 Main Thrusts, 1861–1865 Northern strategists at first believed that the rebellion could be snuffed out quickly by a swift, crushing blow. But the stiffness of Southern resistance to the Union's early probes and the North's inability to strike with sufficient speed and severity revealed that the conflict would be a war of attrition, long and bloody.

encourage foreign intervention but also seduce the still-wavering Border State and its sisters from the Union. The Confederate troops sang lustily,

Thou wilt not cower in the dust,
Maryland! my Maryland!
Thy gleaming sword shall never rust,
Maryland! my Maryland!

But the Marylanders did not respond to the siren song. The presence among the invaders of so many blanketless, hatless, and shoeless soldiers dampened the state's ardor.

Events finally converged toward a critical battle at Antietam Creek, Maryland. Lincoln, yielding to popular pressure, hastily restored "Little Mac" to active command of the main Northern army. His soldiers tossed their caps skyward and hugged his horse as they hailed his return. McClellan succeeded in halting Lee at Antietam on September 17, 1862, in one of the bitterest and bloodiest days of the war. Antietam was more or less a draw militarily. But Lee, finding his thrust parried, retired across the Potomac. McClellan, unaccountably failing to pursue the retreating Confederate army, was removed from command for the second and final time.

The landmark **Battle of Antietam** was one of the most decisive engagements of world history—probably the most decisive of the Civil War. Jefferson Davis was perhaps never again so near victory as on that fateful summer day. The British and French governments were on the verge of diplomatic mediation, and a certain Washington rebuff might well

Battle of Antietam (September 1862)
Landmark battle in the Civil War that essentially ended in a draw but demonstrated the prowess of the Union army, forestalling foreign intervention and giving Lincoln the "victory" he needed to issue the Emancipation Proclamation.

Emancipation Proclamation (1863)
Declared all slaves in rebelling states to be free but did not affect slavery in nonrebelling Border States. The proclamation closed the door on possible compromise with the South and encouraged thousands of Southern slaves to flee to Union lines.

The Killing Fields of Antietam These Confederate corpses testify to the awful slaughter of the battle. The twelve-hour fight at Antietam Creek ranks as the bloodiest single day of the war, with more than ten thousand Confederate casualties and even more on the Union side. "At last the battle ended," one historian wrote, "smoke heavy in the air, the twilight quivering with the anguished cries of thousands of wounded men."

have spurred London and Paris into armed collusion with Richmond. But both Britain and France cooled off when the Union displayed unexpected power at Antietam, and their chill deepened with the passing months.

Bloody Antietam was also the long-awaited "victory" that Lincoln needed for launching his **Emancipation Proclamation**. Abolitionists such as Wendell Phillips had long been clamoring for action. By midsummer of 1862, with the Border States safely in the fold, Lincoln was ready to move. But he believed that issuing such an edict on the heels of military failure would seem like an act of desperation.

Antietam served as the needed emancipation springboard. The halting of Lee's offensive was just enough of a victory to justify Lincoln's issuing, on September 23, 1862, the preliminary Emancipation Proclamation. This hope-giving document announced that on January 1, 1863, the president would issue a final proclamation. On the scheduled date he fully redeemed his promise, and the Civil War became a moral crusade and what Lincoln called a "remorseless revolutionary struggle." After January 1, 1863, Lincoln said, "The character of the war will be changed. It will be one of subjugation.... The [old] South is to be destroyed and replaced by new propositions and ideas."

> *A Confederate soldier assigned to burial detail after the Seven Days' Battles (1862) wrote:*
>
> "The sights and smells that assailed us were simply indescribable... corpses swollen to twice their original size, some of them actually burst asunder with the pressure of foul gasses.... The odors were so nauseating and so deadly that in a short time we all sickened and were lying with our mouths close to the ground, most of us vomiting profusely."

★ A Proclamation Without Emancipation

Lincoln's Emancipation Proclamation of 1863 declared "forever free" the slaves in those Confederate areas still in rebellion. Bondsmen in the loyal Border States were not affected, nor were those in specific conquered areas in the South—all told, about 800,000. The tone of the document was dull and legalistic. But if Lincoln stopped short of a clarion call for a holy war to achieve freedom, he pointedly concluded his historic document by declaring that the Proclamation was an "act of justice" and calling for "the considerate judgment of mankind and the gracious favor of Almighty God."

The presidential pen did not formally strike the shackles from a single slave. Where Lincoln could presumably free the slaves—that is, in the loyal Border States—he refused to do so, lest he spur disunion. Where he could not—that is, in the Confederate states—he tried to. In short, where he *could* he would not, and where he *would* he could not. Thus, the Emancipation Proclamation was stronger on proclamation than emancipation.

Yet much unofficial do-it-yourself liberation did take place. Thousands of jubilant slaves, learning of the proclamation, flocked to the invading Union armies, stripping already rundown plantations of their work force. In this sense the Emancipation Proclamation was heralded by the drumbeat of running feet. The slaves' presence in Union army camps helped put emancipation atop Lincoln's agenda and strengthened the moral cause of the Union at home and abroad. At the same time Lincoln's proclamation clearly foreshadowed the ultimate doom of slavery. This was legally achieved by actions of the individual states and by their ratification of the **Thirteenth Amendment** (see the Appendix) in 1865. The Emancipation Proclamation also fundamentally changed the nature of the war because it effectively removed any chance of a negotiated settlement. Both sides now knew that the war would be a fight to the finish.

Thirteenth Amendment (1865)
Constitutional amendment prohibiting all forms of slavery and involuntary servitude. Former Confederate states were required to ratify the amendment prior to gaining reentry into the Union.

Public reactions to the long-awaited proclamation of 1863 were varied. "God bless Abraham Lincoln," exulted the antislavery editor Horace Greeley in his *New York Tribune*. But many ardent abolitionists complained that Lincoln had not gone far enough. On the other hand, formidable numbers of Northerners, especially in the "Butternut" regions of the Old Northwest and the Border States, felt that he had gone too far. A Democratic rhymester quipped,

> Honest old Abe, when the war first began,
> Denied abolition was part of his plan;
> Honest old Abe has since made a decree,
> The war must go on till the slaves are all free.
> As both can't be honest, will someone tell how,
> If honest Abe then, is he honest Abe now?

Opposition mounted in the North against supporting an "abolition war." Many Boys in Blue, especially from the Border States, had volunteered to fight for the Union, not against slavery. Desertions increased sharply. The crucial congressional elections in the autumn of 1862 went heavily against the administration, particularly in New York, Pennsylvania, and Ohio. Democrats even carried Lincoln's Illinois, although they did not secure control of Congress.

The Emancipation Proclamation caused an outcry to rise from the South that "Lincoln the fiend" was trying to stir up the "hellish passions" of a slave insurrection. Many European aristocrats sympathized with the Southern protests. But the Old World working classes, especially in Britain, reacted otherwise. They sensed that the proclamation spelled the ultimate doom of slavery, and many laborers became more determined than ever to oppose intervention. Gradually the diplomatic position of the Union improved.

Contending Voices

The Controversy over Emancipation

Not everyone in the North welcomed Lincoln's Emancipation Proclamation, as this condemnation from the Cincinnati Enquirer *reveals:*

"The hundreds of thousands, if not millions of slaves [the act] will emancipate will come North and West and will either be competitors with our white mechanics and laborers, degrading them by competition, or they will have to be supported as paupers and criminals at the public expense."

Lincoln defended his policies toward blacks in an open letter to Democrats on August 26, 1863:

"You say you will not fight to free negroes. Some of them seem willing to fight for you; but, no matter. Fight you, then, exclusively to save the Union. I issued the proclamation on purpose to aid you in saving the Union."

How were the causes of emancipating the slaves and saving the Union related in Lincoln's mind and strategy?

The North now had the much stronger moral cause. In addition to preserving the Union, it had committed itself to freeing the slaves. The moral position of the South was correspondingly diminished.

★ Blacks Battle Bondage

As Lincoln moved to emancipate the slaves, he also took steps to enlist blacks in the armed forces. Although some African Americans had served in the Revolution and the War of 1812, the regular army included no blacks at the war's outset, and the War Department refused to accept those free Northern blacks who tried to volunteer. (The Union navy, however, enrolled many blacks, mainly as cooks, stewards, and firemen.)

But as manpower ran low and emancipation was proclaimed, black enlistees were accepted, sometimes over ferocious protests from Northern as well as Southern whites. By war's end some 180,000 blacks served in the Union armies, most of them from the slave states, but many from the free-soil North. Blacks accounted for about 10 percent of the total enlistments in the Union forces on land and sea, and included two black Massachusetts regiments raised largely through the efforts of ex-slave Frederick Douglass.

Black fighting men unquestionably had their hearts in the war against slavery that the Civil War had become after Lincoln proclaimed emancipation. Participating in about five hundred engagements, they received twenty-two Congressional Medals of Honor—the highest military award. Their casualties were extremely heavy; more than thirty-eight thousand died, whether from battle, sickness, or reprisals from vengeful masters. Many, when captured, were put to death as slaves in revolt. In one notorious case, several black soldiers were massacred after they had formally surrendered at Fort Pillow, Tennessee. Thereafter, vengeful black units cried "Remember Fort Pillow!" as they swung into battle and vowed to take no prisoners.

For reasons of pride, prejudice, and principle, the Confederacy could not bring itself to enlist slaves until a month before the war ended. Meanwhile tens of thousands were impressed into building fortifications, supplying armies, and other war-connected activities. Slaves, moreover, were "the stomach of the Confederacy," for they kept the farms going while the white men fought.

In many ways the actions of Southern slaves hamstrung the Confederate war effort and subverted the institution of slavery. Fear of slave insurrection required many eligible young white men to serve as Confederate "home guards" far from the fighting front. Everyday forms of slave resistance and defiance increased, diminishing productivity and undermining discipline. As Union armies approached, escaping slaves served as spies, guides, and scouts. By war's end nearly half a million slaves took the ultimate risk of revolting "with their feet," abandoning their plantations. Although they stopped short of violent uprising, slaves contributed powerfully to the collapse of slavery and the disintegration of the antebellum Southern way of life.

★ Lee's Last Lunge at Gettysburg

After Antietam, Lincoln replaced McClellan as commander of the Army of the Potomac with General A. E. Burnside, whose ornate side-whiskers came to be known as "burnsides" or "sideburns." Protesting his unfitness for this responsibility, Burnside proved it when he launched a rash frontal attack on Lee's strong position at **Fredericksburg**, Virginia, on December 13, 1862. A chicken could not have lived in the line of fire, remarked one Confederate officer. More than ten thousand Northern soldiers were killed or wounded in "Burnside's Slaughter Pen."

A new slaughter pen was prepared when General Burnside yielded his command to General Joseph ("Fighting Joe") Hooker, an aggressive but headstrong officer. At Chancellorsville, Virginia, on May 2–4, 1863, Lee daringly divided his numerically inferior force and sent "Stonewall" Jackson to attack the Union flank. The strategy worked. Hooker, temporarily dazed by a near-hit from a cannonball, was badly beaten but not crushed.

Battle of Fredericksburg (December 1862) *Decisive victory in Virginia for Confederate Robert E. Lee, who successfully repelled a Union attack on his lines.*

Map 21.2 **The Battle of Gettysburg, 1863** With the failure of Pickett's charge, the fate of the Confederacy was sealed—though the Civil War dragged on for almost two more bloody years.

This victory was probably Lee's most brilliant, but it was dearly bought. Jackson was mistakenly shot by his own men in the gathering dusk and died a few days later. "I have lost my right arm," lamented Lee. Southern folklore relates how Jackson outflanked the angels while galloping into Heaven.

Lee now prepared to follow up his brilliant victory by invading the North again, this time through Pennsylvania. A decisive blow would add strength to the noisy peace prodders in the North and would also encourage foreign intervention—still a Southern hope. Quite by accident, the Northern army, now under the scholarly and unspectacular General George G. Meade, took its stand on the rolling hills near quiet little **Gettysburg**, Pennsylvania (see Map 21.2). There his 92,000 men in blue locked horns in furious combat with Lee's 76,000 gray-clad warriors. The battle seesawed across the rolling green slopes for three agonizing days, July 1–3, 1863, and the outcome was in doubt until the very end. The failure of General George Pickett's magnificent but futile charge finally broke the back of the Confederate attack—and broke the heart of the Confederate cause.

Pickett's charge has been called the "high tide of the Confederacy." It defined both the northernmost point reached by any significant Southern force and the last real chance for the Confederates to win the war. After Gettysburg, Lincoln spurned Southern efforts to reach a negotiated peace settlement between the parties. From now on the Southern cause was doomed. Yet the men of Dixie fought for nearly two years longer, through sweat, blood, and weariness of spirit.

Later in that dreary autumn of 1863, with the graves still fresh, Lincoln journeyed to Gettysburg to dedicate the cemetery. Following a two-hour speech by the orator of the

Battle of Gettysburg (July 1863) *Civil War battle in Pennsylvania that ended in Union victory, spelling doom for the Confederacy, which never again managed to invade the North. Site of General George Pickett's daring but doomed charge on the Northern lines.*

Examining the Evidence
Abraham Lincoln's Gettysburg Address

Political speeches are unfortunately all too often composed of claptrap, platitudes, and just plain bunk—and they are frequently written by someone other than the person delivering them. But Abraham Lincoln's address at the dedication of the cemetery at Gettysburg battlefield on November 19, 1863, has long been recognized as a masterpiece of political oratory and as a foundational document of the American political system, as weighty a statement of the national purpose as the Declaration of Independence (which it deliberately echoes in its statement that all men are created equal) or even the Constitution itself. In just 272 simple but eloquent words that Lincoln himself indisputably wrote, he summarized the case for American nationhood.

1. What did Lincoln believe was at stake in the Civil War? (Conspicuously, he made no direct mention of slavery in this address.) Another speech that Lincoln gave in 1861 offers some clues. He said, "I have often inquired of myself what great principle or idea it was that kept this [nation] together. It was not the mere separation of the colonies from the motherland, but that sentiment in the Declaration of Independence which gave liberty not alone to the people of this country, but hope to the world, for all future time."

2. Using the text of the Gettysburg Address, consider: How does Lincoln use language and images of parent and child, conception, rebirth, and sacrifice to present the American nation as a living entity?

3. In Lincoln's view, how does "last full measure of devotion" given by the fallen soldiers "hallow" the cause of liberty and Union and create new obligations for "we the living"?

335

Gettysburg Address (1863) *Abraham Lincoln's oft-quoted speech, delivered at the dedication of the cemetery at Gettysburg battlefield. In the address, Lincoln framed the war as a means to uphold the values of liberty.*

day, Lincoln delivered his two-minute **Gettysburg Address**. Lincoln's noble remarks were branded by the *London Times* as "ludicrous" and by Democratic editors as "dishwatery" and "silly." The address attracted relatively little attention at the time, but the president was speaking for the ages.

★ The War in the West

Events in the western theater of the war at last provided Lincoln with an able general who did not have to be shelved after every reverse. Ulysses S. Grant had been a mediocre student at West Point, although he did do well in mathematics and horsemanship. After fighting creditably in the Mexican War, he was stationed at isolated frontier posts, where boredom and loneliness drove him to drink. Resigning from the army to avoid a court-martial for drunkenness, he failed at various business ventures, and when war came he was working in his father's leather store in Illinois for $50 a month.

Battle of Fort Henry and Fort Donelson (February 1862) *Key victory for Union general Ulysses S. Grant, it secured the North's hold on Kentucky and paved the way for Grant's attacks deeper into Tennessee.*

Battle of Shiloh (April 1862) *Bloody battle on the Tennessee-Mississippi border that left more than twenty-three thousand soldiers dead, wounded, or missing, and ended in a marginal Union victory.*

siege of Vicksburg (1863) *Two-and-a-half-month siege of a Confederate fort on the Mississippi River in Mississippi. Vicksburg finally fell to Ulysses S. Grant in July of 1863, giving the Union army control of the Mississippi River and splitting the South in two.*

Grant did not cut much of a figure. The shy and silent shopkeeper was short, stooped, awkward, stubble-bearded, and sloppy in dress. He managed with some difficulty to secure a colonelcy in the volunteers. From then on his military experience—combined with his boldness, resourcefulness, and doggedness—catapulted him on a meteoric rise.

Grant's first signal success came in the northern Tennessee theater (see Map 21.3). After heavy fighting, he captured **Fort Henry and Fort Donelson** on the Tennessee and Cumberland Rivers in February 1862. When the Confederate commander at Fort Donelson asked for terms, Grant bluntly demanded "an unconditional and immediate surrender."

Grant's triumph in Tennessee was crucial. It not only riveted Kentucky more securely to the Union but also opened the gateway to the strategically important region of Tennessee and eventually to Georgia and the heart of Dixie. Grant next attempted to exploit his victory by capturing the junction of the main Confederate north–south and east–west railroads in the Mississippi Valley at Corinth, Mississippi. But a Confederate force foiled his plans in the gory **Battle of Shiloh**, just over the Tennessee border from Corinth, on April 6–7, 1862. The impressive Confederate showing at Shiloh confirmed that there would be no quick end to the war in the West.

Lincoln resisted all demands for the removal of "Unconditional Surrender" Grant, insisting, "I can't spare this man; he fights." When talebearers later told Lincoln that Grant drank too much, the president allegedly replied, "Find me the brand, and I'll send a barrel to each of my other generals."

Other Union thrusts were in the making. In the spring of 1862, a flotilla commanded by David G. Farragut joined with a Northern army to strike the South a staggering blow by seizing New Orleans. With Union gunboats both ascending and descending the Mississippi, the eastern part of the Confederacy was left with a jeopardized back door. Through this narrowing entrance, between Vicksburg and Port Hudson, flowed herds of vitally needed cattle and other provisions from Louisiana and Texas. The fortress of Vicksburg, located on a hairpin turn of the Mississippi, was the South's sentinel protecting the lifeline to the western sources of supply.

In command of the Union forces attacking Vicksburg, General Grant displayed rare skill and daring in the teeth of grave difficulties. The **siege of Vicksburg** was his best-fought campaign of the war. The beleaguered city at length surrendered on July 4, 1863, with the garrison reduced to eating mules and rats. Five days later came the fall of Port Hudson, the last Southern bastion on the Mississippi. The spinal cord

Map 21.3 The Mississippi River and Tennessee, 1862–1863

General Ulysses S. Grant and General Robert E. Lee Trained at West Point, Grant (left) proved to be a better general than a president. Oddly, he hated the sight of blood and recoiled from rare beef. Lee (right), a gentlemanly general in an ungentlemanly business, remarked when the Union troops were bloodily repulsed at Fredericksburg, "It is well that war is so terrible, or we should get too fond of it."

of the Confederacy was now severed, and, in Lincoln's quaint phrase, the Father of Waters at last flowed "unvexed to the sea."

The Union's victory at Vicksburg (July 4, 1863) came the day after the Confederate defeat at Gettysburg. The political significance of these back-to-back military successes was monumental. Reopening the Mississippi helped to quell strong peace agitation in southern Ohio, Indiana, and Illinois. Confederate control of the Mississippi had cut off that region's usual trade routes down the Ohio–Mississippi River system to New Orleans, thus adding economic pain to that border section's already shaky support for the "abolition war." The twin victories also conclusively tipped the diplomatic scales in favor of the North, as Britain stopped delivery of the Laird rams to the Confederates and as France killed a deal for the sale of six naval vessels to the Richmond government. By the end of 1863 all Confederate hopes for foreign help were irretrievably lost.

★ Sherman Scorches Georgia

General Grant, the victor of Vicksburg, was now transferred to the east Tennessee theater, where Confederates had driven Union forces from the battlefield of Chickamauga into the city of Chattanooga. Grant won a series of desperate engagements in November 1863 in the vicinity of besieged Chattanooga, including Missionary Ridge and Lookout Mountain ("the Battle Above the Clouds"). Chattanooga was liberated, the state was cleared of Confederates, and the way was thus opened for an invasion of Georgia. Grant was rewarded by being made general in chief. Georgia's conquest was entrusted to General William Tecumseh Sherman. Red-haired and red-bearded, grim and ruthless, Sherman captured

Map 21.4 Sherman's March, 1864–1865

Atlanta in September 1864 and burned the city in November of that year. He then daringly left his supply base, lived off the country for some 250 miles, and weeks later emerged at Savannah on the sea.

Sherman's hated "Blue Bellies," sixty thousand strong, cut a sixty-mile-wide swath of destruction through Georgia. They burned buildings, leaving only the blackened chimneys ("Sherman's Sentinels"). They tore up railroad rails, heated them red-hot, and twisted them into "iron doughnuts" and "Sherman's hairpins." They bayoneted family portraits and ran off with valuable "souvenirs." "War . . . is all hell," admitted Sherman later, and he proved it by his efforts to "make Georgia howl." One of the major purposes of **Sherman's march** was to destroy supplies destined for the Confederate army and to weaken the morale of the men at the front by waging war on their homes (see Map 21.4).

Sherman was a pioneer practitioner of total war. His success in "Shermanizing" the South was attested by increasing numbers of Confederate desertions. Although effective, his methods were unquestionably brutal. At times the discipline of his army broke down, as roving riffraff (Sherman's "bummers") engaged in an orgy of pillaging. "Sherman the Brute" was universally damned in the South.

After seizing Savannah as a Christmas present for Lincoln, Sherman's army veered north into South Carolina, where the destruction was even more vicious. Many Union soldiers believed that this state, the "hell-hole of secession," had wantonly provoked the war. The capital city, Columbia, was put to the torch. Crunching northward, Sherman's conquering army had rolled deep into North Carolina by the time the war ended.

★ The Politics of War

Presidential elections come by the calendar and not by the crisis. The election of 1864 fell most inopportunely in the midst of war.

Political infighting in the North added greatly to Lincoln's cup of woe. Factions within his own party, distrusting his ability or doubting his commitment to abolition, sought to tie his hands or even remove him from office. Conspicuous among his critics

Sherman's march (1864–1865) *Union general William Tecumseh Sherman's destructive march through Georgia. An early instance of "total war," purposely targeting infrastructure and civilian property to diminish morale and undercut the Confederate war effort.*

Congressional Committee on the Conduct of the War (1861–1865) *Established by Congress during the Civil War to oversee military affairs. Largely under the control of radical Republicans, the committee agitated for a more vigorous war effort and actively pressed Lincoln on the issue of emancipation.*

Sherman's March to the Sea, 1863–1864 Sherman's army inflicted cruel destruction along its route, an early instance of a tactic that came to characterize modern warfare, in which civilians are considered legitimate targets.

was a group led by the overambitious secretary of the Treasury, Salmon Chase. Especially burdensome to Lincoln was the creation of the **Congressional Committee on the Conduct of the War**, formed in late 1861. It was dominated by "radical" Republicans who pressed Lincoln zealously on emancipation.

Most dangerous of all to the Union cause were the Northern Democrats. Deprived of the talent that had departed with the Southern wing of the party, those Democrats remaining in the North were left with the taint of association with the seceders. Tragedy befell the Democrats—and the Union—when their gifted leader, Stephen A. Douglas, died of typhoid fever seven weeks after the war began. Unshakably devoted to the Union, he probably could have kept much of his following on the path of loyalty.

Lacking a leader, the Democrats divided. A large group of "War Democrats" patriotically supported the Lincoln administration, but tens of thousands of "Peace Democrats" did not. At the extreme were the so-called **Copperheads**, named for the poisonous snake that strikes without a warning rattle. Copperheads openly obstructed the war through attacks against the draft, against Lincoln, and especially, after 1863, against emancipation. They denounced the president as the "Illinois Ape" and condemned the "Nigger War." They commanded considerable political strength in the southern parts of Ohio, Indiana, and Illinois.

Notorious among the Copperheads was Ohio Congressman Clement L. Vallandigham. This tempestuous character possessed brilliant oratorical gifts and unusual talents for

Copperheads *Northern Democrats who obstructed the war effort by attacking Abraham Lincoln, the draft, and, after 1863, emancipation.*

A letter picked up on a dead Confederate in North Carolina and addressed to his "deer sister" concluded that:

it was "dam fulishness" trying to "lick shurmin." He had been getting "nuthin but hell & lots uv it" ever since he saw the "dam yanks," and he was "tirde uv it." He would head for home now, but his old horse was "plaid out." If the "dam yankees" had not got there yet, it would be a "dam wunder." They were thicker than "lise on a hen and a dam site ornerier."

stirring up trouble. A Southern partisan, he publicly demanded an end to the "wicked and cruel" war. In 1863 he was convicted and sentenced to prison by a military tribunal for treasonable utterances. Lincoln decided that if Vallandigham liked the Confederates so much, he ought to be banished to their lines. This was done. But Vallandigham was not so easily silenced. Making his way to Canada, he ran for the governorship of Ohio from foreign soil and polled a substantial but insufficient vote.

★ The Election of 1864

As the election of 1864 approached, Lincoln's precarious authority depended on his retaining Republican support while spiking the threat from the Peace Democrats and the Copperheads. Fearing defeat, the Republican party executed a clever maneuver. Joining with the War Democrats, it proclaimed itself to be the **Union party**. Thus, the Republican party passed temporarily out of existence.

Lincoln's renomination at first encountered surprisingly strong opposition. Hostile factions whipped up considerable agitation to shelve him in favor of Secretary of the Treasury Chase. Lincoln was accused of lacking force, of not having won the war, and of having shocked many sensitive souls by his ill-timed and earthy jokes. But the "ditch Lincoln" move collapsed, and he was nominated by the Union party without serious dissent.

Lincoln's running mate was ex-tailor Andrew Johnson, a loyal War Democrat from Tennessee who had been a small slaveowner when the conflict began. Johnson was placed on the Union party ticket to "sew up" the election by attracting War Democrats and voters in the Border States and, sadly, with no proper regard for the possibility that Lincoln might die in office.

Embattled Democrats—regulars and Copperheads—nominated the deposed and overcautious war hero, General McClellan. The Copperheads managed to force into the Democratic platform a plank denouncing the prosecution of the war as a failure. But McClellan, who could not otherwise have faced his old comrades-in-arms, repudiated this defeatist declaration.

The campaign was noisy and nasty. Lincoln's reelection was at first gravely in doubt. The war was going badly, and Lincoln himself gave way to despondency, fearing that political defeat was imminent. But the atmosphere of gloom was changed electrically, as balloting day neared, by a succession of Northern victories. Admiral Farragut captured Mobile, Alabama, after defiantly shouting the famous order, "Damn the torpedoes! Go ahead." General Sherman seized Atlanta. General ("Little Phil") Sheridan laid waste the verdant Shenandoah Valley of Virginia so thoroughly that in his words, "a crow could not fly over it without carrying his rations with him."

The president pulled through, but nothing more than necessary was left to chance. At election time many Northern soldiers were furloughed home to support Lincoln at the polls. Other Northern soldiers cast their ballots at the front.

Bolstered by the "bayonet vote," Lincoln vanquished General McClellan by 212 electoral votes to 21, losing only Kentucky, Delaware, and New Jersey (see Map 21.5). But "Little Mac" ran a closer race than the electoral count indicates. He netted a healthy 45 percent of the popular vote, 1,803,787 to Lincoln's 2,206,938, piling up much support in the Old Northwest, in New York, and also in his native state of Pennsylvania.

One of the most crushing defeats suffered by the South was the defeat of the Northern Democrats in 1864. The electoral removal of Lincoln was the last ghost of a hope for a Confederate victory, and Southern soldiers would wishfully shout, "Hurrah for McClellan!" When Lincoln triumphed, desertions from the sinking Southern ship increased sharply.

★ Grant Outlasts Lee

After Gettysburg, Grant was brought in from the West over Meade, who was blamed for failing to pursue the defeated but always dangerous Lee. Lincoln needed a general who, employing the superior resources of the North, would have the intestinal stamina to drive straight ahead, regardless of casualties. A soldier of bulldog tenacity, Grant was the man

Union party (1864) A coalition party of prowar Democrats and Republicans formed during the 1864 election to defeat antiwar Northern Democrats.

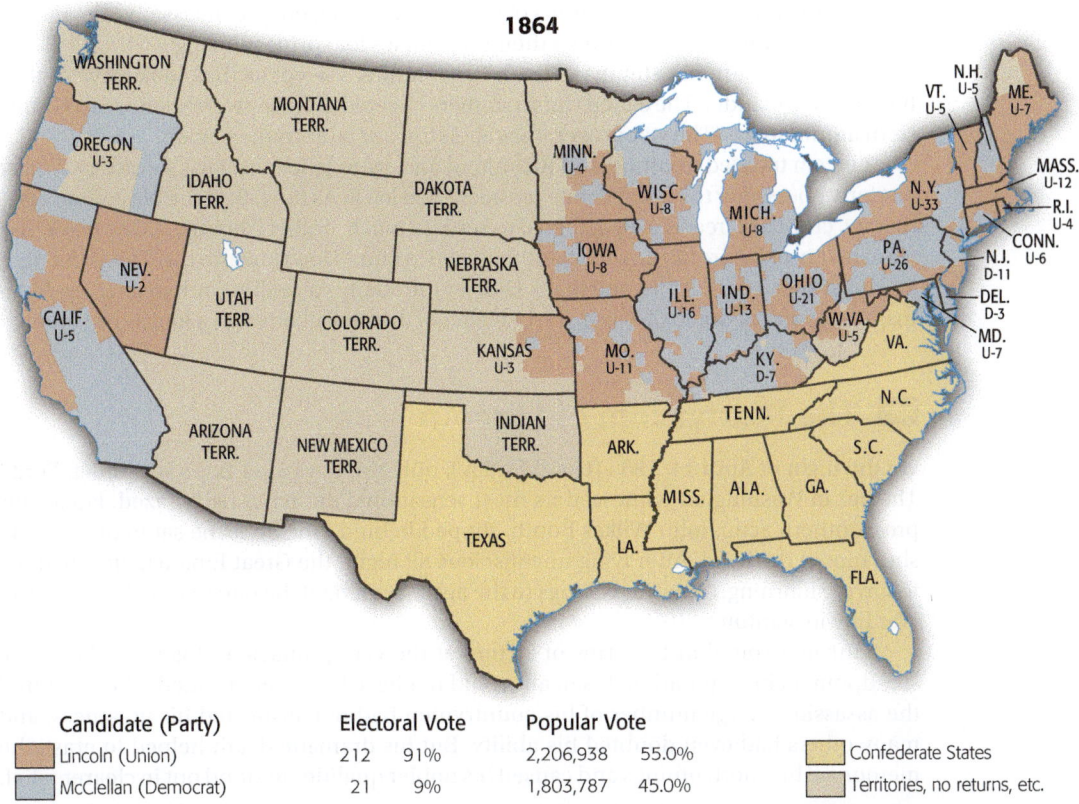

Map 21.5 Presidential Election of 1864 (showing popular vote by county) Lincoln also carried California, Oregon, and Nevada, but there was a considerable McClellan vote in each. Note McClellan's strength in the Border States and in the southern tier of Ohio, Indiana, and Illinois—the so-called "Butternut" region.

for this meat-grinder type of warfare. His overall basic strategy was to assail the enemy's armies simultaneously so that they could not assist one another and hence could be destroyed piecemeal. His personal motto was "When in doubt, fight."

A grimly determined Grant, with more than 100,000 men, struck toward Richmond. He engaged Lee in a series of furious battles in the Wilderness of Virginia during May and June 1864, notably in the leaden hurricane of the "Bloody Angle" and "Hell's Half Acre." In this **Wilderness Campaign** Grant suffered about 50,000 casualties, or nearly as many men as Lee had commanded at the start. But Lee lost about as heavily in proportion.

In a ghastly gamble, on June 3, 1864, Grant ordered a frontal assault on the impregnable Confederate position of Cold Harbor. Union soldiers advanced to almost certain death with papers pinned on their backs bearing their names and addresses. In a few minutes, about seven thousand men were killed or wounded.

Public opinion in the North was appalled by this "blood and guts" fighting, and critics assailed "Grant the Butcher." But Grant's reputation was undeserved, while Lee's was overrated. Lee's rate of loss (one casualty for every five soldiers) was the highest of any general in the war. By contrast, Grant lost one in ten. It was Lee, not Grant, who turned the eastern campaign into a war of attrition fought in the trenches. Lee's new defensive posture in turn forced Grant into some brutal arithmetic. Grant could trade two men for one and still beat the enemy to his knees. "I propose to fight it out on this line," he wrote, "if it takes all summer." It did—and it also took all autumn, all winter, and a part of the spring.

In February 1865, the Confederates, tasting the bitter dregs of defeat, tried desperately to negotiate for peace between the "two countries." But Lincoln could accept nothing short of Union and emancipation, and the Southerners could accept nothing short of independence. So the tribulation wore on—amid smoke and agony—to its terrible climax.

The end came with dramatic suddenness. Rapidly advancing Northern troops captured Richmond and then cornered Lee at **Appomattox Courthouse** in Virginia, in April 1865. Grant—stubble bearded and informally dressed—met with Lee on the ninth, Palm

Wilderness Campaign (1864–1865) *A series of brutal clashes between Ulysses S. Grant's and Robert E. Lee's armies in Virginia, leading up to Grant's capture of Richmond in April of 1865. Having lost Richmond, Lee surrendered to Grant at Appomattox Courthouse.*

Appomattox Courthouse *Site where Robert E. Lee surrendered to Ulysses S. Grant in April 1865 after almost a year of brutal fighting throughout Virginia in the "Wilderness Campaign."*

Sunday, and granted generous terms of surrender. Among other concessions, the hungry Confederates were allowed to keep their own horses for spring plowing.

Tattered Southern veterans—"Lee's Ragamuffins"—wept as they took leave of their beloved commander. The elated Union soldiers cheered, but they were silenced by Grant's stern admonition, "The war is over; the rebels are our countrymen again."

Lincoln traveled to conquered Richmond and sat in Jefferson Davis's evacuated office just forty hours after the Confederate president had left it. As he walked the blasted streets of the city, crowds of freed slaves gathered to see and touch "Father Abraham." One black man fell to his knees before the Emancipator, who said to him, "Don't kneel to me. This is not right. You must kneel to God only, and thank Him for the liberty you will enjoy hereafter." Sadly, as many freed slaves would discover, the hereafter of their full liberty was a long time coming.

★ The Martyrdom of Lincoln

On the night of April 14, 1865 (Good Friday), only five days after Lee's surrender, Ford's Theater in Washington witnessed its most sensational drama. A half-crazed, fanatically pro-Southern actor, John Wilkes Booth, slipped behind Lincoln as he sat in his box and shot him in the head. After lying unconscious all night, the Great Emancipator died the following morning. "Now he belongs to the ages," remarked the once-critical Secretary of War Edwin Stanton.

Lincoln expired in the arms of victory at the very pinnacle of his fame. From the standpoint of his reputation, his death could not have been better timed if he had hired the assassin. A large number of his countrymen had not suspected his greatness, and many others had even doubted his ability. But his dramatic death helped to erase the memory of his shortcomings and caused his nobler qualities to stand out in clearer relief.

New York Mourns Lincoln's Death, April 25, 1865 Lincoln's body traveled by train to lie in state in fourteen cities before arriving at his final resting place of Springfield, Illinois. In New York City, 160,000 mourners accompanied the hearse as the funeral procession slowly made its way down Broadway. Scalpers sold choice window seats for four dollars and up. Blacks were barred from participating, until the mayor changed his mind at the last minute—but only if they marched at the rear.

The full impact of Lincoln's death was not at once apparent to the South. Hundreds of bedraggled ex-Confederate soldiers cheered, as did some Southern civilians and Northern Copperheads, when they learned of the assassination. But as time wore on, increasing numbers of Southerners perceived that Lincoln's death was a calamity for them. Belatedly they recognized that his kindliness and moderation would have been the most effective shields between them and vindictive treatment by the victors. The assassination unfortunately increased the bitterness of the North, partly because of the fantastic rumor that Jefferson Davis had plotted it.

A few historians have argued that if the Great Emancipator had lived, he would have suffered Andrew Johnson's fate of being impeached by the embittered members of his own party who demanded harshness, not forbearance, toward the South. Lincoln no doubt would have clashed with Congress. But the sure-footed and experienced Lincoln could hardly have blundered into the same quicksand that engulfed Johnson. Lincoln was a victorious president, and there is no arguing with victory. In addition to his powers of leadership refined in the war crucible, Lincoln possessed in full measure tact, sweet reasonableness, and an uncommon amount of common sense. Andrew Johnson, hot-tempered and impetuous, lacked all of these priceless qualities. Ford's Theater, with its tragic murder of Lincoln, set the stage for the wrenching ordeal of Reconstruction.

★ The Aftermath of the Nightmare

The Civil War took a grisly toll in gore, about as much as all of America's subsequent wars combined. More than 600,000 men died in action or of disease, and in all over a million were killed or seriously wounded. The numbers of dead greatly exceeded those in World War II. They amounted to 2 percent of the entire nation's population. The modern equivalent would be a loss of some 6 million American lives. To its lasting hurt, the nation lost the cream of its young manhood and potential leadership.

Direct monetary costs of the conflict totaled about $15 billion. But this colossal figure does not include continuing expenses, such as pensions and interest on the national debt. The intangible costs—dislocations, wasted energies, lowered ethics, blasted lives, bitter memories, and burning hates—cannot be calculated.

The greatest constitutional decision of the century, in a sense, was written in blood and handed down at Appomattox Courthouse, near which Lee surrendered. The extreme states' righters were crushed. The national government, tested in the fiery furnace of war, emerged unbroken. Nullification and secession, those twin nightmares of previous decades, were laid to rest.

Beyond doubt the Civil War—the nightmare of the Republic—was the supreme test of American democracy. It finally answered the question, in the words of Lincoln at Gettysburg, whether a nation dedicated to such principles "can long endure." The preservation of democratic ideals, though not an officially announced war aim, was subconsciously one of the major objectives of the North.

Victory for Union arms also provided inspiration to the champions of democracy and liberalism the world over. The great English **Reform Bill of 1867**, under which Britain became a true political democracy, was passed two years after the Civil War ended. American democracy had proved itself, and its success was an additional argument used by the disfranchised British masses in securing similar blessings for themselves.

The "Lost Cause" of the South was lost, but few Americans today would argue that the end result was not for the best. The shameful cancer of slavery was sliced away by the sword, and African Americans were at last in a position to claim their rights to life, liberty, and the pursuit of happiness. The nation was again united politically, though for many generations it was still divided spiritually by the passions of the war. Grave dangers were averted by a Union victory, including the indefinite prolongation of the "peculiar institution," the unleashing of the "slave power" on weak Caribbean neighbors, and the transformation of the area from Panama to Hudson's Bay into an armed camp, with several hostile states constantly snarling and sniping at one another. America still had a long way to go to make the promises of freedom a reality for all its citizens, black and white. But emancipation laid the necessary groundwork, and a united and democratic United States was free to fulfill its destiny as the dominant republic of the hemisphere—and eventually of the world.

Reform Bill of 1867 *Granted suffrage to all male British citizens, dramatically expanding the electorate. The success of the American democratic experiment, reinforced by the Union victory in the Civil War, was used as one of the arguments in favor of the bill.*

Thinking Globally

The Era of Nationalism

The American Civil War was rooted in America's "peculiar institution" of slavery as well as uniquely American controversies about westward expansion. But it was also part of a wider phenomenon that transformed many parts of the world in the mid-nineteenth century: nationalism. To be sure, some ancient societies, such as the Greeks and the Hebrews, had a sense of themselves as distinct peoples who shared a common culture and history. But the creation of robust nation-states with strong central governments ruling over large populations that considered themselves part of an enduring community was of decidedly modern origin. Nationalism was anchored in the French and American Revolutions, with their emphasis on popular sovereignty and on a government that expressed the will of a population that saw itself not just as a random assembly of persons, but as a distinctive and coherent "people," often bonded by religion and language. Nationalism also owed much to modern technologies such as the steamship, railroad, and telegraph, which extended both the emotional range of fellow feeling and the geographical reach of centralized authority. The convergence of these several ninteenth-century developments, intellectual as well as material, made possible the creation of the "imagined communities" called nations.

In the early nineteenth century, only Britain and France could claim to be nation-states in the modern sense. Central Europe remained a patchwork of major and minor principalities. Italy, in the words of the Austrian diplomat Klemens von Metternich, was merely "a geographic expression," as several small duchies and overgrown city-states uneasily coexisted on the Italian peninsula. Both Spain and Japan looked united on the map, but both notoriously lacked internal cohesion. And in the United States, sectional and state loyalties continued to compete with notions of the *national* identity.

But within just a dozen years, between 1859 and 1871, Prince Otto von Bismarck created a modern Germany; Count Camillo di Cavour united Italy ("We have made Italy; now we must make Italians," quipped one Italian wit); a new Meiji emperor launched Japan on a dramatic program of rapid modernization; and the American Civil War, in Abraham Lincoln's words, gave the United States "a new birth of freedom" as a unified country, as well as a significantly invigorated federal government. Before the Civil War, it was said, the United States *were*; after the Civil War, the United States *was*.

These several consolidations created the model for modern states that has prevailed ever since. The rise of nationalism fostered the growth of unprecedentedly powerful governments able to command deep loyalty from millions of people and consequently to marshal enormous economic and military resources—for good or ill. Nationalism was everywhere accompanied by some degree of political democratization and the expansion of public services, as freshly created or reinvigorated central governments sought to secure the loyalty of peoples newly brought under their sways. Bismarck, for example, supported universal suffrage and social insurance for German workers (establishing precedents that would much later be adopted in the United States). The new Italy and Meiji Japan adopted fairly liberal voting laws and programs for universal education. Britain's Reform Bill of 1867 enfranchised 1.5 million adult, male, urban householders, effectively doubling the British electorate.

In the United States, Civil War-era constitutional amendments at least nominally guaranteed the right to vote to adult African American males, while the federal government adopted ambitious plans to facilitate the construction of transcontinental railroads, distribute the public lands under the Homestead Act, and support higher education under the Morrill Land-Grant College Act. The Civil War defined a historic pivot in the role of federal power. Of the twelve amendments to the Constitution passed before 1865, eleven were designed to *limit* the authority of the federal government. Of the fifteen amendments passed since the Civil War, nine include the phrase "Congress shall have the power to *enforce* this article by appropriate legislation."

The words "nation" and "native" derive from the same Latin root, denoting birth or birthplace. Nationalism is at bottom a sentiment of common feeling or shared identity, generally among people born in the same place. The term therefore implies boundaries, territorial as well as psychological. It defines who is included as well as who is excluded. ("No nation imagines itself coterminous with mankind," wrote one scholar of nationalism.) Nationalism can breed exclusionary and nativist pathologies, as well as chauvinism, jingoism, and imperialism. The United States was no exception to these patterns. Nativists mounted increasingly effective anti-immigrant campaigns in the post-Civil War era, beginning with the Chinese Exclusion Act of 1882 and culminating in the highly restrictionist National Origins Act of 1924. As Germany and Italy acquired colonies in Africa and Japan tightened its grip on Taiwan, Korea, and parts of Manchuria, the United States also joined the imperial scramble, annexing the Philippines, Puerto Rico, Guam, and Samoa before the century's end.

Varying Viewpoints

What Were the Consequences of the Civil War?

With the end of the Civil War in 1865, the United States was permanently altered, despite the reunification of the Union and the Confederacy. Slavery was officially banned, secession was a dead issue, and industrial growth surged forward. For the first time, the United States could securely consider itself a singular nation rather than a union of states. Though sectional differences remained, there would be no return to the unstable days of precarious balancing between Northern and Southern interests. With the Union's victory, power rested firmly with the North, and it would orchestrate the future development of the country. According to historian Eric Foner, the war redrew the economic and political map of the country.

The constitutional impact of the terms of the Union victory created some of the most far-reaching transformations. Before the Civil War, all the constitutional amendments has been designed to limit the power of the federal government over citizens. In contrast, the Thirteenth Amendment, which abolished slavery, and the revolutionary Fourteenth Amendment, which conferred citizenship and guaranteed civil rights to all those born in the United States, dramatically expanded federal power and laid the basis for further governmental involvement in the lives of American citizens. Historian James McPherson has noted still other ways in which the Civil War extended the authority of the central government. It expanded federal powers of taxation. It encouraged the government to develop the National Banking System, print currency, and conscript an army. It made the federal courts more influential. And through the Freedmen's Bureau, which aided former slaves in the South, it instituted the first federal social welfare agency. With each of these actions, the nation moved toward a more powerful federal government, invested with the authority to protect civil rights, aid its citizens, and enforce laws in an aggressive manner that superseded state powers.

Yet some scholars have disputed whether the Civil War marked an absolute watershed in American history. They correctly note that racial inequality scandalously persisted after the Civil War, despite the abolition of slavery and the supposed protections extended by federal civil rights legislation. Others have argued that the industrial growth of the post–Civil War era had its real roots in the Jacksonian era, and thus cannot be ascribed solely to war. Thomas Cochran has even argued that the Civil War may have retarded overall industrialization rather than advancing it. Regional differences between North and South endured, moreover, even down to the present day.

Even so, the argument that the Civil War launched a modern America remains convincing. The lives of Americans, white and black, North and South, were transformed by the war experience. Industry entered a period of unprecedented growth, having been stoked by the transportation and military needs of the Union army. The emergence of new, national legal and governmental institutions marked the birth of the modern American state. All considered, it is hard to deny that the end of the Civil War brought one chapter of the nation's history to a close, while opening another.

CHAPTER SUMMARY ★ ★ ★ ★ ★ ★ ★ ★ ★ ★ ★ ★ ★

The Union defeats at Bull Run and the Peninsula Campaign ended Northern complacency about a quick victory and also prevented a quick return of the South to the Union with slavery intact. George McClellan and other early Union generals proved unable to defeat the tactically brilliant Confederate armies under Lee. But the Union naval blockade did place a slowly devastating economic noose around the South.

The political and diplomatic dimensions of the war quickly became critical. In order to retain the Border States, Lincoln first deemphasized any intention to destroy slavery. But the Battle of Antietam in 1862 enabled Lincoln to prevent foreign intervention and turn the struggle into a total war against slavery. Blacks and abolitionists joined enthusiastically in a war for emancipation, but white resentment in part of the North created political problems for Lincoln.

The Union gained military success in the West, taking Vicksburg in 1863 and cutting the Confederacy in half. At the same time, Lee's failed invasion of the North ended at Gettysburg and completely turned the military tide against the South. Southern resistance remained strong, with the hope that politically defeatist "Copperheads" would force a negotiated peace settlement and achieve Confederate independence. But the Union victories at Atlanta and Mobile assured Lincoln's success in the election of 1864 and ended the last Confederate hopes. Shortly after Grant's army forced Lee's surrender at Appomattox, Lincoln's assassination increased bitter sectional feelings. The war ended the issues of disunion and slavery, but at a tremendous cost to both North and South.

KEY TERMS

Battle of Bull Run (Manassas Junction) (327)
Peninsula Campaign (328)
Merrimack and *Monitor* (329)
Second Battle of Bull Run (329)
Battle of Antietam (330)
Emancipation Proclamation (330)
Thirteenth Amendment (332)
Battle of Fredericksburg (333)
Battle of Gettysburg (334)
Gettysburg Address (336)
Battle of Fort Henry and Fort Donelson (336)
Battle of Shiloh (336)
siege of Vicksburg (336)
Sherman's march (338)
Congressional Committee on the Conduct of the War (338)
Copperheads (339)
Union party (340)
Wilderness Campaign (341)
Appomattox Courthouse (341)
Reform Bill of 1867 (343)

PEOPLE TO KNOW

Thomas J. ("Stonewall") Jackson
George B. McClellan
Robert E. Lee
A. E. Burnside
Joseph ("Fighting Joe") Hooker
George G. Meade
George Pickett
Ulysses S. Grant
William Tecumseh Sherman
Salmon Chase
Clement L. Vallandigham
John Wilkes Booth

MindTap is a fully online, highly personalized learning experience built upon Cengage Learning content. MindTap combines student learning tools—readings, multimedia, activities, and assessments—into a singular Learning Path that guides students through the course.

Chapter 22

The Ordeal of Reconstruction
1865–1877

With malice toward none, with charity for all, with firmness in the right as God gives us to see the right, let us strive on to finish the work we are in, to bind up the nation's wounds, to care for him who shall have borne the battle and for his widow and orphan, to do all which may achieve and cherish a just and lasting peace among ourselves and with all nations.

ABRAHAM LINCOLN, SECOND INAUGURAL ADDRESS, MARCH 4, 1865

Chapter Outline

- The Defeated South
- The Freed Slaves
- President Andrew Johnson's Reconstruction Policies
- Moderate and Radical Republicans
- Congressional Reconstruction Policies
- Military Reconstruction, 1867–1877
- Freed People Enter Politics
- "Black Reconstruction" and the Ku Klux Klan
- The Impeachment of Andrew Johnson
- The Legacy of Reconstruction
- *Examining the Evidence: Letter from a Freedman to His Old Master, 1865*
- *Varying Viewpoints: How Radical Was Reconstruction?*

The battle was done, the buglers silent. Bone-weary and bloodied, the American people, North and South, now faced the staggering challenges of peace. Four questions loomed large. How would the South, physically devastated by war and socially revolutionized by emancipation, be rebuilt? How would the liberated blacks fare as free men and women? How would the Southern states be reintegrated into the Union? And who would direct the process of Reconstruction—the Southern states themselves, the president, or Congress?

FOCUS QUESTIONS

1. What were the major problems facing the South and the nation after the Civil War?
2. How did African Americans and whites, Southerners and Northerners, each respond to the end of slavery and approach race relations under new conditions of freedom?
3. How did Andrew Johnson's political incompetence and missteps enable the Radical Republicans to gain control of Reconstruction policy?
4. What were the actual effects of congressional Reconstruction in the South, and how did militant white opposition and growing northern apathy eventually bring an end to Reconstruction in the Compromise of 1877?
5. What were the primary successes and failures of Reconstruction, and what legacy did it leave for later generations of Americans?

CHRONOLOGY

1863	Lincoln announces "10 percent" Reconstruction plan	1867	Reconstruction Act Tenure of Office Act United States purchases Alaska from Russia
1864	Lincoln vetoes Wade-Davis Bill		
1865	Lincoln assassinated Johnson issues Reconstruction proclamation Congress refuses to seat Southern congressmen Freedmen's Bureau established Southern states pass Black Codes	1868	Johnson impeached and acquitted Johnson pardons Confederate leaders
		1870	Fifteenth Amendment ratified
		1870–1871	Force Acts
1866	Congress passes Civil Rights Bill over Johnson's veto Congress passes Fourteenth Amendment Johnson-backed candidates lose congressional election *Ex parte Milligan* case Ku Klux Klan founded	1872	Freedmen's Bureau ended
		1877	Reconstruction ends

★ The Problems of Peace

Other questions also clamored for answers. What should be done with the captured Confederate ringleaders? All Confederate officials were subject to charges of treason, and during the war a popular Northern song had been "Hang Jeff Davis to a Sour Apple Tree." Davis was clapped into prison for two years, but no treason trials were ever held. President Andrew Johnson pardoned all "rebel" leaders as a sort of Christmas present in 1868. Congress removed their civil disabilities thirty years later.

Dismal indeed was the picture presented by the war-wracked South when the rattle of musketry faded. Not only had an age perished, but a civilization had collapsed, in both its economic and its social structure. The moonlight-and-magnolia Old South, largely imaginary in any case, had forever gone with the wind.

Handsome cities of yesteryear, such as Charleston and Richmond, were rubble-strewn and weed-choked. An Atlantan returned to his once-fair hometown and remarked, "Hell has laid her egg, and right here it hatched." Economic life had creaked to a halt. Banks and businesses had locked their doors, ruined by runaway inflation. Factories were smokeless, silent, dismantled. The transportation system had broken down completely. Efforts to untwist the rails corkscrewed by Sherman's soldiers proved bumpily unsatisfactory.

Agriculture—the economic lifeblood of the South—was almost hopelessly crippled. Once-white-carpeted cotton fields yielded a lush harvest of nothing but green weeds. The slave-labor system had collapsed, seed was scarce, and livestock had been driven off by plundering Yankees. Pathetic instances were reported of men hitching themselves to plows, while women and children gripped the handles.

The princely planter aristocrats were humbled by the war—at least temporarily. Reduced to proud poverty, they faced charred and gutted mansions, lost investments, and almost worthless land. Their investment of more than $2 billion in slaves, their primary form of wealth, had evaporated with emancipation.

Beaten but unbent, many high-spirited white Southerners remained dangerously defiant. They cursed the "damn yankees" and spoke of "your government" in Washington instead of "our government." Conscious of no crime, these former Confederates continued to believe that their view of secession was correct and that the "lost cause" was still a just war. One popular anti-Union song ran,

> *I'm glad I fought agin her, I only wish we'd won,*
> *And I ain't axed any pardon for anything I've done.*

Such attitudes boded ill for the prospects of painlessly binding up the Republic's wounds.

⭐ Freedmen Define Freedom

Confusion abounded in the still-smoldering South about the precise meaning of "freedom" for blacks. Emancipation took effect haltingly and unevenly in different parts of the conquered Confederacy. As Union armies marched in and out of various localities, many blacks found themselves emancipated and re-enslaved. A North Carolina slave estimated that he had celebrated freedom about twelve times. In some regions planters stubbornly protested that slavery was legal until state legislatures or the Supreme Court might act. For many slaves the shackles of bondage were not struck off in a single mighty blow; long-suffering blacks often had to pry off their chains link by link.

The variety of responses to emancipation, by whites as well as blacks, illustrated the sometimes startling complexity of the master–slave relationship. Loyalty to the plantation master prompted some slaves to resist the liberating Union armies, while other slaves' pent-up bitterness burst violently forth on the day of liberation. In one instance, a group of Virginia slaves laid twenty lashes on the back of their former master—a painful dose of his own favorite medicine.

Prodded by the bayonets of Yankee armies of occupation, all masters were eventually forced to recognize their slaves' permanent freedom. The once-commanding planter would assemble his former human chattels in front of the porch of the "big house" and announce their liberty. Though some blacks initially responded to news of their emancipation with suspicion and uncertainty, they soon celebrated their newfound freedom. Many took new names in place of the ones given by their masters and demanded that whites formally address them as "Mr." or "Mrs."

Tens of thousands of emancipated blacks took to the roads, some to test their freedom, others to search for long-lost spouses, parents, and children. Emancipation thus strengthened the black family, and many newly freed men and women formalized "slave marriages" for personal and pragmatic reasons, including the desire to make their children legal heirs.

Whole communities sometimes moved together in search of opportunity. From 1878 to 1880, some twenty-five thousand blacks from Louisiana, Texas, and Mississippi surged in a mass exodus to Kansas.

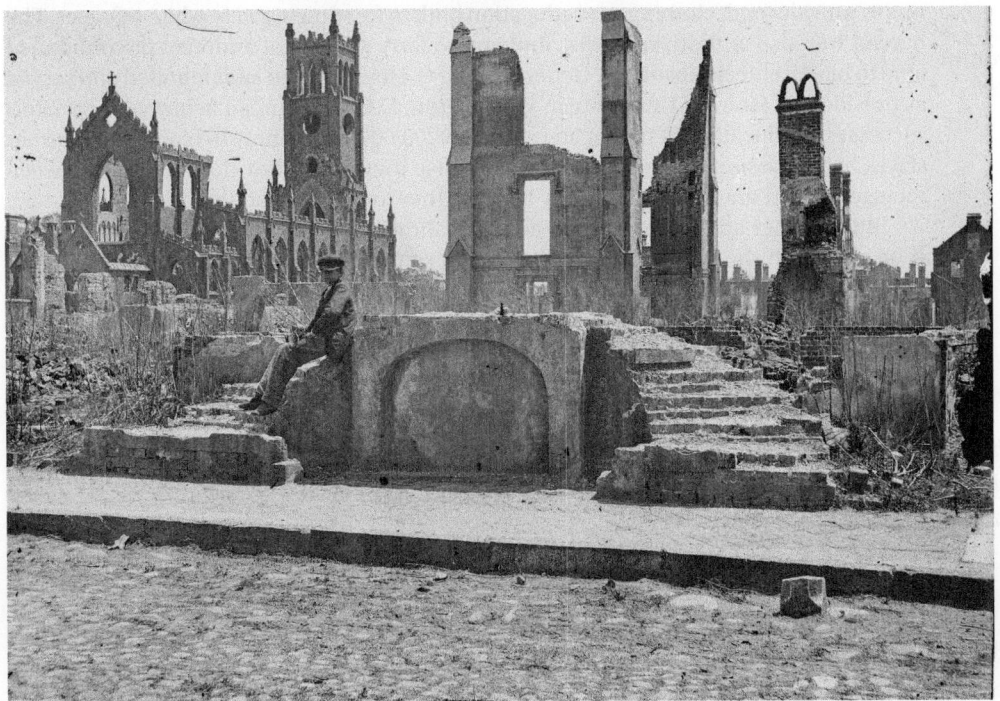

Charleston, South Carolina, in Ruins, April 1865 Rebel troops evacuating Charleston blew up military supplies to deny them to General William Tecumseh Sherman's forces. The explosions ignited fires that all but destroyed the city.

The church became the focus of black community life in the years following emancipation. As slaves, blacks had worshiped alongside whites, but now they formed their own churches pastored by their own ministers. Black churches grew robustly. The 150,000-member black Baptist Church of 1850 reached 500,000 by 1870, while the African Methodist Episcopal Church quadrupled in size from 100,000 to 400,000 in the first decade after emancipation. These churches formed the bedrock of black community life, and they soon gave rise to other benevolent, fraternal, and mutual aid societies. All these organizations helped blacks protect their newly won freedom.

Emancipation also meant education for many blacks. Learning to read and write had been a privilege generally denied to them under slavery. Freedmen wasted no time establishing societies for self-improvement, which undertook to raise funds to purchase land, build schoolhouses, and hire teachers. With qualified black teachers in short supply, they accepted the aid of Northern white women sent by the American Missionary Association. They also turned to the federal government for help. The freed blacks were going to need all the friends—and power—they could muster in Washington.

> *Houston H. Holloway, age twenty at the time of his emancipation, recalled his feelings upon hearing of his freedom:*
>
> *"I felt like a bird out of a cage. Amen. Amen. Amen. I could hardly ask to feel any better than I did that day.... The week passed off in a blaze of glory."*
>
> *The reunion of long-lost relatives also inspired joy; one Union officer wrote home:*
>
> *"Men are taking their wives and children, families which had been for a long time broken up are united and oh! such happiness. I am glad I am here."*

★ The Freedmen's Bureau

Abolitionists had long preached that slavery was a degrading institution. Now the emancipators were faced with the brutal reality that the former slaves were overwhelmingly unskilled, unlettered, without property or money, and with scant knowledge of how to survive as free people. To cope with this problem throughout the conquered South, Congress created the **Freedmen's Bureau** on March 3, 1865.

On paper at least, the bureau was intended to be a kind of primitive welfare agency. It was to provide food, clothing, and education both to freedmen and to white refugees. The bureau was also authorized to distribute up to forty acres of abandoned or confiscated land to black settlers. Headed by General Oliver O. Howard, who later founded and served as president of Howard University in Washington, D.C., the bureau achieved its greatest successes in education. It taught an estimated 200,000 blacks how to read. Many former slaves had a passion for learning, partly because they wanted to close the gap between themselves and the whites and partly because they longed to read the Word of God.

But in other areas the bureau's accomplishments were meager—or even mischievous. Although the bureau was authorized to settle former slaves on forty-acre tracts, little confiscated Confederate land actually passed into black hands. Instead local administrators often collaborated with planters in expelling blacks from towns and cajoling them into signing labor contracts to work for their former masters. Still, the white South resented the bureau as a meddlesome federal interloper that threatened to upset white racial dominance. President Andrew Johnson, who shared the white supremacist views of most white Southerners, repeatedly tried to kill it, and the bureau expired in 1872.

Freedmen's Bureau (1865–1872) *Created to aid newly emancipated slaves by providing food, clothing, medical care, education, and legal support. Its achievements were uneven and depended largely on the quality of local administrators.*

> *Women from the North enthusiastically embraced the opportunity to go south and teach in Freedmen's Bureau schools for emancipated blacks. One volunteer explained her motives:*
>
> *"I thought I must do something, not having money at my command, what could I do but give myself to the work.... I would go to them, and give them my life if necessary."*

★ Johnson: The Tailor President

Few presidents have ever been faced with a more perplexing sea of troubles than that confronting Andrew Johnson. What manner of man was this dark-eyed, black-haired Tennessean, now chief executive by virtue of the bullet that killed Lincoln?

Educating Young Freedmen and Women, 1870s Freed slaves in the South regarded schooling as the key to improving their children's lives and the fulfillment of a long-sought right that had been denied blacks in slavery. These well-dressed school children are lined up outside their rural, one-room schoolhouse alongside their teachers, both black and white.

No citizen, not even Lincoln, has ever reached the White House from humbler beginnings. Born to impoverished parents in North Carolina and orphaned early, Johnson never attended school but was apprenticed to a tailor at age ten. Ambitious to get ahead, he taught himself to read, and later his wife taught him to write and do simple arithmetic. Like many another self-made man, he was inclined to overpraise his maker.

Johnson early became active in politics in Tennessee, where he had moved when seventeen years old. He shone as an impassioned champion of the poor whites against the planter aristocrats, and as a two-fisted stump speaker before angry and heckling crowds. Elected to Congress, he attracted much favorable attention in the North when he refused to secede with his own state. After Tennessee was partially liberated by Union armies, he was appointed war governor of the state.

Political exigency next thrust Johnson into the vice presidency. Lincoln's Union party in 1864 needed to attract support from the War Democrats and other pro-Southern elements, and Johnson, a Democrat, seemed to be the ideal man.

"Old Andy" Johnson was no doubt a man of parts—unpolished parts. He was intelligent, able, forceful, and steadfastly devoted to duty and to the Constitution. Yet the man who had raised himself from the tailor's bench to the president's chair was a misfit. A Southerner who did not understand the North, a Tennessean who had earned the distrust of the South, a Democrat who had never been accepted by the Republicans, a president who had not been elected to the office, he was not at home in a Republican White House. Hotheaded, contentious, and stubborn, Johnson was the wrong man in the wrong place at the wrong time. A Reconstruction policy devised by the angels might well have failed in his tactless hands.

Examining the Evidence

Letter From a Freedman to His Old Master, 1865

What was it like to experience the transition from slavery to freedom? Four million southern blacks faced this exhilarating and formidable prospect with the end of the war. For historians, recovering the African American perspective on emancipation is challenging. Unlike their white masters, freed blacks left few written records. But one former slave captured in a letter to his "Old Master" (whose surname he bore) the heroic determination of many blacks to build new independent and dignified lives for themselves and their families.

During the war Jourdon Anderson escaped slavery in Tennessee with his wife and two daughters. After relocating to the relative safety of Ohio, he received a communication from his former owner asking him to return. In his bold reply, reportedly "dictated by the old servant" himself, Anderson expressed his family's new expectations for life as free people and an uneasiness about his former master's intentions. He made reference to his "comfortable home," his daughters' schooling, the church that he and his wife were free to attend regularly, and the peace of mind that came with knowing that "my girls [would not be] brought to shame by the violence and wickedness of their young masters." To test the white man's sincerity, Anderson and his wife asked for the astronomical figure of $11,680 in back wages from decades as slaves. He closed by reiterating that "the great desire of my life is to give my children an education and have them form virtuous habits." This rare letter demonstrates that many black correspondents may have been illiterate, but they were hardly inarticulate. And they asserted themselves as parents, workers, and citizens not only from the distance of a former free state such as Ohio but also deep within the former slave states of the South.

1. Was the tone of Anderson's letter (and postscript) serious, sarcastic, or tongue-in-cheek? What specific phrases support your answer?

2. How did the eventual accomplishments of Reconstruction correspond with the initial expectations of people like Anderson and his former owner?

3. What does this letter reveal about the complicated relationships between freedmen and their former masters? Is the relationship a "personal" one, or was it entirely dominated by Jourdon Anderson's having been held by Colonel P. H. Anderson as "property"?

Letter from a Freedman to his Old Master.

The following is a genuine document. It was *dictated* by the old servant, and contains his ideas and forms of expression.   [Cincinnati Commercial.

DAYTON, Ohio, August 7, 1865.

To my Old Master, Col. P. H. ANDERSON, Big Spring, Tennessee.

SIR: I got your letter and was glad to find that you had not forgotten Jordan, and that you wanted me to come back and live with you again, promising to do better for me than anybody else can. I have often felt uneasy about you. I thought the Yankees would have hung you long before this for harboring Rebs. they found at your house. I suppose they never heard about your going to Col. Martin's to kill the Union soldier that was left by his company in their stable. Although you shot at me twice before I left you, I did not want to hear of your being hurt, and am glad you are still living. It would do me good to go back to the dear old home again and see Miss Mary and Miss Martha and Allen, Esther, Green and Lee. Give my love to them all, and tell them I hope we will meet in the better world, if not in this. I would have gone back to see you all when I was working in the Nashville Hospital, but one of the neighbors told me Henry intended to shoot me if he ever got a chance.

I want to know particularly what the good chance is you propose to give me. I am doing tolerably well here; I get $25 a month, with victuals and clothing; have a comfortable home for Mandy (the folks here call her Mrs. Anderson), and the children, Milly Jane and Grundy, go to school and are learning well; the teacher says Grundy has a head for a preacher. They go to Sunday-School, and Mandy and me attend church regularly. We are kindly treated; sometimes we over—

As to my freedom, which you say I can have, there is nothing to be gained on that score, as I got my free-papers in 1864 from the Provost-Marshal-General of the Department at Nashville. Mandy says she would be afraid to go back without some proof that you are sincerely disposed to treat us justly and kindly—and we have concluded to test your sincerity by asking you to send us our wages for the time we served you. This will make us forget and forgive old sores, and rely on your justice and friendship in the future. I served you faithfully for thirty-two years, and Mandy twenty years, at $25 a month for me, and $2 a week for Mandy. Our earnings would amount to $11,680. Add to this the interest for the time our wages has been kept back and deduct what you paid for our clothing and three doctor's visits to me, and pulling a tooth for Mandy, and the balance will show what we are in justice entitled to. Please send the money by Adams Express, in care of V. Winters, esq., Dayton, Ohio. If you fail to pay us for faithful labors in the past we can have little faith in your promises in the future.

P. S.—Say howdy to George Carter, and thank him for taking the pistol from you when you were shooting at me.

New York Tribune Tuesday, August 22, 1865

Presidential Reconstruction

Even before the shooting war had ended, the political war over Reconstruction had begun. Abraham Lincoln believed that the Southern states had never legally withdrawn from the Union. Their formal restoration to the Union would therefore be relatively simple. Accordingly, Lincoln in 1863 proclaimed his **"10 percent" Reconstruction plan**. It decreed that a state could be reintegrated into the Union when 10 percent of its voters in the presidential election of 1860 had taken an oath of allegiance to the United States and pledged to abide by emancipation. The next step would be formal erection of a state government. Lincoln would then recognize the purified regime.

Lincoln's proclamation provoked a sharp reaction in Congress, where Republicans feared the restoration of the planter aristocracy to power and the possible re-enslavement of blacks. Republicans therefore rammed through Congress in 1864 the **Wade-Davis Bill**. The bill required that 50 percent of a state's voters take the oath of allegiance and demanded stronger safeguards for emancipation than Lincoln's as the price of readmission. Republicans were outraged when Lincoln "pocket-vetoed" this bill by refusing to sign it after Congress had adjourned.

The controversy surrounding the Wade-Davis Bill had revealed deep differences between the president and Congress. Unlike Lincoln, many in Congress insisted that the seceders had indeed left the Union—had "committed suicide" as republican states—and had therefore forfeited all their rights. They could be readmitted only as "conquered provinces" on such conditions as Congress should decree.

The episode further revealed differences among two emerging Republican factions, moderates and radicals. The majority moderate group tended to agree with Lincoln that the seceded states should be restored to the Union as simply and swiftly as reasonable—though on Congress's terms, not the president's. The minority radical group believed that before the South could be restored, its social structure should be uprooted, the haughty planters punished, and the newly emancipated blacks protected by federal power.

After President Lincoln's assassination in April 1865, some radicals hoped that spiteful Andy Johnson, who shared their hatred for the planter aristocracy, would also share their desire to reconstruct the South with a rod of iron. But Johnson soon disillusioned them. He quickly recognized several of Lincoln's 10 percent governments, and on May 29, 1865, he issued his own Reconstruction proclamation. It disfranchised certain leading Confederates and called for special state conventions, which were required to repeal secession, repudiate all Confederate debts, and ratify the slave-freeing Thirteenth Amendment.

Johnson, savoring his dominance over the high-toned aristocrats who now begged his favor, granted pardons in abundance. Bolstered by the political resurrection of the planter elite, the recently rebellious states moved rapidly in the second half of 1865 to organize governments. But as the pattern of the new governments became clear, Republicans of all stripes grew furious.

"10 percent" Reconstruction plan (1863) Introduced by President Lincoln, it proposed that a state be readmitted to the Union once 10 percent of its voters had pledged loyalty to the United States and promised to honor emancipation.

Wade-Davis Bill Passed by Congressional Republicans in response to Abraham Lincoln's "10 percent plan," but never signed or enacted by Lincoln, it would have required that 50 percent of a state's voters pledge allegiance to the Union, and intended to set stronger safeguards for emancipation. Reflected divisions between Congress and the President, and between radical and moderate Republicans, over the treatment of the defeated South.

The Baleful Black Codes

Among the first acts of the new Southern regimes sanctioned by Johnson was the passage of the iron-toothed **Black Codes**. These laws were designed to regulate the affairs of the emancipated blacks, much as the slave statutes had done in pre-Civil War days. The Black Codes aimed, first of all, to ensure a stable and subservient labor force. Dire penalties were therefore imposed by the codes on blacks who "jumped" their labor contracts, which usually committed them to work for the same employer for one year, and generally at pittance wages.

The codes also sought to restore as nearly as possible the pre-emancipation system of race relations. Freedom was legally recognized, as were some other privileges, such as the right to marry. But all the codes forbade a black to serve on a jury or vote, and some codes even barred blacks from renting or leasing land.

These oppressive laws mocked the ideal of freedom, so recently purchased by buckets of blood. The Black Codes imposed terrible burdens on the unfettered blacks, struggling against mistreatment and poverty to make their way as free people. Thousands of impoverished former slaves slipped into virtual peonage as sharecropper farmers, as did many landless whites.

Black Codes (1865–1866) Laws passed throughout the South to restrict the rights of emancipated blacks, particularly with respect to negotiating labor contracts. Increased Northerners' criticisms of President Andrew Johnson's lenient Reconstruction policies.

Contending Voices

Radical Republicans and Southern Democrats

Representative Thaddeus Stevens (1792–1868), a leading radical Republican, argued in September 1865 for a sweeping plan of compulsory land redistribution and political reform to smash the Southern plantation system:

"The whole fabric of southern society *must* be changed, and never can it be done if this opportunity is lost. . . . If the South is ever to be made a safe republic let her lands be cultivated by the toil of the owners or the free labor of intelligent citizens."

Two months later, the new governor of South Carolina, James Lawrence Orr (1822–1873), voiced elite Southerners' insistence that emancipated slaves must be kept tied to the South's prewar economic system, even if now by contract rather than bondage:

"[Emancipated slaves] must be restrained from theft, idleness, vagrancy and crime, and taught the absolute necessity of strictly complying with their contracts for labor. . . . The labor of every negro in the State is needed, if not to till the soil, in some other useful employment—for the culture of cotton and rice; and, in menial occupations, it is very doubtful whether any laborers in this country or in Europe can supply his place."

> Why were these competing visions of the political future of the post–Civil War South so linked to labor and land policies?

Pacific Railroad Act (1862) *Helped fund the construction of the Union Pacific transcontinental railroad with the use of land grants and government bonds.*

The Black Codes made an ugly impression in the North. If the former slaves were being re-enslaved, people asked one another, had not the Boys in Blue spilled their blood in vain? Had the North really won the war?

★ Congressional Reconstruction

These questions grew more insistent when the congressional delegations from the newly reconstituted Southern states presented themselves in the Capitol in December 1865. To the shock and disgust of the Republicans, many former Confederate leaders were on hand to claim their seats.

The appearance of these ex-rebels was a natural but costly blunder. Voters of the South, seeking able representatives, had turned instinctively to their experienced statesmen. But most of the Southern leaders were tainted by active association with the "lost cause." Among them were four former Confederate generals, five colonels, and various members of the Richmond cabinet and Congress. Worst of all, there was the shrimpy but brainy Alexander Stephens, ex-vice president of the Confederacy, still under indictment for treason.

The presence of these "whitewashed rebels" infuriated the Republicans in Congress. The war had been fought to restore the Union, but not on these kinds of terms. Most Republicans balked at giving up the political advantage they had enjoyed while the South had been "out" from 1861 to 1865. They had passed much legislation that favored the North, such as the Morrill Act, the **Pacific Railroad Act**, and the Homestead Act. On the first day of the congressional session, December 4, 1865, they banged shut the door in the face of the newly elected Southern delegations.

Looking to the future, the Republicans were alarmed to realize that a restored South would be stronger than ever in national politics. Before the war a black slave had counted as three-fifths of a person in apportioning congressional representation. But now, owing to full counting of free blacks, the eleven rebel states were entitled to twelve more votes in Congress and twelve more presidential electoral votes than they had previously enjoyed. Again, angry voices in the North raised the cry, "Who won the war?"

Republicans had good reason to fear that ultimately they might be elbowed aside. Southerners might join hands with Democrats in the North and win control of Congress or maybe even the White House. If that happened, they could perpetuate the Black Codes, virtually re-enslaving the blacks. They could dismantle the economic program of the Republican party and possibly even repudiate the national debt. President Johnson thus deeply disturbed the congressional Republicans when he announced on December 6, 1865, that the recently rebellious states had satisfied his conditions and that in his view the Union was now restored.

★ Johnson Clashes with Congress

A clash between president and Congress was now inevitable. It exploded into the open in February 1866, when the president vetoed a bill (later repassed) extending the life of the controversial Freedmen's Bureau.

Aroused, the Republicans swiftly struck back. In March 1866 they passed the **Civil Rights Bill**, which conferred on blacks the privileges of American citizenship and struck at the Black Codes. President Johnson resolutely vetoed this forward-looking measure, but in April congressmen steamrollered it over his veto—something they repeatedly did henceforth. The hapless president, dubbed "Andy Veto," had his presidential wings clipped short, as Congress increasingly assumed the dominant role in running the government.

The Republicans now undertook to rivet the principles of the Civil Rights Bill into the Constitution as the **Fourteenth Amendment**, so that no future Congress could repeal the law. The proposed amendment, as approved by Congress and sent to the states in June 1866 and ratified in 1868, was sweeping. The amendment (1) conferred civil rights, including citizenship but excluding the franchise, on the freedmen; (2) reduced proportionately the representation of a state in Congress and in the Electoral College if it denied blacks the ballot; (3) disqualified from federal and state office former Confederates who as federal officeholders had once sworn to "support the Constitution of the United States"; and (4) guaranteed the federal debt, while repudiating all Confederate debts. (See the text of the Fourteenth Amendment in the Appendix.)

The radical faction was disappointed that the Fourteenth Amendment did not grant the right to vote, but all Republicans agreed that no state should be welcomed back into the Union fold without first ratifying the Fourteenth Amendment. Yet President Johnson advised the Southern states to reject it, and all of the "sinful eleven," except Tennessee, defiantly spurned the amendment.

Civil Rights Bill (1866) *Passed over Andrew Johnson's veto, the bill aimed to counteract the Black Codes by conferring citizenship on African Americans and making it a crime to deprive blacks of their rights to sue, testify in court, or hold property.*

Fourteenth Amendment (ratified 1868) *Constitutional amendment that extended civil rights to freedmen and prohibited states from taking away such rights without due process.*

★ Swinging 'Round the Circle with Johnson

As 1866 lengthened, the battle grew between Congress and the president. Now the issue was whether Reconstruction was to be carried on with or without the Fourteenth Amendment. The Republicans would settle for nothing less; indeed, they soon insisted on even more.

The crucial congressional elections of 1866—more crucial than some presidential elections—were fast approaching. Johnson was naturally eager to escape from the clutch of Congress by securing a majority favorable to his soft-on-the-South policy. Invited to dedicate a Chicago monument to Stephen A. Douglas, he undertook to speak at various cities en route in support of his views.

Johnson's famous "swing 'round the circle," beginning in the late summer of 1866, was a seriocomedy of errors. The president delivered a series of "give 'em hell" speeches, in which he accused the radicals in Congress of having planned large-scale antiblack riots and murder in the South. As he spoke, hecklers hurled insults at him. Reverting to his stump-speaking days in Tennessee, he shouted back angry retorts, amid cries of "You be damned!" and "Don't get mad, Andy!" The dignity of his high office sank to a new low.

As a vote-getter, Johnson was highly successful—for the opposition. His inept speech-making heightened the cry to "Stand by Congress" against the "Tailor of the Potomac." When the ballots were counted, the Republicans had rolled up more than a two-thirds majority in both houses of Congress.

★ Republican Reconstruction

The Republicans now had a veto-proof Congress and virtually unlimited control of Reconstruction policy. But moderates and radicals still disagreed over the best course to pursue in the South.

The radicals were led in the Senate by the courtly and principled idealist Massachusetts Senator Charles Sumner, who tirelessly labored not only for black freedom but for racial equality. In the House the most powerful radical was crusty and vindictive Pennsylvania Congressman Thaddeus Stevens. An unswerving friend of blacks, he insisted that after his death he be buried in a black cemetery. Still opposed to rapid restoration of the Southern states, the radicals led by Sumner and Stevens wanted to keep them out

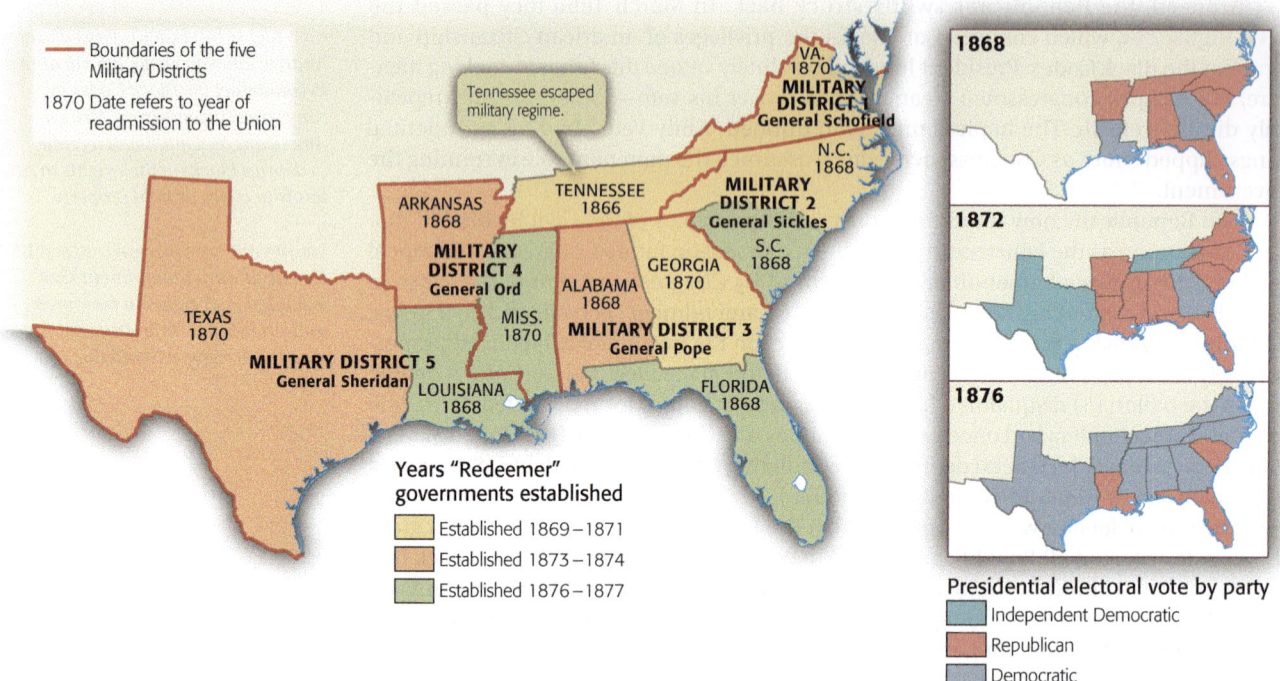

Map 22.1 Military Reconstruction, 1867 (five districts and commanding generals) For many white Southerners, military Reconstruction amounted to turning the knife in the wound of defeat. An often-repeated story of later years had a Southerner remark, "I was sixteen years old before I discovered that damnyankee was two words."

as long as possible and apply federal power to bring about a drastic social and economic transformation in the South.

But moderate Republicans, invoking the principles of states' rights and self-government, preferred policies that restrained the states from abridging citizens' rights, rather than policies that directly involved the federal government in individual lives. The actual policies adopted by Congress showed the influence of both these schools of thought, though the moderates, as the majority faction, had the upper hand. And one thing both groups had come to agree on by 1867 was the necessity to enfranchise black voters, even if it took federal troops to do it.

Against a backdrop of vicious and bloody race riots that had erupted in several Southern cities, Congress passed the **Reconstruction Act** on March 2, 1867 (see Map 22.1). This drastic legislation divided the South into five military districts, each commanded by a Union general and policed by blue-clad soldiers, about twenty thousand all told.

Congress additionally laid down stringent requirements for the readmission of the seceded states. The wayward states were required to ratify the Fourteenth Amendment, giving the former slaves their rights as citizens, and to guarantee in their state constitutions full suffrage for their former adult male slaves. Yet the act, reflecting moderate sentiment, stopped short of giving the freedmen land or education at federal expense. The overriding purpose of the moderates was to create an electorate in Southern states that would vote those states back into the Union on acceptable terms and thus free the federal government from direct responsibility for the protection of black rights. As later events would demonstrate, this approach proved woefully inadequate to the cause of justice for the blacks.

The radical Republicans still worried that once the unrepentant states were readmitted, they would amend their constitutions to withdraw the ballot from the blacks. They therefore sought the ironclad safeguard of incorporating black suffrage in the federal Constitution. This goal was finally achieved by the **Fifteenth Amendment**, passed by Congress in 1869 and ratified by the required number of states in 1870. (See the Appendix.)

Reconstruction Act (1867) *Passed by the newly elected Republican Congress, it divided the South into five military districts, disenfranchised former confederates, and required that Southern states both ratify the Fourteenth Amendment and write state constitutions guaranteeing freedmen the franchise before gaining readmission to the Union.*

Fifteenth Amendment (ratified 1870) *Prohibited states from denying citizens the franchise on account of race. It disappointed feminists who wanted the Amendment to include guarantees for women's suffrage.*

Military Reconstruction of the South not only usurped certain functions of the president as commander in chief but set up a martial regime of dubious legality. The Supreme Court had already ruled, in the case *Ex parte Milligan* (1866), that military tribunals could not try civilians, even during wartime, in areas where the civil courts were open. Peacetime military rule seemed starkly contrary to the spirit of the Constitution, but the circumstances were extraordinary and for the time being the Supreme Court avoided offending the Republican Congress.

Prodded into line by federal bayonets, the Southern states got on with the task of constitution making. By 1870 all of them had reorganized their governments and had been accorded full rights. The hated "bluebellies" (federal troops) remained until the new regimes—usually called "radical" regimes—appeared to be firmly entrenched. Yet when the U.S. Army finally left a state, its government swiftly passed into the hands of white "Redeemer" regimes, which were inevitably Democratic. Finally, in 1877, the last federal muskets were removed from state politics, and the "solid" Democratic South congealed.

The passage of the three Reconstruction-era Amendments—the Thirteenth, Fourteenth, and Fifteenth—delighted former abolitionists but deeply disappointed advocates of women's rights. Women had played a prominent part in the prewar abolitionist movement, and in the eyes of many women the struggle for black freedom and the crusade for women's rights were one and the same. Now, feminist leaders reeled with shock when the Fourteenth Amendment, which defined equal national citizenship, for the first time inserted the word *male* into the Constitution in referring to a citizen's right to vote. When the Fifteenth Amendment proposed to prohibit denial of the vote on the basis of "race, color, or previous condition of servitude," women's rights leaders Susan B. Anthony and Elizabeth Cady Stanton wanted the word *sex* added to the list. They lost this battle, too. Fifty years would pass before the Constitution granted women the right to vote.

> *The prominent suffragist and abolitionist Susan B. Anthony (1820-1906) was outraged over the proposed exclusion of women from the Fourteenth Amendment. In a conversation with her former male allies Wendell Phillips and Theodore Tilton, she reportedly held out her arm and declared:*
>
> "Look at this, all of you. And hear me swear that I will cut off this right arm of mine before I will ever work for or demand the ballot for the negro and not the woman."

Ex parte Milligan (1866) Civil War Era case in which the Supreme Court ruled that military tribunals could not be used to try civilians if civil courts were open.

★ The Realities of Radical Reconstruction in the South

Blacks now had freedom, of a sort. By 1867 Republican hesitation over black voting had given way to a hard determination to enfranchise the former slaves wholesale and immediately, while thousands of white Southerners were being denied the right to vote. By glaring contrast, most of the Northern states, before ratification of the Fifteenth Amendment in 1870, withheld the ballot from their tiny black minorities. White Southerners naturally concluded that the Republicans were hypocritical in insisting that blacks in the South be allowed to vote.

Having gained their right to suffrage, Southern black men seized the initiative and began to organize politically. Their primary vehicle became the Union League, originally a pro-Union organization based in the North. Assisted by Northern blacks, freedmen turned the League into a network of political clubs that educated members in their civic duties and campaigned for Republican candidates. The League's mission soon expanded to include building black churches and schools, representing black grievances before local employers and governments, and recruiting militias to protect black communities from white retaliation.

Though African American women did not obtain the right to vote, they too assumed new political roles. Black women faithfully attended the parades and rallies common in black communities during the early years of Reconstruction and helped assemble mass meetings in the newly constructed black churches. They even showed up at the constitutional conventions held throughout the South in 1867, monitoring the proceedings and participating in informal votes outside the convention halls.

Freedmen Voting, Richmond, Virginia, 1871 The exercise of democratic rights by former slaves constituted a political and social revolution in the South and was bitterly resented by many whites.

But black men elected as delegates to the state constitutional conventions held the greater political authority. They formed the backbone of the black political community. At the conventions, they sat down with whites to hammer out new state constitutions, which most importantly provided for universal male suffrage.

The sight of former slaves holding office deeply offended their onetime masters, who lashed out with fury at the freedmen's white allies, labeling them **scalawags** and **carpetbaggers**. The so-called scalawags were Southerners, often former Unionists and Whigs, whom former Confederates wildly accused of plundering the treasuries of the Southern radical governments. The carpetbaggers were supposedly sleazy Northerners who had packed all their worldly goods into a carpetbag suitcase at war's end and had come South to seek personal power and profit. In fact, most were former Union soldiers and Northern businessmen and professionals who wanted to play a role in modernizing the "New South."

How well or badly did the radical regimes rule? White southerners regularly portrayed the "Black Reconstruction" governments as run by ignorant and corrupt former slaves. Black voters did make up a majority of the electorate in five states, but only in South Carolina did blacks predominate in the lower house of the legislature. Black political participation expanded exponentially during Reconstruction. Many of the newly elected black legislators were literate and able; more than a few came from the ranks of the prewar free blacks who had acquired considerable education. Though no blacks were elected governors of their states, more than a dozen black congressmen and two black United States senators, Hiram Revels and Blanche K. Bruce, both of Mississippi, served in Washington, D.C.

In some radical regimes, there was truth to the charges of graft and corruption. This was especially true in South Carolina and Louisiana, where conscienceless promoters and other pocket-padders used politically inexperienced blacks as cat's-paws. The worst "black-and-white" legislatures purchased as "legislative supplies" such "stationery" as hams, perfumes, suspenders, bonnets, corsets, champagne, and a coffin. Yet this sort of corruption was no more outrageous than the scams and felonies being perpetrated in the North at the same time, especially in Boss Tweed's New York.

---

scalawags *Derogatory term for pro-Union Southerners whom Southern Democrats accused of plundering the resources of the South in collusion with Republican governments after the Civil War.*

carpetbaggers *Pejorative used by Southern whites to describe Northern businessmen and politicians who came to the South after the Civil War to work on Reconstruction projects or invest in Southern infrastructure.*

The radical legislatures also passed much desirable legislation. For the first time in Southern history, steps were taken toward establishing adequate public schools. Tax systems were streamlined; public works were launched; and property rights were guaranteed to women. Many of these welcome reforms were retained by the all-white "Redeemer" governments that later returned to power.

★ The Ku Klux Klan

Deeply embittered, some Southern whites resorted to savage measures against "radical" rule. Many whites resented the success and ability of black legislators as much as they resented alleged "corruption." A number of secret organizations mushroomed forth, the most notorious of which was the "Invisible Empire of the South," or **Ku Klux Klan**, founded in Tennessee in 1866. Hooded nightriders, their horses' hoofs muffled, would hammer on blacks' cabin doors or use other tactics to frighten them. Those stubborn

Ku Klux Klan *An extremist, paramilitary, right-wing secret society founded in the mid-nineteenth century and revived during the 1920s. It was anti-foreign, anti-black, anti-Jewish, anti-pacifist, anti-communist, anti-internationalist, anti-evolutionist, and anti-bootlegger, but pro-Anglo-Saxon and pro-Protestant. Its members, cloaked in sheets to conceal their identities, terrorized freedmen and sympathetic whites throughout the South after the Civil War. By the 1890s, Klan-style violence and Democratic legislation succeeded in virtually disenfranchising all Southern blacks.*

Klansmen in Costume Members of the Ku Klux Klan like these two garbed men utilized terrorist violence on behalf of a political agenda: the disenfranchisement of African Americans and their Republican allies and the reinstatement of white supremacist rule by "Redeemer" governments.

souls who persisted in their "upstart" ways were flogged, mutilated, or even murdered. In one Louisiana parish in 1868, whites in two days killed or wounded two hundred victims; a pile of twenty-five bodies was found half-buried in the woods. By such atrocious terror tactics were blacks "kept in their place"—that is, down.

Congress, outraged by this night-riding lawlessness, passed the harsh **Force Acts** of 1870 and 1871. Federal troops were able to stamp out much of the "lash law," but by this time the Invisible Empire had already done its work of intimidation. The Klan remained a refuge for numerous scoundrels and cutthroats who hid under its sheets, often continuing to operate under the guise of "dancing societies," "missionary clubs," and "rifle clubs."

White resistance undermined attempts to empower blacks politically. The white South for many decades openly flouted the Fourteenth and Fifteenth Amendments. Wholesale disfranchisement of the blacks, starting conspicuously about 1890, was achieved by intimidation, fraud, and trickery. Among various underhanded schemes were the literacy tests, unfairly administered by whites to the advantage of illiterate whites. In the eyes of white Southerners, the goal of white supremacy fully justified these dishonorable devices.

Force Acts (1870–1871) *Passed by Congress following a wave of Ku Klux Klan violence, the acts banned clan membership, prohibited the use of intimidation to prevent blacks from voting, and gave the U.S. military the authority to enforce the acts.*

★ Impeachment and Acquittal for Johnson

Radicals meanwhile had been sharpening their hatchets for President Johnson. Not content with curbing his authority, they decided to remove him altogether by constitutional processes (for impeachment, see Art. I, Sec. II, para. 5, Art. I, Sec. II, paras. 6, 7, Art. II, Sec. IV, in the Appendix).

As an initial step, Congress in 1867 passed the **Tenure of Office Act**—as usual over Johnson's veto. Contrary to precedent, the new law required the president to secure the consent of the Senate before he could remove his cabinet members, including the secretary of war, Edwin M. Stanton, a holdover from the Lincoln administration. Although outwardly loyal to Johnson, Stanton was secretly serving as a spy and informer for the radicals.

Johnson provided the radicals with a pretext to begin impeachment proceedings when he abruptly dismissed Stanton early in 1868. The House of Representatives immediately voted 126 to 47 to impeach Andrew Johnson for "high crimes and misdemeanors," as required by the Constitution, charging him with various violations of the Tenure of Office Act. Two additional articles related to Johnson's verbal assaults on the Congress, involving "disgrace, ridicule, hatred, contempt, and reproach."

With evident zeal the radical-led Senate now sat as a court to try Johnson on the dubious impeachment charges. The House conducted the prosecution. The trial aroused intense public interest and, with only one thousand tickets printed, proved to be the biggest show of 1868. Johnson kept his dignity and maintained a discreet silence. His battery of attorneys argued that the president had fired Stanton merely to put a test case before the Supreme Court. The House prosecutors, including oily-tongued Benjamin F. Butler and embittered Thaddeus Stevens, had a harder time building a compelling case for impeachment.

On May 16, 1868, the day for voting in the Senate, the tension was electric, and heavy breathing could be heard in the galleries. By a margin of only one vote, the radicals failed to muster the two-thirds majority for Johnson's removal. Seven resistant Republican senators, courageously putting country above party, voted "not guilty."

Diehard radicals were infuriated. "The Country is going to the Devil!" cried the crippled Stevens as he was carried

Tenure of Office Act (1867) *Required the President to seek approval from the Senate before removing appointees. When Andrew Johnson removed his secretary of war in violation of the act, he was impeached by the House but remained in office when the Senate fell one vote short of removing him.*

> *The remarkable ex-slave Frederick Douglass (1817?–1895) wrote in 1882:*
>
> "Though slavery was abolished, the wrongs of my people were not ended. Though they were not slaves, they were not yet quite free. No man can be truly free whose liberty is dependent upon the thought, feeling, and action of others, and who has himself no means in his own hands for guarding, protecting, defending, and maintaining that liberty. Yet the Negro after his emancipation was precisely in this state of destitution.... He was free from the individual master, but the slave of society. He had neither money, property, nor friends. He was free from the old plantation, but he had nothing but the dusty road under his feet. He was free from the old quarter that once gave him shelter, but a slave to the rains of summer and the frosts of winter. He was, in a word, literally turned loose, naked, hungry, and destitute, to the open sky."

from the hall. But the nation, though violently aroused, accepted the verdict with a good temper that did credit to its political maturity.

The nation thus narrowly avoided a bad precedent that would have gravely weakened one of the three branches of the federal government. Johnson was clearly guilty of bad speeches, bad judgment, and bad temper, but not of "high crimes and misdemeanors." From the standpoint of the radicals, his greatest crime had been to stand inflexibly in their path.

★ The Purchase of Alaska

Johnson's administration, though largely reduced to a figurehead, achieved its most enduring success in the field of foreign relations. The Russians by 1867 were in a mood to sell the vast and chilly expanse of land now known as Alaska. The region had been ruthlessly "furred out" and was a growing economic liability to them. The Russians were therefore eager to unload their "frozen asset" on the Americans. They preferred the United States to any other purchaser primarily because they wanted to strengthen the American Republic as a barrier against their ancient enemy, Britain.

In 1867 Secretary of State William Seward, an ardent expansionist, signed a treaty with Russia that transferred Alaska to the United States for the bargain price of $7.2 million. But Seward's enthusiasm for these frigid wastes was not shared by his ignorant or uninformed countrymen, who jeered at "Seward's Folly," "Seward's Icebox," and "Walrussia."

Then why did Congress and the American public sanction the purchase? For one thing Russia, alone among the great powers, had been conspicuously friendly to the North during the recent Civil War. Americans did not feel that they could offend their good friend the tsar by hurling his walrus-covered icebergs back into his face. Besides, the territory was rumored to be still teeming with furs, fish, and gold, and it might yet "pan out" profitably—as it later did with natural resources that included vast deposits of oil and gas.

Seward's Folly (1867) *Popular term for Secretary of State William Seward's purchase of Alaska from Russia. The derisive term reflected the anti-expansionist sentiments of most Americans immediately after the Civil War.*

★ The Heritage of Reconstruction

Many white Southerners regarded Reconstruction as a more grievous wound than the war itself. It left a festering scar that would take generations to heal. They resented the upending of their social and racial systems, the political empowerment of blacks, and the insult of federal intervention in their local affairs. Yet given the explosiveness of the issues that had caused the war and the bitterness of the fighting, the wonder is that Reconstruction was not far harsher than it was. Northern policymakers groped for the right policies, influenced as much by Southern responses to defeat and emancipation as by any specific plans of their own.

The Republicans acted from a mixture of idealism and political expediency. They wanted both to protect the freed slaves and to promote the fortunes of the Republican party. In the end their efforts backfired badly. Reconstruction conferred only fleeting benefits on the blacks, and it virtually extinguished the Republican party in the South for nearly one hundred years.

Moderate Republicans never fully appreciated the extensive effort necessary to make the freed slaves completely independent citizens, nor the lengths to which Southern whites would go to preserve their system of racial dominance. Had Thaddeus Stevens's radical program of drastic economic reforms and heftier protection of political rights been enacted, things might well have been different. But deep-seated racism, ingrained American resistance to tampering with property rights, and rigid loyalty to the principle of local self-government, combined with spreading indifference in the North to the plight of blacks, formed too formidable an obstacle. Despite good intentions by Republicans, the Old South was in many ways more resurrected than reconstructed, which spelled continuing woe for generations of Southern blacks.

Varying Viewpoints

How Radical Was Reconstruction?

Few topics have triggered as much intellectual warfare as the "dark and bloody ground" of Reconstruction. The period provoked questions—sectional, racial, and constitutional—about which people felt deeply and remain deeply divided even today. Scholarly argument goes back conspicuously to a Columbia University historian, William A. Dunning, who wrote about Reconstruction as a kind of national disgrace, foisted on a prostrate region by vindictive and self-seeking radical Republican politicians.

In the 1920s, widespread suspicion that the Civil War itself had been a tragic and unnecessary blunder shifted attention to Northern politicians. Scholars such as Howard Beale argued that the radical Republicans had masked a ruthless desire to exploit Southern resources and expand Republican power in the South behind a false "front" of concern for the freed slaves.

Although ignored by his contemporaries, the scholar and founder of the National Association for the Advancement of Colored People W. E. B. Du Bois wrote a sympathetic history of Reconstruction in 1935 that became the basis of historians' interpretations ever since. Following World War II, Kenneth Stampp and others, influenced by the modern civil rights movement, built on Du Bois's argument and claimed that Reconstruction had been a noble though ultimately failed attempt to extend American principles of equity and justice. By the early 1970s, this view had become orthodoxy, and it generally holds sway today. Yet some scholars, such as Michael Benedict and Leon Litwack, disillusioned with the inability to achieve full racial justice in the 1960s and 1970s, claimed to discover that Reconstruction was never really very radical and argued that the Freedmen's Bureau and other agencies had merely allowed white planters to maintain local political and economic control.

More recently, Eric Foner has powerfully reasserted the argument that Reconstruction was a truly radical and noble attempt to establish an interracial democracy. Drawing on the work of Du Bois, Foner has emphasized that Reconstruction allowed blacks to form political organizations and churches and to establish some measure of economic independence. In South Africa, the Caribbean, and other areas once marked by slavery, these opportunities were much harder to come by. Many of the benefits of Reconstruction were erased by white Southerners during the Gilded Age, but in the twentieth century, constitutional principles and organizations developed during Reconstruction provided the foundation for the modern civil rights movement—which some have called the Second Reconstruction.

Steven Hahn's *A Nation Under Our Feet: Black Political Struggles in the Rural South from Slavery to the Great Migration* (2003) is the latest contribution to the literature on Reconstruction. Hahn emphasizes the assertiveness and ingenuity of African Americans in creating new political opportunities for themselves after emancipation.

CHAPTER SUMMARY

With the Civil War over, the nation faced the difficult problems of rebuilding the South, assisting the freed slaves, reintegrating the Southern states into the Union, and deciding who would direct the Reconstruction process.

The South was economically devastated and socially revolutionized by emancipation. As slave owners reluctantly confronted the end of slave labor, blacks took their first steps in freedom. Black churches and freedmen's schools helped the former slaves begin to shape their own destinies.

The new President Andrew Johnson was politically inept and personally contentious. His attempt to implement a moderate plan of Reconstruction, along the lines originally suggested by Lincoln, fell victim to Southern whites' severe treatment of blacks and his own political blunders.

Republicans imposed harsh military Reconstruction on the South after their gains in the 1866 congressional elections. The Southern states reentered the Union with new radical governments, which rested partly on the newly enfranchised blacks, but also had support from some sectors of Southern society. These governments were sometimes corrupt, but they also implemented important reforms, especially in education. For a time, acting from a mixture of idealism and political expediency, Republicans tried seriously to build a new Republican party in the South to guarantee black rights. But the divisions between moderate and radical Republicans meant that Reconstruction's aims were often limited and confused, despite successful passage of the important Fourteenth and Fifteenth Amendments guaranteeing black civil and voting rights.

Embittered whites hated the radical governments and mobilized reactionary terrorist organizations such as the Ku Klux Klan to restore white supremacy. The radical Republican House of Representatives impeached Johnson, but the Senate failed narrowly to convict him. In the end, the inadequate Reconstruction policy, which never really addressed the deep economic and social legacy of slavery and the Civil War, failed disastrously and created as much or more bitterness than the war itself.

KEY TERMS

- Freedmen's Bureau (350)
- "10 percent" Reconstruction plan (353)
- Wade-Davis Bill (353)
- Black Codes (353)
- Pacific Railroad Act (354)
- Civil Rights Bill (355)
- Fourteenth Amendment (355)
- Reconstruction Act (356)
- Fifteenth Amendment (356)
- *Ex parte Milligan* (357)
- scalawags (358)
- carpetbaggers (358)
- Ku Klux Klan (359)
- Force Acts (360)
- Tenure of Office Act (360)
- Seward's Folly (361)

PEOPLE TO KNOW

- General Oliver O. Howard
- Andrew Johnson
- Thaddeus Stevens
- Hiram Revels
- Edwin M. Stanton
- William Seward

MindTap

MindTap is a fully online, highly personalized learning experience built upon Cengage Learning content. MindTap combines student learning tools—readings, multimedia, activities, and assessments—into a singular Learning Path that guides students through the course.

Part 4

FORGING AN INDUSTRIAL SOCIETY

1865–1909

A nation of farmers fought the Civil War in the 1860s. By the time the Spanish-American War broke out in 1898, America was an industrial nation. For generations Americans had plunged into the wilderness and plowed their fields. Now they settled in cities and toiled in factories. Between the Civil War and the century's end, economic and technological change came so swiftly and massively that it seemed to many Americans that a whole new civilization had emerged.

In some ways it had. The sheer scale of the new industrial civilization was dazzling. Transcontinental railroads knit the country together from sea to sea. New industries such as oil and steel grew to staggering sizes—and made mega-millionaires out of entrepreneurs such as oilman John D. Rockefeller and steelmaker Andrew Carnegie.

Drawn by the allure of industrial employment, Americans moved to the city. In 1860 only about 20 percent of the population were city dwellers. By 1900 that proportion had doubled, as rural Americans and European immigrants alike flocked to mill town and metropolis in search of steady jobs.

These sweeping changes challenged the spirit of individualism that Americans had celebrated since the seventeenth century. Even on the western frontier, that historic bastion of rugged loners, the hand of government was increasingly felt, as large armies were dispatched to subdue the Plains Indians and federal authority was invoked to regulate the use of natural resources. The rise of powerful monopolies called into question the government's traditional hands-off policy toward business, and a growing band of reformers increasingly clamored for government regulation of private enterprise. The mushrooming cities, with their needs for transport systems, schools, hospitals, sanitation, and fire and police protection, required bigger governments and budgets than an earlier generation could have imagined. As never before, Americans struggled to adapt old ideals of private autonomy to the new realities of industrial civilization.

With economic change came social and political turmoil. Labor violence brought bloodshed to places such as Chicago and Homestead, Pennsylvania. Small farmers, squeezed by debt and foreign competition, rallied behind the People's, or "Populist," party, a radical movement of the 1880s and 1890s that attacked the power of Wall Street, big business, and the banks. Anti-immigrant sentiment swelled. Bitter disputes over tariffs and monetary policy deeply divided the country, setting debtors against lenders, farmers against manufacturers, the West and South against the Northeast. And in this unfamiliar era of big money and expanding government, corruption flourished, from town hall to Congress, fueling loud cries for political reform.

The bloodiest conflict of all pitted Plains Indians against the relentless push of westward expansion. As railroads drove their iron arrows through the heart of the West, the Indians

Dearborn Street, Chicago Loop, Around 1900 "America is energetic, but Chicago is in a fever," marveled a visiting Englishman about turn-of-the-century Chicago. Street scenes like this were common in America's booming new cities, especially in the "Lord of the Midwest."

lost their land and life-sustaining buffalo herds. By the 1890s, after three decades of fierce fighting with the U.S. Army, the Indians who had once roamed across the vast rolling prairies were struggling to preserve their shattered cultures within the confinement of reservations.

The South remained the one region largely untouched by the Industrial Revolution sweeping the rest of America. For the most part, the South's rural way of life and its peculiar system of race relations were largely unperturbed by the changes happening elsewhere. The post-emancipation era inflicted new forms of racial injustice on African Americans, the vast majority of whom continued to live in the Old South. State legislatures systematically deprived black Americans of their political rights, including the right to vote. Segregation of schools, housing, and all kinds of public facilities made a mockery of African Americans' Reconstruction-era hopes for equality before the law.

The new wealth and power of industrial America nurtured a growing sense of national self-confidence. Literature flowered, and a golden age of philanthropy dawned.

The reform spirit spread. So did a restless appetite for overseas expansion. In a brief war against Spain in 1898, the United States, born in a revolutionary war of independence and long the champion of colonial peoples yearning to breathe free, seized control of the Philippines and itself became an imperial power. Uncle Sam's venture into empire touched off a bitter national debate about America's role in the world and ushered in a long period of argument over the responsibilities, at home and abroad, of a modern industrial state.

What if...?

- What if industrial workers and small farmers in the post–Reconstruction era had joined in a political movement strong enough to challenge the "Captains of Industry" for control of the American economy?

- How would the course of American economic, social, and political development, and the character of America's foreign policy, have been different?

365

Chapter 23

Political Paralysis in the Gilded Age
1869–1896

Grant . . . had no right to exist. He should have been extinct for ages. . . . That, two thousand years after Alexander the Great and Julius Caesar, a man like Grant should be called—and should actually and truly be—the highest product of the most advanced evolution, made evolution ludicrous. . . . The progress of evolution, from President Washington to President Grant, was alone evidence enough to upset Darwin. . . . Grant . . . should have lived in a cave and worn skins.

HENRY ADAMS, THE EDUCATION OF HENRY ADAMS, 1907

Chapter Outline

- Ulysses S. Grant, Soldier-President
- Corruption and Reform in the Post–Civil War Era
- The Depression of the 1870s
- Political Parties and Partisans
- The Compromise of 1877 and the End of Reconstruction
- Class Conflict and Ethnic Clashes
- Civil Service Reform
- Grover Cleveland and the Tariff
- President Harrison and the "Billion-Dollar" Congress
- Populists
- Cleveland and the Depression of the 1890s
- Makers of America: The Chinese
- Varying Viewpoints: The Populists: Radicals or Reactionaries?

The population of the post–Civil War Republic continued to vault upward by vigorous leaps, despite the awful bloodletting in both Union and Confederate ranks. Census takers reported over 39 million people in 1870, a gain of 26.6 percent over the preceding decade, as the immigrant tide surged again. The United States was now the third-largest nation in the Western world, ranking behind Russia and France.

But the civic health of the United States did not keep pace with its physical growth. The Civil War and its aftermath spawned waste, extravagance, speculation, and graft. Disillusionment ran deep among idealistic Americans in the postwar era. They had spilled their blood for the Union, emancipation, and Abraham Lincoln, who had promised "a new birth of freedom." Instead, they got a bitter dose of corruption and political stalemate—beginning with Ulysses S. Grant, a great soldier but an utterly inept politician.

FOCUS QUESTIONS

1. Why was the Gilded Age a period of political patronage, corruption, and stalemate between the two major parties? Given these negative factors, why did political participation achieve such high levels?

2. How did the disputed Hayes–Tilden election of 1877 lead to the Compromise of 1877 and the end of Reconstruction?

3. What did the end of Reconstruction mean for blacks, and how did the South's racial segregation and sharecropping system trap both poor whites and blacks in poverty?

4. What caused the rise of industrial and agricultural conflict in the 1880s–1890s? Why were both Republicans and Democrats unable to address this discontent?

5. How did the severe depression of the 1890s stir growing social protest and class conflict and fuel the rise of the radical Populist party?

CHRONOLOGY

1868	Grant defeats Seymour for the presidency	1883	*Civil Rights Cases*; Pendleton Act sets up Civil Service Commission
1869	Fisk and Gould corner gold market	1884	Cleveland defeats Blaine for presidency
1871	Tweed scandal in New York	1888	Harrison defeats Cleveland for presidency
1872	Crédit Mobilier scandal exposed; Liberal Republicans break with Grant; Grant defeats Greeley for presidency	1890	"Billion-Dollar" Congress; McKinley Tariff Act; Sherman Silver Purchase Act (repealed 1893)
1873	Panic of 1873	1892	Homestead steel strike; Coeur d'Alene (Idaho) silver miners' strike; People's party candidate James B. Weaver wins twenty-two electoral votes; Cleveland defeats Harrison and Weaver to regain presidency
1875	Whiskey Ring scandal; Civil Rights Act of 1875; Resumption Act		
1876	Hayes-Tilden election standoff and crisis		
1877	Compromise of 1877; Reconstruction ends; Railroad strikes paralyze nation	1893	Depression of 1893 begins; Republicans regain House of Representatives
1880	Garfield defeats Hancock for presidency	1895	J. P. Morgan's banking syndicate loans $65 million in gold to federal government
1881	Garfield assassinated; Arthur assumes presidency		
1882	Chinese Exclusion Act	1896	*Plessy v. Ferguson* legitimizes "separate but equal" doctrine

★ The "Bloody Shirt" Elects Grant

Wrangling between Congress and Andrew Johnson had soured the people on professional politicians, and the notion still prevailed that a good general would make a good president. Stubbly bearded General Grant was by far the most popular northern hero to emerge from the war. Grateful citizens of Philadelphia, Washington, and New York showered him with gifts of houses and cash, which the general, silently puffing on his cigar, unapologetically accepted.

Grant was a hapless greenhorn in the political arena. His one presidential vote had been cast for the Democratic ticket in 1856. A better judge of horseflesh than of humans, his cultural background was breathtakingly narrow. He once reportedly remarked that Venice, Italy, would be a fine city if only it were drained.

The Republicans, freed from the Union party coalition of war days, enthusiastically nominated Grant for the presidency in 1868. The party's platform sounded a clarion call for continued Reconstruction of the South under the glinting steel of federal bayonets. Yet Grant, always a man of few words, coined a popular campaign slogan when he declared, "Let us have peace."

Expectant Democrats, meeting in their own nominating convention, denounced military Reconstruction but could agree on little else. Wealthy eastern delegates demanded a platform promising that federal war bonds be redeemed in gold, while the poorer midwesterners backed the "Ohio Idea" calling for redemption in greenbacks. Debt-burdened agrarian Democrats thus hoped to keep more money in circulation and to keep interest rates lower. This dispute introduced a bitter contest over monetary policy that continued to convulse the Republic until the century's end.

Midwestern delegates got the platform but not the candidate. The nominee, former New York governor Horatio Seymour, scuttled the Democrats' faint hope for success by repudiating the Ohio Idea. Republicans whipped up enthusiasm for Grant by energetically **"waving the bloody shirt"**—that is, reviving gory memories of the Civil War—which became for the first time a prominent feature of a presidential campaign.* "Vote as You Shot" was a powerful Republican slogan aimed at Union army veterans.

Grant won, with 214 electoral votes to 80 for Seymour. But despite his great popularity, the former general scored a majority of only 300,000 in the popular vote (3,013,421 to 2,706,829). Most white voters apparently supported Seymour, and the ballots of three still-unreconstructed southern states (Mississippi, Texas, and Virginia) were not counted at all. An estimated 500,000 former slaves gave Grant his margin of victory. To remain in power, the Republican party somehow had to continue to control the South—and to keep the ballot in the hands of the grateful freedmen. Republicans could not take future victories "for Granted."

"waving the bloody shirt" *The use of Civil War imagery by political candidates and parties to draw votes to their side of the ticket.*

★ The Era of Good Stealings

A few skunks can pollute a large area. Although the great majority of businesspeople and government officials continued to conduct their affairs with decency and honor, the whole postwar atmosphere stunk of corruption. The Man in the Moon, it was said, had to hold his nose when passing over America. Freewheeling railroad promoters sometimes left gullible bond buyers with only "two streaks of rust and a right of way." Unethical stock-market manipulators were a cinder in the public eye. Too many judges and legislators put their power up for hire. Cynics defined an honest politician as one who, when bought, would stay bought.

Notorious in the financial world were two millionaire partners, "Jubilee Jim" Fisk and Jay Gould. The corpulent and unscrupulous Fisk provided the "brass," while the undersized and cunning Gould provided the brains. The crafty pair concocted a plot in 1869 to corner the gold market. Their slippery game would work only if the federal Treasury refrained from selling gold. The conspirators worked on President Grant directly, and also through Grant's brother-in-law, who received $25,000 for his complicity. For weeks, Fisk and Gould madly bid the price of gold skyward, so that they could later profit from its heightened value. But on "Black Friday" (September 24, 1869), the bubble burst when the Treasury, contrary to Grant's supposed assurances, was compelled to release gold. The price of gold plunged, and numerous honest businesspeople were driven to the wall. A congressional probe concluded that Grant had done nothing crooked, though he had acted stupidly and indiscreetly.

The infamous **Tweed Ring** in New York City vividly displayed the ethics (or lack of ethics) typical of the age. Burly "Boss" Tweed—240 pounds of rascality—employed bribery, graft, and fraudulent elections to milk the metropolis of as much as $200 million. Honest citizens were cowed into silence. Protesters found their tax assessments raised.

Tweed Ring *A symbol of Gilded Age corruption, "Boss" Tweed and his deputies ran the New York City Democratic party in the 1860s and swindled $200 million from the city through bribery, graft, and vote-buying. Boss Tweed was eventually jailed for his crimes and died behind bars.*

Tweed's luck finally ran out. The *New York Times* secured damning evidence in 1871 and courageously published it, though offered $5 million not to do so. Gifted cartoonist Thomas Nast pilloried Tweed mercilessly, after spurning a heavy bribe to desist. New York attorney Samuel J. Tilden headed the prosecution, gaining fame that later paved the path to his presidential nomination. Unbailed and unwept, Tweed died behind bars.

More serious than Boss Tweed's peccadilloes were the misdeeds of the federal government. President Grant's cabinet was a rodent's nest of grafters and incompetents. Favor seekers haunted the White House, plying Grant himself with cigars, wine, and horses. Several dozen of Grant's in-laws attached themselves to the public payroll.

Crédit Mobilier scandal (1872) *A construction company was formed by owners of the Union Pacific Railroad for the purpose of receiving government contracts to build the railroad at highly inflated prices—and profits. In 1872 a scandal erupted when journalists discovered that the Crédit Mobilier Company had bribed congressmen and even the vice president to allow the ruse to continue.*

The easygoing Grant was first tarred by the **Crédit Mobilier scandal**, which erupted in 1872. Union Pacific Railway insiders had formed the Crédit Mobilier construction

---

*The expression is said to have derived from a speech by Representative Benjamin F. Butler of Massachusetts, who allegedly waved before the House the bloodstained nightshirt of a Klan-flogged carpetbagger.

company and then cleverly hired themselves at inflated prices to build the railroad line, earning dividends as high as 348 percent. Fearing that Congress might blow the whistle, the company furtively distributed shares of its valuable stock to key congressmen. A newspaper exposé and congressional investigation of the scandal led to the formal censure of two congressmen and the revelation that the vice president of the United States had also accepted payments from Crédit Mobilier.

The breath of scandal in Washington also reeked of alcohol. In 1874–1875 a sprawling Whiskey Ring robbed the Treasury of millions in excise-tax revenues. When President Grant's own private secretary turned up among the culprits, the president volunteered a written statement to a jury that helped exonerate the thief. Further rottenness in the Grant administration came to light in 1876, forcing Secretary of War William Belknap to resign after pocketing bribes from suppliers to the Indian reservations. Grant, ever loyal to his crooked cronies, accepted Belknap's resignation "with great regret."

★ The Liberal Republican Revolt of 1872

By 1872 a powerful wave of disgust with Grantism was beginning to build up throughout the nation, even before some of the worst scandals had been exposed. Reform-minded citizens banded together in the Liberal Republican party. Voicing the slogan "Turn the Rascals Out," they urged purification of the Washington administration as well as an end to military Reconstruction.

The Liberal Republicans muffed their chance when their Cincinnati nominating convention astounded the country by nominating the brilliant but erratic Horace Greeley for the presidency. Although Greeley was a fearless editor of the *New York Tribune*, he was dogmatic, emotional, petulant, and notoriously unsound in his political judgments.

Can the Law Reach Him? 1872 Cartoonist Thomas Nast attacked "Boss" Tweed in a series of cartoons like this one that appeared in *Harper's Weekly* in 1872. Here Nast depicts the corrupt Tweed as a powerful giant, towering over a puny law force.

More astonishing still was the action of the office-hungry Democrats, who foolishly proceeded to endorse Greeley's candidacy. In swallowing Greeley the Democrats "ate crow" in large gulps, for the eccentric editor had long blasted them as traitors, slave drivers, saloon keepers, horse thieves, and idiots. Yet Greeley pleased the Democrats, North and South, when he pleaded for clasping hands across "the bloody chasm." The Republicans dutifully renominated Grant. The voters were thus presented with a choice between two candidates who had made their careers in fields other than politics and who were both eminently unqualified, by temperament and lifelong training, for high political office.

In the mud-spattered campaign that followed, regular Republicans denounced Greeley as an atheist, a free-lover, and a vegetarian, while Democrats derided Grant as a drunken swindler. But the regular Republicans, chanting "Grant us another term," pulled the president through. The count in the electoral column was 286 to 66, in the popular column 3,596,745 to 2,843,446.

Liberal Republican agitation frightened the regular Republicans into cleaning their own house before they were thrown out of it. The Republican Congress in 1872 passed a general amnesty act, removing political disabilities from all but some five hundred former Confederate leaders. Congress also moved to reduce high Civil War tariffs and to fumigate the Grant administration with mild civil-service reform. Like many American third parties, the Liberal Republicans left some enduring footprints, even in defeat.

★ Depression and Demands for Inflation

panic of 1873 *A worldwide depression that began in the United States when one of the nation's largest banks abruptly declared bankruptcy, leading to the collapse of thousands of banks and businesses. The crisis intensified debtors' calls for inflationary measures such as the printing of more paper money and the unlimited coinage of silver. Conflicts over monetary policy greatly influenced politics in the last quarter of the nineteenth century.*

Grant's woes deepened in the paralyzing economic **panic of 1873**. Bursting with startling rapidity, the crash was one of those periodic plummets that roller-coastered the economy in this age of unbridled capitalist expansion. Overreaching promoters had laid more railroad track, sunk more mines, erected more factories, and sowed more grain fields than existing markets could bear. Bankers, in turn, had made too many imprudent loans to finance those enterprises. When profits failed to materialize, loans went unpaid, and the whole credit-based house of cards fluttered down. The United States did not suffer alone. Nations worldwide underwent a similar economic collapse in 1873.

Boom times became gloom times as more than fifteen thousand American businesses went bankrupt. In New York City, an army of unemployed riotously battled police. Black Americans were hard hit. The Freedman's Savings and Trust Company had made unsecured loans to several companies that went under. Black depositors, who had entrusted over $7 million to the bank, lost their savings, and black economic development and black confidence in savings institutions went down with the bank.

Hard times inflicted the worst punishment on debtors, who intensified their clamor for inflationary policies. Proponents of inflation breathed new life into the issue of greenbacks. During the war $450 million of the "folding money" had been issued, but it had depreciated under a cloud of popular mistrust and dubious legality.* By 1868 the Treasury had already withdrawn $100 million of the "battle-born currency" from circulation, and "hard-money" people everywhere looked forward to its complete disappearance. But now afflicted agrarian and debtor groups—"cheap-money" supporters—pressed for a reissuance of the greenbacks. With a crude but essentially accurate grasp of monetary theory, they reasoned that more money meant cheaper money and, hence, rising prices and easier-to-pay debts. Creditors, of course, reasoning from the same premises, advocated precisely the opposite policy.

The "hard-money" advocates took a notable step in 1874 when they persuaded Grant to veto a bill to print more paper money. They scored another victory in the Resumption Act of 1875, which pledged the government to the further withdrawal of greenbacks from circulation and to the redemption of all paper currency in gold at face value, beginning in 1879.

Down but not out, debtors now looked for relief to another precious metal, silver. The "sacred white metal," they claimed, had received a raw deal. In the early 1870s, the Treasury stubbornly and unrealistically maintained that an ounce of silver was worth only one-sixteenth as much as an ounce of gold. Silver miners thus stopped selling their shiny product to the federal mints, and Congress dropped the coinage of silver dollars in 1873. Fate then played a sly joke when new silver discoveries later in the 1870s shot production up and forced silver prices down. Westerners from silver-mining states now joined with debtors in assailing the "Crime of '73," demanding a return to the "Dollar of Our Daddies." Like the demand for more greenbacks, the demand for the coinage of more silver was nothing more nor less than another scheme to promote inflation.

Hard-money Republicans resisted this scheme and counted on Grant to hold the line against it. He did not disappoint them. The Treasury began to accumulate gold stocks against the appointed day for resumption of metallic-money payments. Coupled with the reduction of greenbacks, this policy was called "contraction." It had a noticeable deflationary effect—the amount of money per capita in circulation actually decreased between 1870 and 1880, from $19.42 to $19.37. Contraction probably worsened the impact of the depression. But the new policy did restore the government's credit rating, and it brought the embattled greenbacks up to their full face value. When Redemption Day came in 1879, few greenback holders bothered to exchange the lighter and more convenient bills for gold.

Republican hard-money policy had a political backlash. It helped elect a Democratic House of Representatives in 1874, and in 1878 it spawned the Greenback Labor party, which polled over a million votes and elected fourteen members of Congress. The contest over monetary policy was far from over.

---

*The Supreme Court in 1870 declared the Civil War Legal Tender Act unconstitutional. With the concurrence of the Senate, Grant thereupon added to the bench two justices who could be counted on to help reverse that decision, which happened in 1871. This is how the Court grew to its current size of nine justices.

Pallid Politics in the Gilded Age

The political seesaw was delicately balanced throughout most of the **Gilded Age** (a sarcastic name given to the three-decade-long post–Civil War era by Mark Twain in 1873). Even a slight nudge could tip the teeter-totter to the advantage of the opposition party. Every presidential election was a squeaker, and the majority party in the House of Representatives switched six times in the eleven sessions between 1869 and 1891. Wobbling in such shaky equilibrium, politicians tiptoed timidly, producing a political record that was often trivial and petty.

Few significant economic issues separated the major parties. Democrats and Republicans saw very nearly eye-to-eye on questions such as the tariff and civil-service reform, and majorities in both parties substantially agreed even on the much-debated currency question. Yet despite their rough agreement on these national matters, the two parties were ferociously competitive with each other. They were tightly and efficiently organized, and they commanded fierce loyalty from their members. Voter turnouts reached heights unmatched before or since. Nearly 80 percent of eligible voters cast their ballots in presidential elections in the three decades after the Civil War. On election days, droves of the party faithful tramped behind marching bands to the polling places, and "ticket splitting," or failing to vote the straight party line, was as rare as a silver dollar.

How can this apparent paradox of political consensus and partisan fervor be explained? The answer lies in the sharp ethnic and cultural differences in the membership of the two parties—in distinctions of style and tone, and especially of religious sentiment. Republican voters tended to adhere to those creeds that traced their lineage to Puritanism. They stressed strict codes of personal morality and believed that government should play a role in regulating both the economic and the moral affairs of society. Democrats, among whom immigrant Lutherans and Roman Catholics figured heavily, were more likely to adhere to faiths that took a less stern view of human weakness. Their religions professed toleration of differences in an imperfect world, and they spurned government efforts to impose a single moral standard on the entire society. These differences in temperament and religious values often produced raucous political contests at the local level, where issues such as prohibition and education loomed large.

Democrats had a solid electoral base in the South and in the northern industrial cities, teeming with immigrants and controlled by well-oiled political machines. Republican strength lay largely in the Midwest and the rural and small-town Northeast. Grateful freedmen in the South continued to vote Republican in significant numbers. Another important bloc of Republican ballots came from the members of the Grand Army of the Republic (GAR)—a politically potent organization of several hundred thousand Union veterans of the Civil War.

The lifeblood of both parties was **patronage**—disbursing jobs by the bucketful in return for votes, kickbacks, and party service. Boisterous infighting over patronage beset the Republican party in the 1870s and 1880s. A "Stalwart" faction, led by the handsome and imperious Senator Roscoe ("Lord Roscoe") Conkling of New York, unblushingly embraced the time-honored system of swapping jobs for votes. Opposed to the Conklingites were the so-called Half-Breeds, who flirted coyly with civil-service reform, but whose real quarrel with the Stalwarts was over who should grasp the ladle that dished out the spoils. The champion of the Half-Breeds was James G. Blaine, a radiantly personable congressman from Maine with a fine physical presence, a thrilling speaking voice, and an elastic conscience. But despite all the color of their personalities, Conkling and Blaine succeeded only in stalemating each other and deadlocking their party.

> **Gilded Age** *A term originally coined by Mark Twain, given to the period 1865–1896, indicating both the fabulous wealth and the widespread corruption of the era.*

> **patronage** *A system, prevalent during the Gilded Age, in which political parties granted jobs and favors to party regulars who delivered votes on election day. Patronage was both an essential wellspring of support for both parties and a source of conflict within the Republican party.*

The Hayes-Tilden Standoff, 1876

Hangers-on around Grant, like fleas urging their ailing dog to live, begged the "Old Man" to try for a third term in 1876. The general, blind to his own ineptitudes, showed a disquieting willingness. But the House, by a lopsided bipartisan vote of 233 to 18, spiked the third-term boom. It passed a resolution that sternly reminded the country—and Grant—of the antidictator implications of the two-term tradition.

The Political Legacy of the Civil War Union veterans of the Civil War supported Republican candidate Rutherford B. Hayes in 1876. The Grand Army of the Republic (GAR), the Union veterans' organization, voted heavily for the GOP (Grand Old Party) in the post–Civil War years. (Left: The Granger Collection, NYC; Right: Collection of Janice L. and David J. Frent)

With Grant out of the running and with the Conklingites and Blaineites neutralizing each other, the Republicans turned to a compromise candidate, Rutherford B. Hayes, who was obscure enough to be dubbed "the Great Unknown." His foremost qualification was having served as three-term governor of the potent "swing" state of Ohio, which was so crucial to the cliffhanging electoral contests of the day that it regularly produced presidential candidates.

Pitted against the humdrum Hayes was the Democratic nominee, Samuel J. Tilden, who had risen to fame as the man who bagged Boss Tweed in New York. Campaigning against Republican scandal, Tilden racked up 184 electoral votes of the needed 185, with 20 votes in four states doubtful because of irregular returns (see Map 23.1). Oregon eventually fell completely to Hayes, but surely Tilden could pick up at least one of the other three, especially in view of the fact that he had polled 247,448 more popular votes than Hayes, 4,284,020 to 4,036,572.

Both parties scurried to send "visiting statesmen" to the three still-contested southern states of Louisiana, South Carolina, and Florida. These states had all submitted two sets of returns, one Democratic and one Republican. As the weeks drifted by, the paralysis tightened, generating a dramatic constitutional crisis. The Constitution merely specifies that the electoral returns from the states shall be sent to Congress, and in the presence of the House and Senate they shall be opened by the president of the Senate (see the Twelfth Amendment in the Appendix). But who should count them? On this point the Constitution was silent. If counted by the president of the Senate (a Republican), the Republican returns would be selected. If counted by the Speaker of the House (a Democrat), the Democratic returns would be chosen. How could the impasse be resolved?

The Compromise of 1877 and the End of Reconstruction

Clash or compromise was the stark choice. The danger loomed that there would be no president on inauguration day, March 4, 1877. "Tilden or Blood!" cried Democratic hotheads, and some of their "Minute Men" began to drill with arms. But behind the scenes, frantically laboring statesmen gradually hammered out an agreement in the Henry Clay tradition—the **Compromise of 1877**.

The election deadlock itself was to be broken by the Electoral Count Act, which passed Congress early in 1877. It set up an electoral commission consisting of fifteen men selected from the Senate, the House, and the Supreme Court.

In February 1877, about a month before Inauguration Day, the Senate and House met together in an electric atmosphere to settle the dispute. The roll of the states was tolled off alphabetically. When Florida was reached—the first of the three southern states with two sets of returns—the disputed documents were referred to the electoral commission, which sat in a nearby chamber. After prolonged discussion the members agreed, by the partisan vote of eight Republicans to seven Democrats, to accept the Republican returns. Outraged Democrats in Congress, smelling defeat, undertook to launch a filibuster "until hell froze over."

Renewed deadlock was avoided by the rest of the complex Compromise of 1877, already partially concluded behind closed doors. The Democrats reluctantly agreed that Hayes might take office in return for his withdrawing intrusive federal troops from the two states in which they remained, Louisiana and South Carolina. Among various concessions, the Republicans assured the Democrats a place at the presidential patronage trough and support for a bill subsidizing the Texas and Pacific Railroad's construction of a southern transcontinental line. Not all of these promises were kept in later years, including the Texas and Pacific subsidy. But the deal held together long enough to break the dangerous electoral standoff.

The compromise bought peace at a price. Partisan violence was averted by sacrificing the civil rights of southern blacks. With the Hayes-Tilden deal, the Republican party quietly abandoned its commitment to racial equality. That commitment had been weakening in any case. Many Republicans had begun to question the worthiness of Reconstruction and became less willing to send dollars and enlisted sons to bolster southern state governments.

The **Civil Rights Act of 1875** was in a sense the last feeble gasp of the congressional radical Republicans. The act supposedly guaranteed equal accommodations in public places and prohibited racial discrimination in jury selection, but the law was born toothless and stayed that way for nearly a century. The Supreme Court pronounced much of the act unconstitutional in the *Civil Rights Cases* (1883), declaring that the Fourteenth Amendment prohibited only *government* violations of civil rights, not the denial of civil rights by *individuals*. When President Hayes withdrew the blue-clad federal troops that were propping up Reconstruction governments, the bayonet-backed Republican regimes collapsed.

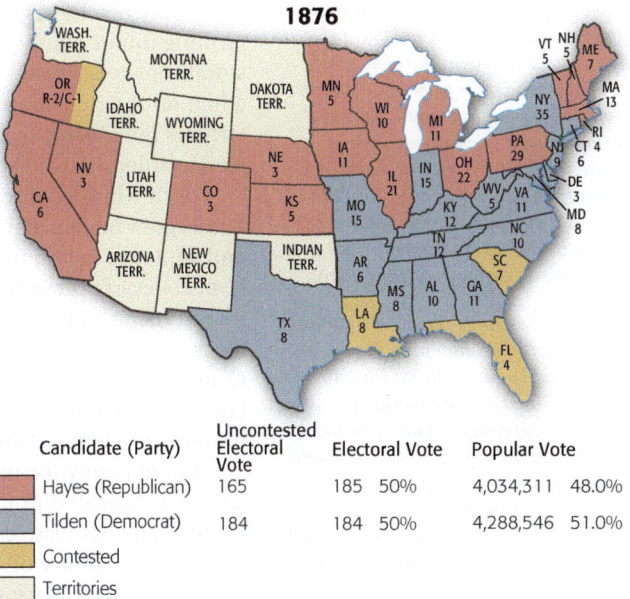

Map 23.1 Hayes-Tilden Disputed Election of 1876 (with electoral vote by state) Nineteen of the twenty disputed votes composed the total electoral count of Louisiana, South Carolina, and Florida. The twentieth was one of Oregon's three votes, cast by an elector who turned out to be ineligible because he was a federal officeholder (a postmaster), contrary to the Constitution (see Art. II, Sec. I, para. 2).

Compromise of 1877 *The agreement that finally resolved the 1876 election and officially ended Reconstruction. In exchange for the Republican candidate, Rutherford B. Hayes, winning the presidency, Hayes agreed to withdraw the last of the federal troops from the former Confederate states. This deal effectively completed the southern return to white-only, Democratic-dominated electoral politics.*

Civil Rights Act of 1875 *The last piece of federal civil rights legislation until the 1950s, the law promised blacks equal access to public accommodations and banned racism in jury selection, but it provided no means of enforcement and was therefore ineffective. In 1883, the Supreme Court declared most of the act unconstitutional.*

The Birth of Jim Crow in the Post-Reconstruction South

Reconstruction was officially ended. Relying shamelessly on fraud and intimidation, white Democrats ("Redeemers") reassumed political power in the South and ruthlessly suppressed the now-friendless blacks. Blacks who tried to assert their rights faced unemployment, eviction, and physical harm.

sharecropping *An agricultural system that emerged after the Civil War in which black and white farmers rented land and residences from a plantation owner in exchange for giving him a certain "share" of each year's crop. Sharecropping was the dominant form of southern agriculture after the Civil War, and landowners manipulated this system to keep tenants in perpetual debt and unable to leave their plantations.*

Jim Crow *System of racial segregation in the American South from the end of Reconstruction until the mid-twentieth century. Based on the concept of "separate but equal" facilities for blacks and whites, the Jim Crow system sought to prevent racial mixing in public, including restaurants, movie theaters, and public transportation. An informal system, it was generally perpetuated by custom, violence, and intimidation.*

Plessy v. Ferguson (1896) *A Supreme Court case that upheld the constitutionality of segregation laws, saying that as long as blacks were provided with "separate but equal" facilities, these laws did not violate the Fourteenth Amendment. This decision provided legal justification for the Jim Crow system until the 1950s.*

Many blacks (as well as poor whites) were forced into **sharecropping** and tenant farming under conditions scarcely better than slavery. Through the "crop-lien" system, storekeepers extended credit to small farmers for food and supplies and in return took a lien on their customers' harvests. Shrewd merchants manipulated the system so that farmers remained perpetually in debt to them. For generations to come, southern blacks were condemned to eke out a harsh and threadbare living.

With white southerners back in the political saddle, daily discrimination against blacks grew increasingly oppressive. What had started as the informal separation of blacks and whites in the immediate postwar years developed by the 1890s into systematic state-level codes of segregation known as **Jim Crow** laws. Southern states also enacted literacy requirements, voter-registration laws, and poll taxes—and tolerated violent intimidation of black voters—to ensure full-scale disfranchisement of the South's freedmen. The Supreme Court validated the South's segregationist social order in the case of *Plessy v. Ferguson* (1896). It ruled that "separate but equal" facilities were constitutional under the "equal protection" clause of the Fourteenth Amendment.

But in reality the quality of African American life was grotesquely unequal to that of whites. Segregated in inferior schools and separated from whites in virtually all public facilities, blacks were assaulted daily by reminders of their second-class citizenship. To ensure the stability of this political and economic "new order," southern whites dealt harshly with any black who dared to violate the South's racial code of conduct. A record number of blacks were lynched during the 1890s, most often for the "crime" of asserting themselves as equals. It would take a second Reconstruction, nearly a century later, to redress the racist imbalance of southern society.

★ Class Conflicts and Ethnic Clashes

The year 1877 marked more than the end of Reconstruction. As the curtains officially closed on regional warfare, they opened on scenes of class struggle. The explosive atmosphere was largely a by-product of the long years of depression and deflation following the panic of 1873. Railroad workers faced particularly hard times, while they watched the railroads continue to rake in huge profits. When the presidents of the nation's four largest railroads collectively decided in 1877 to cut employees' wages by 10 percent, the workers struck back. President Hayes's decision to call in federal troops to quell the unrest brought the striking laborers an outpouring of working-class support. Work stoppages spread like wildfire in cities from Baltimore to St. Louis. When the battling between workers and soldiers ended after several weeks, over one hundred people were dead.

The failure of the great railroad strike exposed the weakness of the labor movement in the face of massive government intervention on the side of the railroads. The federal courts, the United States Army, state militias, and local police all lent their muscle to keeping the engines of big business operating at full throttle, and the workers be damned. Meanwhile, racial and ethnic fissures among workers fractured labor unity. Divisions were particularly acute between the Irish and the Chinese in California (see "Makers of America: The Chinese," p. 375). By 1880 the Golden State counted seventy-five thousand Asian newcomers, about 9 percent of its entire population.

Mostly poor, uneducated, single males from K'uang-t'ung (Guangdong) province in southern China, they had originally come to dig in the gold fields and lay the tracks of the transcontinental railroads across the West. When those jobs ended, the Chinese who remained had to turn to the most menial jobs, often as cooks, laundrymen, or domestic servants. Without women or families, they were deprived of the children who in other immigrant communities eased their parents' assimilation through their exposure to the English language and American customs in school.

In San Francisco, Irish-born demagogue Denis Kearney incited his followers, many of them recently arrived European immigrants, to violent abuse of the hapless Chinese. Taking to the streets, gangs of Kearneyites terrorized the Chinese by shearing off their precious pigtails. Some victims were murdered outright.

Makers of America

The Chinese

Between 1800 and 1925, at least 3 million Chinese left their homeland to labor around the globe. The once great Chinese Empire was disintegrating while its population was exploding, creating severe land shortages and opening up the unstable country to European imperial powers bent on unlocking the riches of a nation closed to outsiders for centuries. Chinese men, faced with economic hardship and political turmoil in their homeland and lured by labor shortages as far afield as Southeast Asia, Australia, and the Americas, migrated by the tens of thousands to work the plantations and dig the mines that fueled a burgeoning global economy. By 1900, more than 300,000 Chinese had entered the United States to contribute their muscle to building the West, wrenching minerals from stubborn rock, and helping to lay the transcontinental railroads that stitched together the American nation.

Chinese emigrants, mostly poor laborers, had set off for destinations as diverse as Vietnam, Cuba, and Peru since the sixteenth century. But until the 1848 discovery of gold in California, there were fewer than 50 Chinese living in the United States. By 1852, at least twenty-five thousand Chinese had arrived in California, which they dubbed the "golden mountain." At that decade's end, Chinese workers made up nearly a quarter of the state's manual laborers, even though they were only a tenth of the population. Employers nationwide viewed the Chinese as cheap labor, recruiting them to cut sugar cane in the South and break strikes in New England shoe factories.

Although Chinese immigrants included a few merchants and artisans, most were unskilled country folk. In some cases families pooled their money to send out a son, but most travelers, desperately poor, obtained their passage through Chinese middlemen, who advanced them ship fare in return for the emigrants' promise to work off their debts after they landed.

The Chinese America of the late-nineteenth-century West was overwhelmingly a bachelor society. Women of good repute rarely made the passage. Of the very few Chinese women who did venture to California at this time, most became prostitutes. Many of them had been deceived by the false promise of honest jobs.

Although a stream of workers returned to China, many Chinese stayed. "Chinatowns" sprang up wherever economic opportunities presented themselves. Chinese in these settlements spoke their own language, enjoyed the fellowship of their own compatriots, and sought safety from prejudice and violence. Many immigrant clubs and associations were American adaptations of Chinese traditions of loyalty to clan. The poorest and most alienated immigrants also established *tongs*—literally, "meeting halls"—secret societies that acquired a sinister reputation among non-Chinese.

Mounting anti-Chinese agitation demanded political action against the immigrants, and in 1882 the Chinese Exclusion Act barred nearly all Chinese from the United States for six decades. Many of the bachelors died or returned home. Slowly, however, those men and the few women who remained raised families and reared a new generation of Chinese Americans. They were joined by thousands more immigrants who made the journey illegally or took advantage of the few exceptions permissible under the Exclusion Act. But this second generation still suffered from discrimination, eking out their living in jobs despised by Caucasian laborers or taking daunting risks in small entrepreneurial ventures. Yet many hard-working Chinese did manage to open their own restaurants, laundries, and other small businesses. Such enterprises formed a solid economic foundation for their small community and remain a source of livelihood for many Chinese Americans even today.

Chinese Butcher Shop, San Francisco, California, c. 1890

Chinese Exclusion Act (1882) *Federal legislation that prohibited most further Chinese immigration to the United States. This was the first major legal restriction on immigration in U.S. history.*

Congress slammed the door on Chinese immigrant laborers when it passed the Chinese Exclusion Act in 1882, prohibiting nearly all further immigration from China. The door stayed shut until 1943. Some exclusionists even tried to strip native-born Chinese Americans of their citizenship, but the Supreme Court ruled in *U.S. v. Wong Kim Ark* in 1898 that the Fourteenth Amendment guaranteed citizenship to all persons born in the United States. This doctrine of "birthright citizenship" provided important protections to Chinese Americans as well as to other immigrant communities.

★ Garfield and Arthur

As the presidential campaign of 1880 approached, "Rutherfraud" Hayes was a man without a party, repudiated by the Republican Old Guard. Seeking a new standard-bearer, the Republicans finally settled on dark-horse candidate Congressman James A. Garfield from the electorally powerful state of Ohio. His vice-presidential running mate was a notorious Stalwart henchman, Chester A. Arthur of New York.

Energetically waving the bloody shirt, Garfield barely squeaked out a victory over the Democratic candidate, Civil War hero Winfield Scott Hancock. Garfield polled only 39,213 more votes than Hancock—4,453,295 to 4,414,082—but his margin in the electoral column was a comfortable 214 to 155.

The new president was an energetic and able man, but he was immediately ensnared in political conflict between his secretary of state, James G. Blaine, and Blaine's Stalwart nemesis, Senator Roscoe Conkling. Then, as the Republican factions dueled, tragedy struck. A disappointed and mentally deranged office seeker, Charles J. Guiteau, shot President Garfield in the back in a Washington railroad station. Garfield died eleven weeks later, on September 19, 1881, and Chester Arthur assumed the presidency.

Garfield's death did have one positive outcome: it shocked politicians into reforming the shameful spoils system. The unlikely instrument of reform was Chester Arthur. Arthur's record of cronyism and fondness for fine wines and elegant clothing (including eighty pairs of trousers) suggested that he was little more than a foppish dandy. But as the new president, Arthur surprised his critics by prosecuting several fraud cases and giving his former Stalwart pals the cold shoulder.

Pendleton Act (1883) *Congressional legislation that established the Civil Service Commission, which granted federal government jobs on the basis of examinations instead of political patronage, thus reining in the spoils system.*

Disgust with Garfield's murder also gave the Republican party itself a previously undetected taste for reform. The medicine finally applied to the long-suffering federal government was the Pendleton Act of 1883—the so-called Magna Carta of civil-service reform. It made compulsory campaign contributions from federal employees illegal, and it established the Civil Service Commission to make appointments to federal jobs on the basis of competitive examinations rather than party pull.

Although at first covering only about 10 percent of federal jobs, civil service reform did rein in the most blatant political abuses. Yet like many well-intentioned reforms, it bred unintended problems of its own. With the "plum" federal posts now beyond their reach, politicians were forced to look elsewhere for money, the "mother's milk of politics." Increasingly, they turned to the bulging coffers of the big corporations. A new breed of boss emerged—less skilled at mobilizing small armies of immigrants and other voters on election day, but more adept at milking dollars from manufacturers and lobbyists.

★ The Blaine-Cleveland Mudslingers of 1884

President Arthur's surprising display of integrity offended too many powerful Republicans, and his ungrateful party refused to nominate him in 1884. Instead they turned to James G. Blaine, whose persistence in pursuit of the presidential nomination finally paid off. The dashing Maine politician, blessed with almost every asset except a reputation for honesty, was the clear choice of the Republican convention in Chicago, though reformers gagged at his candidacy.

Blaine's enemies publicized the Republican nominee's fishy-smelling "Mulligan letters," written by Blaine to a Boston businessman. These damning documents linked Blaine to a corrupt deal involving federal favors to a southern railroad, and one of them ended with the furtive warning "Burn this letter." Some reformers, unable to swallow Blaine, bolted to the Democrats. They were sneeringly dubbed Mugwumps, a word of Indian derivation meaning "sanctimonious" or "holier than thou."

Victory-starved Democrats turned enthusiastically to a noted reformer, Grover Cleveland. A burly bachelor with a soup-straining mustache and a taste for chewing tobacco, Cleveland was a solid but not brilliant lawyer of forty-seven. He had rocketed from the Buffalo mayor's office to the governorship of New York and the presidential nomination in three short years. Known as "Grover the Good," he enjoyed a well-deserved reputation for probity in office.

But Cleveland's admirers soon got a shock. Resolute Republicans, digging for dirt in the past of bachelor Cleveland, unearthed the fact that he had been involved in an amorous affair with a Buffalo widow. Cleveland had provided financial support for her illegitimate son, now eight years old. Demoralized Democratic elders hurried to Cleveland and urged him to lie like a gentleman, but their ruggedly honest candidate insisted, "Tell the truth."

The campaign of 1884 sank to perhaps the lowest level in American experience, as the two parties grunted and shoved for the hog trough of office. Few fundamental differences separated them. Even the bloody shirt had faded to pale pink.* Personalities, not principles, claimed the headlines. Crowds of Democrats surged through city streets, chanting—to the rhythm of left, left, left, right, left—"Burn, burn, burn this letter!" Republicans taunted in return, "Ma, ma, where's my pa?" Defiant Democrats shouted back, "Gone to the White House, ha, ha, ha!"

The contest hinged on the state of New York, where Blaine blundered badly in the closing days of the campaign. A witless Republican clergyman damned the Democrats in a speech as the party of "Rum, Romanism, and Rebellion"— insulting with one swift stroke the culture, the faith, and the patriotism of New York's numerous Irish Americans. Blaine was present at the time but lacked the presence of mind to repudiate the statement immediately. The pungent phrase, shortened to "RRR," stung and stuck. Blaine's silence seemed to give assent, and the wavering Irishmen who then deserted his camp helped to account for Cleveland's paper-thin plurality of about a thousand votes in New York State, enough to give him the presidency. Cleveland swept the solid South and squeaked into office with 219 to 182 electoral votes and 4,879,507 to 4,850,293 popular votes.

---

*Neither candidate had served in the Civil War. Cleveland had hired a substitute to go in his stead while he supported his widowed mother and two sisters. Blaine was the only candidate nominated by the Republicans from Grant through McKinley (1868–1900) who had not been a Civil War officer.

Contending Voices

The Spoils System

In a famous series of newspaper interviews in 1905, George Washington Plunkitt (1842–1924), a political "boss" in the same Tammany Hall Democratic political "machine" that had spawned William Marcy ("Boss") Tweed, candidly described his ethical and political principles, which included a distinction between "honest graft and dishonest graft." Here he condemns civil-service reform while defending the efficacy of the patronage system.

"This civil service law is the biggest fraud of the age. It is the curse of the nation. There can't be no real patriotism while it lasts. How are you goin' to interest our young men in their country if you have no offices to give them when they work for their party? . . . First, this great and glorious country was built up by political parties; second, parties can't hold together if their workers don't get the offices when they win; third, if the parties go to pieces, the government they built up must go to pieces, too; fourth, then there'll be h– to pay."

Future U.S. president Theodore Roosevelt (1858–1919), by contrast, served as a civil-service commissioner and charged the patronage system with "tending to degrade American politics."

"The men who are in office only for what they can make out of it are thoroughly unwholesome citizens, and their activity in politics is simply noxious. . . . Decent private citizens must inevitably be driven out of politics if it is suffered to become a mere selfish scramble for plunder, where victory rests with the most greedy, the most cunning, the most brazen. The whole patronage system is inimical to American institutions; it forms one of the gravest problems with which democratic and republican government has to grapple."

> Who benefited and who lost out in the process of reforming the civil service and curbing political patronage?

"I Want My Pa!" Malicious anti-Cleveland cartoon.

★ "Old Grover" Takes Over

Bull-necked Cleveland in 1885 was the first Democrat to take the oath of presidential office since Buchanan, twenty-eight years earlier. Huge question marks hung over his portly frame (5 feet 11 inches, 250 pounds). Could the "party of disunion" be trusted to govern the Union? Would desperate Democrats, ravenously hungry after twenty-four years of exile, trample the frail sprouts of civil-service reform in a stampede to the patronage trough? Could Cleveland restore a measure of respect and power to the maligned and enfeebled presidency?

Cleveland was a man of principles, most of them safely orthodox by the standards of the day. A staunch apostle of the hands-off creed of laissez-faire, the new president summed up his political philosophy in 1887 when he vetoed a bill to provide seeds for drought-ravaged Texas farmers. "Though the people support the government," he declared, "the government should not support the people." As tactless as a mirror and as direct as a bulldozer, Cleveland was outspoken, unbending, and profanely hot-tempered.

At the outset Cleveland narrowed the North–South chasm by naming to the cabinet two former Confederates. As for the civil service, Cleveland was whipsawed between the demands of the Democratic faithful for jobs and the demands of the Mugwumps, who had helped elect him, for reform. Believing in the merit system, Cleveland at first favored the cause of the reformers, but he eventually caved in to the carpings of Democratic bosses and fired almost two-thirds of the 120,000 federal employees, including 40,000 incumbent (Republican) postmasters, to make room for "deserving Democrats."

Military pensions gave Cleveland some of his most painful political headaches. The politically powerful Grand Army of the Republic (GAR) routinely lobbied hundreds of often questionable private pension bills through a compliant Congress. As a non-veteran, Cleveland was in an awkward position to fight the pension grabbers, but he conscientiously read each bill and ended up vetoing several hundred of them.

Cleveland also risked his political neck by prodding the hornet's nest of the tariff issue. Jacked up to new high levels during the Civil War, the tariff duties were producing enormous revenues while comfortably sheltering American industry. By 1881 the Treasury was running an annual surplus amounting to an embarrassing $145 million. Congress could reduce the surplus either by squandering it on pensions or other "pork-barrel" bills or by lowering the tariff—something big industrialists vehemently opposed.

With his characteristic bluntness, Cleveland tossed an appeal for lower tariffs like a bombshell into the lap of Congress in late 1887. The response was electric. Democrats were deeply frustrated by the obstinacy of their chief. Republicans rejoiced at his apparent recklessness, bellowing loudly that lower tariffs would mean higher taxes, lower wages, and increased unemployment. The old warrior Blaine gloated, "There's one more president for us in [tariff] protection." For the first time in years, a real issue divided the two parties as the 1888 presidential election loomed.

Dismayed Democrats, seeing no alternative, dejectedly renominated Cleveland at their St. Louis convention, while eager Republicans turned to Benjamin Harrison of Indiana, the grandson of former president William Henry ("Tippecanoe") Harrison. The tariff was the prime issue, and the two parties flooded the country with some 10 million pamphlets on the subject. Republicans raised an unprecedented $3 million war chest, largely by "frying the fat" out of nervous industrialists. The money was widely used to line up corrupt "voting cattle," known as "repeaters" or "floaters," especially in crucial swing states like Indiana.

On election day, Harrison nosed out Cleveland, 233 to 168 electoral votes. A change of about 7,000 ballots in New York would have reversed the outcome. Cleveland actually polled more popular votes, 5,537,857 to 5,447,129, but he nevertheless became the first sitting president to be voted out of his chair since Martin Van Buren in 1840.

★ Republicans Return under Harrison

After a four-year famine, the Republicans under Harrison licked their lips hungrily for federal offices to lavish upon the party faithful. But in the House of Representatives they had only three votes more than the necessary quorum of 163 members, and the Democrats were preparing to obstruct all House business by refusing to answer roll calls, demanding roll calls to determine the presence of a quorum, and other similar delaying tactics.

Into this tense cockpit stepped the new Republican Speaker of the House, Thomas B. Reed of Maine. A tall, hulking figure, Reed was a master debater who spoke with a harsh nasal drawl and wielded a verbal harpoon of sarcasm. To one congressman who quoted Henry Clay's saying that he would "rather be right than be president," Reed caustically retorted that he "would never be either." Opponents cringed at the crack of his quip.

"Czar" Reed soon bent the intimidated House to his imperious will. Employing clever parliamentary tactics to the full, Reed utterly dominated the "Billion-Dollar" Congress—the first in history to appropriate that sum. Congress showered pensions on Civil War veterans and increased government purchases of silver. To keep the revenues flowing in—and to protect Republican industrialists from foreign competition—the Billion-Dollar Congress also passed the McKinley Tariff Act of 1890, boosting rates to their highest peacetime level ever (an average of 48.4 percent on dutiable goods).

Sponsored in the House of Representatives by rising Republican star William McKinley of Ohio, the new tariff act brought fresh woes to farmers. Debt-burdened farmers had no choice but to buy high-priced manufactured goods from protected American industrialists, but they were compelled to sell their own agricultural products into highly competitive, unprotected world markets. Mounting discontent against Bill McKinley and his McKinley Bill caused many rural voters to rise in wrath. In the congressional elections of 1890, Republicans lost their precarious majority and were reduced to just 88 seats, compared with 235 Democrats. Ominously for conservatives, the new Congress also included nine members of the Farmers' Alliance, a militant organization of southern and western farmers.

★ The Drumbeat of Discontent

Politics was no longer "as usual" in 1892, when the newly formed People's party, or "Populists," burst upon the scene. Rooted in the Farmers' Alliances in the great agricultural belts of the West and South, the Populists met in Omaha and adopted a scorching platform that denounced the "prolific womb of governmental injustice." They demanded inflation through free and unlimited coinage of silver at the ratio of sixteen ounces of silver to one ounce of gold. They further called for a graduated income tax; government ownership of the railroads, telephone, and telegraph; the direct election of U.S. senators; a one-term limit on the presidency; the adoption of the initiative and referendum to allow citizens to shape legislation more directly; a shorter workday; and immigration restrictions. As their presidential candidate the Populists uproariously nominated the eloquent old Greenbacker, General James B. Weaver.

An epidemic of nationwide strikes in the summer of 1892 raised the prospect that the Populists could weld together a coalition of aggrieved workers and indebted farmers in a revolutionary joint assault on the capitalist order. At Andrew Carnegie's Homestead steel plant near Pittsburgh, company officials called in three hundred armed Pinkerton

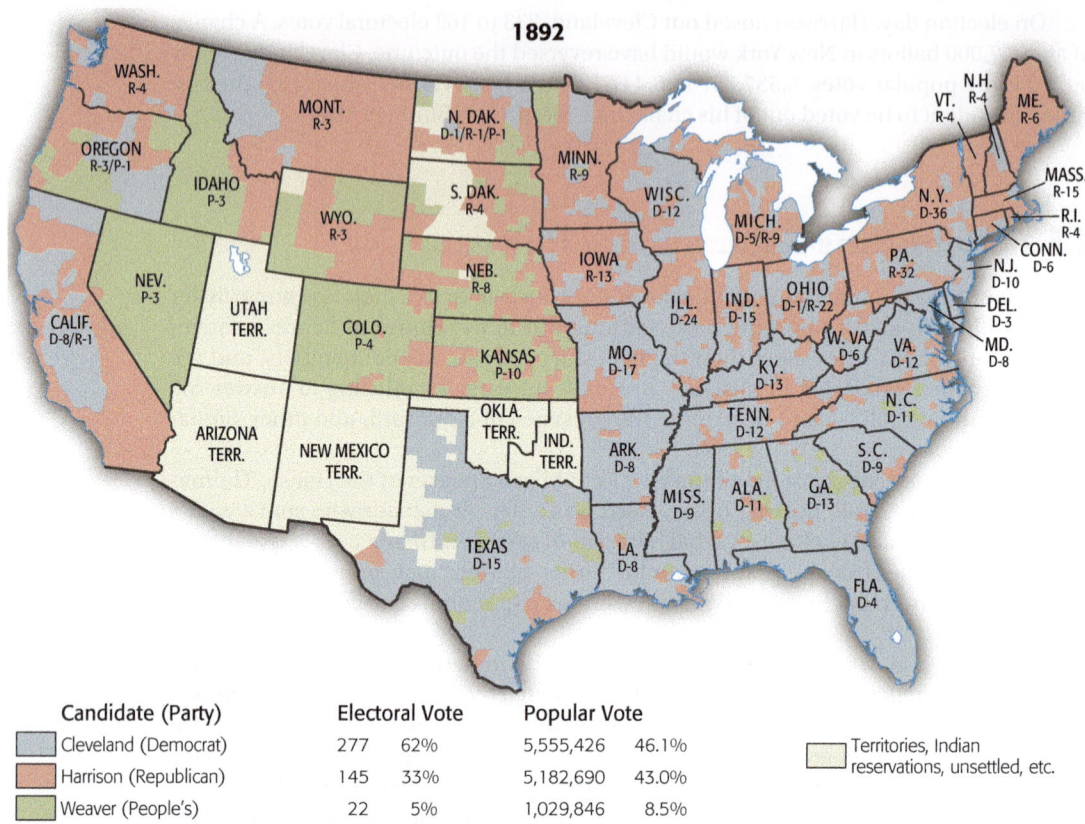

Map 23.2 Presidential Election of 1892 (showing vote by county) Note the concentration of Populist strength in the semiarid farming regions of the western half of the country.

Homestead Strike (1892) *A strike at a Carnegie steel plant in Homestead, Pennsylvania, that ended in an armed battle between the strikers and three hundred armed Pinkerton detectives hired by Carnegie, and federal troops, which killed ten people and wounded more than sixty. The strike was part of a nationwide wave of labor unrest in the summer of 1892 that helped the Populists gain some support from industrial workers.*

detectives in July to crush the obstinate **Homestead Strike** by steelworkers angry over pay cuts. Defiant strikers, armed with rifles and dynamite, forced their assailants to surrender after a vicious battle that left ten people dead and some sixty wounded. Troops were eventually summoned, and both the strike and the union were broken. That same month, federal troops bloodily smashed a strike among silver miners in Idaho's Coeur d'Alene district.

The Populists made a remarkable showing in the 1892 presidential election (see Map 23.2). Singing "Good-bye, Party Bosses," they rolled up 1,029,846 popular votes and 22 electoral votes for General Weaver. They thus became one of the few third parties in U.S. history to break into the electoral column. But they fell far short of an electoral majority. Industrial laborers, especially in the urban East, did not rally to the Populist banner in appreciable numbers. Populist electoral votes came from only six midwestern and western states, four of which (Kansas, Colorado, Idaho, and Nevada) fell completely into the Populist basket.

The South, although a hotbed of agrarian agitation, proved especially unwilling to throw in its lot with the new party. Race was the reason. The more than 1 million southern black farmers, organized in the Colored Farmers' National Alliance, shared a host of complaints with poor white farmers, and for a time their common economic goals promised to overcome their racial differences. Recognizing the crucial edge that black votes could give them in the South, Populist leaders such as Georgia's Tom

A popular protest song of the 1890s among western farmers was titled "The Hayseed." One stanza ran,

I once was a tool of oppression,
And as green as a sucker could be,
And monopolies banded together
To beat a poor hayseed like me.

Watson reached out to the black community. Watson was a wiry redhead who could "talk like the thrust of a Bowie knife." He declared, "There is no reason why the black man should not understand that the law that hurts me, as a farmer, hurts him, as a farmer." Many blacks were disillusioned enough with the Republican party to respond. Alarmed, the conservative white "Bourbon" elite in the South played cynically upon historic racial antagonisms to counter the Populists' appeal for interracial solidarity and woo back poor whites.

Southern blacks were heavy losers. The Populist-inspired reminder of potential black political strength led to the near-total extinction of what little African American suffrage remained in the South. White southerners more aggressively than ever used literacy tests and poll taxes to deny blacks the ballot. The notorious **grandfather clause** exempted from those requirements anyone whose forebear had voted in 1860—when, of course, black slaves had not voted at all. More than half a century would pass before southern blacks could again vote in considerable numbers. Accompanying this disfranchisement were more severe Jim Crow laws designed to enforce racial segregation in public places, including hotels and restaurants, and backed up by atrocious lynchings and other forms of intimidation.

The conservative crusade to eliminate the black vote also had dire consequences for the Populist party itself. Even Tom Watson abandoned his interracial appeals and, in time, became a vociferous racist himself. After 1896 the Populist party lapsed increasingly into vile racism and staunchly advocated black disfranchisement. Such were the bitterly ironic fruits of the Populist campaign in the South.

grandfather clause *A regulation established in many southern states in the 1890s that exempted from voting requirements (such as literacy tests and poll taxes) anyone who could prove that his ancestors ("grandfathers") had been able to vote in 1860. Because slaves could not vote before the Civil War, these clauses guaranteed the right to vote to many whites while denying it to blacks.*

★ Grover, Grim Times, and Gold

With the Populists divided and the Republicans discredited, Grover Cleveland took office once again in 1893, the only president ever reelected after defeat. He was the same old bull-necked and bullheaded Cleveland, with a little more weight, polish, conservatism, and self-assertiveness.

But though it was the same old Cleveland, it was not the same old country. Debtors were up in arms, workers were restless, and the advance shadows of panic were falling. Hardly had Cleveland seated himself back in the presidential chair when the devastating depression of 1893 burst about his burly frame. Lasting for about four years, it was the most punishing economic downturn of the nineteenth century. Contributing causes were the splurge of overbuilding and speculation, labor disorders, and the ongoing agricultural depression. Free-silver agitation—the cry to expand the money supply with unlimited coinage of silver—had also damaged American credit abroad, and the pinch on American finances had come when European banking houses began to call in loans from the United States.

Distress ran deep and far. About eight thousand American businesses collapsed in six months. Dozens of railroad lines went into receivership. Soup kitchens fed the unemployed, while gangs of hoboes ("tramps") wandered aimlessly about the country. Local charities did their feeble best, but the federal government, bound by the let-nature-take-its-course philosophy of the times, saw no legitimate way to relieve the suffering masses.

Cleveland, who had earlier been bothered by a surplus, was now burdened by a deepening deficit and a financial crisis. Owners of the paper currency issued under the Sherman Silver Purchase Act of 1890 were presenting the notes for redemption in gold. By law the notes then had to be reissued, and the new holders would then repeat the process, draining away gold in an "endless chain" operation.

Alarmingly, the gold reserve in the Treasury dropped below the $100 million regarded as the safe minimum for supporting about $350 million in outstanding paper currency. Cleveland saw no alternative but to halt the bleeding away of gold by asking Congress to repeal the Sherman Silver Purchase Act of 1890.

The debate in Congress over repeal of the silver act was heated. A silver-tongued young Democratic congressman from Nebraska, thirty-three-year-old William Jennings Bryan, held the galleries spellbound for three hours as he championed the cause of free silver. The friends of silver announced that "hell would freeze over" before Congress passed the repeal measure. But an angered Cleveland used his patronage power to break the filibuster in the Senate and ram the measure through. He thus alienated Democratic silverites such as Bryan and divided his own his party at the very outset of his second administration.

Repeal of the Sherman Silver Purchase Act only partially stopped the hemorrhaging of gold from the Treasury. In February 1894 the gold reserve sank to a dismaying $41 million. The United States was now in grave danger of going off the gold standard—a move that would render the nation's currency volatile and unreliable and also mortally cripple America's international trade.

Early in 1895 Cleveland turned in desperation to J. P. Morgan, "the bankers' banker" and the head of a Wall Street syndicate. After tense negotiations at the White House, Morgan and his fellow bankers agreed to lend the government $65 million in gold. They were obviously in business for profit, so they charged a commission amounting to about $7 million. The loan, at least temporarily, helped restore confidence in the nation's finances.

But the gold deal stirred up a storm. In the eyes of the silverites and other debtors, the Wall Street ogre represented all that was wicked and grasping in American politics. President Cleveland's secretive dealings with the mighty "Jupiter" Morgan were savagely condemned as a "sellout" of the national government. But Cleveland was certain that he had done no wrong. Sarcastically denying that he was "Morgan's errand boy," Cleveland asserted, "Without shame and without repentance I confess my share of the guilt."

Cleveland suffered further embarrassment with the passage of the Wilson-Gorman Tariff in 1894. The Democrats had pledged to lower tariffs, but by the time the measure made it through Congress, it had been so loaded with special-interest protection that it made scarcely a dent in the high McKinley Tariff rates. An outraged Cleveland grudgingly allowed the bill, which also contained a 2 percent tax on incomes over $4,000, to become law without his signature. When the Supreme Court struck down the income-tax provision in 1895,* the Populists and other disaffected groups found further proof that the courts were only the tools of the plutocrats.

Democratic political fortunes naturally suffered in the face of these setbacks. The tariff dynamite that had blasted the Republicans out of the House in 1890 now dislodged the Democrats, with a strong helping hand from the depression. The revitalized Republicans, singing "Times Are Mighty Hard," won the congressional elections of 1894 in a landslide—244 seats to 105 for the Democrats. Republicans looked forward to the 1896 presidential elections with unconcealed glee.

Despite his gruff integrity and occasional courage, Grover Cleveland failed utterly to cope with the serious economic crisis that befell the country in 1893. He was tied down in office by the same threads that held all the presidents of the day to Lilliputian levels. Grant, Hayes, Garfield, Arthur, Harrison, and Cleveland are often referred to as the "forgettable presidents." Bewhiskered and bland in person, they left mostly blanks—or blots—on the nation's political record, as issues such as the tariff, the money question, and the rights of labor continued to fester. What little political vitality existed in Gilded Age America was to be found in local settings or in Congress, which overshadowed the White House for most of this period. But before the century ended, down-and-out debtors and disgruntled workers would make one last titanic effort to wring reform out of the political system—in the momentous election of 1896.

---

*It violated the "direct tax" clause. See Art. I, Sec. IX, para. 4 in the Appendix. The Sixteenth Amendment of the Constitution, adopted in 1913, permitted an income tax.

Varying Viewpoints

The Populists: Radicals or Reactionaries?

Taking their cue from contemporary satirical commentaries such as Mark Twain and Charles Dudley Warner's *The Gilded Age* (1873), the first historians who wrote about the post–Civil War era judged it harshly. They condemned its politicians as petty and corrupt, lamented the emergence of a new plutocratic class, and railed against the arrogance of corporate power. Such a view is conspicuous in Charles and Mary Beard's *The Rise of American Civilization* (4 vols., 1927–1942), perhaps the most influential American history text ever written.

The Beards were leaders of the so-called progressive school of historical writing that flourished in the early years of the twentieth century. Progressive historians were chillingly antibusiness and warmly pro-labor, pro-farmer, and pro-reform. They identified Populism as virtually the only organized opposition to the social, economic, and political order that took shape in the last decades of the nineteenth century. The Populists thus became heroes to historians such as John D. Hicks, whose work *The Populist Revolt* (1931) is the classic portrayal of the Populists as embattled farmers hurling defiance at Wall Street and the robber barons in defense of their simple, honest way of life. Bowed but unbroken by the defeat of their great champion, William Jennings Bryan, in the presidential election of 1896, the Populists, Hicks claimed, left a reformist legacy that flourished again in the progressive era and the New Deal.

Hicks's point of view was the dominant one until the 1950s, when it was sharply criticized by Richard Hofstadter in *The Age of Reform* (1955). The city-born-and-bred Hofstadter argued that the Populists were best understood not as picturesque protesters, but as "harassed little country businessmen" bristling with provincial prejudices not just against Wall Street, but also irrationally against urbanism, immigrants, the East, and modernity itself. Hofstadter thus exposed a "dark side" of Populism that contained elements of backwoods anti-intellectualism, paranoia, and even anti-Semitism.

In the 1960s several scholars, inspired by the work of C. Vann Woodward, as well as by sympathy with the protest movements of that turbulent decade, began to rehabilitate the Populists as authentic reformers with genuine grievances. Especially notable in this vein was Lawrence Goodwyn's *Democratic Promise: The Populist Movement in America* (1976), which portrayed Populism as the last gasp of popular political revolt against urban industrialism and finance capitalism, a democratic "moment" in American history that expired with the Populists' absorption into the Democratic party.

Two subsequent works, Edward L. Ayers's *Promise of the New South* (1992) and Robert C. McMath's *American Populism* (1993), synthesized many of the older perspectives and presented a balanced view of the Populists as radical in many ways but also limited by their nostalgia for a lost agrarian past. In the last decade Charles Postel's *The Populist Vision* (2007) made the strongest argument yet for the movement's forward-looking elements, while Eric Rauchway's *Blessed Among Nations* (2006) argued that Populism was a reaction to America's increased reliance on foreign investment. Although Hofstadter had made a similar point about resentment of foreign economic control, the impact of the international economy on domestic politics is again a direction for research.

CHAPTER SUMMARY

After the soaring ideals and tremendous sacrifices of the Civil War, the post–Civil War era was generally one of political disillusionment and even cynicism. Politicians from the White House to the courthouse were deeply enmeshed in corruption and scandal, while the actual economic, ethnic, and racial problems afflicting industrializing America festered beneath the surface without being seriously addressed.

The popular war hero Grant was a poor politician and his administration was rife with corruption. Despite occasional futile reform efforts by both high-minded "Mugwumps" and third-party agrarians, politics in the Gilded Age was monopolized by the two patronage-fattened parties, which competed vigorously for spoils while essentially agreeing on most national policies. Cultural and religious differences, different ethnic and regional bases, and deeply felt local issues fueled intense party competition and unprecedented voter participation. Periodic complaints by political reformers and "soft-money" farmers' advocates failed to make much of a dent on politics or the *laissez-faire* business economics of the time.

The deadlocked and bitterly contested 1876 election led to the crass Compromise of 1877, which put an end to Reconstruction at the price of abandoning southern blacks. An oppressive economic system that combined tenant farming and sharecropping with racial segregation and oppression was thereafter fastened on the South, enforced by sometimes lethal violence. Racial prejudice against Chinese immigrants was also linked with labor unrest in the 1870s and 1880s.

Garfield's assassination by a disappointed office seeker spurred the beginnings of civil-service reform but made politics more dependent on big business. Cleveland, the first Democratic president since the Civil War, proposed a lower tariff, creating the first real issue in national politics for some time. But the weakness of conventional politics was exposed by a major economic depression that began in 1893. This crisis, the worst of the nineteenth century, deepened the growing outcry from suffering farmers and workers against a government and economic system that seemed biased toward big business and the wealthy.

KEY TERMS

- "waving the bloody shirt" (368)
- Tweed Ring (368)
- Crédit Mobilier scandal (368)
- panic of 1873 (370)
- Gilded Age (371)
- patronage (371)
- Compromise of 1877 (373)
- Civil Rights Act of 1875 (373)
- sharecropping (374)
- Jim Crow (374)
- *Plessy v. Ferguson* (374)
- Chinese Exclusion Act (376)
- Pendleton Act (376)
- Homestead Strike (380)
- grandfather clause (381)

PEOPLE TO KNOW

- Jay Gould
- Horace Greeley
- Rutherford B. Hayes
- James A. Garfield
- Chester Arthur
- Grover Cleveland
- Thomas B. Reed
- Tom Watson
- William Jennings Bryan
- J. P. Morgan

MindTap is a fully online, highly personalized learning experience built upon Cengage Learning content. MindTap combines student learning tools—readings, multimedia, activities, and assessments—into a singular Learning Path that guides students through the course.

Chapter 24

Industry Comes of Age
1865–1900

The wealthy class is becoming more wealthy, but the poorer class is becoming more dependent. The gulf between the employed and the employer is growing wider; social contrasts are becoming sharper; as liveried carriages appear, so do barefooted children.

HENRY GEORGE, 1879

Chapter Outline

- The Railroad Boom
- Speculators and Financiers
- Early Efforts at Government Regulation
- Lords of Industry
- Industry in the South
- Workers and Unions
- *Examining the Evidence: The Photography of Lewis W. Hine*
- *Varying Viewpoints: Industrialization: Boon or Blight?*

As the nineteenth century drew toward a close, observers were asking, "Why are the best men not in politics?" One answer was that they were being lured away from public life by the lusty attractions of the booming private economy. As America's Industrial Revolution slipped into high gear, talented men ached for profits, not the presidency. They dreamed of controlling corporations, not Congress. What the nation lost in civic leadership, it gained in an astounding surge of economic growth. As late as 1870, agriculture was the nation's biggest business. By 1900 its share of the economy was half that. Until the end of the Civil War the United States imported more merchandise than it exported. By 1900 it annually delivered more than $600 million worth of manufactured goods into the world's marketplace. Americans did not achieve this economic transformation all by themselves. Foreign investment, labor, trade, and technology made it possible. Although in many ways still a political dwarf, the United States was about to stand up before the world as an industrial colossus—and the lives of millions of working Americans would be transformed in the process.

FOCUS QUESTIONS

1. How did the transcontinental railroad network promote the post–Civil War transformation of American industry?
2. How did the American economy come to be dominated by monopolistic corporations in industries such as steel and oil, and what was the public and governmental response to these huge combinations?
3. Why was the South generally excluded from industrial development, and what were the economic, social, and racial problems that the region faced as a result?
4. How did industrialization alter American society, particularly the role of the working class and of women?
5. Why did late-nineteenth-century American labor unions generally fail to mobilize American workers?

CHRONOLOGY

1862	Congress authorizes transcontinental railroad	1876	Bell invents telephone
		1879	Edison invents electric light
1866	National Labor Union organized First working transatlantic telegraph cable	1886	Haymarket Square bombing *Wabash* case American Federation of Labor formed
1869	Transcontinental railroad joined near Ogden, Utah Knights of Labor organized Suez Canal completed	1887	Interstate Commerce Act
		1890	Sherman Anti-Trust Act
1870	Standard Oil Company organized	1901	United States Steel Corporation formed

★ The Iron Colt Becomes an Iron Horse

The government-business entanglements that increasingly shaped politics after the Civil War also undergirded the industrial development of the nation. The unparalleled outburst of railroad construction was a crucial case. When Lincoln was shot in 1865, there were only 35,000 miles of steam railways in the United States, mostly east of the Mississippi. By 1900 the figure had spurted up to 192,556 miles, or more than that for all Europe combined, and much of the new track ran west of the Mississippi.

Transcontinental railroad building was so costly and risky as to require government subsidies, as it had in many other industrializing nations. Everywhere, the construction of railway systems promised greater national unity and economic growth. Congress began to advance liberal loans to two favored cross-continent companies in 1862 and added enormous donations of acreage paralleling the tracks. All told, Washington rewarded the railroads with 155,504,994 acres, and the western states contributed 49 million more—a total area larger than Texas (see Map 24.1).

In later years much criticism was leveled at the "giveaway" of so valuable a birthright to greedy corporations. But the government did receive beneficial returns, including preferential rates for postal service and military traffic. Critics also overlooked the fact that western land had very little value until the railroads made it accessible for settlers and merchants. Little wonder that communities fought one another for the privilege of playing host to the railroads, often offering monetary or other attractions to entice the rail lines to their town.

Deadlock in the 1850s over the location of the proposed transcontinental railroad was broken when the South seceded, leaving the field to the North. In 1862, the year after the guns first spoke at Fort Sumter, Congress made provision for starting the long-awaited line. One weighty argument for action was the urgency of bolstering the Union, already disrupted, by binding the Pacific Coast more securely to the rest of the Republic.

The Union Pacific Railroad—note the word *Union*—was thus commissioned by Congress to thrust westward from Omaha, Nebraska. The laying of rails began in earnest after the Civil War ended in 1865, and with juicy loans and land grants available, the "groundhog" promoters made all possible haste.

Sweaty construction gangs, which included many Irish "Paddies" (Patricks), worked at a frantic pace. On one record-breaking day, a sledge-and-shovel army of some five thousand men laid ten miles of track. A favorite song was:

> *Then drill, my Paddies, drill;*
> *Drill, my heroes, drill;*
> *Drill all day,*
> *No sugar in your tay [tea]*
> *Workin' on the U.P. Railway.*

When hostile Indians attacked, the laborers would drop their picks and seize their rifles. At rail's end, workers tried to find relaxation and conviviality in tented towns known as "hells on wheels," often teeming with as many as ten thousand men and a sprinkling of painted prostitutes and performers.

Rail laying at the California end was undertaken by the Central Pacific Railroad. This line pushed boldly eastward from boomtown Sacramento, over and through the towering, snow-clogged Sierra Nevada. Four farseeing men—the so-called Big Four—were the chief financial backers of the enterprise. The quartet included the heavyset, enterprising ex-governor Leland Stanford of California, who had useful political connections, and the burly, energetic Collis P. Huntington, an adept lobbyist.

The Central Pacific, which was granted the same princely subsidies as the Union Pacific, had the same incentive to haste. Some ten thousand Chinese laborers sweated from dawn to dusk under their basket hats. Hundreds lost their lives in premature explosions and other mishaps. The towering Sierra Nevada presented a formidable barrier; and the nerves of the Big Four were strained when their workers could chip only a few inches a day through solid rock, while the Union Pacific was sledgehammering westward across the plains.

A "wedding of the rails" was finally consummated near Ogden, Utah, in 1869, as the two locomotives gently kissed cowcatchers. The colorful ceremony included the breaking of champagne bottles and the driving of a last ceremonial (golden) spike, with ex-governor Leland Stanford clumsily wielding a silver maul.* In all, the Union Pacific built 1,086 miles, the Central Pacific 689 miles.

---

*The spike was promptly removed and is now exhibited at the Stanford University Museum.

Map 24.1 Federal Land Grants to Railroads The heavy red lines indicate areas within which the railroads might be given specific parcels of land. As shown in the inset, land was reserved in belts of various widths on either side of a railroad's right of way. Until the railroad selected the individual mile-square sections it chose to possess, *all* such sections within the belt were withdrawn from eligibility for settlement. The "time zones" were introduced in 1883 (see p. 389), and their boundaries have since been adjusted.

The Union Pacific and the Central Pacific Link at Promontory Point, Utah, May 10, 1869 Railroad financiers, dignitaries, spectators, and Chinese (Central Pacific) and Irish (Union Pacific) work gangs witnessed the historic joining that created the nation's first transcontinental railroad. After the two locomotives chugged within a few feet of each other, Central Pacific chief and former California governor Leland Stanford tapped a golden spike into a prepared hole on the last tie with a silver-plated maul. The golden spike was whisked away to be preserved for posterity at the Stanford University Museum, but the iron one that replaced it was hardly ordinary. It was wired to a Union Pacific telegraph line, while a copper plate on the maul was connected to a Central Pacific wire. When they touched, they closed a telegraphic circuit that sent the news to cities all over the country.

In 1892 James Baird Weaver (1833–1912), nominee of the Populists, wrote regarding the railroad magnates:

"In their delirium of greed the managers of our transportation systems disregard both private right and the public welfare. Today they will combine and bankrupt their weak rivals, and by the expenditure of a trifling sum possess themselves of properties which cost the outlay of millions. Tomorrow they will capitalize their booty for five times the cost, issue their bonds, and proceed to levy tariffs upon the people to pay dividends upon the fraud."

With the westward trail now blazed, four other transcontinental lines were completed before the century's end. None of them secured monetary loans from the federal government, as had the Union Pacific and the Central Pacific. But all of them except the Great Northern received generous grants of land.

The Northern Pacific Railroad, stretching from Lake Superior to Puget Sound, reached its terminus in 1883. The Atchison, Topeka, and Santa Fe, stretching through the southwestern deserts to California, was completed in 1884. The Southern Pacific ribboned from New Orleans to San Francisco and was consolidated in the same year.

The last of the five nineteenth-century transcontinental railroads, the Great Northern, ran north of the Northern Pacific from Duluth to Seattle. Its creator was James J. Hill, a far-visioned Canadian American who organized his railroad so soundly that it rode through later financial storms with flying colors.

Yet the romance of the rails was not without its sordid side. Pioneer builders were often guilty of gross overoptimism, laying down rails that went "from nowhere to nothing" in order to get the lavish federal land bounties. When prosperity failed to smile, railroad companies went into bankruptcy, carrying down with them the savings of trusting investors. Many of the large railroads in the post–Civil War decades passed through seemingly endless bankruptcies, mergers, or reorganizations.

★ Revolution by Railways

The metallic fingers of the railroads intimately touched countless phases of American life. For the first time, a sprawling nation became physically bound together with ribs of iron and steel. The railroads emerged as the nation's biggest business, employing more people than any other industry and gobbling up nearly 20 percent of investment dollars, from foreign and domestic investors alike.

More than any other single factor, the railroad network spurred the amazing economic growth of the post–Civil War years. By stitching North America together from ocean to ocean, the puffing locomotives opened up the West with its wealth of resources. Trains hauled raw materials to factories and sped them back as finished goods for sale across the continent, making the United States the largest integrated national market in the world. The forging of the rails themselves provided the largest single source of orders for the adolescent steel industry.

The screeching iron horse especially stimulated mining and agriculture, particularly in the West. The railroads took farmers out to their land, carried the fruits of their toil to market, and brought them their manufactured necessities. Clusters of farm settlements paralleled the railroads, just as earlier they had followed the rivers.

Railways were a boon for cities and played a leading role in the great cityward movement of the last decades of the century. The iron monsters could carry food to enormous concentrations of people and at the same time ensure them a livelihood by providing both raw materials and markets.

Railroad companies also stimulated the mighty stream of immigration. Seeking settlers to whom their land grants might be sold at a profit, they advertised seductively in Europe and sometimes offered to transplant the newcomers free to their farms.

The land also felt the impact of the railroad—especially the broad, ecologically fragile midsection of the continent. Settlers following the railroads plowed up the tallgrass prairies of Iowa, Illinois, Kansas, and Nebraska and planted well-drained, rectangular cornfields. On the shortgrass prairies of the high plains in the Dakotas and Montana, range-fed cattle rapidly displaced the buffalo, which were hunted to near- extinction. The white pine forests of Michigan, Wisconsin, and Minnesota disappeared into lumber that was rushed by rail to prairie farmers who used it to build houses and fences.

Time itself was bent to the railroads' needs. Until the 1880s every town in the United States had its own "local" time, dictated by the sun's position. When it was noon in Chicago, it was 11:50 A.M. in St. Louis and 12:18 P.M. in Detroit. For railroad operators worried about keeping schedules and avoiding wrecks, this patchwork of local times was a nightmare. Thus, on November 18, 1883, the major rail lines decreed that the continent would henceforth be divided into four "time zones." Most communities quickly adopted railroad "standard" time.

Finally, the railroad, more than any other single factor, was the maker of millionaires. A raw new aristocracy, consisting of "lords of the rail" such as eastern railroad magnate Cornelius Vanderbilt and "palace car" inventor George Pullman, replaced the old southern "lords of the lash." The multiwebbed lines became the playthings of Wall Street, and colossal wealth was amassed by stock speculators and corporate railroad manipulators.

★ Wrongdoing in Railroading

Corruption lurks nearby when fabulous fortunes can materialize overnight. The fleecings administered by the railroad construction companies, such as the Crédit Mobilier, were but the first of the bunco games that the railroad promoters learned to play. Methods soon became more refined, as fast-fingered financiers executed multimillion-dollar maneuvers beneath the noses of a bedazzled public. Jay Gould was the most adept of these ringmasters of rapacity. For nearly thirty years he boomed and busted the stocks of the Erie, the Kansas Pacific, the Union Pacific, and the Texas and Pacific in an incredible circus of speculative skullduggery.

One of the favorite devices of the moguls of manipulation was "stock watering." The term originally referred to the practice of making cattle thirsty by feeding them salt, and then having them bloat themselves with water before they were weighed in for sale. Using a variation of this technique, railroad stock promoters grossly inflated their claims about a given line's assets and profitability and sold stocks and bonds far in excess of the railroad's actual value. "Promoters' profits" were often the tail that wagged the iron horse itself. Railroad managers were forced to charge extortionate rates and wage ruthless competitive battles in order to pay off the exaggerated financial obligations with which they were saddled.

The public interest was frequently trampled underfoot as the railroad titans waged their brutal wars. Crusty old Cornelius Vanderbilt, when told that the law stood in his way, reportedly exclaimed: "Law! What do I care about the law? Hain't I got the power?" His son, William H. Vanderbilt, when asked in 1883 about public discontent with the discontinuance of a fast mail train, reportedly snorted, "The public be damned!"

While abusing the public, the railroaders blandly bought and sold people in public life. They bribed judges and legislatures, elected their own agents to high office, and showered free passes on journalists and politicians in exchange for favorable treatment.

Railroad kings were, for a time, virtual industrial monarchs. As manipulators of a huge natural monopoly, they exercised more direct control over the lives of more people than did the president of the United States. They increasingly shunned the crude bloodletting of cutthroat competition and began to cooperate with one another to rule the railroad dominion. Sorely pressed to show at least some returns on their bloated investments, they entered into defensive alliances to protect precious profits.

The earliest form of combination was the "pool"—an agreement to divide the business in a given area and share the profits. Other rail barons granted secret rebates or kickbacks to powerful shippers in return for steady and assured traffic. Often they slashed their rates on competing lines, but they more than made up the difference on noncompeting ones, where they might actually charge more for a short haul than for a long one. As a result, small farmers usually paid the highest rates, while large customers got the best deals.

★ Government Bridles the Iron Horse

It was neither healthy nor politically acceptable that so many people should be at the mercy of so few. Impoverished farmers, especially in the Midwest, began to wonder whether the nation had not escaped from the slavery power only to fall into the hands of the money power, as represented by the railroad plutocracy.

But the American people, usually quick to respond to political injustice, were slow to combat economic injustice. Dedicated to free enterprise and to the principle that competition is the soul of trade, they remembered that Jefferson's ideals were hostile to governmental interference with business. Above all, there shimmered the "American dream": the hope that in a catch-as-catch-can economic system, anyone might become a millionaire.

The depression of the 1870s finally goaded the farmers into protesting against being "railroaded" into bankruptcy. Under pressure from organized agrarian groups such as the Grange (see p. 441), many midwestern legislatures tried to regulate the railroad monopoly. The scattered state efforts screeched to a halt in 1886. The Supreme Court, in the case of *Wabash, St. Louis & Pacific Railroad Company v. Illinois*, decreed that individual states had no power to regulate *inter*state commerce. If the mechanical monster were to be corralled, the federal government would have to do the job.

Congress ignored President Cleveland's grumbling indifference to the problem and passed the **Interstate Commerce Act** in 1887, which prohibited rebates and pools and required the railroads to publish their rates openly. The act also forbade unfair discrimination against shippers and outlawed charging more for a short haul than for a long one

---

Wabash, St. Louis & Pacific Railroad Company v. Illinois (1886) *A Supreme Court decision that prohibited states from regulating the railroads because the Constitution grants Congress the power to regulate interstate commerce. As a result, reformers turned their attention to the federal government, which now held sole power to regulate the railroad industry.*

Interstate Commerce Act (1887) *Congressional legislation that established the Interstate Commerce Commission, compelled railroads to publish standard rates, and prohibited rebates and pools. Railroads quickly became adept at using the act to achieve their own ends, but it gave the government an important means to regulate big business.*

over the same line. Most importantly, the Interstate Commerce Act set up the Interstate Commerce Commission (ICC) to administer and enforce the new legislation.

Despite acclaim, the Interstate Commerce Act emphatically did not represent a popular victory over corporate wealth. One of the leading corporation lawyers of the day, Richard Olney, shrewdly noted that the new commission "can be made of great use to the railroads. It satisfies the popular clamor for a government supervision of railroads, at the same time that such supervision is almost entirely nominal.... The part of wisdom is not to destroy the Commission, but to utilize it."

What the new legislation did do was provide an orderly forum where competing business interests could resolve their conflicts in peaceable ways. The country could now avoid ruinous rate wars among the railroads and deflect angry "confiscatory" attacks on the lines by pitchfork-prodded state legislatures. The Interstate Commerce Act tended to stabilize, not revolutionize, the existing business system.

Yet the act still ranks as a red-letter law. It was the first large-scale attempt by Washington to regulate business in the interest of society at large. The act foreshadowed the doom of freewheeling, buccaneering business practices and served full notice that there was a public interest in private enterprise that the government was bound to protect.

★ Miracles of Mechanization

Postwar industrial expansion, partly a result of the railroad network, rapidly began to assume mammoth proportions. When Lincoln was elected in 1860, the Republic ranked only fourth among the manufacturing nations of the world. By 1894 it had bounded into first place. Why the sudden upsurge?

Liquid capital, previously scarce, was now becoming abundant. The word *millionaire* had not been coined until the 1840s, and in 1861 only a handful of individuals were eligible for this class. But the Civil War, partly through profiteering, created immense fortunes, and these accumulations could now be combined with borrowings from foreign capitalists. Investors from abroad loaned more money to the United States in the postwar period than any country had previously received. Unlike in other countries, in America they mostly put the money into private hands, not public coffers. Investors primarily from Britain, but from France, Germany, the Netherlands, and Switzerland as well, sometimes owned all or part of an American business. Other times they simply lent their money to the thousands of European companies set up to manage investment in U.S. industry. Either way, Europeans were usually content to let Americans run the business.

Innovations in transportation fueled growth, too, by bringing the nation's amazingly abundant natural resources—particularly coal, oil, and iron—to the factory door. A shipping system through the Great Lakes carried the rich iron deposits of the Mesabi range of Minnesota to Chicago and Cleveland for refining. This priceless bonanza, where mountains of red-rusted ore could be scooped up by steam shovels, ultimately became a cornerstone of a vast steel empire. Copper, bauxite, and zinc made similar journeys from mine to manufacture.

The sheer size of the American market encouraged innovators to invent mass-production methods. With cheap transportation crisscrossing the nation and an ever larger population able and eager to consume, anyone who could make an appealing new product available for a good price in large quantities—and figure out how to market it—thrived. Industrialists continued to refine the pre–Civil War "American system" of using specialized machinery to make interchangeable parts, culminating in 1913 with Henry Ford's fully developed, moving, assembly line for his Model T (see "The American System" in Chapter 12, p. 178 and "Putting America on Rubber Tires" in Chapter 30, pp. 526–527).

The captains of industry had a major incentive to invent machines: they made it possible to replace expensive, skilled craft labor with unskilled workers, now cheap and plentiful as a result of massive immigration. Steel, the keystone industry, built its strength largely on the sweat of low-priced immigrant labor from eastern and southern Europe, working in two 12-hour shifts, seven days a week.

Just as industry served as a hothouse of invention, brilliant ideas gave rise to whole new lines of business. Between 1860 and 1890, some 440,000 patents were issued. Business operations were facilitated by such machines as the cash register, the stock ticker, and the typewriter ("literary piano"), while the refrigerator car, the electric dynamo, and the electric railway speeded urbanization. One of the most ingenious inventions was the telephone, introduced by Alexander Graham Bell in 1876. America was suddenly turned into a nation of "telephoniacs," as a gigantic communications network was built on Bell's invention. The social impact of the telephone further expanded when it lured "number please" women away from the stove to the switchboard.

The most versatile inventor of all was Thomas Alva Edison (1847–1931), who as a boy had been considered so dull witted that he was taken out of school. Edison was a gifted tinkerer and a tireless worker, not a pure scientist. "Genius," he said, "is 1 percent inspiration and 99 percent perspiration." Wondrous devices poured out of his "invention factory" in New Jersey—the phonograph, the mimeograph, the dictaphone, and the moving picture. He is probably best known for his perfection in 1879 of the electric lightbulb, which turned night into day and transformed ancient human habits as well. People had previously slept an average of nine hours a night; now they slept just a bit more than seven.

★ The Trust Titan Emerges

Despite pious protests to the contrary, competition was the bugbear of most business leaders of the day. Tycoons like Andrew Carnegie, the steel king; John D. Rockefeller, the oil baron; and J. Pierpont Morgan, the bankers' banker, exercised their genius in devising ways to circumvent competition. Carnegie pioneered the "**vertical integration**" of production by directly controlling every phase of his steel-making operation from mining to marketing. His miners dug the ore from Minnesota's Mesabi range; Carnegie ships floated it across the Great Lakes; Carnegie railroads delivered it to blast furnaces at Pittsburgh. When the molten metal finally poured from the glowing crucibles into the waiting ingot molds, no other hands but those in Carnegie's employ had touched the product.

Rockefeller pursued the less economically justifiable technique of "**horizontal integration**," which simply meant allying with competitors to monopolize a given market. He perfected a device for controlling bothersome rivals—the **trust**. Stockholders in various smaller oil companies assigned their stock to the board of directors of Rockefeller's **Standard Oil Company**, formed in 1870, which then consolidated and concerted the operations of the previously competing enterprises. "Let us prey" was said to be Rockefeller's unwritten motto. Ruthlessly wielding vast power, Standard Oil soon cornered virtually the entire world petroleum market. Weaker competitors, left out of the trust agreement, were forced to the wall. Rockefeller's stunning success inspired many imitators, and the word *trust* came to be generally used to describe any large-scale business combination.

The imperial Morgan devised still other schemes for eliminating "wasteful" competition. The depression of the 1890s drove into his welcoming arms many bleeding businesspeople, wounded by cutthroat competition. His prescribed remedy was to consolidate rival enterprises and to ensure future harmony by placing officers of his own banking syndicate on their various boards of directors. These came to be known as **interlocking directorates**.

★ The Supremacy of Steel

"Steel is king!" might well have been the exultant war cry of the new industrialized generation. The mighty metal ultimately held together the new civilization, from skyscrapers to coal scuttles, while providing it with food, shelter, and transportation. Steel making, notably rails for railroads, typified the dominance of heavy industry, which concentrated on making "capital goods," as distinct from the production of "consumer goods" such as clothes and shoes.

Now taken for granted, steel was a scarce commodity in the wood-and-brick America of Abraham Lincoln. Steel was expensive and was used largely for special products

---

vertical integration *The practice perfected by Andrew Carnegie of controlling every step of the industrial production process in order to increase efficiency and limit competition.*

horizontal integration *The practice perfected by John D. Rockefeller of dominating a particular phase of the production process in order to monopolize a market, often by forming trusts and alliances with competitors.*

trust *A mechanism by which one company grants control over its operations, through ownership of its stock, to another company. The Standard Oil Company became known for this practice in the 1870s as it eliminated its competition by taking control of smaller oil companies.*

Standard Oil Company (1870–1911) *John D. Rockefeller's company, formed in 1870, which came to symbolize the trusts and monopolies of the Gilded Age. By 1877 Standard Oil controlled 95 percent of the oil refineries in the United States. It was also one of the first multinational corporations and at times distributed more than half of its kerosene production outside the United States. By the turn of the century it had become a target for trust-busting reformers, and in 1911 the Supreme Court ordered it to break up into several dozen smaller companies.*

interlocking directorates *The practice of having executives or directors from one company serve on the board of directors of another company. J. P. Morgan introduced this practice to eliminate banking competition in the 1890s.*

like cutlery. Yet within an amazing twenty years after 1870, the United States outdistanced all foreign competitors and was pouring out more than one-third of the world's supply of steel. By 1900 the Americans were producing as much as Britain and Germany combined.

What wrought the transformation? Chiefly, the invention in the 1850s of a method of making cheap steel—the Bessemer process. William Kelly, a Kentucky manufacturer of iron kettles, had earlier discovered that cold air blown on red-hot iron caused the metal to become white-hot by igniting the carbon and thus eliminating impurities. But Kelly was unable to win acceptance for the product. Only after Bessemer, a British inventor, joined forces with Kelly did the Bessemer-Kelly process make possible the new steel civilization.

Kingpin among steelmasters was Andrew Carnegie, an undersized, charming Scotsman. As a towheaded lad of thirteen, he was brought to America by his impoverished parents in 1848 and got a job as a bobbin boy at $1.20 a week. Mounting the ladder of success so fast that he was said to have scorched the rungs, he forged ahead by working hard, doing extra chores, cheerfully assuming responsibility, and smoothly cultivating influential people.

After accumulating some capital, Carnegie entered the steel business in the Pittsburgh area. By 1900 he was producing one-fourth of the nation's Bessemer steel, and the partners in these pre-income tax days were dividing profits of $40 million a year as their take-home pay, with the "Napoleon of the Smokestacks" himself receiving a cool $25 million.

Into the picture now stepped the financial giant of the age, J. Pierpont Morgan. "Jupiter" Morgan had made a legendary reputation for himself and his Wall Street banking house by financing the reorganization of railroads, insurance companies, and banks. An impressive figure of a man, with massive shoulders, shaggy brows, piercing eyes, and a bulbous, acne-cursed red nose, he had established an enviable reputation for integrity. Morgan did not believe that "money power" was dangerous, except when in dangerous hands—and he did not regard his own hands as dangerous.

The force of circumstances brought Morgan and Carnegie into collision. By 1900 the canny little Scotsman, weary of turning steel into gold, was eager to sell his holdings. Morgan had meanwhile plunged heavily into the manufacture of steel pipe tubing. Carnegie, cleverly threatening to invade the same business, was ready to ruin his rival if he did not receive his price. The steelmaster's agents haggled with the imperious Morgan for eight agonizing hours, and the financier finally agreed to buy out Carnegie for over $400 million. Fearing that he would die "disgraced" with so much wealth, Carnegie dedicated the remaining years of his life to giving it away for public libraries, pensions for professors, and other such philanthropic purposes—in all disposing of about $350 million.

Morgan moved rapidly to expand his new industrial empire. He took the Carnegie holdings, added others, "watered" the stock liberally, and in 1901 launched the enlarged United States Steel Corporation. Capitalized at $1.4 billion, it was America's first billion-dollar corporation—a larger sum than the total estimated wealth of the nation in 1800. The Industrial Revolution had come into its own.

★ Rockefeller Grows an American Beauty Rose

Another new industry was born almost overnight when in 1859 the first oil well—"Drake's Folly" in Pennsylvania—poured out its liquid "black gold." Kerosene, derived from petroleum, was the first major product of the infant oil industry. Replacing whale oil as the fuel for America's lamps, kerosene became the country's fourth most valuable export by the 1870s.

But what technology gives, technology takes away. By 1885 Thomas Edison's new electric lightbulbs had rendered kerosene largely obsolete. Oil might thus have remained a modest, even a shrinking, industry but for yet another turn of the technological tide—the invention of the automobile. By 1900 the gasoline-burning internal combustion engine had clearly bested its rivals, steam and electricity, and the oil business got a new, long-lasting, and hugely profitable lease on life.

John D. Rockefeller—lanky, shrewd, ambitious, abstemious (he neither drank, smoked, nor swore)—came to dominate the oil industry. Born to a family of precarious income, he became a successful businessman at age nineteen. One upward stride led to another, and in 1870 he organized the Standard Oil Company of Ohio, nucleus of the great trust formed in 1882.

In the jungle world of big business, a kind of primitive savagery prevailed. Rockefeller—"Reckafellow," as Carnegie had once called him—showed little mercy to his competitors. His son later explained that the giant American Beauty rose could be produced "only by sacrificing the early buds that grew up around it." His father pinched off the small buds with complete ruthlessness. By 1877 Rockefeller controlled 95 percent of all the oil refineries in the country. Employing spies and extorting secret rebates from the railroads, he even forced the lines to pay him rebates on the freight bills of his competitors!

Rockefeller thought he was simply obeying a law of nature. "The time was ripe" for aggressive consolidation, he later reflected. "The day of combination is here to stay. Individualism has gone, never to return." On the other side of the ledger, Rockefeller's oil monopoly did turn out a superior product at a relatively cheap price achieved through its large-scale methods of production and distribution. This, in truth, was the tale of the other trusts as well. The efficient use of expensive machinery called for bigness, and consolidation proved more profitable than ruinous price wars.

Other trusts blossomed along with the American Beauty of oil. These included the sugar trust, the tobacco trust, the leather trust, and the harvester trust, which amalgamated some two hundred competitors. The meat industry arose on the backs of bawling western herds, and meat kings such as Gustavus F. Swift and Philip Armour took their places among the new royalty. Wealth was coming to dominate the commonwealth.

These untrustworthy trusts, and the "pirates" who captained them, were disturbingly new. They eclipsed an older American aristocracy of modestly successful merchants and professionals. An arrogant class of "new rich" was now elbowing aside the patrician families in the mad scramble for power and prestige. Not surprisingly, the ranks of the antitrust crusaders were frequently spearheaded by the "best men"—genteel old-family do-gooders who were not radicals but conservative defenders of their own vanishing influence.

Robber Barons Cyrus Field, Jay Gould, Cornelius Vanderbilt, and Russell Sage Kept Afloat on the Broken Backs of America's Workingmen, 1883

⭐ The Gospel of Wealth

Monarchs of yore invoked the divine right of kings, and America's industrial plutocrats took a somewhat similar stance. Some candidly credited heavenly help and justified their social position with what came to be known as the "Gospel of Wealth." "Godliness is in league with riches," preached the Episcopal bishop of Massachusetts, and hardfisted John D. Rockefeller piously declared that "the good Lord gave me my money."

But most defenders of wide-open capitalism relied more heavily on the survival-of-the-fittest theories of English philosopher Herbert Spencer and Yale Professor William Graham Sumner. Later mislabeled **Social Darwinists**, these theorists argued that individuals won their stations in life by competing on the basis of their natural talents. The wealthy and powerful had simply demonstrated greater abilities than the poor. Spencer and Sumner owed less to English evolutionary naturalist Charles Darwin, who stressed the adaptation of organisms, than to British laissez-faire economists David Ricardo and Thomas Malthus. In fact, Spencer, not Darwin, coined the phrase "survival of the fittest." "The millionaires are a product of natural selection," Sumner declared. In 1883 he asked, "What do social classes owe each other?" then answered his own question: nothing. Some Social Darwinists later applied this theory to explain why some nations were more powerful than others or had the right to dominate "lesser peoples," often defined by race.

Self-justification by the wealthy inevitably involved contempt for the poor. Many of the rich, especially the newly rich, had pulled themselves up by their own bootstraps; hence, they concluded that those who stayed poor must be lazy and lacking in enterprise. The Reverend Russell Conwell of Philadelphia became rich by delivering his lecture "Acres of Diamonds" thousands of times. In it he charged, "There is not a poor person in the United States who was not made poor by his own shortcomings." Such attitudes were a formidable roadblock to social reform.

Plutocracy, like the earlier slavocracy, took its stand firmly on the Constitution. The clause that gave Congress sole jurisdiction over interstate commerce was a godsend to the monopolists; their high-priced lawyers used it time and again to thwart controls by the state legislatures. Giant trusts likewise sought refuge behind the Fourteenth Amendment, which had been originally designed to protect the rights of the ex-slaves as persons. The courts ingeniously interpreted a corporation to be a legal "person" and decreed that, as such, it could not be deprived of its property by a state without "due process of law" (see Art. XIV, para. 1 in the Appendix).

⭐ Government Tackles the Trust Evil

At long last the masses of the people began to mobilize against monopoly. They first tried to control the trusts through state legislation, as they had earlier attempted to curb the railroads. Failing here, as before, they were forced

---

Social Darwinists *Believers in the idea, popular in the late nineteenth century, that people gained wealth by "survival of the fittest." Therefore, the wealthy had simply won a natural competition and owed nothing to the poor, and indeed service to the poor would interfere with this organic process. Some Social Darwinists also applied this theory to whole nations and races, explaining that powerful peoples were naturally endowed with gifts that allowed them to gain superiority over others. This theory provided one of the popular justifications for U.S. imperial ventures like the Spanish-American War.*

Contending Voices

Class and the Gilded Age

Industrial millionaires were condemned in the Populist platform of 1892:

"The fruits of the toil of millions are boldly stolen to build up colossal fortunes for a few ... and the possessors of these, in turn despise the Republic and endanger liberty. From the same prolific womb of governmental injustice we breed the two great classes—tramps and millionaires."

But Yale professor William Graham Sumner (1840–1910), in his 1893 book What Social Classes Owe to Each Other, *defended millionaires:*

"In no sense whatever does a man who accumulates a fortune by legitimate industry exploit his employees, or make his capital 'out of' anybody else. The wealth which he wins would not be but for him.... If we should set a limit to the accumulation of wealth, we should say to our most valuable producers, 'We do not want you to do us the services which you best understand how to perform, beyond a certain point.' It would be like killing off our generals in war."

> In what ways did the opening of new class fissures in the Gilded Age challenge traditional American ideals of social opportunity?

Sherman Anti-Trust Act (1890) *A law that forbade trusts or combinations in business, this was landmark legislation because it was one of the first congressional attempts to regulate big business for the public good. At first the law was mostly used to restrain trade unions, as the courts tended to side with companies in legal cases. In 1914 the act was revised so it could more effectively be used against monopolistic corporations.*

to appeal to Congress. After prolonged pulling and hauling, the **Sherman Anti-Trust Act** of 1890 was finally signed into law.

The Sherman Act flatly forbade combinations in restraint of trade, without making any distinction between "good" trusts and "bad" trusts. Bigness, not badness, was the sin. The law proved ineffective, largely because it had only baby teeth or no teeth at all, and because it contained legal loopholes through which clever corporation lawyers could wriggle. But the act was unexpectedly effective in one respect. Contrary to its original intent, the Sherman Act was used to curb labor unions or labor combinations that were deemed to be restraining trade.

Early prosecutions of the trusts by the Justice Department under the Sherman Act of 1890, as it turned out, were neither vigorous nor successful. Not until 1914 were the paper jaws of the Sherman Act fitted with reasonably sharp teeth. Until then, there was some question as to whether the government would control the trusts or the trusts the government.

But the iron grip of monopolistic corporations was being threatened. A revolutionary new principle had been written into the law books by the Sherman Anti-Trust Act of 1890, as well as by the Interstate Commerce Act of 1887. Private greed should henceforth be subordinated to public need.

★ The South in the Age of Industry

The industrial tidal wave that washed over the North after the Civil War caused only feeble ripples in the backwater of the South. The plantation system had degenerated into a pattern of absentee landownership. White and black sharecroppers now tilled the soil for a share of the crop, or they became tenants, in bondage to landlords who controlled needed credit and supplies.

Southern agriculture received a boost in the 1880s, when machine-made cigarettes replaced the roll-your-own variety and tobacco consumption shot up. James Buchanan Duke took full advantage of the new technology to mass produce the dainty "coffin nails." In 1890, in what was becoming a familiar pattern, he absorbed his main competitors into the American Tobacco Company. The cigarette czar later showed such generosity to Trinity College, near his birthplace in Durham, North Carolina, that the trustees gratefully changed its name to Duke University.

Industrialists tried to coax the agricultural South out of the fields and into the factories, but with only modest success. The region remained overwhelmingly rural. Prominent among the boosters of a "new South" was silver-tongued Henry W. Grady, editor of the *Atlanta Constitution*. He tirelessly exhorted the ex-Confederates to become "Georgia Yankees" and outplay the North at the commercial and industrial game.

Yet formidable obstacles lay in the path of southern industrialization. One was the paper barrier of regional rate-setting systems imposed by the northern-dominated railroad interests. Railroads gave preferential rates to manufactured goods moving southward from the North, but in the opposite direction they discriminated in favor of southern raw materials. The net effect was to keep the South in a kind of servitude to the Northeast—as a supplier of raw materials to the manufacturing metropolis, unable to develop a substantial industrial base of its own.

A bitter example of this economic discrimination against the South was the "Pittsburgh plus" pricing system in the steel industry. Rich deposits of coal and iron ore near Birmingham, Alabama, worked by low-wage southern labor, should have given steel manufacturers there a competitive edge, especially in southern markets. But the steel lords of Pittsburgh brought pressure to bear on the compliant railroads. As a result, Birmingham steel, no matter where it was delivered, was charged a fictional fee, as if it had been shipped from Pittsburgh. This stunting of the South's natural economic advantages throttled the growth of the Birmingham steel industry.

In manufacturing cotton textiles, the South fared considerably better. Southerners had long resented shipping their fiber to New England, and now their cry was, "Bring the mills to the cotton." Beginning about 1880, northern capital began to erect cotton mills in the South, largely in response to tax benefits and the prospect of cheap and nonunionized labor.

The textile mills proved a mixed blessing to the economically blighted South. They slowly wove an industrial thread into the fabric of southern life, but at a considerable human cost. Cheap labor was the South's major attraction for potential investors, and keeping labor cheap became almost a religion among southern industrialists. The mills took root in the chronically depressed Piedmont region of southern Appalachia. Blacks were excluded from the mills, so rural southern whites, often derided as "hillbillies" or "lintheads," worked from dawn to dusk amid the whirring spindles. Paid at half the rate of their northern counterparts, most were perpetually in debt to the company store. But despite their depressed working conditions and poor pay, many southerners saw employment in the mills as a salvation. With many mills anxious to tap the cheap labor of women and children, mill work often offered destitute farm-fugitive families their only chance to remain together.

> *Henry W. Grady (1851–1889), editor of the* Atlanta Constitution, *urged the new South to industrialize. In a Boston speech in 1889, he described the burial in Georgia of a Confederate veteran:*
>
> "The South didn't furnish a thing on earth for that funeral but the corpse and the hole in the ground.... They buried him in a New York coat and a Boston pair of shoes and a pair of breeches from Chicago and a shirt from Cincinnati, leaving him nothing to carry into the next world with him to remind him of the country in which he lived, and for which he fought for four years, but the chill of blood in his veins and the marrow in his bones."

★ The Impact of the New Industrial Revolution on America

Economic miracles wrought during the decades after the Civil War enormously increased the wealth of the Republic. The standard of living rose sharply, and well-fed American workers enjoyed more physical comforts than their counterparts in any other industrial nation. Urban centers mushroomed as the insatiable factories demanded more American labor and as immigrants swarmed like honeybees to the new jobs (see "Makers of America: The Poles," p. 523).

Early Jeffersonian ideals were withering before the smudgy blasts from the smokestacks. As agriculture declined in relation to manufacturing, America could no longer aspire to be a nation of small freehold farms. Jefferson's concepts of free enterprise, with neither help nor hindrance by Washington, were being thrown out the factory window.

Older ways of life also wilted in the heat of the factory furnaces. The very concept of time was revolutionized. Rural American migrants and peasant European immigrants, used to living by the languid clock of nature, now had to regiment their lives by the factory whistle. The seemingly arbitrary discipline of industrial labor did not come easily and sometimes had to be forcibly taught by corporate managers.

Probably no single group was more profoundly affected by the new industrial age than women. Propelled into industry by recent inventions, chiefly the typewriter and the telephone switchboard, millions of stenographers and "hello girls" discovered new economic and social opportunities. The "Gibson Girl," a magazine image of an independent and athletic "new woman" created in the 1890s by the artist Charles Dana Gibson, became the romantic ideal of the age. For middle-class women, careers often meant delayed marriages and smaller families. Most women workers, however, toiled neither for independence nor for glamour but out of economic necessity. They faced the same long hours and dangerous working conditions as did their mates and brothers, and they earned less because wages for "women's jobs" were usually set below men's.

The clattering machine age likewise accentuated class division. "Industrial buccaneers" flaunted bloated fortunes, and their rags-to-riches spouses displayed glittering diamonds. Such extravagances evoked bitter criticism. Some of it was envious, but much of the criticism rose from the small and increasingly vocal group of socialists and other radicals, many of whom were recent European immigrants. The existence of an oligarchy of money was amply demonstrated by the fact that in 1900 about one-tenth of the people owned nine-tenths of the nation's wealth.

A nation of farmers and independent producers was becoming a nation of wage earners. In 1860 half of all workers were self-employed; by the century's end, two of every three working Americans depended on wages. Real wages were rising, but with dependence on wages came vulnerability to the swings of the economy and the whims of the employer. Illness or unemployment could mean catastrophe for an entire family. Nothing more sharply defined the growing difference between working-class and middle-class conditions of life than the precariousness of the laborer's lot.

Finally, strong pressures for foreign trade developed as the tireless industrial machine threatened to saturate the domestic market. Aided by developments such as the laying of a transatlantic telegraph in 1866 and the opening of the Suez Canal in 1869, international trade became ever faster, cheaper, and easier. American products and companies like Standard Oil radiated out all over the world. The flag follows trade, and empire tends to follow the flag—a harsh lesson that America was soon to learn.

★ In Unions There Is Strength

The sweat of the laborer lubricated the vast new industrial machine. Yet wage workers did not share proportionately with their employers the benefits of the age of big business.

The worker, suggestive of the Roman galley slave, was becoming a lever puller in a giant mechanism. Individual originality and creativity were being stifled, and less value than ever before was being placed on manual skills. Before the Civil War, the worker might have toiled in a small plant whose owner hailed the employee in the morning by first name and inquired after the family's health. But now the factory hand was employed by a corporation—depersonalized, bodiless, soulless, and often conscienceless. Employers could take advantage of the vast new railroad network and bring in unemployed workers from the four corners of the country and beyond to beat down high wage levels. During the 1880s and 1890s, several hundred thousand unskilled immigrant workers poured into the country from Europe, creating a labor market more favorable to the boss than the worker.

Individual workers were powerless to battle single handedly against giant industry. The corporation could dispense with the individual worker much more easily than the worker could dispense with the corporation. Employers could retain high-priced lawyers, buy up the local press, import strikebreakers ("scabs"), and employ thugs to beat up labor organizers. In 1886 Jay Gould reputedly boasted, "I can hire one-half of the working class to kill the other half."

Corporations had still other weapons in their arsenals. They could call upon conservative federal judges to issue injunctions against strikers, and if defiance continued, the corporations could then request state or federal authorities to send in troops. Employers could lock the doors of their plants—a procedure called the "lockout"—and starve rebellious workers into submission. They could compel them to sign "ironclad oaths" or "yellow dog contracts," both solemn agreements not to join a labor union. They could put the names of labor agitators on a "black list" and circulate it among fellow employers. A corporation might even own the "company town," where high-priced grocery stores and "easy" credit often sank workers into perpetual debt—a status that strongly resembled serfdom.

The middle-class public, annoyed by recurrent strikes, grew deaf to the outcry of the worker. Carnegie and Rockefeller had battled their way to the top, and the view was common that the laborer could do likewise. Somehow the strike seemed like a foreign importation—socialistic and hence unpatriotic. Big business might combine into trusts to raise prices, but the worker must not combine into unions to raise wages. Unemployment seemed to be an act of God, who somehow would take care of the laborer.

★ Labor Limps Along

Labor unions, which had been few and disorganized in 1861, were given a strong boost by the Civil War, when manpower shortages put a premium on labor. By 1872, there were several hundred thousand organized workers and thirty-two national unions, representing such crafts as the bricklayers, typesetters, and shoemakers.

Examining the Evidence
The Photography of Lewis W. Hine

The pell-mell onrush of industrialization after the Civil War spawned countless human abuses, few more objectionable than the employment of children, often in hazardous jobs. For decades, reformers tried to arouse public outrage against child labor, and they made significant headway at last with the help of photography—especially the photographs of Lewis W. Hine (1874–1940). A native of Wisconsin, Hine in 1908 became the staff photographer for the National Child Labor Committee, an organization committed to ending child labor. This 1909 photo of young "doffers," whose job it was to remove fully wound bobbins from textile spinning machines, is typical of Hine's work. He shows the boys climbing dangerously on the whirling mechanism, and his own caption for the photo names the mill—"Bibb Mill No. 1, Macon, Georgia"—but not the boys, as if to underline the impersonal, dehumanizing nature of their work and the specific responsibilities of their employer. His other subjects included child workers on Colorado beet farms, in Pennsylvania coal mines, and Gulf Coast fish canneries, and in the glass, tobacco, and garment trades. Hine's images contributed heavily to the eventual success of the campaign to end child labor in the New Deal era. Hine is also celebrated as one of the fathers of documentary photography.

Library of Congress Prints and Photographs Division [LC-USZ6-1222]

1. Why might Hine's graphic images have succeeded in stirring public opinion more powerfully than factual and statistical demonstrations of the evil of child labor?
2. Given Hine's own reform objectives, can his photographs—or any so-called documentary images—be taken at face value as literal, accurate information about the past?
3. Which details in Lewis Hine's photo especially emphasize the exploitation and dangers experienced by child laborers?

The **National Labor Union**, organized in 1866, represented a giant bootstride by workers. One of the earliest national-scale unions to organize in the Americas or Europe, it aimed to unify workers across locales and trades to challenge their ever more powerful bosses. The union lasted six years and attracted the impressive total of some 600,000 members, including the skilled, unskilled, and farmers, though it excluded the Chinese and made only nominal efforts to include women and blacks. Black workers organized their own Colored National Labor Union, but persistent white racism prevented the two national unions from working together. The National Labor Union agitated for the arbitration of industrial disputes and the eight-hour workday, winning the latter for government workers. But the devastating depression of the 1870s dealt it a knockout blow. Wage reductions in 1877 touched off such disruptive strikes on the railroads that nothing short of federal troops could restore order.

A new organization—the **Knights of Labor**—seized the torch dropped by the defunct National Labor Union. Officially known as the Noble and Holy Order of the Knights of Labor, the organization began inauspiciously in 1869 as a secret society, with a private ritual, passwords, and a special handshake. Secrecy, which continued until 1881, was intended to forestall possible reprisals by employers.

National Labor Union (1866–1872)
This first national labor organization in U.S. history gained 600,000 members from many parts of the work force, although it limited the participation of Chinese, women, and blacks. The organization devoted much of its energy to fighting for an eight-hour workday before it dissolved in 1872.

Knights of Labor *The second national labor organization, organized in 1869 as a secret society and opened for public membership in 1881. The Knights were known for their efforts to organize all workers, regardless of skill level, gender, or race. After the mid-1880s their membership declined for a variety of reasons, including the Knights' participation in violent strikes and discord between skilled and unskilled members.*

The Knights of Labor, like the National Labor Union, sought to include all workers in "one big union." Their slogan was "An injury to one is the concern of all." A welcome mat was rolled out for the skilled and unskilled, for men and women, for whites and blacks, some ninety thousand of whom joined. The Knights barred only liquor dealers, professional gamblers, lawyers, bankers, and stockbrokers.

Setting up broad goals, the embattled Knights campaigned for economic and social reform, including producers' cooperatives and codes for safety and health. The ordinary workday was then ten hours or more, and the Knights waged a determined campaign for the eight-hour stint.

Under the eloquent but often erratic leadership of Terence V. Powderly, an Irish American of nimble wit and fluent tongue, the Knights won a number of strikes for the eight-hour day. When the Knights staged a successful strike against Jay Gould's Wabash Railroad in 1885, membership mushroomed to about three-quarters of a million workers.

⭐ Unhorsing the Knights of Labor

Despite their outward success, the Knights were riding for a fall. They became involved in a number of May Day strikes in 1886, about half of which failed. A focal point was Chicago, home to about eighty thousand Knights. The city was also honeycombed with a few hundred anarchists, many of them foreign-born, who were advocating a violent overthrow of the American government.

Tensions rapidly built up to the bloody **Haymarket Square** episode. Labor disorders had broken out, and on May 4, 1886, the Chicago police advanced on a meeting called to protest alleged brutalities by the authorities. Suddenly a dynamite bomb was thrown that killed or injured several dozen people, including police.

Hysteria swept the Windy City. Eight anarchists were rounded up. Although nobody proved that they had anything to do directly with the bomb, a judge and jury held that since they had preached incendiary doctrines, they could be charged with conspiracy. Five were sentenced to death: one of these men committed suicide, and four were executed. The other three anarchists were given stiff prison terms. They were eventually pardoned in 1892 by Illinois governor John P. Altgeld, a German-born Democrat of strong liberal tendencies.

The Haymarket Square bomb helped blow the props from under the Knights of Labor. They were associated in the public mind, though mistakenly, with the anarchists. The eight-hour movement suffered correspondingly, and subsequent strikes by the Knights met with scant success. By the 1890s the Knights had melted away to only 100,000 members, and these gradually fused with other protest groups of that decade.

Haymarket Square (1886) *A May 4th rally that turned violent when someone threw a bomb into the middle of the meeting, killing several people. Eight anarchists were arrested for conspiracy contributing to the disorder, although evidence linking them to the bombing was thin. Four were executed, one committed suicide, and three were pardoned in 1893.*

⭐ The AF of L to the Fore

The elitist **American Federation of Labor**, born in 1886, was largely the brainchild of squat, square-jawed Samuel Gompers. This colorful Jewish cigar maker, born in a London tenement and removed from school at age ten, was brought to America when thirteen. Taking his turn at reading informative literature to fellow cigar makers in New York, he was pressed into overtime service because of his strong voice. Rising spectacularly in the labor ranks, he was elected president of the American Federation of Labor every year except one from 1886 to 1924.

Gompers adopted a down-to-earth approach, soft-pedaling attempts to engineer sweeping social reform. A bitter foe of socialism, he shunned politics for economic strategies and goals. Gompers had no quarrel with capitalism, but he demanded a fairer share for labor. All he wanted, he said, was "more." Promoting what he called "pure and simple" unionism, he sought better wages, hours, and working conditions.

American Federation of Labor *A national federation of trade unions that included only skilled workers, founded in 1886. Led by Samuel Gompers for nearly four decades, the AFL sought to negotiate with employers for a better kind of capitalism that rewarded workers fairly with better wages, hours, and conditions. The AFL's membership was almost entirely white and male until the middle of the twentieth century.*

The Strike, **by Robert Koehler, 1886** Scenes like this were becoming more typical of American life in the late nineteenth century as industrialism advanced spectacularly and sometimes ruthlessly. Here Koehler (1850–1917) shows an entire community of men, women, and children—many of them apparently immigrant newcomers—challenging the power of the "boss." The scene is tense but orderly, though violence seems to be imminent as one striker reaches for a rock.

The AF of L thus established itself on solid but narrow foundations. Although attempting to speak for all workers, it fell far short of being representative of them. Composed of skilled craftsmen, such as the carpenters and bricklayers, it was willing to let unskilled laborers, including women and especially blacks, fend for themselves. The AF of L weathered the panic of 1893 reasonably well, and by 1900 it could boast a membership of 500,000.

Labor disorders continued, peppering the years from 1881 to 1900 with an alarming total of over 23,000 strikes. These disturbances involved 6,610,000 workers, with a total loss to both employers and employees of $450 million. The strikers lost about half their strikes and won or compromised the remainder. Perhaps the gravest weakness of organized labor was that it still embraced only a small minority of all working people—about 3 percent in 1900.

But attitudes toward labor had begun to change perceptibly by 1900. The public was beginning to concede the right of workers to organize, to bargain collectively, and to strike. As a sign of the times, Labor Day was made a legal holiday by act of Congress in 1894. A few enlightened industrialists had come to perceive the wisdom of avoiding costly economic warfare by bargaining with the unions and signing agreements. But the vast majority of employers continued to fight organized labor, which achieved its grudging gains only after recurrent strikes and frequent reverses. If the age of big business had dawned, the age of big labor was still some distance over the horizon.

Varying Viewpoints

Industrialization: Boon or Blight?

The capitalists who forged an industrial America in the late nineteenth century were once called captains of industry—a respectful title that bespoke awe for their wondrous material accomplishments. But these economic innovators have never been universally admired. During the Great Depression of the 1930s, when the entire industrial order they had created seemed to have collapsed utterly, it was fashionable to speak of them as robber barons—a term implying scorn for their high-handed methods. This sneer often issued from the lips and pens of leftist critics such as Matthew Josephson, who sympathized with the working classes allegedly brutalized by the factory system.

Criticism has also come from writers nostalgic for the preindustrial past. These critics believe that industrialization stripped away the traditions, values, and pride of native farmers and immigrant craftspeople. Conceding that economic development elevated the material standard of living for working Americans, this interpretation contends that the Industrial Revolution diminished their spiritual "quality of life." Accordingly, historians such as Herbert Gutman and David Montgomery portray labor's struggle for control of the workplace as the central drama of industrial expansion.

Nevertheless, even these historians concede that class-based protest has never been as powerful a force in the United States as in certain European countries. Many historians believe that this is so because greater social mobility in America dampened class tensions.

In the 1960s, historians led by Stephan Thernstrom began to test this long-standing belief. Looking at such factors as occupation, wealth, and geographic mobility, they tried to gauge the nature and extent of social mobility in the United States. Most of these historians concluded that, although relatively few Americans made rags-to-riches leaps, large numbers experienced small improvements in their economic and social status. Few sons of laborers became corporate tycoons, but many more became line bosses and white-collar clerks.

Such studies have subsequently been criticized by historians who point out the difficulties involved in defining social status. For instance, some white-collar clerical workers received lower wages than manual laborers did. Were they higher or lower on the social scale? Furthermore, James Henretta has pointed out that different groups defined success differently: whereas Jewish immigrants often struggled to give their sons professional educations, the Irish put more emphasis on acquiring land, and Italians on building small family-run businesses.

Meanwhile, leftist historians such as Michael Katz have argued that the degree of social mobility in America has been overrated. These historians argue that industrial capitalism created two classes: a working class that sold its labor and a business class that controlled resources and bought labor. Although most Americans took small steps upward, they generally remained within the class in which they began. Thus, these historians argue, the inequality of a capitalistic class system persisted in America's seemingly fluid society.

CHAPTER SUMMARY

Aided by government land grant subsidies and loans, the first transcontinental rail line was completed in 1869, soon followed by others. This rail network opened vast new markets and prompted industrial growth. The power and corruption of the railroads led to public demands for regulation. State regulation was declared unconstitutional, but in 1887 the federal government took a small step with the Interstate Commerce Act.

New technology and types of business organization, sometimes employing harsh competitive practices, led to the growth of huge corporate trusts. Andrew Carnegie and John D. Rockefeller led the way in the steel and oil industries. Initially, the oil industry supplied kerosene for lamps; it eventually expanded by providing gasoline to fuel automobiles. Cheap steel transformed industries from construction to rail building, and the powerful railroads dominated the economy and reshaped American society. Many sectors of the economy came to be dominated by monopolistic trusts that used "interlocking directorates" and other pressure tactics to control competitors. Business-oriented ideologies such as the religious "gospel of wealth" and naturalistic "Social Darwinism" celebrated the wealthy as "fittest" to survive and denigrated poverty as a sign of moral and natural failure.

While industrialization did raise the general economy and standard of living, its benefits were very unevenly distributed. The South remained in underdeveloped "Third World" dependence, despite "New South" proclamations, while the industrial working class struggled at the bottom of the growing class divisions of American society. Increasingly transformed from independent producers and farmers to dependent wage earners, America's workers became vulnerable to illness, industrial accidents, and unemployment.

Workers' attempts at labor organization were generally ineffective, hindered by corporate and governmental opposition and their own backward-looking ideologies. The National Labor Union enjoyed brief success but then collapsed, and the Knights of Labor also disappeared after the Haymarket bombing. Gompers's AF of L successfully organized skilled craft laborers but ignored most industrial workers, women, and blacks. Middle class public attitudes toward organized labor slowly became more positive after 1900, but business retained the upper hand and only a small minority of workers were unionized.

KEY TERMS

Wabash, St. Louis & Pacific Railroad Company v. Illinois (390)
Interstate Commerce Act (390)
vertical integration (392)
horizontal integration (392)
trust (392)
Standard Oil Company (392)
interlocking directorates (392)
Social Darwinists (395)
Sherman Anti-Trust Act (396)
National Labor Union (399)
Knights of Labor (399)
Haymarket Square (400)
American Federation of Labor (400)

PEOPLE TO KNOW

Cornelius Vanderbilt
Alexander Graham Bell
Thomas Alva Edison
Andrew Carnegie
John D. Rockfeller
Samuel Gompers

MindTap is a fully online, highly personalized learning experience built upon Cengage Learning content. MindTap combines student learning tools—readings, multimedia, activities, and assessments—into a singular Learning Path that guides students through the course.

Chapter 25

America Moves to the City
1865–1900

What shall we do with our great cities? What will our great cities do with us . . . ? [T]he question . . . does not concern the city alone. The whole country is affected . . . by the condition of its great cities.

LYMAN ABBOT, 1891

Born in the country, America moved to the city in the decades following the Civil War. By the year 1900 the United States' upsurging population nearly doubled from the 40 million people enumerated in the census of 1870. Yet, in the very same period, the population of American cities *tripled*. This cityward drift affected not only the United States but the entire industrializing world. European peasants, pushed off the land in part by competition from cheap American foodstuffs, were pulled into cities—in both Europe and America—by the new lure of industrial jobs. A revolution in American agriculture thus fed the industrial and urban revolutions in Europe, as well as in the United States.

Chapter Outline

- The Rise of the City
- Skyscrapers, Tenements, and Suburbs
- The "New Immigrants"
- New Jobs for Women
- Nativists and Immigration Restriction
- Churches in the City
- Black Leaders: Booker T. Washington and W. E. B. Du Bois
- Literary Achievements
- The "New Woman" and the New Morality
- Art and Entertainment in Urban America
- *Makers of America: The Italians*
- *Examining the Evidence: Manuscript Census Data, 1900*

FOCUS QUESTIONS

1. What features characterized the new industrial city, and what was its impact on American society?

2. Why did the massive "New Immigration" from southern and eastern Europe stir opposition from many native-born Americans, and how did political machines, social reformers, and churches adapt to the new urban and immigrant era?

3. What were the major challenges facing American religious life in the late nineteenth century? How did the growth of Catholicism, Judaism, and other "immigrant" faiths as well as "new" religions alter the character of an historically Protestant America?

4. What were the major changes in American educational and cultural life in the late nineteenth century, and how did the intellectual and literary turn toward "realism" and "pragmatism" reflect the new conditions of an urban and scientific civilization?

5. Why were there such fierce debates over morality in the late nineteenth century, especially over issues concerning sex, women, and the family?

CHRONOLOGY

1859	- Charles Darwin publishes *On the Origin of Species*
1862	- Morrill Act provides public land for higher education
1863	- World's first subway system opens in London
1866	- American Society for the Prevention of Cruelty to Animals (ASPCA) created
1869	- Wyoming Territory grants women the right to vote
1871	- *Woodhull and Claflin's Weekly* published
1872	- Metaphysical Club meets in Cambridge, Massachusetts
1873	- Comstock Law
1874	- Woman's Christian Temperance Union (WCTU) organized - Chautauqua education movement launched - Impressionist artists debut in Paris
1876	- Johns Hopkins University graduate school established
1879	- Henry George publishes *Progress and Poverty* - Dumbbell tenement introduced - Mary Baker Eddy establishes Christian Science - Salvation Army begins work in America
1881	- Booker T. Washington becomes head of Tuskegee Institute - American Red Cross founded - Henry James publishes *The Portrait of a Lady* - Barnum and Bailey first join to stage "Greatest Show on Earth"
1882	- First immigration-restriction laws passed
1883	- Brooklyn Bridge completed - Metropolitan Opera House built in New York
1884	- Mark Twain publishes *The Adventures of Huckleberry Finn*
1885	- Chicago's Home Insurance Building built, the world's first skyscraper - Linotype invented
1886	- Statue of Liberty erected in New York harbor
1887	- American Protective Association (APA) formed - Hatch Act supplements Morrill Act
1888	- Edward Bellamy publishes *Looking Backward* - American all-star baseball team tours world
1889	- Jane Addams founds Hull House in Chicago
1890	- National American Woman Suffrage Association (NAWSA) formed
1891	- Basketball invented
1893	- Lillian Wald opens Henry Street Settlement in New York - Anti-Saloon League formed - World's Columbian Exposition held in Chicago - New Zealand grants women right to vote
1895	- Stephen Crane publishes *The Red Badge of Courage*
1897	- Library of Congress opens - Robert Gould Shaw Memorial erected on Boston Common
1898	- Charlotte Perkins Gilman publishes *Women and Economics*
1899	- Kate Chopin publishes *The Awakening*
1900	- Theodore Dreiser publishes *Sister Carrie*
1907	- Henry Adams privately publishes *The Education of Henry Adams*
1909	- National Association for the Advancement of Colored People (NAACP) founded

⭐ The Urban Frontier

The growth of American metropolises was spectacular. In 1860 no city in the United States could boast a million inhabitants; by 1890 New York, Chicago, and Philadelphia had spurted past the million mark. By 1900 New York, with some 3.5 million people, was the second largest city in the world, outranked only by London. Throughout the world,

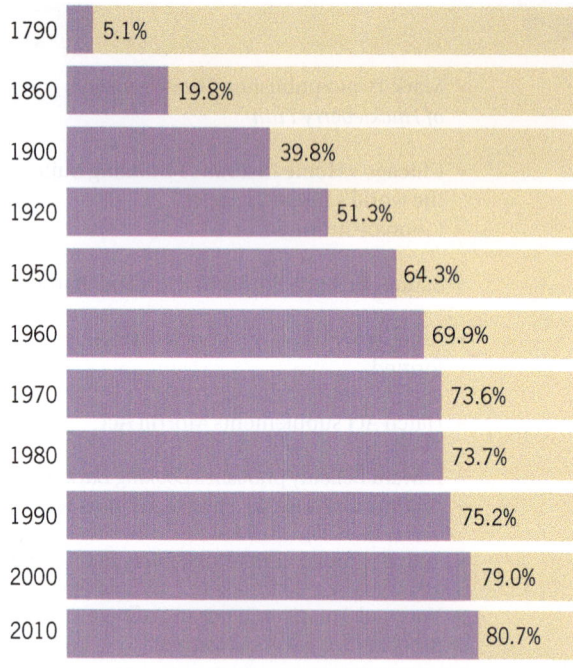

Figure 25.1 The Shift to the American City This chart shows the percentage of total population living in locales with a population of twenty-five hundred or more. Note the slowing of the cityward trend from 1970 on. (Sources: *Historical Statistics of the United States*; U.S. Census Bureau.)

cities were exploding; not only London, but also Paris, Berlin, Tokyo, Moscow, Mexico City, Calcutta, and Shanghai all doubled or tripled in size between 1850 and 1900. The population of Buenos Aires multiplied by more than ten.

American cities grew both up and out. The cloud-brushing skyscrapers allowed more people and workplaces to be packed onto a parcel of land. Appearing first as a ten-story building in Chicago in 1885, the skyscraper was made usable by the perfecting of the electric elevator. An opinionated Chicago architect, Louis Sullivan (1856–1924), contributed formidably to the further development of the skyscraper with his famous principle that "form follows function."

Cities also spread out, turning many Americans into commuters who traveled daily by mass-transit electric trolleys and later subways between their urban job in the central city and their suburban home. The compact and communal "walking city" gave way to the immense and impersonal megalopolis, carved into distinctly different districts for business, industry, and residential neighborhoods—which in turn were segregated by race, ethnicity, and social class.

Rural life could not compete with the siren song of the city (see Figure 25.1). Industrial jobs, above all, drew people off farms in America, as well as abroad, and into factory centers. But the urban lifestyle also held powerful attractions. The predawn milking of cows had little appeal when compared with the late-night glitter of city lights, particularly alluring to young adults yearning for independence. Electricity, indoor plumbing, and telephones all made life in the big city more enticing. Engineering marvels such as the skyscraper and New York's awesome Brooklyn Bridge, a harp-like suspension span dedicated in 1883, further added to the seductive glamour of the gleaming cities.

Cavernous department stores such as Macy's in New York and Marshall Field's in Chicago attracted urban middle-class shoppers and provided urban working-class jobs, many of them for women. The bustling emporiums also heralded a dawning era of consumerism and accentuated widening class divisions. When Carrie Meeber, novelist Theodore Dreiser's fictional heroine in *Sister Carrie* (1900), escapes from rural boredom to Chicago, it is the spectacle of the city's dazzling department stores that awakens her fateful yearning for a richer, more elegant way of life.

The move to the city also introduced Americans to new ways of living. Household products sold in bulk at the local store, without wrapping, gave way to city goods that came in throwaway bottles, boxes, bags, and cans. Cheap ready-to-wear clothing and swiftly changing fashions pushed old suits and dresses out of the closet. And the mountains of waste that city-dwellers generated created a new urban-age issue and testified to a cultural shift away from the virtues of thrift to the convenience of consumerism.

The jagged skyline of America's perpendicular civilization could not fully conceal the canker sores of feverish growth. Criminals flourished like lice in the teeming asphalt jungles. Impure water, uncollected garbage, unwashed bodies, and droppings from draft animals enveloped many cities in a satanic stench.

The cities were monuments of contradiction. They represented "humanity compressed," remarked one observer, "the best and the worst combined, in a strangely composite community." They harbored merchant princes and miserable paupers, stately banks and sooty factories, green-grassed suburbs and treeless ghettos. The glaring contrasts that assaulted the eye in New York reminded one visitor of "a lady in ball costume, with diamonds in her ears, and her toes out at the boots."

Worst of all were the human pigsties known as slums. They seemed to grow ever more crowded, more filthy, and more rat infested, especially after the perfection in 1879 of the "dumbbell" tenement. So named because of the outline of its floor plan, the dumbbell was usually seven or eight stories high, with shallow, sunless, and ill-smelling air shafts providing minimal ventilation. Several families were sardined onto each floor of the barracks-like structures, and they shared a malodorous toilet in the hall. "Flophouses" abounded where the poor and unemployed might sleep for a few cents on verminous

Mulberry Street on New York City's Lower East Side, c. 1900 Population densities in early-twentieth-century American cities were among the highest in the world. Mulberry Street, shown in this photo, was at the heart of New York's "Little Italy" neighborhood.

mattresses. Small wonder that slum dwellers strove mightily to escape their wretched surroundings—as many of them did. But the slums remained, foul places inhabited by successive waves of newcomers.

Cities were dangerous for everyone. In 1871 two-thirds of downtown Chicago burned in a raging fire that left 90,000 people homeless and destroyed more than 15,000 buildings. Closely packed wooden structures fed the insatiable flames, prompting Chicago and other wary cities to require stone and iron buildings downtown. The wealthiest began to leave the risky city behind and head for semirural suburbs. These leafy "bedroom communities" eventually ringed the brick-and-concrete cities with a greenbelt of affluence.

★ The New Immigration

The powerful pull of the American urban magnet was felt even in faraway Europe. A seemingly endless stream of immigrants continued to pour in from the old "mother continent." In each of the three decades from the 1850s through the 1870s, more than 2 million migrants had stepped onto America's shores. By the 1880s the stream had swelled to a rushing torrent, as more than 5 million migrants cascaded into the country.

Until the 1880s most immigrants had come from the British Isles and western Europe, chiefly Germany and Ireland. Also significant were the more than 300,000 Chinese. Many of these earlier immigrants had faced virulent nativism, especially the Irish and Chinese. In fact, the latter were legally excluded in 1882 (see pp. 374–376). But by the last decades of the century, the "old" European immigrants had adjusted well to American life by building supportive ethnic organizations and melding into established farm communities or urban craft unions. Although many still lived, worked, and worshipped among their own, they were largely accepted as "American" by the native-born.

But in the 1880s the character of the immigrant stream changed drastically. The so-called **New Immigrants**—Italians, Croats, Slovaks, Greeks, Poles, Jews, and others—came from southern and eastern Europe. Many of them worshiped in Roman Catholic

New Immigrants *Immigrants from southern and eastern Europe who formed a recognizable wave of immigration from the 1880s until 1924, in contrast to the immigrants from western Europe who had come before them. These new immigrants congregated in ethnic urban neighborhoods, where they worried many native-born Americans, some of whom responded with nativist anti-immigrant campaigns and others of whom introduced urban reforms to help the immigrants assimilate.*

or Eastern Orthodox churches or in Jewish synagogues. They came from countries with little history of democratic government and where opportunities for advancement were few. These new peoples totaled only 19 percent of newcomers in the 1880s; but by the first decade of the twentieth century, they constituted an astonishing 66 percent of the total inflow. They clustered in cities like New York and Chicago, where the "Little Italys" and "Little Polands" soon claimed more inhabitants than the largest cities of the same nationality in the Old World (See "Makers of America: The Italians").

Why were these bright-shawled and quaint-jacketed strangers hammering on the gates? In part they left their native countries because Europe seemed to have no room for them. Rapid population growth, American food imports, and European industrialization shook the peasantry loose from its ancient habitats and customary occupations, creating a vast, footloose army of the unemployed. Europeans by the millions drained out of the countryside and into European cities. Most stayed there, but some kept moving and left Europe altogether. About 60 million Europeans abandoned the Old Continent in the nineteenth and early twentieth centuries. More than half of them moved to the United States, while their compatriots spread out across the globe to South America, Canada, Africa, and Australia. Masses of people were already in motion in Europe before they felt the tug of the American magnet. This European diaspora, dominated by immigration to the United States, was, in many ways, simply a by-product of the urbanization of Europe.

"America fever" proved highly contagious in Europe. The United States was often painted as a land of fabulous opportunity in the "America letters" sent by friends and relatives already transplanted. The land of the free was also blessed with freedom from military conscription and institutionalized religious persecution. Beginning in the 1880s, savage persecution of minorities in Europe, especially of Jews in Russia, drove tens of thousands of battered refugees to American shores. Virtually unique among the New Immigrants, Jews had experienced city life in Europe, and many of them brought their urban skills of tailoring and shopkeeping to America's seaboard Atlantic cities, especially New York. Destitute and devout, eastern European Jews were frequently given a frosty reception not only by old-stock Americans but also by those German Jews who had arrived decades earlier and prospered in the United States, some of them as garment manufacturers who now employed their coreligionists as cheap labor.

The new immigrants struggled heroically to preserve their traditional cultures. Catholics expanded their parochial school system, and Jews established Hebrew schools. Foreign-language newspapers abounded. Yiddish theaters, kosher food stores, Polish parishes, Greek restaurants, and Italian social clubs all attested to the desire to keep old ways alive. Yet time took its toll on these efforts to preserve Old World customs. The children of the immigrants grew up speaking English, and often rejected the Old Country manners of their mothers and fathers in their desire to plunge headlong into the mainstream of American life.

Mary Antin (1881–1949), who came to America from Russian Poland in 1894 when thirteen years of age, later wrote in The Promised Land *(1912):*

"So at last I was going to America! Really, really going, at last! The boundaries burst. The arch of heaven soared. A million suns shone out for every star. The winds rushed in from outer space, roaring in my ears, 'America! America!'"

★ Reactions to the New Immigration

America's government system, nurtured in wide-open spaces, was ill suited to the cement forests of the great cities. Beyond minimal checking to weed out criminals and the insane, the federal government did virtually nothing to ease the assimilation of immigrants into American society. State governments, usually dominated by rural representatives, did even less. City governments, overwhelmed by the sheer scale of rampant urban growth, proved woefully inadequate to the task. By default, the business of ministering to the immigrants' needs fell to the unofficial "governments" of the urban political machines, led by "bosses" such as New York's notorious Boss Tweed.

Makers of America

The Italians

Who were the "New Immigrants," these southern and eastern Europeans who flocked to the United States between 1880 and 1920? Prominent and typical among them were Italians, some 4 million of whom sailed to the United States during the four decades of the New Immigration.

They came from the southern provinces of their native land, the heel and toe of the Italian boot. These areas had lagged behind the prosperous, industrial region of northern Italy. Unification of the nation of Italy had raised hopes of similar progress in the downtrodden south, but it was slow in coming. Southern Italian peasants tilled their fields without fertilizer or machinery, using hand plows and rickety hoes that had been passed down for generations.

From such demeaned conditions, southern Italians set out for the New World. Almost all of them were young men who intended to spend only a few months in America, stuff their pockets with earnings, and return home. At least half of Italian immigrants did indeed repatriate—as did comparable numbers of the other New Immigrants, with the conspicuous exception of the Jews, who had fled their native lands to escape religious persecution. Almost all Italian immigrants sailed through New York harbor, sighting the Statue of Liberty as they debarked from crowded ships. Many soon moved on to other large cities, but so many remained that, in the early years of the twentieth century, more Italians resided in New York than in Florence, Venice, and Genoa combined.

Although most Italian immigrants huddled in the cities, they did not abandon their rural upbringings entirely. Much to their neighbors' consternation, they often kept chickens and raised vegetables in small garden plots nestled between decaying tenement houses.

Those who bade a permanent farewell to Italy clustered in tightly knit communities that boasted opera clubs, Italian-language newspapers, and courts for playing bocci—a version of lawn bowling imported from the Old Country. Pizza emerged from the hot wood-burning ovens of these Little Italys, its aroma and flavor wafting into the hearts and stomachs of all Americans.

Italians typically earned their daily bread as industrial laborers—most famously as longshoremen and construction workers. They owed their prominence in the building trades to the "padrone system." The *padrone*, or labor boss, met immigrants upon arrival and secured jobs for them in New York, Chicago, the West, or wherever there was an immediate demand for industrial labor.

Lacking education, the Italians, as a group, remained in blue-collar jobs longer than some of their fellow New Immigrants. Many Italians, valuing vocation over schooling, sent their children off to work as early in their young lives as possible. Before World War I, less than 1 percent of Italian children enrolled in high school. Over the next fifty years, Italian Americans and their offspring gradually prospered, moving out of the cities into the more affluent suburbs. Many served heroically in World War II and availed themselves of the GI Bill to finance the college educations and professional training their immigrant forebears had lacked.

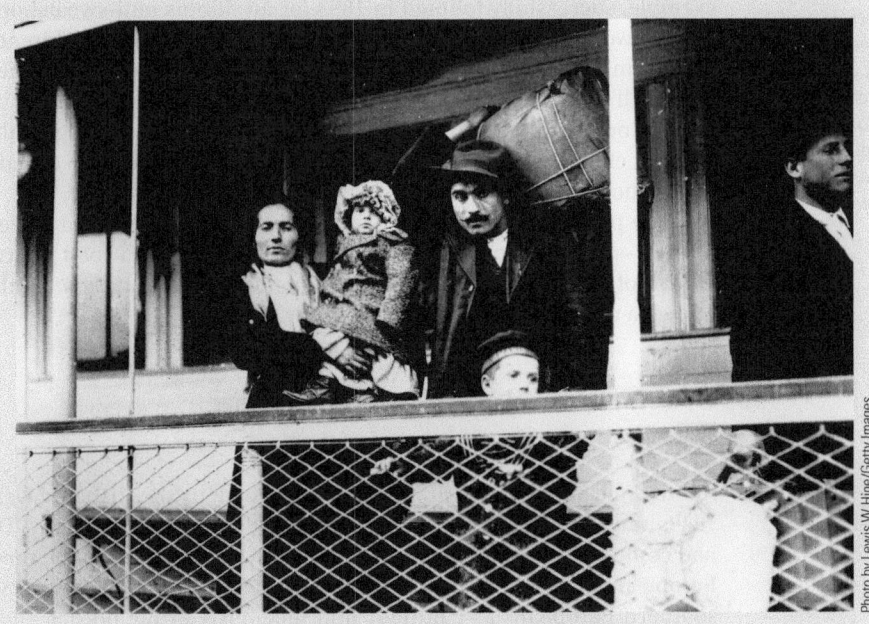

An Italian Immigrant Family Arriving at Ellis Island, ca. 1905

Taking care of the immigrants was big business, indeed. Trading jobs and services for votes, a powerful boss might claim the loyalty of thousands of followers. In return for their support at the polls, the boss provided jobs on the city's payroll, found housing for new arrivals, tided over the needy with gifts of food and clothing, patched up minor scrapes with the law, and helped get schools, parks, and hospitals built in immigrant neighborhoods. Reformers gagged at this cynical exploitation of the immigrant vote, but the political boss gave valuable assistance that was forthcoming from no other source.

The nation's social conscience gradually awakened to the plight of the cities and their immigrant masses. Prominent in this awakening were several Protestant clergymen such as Walter Rauschenbusch of New York City and Washington Gladden of Columbus, Ohio, who both sought to apply the lessons of Christianity to the slums and factories. Preaching the "social gospel," they insisted that churches tackle the burning social issues of the day. The Sermon on the Mount, they declared, was the science of society, and some social gospelers predicted that socialism was the logical outcome of Christianity. These "Christian socialists" did much to prick callous consciences and prepare the path for the later progressive reform movement.

One middle-class woman who was deeply dedicated to uplifting the urban masses was Jane Addams (1860–1935). Born into a prosperous Illinois family, Addams was one of the first generation of college-educated women and sought suitable outlets for her large talents. Inspired by a visit to England, in 1889 she established Hull House in Chicago as the most prominent American settlement house. Soft-spoken but tenacious, Addams became a kind of urban American saint in the eyes of many admirers. The philosopher William James told her, "You utter instinctively the truth we others vainly seek." She was a broad-gauge reformer who courageously condemned war as well as poverty, and she eventually won the Nobel Peace Prize in 1911. But her pacifism also earned her the enmity of some Americans, including the Daughters of the American Revolution, who expelled her from membership in their august organization.

Located in a poor immigrant neighborhood of Greeks, Italians, Russians, and Germans, Hull House offered instruction in English, counseling to help newcomers cope with American big-city life, child-care services for working mothers, and cultural activities for neighborhood residents. Following Jane Addams's lead, women founded **settlement houses** in other cities as well—notably Lillian Wald's Henry Street Settlement in New York, which opened its doors in 1893.

The settlement houses became centers of women's activism and of social reform on behalf of women, children, blacks, and consumers. The women of Hull House, for example, successfully lobbied in 1893 for an Illinois anti-sweatshop law that protected women workers and prohibited child labor. They were led by Florence Kelley, a guerrilla warrior in the urban jungle who battled for decades on behalf of the underprivileged at both Hull House and the Henry Street Settlement. Armed with the insights of socialism and endowed with the voice of an actress, Kelley was a lifelong battler for the welfare of women, children, blacks, and consumers. She served for three decades as general secretary of the National Consumers League.

The pioneering work of Addams, Wald, and Kelley helped blaze the trail that many women—and some men—later followed into careers in urban reform and the new profession of social work. For these female reformers, and for many other women, the city offered a new kind of frontier opportunity.

---

settlement houses *Mostly run by middle-class native-born women, settlement houses in immigrant neighborhoods provided housing, food, education, child care, cultural activities, and social connections for new arrivals to the United States. Many women, both native-born and immigrant, developed lifelong passions for social activism in the settlement houses. Jane Addams's Hull House in Chicago and Lillian Wald's Henry Street Settlement in New York City were two of the most prominent.*

★ Narrowing the Welcome Mat

Antiforeignism, or "nativism," earlier touched off by the Irish and German arrivals in the 1840s and 1850s, bared its ugly face in the 1880s with fresh ferocity. The New Immigrants had come for much the same reasons as the Old—to escape the poverty and squalor of Europe and to seek new opportunities in America. But "nativists" viewed the eastern and southern Europeans as culturally and religiously exotic hordes and often gave them a rude reception. The newest newcomers aroused widespread alarm. Their high birthrate, common among people with a low standard of living, raised worries that the original Anglo-Saxon stock would soon be outbred and outvoted. Still more horrifying was the

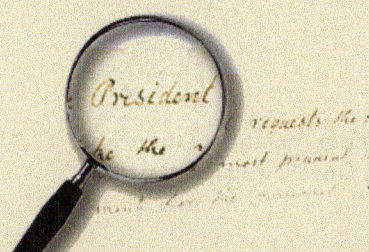

Examining the Evidence

Manuscript Census Data, 1900

Article I of the Constitution requires that a census of the American people be taken every ten years, in order to provide a reliable basis for congressional apportionment. Early censuses gathered little more than basic population numbers, but over the years the census takers have collected information on other matters as well, including occupational categories, educational levels, and citizenship status, yielding copious raw data for historical analysis. The census of 1890 was the first to use punch cards and electric tabulating machines, which greatly expanded the range of data that could be assembled and correlated—though the basic information was still hand recorded by individual canvassers who went door to door to question household members and fill out the census forms. Those handwritten forms, as much as the aggregate numbers printed in the final census tally, can furnish invaluable insights to the historian. Despite its apparent bureaucratic formality, the form shown here richly details the lives of the residents of a tenement house on New York's Lower East Side in 1900. See in particular the entries for the Goldberg family.

1. In what ways does this document reflect the great demographic changes that swept late-nineteenth-century America?
2. What light does the document shed on the character of immigrant "ghettos"?
3. What is the most common occupation of those listed? What is second? What might you conclude about the economic status of these residents of Manhattan?

prospect that it would be "mongrelized" by a mixture of "inferior" southern European blood and that the fairer Anglo-Saxon types would disappear. One New England writer cried out in anguish:

*O Liberty, white Goddess! is it well
To leave the gates unguarded?*

Native-born Americans voiced additional fears. They blamed the immigrants for the degradation of urban government. Some trade unionists assailed the alien arrivals for their willingness to work for "starvation" wages, which seemed to the immigrants like princely sums, and for importing in their intellectual baggage such seemingly dangerous doctrines as socialism, communism, and anarchism. Many business leaders who had welcomed the flood of cheap manual labor began to fear that they had embraced a Frankenstein's monster.

Antiforeign organizations, reminiscent of the "Know-Nothings" of antebellum days, were now revived in a different guise. Notorious among them was the American Protective Association (APA), which was created in 1887 and soon claimed a million members. In pursuing its nativist goals, the APA urged voting against Roman Catholic candidates for office and sponsored the publication of lustful fantasies about runaway nuns.

Organized labor was quick to throw its growing weight behind the move to choke off the rising tide of foreigners. Frequently used as strikebreakers, the wage-depressing immigrants were hard to unionize because of the language barrier. Labor leaders argued, not illogically, that if American industry was entitled to protection from foreign goods, American workers were entitled to protection from foreign laborers.

Congress finally nailed up partial bars against the inpouring immigrants. The first restrictive law, in 1882, banged the gate shut in the faces of paupers, criminals, and convicts, all of whom had to be returned at the expense of the greedy or careless shipper. Congress further responded to pained outcries from organized labor when in 1885 it prohibited the importation of foreign workers under contract—usually for substandard wages.

In later years, other federal laws lengthened the list of undesirables to include the insane, polygamists, prostitutes, alcoholics, anarchists, and people carrying contagious diseases. A proposed literacy test, long a favorite of nativists because it favored the Old Immigrants over the New, met vigorous opposition. The test was not enacted until 1917,

Looking Backward Older immigrants, trying to keep their own humble arrival in America "in the shadows," sought to close the bridge that had carried them and their ancestors across the Atlantic.

after three presidents had vetoed it on the grounds that literacy was more a measure of opportunity than of intelligence.

In 1886, four years after the first immigration restrictions were passed, the Statue of Liberty arose in New York harbor, a gift from the people of France. On its base were inscribed the words of Emma Lazarus:

> *Give me your tired, your poor,*
> *Your huddled masses yearning to breathe free,*
> *The wretched refuse of your teeming shore.*

To many nativists, those noble words described only too accurately the "scum" washed up by the New Immigrant tides. Yet the uprooted immigrants, unlike "natives" lucky enough to have had parents who caught an earlier ship, became American citizens the hard way. These new immigrants stepped off the boat ready to put their shoulders to the nation's industrial wheels. The Republic owes much to these latecomers—for their brawn, their brains, their courage, and the yeasty diversity they brought to American society.

★ Churches Confront the Urban Challenge

The swelling size and changing character of the urban population posed sharp challenges to American churches, which, like other national institutions, had grown up in the country. Protestant churches in particular suffered heavily from the shift to the city, where many of their traditional doctrines and pastoral approaches seemed irrelevant.

As they lost their bearings in the new urban world, some churches were tending to become merely sacred diversions or amusements. Reflecting the wealth of their prosperous parishioners, many of the old-line churches were distressingly slow to raise their voices against social and economic vices. John D. Rockefeller was a pillar of the Baptist Church; J. Pierpont Morgan, of the Episcopal Church. Trinity Episcopal Church in New York City actually owned some of the city's worst slum property. Cynics remarked that the Episcopal Church had become "the Republican party at prayer." The mounting emphasis was on materialism; too many devotees worshiped at the altar of avarice. Money was the accepted measure of achievement, and the new gospel of wealth proclaimed that God caused the righteous to prosper.

Into this spreading moral vacuum stepped a new generation of **liberal Protestants**. With roots in earlier revolts against orthodox Calvinism, liberal ideas came into the mainstream of American Protestantism between 1875 and 1925, leading to frequent and bitter controversies with fundamentalists. Entrenched in the leadership and seminaries of the dominant denominations, liberal Protestants adapted religious ideas to modern culture, attempting to reconcile Christianity with new scientific and economic doctrines. They rejected biblical literalism, urging Christians to view biblical stories as models for Christian behavior rather than as dogma. They stressed the ethical teachings of the Bible and allied themselves with the reform-oriented "social gospel" movement. Friendly to urban revivalists such as Dwight Moody, a former shoe salesman who captivated audiences with his message of forgiveness, optimistic liberal Protestants focused on earthly salvation and personal growth. They helped many Protestant Americans reconcile their religious faith with modern, cosmopolitan ways of thinking.

Contending Voices

The New Immigration

Writing in 1891 in support of a literacy test for immigrants, Massachusetts Republican Henry Cabot Lodge (1850–1924) emphasized a distinction between the recent stream of immigrants from southern and eastern Europe and earlier arrivals from Great Britain and Germany:

"Thus it is proved, first, that immigration to this country is increasing, and, second, that it is making its greatest relative increase from races most alien to the body of the American people and from the lowest and most illiterate classes among those races."

Six years later, Democratic president Grover Cleveland (1837–1908) disputed the merits of just such a distinction:

"It is said . . . that the quality of recent immigration is undesirable. The time is quite within recent memory when the same thing was said of immigrants who, with their descendants, are now numbered among our best citizens."

> What political factors might account for the contrasting positions taken by these two public officials?

---

liberal Protestants *Members of a branch of Protestantism that flourished from 1875 to 1925 and encouraged followers to use the Bible as a moral compass rather than to believe that the Bible represented scientific or historical truth. Many liberal Protestants became active in the "social gospel" and other reform movements of the era.*

Simultaneously, the Roman Catholic and Jewish faiths were gaining enormous strength from the New Immigration. By 1900 Roman Catholics had become the largest single denomination, numbering nearly 9 million communicants. Cardinal James Gibbons (1834–1921) of Baltimore, an urban Catholic leader devoted to American unity, was immensely popular with Roman Catholics and Protestants alike. Acquainted with every president from Andrew Johnson to Warren Harding, he employed his liberal sympathies to assist the American labor movement.

By 1890 the variety-loving Americans could choose from 150 religious denominations, two of them brand new. One was the band-playing Salvation Army, whose soldiers without swords invaded America from England in 1879 and established a beachhead on the street corners. Appealing frankly to the down-and-outers, the boldly named Salvation Army did much practical good, especially with free soup.

The other important new faith was the Church of Christ, Scientist (Christian Science), founded by Mary Baker Eddy in 1879 after she had suffered much ill health. Preaching that the true practice of Christianity heals sickness, she set forth her views in a book entitled *Science and Health with Key to the Scriptures* (1875), which sold an amazing 400,000 copies before her death. A fertile field for converts was found in America's hurried, nerve-wracked, and urbanized civilization. By the time Eddy died in 1910, she had founded an influential church that embraced several hundred thousand devoted worshipers.

Urbanites also participated in a new kind of religious-affiliated organization, the Young Men's and Women's Christian Associations. The YMCA and the YWCA, established before the Civil War, grew by leaps and bounds. Combining physical education with social service and religious instruction, the "Y's" appeared in virtually every major American city by the end of the nineteenth century.

Morning Service at Moody's Church, 1908 Thousands of Chicagoans found the gospel and a helping hand at evangelist Dwight Lyman Moody's church. Although Moody himself died in 1899, his successors continued to attract throngs of worshipers to his church, which could hold up to ten thousand people.

The old-time religion received many blows from modern trends, including a boom sale of books on comparative religion and on historical criticism as applied to the Bible. Most unsettling of all were the writings of the English naturalist Charles Darwin. In the lucid prose of *On the Origin of Species* (1859), Darwin set forth the sensational theory that higher forms of life had slowly evolved from lower forms, through a process of random biological mutation and adaptation.

Darwin's idea of "natural selection" broke new ground. Nature, in his view, blindly selected organisms for survival or death based on random, inheritable variations that they happened to possess. Some traits conferred advantages in the struggle for life and hence better odds of passing them on to offspring. By providing a material explanation for the evolutionary process, Darwin's theory explicitly rejected the "dogma of special creation," which ascribed the design of each fixed species to divine agency.

Darwin's radical ideas evoked the wrath of scientists and laymen alike. Many zoologists, like Harvard's Louis Agassiz, held fast to the old doctrine of "special creation." By 1875, however, the majority of scientists in America and elsewhere had embraced the theory of organic evolution, though not all endorsed natural selection as its agent.

Clergymen and theologians responded to Darwin's theory in several ways. By 1875, after most natural scientists had embraced evolution, the religious community split into two camps. A conservative minority condemned what they thought was the "bestial hypothesis" of Darwinism. Their rejection of scientific consensus spawned a muscular view of biblical authority that eventually gave rise to fundamentalism in the twentieth century.

Most religious thinkers parted company with conservatives, refusing to accept the Bible as either history or science, and sought ways to reconcile Darwinism with Christianity. They heralded the revolutionary theory as a newer and grander revelation of the Almighty. As one commentator observed:

Some call it Evolution,
Others call it God.

While the liberal efforts at compromise did succeed in keeping many Americans in the pews, these compromises also tended to relegate religious teaching to matters of personal faith, private conduct, and family life. As science began to explain more of the external world, commentators on nature and society increasingly refrained from adding religious perspectives to the discussion.

★ The Lust for Learning

Public education continued its upward climb. The ideal of tax-supported elementary schools was still gathering strength. Beginning about 1870, more and more states were making at least a grade-school education compulsory, and this gain, incidentally, helped check the frightening abuses of child labor.

Spectacular indeed was the spread of the high schools, especially by the 1880s and 1890s. By 1900 some six thousand high schools were educating teenage boys and girls. In addition, the states provided free textbooks in increasing numbers during the last two decades of the century.

Teacher-training schools, then called "normal schools," also experienced a striking expansion after the Civil War. In 1860 only twelve normal schools were operating; in 1910, there were more than three hundred. Kindergartens, earlier borrowed from Germany, began to gain strong support. The New Immigration in the 1880s and 1890s brought vast new strength to the private Catholic parochial schools, which were fast becoming a major pillar of the nation's educational structure. In the realm of adult education, the Chautauqua movement, launched in upstate New York in 1874, sponsored public lectures and home study courses that reached hundreds of thousands of participants.

Crowded cities, despite their cancers, generally provided better educational facilities than the old one-room, one-teacher red schoolhouse. The success of the public schools is confirmed by the falling of the illiteracy rate from 20 percent in 1870 to 10.7 percent in 1900. Americans were developing a profound faith, often misplaced, in formal education as the sovereign remedy for their ills.

Booker T. Washington and Education for Black People

War-torn and impoverished, the South lagged far behind other regions in public education, and African Americans suffered most severely. A staggering 44 percent of nonwhites were still illiterate in 1900. Some help came from northern philanthropists, but the foremost champion of black education was an ex-slave, Booker T. Washington, who had slept under a board sidewalk to save pennies for his schooling. Called in 1881 to head the black normal and industrial school at Tuskegee, Alabama, he began with forty students in a tumbledown shanty. Undaunted, he taught black students useful trades so that they could gain self-respect and economic security. But Washington stopped short of advocating *social* equality with whites, acquiescing in segregation in return for the right to develop economic and educational resources of the black community.

Washington's commitment to training young blacks in agriculture and the trades guided the curriculum at the Tuskegee Institute and made it an ideal place for slave-born George Washington Carver to teach and research. After Carver joined the faculty in 1896, he became an internationally famous agricultural chemist who boosted the Southern economy by discovering hundreds of new uses for the lowly peanut (shampoo, axle grease), sweet potato (vinegar), and soybean (paints).

Other black leaders, notably Dr. W. E. B. Du Bois, assailed Booker T. Washington for an approach that would condemn their race to manual labor and perpetual inferiority. Born in Massachusetts, Du Bois was a mixture of African, French, Dutch, and Indian blood ("Thank God, no Anglo-Saxon," he would add). After a determined struggle, he earned a Ph.D. at Harvard, the first of his race to achieve that goal. Du Bois demanded complete equality for blacks, social as well as economic, and helped to found the National Association for the Advancement of Colored People (NAACP) in 1909. Rejecting Washington's gradualism and separatism, he argued that the "talented tenth" of the black community should be given full and immediate access to the mainstream of American life. An exceptionally skilled historian, sociologist, and poet, Du Bois died as a self-exile in Africa in 1963, at the age of ninety-five.

W. E. B. Du Bois (1868–1963) In 1961, at the end of a long lifetime of struggle for racial justice in the United States, Du Bois renounced his American citizenship at the age of ninety-three and took up residence in the newly independent African state of Ghana.

Tuskegee Institute *A normal and industrial school led by Booker T. Washington in Tuskegee, Alabama. It focused on training young black students in agriculture and the trades to help them achieve economic independence. Washington justified segregated, vocational training as a necessary first step on the road to racial equality, although critics accused him of being too "accommodationist."*

W. E. B. Du Bois (1868–1963) wrote in his 1903 classic, The Souls of Black Folk:

"It is a peculiar sensation, this double consciousness, this sense of always looking at one's self through the eyes of others, of measuring one's self through the eyes of others.... One ever feels his two-ness—an American, a Negro; two souls, two thoughts, two unreconciled strivings; two warring ideals in one dark body, whose dogged strength alone keeps it from being torn asunder."

The Hallowed Halls of Ivy

Colleges and universities also shot up like lusty young saplings in the decades after the Civil War (see Table 25.1). Even women and African Americans were finding new opportunities for higher education. The educational battle for women, only partially won before the war, turned into a rout of the masculine diehards. Women's colleges such as Vassar were gaining ground, and universities open to both genders were blossoming, notably in the Midwest. By 1900 every third college graduate was a woman. By the turn of the century the black academies planted during Reconstruction had blossomed into a crop of southern black colleges. Howard University in Washington, D.C., Hampton Institute in Virginia, Atlanta University, and numerous others nurtured higher education for blacks until the civil rights movement of the 1960s made widespread attendance at white institutions possible.

Table 25.1 Educational Levels, 1870–2011

Year	Number Graduating from High School	Number Graduating from College	Median Number of School Years Completed*	High School Graduates as a Percentage of 17-Year-Old Population
1870	16,000	9,371		2.0%
1880	23,634	12,896		2.5%
1890	43,731	15,539		3.5%
1900	94,883	27,410		6.4%
1910	156,429	37,199	8.1	8.8%
1920	311,266	48,622	8.2†	16.8%
1930	666,904	122,484	8.4†	29.0%
1940	1,221,475	186,500	8.6	50.8%
1950	1,199,700	432,058	9.3	59.0%
1960	1,858,023	392,440	10.5	69.5%
1970	2,888,639	792,316	12.2	76.9%
1980	3,042,214	929,417	12.5	71.4%
1990	2,574,162	1,051,344	12.7	73.4%
2000	2,832,844	1,237,875	NA	69.8%
2010	3,434,672	1,650,014	NA	79.7%
2011	3,402,920††	1,715,913	NA	77.9%††

*People twenty-five years and over.
†1910–1930 based on retrogressions of 1940 data; 1940 was the first year measured.
††Projected figure.

Sources: *Digest of Education Statistics*, 2012, a publication of the National Center for Education Statistics; *Statistical Abstract of the United States*, relevant years; Folger and Nam, Education of the American Population, a 1960 Census Monograph.

The truly phenomenal growth of higher education owed much to the Morrill Act of 1862. This enlightened law provided a generous grant of public lands to the states for support of public higher education. The Hatch Act of 1887 extended the Morrill Act by providing federal funds for the establishment of state agricultural experiment stations. Together these two pieces of legislation spawned over a hundred **land-grant colleges** that evolved into state universities, including such institutions as the University of California (1868), Ohio State University (1870), and Texas A&M (1876).

Private philanthropy richly supplemented government grants to higher education. Many of the new industrial millionaires, developing tender social consciences, donated immense fortunes to educational enterprises. In the twenty years from 1878 to 1898 these money barons gave away about $150 million. Among the noteworthy new private universities were Cornell (1865) and Leland Stanford Junior (1891), the latter founded in memory of the deceased fifteen-year-old only child of a builder of the Central Pacific Railroad. The University of Chicago, opened in 1892, speedily forged into a front-rank position, owing largely to the lubricant of John D. Rockefeller's oil millions.

Towering among the new professionalized institutions of higher learning was Johns Hopkins University, opened in 1876, which developed the nation's first high-grade graduate school. Several generations of American scholars, repelled by snobbish English cousins and attracted by painstaking Continental methods, had attended German universities. Reputable scholars no longer had to go abroad for a gilt-edged graduate degree; Dr. Woodrow Wilson, among others, received his Ph.D. from Johns Hopkins.

Homegrown influences shaped the modern American university as much as German models. Antebellum colleges had stressed the "unity of truth," or the idea that knowledge and morality existed in a single system united by theology and moral philosophy. After the Darwinian challenge made religion and science seem less compatible, university reformers struggled to preserve the unity of moral and intellectual purpose. When that effort failed, university educators abandoned moral instruction and divorced "facts" from "values."

land-grant colleges *Colleges and universities created from allocations of public land through the Morrill Act of 1862 and the Hatch Act of 1887. These grants helped fuel the boom in higher education in the late nineteenth century, and many of today's public universities derive from them.*

Other pressures also helped doom the traditional curriculum. Industrialization and science brought insistent demands for "practical" courses, and specialization, not synthesis, became the primary goal of a university education. The turn toward electives and pre-professional training received a powerful boost in the 1870s when Dr. Charles W. Eliot became president of Harvard College. As a sign of the secularizing times, Eliot changed Harvard's motto from *Christo et Ecclesiae* (For Christ and Church) to *Veritas* (Truth).

One of America's most brilliant intellectuals, the slight and sickly William James (1842–1910) served for thirty-five years on the Harvard faculty. Through his numerous writings he made a deep mark on many fields. His *Principles of Psychology* (1890) helped to establish the modern discipline of psychology. In *The Will to Believe* (1897) and *Varieties of Religious Experience* (1902), James explored the philosophy and psychology of religion. In his most famous work, *Pragmatism* (1907), he declared that America's greatest contribution to the history of philosophy was the concept of **pragmatism**—that truth of an idea was to be tested, above all, by its practical consequences.

pragmatism *A distinctive American philosophy that emerged in the late nineteenth century around the theory that the true value of an idea lay in its ability to solve problems. The pragmatists thus embraced the provisional, uncertain nature of experimental knowledge. Among the most well-known purveyors of pragmatism were John Dewey, Oliver Wendell Holmes, Jr., and William James.*

⭐ The Appeal of the Press

Books continued to be a major source of edification and enjoyment for both juveniles and adults. Public libraries—the poor person's university—made encouraging progress in the late nineteenth century, especially in Boston and New York. The magnificent Library of Congress building, which opened its doors in 1897, provided thirteen acres of floor space in the largest and costliest edifice of its kind in the world. A new era was inaugurated by the generous gifts of Andrew Carnegie, who contributed $60 million for the construction of public libraries all across the United States and around the world. By 1900 there were about nine thousand free public libraries in America.

Roaring newspaper presses, spurred by the invention of the Linotype in 1885, more than kept pace with the demands of a word-hungry public. But the heavy investment in machinery and plant was accompanied by a growing fear of offending advertisers and subscribers. Bare-knuckle editorials were, to an increasing degree, being supplanted by feature articles and noncontroversial syndicated material. The day of slashing, journalistic giants such as Horace Greeley was passing.

Sensationalism, at the same time, was capturing the public taste. The semiliterate immigrants, combined with strap-hanging urban commuters, created a profitable market for news that was simply and punchily written. Sex, scandal, and other human-interest stories burst into the headlines, as a vulgarization of the press accompanied the growth of circulation. Critics complained in vain about these "presstitutes."

Two new journalistic tycoons emerged. Joseph Pulitzer, Hungarian born and near blind, was a leader in the techniques of sensationalism in his ownership of the *St. Louis Post-Dispatch* and the *New York World*. His use of colored comics featuring the "Yellow Kid" gave the name **yellow journalism** to his lurid sheets. A close and ruthless competitor was youthful William Randolph Hearst, who had been expelled from Harvard College for a crude prank. Able to draw on his California father's mining millions, Hearst built up a powerful chain of newspapers, beginning with the *San Francisco Examiner* in 1887. Unfortunately, Pulitzer and Hearst both prostituted the press in their struggle for increased circulation; they "stooped, snooped, and scooped to conquer." Their flair for scandal and sensation was happily somewhat offset by the strengthening of the newsgathering Associated Press, which had been founded in the 1840s.

yellow journalism *A scandal-mongering practice of journalism that emerged in New York during the Gilded Age out of the circulation battles between Joseph Pulitzer's New York World and William Randolph Hearst's New York Journal. The expression has remained a pejorative term referring to sensationalist journalism practiced with unethical, unprofessional standards.*

⭐ Apostles of Reform

Magazines partly satisfied the public appetite for good reading, notably old standbys such as *Harper's*, the *Atlantic Monthly*, and *Scribner's Monthly* and new western entrants such as the California-based *Overland Monthly*. Possibly the most influential journal was the liberal and highly intellectual *Nation*, whose modest circulation of ten thousand consisted largely of professors, preachers, and publicists. Launched in 1865 by the Irish-born critic Edwin L. Godkin, the *Nation* crusaded for civil-service reform, honesty in government, and a moderate tariff. Godkin believed that by reaching the most influential readers his ideas might spread to tens of millions.

Another journalist-author, Henry George, was an original thinker who left an enduring mark. Poor in formal schooling, he was rich in idealism and in the milk of human kindness. After seeing poverty at its worst in India and land-grabbing at its greediest in California, George penned his classic treatise *Progress and Poverty* (1879), which undertook to solve "the great enigma of our times"—"the association of progress with poverty." According to George, property owners unjustifiably profited from the pressure of growing population on a fixed supply of land. A single 100 percent tax on those windfall profits would eliminate unfair inequalities and stimulate economic growth.

George's controversial single-tax ideas so horrified the propertied classes that his manuscript was rejected by numerous publishers. Finally published in 1879, the book ultimately sold some 3 million copies. George also lectured widely in America, where he influenced thinking about the maldistribution of wealth, and in Britain, where he left an indelible mark on Fabian socialism. George's proposals resounded for decades, and his concern for the gap between rich and poor inspired numerous later American reformers. Edward Bellamy, a quiet Massachusetts Yankee, was another journalist-reformer of remarkable power. In 1888 he published a socialistic novel, *Looking Backward*, in which the hero, falling into a hypnotic sleep, awakens in the year 2000. The hero "looks backward" and finds that the social and economic injustices of 1887 have melted away under an idyllic government, which has nationalized big business to serve the public interest. To a nation already alarmed by the trust evil, the book had a magnetic appeal and sold over a million copies. Scores of Bellamy Clubs sprang up to discuss this mild utopian socialism, and they heavily influenced American reform movements near the end of the century.

★ The New Morality

Like other radical reformers, Victoria Woodhull shook the pillars of conventional morality when she publicly proclaimed her belief in free love in 1871. Woodhull was a beautiful and eloquent divorcée, sometime stockbroker, and tireless feminist propagandist. Together with her sister Tennessee Claflin she published a far-out periodical, *Woodhull and Claflin's Weekly*. The sisters again shocked "respectable" society in 1872 when their journal struck a blow for the new morality by charging that Henry Ward Beecher, the most famous preacher of his day, had for years been carrying on an adulterous affair.

Pure-minded Americans sternly resisted these affronts to their moral principles. Their foremost champion was a portly crusader, Anthony Comstock, who made lifelong war on the "immoral." Armed after 1873 with a federal statute—the notorious Comstock Law—this self-appointed defender of sexual purity boasted that he had confiscated no fewer than 202,679 "obscene pictures and photos"; 4,185 "boxes of pills, powders, etc., used by abortionists"; and 26 "obscene pictures, framed on walls of saloons."

The antics of the Woodhull sisters and Anthony Comstock exposed to daylight the battle going on in late-nineteenth-century America over sexual attitudes and the place of women. Switchboards and typewriters in the booming cities became increasingly the tools of women's independence. Young workingwomen headed to dance halls and nightclubs when the day was done, enjoying a new sense of freedom in the cities. This "new morality" began to be reflected in soaring divorce rates, the spreading practice of birth control, and increasingly frank discussion of sexual topics. By 1913, said one popular magazine, the chimes had struck "sex o'clock in America."

★ Families and Women in the City

The new urban environment was hard on families. Paradoxically, the crowded cities were emotionally isolating places. Urban families had to go it alone, separated from clan, kin, and village. Many families cracked under the strain of providing the virtually exclusive

> In 1906 progressive reformer Jane Addams (1860–1935) argued that granting women the vote would improve the social and political condition of American cities:
>
> "City housekeeping has failed partly because women, the traditional housekeepers, have not been consulted as to its multiform activities. The men have been carelessly indifferent to much of the civic housekeeping, as they have been indifferent to the details of the household.... City government demands the help of minds accustomed to detail and a variety of work, to a sense of obligation to the health and welfare of young children, and to a responsibility for the cleanliness and comfort of other people."

arena for intimate companionship and emotional satisfaction. The late-nineteenth-century urban era launched the "divorce revolution" that transformed the United States' social landscape in the twentieth century.

Urban life also dictated changes in work habits and even in family size. Not only fathers but mothers and even children as young as ten years old often worked, and usually in widely scattered locations. In the city more children meant more mouths to feed, more crowding in sardine-tin tenements, and more human baggage to carry in the uphill struggle for social mobility. Not surprisingly, birthrates were still dropping, and family size continued to shrink as the nineteenth century lengthened. Marriages were being delayed, and more couples learned the techniques of birth control.

Women were growing more independent in the urban environment, and in 1898 they heard the voice of a major feminist prophet, Charlotte Perkins Gilman. In that year the freethinking and original-minded Gilman published *Women and Economics*. In this classic of feminist literature, Gilman called on women to abandon their dependent status and contribute to the larger life of the community through productive involvement in the economy. Rejecting all claims that biology gave women a fundamentally different character from men, she argued that "our highly specialized motherhood is not so advantageous as believed." She advocated centralized nurseries and cooperative kitchens to facilitate women's participation in the work force—anticipating by more than half a century the day-care centers and convenience-food services of a later day.

Gilman's call for female participation in wage labor reflected epochal changes already under way, but strict codes still prescribed which women might work and what jobs they might hold. Because employment of wives and mothers was considered taboo, the vast majority of working women were single. Race, ethnicity, and class also shaped job opportunities. White-collar jobs like social worker, telephone operator, and department-store clerk were largely reserved for native-born women, while immigrant women clustered in particular industries, as Jewish women did in the garment trade. Black women had few opportunities beyond domestic service.

Beyond addressing the world of work, fiery feminists also continued to insist on the ballot. They had been demanding the vote since before the Civil War, but many high-minded female reformers had temporarily shelved the cause of women to battle for the rights of blacks. In 1890 militant suffragists formed the **National American Woman Suffrage Association (NAWSA)**. Its founders included aging pioneers like Elizabeth Cady Stanton, who had helped organize the first women's rights convention in 1848, and her long-time comrade Susan B. Anthony, the radical Quaker who had courted jail by trying to cast a ballot in the 1872 presidential election.

By 1900 a new generation of women had taken command of the suffrage battle. Their most effective leader was Carrie Chapman Catt, a pragmatic and businesslike reformer of relentless dedication. Significantly, under Catt the suffragists de-emphasized the argument that women deserved the vote as a matter of right, because they were in all respects the equals of men. Instead Catt stressed the desirability of giving women the vote if they were to continue to discharge their traditional duties as homemakers and mothers. Women thus had a special public responsibility for such things as children's education, public health, and safety, the argument ran.

By thus linking the ballot to a traditional definition of women's role, suffragists registered encouraging gains as the new century opened, despite continuing showers of rotten eggs and the jeers of male critics. Women were increasingly permitted to vote in local elections. Wyoming Territory—later called "the Equality State"—granted the first unrestricted suffrage to women in 1869. This important breach in the dike once made, many states followed Wyoming's example. Paralleling these triumphs, most of the states by 1890 had passed laws to permit wives to own or control their property after marriage.

National American Woman Suffrage Association (NAWSA) *An organization founded in 1890 to demand the vote for women. NAWSA argued that women should be allowed to vote because their responsibilities in the home and family made them indispensable in the public decision-making process. During World War I, NAWSA supported the war effort and lauded women's role in the Allied victory, which helped to finally achieve nationwide woman suffrage in the Nineteenth Amendment (1920).*

The reborn suffrage movement and other women's organizations largely excluded black women from their ranks. Fearful that an integrated campaign would handicap its efforts to get the vote, the National American Woman Suffrage Association limited membership to whites. Black women, however, created their own associations. Journalist and teacher Ida B. Wells inspired black women to mount a nationwide antilynching crusade. She also helped launch the black women's club movement, which culminated in the establishment of the National Association of Colored Women in 1896.

Women also took a lead in the growing crusade against alcohol and the saloon. In 1874 the **Woman's Christian Temperance Union (WCTU)** was organized with the white ribbon as its symbol of purity. The saintly Frances E. Willard—also a champion of planned parenthood—was its leading spirit. Less saintly was the mentally deranged "Kansas Cyclone," Carrie A. Nation, who smashed saloon bottles and bars with her hatchet. Female prohibitionists, singing "The Lips That Touch Liquor Must Never Touch Mine," began sweeping new states into the "dry column"—setting the stage for the great, but temporary, triumph of 1919 when the national prohibition amendment (Eighteenth) was attached to the Constitution.

Woman's Christian Temperance Union (WCTU) *Founded in Ohio in the 1870s to combat the evils of excessive alcohol consumption, the WCTU went on to embrace a broad reform agenda, including campaigns to abolish prostitution and gain the right to vote for women.*

★ Postwar Fiction, Lowbrow and High

Not all social activity proved so serious. Post–Civil War Americans devoured millions of "dime novels," usually depicting the wild West. Paint-bedaubed Indians and quick-triggered gunmen such as "Deadwood Dick" shot off vast quantities of gunpowder, and virtue invariably triumphed. These lurid "paperbacks" were frowned on by parents, but goggle-eyed youths read them in haylofts or in schools behind the broad covers of geography books. The king of dime novelists was Harlan F. Halsey, who made a fortune by dashing off about 650 novels, often one in a day.

General Lewis Wallace—lawyer, soldier, and author—was a colorful figure. Having fought with distinction in the Civil War, he sought to combat the prevailing wave of Darwinian skepticism with his novel *Ben Hur: A Tale of the Christ* (1880). A phenomenal success, the book sold an estimated 2 million copies in many languages, including Arabic and Chinese, and later appeared on stage and screen. It was the *Uncle Tom's Cabin* of the anti-Darwinists, who found in it support for the Holy Scriptures.

An even more popular writer was Horatio ("Holy Horatio") Alger, a Puritan-reared New Englander, who in 1866 forsook the pulpit for the pen. He wrote more than a hundred volumes of juvenile fiction that sold over 17 million copies. His stock formula depicted a poor boy, who through a combination of virtue, honesty, hard work, and bravery, achieved success, wealth, and honor—a kind of survival of the purest, especially nonsmokers, nondrinkers, nonswearers, and nonliars.

Literature and the arts were not immune to the era's sweeping changes. Confronted by new cities and industries, American writers and artists forsook the romantic sentimentality of an earlier age and generated three interrelated currents in the arts: **realism**, **naturalism**, and **regionalism**. All three movements responded to the Gilded Age's urban, industrial transformation.

Realism quickly came to dominate post–Civil War American literature. Foregoing romantic pageantry, American authors increasingly found their subjects in the coarse human comedy and material drama of the world around them. William Dean Howells (1837–1920), the celebrated "father of American realism," emerged as the era's preeminent advocate of unsentimental literature. A printer's son from Ohio with limited formal education, he wrote his way into high literary circles of the East and in 1871 became editor of the prestigious Boston-based *Atlantic Monthly*. In his thirty-six novels, Howells wrote about ordinary people and about controversial social themes such as divorce and labor conflict. His most famous novel, *The Rise of Silas Lapham* (1885), describes the trials of a newly rich paint manufacturer caught up in the caste system of Brahmin Boston.

Two recipients of Howells's patronage and friendship—Mark Twain and Henry James—carried literary realism to new heights. With only meager schooling in frontier

realism *Mid-nineteenth-century movement in European and American literature and the arts that sought to depict contemporary life and society as it actually was, in all its unvarnished detail. Adherents eschewed the idealism and nostalgia of the earlier romantic sensibility.*

naturalism *An offshoot of mainstream realism, this late-nineteenth-century literary movement purported to apply detached scientific objectivity to the study of human characters shaped by degenerate heredity and extreme or sordid social environments.*

regionalism *A recurring artistic movement that, in the context of the late nineteenth century, aspired to capture the peculiarities, or "local color," of America's various regions in the face of modernization and national standardization.*

Mark Twain (1835–1910) Born Samuel Langhorne Clemens, he was not only America's most popular author but also a renowned platform lecturer. This photograph was taken in Dublin, New Hampshire, in August 1906 by Albert Bigelow Paine, Mark Twain's biographer.

Missouri, mustachioed Mark Twain (1835–1910) typified a new breed of American authors in revolt against the elegant refinements of the old New England school of writing. Christened Samuel Langhorne Clemens, he had served for a time as a Mississippi river boat pilot. After a stint in the Confederate militia, he journeyed westward to Nevada and California, a trip he described with a mixture of truth and tall tales in *Roughing It* (1872). One year later Twain teamed up with Charles Dudley Warner in 1873 to write *The Gilded Age*, an acid satire on post–Civil War politicians and speculators that gave a name to an era. Many other books flowed from Twain's busy pen. *The Adventures of Tom Sawyer* (1876) preceded *The Adventures of Huckleberry Finn* (1884), an American masterpiece that defied Twain's own definition of a classic as "a book which people praise and don't read." His later years were soured by bankruptcy growing out of unwise investments, and he was forced to take to the lecture platform and amuse what he called "the damned human race." Journalist, humorist, satirist, and foe of social injustice, Twain made his most enduring contribution in capturing frontier realism and humor in the authentic American dialect.

Twain's homegrown vernacular met its match in Henry James's elegant prose. Brother of Harvard philosopher William James, Henry James (1843–1916) was a New Yorker who took as his dominant literary theme the confrontation of innocent Americans with subtle Europeans. James penned a remarkable number of brilliant novels, including *The Portrait of a Lady* (1881) and *The Wings of the Dove* (1902). *The Bostonians* (1886) was one of the first novels about the rising feminist movement. James frequently made women his central characters, exploring their inner reactions to complex situations with a deftness that marked him as a master of "psychological realism." Long resident in England, he became a British subject shortly before his death.

Like her friend James, Edith Wharton (1862–1937) took a magnifying glass to the inner psychological turmoil and moral shortcomings of post–Civil War high society. Born into money, Wharton lived in the blue-blooded social circles of New York and Paris. After an unhappy marriage, she increasingly turned to writing. Her novels, including *The House of Mirth* (1905) and *The Age of Innocence* (1920) exposed the futile struggles and interior costs of striving characters stuck on the social ladder.

While realist authors often treated middle- and upper-class characters in everyday settings, naturalistic novelists placed lower-class or marginal characters in extreme or sordid environments, including the urban jungle. Stephen Crane (1871–1900), the fourteenth son of a Methodist minister, exemplified this naturalistic urge in his writing. His *Maggie: A Girl of the Streets* (1893), a brutal tale about a poor prostitute driven to suicide, proved too grim to find a publisher, so Crane had to have it printed privately. He rose quickly to prominence with *The Red Badge of Courage* (1895), the stirring story of a bloodied young Civil War recruit under the extreme stress of fire. Crane himself had never seen a battle and wrote entirely from the printed Civil War records. Sharing the misfortune of his many characters, he died of tuberculosis in 1900, when only twenty-nine.

Candid, naturalistic portrayals of contemporary life and social problems were the literary order of the day by the turn of the century. Jack London (1876–1916) turned from popular nature books such as *The Call of the Wild* (1903) to depicting a possible fascistic revolution in *The Iron Heel* (1907). Frank Norris (1870–1902), like London a Californian, wrote *The Octopus* (1901), an earthy saga of the stranglehold of the railroad and corrupt politicians on California wheat ranchers.

Conspicuous among the naturalistic novelists rising in the literary firmament was Theodore Dreiser (1871–1945), a homely, gangling writer from Indiana. He burst on the literary scene in 1900 with *Sister Carrie*, a graphic narrative of a poor working girl in Chicago and New York. She becomes one man's mistress, then elopes with another, and finally strikes out on her own to make a career on the stage. The fictional Carrie's disregard for prevailing moral standards so offended Dreiser's publisher that the book was soon withdrawn from circulation, though it later reemerged as an acclaimed American classic.

Sharing a common documentary impulse with realist and naturalistic fiction, regionalism as a movement sought to chronicle the peculiarities of local ways of life before the coming wave of industrial standardization. Regionalist writers accentuated the differences among still-distant American locales, while at the same time partially demystifying regional differences among national audiences bent on postwar reunification.

Twain, London, and Bret Harte, among other western writers, simultaneously popularized and debunked the lusty legends of the Old West. A foppishly dressed New Yorker, Harte (1836–1902) struck it rich in California with his stories of the gold rush, especially "The Luck of Roaring Camp" (1868) and "The Outcasts of Poker Flat" (1869).

Interest in local-color writing about the South also revived in the aftermath of Reconstruction. Two black writers, Paul Laurence Dunbar (1872–1906) and Charles W. Chesnutt (1858–1932), brought their distinctive voices to late-nineteenth-century literature. In Dunbar's acclaimed book of poetry, *Lyrics of Lowly Life* (1896), he used black dialect and folklore to capture the spontaneity and richness of southern black culture. Chesnutt did the same through his short stories, collected in *The Conjure Women* (1899).

Pioneering women also contributed to the post–Civil War southern literary scene. The daring Louisiana feminist author Kate Chopin (1851–1904) wrote candidly about adultery, suicide, and women's ambitions in *The Awakening* (1899). Largely ignored after her death, Chopin was rediscovered by later readers who saw in her work the feminist yearnings that stirred beneath the surface of the Gilded Age.

Some important authors defied categorization. The gifted Henry Adams (1838–1918)—son of Charles Francis Adams, grandson of John Quincy Adams, and great-grandson of John Adams—turned unrivaled family connections into a prolific career as a historian, novelist, and critic. In his nine-volume *History of the United States During the Administrations of Jefferson and Madison* (1889–1891), Adams defended his patrician heritage from posthumous attack. In *Mont-Saint Michel and Chartres* (1905), Adams celebrated the bygone beauty and unity of the High Middle Ages. He channeled his own failure to come to grips with the chaotic modern age into his autobiographical work, *The Education of Henry Adams* (1907).

★ Artistic Triumphs

Realism and regionalism (more so than naturalism) also energized the American art world, much as they did the literary sphere. Philadelphia's native son Thomas Eakins (1836–1920) created a veritable artistic catalogue of his hometown's social, scientific, and sporting life at the end of the nineteenth century. Boston-born Winslow Homer (1836–1910), who as a youth had secretly drawn sketches in school, was perhaps the greatest painter of the group. Earthily American and largely resistant to foreign influences, Homer revealed rugged realism and boldness of conception. His canvases of the sea and of fisherfolk were masterly, and probably no American artist has excelled him in portraying the awesome power of the ocean.

Following in the footsteps of the expatriate writers Henry James and Edith Wharton, prominent American painters working in the realist style made their living abroad. James Whistler (1834–1903) did much of his work, including the celebrated portrait of his mother, in England. This eccentric and quarrelsome Massachusetts Yankee had earlier been dropped from West Point after failing chemistry. "Had silicon been a gas," he later jested, "I would have been a major general." Another gifted portrait painter, likewise self-exiled in Britain, was John Singer Sargent (1856–1925), whose depictions of the British nobility and American nouveau riche were highly prized. Mary Cassatt, an American exile in Paris, painted sensitive portrayals of women and children that earned her a place in the pantheon of the French Impressionist painters.

The most gifted sculptor yet produced by America was Augustus Saint-Gaudens (1848–1907). Born in Ireland of an Irish mother and a French father, he became an adopted American. Among his most moving works is the Robert Gould Shaw memorial, erected in Boston in 1897. It depicts Colonel Shaw, a young white "Boston Brahmin" officer, leading his black troops into battle in the Civil War.

Music, too, was gaining popularity. America of the 1880s and 1890s was assembling high-quality symphony orchestras, notably in Boston, Philadelphia, and Chicago. The famed Metropolitan Opera House of New York was erected in 1883. In its fabled "Diamond Horseshoe" the newly rich, often under the pretense of enjoying the imported singers, would flaunt their jewels, gowns, and furs. While symphonies and operas were devoted to bringing European music to elite American audiences, new strains of home-grown American music were sprouting in the South, another outgrowth of the regionalist trend. Black folk traditions such as spirituals and "ragged music" were evolving into the blues, ragtime, and jazz that would transform American popular music in the twentieth century.

A marvelous invention was the reproduction of music by mechanical means. The phonograph, though a squeakily imperfect instrument when invented by the deaf Edison, had by 1900 reached over 150,000 homes. Americans were rapidly being dosed with "canned music," as the "sitting room" piano increasingly gathered dust.

Wrenching changes to the nation's cities inspired a new generation of architects and planners to reshape American urban space with the **City Beautiful movement**. Its proponents wanted the new American city not just to look beautiful but to convey a confident sense of harmony, order, and monumentality. To achieve these effects they copied European styles of beaux-arts classicism and planning ideas from the master builder of Paris, Baron Georges-Eugène Haussmann. Aiming to assert America's prominence among the greatest urban cultures of the Western world, architects constructed grandiose urban landmarks such as New York's Grand Central Terminal (1913). City planners such as Daniel Burnham redesigned Chicago and Washington, D.C., in the belief they could make them perfect, progressive cities, inspiring civic virtue in their inhabitants. To this end, they joined contemporary landscape architects and park builders like Frederick Law Olmsted, who sought to foster virtue and egalitarian values with his designs for New York's Central Park (1873) as well as the campus of Stanford University (1891).

Burnham's first major project, which came to symbolize the City Beautiful movement, was his design for the great **World's Columbian Exposition**. Held in Chicago in 1893, the exposition, with Burnham's imposing landscape of pavilions and fountains, honored the four-hundredth anniversary of Columbus's first voyage. This so-called dream of loveliness was visited by 27 million people. It did much to raise American artistic standards and promote city planning, although many fair goers proved more interested in the contortions of a hootchy-kootchy dancer named "Little Egypt."

⭐ The Business of Amusement

Fun and frolic were not neglected by the workaday American. People sought their pleasures fiercely, as they had overrun their continent and built their cities fiercely. And now they had more time to play. Varied diversions beckoned. The legitimate stage still flourished, as appreciative audiences responded to the lure of the footlights. Vaudeville, with its coarse jokes and graceful acrobats, continued to be immensely popular during the 1880s and 1890s, as were minstrel shows in the South, now performed by black singers and dancers rather than by whites wearing blackface.

The circus—high tented and multiringed—finally emerged full-blown. Phineas T. Barnum, the master showman who had early discovered that "the public likes to be humbugged," joined hands with James A. Bailey in 1881 to stage the "Greatest Show on Earth."

City Beautiful movement *A turn-of-the-century movement among progressive architects and city planners, who aimed to promote order, harmony, and virtue while beautifying the nation's new urban spaces with grand boulevards, welcoming parks, and monumental public buildings.*

World's Columbian Exposition (1893) *Americans saw this world's fair, held in Chicago, as their opportunity to claim a place among the world's most "civilized" societies, by which they meant the countries of western Europe. The fair honored art, architecture, and science, and its promoters built a mini-city in which to host the fair that reflected all the ideals of city planning popular at the time. For many, this was the high point of the City Beautiful movement.*

Colorful "Wild West" shows, first performed in 1883, were even more distinctively American. Headed by the knightly, goateed, and free-drinking William F. ("Buffalo Bill") Cody, the troupe included war-whooping Indians, live buffalo, and deadeye sharpshooters such as the girlish Annie Oakley. Rifle in hand, she could at thirty paces perforate a tossed-up card half a dozen times before it fluttered to the ground.

Baseball, already widely played before the Civil War, was clearly emerging as the national pastime, if not a national mania. A league of professional players was formed in the 1870s, and in 1888 an all-star baseball team toured the world, using the pyramids as a backstop while in Egypt. Basketball was invented in 1891 by James Naismith, a YMCA instructor in Springfield, Massachusetts. Designed as an active, indoor sport that could be played during the winter months, basketball spread rapidly and enjoyed enormous popularity in the next century.

The trend toward spectator sports was exemplified by football, a rugged game that at first used the dangerous flying-wedge formation. The Yale–Princeton game of 1893 drew fifty thousand cheering fans, while foreigners jeered that the nation was getting "sports on the brain."

Even pugilism, with its long background of bare-knuckle brutality, gained a new gloved respectability in 1892. Agile "Gentleman Jim" Corbett wrested the world championship from the aging and alcoholic John L. Sullivan, the "Boston Strong Boy."

The land of the skyscraper was plainly becoming more standardized, owing largely to the new industrialization. Despite their distinct ethnic and racial neighborhoods, Americans increasingly shared a common culture—playing, reading, shopping, and talking alike. As the century drew to a close, the explosion of cities paradoxically made Americans more diverse and more similar at the same time.

Buffalo Bill's Wild West Show, ca. 1907 By the late 1800s, the "Wild West" was already passing into the realm of myth—and popular entertainment. Famed frontiersman William F. ("Buffalo Bill") Cody (1846–1917) made his fortune showing off his tame cowboys and Indians to enthusiastic urban audiences in Europe as well as the United States. Buffalo Bill's "Wild West"—an extravaganza featuring skilled horsemen from around the globe, including Turks, South American gauchos, Arabs, and Cossacks—was even more motley than the real one.

CHAPTER SUMMARY ★ ★ ★ ★ ★ ★ ★ ★ ★ ★ ★ ★ ★ ★ ★

The United States moved from the country to the city in the post–Civil War decades. Mushrooming urban development was attractive and exciting for many who migrated from farms and small towns, but urban development also created severe social problems, including overcrowding, slums, and a sharp divide between rich and poor.

After the 1880s the cities were also flooded with the "New Immigrants" from southern and eastern Europe. With their culturally different customs and non-Protestant religions, the newcomers often met with nativist hostility and discrimination. Congress began to throw up barriers to immigration, including a complete ban on the Chinese.

Religion had to adjust to social, cultural, and intellectual changes. The immigrant faiths of Roman Catholicism and Judaism gained considerable strength, while conflicts over evolution and biblical interpretation divided American Protestantism into fundamentalist and modernist wings.

American education expanded rapidly, especially at the secondary and collegiate levels; major new research universities were founded, both by state governments and by wealthy industrialists. Women's opportunities for education advanced in both separate institutions and coeducation. Black leaders Washington and Du Bois divided over the question of manual education versus development of an elite "talented tenth."

Significant conflicts over moral values, especially relating to sexuality and the role of women, began to appear. The new urban environment provided expanded opportunities for women but also created difficulties for the family. Families grew more isolated from society, the divorce rate rose, and average family size shrank.

American literature and the arts reflected the social and moral issues of the new urban, industrial age. The major literary and artistic movements of realism, naturalism, and regionalism reflected the new energy and sophistication of American culture, which gained national acclaim and increasing international respect. Leisure-time amusements and sports became enormously popular but also more standardized, in keeping with the new industrial nation.

KEY TERMS

- New Immigrants (407)
- settlement houses (410)
- liberal Protestants (413)
- Tuskegee Institute (416)
- land-grant colleges (417)
- pragmatism (418)
- yellow journalism (418)
- National American Woman Suffrage Association (NAWSA) (420)
- Woman's Christian Temperance Union (WCTU) (421)
- realism (421)
- naturalism (421)
- regionalism (421)
- City Beautiful movement (424)
- World's Columbian Exposition (424)

PEOPLE TO KNOW

- Jane Addams
- Charles Darwin
- Booker T. Washington
- W. E. B. Du Bois
- Joseph Pulitzer
- William Randolph Hearst
- Carrie Chapman Catt
- Mark Twain
- Henry James
- Winslow Homer
- Augustus Saint-Gaudens

MindTap is a fully online, highly personalized learning experience built upon Cengage Learning content. MindTap combines student learning tools—readings, multimedia, activities, and assessments—into a singular Learning Path that guides students through the course.

Chapter 26

The Great West and the Agricultural Revolution
1865–1896

Up to our own day American history has been in a large degree the history of the colonization of the Great West. The existence of an area of free land, its continuous recession, and the advance of American settlement westward, explain American development.

FREDERICK JACKSON TURNER, 1893

The White Man, who possesses this whole vast country from sea to sea, . . . cannot know the cramp we feel in this little spot, with the undying remembrance of the fact . . . that every foot of what you proudly call America, not very long ago belonged to the red man.

WASHAKIE (SHOSHONE INDIAN), 1878

Chapter Outline

- The Conquest of the Indians
- The Mining and Cattle Frontiers
- The Industrialization of Agriculture
- Farmers Protest
- Challenge from the People's Party
- Panic and Depression
- Bryan versus McKinley, 1896
- Makers of America: The Plains Indians
- Examining the Evidence: Robert Louis Stevenson's Transcontinental Journey, 1879
- Thinking Globally: The Great Frontier
- Varying Viewpoints: Was the West Really "Won"?

When the Civil War crashed to a close, the frontier line was still wavering westward. A long fringe of settlement, bulging outward here and there, ran roughly north through central Texas and on to the Canadian border. Between this jagged line and the settled areas on the Pacific slope, there were virtually no white people. The few exceptions were the islands of Mormons in Utah, occasional trading posts and gold camps, and several scattered Mexican settlements throughout the Southwest.

Sprawling in expanse, the Great West was a rough square that measured about a thousand miles on each side. Embracing mountains, plateaus, deserts, and plains, it was the habitat of the Indian, the buffalo, the wild horse, and the coyote. Twenty-five years later—that is, by 1890—the entire domain had been carved into states and the four territories of Utah, Arizona, New Mexico, and "Indian Territory," or Oklahoma. Pioneers flung themselves greedily on this enormous prize, as if to ravish it. Probably never before in human experience had so huge an area been transformed so rapidly.

FOCUS QUESTIONS

1. Why did the western Indians clash with the expanding United States? What were the causes and consequences of their defeat?
2. What were the principal stages of frontier settlement in the West, and how did each affect the region's development?

CHRONOLOGY

c. 1700–1800	New Indian peoples move onto Great Plains	1889–1890	North Dakota, South Dakota, Montana, Washington, Idaho, and Wyoming admitted to Union
1858	Pikes Peak gold rush	1890	Census Bureau declares frontier line ended
1859	Nevada Comstock lode discovered		Emergence of People's party (Populists)
1862	Homestead Act		Battle of Wounded Knee
1864	Sand Creek massacre	1891	Construction of Trans-Siberian Railroad begins
	Nevada admitted to Union		
1867	National Grange organized	1892	Populist party candidate James B. Weaver polls more than 1 million votes in presidential election
1876	Battle of the Little Bighorn		
	Colorado admitted to Union		
1877	Nez Percé War	1893	Frederick Jackson Turner publishes "The Significance of the Frontier in American History"
1881	Helen Hunt Jackson publishes *A Century of Dishonor*		
1884	Federal government outlaws Indian Sun Dance	1894	"Coxey's Army" marches on Washington
			Pullman strike
1885	Canadian Pacific Railway, first transcontinental rail line, completed across Canada	1896	McKinley defeats Bryan for presidency
			Utah admitted to Union
		1897	Dingley Tariff Act
1885–1890	Local chapters of Farmers' Alliances formed	1900	Gold Standard Act
		1907	Oklahoma admitted to Union
1887	Dawes Severalty Act	1924	Indians granted U.S. citizenship
1889	Oklahoma opened to U.S. citizen settlement	1934	Indian Reorganization Act

3. What was the significance of the closing of the frontier in 1890 for American history? Why did the West remain a distinctive American region even as it left its frontier past behind?

4. How did the agricultural revolution transform Great Plains farming? What were the consequences for farmers?

5. What were the causes of western and southern farmers' protests? How were their grievances expressed in the Populist Party?

★ The Clash of Cultures on the Plains

Native Americans numbered about 360,000 in 1860, many of them scattered across the vast grasslands of the trans-Missouri West. But to their misfortune, the Indians stood in the path of the advancing white pioneers. An inevitable clash loomed between an acquisitive, industrializing nation and the Indians' lifeways, highly evolved over centuries to adapt to the demanding environment of the sparsely watered western plains.

Migration and conflict—and sometimes dramatic cultural change—were no strangers to the arid West, even before the whites began to arrive. The Comanches had driven the Apaches off the central plains into the upper Rio Grande valley in the eighteenth century. Harried by the Mandans and Chippewas, the Cheyenne had abandoned their villages along the upper reaches of the Mississippi and Missouri Rivers in the century before the Civil War. The Sioux, displaced from the Great Lakes woodlands in the late eighteenth century, emerged onto the plains to prey upon the Crows, Kiowas, and Pawnees. Mounted on Spanish-introduced horses, peoples like the Cheyenne and the Sioux transformed themselves into wide-ranging nomadic traders and deadly efficient buffalo hunters.

When white soldiers and settlers edged onto the plains just before the Civil War, they accelerated a fateful cycle that exacerbated already fierce enmities among the Indians and ultimately undermined the foundations of Native American culture. White intruders unwittingly spread cholera, typhoid, and smallpox among the native peoples of the plains, with devastating results. Equally harmful, whites put further pressure on the shrinking bison population by hunting and by grazing their own livestock on the prairie grasses. As the once-mammoth buffalo herds dwindled, warfare intensified among the Plains tribes for ever-scarcer hunting grounds.

The federal government tried to sign treaties with various "chiefs" at Fort Laramie in 1851. The treaties marked the beginning of the **reservation system** in the West. But the white treaty makers misunderstood both Indian government and Indian society. "Tribes" and "chiefs" were often fictions of the white imagination, which could not grasp the fact that many Native Americans, living in scattered bands, recognized only the authority of their immediate families or perhaps a band elder. And the nomadic culture of the Plains Indians was utterly alien to the concept of living out one's life in the confinement of a defined territory.

In the 1860s the federal government tried to herd the Plains Indians into confines such as the "Great Sioux Reservation" in the Dakotas and the Indian Territory of present-day

reservation system *The system that allotted land with designated boundaries to Native American tribes in the West, beginning in the 1850s and ending with the Dawes Severalty Act of 1887. Within these reservations, most land was used communally, rather than owned individually. The U.S. government encouraged and sometimes violently coerced Native Americans to stay on the reservations at all times.*

The Buffalo Hunt, by Frederic Remington, 1890 A New Yorker who first went west at the age of nineteen as a cowboy and ranch cook, Remington (1861–1909) became the foremost artist of the vanishing way of life of the old Far West. Once a common sight on the high plains, the kind of buffalo kill that Remington records here was a great rarity by the time he painted this scene in 1890. The once-vast herds of bison had long since been reduced to a pitiful few by the white man's rifles and the increasingly concentrated use of the land by ever more constricted Indians.

> One disheartened Indian complained to the white Sioux Commission created by Congress:
>
> "Tell your people that since the Great Father promised that we should never be removed we have been moved five times.... I think you had better put the Indians on wheels and you can run them about wherever you wish."

Oklahoma, where dozens of southern Plains tribes were forced to move. Promises from Washington that they would be left alone and provided with food, clothing, and other supplies were often violated by corrupt federal agents who regularly cheated the Indians.

For more than a decade after the Civil War, fierce warfare between Indians and the U.S. Army raged in various parts of the West (see Map 26.1). Army troops met formidable adversaries in the Plains Indians, whose superb horsemanship gave them baffling mobility. Fully one-fifth of all U.S. Army personnel on the frontier were African American—dubbed "Buffalo Soldiers" by the Indians.

★ Receding Native Population

The Indian wars in the West were often savage clashes. Aggressive whites sometimes shot peaceful Indians on sight. At Sand Creek, Colorado, in 1864, Colonel J. M. Chivington's militia massacred in cold blood some four hundred Indians who apparently thought they had been promised immunity. Women were shot praying for mercy, children had their brains dashed out, and braves were tortured, scalped, and unspeakably mutilated.

Cruelty begot cruelty. In 1866 a Sioux war party ambushed Captain William Fetterman's command of eighty-one soldiers and civilians in Wyoming's Bighorn Mountains, killing every man and mutilating the corpses. As the cycle of ferocious warfare intensified, the federal government in 1868 abandoned its attempt to construct the Bozeman Trail through Montana. The sprawling "Great Sioux Reservation" was guaranteed to the Sioux tribes.

But in 1874 a new round of warfare with the Plains Indians began when Colonel George Armstrong Custer, a famed Civil War officer, led a "scientific" expedition into the Black Hills of South Dakota and announced that he had discovered gold there. Hordes of greedy gold-seekers soon swarmed into the Sioux lands. The aggrieved Sioux, aided by the Cheyenne and Arapaho, took to the warpath, inspirited by the influential and wily Sitting Bull.

Colonel Custer's Seventh Cavalry set out to suppress the Indians and force them onto the reservation. Attacking what turned out to be a superior force of some 2,500 well-armed warriors along the Little Bighorn River in present-day Montana, the "White Chief with Yellow Hair" and about 250 officers and men were completely wiped out in 1876 when two supporting columns failed to come to their rescue.* But in a series of battles across the northern plains in the ensuing months, the U.S. Army relentlessly hunted down the Indians who had destroyed Custer's troops.

The Nez Percé Indians of northeastern Oregon were goaded into a daring fight in 1877, when U.S. authorities tried to herd them onto a reservation. Chief Joseph finally surrendered his band after a tortuous, seventeen-hundred-mile, three-month trek across the Continental Divide toward Canada. There Chief Joseph hoped to rendezvous with Sitting Bull, who had taken refuge north of the border after the **Battle of the Little Bighorn**. Betrayed into believing that they would be returned to their ancestral lands in Idaho, the Nez Percés instead were sent to a dusty reservation in Kansas, where 40 percent of them perished from disease. The survivors eventually returned to Idaho.

Fierce Apache tribes of Arizona and New Mexico were the most difficult to subdue. Led by Geronimo, whose eyes blazed with hatred of the whites, they were pursued into Mexico by federal troops. Scattered remnants of the warriors were finally persuaded to surrender after the Apache women had been exiled to Florida.

Battle of the Little Bighorn (1876) *A particularly violent example of the warfare between whites and Native Americans in the late nineteenth century, also known as "Custer's Last Stand." In two days, June 25 and 26, 1876, the combined forces of 2,500 Sioux, Cheyenne, and Arapaho Indians defeated and killed more than 250 U.S. soldiers, including Colonel George Custer. The battle came as the U.S. government tried to compel Native Americans to remain on the reservations and Native Americans tried to defend territory from white gold-seekers. This Indian advantage did not last long, however, as the union of these Indian fighters proved tenuous and the U.S. Army soon exacted retribution.*

---

*When whites annihilated Indians, the engagement (in white history books) was usually a "battle"; when Indians slaughtered whites, it was a "massacre." "Strategy," when practiced by Indians, was "treachery."

This relentless fire-and-sword policy of the whites at last shattered the spirit of the Indians. The vanquished Native Americans were finally ghettoized on reservations, where they were compelled to eke out an existence as wards of the government.

The "taming" of the Indians was engineered by a number of factors. Of cardinal importance was the federal government's willingness to back its land claims with military force. Almost as critical was the railroad, which shot an iron arrow through the heart of the West. The Indians were also ravaged by the white people's diseases, to which they showed little resistance, and by their firewater, which they could resist even less.

Above all, the virtual extermination of the buffalo doomed the Plains Indians' nomadic way of life. When the white Americans ventured onto the Great Plains after the Civil War, some 15 million buffalo, or American bison, still blackened the prairies. In 1868 a Kansas Pacific locomotive

> *Civil War veteran and long-time Indian fighter General Philip Sheridan (1831–1888) reflected on the wars against the Indians:*
>
> "We took away their country and their means of support, broke up their mode of living, their habits of life, introduced disease and decay among them, and it was for this and against this they made war. Could anyone expect less?"
>
> *What alternative paths might U.S.-Indian relations have followed during the era of America's intensive westward expansion?*

Map 26.1 Indian Wars, 1860–1890 Surrendering in 1877, Chief Joseph of the Nez Percés declared: "Our chiefs are killed.... The old men are all dead.... The little children are freezing to death.... I want to have time to look for my children.... Hear me, my chiefs. My heart is sick and sad. From where the sun now stands I will fight no more forever."

Contending Voices

The Ghost Dance and the Wounded Knee Massacre

James McLaughlin (1842–1923), a U.S. Indian Service agent involved in events precipitating the bloody 1890 confrontation at Wounded Knee, depicted the Sioux's "Ghost Dance" as a dangerous practice hindering their assimilation and progress:

"The [Ghost Dance] doctrine was artfully framed to appeal to the cupidity of the Indian and to inflame him against the whites, carrying with it promise of return to the free life, with plenty of buffalo and no prospect of work.... A more pernicious system of religion could not have been offered to a people who stood on the threshold of civilization, and who hungered for a realization of dreams that would free them from present poverty, probable hunger, and the prospect of toil."

Oglala Sioux chief Black Elk (1863–1950), meanwhile, recounted the horrifying aftermath of the massacre instigated by that very civilizing impulse:

"[A]fter the soldiers marched away from their dirty work, a heavy snow began to fall.... The snow drifted deep in the crooked gulch, and it was one long grave of butchered women and children and babies, who had never done any harm and were only trying to run away."

Battle of Wounded Knee (1890) *A battle between the U.S. Army and the Dakota Sioux, in which two hundred Native Americans and twenty-nine U.S. soldiers died. Tensions erupted violently over two major issues: the Sioux practice of the "Ghost Dance," which the U.S. government had outlawed, and the dispute over whether Sioux reservation land would be broken up because of the Dawes Act.*

Dawes Severalty Act (1887) *An act that broke up Indian reservations and distributed land to individual households. Leftover land was sold for money to fund U.S. government efforts to "civilize" Native Americans.*

---

had to wait eight hours for a herd to amble across the tracks. These huge, shaggy, lumbering beasts were the staff of life for the Native Americans (see "Makers of America: The Plains Indians," p. 433). Their flesh provided food; their dried dung provided fuel ("buffalo chips"); their hides provided clothing, lariats, and harnesses.

With the building of the railroad, the massacre of the herds began in deadly earnest. The creatures were slain for their hides, for a few choice cuts of meat, or for sheer amusement. The telescope-eyed crack shot William "Buffalo Bill" Cody killed over four thousand buffalo in eighteen months while employed by the Kansas Pacific. "Sportsmen" on lurching railroad trains would lean out the windows and blaze away at the animals to satisfy their lust for slaughter or excitement. Such wholesale butchery left fewer than a thousand buffalo alive by 1885, and the once-numerous beasts were in danger of complete extinction. The whole story is a shocking example of the greed and waste that accompanied the conquest of a continent.

★ The End of the Trail

By the 1880s, the national conscience began to stir uneasily over the plight of the Indians. Helen Hunt Jackson, a Massachusetts writer of children's literature, pricked the moral sense of Americans in 1881 when she published *A Century of Dishonor*. The book chronicled the sorry record of governmental ruthlessness and chicanery in dealing with the Indians. Her later novel *Ramona* (1884), a story of injustice to the California Indians, sold some 600,000 copies and further inspired sympathy for the Indians.

Debate seesawed. Humanitarians wanted to treat the Indians kindly and persuade them thereby to "walk the white man's road." Yet hard-liners insisted on the current policy of forced containment and brutal punishment. Neither side showed much respect for Native American culture. Christian reformers, who often administered educational facilities on the reservations, sometimes withheld food to force the Indians to give up their tribal religion and assimilate to white society. In 1884 these zealous white souls joined with military men in successfully persuading the federal government to outlaw the sacred Sun Dance. When the "Ghost Dance" religious movement later spread to the Dakota Sioux, the army bloodily stamped it out in 1890 at the so-called **Battle of Wounded Knee**. In the fighting thus provoked, an estimated two hundred Indian men, women, and children were killed, as well as twenty-nine invading soldiers.

The misbegotten offspring of the movement to reform Indian policy was the **Dawes Severalty Act** of 1887. Reflecting the forced-civilization views of the reformers, the act dissolved many tribes as legal entities, wiped out tribal ownership of land, and set up individual Indian family heads with 160 free acres. If the Indians behaved themselves like "good white settlers," they would get full title to their holdings, as well as citizenship, in twenty-five years. The probationary period was later extended, but full citizenship was granted to all Indians in 1924.

The federal efforts at forced assimilation included boarding schools for Indian children, beginning in 1879 with the Carlisle Indian School in Pennsylvania. "Kill the Indian and save the man" was the motto for these schools, where Native American children, separated from their tribes, were taught English and inculcated with white values and customs.

Makers of America

The Plains Indians

The last of the native peoples of North America to bow before the military might of the whites, the Indians of the northern Great Plains long defended their lands and their ways of life against the American cavalry. After the end of the Indian wars, toward the close of the nineteenth century, the Plains tribes struggled on, jealously guarding their communities against white encroachment, preserving much of their ancestral culture to this day.

Before Europeans first appeared in North America in the sixteenth century, the vast plain from northern Texas to Saskatchewan was home to some thirty different tribes. There was no typical Plains Indian; each tribe spoke a distinct language, practiced its own religion, and formed its own government.

Indians had first trod the arid plains to pursue sprawling herds of antelope, elk, and especially buffalo, but they were not exclusively hunters. The women were expert farmers, coaxing lush gardens of pumpkins, squash, corn, and beans from the dry but fertile soil. Still, the shaggy pelt and heavy flesh of the buffalo constituted the staff of life on the plains. Hunted by men, the great bison were butchered by women, who used every part of the beast. They fashioned horns into spoons, turned sinews into strong bowstrings, and wove buffalo hair into ropes. Meat not immediately eaten was pounded into pemmican—thin strips of smoked or sun-dried buffalo flesh mixed with berries.

The nomadic Plains Indians had long dispersed in small bands during the winter, gathering together in the summer for larger-scale religious ceremonies, socializing, and communal buffalo hunts. Then in the sixteenth century, the mounted Spanish *conquistadores* ventured into the New World, and their steeds quickly spread over the plains. The horse revolutionized Indian societies, turning the Plains tribes into efficient hunting machines that promised to banish hunger from the prairies. But the plains pony also ignited a furious competition for grazing land and for ever more horses, so wars became increasingly bitter and frequent.

The European invasion soon eclipsed the short-lived era of the horse. After many battles the Plains Indians found themselves crammed together on tiny reservations, clinging with tired but determined fingers to their traditions. Although much of Plains Indian culture persists to this day, the Indians' free-ranging way of life passed into memory. As Black Elk, an Oglala Sioux, put it, "Once we were happy in our own country and we were seldom hungry, for then the two-legged and the four-legged lived together like relatives, and there was plenty for them and for us. But then the Wasichus [white people] came, and they made little islands for us . . . and always these islands are becoming smaller, for around them surges the gnawing flood of Wasichus."

A Comanche Village, by George Catlin, 1834

> *The Indian spokesman Plenty Coups said in 1909:*
>
> *"I see no longer the curling smoke rising from our lodge poles. I hear no longer the songs of the women as they prepare the meal. The antelope have gone; the buffalo wallows are empty. Only the wail of the coyote is heard. The white man's medicine is stronger than ours.... We are like birds with a broken wing."*

The government also sent "field matrons" to the reservations to teach Native American women the art of sewing and to preach the virtues of chastity and hygiene.

The Dawes Act struck directly at tribal organization and tried to make rugged individualists out of the Indians. This legislation ignored the inherent reliance of traditional Indian culture on tribally held land. The forced-assimilation doctrine of the Dawes Act remained the cornerstone of the government's official Indian policy until the Indian Reorganization Act ("the Indian New Deal") of 1934 partially reversed the individualistic approach and belatedly tried to restore the tribal basis of Indian life (see p. 561).

Under these new federal policies, defective though they were, the Indian population started to mount slowly. The total number had been reduced by 1887 to about 243,000—the result of bullets, bottles, and bacteria—but the census of 2010 counted about 5.3 million Native Americans and Alaska Natives, urban and rural.

★ Mining: From Dishpan to Ore Breaker

The conquest of the Indians and the coming of the railroad were life-giving boons to the mining frontier. The golden gravel of California continued to yield "pay dirt," and in 1858 an electrifying discovery of gold convulsed Colorado. Avid "fifty-niners" rushed west with "Pike's Peak or Bust" inscribed on the canvas of their covered wagons. But there were more miners than minerals, and many gold-grubbers creaked wearily back with the added inscription, "Busted, by Gosh." But some bearded fortune seekers stayed on in Colorado to mine silver or extract nonmetallic wealth from the earth in the form of golden grain.

"Fifty-niners" also poured feverishly into Nevada in 1859, after the fabulous Comstock lode had been uncovered. A fantastic amount of gold and silver, worth more than $340 million, was mined by the "Kings of the Comstock" from 1860 to 1890. The scantily populated state of Nevada was prematurely railroaded into the Union in 1864, partly to provide three electoral votes for President Lincoln.

Smaller "lucky strikes" drew frantic gold and silver seekers into Montana, Idaho, and other western states. Boomtowns, known as "Helldorados," sprouted like magic. Every third cabin was a saloon, where sweat-stained miners drank adulterated liquor ("rotgut") in the company of accommodating women. Lynch law and vigilante justice, as in early California, preserved a crude semblance of order. And when the "diggings" petered out, the gold seekers decamped, leaving behind picturesque "ghost towns," such as Virginia City, Nevada. Begun with a boom, these towns ended with a whimper.

Once the loose surface gold was gobbled up, ore-breaking machinery was imported to smash the gold-bearing quartz. This operation was so expensive that it could ordinarily be undertaken only by corporations pooling the wealth of stockholders. Gradually the age of big business came to the **mining industry**. Dusty, bewhiskered miners, dishpans in hand, were replaced by impersonal corporations with their costly machinery and trained engineers.

Yet the mining frontier had played a vital role in conquering the continent. Magnet-like, it attracted population and wealth while advertising the wonders of the Wild West. Women as well as men found opportunity, running boardinghouses or working as prostitutes. They won a kind of equality on the rough frontier that earned them the vote in Wyoming (1869), Utah (1870), Colorado (1893), and Idaho (1896) long before their sisters in the East could cast a ballot. The amassing of precious metals helped finance the Civil War, facilitated the building of railroads, and intensified the already bitter conflict between whites and Indians. The outpouring of silver and gold enabled the Treasury to resume specie payments in 1879 and injected the silver issue into American politics. Finally, the mining frontier added to American folklore and literature, as the writings of Bret Harte and Mark Twain so colorfully attest.

---

mining industry *After gold and silver strikes in Colorado, Nevada, and other western territories in the second half of the nineteenth century, fortune-seekers by the thousands rushed to the West to dig. These metals were essential to U.S. industrial growth and were also sold into world markets. After surface metals were removed, people sought ways to extract ore from under the ground, leading to the development of heavy mining machinery. This, in turn, led to the consolidation of the mining industry, because only big companies could afford to buy and build the necessary machines.*

Beef Bonanzas and the Long Drive

When the Civil War ended, the grassy plains of Texas supported several million tough, longhorn cattle. These scrawny beasts were killed primarily for their hides. There was no way to get their meat profitably to market.

The problem of marketing was neatly solved when the transcontinental railroads thrust their iron fingers into the West. Cattle could now be shipped alive to the stockyards, and "beef barons" such as the Swifts and Armours turned the highly industrialized meatpacking business into a main pillar of the economy. Drawing on the gigantic stockyards at Kansas City and Chicago, the meatpackers could ship their fresh products to the East Coast in the newly perfected refrigerator cars.

A spectacular feeder of the new slaughterhouses was the "Long Drive." Texas cowboys—black, white, and Mexican—drove herds numbering from one thousand to ten thousand head slowly over the unfenced and unpeopled plains until they reached a railroad terminal. The bawling beasts grazed en route on the free government grass. Favorite terminal points were fly-specked "cow towns" such as Dodge City and Abilene (Kansas), Ogallala (Nebraska), and Cheyenne (Wyoming). From 1866 to 1888, bellowing herds totaling over 4 million steers were driven northward from the beef bowl of Texas.

Dressed to Kill Cowboys came in all varieties and sizes in the wild and woolly frontier West—and in all kinds of garb as well.

What the Lord giveth, the Lord also can taketh away. The railroad made the Long Drive; and the railroad unmade the Long Drive, primarily because the locomotives ran both ways. The same rails that bore the cattle from the open range to the kitchen range brought out the sheepherder and the homesteader. Both of these intruders, sometimes amid flying bullets, built barbed-wire fences that were too numerous to be cut down by the cowboys. Furthermore, the terrible winter of 1886–1887, with blinding blizzards and temperatures reaching 68 degrees below zero, left thousands of dazed cattle starving and freezing. The only escape for the stockman was to make cattle raising a big business and avoid the perils of overproduction. Breeders learned to fence their ranches, lay in winter feed, import blooded bulls, and produce fewer and meatier animals. They also learned to organize. The Wyoming Stock-Growers, Association, especially in the 1880s, virtually controlled the territory and its legislature.

This was the heyday of the cowboy. The equipment of the lone cowhand—from "shooting irons" and ten-gallon hat to chaps and spurs—served a useful, not an ornamental, function. A "genuwine" gun-toting cowpuncher, riding where men were men and smelled like horses, could justifiably boast of his toughness.

These bowlegged Knights of the Saddle, with colorful trappings and cattle-lulling songs, became part of American folklore. Many of them, perhaps five thousand, were blacks, who especially enjoyed the new-found freedom of the open range.

The Farmers' Frontier

Miners and cattlemen created the romantic legend of the West, but it was the sober sodbuster who wrote the final chapter of frontier history. A fresh day dawned for western farmers with the **Homestead Act** of 1862. The new law allowed a settler to acquire as much as 160 acres of land (a quarter-section) by living on it for five years, improving it, and paying a nominal fee of about $30.

The Homestead Act marked a drastic departure from previous policy. Before the act, public land had been sold primarily for revenue; now it was to be given away to encourage a rapid filling of empty spaces and to provide a stimulus to the family farm—"the backbone of democracy." During the forty years after its passage, about half a million families took advantage of the Homestead Act to carve out new homes in the vast open stretches. Yet five times that many families *purchased* their land from the railroads, land companies, or the states.

Homestead Act (1862) *A federal law that sold settlers 160 acres of land for about $30 if they lived on it for five years and improved it by, for instance, building a house on it. The act helped make land accessible to hundreds of thousands of westward-moving settlers, but many people also found disappointment when their land was infertile or they saw speculators grabbing up the best land.*

Nebraska Homesteaders in Front of Their Sod House, 1887 These two brothers and their families had escaped to Canada from the slave South during the Civil War. Returning to the United States in the 1880s, they took advantage of the Homestead Act to stake out farms in Custer County, Nebraska.

The Homestead Act often turned out to be a cruel hoax. The standard 160 acres, quite adequate in the well-watered Mississippi basin, frequently proved pitifully inadequate on the rain-scarce Great Plains. Thousands of homesteaders, perhaps two out of three, were forced to give up the one-sided struggle against drought.

Naked fraud was spawned by the Homestead Act and similar laws. Perhaps ten times more of the public domain wound up in the clutches of land-grabbing promoters than in the hands of bona fide farmers. Unscrupulous corporations would use "dummy" homesteaders—often their employees or immigrants bribed with cash or beer—to grab the best properties, containing timber, minerals, and oil. Settlers would later swear that they had "improved" the property by erecting a "twelve-by-fourteen" dwelling, which turned out to measure twelve by fourteen *inches*.

The railways also played a major role in developing the agricultural West, largely through the profitable marketing of crops. Some railroad companies induced Americans and European immigrants to buy the cheap land earlier granted to the railroads by the government. The Northern Pacific Railroad at one time had nearly a thousand paid agents in Europe distributing roseate leaflets in various languages.

Agriculture expanded once the myth of the Great American Desert was shattered. Pioneer explorers had assumed that the soil must be sterile, simply because it was not heavily watered and did not support immense forests. But once the prairie sod was broken with heavy iron plows pulled by four yokes of oxen, the earth proved astonishingly fruitful.

Lured by higher wheat prices resulting from crop failures elsewhere in the world, settlers in the 1870s rashly pushed still farther west, onto the poor, marginal lands beyond the

---

In making the arduous journey across the western prairies, many women settlers discovered new confidence in their abilities. Early on in her trek, Mary Richardson Walker (1811–1897) confided in her diary that:

"my circumstances are rather trying. So much danger attends me on every hand. A long journey before me, going I know not whither, without mother or sister to attend me, can I expect to survive it all?"

Only a month later, she recorded that:

"in the afternoon we rode thirty-five miles without stopping. Pretty well tired out, all of us. Stood it pretty well myself."

100th meridian. Geologist John Wesley Powell, explorer of the Colorado River's Grand Canyon, warned in 1874 that beyond the 100th meridian so little rain fell that agriculture was impossible without massive irrigation. Ignoring Powell's advice, farmers heedlessly chewed up the crusty earth in western Kansas, eastern Colorado, and Montana. They quickly went broke as a six-year drought in the 1880s further desiccated the already dusty region. In the wake of the devastating drought, some pioneers tried the new "dry farming" technique of frequent shallow cultivation. But over time "dry farming" created a finely pulverized surface soil that contributed to the "Dust Bowl" several decades later (see pp. 560-561).

Other adaptations to the western environment were more successful. Tough strains of wheat, resistant to cold and drought, were imported from Russia and blossomed into billowing yellow carpets. Barbed wire, perfected by Joseph F. Glidden in 1874, solved the problem of how to build fences on the treeless prairies. Eventually, federally financed irrigation projects on a colossal scale caused the Great American Desert to bloom. In the long run, hydraulic engineers had more to do with shaping the modern West than all the trappers, miners, cavalrymen, and cowboys ever did.

The Great West experienced a fantastic surge in migration from the 1870s to the 1890s. A parade of new western states proudly joined the Union. Boomtown Colorado, offspring of the Pikes Peak gold rush, was greeted in 1876 as the "Centennial State." In 1889-1890 a Republican Congress, eagerly seeking more Republican electoral and congressional votes, admitted in a wholesale lot six new states: North Dakota, South Dakota, Montana, Washington, Idaho, and Wyoming. The Mormon church—belatedly, in many Americans' eyes—banned polygamy in 1890, but not until 1896 was Utah deemed worthy of admission. Only Oklahoma, New Mexico, and Arizona remained to be lifted into statehood from contiguous territory on the mainland of North America.

In a last gaudy fling, the federal government made available to settlers vast stretches of fertile plains formerly occupied by the Indians in Oklahoma ("the Beautiful Land"). Scores of overeager and well-armed "sooners," illegally jumping the gun, entered Oklahoma Territory before the opening date. They had to be evicted repeatedly by federal troops. On April 22, 1889, all was in readiness for the legal opening, and some fifty thousand "boomers" were poised expectantly on the boundary line. At high noon the bugle shrilled, and a horde of "eighty-niners" poured in on lathered horses or careening vehicles. That night a lonely spot on the prairie had mushroomed into the tent city of Guthrie, with over ten thousand people. By the end of the year Oklahoma boasted 60,000 inhabitants, and Congress made it a territory. In 1907 it became the "Sooner State."

★ The Fading Frontier

In 1890—a watershed date—the superintendent of the census announced that for the first time in America's experience a frontier line was no longer discernible. All the unsettled areas were now broken into by isolated bodies of American settlement. The "closing" of the frontier inspired one of the most influential essays ever written about American history—Frederick Jackson Turner's "The Significance of the Frontier in American History," in 1893.

As the nineteenth century neared its sunset, the westward-tramping American people were disturbed to find that their fabled free land was going or had gone. The secretary of war had prophesied in 1827 that five hundred years would be needed to fill the West. But as the nation finally recognized that its land was not inexhaustible, seeds were planted to preserve the vanishing resource. The government set aside lands for national parks—first Yellowstone in 1872, followed by Yosemite and Sequoia in 1890.

The frontier was more than a place: It was also a state of mind and a symbol of opportunity. Its passing ended a romantic phase of the nation's internal development and created new economic and psychological problems. Traditionally footloose, Americans have been notorious for their mobility. The nation's farmers, unlike the peasants of Europe, seldom remained rooted to their soil.

Much has been said about the frontier as a "safety valve." The theory is that when hard times came, the unemployed who cluttered the city pavements merely moved west, took up farming, and prospered. In truth, relatively few eastern city dwellers migrated to the frontier during depressions. Most of them did not know how to farm; few of them

Examining the Evidence

Robert Louis Stevenson's Transcontinental Journey, 1879

The celebrated Scottish writer Robert Louis Stevenson, author of such enduring classics as *Treasure Island*, *Kidnapped*, and *The Strange Case of Dr. Jekyll and Mr. Hyde*, journeyed from Scotland to California in 1879 to rendezvous with his American fiancée, Frances Osbourne. Between New York and San Francisco, Stevenson traveled on the transcontinental railroad line completed just ten years earlier, and he dutifully recorded his impressions of America, the West in particular, as he made his way toward California. Stevenson's account of his trip provides an unusually gifted writer's vivid portrait of the trans-Mississippi West at the close of the era of the Indian wars. Like all travelogues, Stevenson's colorful tale may reveal as much about the traveler as it does about the things he saw. Yet historians frequently make use of such documents to reconstruct the original appearance and texture of places that were once the exotic destinations of adventurous travelers, before they were transformed by the onrush of modernity.

1. In the passages reproduced here, inspired by the view as Stevenson's train passed through Nebraska and Wyoming, what features of the landscape does the author find most remarkable?

2. What does Stevenson's extended comparison of traveling across the plains to being "at sea" convey about cultured European views of the American West in the late nineteenth century? Why do the buffalo and the cabins he sees not disrupt his perception of the West's "emptiness"?

3. What is Stevenson's view of the Indians, as well of those who built the railroad (including Chinese laborers)?

THE PLAINS OF NEBRASKA

. . . We were at sea—there is no other adequate expression—on the plains of Nebraska. . . . It was a world almost without a feature; an empty sky, an empty earth; front and back, the line of railway stretched from horizon to horizon, like a cue across a billiard-board; on either hand, the green plain ran till it touched the skirts of heaven. . . . [G]razing beasts were seen upon the prairie at all degrees of distance and diminution; and now and again we might perceive a few dots beside the railroad which grew more and more distinct as we drew nearer till they turned into wooden cabins, and then dwindled and dwindled in our wake until they melted into their surroundings, and we were once more alone upon the billiard-board. The train toiled over this infinity like a snail; and being the one thing moving, it was wonderful what huge proportions it began to assume in our regard. . . .

[That] evening we left Laramie [Wyoming]. . . . And yet when day came, it was to shine upon the same broken and unsightly quarter of the world. Mile upon mile, and not a tree, a bird, or a river. Only down the long, sterile cañons, the train shot hooting and awoke the resting echo. That train was the one piece of life in all the deadly land; it was the one actor, the one spectacle fit to be observed in this paralysis of man and nature. And when I think how the railroad has been pushed through this unwatered wilderness and haunt of savage tribes, and now will bear an emigrant for some £12 from the Atlantic to the Golden Gates; how at each stage of the construction, roaring, impromptu cities, full of gold and lust and death, sprang up and then died away again, and are now but wayside stations in the desert; how in these uncouth places pig-tailed Chinese pirates worked side by side with border ruffians and broken men from Europe, talking together in a mixed dialect, mostly oaths, gambling, drinking, quarrelling and murdering like wolves; how the plumed hereditary lord of all America heard, in this last fastness, the scream of the 'bad medicine waggon' charioting his foes; and then when I go on to remember that all this epical turmoil was conducted by gentlemen in frock coats, and with a view to nothing more extraordinary than a fortune and a subsequent visit to Paris, it seems to me, I own, as if this railway were the one typical achievement of the age in which we live, as if it brought together into one plot all the ends of the world and all the degrees of social rank, and offered to some great writer the busiest, the most extended, and the most varied subject for an enduring literary work. . . .

Source: Across the Plains by Robert Louis Stevenson (New York: Charles Scribner's Sons, 1897).

could raise enough money to transport themselves west and then pay for livestock and expensive machinery.

But the safety-valve theory does have some validity. Free acreage did lure to the West a host of immigrant farmers who otherwise might have remained in the eastern cities to clog the job markets and crowd the slums. And the very *possibility* of westward migration may have induced urban employers to maintain wage rates high enough to discourage workers from leaving.

But the real safety valve by the late nineteenth century was in western cities like Denver and San Francisco, where failed farmers, busted miners, and displaced easterners found ways to seek their fortunes. Indeed, after about 1880 the area from the Rocky Mountains to the Pacific Coast was the most urbanized region in America, measured by the percentage of people living in cities.

U.S. history cannot be properly understood unless it is viewed in light of the westward-moving experience. As Frederick Jackson Turner wrote, "American history has been in a large degree the history of the colonization of the Great West." The story of settling and taming the trans-Mississippi West in the late nineteenth century was but the last chapter in the saga of the colonizing of various American "wests" since Columbus's day.

And yet the trans-Mississippi West formed a distinct chapter in that saga and retains even to this day much of its uniqueness. There the Native American peoples waged their last struggle against colonization, and there most Native Americans live today. There "Anglo" culture collided most directly with Hispanic culture, and the Southwest remains the most Hispanicized region in America. There America faced across the Pacific to Asia, and there most Asian Americans dwell today. There the scale and severity of the environment posed their largest challenges to human ambitions, and there the environment continues to mold social and political life, and the American imagination, as in no other part of the nation.

The westward-moving pioneers and the country they confronted have assumed mythic proportions in the American mind. For better or worse, those pioneers planted the seeds of American civilization in the immense western wilderness. The life we live, they dreamed of; the life they lived, we can only dream.

★ The Farm Becomes a Factory

The situation of American farmers, once jacks-and-jills-of-all-trades, was rapidly changing. They had raised their own food, fashioned their own clothing, and bartered for other necessities with neighbors. Now high prices persuaded farmers to concentrate on growing single "cash" crops, such as wheat or corn, and use their profits to buy foodstuffs at the general store and manufactured goods in town or by mail order. The Chicago firm of Aaron Montgomery Ward sent out its first catalogue—a single sheet—in 1872. Farmers were becoming a part of the world economy, as their crops journeyed by rail and ship to distant parts of the globe.

Large-scale farmers were now both specialists and businesspeople. As cogs in the vast industrial machine, they were intimately tied to banking, railroading, and manufacturing. They had to buy expensive machinery to plant and to harvest their crops. The speed of harvesting wheat was immensely increased in the 1870s by the invention of the twine binder and then in the 1880s by the "combine"—the combined reaper-thresher, which was drawn by twenty to forty horses and both reaped and bagged the grain.

This amazing **mechanization of agriculture** in the postwar years was almost as striking as the mechanization of industry. Those who remained on the farms achieved miracles of production, making America the world's breadbasket and butcher shop. The farm was attaining the status of a factory—an outdoor grain factory. The enormous bonanza wheat farms of the Minnesota–North Dakota area foreshadowed the gigantic agribusinesses of the next century. By 1890 at least a half-dozen of them were larger than fifteen thousand acres.

Agriculture was a big business from the outset in California's phenomenally productive (and phenomenally irrigated) Central Valley. California farms, carved out of giant Spanish Mexican land grants and the railroads' huge holdings, were from the outset more

mechanization of agriculture
The development of engine-driven machines, like the combine, which helped to dramatically increase the productivity of land in the 1870s and 1880s. This process contributed to the consolidation of agricultural business that drove many family farms out of existence.

than three times larger than the national average. With the advent of the railroad refrigerator car in the 1880s, California fruits and vegetable crops, raised on sprawling tracts by ill-paid migrant Mexican and Chinese farmhands, sold at a handsome profit in the rich urban markets of the East.

⭐ Deflation Dooms the Debtor

Once the farmers became chained to a one-crop economy—wheat or corn—they were in the same leaky boat with the southern cotton growers. The grain farmers were no longer the masters of their own destinies. They were engaged in one of the most fiercely competitive of businesses, for the price of their product was determined in a world market by the world output. If the wheat fields of Argentina, Russia, and other foreign countries flourished, the price of the farmers' grain would fall and American sodbusters would face ruin, as they did in the 1880s and 1890s.

Low prices and a deflated currency were the chief worries of the frustrated farmer in all regions. If a family had borrowed $1,000 in 1855, when wheat was worth about a dollar a bushel, they expected to pay back the equivalent of one thousand bushels, plus interest, when the mortgage fell due. But if they let their debt run to 1890, when wheat had fallen to about fifty cents a bushel, they would have to pay back the price of two thousand bushels for the $1,000 they had borrowed, plus interest. This unexpected burden struck them as unjust, though their steely-eyed creditors often branded the complaining farmers as slippery and dishonest rascals.

The deflationary pinch on the debtor flowed partly from the static money supply. There were simply not enough dollars to go around, and as a result prices were forced down. In 1870 the currency in circulation for each person was $19.42; in 1890 it was only $22.67. Yet during these twenty years, business and industrial activity, increasing manyfold, had intensified the scramble for available currency.

The forgotten farmers were caught on a treadmill. Despite unremitting toil, they operated year after year at a loss. In a vicious circle, their farm machinery increased their output of grain, lowered the price, and drove them even deeper into debt. Mortgages engulfed homesteads at an alarming rate; by 1890 Nebraska alone reported more than 100,000 farms blanketed with mortgages. The repeated crash of the sheriff-auctioneer's hammer kept announcing to the world that another sturdy American farmer had become landless in a landed nation.

Ruinous rates of interest, running from 8 to 40 percent, were charged on mortgages, largely by agents of eastern loan companies. The windburned sons and daughters of the sod, who felt that they deserved praise for developing the country, cried out in despair against the loan sharks and the Wall Street octopus.

Farm tenancy rather than farm ownership was spreading like stinkweed. The trend was especially marked in the sharecropping South, where cotton prices also sank dismayingly. By 1880 one-fourth of all American farms were operated by tenants. The United States was ready to feed the world, but under the new industrial feudalism the farmers were about to sink into a status suggesting Old World serfdom.

⭐ Unhappy Farmers

Even Mother Nature ceased smiling as her powerful forces conspired against agriculture. Mile-wide clouds of grasshoppers, leaving "nothing but the mortgage," periodically ravaged prairie farms. The terrible cotton boll weevil was also wreaking havoc in the South by the early 1890s.

The good earth was going sour. Floods washed the topsoil off millions of once-lush southern acres. A long succession of droughts seared the trans-Mississippi West, beginning in the summer of 1887. Whole towns were abandoned. "Going home to the wife's folks" and "in God we trusted, in Kansas we busted" were typical laments of many impoverished farmers as they fled their weather-beaten shacks and sunbaked sod houses.

To add to their miseries, the soil-tillers were gouged by their government—local, state, and national. Their land was overassessed, and they paid painful local taxes, whereas wealthy easterners could conceal their stocks and bonds in safe-deposit boxes. High protective tariffs in these years poured profits into the pockets of manufacturers. Farmers, on the other hand, had no choice but to sell their low-priced products in a fiercely competitive, unprotected world market, while buying high-priced manufactured goods in a protected home market.

The farmers were also "farmed" by the corporations. Trusts raised prices on farmers' machinery and supplies to extortionate levels, while operators pushed storage rates to the ceiling at grain warehouses and elevators. The railroad octopus often pushed freight rates so high that the farmers sometimes lost less if they burned their corn for fuel than if they shipped it.

Farmers still made up nearly one-half of the population in 1890, but they were hopelessly disorganized. The manufacturers and the railroad barons knew how to combine to promote their own interests, and so, increasingly, did industrial workers. But the farmers were by nature independent and individualistic—dead set against consolidation or regimentation. They never did organize successfully to restrict production until forced to do so by the federal government nearly half a century later, in Franklin Roosevelt's New Deal days. What they did manage to organize was a monumental political uprising.

★ The Farmers Take Their Stand

Agrarian unrest had flared forth earlier, in the Greenback movement shortly after the Civil War. Prices sagged in 1868, and a host of farmers unsuccessfully sought relief from low prices and high indebtedness by demanding an inflation of the currency with paper money.

The National Grange of the Patrons of Husbandry—better known as the Grange—was organized in 1867. Its leading spirit was Oliver H. Kelley, a shrewd and energetic Minnesota farmer then working as a clerk in Washington. Kelley's first objective was to

The Farmers' Grievances This poster from 1875 expresses one of the agrarian radicals' fundamental premises: that all other walks of life were dependent—or even parasitic—on the indispensable work of farmers. In his famous "Cross of Gold" speech in 1896, Populist presidential candidate William Jennings Bryan put it this way: "Burn down your cities and leave our farms, and your cities will spring up again as if by magic; but destroy our farms and the grass will grow in the streets of every city in the country."

Thinking Globally

The Great Frontier

The American pioneers who surged westward in the nineteenth century were part of a great global land grab that changed lives and landscapes on several continents. From the Australian outback to the Canadian prairies, from the Argentine pampas to the Russian steppes and the African savannas, millions of mostly white settlers poured into vast new territories and claimed them as their own.

Everywhere, the settlers encountered indigenous peoples who had lived on those lands since time immemorial. With their superiority in weaponry, transportation, and political organization, everywhere the newcomers prevailed. By the century's close, they had displaced or destroyed countless native peoples and extended their dominion over parts of the planet once considered too remote or rugged to be habitable.

The American frontier soon became the stuff of legend, and even the subject of a scholarly explanation of American uniqueness—Frederick Jackson Turner's fabled "frontier thesis," which hailed the grit and gumption of the pioneers and commended them as the agents of civilization and democracy. Yet far from being unique, those westering Americans had much in common with settlers in sister societies abroad. Argentina had its cowboys (gauchos), and Australia had its colorful backcountry outlaws, such as Ned Kelly, whose exploits rivaled those of Billy the Kid. The Russians and South Africans had their own versions of "Manifest Destiny," and like the Americans they often cloaked them in the language of racial superiority.

The world's various frontiers also reflected the particularities of geography and history. Australians soon conceded that much of their continent—the world's driest—was too arid for traditional farming. Most of the Outback proved suitable only for enormous "sheep stations," sometimes measuring tens of thousands of acres. Consequently, small-farm homesteading of the American and Canadian type never took root, nor did cities of any consequence emerge in the parched Australian interior.

Canada's westward movement came later than that in the United States and proceeded more peaceably. Only after the Ottawa government promised in 1871 to build a transcontinental railroad connecting eastern Canada to its western provinces did settlement being in earnest. And unlike in America, where restless pioneers typically struck out on their own and made much mischief among themselves and with the Indians they encountered, in Canada, settlers were generally preceded by government authorities—usually the red-jacketed North-West Mounted Police, or "Mounties"—who established at least a semblance of order before large numbers of pioneers appeared on the scene. As a result, Canada's frontier was markedly less violent than America's. Canada, then and now a more law-abiding society than the United States, never had a "Wild West" like that of its southern neighbor.

In Argentina and Russia, inherited patterns of landholding and politics shaped their nineteenth-century frontiers. When Argentina's General Julio Roca vanquished the native Araucanians in 1879, he flung open the horizonless pampas to white settlement. But he also retained the venerable custom, handed down from Spanish colonial times, of apportioning the land in gigantic *estancias* (ranches) to a few favored fellow soldiers and friends. These lordly landowners then employed wage workers, mostly Italian immigrants, who turned the fertile Argentine interior into a beef bowl and breadbasket to the world. The immigrants themselves, however, had little hope of ever possessing land of their own.

Russia's frontier lay to the east and long felt the heavy hand of the tsar. For centuries autocratic rulers had strong-armed landowning nobles to move their serfs onto the "virgin lands" beyond the settled edge of European Russia. By the nineteenth century, imperial Russia had pushed its frontier onto the rolling steppes of central Asia, home to Tartars, Kalmyks, Kazahks, and myriad other indigenous peoples. Only military conquest and a strengthened state bureaucracy made possible European settlement in those regions. Between 1867 and 1897, more than a million of the tsar's subjects left for the hinterland. As elsewhere, the railroad proved essential to the growth of the tsarist empire, especially after the government began construction of the Trans-Siberian line in 1891.

enhance the lives of isolated farmers through social, educational, and fraternal activities. The Grange spread like an old-time prairie fire and by 1875 claimed some 800,000 members, chiefly in the Midwest and South.

The Grangers gradually raised their goals from individual self-improvement to improvement of the farmers' collective plight. In a determined effort to escape the clutches of the trusts, they established cooperatively owned stores, grain elevators, and warehouses, and even made a failed attempt to manufacture harvesting machinery.

Embattled Grangers also went into politics, enjoying their most gratifying success in the grain-growing regions of the upper Mississippi Valley. There, through state legislation,

North-West Mounted Police, c. 1890 Empowered by an act of Parliament in 1873 to establish Canadian authority and order in the Northwest Territories, this force made frontier settlement somewhat more peaceful in Canada than in the United States. In 1920 the North-West Mounted Police absorbed the Dominion Police and became the famed Royal Canadian Mounted Police, or "Mounties."

The Dutch-descended Afrikaners, or Boers, in southern Africa found their frontier to the north, and unlike their American counterparts, they made scant claim to be spreading democracy. Rather, they sought to escape British rule in the Cape Colony—in particular, to escape from the threat of racial equality for blacks after Britain abolished slavery in the 1830s. The Afrikaners' "Great Trek" took them into the land of the Zulus, who ferociously resisted the oncoming Boers but eventually, like indigenous peoples everywhere, were forced to submit to white rule.

In the Americas, Australia, Asia, and Africa, the great frontier of the nineteenth century was the companion of conquest. The frontier brought opportunity to some and oppression to others. In many places it nurtured democracy; elsewhere it invigorated autocracy. And everywhere it expanded the domains of European civilization—for better or worse.

they strove to regulate railway rates and the storage fees charged by railroads and grain elevator operators. Many of the state courts, notably in Illinois, were disposed to recognize the principle of public control of private business for the general welfare. A number of the so-called Granger Laws, however, were bitterly fought through the high courts by the well-paid lawyers of the "interests." Following judicial reverses, most severely at the hands of the Supreme Court in the *Wabash* decision of 1886 (see p. 390), the Grangers' influence faded.

Farmers' grievances likewise found a vent in the Greenback Labor party, which combined the inflationary appeal of the earlier Greenbackers with a program for improving the lot of labor. In 1878, the high-water mark of the movement, the Greenback Laborites polled over a million votes and elected fourteen members of Congress. In the presidential election of 1880 the Greenbackers ran General James B. Weaver, an old Granger who spoke to perhaps half a million citizens but polled only 3 percent of the popular vote.

★ Prelude to Populism

A striking manifestation of rural discontent came through the Farmers' Alliance, founded in Texas in the late 1870s (see p. 379). Farmers came together in the Alliance to socialize, but more importantly they hoped to break the strangling grip of the railroads and manufacturers through cooperative buying and selling. Local chapters spread throughout the South and the Great Plains during the 1880s, until by 1890 members numbered more than a million hard-bitten souls.

Unfortunately, the Alliance weakened itself by ignoring the plight of landless tenant farmers, sharecroppers, and farmworkers. Even more debilitating was the Alliance's exclusion of blacks, who counted for nearly half the agricultural population of the South. In the 1880s a separate Colored Farmers' National Alliance emerged to attract black farmers, and by 1890 membership numbered more than 250,000. The long history of racial division in the South, however, made it difficult for white and black farmers to work together in the same organization.

Out of the Farmers' Alliances a new political party emerged in the early 1890s—the People's Party. Better known as the **Populists**, these frustrated farmers attacked Wall Street and the "money trust." They called for nationalizing the railroads, telephones, and telegraph; instituting a graduated income tax; and building government-owned warehouses where they could store their grain until market prices rose. They also wanted the free and unlimited coinage of silver—yet another of the debtors' demands for inflation that echoed continuously throughout the Gilded Age.

Numerous fiery prophets leapt forward to trumpet the Populist cause. The free coinage of silver struck many Populists as a cure-all, especially after William Hope Harvey produced an enormously popular pamphlet called *Coin's Financial School* (1894). Illustrated by clever woodcuts, the booklet showed how "Coin" Harvey overwhelmed the bankers and professors of economics with his brilliant arguments on behalf of free silver. Another notorious spellbinder was red-haired Ignatius Donnelly of Minnesota, three times elected to Congress. The queen of the Populist "calamity howlers" was Mary Elizabeth ("Mary Yellin") Lease, a tall, athletic woman known as the "Kansas Pythoness." She reportedly demanded that Kansans should raise "less corn and more hell." The *New York Evening Post* snarled, "We don't want any more states until we can civilize Kansas." To many easterners, complaint, not corn, was rural America's staple crop.

Yet the Populists, despite their oddities, were not to be laughed away. They were leading a deadly earnest and impassioned campaign to relieve the farmers' many miseries. Smiles faded from Republican and Democratic faces alike as countless thousands of Populists began to sing "Good-bye, My Party, Good-bye."

In 1892 the Populists had jolted the traditional parties by winning several congressional seats and polling more than 1 million votes for their presidential candidate, James B. Weaver. Racial divisions continued to hobble the Populists in the South, but in the West their ranks were swelling. Could the People's Party now reach beyond its regional bases in agrarian America, join hands with urban workers, and mount a successful attack on the northeastern citadels of power?

Populists *Officially known as the People's Party, the Populists represented Westerners and Southerners who believed that U.S. economic policy inappropriately favored Eastern businessmen instead of the nation's farmers. Their proposals included nationalization of the railroads, a graduated income tax, and, most significantly, the unlimited coinage of silver.*

★ Coxey's Army and the Pullman Strike

The panic of 1893 and the severe ensuing depression strengthened the Populists' argument that farmers and laborers alike were being victimized by an oppressive economic and political system. Ragged armies of the unemployed began marching to protest their plight. In the growing hordes of displaced industrial toilers, the Populists saw potential political allies.

The most famous marcher was "General" Jacob S. Coxey, a wealthy Ohio quarry owner who set out for Washington in 1894 with a small band of supporters. His platform included a demand that the government relieve unemployment by an inflationary $500 million federal public works program. Coxey himself rode in a carriage with his wife and infant son, appropriately named Legal Tender Coxey, while his tiny "army" tramped along behind, singing:

> We're coming, Grover Cleveland,
> 500,000 strong.
> We're marching on to Washington
> to right the nation's wrong.

After the Pullman strike collapsed, Eugene Debs (1855-1926) said:

"No strike has ever been lost."

In 1897 he declared:

"The issue is Socialism versus Capitalism. I am for Socialism because I am for humanity."

The "Commonweal Army" of Coxeyites finally straggled into the nation's capital, but the "invasion" took on the aspects of a comic opera when "General" Coxey and his "lieutenants" were arrested for walking on the grass.

Elsewhere, violent flare-ups accompanied labor protests, notably in Chicago. Most dramatic was the crippling **Pullman strike** of 1894. Eugene V. Debs, a charismatic labor leader, had helped organize the American Railway Union of about 150,000 members. The Pullman Palace Car Company, which maintained a model town near Chicago for its employees, was hit hard by the depression and cut wages by about one-third, while holding the line on rent for company houses. The workers finally struck—in some places overturning Pullman cars—and paralyzed railway traffic from Chicago to the Pacific Coast.

The turmoil in Chicago was serious but not completely out of hand. At least this was the judgment of Governor John Peter Altgeld of Illinois, a friend of the downtrodden, who had pardoned the Haymarket Square anarchists the year before (see p. 400). But U.S. attorney general Richard Olney, an archconservative and an ex-railroad attorney, urged the dispatch of federal troops on the legal grounds that the strikers were interfering with the U.S. mail. President Cleveland supported Olney with the ringing declaration, "If it takes the entire army and navy to deliver a postal card in Chicago, that card will be delivered."

To the delight of conservatives, federal troops, bayonets fixed, crushed the Pullman strike. Debs was sentenced to six months' imprisonment for contempt of court because he had defied a federal court injunction to cease striking. Ironically, the lean labor agitator spent much of his enforced leisure reading radical literature, which led to his later leadership of the socialist movement in America.

Embittered cries of "government by injunction" now burst from organized labor. This was the first time that such a legal weapon had been used conspicuously by Washington to break a strike, and it was all the more distasteful because defiant workers who were held in contempt could be imprisoned without jury trial. Signs multiplied that employers were striving to smash labor unions by court action. Nonlabor elements of the country, including the Populists and other debtors, were likewise incensed. They saw in the brutal Pullman episode further proof of an unholy alliance between business and the courts.

Pullman strike (1894) *A strike by railroad workers upset by drastic wage cuts. The strike was led by socialist Eugene Debs but not supported by the American Federation of Labor. Eventually President Grover Cleveland intervened, and federal troops forced an end to the strike. The strike highlighted both divisions within labor and the government's new willingness to use armed force to combat work stoppages.*

★ Golden McKinley and Silver Bryan

The smoldering grievances of the long-suffering farmers and depression-plagued laborers gave ominous significance to the election of 1896. Conservatives of all stripes feared an impending upheaval, while down-and-out husbandmen and discontented workers cast about desperately for political salvation. Increasingly, monetary policy—whether to maintain the gold standard or inflate the currency by monetizing silver—loomed as the issue on which the election would turn.

The leading candidate for the Republican presidential nomination in 1896 was former congressman William McKinley of Ohio, sponsor of the ill-starred tariff bill of 1890 (see p. 379). He had been a Civil War officer; he hailed from the electorally potent state of Ohio; and he could point to long years of honorable service in Congress.

As a presidential candidate, McKinley was largely the creature of a fellow Ohioan, Marcus Alonzo Hanna, who had made his fortune in the iron business and now coveted

The Sacrilegious Candidate A hostile cartoonist makes sport of Bryan's flamboyant Cross of Gold speech in 1896.

the role of president maker. As a wholehearted Hamiltonian, Hanna believed that a prime function of government was to aid business. Hanna also believed that in some measure prosperity "trickled down" to the laborer, whose dinner pail would be full when business flourished. Critics assailed this idea as equivalent to feeding the horses in order to feed the sparrows.

The hardheaded Hanna, although something of a novice in politics, organized his preconvention campaign for McKinley with consummate skill and a liberal outpouring of his own money. The convention steamroller, well lubricated with Hanna's dollars, nominated McKinley on the first ballot at St. Louis in June 1896. The Republican platform condemned Democratic incapacity in hard times and declared for the gold standard.

Dissension riddled the Democratic camp. Cleveland no longer led his party. The depression had driven the last nail into his political coffin. Dubbed "the Stuffed Prophet," he was undeniably the most unpopular man in the country. Labor-debtor groups remembered too vividly his intervention in the Pullman strike, the backstairs Morgan bond deal, and especially his stubborn hard-money policies. Ultraconservative in finance, Cleveland now looked more like a Republican than a Democrat on the money issue.

Rudderless, the Democratic convention met in Chicago in July 1896, with the silverites lusting for victory. Shouting insults at the absent Cleveland, the delegates refused to endorse their own administration. They had the enthusiasm and the numbers; all they lacked was a leader.

A new Moses suddenly appeared in the person of William Jennings Bryan of Nebraska. Then only thirty-six years of age and known as "the Boy Orator of the Platte,"* Bryan stepped confidently onto the platform before fifteen thousand people. His masterful presence was set off by a peninsular jaw and raven-black hair. He radiated honesty, sincerity, and energy.

The convention-hall setting was made to order for a magnificent oratorical effort. A hush fell over the delegates as Bryan stood before them. With an organ-like voice that rolled into the outer corners of the huge hall, he delivered a fervent plea for silver. Rising to supreme heights of eloquence, he thundered, "We will answer their demands for a gold standard by saying to them: 'You shall not press down upon the brow of labor this crown of thorns, you shall not crucify mankind upon a cross of gold!'"

The Cross of Gold speech was a sensation. Swept off its feet in a tumultuous scene, the Democratic convention nominated Bryan the next day. The platform demanded inflation through the unlimited coinage of silver at the ratio of 16 ounces of silver to 1 of gold, though the market ratio was about thirty-two to one. This meant that the silver in a dollar would be worth about fifty cents.

Democratic "Gold Bugs," unable to swallow Bryan, bolted their party over the silver issue. A conservative senator from New York, when asked if he was a Democrat still, reportedly replied, "Yes, I am a Democrat still—very still." The Democratic minority, including Cleveland, charged that the Populist silverites had stolen both the name and the clothes of their party. Many of them, including Cleveland, not too secretly hoped for a McKinley victory.

The Populists now faced a dilemma because the Democratic majority had appropriated their main plank—"16 to 1," that "heaven-born ratio." The bulk of the Populists, fearing a hard-money McKinley victory, endorsed "fusion" with the Democrats and Bryan for president, sacrificing their identity in the mix. Singing "The Jolly Silver Dollar of the Dads," they became in effect the "Demo-Pop" or "Popocratic" party, though a handful of the original Populists refused to support Bryan and went down with their colors nailed to the mast.

---

*One contemporary sneered that Bryan, like the Platte River, was "six inches deep and six miles wide at the mouth."

★ Class Conflict: Plowholders Versus Bondholders

Mark Hanna smugly assumed that he could make the tariff the focus of the campaign. But Bryan, a dynamo of energy, forced the free-trade issue into a back seat when he took to the stump in behalf of free silver. Sweeping through 27 states and traveling 18,000 miles, Bryan made nearly 600 speeches—36 in one day—and even invaded the East, "the enemy's country." Vachel Lindsay caught the spirit of his oratorical orgy:

> *Prairie avenger, mountain lion,*
> *Bryan, Bryan, Bryan, Bryan,*
> *Gigantic troubadour, speaking like a siege gun,*
> *Smashing Plymouth rock with his boulders from the West.**

Free silver became almost as much a religious as a financial issue. Hordes of fanatical free-silverites, singing "No Crown of Thorns, No Cross of Gold," hailed Bryan as the messiah to lead them out of the wilderness of debt.

Bryan created panic among eastern conservatives with his threat of converting their holdings overnight into fifty-cent dollars. "In God we trust, with Bryan we bust," the Republicans sneered, while one clergyman cried, "That platform was made in Hell." Widespread fear of Bryan and the "silver lunacy" enabled "Dollar Mark" Hanna, now chairman of the Republican National Committee, to shine as a money raiser. He "shook down" the trusts and plutocrats and piled up an enormous "slush fund" for a "campaign of education"—or of propaganda, depending on one's point of view. Republicans appealed to the "belly vote" with their prize slogan, "McKinley and the full dinner pail." The McKinleyites amassed the most formidable political campaign chest thus far in American history—about $16 million, as contrasted with about $1 million for the poorer Democrats (roughly "16 to 1"). With some justification, the Bryanites accused Hanna of "buying" the election and of floating McKinley into the White House on a tidal wave of mud and money.

Bryan's cyclonic campaign began to lose steam as the weeks passed. Fear was probably Hanna's strongest ally, as it was Bryan's worst enemy. Some Republican businesspeople threatened wage reductions or told their workers not to come to work on Wednesday morning if Bryan won. Such were some of the "dirty tricks" of the "Stop Bryan, Save America" crusade.

Hanna's campaign methods paid off. On election day McKinley triumphed decisively. The vote was 271 to 176 in the Electoral College, and 7,102,246 to 6,492,559 in the popular vote. Driven by fear and excitement, an unprecedented outpouring of voters flocked to the polls. McKinley ran strongly in the populous East, where he carried every county of New England, and in the upper Mississippi Valley. Bryan's states, concentrated in the debt-burdened South and the trans-Mississippi West, involved more acreage than McKinley's but less population (see Map 26.2).

The free-silver election of 1896 was perhaps the most significant political turning point since Lincoln's victories in 1860 and 1864. Despite Bryan's strength in the South and West, the results vividly demonstrated his lack of appeal to the unmortgaged farmer and especially to the eastern urban laborer. Many wage earners in the East, threatened as they were by free silver, voted for their jobs and full dinner pails. Living precariously on a fixed wage, the factory workers had no reason to favor inflation, which was the heart of the Bryanites' program.

The Bryan-McKinley battle heralded the advent of a new era in American politics. The outcome represented a resounding victory for big business, the big cities, middle-class values, and financial conservatism. Bryan's defeat marked the last serious effort to win the White House with mostly agrarian votes. The future of presidential politics lay not on the farms, with their dwindling populations, but in the mushrooming cities, with their growing hordes of freshly arriving immigrants.

The Grand Old Party's smashing victory of 1896 also heralded a Republican grip on the White House for sixteen consecutive years—indeed, for all but eight of the next

---

*Reprinted with permission of Macmillan Publishing Company, Inc., from *Collected Poems*, by Vachel Lindsay. Copyright 1920 by Macmillan Publishing Company, Inc., renewed 1948 by Elizabeth C. Lindsay.

448 CHAPTER 26

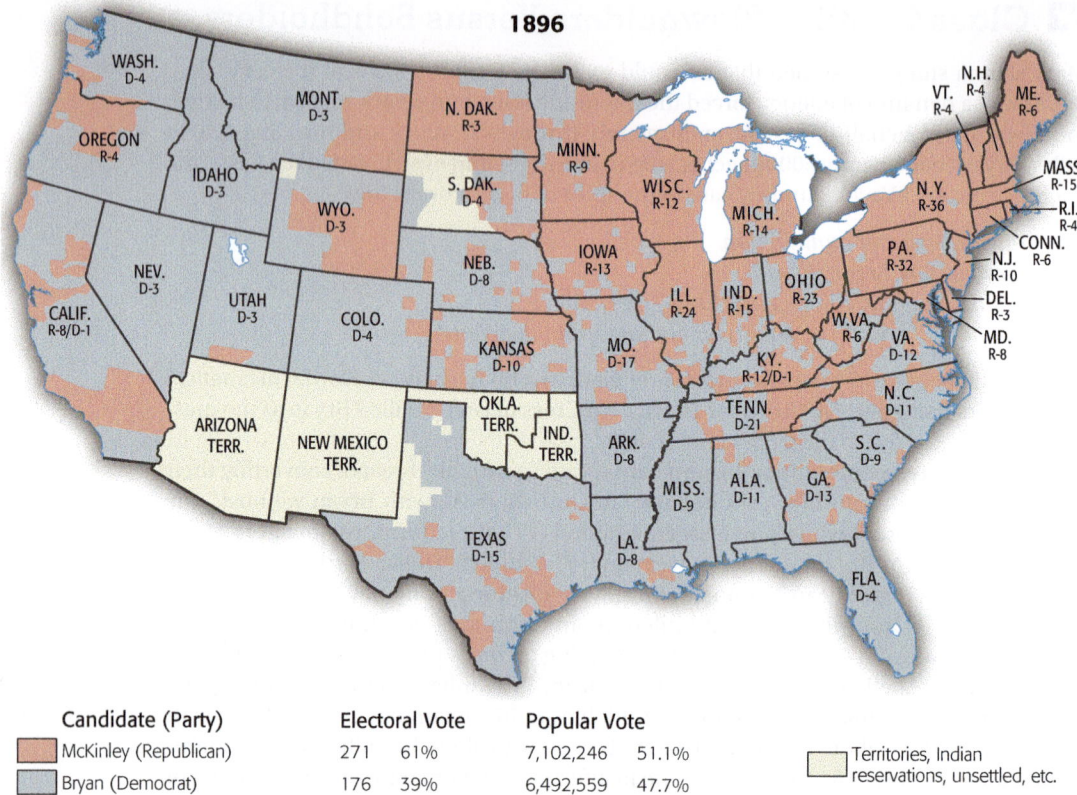

Map 26.2 **Presidential Election of 1896 (with electoral vote by state)** This election tolled the death knell of the Gilded Age political party system, with its razor-close elections, strong party loyalties, and high voter turnouts. Bryans' sweep of the southern states and strong showing in the West gave him only 176 electoral votes to McKinley's 271 from the more populous North and East. For years after 1896, Republicans predominated, and citizens showed declining interest in either joining parties or voting.

fourth party system *A term scholars have used to describe national politics from 1896 to 1932, when Republicans had a tight grip on the White House and issues such as industrial regulation and labor concerns became paramount, replacing older concerns such as civil-service reform and monetary policy.*

thirty-six years. McKinley's election thus imparted a new character to the American political system. The long reign of Republican political dominance that it ushered in was accompanied by diminishing voter participation in elections, the weakening of party organizations, and the fading away of issues such as the money question and civil-service reform, which came to be replaced by concern for industrial regulation and the welfare of labor. Scholars have dubbed this new political era the period of the **fourth party system**, signaling a break with the previous "third party system," in place since 1860, of remarkably high voter turnouts and close contests between Democrats and Republicans.

★ Republican Stand-pattism Enthroned

An eminently "safe" McKinley took the inaugural oath in 1897. Though a man of considerable ability, he was an ear-to-the-ground politician who seldom got far out of line with majority opinion. His cautious, conservative nature caused him to shy away from the flaming banner of reform. Business was given a free rein, and the trusts, which had trusted him in 1896, were allowed to develop more mighty muscles without serious restraints.

Almost as soon as McKinley took office, the tariff issue, which had played second fiddle to silver in the "Battle of '96," quickly forced itself to the fore. In due course the Dingley Tariff Bill was jammed through the House in 1897 under the pounding gavel of the rethroned "Czar" Reed. The proposed new rates were high, but not high enough to satisfy the paunchy lobbyists, who once again descended upon the Senate. Over 850 amendments were tacked onto the overburdened bill. The resulting piece of patchwork finally established the average rates at 46.5 percent, substantially higher than the Democratic Wilson-Gorman Act of 1894 and in some categories even higher than the McKinley Act of 1890.

With the return of prosperity under McKinley in 1897, the money issue that overshadowed politics since the Civil War gradually faded away. The **Gold Standard Act** of 1900, passed over last-ditch silverite opposition, provided that paper currency was to be freely redeemed in gold. Electrifying discoveries of new gold deposits in Canada's fabled Klondike, as well as in Alaska, South Africa, and Australia, brought huge new quantities of gold onto world markets. Moderate inflation thus took care of the currency needs of an explosively expanding nation, as its circulatory system greatly improved. The tide of "silver heresy" rapidly receded, and the "Popocratic" fish were left gasping high and dry on a golden-sanded beach.

Gold Standard Act (1900) *An act that guaranteed that paper currency would be redeemed freely in gold, putting an end to the already dying "free-silver" campaign.*

Varying Viewpoints

Was the West Really "Won"?

For more than half a century, the Turner thesis dominated historical writing about the West. In his famous essay of 1893, "The Significance of the Frontier in American History," historian Frederick Jackson Turner argued that not only the West but the national character had been uniquely shaped by the westward movement. The struggle to overcome the hazards of the western wilderness had transformed *Europeans* into tough, inventive, and self-reliant *Americans*.

Turner's thesis raised a question that Americans found especially intriguing in 1893, just three years after the census superintendent had declared the frontier closed forever. What new forces, Turner asked, would shape a distinctive American national character now that the testing ground of the frontier had been plowed and tamed? Turner's hypothesis that the American character was forged in the western wilderness is surely among the most provocative statements ever made about the nation's formative influences. But as the frontier era recedes ever further into the past, scholars are less persuaded that Turner's thesis adequately explains the national character.

Modern historians like David J. Weber challenge Turner's assumptions by suggesting that the line of the frontier did not define the quavering edge of "civilization," but instead marked the boundary between diverse and equally legitimate cultures. The frontier should therefore be understood not as the place where "civilization" triumphed over "savagery," but as the principal site of interaction between those cultures.

Several so-called New Western historians take this argument still further. Scholars such as Patricia Nelson Limerick, Richard White, and Donald Worster suggest that the cultural and ecological damage inflicted by advancing "civilization" must be reckoned with in any final accounting of what these pioneers accomplished. These same scholars insist that the West did not lose its regional identity after 1890. The West, they argue, is still a unique part of the national mosaic, a region whose history, culture, and identity remain every bit as distinctive as those of New England or the Old South.

But where Turner saw the frontier as the principal shaper of the region's character, the New Western historians emphasize the effects of ethnic and racial confrontation, topography, climate, and the roles of government and big business as the factors that have made the modern West. The pioneer "conquests" of Native Americans and Hispanics were less than complete, they contend, and the West therefore remains, uniquely among American regions, an unsettled arena of commingling and competition among these groups. Moreover, in these accounts the West's distinctively challenging climate and geography yielded to human habitation not through the efforts of heroic individual pioneers, but only through massive corporate—and especially federal government—investments in projects like the transcontinental railroads and irrigation systems. Such developments still give western life its special character today.

CHAPTER SUMMARY

At the close of the Civil War, the Great Plains and Mountain West were still controlled by Indians who hunted buffalo on horseback and fiercely resisted white encroachment on their land and way of life. But the whites' railroads, mining, and livestock activities gradually broke up the Indians' land, while disease and the destruction of the buffalo reduced their numbers and ended their way of life. After a series of sharp military clashes, the federal government eventually forced the Indians onto largely barren reservations.

Attempting to coerce Indians into adopting white ways, the government passed the Dawes Act, which eliminated tribal ownership of land, while often insensitive "humanitarians" created a network of Indian boarding schools that further assaulted traditional culture.

The mining and cattle frontiers created colorful chapters in western history. Farmers carried out the final phase of settlement, lured by free homesteads, railroads, and irrigation. The census declared the end of the frontier in 1890, concluding a formative phase of American history. The frontier was less of a "safety valve" for American class conflict than many believed, but it may have had some impact on keeping American wage rates relatively high. The newest western frontier was actually in western cities, which helped make the West the most urbanized (by percentage) region of the United States by the 1890s.

Beginning in the 1870s, farmers began pushing onto the treeless prairies beyond the 100th meridian, using techniques of dry farming that gradually contributed to soil erosion. Irrigation projects, later financed by the federal government, allowed specialized farming in some areas of the arid West, including California. The "closing" of the frontier in 1890 signified the end of traditional westward expansion, but the Great West remained a unique social and environmental region.

As the farmers opened vast new lands, agriculture was becoming a mechanized business dependent on specialized production and international markets. Once declining prices and other woes doomed the farmers to permanent debt and dependency, they began to protest their lot, first through the Grange and then through the Farmers' Alliances, the prelude to the People's (Populist) Party. The Populists made spectacular gains in the West and the South, but racial divisions undermined southern Populism.

The major depression of the 1890s accelerated farmer protest and labor unrest and strikes, leading to a growing class conflict. In 1896 pro-silver hero William Jennings Bryan captured the Democratic Party's nomination, and with Populist support as well led a fervent campaign against the "goldbug" Republicans and their candidate William McKinley. McKinley's success in winning urban workers away from Bryan proved a turning point in American politics, signaling the triumph of the city, the middle class, and a new party system. The return of prosperity in McKinley's first term ended the late-nineteenth-century preoccupation with monetary issues and made Republicans the dominant party for two generations.

KEY TERMS

- reservation system (429)
- Battle of the Little Bighorn (430)
- Battle of Wounded Knee (432)
- Dawes Severalty Act (432)
- mining industry (434)
- Homestead Act (435)
- mechanization of agriculture (439)
- Populists (444)
- Pullman strike (445)
- fourth party system (448)
- Gold Standard Act (449)

PEOPLE TO KNOW

- Frederick Jackson Turner
- Jacob S. Coxey
- William McKinley
- Marcus Alonzo Hanna

 MindTap is a fully online, highly personalized learning experience built upon Cengage Learning content. MindTap combines student learning tools—readings, multimedia, activities, and assessments—into a singular Learning Path that guides students through the course.

Chapter 27

Empire and Expansion
1890–1909

We assert that no nation can long endure half republic and half empire, and we warn the American people that imperialism abroad will lead quickly and inevitably to despotism at home.

DEMOCRATIC NATIONAL PLATFORM, 1900

Chapter Outline

- The Sources of American Expansionism
- Cleveland and the Venezuelan Boundary Dispute, 1895–1896
- The Hawaii Question
- The Explosion of the Maine, February 15, 1898
- The Spanish-American War, 1898
- The Invasion of Cuba
- Acquiring Puerto Rico (1898) and the Philippines (1899)
- Crushing the Filipino Insurrection
- The Open Door Notes, 1899 and 1900
- TR Becomes President, 1901
- The Panama Canal
- The Roosevelt Corollary to the Monroe Doctrine, 1904
- Roosevelt and East Asia
- *Makers of America: The Puerto Ricans*
- *Makers of America: The Filipinos*
- *Thinking Globally: The Age of Empire*
- *Varying Viewpoints: Why Did America Become a World Power?*

In the years immediately following the Civil War, Americans remained astonishingly indifferent to the outside world. Enmeshed in struggles over Reconstruction and absorbed in efforts to heal the wounds of civil war, build an industrial economy, make their cities habitable, and settle the sprawling West, most citizens took little interest in international affairs. But the sunset decades of the nineteenth century witnessed a momentous shift in U.S. foreign policy. America's new diplomacy reflected the far-reaching changes that were reshaping agriculture, industry, and the social structure. American statesmen also responded to the intensifying scramble of other nations for international advantage in the dawning "age of empire." By the beginning of the twentieth century, America had acquired its own empire, an astonishing departure from its venerable anticolonial traditions. The world now had to reckon with a new great power, potentially powerful but with diplomatic ambitions and principles that remained to be defined.

FOCUS QUESTIONS

1. Why did the United States abandon its historic isolationism and turn outward to develop imperial great power ambitions at the end of the nineteenth century?
2. What were the causes of the Spanish-American War, and how did the war lead to the acquisition of an American empire in the Philippines, Guam, and Puerto Rico?
3. Why was there such a vigorous national debate over imperialism, and how did the Filipino rebellion against U.S. rule contribute to doubts about America's overseas role?
4. How did the United States become increasingly involved in China and the rest of East Asia, and what were the Open Door policy toward China and Theodore Roosevelt's diplomacy with Japan intended to achieve?
5. How did Theodore Roosevelt vigorously assert American power in Panama and elsewhere in Latin America, and why did the "Roosevelt Corollary" to the Monroe Doctrine stir controversy?

CHRONOLOGY

1820	New England missionaries arrive in Hawaii	1901	Supreme Court *Insular Cases* Platt Amendment McKinley assassinated; Roosevelt becomes president Filipino rebellion suppressed Hay-Pauncefote Treaty with Britain gives United States exclusive right to build Panama Canal
1889	Samoa crisis with Germany Pan-American Conference		
1890	Mahan publishes *The Influence of Sea Power upon History*		
1891	New Orleans crisis with Italy	1902	U.S. troops leave Cuba Colombian senate rejects U.S. proposal for canal across Panama
1892	Valparaiso crisis with Chile		
1893	White planter revolt in Hawaii Cleveland refuses Hawaii annexation	1903	Panamanian revolution against Colombia Hay-Bunau-Varilla Treaty gives United States control of Canal Zone in newly independent Panama
1895	Cubans revolt against Spain		
1895–1896	Venezuelan boundary crisis with Britain	1904	Roosevelt Corollary to the Monroe Doctrine
1898	*Maine* explosion in Havana harbor Spanish-American War Teller Amendment Dewey's victory at Manila Bay Hawaii annexed	1904–1914	Construction of the Panama Canal
		1905	United States takes over Dominican Republic customs service Roosevelt mediates Russo-Japanese peace treaty
1899	Senate ratifies treaty acquiring Philippines Aguinaldo launches rebellion against United States in the Philippines First American Open Door note	1906	San Francisco Japanese education crisis Roosevelt arranges Algeciras conference
		1906–1909	U.S. Marines occupy Cuba
1900	Hawaii receives full territorial status Foraker Act for Puerto Rico Boxer Rebellion and U.S. military expedition to China Second Open Door note McKinley defeats Bryan for presidency	1907	Great White Fleet makes world voyage
		1907–1908	"Gentlemen's Agreement" with Japan
		1908	Root-Takahira agreement
		1917	Puerto Ricans granted U.S. citizenship

★ Imperialist Stirrings

Many developments fed the nation's ambition for overseas expansion. Both farmers and factory owners began to look beyond American shores as agricultural and industrial production boomed. Many Americans believed that the United States had to expand or explode. Their country was bursting with a new sense of power generated by the robust growth in population, wealth, and productive capacity—and it was trembling from the hammer blows of labor violence and agrarian unrest. Overseas markets might provide a safety valve to relieve those pressures.

Other forces whetted the popular appetite for overseas involvement. The lurid "yellow press" of Joseph Pulitzer and William Randolph Hearst described foreign exploits as manly adventures, the kind of dashing derring-do that was the stuff of young boys' dreams. Pious missionaries, inspired by books such as the Reverend Josiah Strong's *Our Country: Its Possible Future and Its Present Crisis*, looked overseas for new souls to harvest. Strong trumpeted the superiority of Anglo-Saxon civilization and summoned Americans to spread their religion and their values to "backward" peoples. At the same time, aggressive Americans such as Theodore Roosevelt and Congressman (later Senator) Henry Cabot Lodge were interpreting Darwinism to mean that the earth belonged to the strong and the fit—that is, to Uncle Sam. This view was strengthened as latecomers to the colonial scramble began to scoop up leavings from the banquet table of earlier diners in Africa, China, and elsewhere. If America was to survive in the competition of modern nation-states, perhaps it, too, would have to become an imperial power.

The development of a new steel navy also focused attention overseas. Captain Alfred Thayer Mahan's book of 1890, *The Influence of Sea Power upon History, 1660–1783*, argued that control of the sea was the key to world dominance. Mahan helped stimulate the naval race among the great powers that gained momentum around the turn of the century. Red-blooded Americans joined in the demands for a mightier navy and for an American-built isthmian canal between the Atlantic and the Pacific.

> *The undiplomatic note to Britain by Secretary of State Richard Olney (1835–1917) read:*
>
> *"Today the United States is practically sovereign on this continent, and its fiat is law upon the subjects to which it confines its interposition.... Its infinite resources combined with its isolated position render it master of the situation and practically invulnerable as against any or all other powers."*

America's new international assertiveness manifested itself in a number of diplomatic crises or near-wars in the late 1880s and early 1890s. The American and German navies nearly came to blows in 1889 over the faraway Samoan Islands in the South Pacific, which were formally divided between the two nations in 1899. (German Samoa eventually became an independent republic; American Samoa remains an American territory.) The lynching of eleven Italians in New Orleans in 1891 brought America and Italy to the brink of war, until the United States agreed to pay compensation. In the ugliest affair, American demands on Chile after the deaths of two American sailors in the port of Valparaiso in 1892 made hostilities between the two countries seem inevitable. The threat of attack by Chile's modern navy spread alarm on the Pacific Coast, until the Chileans finally agreed to pay an indemnity. The willingness of Americans to risk war over such distant and minor disputes demonstrated the aggressive new national mood.

America's new belligerence combined with old-time anti-British feeling to create a serious crisis between the United States and Britain in 1895–1896. The jungle boundary between British Guiana and Venezuela had long been in dispute, but the discovery of gold in the contested area brought the conflict between Britain and Venezuela to a head. President Cleveland and his pugnacious secretary of state, Richard Olney, stepped into the affair with a combative note to Britain invoking the Monroe Doctrine and declaring that the United States was now calling the tune in the Western Hemisphere. Unimpressed British officials shrugged off Olney's salvo as just another twist of the lion's tail and replied that the affair was none of Uncle Sam's business. President Cleveland—"mad clear through," as he put it—sent a bristling special message to Congress that called for a U.S. commission to determine where the line ought to go and threatened war if the British would not accept the boundary it set.

The entire country, irrespective of political party, was swept off its feet in an outburst of hysteria. War seemed inevitable. Fortunately, sober second thoughts prevailed on both sides of the Atlantic. A rising challenge from Kaiser Wilhelm's Germany and a looming war with the Dutch-descended Boers in South Africa left Britain in no mood for war with America. London backed off and consented to arbitration.

The chastened British, their eyes fully opened to the European peril, now cultivated Yankee friendship and inaugurated an era of "patting the Eagle's head," which replaced a century or so of America's "twisting the lion's tail." Sometimes called the Great Rapprochement—or reconciliation—between the United States and Britain, the new Anglo-American cordiality became a cornerstone of both nations' foreign policies as the twentieth century opened.

Great Rapprochement *After decades of occasionally "twisting the lion's tail," American diplomats began to cultivate close, cordial relations with Great Britain at the end of the nineteenth century—a relationship that would intensify further during World War I.*

★ Spurning the Hawaiian Pear

Enchanted Hawaii had early attracted the attention of Americans. In the morning years of the nineteenth century, the breeze-brushed islands were a way station and provisioning point for Yankee shippers, sailors, and whalers. In 1820 the first New England missionaries arrived, preaching the twin blessings of Protestant Christianity and protective calico. Soon American sugar production flourished on the Hawaiian Islands, and the U.S. government assumed a greater interest. The State Department, beginning in the 1840s, sternly warned other powers to keep their hands off the islands. America's grip was further tightened in 1887 by a treaty with the native government guaranteeing priceless naval-base rights at spacious Pearl Harbor.

But trouble was brewing in the insular paradise. Old World pathogens had scythed the indigenous Hawaiian population to one-sixth of its size at the time of first European contact, leading the American sugar lords to import large numbers of Asian laborers. By century's end Chinese and Japanese immigrants outnumbered both whites and native Hawaiians, prompting fears that Tokyo might intervene on behalf of its often-abused nationals. Then sugar markets went sour in 1890 when the **McKinley Tariff** Act raised barriers against the Hawaiian product. White American planters' mounting efforts to secure annexation by the United States were blocked by Queen Liliuokalani, who insisted that native Hawaiians should control the islands. Though only a tiny minority, the white planters staged a successful coup early in 1893. They were openly assisted by American troops, who landed under the unauthorized orders of the expansionist American minister to Honolulu. "The Hawaiian pear is now fully ripe," he wrote exultantly to his superiors in Washington, "and this is the golden hour for the United States to pluck it."

A treaty of annexation was rushed to Washington, but before it could be railroaded through the Senate, Republican president Harrison's term expired and Democratic president Cleveland came in. Suspecting that his powerful nation had gravely wronged the deposed Queen Liliuokalani and her people, "Old Grover" abruptly withdrew the treaty. A subsequent investigation determined that a majority of Hawaiian natives opposed annexation. Although Queen Liliuokalani could not be reinstated, the sugarcoated move for annexation had to be temporarily abandoned. The Hawaiian pear continued to ripen until 1898, when the United States acquired its overseas empire (see Map 27.1).

★ War with Spain over Cuba

Cuba's masses, frightfully misgoverned, again rose against their Spanish oppressors in 1895. The roots of their revolt were partly economic. Sugar production—the backbone of the island's prosperity—was crippled when the American tariff of 1894 restored high duties on the toothsome product.

The desperate *insurrectos* sought to drive out their Spanish overlords by adopting a scorched-earth policy, torching cane fields and sugar mills and dynamiting passenger trains. American sympathies went out to the Cuban underdogs. Sentiment aside, American business had about $50 million of investment in Cuba and conducted annual trade of about $100 million.

Fuel was added to the Cuban conflagration in 1896 with the coming to power of the Spanish General ("Butcher") Weyler. He undertook to crush the rebellion by herding many civilians into barbed-wire reconcentration camps, where they could not give assistance to the armed *insurrectos*. Lacking proper sanitation, these enclosures turned into deadly pestholes where the victims died miserably.

Atrocities in Cuba were red meat for the sensational new "yellow journalism." William Randolph Hearst and Joseph Pulitzer engaged in a titanic duel for circulation, each attempting to outdo the other with screeching headlines and hair-raising "scoops." Where atrocity stories did not exist, they were invented. Hearst sent the gifted artist Frederic Remington to Cuba to draw sketches, allegedly with the pointed admonition, "You furnish the pictures and I'll furnish the war." Among other outrages, Remington depicted Spanish customs officials brutally disrobing and searching an American woman. Most readers of Hearst's *Journal*, their indignation soaring, had no way of knowing that such tasks were performed by female attendants.

Then early in 1898 Washington sent the battleship *Maine* to Cuba, ostensibly for a "friendly visit" but actually to protect and evacuate Americans if a dangerous flare-up

---

McKinley Tariff (1890) *Shepherded through Congress by President William McKinley, this tariff raised duties on Hawaiian sugar and set off renewed efforts to secure the annexation of Hawaii to the United States.*

insurrectos *Cuban insurgents who sought freedom from colonial Spanish rule. Their destructive tactics threatened American economic interests in Cuban plantations and railroads.*

Maine (1898) *American battleship dispatched to keep a "friendly" watch over Cuba in early 1898. It mysteriously blew up in Havana harbor on February 15, 1898, with a loss of 260 sailors. Later evidence confirmed that the explosion was accidental, resulting from combustion in one of the ship's internal coal bunkers. But many Americans, eager for war, insisted that it was the fault of a Spanish submarine mine.*

Map 27.1 United States Expansion, 1857–1917 With the annexation of the Philippines, Hawaii, and Puerto Rico in 1898, the United States became an imperial power.

should occur. Tragedy struck on February 15, 1898, when the *Maine* mysteriously blew up in Havana harbor, with a loss of 260 sailors.

Two investigations of the iron coffin ensued, one by U.S. naval officers and the other by Spanish officials. The Spaniards concluded that the explosion had been internal and presumably accidental; the Americans argued that the blast had been caused by a submarine mine. Not until 1976 did U.S. Navy Admiral H. G. Rickover confirm the original Spanish finding with overwhelming evidence that the initial explosion had resulted from spontaneous combustion in one of the coal bunkers adjacent to a powder magazine.

But Americans in 1898, now mad for war, blindly embraced the less likely explanation. Lashed to fury by the yellow press, they leapt to the inaccurate conclusion that the Spanish government had been guilty of intolerable treachery. The battle cry of the hour became:

Remember the Maine!
To hell with Spain!

Nothing would do but to hurl the "dirty" Spanish flag from the hemisphere.

The national war fever burned ever higher, even though American diplomats had already gained Madrid's agreement to Washington's two basic demands: an end to reconcentration and an armistice with the Cuban rebels. The cautious McKinley found himself in a jam. He did not want hostilities, but neither did he want continuing Spanish control nor a fully independent Cuba. More impetuous souls denounced the president as "Wobbly Willy" McKinley. Fight-hungry Theodore Roosevelt reportedly snarled

The Explosion of the *Maine*, February 15, 1898 Encouraged and amplified by the "yellow press," the outcry over the tragedy of the *Maine* helped drive the country into an impulsive war against Spain.

that the "white-livered" occupant of the White House did not have "the backbone of a chocolate éclair."

McKinley, recognizing the inevitable, eventually yielded and gave the people what they wanted. But public pressure did not fully explain McKinley's course. He did not trust Spanish promises, and he worried that Democrats would win the upcoming presidential election of 1900 if he remained indecisive. On April 11, 1898, McKinley sent his war message to Congress, urging armed intervention to free the oppressed Cubans. The legislators responded uproariously with what was essentially a declaration of war. In a burst of self-righteousness, they likewise adopted the hand-tying **Teller Amendment**. This proviso proclaimed to the world that when the United States had overthrown Spanish misrule, it would give the Cubans their freedom—a declaration that caused imperialistic Europeans to smile skeptically.

Teller Amendment (1898) *A proviso to President William McKinley's war plans that proclaimed to the world that when the United States had overthrown Spanish misrule, it would give Cuba its freedom. The amendment testified to the ostensibly "anti-imperialist" designs of the initial war plans.*

★ Dewey's May Day Victory at Manila

The American people plunged into the war lightheartedly, like schoolchildren off to a picnic. Bands blared incessantly "There'll Be a Hot Time in the Old Town Tonight" and "Hail, Hail, the Gang's All Here," thus leading some foreigners to believe that those were the national anthems.

The war got off to a giddy start for American forces. Even before the declaration of war, on February 25, 1898, while Navy Secretary John D. Long was away from the office, his hot-blooded assistant secretary Theodore Roosevelt took matters into his own hands. Roosevelt cabled Commodore George Dewey, commanding the American Asian squadron, to descend upon Spain's Philippines in the event of war.

Dewey carried out his orders magnificently on May 1, 1898. Sailing boldly with his six warships at night into the fortified harbor of Manila, he trained his guns the next morning on the Spanish fleet. The entire collection of antiquated and overmatched vessels was quickly destroyed.

Taciturn George Dewey became a national hero overnight. An amateur poet blossomed forth with this:

Oh, dewy was the morning
Upon the first of May,
And Dewey was the Admiral
Down in Manila Bay.
And dewy were the Spaniards' eyes,
Them orbs of black and blue;
And dew we feel discouraged?
I dew not think we dew!

Yet Dewey was in a perilous position. He had destroyed the enemy fleet, but he could not storm the forts of Manila with his sailors. His nerves frayed, he was forced to wait in the sweltering bay while troop reinforcements were slowly assembled in America. The appearance of German warships in Manila harbor added to the tension.

Long-awaited American troops, finally arriving in force, captured Manila on August 13, 1898, in collaboration with Filipino insurgents commanded by their well-educated, part-Chinese leader, Emilio Aguinaldo. Dewey, to his later regret, had brought this shrewd and magnetic revolutionary from exile in Asia so that he might weaken Spanish resistance.

These thrilling events in the Philippines had meanwhile focused attention on Hawaii. An impression spread that America needed the archipelago as a coaling and provisioning way station in order to send supplies and reinforcements to Dewey. A joint resolution of annexation was rushed through Congress and approved by McKinley on July 7, 1898. Hawaii received full territorial status in 1900.

★ The Confused Invasion of Cuba

Shortly after the outbreak of war, the Spanish government ordered a fleet of warships to Cuba. But the decrepit Spanish "armada" was soon forced into bottle-shaped Santiago harbor, where it was blockaded by the much more powerful American fleet. Sound strategy seemed to dictate that an American army be sent in from the rear to drive out the Spanish ships. Leading the ill-equipped American invading force was the grossly overweight General William R. Shafter, a would-be warrior so blubbery that he had to be carried about on a door.

The **Rough Riders**, a part of the invading army, now charged onto the stage of history. This colorful regiment of volunteers, short on discipline but long on dash, consisted largely of western cowboys and other hardy characters, with a sprinkling of ex-polo players and ex-convicts. Commanded by Colonel Leonard Wood, the group was organized principally by the glory-chasing Theodore Roosevelt, who had resigned from the Navy Department to serve as lieutenant colonel.

About the middle of June a bewildered American army of seventeen thousand men finally embarked from Tampa, Florida, amid scenes of indescribable confusion. Shafter's landing near Santiago, Cuba, met little opposition. Brisk fighting broke out on July 1 at El Caney and Kettle Hill, up which Colonel Roosevelt and his Rough Riders charged, with strong support from two crack black regiments. They suffered heavy casualties, but the colorful colonel, having the time of his life, shot a Spaniard with his revolver and rejoiced to see his victim double up like a jackrabbit. He later wrote a book on his exploits, which the famed satirist Finley Peter Dunne's character "Mr. Dooley" remarked ought to have been entitled *Alone in Cubia* [sic].

The American army, fast closing in on Santiago, spelled doom for the Spanish fleet. On July 3 the Spanish ships steamed out of the harbor and into the teeth of the waiting American warships. "Don't cheer, men," Captain Philip of the *Texas* admonished his seamen. "The poor devils are dying." Shortly thereafter Santiago surrendered.

Rough Riders (1898) *Organized by Theodore Roosevelt, this was a colorful, motley regiment of Cuban war volunteers consisting of western cowboys, ex-convicts, and effete Ivy Leaguers. Roosevelt emphasized his experience with the regiment in subsequent campaigns for governor of New York and vice president under William McKinley.*

Contending Voices

Debating Imperialism

The contest over American imperialism took place on the Senate floor as well as around the globe. In 1900 Senator Albert J. Beveridge (1862–1927), Republican from Indiana, returned from an investigative trip to the Philippines to defend its annexation:

"The Philippines are ours forever. . . . And just beyond the Philippines are China's illimitable markets. We will not retreat from either. We will not abandon our opportunity in the Orient. We will not renounce our part in the mission of our race: trustee, under God, of the civilization of the world."

Two years later Senator George F. Hoar (1826–1904), Republican from Massachusetts, broke with his party to denounce American annexation of the Philippines and other territories:

"You cannot maintain despotism in Asia and a republic in America. If you try to deprive even a savage or a barbarian of his just rights you can never do it without becoming a savage or a barbarian yourself."

> Was the alleged conflict between American power and American democratic ideals a fundamentally new problem at the turn of the twentieth century, or a new variation on a recurring tension in the country's history?

Hasty preparations were then made for a descent on Puerto Rico before the war should end. There the American army met even less resistance. By this time Spain was ready for an armistice, which was signed on August 12, 1898.

If the Spaniards had held out a few months longer in Cuba, the American army might have melted away. Malaria, typhoid fever, dysentery, and yellow fever incapacitated numerous soldiers and sailors. Others suffered from fetid canned meat known as "embalmed beef." All told, nearly four hundred men lost their lives to bullets; over five thousand succumbed to bacteria and other causes.

★ America's Course (Curse?) of Empire

Late in 1898 Spanish and American negotiators met in Paris. War-racked Cuba, as expected, was freed from its Spanish overlords. The Americans had little difficulty in securing the remote Pacific island of Guam, which they had captured early in the conflict from astonished Spaniards who had not even known that a war was on. Spain also ceded Puerto Rico to the United States. Ironically, the last remnant of Spain's vast New World empire thus became the first territory ever annexed to the United States without the express promise of eventual statehood. In the decades to come, American investment in the island and Puerto Rican immigration to the United States would make this acquisition one of the weightier consequences of this somewhat carefree war (see "Makers of America: The Puerto Ricans," pp. 460–461).

Knottiest of all was the problem of the Philippines, a veritable apple of discord. These lush islands not only embraced an area larger than the British Isles but also contained an ethnically diverse population of some 7 million souls. McKinley was confronted with a devil's dilemma. He did not feel that America could honorably give the islands back to Spanish misrule, especially after it had fought a war to free Cuba. And America would be turning its back on its responsibilities, he believed, if it simply pulled up anchor and sailed away.

McKinley viewed all the choices open to him as trouble-fraught. The Filipinos, if left to govern themselves, might fall into anarchy. One of the major powers, possibly aggressive Germany or Japan, might then seize them and suck the United States into a major war. Seemingly the least of the evils was to acquire all the Philippines and then perhaps give the Filipinos their freedom later.

President McKinley, ever sensitive to public opinion, kept a carefully attuned ear to the ground. The rumble that he heard seemed to call for taking possession of the entire group of islands. Zealous Protestant missionaries were eager to win Filipino converts from Catholicism. (The Philippines had been substantially Christianized by Spanish Catholics before the founding of Jamestown in 1607.) Wall Street had generally opposed the war; but awakened by the booming of Dewey's guns, it was clamoring for profits in the Philippines.

A tormented McKinley later claimed that he went down on his knees seeking divine guidance and heard an inner voice telling him to take all the Philippines and Christianize and civilize them. Accordingly, he decided for outright annexation of the islands. Because Manila had been captured *after* the armistice was signed, the Americans agreed to pay Spain $20 million for the Philippine Islands—the last great Spanish haul from the New World.

The signing of the pact of Paris touched off one of the most impassioned foreign-policy debates in American history. Except for glacial Alaska, coral-reefed Hawaii, and a handful of Pacific atolls, the Republic had hitherto absorbed only contiguous territory on the North American continent. All previous acquisitions had been thinly peopled and eligible for ultimate statehood. But in the Philippines the nation had on its hands a distant tropical area, thickly populated by Asians of a different culture, tongue, and government institutions.

Opponents of annexation argued that such a step would dishonor and ultimately destroy American's venerable commitments to self-determination and anticolonialism. "Goddamn the United States for its vile conduct in the Philippine Isles!" burst out the usually mild-mannered Professor William James. The Harvard philosopher could not believe that the United States could "puke up its ancient soul in five minutes without a wink of squeamishness." The **Anti-Imperialist League** sprang into being to fight the McKinley administration's expansionist moves. The organization counted among its members some of the most prominent people in the United States, including the presidents of Stanford and Harvard Universities and the novelist Mark Twain. The anti-imperialist blanket even stretched over such strange bedfellows as the labor leader Samuel Gompers and the steel titan Andrew Carnegie.

Anti-imperialists raised many objections. The Filipinos thirsted for freedom; to annex them would violate the "consent of the governed" philosophy of the Declaration of Independence and the Constitution. Despotism abroad might well beget despotism at home. Imperialism was costly and unlikely ever to turn a profit. Finally, annexation would propel the United States into the political and military cauldron of East Asia.

Yet the expansionists or imperialists could sing a seductive song. They appealed to patriotism, invoked America's "civilizing mission," and played up possible trade profits. Manila, they claimed, might become another Hong Kong. Rudyard Kipling, the British poet laureate of imperialism, urged America down the slippery path with a quotable poem:

> *Take up the White Man's burden—*
> *Ye dare not stoop to less—*
> *Nor call too loud on Freedom*
> *To cloak your weariness.*

In short, the wealthy Americans must help to uplift (and exploit) the underprivileged, underfed, and underclad of the world.

Over heated protests, the Senate approved the treaty with Spain with just one vote to spare on February 6, 1898. America was now officially an empire.

President William McKinley (1843–1901) later described his decision to annex the Philippines:

"When next I realized that the Philippines had dropped into our laps, I confess I did not know what to do with them.... I went down on my knees and prayed Almighty God for light and guidance.... And one night late it came to me this way.... That there was nothing left for us to do but to take them all, and to educate the Filipinos, and uplift and civilize and Christianize them and by God's grace do the very best we could by them, as our fellow men, for whom Christ also died. And then I went to bed and went to sleep, and slept soundly."

Anti-Imperialist League (1898–1921) *A diverse group formed to protest American colonial oversight in the Philippines. It included university presidents, industrialists, clergymen, and labor leaders. Strongest in the Northeast, the Anti-Imperialist League was the largest lobbying organization on a U.S. foreign-policy issue up to that time. It declined in strength after the United States signed the Treaty of Paris (which approved the annexation of the Philippines), and especially after hostilities broke out between Filipino nationalists and American forces.*

★ Perplexities in Puerto Rico and Cuba

From the outset, the status of Puerto Rico was anomalous—neither a state nor a territory, and with little prospect of eventual independence. The **Foraker Act** of 1900 accorded the Puerto Ricans a limited degree of popular government, and in 1917 Congress granted Puerto Ricans U.S. citizenship but withheld full self-rule. Although the American regime worked wondrous improvements in education, sanitation, and transportation, many of the inhabitants still aspired to independence. Great numbers of Puerto Ricans ultimately moved to New York City, where they added to the complexity of the melting pot.

The annexation of Puerto Rico (and the Philippines) posed a thorny legal problem: Did the Constitution follow the flag? Did American laws, including tariff laws and the Bill of Rights, apply with full force to the newly acquired possessions? "Who are we?" a group

Foraker Act (1900) *Sponsored by Senator Joseph B. Foraker, a Republican from Ohio, this accorded Puerto Ricans a limited degree of popular government. The first comprehensive congressional effort to provide for governance of territories acquired after the Spanish-American War, it served as a model for a similar act adopted for the Philippines in 1902.*

Makers of America

The Puerto Ricans

At dawn on July 26, 1898, the U.S. warship *Gloucester* steamed into Puerto Rico's Guanica harbor, fired at the Spanish blockhouse, and landed some thirty-three hundred troops. Within days, the Americans had taken possession of the Caribbean island a thousand miles southeast of Florida. In so doing they set in motion changes on the island that ultimately brought a new wave of immigrants to U.S. shores.

Puerto Rico had been a Spanish possession since Christopher Columbus claimed it in 1493. The Spaniards enslaved many of the island's forty thousand Taino Indians and set them to work on farms and in mines. Many Tainos died of exhaustion and disease, and in 1511 the Indians rebelled. The Spaniards crushed the uprising, killed thousands of Indians, and began importing African slaves—thus establishing the basis for Puerto Rico's multiracial society.

The first Puerto Rican immigrants to the United States arrived as political exiles in the nineteenth century. From their haven in America, they agitated for the island's independence from Spain. The Puerto Rican political émigrés in the United States returned home after the Americans conquered the island in 1898. But they were soon replaced by poor islanders looking for work. When Congress granted Puerto Ricans U.S. citizenship in 1917, thereby eliminating immigration hurdles, many islanders hurried north to find jobs. Over the ensuing decades, Puerto Ricans went to work in Arizona cotton fields, New Jersey soup factories, and Utah mines. The majority, however, clustered in New York City and found work in the city's cigar factories, shipyards, and garment industry. Migration slowed somewhat after the 1920s as the Great Depression shrank the job market on the mainland and as World War II made travel hazardous.

When World War II ended in 1945, the sudden advent of cheap air travel sparked an emigration explosion. As late as the 1930s, the tab for a boat trip to the mainland exceeded the average Puerto Rican's yearly earnings. But with an airplane surplus after World War II, the six-hour flight from Puerto Rico to New York cost under fifty dollars. The Puerto Rican population on the mainland quadrupled between 1940 and 1950 and tripled again by 1960. In 1970, 1.5 million Puerto Ricans lived in the United States, one-third of the island's total population.

United States citizenship and affordable air travel made it easy for Puerto Ricans to return home. Thus to a far greater degree than most immigrant groups, Puerto Ricans kept one foot in the United States and the other on their native island. By some estimates, 2 million people a year journeyed to and from the island during the postwar period. This transience worked to keep Puerto Ricans' educational attainment and English proficiency far below the national average. At the same time, the immigrants encountered a deep-seated racism in America unlike anything on their multiracial island. Throughout the postwar years, Puerto Ricans remained one of the poorest groups in the United States. Still, Puerto Ricans have fared better economically in the United States than on the island, where, in 1970, 60 percent of all inhabitants lived below the poverty line. In recent years Puerto Ricans have attained more schooling, and many have attended college. Invigorated by the civil rights movement of the 1960s, Puerto Ricans also became more politically active, electing growing numbers of congressmen and state and city officials.

Insular Cases (1901–1904) *Beginning in 1901, a badly divided Supreme Court decreed in these cases that the Constitution did not follow the flag. In other words, Puerto Ricans and Filipinos would not necessarily enjoy all American rights.*

Platt Amendment (1901) Following its military occupation, the United States successfully pressured the Cuban government to write this amendment into its constitution. It limited Cuba's treaty-making abilities, controlled its debt, and stipulated that the United States could intervene militarily to restore order when it saw fit.

of Puerto Rican petitioners asked Congress in 1900. "Are we citizens or are we subjects?" Beginning in 1901 with the *Insular Cases*, a badly divided Supreme Court decreed, in effect, that the flag did outrun the Constitution, and that the outdistanced document did not necessarily extend with full force to the new windfall. Puerto Ricans (and Filipinos) might be subject to American rule, but they did not enjoy all American rights.

Cuba, scorched and chaotic, presented another challenge. However, an American military government under General Leonard Wood of Rough Rider fame wrought miracles in governance, finance, education, agriculture, and public health. Wood and Colonel William C. Gorgas also launched a frontal attack on yellow fever. Spectacular experiments performed by Dr. Walter Reed and others on American soldiers, who volunteered as human guinea pigs, proved that the stegomyia mosquito was the lethal carrier. Cleaning up breeding places for mosquitoes wiped out yellow fever in Havana.

The United States, honoring its self-denying Teller Amendment of 1898, withdrew from Cuba in 1902. Old World imperialists could scarcely believe their eyes. But the Washington government feared that if Cuba were left on its own a grasping power like Germany might secure dangerous lodgment near America's soft underbelly. The Cubans were therefore forced to write into their own constitution of 1901 the so-called **Platt Amendment**.

The First Puerto Ricans The Spanish conquistadores treated the native Taino Indian peoples in Puerto Rico with extreme cruelty, and the Indians were virtually extinct by the mid-1500s.

The Platt Amendment placed restrictions on Cubans' political and financial autonomy and permitted the United States to intervene with troops to restore order when it saw fit. The Cubans also promised to sell or lease coaling or naval stations to their powerful "benefactor." The Cubans loathed the amendment, which served McKinley's ultimate purpose of bringing Cuba under American control. ("Plattism" survives as a colloquial term of derision even in modern-day Cuba.) The United States finally abrogated the amendment in 1934, although Uncle Sam still occupies one remaining base, Guantanamo, under an agreement that can be revoked only by the consent of both parties (see p. 572).

★ New Horizons in Two Hemispheres

In essence, the Spanish-American War was a kind of colossal coming-out party. Dewey's thundering guns merely advertised the fact that the nation was already a world power. The war itself was short (113 days), spectacular, low in casualties, and theatrically successful—despite the bungling. Secretary of State John Hay called it a "splendid

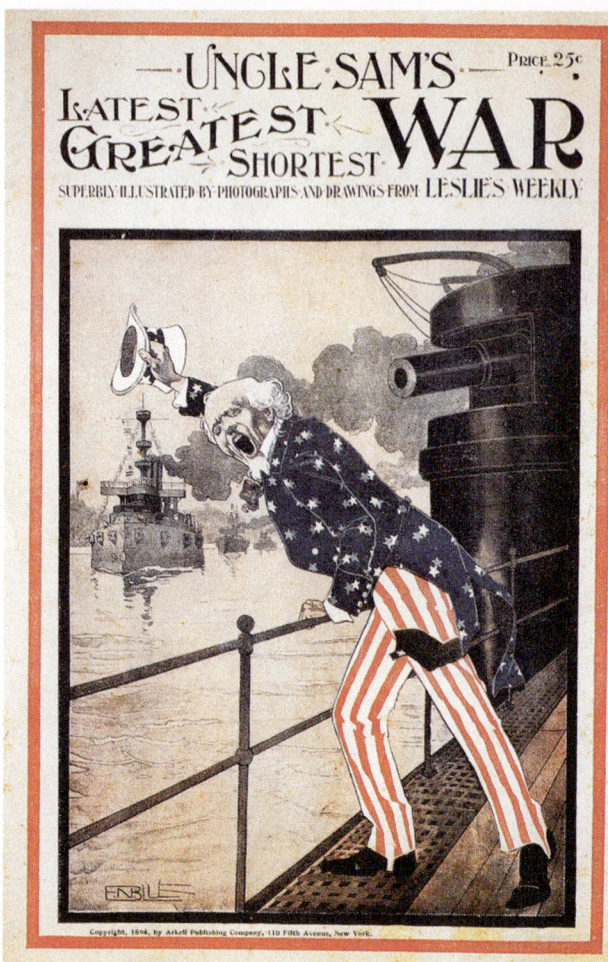

The New Jingoism An enthusiastic Uncle Sam cheers the U.S. Navy in the "splendid little war" of 1898. Many Americans, however, were less than enthused about America's new imperial adventure.

little war." American prestige rose sharply, and the European great powers grudgingly accorded the Republic more respect.

An exhilarating new martial spirit thrilled America, buoyed along by the newly popular military marching-band music of John Philip Sousa. Most Americans did not start the war with consciously imperialistic motives, but after falling through the cellar door of imperialism in a drunken fit of idealism, they wound up with imperialistic and colonial fruits in their grasp. Captain Mahan's big-navyism seemed vindicated, and popular support grew for more and better battleships. A masterly organizer, Secretary of War Elihu Root, established a general staff and founded the War College in Washington.

One of the most beneficial results of the conflict was the further closing of the "bloody chasm" between North and South. Thousands of patriotic southerners had flocked to the Stars and Stripes, and gray-bearded General Joseph ("Fighting Joe") Wheeler—a Confederate cavalry hero—was given a command in Cuba. He allegedly cried, in the heat of battle, "To hell with the Yankees! Dammit, I mean the Spaniards!"

Even so, the newly imperial nation was not yet prepared to pay the full bill for its new status. By taking on the Philippine Islands, the United States became a full-fledged East Asian power. But the distant islands eventually became a "heel of Achilles"—a kind of indefensible hostage given to Japan, as events proved in World War II. Here and elsewhere, the Americans had short-sightedly assumed burdensome commitments that they proved unwilling to defend with appropriate naval and military outlays.

★ "Little Brown Brothers" in the Philippines

The liberty-loving Filipinos assumed that they, like the Cubans, would be granted their freedom after the Spanish-American War. They were tragically deceived. Washington excluded them from the peace negotiations with Spain and made clear its intention to stay in the Philippines indefinitely. Bitterness toward the occupying American troops erupted into open insurrection on February 4, 1899, under Emilio Aguinaldo. Having plunged into war with Spain to free Cuba, the United States was now forced to deploy some 126,000 troops ten thousand miles away to rivet shackles onto a people who asked for nothing but freedom—in the American tradition.

The poorly equipped Filipino rebels soon melted into the jungle to wage vicious guerrilla warfare. Just months earlier, American soldiers had believed they were rescuing innocent Philippine victims of Spanish tyranny. Now they were fighting the Filipinos, whom they came to see as dangerous enemies of the United States. This shift contributed to a mounting "race war" in which both sides perpetrated sordid atrocities. Uncle Sam's soldiers adopted the "water cure"—forcing water down victims' throats until they yielded information or died. American-built reconcentration camps rivaled those of "Butcher" Weyler in Cuba. Having begun the Spanish war with noble ideals, America now dirtied its hands. One New York newspaper published a reply to Rudyard Kipling's famous poem:

> We've taken up the white man's burden
> Of ebony and brown;
> Now will you kindly tell us, Rudyard,
> How we may put it down?

The Americans broke the back of the Filipino insurgency in 1901 when they captured Aguinaldo. But sporadic fighting dragged on for many dreary months, eventually claiming the lives of 4,234 Americans and as many as 200,000 Filipinos.

Future president William H. Taft, an able and amiable Ohioan who weighed some 350 pounds, became civil governor of the Philippines in 1901. Forming a strong attachment to the Filipinos, he called them his "little brown brothers." But McKinley's "benevolent assimilation" of the Philippines proceeded with painful slowness. Millions of American dollars did lead to better roads, improved public sanitation, and an unusually good school system. But all this vast expenditure was ill received. The Filipinos hated compulsory Americanization and pined for liberty. They finally got their freedom on the Fourth of July, 1946. In the meantime, thousands of Filipinos emigrated to the United States (see "Makers of America: The Filipinos," p. 464).

⭐ Hinging the Open Door in China

Ominous events had meanwhile been brewing in enfeebled China. After its defeat by Japan in 1894–1895, the imperialistic European powers, notably Russia and Germany, moved in. Like vultures descending upon a wounded animal, they began to tear away valuable leaseholds and economic spheres of influence from the Manchu government.

A growing group of Americans viewed the vivisection of China with alarm. Churches were worried about their missionary strongholds. Merchants feared that Europeans would monopolize Chinese markets. An alarmed American public demanded that Washington do something. Secretary of State John Hay, a witty poet-novelist-diplomat, finally decided upon a dramatic move.

In the summer of 1899, Hay dispatched to all the great powers a communication soon known as the **Open Door note**. He urged them to announce that in their leaseholds or spheres of influence they would respect certain Chinese rights and the ideal of fair competition. Tellingly, Hay had not bothered to consult the Chinese themselves.

Open Door note (1899–1900) *A set of diplomatic letters in which Secretary of State John Hay urged the great powers to respect Chinese rights and free and open competition within their spheres of influence. The notes established the "Open Door policy," which sought to ensure access to the Chinese market for the United States, despite the fact that it did not have a formal sphere of influence in China.*

American Missionary Grace Roberts Teaching in China, 1903 A long history of American missionary involvement in China nurtured a sentimental affection for that country among Americans that persisted well into the twentieth century.

Makers of America

The Filipinos

At the beginning of the twentieth century, the United States, its imperial muscles just flexed in the war with Spain, found itself in possession of the Philippines. Uncertain of how to manage this empire, which seethed resentfully against its new masters, the United States promised to build democracy in the Philippines and to ready the islanders for home rule. Almost immediately after annexation, the American governor of the archipelago sent a corps of Filipino students to the United States, hoping to forge future leaders steeped in American ways who would someday govern an independent Philippines.

Most Filipino immigrants to the United States in these years, however, came not to study but to toil. With Chinese immigration banned, Hawaii and the Pacific Coast states turned to the Philippines for cheap agricultural labor. Beginning in 1906, the Hawaiian Sugar Planters Association aggressively recruited Filipino workers. By the 1920s thousands of young Filipino men had reached the Hawaiian Islands and been assigned to sugar plantations or pineapple fields.

Those Filipinos venturing as far as the American mainland found work less arduous but also less certain than did their countrymen on Hawaiian plantations. Many mainlanders worked seasonally—in winter as domestic servants, busboys, or bellhops; in summer journeying to the fields to harvest lettuce, strawberries, sugar beets, and potatoes. Eventually Filipinos, along with Mexican immigrants, came to make up the largest share of California's agricultural work force.

A mobile society, Filipino Americans also were overwhelmingly male; there was only one Filipino woman for every fourteen Filipino men in California in 1930. Thus, the issue of intermarriage became acutely sensitive. California and many other states prohibited the marriage of Asians and Caucasians in demeaning laws that remained on the books until 1948. Undeterred by such overt discrimination and the vigilante violence sometimes directed at them, especially in Washington and California, Filipinos challenged restrictive state laws and the hooligans who found in them an excuse for mayhem. But Filipinos, who did not become eligible for American citizenship until 1946, long lacked political leverage.

After World War II, Filipino immigration accelerated. Between 1950 and 1970, the number of Filipinos in the United States nearly doubled, with women and men stepping aboard the new transpacific airliners in roughly equal numbers. Many of these recent arrivals were solidly middle class and sought in America a better life for their children. Today, the Philippines sends more immigrants to American shores than does any other Asian nation.

Filipino Laborers at Work on a Hawaiian Pineapple Plantation, Between 1910 and 1925

The phrase *Open Door* quickly caught the American public's fancy. But Hay's proposal caused much squirming in the leading world capitals, though all the great powers except Russia eventually agreed to it.

Open Door or not, patriotic Chinese did not care to be used as a doormat by the Europeans. In 1900 a superpatriotic group, known as the "Boxers" for their training in martial arts, broke loose with the cry, "Kill Foreign Devils." In what became known as the **Boxer Rebellion**, they murdered more than two hundred foreigners and thousands of Chinese Christians and besieged the foreign diplomatic community in the capital, Beijing (Peking).

A multinational rescue force of some eighteen thousand soldiers, including several thousand Americans, arrived in the nick of time to quell the rebellion and prop the Open Door open. The victorious allied invaders acted angrily and vindictively. They assessed prostrate China an excessive indemnity of $333 million, of which America's share was to be $24.5 million. When Washington discovered that this sum was much more than enough to pay damages and expenses, it remitted about $18 million to be used for the education of a selected group of Chinese students in the United States—a not-so-subtle initiative to further the westernization of Asia.

Secretary Hay let fly another paper broadside in 1900, announcing that henceforth the Open Door would embrace the territorial integrity of China. Those principles helped spare China from possible partition in those troubled years and were formally incorporated into the Nine-Power Treaty of 1922, only to be callously violated by Japan's takeover of Manchuria a decade later (see pp. 537–538).

Boxer Rebellion (1900) *An uprising in China directed against foreign influence. It was suppressed by an international force of some eighteen thousand soldiers, including several thousand Americans. The Boxer Rebellion paved the way for the revolution of 1911, which led to the establishment of the Republic of China in 1912.*

⭐ Imperialism or Bryanism in 1900?

President McKinley's renomination by the Republicans in 1900 was a foregone conclusion. He had won a war, acquired rich though burdensome colonial territories for the United States, safeguarded the gold standard, and brought the promised prosperity of the full dinner pail. An irresistible vice-presidential boom had developed for "Teddy" Roosevelt (TR), the cowboy-hero of the Cuban campaign. Capitalizing on his war-born popularity, he had been elected governor of New York, where the local political bosses had found him headstrong and difficult to manage. They therefore devised a scheme to kick the colorful colonel upstairs into the vice presidency.

This plot to railroad Roosevelt worked beautifully. Gesticulating wildly, Roosevelt sported a cowboy hat that made him stand out like a white crow at the Republican convention. To cries of "We Want Teddy!" he was handily nominated. A wary Mark Hanna reportedly moaned that there would now be only one heartbeat between "that damned cowboy" and the presidency of the United States.

William Jennings Bryan was the odds-on choice of the Democrats, meeting at Kansas City. Their platform proclaimed that the paramount issue was Republican overseas imperialism.

McKinley, the soul of dignity, once again campaigned safely from his front porch. Bryan again took to the stump in a cyclonic campaign. Lincoln, he charged, had abolished slavery for 3.5 million Africans; McKinley had reestablished it for 7 million Filipinos. Roosevelt out-Bryaned Bryan, touring the country with revolver-shooting cowboys. Flashing his monumental teeth and pounding his fist into his palm, Roosevelt denounced all the dastards who would haul down Old Glory.

McKinley handily triumphed by a much wider margin than in 1896: 7,218,491 to 6,356,734 popular votes, and 292 to 155 electoral votes. But victory for the Republicans was not a mandate for imperialism. If there was any mandate at all, it was for the two *P*s: prosperity and protectionism. Meanwhile, the New York bosses gleefully looked forward to watching the nettlesome Roosevelt "take the veil" as vice president.

⭐ TR: Brandisher of the Big Stick

Kindly William McKinley had scarcely served another six months when, in September 1901, he was murdered by a deranged anarchist in Buffalo, New York. Roosevelt rode a buckboard out of his campsite in the Adirondack Mountains to take the oath of office, becoming, at age forty-two, the youngest president thus far in American history.

Born into a wealthy and distinguished New York family, Roosevelt, a red-blooded blue blood, had fiercely built up his spindly, asthmatic body by a stern and self-imposed routine of exercise. He graduated from Harvard with Phi Beta Kappa honors and published, at the age of twenty-four, the first of some thirty volumes of muscular prose. He worked as a ranch owner and cowboy in the Dakotas before pursuing his political career full time. Barrel-chested, bespectacled, with mulelike molars, squinty eyes, droopy mustache, and piercing voice, he was ever the delight of cartoonists.

The Rough Rider's high-voltage energy was electrifying. Believing that it was better to wear out than to rust out, he would shake the hands of some six thousand people at one stretch or ride long miles on horseback. Incurably boyish and bellicose, Roosevelt ceaselessly preached the virile virtues and denounced pacifist "flubdubs" and "mollycoddles." An ardent champion of military and naval preparedness, he adopted as his pet proverb, "Speak softly and carry a big stick, [and] you will go far."

His outsized ego caused it to be said of him that he wanted to be the bride at every wedding and the corpse at every funeral. He loved people and mingled with those of all ranks, from Catholic cardinals to professional prizefighters. "TR" commanded an idolatrous personal following. After visiting him, a journalist wrote, "You go home and wring the personality out of your clothes."

Above all, TR believed that the president should lead boldly. He had no real respect for the delicate checks and balances among the three branches of government. The president, he felt, may take any action in the general interest that is not specifically forbidden by the laws or the Constitution.

★ Building the Panama Canal

Roosevelt soon applied his bullish energy to foreign affairs. The Spanish-American War had reinvigorated interest in the long-talked-about canal across the Central American isthmus. An isthmian canal would plainly augment the strength of the navy by increasing its mobility. Such a waterway would also make easier the defense of such recent acquisitions as Puerto Rico, Hawaii, and the Philippines (see Map 27.2).

Map 27.2 Big Stick in the Caribbean In 1901 Roosevelt declared: "If a man continually blusters . . . a big stick will not save him from trouble; and neither will speaking softly avail, if back of the softness there does not lie strength, power. . . . If the boaster is not prepared to back up his words his position becomes absolutely contemptible."

Initial obstacles in the path of the canal builders were legal rather than geographical. By the terms of the ancient Clayton-Bulwer Treaty, concluded with Britain in 1850, the United States could not secure exclusive control over an isthmian route. But by 1901 America's British cousins were willing to yield ground. Confronted with an unfriendly Europe and bogged down in the South African Boer War, they consented to the Hay-Pauncefote Treaty in 1901. It not only gave the United States a free hand to build the canal but conceded the right to fortify it as well.

But where exactly should the canal be dug? Many American experts favored a route across Nicaragua, but agents of an old French canal company were eager to salvage something from their costly failure in S-shaped Panama. Represented by a young, energetic, and unscrupulous engineer, Philippe Bunau-Varilla, the New Panama Canal Company suddenly dropped the price of its holdings from $109 million to the fire sale price of $40 million.

Congress in June 1902 finally decided on the Panama route. The scene now shifted to Colombia, of which Panama was a restive part. The Colombian senate rejected an American offer of $10 million and annual payment of $250,000 for a six-mile-wide zone across Panama. Roosevelt railed against "those dagos" who were frustrating his ambitions. Meanwhile, impatient Panamanians were ripe for a revolt. Scheming Bunau-Varilla was no less disturbed by the prospect of losing the company's $40 million if the Americans should turn to the Nicaraguan route. Working hand in glove with the Panama revolutionists, Bunau-Varilla helped incite a rebellion on November 3, 1903. United States naval forces prevented Colombian troops from crossing the isthmus to quell the uprising.

Roosevelt moved rapidly to make steamy Panama a virtual outpost of the United States. Just three days after the insurrection, he hastily extended the right hand of recognition. Fifteen days later, Bunau-Varilla, who was now the Panamanian minister despite his French citizenship, signed the Hay–Bunau-Varilla Treaty in Washington. The price of the canal strip was left the same, but the zone was widened from six to ten miles. The French company gladly pocketed its $40 million from the U.S. Treasury.

Hay-Pauncefote Treaty (1901) *A treaty signed between the United States and Great Britain giving Americans a free hand to build a canal in Central America. The treaty nullified the Clayton-Bulwer Treaty of 1850, which prohibited Britain or the United States from acquiring territory in Central America.*

Theodore Roosevelt and His Big Stick in the Caribbean, 1904 Roosevelt's policies seemed to be turning the Caribbean into a Yankee pond.

Roosevelt, it seems clear, did not actively plot to tear Panama from the side of Colombia. But the conspirators knew of his angrily expressed views, and they counted on his using the big stick to hold Colombia at bay. The Rough Rider became so indiscreetly involved in the Panama affair as to create the impression that he had been a secret party to the intrigue, and the so-called rape of Panama marked an ugly downward lurch in U.S. relations with Latin America.

Canal construction began in 1904, in the face of daunting difficulties ranging from labor troubles to landslides and lethal tropical diseases. Colonel William C. Gorgas, the quiet and determined exterminator of yellow fever in Havana, ultimately made the Canal Zone "as safe as a health resort." At a cost of some $400 million, an autocratic West Point engineer, Colonel George Washington Goethals, ultimately brought the project to completion in 1914, just as World War I was breaking out.

⭐ TR's Perversion of Monroe's Doctrine

Latin American debt defaults prompted further Rooseveltian involvement in affairs south of the border. Nations such as Venezuela and the Dominican Republic were chronically in arrears in their payments to European creditors.

Roosevelt feared that if the Germans or British got their foot in the door as bill collectors, they might remain in Latin America, in flagrant violation of the Monroe Doctrine. He therefore declared a brazen policy of "preventive intervention," better known as the **Roosevelt Corollary** to the Monroe Doctrine. He announced that in the event of future financial malfeasance by the Latin American nations, the United States itself would intervene, take over the customshouses, pay off the debts, and keep the troublesome Europeans on the other side of the Atlantic. In short, no outsiders could push around the Latin American nations except Uncle Sam, Policeman of the Caribbean. This new brandishing of the big stick in the Caribbean became effective in 1905 when the United States took over the Dominican Republic's tariff collections. The big stick was vigorously wielded again in 1906 when revolutionary disorders in Cuba led to the sending of the U.S. Marines, who policed the country until they were temporarily withdrawn in 1909. In Latin American eyes this episode was but another example of the creeping power of the Colossus of the North.

TR's rewriting of the Monroe Doctrine probably did more than any other single step to promote the "Bad Neighbor" policy begun in these years. As time wore on, the new corollary was used to justify wholesale interventions and repeated landings of the Marines, all of which helped turn the Caribbean into a "Yankee lake." To Latin Americans it seemed as though the revised Monroe Doctrine, far from providing a shield, was a cloak behind which the United States sought to strangle them.

Roosevelt Corollary (1904) A brazen policy of "preventive intervention" advocated by Theodore Roosevelt in his Annual Message to Congress in 1904. Adding ballast to the Monroe Doctrine, his corollary stipulated that the United States would retain a right to intervene in the domestic affairs of Latin American nations in order to restore military and financial order.

⭐ Roosevelt on the World Stage

Booted and spurred, Roosevelt charged into international affairs far beyond Latin America. The outbreak of war between Russia and Japan in 1904 gave him a chance to perform as a global statesman. The Russians' threatened seizure of China's Manchuria would be a pistol pointed at Japan's strategic heart. The Japanese responded in 1904 with a devastating surprise pounce on the Russian fleet. They proceeded to administer a humiliating series of beatings to the inept Russians—the first serious military setback to a major European power since the sixteenth century. But as the war dragged on, Japan began to run short of men and yen. Tokyo officials therefore approached Roosevelt in the deepest secrecy and asked him to help sponsor peace negotiations.

Roosevelt was happy to oblige, as he wanted to avoid a complete Russian collapse so that the tsar's empire could remain a counterweight to Japan's growing power. At Portsmouth, New Hampshire, in 1905, TR guided the warring parties to a settlement that satisfied neither side. Japan was forced to drop its demands for a cash indemnity and Russian evacuation of Sakhalin Island, though it did gain effective control over Korea, which it formally annexed in 1910.

For achieving this agreement, as well as for helping arrange an international conference at Algeciras, Spain, in 1906 to mediate North African disputes, TR received the Nobel Peace Prize in 1906. But the price of his diplomatic glory was high for U.S. foreign relations. Two historic friendships withered on the windswept plains of Manchuria. America's relations with Russia, once friendly, soured as the Russians implausibly accused Roosevelt of robbing them of military victory. Japan, once America's protégé, felt robbed of its due compensation. Both newly powerful, Japan and America now became rivals in Asia, as fear and jealousy between them grew.

Japanese Laborers in California

America's Pacific Coast soon felt the effects of the Russo-Japanese War. The conflict's dislocations and tax burdens sent a new wave of Japanese immigrants into the spacious valleys of California. Although Japanese residents never amounted to more than 3 percent of the state's population, white Californians ranted about a new "yellow peril" and feared being drowned in an Asian sea.

A showdown on the influx came in 1906 when San Francisco's school board, coping with the aftermath of a frightful earthquake and fire, ordered the segregation of Chinese, Japanese, and Korean students in a special school to free more space for whites. Instantly the incident boiled into an international crisis. The people of Japan, understandably sensitive on questions of race, regarded this discrimination as an insult to them and their beloved children. On both sides of the Pacific, irresponsible war talk sizzled in the yellow press—the real "yellow peril." Roosevelt, the often-bellicose Rough Rider, was in this case

Japanese Workers Building a Road in California, c. 1910

Thinking Globally

The Age of Empire

The closing years of the nineteenth century witnessed an unprecedented explosion of imperialism, roughly defined as the forcible imposition of one country's rule on the unwilling inhabitants of another. Between 1870 and the outbreak of World War I in 1914, a handful of European states extended their sway over nearly one-quarter of the earth's surface. Other countries followed suit, notably Japan and eventually the United States.

All the imperial powers had in common a heritage of nationalism and a high degree of industrialization. They commanded the elaborate administrative apparatus of large unified states, along with quantities of wealth, technology, and murderous firepower utterly beyond the capacity of the so-called backward peoples they sought to dominate. As a result, imperialism was, from the start, a lopsided game. As one English wit mordantly noted in 1898:

> *Whatever happens, we have got*
> *The Maxim gun, and they have not.*

Yet ultimately, even with their enormously disproportionate advantages, the imperial states were unable to sustain the age of imperialism for much more than a century.

In many ways, modern imperialism resembled eighteenth-century mercantilism, as economically advanced states backed away from the free-trade doctrines that had energized the early stages of the Industrial Revolution and sought instead to create what one British imperialist called "a great self-sustaining and self-protecting empire." The new imperialism also differed from older colonialism in that the imperial powers sought not merely to exploit but also to transform, modernize, and "westernize" the "backward" societies under their control.

Imperialists often justified their dominion over less-developed societies with high-toned slogans. The British professed to be nobly shouldering "the white man's burden." The French piously invoked their *mission civilisatrice* (civilizing mission). The Germans touted the benefits of spreading their vaunted *Kultur* (culture). The Americans prated about the superiority of the Anglo-Saxons, as the Japanese did about their own "Yamato" race.

These protestations may have been sincere, but other motives more powerfully propelled the imperial enterprise. Prominent among them was the quest for new markets, as maturing industrial economies appeared to be exhausting the possibilities for economic growth at home. The need for reliable sources of products such as cotton, sugar, copper, coffee, and tea also figured conspicuously. An even more compelling incentive was the need to protect the huge investments of capital that built the railroads, highways, bridges, ports, mills, foundries, mines, smelters, and telegraphs of the developing world. By the eve of World War I, fully one-quarter of Britain's accumulated wealth was invested overseas.

But perhaps the most important factor driving the imperialist venture was simply the competitive nature of the international system itself. In an unstable, unpredictable world inhabited by ambitious and wary powers, no state thought it could afford to cede an advantage, however ill defined, to any real or imagined rival. Indeed, quite independently of their hard economic value, colonies came to be considered the necessary symbols of great-power status. This perverse logic proved to be a powerful dynamite: Once the imperial race began, it was difficult to stop. As Cecil Rhodes, the fabled British colonizer in southern Africa, once said, "I would annex the planets, if I could." So when Belgium's King Leopold took an interest in Africa's Congo basin in the 1870s, he touched off a mad imperial scramble that eventually involved Belgium, Britain, Germany, France, Italy, and Portugal. Less than two decades later, with the exceptions of Ethiopia and Liberia, the entire continent, much of it unexplored and of dubious economic value, lay under European domination.

In Asia, Germany annexed part of New Guinea in 1884. France completed its annexation of Indochina (present-day Vietnam, Laos, and Cambodia) that same year. Britain acquired Burma (now Myanmar) in 1885 and parts of Borneo and the Malay Peninsula soon after. Japan closed its grip on Okinawa in 1872, Formosa (Taiwan) in 1895, and Korea

unhappy that California might stir up a war. He therefore invited the entire San Francisco Board of Education to the White House.

TR finally broke the deadlock, but not until he had brandished his big stick and bared his big teeth. The Californians were induced to repeal the offensive school order and to accept what came to be known as the "Gentlemen's Agreement." By this secret understanding, worked out during 1907–1908, Tokyo agreed to stop the flow of laborers to the American mainland by withholding passports.

Worried that his intercession might be interpreted in Tokyo as prompted by fear, Roosevelt hit upon a dramatic scheme to impress the Japanese with the heft of his big stick. He daringly decided to send the entire U.S. battleship fleet on a highly visible voyage around the world.

A Young Ho Chi Minh Ho Chi Minh (1890–1969) attended the Congress of the Socialist Party in Tours, France, where the French Communist party was created in late December 1920.

in 1910. All those powers, in addition to Russia, also had designs on China. In the Open Door notes of 1899 and 1900 (see p. 463), the United States tried to temper the imperialists' appetites for Chinese territory and concessions, while at the same time America was becoming an imperial power itself with the takeover of the Philippines and Puerto Rico.

The imperialists brought not only their might and their majesty, their capital and their Maxim guns. They also brought their ideas, including concepts of nationalism, self-determination, and democracy. In 1919 a young Vietnamese nationalist named Nguyen Sinh Cung unsuccessfully petitioned the post–World War I peacemakers at Versailles for his country's right to self-determination. A little more than half a century later, under the name Ho Chi Minh, he secured Vietnam's independence by prevailing in a war first against the French and then against the Americans. By that time the United States had long since voluntarily relinquished the Philippines (in 1946, though Puerto Rico remains an American possession), and virtually all of Africa and Asia had been decolonized. With the handover of Hong Kong (1997) and Macao (1999) to the People's Republic of China, the age of empire effectively ended.

Late in 1907, sixteen sparkling-white smoke-belching battleships started from Virginia waters. Their commander pointedly declared that he was ready for "a feast, a frolic, or a fight." The Great White Fleet received tumultuous welcomes in Latin America, Hawaii, New Zealand, and Australia. The high point of the trip was an overwhelming reception in Japan, as tens of thousands of kimonoed schoolchildren turned out to wave tiny American flags and sing "The Star Spangled Banner."

In the warm diplomatic atmosphere created by the visit of the fleet, the United States signed the Root-Takahira agreement with Japan in 1908. The agreement pledged both powers to respect each other's territorial possessions in the Pacific and to uphold the Open Door in China. For the moment, at least, the two rising rival powers had found a means to maintain the peace.

Root-Takahira agreement (1908)
Agreement by which the United States and Japan agreed to respect each other's territorial possessions in the Pacific and to uphold the Open Door in China. The agreement was credited with easing tensions between the two nations, but it also resulted in a weakened American influence over further Japanese hegemony in China.

Varying Viewpoints

Why Did America Become a World Power?

American imperialism has long been an embarrassing topic for students of American history, who remember the Republic's own revolutionary origins and anticolonial tradition. Perhaps for that reason, many historians have tried to explain the dramatic overseas expansionism of the 1890s as some kind of aberration—a sudden, singular, and short-lived departure from time-honored American principles and practices. Various explanations have been offered to account for this spasmodic lapse. Scholars such as Julius Pratt pointed to the irresponsible behavior of the yellow press. Richard Hofstadter ascribed America's imperial fling to the "psychic crisis of the 1890s," a crisis brought on, he argued, by the strains of the decade's economic depression and the Populist upheaval. Howard K. Beale emphasized the contagious scramble for imperial possessions by the European powers, as well as Japan, in these years.

In Beale's argument, the United States—and Theodore Roosevelt in particular—succumbed to a kind of international peer pressure: if other countries were expanding their international roles and even establishing colonies around the globe, could the United States safely refrain from doing the same? More recent scholars like Paul Kramer stress the degree to which American imperialists turned to European precedents for guidance and inspiration. Thus U.S. colonial officials in the Philippines and Puerto Rico studied and selectively adapted elements of British imperial policy.

Perhaps the most controversial interpretation of American imperialism has come from a so-called New Left school of writers, inspired by William Appleman Williams (and before him by V. I. Lenin's 1916 book *Imperialism: The Highest Stage of Capitalism*). Historians such as Williams and Walter LaFeber argue that the explanation for political and military expansion abroad is to be found in economic expansion at home. Increasing industrial output, so the argument goes, required ever more raw materials and, especially, overseas markets. That "revisionist" interpretation, in turn, has been sharply criticized by scholars who point out that foreign trade accounted for only a tiny share of American output and that the diplomacy of this period was far too complex to be reduced to "economic need."

Most recently, historians have highlighted the importance of race and gender in the march toward empire. Roosevelt and other imperialists perceived their world in gendered terms. Many feared American society had lost touch with manly virtues and grown soft and "feminine" since the closing of the frontier. Imperialists also saw the nations of the world in a strict racial hierarchy, with "primitive" blacks and Indians at the bottom and "civilized" Anglo-Saxons at the top. In this world view the conquest of "inferior" peoples seemed a natural tonic to restore the nation's masculine virility. Scholars who emphasize these explanations of imperialism are less likely to see the expansionism of the 1890s as an aberration in American history. Instead, they argue, these overseas adventures were part of a long tradition of race-fueled militarism, from the nation's earliest Indian wars to Cold War engagements in Korea and Vietnam.

CHAPTER SUMMARY

The previously isolated United States dramatically turned its attention overseas in the 1890s, leading to a sudden burst of imperialism. Among the stimuli for the new imperialism were the desire for new economic markets, the sensationalistic "yellow press," Protestant missionary fervor, "Social Darwinist" ideology, great-power rivalry, and naval competition.

American intervention in the Venezuelan boundary dispute of 1895–1896 demonstrated an aggressive new assertion of the Monroe Doctrine and led to an American-British rapprochement after a severe war scare. Longtime American involvement in Hawaii climaxed in 1893 with a revolution against native rule by white American planters. The new government sought annexation by the United States, but President Cleveland blocked the effort.

The "splendid little" Spanish-American War began in 1898 over American outrage about Spanish oppression of Cuba. American support for the Cuban rebellion was whipped into intense popular fervor by the "yellow press." After the mysterious *Maine* explosion in February 1898, this public passion pushed a reluctant President McKinley into war, even though Spain was ready to concede on the major issues.

An astounding first development of the war was Admiral Dewey's naval victory in May 1898 in the rich Spanish islands of the Philippines in the Pacific. American troops, assisted by Filipino rebels, captured the Philippine city of Manila in another dramatic victory. Despite military confusion and many deaths from disease, American forces also easily and quickly overwhelmed the Spanish in Cuba and Puerto Rico.

McKinley's decision to take the Philippines precipitated a long and bitter national debate in Congress and the country over the wisdom and justice of American imperialism. The narrow pro-imperialist victory in the Senate made the Philippines, Guam, and Puerto Rico American colonial possessions. Despite continuing doubts about the wisdom of imperialism, the United States had asserted itself as a new international power, including in East Asia.

Empire and Expansion 473

America's decision to take the Philippines stirred violent resistance from the Filipinos, who had expected independence. The brutal war to defeat the Filipino rebels was longer and costlier than the Spanish-American conflict.

Economic interests, missionary efforts, and European imperialistic intrusion led to growing American involvement in China and East Asia. Hay's Open Door policy helped prevent the European great powers from dismembering and colonizing China. The United States joined the international expedition to suppress the Boxer Rebellion.

McKinley readily defeated Bryan's anti-imperialist campaign in 1900 to win reelection. Assuming the presidency after McKinley's death, Theodore Roosevelt brought a new energy and assertiveness to American foreign policy. When his plans to build a canal in Panama were frustrated by the Colombian Senate, he supported a Panamanian revolt that enabled the strategically important canal to be built. He also revised the Monroe Doctrine by adding a "Roosevelt Corollary" that declared an American right to intervene in Latin America, stirring considerable resentment south of the U.S. border.

Roosevelt successfully negotiated an end to the Russo-Japanese War but angered both parties in the process. The United States and Japan were now competitors in the Pacific. Japanese immigration and Pacific Coast fears of a "yellow peril" added to tensions, but Roosevelt's diplomacy enabled the two countries to maintain a fragile peace.

KEY TERMS

- Great Rapprochement (453)
- McKinley Tariff (454)
- *insurrectos* (454)
- *Maine* (454)
- Teller Amendment (456)
- Rough Riders (457)
- Anti-Imperialist League (459)
- Foraker Act (459)
- *Insular Cases* (460)
- Platt Amendment (460)
- Open Door note (463)
- Boxer Rebellion (465)
- Hay-Pauncefote Treaty (467)
- Roosevelt Corollary (468)
- Root-Takahira agreement (471)

PEOPLE TO KNOW

- Josiah Strong
- Alfred Thayer Mahan
- Richard Olney
- Liliuokalani
- "Butcher" Weyler
- George Dewey
- Emilio Aguinaldo
- William H. Taft
- John Hay
- Theodore "Teddy" Roosevelt

MindTap is a fully online, highly personalized learning experience built upon Cengage Learning content. MindTap combines student learning tools—readings, multimedia, activities, and assessments—into a singular Learning Path that guides students through the course.

Part 5

STRUGGLING FOR JUSTICE AT HOME AND ABROAD

1901–1945

The new century brought astonishing changes to the United States. Victory in the Spanish-American War made it clear that the United States was a world power. Industrialization ushered in giant corporations, sprawling factories, sweatshop labor, and the ubiquitous automobile. A huge wave of immigration was altering the face of the nation, especially the cities, where a majority of Americans lived by 1920. With bigger cities came bigger fears—of crime, vice, poverty, and disease.

Changes of such magnitude raised vexing questions. What role should the United States play in the world? How could the enormous power of industry be controlled? How would the millions of new immigrants make their way in America? What should the country do about poverty, disease, and the continuing plague of racial inequality? All these issues turned on a fundamental point: should government remain narrowly limited in its powers, or did the times require a more potent government that would actively shape society and secure American interests abroad?

The progressive movement represented the first attempt to answer those questions. Reform-minded men and women from all walks of life and from both major parties shared in the progressive crusade for greater government activism. Buoyed by this outlook, Presidents Theodore Roosevelt, William Howard Taft, and Woodrow Wilson enlarged the capacity of government to fight graft, "bust" business trusts, regulate corporations, and promote fair labor practices, child welfare, conservation, and consumer protection. Progressive reformers, convinced that women would bring greater morality to politics, bolstered the decades-long struggle for female suffrage. Women finally secured the vote in 1920 with the ratification of the Nineteenth Amendment.

The progressive-era presidents also challenged America's tradition of isolationism in foreign policy. They felt the country had a moral obligation to spread democracy and an economic opportunity to reap profits in foreign markets. Roosevelt and Taft launched diplomatic initiatives in the Caribbean, Central America, and East Asia. Wilson aspired to "make the world safe for democracy" by rallying support for American intervention in the First World War.

The progressive spirit waned, however, as the United States retreated during the 1920s into what President Harding called "normalcy." Isolationist sentiment revived with a vengeance. Blessed with a booming economy, Americans turned their gaze inward to baseball heroes, radio, jazz, movies, and the first mass-produced American automobile, the Model T Ford. Presidents Harding, Coolidge, and Hoover backed off from the economic regulatory zeal of their predecessors.

"Normalcy" also had a brutal side. Thousands of suspected radicals were jailed or deported in the red scare of 1919 and 1920. Anti-immigrant passions flared until immigration quotas in 1924 squeezed the flow of newcomers to a trickle. Race riots scorched several northern cities in the

Marching for Suffrage Prominent New York socialite Mrs. Herbert Carpenter, bearing an American flag, marches in a parade for women's suffrage on Manhattan's Fifth Avenue, 1912.

summer of 1919, a sign of how embittered race relations had become in the wake of the migration of southern blacks to wartime jobs in northern industry. A reborn Ku Klux Klan staged a comeback, not just in the South but in the North and West as well.

"Normalcy" itself soon proved short lived, a casualty of the stock-market crash of 1929 and the Great Depression that followed. As Americans watched banks fail, businesses collapse, and millions of people lose their jobs, they asked with renewed urgency what role the government should play in rescuing the nation. President Franklin D. Roosevelt's answer was the "New Deal"—an ambitious array of relief programs, public works, and economic regulations that failed to cure the depression but furnished an impressive legacy of social reforms.

Most Americans came to accept an expanded federal governmental role at home under FDR's leadership in the 1930s, but they still clung stubbornly to isolationism. The United States did little in the 1930s to check the rising military aggression of Japan and Germany. By the early 1940s, events forced Americans to reconsider. Once Hitler's Germany had seized control of most of Europe, Roosevelt, who had long opposed the isolationists, found ways to aid a beleaguered Britain. When Japan attacked the American naval base at Pearl Harbor, Hawaii, in December 1941, isolationists at last fell silent. Roosevelt led a stunned but determined nation into the Second World War, and victory in 1945 positioned the United States to assume a commanding position in the postwar world order.

The Great Depression and the Second World War brought to a head a half-century of debate over the role of government and the place of the United States in the world. In the name of a struggle for justice, FDR established a new era of government activism at home and internationalism abroad. The New Deal's legacy set the terms of debate in American political life for the rest of the century.

What if . . . ?

■ What if the Great Depression had never occurred, or had been swiftly overcome, in America and abroad?

■ Would there then have been a New Deal—or a Second World War?

475

Chapter 28

Progressivism and the Republican Roosevelt
1901–1912

When I say I believe in a square deal I do not mean . . . to give every man the best hand. If the cards do not come to any man, or if they do come, and he has not got the power to play them, that is his affair. All I mean is that there shall be no crookedness in the dealing.

THEODORE ROOSEVELT, 1905

Chapter Outline

- The Origins of Progressivism
- Progressive Political Reforms
- Progressive Women at the Forefront
- Roosevelt, Labor, and the Trusts
- Consumer Protection and Conservation
- The Roosevelt Legacy
- The Troubled Presidency of William Howard Taft
- Roosevelt's Progressive Revolt
- Roosevelt's New Nationalism vs. Wilson's New Freedom, 1912
- *Examining the Evidence:* Muller v. Oregon, 1908
- *Makers of America:* The Environmentalists

Nearly 76 million Americans greeted the new century in 1900. Almost one in seven of them was foreign born. In the fourteen years of peace that remained before the Great War of 1914 engulfed the globe, 13 million more migrants would carry their bundles down the gangplanks to the land of promise.

Hardly had the twentieth century dawned on the ethnically and racially mixed American people than they were convulsed by a reform movement, the likes of which the nation had not seen since the 1840s. The new crusaders, who called themselves "progressives," waged war on many evils, notably monopoly, corruption, inefficiency, and social injustice. The progressive army was large, diverse, and widely deployed, but it had a single battle cry: "Strengthen the State." The "real heart of the movement," explained one progressive reformer, was to "use government as an agency of human welfare."

FOCUS QUESTIONS

1. What were the origins and central principles of the progressive movement?
2. What were the primary achievements of progressivism at the local, state, and national levels, and why were female reformers so important to its success?
3. How did President Theodore Roosevelt apply progressive principles to the American economy, and why were consumer protection and conservation such important progressive causes for Roosevelt?
4. How did William Howard Taft's policies split the Republican party and inspire Theodore Roosevelt's progressive revolt?
5. What made the election of 1912 a contest of ideologies as well as of candidates Roosevelt, Taft, and Wilson? Why did Wilson win the election?

CHRONOLOGY

1892	Sierra Club founded	1908	*Muller* v. *Oregon*
			Taft defeats Bryan for presidency
1899	National Consumers League founded	1909	Payne-Aldrich Tariff
1901	Commission system established in Galveston, Texas	1910	Ballinger-Pinchot affair
	Progressive Robert La Follette elected governor of Wisconsin		Washington State grants woman suffrage
	Socialist Party of America formed	1911	Triangle Shirtwaist Company fire
1902	Lincoln Steffens and Ida Tarbell publish muckraking exposés		Standard Oil antitrust case
	Anthracite coal strike		U.S. Steel Corporation antitrust suit
	Newlands Act		California grants woman suffrage
1903	Department of Commerce and Labor established	1912	Taft wins Republican nomination over Roosevelt
	Elkins Act		Wilson defeats Taft and Roosevelt for presidency
	Women's Trade Union League founded		Arizona, Kansas, and Oregon grant woman suffrage
1904	*Northern Securities* case		Children's Bureau established in Department of Labor
	Roosevelt wins election to a first full term as president	1913	Seventeenth Amendment passed (direct election of U.S. senators)
1905	*Lochner* v. *New York*		Federal Reserve Act
1906	Hepburn Act		San Francisco decides to build Hetch Hetchy Reservoir
	Upton Sinclair publishes *The Jungle*	1920	Women's Bureau established in Department of Labor
	Meat Inspection Act		
	Pure Food and Drug Act		
1907	"Roosevelt panic"		

⭐ Progressive Roots

The groundswell of the new reformist wave went far back—to the Greenback Labor party of the 1870s and the Populists of the 1890s, to the mounting unrest throughout the land as grasping industrialists concentrated more and more power in fewer and fewer hands. An outworn philosophy of hands-off individualism seemed increasingly out of place in the modern machine age. Progressive theorists were insisting that society could no longer afford the luxury of a limitless "let-alone" (laissez-faire) policy and a feeble Jeffersonian government. The people, through government, must substitute mastery for drift.

Well before 1900, perceptive politicians and writers had begun to pinpoint targets for the progressive attack. William Jennings Bryan, John Peter Altgeld, and the Populists loudly branded the "bloated trusts" with the stigma of corruption and wrongdoing. In 1894 Henry Demarest Lloyd charged headlong into the Standard Oil Company with his book entitled *Wealth Against Commonwealth*. Eccentric economist Thorstein Veblen assailed the new rich with his prickly pen in *The Theory of the Leisure Class* (1899), a savage attack on "predatory wealth" and "conspicuous consumption."

Other pen-wielding knights likewise entered the fray. The keen-eyed Danish immigrant Jacob A. Riis, a reporter for the *New York Sun*, shocked middle-class Americans in 1890 with *How the Other Half Lives*. His account was a damning indictment of the dirt, disease, vice, and misery of those rat-gnawed human rookeries known as the New York

Room in a Tenement Flat, 1910 Tenement life on the Lower East Side of New York City was exposed by the camera of Jacob Riis, who compiled a large photographic archive of turn-of-the-century urban life. Many families counted themselves lucky to share a single room, no matter how squalid.

slums. Novelist Theodore Dreiser used his blunt prose to batter promoters and profiteers in *The Financier* (1912) and *The Titan* (1914).

Socialists, many of whom were European immigrants inspired by the strong movements for state socialism in the Old World, began to register appreciable strength at the ballot box. High-minded messengers of the **social gospel** drew on their religious beliefs to demand better housing and living conditions for the urban poor. University-based economists urged new reforms modeled on European examples, importing policy ideas from Berlin to Baltimore. Feminists in multiplying numbers added social justice to suffrage on their list of needed reforms. With urban pioneers such as Jane Addams in Chicago and Lillian Wald in New York city blazing the way, women entered the fight to improve the lots of families living and working in the festering cities.

social gospel *A reform movement led by Protestant ministers who used religious doctrine to demand better housing and living conditions for the urban poor. Popular at the turn of the twentieth century, it was closely linked to the settlement-house movement, which brought middle-class, Anglo-American service volunteers into contact with immigrants and working people.*

★ Raking Muck with the Muckrakers

Beginning about 1902 the exposing of evil became a flourishing industry among American publishers. A group of aggressive popular magazines surged to the front, notably *McClure's, Cosmopolitan, Collier's,* and *Everybody's*. Waging fierce circulation wars, these magazines dug deep for the dirt that the public loved to hate. Enterprising editors financed extensive research and encouraged pugnacious writing by their bright young reporters, whom President Roosevelt branded as **muckrakers** in 1906.

Despite presidential scolding, these muckrakers boomed circulation, and some of their most scandalous exposures were published as best-selling books. In 1902 a brilliant New York reporter, Lincoln Steffens, launched a series of articles in *McClure's* titled "The Shame of the Cities." He fearlessly unmasked the corrupt alliance between big business and municipal government. Steffens was followed in the same magazine by Ida M. Tarbell, a pioneering woman journalist who published a devastating factual exposé of the Standard Oil Company. (Her father had been ruined by the oil interests.)

muckrakers *Bright young reporters at the turn of the twentieth century who won this unfavorable moniker from Theodore Roosevelt but boosted the circulations of their magazines by writing exposés of widespread corruption in American society. Their subjects included business manipulation of government, white slavers, child labor, and the illegal deeds of the trusts. These reports helped spur the passage of reform legislation.*

Plucky muckrakers fearlessly tilted their pen-lances at varied targets. They assailed the malpractices of life insurance companies and tariff lobbies. They roasted the beef trust, the "money trust," the railroad barons, and the corrupt amassing of American fortunes. David G. Phillips shocked an already startled nation by his series in *Cosmopolitan* titled "The Treason of the Senate" (1906). He boldly charged that seventy-five of the ninety senators did not represent the people at all but the railroads and trusts.

Some of the most effective fire of the muckrakers was directed at social evils. The ugly list included the immoral "white slave" traffic in women, the rickety slums, and the appalling number of industrial accidents. The sorry subjugation of America's 9 million blacks—of whom 90 percent still lived in the South and one-third were illiterate—was spotlighted in Ray Stannard Baker's *Following the Color Line* (1908). The abuses of child labor were brought luridly to light by John Spargo's *The Bitter Cry of the Children* (1906).

Vendors of potent patent medicines (often heavily spiked with alcohol) likewise came in for bitter criticism. These conscienceless vultures sold incredible quantities of adulterated or habit-forming drugs. Muckraking attacks in *Collier's* were substantiated by Dr. Harvey W. Wiley, chief chemist of the Department of Agriculture, who even performed experiments on himself.

Full of sound and fury, the muckrakers signified much about the nature of the progressive reform movement. They were long on lamentation but stopped short of revolutionary remedies. To right social wrongs they counted on publicity and an aroused public conscience, not drastic political change. They sought not to overthrow capitalism but to cleanse it. The cure for the ills of American democracy, they earnestly believed, was more democracy.

Contending Voices

Debating the Muckrakers

In his muckraker speech (1906), Theodore Roosevelt (1858–1919) chastised the new investigative journalists for being excessively negative and sensational:

"Now, it is very necessary that we should not flinch from seeing what is vile and debasing. There is filth on the floor and it must be scraped up with the muck-rake; and there are times and places where this service is the most needed of all the services that can be performed. But the man who never does anything else, who never thinks or speaks or writes, save of his feats with the muck-rake, speedily becomes, not a help to society, not an incitement to good, but one of the most potent forces for evil."

Years later, leading muckraker Ida Tarbell (1857–1944) offered her own take on Roosevelt's consternation:

"I felt at the time that Mr. Roosevelt had a good deal of the usual conviction of the powerful man in public life that correction should be left to him, a little resentment that a profession outside his own should be stealing his thunder."

> Were the muckrakers ultimately a help or a hindrance to reform?

★ Political Progressivism

The question, "Who were the progressives?" evokes contradictory answers. Progressive reformers included militarists such as Theodore Roosevelt, who thrilled to the strenuous life, as well as pacifists such as Jane Addams, whose loftiest goals included the abolition of war. Female settlement workers hoping to "Americanize" recent immigrants mobilized alongside labor unionists and enlightened businessmen to strengthen the helping hand of government. In diverse ways, and sometimes with divergent aims, the progressives sought to modernize American institutions to achieve two chief goals: to use the state to curb monopoly power and to improve the common person's conditions of life and labor. Progressives emerged in both major parties, in all regions, and at all levels of government. The truth is that progressivism was less a monolithic minority movement and more a broadly dispersed majority mood.

One of the first objectives of progressives was to regain the power that had slipped from the hands of the people into those of the "interests." These ardent reformers pushed for direct primary elections so as to undercut power-hungry party bosses. They favored the **initiative** so that voters could directly propose legislation themselves, thus bypassing the boss-bought state legislatures. Progressives also agitated for the **referendum**, which would give the people the right to reject laws pushed through compliant legislatures by free-spending agents of big business. The **recall** would enable the voters to remove faithless elected officials who had been bribed

initiative *A progressive reform measure allowing voters to petition to have a law placed on the general ballot. Like the referendum and recall, it brought democracy directly "to the people" and helped foster a shift toward interest group politics and away from old political "machines."*

referendum *A progressive reform procedure allowing voters to place a bill on the ballot for final approval, even after being passed by the legislature.*

recall *A progressive ballot procedure allowing voters to remove elected officials from office.*

> The suffrage campaign of the early twentieth century benefited from a new generation of women who considered themselves "feminists." At a mass meeting in New York in 1914, Marie Jenny Howe (1870–1934), a minister by training as well as a prominent early feminist, proclaimed:
>
> "We intend simply to be ourselves, not just our little female selves, but our whole big human selves."

Australian ballot *A system that allows voters privacy in marking their ballot choices. Developed in Australia in the 1850s, it was introduced to the United States during the progressive era to help counteract boss rule.*

by bosses or lobbyists. The secret **Australian ballot** was likewise introduced in the states to counteract boss rule.

Direct election of U.S. senators became a favorite goal of progressives, especially after muckrakers had exposed the scandalous intimacy between greedy corporations and Congress. By 1900 the Senate had so many rich men that it was often sneered at as the "Millionaires' Club." Direct election was finally achieved by the Seventeenth Amendment to the Constitution, approved in 1913 (see the Appendix). But the expected improvement in caliber was slow in coming.

Woman suffrage, the goal of female reformers for many decades, likewise received powerful new support from the progressives early in the 1900s. The political reformers believed that women's votes would elevate the political tone, and the foes of the saloon felt that they could count on the support of enfranchised females. Many of the states, especially the more liberal ones in the West like Washington, California, and Oregon, gradually extended the vote to women. But by 1910 nationwide female suffrage was still a decade away.

★ Progressivism in the Cities and States

Progressives scored some of their most impressive gains in the cities. Frustrated by the inefficiency and corruption of machine-oiled city government, many localities followed the pioneering example of Galveston, Texas. In 1901 it had appointed expert-staffed commissions to manage urban affairs. Other communities adopted the city manager system, also designed to take politics out of municipal administration. Some of these "reforms" obviously valued efficiency more highly than democracy, as control of civic affairs was further removed from the people's hands.

Urban reformers likewise attacked "slumlords," juvenile delinquency, and wide-open prostitution (vice-at-a-price), which flourished in red-light districts unchallenged by bribed police. Public-spirited Americans looked to British and German cities for lessons on how to clean up their water supplies, light their streets, and run their trolley cars. The vogue of public ownership of utilities swept the nation as local governments tried to halt the corrupt sale of franchises.

Progressivism naturally bubbled up to the state level, notably in Wisconsin, which became a yeasty laboratory of reform. Pompadoured Governor Robert M. ("Fighting Bob") La Follette emerged as the most militant of the progressive Republican leaders. Elected governor in 1901, he waged a desperate fight with entrenched monopolies to win control of Wisconsin from crooked lumber and railroad interests and return it to the people. He also perfected a scheme for regulating public utilities while laboring in close association with experts on the faculty of the University of Wisconsin at Madison.

Other states marched steadily toward the progressive camp, as they undertook to regulate railroads and trusts, chiefly through public utilities commissions. Oregon was not far behind Wisconsin, and California made giant boot strides under the stocky Hiram W. Johnson. Elected Republican governor in 1910, this dynamic prosecutor of grafters helped break the dominant grip of the Southern Pacific Railroad on California politics and then, like La Follette, set up a political machine of his own.

★ Progressive Women

Women proved themselves an indispensable part of the progressive army. A crucial focus for women's activism was the settlement house movement (see p. 410). At a time when women could neither vote nor hold political office, settlement houses offered a side door to public life. They exposed middle-class women to the numerous problems plaguing

American cities and gave them the skill and confidence to tackle those evils. The women's club movement also turned from literary self-improvement to engagement with social issues and current events. "Dante has been dead for several centuries," observed the president of the General Federation of Women's Clubs in 1904. "I think it is time that we dropped the study of his *Inferno* and turned our attention to our own."

Nineteenth-century notions of "separate spheres" dictated that a woman's place was in the home, so most female progressives defended their new activities as an extension—not a rejection—of the traditional roles of wife and mother. Thus they were often drawn to moral and "maternal" issues such as keeping children out of sweltering sweatshops or ensuring that only safe food products found their way to the family table. Female activists agitated through organizations such as the National Consumers League (1899) and the Women's Trade Union League (1903) and through two new federal agencies, the Children's Bureau (1912) and the Women's Bureau (1920), both in the Department of Labor.

Campaigns for factory reform and temperance particularly attracted women foot soldiers. Unsafe and unsanitary sweatshops—factories where workers toiled long hours for low wages—were a public scandal in many cities. Florence Kelley, a former resident of Jane Addams's Hull House, became the state of Illinois's first chief factory inspector and one of the leading advocates for improved factory conditions. In 1899 Kelley took control of the newly founded National Consumers League, which mobilized female consumers to pressure for laws safeguarding women and children in the workplace. In the landmark case *Muller v. Oregon* (1908), crusading attorney Louis D. Brandeis persuaded the Supreme Court to accept the constitutionality of laws protecting women workers by presenting evidence of the harmful effects of factory labor on women's bodies. Although this argument calling for special protection for women seemed discriminatory by later standards and closed many "male" jobs to women, progressives at the time hailed Brandeis's achievement as a triumph. The American welfare state that emerged from female activism focused more on protecting women and children than on granting benefits to everyone, as was the case in much of western Europe, with its stronger labor overtones.

Muller v. Oregon (1908) *A landmark Supreme Court case in which crusading attorney (and future Supreme Court justice) Louis D. Brandeis persuaded the Supreme Court to accept the constitutionality of limiting the hours of women workers. Coming on the heels of* Lochner v. New York, *it established a different standard for male and female workers.*

The Wages of Negligence Family members arrive at the morgue to identify the bodies of victims of the Triangle Shirtwaist Company fire in 1911. Outrage over this calamity galvanized a generation of reformers to fight for better workplace safety rules.

Lochner v. New York (1905) *A setback for labor reformers, this Supreme Court decision invalidated a state law establishing a ten-hour day for bakers. It held that the "right to free contract" was implicit in the due process clause of the Fourteenth Amendment.*

Crusaders for these humane measures did not always have smooth sailing. One dismaying setback came in 1905, when the Supreme Court in *Lochner v. New York* invalidated a New York law establishing a ten-hour day for bakers. Yet the reformist progressive wave finally washed up into the judiciary, and in 1917 the Court upheld a ten-hour law for factory workers.

Laws regulating factories were worthless if not enforced, a truth horribly demonstrated by a lethal fire in 1911 at the Triangle Shirtwaist Company in New York City. Locked doors and other flagrant violations of the fire code turned the factory into a death trap, incinerating one hundred forty-six workers, most of them young immigrant women. Lashed by the public outcry, including a massive strike of women in the needle trades, the New York legislature passed much stronger laws regulating the hours and conditions of sweatshop toil. By 1917 thirty states had put workers' compensation laws on their books, providing insurance to workers injured in industrial accidents. Gradually, the concept of the employer's responsibility to society was replacing the old dog-eat-dog philosophy of unregulated free enterprise.

Corner saloons naturally attracted the ire and fire of progressives, especially because the sale of alcohol was often intimately connected with prostitution and voter corruption. By 1900 cities such as New York and San Francisco had one saloon for about every two hundred people. Antiliquor campaigners received powerful support from several militant organizations, notably the Woman's Christian Temperance Union (WCTU). Founder Frances E. Willard, who would fall on her knees in prayer on saloon floors, mobilized nearly 1 million women to "make the world homelike" and built the WCTU into the largest organization of women in the world. She found a vigorous ally in the Anti-Saloon League, which was aggressive, well organized, and well financed.

Caught up in the crusade, some states and counties passed "dry" laws to control, restrict, or abolish alcohol. The big cities were generally "wet," for they had a large immigrant vote accustomed in the Old Country to the free flow of wine and beer. When World War I erupted in 1914, nearly one-half of the population lived in "dry" territory. Demon Rum was groggy and about to be floored—temporarily—by the Eighteenth Amendment in 1919.

★ TR's Square Deal for Labor

Theodore Roosevelt, although something of an imperialistic busybody abroad, was touched by the progressive wave at home. Like other reformers, he feared that the "public interest" was being submerged in the drifting seas of indifference. Everybody's interest was nobody's interest. Roosevelt decided to make it his. His sportsman's instincts spurred him into demanding a "square deal" for capital, labor, and the public at large. Broadly speaking, his program embraced three C's: control of the corporations, consumer protection, and conservation of natural resources.

The Square Deal for labor received its acid test in 1902, when a crippling strike broke out in the anthracite coal mines of Pennsylvania. Some 140,000 sooty workers, many of them illiterate immigrants, had long been frightfully exploited and accident-plagued. They demanded, among other improvements, a 20 percent increase in pay and a reduction of the working day from ten to nine hours.

Unsympathetic mine owners, confident that a chilled public would react against the miners, refused to arbitrate or even negotiate. One of their spokesmen, multimillionaire George F. Baer, wrote that workers would be cared for "not by the labor agitators, but by the Christian men to whom God in his infinite wisdom has given the control of the property interests of this country."

As coal supplies dwindled, factories and schools were forced to shut down, and even hospitals felt the icy grip of winter. Profoundly annoyed by the "extraordinary stupidity and bad temper" of the "wooden-headed" mine owners, Roosevelt threatened to seize the mines and operate them with federal troops. Faced with this first-time-ever threat to use federal bayonets against capital, rather than labor, the owners grudgingly consented to arbitration. A compromise decision ultimately gave the miners a 10 percent pay boost and a working day of nine hours. But their union was not officially recognized as a bargaining agent.

Keenly aware of the mounting antagonisms between capital and labor, Roosevelt urged Congress to create the new Department of Commerce and Labor. This goal was achieved in 1903. (Ten years later the agency was split in two.) An important arm of the new cabinet agency was the Bureau of Corporations, which was authorized to probe businesses engaged in interstate commerce. The bureau was highly useful in helping to break the stranglehold of monopoly and in clearing the road for the era of "trustbusting."

★ TR Corrals the Corporations

The sprawling railroad octopus sorely needed restraint. The Interstate Commerce Commission, created in 1887 as a feeble sop to the public, had proved woefully inadequate. Railroad barons could simply appeal the commission's decisions on rates to the federal courts—a process that might take ten years.

Spurred by the former-cowboy president, Congress passed effective railroad legislation, beginning with the **Elkins Act** of 1903. This curb was aimed primarily at the rebate evil. Heavy fines could now be imposed both on the railroads that gave rebates and on the shippers that accepted them.

Still more effective was the Hepburn Act of 1906. Free passes, with their hint of bribery, were severely restricted. The once-infantile Interstate Commerce Commission was expanded, and its reach was extended to include express companies, sleeping-car companies, and pipelines. For the first time, the commission was given real molars when it was authorized to nullify existing shipping rates and stipulate maximum rates.

Railroads also provided Roosevelt with an opportunity to brandish his antitrust bludgeon. *Trusts* had come to be a fighting word in the progressive era. TR was determined to respond to the public outcry against the trusts by curbing but not eliminating them. He believed that there were "good" trusts with public consciences and "bad" trusts greedy for power, and that the goal was not to throw out the baby with the bathwater.

Roosevelt as a trustbuster first burst into the headlines in 1902 with an attack on the Northern Securities Company, a railroad holding company organized by financial titan J. P. Morgan and empire builder James J. Hill. These Napoleonic moguls of money sought to achieve a virtual monopoly of the railroads in the Northwest. Roosevelt was therefore challenging the most regal potentates of the industrial aristocracy.

The railway promoters appealed to the Supreme Court, which in 1904 upheld Roosevelt's antitrust suit and ordered the Northern Securities Company to be dissolved. The *Northern Securities* decision jolted Wall Street and angered big business but greatly enhanced Roosevelt's reputation as a trust smasher. Roosevelt's big stick crashed down on other giant monopolies, as he initiated over forty legal proceedings against the beef, sugar, fertilizer, harvester, and other monopolies.

Much mythology has inflated Roosevelt's reputation as a trustbuster. The Rough Rider understood the political popularity of monopoly smashing, but he did not consider it sound economic policy. Combination and integration, he felt, were the hallmarks of the age, and to try to stem the tide of economic progress by political means he considered the rankest folly. Bigness was not necessarily badness, so why punish success? Roosevelt's real purpose in assaulting the Goliaths of industry was to prove conclusively that the government, not private business, ruled the country. He believed in regulating, not fragmenting, the big business combines. The threat of dissolution, he felt, might make the sultans of the smokestacks more amenable to federal regulation—and it did.

In truth, Roosevelt never swung his trust-crushing stick with maximum force. His successor, William Howard Taft, actually "busted" more trusts than TR did. In one celebrated instance in 1907, Roosevelt even gave his personal blessing to J.P. Morgan's plan to have the U.S. Steel Corporation absorb the Tennessee Coal and Iron Company without fear of antitrust reprisals. When Taft then launched a suit against United States Steel in 1911, the political reaction from TR was explosive (see p. 490).

Elkins Act (1903) *Law passed by Congress to impose penalties on railroads that offered rebates and customers who accepted them. The law strengthened the Interstate Commerce Act of 1887. The Hepburn Act of 1906 added free passes to the list of railroad no-no's.*

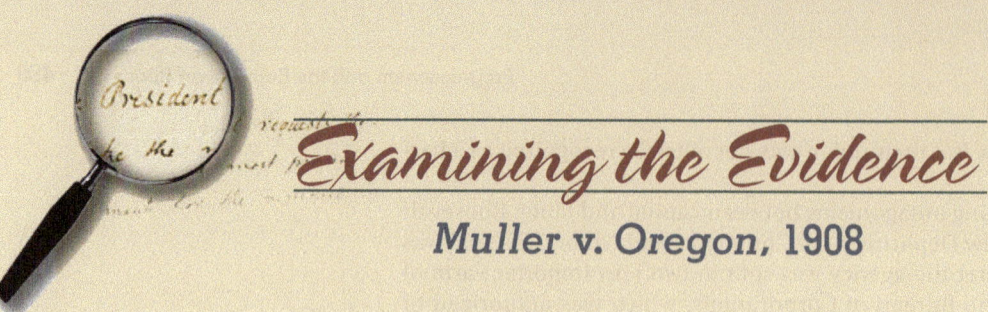

Examining the Evidence

Muller v. Oregon, 1908

Court records provide notably fruitful sources for historians. They not only tell often-colorful stories about the lives of ordinary men and women caught up in the legal system; they also by their very nature testify to the norms and values that lawyers employ to make their cases and that judges invoke to explain their decisions. The case of *Muller* v. *Oregon* (see p. 481) is especially instructive on both counts. The official Supreme Court records tell how on September 4, 1905, Joe Haselbock, a supervisor in Curt Muller's Grand Laundry in Portland, Oregon, asked an employee, Mrs. E. Gotcher, to remain after hours to do an extra load of laundry. That request violated Oregon's law prohibiting women from working more than ten hours per day. Mrs. Gotcher later complained to the authorities, and Muller was fined $10.

Muller refused to pay and took his case all the way to the U.S. Supreme Court. In its landmark decision (below), the Court upheld the constitutionality of the Oregon statute, and Muller at last had to cough up his fine.

1. On what grounds did the Court justify its ruling?
2. What does Justice David J. Brewer's argument on behalf of the Court's decision suggest about the cultural identity and social role of women in early-twentieth-century American society?
3. Was Brewer's ruling really a "progressive" one? Why might progressives in the early twentieth century have regarded *Muller* as a great step forward, while Americans of the early twenty-first century might not?

(208 U.S. 412)
CURT MULLER, Plff. in Err.,
v.
STATE OF OREGON.

... That woman's physical structure and the performance of material functions place her at a disadvantage in the struggle for subsistence is obvious. This is especially true when the burdens of motherhood are upon her.... and as healthy mothers are essential to vigorous offspring, the physical well-being of woman becomes an object of public interest and care in order to preserve the strength and vigor of the race.

Still again, history discloses the fact that woman has always been dependent upon man. He established his control at the outset by superior physical strength, and this control in various forms, with diminishing intensity, has continued to the present.... It is still true that in the struggle for subsistence she is not an equal competitor with her brother.... Differentiated by these matters from the other sex, she is properly placed in a class by herself, and legislation designed for her protection may be sustained, even when like legislation is not necessary for men, and could not be sustained. It is impossible to close one's eyes to the fact that she still looks to her brother and depends upon him.... The two sexes differ in structure of body, in the functions to be performed by each, in the amount of physical strength, in the capacity for long continued labor, particularly when done standing, the influence of vigorous health upon the future well-being of the race, the self-reliance which enables one to assert full rights, and in the capacity to maintain the struggle for subsistence. This difference justifies a difference in legislation, and upholds that which is designed to compensate for some of the burdens which rest upon her.

We have not referred in this discussion to the denial of the elective franchise in the state of Oregon, for while that may disclose a lack of political equality in all things with her brother, that is not of itself decisive. The reason runs deeper, and rests in the inherent difference between the two sexes, and in the different functions in life which they perform....

★ Caring for the Consumer

Roosevelt backed a noteworthy measure in 1906 that benefited both corporations and consumers. Big meatpackers were being shut out of certain European markets because some American meat had been found to be tainted. Foreign governments were threatening to ban all American meat imports.

At the same time, American consumers hungered for safer products. Their appetite for reform was whetted by Upton Sinclair's sensational novel *The Jungle*, published in 1906. Sinclair, a dedicated Socialist, intended his revolting tract to focus attention on the plight of the workers in the big meat-canning factories, but instead he appalled the public with his description of disgustingly unsanitary food products. (As he put it, he aimed for the nation's heart but hit its stomach.) The book described in noxious detail the filth, disease, and putrefaction in Chicago's damp, ill-ventilated slaughterhouses. A cynical jingle of the time ran:

> *Mary had a little lamb,*
> *And when she saw it sicken,*
> *She shipped it off to Packingtown,*
> *And now it's labeled chicken.*

Backed by a nauseated public, Roosevelt induced Congress to pass the **Meat Inspection Act** of 1906. The act decreed that the preparation of meat shipped over state lines would be subject to federal inspection from corral to can. The largest packers eventually accepted the act as an opportunity to drive their smaller, fly-by-night competitors out of business. At the same time, they could receive the government's seal of approval on their exports. As a companion to the Meat Inspection Act, the **Pure Food and Drug Act** of 1906 was designed to prevent the adulteration and mislabeling of foods and pharmaceuticals.

★ Earth Control

Wasteful Americans, assuming that their natural resources were inexhaustible, had looted and polluted their incomparable domain with unparalleled speed and greed. Western ranchers and timber men were especially eager to accelerate the destructive process, for they panted to build up the country, and the environmental consequences be hanged. But even before the end of the nineteenth century, far-visioned leaders saw that such a squandering of the nation's birthright would have to be halted or America would sink from resource richness to despoiled dearth.

A first serious step toward conservation was the Forest Reserve Act of 1891, authorizing the president to set aside public forest land as national forests and other reserves. Under this statute some 46 million acres of magnificent trees were rescued from the lumberman's saw in the 1890s and preserved for posterity.

A new day in the history of conservation dawned with Roosevelt (see "Makers of America: The Environmentalists," p. 486). Huntsman, naturalist, rancher, lover of the great outdoors, he was appalled by the pillaging of timber and mineral resources. Other dedicated conservationists, notably Gifford Pinchot, head of the federal Division of Forestry, had broken important ground before him. But Roosevelt seized the banner of leadership and charged into the fray with all the weight of his prestige, his energy, his firsthand knowledge, and his slashing invective.

Congress responded to the whip of the Rough Rider by passing the Newlands Act of 1902, which authorized Washington to use funds from the sale of public lands in the sun-baked western states for irrigation projects. Settlers repaid the cost of reclamation from their now-productive soil, and the money was put into a revolving fund to finance more

---

Meat Inspection Act (1906) *A law passed by Congress to subject meat shipped over state lines to federal inspection. The publication of Upton Sinclair's novel* The Jungle *earlier that year so disgusted American consumers with its description of conditions in slaughterhouses and meatpacking plants that it mobilized public support for government action.*

Pure Food and Drug Act (1906) *A law passed by Congress to inspect and regulate the labeling of all foods and pharmaceuticals intended for human consumption. This legislation, and additional provisions passed in 1911 to strengthen it, aimed particularly at the patent medicine industry. The more comprehensive Food, Drug, and Cosmetic Act of 1938 largely replaced this legislation.*

In his annual message to Congress in 1907, Roosevelt declared prophetically:

"We are prone to speak of the resources of this country as inexhaustible; this is not so. The mineral wealth of the country, the coal, iron, oil, gas, and the like, does not reproduce itself, and therefore is certain to be exhausted ultimately; and wastefulness in dealing with it today means that our descendants will feel the exhaustion a generation or two before they otherwise would."

Makers of America

The Environmentalists

Humans have long been awed by nature, but they have also yearned to be its masters. The earliest European colonists saw North America as a "howling wilderness" and toiled mightily with ax and plow to tame it. By the mid-nineteenth century, Americans commanded powerful new technologies that promised unbridled dominion over the natural world. Only then did voices begin to be heard in defense of the wounded earth—the first faint stirrings of what would come to be called "environmentalism."

In a pattern that would often be repeated, nature's earliest defenders tended to be well-off townsfolk and city dwellers such as Henry David Thoreau and Ralph Waldo Emerson. The Americans most likely to appreciate the value of pristine wilderness, it seemed, were those who had ceased to struggle against it. For the loggers, miners, and farmers who continued to sweat their living out of nature's grudging embrace, concern for environmental niceties often seemed like the sanctimonious piety of a privileged elite.

By the dawn of the twentieth century, many genteel, urban Americans had come to romanticize their pioneer forebears. Preservationists such as John Muir waxed lyrical about the mystic allure of unspoiled nature. Seizing the popular mood, Theodore Roosevelt deliberately constructed an image of himself as a manly outdoorsman, and as president he greatly expanded the system of national forests.

But Roosevelt was also a pioneer of another sort—as a prominent promoter of the progressive-era "conservation" movement, composed of a loose coalition of scientists, bureaucrats, and businesspeople dependent on stable access to America's rich endowment of natural resources. Progressive conservationists believed that nature must be neither uncritically reverenced nor wastefully exploited, but must instead be efficiently utilized. Thus the same TR who admired the wonders of Yosemite Valley in the company of John Muir also promoted the "rational use" philosophy that justified the systematic harvesting of millions of trees and the drowning of vast river valleys behind massive dams. This attitude toward nature triumphed in the New Deal era of the 1930s, when the federal government initiated colossal projects that undertook nothing less than reengineering the face of the continent—including the Tennessee Valley Authority, the Soil Conservation Service, and the Shelterbelt tree planting on the Great Plains.

The rise of ecological science in the post–World War II era fundamentally changed the debate about the relation of nature to civilization. Ecologists charged that the apparent "rationality" of the earlier conservationists dangerously neglected the stunningly complex interrelationships that linked together seemingly unrelated organisms—and to the perils of tampering even slightly with the delicate biological fabrics that nature had taken millennia to weave. Rachel Carson helped to popularize this new outlook in her sensational 1962 exposé, *Silent Spring*, about the far-reaching effects of pesticides on birds, plants, and animals—including humans.

The advent of ecological studies coincided with a revival of preservationist sentiment, especially in the suburbs, where Americans increasingly dwelled. Membership in environmental organizations such as the Sierra Club and the Audubon Society soared, as a generation infatuated with nature demanded a clean and green world. The first celebration of Earth Day on April 22, 1970 marked the maturation of modern-day environmentalism, which wedded scientific analysis with respect for nature's majesty. That same year saw the creation of the federal Environmental Protection Agency (EPA), soon to be followed by the Endangered Species Act and other legislation designed to regulate the relationship between humans and nature.

At the outset of the twenty-first century, developments like global warming served dramatic notice that planet Earth was an ecological system that did not recognize national boundaries. Yet while Americans took pride in the efforts they had made to clean up their own turf, who were they, having long since consumed their timberlands and tamed their free-flowing waters, to tell the Brazilians that they should not cut down their Amazon forest or the Chinese that they should not dam their rivers? For the peoples of the developing world, struggling to match America's standard of living, environmentalists often seemed like spoiled spoilers, preaching the same privileged pieties that had infuriated generations of working Americans.

Pinchots in the Great Outdoors Gifford Pinchot, the father of the modern Forest Service, poses with his family of fellow nature-lovers. His wife Cornelia was a driven feminist, political activist, and, as a passionate gardener, a proponent in her own right of people's "rational use" of the natural world.

such enterprises. Thanks to this epochal legislation, dozens of dams were thrown across virtually every major western river in the ensuing decades.

Roosevelt pined to preserve the nation's shrinking forests. By 1900 only about a quarter of the once-vast virgin timberlands remained standing. Lumbermen had already logged off most of the first-growth timber from Maine to Michigan, and the sharp thud of their axes was beginning to split the silence in the great fir forests of the Pacific slope. Roosevelt proceeded to set aside in federal reserves some 125 million acres, or almost three times the acreage thus saved from the saw by his three predecessors. He similarly earmarked millions of acres of coal deposits, as well as water resources useful for irrigation and power.

Conservation may have been Roosevelt's most enduring tangible achievement. He was buoyed in this effort by an upwelling national mood of concern about the disappearance of the frontier. An increasingly citified people worried that too much civilization might not be good for the national soul. City dwellers snapped up Jack London's *Call of the Wild* (1903) and other books about nature, and urban youngsters made the outdoor-oriented Boy Scouts of America the country's largest youth organization. Middle-class clubwomen raised money for nature preserves and organized the Massachusetts—and later National—Audubon Society to save wild native birds by banning the use of plumes to ornament fashionable ladies' hats. The Sierra Club, founded in 1892, dedicated itself to preserving the wildness of the western landscape.

The preservationists lost a major battle in 1913 when the federal government allowed the city of San Francisco to build a dam for its municipal water supply in the spectacular, high-walled **Hetch Hetchy Valley** in Yosemite National Park. The Hetch Hetchy controversy laid bare a deep division among conservationists that persists to the present day. To the preservationists of the Sierra Club, including famed naturalist John Muir, Hetch Hetchy was a "temple" of nature that should be held inviolable by the civilizing hand of humanity. But other conservationists, including President Roosevelt and his chief forester, Gifford Pinchot, wanted to *use* the nation's natural endowment intelligently rather than lock it away as wilderness. With a policy of "multiple-use resource management," they sought to combine recreation, sustained-yield logging, watershed protection, and summer stock grazing on the same expanse of federal land.

At first many westerners resisted the federal management of natural resources, but they soon learned how to take advantage of new agencies like the Forest Service and especially the Bureau of Reclamation. The largest ranches and timber companies in particular figured out how to work hand in glove with federal conservation programs devoted to the rational, large-scale, and long-term use of natural resources. The one-man-and-a-mule logger or the one-man-and-a-dog sheepherder had little clout in the new resources bureaucracy. Single-person enterprises were shouldered aside, in the interest of efficiency, by the combined bulk of big business and big government.

High Point for Conservation Roosevelt and famed naturalist-conservationist John Muir visit Glacier Point, on the rim of Yosemite Valley, California. In the distance is Yosemite Falls; a few feet behind Roosevelt is a sheer drop of 3,254 feet.

Hetch Hetchy Valley *The federal government allowed the city of San Francisco to build a dam here in 1913. This was a blow to preservationists, who wished to protect the Yosemite National Park, where the dam was located.*

⭐ The Rough Rider Thunders Out

Roosevelt was handily elected president in 1904 and entered his new term buoyed by his enormous personal popularity. Yet the conservative Republican bosses grew increasingly restive as Roosevelt in his second term called ever more loudly for regulating corporations, taxing incomes, and protecting workers. Roosevelt, meanwhile, had

Baby, Kiss Papa Good-bye Theodore Roosevelt leaves his baby, "My Policies," in the hands of his chosen successor, William Howard Taft. Friction between Taft and Roosevelt would soon erupt, however, prompting Roosevelt to return to politics and challenge Taft for the presidency.

partly defanged himself after his election in 1904 by announcing that under no circumstances would he be a candidate for a third term.

Roosevelt suffered a sharp setback in 1907, when a short but punishing panic descended on Wall Street. The financial flurry featured frightened "runs" on banks, suicides, and criminal indictments against speculators. The financial world hastened to blame Roosevelt for the storm. It cried that this "quack" had unsettled industry with his boat-rocking tactics and branded the current distress the "Roosevelt panic." The hot-tempered president angrily lashed back at his critics when he accused "certain malefactors of great wealth" of having deliberately engineered the crisis to force the government to relax its assaults on trusts.

Still warmly popular in 1908, Roosevelt could easily have won a second presidential nomination and almost certainly the election. But he felt bound by his impulsive postelection promise after his victory in 1904. The departing president thus naturally sought a successor who would carry out "my policies." The man of his choice was amiable and ample-girthed William Howard Taft, his secretary of war and a mild progressive.

As the heir apparent, Taft had often been called upon in Roosevelt's absence to "sit on the lid"—all 350 pounds of him. At the Republican convention of 1908 in Chicago, Roosevelt used his control of the party machinery—the "steamroller"—to push through Taft's nomination on the first ballot. Three weeks later, in mile-high Denver in the heart of silver country, the Democrats again nominated twice-beaten William Jennings Bryan.

The dull campaign of 1908 featured the rotund Taft and the now-balding "Boy Orator" both trying to don the progressive Roosevelt mantle. The solid Judge Taft read cut-and-dried speeches, while Bryan griped that Roosevelt had stolen his policies from the Bryanite camp. A majority of voters chose stability with Roosevelt-endorsed Taft, who polled 321 electoral votes to 162 for Bryan. The victor's popular count was 7,675,320 to 6,412,294. The election's only surprise came from the Socialists, who amassed 420,793 votes for Eugene V. Debs, the hero of the Pullman strike of 1894 (see pp. 444–445).

Roosevelt, ever in the limelight, left soon after the election for a lion hunt in Africa. His numerous enemies clinked glasses while toasting "Health to the lions," and a few irreverently prayed that some big cat would "do its duty." But TR survived, still bursting with energy at the age of fifty-one in 1909.

Roosevelt was branded by his adversaries as a wild-eyed radical, but his reputation as an eater of errant industrialists now seems inflated. He fought many a sham battle, and the number of laws that he inspired was certainly not in proportion to the amount of noise he emitted. He was often under attack from the reigning business lords, but the more enlightened of them knew that they had a friend in the White House. Roosevelt should be remembered first and foremost as the cowboy who started to tame the bucking bronco of adolescent capitalism, thus ensuring it a long adult life.

TR's enthusiasm and perpetual youthfulness, like an overgrown Boy Scout's, appealed to the young of all ages. "You must always remember," a British diplomat cautioned his colleagues, "that the president is about six." He served as a political lightning rod to protect capitalists against popular indignation—and against socialism, which Roosevelt regarded as "ominous." He strenuously sought the middle road between unbridled individualism and paternalistic collectivism. His conservation crusade, which tried to mediate between the romantic wilderness-preservationists and the rapacious resource-predators, was probably his most typical and his most lasting achievement.

Several other contributions of Roosevelt lasted beyond his presidency. First, he greatly enlarged the power and prestige of the presidential office—and masterfully developed the technique of using the big stick of publicity as a political bludgeon. Second, he helped shape the progressive movement and beyond it the liberal reform campaigns later in the century. His Square Deal, in a sense, was the grandfather of the New Deal later launched by his fifth cousin, Franklin D. Roosevelt. Finally, to a greater degree than any of his predecessors, TR opened the eyes of Americans to the fact that they shared the world with other nations. As a great power, they had fallen heir to great responsibilities—and had been seized by great ambitions—from which there was no escaping.

★ Taft: A Round Peg in a Square Hole

William Howard Taft, with his ruddy complexion and upturned mustache, at first inspired widespread confidence. "Everybody loves a fat man," the saying goes, and the jovial Taft, with "mirthquakes" of laughter bubbling up from his abundant abdomen, was personally popular. He had graduated second in his class at Yale and established an admirable reputation as a lawyer and judge, though he was widely regarded as hostile to labor unions. He had served as a trusted administrator and troubleshooter under Roosevelt—in the Philippines, at home, and in Cuba.

But "good old Will" suffered from lethal political handicaps. Roosevelt had led the conflicting elements of the Republican party by the sheer force of his personality. Taft, in contrast, had none of the arts of a dashing political leader and none of Roosevelt's zest for the fray. Recoiling from the clamor of controversy, he generally adopted an attitude of passivity toward Congress. He was a poor judge of public opinion, and his candor made him a chronic victim of "foot-in-mouth" disease.

"Peaceful Bill" was no doubt a mild progressive, but at heart he was more wedded to the status quo than to change. Significantly, his cabinet did not contain a single representative of the party's "insurgent" wing, which was on fire for reform of current abuses, especially the tariff.

★ The Dollar Goes Abroad as a Diplomat

Though ordinarily lethargic, Taft bestirred himself to use the lever of American investments to boost American political interests abroad. Washington warmly encouraged Wall Street bankers to sluice their surplus dollars into foreign areas of strategic concern to the United States. New York bankers would thus strengthen American defenses and foreign policies while bringing further prosperity to their homeland—and to themselves. The almighty dollar thereby supplanted the big stick.

China's Manchuria was the object of Taft's most spectacular effort to practice **dollar diplomacy**. Newly ambitious Japan and imperialistic Russia, recent foes, controlled the railroads of this strategic province. President Taft saw in the Manchurian railway monopoly a possible slamming of the Open Door in the faces of U.S. merchants. But Secretary of State Philander Knox's attempt in 1909 to persuade U.S. investors to buy the Manchurian railroads and then turn them over to China ran into blunt Japanese and Russian opposition. Taft was showered with ridicule.

Another dangerous new trouble spot was the revolution-riddled Caribbean—now virtually a Yankee lake. Hoping to head off trouble, Washington urged Wall Street bankers to pump dollars into the financial vacuums in Honduras and Haiti. Again necessity was the mother of armed Caribbean intervention. Sporadic disorders in palm-fronded Cuba, Honduras, and the Dominican Republic brought American forces to these countries to restore order and protect American investments. A revolutionary upheaval in Nicaragua, partly fomented by American interests, resulted in the landing of twenty-five hundred Marines in 1912. The Marines remained in Nicaragua for thirteen years (see Map 29.1 on p. 499).

dollar diplomacy Name applied by President Taft's critics to the policy of supporting U.S. investments and political interests abroad. First applied to the financing of railways in China after 1909, the policy then spread to Haiti, Honduras, and Nicaragua. President Woodrow Wilson disavowed the practice, but his administration undertook comparable acts of intervention in support of U.S. business interests, especially in Latin America.

Taft the Trustbuster

Taft managed to gain some fame as a smasher of monopolies. The ironic truth is that the colorless Taft brought ninety suits against the trusts during his four years in office, compared with some forty-four for Roosevelt in seven and a half years.

The most sensational judicial actions during the Taft regime came in 1911. In that year the Supreme Court ordered dissolution of the mighty Standard Oil Company, which was judged to be a combination in restraint of trade in violation of the Sherman Anti-Trust Act of 1890. At the same time the Court handed down its famous "rule of reason." This doctrine held that only those combinations that "unreasonably" restrained trade were illegal. This fine-point proviso ripped a huge hole in the government's antitrust net.

Even more explosively, in 1911 Taft decided to press an antitrust suit against the U.S. Steel Corporation. This initiative infuriated Roosevelt, who had personally been involved in one of the mergers that prompted the suit. Once Roosevelt's protégé, President Taft was increasingly taking on the role of his antagonist. The stage was being set for a bruising confrontation.

Taft Splits the Republican Party

Lowering the barriers of the formidable protective tariff—the "Mother of Trusts"—was high on the agenda of the progressive members of the Republican party, and they at first thought they had a friend and ally in Taft. When the president called Congress into special session in March 1909, the House passed a moderately reductive bill. But senatorial reactionaries, led by Senator Nelson Aldrich of Rhode Island, tacked on hundreds of upward tariff revisions. Only such items as hides, sea moss, and canary seed were left on the duty-free list.

Taft nevertheless signed the **Payne-Aldrich Bill**, thus betraying his campaign promises and outraging the progressive wing of his party, heavily drawn from the Midwest. Taft rubbed salt in the wound by proclaiming it "the best bill that the Republican party ever passed."

Taft revealed a further knack for shooting himself in the foot in his handling of conservation. The portly president was a dedicated conservationist, and his contributions—like the establishment of the Bureau of Mines to control mineral resources—actually equaled or surpassed those of Roosevelt. But his praiseworthy accomplishments were largely erased in the public mind by the noisy Ballinger-Pinchot quarrel that erupted in 1910.

When Secretary of the Interior Richard Ballinger opened public lands in Wyoming, Montana, and Alaska to corporate development, he was sharply criticized by Gifford Pinchot, chief of the Agriculture Department's Division of Forestry and a stalwart Rooseveltian. When Taft dismissed Pinchot on the narrow grounds of insubordination, a storm of protest arose from conservationists and from Roosevelt's friends, who were legion. The whole unsavory episode further widened the growing rift between the president and the former president, onetime bosom political partners.

The reformist wing of the Republican party was now up in arms, while Taft was being pushed increasingly into the embrace of the stand-pat Old Guard. By the spring of 1910, the Grand Old Party was split wide open, owing largely to the clumsiness of Taft. A suspicious Roosevelt returned triumphantly to New York in June 1910 and shortly thereafter stirred up a tempest. In a flaming speech at Osawatamie, Kansas, he proclaimed a doctrine—popularly known as the **New Nationalism**—that urged the national government to increase its power to remedy economic and social abuses.

Weakened by these internal divisions, the Republicans lost badly in the congressional elections of 1910. The Democrats emerged from their landslide victory with 228 seats to only 161 for the once-dominant Republicans. In a further symptom of the reforming temper of the times, a Socialist representative, Austrian-born Victor L. Berger, was elected from Milwaukee. The Republicans, by virtue of holdovers, retained the Senate, 51 to 41, but the insurgents in their midst were numerous enough to make that hold precarious.

Payne-Aldrich Bill (1909) *While intended to lower tariff rates, this bill was eventually revised beyond all recognition, retaining high rates on most imports. President Taft angered the progressive wing of his party when he declared it "the best bill that the Republican party ever passed."*

New Nationalism (1912) *State-interventionist reform program devised by journalist Herbert Croly and advocated by Theodore Roosevelt during his Bull Moose presidential campaign. Roosevelt did not object to continued consolidation of trusts and labor unions. Rather, he sought to create stronger regulatory agencies to ensure that they operated to serve the public interest, not just private gain.*

Ex-President Theodore Roosevelt Watches President Taft Struggle with the Demands of Government, 1910

⭐ The Taft-Roosevelt Rupture

The sputtering uprising in Republican ranks had now blossomed into a full-fledged revolt. Early in 1911 the National Progressive Republican League was formed, with the fiery, white-maned Senator Robert La Follette of Wisconsin its leading candidate for the Republican presidential nomination. The assumption was that Roosevelt, an anti–third-termer, would not permit himself to be "drafted."

But the restless Rough Rider began to change his views about third terms as he saw Taft, hand in glove with the hated Old Guard, discard "my policies." In February 1912 Roosevelt formally wrote to seven state governors that he was willing to accept the Republican nomination. His reasoning was that the third-term tradition applied to three *consecutive elective* terms. Exuberantly he cried, "My hat is in the ring!" and "The fight is on and I am stripped to the buff!"

Roosevelt forthwith seized the Progressive banner, while La Follette, who had served as a convenient pathbreaker, was protestingly elbowed aside. Girded for battle, the Rough Rider came clattering into the presidential primaries then being held in many states. He shouted through half-clenched teeth that the president had fallen under the thumb of the reactionary bosses and that although Taft "means well, he means well feebly." The once-genial Taft, now in a fighting mood, retorted by branding Roosevelt supporters "emotionalists and neurotics."

A Taft-Roosevelt explosion was near in June 1912, when the Republican convention met in Chicago. The Rooseveltites, who were about 100 delegates short of winning the nomination, challenged the right of some 250 Taft delegates to be seated. Most of these contests were arbitrarily settled in favor of Taft, whose supporters held the throttle of the convention steamroller. The Roosevelt adherents, crying "fraud" and "naked theft," in the end refused to vote, and Taft won the Republican nomination. But Roosevelt, the supposedly good sportsman, refused to quit the game. Having tasted for the first time the bitter cup of defeat, he was now on fire to lead a third-party crusade.

The "Bull Moose" Campaign of 1912

Office-hungry Democrats, the "outs" since 1897, were jubilant over the disruptive Republican brawl in Chicago. If they could come up with an outstanding reformist leader, they had an excellent chance to win the White House. Such a leader appeared in New Jersey Governor Woodrow Wilson, once a mild conservative but now a militant progressive. Beginning professional life as a brilliant academic scholar of government, Wilson had risen in 1902 to the presidency of Princeton University, where he had achieved sweeping educational reforms.

Wilson entered politics in 1910 when New Jersey bosses nominated him for governor, expecting the novice to serve as a respectable "front" man who could be led around by the nose. But Wilson instead ran a passionate reform campaign in which he assailed the "predatory" trusts and promised to return state government to the people. As governor, Wilson drove through a sheaf of forward-looking measures that made reactionary New Jersey one of the more liberal states—and its zealous chief executive a leading contender for the presidency.

When the Democrats met in Baltimore in 1912, Wilson was nominated on the forty-sixth ballot, aided by William Jennings Bryan's switch to his side. The Democrats gave Wilson a strong progressive platform to run on, dubbed the **New Freedom** program.

Surging events had meanwhile been thrusting Roosevelt to the fore as a candidate for the presidency on a third-party Progressive ticket. The fighting ex-cowboy, angered by his recent rebuff, was eager to lead the charge. A pro-Roosevelt Progressive convention assembled in Chicago in August 1912. Dramatically symbolizing the rising political status of women, as well as Progressive support for the cause of social justice, settlement-house pioneer Jane Addams placed Roosevelt's name in nomination for the presidency. Thunderous applause erupted when Roosevelt fervently cried, "We stand at Armageddon, and we battle for the Lord!" A religious revival atmosphere suffused the convention, as the hoarse delegates sang "Onward Christian Soldiers" and the "Battle Hymn of the Republic." William Allen White, the caustic Kansas journalist, later wrote, "Roosevelt bit me and I went mad."

New Freedom (1912) *Platform of reforms advocated by Woodrow Wilson in his first presidential campaign, including stronger antitrust legislation to protect small business enterprises from monopolies, banking reform, and tariff reductions. Wilson's strategy involved taking action to increase opportunities for capitalist competition rather than increasing government regulation of large trusts.*

The Finishing Touch, 1912 Despite the excitement generated by Roosevelt's Progressive Party challenge in 1912, the GOP split that year helped to hand victory to the Democrats. This election-eve cartoon depicts Woodrow Wilson, attired in academic garb, preparing to slay Roosevelt the charging bull moose. The latter had already been injured by a slew of controversies, including allegations of improper campaign contributions during a previous election. Wilson's campaign manager and future treasury secretary, William McAdoo, holds the cape.

Fired-up Progressives entered the campaign with righteousness and enthusiasm. Roosevelt boasted that he felt "as strong as a bull moose," so the bull moose took its place with the donkey and the elephant in the American political zoo. As one poet whimsically put it:

I want to be a Bull Moose,
And with the Bull Moose stand
With antlers on my forehead
And a Big Stick in my hand.

The overshadowing question of the 1912 campaign was which of two varieties of progressivism would prevail—Roosevelt's New Nationalism or Wilson's New Freedom. Both men favored a more active government role in economic and social affairs, but they disagreed sharply over specific strategies. Roosevelt preached the theories spun out by the progressive thinker Herbert Croly in his book *The Promise of American Life* (1910). Croly and TR both favored continued consolidation of trusts and labor unions, paralleled by the growth of powerful regulatory agencies in Washington. Roosevelt and his "bull moosers" also campaigned for woman suffrage and a broad program of social welfare, including minimum-wage laws and publicly supported health care. Clearly, the bull moose Progressives looked forward to the kind of activist welfare state that Franklin Roosevelt's New Deal would one day make a reality.

Wilson's New Freedom, by contrast, favored small enterprise, entrepreneurship, and the free functioning of unregulated and unmonopolized markets. The Democrats shunned social-welfare proposals and pinned their economic faith on competition—on the "man on the make," as Wilson put it. The New Freedom Program called for banking reform and tariff reductions. But the keynote of Wilson's program was not regulation but fragmentation of the big industrial combines, chiefly by means of vigorous enforcement of the antitrust laws. The election of 1912 thus offered the voters a choice not merely of policies but of political and economic philosophies—a rarity in United States history.

Former professor Wilson won handily, with 435 electoral votes and 6,296,547 popular votes. The "third-party" candidate, Roosevelt, finished second, with 88 electoral votes and 4,118,571 popular votes. Taft won only 8 electoral votes and 3,486,720 popular votes. To the progressive tally must be added some support for the Socialist candidate, persistent Eugene V. Debs, who rolled up 900,672 votes, 6 percent of the total cast, or more than twice as many as he had netted four years earlier. Starry-eyed Socialists dreamed of being in the White House within eight years.

Taft went on to a fruitful old age. He taught law for eight pleasant years at Yale University and in 1921 became chief justice of the Supreme Court—a job for which he was far more happily suited than the presidency.

CHAPTER SUMMARY

The progressive movement of the early twentieth century became the greatest American reform crusade since abolitionism. Inaugurated by Populists, socialists, social gospelers, female reformers, and muckraking journalists, progressivism became a widely popular effort to strengthen government's power to correct the many social and economic problems associated with industrialization and urbanization.

Progressivism began at the city and state level, where it initially focused on "good government" political reforms to corral corrupt bosses. It then turned to correcting a host of social and economic evils that seemed to require national action by the federal government. Women played an especially critical role in galvanizing progressive social concern. Seeing involvement in such issues as reforming child labor, poor tenement housing, and consumer causes as a natural extension of their traditional roles as wives and mothers, female activists brought significant changes in both law and public attitudes in these areas.

At the national level, Roosevelt's Square Deal vigorously deployed the federal government to promote the public interest and mediate conflicts between labor interests on the one hand and the corporate trusts on the other. Rooseveltian progressivism also inspired attention to consumer and environmental concerns. Conservation became an important public crusade under Roosevelt, although sharp disagreements divided wilderness "preservationists" from moderate conservationists such as Roosevelt who favored the "multiple use" of nature.

Roosevelt personally selected his longtime subordinate Taft as his political successor, expecting him to carry out "my policies." But Taft proved to be a poor politician who fell under the thumb of the conservative Republican Old Guard and rapidly lost public support. The progressives' hostility to Taft split the Republican party, and when Roosevelt failed to win the nomination he launched a fiery third-party crusade in the 1912 election under the banner of his new Progressive party.

Delighted at the Republican split, Democrats nominated New Jersey Governor Woodrow Wilson, a strong reformer. Roosevelt and Wilson offered competing progressive visions in the campaign. Roosevelt's New Nationalism stressed regulation and social welfare, while Wilson's New Freedom promoted economic fairness and competition. Wilson won the fiercely contested election, with Roosevelt second, Taft third, and Socialist Eugene Debs fourth.

KEY TERMS

- social gospel (478)
- muckrakers (478)
- initiative (479)
- referendum (479)
- recall (479)
- Australian ballot (480)
- *Muller v. Oregon* (481)
- *Lochner v. New York* (482)
- Elkins Act (483)
- Meat Inspection Act (485)
- Pure Food and Drug Act (485)
- Hetch Hetchy Valley (487)
- dollar diplomacy (489)
- Payne-Aldrich Bill (490)
- New Nationalism (490)
- New Freedom (492)

PEOPLE TO KNOW

- Ida Tarbell
- Henry Demarest Lloyd
- Thorstein Veblen
- Jacob A. Riis
- Robert M. ("Fighting Bob") La Follette
- Hiram W. Johnson
- Florence Kelley
- Frances E. Willard
- Gifford Pinchot
- John Muir

MindTap is a fully online, highly personalized learning experience built upon Cengage Learning content. MindTap combines student learning tools—readings, multimedia, activities, and assessments—into a singular Learning Path that guides students through the course.

Chapter 29

Wilsonian Progressivism in Peace and War
1913–1920

American enterprise is not free; the man with only a little capital is finding it harder and harder to get into the field, more and more impossible to compete with the big fellow. Why? Because the laws of this country do not prevent the strong from crushing the weak.

Woodrow Wilson, The New Freedom, 1913

Woodrow Wilson's two tumultuous presidential terms saw the apex of progressive achievements, as well as entanglement in a global war that helped snuff out the reform fires at home. That outcome was ironic because America entered the conflict buoyed by the same crusading idealism and confidence that had driven domestic progressivism.

Chapter Outline

- Wilsonian Progressivism: Reforming the Tariff, the Banks, and the Trusts
- Wilson's Diplomacy in Mexico and Latin America
- War in Europe and American Neutrality
- The Reelection of Wilson, 1916
- German Submarines Push America into War, 1917
- Wilsonian Idealism and the Fourteen Points
- Wartime Propaganda and the Stifling of Dissent
- Workers, Blacks, and Women on the Home Front
- The American Doughboys
- The American Forces Fight in France
- Wilsonian Peacemaking in Paris
- The Senate Rejects the Versailles Treaty
- *Examining the Evidence:* "Mademoiselle from Armentières"
- *Varying Viewpoints:* Woodrow Wilson: Realist or Idealist?

FOCUS QUESTIONS

1. How did Wilsonian progressivism overcome the "triple wall of privilege"?
2. What were the central features of Wilson's moralistic foreign policy? How did he apply those principles to Latin America and then to Europe in World War I?
3. What was America's response to the outbreak of World War I? Why did Wilson's attempt to maintain neutrality turn into a critical stance toward Germany?
4. Why did America enter World War I?
5. Why did Woodrow Wilson proclaim America's entry into the war as an ideological crusade for universal democracy and freedom, rather than simply an attempt to curb German military power?
6. How did America mobilize for war, and what was the war's impact on labor, women, and African Americans?
7. Why was Wilson forced to compromise his idealistic Fourteen Points plan for peace at the Versailles Conference? Why was the battle over ratifying the Treaty of Versailles so bitter, and why was the Treaty defeated?

CHRONOLOGY

1913	- Underwood Tariff Act - Sixteenth Amendment (income tax) - Federal Reserve Act - Huerta takes power in Mexico		- United States enters World War I - Espionage Act of 1917 - Wilson calls for "peace without victory" - Bolshevik Revolution
1914	- Clayton Anti-Trust Act - Federal Trade Commission established - U.S. seizes port of Veracruz, Mexico - World War I begins in Europe	**1918**	- Wilson proposes Fourteen Points - Sedition Act of 1918 - Battle of Château-Thierry - Second Battle of the Marne - Meuse-Argonne offensive
1915	- La Follette Seamen's Act - *Lusitania* torpedoed and sunk by German U-boat - Germany declares submarine war area around British Isles	**1918–1919**	- Armistice ends World War I - Worldwide influenza pandemic
1916	- *Sussex* ultimatum and pledge - U.S. exports to European belligerents skyrocket - Workingmen's Compensation Act - Federal Farm Loan Act - Adamson Act - Pancho Villa raids New Mexico - Brandeis appointed to Supreme Court - Jones Act - Wilson defeats Hughes for presidency	**1919**	- Paris Peace Conference and Treaty of Versailles - Wilson's pro-League tour and collapse - Eighteenth Amendment (prohibition of alcohol) passed - First Senate defeat of Versailles Treaty
1917	- Germany resumes unrestricted submarine warfare - Zimmermann note - Railroads placed under federal control	**1920**	- Final Senate defeat of Versailles Treaty after reconsideration - Nineteenth Amendment (woman suffrage) passed - Harding defeats Cox for presidency

★ Wilson: The Idealist in Politics

(Thomas) Woodrow Wilson, the second Democratic president since 1861, looked like the ascetic intellectual he was, with his clean-cut features, pinch-nose eyeglasses, and trim figure. Born in Virginia shortly before the Civil War and reared in Georgia and the Carolinas, the professor-politician was the first man from one of the seceded southern states to reach the White House since Zachary Taylor, sixty-four years earlier. Wilson's admiration for the Confederacy's attempt to win independence partly inspired his ideal of self-determination for people in other countries. Steeped in the traditions of Jeffersonian democracy, he shared Jefferson's faith in the masses—if they were properly informed.

Son of a Presbyterian minister, Wilson was reared in an atmosphere of fervent piety, and he deftly used the presidential pulpit to preach his inspirational political sermons. Convinced that Congress could not function properly unless the president got out in front and provided leadership, Wilson repeatedly relied on his eloquence to appeal over the heads of legislators to the sovereign people.

Splendid though Wilson's intellectual equipment was, he suffered from serious defects of personality. Incapable of acting the showman, like "Teddy" Roosevelt, Wilson lacked the common touch and knew it. Roosevelt "appeals to [the voters'] imagination; I do not," Wilson reflected. "I am a vague, conjectural personality, more made up of opinions and academic prepossessions than of human traits and red corpuscles."

⭐ Wilson Attacks the "Triple Wall of Privilege"

Few presidents have arrived at the White House with a clearer program than Wilson's or one destined to be so completely achieved. The new president called for an all-out assault on what he called the "triple wall of privilege": the tariff, the banks, and the trusts.

He tackled the tariff first. In a precedent-shattering move, he appeared in person before a joint session of Congress in 1913 and presented his appeal with stunning eloquence and effectiveness. Moved by Wilson's aggressive leadership, the House swiftly passed the **Underwood Tariff** Bill, which provided for a substantial reduction of rates. The bill was also a landmark in tax legislation. Under authority granted by the recently ratified Sixteenth Amendment, Congress enacted a graduated income tax, beginning with a modest levy on incomes over $3,000 (then considerably higher than the average family's income). By 1917 revenue from the income tax shot ahead of receipts from the tariff, a gap that has since vastly widened.

A second bastion of the "triple wall of privilege" was the antiquated and inadequate banking and currency system, long since outgrown by the Republic's lusty economic expansion. The most serious shortcoming of the country's financial structure, still creaking along under the Civil War National Banking Act, was the inelasticity of the currency. Banking reserves were heavily concentrated in New York and a handful of other large cities and could not be mobilized in times of financial stress into areas that were badly pinched.

A House committee chaired by Congressman Arsene Pujo had already stirred public concern about the concentration of financial power by tracing the tentacles of the "money monster" into the hidden vaults of American banking and business. President Wilson's confidant, progressive-minded Massachusetts attorney Louis D. Brandeis, further fanned the flames of reform with his incendiary though scholarly book *Other People's Money and How the Bankers Use It* (1914).

In June 1913, in a second dramatic personal appearance before Congress, the president issued a ringing call for a decentralized bank in government hands, as opposed to Republican demands for a huge private bank. Again appealing to the sovereign people, Wilson scored another triumph. In 1913 he signed the **Federal Reserve Act**, the most important piece of economic legislation between the Civil War and the New Deal.

The new Federal Reserve Board, appointed by the president, oversaw a nationwide system of twelve regional reserve banks. These regional banks were owned by member financial institutions, but the final authority of the Federal Reserve Board guaranteed public control. The board was also empowered to issue paper money—"Federal Reserve Notes"—backed by commercial paper, such as the promissory notes of businesspeople. Thus the amount of money in circulation could be swiftly increased as needed for the legitimate requirements of business.

Without pausing for breath, Wilson pushed toward the last remaining rampart in the "triple wall of privilege"—the trusts. His third personal appearance before Congress in 1914 led to passage of the **Federal Trade Commission Act** of 1914. The new law empowered a presidentially appointed commission to turn a searchlight on industries engaged in interstate commerce, such as the meatpackers. The commissioners were expected to crush monopoly at the source by rooting out unfair trade practices, including unlawful competition, false advertising, mislabeling, adulteration, and bribery.

The knot of monopoly was further cut by the **Clayton Anti-Trust Act** of 1914. This act lengthened the Sherman Act's list of objectionable business practices to include price discrimination and interlocking directorates (whereby the same individuals served as directors of supposedly competing firms), an end often achieved through **holding companies**.

The Clayton Act also conferred long-overdue benefits on workers by exempting labor and agricultural organizations from antitrust prosecution under the Sherman Act, while explicitly legalizing strikes and peaceful picketing. Union leader Samuel Gompers hailed the act as the Magna Carta of labor because it legally lifted human labor out of the category of "a commodity or article of commerce." But the rejoicing was premature, as conservative judges in later years continued to clip the wings of the union movement.

Underwood Tariff (1913) *This tariff provided for a substantial reduction of rates and enacted an unprecedented, graduated federal income tax. By 1917, revenue from the income tax surpassed receipts from the tariff, a gap that has since been vastly widened.*

Federal Reserve Act (1913) *An act establishing twelve regional Federal Reserve Banks and a Federal Reserve Board, appointed by the president, to regulate banking and create stability on a national scale in the volatile banking sector. The law carried the nation through the financial crises of the First World War of 1914-1918.*

Federal Trade Commission Act (1914) *A banner accomplishment of Woodrow Wilson's administration, this law empowered a standing, presidentially appointed commission to investigate illegal business practices in interstate commerce like unlawful competition, false advertising, and mislabeling of goods.*

Clayton Anti-Trust Act (1914) *Law extending the anti-trust protections of the Sherman Anti-Trust Act and exempting labor unions and agricultural organizations from antimonopoly constraints. The act conferred long-overdue benefits on labor.*

holding companies *Companies that own part or all of other companies' stock in order to extend monopoly control. Often, a holding company does not produce goods or services of its own but only exists to control other companies. The Clayton Anti-Trust Act of 1914 sought to clamp down on these companies when they obstructed competition.*

Reading the Death Warrant This cartoon appeared in a New York newspaper soon after Woodrow Wilson called for dramatic reform of the banking system before both houses of Congress. With the "money trust" of bankers and businessmen cowed, Wilson was able to win popular and congressional support for the Federal Reserve Act of 1913.

Workingmen's Compensation Act (1916) *Passed under Woodrow Wilson, this law granted assistance to federal civil-service employees during periods of disability. It was a precursor to labor-friendly legislation passed during the New Deal.*

Adamson Act (1916) *This law established an eight-hour day for all employees on trains involved in interstate commerce, with extra pay for overtime. The first federal law regulating the hours of workers in private companies, it was upheld by the Supreme Court in* Wilson v. New *(1917).*

Jones Act (1916) *Law according territorial status to the Philippines and promising independence as soon as a "stable government" could be established. The United States did not grant the Philippines independence until July 4, 1946.*

Wilson at the Peak

Having treated the nation to a dazzling demonstration of vigorous presidential leadership, Wilson pressed ahead with further reforms. The Federal Farm Loan Act of 1916 made credit available to farmers at low rates of interest—as long demanded by the Populists. The La Follette Seamen's Act of 1915 required decent treatment and a living wage for often-mistreated sailors on American merchant ships.

Wilson further helped workers with the **Workingmen's Compensation Act** of 1916, granting assistance to federal civil-service employees during periods of disability. In the same year the president endorsed an act restricting child labor on products flowing into interstate commerce, though the stand-pat Supreme Court soon invalidated the law. The **Adamson Act** of 1916 established an eight-hour day for all railroad employees on trains in interstate commerce, with extra pay for overtime.

Wilson earned the enmity of businesspeople and bigots but endeared himself to progressives when in 1916 he nominated for the Supreme Court the prominent reformer Louis D. Brandeis—the first Jew to be called to the high bench. Yet Wilson's progressivism had its limits, and it clearly stopped short of better treatment for blacks. The southern-bred Wilson actually presided over accelerated segregation in the federal bureaucracy. When a delegation of black leaders personally protested to him, the schoolmasterish president virtually froze them out of his office.

New Directions in Foreign Policy

In one important area, Wilson chose not to answer the trumpet call of the bull moosers. In contrast to Roosevelt and even Taft, Wilson recoiled from an aggressive foreign policy. Hating imperialism, he was repelled by TR's big stickism. Suspicious of Wall Street, he detested the so-called dollar diplomacy of Taft.

In office only a week, Wilson declared war on dollar diplomacy. He proclaimed that the government would no longer support American investors in Latin America and China. Shivering from this Wilsonian bucket of cold water, American bankers pulled out of the Taft-engineered six-nation loan to China the next day. Wilson's anti-imperialism also produced the **Jones Act** of 1916, which granted territorial status to the Philippines and promised independence as soon as a "stable government" could be established. Wilson's racial prejudices, however, made it difficult for him to anticipate anything other than a long political tutelage for the Filipinos. Indeed, not until July 4, 1946—thirty years later—did the United States accept Philippine independence.

Events in the Caribbean soon forced Wilson to eat some of his anti-imperialist words. In response to disorders in Haiti in 1914–1915, the president reluctantly dispatched marines to protect American lives and property. In 1916 he stole a page from the Roosevelt Corollary to the Monroe Doctrine as the United States took over supervision of Haiti's finances and police. In the same year, Wilson sent the leatherneck marines to quell riots in the Dominican Republic, which then came under the shadow of the American eagle's wings for the next eight years. In 1917 Wilson purchased from Denmark the Virgin Islands in the West Indies. Increasingly, the Caribbean Sea, with its vital approaches to the now-navigable Panama Canal, was taking on the earmarks of a Yankee preserve (see Map 29.1).

★ Moralistic Diplomacy in Mexico

Rifle bullets whining across the southern border served as a constant reminder that all was not quiet in Mexico. For decades Mexico had been sorely exploited by foreign investors in oil, railroads, and mines. By 1913 American capitalists had sunk about a billion dollars into the underdeveloped but generously endowed country.

But if Mexico was rich, the Mexicans were poor. Fed up with their miserable lot, the Mexicans at last revolted. Their revolution took an ugly turn in early 1913, when a conscienceless clique (with the support of President Taft's ambassador to Mexico) murdered the popular new revolutionary president and installed General Victoriano Huerta, a Huichol Indian, in the president's chair. All this chaos accelerated a massive migration of Mexicans to the United States. More than a million Spanish-speaking newcomers tramped across the southern border in the first three decades of the twentieth century. Settling mostly in Texas, New Mexico, Arizona, and California, they helped to create a unique borderland culture that blended Mexican and American folkways.

The revolutionary bloodshed also menaced American lives and property in Mexico. Cries for intervention burst from the lips of American jingoes such as publisher William Randolph Hearst, who owned a Mexican ranch larger than Rhode Island. Yet once again, President Wilson refused to practice the same old dollar diplomacy of his predecessors, deeming it "perilous" to determine foreign policy "in the terms of material interest."

Wilson strove as best he could to steer a moral course in Mexico. He sent his aggressive ambassador packing, imposed an arms embargo, and refused to recognize officially the murderous government of "that brute" Huerta, even though most foreign powers

Map 29.1 The United States in the Caribbean, 1898–1941 This map explains why many Latin Americans accused the United States of turning the Caribbean Sea into a "Yankee lake." The map also suggests that Uncle Sam was much less "isolationist" in his own backyard than he was in faraway Europe or Asia.

acknowledged Huerta's bloody-handed regime. "I am going to teach the South American republics to elect good men," the former professor declared. He put his munitions where his mouth was in 1914, when he allowed American arms to flow to Huerta's principal rivals, white-bearded Venustiano Carranza and the firebrand Francisco ("Pancho") Villa.

The Mexican volcano erupted at the Atlantic seaport of Tampico in April 1914, when a small party of American sailors was arrested. The Mexicans promptly released the captives and apologized, but they refused the affronted American admiral's demand for a twenty-one gun salute. Wilson ordered the navy to seize the Mexican port of Veracruz to thwart the arrival of a German steamer carrying Huerta-bound guns and ammunition.

Just as a full-dress shooting conflict seemed inevitable, Wilson was rescued by an offer of mediation from the ABC powers—Argentina, Brazil, and Chile. Huerta collapsed in July 1914 under pressure from within and without. He was succeeded by his archrival Carranza, who hotly resented Wilson's military meddling. The whole sorry **Tampico Incident** did not augur well for the future of United States–Mexican relations.

"Pancho" Villa, a combination of bandit and Robin Hood, had meanwhile emerged as the chief rival of President Carranza, whom Wilson now reluctantly supported. Challenging Carranza's authority while also punishing the gringos, Villa's men ruthlessly killed sixteen American mining engineers in northern Mexico in January 1916. A month later Villa and his followers, hoping to provoke a war between Wilson and Carranza, blazed across the border into Columbus, New Mexico, and murdered another nineteen Americans.

General John J. ("Black Jack," so called from his earlier service as an officer with the crack black Tenth Cavalry) Pershing, a ramrod-erect veteran of the Cuban and Philippine campaigns, was ordered to break up the bandit band. His hastily organized force of several thousand mounted troops penetrated deep into rugged Mexico with surprising speed. They clashed with Carranza's forces and mauled the Villistas but failed to capture Villa himself. As the threat of war with Germany loomed larger, the invading army was withdrawn in January 1917.

★ Thunder Across the Sea

Europe's powder magazine, long smoldering, blew up in the summer of 1914, when the flaming pistol of a Serb patriot killed the heir to the throne of Austria-Hungary in Sarajevo. An outraged Vienna government, backed by Germany, forthwith presented a stern ultimatum to Serbia.

An explosive chain reaction followed. Russia's mobilization in support of Serbia threatened Germany in the east, even as the tsar's ally, France, confronted Germany in the west. In alarm, the Germans struck suddenly at France through unoffending Belgium. Great Britain in turn was sucked into the conflagration on the side of France.

Almost overnight most of Europe was locked in a fight to the death. On one side were arrayed the **Central Powers**: Germany and Austria-Hungary, and later Turkey and Bulgaria. On the other side were the **Allies**, principally France, Britain, and Russia, and later Japan and Italy. Americans thanked God for the ocean moats and self-righteously congratulated themselves on having had ancestors wise enough to have abandoned the hell pits of Europe. Americans felt strong, snug, smug, and secure—but not for long.

President Wilson issued the routine neutrality proclamation and called on Americans to be neutral in thought as well as deed. But such scrupulous evenhandedness proved difficult. Both sides wooed the United States, the great neutral in the West. The British enjoyed the boon of close cultural, linguistic, and economic ties with America and had the added advantage of controlling most of the transatlantic cables. Their censors sheared away war stories harmful to the Allies and drenched the United States with tales of German bestiality. Germany in turn looked for support from some 11 million Americans of German descent. Some recent immigrants did express noisy support for the Fatherland, but most were simply grateful to be so distant from the fray.

The majority of Americans were anti-German from the outset. With his villainous upturned mustache, Kaiser Wilhelm II seemed the embodiment of arrogant autocracy, an impression strengthened by Germany's ruthless strike at neutral Belgium. The discovery

Tampico Incident (1914) An arrest of American sailors by the Mexican government that spurred Woodrow Wilson to dispatch the American navy to seize the port of Veracruz in April 1914. Although war was avoided, tensions grew between the United States and Mexico.

Central Powers Germany and Austria-Hungary, later joined by Turkey and Bulgaria, made up this alliance against the Allies in World War I.

Allies Great Britain, Russia, and France, later joined by Italy, Japan, and the United States, formed this alliance against the Central Powers in World War I.

U-boats German submarines, named for the German Unterseeboot, or "undersea boat," proved deadly for Allied ships in the war zone. U-boat attacks played an important role in drawing the United States into the First World War.

in 1915 of German plans for industrial sabotage of American factories and ports further inflamed opinion against the kaiser and Germany. Still, most Americans earnestly hoped to stay out of the horrible war.

★ America Earns Blood Money

When Europe burst into flames in 1914, the United States was bogged down in a worrisome business recession. But British and French war orders soon pulled American industry out of the morass of hard times and onto a peak of war-born prosperity. Part of this boom was financed by American bankers, notably the Wall Street firm of J.P. Morgan and Company, which eventually advanced to the Allies the enormous sum of $2.3 billion during the period of American neutrality.

American trade with Germany could legally have rivaled that of the Allies. But the British threw a noose-tight blockade around the German North Sea ports and began forcing American merchant vessels into their own ports. As a result trade between Germany and the United States virtually ceased.

Hard-pressed Germany did not tamely consent to being starved out. In retaliation for the British blockade, in February 1915 Berlin announced a submarine war area around the British Isles. The submarine was a weapon so new that existing international law could not be made to fit it. The old rule that a warship must stop and board merchant ships could hardly apply to submarines, which could easily be rammed or sunk if they surfaced.

The cigar-shaped marauders posed a dire threat to the United States—so long as Wilson insisted on maintaining America's neutral rights. Berlin officials declared that they would try not to sink *neutral* shipping, but they warned that mistakes would probably occur. Wilson now determined on a policy of calculated risk. He would continue to claim profitable neutral trading rights while hoping that no high-seas incident would force his hand to grasp the sword of war. The German submarines (known as U-boats, from the German *Unterseeboot*, or "undersea boat") meanwhile began their deadly work. In the first months of 1915, they sank about ninety ships in the war zone. Then the submarine issue became acute when the British passenger liner *Lusitania* was torpedoed and sank off the coast of Ireland on May 7, 1915, with the loss of 1,198 lives, including 128 Americans.

The *Lusitania* was carrying forty-two hundred cases of small-arms ammunition, a fact the Germans used to justify the sinking. But Americans were swept by a wave of shock and anger at this act of "mass murder" and "piracy." The eastern United States, closer to the war, seethed with talk of fighting, but the rest of the country showed a strong distaste for hostilities. The peace-loving Wilson had no stomach for leading a disunited nation into war and relied instead on a series of increasingly strong notes to take the German warlords sharply to task. "There is such a thing," he said, "as a man being too proud to fight." Wilson's policies incensed the war-thirsty Theodore Roosevelt, who assailed what he saw as the "weasel words" and spinelessness of the peace-loving professor in the White House.

Yet Wilson, sticking to his verbal guns, made some diplomatic progress. After another British liner, the *Arabic*, was sunk in August 1915, with the loss of two American lives, Berlin reluctantly agreed not to sink unarmed and unresisting passenger ships *without warning*. This pledge appeared to be violated in March 1916, when the Germans torpedoed a French passenger steamer, the *Sussex*. The infuriated Wilson informed the Germans that unless they renounced the inhuman practice of sinking merchant ships without warning he would break diplomatic relations—an almost certain prelude to war.

Germany reluctantly knuckled under to President Wilson's *Sussex* ultimatum, agreeing not to sink passenger ships and merchant vessels without giving warning. But the Germans attached a long string to their *Sussex* pledge: the United States would have to persuade the Allies to modify what Berlin regarded as their illegal blockade. This, obviously, was something that Washington could not do. Wilson promptly accepted the

> The Fatherland, *the chief German-American propaganda newspaper in the United States, cried:*
>
> "We [Americans] prattle about humanity while we manufacture poisoned shrapnel and picric acid for profit. Ten thousand German widows, ten thousand orphans, ten thousand graves bear the legend 'Made in America.'"

Lusitania British passenger liner that sank after it was torpedoed by Germany on May 7, 1915. It ended the lives of 1,198 people, including 128 Americans, and pushed the United States closer to war.

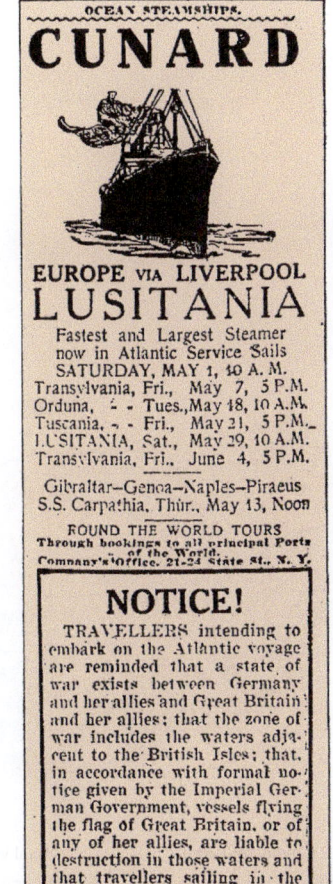

Advertisement from the *New York Herald*, May 1, 1915 Six days later the *Lusitania* was sunk. Notice the German warning.

German pledge, without accepting the "string." He thus won a temporary but precarious diplomatic victory—precarious because Germany could pull the string whenever it chose, and the president might suddenly find himself tugged over the cliff of war.

★ Wilson Wins Reelection in 1916

Against this ominous backdrop, the presidential campaign of 1916 gathered speed. Both the bull moose Progressives and the Republicans met in Chicago. The Progressives uproariously renominated Theodore Roosevelt, but the Rough Rider, who loathed Wilson and all his works, had no stomach for splitting the Republicans again and ensuring the reelection of his hated rival. In refusing to run, he sounded the death knell of the Progressive party.

The Republicans drafted Supreme Court Justice Charles Evans Hughes, the cold, intellectual former governor of New York. The Republican platform condemned the Democratic tariff, assaults on the trusts, and Wilson's wishy-washiness in dealing with Mexico and Germany.

For his part, Wilson knew that his election in 1912 had owed largely to the Taft-Roosevelt split in the GOP. He had used his first term to identify himself as the candidate of progressivism and woo bull moose voters into the Democratic fold. Nominated by acclamation at the Democratic convention in St. Louis, Wilson now built his 1916 campaign on the slogan "He Kept Us Out of War."

On election day, Hughes swept the East and looked like a surefire winner. Wilson went to bed that night prepared to accept defeat, while New York newspapers displayed huge portraits of "The President-Elect—Charles Evans Hughes." But the rest of the country turned the tide. Midwesterners and westerners, attracted by Wilson's progressive reforms and antiwar policies, flocked to the polls for the president. The final result, in doubt for several days, hinged on California, which Wilson carried by some 3,800 votes out of about a million cast.

Wilson barely squeaked through, with a final vote of 277 to 254 in the Electoral College and 9,127,695 to 8,533,507 in the popular column (see Map 29.2). The pro-labor Wilson received strong support from the working class and from renegade bull moosers, whom Republicans failed to lure back into their camp. Wilson had not specifically promised to keep the country out of war, but probably enough voters relied on such implicit assurances to ensure his victory. Their hopeful expectations were soon rudely shattered.

Map 29.2 Presidential Election of 1916 (with electoral vote by state) Wilson was so worried about being a lame-duck president in a time of great international tensions that he drew up a plan whereby Hughes, if victorious, would be appointed secretary of state, Wilson and the vice president would resign, and Hughes would thus succeed immediately to the presidency.

★ War by Act of Germany

Destiny dealt cruelly with Woodrow Wilson. The lover of peace, as fate would have it, was forced to lead a hesitant and peace-loving nation into war. As the last days of 1916 slipped through the hourglass, the president made one final, futile attempt to mediate between the embattled belligerents. On January 22, 1917, he delivered one of his most moving addresses, restating America's conviction that only a negotiated "peace without victory" would prove durable.

Germany's warlords responded with a blow of the mailed fist. On January 31, 1917, they announced to an astonished world that they intended to wage *unrestricted* submarine warfare, sinking *all* ships, including America's, in the war zone.

Why this rash act? War with America was the last thing Germany wanted. But after three ghastly years in the trenches, Germany's leaders decided that making distinctions between combatants and noncombatants was a luxury they could no longer afford. Thus they jerked on the string they had attached to their *Sussex* pledge in 1916, desperately hoping to bring Britain to its knees before the United States entered the war.

Wilson, his bluff called, broke diplomatic relations with Germany but refused to move closer to war unless the Germans undertook "overt" acts against American lives. To defend American interests short of war, the president asked Congress for authority to arm American merchant ships. When a band of midwestern senators launched a filibuster to block the measure, Wilson denounced them as a "little group of willful men" who were rendering a great nation "helpless and contemptible." But their obstructionism was a powerful reminder of the continuing strength of American isolationism.

Meanwhile, the sensational **Zimmermann note** was intercepted and published on March 1, 1917, infuriating Americans, especially westerners. German foreign secretary Arthur Zimmermann had secretly proposed a German-Mexican alliance, tempting anti-Yankee Mexico with veiled promises of recovering Texas, New Mexico, and Arizona.

On the heels of this provocation came the long-dreaded "overt" acts in the Atlantic, where German U-boats sank four unarmed American merchant vessels in the first two weeks of March. As one Philadelphia newspaper observed, "The difference between war and what we have now is that now we aren't fighting back." Simultaneously came the rousing news that a revolution in Russia had toppled the cruel regime of the tsars. America could now fight foursquare for democracy on the side of the Allies without the black sheep of Russian despotism in the Allied fold.

Subdued and solemn, Wilson at last stood before a hushed joint session of Congress on the evening of April 2, 1917, and asked for a declaration of war. He had lost his gamble that America could pursue the profits of neutral trade without being sucked into the ghastly maelstrom. A myth developed in later years that America was dragged unwittingly into war by munitions makers and Wall Street bankers, desperate to protect their profits and loans. Yet the weapons merchants and financiers were already thriving, unhampered by wartime government restrictions and heavy taxation. The simple truth is that British harassment of American commerce had been galling but endurable; Germany had resorted to the mass killing of civilians. President Wilson had drawn a clear, if risky, line against the depredations of the submarine. The German high command, in a last desperate throw of the dice, chose to cross it. In a figurative sense, America's war declaration of April 6, 1917, bore the unambiguous trademark "Made in Germany."

Zimmermann note (1917) *Secret proposal by German foreign secretary Arthur Zimmerman for a German-Mexican alliance against the United States. When the note was intercepted and published in March 1917, it caused an uproar that made some Americans more willing to enter the war.*

★ Wilsonian Idealism Enthroned

"It is a fearful thing to lead this great peaceful people into war," Wilson said in his war message. It proved fearful indeed. How could the president arouse the American people to shoulder this unprecedented burden? For more than a century, they had prided themselves on their isolation from the periodic outbursts of militarized violence that afflicted the Old World. Ominously, no fewer than six senators and fifty representatives (including the first congresswoman, Jeannette Rankin of Montana) had voted against the war resolution. Wilson could whip up no enthusiasm, especially in the landlocked Midwest, by calling on the nation to fight to make the world safe from the submarine.

To galvanize the country, Wilson would have to proclaim more glorified aims. Radiating the spiritual fervor of his Presbyterian ancestors, he declared the supremely ambitious goal of a crusade "to make the world safe for democracy." Brandishing the sword of righteousness, Wilson virtually hypnotized the nation with his lofty ideals. He contrasted the selfish war aims of the other belligerents, Allied and enemy alike, with America's shining altruism. America, he preached, did not fight for the sake of riches or territorial conquest. The Republic sought only to shape an international order in which democracy could flourish without fear of power-crazed autocrats and militarists.

In Wilsonian idealism the personality of the president and the necessities of history were perfectly matched. The high-minded Wilson genuinely believed in the principles he so eloquently intoned—especially that the modern world could not afford the kind of hyper-destructive war that advanced industrial states were now capable of waging. In this, Wilson's vision was prophetic. In any case, probably no other argument could have successfully converted the American people from their historic hostility to involvement in European squabbles. Americans, it seemed, could be either isolationists or crusaders, but nothing in between.

Wilson's appeal worked—perhaps too well. Holding aloft the torch of idealism, the president fired up the public mind to a fever pitch. "Force, force to the utmost, force without stint or limit," he cried, while the country responded less elegantly with, "Hang the kaiser!" Lost on the gale was Wilson's earlier plea for "peace without victory."

Fourteen Points (1918) *Woodrow Wilson's proposal to ensure peace after World War I, calling for an end to secret treaties, widespread arms reduction, national self-determination, and a new league of nations.*

Committee on Public Information (1917) *A government office during World War I known popularly as the Creel Committee for its chairman George Creel, dedicated to winning everyday Americans' support for the war effort. It regularly distributed prowar propaganda and sent out an army of "four-minute men" to rally crowds and deliver "patriotic pep."*

★ Wilson's Fourteen Potent Points

Wilson quickly came to be recognized as the moral leader of the Allied cause. He scaled a summit of inspiring oratory on January 8, 1918, when he delivered his famed **Fourteen Points** Address to an enthusiastic Congress. Wilson's vision inspired all the drooping Allies to make mightier efforts and demoralized the enemy governments by holding out alluring promises to their dissatisfied minorities.

The first five of the Fourteen Points were broad in scope: (1) A proposal to abolish secret treaties pleased liberals of all countries. (2) Freedom of the seas appealed to the Germans, as well as to Americans who distrusted British sea power. (3) A removal of economic barriers among nations had long been the goal of liberal internationalists everywhere. (4) Reduction of armament burdens was gratifying to taxpayers of all countries. (5) An adjustment of colonial claims in the interests of both native peoples and the colonizers was a potentially revolutionary appeal that helped delegitimize old empires and inspire "subject peoples."

Other points among the fourteen proved to be no less seductive. They held out the promise of independence ("self-determination") to oppressed minority groups, such as the Poles, millions of whom lay under the heel of Germany and Austria-Hungary. The capstone point, number fourteen, foreshadowed the League of Nations—an international organization that Wilson dreamed would provide a system of collective security.

Yet Wilson's appealing points, though raising hopes the world over, were not everywhere applauded. Certain leaders of the Allied nations, with an eye to territorial booty, were less than enthusiastic. Hard-nosed Republicans at home grumbled, and some openly mocked the "fourteen commandments" of "God Almighty Wilson."

Anti-German Propaganda The government relied extensively on emotional appeals and hate propaganda to rally support for the First World War, which most Americans regarded as a distant "European" affair. This poster used gendered imagery to evoke the brutal German violation of Belgian neutrality in August 1914.

★ Manipulating Minds and Stifling Dissent

Mobilizing people's minds for war, both in America and abroad, was an urgent task facing the Washington authorities. The **Committee on Public Information**, headed by journalist George Creel, was therefore created to sell America on the war and to sell the world on Wilsonian war aims. Creel's organization, employing 150,000 workers at home and overseas, proved that words were indeed weapons. It sent out an army of 75,000 "four-minute men"—often longer-winded than that—who delivered countless speeches full of "patriotic pep."

Creel's propaganda took varied forms. Posters were splashed on billboards in the "Battle of the Fences," as artists "rallied to the colors." Millions of pamphlets containing the most pungent Wilsonisms were showered like confetti upon the world. Hang-the-kaiser movies, carrying such titles as *The Kaiser, The Beast of Berlin* and *To Hell with the Kaiser*, portrayed the helmeted "Hun" at his bloodiest. Arm-waving conductors by the thousands led huge audiences in songs that poured scorn on the enemy and glorified the "boys" in uniform.

The entire nation, catching the frenzied spirit of a religious revival, burst into song. Most memorable of many anthems was George M. Cohan's spine-tingling "Over There":

Over there, over there
Send the word, send the word over there,
That the Yanks are coming, the Yanks are coming
The drums rum-tumming ev'rywhere.

Creel typified American war mobilization, which relied more on aroused passion and voluntary compliance than on formal laws. But he oversold the ideals of Wilson and led the world to expect too much. When the president proved to be a mortal and not a god, the resulting disillusionment at home and abroad was disastrous.

Patriotic fervor also had a darker side. German Americans numbered over 8 million, counting those with at least one parent foreign-born, out of a total population of 100 million. Most proved to be loyal to the United States. But as emotion mounted, hysterical hatred of Germans and things Germanic swept the nation. Orchestras found it unsafe to present German-composed music, like that of Wagner and Beethoven. German books were removed from library shelves, and German classes were canceled in high schools and colleges. Sauerkraut became "liberty cabbage" and hamburger "liberty steak." Even beer became suspect, as patriotic Americans fretted over the loyalty of breweries with names like Schlitz or Pabst.

Both the **Espionage Act** of 1917 and the Sedition Act of 1918 reflected current fears about Germans and antiwar Americans. Especially visible among the nineteen hundred prosecutions undertaken under these laws were antiwar Socialists and members of the radical union Industrial Workers of the World (IWW). Kingpin Socialist Eugene V. Debs was tried under the Espionage Act in 1918 and sentenced to ten years in a federal penitentiary. IWW leader William D. ("Big Bill") Haywood and ninety-nine associates were similarly convicted. Virtually any criticism of the government could be censored and punished. Some critics claimed the new laws were bending, if not breaking, the First Amendment. But in ***Schenck v. United States*** (1919), the Supreme Court affirmed their legality, arguing that freedom of speech could be revoked when such speech presented a "clear and present danger" to the nation.

These prosecutions form an ugly chapter in the history of American civil liberty. With the dawn of peace, presidential pardons were rather freely granted, including President Harding's to Eugene Debs in 1921. Yet a few victims lingered behind bars into the 1930s.

Patriotic Persuasion Worried about the public's enthusiasm for the war, the government employed all the arts of psychology and propaganda to sustain the martial spirit. The prewar song "I Didn't Raise My Boy to Be a Soldier" was changed to "I Didn't Raise My Boy to Be a Slacker," which in turn inspired the cruel parody "I Didn't Raise My Boy to Be a Sausage."

Espionage Act (1917) *A law prohibiting interference with the draft and other acts of national "disloyalty." Together with the Sedition Act of 1918, which added penalties for abusing the government in writing, it created a climate that was unfriendly to civil liberties.*

***Schenck* v. *United States* (1919)** *A Supreme Court decision that upheld the Espionage and Sedition Acts, reasoning that freedom of speech could be curtailed when it posed a "clear and present danger" to the nation.*

★ Forging a War Economy

Victory was no foregone conclusion, especially because the Republic was caught flatfootedly unready for its leap into global war. Wilson had only belatedly backed some mild preparedness measures beginning in 1915. It would take a herculean effort to mobilize America's daunting but disorganized resources and throw them into the field quickly enough to bolster the Allied war effort.

Towering obstacles confronted economic mobilizers. Sheer ignorance was among the biggest roadblocks. No one knew precisely how much steel or explosive powder the country was capable of producing. Traditional fears of big government hamstrung efforts to orchestrate the economy from Washington. The largely voluntary character of economic war organization testified to ocean-insulated America's safe distance from the fighting—as well as to the still-modest scale of government powers in the progressive-era Republic.

Late in the war, Wilson finally succeeded in imposing some order on this economic confusion. In March 1918 he appointed Wall Street's Bernard Baruch to head the **War Industries Board**. Although the board had only feeble formal powers, it set a precedent for the federal government to take a central role in economic planning in moments of crisis.

As the larder of democracy, America had to feed itself and its allies. Herbert C. Hoover, the Quaker-humanitarian head of the Food Administration, shared his fellow war administrators' preference for relying on voluntary compliance rather than compulsory edicts. Instead of rationing food supplies, he waged a whirlwind propaganda campaign through posters, billboards, newspapers, pulpits, and movies. To save food for export, Hoover proclaimed wheatless Wednesdays and meatless Tuesdays—all on a voluntary basis. Even children, when eating apples, were urged to be "patriotic to the core." The country soon broke out in a rash of vegetable "victory gardens." Thanks to the fervent patriotic wartime spirit, Hoover's voluntary approach worked, greatly increasing farm production and food exports to the Allies.

Congress severely restricted the use of foodstuffs for manufacturing alcoholic beverages. The wartime drive against German-descended brewers aided in the passage of the Eighteenth Amendment in 1919, which prohibited not only beer but all alcoholic drinks.

As prohibition indicated, despite the Wilson administration's preference for voluntary means of mobilizing the economy, over the course of the war the federal government expanded in size and power. The War Industries Board eventually issued production quotas, allocated raw materials, and set prices for government purchases. Following indescribably tangled traffic snarls in late 1917, Washington took over the railroads. Time itself came under Uncle Sam's control when the entire country was ordered to observe daylight saving time to extend the workday and save on fuel.

★ Workers in Wartime

Spurred by the slogan "Labor Will Win the War," American workers sweated their way to victory. In 1918 the War Department threatened to draft any unemployed male, but for the most part the government tried to treat labor fairly. Samuel Gompers and his American Federation of Labor (AF of L) loyally supported the war and were rewarded for it. At war's end, the AF of L had more than doubled its membership, to over 3 million. In the most heavily unionized industries, wages had risen by more than 20 percent over prewar levels.

Yet labor still harbored grievances. Six thousand strikes, several bloody, broke out in the war years. The radical antiwar **Industrial Workers of the World**, known as the "Wobblies," engineered some damaging industrial sabotage, and not without reason. Transient laborers in such industries as fruit and lumber, the Wobblies were victims of some of the shabbiest working conditions in the country.

In 1919, the greatest strike in American history rocked the steel industry. More than a quarter of a million workers walked off the job in a bid to force their employers to recognize their right to bargain collectively. The steel companies refused to negotiate and brought in thirty thousand African American strikebreakers to keep the mills running. After bitter confrontations that left more than a dozen workers dead, the steel strike collapsed, a grievous setback that crippled the union movement for more than a decade.

The black workers who entered the steel mills in 1919 were but a fraction of the tens of thousands of southern blacks drawn to the North by the magnet of war-industry employment. These migrants made up the small-scale beginnings of the **Great Migration**, a northward trek that would eventually grow to massive proportions. Their sudden appearance in previously all-white areas sometimes sparked interracial violence. An explosive

---

War Industries Board (1917) *Federal agency, headed by Bernard Baruch, that coordinated industrial production during World War I, setting production quotas, allocating raw materials, and pushing companies to increase efficiency and eliminate waste. Under the economic mobilization of the War Industries Board, industrial production in the United States increased 20 percent during the war.*

Industrial Workers of the World (1905) *Also known as the "Wobblies," a radical organization that sought to build "one big union" and advocated industrial sabotage to advance that goal. At its peak in 1923, it claimed 100,000 members and was supported by 300,000. The IWW particularly appealed to migratory workers in agriculture and lumbering and to miners, all of whom suffered from horrific working conditions.*

Great Migration *The movement of 6 million African Americans from the rural South to the urban North and West in two major waves. The first, from World War I until the onset of the Great Depression, brought more than 1.5 million migrants to northern cities. From 1940 to 1970, another 5 million left the South, pushed off the land by the mechanization of cotton farming and lured north and west by hopes for greater economic opportunity and more equitable political participation. After 1970, increasing numbers of African Americans trekked back to the South in what was called the New Great Migration, as new jobs became more plentiful in the South than in the older industrial cities of the North and racial relations improved in the South.*

Nineteenth Amendment (1920) *Gave women the right to vote, more than seventy years after the first organized calls for woman's suffrage in Seneca Falls, New York.*

riot in East St. Louis, Illinois, in July 1917 left nine whites and at least forty blacks dead. An equally gruesome riot ripped through Chicago in July 1919, fanned by tensions between white working-class neighborhoods and African Americans toiling as strikebreakers in meatpacking plants. Fifteen whites and twenty-three blacks were killed during nearly two weeks of terror.

★ Suffering Until Suffrage

Women also heeded the call of patriotism and opportunity. Thousands of female workers flooded into factories and fields, taking up jobs vacated by men who left the assembly line for the front line. But the war split the women's movement deeply. Many progressive feminists were pacifists, inclined to oppose both the participation of America in the war and women in the war effort. This group found a voice in the National Woman's party, led by Quaker activist Alice Paul, which demonstrated against "Kaiser Wilson" with marches and hunger strikes.

But the larger part of the suffrage movement, represented by the National American Woman Suffrage Association, supported Wilson's war. Leaders echoed Wilson's justification for fighting by arguing that women must take part in the war effort to earn a role in shaping the peace. The fight for democracy abroad was women's best chance for winning true democracy at home.

War mobilization gave new momentum to the suffrage fight. Impressed by women's war work, President Wilson endorsed woman suffrage as "a vitally necessary war measure." In 1917 New York voted for suffrage at the state level; Michigan, Oklahoma, and South Dakota followed. The next year, governments in Great Britain, Austria-Hungary, and Germany extended the suffrage to women. Not long after, the United States followed suit. In 1920, more than seventy years after the first calls for suffrage at Seneca Falls, the **Nineteenth Amendment** was ratified, giving all American women the right to vote. (See the Appendix.)

Despite political victory, women's wartime economic gains proved fleeting. When peace arrived, most women workers soon gave up their war jobs. Meanwhile, Congress reaffirmed its support for women in their traditional role as mothers when it passed the **Sheppard-Towner Maternity Act** of 1921, providing federally financed instruction in maternal and infant health care. In doing so, Congress also expanded the responsibility of the federal government for family welfare. Partial though the feminist victories were, the developments of the World War I era foreshadowed a future when women's wage-labor and political power would reshape the American way of life.

Contending Voices

Battle of the Ballot

In an open address to Congress in 1917, suffragist Carrie Chapman Catt (1859–1947) capitalized on the idealism of the day and invoked the founding principles of American democracy in arguing the case for women's right to vote:

"How can our nation escape the logic it has never failed to follow, when its last unenfranchised class calls for the vote? Behold our Uncle Sam floating the banner with one hand, 'Taxation without representation is tyranny,' and with the other seizing the billions of dollars paid in taxes by women to whom he refuses 'representation.' ... Is there a single man who can justify such inequality of treatment, such outrageous discrimination? Not one."

Female anti-suffrage activists, for their part, often depicted their opposition to the ballot as a means to protect women's unique role in promoting reform free of corrupt politics, as Mrs. Barclay Hazard (1861–1938) explained in a 1907 speech:

"[We] must accept partisanship, political trickery, and office-seeking as necessary evils inseparable from modern conditions, and the question arises what can be done to palliate the situation. To our minds, the solution has been found by the entrance of women into public life. Standing in an absolutely independent political position, freed from all partisan affiliations, untrammeled by any political obligations, the intelligent, self-sacrificing women of today are ... a third party whose disinterestedness none can doubt."

> How did progressive-era notions inform the debate over suffrage?

★ Making Plowboys into Doughboys

Most citizens, at the outset, did not dream of sending a mighty force to France, assuming American naval power and material support would suffice. But in April and May of 1917, the Europeans confessed that they were scraping the bottom not only of their money

Sheppard-Towner Maternity Act (1921) *Designed to appeal to new women voters, provided federally financed instruction in maternal and infant health care and expanded the role of government in family welfare.*

In the Trenches and to the Polls Wars often bring opportunities and innovations as well as danger and destruction. As U.S. Army nurses went into harm's way at the fighting front in France, the century-long struggle for women's suffrage intensified on the home front, culminating in the Nineteenth Amendment in 1920.

chests but, more ominously, of their manpower barrels. A huge American army would have to be raised, trained, and transported, or the whole western front would collapse. And America's small existing army of 100,000 regulars ranked only fifteenth among the armies of the world.

Conscription was the only answer to the need for raising an immense army with all possible speed. Wilson disliked a draft, but he eventually accepted and eloquently supported conscription as a disagreeable and temporary necessity. Six weeks after declaring war, Congress grudgingly passed conscription to supply manpower for the American Expeditionary Forces (AEF) in Europe.

The draft machinery, on the whole, worked effectively. Within a few frantic months the army grew to over 4 million men. For the first time, women were admitted to the armed forces: some 11,000 to the navy and 269 to the marines. African Americans also served in the AEF, though in strictly segregated units and usually under white officers.

Recruits were supposed to receive six months of training in America and two more months overseas. But so great was the urgency that many doughboys were swept swiftly into battle scarcely knowing how to handle a rifle, much less a bayonet.

Ignoring grisly tales of the agonies of trench warfare, many young American men saw an opportunity for adventure and seized it. Author John Dos Passos (1896–1970) recollected how he felt going off to war in 1917:

"We had spent our boyhood in the afterglow of the peaceful nineteenth century.... What was war like? We wanted to see with our own eyes. We flocked into the volunteer services. I respected the conscientious objectors, and occasionally felt I should take that course myself, but hell, I wanted to see the show."

⭐ America Helps Hammer the Hun

Russia's collapse underscored the need for haste. After the communist Bolsheviks withdrew their beaten country from the "capitalist" war early in 1918, Germany moved hundreds of thousands of its battle-tested soldiers from the eastern front facing Russia to the western front in France, where, for the first time in the war, they were developing a dangerous superiority in manpower—and the Yanks were yet to arrive.

France gradually began to bustle with American doughboys (see Map 29.3). The first trainees to reach the

Map 29.3 Major U.S. Operations in France, 1918 One doughboy recorded in his diary his baptism of fire at St. Mihiel: "Hiked through dark woods. No lights allowed, guided by holding on the pack of the man ahead. Stumbled through underbrush for about half mile into an open field where we waited in soaking rain until about 10:00 P.M. We then started on our hike to the St. Mihiel front, arriving on the crest of a hill at 1:00 A.M. I saw a sight which I shall never forget. It was the zero hour and in one instant the entire front as far as the eye could reach in either direction was a sheet of flame, while the heavy artillery made the earth quake."

front were used as replacements in the Allied armies. The newcomers soon made friends with the French girls—or tried to. One of the most sung-about women in history was the fabled "Mademoiselle from Armentières." A printable stanza ran

> *She was true to me, she was true to you,*
> *She was true to the whole damned army, too.*

Not surprisingly, American soldiers suffered from high rates of venereal disease.

The dreaded German drive on the western front exploded in the spring of 1918. Spearheaded by about half a million troops, the enemy rolled forward with terrifying momentum. So dire was the peril that the Allied nations for the first time united under a supreme commander, the quiet French Marshal Ferdinand Foch, whose axiom was "To make war is to attack."

At last the ill-trained "Yanks" were coming—and not a moment too soon. Late in May 1918, the German juggernaut, smashing to within forty miles of Paris, threatened to knock out France. Newly arrived American troops, numbering fewer than thirty thousand, were thrown into the breach at the **Battle of Château-Thierry**, right in the teeth of the German advance. This was a historic moment—the first significant engagement of American troops in a European war. Battle-fatigued French soldiers gaped as the roads filled with inexhaustible truckloads of American doughboys. With their arrival, it was clear that a new American giant had arisen in the West to replace the dying Russian titan in the East.

America had now put decisive military weight on the scales. By July 1918 the awesome German drive had spent its force, and the AEF joined a Foch counteroffensive in the Second Battle of the Marne. This engagement marked the beginning of a German

Château-Thierry, Battle of (1918)
The first significant engagement of American troops in World War I—and, indeed, in any European war. To weary French soldiers, the American doughboys were an image of fresh and gleaming youth.

Examining the Evidence
"Mademoiselle From Armentières"

Some familiar songs, such as Julia Ward Howe's stirring Civil War–era melody "Battle Hymn of the Republic," were penned by known composers and have well-established scores and lyrics. But many ballads have no specific author. Songwriters may fit new verses to known tunes, but the songs essentially grow out of the soil of popular culture and take on a life of their own. "Yankee Doodle Dandy," for example, originated during the seventeenth-century English Civil War, was adapted by the American revolutionaries more than a century later, and was parodied by Southerners during the American Civil War:

> Yankee Doodle had a mind
> To whip the Southern "traitors,"
> Because they didn't choose to live
> On codfish and potaters.

"Stagger Lee," or "Stagolee," a blues ballad supposedly based on a murder in Memphis in the 1930s, has been played in countless renditions, with its homicidal subject variously portrayed as a ruthless badman or a civil rights hero.

This process of accretion and adaptation can furnish valuable clues to historians about changing sentiments and sensibilities, just as the ballads themselves give expression to feelings not always evident in the official record. Folklorist Alan Lomax spent a lifetime tracking down American ballads, documenting layers of life and experience not usually excavated by traditional scholars. In the case of the First World War's most notorious song, "Mademoiselle from Armentières" (or "Hinky Dinky, Parley-Voo?"), Lomax compiled from various sources more than six hundred soldier-authored stanzas, some of which are reproduced here (others he delicately described as "not mailable").

> Mademoiselle from Armentières,
> She hadn't been kissed in forty years.

> She might have been young for all we knew,
> When Napoleon flopped at Waterloo....
> You'll never get your croix de Guerre,
> If you never wash your underwear....

> The French, they are a funny race,
> They fight with their feet and save their face.

> The cootie [louse] is the national bug of France.
> The cootie's found all over France,
> No matter where you hang your pants....

> Oh, the seventy-seventh went over the top,
> A sous lieutenant, a Jew, and a Wop....

> The officers get all the steak,
> And all we get is the belly-ache.

> The general got a Croix de Guerre,
> The son-of-a-gun was never there....

> There's many and many a married man,
> Wants to go back to France again.

> 'Twas a hell of a war as we recall,
> But still 'twas better than none at all.

1. What fresh—and irreverent—perspectives do these stanzas reveal about the soldier's-eye view of military life?
2. What view of France and the French people is implied in the lyrics? How do the ordinary American soldiers view their own experience of being in France?
3. What does the implied sexual content of the song and the "Mademoiselle" who supposedly inspired it reveal about this war as a "gendered" activity?

From John A. Lomax and Alan Lomax, *American Ballads and Folksongs*, pp. 558–560. Reprinted by permission of Odyssey Productions, Inc.)

withdrawal that was never effectively reversed. In September 1918 nine American divisions (about 243,000 men) joined four French divisions to push the Germans from the St. Mihiel salient, a German dagger in France's flank.

The Americans meanwhile demanded and got a separate army under their own command. General John J. Pershing was assigned a front stretching northwestward from the Swiss border to the French lines. As part of the last mighty Allied assault, Pershing's army undertook the **Meuse-Argonne offensive**, from September 26 to November 11, 1918. This battle, the most gargantuan thus far in American history, lasted forty-seven days and engaged 1.2 million American troops. With especially heavy fighting in the rugged Argonne Forest, the killed and wounded mounted to 120,000.

Victory was in sight—and fortunately so. The slowly advancing American armies in France were eating up their supplies so rapidly that they were in grave danger of running short. But the battered Germans were staggering under the sledgehammer blows of the Allies and suffering from critical food shortages caused by the British blockade. Propaganda leaflets containing seductive Wilsonian promises rained upon their crumbling lines from balloons, shells, and rockets.

Berlin was now ready to hoist the white flag. In October 1918 the Germans first sought a peace based on the Fourteen Points. But Wilson made it clear that the kaiser must be thrown overboard before an armistice could be negotiated. The war-weary Germans took the hint and forced the kaiser to flee to Holland.

The exhausted Germans laid down their arms at eleven o'clock on the eleventh day of the eleventh month of 1918, and an eerie, numbing silence fell over the western front. War-taut America burst into a delirium of around-the-clock rejoicing, the streets jammed with laughing, whooping, milling, dancing masses as the "war to end wars" had ended. But the costs exceeded comprehension: nearly 9 million soldiers had died and more than 20 million had suffered grievous wounds. To make matters even worse, some 30 million people perished in a worldwide influenza pandemic in 1918-1919. Over 550,000 Americans—more than ten times the number of U.S. combat casualties—died from flu.

The United States' main contribution to the ultimate victory had been foodstuffs, munitions, credits, oil, and manpower—but not battlefield victories. The AEF fought only two major battles, St. Mihiel and the Meuse-Argonne. It was the *prospect* of endless U.S. troop reserves, rather than America's actual military performance, that eventually demoralized the Germans.

General Pershing's army itself, meanwhile, purchased more of its supplies in Europe than it shipped from the United States, including most of its artillery and nearly all of its aircraft. America was no arsenal of democracy in this war; that role awaited it in the next global conflict, two decades later.

Meuse-Argonne offensive (1918)
Effort led by General John J. ("Black Jack") Pershing to cut the German railroad lines supplying the western front. One of the few major battles that Americans participated in during the entire war, it was still under way when the war ended.

★ Wilson Steps Down from Olympus

Woodrow Wilson had helped to win the war. What part would he now play in shaping the peace? Expectations ran extravagantly high. As the fighting in Europe crashed to a close, the American president towered at the summit of his popularity and power. No other man had ever occupied so dizzy a pinnacle as moral leader of the world. Wilson also had behind him the prestige of victory and the economic resources of the mightiest nation on earth. But at this fateful moment, his sureness of touch deserted him, and he began to make a series of tragic fumbles.

Hoping to strengthen his hand at the Paris peace table, Wilson personally appealed for a Democratic victory in the congressional elections of November 1918. But the maneuver backfired when voters instead returned a narrow Republican majority to Congress. Having staked his reputation on the outcome, Wilson went to Paris as a diminished leader. Unlike all the parliamentary statesmen at the table, he did not command a legislative majority at home.

Wilson's decision to go in person to Paris to help make the peace infuriated Republicans, who saw it as flamboyant grandstanding. He further ruffled Republican feathers when he neglected to include a single Republican senator in his official peace delegation. The logical choice was the new chairman of the Senate Committee on Foreign

> The English science fiction writer H. G. Wells (1866–1946), soon a strong proponent of the League of Nations, spoke for many Europeans when he praised Woodrow Wilson in 1917:
>
> "In all the world there is no outstanding figure to which the world will listen, there is no man audible in all the world, in Japan as well as Germany and Rome as well as Boston—except the President of the United States."

Relations, slender and aristocratically bewhiskered Henry Cabot Lodge of Massachusetts. But Wilson loathed him, and the feeling was hotly reciprocated. An accomplished author with a Harvard Ph.D., Lodge had been known as "the scholar in politics" until Wilson came on the scene. The two men were at daggers drawn, personally and politically.

★ An Idealist amid the Imperialists

Idealist Woodrow Wilson received tumultuous welcomes from the masses of France, Britain, and Italy, even as their wary statesmen tried to keep the new messiah at arm's length from worshipful crowds. When it came to negotiating the shape of the postwar world at the Paris Conference of great and small nations begun on January 18, 1919, the Allies formed an inner circle known as the Big Four, with Wilson, representing the richest and freshest great power, more or less in charge. He was joined by genial Premier Vittorio Orlando of Italy, Prime Minister David Lloyd George of Britain, and cynical, hard-bitten Premier Georges Clemenceau of France, known as "the Tiger."

Wilson first bent his energies to preventing any vengeful parceling out of the former colonies of the vanquished powers. He tried to force through a compromise between naked imperialism and idealism. The victors would not take possession of conquered territories, like Syria and Iraq, but would receive them as trustees of the League of Nations. In practice this half-loaf solution was little more than the old colonialism, thinly disguised. But in decades to come anticolonial independence movements would wield the Wilsonian ideal of self-determination against their imperial occupiers.

Meanwhile, Wilson had been serving as midwife for a world parliament known as the **League of Nations**, which he envisioned as containing an assembly with seats for all nations and a council to be controlled by the great powers. To his great satisfaction, in February 1919, his fellow treatymakers agreed to make the League Covenant, Wilson's brainchild, an integral part of the final peace treaty. But tough bargains and grinding compromises loomed ahead in Paris.

The hardheaded Clemenceau pressed French demands for the German-inhabited Rhineland and the Saar Valley, a rich coal area. Faced with fierce Wilsonian opposition to this violation of self-determination, France settled for a compromise whereby the Saar basin would remain under the League of Nations for fifteen years, and then a popular vote would determine its fate. (The Saar population voted overwhelmingly to rejoin Germany in 1935.) Wilson's next battle was with Italy over Fiume, a valuable seaport inhabited by both Italians and Yugoslavs. When Italy demanded Fiume, Wilson insisted that the seaport go to Yugoslavia and appealed over the heads of Italy's leaders to the country's masses. The maneuver fell flat. The Italian delegates went home in a huff, while the Italian masses turned savagely against Wilson.

Another crucial struggle was with Japan over China's Shandong (Shantung) Peninsula and the German islands in the Pacific, which the Japanese had seized during the war. Japan received the strategic Pacific islands under a League of Nations mandate,* But Wilson staunchly opposed Japanese control of Shandong as a violation of self-determination for its 30 million Chinese residents. When the Japanese threatened to walk out, however, Wilson reluctantly accepted a compromise whereby Japan kept Germany's economic holdings in Shandong and pledged to return the peninsula to China at a later date. The Chinese were outraged by this imperialistic solution, while Clemenceau jeered that Wilson "talked like Jesus Christ and acted like Lloyd George."

League of Nations (1919) *A world organization of national governments proposed by President Woodrow Wilson and established by the Treaty of Versailles in 1919. It worked to facilitate peaceful international cooperation. Despite emotional appeals by Wilson, isolationists' objections to the League created the major obstacle to American signing of the Treaty of Versailles.*

---

*In due time the Japanese illegally fortified these islands—the Marshalls, Marianas, and Carolines—and used them as bases against the United States in World War II.

Wilson in Dover, England, 1919 Hailed by many Europeans in early 1919 as the savior of the Western world, Wilson was a fallen idol only a few months later, when his own countrymen repudiated the peace treaty he had helped to craft.

A completed **Treaty of Versailles** was handed to the Germans in June 1919—almost literally on the point of a bayonet. Excluded from the settlement negotiations in Paris, Germany had capitulated in the hope that it would be granted a peace based on the Fourteen Points. A careful analysis of the treaty shows that only four of the original Wilsonian points were fully honored. Vengeance, not reconciliation, was the treaty's dominant tone. Loud and bitter cries of betrayal burst from German throats—charges that Adolf Hitler would soon reiterate during his meteoric rise to power in Germany.

Wilson was guilty of no conscious betrayal. But the Allied powers were torn by conflicting aims, many of them sanctioned by secret treaties. There had to be compromise at Paris, or there would be no agreement. Faced with hard realities, Wilson was forced to abandon some of his less-cherished Fourteen Points in order to salvage the more precious League of Nations. All the same, the loudly condemned treaty actually had much to commend it. Not least among its merits was its liberation of many oppressed peoples, such as the Poles, from the yoke of imperial dynasties.

Treaty of Versailles (1919) *Treaty signed after six months of tough negotiations, establishing terms of settlement of the First World War. Article 231, "the war guilt clause," blamed the war on Germany, forcing German disarmament and saddling Germany with heavy reparations payments. Germans detested the treaty as too harsh, the French feared it was too weak, and the U.S. Senate rejected it, largely because it obliged the United States to join the League of Nations.*

★ Wilson's Battle for Ratification

Returning to America, Wilson sailed straight into a political typhoon. Isolationists raised a whirlwind of protest against the treaty, especially against Wilson's commitment to ushering the United States into his newfangled League of Nations, which they regarded as either a useless "sewing circle" or an overpotent "superstate." The opposition's hard core

irreconcilables *Hardcore group of militant isolationists, led by Senators William Borah of Idaho and Hiram Johnson of California, who opposed Wilson's dream of international cooperation in the League of Nations after World War I. Played an important part in preventing American participation in the organization.*

was composed of a dozen or so militants, led by Idaho Senator William Borah and California Senator Hiram Johnson, known as **irreconcilables**. Invoking the revered advice of Washington and Jefferson, they wanted no part of any "entangling alliance."

Nor were isolationists Wilson's only problem. Critics showered the Treaty of Versailles with abuse from all sides. Rabid Hun-haters regarded the pact as not harsh enough. Principled liberals thought it too punitive. German Americans, Italian Americans, and others whom Wilson had termed "hyphenated Americans" were aroused because the peace settlement was not sufficiently favorable to their native lands. Irish Americans in particular feared that the League would empower Britain in the face of any movement for Irish independence.

Despite mounting discontent, a strong majority of the people still seemed favorable to the treaty, with the "Wilson League" firmly riveted as Part I. At this time—early July 1919—Senator Lodge had no real hope of defeating the Treaty of Versailles. His strategy was merely to amend it in such a way as to "Americanize," "Republicanize," or "senatorialize" it.

Lodge effectively used delay to muddle and divide public opinion. He read the entire 264-page treaty aloud in the Senate Foreign Relations Committee and held protracted hearings in which people of various nationalities aired their grievances. Wilson fretted increasingly as the hot summer of 1919 wore on. The pact was bogged down in the Senate, while the nation was drifting into confusion and apathy. He therefore decided to take his case to the country in a spectacular speechmaking tour. Wilson undertook his strenuous barnstorming campaign despite protests from physicians and friends. Never robust, Wilson's frail body had begun to sag under the strain of his first wife's death in 1914, partisan strife, a global war, and a stressful peace conference. But he declared that he was willing to die, like the soldiers he had sent into battle, for the sake of the new world order.

The presidential tour, begun in September 1919, started off shakily in the Midwest, but the reception improved in the Rocky Mountain region and the Pacific Coast. The high point—and the breaking point—of the return trip came in Pueblo, Colorado, on September 25, 1919. With tears coursing down his cheeks, Wilson pleaded for the League of Nations as the only real hope of preventing future wars. That night he collapsed from physical and nervous exhaustion. A "funeral train" whisked him back to Washington, where several days later a stroke paralyzed one side of his body. During the next few weeks he lay in a darkened room in the White House. For more than seven months he did not meet his cabinet.

Senator Lodge was now at the helm. After failing to amend the treaty outright, he finally came up with fourteen formal reservations to it—a sardonic slap at Wilson's Fourteen Points. These safeguards reserved the rights of the United States under the Monroe Doctrine and otherwise sought to protect American sovereignty. Wilson, hating Lodge, saw red at the mere suggestion of the Lodge reservations.

Too feeble to lead, Wilson remained strong enough to obstruct. When the day finally came for the Senate vote, he sent word to all true Democrats to vote *against* the treaty with the odious Lodge reservations attached. On November 19, 1919, loyal Democrats in the Senate did Wilson's bidding, helping to reject the treaty, by a vote of 55 to 39. So strong was public indignation at the vote that the Senate was forced to act a second time. In March 1920 the treaty was brought up again, with the Lodge reservations tacked on. There was only one possible path to success—passing the pact with the reservations included. But the sickly Wilson again sent word to all loyal Democrats to vote down the treaty with the obnoxious reservations. He thus signed the death warrant of the treaty as far as America was concerned. On March 19, 1920, the treaty netted a simple majority but failed to get the necessary two-thirds majority by a count of 49 yeas to 35 nays.

Who defeated the treaty? The Lodge-Wilson personal feud, traditionalism, isolationism, disillusionment, and partisanship all contributed to the confused picture. But Wilson himself must bear a substantial share of the responsibility. He asked for all or nothing—and got nothing.

★ The "Solemn Referendum" of 1920

Wilson proposed to settle the treaty issue in the forthcoming presidential campaign by appealing to the people for a "solemn referendum." This was sheer folly, for a true mandate on the League in the noisy arena of politics was clearly impossible.

Jubilant Republicans gathered in Chicago in June 1920 with wayward bull moosers back in the corral (after Theodore Roosevelt's death in 1919) and the senatorial Old Guard back in the saddle. A group of Senate bosses meeting in the historic "smoke-filled" Room 404 of the Hotel Blackstone, informally decided on affable and malleable Senator Warren G. Harding of Ohio as the party's presidential nominee. To run with the "folksy," back-slapping former newspaper editor, the party nominated for vice president frugal, grim-faced Governor Calvin ("Silent Cal") Coolidge of Massachusetts. Meeting in San Francisco, Democrats nominated earnest Governor James M. Cox of Ohio, who strongly supported the League. His running mate was Assistant Navy Secretary Franklin D. Roosevelt, a young, handsome, vibrant New Yorker.

Democratic attempts to make the campaign a referendum on the League were thwarted by Senator Harding, who offered muddled and contradictory statements on the issue from his front porch. With newly enfranchised women swelling the vote totals, Harding was swept into power with a prodigious plurality of over 7 million votes—16,143,407 to 9,130,328 for Cox, the largest victory margin to that date in a presidential election. The electoral count was 404 to 127. Eugene V. Debs, federal prisoner number 9653 in the Atlanta Penitentiary, rolled up the largest vote ever for the left-wing Socialist party—919,799.

Public desire for a change found vent in a resounding repudiation of "high and mighty" Wilsonianism. Tired of star-reaching idealism, and soothed by Harding's promise of a return to "normalcy," voters were willing to accept a second-rate president—and they got a third-rate one.

Republican isolationists successfully turned Harding's victory into a death sentence for the League. Politicians increasingly shunned the League as they would a leper. When the legendary Wilson died in 1924, admirers knelt in the snow outside his Washington home. His "great vision" of a league for peace had perished long before.

★ The Betrayal of Great Expectations

America's spurning of the League was tragically short-sighted. The Republic had helped to win a costly war, but it foolishly kicked the fruits of victory under the table. Whether a strong international organization would have averted World War II in 1939 will always be a matter of dispute. But there can be no doubt that the orphaned League of Nations was undercut at the start by the refusal of the mightiest power on the globe to join it.

The ultimate collapse of the Treaty of Versailles must be laid, at least in some degree, at America's doorstep. This complicated pact, tied in with the four other peace treaties through the League Covenant, was a top-heavy structure designed to rest on a four-legged table. When the fourth leg, the United States, was never put into place the rickety contraption teetered for over a decade and then crashed in ruins—a debacle that played into the hands of the German demagogue Adolf Hitler.

The United States hurt its own cause when it buried its head in the sand. Granted that the conduct of its Allies had been disillusioning, carrying through the Wilsonian program would have served its own interests. By embracing the role of global leader, the United States could have used its enormous strength to shape the world's future. Instead it permitted the warring nations of World War I blithely to drift toward the abyss of a second and even more bloody international disaster.

Varying Viewpoints

Woodrow Wilson: Realist or Idealist?

As the first president to take the United States into a foreign war, Woodrow Wilson was obliged to make a systematic case to the American people to justify his unprecedented European intervention. His ideas have largely defined the character of American foreign policy ever since—for better or worse.

"Wilsonianism" comprised three closely related principles: (1) the era of American isolation from world affairs had irretrievably ended; (2) the United States must infuse its own founding political and economic ideas—including democracy, the rule of law, free trade, and national self-determination (or anticolonialism)—into the international order; and (3) American influence could eventually steer the world away from rivalry and warfare and toward a cooperative and peaceful international system, maintained by the League of Nations or, later, the United Nations.

Whether that Wilsonian vision constituted hard-nosed realism or starry-eyed idealism has excited scholarly debate for nearly a century. "Realists," such as George F. Kennan and Henry Kissinger, insist that Wilson was anything but a realist. They criticize the president as a naïve, impractical dreamer who failed to understand that the international order was, and always will be, an anarchic, unruly arena, outside the rule of law, where only military force can effectively protect the nation's security. In a sharp critique in his 1950 study, *American Diplomacy*, Kennan condemned Wilson's vision as "moralism-legalism." In this view Wilson dangerously threatened to sacrifice American self-interests on the altar of his admirable but ultimately unworkable ideas.

Wilson's defenders, including his biographers Arthur S. Link and Thomas J. Knock, argue that Wilson's idealism was in fact a kind of higher realism, recognizing as it did that armed conflict on the scale of World War I could never again be tolerated and that some framework of peaceful international relations simply had to be found. The development of nuclear weapons in a later generation gave this argument more force. This "liberal" defense of Wilsonianism derives from the centuries-old liberal faith that, given sufficient intelligence and willpower, the world can be made a better place. Realists reject this notion of moral and political progress as hopelessly innocent, especially as applied to international affairs.

Some leftist scholars, such as William Appleman Williams, have argued that Wilson was in fact a realist of another kind: a subtle and wily imperialist whose stirring rhetoric cloaked a grasping ambition to make the United States the world's dominant economic power. Sometimes called "the imperialism of free trade," this strategy allegedly sought not to decolonialize the world and open up international commerce for the good of peoples elsewhere, but to create a system in which American economic might would irresistibly prevail. Wilson's defenders would claim that in a Wilsonian world, *all* parties would be better off because of free trade and international competition. Still other scholars, especially John Milton Cooper, Jr., have emphasized the absence of economic factors in shaping Wilson's diplomacy. Isolationism, so this argument goes, held such sway over American thinking precisely because the United States had such a puny financial stake abroad—no hard American economic interests were mortally threatened in 1917, nor for a long time thereafter. In these circumstances Wilson—and the Wilsonians who came after him, such as Franklin D. Roosevelt—had no choice but to appeal to abstract ideals and high principles. The "idealistic" Wilsonian strain in American diplomacy, in this view, may have been an unavoidable heritage of America's historically isolated situation. If so, it was Wilson's genius to make practical use of those ideas in his bid for popular support of his diplomacy.

A new generation of scholars has begun to explore the influence of Wilsonian ideals on social movements outside the United States and Europe. Erez Manela has argued that emerging anticolonial and nationalist movements appropriated Wilsonian ideals and adapted them to their own political ends, challenging forms of colonialism that Wilson himself failed to criticize. In this view the legacy of Wilsonian foreign policy may have been felt most strongly outside the United States.

CHAPTER SUMMARY

As soon as he assumed the presidency, the eloquent, idealistic, but often ideologically self-righteous Woodrow Wilson successfully carried out a sweeping progressive program of economic reform of the tariff, money and banking, and the trusts—what Wilson called the "triple wall of privilege." He also achieved substantial social reforms that benefited women and the working classes, but his lack of sympathy for blacks actually furthered segregation.

Wilson's attempt to implement similar progressive moral goals in foreign policy was less successful, as he stumbled into military involvements in the Caribbean and revolutionary Mexico. The outbreak of World War I in Europe brought growing risks of American involvement, especially because of the threat to neutral shipping from German submarine warfare. Led by President Wilson, most Americans earnestly sought to stay clear of the war, though all but a minority sympathized more with the Allies than the Germans.

Wilson temporarily avoided war by extracting the precarious *Sussex* pledge from Germany. His progressive campaign of 1916, appealing to workers and former bull moose supporters, narrowly won him reelection over Charles Evans Hughes and the Republicans. While Wilson never promised to stay out of war, many voters were also attracted by his emphasis on peace.

Germany's declaration of unlimited submarine warfare in January 1917, as well as the Zimmermann note proposing a German alliance with Mexico, finally caused the United States to declare war. Wilson aroused the country to patriotic heights by declaring the war an idealistic crusade for democracy and a just peace, based on his ideologically liberal Fourteen Points.

Vigorous wartime propaganda stirred voluntary commitment to the war effort, but at the cost of stifling dissent and curtailing civil liberties. American voluntary mobilization worked wonders in organizing industry, producing food, and financing the war. Labor, including women, made substantial wartime gains, though numerous strikes and the radical Industrial Workers of the World caused disruptions. Some progressive women opposed the war, but the majority of women's wartime efforts helped spur passage of the Nineteenth (Suffrage) Amendment. The beginnings of the Great Migration of blacks from the South to northern cities, sometimes as strikebreakers, led to racial tensions and riots.

Despite the emphasis on voluntarism, the federal government turned to the coercive military draft to produce the vast American Expeditionary Force in a brief time. America's soldiers took nearly a year to arrive in Europe, and they fought in only two major battles at the end of the war. America's main contribution to the Allied victory was to provide new enthusiasm and morale, along with the threat of endless supplies of men and *matériel* to follow. Wilson's immense prestige created high expectations for an idealistic peace based on his Fourteen Points. But his own political blunders and the clever, stubborn opposition of European statesmen forced him to compromise his lofty aims and made the Versailles Treaty considerably harsher than he intended.

Opposition to Wilson and the League of Nations arose not only from traditional isolationists but from militant anti-Germans, liberals, and diverse ethnic groups. As Henry Cabot Lodge stalled the treaty in the U.S. Senate, Wilson tried to rouse the country on behalf of his cherished League. A stroke ended Wilson's pro-League speaking tour, and his stubborn refusal to compromise with Lodge and the Republicans finally killed the treaty and the League. Wilson sought a "solemn referendum" on the League in the election of 1920, but the public delivered a harsh repudiation of Wilsonianism. Republican isolationists turned Harding's victory into a death sentence for the League. America thus turned its back on international affairs and harmed its own best interests in shaping a global order.

KEY TERMS

Underwood Tariff (497)
Federal Reserve Act (497)
Federal Trade Commission Act (497)
Clayton Anti-Trust Act (497)
holding companies (497)
Workingmen's Compensation Act (498)
Adamson Act (498)
Jones Act (498)
Tampico Incident (500)
Central Powers (500)
Allies (500)
U-boats (500)
Lusitania (501)
Zimmermann note (503)
Fourteen Points (504)
Committee on Public Information (504)
Espionage Act (505)
Schenck v. United States (505)
War Industries Board (506)
Industrial Workers of the World (506)
Great Migration (506)
Nineteenth Amendment (506)
Sheppard-Towner Maternity Act (507)
Château-Thierry, Battle of (509)
Meuse-Argonne offensive (511)
League of Nations (512)
Treaty of Versailles (513)
irreconcilables (514)

PEOPLE TO KNOW

Louis D. Brandeis
Francisco ("Pancho") Villa
Arthur Zimmermann
George Creel
Eugene V. Debs
William D. ("Big Bill") Haywood
Herbert C. Hoover
Alice Paul
Henry Cabot Lodge

MindTap is a fully online, highly personalized learning experience built upon Cengage Learning content. MindTap combines student learning tools—readings, multimedia, activities, and assessments—into a singular Learning Path that guides students through the course.

Chapter 30

American Life in the "Roaring Twenties"
1920–1929

• • •

America's present need is not heroics but healing; not nostrums but normalcy; not revolution but restoration; . . . not surgery but serenity.

WARREN G. HARDING, 1920

Chapter Outline

- The Red Scare and the Ku Klux Klan
- Immigration Restriction, 1921–1924
- Prohibition and Gangsterism
- Cultural Conflict and the Scopes Trial
- The Mass-Consumption Economy and the Automobile Age
- Radio, Film, and Music in the Jazz Age
- Changes in Sexuality and Race
- The Economic Boom
- Makers of America: The Poles
- Examining the Evidence: The Jazz Singer, 1927

Bloodied by the war and disillusioned by the peace, Americans turned inward in the 1920s. Shunning diplomatic commitments to foreign countries, they also denounced "radical" foreign ideas, condemned "un-American" lifestyles, and clanged shut the immigration gates against foreign peoples. They partly sealed off the domestic economy from the rest of the world and plunged headlong into a dizzying decade of homegrown prosperity.

The boom of the golden twenties showered genuine benefits on Americans, as incomes and living standards rose for many. But there seemed to be something incredible about it all, even as people sang:

> My sister she works in the laundry,
> My father sells bootlegger gin,
> My mother she takes in the washing,
> My God, how the money rolls in!

New technologies, new consumer products, and new forms of leisure and entertainment made the twenties roar. Yet just beneath the surface lurked widespread anxieties about the future and fears that America was losing sight of its traditional ways.

FOCUS QUESTIONS

1. Why did the United States turn so sharply inward and embrace social conservatism in the wake of World War I?

2. What were the major cultural conflicts that occurred over immigration, cultural pluralism, prohibition, and evolution in the 1920s? Why did these issues create such strong polarization among Americans?

3. What were the major features of the new "mass consumer economy," and what effects did it have on the way Americans lived?

4. How did the "new media" of radio, film, and recorded music help transform sexuality and mass popular culture?

5. How were the new ideas of the times reflected in the American literary renaissance of the 1920s? How was the Harlem Renaissance of black writers similar to and different from artistic movements in the white literary world?

CHRONOLOGY

1903	Wright brothers fly first airplane First story-sequence motion picture	1923	Equal Rights Amendment (ERA) proposed
1908	Henry Ford introduces Model T	1924	Immigration Act of 1924
1914	W.C. Handy's "St. Louis Blues" debuts	1925	Scopes trial Florida real estate boom Fitzgerald publishes *The Great Gatsby* Dreiser publishes *An American Tragedy*
1917	Bolshevik Revolution in Russia		
1919	Eighteenth Amendment (prohibition) Volstead Act Seattle general strike Anderson publishes *Winesburg, Ohio*	1926	Hughes publishes *The Weary Blues* Hemingway publishes *The Sun Also Rises*
1919–1920	"Red scare"	1927	Lindbergh flies solo across Atlantic First talking motion picture, *The Jazz Singer* Sacco and Vanzetti executed
1920	Radio broadcasting begins Fitzgerald publishes *This Side of Paradise* Lewis publishes *Main Street*	1928	Eugene O'Neill's *Strange Interlude* debuts on Broadway
1921	Sacco-Vanzetti trial Emergency Quota Act Bureau of the Budget created	1929	Faulkner publishes *The Sound and the Fury* Hemingway publishes *A Farewell to Arms*
1922	Lewis publishes *Babbitt* Eliot publishes *The Waste Land*	1932	Al Capone imprisoned

★ Seeing Red

Hysterical fears of red Russia continued to color American thinking for several years after Communists came to power in the **Bolshevik Revolution** of 1917, which spawned a tiny Communist party in America. Tensions were heightened by an epidemic of strikes that convulsed the Republic at war's end, many of them the result of high prices and frustrated union-organizing drives. Upstanding Americans jumped to the conclusion that labor troubles were fomented by bomb-and-whisker Bolsheviks. A general strike in Seattle in 1919, though modest in its demands and orderly in its methods, prompted a call from the mayor for federal troops to head off "the anarchy of Russia." Fire-and-brimstone evangelist Billy Sunday said he would like to "fill the jails so full of [Bolsheviks] that their feet would stick out the window."

The big **red scare** of 1919–1920 resulted in a nationwide crusade against left-wingers whose Americanism was suspect. Attorney General A. Mitchell Palmer earned the title of the "Fighting Quaker" for his excess zeal in rounding up about six thousand suspects. When a bomb shattered both the nerves and the Washington home of Palmer in June 1919, the "Fighting Quaker" was dubbed the "Quaking Fighter." Late in December 1919, a shipload of 249 alleged alien radicals was deported on the *Buford* ("the Soviet Ark") to the "workers' paradise" of Russia. Hysteria was revived in September 1920 when a still-unexplained bomb blast on Wall Street killed thirty-eight people and wounded more than a hundred others.

Various states joined the pack in the outcry against radicals. In 1919–1920 a number of legislatures passed **criminal syndicalism laws** that outlawed the mere *advocacy* of violence to secure social change. Critics protested that mere words were not criminal deeds, that there was a great gulf between throwing fits and throwing bombs, and that "free screech" was for the nasty as well as the nice. Violence was done to traditional American concepts of free speech as IWW members and other radicals were vigorously prosecuted.

Bolshevik Revolution (1917) *The second stage of the Russian Revolution in November 1917 when Vladimir Lenin and his Bolshevik party seized power and established a communist state. The first stage had occurred the previous February when more moderate revolutionaries overthrew the Russian czar.*

red scare (1919–1920) *A period of intense anticommunism. The "Palmer raids" of Attorney General A. Mitchell Palmer resulted in about six thousand deportations of people suspected of "subversive" activities.*

criminal syndicalism laws (1919–1920) *Laws passed by many states during the red scare outlawing the mere advocacy of violence to secure social change. Stump speakers for the Industrial Workers of the World were special targets.*

The hysteria went so far that in 1920 five members of the New York legislature, all lawfully elected, were denied their seats simply because they were Socialists.

The red scare was a godsend to conservative businesspeople, who used it to break the backs of the fledgling unions. Labor's call for the "closed," or all-union, shop was denounced as "Sovietism in disguise." Employers, in turn, hailed their own antiunion campaign for the "open" shop as the **American plan**.

Anti-redism and antiforeignism were reflected in a notorious case regarded by liberals as a "judicial lynching." Nicola Sacco, a shoe-factory worker, and Bartolomeo Vanzetti, a fish peddler, were convicted in 1921 of the murder of a Massachusetts paymaster and his guard. The jury and judge were prejudiced in some degree against the defendants because they were Italians, atheists, anarchists, and draft dodgers.

Liberals and radicals the world over rallied to the defense of the two aliens doomed to die. The case dragged on for six years until 1927, when the condemned men were electrocuted. Communists and other radicals were thus presented with two martyrs in the "class struggle," while many American liberals hung their heads.

American plan *A business-oriented approach to worker relations popular among firms in the 1920s to defeat unionization. Managers sought to strengthen their communication with workers and to offer benefits like pensions and insurance. They insisted on an "open shop" in contrast to the mandatory union membership through the "closed shop" that many labor activists had demanded in the strike wave after World War I.*

★ Hooded Hoodlums of the KKK

A new Ku Klux Klan, spawned by the postwar reaction, mushroomed fearsomely in the early 1920s. Despite the familiar sheets and hoods, it more closely resembled the antiforeign nativist movements of the 1850s than the antiblack nightriders of the 1860s. The new KKK was antiforeign, anti-Catholic, antiblack, anti-Jewish, antipacifist, anti-Communist, anti-internationalist, anti-evolutionist, anti-adultery, and anti–birth control. It was also pro–Anglo Saxon, pro–"native" American, and pro-Protestant. In short, the besheeted Klan betokened an extremist, ultraconservative uprising against many of the forces of diversity and modernity that were transforming American culture.

As reconstituted, the Klan spread with astonishing rapidity, especially among some white Protestants in the Midwest and South. At its peak in the mid-1920s, the Klan claimed about 5 million dues-paying members and wielded potent political influence. The "Knights of the Invisible Empire" included among their officials Imperial Wizards, Grand Goblins, and King Kleagles. The Klan's most impressive displays were "konclaves" and huge flag-waving parades. Their chief warning was the blazing cross, and their weapon the bloodied lash, supplemented by tar and feathers.

This reign of hooded horror, so repulsive to the best American ideals, collapsed rather suddenly in the late 1920s. The Klan's bubble burst as decent people at last recoiled from its terrorism, while scandalous embezzling by Klan officials launched a congressional investigation that exposed the movement as a vicious racket. The KKK was an alarming manifestation of the intolerance and prejudice plaguing people anxious about the dizzying pace of social change in the 1920s. Despite the Klan's decline, civil rights activists fought in vain for legislation making lynching a federal crime, as lawmakers feared alienating white southern voters.

Hiram Wesley Evans (1881–1966), imperial wizard of the Ku Klux Klan, in 1926 poignantly described the cultural grievances that fueled the Klan and lay behind much of the Fundamentalist revolt against "Modernism":

"Nordic Americans for the last generation have found themselves increasingly uncomfortable and finally deeply distressed.... One by one all our traditional moral standards went by the boards, or were so disregarded that they ceased to be binding. The sacredness of our Sabbath, of our homes, of chastity, and finally even of our right to teach our own children in our own schools fundamental facts and truths were torn away from us. Those who maintained the old standards did so only in the face of constant ridicule.... We found our great cities and the control of much of our industry and commerce taken over by strangers.... We are a movement of the plain people, very weak in the matter of culture, intellectual support, and trained leadership.... This is undoubtedly a weakness. It lays us open to the charge of being 'hicks' and 'rubes' and 'drivers of second-hand Fords.'"

★ Stemming the Foreign Flood

Isolationist America of the 1920s, ingrown and provincial, had little use for the immigrants who began to flood into the country again as peace settled on the war-torn world. Some 800,000 stepped ashore in 1920–1921, about two-thirds of

Klanswomen on Parade, 1928 Founded in the Reconstruction Era, the Ku Klux Klan enjoyed a remarkable resurgence in the 1920s. Here, women members, unmasked and unapologetic, march down Pennsylvania Avenue under the very shadow of the Capitol Dome.

them from southern and eastern Europe. The "one-hundred-percent Americans," recoiling at the sight of this resumed "New Immigration," once again cried that the famed poem at the base of the Statue of Liberty was all too literally true: they claimed that a sickly Europe was indeed vomiting on America "the wretched refuse of its teeming shore."

Congress temporarily plugged the breach with the Emergency Quota Act of 1921. This stopgap legislation was soon replaced by the **Immigration Act of 1924**. Quotas for foreigners were drastically cut to 2 percent of persons of each nationality living in the United States in 1890, when comparatively few southern Europeans had arrived.* The purpose was clearly to freeze America's existing ethnic composition, which was largely northern European. A flagrantly discriminatory section of the Immigration Act of 1924 slammed the door absolutely against Japanese immigrants. Only Canadians and Latin Americans were exempt from the quota system.

The quota system effected a pivotal departure in American policy, as the country sacrificed something of its tradition of freedom and opportunity, as well as future ethnic diversity. The Immigration Act of 1924 marked the end of an era—a period of virtually unrestricted immigration that in the previous century had brought some 35 million newcomers to the United States, mostly from Europe (see Figure 30.1). The immigrant tide now dwindled to a mere trickle, but it left on American shores by the 1920s a patchwork of ethnic communities separated from the larger society and from each other by language, religion, and customs. Many Italians, Jews, Poles, and others lived in isolated enclaves

Immigration Act of 1924 Established quotas for immigration to the United States. Also known as the "National Origins Act." Immigration from southern and eastern Europe was sharply curtailed, while immigrants from Asia were shut out altogether.

---

*Five years later the Immigration Act of 1929, using 1920 as the quota base, virtually cut immigration in half by limiting the total to 152,574 a year. In 1965 Congress abolished the national-origins quota system.

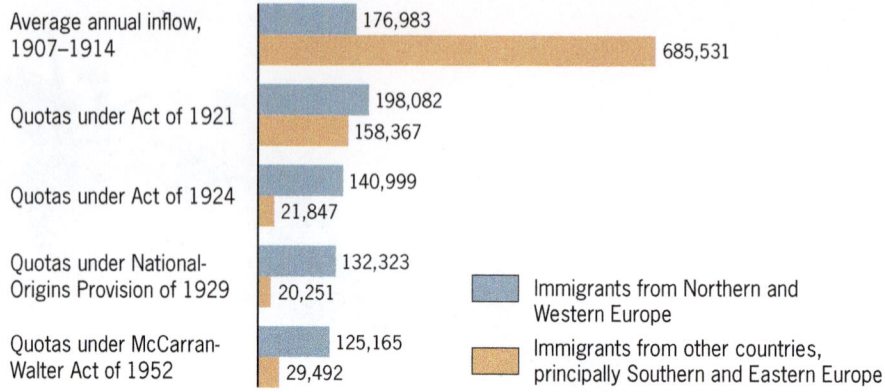

Figure 30.1 Annual Immigration and the Quota Laws

with their own houses of worship, newspapers, and theaters (see "Makers of America: The Poles," p. 523). Efforts to organize labor unions repeatedly foundered on the rocks of ethnic rivalries, which were often played upon by cynical employers. Ethnic variety thus undermined class and political solidarity in America.

Reformers opposed immigration restriction. A chorus of "cultural pluralists" had long criticized the idea that an American "melting pot" would eliminate ethnic differences. Two intellectuals, the philosopher Horace Kallen and critic Randolph Bourne, championed alternative conceptions of the immigrant role in American society. Kallen defended immigrants' right to practice their ancestral customs and preserve their cultural uniqueness. In Kallen's vision, America's ethnic groups should be like the instruments in a symphony orchestra, with each harmonizing with the others while retaining its own identity.

If Kallen stressed the preservation of identity, Bourne advocated greater cross-fertilization among immigrants. Cosmopolitan interchange, Bourne believed, was destined to make America "not a nationality but a trans-nationality, a weaving back and forth … of many threads of all sizes and colors." In this view the United States should serve as the vanguard of a more internationalized and multicultural age.

Other intellectuals, including progressives such as John Dewey, Jane Addams, and Louis Brandeis, joined Kallen and Bourne in their defense of ethnic diversity. Vastly outnumbered in the debate over immigration in the 1920s, these early proponents of "cultural pluralism" planted the seeds for the blooming of "multiculturalism" in the last quarter of the twentieth century.

★ The Prohibition Experiment

One of the last peculiar spasms of the progressive reform movement was prohibition, loudly supported by crusading churches and by many women. The arid new order was authorized in 1919 by the **Eighteenth Amendment** (see the Appendix), as implemented by the **Volstead Act** passed by Congress later that year. Together these laws made the world "safe for hypocrisy."

The legal abolition of alcohol was especially popular in the South and the West. Southern whites were eager to keep stimulants out of the hands of blacks, lest they burst out of "their place." In the West, prohibition represented an attack on all the vices associated with the ubiquitous western saloon: public drunkenness, prostitution, and crime. But despite the overwhelming ratification of the "dry" amendment, strong opposition persisted in the larger eastern cities. For many "wet" foreign-born people, sociability was built around drinking in beer gardens and corner taverns.

Prohibitionists were naïve in the extreme. They overlooked the tenacious American tradition of weak control by the central government, especially over private lives. They forgot that the federal authorities had never satisfactorily enforced a law if the majority of

Eighteenth Amendment (1919) *Prohibited the manufacture, sale, and transportation of alcoholic beverages, ushering in the era known as prohibition.*

Volstead Act (1919) *A federal act enforcing the Eighteenth Amendment, which prohibited the manufacture, sale, and transportation of alcoholic beverages.*

Makers of America

The Poles

The Poles were among the largest immigrant groups to respond to industrializing America's call for badly needed labor after the Civil War. Between 1870 and World War I, some 2 million Polish-speaking peasants boarded steamships bound for the United States. By the 1920s, when antiforeign feeling led to restrictive legislation that choked the immigrant stream to a trickle, Polish immigrants and their American-born children began to develop new identities as Polish Americans.

The first Poles to arrive in the New World had landed in Jamestown in 1608 and helped to develop that colony's timber industry. Over the ensuing two and a half centuries, scattered religious dissenters and revolutionary nationalists also made their way from Poland to America. During the Revolution about one hundred Poles, including two officers recruited by Benjamin Franklin, served in the Continental Army.

But the Polish hopefuls who poured into the United States in the late nineteenth century came primarily to stave off starvation and to earn money to buy land. Known in their homeland as *za chlebem* ("for bread") emigrants, they belonged to the mass of central and eastern European peasants who had been forced off their farms by growing competition from large-scale, mechanized agriculture. An exceptionally high birthrate among the Catholic Poles compounded this economic pressure, creating an army of the land-poor and landless. With wages in the United States more than eight times higher than in Poland, the American magnet was irresistible.

Many Polish immigrants were also lured by glowing letters from friends and relatives already living in the United States. The first wave of Polish immigrants had established a thriving network of self-help and fraternal associations, organized around Polish Catholic parishes. Often, Polish American entrepreneurs helped their European compatriots make travel arrangements or find jobs in the United States. One of the most successful of these, the energetic Chicago grocer Anton Schermann, is credited with "bringing over" a hundred thousand Poles and causing the Windy City to earn the nickname "the American Warsaw."

Most of the Poles arriving in the United States in the late nineteenth century headed for booming industrial cities such as Buffalo, Pittsburgh, Detroit, Milwaukee, and Chicago. In 1907 four-fifths of the men toiled as unskilled laborers in coal mines, meatpacking factories, textile and steel mills, oil refineries, and garment-making shops. Although married women usually stayed home and contributed to the family's earnings by taking in laundry and boarders, children and single girls often joined their fathers and brothers on the job.

When an independent Poland was created after World War I, few Poles chose to return to their Old World homeland. Instead, like other immigrant groups in the 1920s, they redoubled their efforts to integrate into American society. Polish institutions such as churches and fraternal organizations, which had served to perpetuate a distinctive Polish culture in the New World, now facilitated the transformation of Poles into Polish Americans. When Poland was absorbed into the Communist bloc after World War II, Polish Americans clung still more tightly to their American identity, pushing for landmarks such as Chicago's Pulaski Road to memorialize their culture in the New World.

A Polish Child Laboring Among Men In his notes on this 1910 image of workers at an Illinois Glass Company factory in Alton, Illinois, the renowned photographer Lewis Hine recorded: "Even the tiny chap on left end of photo was working. He is a Polish boy who cannot understand English." Poles' traditionally high birthrates in Europe were replicated in the United States during the great wave of Polish immigration in the late nineteenth and early twentieth centuries. Large families put further pressure on children to contribute economically. (For more on Hine's work chronicling child labor, see "Examining the Evidence: The Photography of Lewis W. Hine," p. 399.)

the people—or a strong minority—were hostile to it. Prohibition simply did not prohibit. The old-time "men-only" corner saloons were replaced by thousands of "speakeasies," each with its tiny grilled window through which the thirsty spoke softly before the barred door was opened. Because of the difficulty of transporting and concealing bottles, hard liquor of high alcoholic content gained in popularity. Illegal rumrunners operating from the West Indies or Canada had their inning. "Home brew" and "bathtub gin" became popular, as law-evading adults engaged in "alky cooking" with toy stills.

Yet the "noble experiment" was not entirely a failure. Bank savings increased, and absenteeism in industry decreased, presumably because of the newly sober ways of formerly soused barflies. On the whole, less alcohol was consumed than in the days before prohibition, though strong drink continued to be available. As a legendary tippler remarked, prohibition was "a darn sight better than no liquor at all."

Prohibition also spawned shocking crimes. The lush profits of illegal alcohol led to bribery of the police. Violent wars broke out in the big cities between rival gangs—often rooted in immigrant neighborhoods—who sought to corner the rich market in booze. Rival triggermen used their sawed-off shotguns and chattering "typewriters" (machine guns) to "erase" bootlegging competitors who were trying to "muscle in" on their "racket." In the gang wars of the 1920s in Chicago, about five hundred mobsters were murdered.

Chicago was by far the most spectacular example of lawlessness. In 1925 "Scarface" Al Capone, a grasping and murderous booze distributor, began six years of gang warfare that netted him millions of blood-spattered dollars. He zoomed through the streets in an armor-plated car with bulletproof windows. Capone could not be convicted of the cold-blooded massacre, on St. Valentine's Day in 1929, of seven rival gang members, but he was finally sent to jail in 1932 for income tax evasion.

Gangsters rapidly moved into other profitable and illicit activities: prostitution, gambling, and narcotics. Honest merchants were forced to pay "protection money" to prevent thugs from destroying their property or beating up their employees. Racketeers even invaded the ranks of labor unions as organizers and promoters. Organized crime had come to be one of the nation's most gigantic businesses. By 1930 the annual "take" of the underworld was estimated to be from $12 billion to $18 billion—several times the income of the Washington government.

Racketeers *People who obtain money illegally by fraud, bootlegging, gambling, or threats of violence. Racketeers invaded the ranks of labor during the 1920s, a decade when gambling and gangsterism were prevalent in American life.*

⭐ Monkey Business in Tennessee

Education in the 1920s continued to make giant boot-strides. More and more states were requiring young people to remain in school until age sixteen or eighteen, or until graduation from high school. The proportion of seventeen-year-olds who finished high school almost doubled in the 1920s, to more than one in four.

The most revolutionary contribution to educational theory during these yeasty years was made by mild-mannered Professor John Dewey, who served on the faculty of Columbia University from 1904 to 1930. By common consent one of America's few front-rank philosophers, he set forth the principles of "learning by doing" that formed the foundation of so-called progressive education, with its greater "permissiveness." Dewey believed that the workbench was as essential as the blackboard and that "education for life" should be a primary goal of the teacher.

Science also scored wondrous advances in these years. A massive public health program, launched by the Rockefeller Foundation in the South in 1909, had virtually wiped out the ancient affliction of hookworm by the 1920s. Better nutrition and health care helped to increase the life expectancy of a newborn infant from fifty years in 1901 to fifty-nine years in 1929.

Yet both science and progressive education in the 1920s were subjected to unfriendly fire from Fundamentalists. These devoted religionists charged that the teaching of Darwinian evolution was destroying faith in God and the Bible while contributing to the moral breakdown of youth in the jazz age. Numerous attempts were made to secure

The bombastic Fundamentalist evangelist W. A. (Billy) Sunday (1862–1935) declared in 1925:

"If a minister believes and teaches evolution, he is a stinking skunk, a hypocrite, and a liar."

The Battle over Evolution Opponents of Darwin's theories set up shop at the opening of the famed "Scopes Trial" in Dayton, Tennessee, in 1925. The trial was an early battle in an American "culture war" that was still being waged nearly a century later.

laws prohibiting the teaching of evolution, "the bestial hypothesis," in the public schools, and three southern states adopted such shackling measures. The trio of states included Tennessee, in the heart of the so-called **Bible Belt** South, where evangelical religion was especially robust.

The stage was set for the memorable "Monkey Trial" in the hamlet of Dayton, Tennessee, in 1925. A likable high school biology teacher, John T. Scopes, was indicted for teaching evolution. Batteries of newspaper reporters, armed with notebooks and cameras, descended upon the quiet town to witness the spectacle. Scopes was defended by nationally known attorneys, while former presidential candidate William Jennings Bryan, an ardent Presbyterian Fundamentalist, joined the prosecution. Taking the stand as an expert on the Bible, Bryan was made to appear foolish by the famed criminal lawyer Clarence Darrow. Five days after the trial was over, Bryan died of a stroke, no doubt brought on by the wilting heat and witness-stand strain.

This historic clash between theology and biology proved inconclusive. Scopes, the forgotten man of the drama, was found guilty and fined $100. But the supreme court of Tennessee, while upholding the law, set aside the fine on a technicality. The Fundamentalists at best won only a hollow victory, for the absurdities of the trial cast ridicule on their cause. Yet even though increasing numbers of Christians were coming to reconcile the revelations of religion with the findings of modern science, **Fundamentalism**, with its emphasis on literal reading of the Bible, remained a vibrant force in American spiritual life. It was especially strong in the Baptist Church and in the rapidly growing Churches of Christ, organized in 1906.

Bible Belt *The region of the American South, extending roughly from North Carolina west to Oklahoma and Texas, where Protestant Fundamentalism and belief in literal interpretation of the Bible were traditionally strongest.*

Fundamentalism *A Protestant Christian movement emphasizing the literal truth of the Bible and opposing religious modernism, which sought to reconcile religion and science. It was especially strong in the Baptist Church and the Church of Christ, first organized in 1906.*

★ The Mass-Consumption Economy

Prosperity—real, sustained, and widely shared—put much of the roar into the twenties. The economy kicked off its war harness in 1919, faltered a few steps in the recession of 1920–1921, and then sprinted forward for nearly seven years. Both the recent war and

Treasury Secretary Andrew Mellon's tax policies favored the rapid expansion of capital investment. Ingenious machines, powered by cheap energy from newly tapped oil fields, dramatically increased the productivity of the laborer. Assembly-line production was so advanced at Henry Ford's famed Rouge River plant near Detroit that a finished automobile emerged every ten seconds.

Great new industries suddenly sprouted forth. Supplying electrical power for the humming new machines became a giant business in the 1920s. Above all, the automobile, once the horseless chariot of the rich, now became the carriage of the common citizen. By 1930 Americans owned almost 30 million cars.

The nation's deepening love affair with the automobile headlined a momentous shift in the character of the economy. American manufacturers seemed to have mastered the problems of production; their worries now focused on consumption. Could they find the mass markets for the goods they had contrived to spew forth in such profusion?

Responding to this need, a new arm of American commerce came into being: advertising. By persuasion and ploy, allure and sexual suggestion, advertisers sought to make Americans chronically discontented with their paltry possessions and want more, more, more. A founder of this new Madison Avenue "profession" was Bruce Barton, who published a best seller, *The Man Nobody Knows* (1925), portraying Jesus Christ as the greatest adman of all time. Christ was also an executive who "picked up twelve men from the bottom ranks of business and forged them into an organization that conquered the world."

Sports became big business in the consumer economy of the 1920s. Ballyhooed by the "image makers," home-run heroes such as George H. ("Babe") Ruth were far better known than most statesmen. In 1921 a Jersey City crowd paid more than a million dollars to watch heavyweight champion Jack Dempsey knock out challenger George Carpentier—the first in a series of million-dollar gates in the golden 1920s.

Buying on credit was another innovative feature of the postwar economy. "Possess today and pay tomorrow" was the message directed at buyers. Once-frugal descendants of Puritans went ever deeper into debt to own all kinds of newfangled marvels—refrigerators, vacuum cleaners, and especially cars and radios—*now*. Prosperity thus accumulated an overhanging cloud of debt, and the economy became increasingly vulnerable to disruptions of the credit structure.

★ Putting America on Rubber Tires

A new industrial revolution slipped into high gear in America in the 1920s. Machinery was the new messiah—and the automobile was its principal prophet. The manufacture of millions of private vehicles heralded an amazing new industrial system based on assembly-line methods and mass-production techniques.

Europeans invented the gasoline engine, but Americans quickly adapted it. By the 1890s a few daring American inventors and promoters, including Henry Ford and Ransom E. Olds (Oldsmobile), were developing the infant automotive industry. By 1910 sixty-nine car companies rolled out a total annual production of 181,000 units. Soon an enormous industry sprang into being, as Detroit became the motorcar capital of America. The mechanized colossus owed much to the stopwatch efficiency techniques of Frederick W. Taylor, a prominent engineer and inventor who became known as the "Father of Scientific Management."

The mechanical genius who put America on rubber tires was the lean and silent Henry Ford. This ill-educated, multimillionaire mechanic was socially and culturally narrow. "History is bunk," he once testified. But he dedicated himself with one-track devotion to the gospel of standardization. After two early failures, he grasped and applied fully the techniques of standardization and moving assembly-line production—Fordism. He is supposed to have remarked that the purchaser could have his Model T car in any color he desired—just as long as it was black.

The flood of Fords was phenomenal. In 1914 the "Automobile Wizard" turned out his 500,000th Model T. By 1929, when the great bull market collapsed, Ford had produced nearly 20 million vehicles, and a total of 26 million were registered in the United States. This figure, averaging 1 for every 4.9 Americans, represented far more automobiles than existed in all the rest of the world.

Scientific Management *A system of industrial management created and promoted in the early twentieth century by Frederick W. Taylor, emphasizing stopwatch efficiency to improve factory performance. The system gained immense popularity across the United States and Europe.*

Fordism *A system of assembly-line manufacturing and mass production named after Henry Ford, founder of the Ford Motor Company and developer of the Model T car.*

The impact of the self-propelled carriage on various aspects of American life was tremendous. A gigantic new industry emerged, employing directly or indirectly about 6 million people by 1930. Thousands of new jobs, moreover, were created in supporting industries such as rubber, glass, and fabrics, to say nothing of highway construction and thousands of service stations and garages. America's standard of living, responding to this infectious vitality, rose to an enviable level.

Zooming motorcars were agents of social change. At first a luxury, they rapidly became a necessity. Essentially devices for transportation, they soon developed into a badge of freedom and equality—a necessary prop for self-respect. Women were further freed from their dependence on men. Buses made possible the consolidation of schools and to some extent of churches.

Virtuous home life partially broke down as joyriders of all ages forsook the parlor for the highway. What might young people get up to in the privacy of a closed-top Model T? An Indiana juvenile judge voiced parents' worst fears when he condemned the automobile as "a house of prostitution on wheels." Yet no sane American would plead for a return of the old horse and buggy, complete with fly-breeding manure. Life might be cut short on the highways, and smog might poison the air, but the automobile brought more convenience, pleasure, and excitement into more people's lives than almost any other single invention.

★ Humans Develop Wings

Gasoline engines also provided the power that enabled humans to fulfill the age-old dream of sprouting wings. After near-successful experiments by others with heavier-than-air craft, the Wright brothers, Orville and Wilbur, performed "the miracle at Kitty Hawk," North Carolina. On a historic day—December 17, 1903—Orville Wright took aloft a feebly engined plane that stayed airborne for 12 seconds and 120 feet. Thus the air age was launched by two obscure bicycle repairmen.

Airplanes, once "flying coffins" for stuntmen, were first used with marked success for a serious purpose during the Great War of 1914–1918. Shortly thereafter private companies began to operate passenger lines with airmail contracts, which were in effect a subsidy from Washington. The first transcontinental airmail route was established from New York to San Francisco in 1920.

In 1927 modest and skillful Charles A. Lindbergh electrified the world with the first solo west-to-east conquest of the Atlantic. Seeking a prize of $25,000, the lanky flier courageously piloted his single-engine plane, the *Spirit of St. Louis*, from New York to Paris in a grueling thirty-three hours and thirty-nine minutes.

Lindbergh's exploit swept Americans off their feet. Fed up with the cynicism and debunking of the jazz age, they found in this wholesome and handsome youth a genuine hero. "Lucky Lindy" received an uproarious welcome in the canyons of lower Broadway, as eighteen hundred tons of ticker tape and other confetti showered upon him. Lindbergh's achievement did much to dramatize and popularize flying while giving a strong boost to the infant aviation industry.

The impact of the airplane was tremendous. The floundering railroads received another sharp setback through the loss of passengers and mail. A lethal new weapon was given to the gods of war with the coming of city-busting aerial bombs. The Atlantic Ocean was shriveling to about the size of the Aegean Sea in the days of Socrates, while isolation behind ocean moats was becoming a bygone dream.

★ The Radio and Film Revolutions

The speed of the airplane was far eclipsed by the speed of radio waves. Guglielmo Marconi, an Italian, invented wireless telegraphy in the 1890s, and his brainchild was used for long-range communication during World War I. Next came the voice-carrying radio, a triumph of many minds. In November 1920 Pittsburgh station KDKA made history with a live broadcast of the news of the Harding landslide. Radio knitted the nation together and, unlike the automobile, lured the American family back home. By the late 1920s, national commercial networks gained control of the new industry and drowned out much local programming. Various regions heard voices with standardized accents, and countless millions tuned in to perennial comedy favorites such as "Amos 'n' Andy." Advertising "commercials" made radio another vehicle for American free enterprise, and brand-named programs such as the "A&P Gypsies" and the "Eveready Hour" helped make radio-touted labels household words and purchases.

The flickering movie, the inventive fruit of Thomas Edison and others, first attracted attention in the naughty peep-show arcades in the 1890s. The first story-sequence movie, a breathless melodrama called *The Great Train Robbery*, was featured in the five-cent theaters, popularly called "nickelodeons." Spectacular among the first full-length classics was D. W. Griffith's *The Birth of a Nation* (1915), which glorified the Ku Klux Klan of Reconstruction days and defamed both blacks and Northern carpetbaggers. White southerners reputedly fired guns at the screen during the attempted "rape" scene. African Americans were outraged at the film and angrily organized protest marches, petition campaigns, and public hearings.

A fascinating industry was thus launched. Hollywood, California, quickly became the movie capital of the world, for it enjoyed a maximum of sunshine and other advantages. Early movies featured nudity and heavy-lidded female vampires ("vamps"), and an offended public forced the screen magnates to set up their own rigorous code of censorship. The motion picture really arrived during World War I, when it was used as an engine of anti-German propaganda.

A new era began in 1927 with the first "talkie"—*The Jazz Singer*, starring white performer Al Jolson in blackface. About the same time, color films began to be produced. Movies eclipsed all other new forms of amusement in the phenomenal growth of their popularity. Movie "stars" of the first pulchritude commanded much larger salaries than the president of the United States, in some cases as much as $100,000 for a single picture.

Critics bemoaned the vulgarization of popular taste wrought by the technologies of radio and movies. But the effects of the new mass media were not all negative. The insularity of ethnic communities eroded as the immigrants' children, especially, forsook the neighborhood vaudeville theater for the downtown movie palace or turned away from Grandma's Yiddish storytelling to tune in "Amos 'n' Andy." If some of the rich diversity of immigrants' cultures was lost, the standardization of tastes and language hastened entry into the American mainstream—and set the stage for the emergence of a working-class political coalition that, for a time, would overcome the divisive ethnic differences of the past.

★ The Dynamic Decade

Far-reaching changes in lifestyles and values paralleled the dramatic upsurge of the economy. The census of 1920 revealed that for the first time most Americans no longer lived in the countryside but in urban areas. Women continued to find new opportunities for employment in the cities, though they tended to cluster in a few low-paying jobs (such as retail clerking and office typing) that became classified as "women's work." An organized birth control movement, led by the fiery feminist Margaret Sanger, openly championed the use of contraceptives. Alice Paul's National Woman's party began in 1923 to campaign for an Equal Rights Amendment to the Constitution. To some defenders of traditional ways, it seemed that the world had suddenly gone mad.

Even the churches were affected. Fundamentalists lost ground to Modernists, who liked to think that God was a "good guy." To compete with automobiles and golf, some churches turned to providing entertainment of their own, including wholesome moving pictures for young people.

Even before the war, one observer thought the chimes had struck "sex o'clock in America," and the 1920s witnessed what many old-timers thought was a veritable erotic eruption. Advertisers exploited sexual allure to sell everything from soap to car tires.

Examining the Evidence

The Jazz Singer, 1927

The Jazz Singer was the first feature-length "talkie," a motion picture in which the characters actually speak, and its arrival spelled the end for "silent" films in which the audience read subtitles with live or recorded music as background. Although moviegoers flocked to *The Jazz Singer* to hear recorded sound, when they got there they found a movie concerned with themes of great interest to the urban, first- or second-generation immigrant audiences who were Hollywood's major patrons. *The Jazz Singer* told the story of a poor, assimilating Jewish immigrant torn between following his father's wish that he train as an Orthodox cantor and his own ambition to make a success for himself as a jazz singer, performing in the popular blackface style. The movie's star, Al Jolson, was himself an immigrant Jew who had made his name as a blackface performer. White actors had gradually taken over the southern black minstrel show during the nineteenth century. By the early twentieth century, Jewish entertainers had entirely monopolized these roles. Jolson, like other Jewish blackface performers, used his ability to impersonate a black person to force his acceptance into mainstream white American society. This use of blackface seems ironic because black Americans in the 1920s were struggling with their own real-life battles against Jim Crow–era segregation, a blatant form of exclusion from American society.

1. Besides the novelty of being a "talkie," what may have made *The Jazz Singer* a box office hit in 1927?
2. How might different types of viewers in the audience have responded to the story?
3. Was the "blackface" tradition of performance by white actors an entirely racist one? Or is there a way in which it acknowledges the great importance of blacks within the wider American culture?

529

Contending Voices

All that Jazz

Not all Americans welcomed the rising popularity of jazz music. For some stuffy traditionalists, including clergyman and writer Henry van Dyke (1852–1933), jazz symbolized the excessive liberation and dangerous exuberance of modern society.

"As I understand it, [jazz] is not music at all. It is merely an irritation of the nerves of hearing, a sensual teasing of the strings of physical passion.... '[J]azz' is an unmitigated cacophony, a combination of disagreeable sounds in complicated discords, a willful ugliness and a deliberate vulgarity."

But for a musical innovator like Duke Ellington (1899–1974), jazz's connection to the modern temper was the key to its authenticity and importance.

"I am trying to play the natural feelings of a people.... Beethoven, Wagner, and Bach are geniuses; no one can rob their work of the merit that is due it, but these men have not portrayed the people who are about us today, and the interpretation of these people is our future music."

[How do music and other artistic genres reflect "the people who are about us today"?

Once-modest maidens now proclaimed their new freedom as "flappers" in bobbed tresses and dresses. Young women appeared with hemlines elevated, stockings rolled, breasts taped flat, cheeks rouged, and lips a "crimson gash" that held a dangling cigarette. Thus did the "flapper" symbolize a yearned-for and devil-may-care independence (some said wild abandon) in some American women.

Justification for this new sexual frankness could be found in the recently translated writings of Dr. Sigmund Freud. This Viennese physician appeared to argue that sexual repression was responsible for a variety of nervous and emotional ills. Thus not pleasure alone but health demanded sexual gratification and liberation.

Many taboos flew out the window as sex-conscious Americans let themselves go. As unknowing Freudians, teenagers pioneered the sexual frontiers. Glued together in rhythmic embrace, they danced to jazz music squeaking from phonographs. The youthful "neckers" and "petters" also poached upon the forbidden territory of each others' bodies in darkened movie houses or in automobiles.

If the flapper was the goddess of the era, jazz was its sacred music. With its virtuoso wanderings and tricky syncopation, jazz moved up from New Orleans along with migrating blacks during World War I. Tunes such as W. C. Handy's "St. Louis Blues" became instant classics, as the wailing saxophone became the trumpet of the new era. Black performers such as Handy, "Jelly Roll" Morton, Louis Armstrong, and Joseph "King" Oliver gave birth to jazz, but the entertainment industry soon spawned all-white bands—notably Paul Whiteman's. Caucasian impresarios cornered the profits, though not the creative soul, of America's most native music.

A new racial pride also blossomed in the northern black communities that burgeoned during and after the war. Harlem in New York City, counting some 150,000 African American residents in the 1920s, was one of the largest black communities in the world. Harlem sustained a vibrant, creative culture that nourished poets such as Langston Hughes, whose first volume of verse, *The Weary Blues*, appeared in 1926.

Harlem in the 1920s also spawned a charismatic leader, Marcus Garvey. The Jamaican-born Garvey founded the **United Negro Improvement Association (UNIA)** to promote the resettlement of American blacks in Africa. His Black Star Line Steamship Company and other enterprises eventually failed financially, and Garvey himself was convicted of alleged mail fraud in 1927 and deported by a nervous U.S. government. But the race pride that Garvey inspired among his 4 million UNIA followers helped these newcomers to northern cities gain self-confidence and self-reliance. And his example proved important to the later founding of the Nation of Islam (Black Muslim) movement.

United Negro Improvement Association (UNIA) *A black nationalist organization founded in 1914 by the Jamaican-born Marcus Garvey in order to promote resettlement of African Americans to their "African homeland" and to stimulate a vigorous separate black economy within the United States.*

★ Literary Liberation

Likewise in literature, an older era seemed to have ground to a halt with the recent war. By the dawn of the 1920s, most of the custodians of an aging genteel culture had died—Henry James in 1916, Henry Adams in 1918, and William Dean Howells ("the Dean of American literature") in 1920. A few novelists who had been popular in the previous decades continued to thrive, notably the well-to-do, cosmopolitan New Yorker Edith Wharton and the Virginia-born Willa Cather, esteemed for her stark but sympathetic portrayals of pioneering on the prairies.

But in the decade after the war, a new generation of writers burst on the scene. Many of them hailed from ethnic and regional backgrounds different from that of the Protestant New Englanders who traditionally had dominated American cultural life. The newcomers exhibited the energy of youth, the ambition of excluded outsiders, and, in many cases the smoldering resentment of ideals betrayed. Animated by the spark of the international modernist movement, they bestowed on American literature a new vitality, imaginativeness, and artistic quality.

Central to **modernism** was its questioning of social conventions and traditional authorities. No one personified this iconoclasm better than H. L. Mencken, the "Bad Boy of Baltimore." As the era's most influential critic, Mencken promoted modernist causes in politics and literature. With his acidic wit, Mencken assailed marriage, patriotism, democracy, prohibition, Rotarians, and the middle-class American "booboisie." The provincial South he contemptuously dismissed as "the Sahara of the Bozart" (a bastardization of *beaux arts*, French for fine arts), and he scathingly attacked do-gooders as "Puritans." Puritanism, he jibed, was "the haunting fear that someone, somewhere, might be happy."

King Oliver's Creole Jazz Band, Early 1920s Joseph "King" Oliver arrived in Chicago from New Orleans in 1918. His band became the first important black jazz ensemble and made Chicago's Royal Garden Café a magnet for jazz lovers. Left to right: Honoré Dutrey, trombone; Baby Dodds, drums; King Oliver, cornet; Lil Hardin, piano; Bill Johnson, banjo; and Johnny Dodds, clarinet. Kneeling in the foreground is the young Louis Armstrong, playing a trombone.

modernism *An artistic and cultural movement that revolted against comfortable Victorian standards and accepted chance, change, contingency, uncertainty, and fragmentation. Originating among avant-garde artists and intellectuals around the turn of the twentieth century, modernism blossomed into a full-fledged cultural movement in art, music, literature, and architecture.*

The war had jolted many young writers out of their complacency about traditional values and literary standards. With their pens they probed for new codes of morals and understanding, as well as fresh forms of expression. F. Scott Fitzgerald, a handsome, Minnesota-born Princetonian then only twenty-four years old, became an overnight celebrity when he published *This Side of Paradise* in 1920. The book became a kind of Bible for the young. It was eagerly devoured by aspiring flappers and their ardent wooers, many of whom affected an air of bewildered abandon toward life. Catching the spirit of the hour (often about 4 A.M.), Fitzgerald found "all gods dead, all wars fought, all faiths in man shaken." He followed this melancholy success with *The Great Gatsby* (1925), a brilliant commentary on the illusory American ideal of the self-made man. Theodore Dreiser's masterpiece of 1925, *An American Tragedy*, similarly explored the pitfalls of social striving, as it dealt with the murder of a pregnant working girl by her socially ambitious young lover.

Ernest Hemingway, who had seen action on the Italian front in 1917, was among the writers most affected by the war. He responded to pernicious propaganda and the overblown appeal of patriotism by devising his own lean, word-sparing but word-perfect style. In *The Sun Also Rises* (1926) Hemingway told of disillusioned, spiritually numb American expatriates in Europe. In *A Farewell to Arms* (1929) he crafted one of the finest novels in any language about the war experience. Hemingway's literary successes and flamboyant personal life made him one of the most famous writers in the world. He won the Nobel Prize in literature in 1954—and blew out his brains with a shotgun blast in 1961.

Hemingway, Fitzgerald, and many other writers and painters found shelter and inspiration in the Paris salon of brainy and eccentric Gertrude Stein, an expatriate American. A literary innovator in her own right, Stein wrote experimental poetry and prose, including *Three Lives* (1909), *Tender Buttons* (1914), and most famously, *The Autobiography of Alice B. Toklas* (1933), named for her lifelong partner.

Stein joined fellow American poets Ezra Pound and T.S. Eliot in the vanguard of modernist literary innovation. These "high modernists" experimented with the breakdown

F. Scott Fitzgerald and His Wife, Zelda They are shown here in the happy, early days of their stormy marriage.

Harlem Renaissance *A creative outpouring among African American writers, jazz musicians, and social thinkers, centered around Harlem in the 1920s, that celebrated black culture and advocated for a "New Negro" in American social, political, and intellectual life.*

of traditional literary forms and wrote in a self-consciously internationalist mode. Pound, a brilliantly erratic Idahoan who deserted America for Europe, rejected what he called "an old bitch civilization, gone in the teeth," and proclaimed his doctrine: "Make It New." Pound strongly influenced the Missouri born and Harvard-educated T. S. Eliot. After taking up permanent residence in England, Eliot produced *The Waste Land* (1922), one of the most influential poems of the century.

Not all literary efforts of the era proved so radical. Robert Frost, a San Francisco-born poet, wrote hauntingly about the nature and folkways of his adopted New England. Other writers turned to a caustic probing of American small-town life. Sherwood Anderson dissected various fictional personalities in *Winesburg, Ohio* (1919), finding them all in some way warped by their cramped psychological surroundings. Sinclair Lewis, a hotheaded, heavy-drinking writer from Sauk Centre, Minnesota, sprang into prominence in 1920 with *Main Street*, the story of one woman's unsuccessful revolt against provincialism. In *Babbitt* (1922) Lewis affectionately pilloried George F. Babbitt, a prosperous, vulgar, slavishly conformist real estate broker. The word *Babbittry* was quickly coined to describe his all-too-familiar lifestyle.

William Faulkner, a dark-eyed, pensive Mississippian, offered a fictional chronicle of an imaginary, history-rich Deep South county he named "Yoknapatawpha." In powerful books such as *The Sound and the Fury* (1929) and *As I Lay Dying* (1930), Faulkner peeled back layers of time and consciousness from the constricted souls of his ingrown southern characters. His extended meditations on "the rag-tag and bob-ends of old tales and talkings" culminated in what some readers consider his greatest work, *Absalom, Absalom* (1936).

On the stage, Eugene O'Neill, a restless Princeton dropout, emerged as America's first world-class playwright. O'Neill laid bare Freudian notions of sex and the subconscious in plays like *Strange Interlude* (1928). A prodigious playwright, he authored more than a dozen productions in the 1920s and garnered the Nobel Prize in literature in 1936.

O'Neill arose from New York's Greenwich Village, which before and after the war was a seething cauldron of writers, painters, musicians, actors, and other would-be artists. After the war a black cultural renaissance also took root uptown in Harlem, led by such gifted writers as Claude McKay, Langston Hughes, and Zora Neale Hurston, and by jazz artists such as Louis Armstrong and Eubie Blake. In an outpouring of creative expression called the Harlem Renaissance, they proudly exulted in their black culture and argued for a "New Negro" who was a full citizen and a social equal to whites.

★ Wall Street's Big Bull Market

Signals abounded that the economic joyride might end in a crash. This something-for-nothing craze was well illustrated by real estate speculation, especially the fantastic Florida boom that culminated in 1925. Numerous underwater lots were sold to eager purchasers for preposterous sums. The whole wildcat scheme collapsed when the peninsula was devastated by a hurricane.

The stock exchange provided even greater sensations. Speculation ran wild. An orgy of boom-or-bust trading pushed the bull market to dizzying peaks, as Wall Street gamblers gored one another and fleeced greedy lambs. The stock market became a veritable gambling den.

As the 1920s lurched forward, everybody seemed to be buying stocks "on margin"—that is, with a small down payment. Barbers, stenographers, and elevator boys cashed in on "hot tips" picked up while on duty. One valet was reported to have parlayed his wages into a quarter of a million dollars. Rags-to-riches Americans eagerly worshiped at the altar of the ticker-tape machine. So powerful was the intoxicant of quick profits that few heeded the warnings raised in certain quarters that this kind of tinsel prosperity could not last forever.

Little was done by Washington to curb money-mad speculators. In the wartime days of Wilson, the national debt had rocketed from the 1914 figure of $1,188,235,400 to the 1921 peak of $23,976,250,608. Conservative principles of money management pointed to a diversion of surplus funds to reduce this financial burden. But to Secretary of the Treasury Andrew Mellon and his fellow millionaires, the burdensome taxes inherited from the war were especially distasteful. Their theory was that such high levies forced the rich to invest in tax-exempt securities rather than in factories that dispensed prosperous payrolls. The Mellonites also argued, with considerable persuasiveness, that high taxes not only discouraged business but also brought a smaller net return to the Treasury than moderate taxes.

Seeking to succor the "poor" rich people, Mellon helped engineer a series of tax reductions from 1921 to 1926. Congress followed his lead by repealing the excess-profits tax, abolishing the gift tax, and reducing excise taxes, the surtax, the income tax, and estate taxes. In 1921 a wealthy person with an income of $1 million had paid $663,000 in income taxes; in 1926 the same person paid about $200,000. Mellon's spare-the-rich policies thus shifted much of the tax burden from the wealthy to middle-income groups.

Mellon, lionized by conservatives as "the greatest secretary of the Treasury since Hamilton," remains a controversial figure. True, he reduced the national debt by $10 billion—from about $26 billion to $16 billion. But foes of the emaciated multimillionaire charged that he should have bitten an even larger chunk out of the debt, especially while the country was pulsating with prosperity. He was also accused of indirectly encouraging the bull market. If he had absorbed more of the national income in taxes, there would have been less money left for frenzied speculation. His refusal to do so typified the single-mindedly probusiness regime that dominated the political scene throughout the postwar decade.

> *Langston Hughes (1902–1967) celebrated Harlem's role in energizing a generation of artists and writers in his poem "Esthete in Harlem" (1930):*
>
> "Strange,
> That in this nigger place
> I should meet life face to face;
> When, for years, I had been seeking
> Life in places gentler-speaking,
> Until I came to this vile street
> And found Life stepping on my feet!"*
>
> ---
>
> *"Aesthete in Harlem," from *The Collected Poems of Langston Hughes* by Langston Hughes, edited by Arnold Rampersad with David Roessel, Associate Editor, copyright ©1994 by the Estate of Langston Hughes. Used by permission of Alfred A. Knopf, an imprint of the Knopf Doubleday Publishing Group, a division of Random House LLC and Harold Ober Associates, Inc. All rights reserved. Any third party use of this material, outside of this publication, is prohibited. Interested parties must apply directly to Random House LLC and Harold Ober Associates for permission.

CHAPTER SUMMARY ★ ★ ★ ★ ★ ★ ★ ★ ★ ★ ★ ★ ★ ★

After the crusading idealism of World War I, America sharply turned inward, as many citizens became hostile to anything foreign or different. Radicals and immigrants were targeted in the red scare and the Sacco-Vanzetti case, while the resurgent Ku Klux Klan reflected many Protestant Americans' fears of change. New restrictions on immigration reflected prejudice against "non-Anglo-Saxon" groups. Sharp cultural and religious conflicts also occurred over the prohibition experiment and evolution.

A new mass-consumption economy fueled the spectacular prosperity of the 1920s. The automobile industry, led by Henry Ford, transformed the economy and altered American lifestyles. Charles Lindbergh's flight symbolized the persistence of individual heroism in an age of cynicism and mass standardization.

The pervasive media of radio and film dramatically altered popular culture and values. Jazz music, the Harlem Renaissance, and Marcus Garvey's movement all reflected African Americans' new cultural energy. Birth control and Freudian psychology overturned traditional sexual standards, especially for women. Young literary rebels, many originally from the Midwest, scorned genteel New England and small-town culture and searched for new values, sometimes as expatriates in Europe. An international modernist movement in the arts and culture self-consciously broke from the past by criticizing traditional authorities and social conventions. The stock-market boom symbolized the free-wheeling spirit of the decade.

KEY TERMS

Bolshevik Revolution (519)
red scare (519)
criminal syndicalism laws (519)
American plan (520)
Immigration Act of 1924 (521)
Eighteenth Amendment (522)
Volstead Act (522)
Racketeers (524)
Bible Belt (525)
Fundamentalism (525)
Scientific Management (526)
Fordism (526)
United Negro Improvement Association (UNIA) (530)
modernism (531)
Harlem Renaissance (532)

PEOPLE TO KNOW

A. Mitchell Palmer
Frederick W. Taylor
Nicola Sacco
Bartolomeo Vanzetti
Horace Kallen
Randolph Bourne
Al Capone
John T. Scopes
Henry Ford
Charles A. Lindbergh
Margaret Sanger
Sigmund Freud
H. L. Mencken
F. Scott Fitzgerald
Ernest Hemingway
T. S. Eliot
William Faulkner
Langston Hughes

MindTap is a fully online, highly personalized learning experience built upon Cengage Learning content. MindTap combines student learning tools—readings, multimedia, activities, and assessments—into a singular Learning Path that guides students through the course.

Chapter 31

The Politics of Boom and Bust
1920–1932

> *We in America today are nearer to the final triumph over poverty than ever before in the history of any land. We have not yet reached the goal—but . . . we shall soon, with the help of God, be in sight of the day when poverty will be banished from this nation.*
>
> HERBERT HOOVER, 1928

Chapter Outline

- Conservative Republicans Take Power
- Disarmament and Isolation
- The Harding Scandals
- Calvin Coolidge and the Election of 1924
- Foreign Policy and the International Debt Tangle
- Herbert Hoover's Competing Ideologies
- The Great Crash, 1929
- Hoover and the Great Depression
- *Examining the Evidence: Lampooning Hoover, 1932*

Three Republican presidents—Warren G. Harding, Calvin Coolidge, and Herbert Hoover—steered the nation on the roller-coaster ride of the 1920s, a thrilling ascent from the depths of post–World War I recession to breathtaking heights of prosperity, followed by a terrifying crash into the Great Depression. In a retreat from progressive reform, Republicans sought to serve the public good less by direct government action and more through cooperation with big business. Some corrupt officials served themselves as well, exploiting public resources for personal profit. Meanwhile, the United States retreated from its brief international fling during World War I and resumed with a vengeance its traditional foreign policy of military unpreparedness and political isolationism.

FOCUS QUESTIONS

1. How did the political conservatism and economic prosperity of the 1920s lead to policies that attempted to advance the interests of business and isolate America from the world?

2. What was consistent and what was different in the leadership and policies of the three Republican presidents of the 1920s—Harding, Coolidge, and Hoover?

3. How did the United States eventually address the international economic tangle of loans, war debts, and reparations? Why was there so much resentment of America's actions in Europe?

4. What were the immediate and more fundamental causes of the stock market crash and the broader Great Depression?

5. In what ways was Hoover's response to the Great Depression a reflection of the older ideology of individualism and *laissez-faire*, and in what ways did his actions reflect a newer view of government responsibility for the nation's collective economic well-being?

CHRONOLOGY

1919	American Legion founded	1926	U.S. troops occupy Nicaragua
1920	Esch-Cummins Transportation Act	1928	Kellogg-Briand Pact Hoover defeats Smith for presidency
1921	Veterans Bureau created Capper-Volstead Act	1929	Agricultural Marketing Act sets up Federal Farm Board Stock-market crash
1922	Five-Power Naval Treaty signed Four-Power and Nine-Power Treaties on the Far East Fordney-McCumber Tariff Law	1930	Hawley-Smoot Tariff
		1931	Japanese invade Manchuria
1923	*Adkins v. Children's Hospital* Teapot Dome scandal Harding dies; Coolidge assumes presidency	1932	Reconstruction Finance Corporation (RFC) established Norris-La Guardia Anti-Injunction Act "Bonus Army" dispersed from Washington, D.C.
1924	Adjusted Compensation Act for veterans Dawes Plan for international finance U.S. troops leave Dominican Republic Coolidge wins three-way presidential election		

★ The Republican "Old Guard" Returns

Warren G. Harding, inaugurated in 1921, *looked* presidential. With erect figure, broad shoulders, bushy eyebrows, and graying hair, he was one of the best-liked men of his generation. An easygoing, warm-handed backslapper, he exuded graciousness and love of people. Yet the charming, smiling exterior concealed a weak, inept interior. With a mediocre mind, Harding quickly found himself beyond his depth in the presidency. "God! What a job!" was his anguished cry on one occasion.

Harding, like Grant, was unable to detect moral halitosis in his associates, and he was soon surrounded by his poker-playing, shirt-sleeved cronies of the "Ohio gang." Harding hated to hurt his friends' feelings by saying no, and designing political leeches capitalized on this weakness. He "was not a bad man," said one Washington observer. "He was just a slob."

Admitting his own scanty mental furnishings, Harding appointed to his cabinet some strong and capable Republicans: imperious and brilliant Charles Evans Hughes as secretary of state; lean and elderly Andrew W. Mellon as secretary of the treasury; and chubby-faced Herbert Hoover, famed wartime feeder of the Belgians, as secretary of commerce. But Harding also brought into his cabinet such corrupt characters as Secretary of the Interior Albert B. Fall, a scheming anticonservationist, and Attorney General Harry M. Daugherty, a member of the "Ohio gang" and a big-time crook.

Well intentioned but weak-willed, Harding was a perfect "front" for enterprising industrialists. A McKinley-style old order settled back into place at war's end, crushing the reform seedlings that had sprouted in the progressive era. This new Old Guard hoped to improve on the old business doctrine of laissez-faire. Their plea was not simply for government to keep its hands off business but for government to help guide business along the path to profits. They subtly and effectively achieved their ends by putting the courts and the administrative bureaus into the safekeeping of fellow stand-patters for the duration of the decade.

The Supreme Court was a striking example of this trend. In his short presidency, Harding appointed four justices who were or became deep-dyed reactionaries. In the first years of the 1920s, the Supreme Court axed progressive legislation. It killed a federal child-labor law, stripped away many of labor's hard-won gains, and rigidly restricted governmental intervention in the economy. In the landmark case of *Adkins v. Children's Hospital* (1923), the Court reversed its own reasoning in *Muller* v. *Oregon* (see p. 481) and

Adkins v. Children's Hospital (1923)
A landmark Supreme Court decision reversing the ruling in Muller v. Oregon, *which had declared women to be deserving of special protection in the workplace.*

invalidated a minimum-wage law for women. Its strained ruling was that, because females now had the vote (Nineteenth Amendment), they were the legal equals of men and could no longer be protected by special legislation. The contradictory premises of the *Muller* and *Adkins* cases framed a debate over gender differences that would continue for the rest of the century: were women sufficiently different from men that they merited special legal and social treatment, or were they effectively equal in the eyes of the law and therefore undeserving of special protection and preferences?

Under Harding, corporations could once more relax and expand. Antitrust laws were often ignored, circumvented, or feebly enforced by friendly prosecutors in the attorney general's office. The Interstate Commerce Commission, to single out one agency, came to be dominated by members sympathetic to the railroad managers.

> *Justice Oliver Wendell Holmes (1841–1935), wryly dissenting in the* Adkins *case, said:*
>
> "It would need more than the Nineteenth Amendment to convince me that there are no differences between men and women, or that legislation cannot take those differences into account."

Big industrialists, striving to lessen competition, now had a free hand to set up trade associations. Cement manufacturers, for example, would use these agencies to agree upon standardization of product, publicity campaigns, and a united front in dealing with the railroads and labor. Although many of these associations ran counter to the spirit of existing antitrust legislation, their formation was encouraged by Secretary of Commerce Herbert Hoover. His sense of engineering efficiency led him to condemn the waste resulting from cutthroat competition and to encourage business self-regulation.

★ The Aftermath of War

Wartime government controls on the economy were swiftly dismantled. The War Industries Board disappeared with almost indecent haste. With its passing, progressive hopes for more government regulation of big business evaporated.

Washington likewise returned the railroads to private management in 1920. The Esch-Cummins Transportation Act of 1920 encouraged private consolidation of the railroads and pledged the federal Interstate Commerce Commission to guarantee their profitability.

Labor, suddenly deprived of its wartime crutch of friendly government support, limped along badly in the postwar decade. A bloody strike in the steel industry was ruthlessly broken in 1919, partly by exploiting ethnic and racial divisions among the steelworkers and by branding the strikers as dangerous "reds." The Railway Labor Board, a successor body to the wartime labor boards, ordered a wage cut of 12 percent in 1922, provoking a two-month strike. It ended when Attorney General Daugherty, who fully shared Harding's big-business bias, clamped on the strikers one of the most sweeping injunctions in American history. Unions wilted in this hostile political environment, and membership shriveled by nearly 30 percent between 1920 and 1930.

Needy veterans were among the few nonbusiness groups to reap lasting gains from the war. In 1921 Congress created the Veterans Bureau to operate hospitals and provide vocational rehabilitation for the disabled. The American Legion, founded in Paris in 1919 by Colonel Theodore Roosevelt, Jr., became known for its militant conservative patriotism and aggressive lobbying for veterans' benefits. The Legion demanded "adjusted compensation" to make up for the wages veterans had "lost" while in uniform. Harding vetoed one such bill in 1922, but in 1924 Congress passed the Adjusted Compensation Act over President Calvin Coolidge's veto. This Act gave every former soldier a paid-up insurance policy due in twenty years—adding about $3.5 billion to the total cost of the war.

★ America Seeks Benefits Without Burdens

Isolation was enthroned in Washington. The Harding administration, with the Senate "irreconcilables" holding a hatchet over its head, continued to regard the League of Nations as a thing unclean.

But disarmament was one international issue on which Harding set isolationism aside and seized the initiative. He was prodded by businesspeople unwilling to dig deeper into their pockets for money to finance the ambitious naval-building program started during the war. A deadly contest was shaping up with Britain and Japan, which watched with alarm as the oceans filled with American vessels. Public agitation in America, fed by worries about British and Japanese cooperation in the Pacific, brought about the headline-making Washington "Disarmament" Conference in 1921–1922. The double agenda included naval disarmament and the situation in East Asia.

At the outset, Secretary of State Charles Evans Hughes dramatically proposed a ten-year "holiday" on construction of battleships and even the scrapping of some of the huge dreadnoughts already built or being built. Hughes proposed that the scaled-down navies of America and Britain should enjoy parity in battleships and aircraft carriers, with Japan on the small end of a 5-5-3 ratio.

The conference's Five-Power Naval Treaty of 1922 embodied Hughes's ideas on ship ratios, but only after face-saving compensation for the insecure Japanese. The British and Americans both conceded that they would refrain from fortifying their East Asian possessions, including the Philippines. The Japanese were not subjected to such restraints in their possessions. In addition, a Four-Power Treaty bound Britain, Japan, France, and the United States to preserve the status quo in the Pacific—another concession to the Japanese. Finally, the Washington Conference gave chaotic China—"the Sick Man of East Asia"—a shot in the arm with the **Nine-Power Treaty** of 1922, whose signatories agreed to nail wide open the Open Door in China.

The Hardingites boasted of this globe-shaking achievement in disarmament, but their satisfaction was somewhat illusory. No restrictions had been placed on small warships, and the other powers churned ahead with the construction of cruisers, destroyers, and submarines, while penny-pinching Uncle Sam lagged dangerously behind. Ominously, the American people seemed content to rely for their security on words and wishful thinking rather than on weapons and hardheaded realism.

A similar sentimentalism welled up later in the decade, when Americans clamored for the "outlawry of war." Calvin Coolidge's secretary of state, Frank B. Kellogg, signed with the French foreign minister in 1928 the **Kellogg-Briand Pact**, which was ultimately ratified by sixty-two nations. Lacking both muscles and teeth, this parchment peace was a diplomatic derelict—and virtually useless in a showdown. Yet it accurately—and dangerously—reflected the American mind in the 1920s, which was all too ready to be lulled into a false sense of security. This mood took even deeper hold in the ostrich-like neutralism of the 1930s.

★ Hiking the Tariff Higher

A comparable lack of realism afflicted foreign economic policy in the 1920s. Businesspeople, shortsightedly obsessed with the dazzling prospects in the prosperous home market, sought to keep that market to themselves by flinging up insurmountable tariff walls around the United States. In 1922 Congress passed the **Fordney-McCumber Tariff Law**, which boosted schedules from the average of 27 percent under Wilson's Underwood Tariff of 1913 to an average of 38.5 percent.

The high-tariff course thus charted by the Republican regimes set off an ominous chain reaction. European producers felt the squeeze, for the American tariff walls prolonged the postwar chaos. An impoverished Europe needed to sell manufactured goods to the United States, particularly if it hoped to achieve economic recovery and to pay its huge war debt to Washington. America needed to give foreign nations a chance to make a profit from it so that they could buy U.S. manufactured articles and repay debts. International trade, Americans were slow to learn, is a two-way street.

Erecting tariff walls was a game that two could play. The American example spurred European nations, throughout the feverish 1920s, to pile up higher barriers themselves. The whole vicious circle further deepened the international economic distress, providing one more rung on the ladder by which Adolf Hitler scrambled to power.

Nine-Power Treaty (1922) *Agreement coming out of the Washington "Disarmament" Conference of 1921–1922 that pledged Britain, France, Italy, Japan, the United States, China, the Netherlands, Portugal, and Belgium to abide by the Open Door policy in China. The Five-Power Naval Treaty on ship ratios and the Four-Power Treaty to preserve the status quo in the Pacific also came out of the conference.*

Kellogg-Briand Pact (1928) *A sentimental triumph of the 1920s peace movement, this 1928 pact linked sixty-two nations in the supposed "outlawry of war."*

Fordney-McCumber Tariff Law (1922) *A comprehensive bill passed to protect domestic production from foreign competitors. As a direct result, many European nations were spurred to increase their own trade barriers.*

⭐ The Stench of Scandal

The loose morality and get-rich-quickism of the Harding era manifested themselves spectacularly in a series of scandals. Early in 1923 the head of the Veterans Bureau, Colonel Charles R. Forbes, was caught with his hand in the till. An appointee of the gullible Harding, he and his accomplices looted the government to the tune of about $200 million, chiefly in connection with the building of veterans' hospitals. Forbes was convicted and sentenced to two years in a federal penitentiary.

Most shocking of all was the **Teapot Dome scandal**, an affair that involved priceless naval oil reserves at Teapot Dome (Wyoming) and Elk Hills (California). In 1921 the slippery secretary of the interior, Albert B. Fall, induced his careless colleague, the secretary of the navy, to transfer these valuable properties to the Interior Department. Harding indiscreetly signed the secret order. Fall then quietly leased the lands to oilmen Harry F. Sinclair and Edward L. Doheny, but not until they had paid him some $400,000 in bribes ("loans").

Teapot Dome, no tempest in a teapot, finally came to a whistling boil. Details of the crooked transaction leaked out in March 1923. Fall, Sinclair, and Doheny were indicted in 1924. Fall was found guilty of taking a bribe and sentenced to one year in jail. The two bribe givers were acquitted, though Sinclair served time in jail for "shadowing" jurors and for refusing to testify before a Senate committee.

Still more scandals erupted. Persistent reports about the underhanded doings of Attorney General Daugherty brought a Senate investigation in 1924 of the illegal sale of pardons and liquor permits. Forced to resign, the accused official was tried in 1927 but released after a jury twice failed to agree. During the trial, Daugherty hid behind the trousers of Harding by implying that persistent probing might uncover crookedness in the White House.

Harding was mercifully spared the full revelation of these iniquities. Just as news of the scandals was beginning to break, he died in San Francisco on August 2, 1923, of pneumonia and thrombosis. Mourning millions, not yet fully aware of the graft in Washington, expressed genuine sorrow.

The brutal fact is that Harding simply was not a strong enough man for the presidency—as he himself privately admitted. Such was his weakness that he tolerated people and conditions that subjected the Republic to its worst disgrace since the days of President Grant.

The Harding Scandals This 1924 cartoon satirizing the misdemeanors of the Harding administration shows the sale of the Capitol, the White House, and even the Washington Monument.

Teapot Dome scandal (1921) A tawdry affair involving the illegal lease of priceless naval oil reserves in Teapot Dome, Wyoming, and Elk Hills, California. The scandal, which implicated President Harding's secretary of the interior, was one of several that gave his administration a reputation for corruption.

⭐ "Silent Cal" Coolidge

News of Harding's death was sped to Vice President Coolidge, then visiting at his father's New England farmhouse. By the light of two kerosene lamps the elder Coolidge, a justice of the peace, used the old family Bible to administer the presidential oath to his son.

This homespun setting was symbolic of Coolidge. Quite unlike Harding, the stern-faced Vermonter, with his thin nose and tightly set lips, embodied the New England virtues of honesty, morality, industry, and frugality. His dour visage prompted the acerbic observation that he had been "weaned on a pickle."

Coolidge seemed to be a crystallization of the commonplace. Painfully shy, he was blessed with only mediocre powers of leadership. He would occasionally display a dry wit in private; but his speeches, delivered in a nasal New England twang, were invariably boring.

A staunch apostle of the status quo, he became the "high priest of the great god Business." He believed that "the man who builds a factory builds a temple" and that "the man who works there worships there." The hands-off temperament of "Cautious Cal" perfectly suited the times, and Coolidge "luck" held during his five and a half prosperity-blessed years.

Ever a profile in caution, Coolidge slowly gave the Harding regime a badly needed moral fumigation. Teapot Dome had scalded the Republican party badly, but so transparently honest was the vinegary Vermonter that the scandalous oil did not rub off on him.

★ Frustrated Farmers

Sun-bronzed farmers were caught squarely in a boom-or-bust cycle in the postwar decade. While the fighting had raged, they had raked in money, hand over gnarled fist. But peace brought an end to high farm prices and to massive purchases by other nations, as foreign production reentered the stream of world commerce.

Machines also threatened to plow the farmer under an avalanche of his own overabundant crops. Aided by the efficiency of the new gasoline-engine tractor, agricultural production expanded and piled up more price-dampening surpluses. A withering depression swept through agricultural districts in the 1920s, when one farm in four was sold for debt or taxes.

Schemes abounded for bringing relief to the hard-pressed farmers. A bipartisan "farm bloc" from the agricultural states coalesced in Congress in 1921 and succeeded in driving through some helpful laws. Noteworthy was the Capper-Volstead Act, which exempted farmers' marketing cooperatives from antitrust prosecution. The farm bloc's favorite proposal was the **McNary-Haugen Bill**, pushed energetically from 1924 to 1928. It sought to keep agricultural prices high by authorizing the government to buy up surpluses and sell them abroad. Congress twice passed the bill, but frugal Coolidge twice vetoed it. Farm prices stayed low, and the farmers' political temperatures stayed high, reaching fever pitch in the election of 1924.

McNary-Haugen Bill (1924–1928)
A farm-relief bill that was championed throughout the 1920s and aimed to keep agricultural prices high by authorizing the government to buy up surpluses and sell them abroad. Congress twice passed the bill, but President Calvin Coolidge vetoed it in 1927 and 1928.

★ A Three-Way Race for the White House in 1924

Self-satisfied Republicans, chanting "Keep Cool and Keep Coolidge," nominated "Silent Cal" for the presidency at their convention in Cleveland in the simmering summer of 1924. Squabbling Democrats had more difficulty choosing a candidate when they met in New York's sweltering Madison Square Garden. Reflecting many of the cultural tensions of the decade, the party was hopelessly split between "wets" and "drys," urbanites and farmers, Fundamentalists and Modernists, northern liberals and southern stand-patters, immigrants and old-stock Americans. Deadlocked for an unprecedented 102 ballots, the convention at last turned wearily, sweatily, and unenthusiastically to John W. Davis. A wealthy Wall Street lawyer, the polished nominee was no less conservative than cautious Calvin Coolidge.

The field was now wide open for a liberal candidate, and white-pompadoured Senator Robert ("Fighting Bob") La Follette of Wisconsin sprang forward to lead a new Progressive party. He gained the support of both the American Federation of Labor and the Socialist party, but his major constituency was the price-pinched farmers. La Follette's new Progressive party, only a shadow of the robust progressive coalition of prewar days, called for government ownership of railroads and relief for farmers, lashed out at monopoly and antilabor injunctions, and urged a constitutional amendment to limit the Supreme Court's power to invalidate laws passed by Congress.

La Follette turned in a respectable showing, polling nearly 5 million votes. But "Cautious Cal" and the oil-smeared Republicans slipped easily back into office, overwhelming Davis, 15,718,211 votes to 8,385,283. The electoral count stood at 382 for Coolidge, 136 for Davis, and 13 for La Follette, all from his home state of Wisconsin (see Map 31.1).

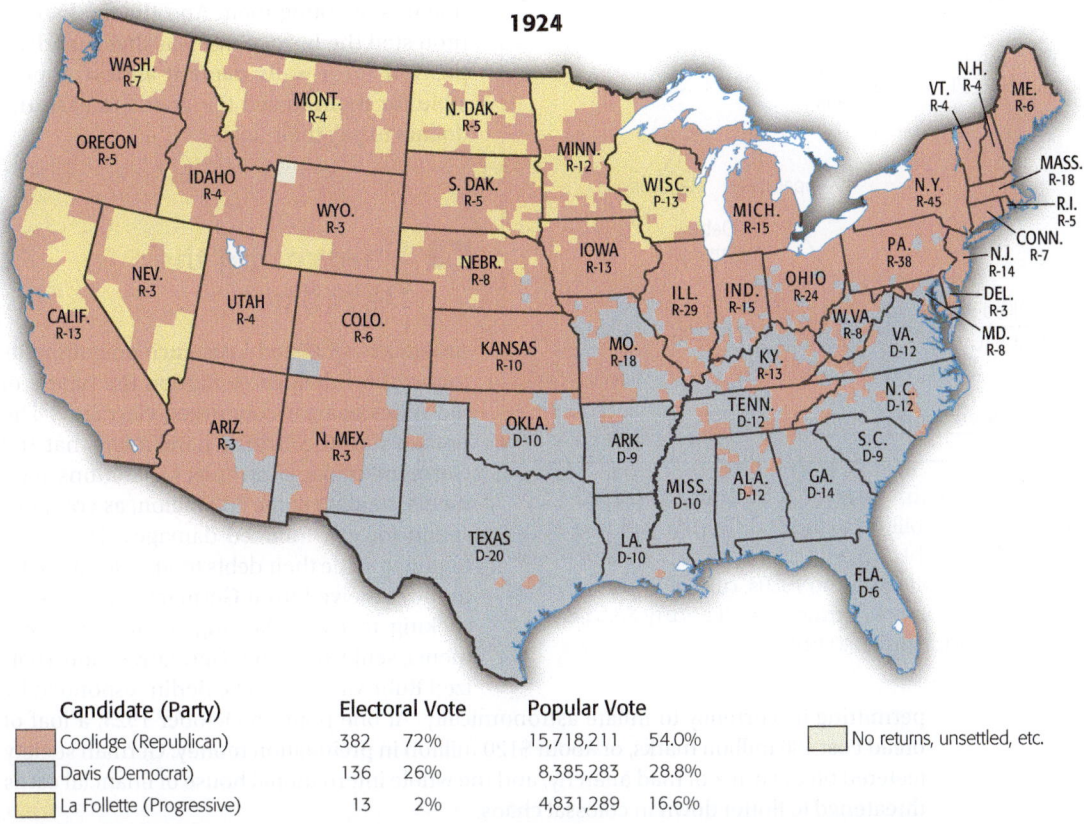

Map 31.1 **Presidential Election of 1924 (showing popular vote by county)** Note the concentration of La Follette's votes in the old Populist strongholds of the Midwest and the mountain states. His ticket did especially well in the grain-growing districts battered by the postwar slump in agricultural prices.

★ Foreign-Policy Flounderings

Isolation continued to reign in the Coolidge era. Despite presidential proddings, the Senate proved unwilling to allow America to adhere to the World Court—the judicial arm of the still-suspect League of Nations. Coolidge only halfheartedly—and unsuccessfully—pursued further naval disarmament after the loudly trumpeted agreements worked out at the Washington Conference in 1922.

A glaring exception to the United States' inward-looking indifference to the outside world in the 1920s was the armed interventionism in the Caribbean and Central America. American troops were withdrawn (after an eight-year stay) from the Dominican Republic in 1924, but they remained in Haiti from 1914 to 1934. President Coolidge in 1925 briefly removed American bayonets from troubled Nicaragua, where they had glinted intermittently since 1909, but in 1926 he sent them back, five thousand strong, and they stayed until 1933. When U.S. oil companies clamored for intervention in Mexico in 1926 to protect their interests there, Coolidge kept cool and defused the crisis with some skillful diplomatic negotiating. But his mailed-fist tactics elsewhere bred sore resentments south of the Rio Grande, where angry critics loudly assailed "*yanqui* imperialism."

Overshadowing all other foreign-policy problems in the 1920s was the knotty issue of international debts, a complicated tangle of private loans, Allied war debts, and German reparations (see Figure 31.1). The key knot in the debt tangle was the $10 billion that the U.S. Treasury had loaned to the Allies during and immediately after the war. Uncle Sam held their IOUs—and he wanted to be paid. The Allies, in turn, protested that this was unfair because they had held up a wall of flesh and bone against the common foe until America the Unready had finally entered the fray. America, they argued, should write off its loans as war costs, just as the Allies had been tragically forced to write off the lives of

Figure 31.1 Aspects of the Financial Merry-Go-Round, 1921–1933
Great Britain, with a debt of over $4 billion to the U.S. Treasury, had a huge stake in proposals for inter-Allied debt cancellation, but France's stake was even larger. Less prosperous than Britain in the 1920s, and more battered by the war, which had been fought on its soil, France owed nearly $3.5 billion to the United States and additional billions to Britain.

Dawes Plan (1924) *An arrangement negotiated in 1924 to reschedule German reparations payments. It stabilized the German currency and opened the way for further American private loans to Germany.*

millions of young men. And the final straw, protested the Europeans, was that America's postwar tariff walls made it almost impossible for them to sell the goods to earn the dollars to pay their debts.

★ Unraveling the Debt Knot

America's tightfisted insistence on getting its money back helped to harden the hearts of the Allies against conquered Germany. The French and the British demanded that the Germans make enormous reparations payments, totaling some $32 billion, as compensation for war-inflicted damages. The Allies hoped to settle their debts to America with the money received from Germany. The French, seeking to extort lagging reparations payments, sent troops into Germany's industrialized Ruhr Valley in 1923. Berlin responded by permitting its currency to inflate astronomically. At one point in October 1923, a loaf of bread cost 480 million marks, or about $120 million in preinflation money. German society teetered on the brink of mad anarchy, and the whole international house of financial cards threatened to flutter down in colossal chaos.

Sensible statesmen now urged that the war debts and reparations alike be drastically scaled down or canceled outright. But to Americans such proposals smacked of "welshing" on a debt. Scroogelike Calvin Coolidge turned aside suggestions of debt cancellation with a typically terse question: "They hired the money, didn't they?"

Reality finally dawned in the **Dawes Plan** of 1924. Negotiated largely by Charles Dawes, about to be Coolidge's running mate, it rescheduled German reparations payments and opened the way for further American private loans to Germany. The whole financial cycle now became still more complicated as U.S. bankers loaned money to Germany, Germany paid reparations to France and Britain, and the former Allies paid war debts to the United States. Clearly the source of this monetary merry-go-round was the flowing well of American credit. When that well dried up after the great crash in 1929, the tangled jungle of international finance quickly turned into a desert.

The United States never did get its money, but it harvested a bumper crop of ill will. Throughout Europe Uncle Sam was caricatured as Uncle Shylock, greedily whetting his knife for the last pound of Allied flesh. The bad taste left in American mouths by the whole sorry episode contributed powerfully to the storm-cellar neutrality legislation passed by Congress in the 1930s.

★ The Triumph of Herbert Hoover in 1928

Poker-faced Calvin Coolidge, the tight-lipped "Sphinx of the Potomac," bowed out of the 1928 presidential race when he announced, "I do not choose to run." His logical successor was super-Secretary (of Commerce) Herbert Hoover. He was nominated on a platform that clucked contentedly over both prosperity and prohibition.

Still-squabbling Democrats nominated Alfred E. Smith, the wisecracking, glad-handing governor of New York and one of the most colorful personalities in American politics. "Al (cohol)" Smith was soakingly "wet" on prohibition, abrasively urban, and Roman Catholic in an overwhelmingly Protestant—and unfortunately prejudiced—land. Many dry, rural, and Fundamentalist Democrats gagged on his candidacy, and they saddled the wet Smith with a dry running mate and a dry platform.

Radio figured prominently in this campaign for the first time, and it helped Hoover more than Smith. The New Yorker had more personal sparkle, but he could not project it through the radio. Iowa-born Hoover, with his double-breasted dignity, came out of the microphone better than he went in.

Chubby-faced, ruddy-complexioned Herbert Hoover, with his painfully high starched collar, was a living example of the American success story and an intriguing mixture of two centuries. As a poor orphan boy who had worked his way through Stanford University, he had absorbed the nineteenth-century copybook maxims of industry, thrift, and self-reliance. As a fabulously successful mining engineer and businessman, he had honed to a high degree the efficiency doctrines of the progressive era.

A small-town boy from Iowa and Oregon, Hoover had traveled and worked abroad extensively. His experiences there had further strengthened his faith in American individualism, free enterprise, and small government. With his unshaken dignity and Quaker restraint, Hoover was a far cry from the typical backslapping politician. Personally colorless in public, he had been accustomed during much of his life to giving orders to subordinates and did not adapt readily to the necessary give-and-take of political accommodation.

As befitted America's newly mechanized civilization, Hoover was the ideal businessperson's candidate. A self-made millionaire, he recoiled from anything suggesting socialism, paternalism, or "planned economy." Yet as secretary of commerce, he had exhibited some progressive instincts. He endorsed labor unions and supported federal regulation of the new radio broadcasting industry. He even flirted for a time with the idea of government-owned radio, similar to the British Broadcasting Corporation (BBC).

Despite the best efforts of Hoover and Smith, below-the-belt tactics were employed to a disgusting degree by lower-level campaigners. Religious bigotry raised its hideous head over Smith's Catholicism. An irresponsible whispering campaign claimed that "A vote for Al Smith is a vote for the Pope" and that the White House, under Smith, would become a branch of the Vatican.

Hoover triumphed in a landslide. He bagged 21,391,993 popular votes to 15,016,169 for his embittered opponent, while rolling up an electoral count of 444 to 87. A huge Republican majority was returned to the House of Representatives. Tens of thousands of dry southern Democrats—"Hoovercrats"—rebelled against Al Smith. Hoover carried all the Border States and five states of the former Confederacy, the first Republican candidate in fifty-two years to carry multiple states that had seceded.

Contending Voices

Depression and Protection

Republican co-sponsor Willis Hawley (1864–1941) touted the Hawley-Smoot Tariff in the House, emphasizing his party's long-standing commitment to protectionism. (Indeed, the idea for this bill originated in 1928, prior to the onset of the depression.)

"[I]f this bill is enacted into law . . . we will have a new era of prosperity such as followed the enactment of every Republican tariff bill, in which all of the people of the United States in every occupation, every industry, and every employment will share as they have always shared."

A petition signed by 1,028 economists and published in the New York Times, *meanwhile, argued strenuously against the bill.*

"The proponents of higher tariffs claim that an increase in rates will give work to the idle. This is not true. We cannot increase employment by restricting trade. . . . Finally, we would urge our government to consider the bitterness which a policy of higher tariffs would inevitably inject into our international relations. . . . A tariff war does not furnish good soil for the growth of world peace."

What might account for the crisis-era enactment of a policy conceived under radically different economic conditions?

★ President Hoover's First Moves

Prosperity in the late 1920s smiled broadly as the Hoover years began. Soaring stocks on the bull market continued to defy the laws of financial gravitation. But two immense groups of citizens were not getting their share of the riches flowing from the national cornucopia: the unorganized wage earners and especially the disorganized farmers.

Hoover's administration, in line with its philosophy of promoting self-help, responded to the outcry of the farmers with the **Agricultural Marketing Act**. Passed by Congress in

Agricultural Marketing Act (1929)
This act established the Federal Farm Board, a lending bureau for hard-pressed farmers. The act also aimed to help farmers help themselves through new producers' cooperatives. As the depression worsened in 1930, the Board tried to bolster falling prices by buying up surpluses, but it was unable to cope with the flood of farm produce to market.

June 1929, it was designed to help the farmers help themselves, largely through producers' cooperatives.

Farmers also clutched at the tariff as a possible straw to keep their heads above the water of financial ruin. But the **Hawley-Smoot Tariff** of 1930, which started out in the House as a fairly reasonable measure designed to assist farmers, acquired more than a thousand amendments in the Senate and turned into the highest protective tariff in the nation's peacetime history. The average duty was raised from 38.5 percent to nearly 60 percent. To angered foreigners, the Hawley-Smoot Tariff seemed like a declaration of economic warfare on the entire outside world. It widened the yawning trade gaps and plunged both America and other nations deeper into the terrible depression that had already begun. The Hawley-Smoot Tariff increased international financial chaos and forced the United States further into the bog of economic isolationism, playing directly into the hands of the hate-filled German demagogue Adolf Hitler.

Hawley-Smoot Tariff (1930) *The highest protective tariff in the peacetime history of the United States, passed as a result of good old-fashioned horse trading. To the outside world, it smacked of ugly economic warfare.*

★ The Great Crash Ends the Golden Twenties

When Herbert Hoover confidently took the presidential oath on March 4, 1929, America's productive colossus—stimulated by the automobile, radio, movie, and other new industries—was roaring along at a breathtaking speed that suggested a permanent plateau of prosperity. Prices on the stock exchange continued to spiral upward and create a fool's paradise of paper profits. A few prophets of disaster sounded warnings, but they were drowned out by the mad chatter of the ticker-tape machine.

A catastrophic crash came on **Black Tuesday**, October 29, 1929, when 16,410,030 shares of stock were sold in a save-who-may scramble. Wall Street became a wailing wall as gloom and doom replaced boom and suicides increased alarmingly. Losses, even in blue-chip securities, were unbelievable. By the end of 1929—two months after the initial crash—stockholders had lost $40 billion in paper values, or more than the total cost of World War I to the United States (see Figure 31.2).

Black Tuesday (1929) *The dark, panicky day of October 29, 1929, when over 16,410,000 shares of stock were sold on Wall Street. It was a trigger that helped bring on the Great Depression.*

The stock-market collapse heralded a business depression, at home and abroad, that was the most prolonged and prostrating in American or world experience. No other industrialized nation suffered so severe a setback. By the end of 1930, more than 4 million workers in the United States were jobless; two years later the figure had about tripled. Hungry and despairing workers pounded pavements in search of nonexistent jobs. Where employees were not discharged, wages and salaries were often slashed. A current jingle ran:

> *Mellon pulled the whistle,*
> *Hoover rang the bell*
> *Wall Street gave the signal*
> *And the country went to hell.*

The misery and gloom were incalculable, as forests of dead chimneys stood stark against the sky. Over five thousand banks collapsed in the first three years of the depression, carrying down with them the life savings of tens of thousands of ordinary citizens. Countless thousands of honest, hard-working people lost their homes and farms to the forecloser's hammer. Breadlines formed, soup kitchens dispensed food, and apple sellers stood shivering on street corners trying to peddle their wares for five cents.

Families felt the stress, as jobless fathers nursed their guilt and shame at not being able to provide for their households. Breadless breadwinners often blamed themselves for their plight, despite abundant evidence that the economic system, not individual initiative, had broken down. Mothers meanwhile nursed fewer babies as hard

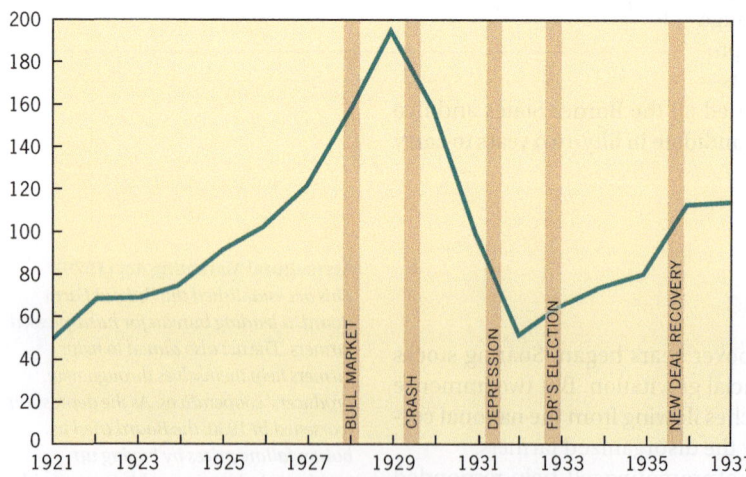

Figure 31.2 Index of Common Stock Prices (1926 = 100)

times reached even into the nation's bedrooms, precipitating a decade-long dearth of births. As cash registers gathered cobwebs, the song "My God, How the Money Rolls In" was replaced with "Brother, Can You Spare a Dime?"

★ Hooked on the Horn of Plenty

What caused the Great Depression? One basic explanation is overproduction by both farm and factory. Ironically, the depression of the 1930s was one of abundance, not want. It was the "great glut" or the "plague of plenty."

The nation's ability to produce goods had clearly outrun its capacity to consume or pay for them. Too much money was going into the hands of a few wealthy people, who invested it in factories and other agencies of production. Not enough was going into salaries and wages, where revitalizing purchasing power could be more quickly felt. Overexpansion of credit on so-called easy terms also caused many consumers to dive in beyond their depth.

This already bleak picture was further darkened by economic anemia abroad. Britain and the Continent had never fully recovered from the upheaval of World War I. A drying up of international trade, moreover, had been hastened by the shortsighted Hawley-Smoot Tariff of 1930.

By 1930 the depression had become a national calamity. Through no fault of their own, a host of industrious citizens had lost everything. They wanted to work—but there was no work. The insidious effect of all this dazed despair on the nation's spirit was incalculable and long lasting. Hitherto the people had grappled with the physical obstacles of

> *The Depression spectacle of want in the shadow of surplus moved an observer to write in* Current History *(1932):*
>
> "We still pray to be given each day our daily bread. Yet there is too much bread, too much wheat and corn, meat and oil and almost every commodity required by man for his subsistence and material happiness. We are not able to purchase the abundance that modern methods of agriculture, mining and manufacture make available in such bountiful quantities. Why is mankind being asked to go hungry and cold and poverty stricken in the midst of plenty?"

"Hooverville" in Seattle, 1934 In the early years of the depression, desperate, homeless people constructed shacks with scavenged materials. These shantytowns sprang up in cities across the country.

> Herbert Hoover (1874–1964) spoke approvingly in a campaign speech in 1928 of "the American system of Rugged Individualism." In 1930 he referred to Cleveland's 1887 veto of a bill to appropriate seed grain for the drought-stricken farmers of Texas:
>
> "I do not believe that the power and duty of the General Government ought to be extended to the relief of individual suffering.... The lesson should be constantly enforced that though the people support the Government the Government should not support the people."

nature. But the depression was a baffling wraith they could not grasp. Initiative and self-respect were stifled. In extreme cases "ragged individualists" slept under "Hoover blankets" (old newspapers), fought over the contents of garbage cans, or cooked their findings in old oil drums in tin-and-paper shantytowns cynically named **Hoovervilles**. The very foundations of America's social and political structure trembled.

Hoover's exalted reputation as a wonder-worker and efficiency engineer crashed about as dismally as the stock market. The perplexed president was impaled on the horns of a cruel dilemma. As a deservedly famed humanitarian, he was profoundly distressed by the widespread misery about him. Yet as a "rugged individualist," deeply rooted in an earlier era of free enterprise, he shrank from the heresy of government handouts. Convinced that industry, thrift, and self-reliance were the virtues that had made America great, President Hoover feared that a government doling out doles would weaken, perhaps destroy, the national fiber.

Hoovervilles *Grim shantytowns where impoverished victims of the Great Depression slept under newspapers and in makeshift tents. Their visibility (and sarcastic name) tarnished the reputation of the Hoover administration.*

As the depression nightmare steadily worsened, Hoover was finally forced to turn reluctantly from his doctrine of log-cabin individualism and accept the proposition that the welfare of the people in a nationwide catastrophe is a direct concern of the national government. The president at last worked out a compromise between the old hands-off philosophy and the "soul-destroying" direct dole then being used in Britain. He would assist the hard-pressed railroads, banks, and rural credit corporations, in the hope that, if financial health were restored at the top of the economic pyramid, unemployment would be relieved at the bottom on a trickle-down basis.

Early in 1932 Congress, responding to Hoover's belated appeal, established the **Reconstruction Finance Corporation (RFC)**. With an initial working capital of half a billion dollars, this agency became a government lending bank that provided indirect relief to insurance companies, banks, agricultural organizations, railroads, and even hard-pressed state and local governments. But to preserve individualism and character, there would be no loans to individuals from this "billion-dollar soup kitchen."

Reconstruction Finance Corporation (RFC) (1932) *A government lending agency established under the Hoover administration in order to assist insurance companies, banks, agricultural organizations, railroads, and local governments. It was a precursor to later agencies that grew out of the New Deal and symbolized a recognition by the Republicans that some federal action was required to address the Great Depression.*

"Pump-priming" loans by the RFC were of widespread benefit, but the organization was established many months too late for maximum usefulness. RFC projects were largely self-liquidating, and the government as a banker actually profited to the tune of many millions of dollars. Giant corporations so obviously benefited from this assistance that the RFC was dubbed—rather unfairly—"the millionaires' dole."

Hoover's administration also provided some indirect benefits for labor. After stormy debate, Congress passed the **Norris–La Guardia Anti-Injunction Act** in 1932, and Hoover signed it. The measure outlawed "yellow dog" (antiunion) contracts and forbade the federal courts from issuing injunctions to restrain strikes, boycotts, and peaceful picketing.

Norris–La Guardia Anti-Injunction Act (1932) *This law banned "yellow-dog," or antiunion, work contracts and forbade federal courts from issuing injunctions to quash strikes and boycotts. It was an early piece of labor-friendly federal legislation.*

The truth is that Herbert Hoover, despite criticism of his "heartlessness," did inaugurate a significant new policy. In previous panics the masses had been forced to "sweat it out." Slow though Hoover was to abandon this nineteenth-century bias, by the end of his term he had started down the road toward government assistance for needy citizens—a road that Franklin Roosevelt would travel much further.

Many veterans of World War I were numbered among the hard-hit victims of the depression. A drive developed for the premature payment of the deferred bonus voted by Congress in 1924 and payable in 1945. Thousands of impoverished veterans, both of war and of unemployment, prepared to move on Washington, there to demand of Congress the immediate payment of their *entire* bonuses. The "Bonus Expeditionary Force" of about twenty thousand men converged on the capital in the summer of 1932. These supplicants promptly set up unsanitary public camps on vacant lots—a gigantic "Hooverville."

Bonus Army (1932) *Officially known as the Bonus Expeditionary Force (BEF), this rag-tag group of twenty thousand veterans marched on Washington to demand immediate payment of bonuses earned during World War I. General Douglas MacArthur dispersed the veterans with tear gas and bayonets.*

Following riots that cost two lives, Hoover ordered the army to evacuate the remaining members of the **Bonus Army**. The eviction was carried out by General Douglas MacArthur

Examining the Evidence
Lampooning Hoover, 1932

The pages of *The American Pageant* are filled with political cartoons that provide pungent commentary on historical events. With one image rather than many words, a cartoonist can convey a point of view much the way an editorial writer does. This cartoon appeared in the *Washington Daily News* on July 25, 1932, three and a half months before Republican president Hoover lost the presidential election to his Democratic challenger, Franklin D. Roosevelt. The cartoonist foretells Hoover's defeat in November and departure from the White House the following March (not January, as at present) and expresses his support for the Home Loan Bank Bill. With this proposal, Hoover sought to come to the aid of home mortgage lenders in order to forestall them from foreclosing on homeowners. The cartoonist jokes that Hoover supported this bill because he identified with homeowners about to lose their homes, but he also cleverly insinuates that Hoover's banking reform was motivated by electoral opportunism. Surely Hoover sought to win public support in return for his new banking program as he battled for reelection, but the Home Loan Bank Bill also reflected Hoover's growing recognition that the federal government had to take direct action to remedy flaws that had precipitated the crisis of the Great Depression. As Hoover later recorded in his memoirs, "All this seems dull economics, but the poignant American drama revolving around the loss of the old homestead had a million repetitions straight from life, not because of the designing villain but because of a fault in our financial system."

1. How does the cartoonist use caricature to make his point?
2. What accounts for the political cartoon's special power?
3. Are there limitations to this genre? Find another cartoon in this book, and subject it to similar analysis.

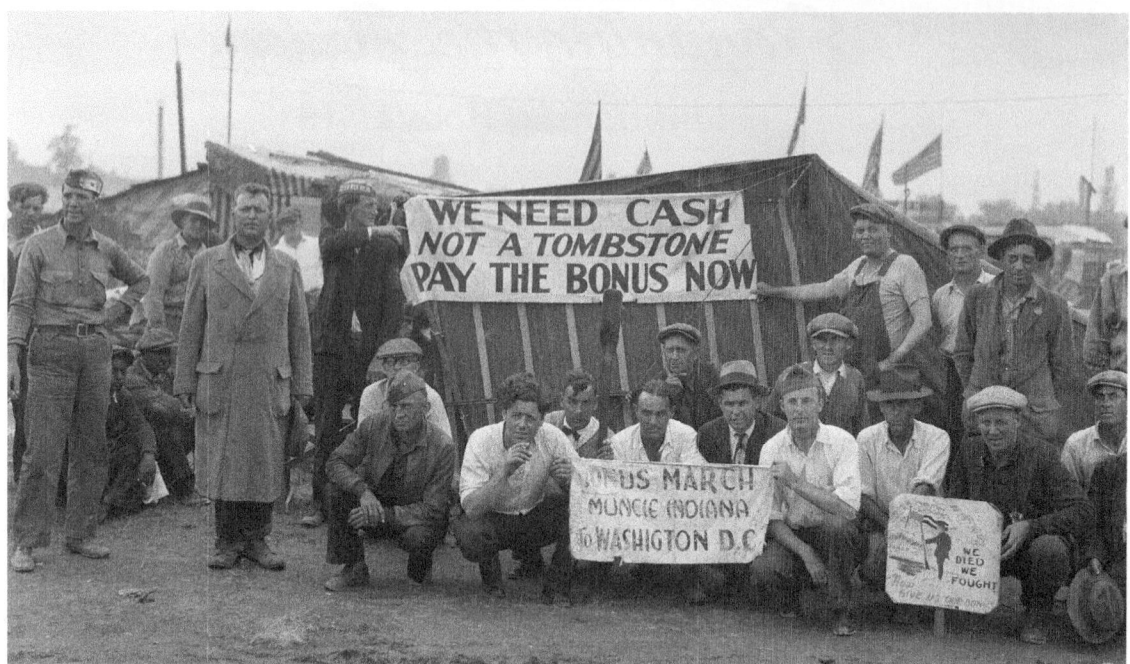

The Bonus Army in Washington, D.C., 1932 World War I veterans from Muncie, Indiana were among many contingents to set up camp in the capital during the summer of 1932, determined to remain there until they received full payment of their promised bonuses.

with bayonets and tear gas in the inglorious "Battle of Anacostia Flats." The veterans' shantytown was put to the torch, a few of the former soldiers were injured, and an eleven-month-old "bonus baby" allegedly died from exposure to tear gas.

This brutal episode brought down additional abuse on the once-popular Hoover, who by now was the most loudly booed man in the country. Cynics sneered that the "Great Engineer" had in a few months "ditched, drained, and damned the country." The existing panic was unfairly branded "the Hoover depression." In truth, Hoover had been oversold as a wizard, and the public grumbled when his magician's wand failed to produce rabbits. The time was ripening for the Democratic party—and Franklin D. Roosevelt—to cash in on Hoover's calamities.

Japanese Aggression

The Great Depression, which brewed enough distress at home, added immensely to difficulties abroad. Militaristic Japan stole the East Asian spotlight. In September 1931 the Japanese imperialists, noting that the Western world was badly mired in depression, plunged into Manchuria. Alleging provocation, they rapidly overran the coveted Chinese province and proceeded to bolt shut the Open Door in the conquered area.

Americans were stunned by this act of naked aggression. Many, though by no means a majority, urged strong measures, ranging from boycotts to a blockade backed by the League of Nations. But the League was handicapped in taking two-fisted action by the nonmembership of the United States. Washington and Secretary of State Henry L. Stimson, in the end, decided to fire only paper bullets at the Japanese aggressors. The so-called Stimson Doctrine, proclaimed in 1932, declared that the United States would not recognize any territorial acquisitions achieved by force. This verbal slap on the wrist did not at all deter the march of the Japanese militarists. But there was no real sentiment for stronger measures among the depression-ridden American people, who remained strongly isolationist during the 1930s.

CHAPTER SUMMARY ★★★★★★★★★★★★

The Republican governments of the 1920s carried out active, probusiness policies while undermining much of the progressive legacy by neglect or lack of enforcement. The Washington Naval Conference indicated America's strong desire in the 1920s to withdraw from international involvements. Sky-high tariffs protected America's booming industry but caused severe economic troubles elsewhere in the world and deepened the woes of farmers, who did not share in the nation's prosperity.

As the Harding scandals broke, Harding died and the puritanical Calvin Coolidge took office, thus avoiding political repercussions for the Republicans. Bitterly feuding Democrats—divided by region, religion, and culture—and La Follette Progressives fell easy victims to Republican-managed prosperity in the election of 1924.

American demands for strict repayment of war debts created international economic difficulties and resentment of the United States. The Dawes Plan provided temporary relief, but the Hawley-Smoot Tariff proved another devastating blow to international trade. Herbert Hoover, a renowned businessman and humanitarian, won a landslide victory over Catholic Al Smith in 1928.

The stock-market crash of 1929 brought a sudden end to prosperity and plunged America into a horrible depression. Herbert Hoover's reputation collapsed as he failed to relieve national suffering, although he did make unprecedented but limited efforts to revive the economy through federal assistance. The global depression and American isolationism encouraged Japanese aggression in Chinese Manchuria, which neither the United States nor the feeble League of Nations could thwart.

KEY TERMS

Adkins v. Children's Hospital (536)
Nine-Power Treaty (538)
Kellogg-Briand Pact (538)
Fordney-McCumber Tariff Law (538)
Teapot Dome scandal (539)
McNary-Haugen Bill (540)
Dawes Plan (542)
Agricultural Marketing Act (543)
Hawley-Smoot Tariff (544)
Black Tuesday (544)
Hoovervilles (546)
Reconstruction Finance Corporation (RFC) (546)
Norris–La Guardia Anti-Injunction Act (546)
Bonus Army (546)

PEOPLE TO KNOW

Warren G. Harding
Albert B. Fall
Calvin Coolidge
John W. Davis
Robert M. ("Fighting Bob") La Follette
Alfred E. Smith

MindTap is a fully online, highly personalized learning experience built upon Cengage Learning content. MindTap combines student learning tools—readings, multimedia, activities, and assessments—into a singular Learning Path that guides students through the course.

Chapter 32

The Great Depression and the New Deal
1933–1939

The country needs and... demands bold, persistent experimentation. It is common sense to take a method and try it. If it fails, admit it frankly and try another. But above all, try something.

FRANKLIN D. ROOSEVELT, CAMPAIGN SPEECH, 1932

Chapter Outline

- Franklin D. Roosevelt as President
- The Hundred Days Congress, 1933
- The National Recovery Administration, 1933–1935
- The Agricultural Adjustment Administration, 1933–1936
- The Tennessee Valley Authority
- The Social Security Act, 1935
- Gains for Organized Labor
- The Election of 1936 and the "Roosevelt Coalition"
- The Supreme Court Fight, 1937
- The New Deal Assessed
- *Varying Viewpoints: How Radical Was the New Deal?*

Voters were in an ugly mood as the presidential campaign of 1932 neared. Countless factory chimneys remained ominously cold, while more than 11 million unemployed workers and their families sank ever deeper into the pit of poverty.

Hoover, sick at heart, was renominated by the Republican convention in Chicago without great enthusiasm. The rising star in the Democratic firmament was Governor Franklin Delano Roosevelt of New York, a fifth cousin of Theodore Roosevelt. Like the Rough Rider, Franklin Roosevelt had been born to a wealthy New York family, had graduated from Harvard, had been elected as a kid-gloved politician to the New York legislature, had served as governor of the Empire State, had been nominated for the vice presidency (though not elected), and had served capably as assistant secretary of the navy. Although both men were master politicians, adept with the colorful phrase, TR was pugnacious and confrontational, whereas FDR was suave and conciliatory—qualities that appealed strongly to a people traumatized by one of the greatest crises in American history.

FOCUS QUESTIONS

1. What personal qualities did Franklin Roosevelt bring to the presidency, and how did these shape both public attitudes and the New Deal policies designed to combat the Great Depression?
2. What were the primary New Deal efforts to achieve relief, recovery, and reform? Which were most successful and enduring, and which largely failed?
3. How did the early New Deal affect business, agriculture, and labor? Why did it meet such strong opposition from some quarters, including the Supreme Court?
4. How did Roosevelt politically mobilize the "New Deal coalition" of Southerners, Catholics, Jews, African Americans, and women to achieve his goals and lay the foundations for two generations of Democratic party dominance?
5. What did the New Deal truly accomplish? Is the idea of a large federal government role in the economy best understood as a response to an emergency, or a necessary feature of modern industrial life?

CHRONOLOGY

1932	■ Roosevelt defeats Hoover for presidency	1935	■ WPA established
			■ Wagner Act
1933	■ Bank holiday		■ Resettlement Administration
	■ Emergency Banking Relief Act		■ Social Security Act
	■ Beer and Wine Revenue Act		■ Public Utility Holding Company Act
	■ Hundred Days Congress enacts HOLC, AAA, NRA, PWA, and TVA		■ *Schechter* "sick chicken" case
	■ Federal Securities Act		■ CIO organized
	■ Glass-Steagall Banking Reform Act	1936	■ Soil Conservation and Domestic Allotment Act
	■ CWA established		■ Roosevelt defeats Landon for presidency
	■ Twentieth Amendment (changed calendar of congressional sessions and date of presidential inauguration)	1937	■ USHA established
	■ Twenty-first Amendment (prohibition repealed)		■ Roosevelt announces "court-packing" plan
1934	■ Gold Reserve Act	1938	■ Second AAA
	■ Securities and Exchange Commission authorized		■ Fair Labor Standards Act
	■ Indian Reorganization Act	1939	■ Hatch Act
	■ FHA established		■ Reorganization Act
	■ Frazier-Lemke Farm Bankruptcy Act		

★ FDR: Politician in a Wheelchair

Infantile paralysis, while putting steel braces on Franklin Roosevelt's legs, put additional steel into his soul. Until 1921, when the dread disease struck, young Roosevelt—tall, athletic, and handsome—impressed observers as charming and witty yet at times as a superficial and arrogant "lightweight." But suffering humbled him to the level of common clay. In courageously fighting his way back from complete helplessness to a hobbling mobility, he schooled himself in patience, tolerance, compassion, and strength of will. He once remarked that, after trying for two years to wiggle one big toe, all else seemed easy.

Another of Roosevelt's great personal and political assets was his wife, Eleanor Roosevelt. The niece of Theodore Roosevelt, she was Franklin Roosevelt's distant cousin as well as his spouse. Tall, ungainly, and toothy, she overcame the misery of an unhappy childhood and emerged as a champion of the dispossessed—and ultimately as the "conscience of the New Deal." Through her lobbying of her husband, her speeches, and her syndicated newspaper column, Eleanor powerfully influenced the policies of the national government. Always she battled for the impoverished and the oppressed. At one meeting in Birmingham, Alabama, she confounded local authorities and flouted the segregation statutes by deliberately straddling the aisle that separated the black and white seating sections.

Eleanor Roosevelt marched to her own drummer. As a young woman she had worked in a New York settlement house, and later on she joined the Women's Trade Union League and the League of Women Voters. When she and Franklin moved into the White House, she brought an unprecedented number of women activists with her to Washington. This network of reformers helped make her the most active First Lady in history. Sadly, her personal relationship with her husband was often rocky due to his occasional infidelity. Condemned by conservatives and

> *In his successful campaign for the governorship of New York in 1928, Franklin Roosevelt (1882–1945) had played down alleged Democratic "socialism":*
>
> "We often hear it said that government operation of anything under the sun is socialistic. If that is so, our postal service is socialistic, so is the parcel post which has largely taken the place of the old express companies; so are the public highways which took the place of the toll roads."

loved by liberals, Eleanor was one of the most controversial—and consequential—public figures of the twentieth century.

Franklin Roosevelt's political appeal was amazing. His commanding presence and his golden speaking voice, despite a sophisticated accent, combined to make him the premier American orator of his generation. He could turn on charm in private conversations as one would turn on a faucet. As a popular depression governor of New York, he had sponsored heavy state spending to relieve human suffering. Though favoring frugality, he believed that money, rather than humanity, was expendable. Roosevelt revealed a deep concern for the plight of the "forgotten man"—a phrase he used in a 1932 speech—although he was assailed by the rich as a "traitor to his class."

Exuberant Democrats met in Chicago in June 1932 and speedily nominated Roosevelt, who flew daringly through stormy weather to Chicago where he smashed precedent to accept the nomination in person. He electrified the delegates and the public with these words: "I pledge you, I pledge myself to a new deal for the American people."

Eleanor Roosevelt (1884–1962) America's most active First Lady, she commanded enormous popularity and influence during FDR's presidency. Here she emerges, miner's cap in hand, from an Ohio coal mine.

Brain Trust *Specialists in law, economics, and welfare, many of them young university professors, who advised President Franklin D. Roosevelt and helped develop the policies of the New Deal.*

New Deal *The economic and political policies of Franklin Roosevelt's administration in the 1930s, which aimed to solve the problems of the Great Depression by providing relief for the unemployed and launching efforts to stimulate economic recovery. The New Deal built on reforms of the progressive era to expand greatly an American-style welfare state.*

★ Roosevelt Routs Hoover in 1932

In the campaign that followed, Roosevelt consistently preached a New Deal for the "forgotten man," but he was annoyingly vague and somewhat contradictory. Many of his speeches were ghostwritten by the "Brains Trust" (popularly the **Brain Trust**), a small group of reform-minded intellectuals. They were predominantly young college professors who, as a kind of kitchen cabinet, later authored much of the **New Deal** legislation. Roosevelt rashly promised a balanced budget and denounced deficits. All of this was to make ironic reading in later months.

The high spirits of the Democrats found expression in the catchy air, "Happy Days Are Here Again." This theme song fit FDR's indestructible smile, his jauntily angled cigarette holder, his breezy optimism, and his promises to do something, even at the risk of bold experimentation. Meanwhile, grim-faced Herbert Hoover predicted on the campaign trail that if the Hawley-Smoot Tariff were repealed, the grass would grow "in the streets of a hundred cities." Such down-at-the-mouth gloom contrasted sharply with Roosevelt's tooth-flashing optimism and sparkling promises.

Hoover had been swept into office on the rising tide of prosperity; he was swept out by the receding tide of depression. The flood of votes totaled 22,809,638 for Roosevelt and 15,758,901 for Hoover; the electoral count stood at 472 to 59. In all, the loser carried only six rock-ribbed Republican states.

One striking feature of the election was a distinct shift of blacks from their traditional home in the Republican party of Lincoln to the Roosevelt camp. Beginning with the election of 1932, they became, notably in the great urban centers of the North, a vital element in the Democratic party.

Defeated and repudiated, Hoover continued to be president for four long months, until March 4, 1933. But he was helpless to embark on any long-range policies without the cooperation of Roosevelt. In two meetings with Roosevelt, Hoover tried to bind his successor to an anti-inflationary policy that would have made impossible many of the later New Deal experiments. But Roosevelt refused to assume responsibility without authority and airily remarked to the press, "It's not my baby."

With Washington deadlocked, the vast and vaunted American economic machine clanked to a virtual halt. One worker in four tramped the streets, feet weary and hands idle. Banks were locking their doors all over the nation as people nervously stuffed paper money under their mattresses.

★ FDR and the Three Rs: Relief, Recovery, and Reform

Great crises often call forth gifted leaders, and the hand of destiny tapped Roosevelt on the shoulder. On a dreary inauguration day, March 4, 1933, his vibrant voice provided the American people with inspirational new hope. He denounced the "money changers" who had brought on the calamity, and he declared that the government must wage war on the Great Depression as it would wage war on an armed foe. His clarion note was, "Let me assert my firm belief that the only thing we have to fear is fear itself."

Roosevelt moved decisively. Now that he had full responsibility, he boldly declared a nationwide bank holiday, March 6–10, as a prelude to opening the banks on a sounder basis. He then summoned the overwhelmingly Democratic Congress into special session to cope with the national emergency. For the so-called **Hundred Days** (March 9–June 16, 1933), members hastily ground out an unprecedented basketful of remedial legislation (see Table 32.1).

Hundred Days (1933) *The first hundred days of Franklin D. Roosevelt's administration, stretching from March 9 to June 16, 1933, when an unprecedented number of reform bills were passed by a Democratic Congress to launch the New Deal.*

Table 32.1 Principal New Deal Acts During Hundred Days Congress, 1933
(items in parentheses indicate secondary purposes)

Recovery	Relief	Reform
FDR closes banks, March 6, 1933 Emergency Banking Relief Act, March 9, 1933		
(Beer Act)	(Beer Act)	Beer and Wine Revenue Act, March 22, 1933
(CCC)	Unemployment Relief Act, March 31, 1933, creates Civilian Conservation Corps (CCC)	
FDR orders gold surrender, April 5, 1933 FDR abandons gold standard, April 19, 1933		
(FERA)	Federal Emergency Relief Act, May 12, 1933, creates Federal Emergency Relief Administration (FERA)	
(AAA)	Agricultural Adjustment Act (AAA), May 12, 1933	
(TVA)	(TVA)	Tennessee Valley Authority Act (TVA), May 18, 1933 Federal Securities Act, May 27, 1933
Gold-payment clause repealed, June 5, 1933		
(HOLC)	Home Owners' Refinancing Act, June 13, 1933, creates Home Owners' Loan Corporation (HOLC)	
National Industrial Recovery Act, June 16, 1933, creates National Recovery Administration (NRA), Public Works Administration (PWA)	(NRA, PWA)	(NRA)
(Glass-Steagall Act)	(Glass-Steagall Act)	Glass-Steagall Banking Reform Act, June 16, 1933, creates Federal Deposit Insurance Corporation

For later New Deal measures, see Table 32.2, p. 556

Roosevelt's New Deal program aimed at three *R*'s—relief, recovery, and reform. Short-range goals were relief and immediate recovery, especially in the first two years. Long-range goals were permanent recovery and reform of current abuses, particularly those that had produced the boom-or-bust catastrophe. The three-*R* objectives often overlapped and got in one another's way. But amid all the topsy-turvy haste, the gigantic New Deal program lurched forward.

Firmly ensconced in the driver's seat, President Roosevelt cracked the whip. A green Congress so fully shared the panicky feeling of the country that it was ready to rubber-stamp bills drafted by White House advisers. More than that, Congress gave the president extraordinary blank-check powers: some laws it passed expressly delegated legislative authority to the chief executive.

Roosevelt was delighted to exert executive leadership. He was inclined to do things by intuition—off the cuff. He was like the quarterback, as he put it, whose next play depends on the outcome of the previous play. So desperate was the mood of an action-starved public that any movement, even in the wrong direction, seemed better than no movement at all.

The frantic Hundred Days Congress passed many essentials of the New Deal's "three *R*'s," though important long-range measures were added in later sessions. These reforms owed much to the legacy of the pre–World War I progressive movement. Many of them were long overdue, sidetracked by the war in Europe and the Old Guard reaction of the 1920s. In an explosive burst of pent-up energy, New Dealers raided file cabinets full of old pamphlets on German social insurance, English housing and garden cities, Danish agricultural recovery, and American World War I collectivization. In time, the New Dealers

The Champ: FDR Chatting with Reporters Roosevelt mastered the press as few presidents before or since have been able to do. He was also ingenious in finding opportunities to converse with reporters without revealing his physical limitations.

embraced progressive ideas such as unemployment insurance, old-age insurance, minimum-wage regulations, conservation and development of natural resources, and restrictions on child labor. They also invented some new schemes, such as the Tennessee Valley Authority (see pp. 561–562). Soon, depression-weary Europeans came to marvel at the exciting din of reform activity underway in the United States.

★ Roosevelt Tackles Money and Banking

Banking chaos cried aloud for immediate action. Congress pulled itself together and in an incredible eight hours had the Emergency Banking Relief Act of 1933 ready for Roosevelt's busy pen. The new law invested the president with power to regulate banking transactions and foreign exchange and to reopen solvent banks.

Roosevelt, the master showman, next turned to the radio to deliver the first of thirty famous "fireside chats." As some 35 million people hung on his soothing words, he gave assurances that it was now safer to keep money in a reopened bank than "under the mattress." Confidence returned with a gush, and the banks unlocked their doors.

The Hundred Days Congress also buttressed public reliance on the banking system by enacting the memorable **Glass-Steagall Banking Reform Act**. This measure provided for the Federal Deposit Insurance Corporation, which insured individual deposits up to $5,000 (later raised).

Roosevelt moved swiftly elsewhere on the financial front, seeking to protect the melting gold reserve and to prevent panicky hoarding. He ordered all private holdings of gold to be surrendered to the Treasury in exchange for paper currency and then took the nation off the gold standard.

The goal of Roosevelt's "managed currency" was inflation, which he believed would relieve debtors' burdens and stimulate new production. Roosevelt's principal instrument for achieving inflation was gold buying. He instructed the Treasury Department to purchase gold, ratcheting its price up from $21 an ounce in 1933 to $35 an ounce in 1934, a price that held for nearly four decades. This policy did increase the amount of dollars in circulation, as holders of gold cashed it in at the newly elevated prices, although "sound-money" critics gagged on the "baloney dollar." The gold-buying scheme came to an end in February 1934, when FDR returned the nation to a limited gold standard of $35 an ounce for purposes of international trade only. The Treasury thereafter stopped minting gold coins for domestic circulation.

Glass-Steagall Banking Reform Act (1933) *A law creating the Federal Deposit Insurance Corporation, which insured individual bank deposits and ended a century-long tradition of unstable banking that had reached a crisis in the Great Depression.*

★ Creating Jobs for the Jobless

Overwhelming unemployment clamored for prompt remedial action. One out of every four workers was jobless when FDR took his inaugural oath—the highest level of unemployment in the nation's history. Roosevelt had no hesitancy about using federal money to assist the unemployed and at the same time to "prime the pump" of industrial recovery. (A farmer has to pour a little water into a dry pump—that is, "prime it"—to start the flow.)

The Hundred Days Congress responded to Roosevelt's spurs when it created the **Civilian Conservation Corps (CCC)**. This agency provided employment in fresh-air government camps for about 3 million uniformed young men. Their useful work included reforestation, fire fighting, flood control, and swamp drainage. The recruits were required to help their parents by sending home most of their pay. Both human resources and natural resources were thus conserved.

The first major effort of the new Congress to grapple with the millions of adult unemployed was the Federal Emergency Relief Act. Its chief aim was immediate relief rather than long-range recovery. The resulting Federal Emergency Relief Administration (FERA) was handed over to zealous Harry L. Hopkins, a painfully thin, shabbily dressed, chain-smoking New York social worker who became one of Roosevelt's closest friends and most influential advisers. Hopkins's agency finally granted about $3 billion to the states for direct dole payments or preferably for wages on work projects.

Civilian Conservation Corps (CCC) (1933) *A government program created by Congress to hire young unemployed men to improve the rural, out-of-doors environment with such work as planting trees, fighting fires, draining swamps, and maintaining national parks. The CCC proved to be an important foundation for the post–World War II environmental movement.*

Table 32.2 Later Major New Deal Measures, 1933–1939
(items in parentheses indicate secondary purposes)

Recovery	Relief	Reform
(CWA)	FDR establishes Civil Works Administration (CWA), November 9, 1933	
		Securities and Exchange Commission (SEC) authorized by Congress, June 6, 1934 Indian Reorganization Act, June 18, 1934
(FHA)	National Housing Act, June 28, 1934, authorizes Federal Housing Administration (FHA)	(FHA)
(Frazier-Lemke Act)	Frazier-Lemke Farm Bankruptcy Act, June 28, 1934	
(Resettlement Administration)	FDR creates Resettlement Administration, April 30, 1935	
(WPA)	FDR creates Works Progress Administration (WPA), May 6, 1935, under act of April 8, 1935	
(Wagner Act)	(Wagner Act)	(Wagner) National Labor Relations Act, July 5, 1935 Social Security Act, August 14, 1935 Public Utility Holding Company Act, August 26, 1935
(Soil Conservation Act)	Soil Conservation and Domestic Allotment Act, February 29, 1936	
(USHA)	(USHA)	United States Housing Authority (USHA) established by Congress, September 1, 1937
(Second AAA)	Second Agricultural Adjustment Act, February 16, 1938	
(Fair Labor Standards)	(Fair Labor Standards)	Fair Labor Standards Act (Wages and Hours Bill), June 25, 1938 Reorganization Act, April 3, 1939 Hatch Act, August 2, 1939

Immediate relief was also given to two large and hard pressed special groups by the Hundred Days Congress. One section of the Agricultural Adjustment Act (AAA) made available many millions of dollars to help farmers meet their mortgages. Another law created the Home Owners' Loan Corporation (HOLC). Designed to refinance mortgages on nonfarm homes, it ultimately assisted about a million badly pinched households while simultaneously bailing out mortgage-holding banks.

Harassed by the continuing plague of unemployment, FDR himself established the Civil Works Administration (CWA) under Hopkins's direction late in 1933 (see Table 32.2). Designed to provide temporary jobs during the cruel winter emergency, it employed tens of thousands of jobless people in leaf raking and other make-work tasks. The CWA served a useful purpose, although it was heavily criticized as "boondoggling."

Direct relief from Washington to needy families helped pull the nation through the ghastly winter of 1933–1934. But the disheartening persistence of unemployment and suffering demonstrated that emergency relief measures must be not only continued but supplemented.

> *In 1935 Father Charles Coughlin (1891–1979) single-handedly defeated President Roosevelt's effort to win Senate ratification of a treaty providing for American membership in the World Court, a judicial body of limited authority established by the League of Nations. What FDR saw as a symbolic embrace of international responsibility Coughlin convinced his radio listeners was a conspiracy of international moneyed interests against American sovereignty:*
>
> **"Our thanks are due to Almighty God in that America retains her sovereignty. Congratulations to the aroused people of the United States who, by more than 200,000 telegrams containing at least 1,000,000 names, demanded that the principles established by Washington and Jefferson shall keep us clear from foreign entanglements and European hatreds."**

★ A Day for Every Demagogue

One danger signal was the appearance of various demagogues, notably a magnetic "microphone messiah," Father Charles Coughlin, a Catholic priest in Michigan who began broadcasting in 1930 with the slogan "Social Justice." His anti–New Deal harangues to some 40 million radio fans finally became so anti-Semitic, fascistic, and demagogic that he was silenced in 1942 by his ecclesiastical superiors.

Also notorious among the new brood of agitators were those who capitalized on popular discontent to make pie-in-the-sky promises. Most conspicuous of these individuals were Dr. Francis E. Townsend, a retired California physician who promised everyone over sixty $200 a month, and Senator Huey P. ("Kingfish") Long of Louisiana, who was said to have more brass than a government mule. Long used his abundant rabble-rousing talents to publicize his "Share Our Wealth" program, which promised to make "Every Man a King." Every family was to receive $5,000, supposedly at the expense of the prosperous. H. L. Mencken called Long's chief lieutenant, former clergyman Gerald L. K. Smith, "the deadliest and damndest orator ever heard on this or any other earth, the champion boob-bumper of all time." Fear of Long's becoming a fascist dictator ended when he was shot by an assassin in the Louisiana state capitol in 1935.

Father Coughlin and Huey Long frightened many Americans because they raised troubling questions about the link between fascism and economic crisis. Danger seemed to be lurking ominously in many corners of the world. Authoritarian rule was strengthening in Japan, while Adolf Hitler was acquiring absolute authority in Germany. Some even worried that Franklin Roosevelt himself would turn into a dictator.

Partly to quiet the groundswell of unrest that might lead to a political explosion, Congress authorized the Works Progress Administration (WPA) in 1935. The objective was employment on useful projects. Launched under the supervision of the energetic Hopkins, this remarkable agency ultimately spent about $11 billion on thousands of public buildings, bridges, and hard-surfaced roads. One of the best-loved WPA programs was the Federal Art Project, which hired artists to create posters and murals—many still adorning post office walls. Critics sneered that WPA meant "We Provide Alms." But the fact is that over a period of eight years, nearly 9 million people were given jobs, not handouts.

Agencies of the WPA also found part-time occupations for needy high school and college students and for such unemployed white-collar workers as actors, musicians, and writers. John Steinbeck, later a Nobel Prize novelist, counted dogs in his California county. Cynical taxpayers condemned lessons in tap dancing, as well as the painting of scenes on post office walls. But much precious talent was nourished, self-respect was preserved, and more than a million pieces of art were created, many of them publicly displayed.

★ New Visibility for Women

Just over a decade after the ratification of the Nineteenth Amendment, American women began to carve a larger space for themselves in the nation's political and intellectual life. First Lady Eleanor Roosevelt may have been the most visible woman in the Roosevelt

White House, but she was hardly the only female voice. Secretary of Labor Frances Perkins (1880–1965) became the first woman cabinet member. Mary McLeod Bethune (1875–1955), director of the Office of Minority Affairs in the National Youth Administration, served as the highest ranking African American in the Roosevelt administration.

Women also made important contributions in the social sciences, and especially in the relatively new field of anthropology. The landmark book by Ruth Benedict (1887–1948), *Patterns of Culture*, established the study of cultures as collective personalities. One of Benedict's students, Margaret Mead (1901–1978), drew from her own scholarly studies of adolescence among Pacific island peoples to advance bold new ideas about sexuality, gender roles, and intergenerational relationships.

Pearl S. Buck, raised in China by missionary parents, gained fame as a novelist by introducing American readers to Chinese peasant society. Her best-selling novel, *The Good Earth* (1931), earned her the Nobel Prize for literature in 1938.

⭐ Helping Industry and Labor

A daring attempt to stimulate a nationwide comeback was initiated when the Hundred Days Congress authorized the **National Recovery Administration (NRA)**. This ingenious scheme was by far the most complex and far-reaching effort by the New Dealers to combine immediate relief with long-range recovery and reform. Triple-barreled, the NRA was designed to assist industry, labor, and the unemployed.

Individual industries—over two hundred in all—were to work out codes of "fair competition," under which hours of labor would be reduced so that employment could be spread over more people. A ceiling was placed on the maximum hours of labor; a floor was placed under wages to establish minimum levels.

Labor, under the NRA, was granted additional benefits. Workers were formally guaranteed the right to organize and bargain collectively through representatives *of their own choosing*. The hated "yellow dog," or antiunion, contract was expressly forbidden, and certain safeguarding restrictions were placed on the use of child labor.

Enthusiasm for industrial recovery through the NRA was stirred by patriotic mass meetings and huge parades, which included 200,000 marchers on New York City's Fifth Avenue. A handsome blue eagle was designed as the symbol of the NRA, and Philadelphia's newly formed professional football team was named the Eagles. Such was the enthusiasm for the NRA that for a brief period there was a marked upswing of business activity.

But the high-flying eagle gradually fluttered to earth. The "fair competition" codes required too much sacrifice by labor, industry, and the public for such a scheme to work. Critics began to brand the NRA "Nuts Running America," symbolized by what Henry Ford called "that damn Roosevelt buzzard." Complete collapse was imminent when, in 1935, the Supreme Court shot down the dying eagle in the *Schechter* "sick chicken" decision. The learned justices unanimously held that Congress could not "delegate legislative powers" to the executive. They further declared that congressional control of interstate commerce could not properly apply to a local fowl business, such as that of the Schechter brothers in Brooklyn. Roosevelt was incensed by this "horse and buggy" interpretation of the Constitution, but actually the Court helped him out of a bad jam.

The same act of Congress that hatched the NRA eagle also authorized the Public Works Administration (PWA), likewise intended both for industrial recovery and for unemployment relief. The agency was headed by acid-tongued Secretary of the Interior Harold L. Ickes, a free-swinging former bull mooser. Long-range recovery was the primary purpose of the new agency, and in time over $4 billion was spent on some thirty-four thousand projects, which included public buildings, highways, and parkways.

One spectacular PWA achievement was the Grand Coulee Dam on the Columbia River. In the depths of the depression, the towering dam seemed the height of folly. It made possible the irrigation of millions of acres of new farmland—at a time when the government was desperately trying to reduce farm surpluses. It created vast amounts of electrical power—in a region with little industry and virtually no market for additional power. But with the outbreak of World War II and then postwar prosperity, the dam would come to seem a stroke of genius, transforming the entire region with abundant water and power.

National Recovery Administration (NRA) (1933) *An early New Deal program designed to assist industry, labor, and the unemployed through centralized planning mechanisms that monitored workers' earnings and working hours to distribute work and established codes for "fair competition" to ensure that similar procedures were followed by all firms in any particular industrial sector.*

Grand Coulee Dam on the Columbia River, Washington State The Grand Coulee Dam was one of the most ambitious projects of the New Deal's Public Works Administration. It is one of the few man-made constructions visible from outer space, the largest concrete structure in the United States, and the central facility in the Columbia Basin Project, which generates electricity for the Pacific Northwest and provides irrigation for half a million acres of Columbia Valley farmland—services that have transformed the life of the region.

Special stimulants aided the recovery of one segment of business—the liquor industry. The Hundred Days Congress, in one of its earliest acts, legalized and taxed "light" wine and beer (3.2 percent alcohol), providing new employment and federal revenue. Prohibition was officially repealed by the Twenty-first Amendment late in 1933 (see Appendix), and the saloon doors swung open.

★ Paying Farmers Not to Farm

Ever since the war-boom days of 1918, farmers had suffered from low prices and overproduction, especially of grain. During the depression, conditions became desperate as innumerable mortgages were foreclosed, corn was burned for fuel, and embattled farmers tried to prevent shipment of crops to glutted markets. In Iowa several volatile counties were placed under martial law.

A radical new approach to farm recovery was embraced when the Hundred Days Congress established the **Agricultural Adjustment Administration (AAA)**. Through "artificial scarcity" this agency was to establish "parity prices" for basic commodities. "Parity" was the price set for a product that gave it the same real value, in purchasing power, that it had enjoyed during the prosperous period from 1909 to 1914. The AAA would eliminate price-depressing surpluses by paying growers to reduce their crop acreage.

Unhappily, the AAA got off to a wobbly start. It was begun after much of the cotton crop for 1933 had been planted, and balky mules, trained otherwise, were forced to plow under countless young plants. Several million squealing pigs were purchased and

Agricultural Adjustment Administration (AAA) (1933)
A New Deal program designed to raise agricultural prices by paying farmers not to farm. It was based on the assumption that higher prices would increase farmers' purchasing power and thereby help alleviate the Great Depression.

> *Novelist John Steinbeck (1902–1968) related in his novel* The Grapes of Wrath *(1939) that when the "Okies" and "Arkies" reached California, they found the big growers unwilling to pay more than twenty-five cents an hour for work in the fields. One owner mutters:*
>
> **"A Red is any son-of-a-bitch that wants thirty cents an hour when we're paying twenty-five!"**

slaughtered. Much of their meat was distributed to persons on relief, but some of it was used for fertilizer. This "sinful" destruction of food, at a time when thousands of citizens were hungry, increased condemnation of the American economic system by many left-leaning voices. When the Supreme Court finally killed the AAA in 1936 by declaring its regulatory tax unconstitutional, foes of the plow-under program rejoiced loudly.

The New Deal quickly recovered from this blow by passing the Soil Conservation and Domestic Allotment Act (1936), which paid subsidies to farmers if they planted soil-conserving crops, like soybeans, or let their land lie fallow. The Second Agricultural Adjustment Act of 1938 permitted parity payments if farmers observed acreage restrictions on commodities like cotton and wheat. Other provisions of the new AAA were designed to give farmers not only a fairer price but a more substantial share of the national income. Both goals were partially achieved.

★ Dust Bowls and Black Blizzards

Dust Bowl *Grim nickname for the Great Plains region devastated by drought and dust storms during the 1930s. The disaster led to the migration into California of thousands of displaced "Okies" and "Arkies."*

Nature meanwhile had been providing some unplanned scarcity. Late in 1933 a prolonged drought struck the states of the trans-Mississippi Great Plains. Rainless weeks were followed by furious, whining winds, while the sun was darkened by millions of tons of powdery topsoil torn from homesteads that stretched from eastern Colorado to western Missouri—soon to be dubbed the **Dust Bowl** (see Map 32.1). Despondent citizens sat on front porches with protective masks on their faces, watching their farms swirl by.

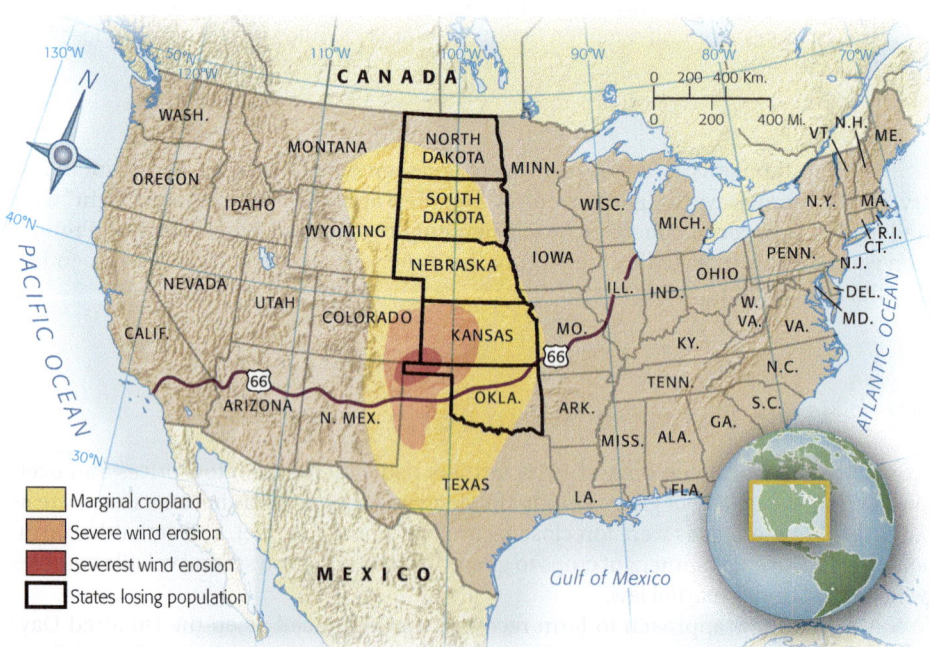

Map 32.1 The Extent of Erosion in the 1930s Note the extensive wind erosion in the western Oklahoma panhandle region, which was dubbed the "Dust Bowl" in the 1930s. Mechanized farmers had "busted" the sod of the southern plains so thoroughly that they literally broke the back of the land. Tons of dust blew out of the Dust Bowl in the 1930s and blotted the sun from the skies as far away as New York. A Kansas newspaperman reported in 1935 that in his dust-darkened town, "Lady Godiva could ride through streets without even the horse seeing her."

Overawed victims of the Dust Bowl disaster predicted the end of the world or the second coming of Christ.

Burned and blown out of the Dust Bowl, tens of thousands of refugees fled their ruined acres. In five years about 350,000 Oklahomans and Arkansans—"Okies" and "Arkies"— trekked to southern California in "junkyards on wheels." Undeterred by signs telling them to "KEEP OUT," many found new homes in the San Joaquin Valley, which shared much in common with the southern plains—arid climate, cotton growing, newfound oil deposits, and abundant land. Yet the transition was cruel. Food, shelter, and clothing were scarce; the winter months, without work and heat, proved nearly unendurable for the migrants. The dismal story of these human tumbleweeds was realistically portrayed in John Steinbeck's best-selling novel *The Grapes of Wrath* (1939), which proved to be the *Uncle Tom's Cabin* of the Dust Bowl.

Zealous New Dealers, sympathetic toward these desperate soil-tillers, made various efforts to relieve their burdens. The Frazier-Lemke Farm Bankruptcy Act, passed in 1934, made possible a suspension of mortgage foreclosures for five years; a revised version was upheld by the Supreme Court. In 1935 the president set up the Resettlement Administration to help farmers move to better land. And more than 200 million young trees were successfully planted on the bare prairies as windbreaks by the young men of the Civilian Conservation Corps.

Native Americans also felt the far-reaching hand of New Deal reform. Commissioner of Indian Affairs John Collier ardently sought to reverse the forced-assimilation policies in place since the Dawes Act of 1887. The Indian Reorganization Act of 1934 (the "Indian New Deal") encouraged tribes to establish local self-government, helped stop the loss of Indian lands, and revived tribes' interest in their identities and cultures. Nearly two hundred tribes established governments under its provisions, though seventy-seven others refused to organize.

★ Reforming Business and Creating Public Power

Reformist New Dealers were determined from the outset to curb the "money changers" who had played fast and loose with gullible investors before the Wall Street crash of 1929. The Hundred Days Congress passed the "Truth in Securities Act" (Federal Securities Act), which required promoters to transmit to the investor sworn information regarding the soundness of their stocks and bonds. In 1934 Congress took further steps to protect the public against fraud, deception, and inside manipulation. It authorized the Securities and Exchange Commission (SEC), which was designed as a watchdog administrative agency. Stock markets henceforth were to operate more as trading marts and less as gambling casinos.

New Dealers likewise directed their fire at public utility holding companies, those supercorporations. When Chicagoan Samuel Insull's multibillion-dollar financial empire crashed in 1932, citizens rebelled against such pyramided layers of big business. The Public Utility Holding Company Act of 1935 delivered a "death sentence" to this type of bloated growth.

Inevitably, the sprawling electric-power industry attracted the fire of New Deal reformers. Within a few decades it had risen from nothingness to a behemoth with an investment of $13 billion. As a public utility, it reached directly and regularly into the pocketbooks of millions of consumers for vitally needed services. Ardent New Dealers accused the electric-power industry of gouging the public with excessive rates, especially because it owed its success to having secured, often for a song, priceless water-power sites from the public domain.

The tempestuous Tennessee River provided New Dealers with a rare opportunity. With its tributaries, the river drained a badly eroded area about the size of England, containing some 2.5 million of the most poverty-stricken people in America. The federal government already owned valuable properties at Muscle Shoals, where it had erected plants for needed nitrates in World War I. By developing the hydroelectric potential of the entire area, Washington could combine the immediate advantage of putting thousands of people to work with a long-term project for reforming the power monopoly.

Tennessee Valley Authority (TVA) (1933) *One of the most revolutionary of the New Deal public works projects, which brought cheap electric power, full employment, low-cost housing, and environmental improvements to Americans in the Tennessee Valley.*

An act that created the **Tennessee Valley Authority (TVA)** was passed in 1933 by the Hundred Days Congress. This far-ranging enterprise was largely a result of the steadfast vision and unflagging zeal of Senator George W. Norris of Nebraska, after whom one of the mighty dams was named. From the standpoint of "planned economy," the TVA was by far the most revolutionary of all New Deal schemes.

New Dealers pointed a prideful finger at the amazing achievements of the TVA, despite critics who called it "creeping socialism." The gigantic project brought to the area not only cheap electric power but full employment, low-cost housing, abundant cheap nitrates, restoration of eroded soil, reforestation, improved navigation, and flood control.

Exulting New Dealers agitated for parallel enterprises in the valleys of the Columbia, Colorado, and Missouri Rivers. Hydroelectric power from federally built dams would drive the growth of the urban West, and the waters the dams diverted would nurture agriculture in the previously bone-dry western deserts. But conservative reaction against the "socialistic" New Deal confined the TVA's brand of federally guided resource management and comprehensive regional development to the Tennessee Valley.

★ Housing and Social Security

The New Deal had meanwhile framed sturdy new policies for housing construction. To speed recovery and improve homes, Roosevelt set up the Federal Housing Administration (FHA) as early as 1934. The building industry was to be stimulated by small loans to householders. So popular did the FHA prove to be that it was one of the few "alphabetical agencies" to outlast the age of Roosevelt.

Congress bolstered the program in 1937 by authorizing the United States Housing Authority (USHA)—an agency designed to lend money to states or communities for low-cost construction. Although units for about 650,000 low-income people were started, new building fell tragically short of needs. New Deal efforts to expand the project collided with brick-wall opposition from real estate promoters, builders, and landlords ("slumlords"), to say nothing of anti–New Dealers who attacked what they considered down-the-rathole spending. Nonetheless, for the first time in a century the slum areas in America ceased growing and even shrank.

Social Security Act (1935) *A flagship accomplishment of the New Deal, providing for unemployment and old-age insurance financed by a payroll tax on employers and employees. It has long remained a pillar of the "New Deal Order."*

Incomparably more important was the success of New Dealers in the field of unemployment insurance and old-age pensions. Their greatest victory was the **Social Security Act** of 1935—one of the most complicated and far-reaching laws ever to pass Congress. To cushion future depressions, the measure provided for federal-state unemployment insurance. To provide security for old age, specified categories of retired workers were to receive regular payments from Washington, ranging from $10 to $85 a month (raised periodically). These pensions were financed by a payroll tax on both employers and employees. Provision was also made for the blind, the physically handicapped, and dependent children.

Social Security was largely inspired by the example of some of the more highly industrialized nations of Europe. The United States government was now recognizing its responsibility for the economic welfare of its citizens. By 1939 more than 45 million people were eligible for Social Security benefits. In subsequent years further categories of workers were added, including, belatedly, farm and domestic workers. For decades, millions of poor men and women were excluded from Social Security. In contrast to Europe, where welfare programs generally were universal, American workers had to be employed and in certain kinds of jobs to get coverage.

★ A New Deal for Labor

The NRA blue eagles, with their call for collective bargaining, had been a godsend to organized labor. As New Deal expenditures brought some slackening of unemployment, labor began to feel more secure and hence more self-assertive. A rash of walkouts occurred in the summer of 1934, including a paralyzing general strike in San Francisco. When the Supreme Court axed the blue eagle, a Congress sympathetic to labor unions undertook to fill the vacuum. The fruit of its deliberations was the National Labor Relations Act of 1935, more commonly known as the **Wagner Act** after its congressional sponsor, New York Senator Robert F. Wagner. This trailblazing law created a powerful new National Labor Relations Board and reasserted the right of labor to organize and bargain collectively through representatives of its own choice. Considered the Magna Carta of American labor, the Wagner Act proved to be a major milestone for American workers.

Under the encouragement of a highly sympathetic National Labor Relations Board, a host of unskilled workers began to organize themselves into effective unions. The leader of this drive was beetle-browed, domineering, and melodramatic John L. Lewis, boss of the United Mine Workers. In 1935 he succeeded in forming the Committee for Industrial Organization (CIO) within the ranks of the skilled-craft American Federation of Labor. But skilled workers, ever since the days of the ill-fated Knights of Labor in the 1880s, had shown only lukewarm sympathy for the cause of unskilled labor, especially blacks. In 1936, following inevitable friction with the CIO, the older federation suspended the upstart unions associated with the newer organization.

Undaunted, the rebellious CIO moved on a concerted scale into the huge automobile industry. Late in 1936 the workers resorted to a revolutionary technique known as the sit-down strike: they refused to leave the factory buildings of General Motors at Flint, Michigan, and thus prevented the importation of strikebreakers. Conservative respecters of private property were scandalized. The CIO finally won a resounding victory when its union, after heated negotiations, was recognized by General Motors as the sole bargaining agency for its employees.

Wagner Act (1935) *Also known as the National Labor Relations Act, protected the right of labor to organize in unions and bargain collectively with employers and established the National Labor Relations Board to monitor unfair labor practices on the part of employers. Its passage marked the culmination of decades of labor protest.*

★ Roosevelt's "Coddling" of Labor

Unskilled workers now pressed their advantage. The United States Steel Corporation, previously an impossible nut for labor to crack, averted a costly strike when it voluntarily granted rights of unionization to its CIO-organized employees. But the "little steel" companies fought back savagely. Citizens were shocked in 1937 by the Memorial Day massacre at the plant of the Republic Steel Company in Chicago, where police gunfire killed or wounded several score picketers.

A better deal for labor continued when Congress, in 1938, passed the memorable **Fair Labor Standards Act** (Wages and Hours Bill). Industries involved in interstate commerce were to set up minimum-wage and maximum-hour levels. The eventual standards were forty cents an hour (later raised) and a forty-hour week. Labor by children under sixteen (under eighteen if the occupation was dangerous) was forbidden. But the exclusion of agricultural, service, and domestic workers meant that blacks, Mexican Americans, and women, who were concentrated in these fields, did not benefit from the act.

In later New Deal days, labor unionization thrived. "Roosevelt wants you to join a union" was the rallying cry of professional organizers. The president received valuable support at the ballot-box from labor leaders and many appreciative working people. One mill worker remarked that Roosevelt was "the only man we ever had in the White House who would know that my boss is an s.o.b."

The CIO surged forward, breaking completely with the AF of L in 1938. On that occasion the *Committee* for Industrial Organization was formally reconstituted as the **Congress of Industrial Organizations** (the new **CIO**), under the visionary though highhanded presidency of John L. Lewis. By 1940 the CIO could claim about 4 million members in its constituent unions, including some 200,000 blacks.

Fair Labor Standards Act (1938) *Important New Deal labor legislation that regulated minimum wages and maximum hours for workers involved in interstate commerce. The law also outlawed labor by children under sixteen. The exclusion of agricultural, service, and domestic workers meant that many blacks, Mexican Americans, and women—who were concentrated in these sectors—did not benefit from the act's protection.*

Congress of Industrial Organizations (CIO) *A New Deal–era labor organization that broke away from the American Federation of Labor (AFL) in order to organize unskilled industrial workers regardless of their particular economic sector or craft. The CIO gave a great boost to labor organizing in the midst of the Great Depression and during World War II. In 1955, the CIO merged with the AFL.*

★ Landon Challenges "the Champ" in 1936

As the presidential campaign of 1936 neared, the New Dealers were on top of the world. They had achieved considerable progress, and millions of "reliefers" were grateful to their bountiful government. The exultant Democrats renominated Roosevelt on a platform squarely endorsing the New Deal.

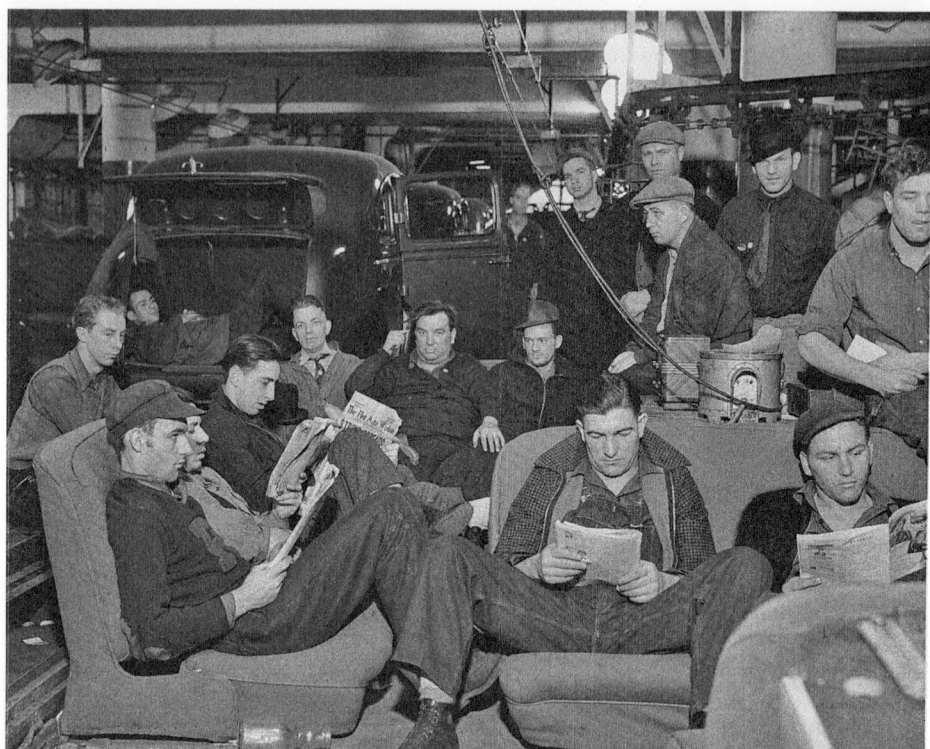

General Motors Sit-Down Strikers, Flint, Michigan, 1937 Strikers like these sometimes kept their spirits up with the song "Sit Down":

When the boss won't talk
Don't take a walk;
Sit down, sit down.

The Republicans were hard pressed to find someone to feed to "the Champ." They finally settled on the colorless but homespun and honest governor of Kansas, Alfred M. Landon. Landon himself was a moderate who accepted some New Deal reforms, although not the popular Social Security Act. But the Republican platform vigorously condemned the New Deal for its radicalism, experimentation, confusion, and "frightful waste." Backing Landon, ex-president Hoover called for a "holy crusade for liberty," echoing the cry of the American Liberty League, a group of wealthy conservatives organized to fight "socialistic" New Deal schemes.

Roosevelt gave as good as he got. Angry enough to stretch sheet iron, Roosevelt took to the stump and denounced the "economic royalists" who sought to "hide behind the flag and the Constitution." "I welcome their hatred," he proclaimed.

A landslide overwhelmed Landon as the demoralized Republicans carried only two states, Maine and Vermont. The popular vote was 27,752,869 to 16,674,665; the electoral count was 523 to 8—the most lopsided in 116 years. A good-humored newspaper columnist quipped, "If Landon had given one more speech, Roosevelt would have carried Canada, too." Democratic majorities were again returned to Congress. Jubilant Democrats could now claim more than two-thirds of the seats in the House and a like proportion in the Senate.

The battle of 1936, perhaps the most bitter since Bryan's defeat in 1896, partially bore out Republican charges of class warfare. Even more than in 1932, the needy economic groups were lined up against the so-called greedy economic groups. CIO units contributed generously to FDR's campaign chest. Many left-wingers turned to Roosevelt, as the customary third-party protest vote sharply declined. Blacks, several million of whom had also appreciated relief checks, had by now largely shaken off their traditional allegiance to the Republican party. To them, Lincoln was "finally dead."

FDR won primarily because he appealed to the "forgotten man," whom he never forgot. Roosevelt in fact had forged a powerful and enduring coalition of southerners, blacks, urbanites, and the poor. He proved especially effective in marshaling the support of the multitudes of "New Immigrants"—mostly Catholics and Jews who had swarmed into the great cities since the turn of the century. These once-scorned newcomers, with their now-numerous sons and daughters, had at last come politically of age. In the 1920s, one out of every twenty-five federal judgeships went to a Catholic; Roosevelt appointed Catholics to one out of every four.

★ Nine Old Men on the Bench

Bowing his head to the sleety blasts, Roosevelt took the presidential oath on January 20, 1937, instead of the traditional March 4. The Twentieth Amendment to the Constitution had been ratified in 1933. (See the Appendix.) It swept away the postelection lame duck session of Congress and shortened by six weeks the awkward period before inauguration.

Flushed with victory, Roosevelt interpreted his reelection as a mandate to continue New Deal reforms. But in his eyes the cloistered old men on the supreme bench, like fossilized stumbling blocks, stood stubbornly in the pathway of progress. In nine major cases involving the New Deal, the Roosevelt administration had been thwarted seven times. The Supreme Court was ultraconservative, and six of the nine oldsters in black were over seventy. As luck would have it, not a single member had been appointed by FDR in his first term.

Roosevelt, his "Dutch up," viewed with mounting impatience what he regarded as the obstructive conservatism of the Court. To overcome such obstructionism, Roosevelt finally hit upon a Court scheme that he regarded as "the answer to a maiden's prayer." In fact, it proved to be one of the most costly political misjudgements of his career. Roosevelt's brainstorm, which surprised and shocked the country, asked Congress for legislation to permit him to add a new justice to the Supreme Court for every member over seventy who would not retire. The maximum membership could then be fifteen.

Congress and the nation were promptly convulsed over Roosevelt's **Court-packing plan** to expand the Supreme Court. Franklin "Double-crossing" Roosevelt was savagely condemned for attempting to break down the delicate checks and balances among the three branches of the government.

The Court had meanwhile seen the ax hanging over its head. Whatever his motives, Justice Owen J. Roberts, formerly regarded as a conservative, began to vote on the side of his liberal colleagues. "A switch in time saves nine" was the classic witticism inspired by this change. By a five-to-four decision, the Court, in March 1937, upheld the principle of a state minimum wage for women, thereby reversing its stand on a different case a year earlier. In succeeding decisions a Court more sympathetic to the New Deal upheld the National Labor Relations Act (Wagner Act) and the Social Security Act.

With these changes under way, Congress refused to endorse the court-packing scheme, and Roosevelt suffered his first major legislative defeat at the hands of his

---

Contending Voices

The New Deal at High Tide

Three days before the 1936 election, President Franklin Roosevelt (1882–1945) took the moral high ground in his fiery speech at New York's Madison Square Garden:

"I should like to have it said of my first Administration that in it the forces of selfishness and of lust for power met their match. I should like to have it said of my second Administration that in it these forces met their master."

One day prior to that, his predecessor Herbert Hoover (1874–1964) voiced the sentiments of many conservatives when he depicted the New Deal as a dangerous power grab:

"Through four years of experience this New Deal attack upon free institutions has emerged as the transcendent issue in America. All the men who are seeking for mastery in the world today are using the same weapons. They sing the same songs. They all promise the joys of Elysium without effort. But their philosophy is founded on the coercion and compulsory organization of men."

> What ideologies about the nature of government lay behind Roosevelt's and Hoover's very different opinions of the New Deal? In what ways have their respective views persisted in American political life?

Court-packing plan (1937) *Franklin Roosevelt's politically motivated and ill-fated scheme to add a new justice to the Supreme Court for every member over seventy who would not retire. His objective was to overcome the Court's objections to New Deal reforms.*

own party. Yet in losing this battle, Roosevelt incidentally won his campaign. The Court, as he had hoped, became markedly more friendly to New Deal reforms. Furthermore, a succession of deaths and resignations enabled him to make nine appointments to the tribunal.

Yet in a sense FDR lost both the Court battle and the war. He so aroused conservatives of both parties in Congress that few New Deal reforms were passed after 1937, the year of the fight to "pack" the Supreme Court. With this catastrophic miscalculation, he squandered much of the political goodwill that had carried him to such a resounding victory in the 1936 election.

★ The Twilight of the New Deal

Roosevelt's first term, from 1933 to 1937, did not banish the depression from the land. Unemployment stubbornly persisted in 1936 at about 15 percent, down from the grim 25 percent of 1933 but still miserably high. Despite the inventiveness of New Deal programs and the billions of dollars in "pump priming," recovery had been dishearteningly modest, though the country seemed to be inching its way back to economic health.

Then, in 1937, the economy took another sharp downturn, a surprisingly severe depression-within-the-depression that the president's critics quickly dubbed the "Roosevelt recession." In fact, government policies had caused the nosedive, as new Social Security taxes began to bite into payrolls and as the administration cut back on spending out of continuing reverence for the orthodox economic doctrine of the balanced budget.

Only at this late date did Roosevelt at last frankly and deliberately embrace the recommendations of the British economist John Maynard Keynes. The New Deal had run deficits for several years, but all of them had been rather small and none was intended. Now, in April 1937, FDR announced a bold program to stimulate the economy by planned deficit spending. Although the deficits were still undersized for the herculean task of conquering the depression, this abrupt policy reversal marked a turning point in the government's relation to the economy. **Keynesianism**—the use of government spending and fiscal policy to "prime the pump" of the economy and encourage consumer spending—became the new economic orthodoxy and remained so for decades.

Roosevelt had meanwhile been pushing the remaining reform measures of the New Deal. But only a few of his proposals made it through an increasingly conservative Congress. The Reorganization Act gave him limited power for administrative reforms, including the key new Executive Office in the White House. The Hatch Act of 1939 barred federal officials from political campaigning or using government funds for political purposes. But such clever ways of getting around it were found that the legislation proved disappointing.

By 1938 the New Deal had clearly lost most of its early momentum. Magician Roosevelt could find few dazzling new reform rabbits to pull out of his tall silk hat. In the congressional elections of 1938 the Republicans, for the first time, cut heavily into the New Deal majorities in Congress, though failing to gain control of either house. The international crisis that came to a boil in 1938–1939 shifted public attention away from domestic reform and no doubt helped save the political hide of the Roosevelt "spendocracy." The New Deal, for all practical purposes, had shot its bolt.

Keynesianism An economic theory based on the work of British economist John Maynard Keynes, holding that central banks should adjust interest rates and governments should use deficit spending and tax policies to increase purchasing power and hence prosperity.

> *A basic objective of the New Deal was featured in Roosevelt's second inaugural address (1937):*
>
> "I see one-third of a nation ill-housed, ill-clad, ill-nourished.... The test of our progress is not whether we add more to the abundance of those who have much; it is whether we provide enough for those who have too little."

★ New Deal or Raw Deal?

Foes of the New Deal condemned its alleged radicalism, incompetence, confusion, and cross-purposes. New Dealers conceded some weaknesses but defended their record as a necessary and effective response to the depression.

To some conservatives, the New Deal was a radical attempt to make America over in a Bolshevik-Marxist image. They condemned "Rooseveltski" for bringing to Washington "crackpot" college professors, leftist "pinkos," and outright Communists. The Hearst newspapers lambasted:

The Red New Deal with a Soviet seal
Endorsed by a Moscow hand,
The strange result of an alien cult
In a liberty-loving land.

Roosevelt was further accused by conservatives of tapping too many bright young leftists for his "Jew Deal," or even of being Jewish himself ("Rosenfeld").

More widespread was the charge that the New Deal brought bureaucracy, waste, and a welfare-state mentality that undermined the old American virtues of individualism, thrift, self-reliance, and limited government. The federal government, with its hundreds of thousands of employees, became incomparably the largest single business in the country, as the states faded further into the background. Promises of budget balancing went out the window as the national debt skyrocketed from $19,487,000,000 in 1932 to $40,440,000,000 by 1939. Critics charged that the lavish benefactions of the "handout state" were turning once self-reliant Americans into relief-seeking loafers, with wishbones larger than their backbones.

Business was bitter. Accusing the New Deal of fomenting class strife, countless businesspeople, especially Republicans, declared that they could pull themselves out of the depression if they could only get an interventionist big government off their backs. Private enterprise, they charged, was being stifled by a "planned economy" and "creeping socialism." Roosevelt's aggressive leadership also came in for denunciation and charges that he was trying to create a "one-man supergovernment."

The most damning indictment of the New Deal was that it failed to cure the depression. Despite some $20 billion poured out in six years of deficit spending and lending, many economists came to believe that better results would have been achieved by much greater deficit spending. The New Deal had merely administered aspirin, sedatives, and Band-Aids, with the result that in 1939 millions of dispirited men and women were still unemployed. Not until World War II increased the national debt from $40 billion in 1939 to $258 billion in 1945 was the unemployment headache solved.

New Dealers staunchly defended their record. Admitting imperfection, they argued that the bureaucratic inefficiency and waste had been trivial in view of the immense sums spent and the obvious need for haste. The New Deal, they insisted, relieved a crisis by demonstrating that the Washington regime was to be used, not feared. The collapse of America's economic system was averted; a fairer distribution of the national income was achieved; and the citizens were enabled to regain and retain their self-respect.

Though hated by business tycoons, FDR should have been their patron saint, so his admirers claimed. He deflected popular resentments against business and may have saved the American system of free enterprise. Roosevelt's quarrel was not with capitalism but with capitalists; he purged American capitalism of some of its worst abuses so that it might be saved from itself. He may even have headed off a more radical swing to the left by a mild dose of what was mistakenly reviled as "socialism." The head of the American Socialist party, when once asked if the New Deal had carried out the Socialist program, reportedly replied that it had indeed—on a stretcher.

Roosevelt, like Jefferson, provided reform without a bloody revolution—at a time in history when some foreign nations were suffering armed uprisings and when many Europeans were predicting either communism or fascism for America. He was upbraided by the left-wing radicals for not going far enough, by the right-wing radicals for going too far. Choosing the middle road, he has been called the greatest American conservative since Hamilton. He was in fact Hamiltonian in his espousal of big government, but Jeffersonian in his concern for the "forgotten man." Demonstrating anew the value of powerful presidential leadership, he exercised that power to relieve the erosion of the nation's greatest physical resource—its people. He helped preserve democracy in America at a time when democracies abroad were disappearing down the sinkhole of dictatorship. And in playing this role, he unwittingly girded the nation for its part in the titanic war that loomed on the horizon—a war in which democracy the world over would be at stake.

Varying Viewpoints

How Radical Was the New Deal?

The Great Depression was both a great calamity and a great opportunity. How effectively Franklin Roosevelt responded to the calamity and what use he made of the opportunity are the two questions that have animated historical debate about the New Deal.

Some historians have denied that there was much of a connection between the depression and the New Deal. Arthur M. Schlesinger, Jr., for example, who believed in "cycles" of reform and reaction in American history, wrote that "there would very likely have been some sort of New Deal in the 1930s even without the Depression." But most of the first generation of historians who wrote about the New Deal (in the 1940s, 1950s, and early 1960s) agreed with Carl Degler's judgment that the New Deal was "a revolutionary response to a revolutionary situation." In this view, though Roosevelt never found a means short of war to bring about economic recovery, he shrewdly utilized the stubborn economic crisis as a means to enact sweeping reforms.

Some leftist scholars writing in the 1960s, however, notably Barton J. Bernstein, charged that the New Deal did not reach far enough. This criticism echoed the socialist complaint in the 1930s that the depression represented the total collapse of American capitalism and that the New Deal muffed the chance truly to remake American society. Roosevelt had the chance, these historians argue, to redistribute wealth, improve race relations, and bring the giant corporations to heel. Instead, said these critics, the New Deal simply represented a conservative holding action to shore up a sagging and corrupt capitalist order.

Those charges against the New Deal stimulated another generation of scholars in the 1970s, 1980s, and 1990s to look closely at the concrete institutional, attitudinal, and economic circumstances in which the New Deal unfolded. Historians such as James Patterson, Alan Brinkley, Kenneth Jackson, Harvard Sitkoff, and Lizabeth Cohen—sometimes loosely referred to as the "constraints school"—concluded that the New Deal offered just about as much reform as circumstances allowed and as the majority of Americans wanted. The findings of these historians are impressive: the system of checks and balances limited presidential power; the disproportionate influence of southern Democrats in Congress stalled attempts to move toward racial justice; the federal system, in fact, inhibited all efforts to initiate change from Washington.

Most important, a majority of the American people at the time wanted to reform capitalism, not overthrow it. Industrial workers, for example, were not hapless pawns upon whom the New Deal was foisted, frustrating their yearning for more radical change. Instead, as David Kennedy has argued, they sought security and self-determination in ways quite compatible with the New Deal's programs for unemployment insurance, old-age pensions, and guarantees of labor's right to organize.

More recently, scholars such as Alice Kessler-Harris, Linda Gordon, and Susan Mettler have argued that the New Deal had a more radical effect on men than women. Social Security, for example, was designed to assist male breadwinners, who were then expected to share their benefits with their dependent wives and children. Ira Katznelson, meanwhile, has re-centered scholarly attention on the key role of southern Democrats in Congress in constricting the New Deal along racial lines.

Perhaps William Leuchtenburg summed it up best when he described the New Deal as a "half-way revolution," neither radical nor conservative but accurately reflecting the American people's needs and desires in the 1930s—and for a long time thereafter. The great "New Deal coalition" that dominated American politics for nearly four decades after Roosevelt's election in 1932 represented a broad consensus in American society about the opportunities and legitimate limits of government efforts to shape the social and economic order.

CHAPTER SUMMARY ★ ★ ★ ★ ★ ★ ★ ★ ★ ★ ★ ★ ★

Franklin Roosevelt, a confident aristocrat with a common touch, swept into office with an urgent mandate to cope with the depression emergency. His bank holiday and frantic Hundred Days legislation lifted America's spirits and created a host of new agencies to provide relief to the unemployed, economic recovery, and hoped-for permanent reform of a largely unregulated capitalist system.

Roosevelt's early programs put millions of the unemployed back on the job through federal action, but failed to achieve the full economic recovery he sought. As popular demagogues such as Senator Huey Long and Father Charles Coughlin gained followings among the suffering population, Roosevelt developed further ambitious programs to reform American industry, labor, and agriculture. The Supreme Court declared unconstitutional the most sweeping effort, the National Recovery Administration, and farmers continued to suffer from the Dust Bowl. But the TVA, Social Security, and the Wagner Act brought far-reaching social changes that especially benefited the economically disadvantaged.

Conservatives furiously denounced the New Deal, but Roosevelt formed a powerful coalition of urbanites, labor, "new immigrants," blacks, and southerners that swept him to victory in 1936. FDR and especially his vigorously reformist wife Eleanor brought new visibility to women in his administration and the country.

Roosevelt's overreaching court-packing plan failed, but the Supreme Court finally began approving New Deal legislation. The later New Deal encountered mounting conservative opposition and the stubborn persistence of unemployment. Although the New Deal was highly controversial, it steered a middle course between unregulated capitalism and socialism that prevented America from turning toward dictatorship or extreme right-wing or left-wing solutions.

KEY TERMS

Brain Trust (552)
New Deal (552)
Hundred Days (553)
Glass-Steagall Banking Reform Act (555)
Civilian Conservation Corps (CCC) (555)
National Recovery Administration (NRA) (558)
Agricultural Adjustment Administration (AAA) (559)
Dust Bowl (560)
Tennessee Valley Authority (TVA) (562)
Social Security Act (562)
Wagner Act (563)
Fair Labor Standards Act (563)
Congress of Industrial Organizations (CIO) (563)
Court-packing plan (565)
Keynesianism (566)

PEOPLE TO KNOW

Franklin Delano Roosevelt
Eleanor Roosevelt
Harry L. Hopkins
Father Charles Coughlin
Francis E. Townsend
Huey P. ("Kingfish") Long
Frances Perkins
Mary McLeod Bethune
Robert F. Wagner

MindTap is a fully online, highly personalized learning experience built upon Cengage Learning content. MindTap combines student learning tools—readings, multimedia, activities, and assessments—into a singular Learning Path that guides students through the course.

Chapter 33

Franklin D. Roosevelt and the Shadow of War
1933–1941

* * *

The epidemic of world lawlessness is spreading. When an epidemic of physical disease starts to spread, the community approves and joins in a quarantine of the patients in order to protect the health of the community against the spread of the disease. . . . There must be positive endeavors to preserve peace.

FRANKLIN D. ROOSEVELT, CHICAGO "QUARANTINE SPEECH," 1937

Chapter Outline

- Roosevelt's Early Foreign Policies
- The Rise of Fascism and American Isolationism
- War in Europe and the Debate over American Neutrality
- Roosevelt's Third-Term Victory and Lend-Lease Aid to Britain
- Refugees from Hitler's Holocaust
- The Japanese Attack on Pearl Harbor, December 7, 1941
- *Examining the Evidence: Public Opinion Polling in the 1930s*

Americans in the 1930s tried to turn their backs on the world's problems. Their president at first seemed to share these views. The only battle Roosevelt sought was against the Depression. America had its own burdens to shoulder, and the costs of foreign involvement, whether in blood or treasure, simply seemed too great.

But as the clouds of war gathered over Europe, Roosevelt eventually concluded that the United States could no longer remain aloof. Events gradually brought the American people around to his thinking: No nation was safe in an era of international anarchy, and the world could not remain half-enchained and half-free.

FOCUS QUESTIONS

1. What were the goals and results of Franklin Roosevelt's early foreign policy?
2. How and why did isolationism come to dominate American public opinion and foreign policy in the 1930s?
3. How did the United States gradually awaken to the threat of totalitarian aggression in the late 1930s while still attempting to avoid foreign entanglements?
4. Why did FDR's increasingly bold moves to aid Britain in the fight against Hitler stir a fierce national debate over the risk of being drawn into war and the best way to preserve America's security?
5. What issues and developments in Japanese-American relations led up to the surprise Japanese attack on Pearl Harbor?

CHRONOLOGY

1933	▪ FDR torpedoes London Economic Conference ▪ United States recognizes Soviet Union ▪ FDR declares Good Neighbor policy toward Latin America ▪ Hitler becomes German chancellor ▪ Germany quits League of Nations	1938	▪ Hitler seizes Austria ▪ Munich Conference ▪ *Kristallnacht* in Germany
1934	▪ Tydings-McDuffie Act provides for Philippine independence on July 4, 1946 ▪ U.S. Marines vacate Haiti	1939	▪ Hitler seizes all of Czechoslovakia ▪ Nazi-Soviet pact ▪ World War II begins in Europe with Hitler's invasion of Poland ▪ U.S. Neutrality Act of 1939
1935	▪ Mussolini invades Ethiopia ▪ U.S. Neutrality Act of 1935 ▪ Japan quits League of Nations	1940	▪ Hitler invades Denmark, Norway, Netherlands, and Belgium ▪ Fall of France ▪ United States institutes first peacetime draft ▪ Battle of Britain ▪ Bases-for-destroyers deal with Britain ▪ FDR defeats Willkie for presidency
1936	▪ U.S. Neutrality Act of 1936 ▪ Mussolini and Hitler form Rome-Berlin Axis ▪ Stalin begins Great Purge ▪ German troops invade Rhineland	1941	▪ Lend-Lease Act ▪ Hitler attacks Soviet Union ▪ Atlantic Charter ▪ Japan attacks Pearl Harbor
1936–1939	▪ Spanish Civil War		
1937	▪ U.S. Neutrality Act of 1937 ▪ *Panay* incident ▪ Japan invades China		

★ Roosevelt's Early Foreign Policies

The sixty-six nation **London Economic Conference** in the summer of 1933 revealed how thoroughly Roosevelt's early foreign policy was subordinated to his strategy for domestic economic recovery. The delegates hoped to organize a coordinated international attack on the global depression by stabilizing national currencies and exchange rates. But Roosevelt, unwilling to subordinate his gold-juggling and other inflationary policies to an international agreement that might tie his hands, torpedoed the conference with a bombshell message that scolded the delegates for even trying to stabilize currencies and withdrew America from the negotiations.

Whether the conference could have arrested the worldwide economic slide is debatable, but Roosevelt's every-man-for-himself attitude plunged the planet even deeper into economic crisis. The collapse of the London Conference also strengthened the global trend toward extreme nationalism—a trend that played directly into the hands of power-mad dictators who were determined to shatter the peace of the world.

Roosevelt matched isolationism from Europe with withdrawal from Asia. With the descent into hard times, American taxpayers were eager to throw overboard their expensive tropical liability in the Philippine Islands. Congress passed the Tydings-McDuffie Act in 1934, which provided for the future independence of the Philippines in 1946. In truth, the American people were not so much giving freedom to the Philippines as they were freeing themselves *from* the Philippines by imposing economic terms so ungenerous as to threaten the islands with economic prostration. American isolationists rejoiced once again, and Japanese militarists calculated that they had little to fear from an inward-looking America.

Closer to home, Roosevelt inaugurated a refreshing new era in relations with Latin America. He proclaimed in his inaugural address, "I would dedicate this nation to the policy of the Good Neighbor." Roosevelt's hope-inspiring **Good Neighbor policy** renounced

London Economic Conference (1933) *A sixty-six-nation economic conference organized to stabilize international currency rates. Franklin Roosevelt's decision to revoke American participation contributed to a deepening world economic crisis.*

Good Neighbor policy *A policy stressing nonintervention in Latin America, a major departure from the Roosevelt Corollary to the Monroe Doctrine. It was begun by Herbert Hoover but is most strongly associated with Franklin D. Roosevelt, who put it into practice in Mexico and elsewhere.*

further armed intervention in Latin America, particularly the vexatious corollary to the Monroe Doctrine devised by his cousin Theodore Roosevelt. It also sought a new attitude of friendliness and consultation with America's southern neighbors rather than aggressive assertion of U.S. economic interests.

Accordingly, the United States withdrew the last marines from Haiti in 1934. That same year, after military strongman Fulgencia Batista came to power, restive Cuba was released from the worst hobbles of the interventionist Platt Amendment, although the United States retained its naval base at Guantanamo (see p. 461). The United States similarly relaxed its grip on Panama in 1936. The acid test of the Good Neighbor policy came when the Mexican government seized Yankee oil properties in 1938. Roosevelt successfully resisted strong business badgering to intervene and eventually threshed out a settlement in 1941. These earnest acts of friendliness paid rich dividends in goodwill among the peoples to the south, and Roosevelt was cheered with tremendous enthusiasm when he traveled to an Inter-American Conference at Buenos Aires, Argentina, in 1936. The Colossus of the North now seemed less a vulture and more an eagle.

Rome-Berlin Axis (1936) *Treaty by which Nazi Germany, under Adolf Hitler, and Fascist Italy, led by Benito Mussolini, allied themselves together. The pact was signed after both countries had intervened on behalf of the fascist leader Francisco Franco during the Spanish Civil War.*

★ Turning Toward Isolationism

Post-1918 chaos in Europe, followed by the Great Depression, spawned the ominous spread of totalitarianism. The individual was nothing; the state was everything. The communist USSR led the way, with the crafty and ruthless Joseph Stalin finally emerging as dictator. In 1936, Stalin began to purge his communist state of all suspected dissidents, ultimately executing hundreds of thousands and banishing millions to remote Siberian forced-labor camps. Blustery Benito Mussolini, a swaggering Fascist, seized the reins of power in Italy during 1922. And Adolf Hitler, a fanatic with a toothbrush mustache, plotted and harangued his way into control of Germany in 1933 with liberal use of the "big lie."

Hitler was the most dangerous of the dictators because he combined tremendous power with impulsiveness. A frustrated Austrian painter, with hypnotic talents as an orator and leader, Hitler had led the Nazi party to power in Germany by making political capital of the Treaty of Versailles and Germany's depression-spawned unemployment. The desperate German people had fallen in behind the new Pied Piper, for they saw no other hope of escape from the plague of economic chaos and national disgrace. Hitler began clandestinely (and illegally) rearming in 1933, and in 1936 the Nazi Hitler and the Fascist Mussolini allied themselves in the **Rome-Berlin Axis**.

International gangsterism was likewise spreading in East Asia, where imperial Japan was on the make. Like Germany and Italy, Japan was a so-called have-not power. Like them, Japan resented the ungenerous Treaty of Versailles. Like them, Japan demanded additional space for its teeming millions, cooped up in their crowded island nation. Determined to find a place in the Asian sun, Tokyo terminated the Washington Naval Treaty in 1934, and in the following year accelerated its construction of giant battleships. In 1940 Japan joined arms with Germany and Italy in the Tripartite Pact.

Jut-jawed Mussolini, seeking both glory and empire in Africa, brutally attacked Ethiopia in 1935. The members of the League of Nations could have halted Mussolini's war machine with an oil embargo. But fearing global hostilities they failed to act, and the brave but poorly armed Ethiopians were speedily crushed by Mussolini's bombers and tanks.

Isolationism, long festering in America, received a strong boost from these alarms abroad. Though disapproving the

The Wages of Despair Disillusioned and desperate, millions of Germans in the 1930s looked to Adolf Hitler as their savior from the harsh terms of the Treaty of Versailles, which had concluded World War I. This Nazi poster reads, "Our Last Hope: Hitler."

dictators, Americans still believed that their encircling seas conferred a kind of mystic immunity. They were continuing to suffer the disillusionment born of their participation in World War I, which they now regarded as a colossal blunder. Americans likewise nursed bitter memories of the ungrateful and defaulting debtors. As early as 1934, a spiteful Congress passed the **Johnson Debt Default Act**, which prevented debt-dodging nations from borrowing further in the United States.

Mired down in the Great Depression, Americans had no real appreciation of the revolutionary forces being harnessed by the dictators. Americans were not so much afraid that totalitarian aggression would cause trouble as they were fearful that they might be drawn into it. Strong nationwide sentiment welled up for a constitutional amendment to forbid a declaration of war by Congress—except in case of invasion—unless there was a favorable popular referendum.

As the gloomy 1930s lengthened, an avalanche of lurid articles and books condemning the munitions manufacturers as war-fomenting "merchants of death" poured from American presses. A Senate committee headed by Senator Gerald Nye of North Dakota sensationalized evidence regarding America's entry into World War I, shifting the blame away from German submarines onto American bankers and arms manufacturers. Because the munitions makers had obviously made money out of the war, many a naïve citizen leaped to the illogical conclusion that these soulless scavengers had *caused* the war in order to make money. This kind of reasoning suggested that if the profits could only be removed from the arms traffic—"one hell of a business"—the country could steer clear of any future world conflict.

Responding to overwhelming popular pressure, Congress made haste to legislate the nation out of war. Action was spurred by the danger that Mussolini's Ethiopian assault would plunge the world into a new bloodbath. The **Neutrality Acts of 1935, 1936, and 1937**, taken together, stipulated that *when the president proclaimed* the existence of a foreign war, certain restrictions would automatically go into effect: No American could legally sail on a belligerent ship, sell or transport munitions to a belligerent, or make loans to a belligerent.

This storm-cellar neutrality proved to be tragically shortsighted. Through its neutrality laws, America served notice that it would make no distinction between brutal aggressors and innocent victims. By striving to hold the scales even, America actually overbalanced them in favor of the dictators, who had armed themselves to the teeth. By declining to use its vast industrial strength to aid its democratic friends and defeat its totalitarian foes, America helped goad the aggressors along their blood-spattered path of conquest.

The Spanish Civil War of 1936–1939—a proving ground and dress rehearsal in miniature for World War II—was a painful object lesson in the folly of neutrality-by-legislation. Spanish rebels, who rose against the left-leaning republican government in Madrid, were headed by fascistic General Francisco Franco. Generously aided by his fellow conspirators Hitler and Mussolini, he undertook to overthrow the established Loyalist regime, which in turn was assisted on a smaller scale by the Soviet Union. This pipeline from communist Moscow chilled the natural sympathies of many Americans, especially Roman Catholics, for the republican Loyalists. But other Americans burned with passion to defend the struggling republic against Franco's fascist coup. Some three thousand young men and women headed to Spain to fight as volunteers in the **Abraham Lincoln Brigade**.

Washington continued official relations with the Loyalist government. But Congress, with the encouragement of Roosevelt and with only one dissenting vote, amended the existing neutrality legislation so as to apply an arms embargo to both Loyalists and rebels.

Uncle Sam thus sat on the sidelines while Franco, abundantly supplied with arms and men by his fellow dictators, strangled the republican government of Spain. The democracies, including the United States, were so determined to stay out of war that they helped to condemn a fellow democracy to death. In so doing they further encouraged the dictators to take the dangerous road that led over the precipice to World War II.

The thirst of Benito Mussolini (1883–1945) for national glory in Ethiopia is indicated by his remark in 1940:

"To make a people great it is necessary to send them to battle even if you have to kick them in the pants."

(The Italians were notoriously unwarlike.)

In 1934 Mussolini proclaimed in a public speech:

"We have buried the putrid corpse of liberty."

Johnson Debt Default Act (1934) *A spiteful act, steeping in ugly memories of World War I, that prevented debt-ridden European nations from borrowing further from the United States.*

Neutrality Acts of 1935, 1936, and 1937 *Short-sighted acts passed to prevent American participation in a European war. Among other restrictions, they prevented Americans from selling munitions to foreign belligerents.*

Abraham Lincoln Brigade *Idealistic American volunteers who served in the Spanish Civil War, defending Spanish republican forces from the fascist General Francisco Franco's nationalist coup. Some three thousand Americans served alongside volunteers from other countries.*

⭐ Appeasing Japan and Germany

Sulfurous war clouds had meanwhile been gathering in tension-taut East Asia. In 1937 the Japanese militarists, at the Marco Polo Bridge near Beijing (Peking), touched off the explosion that led to an all-out invasion of China. In a sense this attack was the curtain-raiser of World War II.

Roosevelt shrewdly declined to invoke the recently passed neutrality legislation by refusing to call the China incident an officially declared war. If he had put the existing restrictions into effect, he would have cut off the tiny trickle of munitions on which the Chinese were desperately dependent. The Japanese, of course, could continue to buy mountains of war supplies in the United States.

In Chicago—unofficial isolationist "capital" of America—President Roosevelt delivered his sensational **Quarantine Speech** in the autumn of 1937. Alarmed by the recent aggression of Italy and Japan, he called for "positive endeavors" to "quarantine" the aggressors—presumably by economic embargoes. The speech triggered a cyclone of protest from isolationists and other foes of involvement; they feared that a moral quarantine would lead to a shooting quarantine. Startled by this angry response, Roosevelt retreated and sought less direct means to curb the dictators.

America's isolationist mood intensified in December 1937 when Japanese aviators bombed and sank an American gunboat, the *Panay*, in Chinese waters. After Tokyo apologized and paid an indemnity, Americans breathed a deep sigh of relief that they need not respond to the outrage.

Adolf Hitler meanwhile grew louder and bolder in Europe. In 1935 he had openly flouted the Treaty of Versailles by introducing compulsory military service in Germany. The next year he brazenly marched into the demilitarized German Rhineland, likewise contrary to the detested treaty, while France and Britain looked on in an agony of indecision. Lashing his following to a frenzy, Hitler undertook to persecute and then exterminate the Jewish population in the areas under his control. In the end, he wiped out about 6 million innocent victims, mostly in gas chambers. Calling upon his people to sacrifice butter for guns, he whipped the new German air force and mechanized ground divisions into the most devastating military machine the world had yet seen.

Suddenly, in March 1938, Hitler bloodlessly occupied German-speaking Austria, his birthplace. The democratic powers, wringing their hands in despair, prayed that this last grab would satisfy his passion for conquest. But like a drunken reveler calling for madder music and stronger wine, Hitler could not stop. Intoxicated by his recent gains, he began to make bullying demands for the German-inhabited Sudetenland of neighboring Czechoslovakia.

British and French leaders, eager to appease Hitler, frantically arranged a conference with Hitler and Mussolini at Munich, Germany, in September 1938. There they betrayed Czechoslovakia to Germany when they consented to the shearing away of the Sudetenland. Europeans and Americans alike hoped that these concessions would bring "peace in our time." Indeed, Hitler publicly promised that the Sudetenland "is the last territorial claim I have to make in Europe."

Appeasement of the dictators, symbolized by the ugly word *Munich*, turned out to be merely surrender on the installment plan. It was like giving a cannibal a finger in the hope of saving an arm. In March 1939, scarcely six months later, Hitler suddenly erased the rest of Czechoslovakia from the map, contrary to his solemn vows. The democratic world was again stunned.

⭐ Hitler's Belligerency and U.S. Neutrality

Joseph Stalin, the sphinx of the Kremlin, was a key to the peace puzzle. When his efforts to secure a mutual defense treaty with Britain and France fell through in the summer of 1939, the Soviet Union astounded the world by signing, on August 23, 1939, a nonaggression treaty with the German

---

Quarantine Speech (1937) *An important speech delivered by Franklin Roosevelt in which he called for "positive endeavors" to "quarantine" land-hungry dictators, presumably through economic embargoes. The speech flew in the face of isolationist politicians.*

Appeasement (1938) *The policy followed by leaders of Britain and France at the 1938 conference in Munich. Their purpose was to avoid war, but they allowed Germany to take the Sudetenland from Czechoslovakia.*

Hitler-Stalin pact (1939) *Treaty signed on August 23, 1939, in which Germany and the Soviet Union agreed not to fight each other. The fateful agreement paved the way for German aggression against Poland and the Western democracies.*

Neutrality Act of 1939 *Act stipulating that European democracies might buy American munitions, but only if they could pay in cash and transport them in their own ships, a policy known as "cash-and-carry." It represented an effort to avoid war debts and protect American arms-carriers from torpedo attacks.*

President Roosevelt was roused at 3 A.M. on September 1, 1939, by a telephone call from Ambassador William Bullitt (1891–1967) in Paris:

"Mr. President, several German divisions are deep in Polish territory.... There are reports of bombers over the city of Warsaw."

"Well, Bill," FDR replied, "it has come at last. God help us all."

dictator. The notorious **Hitler-Stalin pact** meant that, contrary to hopes of wishful thinkers in Western Europe, the two menaces would not bleed each other to death, but rather join hands to share the spoils.

With the signing of the Nazi-Soviet pact, World War II was only hours away. Hitler now demanded from neighboring Poland a return of the areas wrested from Germany after World War I. Failing to secure satisfaction, he sent his mechanized divisions crashing into Poland at dawn on September 1, 1939. Honoring their commitments, Britain and France promptly declared war. But they were powerless to aid Poland, which was quickly divided between Hitler and his partner in crime, Stalin. Long-dreaded World War II was now fully launched, and the long truce of 1919–1939 had come to an end.

Americans were overwhelmingly anti-Nazi and anti-Hitler, but they were desperately determined to stay out of war; they were not going to be "suckers" again. Neutrality promptly became a heated issue in the United States. Britain and France urgently needed American airplanes and other weapons, but the Neutrality Act of 1937 raised a sternly forbidding hand. Roosevelt summoned Congress into special session, and after six weeks of hectic debate it came up with the makeshift **Neutrality Act of 1939**. This law provided that henceforth the European democracies might buy American war materials, but only on a "cash-and-carry" basis. This meant that they would have to pay for munitions in cash and transport them in their own ships. America would thus avoid loans, war debts, and the torpedoing of American arms-carriers.

Despite its defects, this unneutral neutrality law clearly favored the European democracies against the dictators. Because the British and French navies controlled the Atlantic, the European aggressors could not send their ships to buy America's munitions. The United States not only improved its moral position but simultaneously helped its economic position. Overseas demand for war goods brought a sharp upswing from the recession of 1937–1938 and ultimately solved the decade-long unemployment crisis.

★ The Fall of France

The months following the collapse of Poland, while France and Britain marked time, were known as the "phony war." An ominous silence fell on Europe as Hitler shifted his victorious divisions from Poland for a knockout blow at France. Inaction during this anxious period was relieved by the Soviets, who wantonly attacked neighboring Finland in an effort to secure strategic buffer territory.

An abrupt end to the "phony war" came in April 1940 when Hitler, again without warning, overran his weaker neighbors Denmark and Norway. Hardly pausing for breath, the next month Hitler attacked the Netherlands and Belgium, followed by a paralyzing blow at France. By late June France was forced to surrender, but not until Mussolini had pounced on its rear for a jackal's share of the loot. In a pell-mell but successful evacuation from the French port of Dunkirk, the British managed to salvage the bulk of their shattered army. The crisis providentially brought forth an inspired leader in Prime

---

Contending Voices

To Intervene or Not to Intervene

Chicago industrialist Sterling Morton (1885–1961), a backer of the isolationist America First Committee, emphasized the American tradition of nonintervention in an August 1940 speech:

"We should follow the advice of [George] Washington: We should maintain friendly relations with all nations, grant special favors to none. We should remember that the Monroe Doctrine was just as emphatic against American interference in Europe as against European interference in the Americas. We should not meddle in the affairs of other nations.... We have no mission to impose our ideas of government on others."

That same summer President Franklin Roosevelt (1882–1945) made a compelling case against the isolationists in a speech at the University of Virginia:

"Some indeed still hold to the now somewhat obvious delusion that we of the United States can safely permit the United States to become a lone island, a lone island in a world dominated by the philosophy of force. Such an island may be the dream of those who still talk and vote as isolationists. Such an island represents to me and to the overwhelming majority of Americans today a helpless nightmare of a people without freedom—the nightmare of a people lodged in prison, handcuffed, hungry, and fed through the bars from day to day by the contemptuous, unpitying masters of other continents."

> What factors might explain the intense divisions in American opinion about intervening in the war?

> *Adolf Hitler (1889-1945) promised to win his fellow Germans* Lebensraum, *or "living space," and to win it by war if necessary. In his eyes, his nationalist and racist crusade justified every violent means at hand. As he told his commanders:*
>
> "When you start a war, what matters is not who is right, but who wins. Close your hearts to pity. Act with brutality. Eighty million Germans must get what is their due. Their existence must be made secure. The stronger man is in the right."

Minister Winston Churchill, the bulldog-jawed orator who nerved the British to fight off the fearful air bombings of their cities.

France's sudden collapse shocked Americans out of their daydreams. Stouthearted Britons, singing "There'll Always Be an England," were all that stood between Hitler and the death of constitutional government in Europe. If Britain went under, Hitler would have at his disposal the workshops, shipyards, and slave labor of Western Europe. He might even have the powerful British fleet as well. This frightening possibility, which seemed to pose a dire threat to American security, steeled the American people to a tremendous effort.

Roosevelt moved with electrifying energy and dispatch. He called upon an already debt-burdened nation to build huge airfleets and a two-ocean navy, which could also check Japan. Congress, jarred out of its apathy toward preparedness, within a year appropriated the astounding sum of $37 billion, more than the total cost of fighting World War I. Congress also passed a conscription law on September 6, 1940, America's first peacetime draft.

★ Refugees from the Holocaust

Aroused by Adolf Hitler, the ancient demon of anti-Semitism brutally bared its fangs. In modern Germany primeval violence reappeared with shocking efficiency on the night of November 9, 1938. Instigated by a speech by Nazi propagandist Joseph Goebbels, mobs ransacked more than seven thousand Jewish shops and almost all of Germany's synagogues. At least ninety-one Jews lost their lives and about thirty thousand were sent to concentration camps in the turbulent wake of **Kristallnacht** (the "night of broken glass").

Kristallnacht *German for "night of broken glass," the murderous pogrom that destroyed Jewish businesses and synagogues and sent thousands to concentration camps on the night of November 9, 1938. Thousands more attempted to find refuge in the United States but were ultimately turned away due to restrictive immigration laws.*

Many Jews attempted to escape from Hitler's racist juggernaut. To take one poignant case, in May 1939, 937 passengers, almost all of them Jewish refugees, boarded the ship *St. Louis* in Hamburg and departed for Havana, Cuba. Most, however, were denied entry for lack of valid Cuban visas. The *St. Louis* then sailed to Miami, which proved no more hospitable. President Roosevelt briefly showed some interest in accepting the beleaguered passengers, but restrictive immigration laws, together with opposition from southern Democrats and Secretary of State Cordell Hull, convinced him otherwise. The *St. Louis* eventually deposited its passengers in England, France, Belgium, and the Netherlands, where many of them subsequently perished under the Nazi heel.

After reports of Nazi genocide began to be verified in 1942, Roosevelt created the **War Refugee Board**, which saved thousands of Hungarian Jews from deportation to the notorious death camp at Auschwitz. But all told, only 150,000 Jews—mostly Germans and Austrians—found refuge in the United States. By the end of the war, some 6 million Jews had been murdered in the Holocaust.

War Refugee Board *A U.S. agency formed to help rescue Jews from German-occupied territories and to provide relief to inmates of Nazi concentration camps. The agency performed noble work, but it did not begin operations until very late in the war, after millions had already been murdered.*

★ Bolstering Britain

Before the fall of France in June 1940, Washington had generally observed a technical neutrality. But now, as Britain alone stood between Hitler and his dream of world domination, the wisdom of neutrality seemed increasingly questionable. Hitler launched air attacks against Britain in August 1940, preparatory to an invasion scheduled for September. For months the Battle of Britain raged in the air over the British Isles. The Royal Air Force's tenacious defense of its native islands eventually led Hitler to postpone his planned invasion indefinitely.

Examining the Evidence

Public Opinion Polling in the 1930s

In 1936 the prominent news publication *Literary Digest* made a monumental gaffe when it relied on public-opinion polling data to forecast a victory for the Republican candidate, Alf Landon, over the incumbent, Franklin D. Roosevelt. As it happened, Roosevelt racked up a monstrous majority, winning the electoral votes of all but two states. The *Digest*'s error had been to compile its polling lists from records of automobile registration and telephone directories—unwittingly skewing its sample toward relatively well-off voters in an era when fewer than half of American families owned either a car or a telephone. The *Digest*'s embarrassing mistake ended an era of informal polling techniques, as new, scientifically sophisticated polling organizations founded by George Gallup and Elmo Roper forged to the fore. From this date forward, polling became a standard tool for marketers and advertisers—as well as for political strategists and historians. Yet controversy has long clouded the relationship between pollsters and politicians, who are often accused of abdicating their roles as leaders and slavishly deferring to public opinion, rather than trying to shape it. Franklin Roosevelt confronted this issue in the 1930s, as polls seemed to confirm the stubborn isolationism of the American people, even as the president grew increasingly convinced that the United States must play a more active international role.

1. What do the poll results suggest about Roosevelt's handling of this issue? What do the results suggest about the reliability of polling data?

2. What are the legitimate political uses of public-opinion polls? How valuable are they to the historian?

3. How might the pollsters' wording of the questions have influenced the results or made them difficult to interpret? Is it possible for polls to avoid terms such as "everything possible" (Question #1) or "becomes necessary" (Question #6) that contain elements of subjective interpretation?

[1.] (U.S. Oct 3 '39) Do you think the United States should do everything possible to help England and France win the war, except go to war ourselves? (AIPO)

        Yes 62%   No 38%

[2.] (U.S. Oct 3 '39) If it appears that Germany is defeating England and France, should the United States declare war on Germany and send our army and navy to Europe to fight? (AIPO)

	Yes	No
National total	29%	71%
BY GEOGRAPHICAL SECTION		
New England	33%	67%
Middle Atlantic	27	73
East central	25	75
West central	26	74
South	47	53
West	28	72
(Jan 30 '40) National total	23%	77%

[3.] (U.S. May 29 '40) If the question of the United States going to war against Germany came up for a national vote to go to war (go into the war or stay out of the war)? (AIPO)

        Yes 16%   No 84%
(June 11 '40).......... Go in 19%   Stay out 81%

[4.] (U.S. Aug 5 '41) Should the United States go to war now against Japan? (AIPO)

	Yes	No	No opinion
	22%	78% = 100%	11%
(Oct 22 '41)	13	74	13

[5.] (U.S. Sept 17 '41) Should the United States go into the war now and send an army to Europe to fight? (AIPO)

Yes 9%   No 87%   No opinion 4%

[6.] (U.S. Nov 5 '41) If, in trying to defeat Germany, it becomes necessary to send a large American army to Europe, would you favor this step? (AIPO)

Yes 47%   No 46%   No opinion 7%

Source: From Hadley Cantril, ed. *Public Opinion, 1935–1946* (Princeton: Princeton University Press, 1951).

During the precarious months of the Battle of Britain, debate intensified in the United States over what foreign policy to embrace. Radio broadcasts from London brought the drama of German air raids directly into millions of American homes. Sympathy for Britain grew, but it was not yet sufficient to push the United States into war. Roosevelt faced a historic decision: whether to hunker down in a "Fortress America" posture in the Western Hemisphere, or to bolster beleaguered Britain by all means short of war itself.

Both sides had their advocates. Supporters of aid to Britain formed the Committee to Defend America by Aiding the Allies. It proclaimed the slogan that "Britain is Fighting Our Fight," while implying that assisting the democracies could keep the terrible conflict in faraway Europe.

The isolationists, both numerous and sincere, were by no means silent. Determined to avoid American bloodshed at all costs, they organized the America First Committee and proclaimed, "England Will Fight to the Last American." Their basic philosophy was "The Yanks Are Not Coming," and their most effective speechmaker was the famed aviator Colonel Charles A. Lindbergh, who, ironically, had narrowed the Atlantic in 1927.

Britain was in critical need of destroyers, for German submarines were again threatening to starve it out with attacks on shipping. Roosevelt moved boldly when, on September 2, 1940, he agreed to transfer to Great Britain fifty old destroyers left over from World War I. In return, the British promised to hand over to the United States eight valuable defensive bases, stretching from Newfoundland to South America, for ninety-nine years.

Shifting warships from a neutral United States to a belligerent Britain was, beyond question, a flagrant violation of neutral obligations. But public-opinion polls demonstrated that a majority of Americans were determined, even at the risk of armed hostilities, to provide the battered British with "all aid short of war."

★ Shattering the Two-Term Tradition

In the midst of this crisis came the distracting presidential election of 1940. The two leading Republican aspirants were Senator Robert Taft of Ohio, son of the former president, and the energetic boy wonder Governor Thomas E. Dewey of New York. But in one of the miracles of American political history, the Philadelphia convention was swept off its feet by Wendell L. Willkie, a colorful German-descended son of Hoosier Indiana. This dynamic lawyer and public utilities corporation executive—tousle-headed, broad-faced, and large-framed—was a complete novice in politics. With the convention galleries wildly chanting "We Want Willkie," the delegates finally accepted this magnetic, homespun political upstart as the only candidate who could possibly beat Roosevelt. The outspoken Willkie was opposed not so much to the New Deal as to its extravagances and inefficiencies. Democratic critics branded him "the simple barefoot Wall Street lawyer."

Roosevelt delayed to the last minute the announcement of his decision to challenge the sacred two-term tradition. Despite what he described as his personal yearning for retirement, he avowed that in so grave a crisis he owed his experienced hand to the service of his country and humanity.

Burning with sincerity and energy, Willkie launched a whirlwind, Bryanesque campaign in which he delivered over five hundred speeches. With the country already badly split between interventionists and isolationists, Willkie might have widened the breach dangerously by a violent attack on Roosevelt's aid-to-Britain policies. But the statesmanlike Republican candidate refrained from assailing the president's interventionism and accepted the essential premises of an internationalist foreign policy.

Willkie hit hard against Rooseveltian "dictatorship" and the third term. Roosevelt, busy at his desk with mounting problems, made only a few speeches. But stung by taunts that he was leading the nation by the back door into the European slaughterhouse, he emphatically declared in a Boston speech, "Your boys are not going to be sent into any foreign wars"—a pledge that later came back to plague him.

The time-honored argument that one should not change horses in the middle of a stream was strong, especially in an era of war-pumped prosperity. Roosevelt triumphed, although Willkie ran a strong race. The electoral count was 449 to 82. The popular vote was much closer—27,307,819 to 22,321,018. Democratic majorities in Congress remained about the same.

★ A Landmark Lend-Lease Law

By late 1940 embattled Britain was nearing the end of its financial tether. But Roosevelt, who had bitter memories of the wrangling over the Allied debts of World War I, was determined, as he put it, to eliminate "the silly, foolish, old dollar sign." He finally hit on the scheme of lending or leasing American arms to the reeling democracies. When the shooting was over, to use his comparison, the guns and tanks could be returned, just as one's next-door neighbor would return a garden hose when a threatening fire was put out. But isolationist Senator Robert Taft retorted that lending arms was like lending chewing gum: "You don't want it back."

The **Lend-Lease Bill**, patriotically numbered 1776, was entitled "An Act Further to Promote the Defense of the United States." The underlying concept was "Send guns, not sons" or "Billions, not bodies." America, so President Roosevelt promised, would be the "arsenal of democracy." It would send a limitless supply of arms to the victims of aggression, who in turn would finish the job and keep the war on their side of the Atlantic. Isolationists assailed the lend-lease scheme as "the blank-check bill." Isolationist Senator Burton Wheeler called it "the new triple-A [Agricultural Adjustment Act] bill"—a measure designed to "plow under every fourth American boy." Nevertheless, lend-lease was finally approved in March 1941 by sweeping majorities in both houses of Congress.

Lend-lease was one of the most momentous laws ever to pass Congress; it was a challenge hurled squarely into the teeth of the Axis dictators. America eventually sent about $50 billion worth of arms and equipment to those nations fighting aggressors (see Map 33.1). By its very nature, the Lend-Lease Bill marked the abandonment of any pretense of neutrality. It was no destroyer deal arranged privately by President Roosevelt. The bill was universally debated over drugstore counters and cracker barrels from California to Maine, and the sovereign citizens at last spoke through convincing majorities in Congress. Lend-lease had the somewhat incidental result of gearing U.S. factories for all-out war production. The enormously increased capacity thus achieved helped to save America's own skin when, at long last, the shooting war burst around its head.

Lend-Lease Bill (1941) *Abandoned pretenses of neutrality by allowing Americans to sell unlimited supplies of arms to any nation defending itself against Axis powers. Based on the motto "Send guns, not sons" and patriotically numbered 1776, the bill was praised as a device for keeping the nation out of World War II.*

Map 33.1 Main Flow of Lend-Lease Aid (width of arrows indicates relative amount) The proud but desperate British prime minister, Winston Churchill, declared in early 1941: "Give us the tools and we will finish the job." Lend-lease eventually provided the British and other Allies with $50 billion worth of "tools."

> *Senator (later president) Harry S. Truman (1884–1972) expressed a common reaction to Hitler's invasion of the Soviet Union in 1941:*
>
> "If we see that Germany is winning, we ought to help Russia, and if we see Russia is winning, we ought to help Germany, and that way let them kill as many as possible."

Hitler evidently recognized lend-lease as an unofficial declaration of war. Until then Germany had avoided attacking U.S. ships; memories of America's decisive intervention in 1917–1918 were still fresh in German minds. But after the passing of lend-lease there was less point in trying to curry favor with the United States. On May 21, 1941, the *Robin Moor*, an unarmed American merchant ship, was torpedoed and destroyed by a German submarine in the South Atlantic, outside a war zone. The sinkings had started, but on a limited scale.

★ Charting a New World

Two globe-shaking events marked the course of World War II before the assault on Pearl Harbor in December 1941. One was the fall of France in June 1940; the other was Hitler's invasion of the Soviet Union, almost exactly one year later, in June 1941.

The scheming dictators Hitler and Stalin had been uneasy yoke-fellows under the Nazi-Soviet pact of 1939. As masters of the double cross, neither trusted the other. Believing that his invincible armies would subdue Stalin's "Mongol half-wits" in a few short weeks, Hitler launched a devastating attack on his Soviet neighbor on June 22, 1941.

This assault seemed an incredible stroke of good fortune for the democratic world—if the Soviets did not quickly collapse, as many military experts predicted. Sound American strategy seemed to dictate speedy aid to Moscow while it was still afloat. Roosevelt promised immediate assistance, and a few months later extended $1 billion in lend-lease aid to the USSR—the first installment on an ultimate total of $11 billion.

With the surrender of the Soviet Union still a possibility, Franklin Roosevelt and cherub-faced British Prime Minister Winston Churchill secretly met on a warship off the foggy coast of Newfoundland in August 1941. This was the first of a series of history-making conferences between the two statesmen for the discussion of common problems, including the menace of Japan.

The most memorable offspring of this get-together was the eight-point **Atlantic Charter**. This covenant, suggestive of Wilson's Fourteen Points, outlined the aspirations of the democracies for a better world at war's end. Arguing for the rights of individuals rather than nations, the Atlantic Charter laid the groundwork for later advocacy on behalf of universal human rights.

Many people were surprised by how specific the document was. Among its key features were self-determination for all peoples, disarmament, and eventually a "permanent system of general security" (a new League of Nations). The Atlantic Charter was cheered by liberals and subject peoples the world over, although roundly condemned by isolationists in the United States.

But the hope of isolating America from the conflict was rapidly slipping away. Lend-lease shipments of arms to Britain on British ships were bound to be sunk by German wolf-pack submarines. If the intent was to get the munitions to Britain, not to dump them into the ocean, the freighters would have to be escorted by U.S. warships. Britain simply did not have enough destroyers. Roosevelt made the fateful decision to convoy in July 1941, ordering the U.S. Navy to escort lend-lease shipments as far as Iceland. The British would then shepherd them the rest of the way.

Inevitable clashes with submarines ensued on the Iceland run. In September 1941, the U.S. destroyer *Greer*, provocatively trailing a German U-boat, was attacked by the undersea craft, without damage to either side. Roosevelt then proclaimed a shoot-on-sight policy. On October 17, 1941, the escorting destroyer *Kearny*, while engaged in a battle with U-boats, lost eleven men when it was crippled but not sent to the bottom. Two weeks later the destroyer *Reuben James* was torpedoed and sunk off southwestern Iceland, with the loss of more than a hundred officers and enlisted men.

Atlantic Charter (1941) *Covenant signed by Franklin Roosevelt and British prime minister Winston Churchill on a warship off the coast of Newfoundland, outlining the future path toward disarmament, peace, and a permanent system of general security. Its spirit would animate the founding of the United Nations and raise awareness of individual human rights after World War II.*

Neutrality was still inscribed on the statute books, but not on American hearts. Congress, responding to public pressures and confronted with a shooting war, voted in mid-November 1941 to pull the teeth from the now-useless Neutrality Act of 1939. Merchant ships could henceforth be legally armed. Americans braced themselves for wholesale attacks by Hitler's submarines.

Surprise Assault at Pearl Harbor

The blowup came not in the Atlantic but in the faraway Pacific. This explosion should have surprised no close observer, for Japan, since September 1940, had been a formal military ally of Nazi Germany.

Japan's position in East Asia had grown more perilous by the hour. It was still mired down in the costly and exhausting "China incident," from which it could extract neither honor nor victory. Its war machine was fatally dependent on immense shipments of steel, scrap iron, oil, and aviation gasoline from the United States. Such assistance to the Japanese aggressor was highly unpopular in America. But Roosevelt had resolutely held off an embargo, lest he goad the Tokyo warlords into a descent upon the oil-rich but defense-poor Dutch East Indies (present-day Indonesia).

Washington, late in 1940, finally imposed the first of its embargoes on Japan-bound supplies. This blow was followed in mid-1941 by a freezing of Japanese assets in the United States and a cessation of all shipments of gasoline and other sinews of war. As the oil gauge dropped, the squeeze on Japan grew steadily more nerve-racking. Japanese leaders were faced with two painful alternatives. They could either knuckle under to the Americans or break out of the embargo ring by a desperate attack on the oil supplies and other riches of Southeast Asia.

Final tense negotiations with Japan took place in Washington during November and early December of 1941. The State Department insisted that the Japanese clear out of China, but to sweeten the pill offered to renew limited trade relations. Japanese imperialists, after waging a bitter war against the Chinese for more than four years, were unwilling to lose face by withdrawing at the behest of the United States. Faced with capitulation or continued conquest, they chose the sword.

Officials in Washington, having "cracked" the top-secret code of the Japanese, knew that Tokyo's decision was for war. But the United States, as a democracy committed to public debate and action by Congress, could not shoot first. Roosevelt and other officials, misled by Japanese ship movements in the western Pacific, evidently expected the blow to fall on British Malaya or on the Philippines. No one in high authority in Washington evidently believed that the Japanese were either strong enough or foolhardy enough to strike Hawaii.

But the paralyzing blow struck **Pearl Harbor**, while Tokyo was deliberately prolonging negotiations in Washington. Japanese bombers, winging in from distant aircraft carriers, attacked without warning on the "Black Sunday" morning of December 7, 1941. It was a date, as Roosevelt told Congress, "which will live in infamy." About three thousand casualties were inflicted on American personnel, many aircraft were destroyed, and the battleship fleet was virtually wiped out.

The next day an angered Congress, with only one dissenting vote, officially recognized that war had been "thrust" upon the United States. When Japan's allies, Germany and Italy, also declared war on December 11, 1941, the challenge was unanimously accepted by Congress the same day. The unofficial war was now official.

Japan's hara-kiri gamble in Hawaii paid off only in the short run. True, the Pacific fleet was largely destroyed or immobilized, but the sneak attack aroused and united America as almost nothing else could have done. To the very day of the blowup, a strong majority of Americans still wanted to keep out of war. But the bombs that pulverized Pearl Harbor blasted the isolationists into silence. The only thing left to do, growled isolationist Senator Wheeler, was "to lick hell out of them."

But Pearl Harbor was not the full answer to the question as to why the United States went to war. This treacherous attack was but the last explosion in a long chain reaction.

Pearl Harbor (1941) *An American naval base in Hawaii where Japanese warplanes destroyed numerous ships and caused three thousand casualties on December 7, 1941—a day that, in President Roosevelt's words, was to "live in infamy." The attack brought the United States into World War II.*

The Battleship *West Virginia* The shocking Japanese attack on Pearl Harbor on December 7, 1941, propelled the United States into World War II. One of the first ships to be hit, the USS *West Virginia* quickly sank at its mooring, taking at least seventy sailors down with it. By September 1944 the *West Virginia* had been repaired and was back in service.

Following the fall of France, Americans were confronted with a devil's dilemma. They desired above all to stay out of the conflict, yet they did not want Britain to be knocked out of the war. They also wished to halt Japan, which menaced American trade, security, and international peace. To keep Britain from collapsing, the Roosevelt administration felt compelled to extend the unneutral aid that invited attacks from German submarines. To keep Japan from expanding, Washington undertook to cut off vital Japanese supplies with embargoes that invited possible retaliation. Rather than let democracy die and dictatorship rule supreme, most citizens were evidently determined to support a policy that might lead to war. It did.

CHAPTER SUMMARY ★ ★ ★ ★ ★ ★ ★ ★ ★ ★ ★ ★ ★ ★

Roosevelt's early foreign policies, such as wrecking the London economic conference and establishing the Good Neighbor policy in Latin America, were governed by his determination to make domestic recovery the national priority and to turn the United States away from commitments elsewhere in the world. America virtually withdrew from all European affairs and promised independence to the Philippines in an attempt to avoid future involvement in East Asia.

Depression-spawned chaos and war in Europe and Asia strengthened the isolationist impulse, as Congress passed a series of Neutrality Acts designed to prevent America from being drawn into foreign wars. The United States adhered to this policy for a time, despite the spreading aggression of Italy, Germany, and Japan. But after the outbreak of World War II in Europe, Roosevelt cautiously began to provide some aid to the Allies.

After the fall of France in June 1940, Roosevelt provided greater assistance to desperate Britain in the destroyers-for-bases deal, and Congress passed the lend-lease program. Still-powerful isolationists protested these measures, but dark-horse Republican nominee Wendell Willkie refrained from attacking Roosevelt's foreign policy in the 1940 campaign.

Roosevelt won an unprecedented third term, but by a closer margin than his previous victories.

The fall of France in June 1940 and Hitler's invasion of the Soviet Union in June 1941 made apparent the threat to the survival of Western democracies. To help prevent a German victory over the USSR, Roosevelt extended lend-lease aid to Stalin. In August 1941 Roosevelt and Winston Churchill issued the Atlantic Charter upholding shared democratic principles and outlining plans for future peace and security. By the summer of 1941, the United States was fighting an undeclared naval war with Nazi Germany in the North Atlantic.

Meanwhile, American economic embargoes against Japan made Japanese militarists desperate. With the United States insisting on Japanese withdrawal from China as a condition of resuming trade, the Japanese leaders decided that only a war with the United States would achieve their goals. The surprise attack on Pearl Harbor in December 1941 united the American people and plunged the United States into World War II.

KEY TERMS

- London Economic Conference (571)
- Good Neighbor policy (571)
- Rome-Berlin Axis (572)
- Johnson Debt Default Act (573)
- Neutrality Acts of 1935, 1936, and 1937 (573)
- Abraham Lincoln Brigade (573)
- Quarantine Speech (574)
- Appeasement (574)
- Hitler-Stalin pact (574)
- Neutrality Act of 1939 (574)
- Kristallnacht (576)
- War Refugee Board (576)
- Lend-Lease Bill (579)
- Atlantic Charter (580)
- Pearl Harbor (581)

PEOPLE TO KNOW

- Benito Mussolini
- Adolf Hitler
- Francisco Franco
- Wendell L. Willkie

MindTap is a fully online, highly personalized learning experience built upon Cengage Learning content. MindTap combines student learning tools—readings, multimedia, activities, and assessments—into a singular Learning Path that guides students through the course.

Chapter 34

America in World War II
1941–1945

Never before have we had so little time in which to do so much.

FRANKLIN D. ROOSEVELT, 1942

The United States was plunged into the inferno of World War II with the most stupefying and humiliating military defeat in its history. In the dismal months that ensued, the democratic world teetered on the edge of disaster.

Japan's fanatics forgot that whoever stabs a king must stab to kill. A wounded but still potent American giant pulled itself out of the mud of Pearl Harbor, grimly determined to avenge the bloody treachery. "Get Japan first" was the cry that rose from millions of infuriated Americans, especially on the Pacific Coast. These outraged souls regarded America's share in the global conflict as a private war of vengeance in the Pacific, with the European front a kind of holding operation.

But Washington, in the so-called **ABC-1 agreement** with the British, had earlier and wisely adopted the grand strategy of "getting Germany first." If America diverted its main strength to the Pacific, Hitler might crush both the Soviet Union and Britain and then emerge unconquerable in Fortress Europe. But if Germany was knocked out first, the combined Allied forces could be concentrated on Japan, and its daring game of conquest would be up. Meanwhile, just enough American strength would be sent to the Pacific to prevent Japan from digging in too deeply.

Chapter Outline

- The Grand American Strategy for War
- Mobilizing for War
- Women in Wartime
- Changes for African Americans, Native Americans, and Mexican Americans
- The Social and Economic Impact of War
- Turning the Japanese Tide in the Pacific
- Campaigns in North Africa (1942) and Italy (1943)
- D-Day and the German Surrender
- The Atomic Bomb Ends the War with Japan
- *Makers of America: The Japanese*
- *Examining the Evidence: Franklin Roosevelt at Tehran, 1943*
- *Thinking Globally: America and the World in Depression and War: A Study in Contrasts*
- *Varying Viewpoints: The Atomic Bombs: Were They Justified?*

FOCUS QUESTIONS

1. How did the government and the American people mobilize to wage a total war against both Germany and Japan?
2. What was the war's impact on American society, including changing gender roles, regional migration, and race relations?
3. How did the strategy of "island hopping" enable the United States to turn the Japanese tide in the Pacific and advance to within striking distance of the Japanese home islands?
4. How did the British-American and Soviet armies together conquer Nazi Germany and force its surrender?
5. How did the United States develop the atomic bomb, and why was the dropping of two bombs on Japan controversial, despite its immediate ending of the war?

CHRONOLOGY

1941	- United States declares war on Japan - Germany declares war on United States - Randolph plans black march on Washington - Fair Employment Practices Commission (FEPC) established - Roosevelt delivers "four freedoms" speech		- "Zoot-suit" riots in Los Angeles - Race riot in Detroit - Japanese driven from Guadalcanal - Tehran conference
1942	- Japanese Americans sent to internment camps - Japan conquers the Philippines - Battle of the Coral Sea - Battle of Midway - United States invades North Africa - Congress of Racial Equality (CORE) founded	1944	- *Korematsu* v. *U. S.* - D-Day invasion of France - Battle of Marianas - Roosevelt defeats Dewey for presidency
		1944–1945	- Battle of the Bulge
1943	- Allies hold Casablanca conference - Allies invade Italy - Smith-Connally Anti-Strike Act	1945	- Roosevelt dies; Truman assumes presidency - Germany surrenders - Battles of Iwo Jima and Okinawa - Potsdam conference - Atomic bombs dropped on Hiroshima and Nagasaki - Japan surrenders

The get-Germany-first strategy was the solid foundation on which all American military strategy was built. But it encountered much ignorant criticism from two-fisted Americans who thirsted for revenge against Japan. Aggrieved protests were also registered by short-handed American commanders in the Pacific and by Chinese and Australian allies. But President Roosevelt, a competent strategist in his own right, wisely resisted these pressures.

★ The Allies Trade Space for Time

Given time, the Allies seemed bound to triumph. But would they be given time? True, they had on their side the great mass of the world's population, but the wolf is never intimidated by the number of the sheep.

Time, in a sense, was the most needed munition. Expense was no limitation. The overpowering problem confronting America was to retool itself for all-out war production, while praying that the dictators would not meanwhile crush their adversaries who remained in the field—notably Britain and the Soviet Union. Haste was all the more imperative because the highly skilled German scientists might turn up with unbeatable secret weapons, including rocket bombs and perhaps even atomic arms.

America's task was far more complex and backbreaking than during World War I. It had to feed, clothe, and arm itself, as well as transport its forces to regions as far separated as Britain and Burma. More than that, it had to send a vast amount of food and munitions to its hard-pressed allies, who stretched all the way from the USSR to Australia. Could the American people, reputedly "gone soft," measure up to this herculean task? Was democracy "rotten" and "decadent," as the dictators sneeringly proclaimed?

★ The Shock of War

National unity was no worry, thanks to the electrifying blow by the Japanese at Pearl Harbor. American Communists had denounced the Anglo-French "imperialist" war before Hitler attacked Stalin in 1941, but they now clamored for an unmitigated assault

ABC-1 agreement (1941) *An agreement between Britain and the United States developed at a conference in Washington, D.C., between January 29 and March 27, 1941, that should the United States enter World War II, the two nations and their allies would coordinate their military planning, making a priority of protecting the British Commonwealth. That would mean "getting Germany first" in the Atlantic and the European theater and fighting more defensively on other military fronts.*

> Monica Sone (b. 1919), a college-age Japanese American woman in Seattle, recorded the shock she and her brother felt when they learned of Executive Order No. 9066, which authorized the War Department to remove Japanese—aliens and citizens alike—from their homes:
>
> "In anger, Henry and I read and reread the Executive Order. Henry crumbled the newspaper in his hand and threw it against the wall. 'Doesn't my citizenship mean a single blessed thing to anyone? Why doesn't somebody make up my mind for me? First they want me in the army. Now they're going to slap an alien 4-C on me because of my ancestry....' Once more I felt like a despised, pathetic two-headed freak, a Japanese and an American, neither of which seemed to be doing me any good."

on the Axis powers. The handful of strutting pro-Hitlerites in the United States melted away, while millions of Italian Americans and German Americans loyally supported the nation's war program. In contrast to World War I, when the patriotism of millions of immigrants was hotly questioned, World War II actually speeded the assimilation of many ethnic groups into American society. Immigration had been choked off for almost two decades before 1941, and America's ethnic communities were now composed of well-settled members, whose votes were crucial to Franklin Roosevelt's Democratic party. Consequently, there was virtually no governmental witch-hunting of minority groups, as had happened in World War I.

A painful exception was the plight of some 110,000 Japanese Americans, concentrated on the Pacific Coast (see "Makers of America: The Japanese," p. 587). The Washington top command, fearing that they might act as saboteurs for Japan in case of invasion, forcibly herded them together in concentration camps, though about two-thirds of them were American-born U.S. citizens. This brutal precaution, authorized under **Executive Order No. 9066**, was both unnecessary and unfair, as the loyalty and combat record of Japanese Americans proved to be admirable. But a wave of post–Pearl Harbor hysteria, backed by the long historical swell of anti-Japanese prejudice on the West Coast, temporarily robbed many Americans of their good sense—and their sense of justice. The internment camps deprived these uprooted Americans of dignity and basic rights; the internees also lost hundreds of millions of dollars in property and foregone earnings. The wartime Supreme Court in 1944 upheld the constitutionality of the Japanese relocation in *Korematsu v. United States*. But more than four decades later in 1988, the U.S. government officially apologized for its actions and approved the payment of reparations of $20,000 to each camp survivor.

The war prompted other changes in the American mood. Many programs of the once-popular New Deal were wiped out by the conservative Congress elected in 1942, and even President Roosevelt declared in 1943 that "Dr. New Deal" was going into retirement to be replaced by "Dr. Win-the-War." The era of New Deal reform was over.

World War II was no idealistic crusade, as World War I had been. The Washington government emphasized action rather than propaganda. According to opinion polls during the war, a majority or near-majority of citizens confessed to having "no clear idea what the war is about." All Americans knew was that they had a dirty job on their hands and that the only way out was forward. They went about their bloody task with astonishing efficiency.

⭐ Building the War Machine

The war crisis snapped the drooping American economy to attention. Massive military orders—over $100 billion in 1942 alone—almost instantly soaked up the idle industrial capacity of the still-lingering Great Depression. Orchestrated by the **War Production Board (WPB)**, American factories poured forth an avalanche of weaponry: 40 billion bullets, 300,000 aircraft, 76,000 ships, 86,000 tanks, and 2.6 million machine guns. Farmers, too, rolled up their sleeves and increased their output. The armed forces drained the farms of workers, but heavy new investment in agricultural machinery and improved fertilizers more than made up the difference. In 1944 and 1945, blue-jeaned farmers hauled in record-breaking billion-bushel wheat harvests.

Executive Order No. 9066 Order signed by President Roosevelt on February 19, 1942, authorizing the secretary of war to designate military zones from which certain categories of people could be excluded. Fueled by historic anti-Japanese sentiment as well as panic following the December 7, 1941, attack on Pearl Harbor, the order led to the forced removal of some 120,000 persons of Japanese ancestry (70,000 of them U.S. citizens) from the Western Military Zone (the coastal sections of Washington, Oregon, and California). Most but not all of those removed were interned in relocation camps in the interior West. The order was rescinded in December 1944, and legislation passed in 1988 offered an official government apology and modest financial compensation to surviving citizen internees.

War Production Board (WPB) Established in 1942 by executive order to direct all war production, including procuring and allocating raw materials, to maximize the nation's war machine. The WPB had sweeping powers over the U.S. economy and was abolished in November 1945 soon after Japan's defeat.

Makers of America

The Japanese

In 1853 the American commodore Matthew Perry sailed four gunboats into Japan's Uraga Bay and demanded that the nation open itself to diplomatic and commercial exchange with the United States. Within two decades of Perry's arrival, Japan's new "Meiji" government had launched the nation on an ambitious program of industrialization and militarization designed to make it the economic and political equal of the Western powers.

As Japan rapidly modernized, its citizens increasingly took ship for America. A steep land tax drove more than 300,000 Japanese farmers off their land. In 1884 the Meiji government permitted Hawaiian planters to recruit contract laborers from among this displaced population. By the 1890s many Japanese were sailing beyond Hawaii to the ports of Long Beach, San Francisco, and Seattle.

Between 1885 and 1924, roughly 200,000 Japanese migrated to Hawaii, and around 180,000 more ventured to the U.S. mainland. They were a select group: because the Meiji government saw overseas Japanese as representatives of their homeland, it strictly regulated emigration. Thus Japanese immigrants to America arrived with more money and better education than their European counterparts.

Women as well as men migrated. The Japanese government, wanting to avoid the problems of an itinerant bachelor society that it observed among the Chinese in the United States, actively promoted women's migration. Although most Japanese immigrants were young men in their twenties and thirties, thousands of women also ventured to Hawaii and the mainland as contract laborers or "picture brides," so called because their courtships had consisted exclusively of exchanges of photographs with their prospective husbands.

In Hawaii most Japanese labored on the vast sugar cane plantations. On the mainland they initially found migratory work on the railroads or in fish, fruit, or vegetable canneries. A separate Japanese economy of restaurants, stores, and boardinghouses soon sprang up in cities to serve the immigrants' needs.

From such humble beginnings, many Japanese—particularly those on the Pacific Coast—quickly moved into farming. In the late nineteenth century, the spread of irrigation shifted California agriculture from grain to fruits and vegetables, and the invention of the refrigerated railcar opened hungry new markets in the East. The Japanese, with centuries of experience in intensive farming, arrived just in time to take advantage of these developments. By 1940 Japanese farmers produced most of the state's strawberries, beans, and tomatoes.

But the very success of the Japanese proved a lightning rod for trouble. On the West Coast, Japanese immigrants had long endured racist barbs and social segregation. Increasingly, white workers and farmers, jealous of Japanese success, pushed for immigration restrictions. Bowing to this pressure, President Theodore Roosevelt in 1908 negotiated the "Gentlemen's Agreement," under which the Japanese government voluntarily agreed to limit emigration. In 1913 the California legislature denied Japanese immigrants already living in the United States the right to own land.

Legally barred from becoming citizens, Japanese immigrants (the "Issei," from the Japanese word for *first*) became more determined than ever that their American-born children (the "Nissei," from the Japanese word for *second*) would reap the full benefits of their birthright. Japanese parents encouraged their children to learn English, to excel in school, and to get a college education. Many Nissei grew up in two worlds, a fact they often recognized by Americanizing their Japanese names. Although education and acculturation did not protect the Nissei from the hysteria of World War II, those assets did give them a springboard to success in the postwar era.

Japanese American Evacuees, 1942 After the U.S. Army's Western Defense Command ordered the forced evacuation of all Japanese and Japanese Americans living on the Pacific Coast, families had no choice but to pack up whatever they could carry and move to the "relocation centers" hastily erected farther inland.

Office of Price Administration (OPA) (1941–1947) *A critically important wartime agency charged with regulating the consumer economy by rationing scarce supplies, such as automobiles, tires, fuel, nylon, and sugar, and by curbing inflation by setting ceilings on the price of goods. Rents were controlled as well in parts of the country overwhelmed by war workers. The OPA was extended after World War II ended to continue the fight against inflation.*

National War Labor Board (NWLB) *Established by President Franklin D. Roosevelt to act as an arbitration tribunal and mediate disputes between labor and management that might have led to war stoppages and thereby undermined the war effort. The NWLB was also charged with adjusting wages with an eye to controlling inflation.*

Smith-Connally Anti-Strike Act (1943) *Allowed the federal government to seize and operate plants threatened by labor disputes. Passed amidst worries about the effects that labor strikes would have on war production, it also criminalized strike action against government-run companies.*

WACs (Women's Army Corps) *The women's branch of the U.S. Army established during World War II to employ women in noncombatant jobs. Women now participated in the armed services in ways that went beyond their traditional roles as nurses.*

WAVES (Women Accepted for Voluntary Emergency Service) *The women's branch of the U.S. Navy established during World War II to employ women in noncombatant jobs.*

SPARs (U.S. Coast Guard Women's Reserve) *The women's branch of the U.S. Coast Guard established during World War II to employ women in noncombatant jobs.*

Bracero program (1942) *Program established by agreement with the Mexican government to recruit temporary Mexican agricultural workers to the United States to make up for wartime labor shortages in the Far West. The program persisted until 1964, by which time it had sponsored 4.5 million border crossings.*

These wonders of production also brought economic strains. Full employment and scarce consumer goods fueled a sharp inflationary surge in 1942. The **Office of Price Administration (OPA)** eventually brought ascending prices under control with extensive regulations. Rationing held down the consumption of critical goods such as meat and butter, though some "black marketeers" and "meatleggers" cheated the system. The **National War Labor Board (WLB)** imposed ceilings on wage increases.

Labor unions, whose memberships grew from about 10 million to more than 13 million workers during the war, fiercely resented the government-dictated wage ceilings. Despite the no-strike pledges of most major unions, a rash of labor walkouts plagued the war effort. Threats of lost production through strikes became so worrisome that Congress, in June 1943, passed the **Smith-Connally Anti-Strike Act**, which authorized the federal government to seize and operate tied-up industries. Under the act, Washington took over the coal mines and, for a brief period, the railroads. Yet work stoppages accounted for less than 1 percent of the total working hours of the United States' wartime laboring force.

★ Manpower and Womanpower

The armed services enlisted nearly 15 million men in World War II, and some 216,000 women, who were employed for noncombat duties. Best known of these "women in arms" were the **WACS (Women's Army Corps), WAVES (Women Accepted for Voluntary Emergency Service)** (navy), and **SPARS (U.S. Coast Guard Women's Reserve)**.

Despite exemptions for key categories of industrial and agricultural workers, the draft left the nation's farms and factories so short of personnel that new workers had to be found. An agreement with Mexico in 1942 brought thousands of Mexican agricultural workers, called *braceros*, across the border to harvest the fruit and grain crops of the West. The ***Bracero* program** outlived the war by some twenty years, becoming a fixed feature of the agricultural economy in many western states.

Even more dramatic was the march of women onto the factory floor. More than 6 million women took up jobs outside the home; over half of them had never before worked for wages. Many of them were mothers, and the government was obliged to set up some three thousand day-care centers to care for "Rosie the Riveter's" children while she drilled the fuselage of a heavy bomber or joined the links of a tank track. When the war ended, Rosie and many of her sisters wanted to keep on working and often did. The war thus foreshadowed an eventual revolution in the roles of women in American society.

Yet the war's immediate impact on women's lives has frequently been exaggerated. The great majority of women—especially those with husbands present in the home or with small children to care for—did not work for wages in the wartime economy but continued in their traditional roles. In both Britain and the Soviet Union, a far greater percentage of women, including mothers, were pressed into industrial employment as the gods of war laid a much heavier hand on those societies than they did on the United States.

At war's end, two-thirds of women war workers left the labor force. Many of them were forced out of their jobs by employers or unions, but half of them quit their jobs voluntarily because of family obligations. The immediate postwar period witnessed not a permanent widening of women's employment opportunities but a widespread rush into suburban domesticity and the mothering of the "baby boomers," who were born by the tens of millions in the decade and a half after 1945. America was destined to experience a revolution in women's status later in the postwar period, but that epochal change was only beginning to gather momentum in the war years.

★ Wartime Migrations

The war also proved to be a demographic cauldron, churning and shifting the American population. Many of the 15 million men and women in uniform, having seen new sights and glimpsed new horizons, chose not to go home again at war's end. War industries sucked people into boomtowns like Los Angeles, Detroit, Seattle, and Baton Rouge. California's population grew by nearly 2 million. The South experienced especially dramatic changes. The states of the old Confederacy received a disproportionate share of defense contracts, including nearly $6 billion of federally financed industrial facilities. Here were the seeds of the postwar blossoming of the "Sunbelt" (see Map 34.1).

Despite this economic stimulus in the South, some 1.6 million blacks left the land of their past enslavement to seek jobs in the war plants of the West and North. Forever after, race relations constituted a national, not a regional, issue. Explosive tensions developed over employment, housing, and segregated facilities. Black leader A. Philip Randolph, head of the Brotherhood of Sleeping Car Porters, threatened a massive "Negro March on Washington" in 1941 to demand equal opportunities for blacks in war jobs and in the armed forces. Roosevelt's response was to issue an executive order forbidding discrimination in defense industries and to establish the **Fair Employment Practices Commission (FEPC)** to monitor compliance with his edict.

Blacks were also drafted into the armed forces, though they were generally assigned to service branches rather than combat units. But in general the war helped to embolden blacks in their long struggle for equality. Membership in the National Association for the Advancement of Colored People (NAACP) shot up almost to the half-million mark, and a new militant organization committed to nonviolent "direct action," the **Congress of Racial Equality (CORE)**, was founded in 1942.

The northward migration of African Americans accelerated after the war, thanks to the advent of the mechanical cotton picker—an invention whose impact rivaled that of Eli Whitney's cotton gin. Overnight, the Cotton South's historic need for cheap labor disappeared. Their muscle no longer required in Dixie, some 5 million black tenant farmers and sharecroppers headed north in the three decades after the war. Within a single generation, a near-majority of African Americans gave up their historic homeland and their rural way of life. By 1970 half of all blacks lived outside the South. The speed and scale of these changes jolted the migrants and sometimes convulsed the communities that received them.

The war also prompted an exodus of Native Americans from the reservations. Thousands of Indian men and women found war work in the major cities, and thousands more answered Uncle Sam's call to arms. More than 90 percent of Indians resided on reservations in 1940; seven decades later more than half lived in cities. Some twenty-five thousand Native American men served in the armed forces. Comanches in Europe and Navajos in the Pacific made especially valuable contributions as "**code talkers**," who transmitted radio messages in their native languages.

The sudden rubbing against one another of unfamiliar peoples produced some distressingly violent friction. In 1943 young "zoot-suit"–clad Mexicans and Mexican Americans in Los Angeles were viciously attacked by Anglo sailors who cruised the streets in taxicabs, searching for victims. At almost the same time, an even more brutal race riot erupted in Detroit, killing twenty-five blacks and nine whites.

★ Holding the Home Front

Despite these ugly episodes, Americans on the home front suffered little from the war compared with the peoples of the other fighting nations. By war's end much of the planet was a smoking ruin. But in America the war invigorated the economy and lifted the

Workers in Wartime—and Beyond? More than 6 million women—more than 3 million of them homemakers who had never before worked for wages—entered the work force during World War II. That work was valued and encouraged during the war years.

Fair Employment Practices Commission (FEPC) (1941) *Set up to monitor compliance with Franklin D. Rooosevelt's executive order forbidding racial discrimination in all defense plants operating under contract with the federal government. The order came in response to the threat of a massive "Negro March on Washington" to demand equal opportunities in war jobs and in the military.*

Congress of Racial Equality (CORE) (1942) *Nonviolent civil rights organization founded in 1942 and committed to the "Double V"—victory over fascism abroad and racism at home. After World War II, CORE would become a major force in the civil rights movement.*

code talkers *Native American men who served in the military by transmitting radio messages in their native languages, which were undecipherable by German and Japanese spies.*

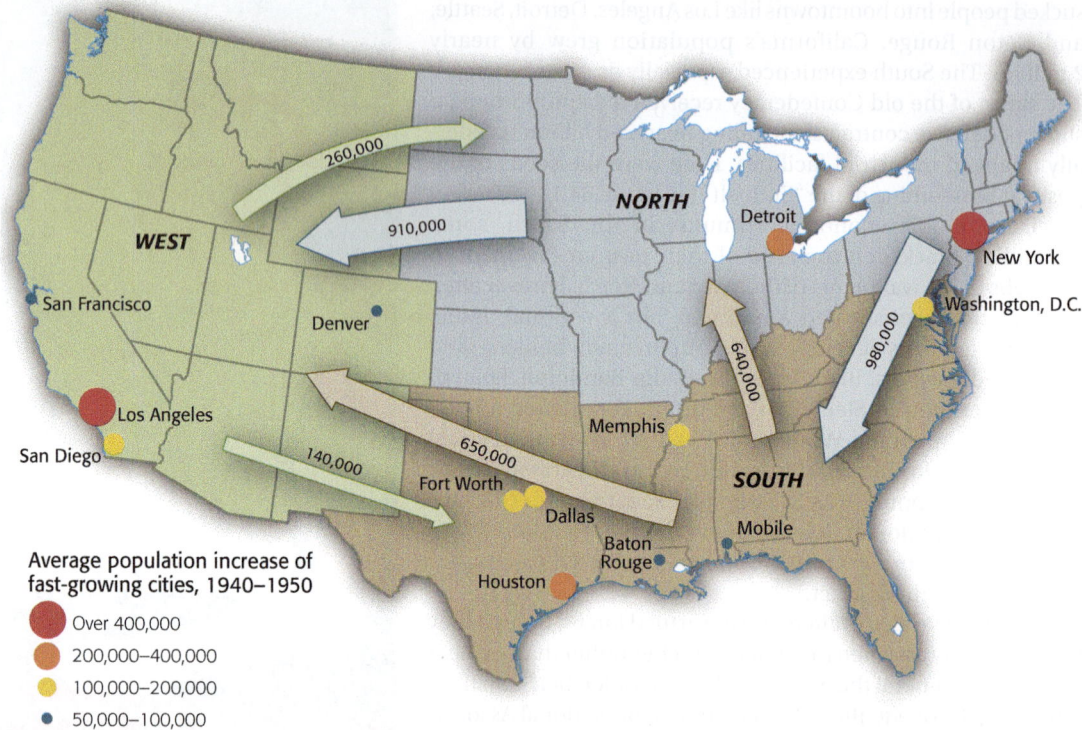

Map 34.1 Internal Migration in the United States during World War II Few events in American history have moved the American people about so massively as World War II. The West and the South boomed, and several war-industry cities grew explosively. A majority of migrants from the South were blacks; 1.6 million African Americans left the region in the 1940s. (Source: United States Department of Labor, Bureau of Labor Statistics.)

country out of a decade-long depression. The gross national product vaulted from less than $100 billion in 1940 to more than $200 billion in 1945. Corporate profits nearly doubled during the war. Despite wage ceilings, overtime pay fattened pay envelopes. On December 7, 1944, the third anniversary of Pearl Harbor, Macy's department store rang up the biggest sales day in its history. Americans had never had it so good—and they wanted it a lot better.

The hand of government touched more American lives more intimately during the war than ever before. The war, perhaps even more than the New Deal, pointed the way to the post-1945 era of big-government interventionism. Millions of men and women worked for Uncle Sam in the armed forces or in defense industries, and their personal needs were cared for by government-sponsored housing projects, day-care facilities, and health plans. The Office of Scientific Research and Development channeled hundreds of millions of dollars into university-based scientific research, establishing the partnership between the government and universities that underwrote America's technological and economic leadership in the postwar era.

The flood of war dollars—not the relatively modest rivulet of New Deal spending—at last swept the plague of unemployment from the land. War, not enlightened social policy, cured the depression. As the postwar economy continued to depend dangerously on military spending for its health, many observers looked back to the years 1941–1945 as the origins of a "warfare-welfare state."

The conflict was phenomenally expensive. The wartime bill amounted to more than $330 billion—ten times the direct cost of World War I and twice as much as *all* previous federal spending since 1776. Despite an expanded income tax and higher tax rates, only about two-fifths of the war costs were paid from current revenues. The remainder was borrowed. The national debt skyrocketed from $49 billion in 1941 to $259 billion in 1945.

⭐ The Rising Sun in the Pacific

Early successes of the efficient Japanese militarists were breathtaking: they realized that they would have to win quickly or lose slowly. Simultaneously with the assault on Pearl Harbor, the Japanese launched widespread and uniformly successful attacks on various bastions across the Pacific and East Asia. These included the American outposts of Guam, Wake, and the Philippines, as well as Hong Kong and British Malaya, with its critically important supplies of rubber and tin.

Nor did the Japanese tide stop there. The soldiers of the emperor, plunging into the snake-infested jungles of Burma, cut the famed Burma Road. This was the route over which the United States had been trucking a trickle of munitions to the armies of Chinese generalissimo Jiang Jieshi (Chiang Kai-shek), who was still resisting the Japanese invader in China. Thereafter, intrepid American aviators were forced to fly a handful of war supplies to Jiang "over the hump" of the towering Himalaya Mountains from the India-Burma theater. Meanwhile, the Japanese had lunged southward against the oil-rich Dutch East Indies, which speedily fell to the assailants.

In the Philippines General Douglas MacArthur, the eloquent and egotistical American commander, slowed the invading Japanese army's advance for five months. Twenty thousand American troops and a larger force of Filipinos withdrew to a strong defensive position at Bataan, near Manila, where they held off violent Japanese attacks until April 9, 1942. Before the inevitable American surrender, MacArthur was ordered by Washington to depart secretly for Australia, but he proclaimed as he departed, "I shall return." The battered remnants of his army were treated with vicious cruelty in the infamous eighty-mile Bataan Death March to prisoner-of-war camps. The island fortress of Corregidor, in Manila harbor, held out until May 6, 1942, when it too surrendered and left Japanese forces in complete control of the Philippine archipelago (see Map 34.2).

⭐ Japan's High Tide at Midway

The aggressive warriors from Japan, making hay while the Rising Sun shone, pushed relentlessly southward. They invaded the turtle-shaped island of New Guinea, north of Australia, and landed on the Solomon Islands, from which they threatened Australia itself. Their onrush was finally checked by a crucial naval battle in the Coral Sea, in May 1942. An American carrier task force, with Australian support, inflicted heavy losses on the victory-flushed Japanese. For the first time in history, the fighting was all done by carrier-based aircraft.

Japan next undertook to seize Midway Island, more than a thousand miles northwest of Honolulu. From this strategic base, it could launch devastating assaults on Pearl Harbor and perhaps force the weakened American Pacific fleet into destructive combat. The epochal **Battle of Midway** was fought on June 3–6, 1942. Admiral Chester W. Nimitz, a high-grade naval strategist, directed a smaller but skillfully maneuvered carrier force against the powerful invading fleet. The fighting was all done by aircraft, and the Japanese broke off action after losing four vitally important carriers.

Contending Voices

War and the Color Line

Activist pressure as well as the need to frame the war as a fight for freedom compelled President Franklin Roosevelt (1882–1945) to support civil rights, as indicated in a 1944 speech endorsing a permanent Fair Employment Practices Commission (FEPC):

"The American people are resolved that when our men and women return home from this war, they shall come back to a place where all persons, regardless of race, color, creed or place of birth, can live in peace, honor and human dignity."

But, with the armed forces still segregated and the home front riven by discrimination, African Americans like this unnamed soldier remained disappointed, even embittered:

"Why is it we Negro soldiers who are as much a part of Uncle Sam's great military machine as any cannot be treated with equality and the respect due us? The same respect which white soldiers expect and demand from us? . . . There is great need for drastic change in this man's Army! How can we be trained to protect America, which is called a *free* nation, when all around us rears the ugly head of segregation?"

[How might this contradiction between ideal and reality have mobilized African Americans to take a more politically activist path after World War II?

Battle of Midway (1942) *A pivotal naval battle fought near the island of Midway on June 3–6, 1942. The victory halted Japanese advances in the Pacific.*

Map 34.2 United States Thrusts in the Pacific, 1942–1945 American strategists had to choose among four proposed plans for waging the war against Japan:

1. Defeating the Japanese in China by funneling supplies over the Himalayan "hump" from India.
2. Carrying the war into Southeast Asia (a proposal much favored by the British, who could thus regain Singapore).
3. Heavy bombing of Japan from Chinese air bases.
4. "Island-hopping" from the South Pacific to within striking distance of the Japanese home islands. The fourth strategy, favored by General Douglas MacArthur, was the one finally emphasized.

The Battle of Midway was a pivotal victory. Combined with the Battle of the Coral Sea, the U.S. success at Midway halted Japan's juggernaut. But the thrust of the Japanese into the eastern Pacific did net them America's fog-girt islands of Kiska and Attu in the Aleutian archipelago, off Alaska. This easy conquest aroused fear of an invasion of the United States from the northwest. Much American strength was consequently diverted to the defense of Alaska.

Yet the Japanese imperialists, overextended in 1942, suffered from "victory disease." Their appetites were bigger than their stomachs. If they had only dug in and consolidated their gains, they would have been much more difficult to dislodge once the tide turned.

★ American Leapfrogging Toward Tokyo

Following the heartening victory at Midway, the United States for the first time was able to seize the initiative in the Pacific. In August 1942 American ground forces gained a toehold on Guadalcanal Island, in the Solomons, in an effort to protect the lifeline from America to Australia through the Southwest Pacific. After several desperate sea battles for naval control of the area, the Japanese troops evacuated Guadalcanal in February 1943.

American and Australian forces, under General MacArthur, meanwhile had been hanging on courageously to the southeastern tip of New Guinea, the last buffer protecting Australia. Aided by American naval forces, MacArthur eventually fought his way westward through the tropical jungle hells and completed the conquest of New Guinea by August 1944.

The U.S. Navy, with marines and army divisions doing the meat-grinder fighting, had meanwhile been "leapfrogging" the Japanese-held islands in the Pacific. Old-fashioned strategy dictated that the American forces, as they drove toward Tokyo, should reduce the fortified Japanese outposts on their flank. The new American strategy of island-hopping called for bypassing some of the most heavily fortified Japanese posts, capturing nearby islands, setting up airfields on them, and then neutralizing the enemy bases through heavy bombing. Deprived of essential supplies from the homeland, Japan's outposts would slowly wither on the vine—as they did.

With Admiral Nimitz skillfully coordinating the efforts of naval, air, and ground units, the American attacks achieved brilliant success. In May and August 1943, Attu and Kiska in the Aleutians were easily retaken. In November 1943 "bloody Tarawa" and Makin in the Gilbert Islands fell after suicidal resistance. Key outposts in the Marshall Islands succumbed after savage fighting in January and February 1944. The conquest of Guam and other islands in the Marianas in July and August 1944 provided airfields for America's new B-29 super-bombers to carry out round-trip bombing raids on Japan's home islands. With these unsinkable aircraft carriers now available, virtual around-the-clock bombing of Japan began in November 1944.

★ The Allied Halting of Hitler

Early setbacks for America in the Pacific were paralleled in the Atlantic. Hitler had entered the war with a formidable fleet of ultramodern submarines, which ultimately operated in "wolf packs" with frightful effect. During ten months of 1942 more than five hundred merchant ships were lost. Not until the spring of 1943 did the Allies clearly gain the upper hand against the U-boat. Their antisubmarine tactics were substantially aided by British code breakers, who had cracked the Germans' "Enigma" codes and could therefore pinpoint the locations of the U-boats lurking in the North Atlantic.

The turning point of the land-air war against Hitler came late in 1942. The British launched a thousand-plane raid on Cologne in May, and in August they were joined by the American air force in cascading bombs on German cities. In North Africa, the Germans under Marshal Erwin Rommel—the "Desert Fox"—had driven eastward across the hot sands into Egypt, perilously close to the Suez Canal. A breakthrough would have spelled disaster for the Allies. But late in October 1942, British general Bernard Montgomery delivered a withering attack at El Alamein, west of Cairo. With the aid of several hundred hastily shipped American Sherman tanks, he speedily drove the enemy back to Tunisia, more than a thousand miles away.

On the Soviet front, the unexpected successes of the red army gave a new lift to the Allied cause. In September 1942 the Russians stalled the German steamroller at rubble-strewn Stalingrad, graveyard of Hitler's hopes. In November 1942 the resilient Russians unleashed a crushing counteroffensive, which was never seriously reversed. A year later, Stalin had regained about two-thirds of the blood-soaked Soviet motherland wrested from him by the German invader.

★ A Second Front from North Africa to Rome

Soviet losses were already staggering in 1942; millions of soldiers and civilians lay dead, and Hitler's armies had laid waste a vast territory equivalent in the United States to the area from Chicago to the Atlantic seaboard. Small wonder that Kremlin leaders clamored for a second front to divert the German strength westward.

Many Americans, including FDR, were eager to begin an invasion of France in 1942 or 1943. They feared that the Soviets might make a separate peace with Germany, as they had in 1918, and leave the Western Allies to face Hitler's fury alone. But British military planners, remembering their appalling losses in France in 1914–1918, preferred to attack Hitler's Fortress Europe through the "soft underbelly" of the Mediterranean. Faced with British boot-dragging, the Americans reluctantly agreed to postpone a massive invasion of Europe.

An assault on French-held North Africa was a compromise second front. The highly secret attack, launched in November 1942, was headed by a gifted and easy-smiling American general, Dwight D. ("Ike") Eisenhower, a master of organization and conciliation. The joint Allied operation, ultimately involving some 400,000 men and about 850 ships, was highly successful. After savage fighting, the remnants of the German-Italian army were finally trapped in Tunisia and surrendered in May 1943.

At Casablanca, in newly occupied French Morocco, President Roosevelt met with Winston Churchill in January 1943 to plan new blows. The Big Two agreed to step up the Pacific war, invade Sicily, increase pressure on Italy, and insist on "unconditional surrender" by the enemy. Designed to hearten the ultra-suspicious Soviets, who professed to fear separate Allied peace negotiations, "unconditional surrender" proved to be one of the most controversial moves of the war. The main criticism was that it steeled the enemy to fight to a last-bunker resistance, while discouraging antiwar groups in Germany from revolting. Although there was some truth in these charges, no one can prove that "unconditional surrender" either shortened or lengthened the war. But this is known: by helping to destroy the German government utterly, the harsh policy forced a thorough postwar reconstruction.

The Allied forces, victorious in Africa, now turned against the not-so-soft underbelly of Europe. Sicily fell in August 1943 after sporadic but sometimes bitter resistance. Shortly before the conquest of the island, Mussolini was deposed, and Italy surrendered unconditionally soon thereafter, in September 1943.

But if Italy dropped out of the war, the Germans did not drop out of Italy. Hitler's well-trained troops stubbornly resisted the Allied invaders now pouring into the toe of the Italian boot. "Sunny Italy" proceeded to belie its name, for in the snow-covered and mud-caked mountains of its elongated peninsula occurred some of the filthiest, bloodiest, and most frustrating fighting of the war.

After a touch-and-go assault on the Anzio beachhead, Rome was finally taken on June 4, 1944. But slow and painful fighting continued in northern Italy, and not until May 2, 1945, only five days before Germany's official surrender, did several hundred thousand Axis troops in Italy lay down their arms. While the Italian second front opened the Mediterranean and diverted some German divisions from the blazing Soviet and French battle lines, it also may have delayed the main Allied invasion of France by many months—allowing more time for the Soviet army to advance into Eastern Europe.

⭐ D-Day: June 6, 1944

The Soviets never ceased their clamor for an all-out second front. Plans for a major Allied invasion were finally settled at a conference of Stalin, Churchill, and Roosevelt held in Tehran, the capital of Iran, from November 28 to December 1, 1943. The Soviets agreed to launch attacks on Germany from the east simultaneously with the prospective Allied assault from the west.

Preparations for the cross-channel invasion of France were gigantic. Britain's fast-anchored isle virtually groaned with munitions, supplies, and troops, as nearly 3 million fighting men were readied. Because the United States was to provide most of the Allied warriors, the overall command was entrusted to an American, General Eisenhower.

French Normandy, less heavily defended than other parts of the European coast, was pinpointed for the invasion assault. On **D-Day**, June 6, 1944, the enormous operation, which involved some forty-six hundred vessels, unwound. Stiff resistance was encountered from the Germans, who had been misled by a feint into expecting the blow to fall farther north.

The Allied beachhead, at first clung to with fingertips, was gradually enlarged, consolidated, and reinforced. After desperate fighting, the invaders finally broke out of the German iron ring that enclosed the Normandy landing zone. Most spectacular were the lunges across France by American armored divisions, brilliantly commanded by blustery and profane General George S. ("Blood 'n' Guts") Patton. The retreat of the German defenders was hastened when an American-French force landed in August 1944 on the southern

D-Day (1944) *A massive military operation led by American forces in Normandy beginning on June 6, 1944. The pivotal battle led to the liberation of France and brought on the final phases of World War II in Europe.*

Allies Landing in Normandy, June 6, 1944 Nine-foot ocean swells on invasion day made loading the assault landing craft, such as the one pictured here, treacherous business. Many men were injured or tossed into the sea as the bathtub-like amphibious vessels bobbed wildly up and down alongside the troop transports. As the vulnerable boats churned toward the beach, some officers led their tense, grim-faced troops in prayer. One major, recalling the remarkable Battle of Agincourt in 1415, quoted from Shakespeare's *Henry V*: "He that outlives this day, and comes safe home / Will stand a tip-toe when this day is named."

coast of France and swept northward. With the assistance of the French "underground," Paris was liberated in August 1944, amid exuberant manifestations of joy and gratitude.

Allied forces rolled irresistibly across France toward Germany. "Lafayette, we are here again," proclaimed American soldiers. The first important German city (Aachen) fell to the Americans in October 1944, and the days of Hitler's "thousand-year Reich" were numbered (see Map 34.3).

★ FDR: The Fourth-Termite of 1944

The presidential campaign of 1944 came awkwardly as the awful conflict roared to its climax. Meeting in Chicago, victory-starved Republicans nominated short, mustachioed, and dapper Thomas Dewey, the popular governor of New York. A former prosecutor, Dewey was only forty-two years of age, causing one veteran New Dealer to sneer that the candidate had cast his diaper into the ring. To offset Dewey's mild internationalism, the convention nominated for the vice presidency a strong isolationist, Senator John W. Bricker of Ohio.

FDR, aging under the strain, was still the Democrats' "indispensable man." He was nominated by acclamation for a fourth term. The scramble for the vice-presidential plum turned into a free-for-all. Roosevelt's third-term vice president, former agriculture secretary Henry A. Wallace, was a committed liberal who desired renomination. But conservative Democrats who distrusted him as ill-balanced and unpredictable concocted a "ditch Wallace" movement that developed momentum and finally won Roosevelt's blessing.

Map 34.3 World War II in Europe and North Africa, 1939–1945

The vice presidential nomination then went to smiling and self-assured Senator Harry S. Truman of Missouri, who had recently attained national visibility as the efficient chairman of a Senate committee investigating wasteful war expenditures.

A dynamic Dewey took the offensive in the campaign, proclaiming in his beautiful baritone voice that it was "time for a change" after "twelve long years" of New Dealism. In the closing weeks of the campaign, Roosevelt left his desk for the stump. He was eager to show himself, even in chilling rains, to spike well-founded rumors of failing health.

Democrats relied heavily on the new political action committee of the CIO, which provided substantial funds and zealous campaign workers for FDR. Roosevelt, as customary, won a sweeping victory: 432 to 99 in the Electoral College, 25,606,585 to 22,014,745 in the popular totals. Elated, Roosevelt quipped that "the first twelve years are the hardest."

★ The Last Days of Hitler

By mid-December 1944, the month after Roosevelt's fourth-term victory, Germany seemed to be wobbling on its last legs. The Soviet surge had penetrated eastern Germany. Allied aerial "blockbuster" bombs, making the "rubble bounce" with around-the-clock attacks, were falling like giant explosive hailstones on cities, factories, and transportation arteries. The German western front seemed about to buckle under the sledgehammer blows of the United States and its Allies.

Examining the Evidence
Franklin Roosevelt at Tehran, 1943

In late 1943 the "Big Three" wartime leaders—British prime minister Winston Churchill, American president Franklin Roosevelt, and Soviet leader Marshal Joseph Stalin—gathered together for the first time. They met amid growing Soviet frustration with the British and the Americans for their failure thus far to open a "second front" against Germany in Western Europe, while the Soviets continued to suffer horrendous losses in the savage fighting in Eastern Europe. American military planners were eager to open a second front as soon as possible, but the British, who would necessarily have to supply most of the troops until America was fully mobilized, balked. Tension among the three leaders over the second-front plan—code-named OVERLORD, the operation that resulted in the Anglo-American invasion of Normandy on "D-Day," June 6, 1944—is evident in this report of their discussions in the Iranian city of Tehran on November 28, 1943. The excerpts printed here are actually taken from two separate accounts: one composed by the American diplomat and Roosevelt's official translator Charles Bohlen, the other written by a military officer on behalf of the United States Joint Chiefs of Staff. Both versions were published in *Foreign Relations of the United States*, a compilation of American diplomatic records since 1861. The Soviets and the British also kept their own records of the Tehran meetings, giving historians remarkably rich sources with which to reconstruct the crucial negotiations and decisions that shaped wartime diplomacy.

1. Why might the history of diplomacy be so lavishly documented?
2. At this meeting, what were the principal objectives that each leader pursued? How did each man address his task?
3. In what ways was the future of the war—and the postwar world—here foreshadowed?

FIRST PLENARY MEETING, NOVEMBER 28, 1943, 4 P.M., CONFERENCE ROOM, SOVIET EMBASSY

Bohlen Minutes

SECRET

THE PRESIDENT said as the youngest of the three present he ventured to welcome his elders. He said he wished to welcome the new members to the family circle and tell them that meetings of this character were conducted as between friends with complete frankness on all sides with nothing that was said to be made public. . . .

Chief of Staff Minutes

MARSHAL STALIN asked who will be the commander in this Operation Overlord. (THE PRESIDENT and PRIME MINISTER interpolated this was not yet decided.) MARSHAL STALIN continued, "Then nothing will come out of these operations." . . .

THE PRESIDENT said we again come back to the problem of the timing for OVERLORD. It was believed that it would be good for OVERLORD to take place about 1 May, or certainly not later than 15 May or 20 May, if possible.

THE PRIME MINISTER said that he could not agree to that. . . .

. . . He said he (the Prime Minister) was going to do everything in the power of His Majesty's Government to begin OVERLORD at the earliest possible moment. However, he did not think that the many great possibilities in the Mediterranean should be ruthlessly cast aside as valueless merely on the question of a month's delay in OVERLORD.

MARSHAL STALIN said all the Mediterranean operations are diversions, . . .

THE PRESIDENT said he found that his staff places emphasis on OVERLORD. While on the other hand the Prime Minister and his staff also emphasize OVERLORD, nevertheless the United States does not feel that OVERLORD should be put off.

THE PRESIDENT questioned whether it would not be possible for the *ad hoc* committee to go ahead with their deliberations without any further directive and to produce an answer by tomorrow morning.

MARSHAL STALIN questioned, "What can such a committee do?" He said, "We Chiefs of State have more power and more authority than a committee. General Brooke cannot force our opinions and there are many questions which can be decided only by us." He said he would like to ask if the British are thinking seriously of OVERLORD only in order to satisfy the U.S.S.R.

THE PRIME MINISTER replied that if the conditions specified at Moscow regarding OVERLORD should exist, he firmly believed it would be England's duty to hurl every ounce of strength she had across the Channel at the Germans.

THE PRESIDENT observed that in an hour a very good dinner would be awaiting all and people would be very hungry. He suggested that the staffs should meet tomorrow morning and discuss the matter. . . .

Source: FDR Library

Hitler then staked everything on one last throw of his reserves. Secretly concentrating a powerful force, he hurled it, on December 16, 1944, against the thinly held American lines in the heavily befogged and snow-shrouded Ardennes Forest. Caught off guard, the outmanned Americans were driven back, creating a deep "bulge" in the Allied line. The ten-day penetration was finally halted after the 101st Airborne Division stood firm at the vital bastion of Bastogne. The commander, Brigadier General A. C. McAuliffe, defiantly answered the German demand for surrender with one word: "Nuts." Reinforcements were rushed up, and the last-gasp Hitlerian offensive was at length bloodily stemmed in the Battle of the Bulge.

In March 1945, forward-driving American troops reached Germany's Rhine River, where, by incredibly good luck, they found one strategic bridge not demolished. Pressing their advantage, General Eisenhower's troops reached the Elbe River in April 1945. There, a short distance south of Berlin, American and Soviet advance guards dramatically clasped hands amid cries of "*Amerikanskie tovarishchi*" (American comrades).

The conquering Americans were horrified to find blood-bespattered concentration camps, where the German Nazis had engaged in scientific mass murder of "undesirables," including an estimated 6 million Jews. The Washington government had long been informed about Hitler's campaign of genocide against the Jews and had been reprehensibly slow to take steps against it. Roosevelt's administration had bolted the door against large numbers of Jewish refugees, and his military commanders declined even to bomb the rail lines that carried the victims to the camps. But until the war's end, the full dimensions of the "Holocaust" were not known. When the details were revealed, the whole world was aghast.

The vengeful Soviets, clawing their way forward from the east, reached Berlin in April 1945. After desperate house-to-house fighting, followed by an orgy of pillage and rape, they captured the bomb-shattered city. Adolf Hitler, after a hasty marriage to his mistress, committed suicide in an underground bunker on April 30, 1945.

Tragedy had meanwhile struck the United States. President Roosevelt, while relaxing at Warm Springs, Georgia, suddenly died from a massive cerebral hemorrhage on April 12, 1945. Knots of confused, leaderless citizens gathered to discuss the future anxiously, as bewildered, unbriefed Vice President Truman took the helm.

On May 7, 1945, what was left of the German government surrendered unconditionally. May 8 was officially proclaimed **V-E (Victory in Europe) Day** and was greeted with frenzied rejoicing in the Allied countries.

V-E (Victory in Europe) Day *The official end to the war in Europe, marked on May 8, 1945, following the unconditional surrender of what remained of the German government.*

★ Japan Dies Hard

Japan's rickety bamboo empire meanwhile was tottering to its fall. American submarines—"the silent service"—were sending the Japanese merchant marine to the bottom so fast they were running out of prey. All told, these undersea craft destroyed 1,042 ships, or about 50 percent of Japan's entire life-sustaining merchant fleet.

Meanwhile, giant bomber attacks launched from Saipan and other captured Mariana islands were reducing the enemy's fragile cities to cinders. The massive firebomb raid on Tokyo, March 9–10, 1945 destroyed over 250,000 buildings, gutted a quarter of the city, and killed an estimated 83,000 people—a loss comparable to that later inflicted by the atomic bombs.

General MacArthur was also on the move. Completing the conquest of jungle-draped New Guinea, he headed northwest for the Philippines, en route to Japan, with 600 ships and 250,000 men. In a scene well staged for the photographers, he splashed ashore at Leyte Island, on October 20, 1944, with the summons, "People of the Philippines, I have returned . . . Rally to me." The ravaged city of Manila on the main island of Luzon fell in March 1945, but the Philippines were not finally conquered until July, after bitter fighting against holed-in Japanese, who took a toll of over sixty thousand American casualties.

America's steel vise was tightening mercilessly around Japan. The tiny island of Iwo Jima was captured in March 1945, after a desperate twenty-five day assault that cost over four thousand American dead. The island of Okinawa, well defended by Japanese soldiers who fought with incredible courage from their caves, was finally taken in June 1945, at the cost of fifty thousand American casualties and far heavier Japanese losses. The U.S. Navy, which covered the invasion of Okinawa, sustained severe damage. Japanese suicide pilots ("kamikazes"), in an exhibition of mass hara-kiri for their emperor, smashed their bomb-laden planes onto the decks of the invading fleet, sinking over thirty ships and damaging scores more.

★ The Atomic Bombs

Strategists in Washington were meanwhile planning an all-out invasion of the main islands of Japan—an invasion that presumably would cost hundreds of thousands of American (and even more Japanese) casualties. Tokyo, recognizing imminent defeat, had secretly sent peace feelers to Moscow, which had not yet entered the East Asian war. But bomb-scorched Japan still showed no outward willingness to surrender *unconditionally* to the Allies.

> *The scientific director of the Manhattan Project, J. Robert Oppenheimer (1904–1967), recalled his reaction as he witnessed the detonation of the first atomic bomb at the Trinity test site in Alamogordo, New Mexico, in July 1945. He was not only awed by the extraordinary force of this new weapon. He also feared the power to do harm that it gave to humans:*
>
> "I remembered the line from the Hindu scripture, the *Bhagavad-Gita*: 'Now I am become Death, the destroyer of Worlds.'"

The **Potsdam conference**, held near Berlin in July 1945, sounded the death knell of the Japanese. There President Truman, still new on his job, met in a seventeen-day parley with Joseph Stalin and the British leaders. The conferees issued a stern ultimatum to Japan: surrender or be destroyed. But no encouraging response was forthcoming.

America had a fantastic ace up its sleeve. Early in 1940, after Hitler's wanton assault on Poland, Roosevelt was persuaded by American and exiled scientists, notably German-born Albert Einstein, to push ahead with preparations for unlocking the secret of an atomic bomb. Congress, at Roosevelt's blank-check request, blindly made available nearly $2 billion.

What was called the **Manhattan Project** pushed feverishly forward, as American know-how and industrial power were combined with the most advanced scientific knowledge. Much technical skill was provided by British and refugee scientists, who had fled to America to escape the torture chambers of the dictators. Finally, in the desert near Alamogordo, New Mexico, on July 16, 1945, the experts detonated the first awesome and devastating atomic device.

With Japan still refusing to surrender, the Potsdam threat was fulfilled. On August 6, 1945, a lone American bomber dropped one atomic bomb on the city of Hiroshima, Japan. In a blinding flash of death, followed by a funnel-shaped cloud, about 180,000 people were left killed, wounded, or missing. Some 70,000 of them died instantaneously. Sixty thousand more soon perished from burns and radiation disease.

Two days later, on August 8, Stalin entered the war against Japan, exactly on the deadline date previously agreed upon with his allies. Soviet armies speedily overran the depleted Japanese defenses in Manchuria and Korea. Stalin was evidently determined to be in on the kill, lest he lose a voice in the final division of Japan's holdings.

Fanatically resisting Japanese, though facing atomization, still did not surrender. On August 9, American aviators dropped a second atomic bomb on the city of Nagasaki. The explosion took a horrible toll of about eighty thousand people killed or missing (see "Varying Viewpoints," p. 602). The Japanese nation could endure no more. On August 10, 1945, Tokyo sued for peace on one condition: that Hirohito, the bespectacled Son of Heaven, be allowed to remain on his ancestral throne as nominal emperor. Despite their "unconditional surrender" policy, the Allies accepted this condition on August 14, 1945. The official surrender ceremonies took place on the battleship *Missouri* in Tokyo Bay on September 2, 1945. At the same time, Americans at home hysterically celebrated **V-J (Victory in Japan) Day**, after the most horrible war in history had ended in mushrooming atomic clouds.

Potsdam conference (1945) Meeting from July 17 to August 2, 1945 among President Harry S. Truman, Soviet leader Joseph Stalin, and British leaders Winston Churchill and later Clement Attlee (when the Labour party defeated Churchill's Conservative party) near Berlin to deliver an ultimatum to Japan: surrender or be destroyed.

Manhattan Project (1942) Code name for the American commission established in 1942 to develop the atomic bomb. The first experimental bomb was detonated on July 16, 1945, in the desert of New Mexico. Atomic bombs were then dropped on two cities in Japan in hopes of bringing the war to an end: Hiroshima on August 6, 1945, and Nagasaki on August 9, 1945.

V-J (Victory in Japan) Day August 15, 1945, marking the surrender of Japan and the final end to World War II.

★ The Allies Triumphant

World War II proved to be terribly costly (see Thinking Globally). American forces suffered some 1 million casualties, more than one-third of which were deaths. Compared with other wars, the proportion killed by wounds and disease was sharply reduced, owing in part to the use of blood plasma and "miracle" drugs, notably penicillin.

Thinking Globally

America and the World in Depression and War: A Study in Contrasts

The Great Depression of the 1930s was a monstrous, planetary-scale economic hurricane that wreaked havoc around the globe. All nations were walloped by its destructive force, but two were especially hard hit: the United States and Germany. In both countries production of goods declined by nearly 50 percent, and unemployment approached 25 percent. Also, in both countries the depression discredited existing political regimes and created opportunities for new leadership to emerge. Fatefully, Germany got Adolf Hitler, while the United States got Franklin D. Roosevelt.

Roosevelt and Hitler were of the same generation, both born in the 1880s. They came to power within weeks of each other—Hitler as Germany's chancellor on January 30, 1933, and Roosevelt as U.S. president on March 4, 1933. Both achieved office through democratic elections, though democracy soon withered under one's hand and flourished under the other's.

Roosevelt's entire presidency unfolded under the looming threat, and eventually the armed challenge, of Hitler's Nazi regime. FDR's record, as well as the very character of American democracy in the mid-twentieth century, can only be properly understood in that larger context.

Consider: In the spring of 1933, Roosevelt was coaxing legislation out of the Hundred Days Congress, forging labor unions and sundry ethnic and racial minorities into a long-lasting Democratic party coalition, and making innovative use of the radio to outflank the hostile media magnates who controlled the nation's newspapers. In those same months, Hitler was dissolving German labor unions and ruthlessly censoring the German press. Soon he declared the Nazis the only legal political party in Germany and proceeded to impose on the German people a reign of terror cruelly enforced by the Gestapo, the Nazis' grimly efficient secret police.

A year later, while Roosevelt worried about a possible political challenge from the swashbuckling Louisiana Senator Huey P. Long, Hitler dispatched with his main Nazi rival, Ernst Rohm, by ordering his execution.

The following year, 1935, Roosevelt shepherded his sweeping reform program through Congress, notably including the Social Security Act, which helped to usher millions of Americans into the mainstream of American life, especially members of the great immigrant communities that had arrived a generation or so earlier. "We are going to make a country," Roosevelt said, "in which no one is left out." That same year Hitler codified the Nazis' viciously anti-Semitic policies in the notorious Nuremberg Laws, stripping German Jews of their citizenship, barring them from the professions and military service, and prohibiting marriage between Jews and "Aryans" (defined by the Nazis as a master race of non-Jewish Caucasians, especially those having Nordic features)—all gruesome steps on the road to the genocidal wartime Holocaust, which would eventually murder some 6 million Jews.

Meanwhile, Hitler was relentlessly building his war machine, while FDR's America clung stubbornly to its traditional isolationism. And when the great conflict of World War II finally erupted, Hitler's Germany and Roosevelt's America fought decidedly different wars. Indeed the United States' experience in the war stands in vivid contrast to the experience of *all* other combatants, including not only Germany but also America's allies in the "Grand Alliance."

Hitler's vaunted "thousand-year Reich" lay in smoldering ruins at war's end, his people dazed, demoralized, and starving. The strutting Führer had brewed a catastrophe so vast that its conclusion seemed to sunder the web of time itself. Germans remember the moment of their surrender on May 7, 1945, as the *Stunde null*, or "zero hour," when history's clock came to a fearful halt. Elsewhere, even America's main wartime partners, Great Britain and the Soviet Union, had paid a far greater price in blood and treasure than the United States. Uniquely among all the belligerents in World War II—perhaps uniquely in the history of warfare—the

Franklin Delano Roosevelt, Thirty-second President of the United States

United States had managed to grow its civilian economy even while waging a hugely costly war. In Germany, Britain, and the Soviet Union, the civilian standard of living had gone down by approximately one-third. In the United States, the civilian economy had actually expanded by 15 percent, preparing the way for phenomenal prosperity in the postwar decades.

And though 405,399 brave American service members died in World War II, proportionate to population American losses were about one-third those of Britain and about one-sixtieth those of the Soviet Union, where some 10 million soldiers and a staggering 17 million civilians perished (see Table 34.1). By glaring contrast, in the forty-eight states in 1945, the U.S. civilian death toll due to enemy action was just six persons, all of them the victims of a crude Japanese balloon-borne firebomb that exploded in their faces near the hamlet of Bly, Oregon, on May 5, 1945.

For all the misery that depression and war visited upon the United States, Americans could count their blessings that fortune had spared them the enormous deprivations and horrors that were all too common elsewhere. Yet some observers worried that America was now assuming leadership in a world where the depths of other peoples' wounds and woes could scarcely be imagined.

German Chancellor Adolf Hitler

Table 34.1 The Comparative Costs of World War II

Country	Military Deaths	Civilian Deaths	Government Expenditures	Damage to Civilian Property
China	2,000,000	7,750,000		
France	250,000	350,000		
Poland	123,000	6,000,000		
USSR	10,000,000	17,000,000	$192 billion	$128 billion
United Kingdom	300,000	60,600	$120 billion	$5 billion
United States	405,399	6*	$317 billion	
Germany (including Austria)	3,500,000	1,600,000	$272 billion	$50–$75 billion
Italy	242,000	60,000	$94 billion	
Japan	2,000,000	650,000		

*In the forty-eight states; additional civilian deaths occurred in Hawaii, Alaska, and the Philippines.

Sources: World War II casualty estimates vary widely. The figures here are largely taken from David M. Kennedy, ed., *The Library of Congress World War II Companion*; I. C. B. Dear, ed., *The Oxford Companion to the Second World War*; Louis L. Snyder, *Historical Guide to World War II*; and John Ellis, *World War II: A Statistical Survey*.

America was fortunate in emerging with its mainland virtually unscathed. Much of the rest of the world was utterly destroyed and destitute. America alone was untouched and healthy—oiled and muscled like a prize bull, standing astride the world's ruined landscape.

This complex conflict was the best-fought war in America's history. Though unprepared for it at the outset, the nation was better prepared than for the others, partly because America had begun to buckle on its armor about a year and a half before the war officially began. In the end the United States showed itself to be resourceful, tough, adaptable—able to accommodate itself to the tactics of an enemy who was relentless and ruthless.

American military leadership proved to be of the highest order. A new crop of war heroes emerged in brilliant generals such as Eisenhower, MacArthur, and George Marshall (chief of staff) and in imaginative admirals like Nimitz. President Roosevelt and Prime Minister Churchill, as kindred spirits, collaborated closely in planning strategy. Industrial leaders were no less skilled, for marvels of production were performed almost daily. Assembly lines proved as important as battle lines, and victory went again to the side with the most smokestacks. The enemy was almost literally smothered by bayonets, bullets, bazookas, and bombs. Hitler and his Axis co-conspirators had chosen to make war with machines, and the ingenious Yankees could ask for nothing better. They demonstrated again, as they had in World War I, that the American way of war was simply more—more men, more weapons, more machines, more technology, and more money than any enemy could hope to match. From 1940 to 1945, the output of American factories was simply phenomenal.

Hermann Goering, a Nazi leader, had sneered, "The Americans can't build planes—only electric iceboxes and razor blades." Democracy had given its answer, as the dictators, despite long preparation, were overthrown and discredited. It is true that an unusual amount of direct control was exercised over the individual by the Washington authorities during the war emergency. But the American people preserved their precious liberties without serious impairment.

Varying Viewpoints

The Atomic Bombs: Were They Justified?

No episode of the World War II era has provoked sharper controversy than the atomic bombings of Japan in August 1945. Lingering moral misgivings about the nuclear incineration of Hiroshima and Nagasaki have long threatened to tarnish America's crown of military victory. Some critics have accused the United States of racist motives because the bombs were dropped on a non-white people. Other commentators believe the bombs—especially the second bomb dropped on Nagasaki—were unnecessary because the Japanese were already on the verge of collapse. Still other scholars, notably Gar Alperovitz, have charged that the atomic bombs were not the last shots of World War II but the first salvos in the emerging Cold War. Alperovitz argues that President Truman dropped the bomb not simply to defeat Japan but because he wanted to intimidate and isolate the Soviet Union.

Each of these accusations has been vigorously rebutted. Richard Rhodes's history of the making of the atomic bomb emphasizes that the Anglo-American atomic project began as a race against the Germans, who were known to be pursuing a nuclear weapons program. From the outset both British and American planners believed this ultimate weapon of destruction would deliver victory into the hands of whoever possessed it. They consequently assumed that it would be used at the earliest possible moment, and German cities could well have been the target if the European war had lasted longer.

It is true that American intelligence sources knew in the early summer of 1945 that some Japanese statesmen were trying to use the Russians' good offices to negotiate a surrender. But as R. J. C. Butow's fine-grained study of Japan's decision to surrender demonstrates, the Japanese clung to several unacceptable conditions, including no military occupation of the home islands and no international trials of alleged war criminals. All this flew squarely in the face of America's demand for nothing less than an *unconditional* surrender. As for the Nagasaki bomb (dropped on August 9), Butow notes that it conclusively dispelled the Japanese government's original assessment that the Hiroshima attack on August 6 was a one-time-only stunt.

Could the use of the atomic bombs have been avoided? Martin J. Sherwin, Barton J. Bernstein, and McGeorge Bundy have shown that few policymakers of the time seriously asked that question. In fact, the "decision" to use the bomb was not made in 1945, but in 1942, when the United States committed itself to a crash program to build—and use—a nuclear weapon as swiftly as possible. Intimidating the Soviets might have been a "bonus" to using the bomb against Japan, but influencing Soviet behavior was never the *primary* reason for the fateful decision.

Doubt and remorse about the atomic conclusion of World War II have plagued the American conscience ever since. Less often remarked on are the deaths of four times more Japanese noncombatants than died at Hiroshima and Nagasaki in the so-called conventional fire-bombing of some five dozen Japanese cities in 1945. Those deaths suggest that the deeper moral questions should perhaps not be addressed to the particular technology of nuclear weaponry, but to the quite deliberate decision, made by several combatants—including the Germans, the British, the Americans, and the Japanese themselves—to designate civilian populations as legitimate military targets.

CHAPTER SUMMARY

America was badly wounded but roused to national unity and determination by Pearl Harbor. Roosevelt and Churchill settled on a fundamental strategy of dealing with Hitler first, while doing just enough in the Pacific to block the Japanese advance.

With the ugly exception of the Japanese-American concentration camps, World War II proceeded in the United States without the fanaticism and violations of civil liberties that occurred in World War I. The economy was effectively mobilized, using new sources of labor such as women and Mexican *braceros*. Numerous African Americans and Indians also left their traditional rural homelands and migrated to war-industry jobs in the cities of the North and West. The war brought full employment and prosperity, as well as enduring social changes, as millions of Americans were uprooted and thrown together in the military and in new communities across the country. Unlike European and Asian nations, however, the United States experienced relatively little economic and social devastation from the war. The federal government became vastly more powerful, and touched Americans' lives in numerous new ways.

The tide of Japanese conquest was stemmed at the Battles of Midway and the Coral Sea, and American forces then began a slow strategy of "island hopping" toward Tokyo. Allied troops first invaded North Africa and Italy in 1942–1943, providing a small, compromise "second front" that attempted to appease both the desperate Soviet Union as well as the anxious British. The real second front came in June 1944 with the D-Day invasion of France. The Allies moved rapidly across France, but faced a temporary setback in the Battle of the Bulge in the Low Countries.

Meanwhile, American capture of the Marianas Islands enabled the use of ground bases for extensive bombing of the Japanese home islands. The seriously ill Roosevelt defeated Thomas Dewey and won a fourth term in 1944 just as Allied troops entered Germany. Soon after FDR's death in April 1945 American troops finally met the Russians, bringing an end to Hitler's rule in May 1945. After a last round of brutal warfare on Okinawa and Iwo Jima, the dropping of two atomic bombs ended the war against Japan in August 1945.

KEY TERMS

ABC-1 agreement (585)
Executive Order No. 9066 (586)
War Production Board (WPB) (586)
Office of Price Administration (OPA) (588)
National War Labor Board (NWLB) (588)
Smith-Connally Anti-Strike Act (588)
WACs (Women's Army Corps) (588)
WAVES (Women Accepted for Volunteer Emergency Service) (588)
SPARs (U.S. Coast Guard Women's Reserve) (588)
Bracero program (588)
Fair Employment Practices Commission (FEPC) (589)
Congress of Racial Equality (CORE) (589)
code talkers (589)
Battle of Midway (591)
D-Day (594)
V-E (Victory in Europe) Day (598)
Potsdam conference (599)
Manhattan Project (599)
V-J (Victory in Japan) Day (599)

PEOPLE TO KNOW

Douglas MacArthur
Chester Nimitz
Dwight D. "Ike" Eisenhower
Harry S. Truman
Albert Einstein

MindTap is a fully online, highly personalized learning experience built upon Cengage Learning content. MindTap combines student learning tools—readings, multimedia, activities, and assessments—into a singular Learning Path that guides students through the course.

Part 6

MAKING MODERN AMERICA
1945 To The Present

World War II broke the back of the Great Depression in the United States and also ended the century-and-a-half-old American tradition of isolationism in foreign affairs. Alone among the warring powers, the United States managed to emerge from the great conflict physically unscarred, economically healthy, and militarily muscled up, especially with nuclear weapons. For more than two decades after 1945, Americans enjoyed an exceptional era of broadly shared prosperity at home and dominance abroad, challenged only by the Soviet Union in a protracted confrontation known as the Cold War. But setbacks both domestic and foreign began to bring that era to a close by the 1970s. At home, sustained economic growth in the postwar quarter century nourished a robust sense of national self-confidence and fed a revolution of rising expectations. The lingering ravages of World War II abroad largely insulated American industries from foreign competition, while the Cold War conflict with the Soviet Union spurred huge public investments in infrastructure, scientific research, and human capital. The result was what economists term "The Great Compression"—a generation or more of rising living standards, relative income equality, and a remarkable measure of social peace. Anything and everything seemed possible. Invigorated by the prospect of endlessly spreading affluence, Americans in the postwar years had record numbers of babies, moved by the millions to spanking-new suburbs, generously expanded the welfare state, widened opportunities for women, and even found the will to grapple at long last with the nation's grossest legacy of injustice, its treatment of African Americans. Citizens trusted their government and had faith in the American dream that their children's lives would be richer than their own.

The rising curve of expectations peaked in the 1960s, a stormy decade that saw great gains for civil rights and efforts to abolish poverty through President Lyndon Johnson's "Great Society" initiatives, but also brought turbulent social unrest driven by racial conflict, a rising generation's challenges to cultural mores, and protest against the Vietnam War. As government lost credibility, economic growth flattened in the 1970s, shrinking the horizon of hope in the future that had beckoned over the previous three decades. The seeds of America's economic predicament could be found in the very postwar international order that America had helped to build. Competition from reconstructed European and Japanese economies put new pressure on domestic industries and their unionized workers. Meanwhile, America's vexed Cold War venture in Vietnam unleashed a vicious inflationary cycle that further stressed the American economy. Americans now faced slower and more fitful economic growth, starkly rising income inequality, loss of faith in institutions from government to the media and even churches, intensifying social conflict, and a resurgence of free-market ideas and practices.

Paradoxically, this era of mounting economic inequality also saw widening social inclusion. "Second-wave feminism" enabled women to burst through the barriers that had long excluded them from traditional male domains. The long-reverberating civil rights movement brought greater acceptance in a multicultural America for African Americans and other minorities, including waves of new immigrants and, eventually, gays and lesbians.

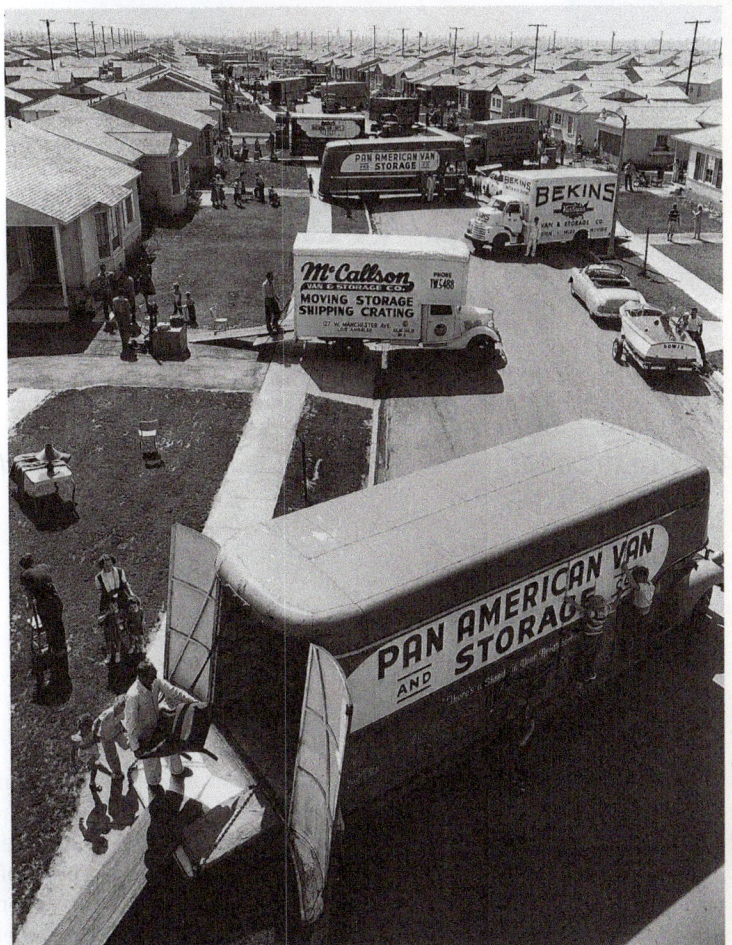

A Suburban Society In the phenomenally affluent post-WWII years, newly prosperous Americans flocked to new suburban housing developments. By the twentieth century's end, a majority of Americans were suburbanites.

The odd combination of deepening income disparity alongside widening social inclusion profoundly shaped American politics in the post-1970s era. A resurgent conservative movement helped secure Ronald Reagan's election to the presidency in 1980, inaugurating an epoch of cultural, ideological, and political contestation that increasingly divided the country and all but paralyzed the political system. Both Democratic and Republican presidents struggled to achieve lasting accomplishments in the face of a mistrustful public, anemic economy, and a polarized Congress.

For more than forty years after World War II, the fierce competition with the Soviet Union colored almost every aspect of America's foreign relations. When the Cold War ended with the collapse of the Soviet Union in 1991, the United States enjoyed a decade of unchallenged international supremacy. But terrorist attacks on American soil on September 11, 2001 brought the brief moment to a close, leading to wars in Iraq and Afghanistan and a new cycle of domestic conflict over national security, civil liberties, and the role of a superpower in the post-Cold War world.

The attacks of 9/11 brought Americans together for a time in grief and anger. But the "Great Recession" that walloped the American and global economy in 2008 further intensified partisan divisions and threatened to put a permanent end to dreams of ever-expanding personal opportunity and American global hegemony.

What if...?

- What if the United States had not fought the Vietnam War?
- Would the modern American conservative movement have risen to power over a weakened liberalism in the 1980s?
- Would American politics have become so sharply polarized in the 1990s and 2000s?

605

Chapter 35

The Cold War Begins
1945–1952

America stands at this moment at the summit of the world.

WINSTON CHURCHILL, 1945

The American people, 140 million strong, cheered their nation's victories in Europe and Asia at the conclusion of World War II. But before the shouting had even faded, many Americans began to worry about their futures. Four fiery years of global war had not entirely driven from their minds the painful memories of twelve desperate years of the Great Depression. Still more ominously, victory celebrations had barely ended before America's crumbling relations with its wartime ally, the Soviet Union, threatened a new and even more terrible international conflict.

Chapter Outline

- Harry S. Truman as President
- The Yalta Conference, February 1945
- Origins of the Cold War
- The Cold War in East Asia
- The Korean War, 1950–1953
- Anticommunism at Home
- Truman Defeats Dewey, 1948
- Postwar Prosperity
- The Rise of the "Sunbelt" and the Suburbs
- The Postwar Baby Boom
- *Makers of America: The Suburbanites*
- *Varying Viewpoints: Who Was to Blame for the Cold War?*

FOCUS QUESTIONS

1. What were the primary causes of the Cold War between the United States and the Soviet Union, and how did the confrontation with communism spread to China and Korea?
2. How did the Cold War affect domestic American society, and what were the results of the widespread fear of both Soviet spying and Communist subversion inside the United States?
3. What were the principal causes of the sustained period of postwar prosperity that began in the late 1940s?
4. How did the postwar "baby boom" and the mass migrations to the suburbs and the Sunbelt alter the character and concerns of American society?
5. How did Harry Truman successfully transform himself from a seemingly unprepared accidental president into a vigorous foreign policy leader and underdog victor in the election of 1948?

CHRONOLOGY

1944	• Servicemen's Readjustment Act (GI Bill) • Bretton Woods economic conference	1948–1949	• Berlin blockade
1945	• Spock publishes *The Common Sense Book of Baby and Child Care* • Yalta conference • United States ends lend-lease to USSR • United Nations established	1949	• NATO established • Communists defeat Nationalists in China • Soviets explode their first atomic bomb
1945–1946	• Nuremberg war crimes trial in Germany	1950	• American economy begins postwar growth • McCarthy red hunt begins • McCarran Internal Security Act passed by Congress over Truman's veto
1946	• Employment Act creates Council of Economic Advisers • Iran crisis • Kennan develops containment doctrine	1950–1953	• Korean War
1947	• Truman Doctrine • Marshall Plan • Taft-Hartley Act • National Security Act creates Department of Defense, National Security Council (NSC), and Central Intelligence Agency (CIA)	1951	• Truman fires MacArthur • Rosenbergs convicted of treason
		1952	• United States explodes first hydrogen bomb
		1957	• Postwar peak of U.S. birthrate
1948	• Israel founded; United States recognizes it • Alger Hiss case begins • Truman defeats Dewey for presidency	1973	• U.S. birthrate falls below replacement level

★ Truman: The "Gutty" Man from Missouri

Presiding over the opening of the postwar period was the "accidental president"—Harry S. Truman. Trim and owlishly bespectacled, with his graying hair and a friendly, toothy grin, Truman was called "the average man's average man." The first president in many years without a college education, he had farmed, served as an artillery officer in France during World War I, and failed as a haberdasher. He then tried his hand at precinct-level Missouri politics, through which he rose from a judgeship to the U.S. Senate. Though a protégé of a notorious political machine in Kansas City, Truman had managed to keep his own hands clean.

The problems of the postwar period were staggering, and the suddenly burdened new president at first approached his tasks with humility. But he gradually evolved from a shrinking pipsqueak into a scrappy little cuss, gaining confidence to the point of cockiness. When the Soviet foreign minister complained, "I've never been talked to like that in my life," Truman shot back, "Carry out your agreements and you won't get talked to like that."

A smallish man thrust suddenly into a giant job, Truman permitted designing old associates of the "Missouri gang" to gather around him and, like Ulysses Grant, was stubbornly loyal to them when they were caught with cream on their whiskers. On occasion he would send critics hot-tempered and profane "s.o.b." letters. Most troubling, in trying to demonstrate to a skeptical public his decisiveness and power of command, he was inclined to go off half cocked or stick mulishly to some wrongheaded notion.

But if Truman was sometimes small in the small things, he was often big in the big things. He had down-home authenticity, few pretensions, rock-solid probity, and a lot of that old-fashioned character trait called moxie. Not one to dodge responsibility, he placed a sign on his White House desk that read, "The buck stops here." Among his favorite sayings was, "If you can't stand the heat, get out of the kitchen."

★ Yalta: Bargain or Betrayal?

Vast and silent, the Soviet Union continued to be the great enigma. The conference in Tehran in 1943, where Roosevelt had first met Joseph Stalin man to man, had cleared the air somewhat, but much had remained unresolved—especially questions about the postwar fates of Germany, Eastern Europe, and Asia.

The **Yalta conference**, the final fateful conference of the Big Three, took place in February 1945. At this former tsarist resort on the relatively warm shores of the Black Sea, Stalin, Churchill, and the fast-failing Roosevelt reached momentous agreements after pledging their faith with vodka. Stalin agreed that Poland, with revised boundaries, should have a representative government based on free elections—a pledge he soon broke. Bulgaria and Romania were likewise to have free elections—a promise also flouted. The Big Three further announced plans for fashioning a new international peace-keeping organization, the United Nations.

The most controversial decision at Yalta concerned Moscow's entry into the war against Japan. The atomic bomb had not yet been tested, and Washington strategists expected frightful American casualties in the projected assault on Japan. Roosevelt was therefore willing to offer inducements to the Soviets to enter the Asian war and pin down Japanese troops in Manchuria and Korea. Stalin, striking a hard bargain, agreed to attack Japan within three months after the collapse of Germany. In return the Soviets were promised the southern half of Sakhalin Island, Japan's Kurile Islands, and control of key railroads and seaports in China's Manchuria. As it turned out, Moscow's muscle was not necessary to knock out Japan. Critics later charged that Roosevelt had sold Jiang Jieshi (Chiang Kai-shek) down the river and contributed powerfully to his overthrow by the Chinese communists four years later. Roosevelt's defenders countered that Stalin's mighty red army could have secured much more of China if he had wished and that the Yalta conference really set limits to his ambitions. Apologists for Roosevelt also noted that Soviet troops had already occupied much of Eastern Europe, and a war to throw them out was unthinkable.

The fact is that the Big Three at Yalta were not drafting a comprehensive peace settlement; at most they were sketching general intentions and testing one another's reactions. Later critics who howled about the broken promises overlooked that fundamental point. More specific understandings among the wartime allies—especially the two emerging superpowers, the United States and the Soviet Union—awaited the arrival of peace.

Yalta conference (1945) *Meeting of Franklin Roosevelt, Winston Churchill, and Joseph Stalin in February 1945 at an old tsarist resort on the Black Sea, where the Big Three leaders laid the foundations for the postwar division of power in Europe, including a divided Germany and territorial concessions to the Soviet Union.*

★ The United States and the Soviet Union

History provided little hope that the United States and the Soviet Union would reach cordial understandings about the shape of the postwar world. Mutual suspicions were ancient, abundant, and deep. Communism and capitalism were historically hostile social philosophies. The United States had refused officially to recognize the Bolshevik revolutionary government in Moscow until 1933. Soviet skepticism was nourished by American delays in opening a second front against Germany, by the abrupt termination of vital lend-lease aid in 1945, and by U.S. refusal of Moscow's plea for a $6 billion reconstruction loan—while approving a similar loan of $3.75 billion to Britain in 1946.

Different visions of the postwar world also separated the two superpowers. Stalin aimed above all to guarantee the security of the Soviet Union by establishing friendly governments along its western border, especially in Poland. By maintaining an extensive Soviet sphere of influence in Eastern and Central Europe, the USSR could protect itself and consolidate its revolutionary base as the world's leading communist country.

To many Americans, that "sphere of influence" looked like an ill-gained "empire." Doubting that Soviet goals were purely defensive, they remembered the earlier Bolshevik call for world revolution. Stalin's emphasis on "spheres" also clashed with Franklin Roosevelt's Wilsonian dream of an "open world"—decolonized, demilitarized, and democratized, with a strong international organization to oversee global peace.

Even the ways in which the United States and the Soviet Union resembled each other were troublesome. Both countries had been largely isolated from world affairs

The Communist Menace First appearing in the *New York Daily News* on January 6, 1946, this map reflected the rising anxiety in post–World War II America that the Soviet Union was an aggressively expansionist power, relentlessly gobbling up territory and imposing its will across both Europe and Asia.

before World War II. Both nations also had a history of conducting a kind of "missionary" diplomacy—of trying to export to all the world the political doctrines precipitated out of their respective revolutionary origins.

Unaccustomed to their great-power roles, America and the USSR suddenly found themselves staring eyeball-to-eyeball over the prostrate body of battered Europe. The wartime "Grand Alliance" of the United States, the Soviet Union, and Britain had been a misbegotten child of necessity. When the hated Hitler fell, suspicion and rivalry between communistic, despotic Russia and capitalistic, democratic America were all but inevitable. In a fateful progression of events, marked often by misperceptions as well as by genuine conflicts of interest, the two powers provoked each other into a tense standoff known as the **Cold War**. Enduring four and a half decades, the Cold War not only shaped Soviet-American relations; it overshadowed the entire postwar international order in every corner of the globe.

★ Shaping the Postwar World

Despite these obstacles, the United States did manage at war's end to erect some of the structures that would support Roosevelt's vision of an open world. At the **Bretton Woods Conference** in Bretton Woods, New Hampshire in 1944, the Western Allies established the International Monetary Fund (IMF) to encourage world trade and the World Bank to promote economic growth in war-ravaged and underdeveloped areas. Three years

Cold War (1946–1991) *The forty-five-year-long diplomatic tension between the United States and the Soviet Union that divided much of the world into polarized camps, capitalist against communist. Most of the international conflicts during that period, particularly in the developing world, can be traced to the competition between the United States and the Soviet Union.*

Bretton Woods Conference (1944) *Meeting of Western allies to establish a postwar international economic order to avoid crises like the one that spawned World War II. Led to the creation of the International Monetary Fund (IMF) and the World Bank, designed to regulate currency levels and provide aid to underdeveloped countries.*

> *Former British prime minister Winston Churchill (1874–1965), in a highly controversial speech at Fulton, Missouri (March 1946), warned of Soviet expansionism in language that would frame the Cold War in Europe for decades:*
>
> "From Stettin in the Baltic to Trieste in the Adriatic an iron curtain has descended across the Continent."

United Nations (U.N.) *International body formed in 1945 to bring nations into dialogue in hopes of preventing further world wars. Much like the former League of Nations in ambition, the U.N. was more realistic in recognizing the authority of the Big Five powers in keeping peace in the world. Thus, it guaranteed veto power to all permanent members of its Security Council—Britain, China, France, the Soviet Union, and the United States.*

Nuremberg war crimes trial (1945–1946) *Highly publicized proceedings against former Nazi leaders for war crimes and crimes against humanity in postwar Germany. The trials led to several executions and long prison sentences.*

later, the General Agreement on Tariffs and Trade (GATT) reduced trade barriers among member nations, helping spread the economic globalization of the last half of the century. In contrast to its behavior after World War I, the United States took the lead in creating these important international bodies (see "Thinking Globally: The Era of Globalization," pp. 674–675).

Meeting in San Francisco in April 1945, representatives from fifty nations fashioned the United Nations Charter. The **United Nations (U.N.)** was a successor to the old League of Nations, but it differed from its predecessor in significant ways. The League had adopted rules denying veto power to any party in a dispute. The U.N., by contrast, more realistically provided that no member of the Security Council, dominated by the Big Five powers (the United States, Britain, the USSR, France, and China), could have action taken against it without its consent. The League, in short, presumed great-power conflict; the U.N. presumed great-power cooperation. The U.N. also featured the General Assembly, which could be controlled by smaller countries. In contrast to the U.S. rejection of the League in 1919, the Senate overwhelmingly approved the U.N. Charter on July 28, 1945, by a vote of 89 to 2.

The United Nations had some gratifying initial successes. It helped preserve peace in Iran, Kashmir, and other trouble spots. It played a large role in creating the new Jewish state of Israel. The U.N. Trusteeship Council guided former colonies to independence. Through such arms as UNESCO (United Nations Educational, Scientific, and Cultural Organization), FAO (Food and Agricultural Organization), and WHO (World Health Organization), the U.N. brought benefits to peoples the world over.

But it proved far less successful in controlling the fearsome new technology of the atom. The suspicious Soviets vetoed an American proposal in 1946 for a U.N. agency to be charged with worldwide authority over atomic energy, weapons, and research. A priceless opportunity to tame the nuclear monster in its infancy was lost.

★ The Problem of Germany

Hitler's ruined Reich posed especially thorny problems for all the wartime Allies. They agreed only that the cancer of Nazism had to be cut out of the German body politic, which involved punishing Nazi leaders for war crimes. The Allies joined in trying twenty-two top culprits at the **Nuremberg war crimes trial** during 1945–1946. Accusations included committing crimes against the laws of war and humanity and plotting aggressions contrary to solemn treaty pledges. Justice, Nuremberg-style, was harsh. Twelve of the accused Nazis swung from the gallows, and seven were sentenced to long jail terms.

Beyond punishing the top Nazis, the Allies could agree on little about postwar Germany. Some American Hitler-haters wanted to completely dismantle all German factories, while the Soviets sought to extract enormous reparations from the Germans. Both these desires clashed headlong with the reality that an industrial, healthy German economy was indispensable to the recovery of Europe. Along with Austria, Germany had been divided at war's end into four military occupation zones, each assigned to one of the Big Four powers (France, Britain, America, and the USSR) (see Map 35.1). Before long, it was apparent that Germany would remain indefinitely divided. West Germany eventually became an independent country, wedded to the West. East Germany and the other Soviet-dominated Eastern European countries, such as Poland and Hungary, became nominally independent "satellite" states, bound to the Soviet Union. Eastern Europe virtually disappeared from Western sight behind the "iron curtain" of secrecy and isolation that Stalin clanged down across Europe from the Baltic to the Adriatic. This division of Europe would endure for more than four decades.

With Germany now split in two, there remained the problem of the rubble heap known as Berlin. Lying deep within the Soviet zone, this beleaguered isle in a red sea had been broken, like Germany as a whole, into sectors occupied by troops of each of the four

Map 35.1 Postwar Partition of Germany Germany lost much of its territory in the east to Poland and the Soviet Union. The military occupation zones were the bases for the formation of two separate countries in 1949, when the British, French, and American zones became West Germany, and the Soviet zone became East Germany. (The two Germanies were reunited in 1990.) Berlin remained under joint four-power occupation from 1945 to 1990 and became a focus and symbol of Cold War tensions.

victorious powers. In 1948 the Soviets abruptly choked off all rail and highway access to Berlin, evidently reasoning that the Allies would be starved out.

Berlin became a hugely symbolic issue as well as a test of wills for both Moscow and Washington. The Americans organized the gigantic **Berlin airlift** in the midst of hair-trigger tension. For nearly a year American pilots ferried thousands of tons of supplies to the grateful Berliners, their former enemies. The Soviets, their bluff dramatically called, finally lifted their blockade in May 1949. In the same year the governments of the two Germanys, East and West, were formally established. The Cold War had icily congealed.

Berlin airlift (1948–1949) *Year-long mission of flying food and supplies to blockaded West Berliners, whom the Soviet Union cut off from access to the West in the first major crisis of the Cold War.*

★ The Cold War Deepens

A crafty Stalin also probed the West's resolve at other sensitive points, including oil-rich Iran. In 1946 he broke an agreement to remove his troops from Iran's northernmost province, which the USSR had occupied during World War II. Truman sent off a stinging protest, and the Soviet dictator backed down.

Moscow's hard-line policies in Germany, Eastern Europe, and the Middle East wrought a psychological Pearl Harbor. Any remaining goodwill from the period of comradeship-in-arms evaporated in a cloud of dark distrust. "I'm tired of babying the Soviets," Truman remarked privately in 1946, as attitudes on both sides began to harden frostily.

Truman's piecemeal responses to various Soviet challenges took on intellectual coherence in 1947 with the formulation of the **containment doctrine**. Crafted by

containment doctrine *America's strategy against the Soviet Union based on ideas of George Kennan. The doctrine declared that the Soviet Union and communism were inherently expansionist and had to be stopped from spreading through both military and political pressure. Containment guided American foreign policy throughout most of the Cold War.*

Contending Voices

Debating the Cold War

In February 1946 Kremlin specialist George F. Kennan (1904–2005) sent his landmark "Long Telegram" to the State Department. In the eight-thousand-word message, Kennan assessed the Soviet threat and called for a new kind of response, which would eventually become known as the "containment doctrine."

"In summary, we have here a political force [Stalin's regime] committed fanatically to the belief that with [the] US there can be no permanent *modus vivendi*, that it is desirable and necessary that the internal harmony of our society be disrupted, our traditional way of life be destroyed, the international authority of our state be broken, if Soviet power is to be secure."

Six months later, former Vice President-turned-Secretary of Commerce Henry A. Wallace (1888–1965) wrote to President Truman to urge a more conciliatory policy. Wallace's lonely opposition to America's emerging Cold War policy would propel him into the top spot of a left-wing third-party presidential campaign in 1948.

"How do American actions since V-J Day appear to other nations? I mean by actions the concrete things like $13 billion for the War and Navy Departments, the Bikini tests of the atomic bomb, . . . and the effort to secure air bases spread over half the globe from which the other half of the globe can be bombed. . . . . How would it look to us if Russia had the bomb and we did not, if Russia had 10,000-mile bombers and air bases within a thousand miles of our coast lines and we did not?"

> How inevitable was the Cold War between the United States and the Soviet Union and their respective spheres of influence?

a brilliant young diplomat and Soviet specialist, George F. Kennan, this concept held that Russia, whether tsarist or communist, was relentlessly expansionary. But the Kremlin was also cautious, Kennan argued, and the flow of Soviet power into "every nook and cranny available to it" could be stemmed by "firm and vigilant containment."

Truman embraced Kennan's advice when he formally and publicly adopted a "get-tough-with-Russia" policy in 1947. His first dramatic move was triggered by word that heavily burdened Britain could no longer bear the financial and military load of defending Greece against communist pressures. If Greece fell, Turkey would presumably collapse, and the strategic eastern Mediterranean would pass into the Soviet orbit.

In a surprise appearance before Congress on March 12, 1947, the president requested support for what came to be called the **Truman Doctrine**. Specifically, he asked for $400 million to bolster Greece and Turkey, which Congress quickly granted. More generally, he declared that "it must be the policy of the United States to support free peoples who are resisting attempted subjugation by armed minorities or outside pressures"—a sweeping and open-ended commitment of vast and worrisome proportions.

Critics then and later charged that the Truman Doctrine committed the United States to backing any tinhorn despot who claimed to be resisting "Communist aggression," needlessly polarized the world into pro-Soviet and pro-American camps, and unwisely construed the Soviet threat as primarily military in nature. Apologists for Truman have explained that it was Truman's fear of a revived isolationism that led him to exaggerate the Soviet threat and to pitch his message in the charged language of a holy global war against godless communism.

Meanwhile, a threat of a different sort loomed in Western Europe—especially France and, Italy. Still suffering from the hunger and economic chaos spawned by the war, these key nations were in grave danger of being taken over from the inside by Communist parties that could exploit these hardships. President Truman responded with a bold policy, in keeping with America's desire for a liberalized global economy. In an address at Harvard University on June 5, 1947, Secretary of State George C. Marshall invited the Europeans to work out a *joint* plan for their economic recovery. If they did so, then the United States would provide substantial financial assistance. The democratic nations of Europe enthusiastically accepted this life-giving **Marshall Plan** at a Paris conference in July 1947. Marshall offered the same aid to the Soviet Union and its allies, but nobody was surprised when the Soviets denounced the "Martial Plan" as one more capitalist trick.

Congress at first balked at the Marshall Plan's proposal for spending the mammoth sum of $12.5 billion over four years in sixteen countries. But a Soviet-sponsored communist coup in Czechoslovakia finally awakened the legislators to reality, and they voted the initial appropriations in April 1948. Truman's Marshall Plan was a spectacular success. American dollars pumped reviving blood into the economic veins of the anemic Western European nations. Within a few years, an "economic miracle" drenched Europe in prosperity. The Communist parties in Italy and France lost ground, and these two keystone countries were saved from the westward thrust of communism.

A resolute Truman made another fateful decision in 1948. Access to Middle Eastern oil was crucial to the European recovery program and, increasingly, to the health of the U.S. economy, given finite American oil reserves. Yet the Arab oil countries adamantly opposed the creation of the Jewish state of Israel in the British mandate territory of Palestine. Defying Arab wrath and his own State and Defense Departments, Truman officially recognized the state of Israel on the day of its birth, May 14, 1948. Humanitarian sympathy for the Jewish survivors of the Holocaust ranked high among his reasons, as did his wishes to preempt Soviet influence in the Jewish state and to retain the support of American Jewish voters. Truman's policy of strong support for Israel would vastly complicate U.S. relations with the Arab world in the decades ahead.

★ America Begins to Rearm

The Cold War—the struggle to contain Soviet communism—was not war, yet it was not peace. The standoff with the Kremlin banished the dreams of tax-fatigued Americans that tanks could be beaten into automobiles.

The Soviet menace spurred the unification of the armed services as well as the creation of a huge new national security apparatus. Congress in 1947 passed the National Security Act, creating the Department of Defense. The uniformed heads of each service were brought together as the Joint Chiefs of Staff. The National Security Act also established the National Security Council (NSC) to advise the president on security matters and the Central Intelligence Agency (CIA) to coordinate the government's foreign fact gathering. In the same year, Congress resurrected the military draft, providing for the conscription of selected young men from nineteen to twenty-five years of age. The forbidding presence of the Selective Service System shaped millions of young people's educational, marital, and career plans in the following quarter century. The Soviet threat was also forcing the democracies of Western Europe into an unforeseen degree of unity. Proposing a treaty of defensive alliance, five Western European nations invited the United States to join them. American had traditionally avoided entangling alliances, but the emerging coalition could contain the Soviet Union, reintegrate Germany into the European family, and reassure jittery Europeans that a traditionally isolationist Uncle Sam would not abandon them. On April 4, 1949, twelve nations signed the North Atlantic Treaty, which pledged the signatories to regard an attack on one as an attack on all and to respond with "armed force," if necessary. Despite last-ditch howls from immovable isolationists, the U.S. Senate approved the treaty on July 21, 1949, by a vote of 82 to 13.

The NATO pact was epochal. The formation of the **North Atlantic Treaty Organization (NATO)** marked a dramatic departure from American diplomatic convention, a gigantic boost for European unification, and a significant step in the militarization of the Cold War. NATO became the cornerstone of all Cold War American policy toward Europe. With good reason, pundits summed up NATO's threefold purpose: "to keep the Russians out, the Germans down, and the Americans in."

★ Reconstruction and Revolution in Asia

Reconstruction in Japan was simpler than in Germany, primarily because it was largely a one-man show. Under General Douglas MacArthur, the occupying American army went inflexibly ahead with his program for the democratization of Japan, which enjoyed stunning success. The Japanese cooperated to an astonishing degree. They saw that good behavior and the adoption of democracy would speed the end of occupation—and it did. A MacArthur-dictated constitution, adopted in 1946, paved the way for a phenomenal economic recovery that within a few decades made Japan one of the world's mightiest industrial powers.

If Japan proved a postwar success story for American policymakers, the opposite was true in China, where a bitter civil war had raged for years between Nationalists and communists. Washington had halfheartedly supported the Nationalist government of

Truman Doctrine (1947) *President Truman's universal pledge of support for any people fighting any communist or communist-inspired threat. Truman presented the doctrine to Congress in 1947 in support of his request for $400 million to defend Greece and Turkey against Soviet-backed insurgencies.*

Marshall Plan (1948) *Massive transfer of aid money to help rebuild postwar Western Europe, intended to bolster capitalist and democratic governments and prevent domestic communist groups from riding poverty and misery to power. The plan was first announced by Secretary of State George Marshall at Harvard's commencement in June 1947.*

North Atlantic Treaty Organization (NATO) *Military alliance of Western European powers and the United States and Canada established in 1949 to defend against the common threat from the Soviet Union, marking a giant stride forward for European unity and American internationalism.*

Generalissimo Jiang Jieshi in his struggle with the communists under Mao Zedong (Mao Tse-tung). But ineptitude and corruption within the generalissimo's regime eroded his people's confidence. The communist armies swept to victory late in 1949. Jiang was forced to flee with the remnants of his force to the island of Taiwan.

The collapse of Nationalist China was a depressing defeat for America and its allies in the Cold War. At one fell swoop nearly one-fourth of the world's population—some 500 million people—was swept into the communist camp. The so-called "fall of China" became a bitterly partisan issue in the United States. Seeking scapegoats, the Republicans charged that President Truman and his bristly mustached secretary of state, Dean Acheson, had "lost China." They insisted that Democratic agencies, wormy with communists, had deliberately withheld aid from Jiang Jieshi and caused his fall.

More bad news came in September 1949 when President Truman shocked the nation by announcing that the Soviets had exploded an atomic bomb—approximately three years earlier than many experts had thought possible. To outpace the Soviets in nuclear weaponry, Truman ordered the development of the "H-bomb" (hydrogen bomb)—a city-smashing thermonuclear weapon that was a thousand times more powerful than the atomic bomb. Physicists Albert Einstein and J. Robert Oppenheimer, former scientific director of the Manhattan Project and current chair of the Atomic Energy Commission, led a group of scientists in opposition to the crash program to design thermonuclear weapons.

But Einstein and Oppenheimer, the nation's two most famous scientists, could not dissuade Truman, anxious over communist threats in East Asia, from proceeding with the H-bomb. The United States exploded its first hydrogen device on a South Pacific atoll in 1952. Not to be outdone, the Soviets exploded their first H-bomb in 1953, and the nuclear arms race entered a perilously competitive cycle, spurred by massive state support for defense-related scientific research in both countries. It was only constrained by the recognition that a truly hot Cold War would leave no world for the communists to communize or the democracies to democratize. Peace through mutual terror brought a shaky stability to the superpower standoff.

★ The Korean Volcano Erupts

Korea, the Land of the Morning Calm, heralded a new and more ominous phase of the Cold War—a shooting phase—in June 1950. When Japan collapsed in 1945, Soviet troops had accepted the Japanese surrender north of the thirty-eighth parallel on the Korean peninsula, and American troops had done likewise south of that line. Both superpowers professed to want the reunification and independence of Korea, a Japanese colony since 1910. But, as in Germany, each helped to set up rival regimes above and below the parallel.

By 1949, when the Soviets and Americans withdrew, the entire peninsula was a bristling armed camp, with two hostile regimes eyeing each other suspiciously. The explosion came on June 25, 1950, when North Korean army columns with Soviet-made tanks rumbled across the thirty-eighth parallel. Caught flat-footed, the South Koreans were shoved back southward to a dangerously tiny defensive area around Pusan, their weary backs to the sea.

President Truman sprang quickly into the breach. The invasion seemed to provide devastating proof of a fundamental premise in the "containment doctrine" that shaped Washington's foreign policy: even a slight relaxation of America's guard was an invitation to communist aggression somewhere.

The Korean invasion prompted a massive expansion of the American military. A few months before, Truman's National Security Council had issued its famous **National Security Council Memorandum Number 68 (NSC-68)**, recommending that the United States quadruple its defense spending. Ignored at first because it seemed politically impossible to implement, NSC-68 got a new lease on life from the Korean crisis. "Korea saved us," Secretary of State Acheson later commented. Truman now ordered a massive military buildup, well beyond what was necessary for Korea. Soon the United States had 3.5 million men under arms and was spending $50 billion per year on the defense budget—some 13 percent of the GNP.

National Security Council Memorandum Number 68 (NSC-68) (1950) *National Security Council recommendation to quadruple defense spending and rapidly expand peacetime armed forces to address Cold War tensions. It reflected a new militarization of American foreign policy, but the huge costs of rearmament were not expected to interfere with what seemed like the limitless possibilities of postwar prosperity.*

NSC-68 was a key document of the Cold War period, not only because it marked a major step in the militarization of American foreign policy, but also because it vividly reflected the sense of almost limitless possibility that pervaded postwar American society. NSC-68 rested on the assumption that the enormous American economy could bear without strain the huge costs of a gigantic rearmament program.

Truman took full advantage of a temporary Soviet absence from the United Nations Security Council on June 25, 1950, to obtain a unanimous condemnation of North Korea as an aggressor. Two days later, without consulting Congress, Truman ordered American armed forces under General Douglas MacArthur to support South Korea. So began the ill-fated **Korean War**. Officially, the United States was simply participating in a United Nations "police action," but in fact the United States provided 88 percent of the U.N. contingents, and General MacArthur took his orders from Washington, not from the Security Council.

★ The Military Seesaw in Korea

Rather than fight his way out of the southern Pusan perimeter, MacArthur launched a daring amphibious landing behind the enemy's lines at Inchon. This bold gamble on September 15, 1950, succeeded brilliantly; within two weeks the North Koreans had scrambled back behind the "sanctuary" of the thirty-eighth parallel. Truman's avowed intention was to restore South Korea to its former borders, but there seemed little point in permitting the North Koreans to regroup north of the parallel and come again. The U.N. General Assembly tacitly authorized a crossing by MacArthur, whom President Truman ordered northward, provided that there was no intervention in force by the Chinese or Soviets (see Map 35.2).

The Americans thus raised the stakes in Korea, and in so doing quickened the fears of another potential player in this dangerous game. The Chinese had publicly warned that they would not sit idly by and watch hostile troops approach the strategic Yalu River boundary between Korea and China. But MacArthur pooh-poohed all predictions of an effective intervention by the Chinese and reportedly boasted that he would "have the boys home by Christmas."

MacArthur erred badly. In November 1950 tens of thousands of Chinese fell upon his rashly overextended lines and hurled the U.N. forces reeling back down the peninsula. The fighting then sank into a frostbitten stalemate on the icy terrain near the thirty-eighth parallel.

An imperious MacArthur, humiliated by this rout, pressed for drastic retaliation. He favored a blockade of the China coast and bombardment of Chinese bases in Manchuria. He even suggested that the United States use nuclear weapons on the advancing Chinese. But Washington policymakers, with anxious eyes on Moscow, refused to enlarge the already costly conflict. The chairman of the Joint Chiefs of Staff declared that a wider clash in Asia would be "the wrong war, at the wrong place, at the wrong time, and with the wrong enemy." Europe, not Asia, was the administration's first concern; and the USSR, not China, loomed as the more sinister foe.

Two-fisted General MacArthur felt that he was being asked to fight with one hand tied behind his back. He sneered at the concept of a "limited war" and insisted that "there is no

Map 35.2 The Shifting Front in Korea

Korean War (1950–1953) First "hot war" of the Cold War. It began when the Soviet-backed North Koreans invaded South Korea and U.N. forces, dominated by the United States, launched a counteroffensive. The war ended in stalemate in 1953.

Truman Takes the Heat

substitute for victory." Truman bravely resisted calls for nuclear escalation. When MacArthur began to criticize the president's policies publicly, Truman had no choice but to remove the insubordinate general from command on April 11, 1951. By July, truce discussions began near the firing line. Snagged by the issue of prisoner exchange, the talks dragged on for nearly two years while men continued to die.

Meanwhile, MacArthur, a legend in his own mind, returned to an uproarious American welcome, whereas Truman was condemned in many circles as a "pig," an "imbecile," a "Judas," and an appeaser of communism. The domestic response to the Truman-MacArthur conflict offered a hint of the depth of popular passions coursing through the Cold War at home.

★ The Cold War Home Front

As never before, international events deeply shaped American political and economic developments at home in the years after World War II. The solidifying Cold War with Russia fueled domestic political conflict and drew new boundaries for acceptable political opinion. Meanwhile, the postwar economic order that the United States helped to forge, combined with Cold War spending and investment, laid the foundations for a Long Boom that transformed the country over the next several decades.

A new anti-red chase accelerated within America's borders as U.S.-Soviet relations froze. Many nervous citizens feared that communist spies, paid with Moscow gold, were undermining the government and treacherously misdirecting foreign policy. In 1947 Truman launched a massive "loyalty" program. The attorney general drew up a list of ninety supposedly disloyal organizations. A Loyalty Review Board investigated more than 3 million federal employees, some 3,000 of whom either resigned or were dismissed, none under formal indictment.

Individual states likewise became intensely security-conscious. Loyalty oaths in increasing numbers were demanded of employees, especially teachers. The gnawing question for many earnest Americans was whether the nation could continue to enjoy traditional freedoms—especially freedom of speech and the right of political dissent-in a Cold War climate.

In 1949 eleven communists were convicted of advocating the overthrow of the American government under the Smith Act of 1940 and sent to prison. In 1948 Congressman Richard M. Nixon, a member of the **House Un-American Activities Committee (HUAC)** and an ambitious red-catcher, led the chase after Alger Hiss, a prominent ex–New Dealer and a distinguished member of the "eastern establishment." Accused of being a communist agent in the 1930s, Hiss dramatically confronted his chief accuser before HUAC and denied everything. But Hiss was caught in embarrassing falsehoods, convicted of perjury in 1950, and sentenced to five years in prison.

The stunning success of Soviet scientists in developing an atomic bomb was attributed by many to the cleverness of communist spies in stealing American secrets. In 1951 two American citizens, Julius and Ethel Rosenberg, were convicted in a sensational trial of leaking atomic data to Moscow and eventually sent to the electric chair in 1953. Though declassified evidence has subsequently strengthened the case against the Rosenbergs, some citizens at the time believed in their innocence and began to sour on the excesses of the red-hunters.

Was America really riddled with Soviet spies? Soviet agents did infiltrate certain government agencies, and espionage may have helped the Soviets develop an atomic bomb somewhat sooner than they would have otherwise. But for many ordinary Americans, the hunt for communists was not just about fending off the military threat of the Soviet Union. Unsettling dangers lurked closer to home. While men such as Nixon and Senator Joseph

---

House Un-American Activities Committee (HUAC) *Investigatory body established in 1938 to root out "subversion." Sought to expose communist influence in American government and society, in particular through the case of Alger Hiss.*

McCarthy led the search for communists in Washington, conservative politicians at the state and local levels discovered that all manner of real or perceived social changes—including declining religious sentiment, increased sexual freedom, and agitation for civil rights—could be tarred with a red brush. Anticommunist crusaders ransacked school libraries for "subversive" books and drove debtors, drinkers, and homosexuals, all alleged to be security risks, from their jobs.

Some Americans, including President Truman, realized that the red hunt was turning into a witch hunt. In 1950 Truman vetoed the McCarran Internal Security Bill, which authorized the president to arrest and detain suspicious persons during an "internal security emergency." But the congressional guardians of the Republic's liberties enacted the bill over Truman's veto.

The demagogic politics of anticommunism found its most dangerous practitioner in Joseph R. McCarthy, an obstreperous Republican senator from Wisconsin. The swaggering senator crashed into the limelight in February 1950 when he accused Secretary of State Dean Acheson of knowingly employing 205 Communist party members—though in the end he failed to identify even one. Some of McCarthy's Republican colleagues realized the partisan usefulness of this kind of attack on the Democratic administration. Ohio Senator John Bricker reportedly said, "Joe, you're a dirty s.o.b. But there are times when you've got to have an s.o.b. around, and this is one of them."

McCarthy's rhetoric grew ever bolder and his accusations wilder over the next several years. Incredibly, he even denounced General George Marshall, former army chief of staff and ex-secretary of state, as "part of a conspiracy so immense and an infamy so black as to dwarf any previous venture in the history of man."

McCarthy—and what became known as **McCarthyism**—flourished in the seething Cold War atmosphere of suspicion and fear. McCarthy was the most ruthless of the red-hunters, and did the most damage to American traditions of fair play and free speech. The careers of countless officials, writers, and actors were ruined after "Low-Blow Joe" had "named" them as communists or communist sympathizers.

At the peak of his powers McCarthy effectively controlled personnel policy at the State Department, causing severe damage to the effectiveness and morale of the professional foreign service. In particular, McCarthyite purges deprived the government of a number of Asian specialists who might have counseled a wiser course in Vietnam in the fateful decade that followed.

McCarthy finally bent the bow too far when he attacked the U.S. Army. Up to 20 million Americans watched the televised **Army-McCarthy hearings** in fascination as a boorish, surly McCarthy publicly cut his own throat by parading his essential meanness and irresponsibility. A few months later the Senate formally condemned him, and he died three years later of chronic alcoholism. But "McCarthyism" has passed into the English language as a label for dangerous forces of unfairness and fear.

Beyond fights over security and civil liberties, the Cold War shaped American culture in complex and profound ways. Many Americans interpreted the conflict between the West and the communist East in religious terms. They received support from theologians like the influential liberal Protestant clergyman Reinhold Niebuhr (1892–1971). A vocal enemy of fascism, communism, *and* pacifism in the 1940s and 1950s, Niebuhr divided the world into two polarized camps, the "children of light" and the "children of darkness." For Niebuhr, Christian justice required a "realist" response, including force if necessary, to "children of darkness" like Hitler and Stalin. But Niebuhr's realism also emphasized the dangers of fallibility and the limits of power, in contrast to the crusading spirit of conservative Christian anticommunists. The postwar decades saw an emphasis on religious belief as a distinguishing feature of the "American Way" against atheistic communism. Congress's insertion of the words "under God" into the Pledge of Allegiance in 1954 epitomized this Cold War impulse.

The Cold War influenced domestic politics and society in still other ways. Forceful advocates for racial justice and civil rights in unions, universities, and churches were often slandered as communists and fellow travelers. But at the same time competition with the Soviets for international support placed pressure on the United States to live up to its own stated democratic ideals. An example of the new international politics of civil rights came in 1948, when President Truman issued his landmark **Executive Order 9981** desegregating the armed forces.

McCarthyism *A brand of vitriolic, fear-mongering anticommunism associated with the career of Senator Joseph McCarthy. In the early 1950s, Senator McCarthy used his position in Congress to baselessly accuse high-ranking government officials and other Americans of conspiracy with communism. The term named after him refers to the dangerous forces of unfairness and fear wrought by anticommunist paranoia.*

Army-McCarthy hearings (1954) *Congressional hearings called by Senator Joseph McCarthy to accuse members of the army of communist ties. In this widely televised spectacle, McCarthy finally went too far for public approval. The hearings exposed the senator's extremism and led to his eventual disgrace.*

Executive Order 9981 (1948) *Order issued by President Truman to desegregate the armed forces. The president's action resulted from a combination of pressure from civil rights advocates, election-year political calculations, and the new geopolitical context of the Cold War.*

★ Postwar Economic Anxieties

The communist menace was not the only specter haunting Americans after World War II. The decade of the 1930s had left deep scars. Joblessness and insecurity had pushed up the suicide rate and dampened the marriage rate. Babies went unborn as pinched budgets and sagging self-esteem wrought a sexual depression in American bedrooms. The war had banished the blight of depression, but grim-faced observers warned that peace would bring the return of hard times.

The faltering economy in the initial postwar years threatened to confirm the worst predictions of the doomsayers who foresaw another Great Depression. Real gross national product (GNP) slumped sickeningly in 1946 and 1947 from its wartime peak. With the removal of wartime price controls, prices giddily levitated by 33 percent in 1946–1947. An epidemic of strikes swept the country. During 1946 alone some 4.6 million laborers laid down their tools, fearful that soon they would barely be able to afford the autos and other consumer goods their war-commandeered factories would soon manufacture.

The growing muscle of organized labor deeply annoyed many conservatives. They had their revenge against labor's New Deal gains in 1947, when a Republican-controlled Congress (the first in fourteen years) passed the **Taft-Hartley Act** over President Truman's vigorous veto. Labor leaders condemned the Taft-Hartley Act as a "slave-labor law." It outlawed the "closed" (all-union) shop, made unions liable for damages resulting from jurisdictional disputes, and required union leaders to take a noncommunist oath.

Taft-Hartley was one of several obstacles that slowed the growth of organized labor in the years after World War II. The unions' efforts to spread the triumph of their New Deal success in the North to historically antiunion regions of the South and West proved frustrating. The CIO's **Operation Dixie**, aimed at unionizing southern textile workers and steelworkers in 1948, failed miserably, partly due to white workers' fears of racial mixing. Organized labor continued to play a significant role in shaping the American social and economic order for several decades after World War II, but private-sector union membership peaked in the 1950s and then began a long, slow decline.

The Democratic administration meanwhile took steps of its own to forestall an economic downturn. It sold war factories and other government installations to private businesses at fire-sale prices. It secured passage of the **Employment Act of 1946**, which created a three-member Council of Economic Advisers to advise the president on government policy and to "promote maximum employment, production, and purchasing power."

Most dramatic was the passage of the Servicemen's Readjustment Act of 1944—better known as the GI Bill of Rights, or the **GI Bill**. Enacted partly out of fear that the employment markets would never be able to absorb 15 million returning veterans at war's end, the GI Bill made generous provisions for sending the former soldiers to school. In the postwar decade, some 8 million veterans advanced their educations at Uncle Sam's expense. The majority attended technical and vocational schools, but colleges and universities were crowded to the blackboards as more than 2 million ex-GIs stormed the halls of higher learning. The total eventually spent for education was some $14.5 billion in taxpayer dollars. The act also enabled the Veterans Administration (VA) to guarantee about $16 billion in loans for veterans to buy homes, farms, and small businesses. By raising educational levels and stimulating the construction industry, the GI Bill powerfully nurtured the robust and long-lived economic expansion that eventually took hold in the late 1940s and that profoundly shaped the postwar era.

★ Democratic Divisions in 1948

Attacking high prices and "High-Tax Harry" Truman, the Republicans had won control of Congress in the congressional elections of 1946. Their prospects had seldom looked rosier as they gathered in Philadelphia to choose their 1948 presidential candidate. They noisily renominated New York governor Thomas E. Dewey, still as debonair as if he had stepped out of a bandbox.

Also gathering in Philadelphia, Democratic politicos looked without enthusiasm on their hand-me-down president and sang "I'm Just Mild About Harry." But a "dump

---

Taft-Hartley Act (1947) *Republican-promoted, antiunion legislation passed over President Truman's vigorous veto that weakened many of labor's New Deal gains by banning the closed shop and other strategies that helped unions organize. It also required union leaders to take a noncommunist oath, which purged the union movement of many of its most committed and active organizers.*

Operation Dixie (1948) *Failed effort by the CIO after World War II to unionize southern workers, especially in textile factories.*

Employment Act of 1946 *Legislation declaring that the government's economic policy should aim to promote maximum employment, production, and purchasing power, as well as to keep inflation low. This general commitment was much shorter on specific targets and rules than its liberal creators had wished. The act created the Council of Economic Advisers to provide the president with data and recommendations to make economic policy.*

GI Bill (1944) *Known officially as the Servicemen's Readjustment Act and more informally as the GI Bill of Rights, this law helped returning World War II soldiers reintegrate into civilian life by securing loans to buy homes and farms and set up small businesses. It also made tuition and stipends available for them to attend college, as well as job training programs. The act was intended to cushion the blow of 15 million returning servicemen on the employment market and to nurture the postwar economy.*

Going to College on the GI Bill Financed by the federal government, thousands of World War II veterans crowded into college classrooms in the late 1940s. Universities struggled to house these older students, many of whom already had families. Pennsylvania State College resorted to setting up hundreds of trailers.

Truman" movement collapsed when war hero Dwight D. Eisenhower refused to be drafted. The peppery president, unwanted but undaunted, was then chosen in the face of vehement opposition by southern delegates, alienated by his strong stand in favor of civil rights for blacks, especially his desegregation of the military.

Truman's nomination split the party wide open. Embittered southern Democrats from thirteen states, like their fire-eating forebears of 1860, met in their own convention in Birmingham, Alabama, with Confederate flags brashly in evidence. Amid scenes of heated defiance, these "Dixiecrats" nominated Governor J. Strom Thurmond of South Carolina on a States' Rights party ticket.

To add to the confusion within Democratic ranks, former vice president Henry A. Wallace threw his hat into the ring. Having parted company with the administration over its get-tough-with-Russia policy, he was nominated by the new Progressive party—a bizarre collection of disgruntled former New Dealers, starry-eyed pacifists, well-meaning liberals, and communist-fronters.

Wallace, a vigorous if misguided liberal, assailed Uncle Sam's "dollar imperialism" from the stump. This so-called Pied Piper of the Politburo took a Soviet-friendly line that earned him drenchings with rotten eggs in hostile cities. But to his supporters, Wallace raised the only hopeful voice in the deepening gloom of the Cold War.

With the Democrats ruptured three ways and the Republican congressional victory of 1946 just past, Dewey's victory seemed assured. Cold, smug, and overconfident, Dewey confined himself to dispensing soothing-syrup trivialities like "Our future lies before us."

The seemingly doomed Truman, with little money and few active supporters, had to rely on his "gut-fighter" instincts and folksy personality. Traveling the country by train to deliver some three hundred "give 'em hell" speeches, he lashed out at the Taft-Hartley "slave labor" law and the "do-nothing" Republican Congress while whipping up

> *In his inaugural address, January 1949, President Harry S. Truman (1884–1972) said:*
>
> **"Communism is based on the belief that man is so weak and inadequate that he is unable to govern himself, and therefore requires the rule of strong masters.... Democracy is based on the conviction that man has the moral and intellectual capacity, as well as the inalienable right, to govern himself with reason and justice."**

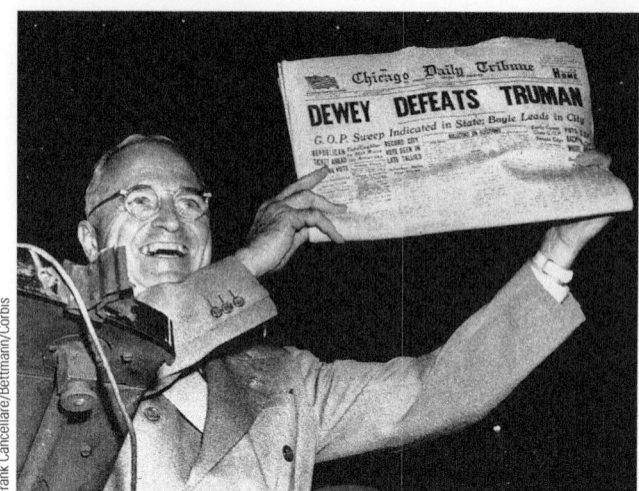

That Ain't the Way I Heard It! Truman wins.

support for his program of civil rights, improved labor benefits, and health insurance. "Pour it on 'em, Harry!" cried increasingly large and enthusiastic crowds as the pugnacious president rained a barrage of verbal uppercuts on his opponent.

On election night the *Chicago Tribune* ran off an early edition with the headline "DEWEY DEFEATS TRUMAN." But in the morning it turned out that "President" Dewey had embarrassingly snatched defeat from the jaws of victory. Truman had swept to a stunning triumph, to the complete bewilderment of politicians, pollsters, prophets, and pundits. Even though Thurmond took away 39 electoral votes in the South, Truman won 303 electoral votes, primarily from the South, Midwest, and West, besting Dewey's largely Eastern-based total of 189. To make the victory sweeter, the Democrats regained control of Congress as well, thanks especially to support from Republican-wary farmers, workers, and African Americans.

Smiling and self-assured, Truman sounded a clarion note in the fourth point of his inaugural address, known thereafter as "Point Four." The plan was to lend U.S. money and technical aid to underdeveloped lands to help them help themselves. This farseeing program was officially launched in 1950, and it brought badly needed assistance to impoverished countries, notably in Latin America, Africa, the Middle East, and Asia.

At home Truman outlined a sweeping **Fair Deal** program in his 1949 message to Congress. The program called for improved housing, full employment, a higher minimum wage, better farm price supports, new TVAs, and an extension of Social Security. But most of the Fair Deal fell victim to congressional opposition from Republicans and southern Democrats. The only major successes came in raising the minimum wage, providing for public housing in the Housing Act of 1949, and extending old-age insurance to many more beneficiaries in the Social Security Act of 1950. Short-term legislative obstacles to reform, however, paled against the seismic shifts in the domestic economy that brought substantial improvements to many Americans' lives.

Fair Deal *President Truman's extensive social program introduced in his 1949 message to Congress. Republicans and southern Democrats kept much of his vision from being enacted, except for raising the minimum wage, providing for more public housing, and extending old-age insurance to many more beneficiaries under the Social Security Act.*

★ The Long Economic Boom, 1950–1970

Gross national product began to climb haltingly in 1948. Then, beginning about 1950, the American economy surged onto a dazzling plateau of sustained growth that was to last virtually uninterrupted for two decades. America's economic performance became the envy of the world. National income nearly doubled in the 1950s and almost doubled again in the 1960s, shooting through the trillion-dollar mark in 1973. Americans, some 6 percent of the world's people, were enjoying about 40 percent of the planet's wealth.

Nothing loomed larger in the history of the post–World War II era than this fantastic eruption of affluence. It did not enrich all Americans, and it did not touch all people evenly, but it transformed the lives of a majority of citizens and molded the agenda of politics and society for at least two generations. Prosperity underwrote social mobility, paved the way for the civil rights movement, funded vast new welfare programs like Medicare, and gave Americans the confidence to exercise unprecedented international leadership in the Cold War era.

As the gusher of prosperity poured forth its riches, Americans drank deeply from the gilded goblet. Millions of depression-pinched souls sought to make up for the sufferings of the 1930s. They determined to "get theirs" while the getting was good. A people who had once considered a chicken in every pot the standard of comfort and security now hungered for two cars in every garage, swimming pools in their backyards, vacation homes, and gas-guzzling recreational vehicles. The size of the "middle class," defined as households earning between $3,000 and $10,000 a year, doubled from pre–Great Depression days and included 60 percent of the American people by the mid-1950s. By the end of that decade, the vast majority of American families owned their own cars and washing machines, and nearly 90 percent owned a television set. In another revolution of sweeping consequences, almost 60 percent of American families owned their own homes by 1960, compared with less than 40 percent in the 1920s.

Of all the beneficiaries of postwar prosperity, none reaped greater rewards than women. More than ever, urban offices and shops provided a bonanza of employment for female workers, as the service sector of the economy dramatically outgrew the old industrial and manufacturing sectors. Women accounted for a quarter of the American work force at the end of World War II and for nearly half the labor pool five decades later. Yet even as women continued their march into the workplace in the 1940s and 1950s, popular culture glorified the traditional feminine roles of homemaker and mother. The clash between the demands of suburban housewifery and the realities of employment eventually sparked a feminist revolt in the 1960s.

What propelled this unprecedented economic explosion? The Second World War itself provided a powerful stimulus. While other countries had been ravaged by years of fighting, the United States had used the war crisis to fire up its smokeless factories and rebuild its depression-plagued economy. America had almost effortlessly come to dominate the ruined global landscape of the postwar period.

Ominously, much of the glittering prosperity of the 1950s and 1960s rested on the underpinnings of colossal military budgets, leading some critics to speak of a "permanent war economy." The economic upturn of 1950 was fueled by massive appropriations for the Korean War, and defense spending accounted for some 10 percent of the GNP throughout the ensuing decade. Pentagon dollars primed the pumps of high-technology industries such as aerospace, plastics, and electronics and also financed much of the scientific research and development ("R and D") that spurred the economy.

Cheap energy also fed the economic boom. Americans doubled their consumption of inexpensive and seemingly inexhaustible oil from the Middle East and elsewhere in the quarter century after the war. Anticipating a limitless future of low-cost fuels, they flung out endless ribbons of highways, installed air conditioning in their homes, and engineered a sixfold increase in the country's electricity-generating capacity between 1945 and 1970.

With the forces of nature increasingly harnessed in their hands, workers chalked up spectacular gains in productivity. In the two decades after the outbreak of the Korean War in 1950, productivity increased at an average rate of more than 3 percent per year. Gains in productivity were also enhanced by the rising educational level of the work force. By 1970 nearly 90 percent of the school-age population were enrolled in educational institutions. Better educated and better equipped, American workers in 1970 could produce nearly twice as much in an hour's labor as they had in 1950. Productivity was the key to prosperity. Rising productivity in the 1950s and 1960s virtually doubled the average American's standard of living in the postwar quarter century.

Also contributing to the vigor of the postwar economy was the accelerating shift of the workforce out of agriculture into industry. Agriculture achieved spectacular gains in productivity, thanks largely to mechanization and rich new fertilizers. Giant agribusinesses replaced the family farm, and farmers whose forebears had busted sod with horses now plowed their fields in air-conditioned cabs. Still some 15 percent of the labor force at the end of World War II, farmers made up a slim 2 percent of working Americans by the turn of the twenty-first century—yet they fed much of the world.

★ The Smiling Sunbelt

The convulsive economic changes of the post-1945 period shook and shifted the American people, amplifying the population redistribution set in motion by World War II. As immigrants and westward-trekking pioneers, Americans had always been a people on the move, but they were astonishingly footloose in the postwar years. For some three decades after 1945, an average of 30 million persons changed residences every year. Families especially felt the strain, as distance divided parents from children, and brothers and sisters from one another. One sign of this sort of stress was the phenomenal popularity of advice books on child rearing, especially Dr. Benjamin Spock's *The Common Sense Book of Baby and Child Care*. First published in 1945, the book instructed millions of parents during the

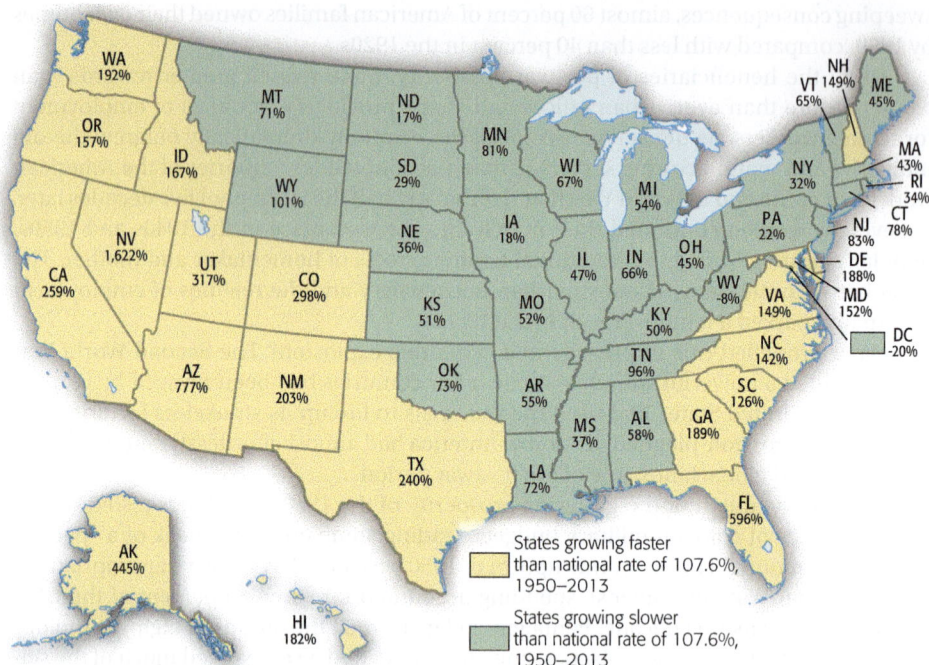

Map 35.3 Distribution of Population Increase, 1950–2013 States with figures higher than 106.7 percent were growing faster than the national average between 1950 and 2013. Note that much of the growth was in the "Sunbelt," a loose geographical concept, as some Deep South states had very little population growth, whereas the mountain and Pacific states were booming.

Sunbelt *The fifteen-state crescent through the American South and Southwest that experienced terrific population and productivity expansion during World War II and particularly in the decades after the war, eclipsing the old industrial Northeast (the "Frostbelt").*

ensuing decades in the kind of homely wisdom that was once transmitted naturally from grandparent to parent, and from parent to child.

Especially striking was the growth of the **Sunbelt**—a fifteen-state area stretching in a smiling crescent from Virginia through Florida and Texas to Arizona and California. This region increased its population at a rate nearly double that of the old industrial zones of the Northeast (the "Frostbelt"). In the 1950s California alone accounted for one-fifth of the entire nation's population growth and by 1963 had outdistanced New York as the most populous state—a position it still holds in the early years of the twenty-first century, with more than 38 million people, or more than one out of every eight Americans.

A Niagara of federal dollars accounted for much of the Sunbelt's prosperity, though, ironically, southern and western politicians led the cry against government spending. By the early twenty-first century, states in the South and West were annually receiving some $444 billion more in federal funds than those in the Northeast and Midwest. Northeasterners and their allies from the hard-hit region of the Ohio Valley tried to rally political support with the sarcastic slogan "The North shall rise again."

These dramatic shifts of population and wealth further broke the historic grip of the North on the nation's political life. Every elected occupant of the White House from 1964 to 2008 hailed from the Sunbelt, and the region's congressional representation rose as its population grew.

★ The Rush to the Suburbs

In all regions, America's modern migrants—if they were white—fled from the cities to the burgeoning new suburbs (see "Makers of America: The Suburbanites," p. 623). While other industrial countries struggled to rebuild their war-ravaged cities, government policies in the United States encouraged movement away from urban centers. Federal

Makers of America

The Suburbanites

Few images evoke more vividly the prosperity of the postwar era than aerial photographs of sprawling suburbs. Neat rows of look-alike tract houses, each with driveway and lawn and here and there a backyard swimming pool, came to symbolize the capacity of the economy to deliver the "American dream" to millions of families.

Suburbanization was hardly new. Well-off city dwellers had beaten paths to leafy outlying neighborhoods since the nineteenth century. But after 1945 the steady flow became a stampede. The baby boom, new highways, government guarantees for mortgage lending, and favorable tax policies all made suburbia blossom.

Who were the Americans racing to the new postwar suburbs? War veterans led the way in the immediate postwar years, aided by low-interest Veterans Administration mortgages. People of all kinds followed, heading for neighborhoods that varied from the posh to the plain. Yet the overwhelming majority of suburbanites were white and middle class. In 1967 sociologist Herbert Gans published *The Levittowners*, based on his own move to a Levitt-built community outside Philadelphia. He described suburban families in tract developments as predominantly third- or fourth-generation Americans with some college education and at least two children. Men tended to work in either white-collar jobs or upper-level blue-collar positions. Women usually worked in the home, so much so that suburbia came to symbolize domestic confinement for feminists of the 1960s and 1970s.

The house itself became more important than ever as postwar suburbanites built their leisure lives around television, home improvement projects, and barbecues on the patio. The center of family life shifted to the fenced-in backyard, and institutions that had thrived as social centers in the city—churches, women's clubs, fraternal organizations, taverns—had a tougher time attracting patrons in the privatized world of postwar surburbia.

Life in the suburbs was a boon to the automobile, as parents jumped behind the wheel to shuttle children, groceries, and golf clubs to and fro. Drive-thru restaurants and drive-in movies sprang up, and roadside shopping centers edged out downtowns as places to shop. Meanwhile, the new interstate highway system enabled breadwinners to live farther from their jobs and still commute to work daily.

Many suburbanites continued to depend on cities for jobs, though by the 1980s the suburbs themselves became important sites of employment. Wherever they worked, suburbanites turned their backs on the city and its problems. They fought to maintain their independent municipalities as secluded retreats, with their own taxes, schools, and zoning restrictions designed to keep out public housing and the poor. Even the naming of towns reflected the pastoral ideal.

East Paterson, New Jersey, was renamed Elmwood Park in 1973. With a majority of Americans living in suburbs by the 1980s, cities lost their political clout. Bereft of state and federal aid, cities festered with worsening social problems: poverty, drug addiction, and crime.

Middle-class African Americans began to move to the suburbs in substantial numbers by the 1980s, but even that migration failed to alter dramatically the racial divide of metropolitan America. Black suburbanites settled in black middle-class suburbs within white-majority counties. By the beginning of the twenty-first century, suburbia as a whole was more racially diverse than at midcentury. But the old patterns of residential segregation endured, and economic inequality increasingly separated older and poorer "inner-ring" suburbs from new more middle-class ones.

Drive-in Café in Los Angeles, the Mother and Model of All Suburbias

Housing Authority (FHA) and Veterans Administration (VA) home-loan guarantees made it more economically attractive to own a home in the suburbs than to rent an apartment in the city. Tax deductions for interest payments on home mortgages provided additional financial incentive. And government-built highways that sped commuters from suburban homes to city jobs further facilitated this mass migration. By 1960 one in every four Americans dwelt in suburbia, and a half-century later, more than half the nation's population did.

The construction industry boomed in the 1950s and 1960s to satisfy this demand. Pioneered by innovators such as the Levitt brothers, whose first **Levittown** sprouted on New York's Long Island in the 1940s, builders revolutionized the techniques of mass-produced housing construction. Snooty critics wailed about the aesthetic monotony of the suburban "tract" developments, but eager homebuyers nevertheless moved into them by the millions.

"White flight" to the leafy green suburbs left the inner cities—especially in the Northeast and Midwest—black, brown, and broke. Migrating blacks from the South filled up the urban neighborhoods abandoned by the departing white middle class (see "Makers of America: The Great African American Migration," p. 633). Taxpaying businesses fled with their affluent customers from downtown shops to suburban shopping malls.

Government policies sometimes aggravated this spreading pattern of residential segregation. FHA administrators often refused home mortgage loans to blacks and "other unharmonious racial or nationality groups," thus limiting black mobility out of the inner cities. Even public housing programs frequently built housing for blacks in neighborhoods that were already predominantly black—thus solidifying racial separation. Government-supported residential discrimination not only worsened segregation, but also fed the long-term "wealth gap" between whites and blacks, since most Americans' wealth consists primarily of the value of their home.

Levittown *Suburban communities with mass-produced tract houses built in the New York and Philadelphia metropolitan areas in the 1950s by William Levitt and Sons. Typically inhabited by white middle-class people who fled the cities in search of homes to buy for their growing families.*

⭐ The Postwar Baby Boom

Alongside its economic boom, America experienced an equally dramatic **baby boom**—the huge leap in the birthrate in the decade and a half after 1945. Confident young men and women tied the nuptial knot in record numbers at war's end, and they began immediately to fill the nation's empty cradles. They thus touched off a demographic explosion that added more than 50 million bawling babies to the nation's population by the end of the 1950s. The soaring birthrate finally crested in 1957 and was followed by a deepening birth dearth. By 1973 fertility rates had dropped below the point necessary to maintain existing population figures without further immigration.

This boom-or-bust cycle of births begat a bulging wave along the American population curve. As the oversize postwar generation grew to maturity, it was destined—like the fabled pig passing through the python—to strain and distort many aspects of American life. Elementary-school enrollments, for example, swelled to nearly 34 million pupils in 1970. Then began a steady decline, as the onward-marching age group left in its wake closed schools and unemployed teachers.

The maturing babies of the postwar boom sent economic shock waves undulating through the decades. The baby boomers created lucrative markets for toys and baby food in the 1940s and 1950s and for clothes and recorded rock music in the 1960s. In the 1980s the hordes of baby boomers bumped and jostled one another in the job market, struggling to get a foothold on the crowded ladder of social mobility. As the boomers entered middle age, a "secondary boom" of children peaked in the early 1990s—a faint demographic echo of the postwar population explosion. The impact of the huge postwar generation will continue to ripple through American society well into the twenty-first century, as members pass into retirement and place enormous strains on the Social Security and Medicare systems.

baby boom (1946–1964) *Demographic explosion from births to returning soldiers and others who had put off starting families during the war. This large generation of new Americans forced the expansion of many institutions such as schools and universities.*

Varying Viewpoints

Who Was to Blame for the Cold War?

Whose fault was the Cold War? (And, for that matter, who should get credit for ending it?) For two decades after World War II, American historians generally agreed that the aggressive Soviets were solely responsible. This "orthodox" or "official" appraisal squared with the traditional view of the United States as a virtuous, innocent land with an idealistic foreign policy. This point of view also justified America's Cold War containment policy, which cast the Soviet Union as an aggressor that must be confined by an ever-vigilant United States. America supposedly had only defensive intentions, with no expansionary ambitions of its own.

In the 1960s a vigorous revisionist interpretation flowered, powerfully influenced by disillusion over U.S. involvement in Vietnam. The revisionists stood the orthodox view on its head. The Soviets, they argued, had only defensive intentions at the end of World War II; it was the Americans who behaved provocatively by brandishing their new atomic weaponry. Some of these critics pointed an accusing finger at President Truman, alleging that he abandoned Roosevelt's conciliatory approach to the Soviets and adopted a bullying attitude, emboldened by the American atomic monopoly.

More radical revisionists such as Gabriel and Joyce Kolko even claimed to have found the roots of Truman's alleged belligerence in long-standing American policies of economic imperialism—policies that eventually resulted in the tragedy of Vietnam. In this view the Vietnam War followed logically from America's insatiable "need" for overseas markets and raw materials. Vietnam itself may have been economically unimportant, but revisionists believed that losing in Vietnam would have undermined American hegemony and eventually unraveled the American economy.

In the 1970s a "postrevisionist" interpretation emerged that is widely agreed upon today. Historians such as John Lewis Gaddis and Melvyn Leffler pooh-pooh the economic determinism of the revisionists, while frankly acknowledging that the United States did have vital security interests at stake in the post–World War II era. The postrevisionists analyze the ways in which inherited ideas (such as isolationism) and the contentious nature of post–World War II domestic politics, as well as miscalculations by American leaders, led a nation in search of security into seeking not simply a sufficiency but a "preponderance" of power. The American *overreaction* to its security needs, these scholars suggest, exacerbated U.S.-Soviet relations and precipitated the four-decade-long nuclear arms race that formed the centerpiece of the Cold War.

In the case of Vietnam, the postrevisionist historians focus not on economic necessity but on a failure of political intelligence, induced by the stressful conditions of the Cold War, that made the dubious domino theory—the belief that failure in Vietnam would cause other nations to tumble like dominoes into the Soviet camp—seem plausible. Misunderstanding Vietnamese intentions, exaggerating Soviet ambitions, and fearing to appear "soft on communism" in the eyes of their domestic political rivals, American leaders plunged into Vietnam, sadly misguided by their own Cold War obsessions.

Most postrevisionists, however, still lay the lion's share of the blame for the Cold War on the Soviet Union. By the same token, they credit the Soviets with ending the Cold War—a view hotly disputed by Ronald Reagan's champions, who claim it was his anti-Soviet policies in the 1980s that brought the Russians to their knees (see p. 690). The great unknown, of course, is the precise nature of Soviet thinking in the Cold War years. Were Soviet aims predominantly defensive, or did the Kremlin incessantly plot world conquest? Was there an opportunity for reconciliation with the West following Stalin's death in 1953? Should Mikhail Gorbachev or Ronald Reagan be remembered as the leader who ended the Cold War? With the opening of Soviet archives, scholars are eagerly pursuing answers to such questions.

CHAPTER SUMMARY ★ ★ ★ ★ ★ ★ ★ ★ ★ ★ ★ ★

With the death of Franklin Roosevelt as World War II came to a close, Harry S. Truman was suddenly launched into the presidency. Regarded at first as a weak and fumbling figure, Truman evolved into a courageous statesman who boldly addressed unprecedented international and domestic challenges. The Yalta agreement near the end of World War II left major issues undecided and created growing controversy over postwar relations with the Soviet Union. The two new ideologically incompatible superpowers soon found themselves at odds over Eastern Europe, Germany, and the Middle East. A battered Europe, especially in Italy and France, threatened to succumb to powerful internal Communist parties.

The Truman Doctrine announced military aid to threatened noncommunist nations and an ideological crusade against international communism. The Marshall Plan provided economic assistance to starving and communist-threatened Europe, which soon joined the United States in the permanent NATO military alliance. But the triumph of communism in China created bitter divisions within the United States. Communist North Korea's unprovoked attack on pro-Western South Korea in 1950 led to the seesaw Korean War and to a massive American military buildup. General Douglas MacArthur's insubordination and threats to expand the war to China led Truman to fire him.

The Cold War and revelations of Soviet spying aroused deep fears of communist subversion at home, which spread into a general assault on the socially "deviant." Issues of the Cold War and civil rights fractured the Democratic party three ways in 1948, but a gutsy Truman campaign overcame the divisions to win a triumphant underdog victory over Dewey, Thurmond, and Wallace.

The Cold War and revelations of Soviet spying aroused deep fears of communist subversion at home, which spread into a general assault on alleged communist sympathizers as well as the socially marginal. Demagogic Wisconsin Senator Joseph McCarthy gained immense power with his irresponsible attacks, but finally collapsed after attacking the U.S. Army.

In the immediate postwar years there were widespread fears of a return to depression. But fueled by cheap energy, increased worker productivity, and government programs such as the GI Bill of Rights, the economy began a spectacular expansion that lasted from 1950 to 1970. This burst of affluence transformed American industry and society. More women joined the work force even as popular culture glorified the roles of mother and homemaker.

Footloose Americans migrated to the Sunbelts of the South and West and to the growing suburbs, leaving the northeastern cities with poorer populations. Families grew rapidly, as the "baby boom" created a population bulge that would last for decades.

KEY TERMS

- Yalta conference (608)
- Cold War (609)
- Bretton Woods Conference (609)
- United Nations (U.N.) (610)
- Nuremberg war crimes trial (610)
- Berlin airlift (611)
- containment doctrine (611)
- Truman Doctrine (613)
- Marshall Plan (613)
- North Atlantic Treaty Organization (NATO) (613)
- National Security Council Memorandum Number 68 (NSC-68) (614)
- Korean War (615)
- House Un-American Activities Committee (HUAC) (616)
- McCarthyism (617)
- Army-McCarthy hearings (617)
- Executive Order 9981 (617)
- Taft-Hartley Act (618)
- Operation Dixie (618)
- Employment Act of 1946 (618)
- GI Bill (618)
- Fair Deal (620)
- Sunbelt (622)
- Levittown (624)
- baby boom (624)

PEOPLE TO KNOW

- Joseph Stalin
- Jiang Jieshi
- George F. Kennan
- George C. Marshall
- Joseph McCarthy
- Reinhold Niebuhr
- Benjamin Spock

MindTap is a fully online, highly personalized learning experience built upon Cengage Learning content. MindTap combines student learning tools—readings, multimedia, activities, and assessments—into a singular Learning Path that guides students through the course.

Chapter 36

American Zenith
1952–1963

Our soil is fertile, our agriculture productive. The air rings with the song of our industry—rolling mills and blast furnaces, dynamos, dams and assembly lines—the chorus of America the bountiful. . . . We live in a land of plenty, but rarely has this earth known such peril as today.

Dwight D. Eisenhower, January 21, 1957

Unmatched in power or plenty, the United States bestrode the world like a colossus as the 1950s began to unfold. Broadly shared prosperity fueled confidence in the country's capacity to tackle major problems at home and abroad. But problems abounded nonetheless. Americans at midcentury were dug into the frontlines of the global Cold War while bitterly divided at home over the explosive issues of communist subversion and civil rights.

Chapter Outline

- Affluence and Consumer Culture
- Eisenhower Republicanism
- Martin Luther King, Jr., and the Early Civil Rights Movement
- Eisenhower's Domestic and Foreign Policies
- The Fluctuating Cold War
- John F. Kennedy Defeats Richard Nixon, 1960
- Postwar Literature and Culture
- The Kennedy Promise
- Ventures in Vietnam and Cuba
- Civil Rights Rising
- *Makers of America: The Great African American Migration*
- *Examining the Evidence: The Shopping Mall as New Town Square, 1960*

FOCUS QUESTIONS

1. What changes in the American economy and work force fueled the rise of a mass, popular consumer culture in the 1950s?

2. What were the origins of the modern American civil rights movement, and what challenges did it face amidst the generally conservative political and social environment of the 1950s? What enabled the movement to gain political momentum in the early 1960s?

3. What were the fundamental principles of "Eisenhower Republicanism" at home and abroad? How did Eisenhower manage to address numerous Cold War crises while avoiding war?

4. How did the American cultural "renaissance" of the 1950s and early 1960s reflect American affluence and prestige? Which writers and artists were more critical of America and the "American dream"?

5. Why did John F. Kennedy's "New Frontier" raise such high expectations, and to what extent were those expectations met?

CHRONOLOGY

1952	• Eisenhower defeats Stevenson for presidency • Ellison publishes *Invisible Man*	1958	• NDEA authorizes loans and grants for science and language education • Galbraith publishes *The Affluent Society*
1953	• CIA-engineered coup installs shah of Iran • Joseph Stalin dies	1958–1959	• Berlin crisis
1954	• French defeated at Dien Bien Phu in Vietnam • *Brown v. Board of Education*. • Nasser becomes president of Egypt • CIA-sponsored coup in Guatemala	1959	• Castro seizes power in Cuba • Landrum-Griffin Act • Alaska and Hawaii attain statehood
		1960	• Sit-in movement for civil rights begins • U-2 incident sabotages Paris summit • OPEC formed • Kennedy defeats Nixon for presidency • Updike publishes *Rabbit, Run*
1955	• Montgomery bus boycott by blacks begins; emergence of Martin Luther King, Jr. • Geneva summit meeting on Vietnam • AF of L merges with CIO • Tennessee Williams's *Cat on a Hot Tin Roof* first performed	1961	• Heller publishes *Catch-22* • Berlin Wall built • Alliance for Progress • Bay of Pigs invasion • Kennedy sends "military advisers" to South Vietnam
1956	• Soviets crush Hungarian revolt • Suez crisis • Eisenhower defeats Stevenson for presidency • Ginsberg publishes *Howl and Other Poems*	1962	• Pressure from Kennedy results in rollback of steel prices • Trade Expansion Act • Cuban missile crisis
1957	• Little Rock school desegregation crisis • Civil Rights Act passed • Southern Christian Leadership Conference (SCLC) formed • Soviet Union launches *Sputnik* satellites • European Economic Community (EEC, Common Market) created	1963	• Plath publishes *The Bell Jar* • Anti-Diem coup in South Vietnam • Civil rights march in Washington, D.C. • Kennedy assassinated; Johnson assumes presidency

★ Affluence and Its Anxieties

The continuing post–World War II economic boom wrought wondrous changes in American society in the 1950s. Prosperity triggered a fabulous surge in home construction: One of every four homes standing in America in 1960 had been built in the 1950s, and 83 percent of those new homes were in the suburbs.

In a period marked by massive military spending and public investment in research, science and technology drove economic growth more than ever. The invention of the transistor in 1948 sparked a revolution in electronics, and especially in computers. The first electronic computers in the 1940s were massive machines with fickle cathode ray tubes, but transistors and, later, printed circuits on silicon wafers made possible dramatic miniaturization and phenomenal computational speed. Computer giant International Business Machines (IBM) became the prototype of the "high-tech" corporation in the dawning "information age." Aerospace industries also grew fantastically in the 1950s, thanks both to the government's building of the Strategic Air Command and to a robustly expanding passenger airline business—as well as to connections between military and civilian aircraft production. Seattle-based Boeing Company brought out the first large passenger jet, the "707," in 1957, whose design owed much to the previous development of SAC's long-range strategic bomber.

The nature of the work force was also changing. A quiet revolution was marked in 1956 when "white-collar" workers for the first time outnumbered "blue-collar" workers, signaling the passage from an industrial to a postindustrial or service-based economy.

Keeping pace with that fundamental transformation, organized labor withered as a percentage of the labor force, after peaking at about 35 percent in 1954.

The surge in white-collar employment opened special opportunities for women. When many women left the work force at the end of World War II, postwar popular culture developed a "cult of domesticity" celebrating the conventional female roles of wife and mother. When popular television programs like "Ozzie and Harriet" and "Leave It to Beaver" depicted idyllic suburban families with a working husband, two children, and a housebound wife they did so without irony; much of middle-class America really did live that way. But as the 1950s progressed, another quiet revolution was gaining momentum that was destined to transform women's roles and even the character of the American family.

Of some 40 million new jobs created in the three decades after 1950, more than 30 million were in clerical and service work. Women filled the huge majority of these new positions. These exploding employment opportunities for women unleashed a groundswell of social and psychological change that mounted to tidal-wave proportions in the decades that followed. In the new urban age, women's dual role as *both* workers and homemakers raised urgent questions about family life and about traditional definitions of gender differences.

Feminist Betty Friedan gave focus and fuel to women's feelings in 1963 when she published *The Feminine Mystique*, a runaway best-seller and a classic of the modern feminist movement. Friedan spoke in rousing accents to millions of able, educated women who applauded her indictment of the stifling boredom of suburban housewifery.

The Feminine Mystique (1963) *Best-selling book by feminist thinker Betty Friedan. This work challenged women to move beyond the drudgery of suburban housewifery and helped launch what would become second-wave feminism.*

★ Consumer Culture in the Fifties

The 1950s witnessed a huge expansion of the middle class and the blossoming of a consumer culture that defined a distinctive lifestyle. Diner's Club introduced the plastic credit card in 1949, just one year after the first "fast-food" McDonald's hamburger stand opened in San Bernardino, California. In 1955 Disneyland opened its doors in Anaheim, California. Easy credit, high-volume "fast-food" production, and new forms of leisure marked an emerging culture of consumption that soon moved beyond America's borders.

Crucial to the development of consumerism was the rapid rise of the new technology of television. Only 6 TV stations were broadcasting in 1946; a decade later 442 stations were operating. TV sets were rich people's novelties in the 1940s, but 7 million sets were sold in 1951. By 1960 virtually every American home had one, in a stunning display of the speed with which new technologies can pervade and transform modern societies. By the mid-1950s advertisers annually spent $10 billion to hawk their wares on television, while critics fumed that the wildly popular new mass medium was degrading the public's aesthetic, moral, political, and educational standards.

Even religion capitalized on the powerful new electronic pulpit. Celebrity preachers and priests like the Baptist Billy Graham, the Pentecostal Oral Roberts, and the Roman Catholic Fulton J. Sheen took to the airwaves to spread the Christian gospel. Television also catalyzed the commercialization of professional sports, as viewing audiences that once numbered in the stadium-capacity thousands could now be counted in the couch-potato millions.

Sports also reflected the shift in population toward the West and South. In 1958 baseball's New York Giants moved to San Francisco, and the Brooklyn Dodgers abandoned Flatbush for Los Angeles. Those moves touched off a new westward and southward movement of sports franchises. Shifting population and spreading affluence led eventually to substantial expansion of the major baseball leagues and the principal football and basketball leagues as well.

Popular music was also dramatically transformed in the 1950s. The chief revolutionary was Elvis Presley, a white singer born in 1935 in Tupelo, Mississippi. Fusing black rhythm and blues with white bluegrass and country styles, Elvis created a new musical idiom known forever after as **rock 'n' roll**. Listening and dancing to rock n' roll became a rite of passage for millions of young people around the world, from Japan to working-class Liverpool, England, where Elvis's music inspired teenagers John Lennon and Paul McCartney to form a band that would become the Beatles.

rock 'n' roll *"Crossover" musical style that rose to dominance in the 1950s, merging black rhythm and blues with white bluegrass and country. Featuring a heavy beat and driving rhythm, rock 'n' roll music became a defining feature of the 1950s youth culture.*

The King With his fleshy face, pouting lips, and antic, sexually suggestive gyrations, Elvis Presley became the high priest of rock 'n' roll in the 1950s, to the chagrin of parents everywhere. Bloated by fame, fortune, and drugs, he died in 1977 at the age of forty-two.

Traditionalists were repelled by Presley and much else in the affluent fifties. Movie star Marilyn Monroe, with her ingenuous smile and dangerous curves, helped to popularize—and commercialize—new standards of sensuous sexuality. So did *Playboy* magazine, whose first issue Monroe graced in 1953. As the decade closed, Americans were well on their way to becoming free-spending consumers of mass-produced, standardized products advertised on the electronic medium of television and often sold for their alleged sexual allure.

Many critics lamented the implications of this new consumerist lifestyle. Harvard sociologist David Riesman portrayed the postwar generation as a pack of conformists in *The Lonely Crowd* (1950), as did William H. Whyte, Jr., in *The Organization Man*. Harvard economist John Kenneth Galbraith bemoaned the spectacle of private opulence amidst public squalor in a series of books beginning with *The Affluent Society* (1958). But Galbraith's call to invest in the public good fell on mostly deaf ears in the giddily affluent 1950s.

★ The Advent of Eisenhower

Democratic prospects in the presidential election of 1952 were blighted by the military deadlock in Korea, Truman's clash with MacArthur, and war-bred inflation. Dispirited Democrats nominated Adlai E. Stevenson, the eloquent governor of Illinois. Republicans enthusiastically chose war hero General Dwight D. Eisenhower. Ike's running mate was California Senator Richard M. Nixon, who had gained notoriety as a relentless red-hunter.

Eisenhower was already the most popular American of his time, as "I Like Ike" buttons everywhere testified. Striking a grandfatherly, nonpartisan pose, Eisenhower left the rough campaigning to Nixon, who relished bare-knuckle political combat. The vice-presidential candidate lambasted his opponents with charges that they had cultivated corruption, caved in on Korea, and coddled communists. He particularly blasted the cerebral Stevenson as "Adlai the appeaser," with a "Ph.D. from [Secretary of State] Dean Acheson's College of Cowardly Communist Containment."

Nixon himself faltered late in the campaign amid accusations that he had accepted illegal donations. Responding with a self-pitying live address on television, Nixon denied the charges and solemnly declared that the only campaign gift he had ever received was the family cocker spaniel, Checkers. The shameless and mawkish **Checkers Speech** saved Nixon's spot on the ticket and spotlighted a fundamental change in American politics. Television allowed candidates to bypass traditional political party machinery and speak directly to voters.

The outcome of the presidential election of 1952 was never really in doubt. Given an extra prod by Eisenhower's last-minute pledge to go personally to Korea to end the war, the voters overwhelmingly declared for Ike. He garnered 33,936,234 votes to Stevenson's 27,314,992, ringing up 442 electoral votes to 89 for his opponent. Ike also managed to pull enough Republican legislators into office to gain GOP control of the new Congress by a hairbreadth.

True to his campaign pledge, president-elect Eisenhower flew to Korea in December 1952. Seven months later an armistice was finally signed. The brutal and futile fighting had lasted three years. More than thirty thousand Americans lay dead, joined by perhaps more than a million Chinese, North Koreans, and South Koreans. Tens of billions of American dollars had been poured down the Asian sinkhole. Yet this terrible toll in blood and treasure bought only a return to the conditions of 1950; Korea remained divided at the thirty-eighth parallel, while the broader Cold War remained frigidly frozen. Both in the military and civilian realms, Eisenhower had long cultivated a leadership style that self-consciously projected an image of sincerity, fairness, and optimism. Ike thus seemed

Checkers Speech (1952) *Nationally televised address by vice-presidential candidate Richard Nixon during which he defended himself against allegations of corruption. Using the new mass medium of television shortly before the 1952 election, Nixon saved his place on the ticket by saying the only campaign gift he had received was a cocker spaniel named Checkers.*

ideally suited to soothe the anxieties of troubled Americans who yearned for a period of calm. Ably playing this reassuring role, he presided over a decade of shaky peace and shining prosperity. Yet critics charged that he unwisely hoarded the "asset" of his immense popularity, rather than spend it for a good cause (especially civil rights), and that he displayed opportunism by initially failing to stand up to McCarthyist demagoguery.

★ Desegregating American Society

America counted some 15 million black citizens in 1950, two-thirds of whom still made their homes in the South. There they lived bound by the iron set of antiquated rules known as "Jim Crow" laws. Every day of their lives, southern blacks dealt with a bizarre array of separate arrangements that kept them socially insulated from whites, economically inferior, and politically powerless. Blacks in the South not only attended segregated schools but were compelled to use separate public toilets, drinking fountains, restaurants, and waiting rooms. Trains and buses had "whites only" and "colored only" seating. Only about 20 percent of eligible southern blacks were registered to vote, fewer than 5 percent in some Deep South states like Mississippi and Alabama.

Where the law proved insufficient to enforce this regime, vigilante violence did the job. Six black war veterans, claiming the rights for which they had fought overseas, were murdered in the summer of 1946. A Mississippi mob lynched black fourteen-year-old Emmett Till for allegedly leering at a white woman. It is small wonder that a black clergyman declared that "everywhere I go in the South the Negro is forced to choose between his hide and his soul."

Segregation tarnished America's international image, much as McCarthyism did. After the war, African American entertainers like Paul Robeson and Josephine Baker toured widely in Europe and Latin America, informing audiences about the horrors of Jim Crow and raising doubts about America's reputation as the beacon of freedom against Soviet communism. In response, the State Department confiscated Robeson's passport but had to find other ways to silence Baker, who had assumed French citizenship. Intellectuals poured on criticism as well. Swedish scholar Gunnar Myrdal published his landmark book, *An American Dilemma*, exposing the scandalous contradiction between the liberty-loving "American Creed" and the nation's shameful treatment of black citizens.

International pressure combined with grassroots and legal activism to propel some racial progress in the North after World War II. In a growing number of northern cities and states, African Americans battled for—and won—equal access to public accommodations like restaurants, hotels, theaters, and beaches (see "Makers of America: The Great African American Migration," p. 633). Jackie Robinson cracked baseball's color barrier when the Brooklyn Dodgers signed him in 1946. The repeal of the Chinese Exclusion Act in 1943 and the repeal of many state-level anti-miscegenation laws signaled the decline of legal discrimination against not only African Americans but other racial and ethnic minorities as well.

A black woman described the day-in, day-out humiliations of life in a Jim Crow South:

"You could not go to a white restaurant; you sat in a special place at the movie house; and Lord knows, you sat in the back of the bus. It didn't make any difference if you were rich or poor, if you were black you were nothing. You might have a hundred dollars in your pocket, but if you went to the store you would wait at the side until all the clerks got through with all the white folks, no matter if they didn't have change for a dollar. Then the clerk would finally look at you and say, 'Oh, did you want something? I didn't see you there.'"

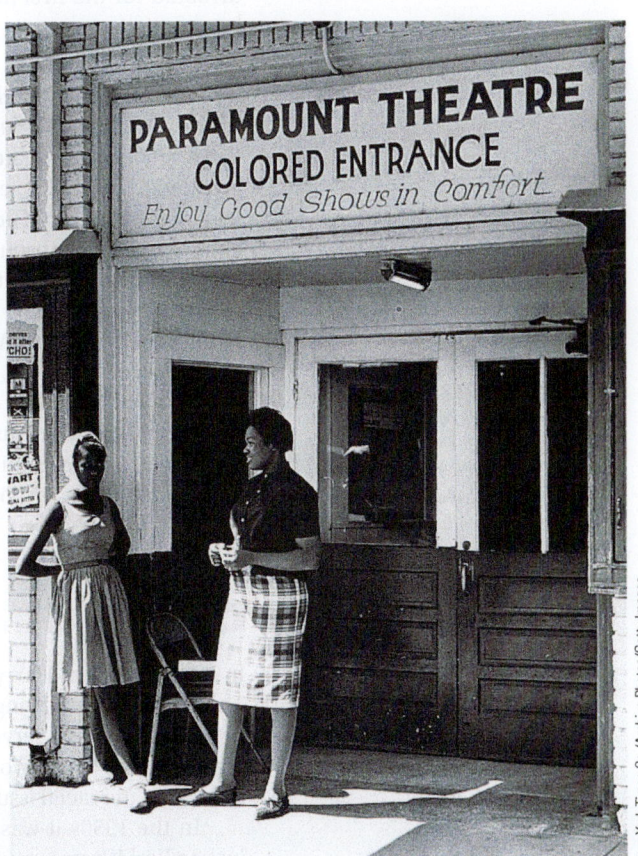

The Face of Segregation These women in the segregated South of the 1950s were compelled to enter the movie theater through the "Colored Entrance." Once inside, they were restricted to a separate seating section, usually in the rear of the theater.

Martin Luther King, Jr., and His Wife, Coretta, Arrested King and his wife were arrested for the first time in Montgomery, Alabama, in 1955 while organizing a bus boycott.

The South saw little of that progress in the early postwar years—but increasingly, African Americans refused to suffer in silence. On a chilly day in December 1955, Rosa Parks, a college-educated black seamstress, made history in Montgomery, Alabama. She boarded a bus, took a seat in the "whites only" section, and refused to give it up. Her arrest for violating the city's Jim Crow statutes sparked a yearlong black boycott of the city buses and served notice throughout the South that blacks would no longer submit meekly to the absurdities and indignities of segregation.

Montgomery bus boycott (1955) *Protest by black Alabamians against segregated seating on city buses, sparked by Rosa Parks's defiant refusal to move to the back of the bus. The bus boycott lasted from December 1, 1955, until December 26, 1956, and became one of the foundational moments of the civil rights movement. It led to the rise of Martin Luther King, Jr., and ultimately to a Supreme Court decision opposing segregated busing.*

The Montgomery bus boycott also catapulted to prominence a young pastor at Montgomery's Dexter Avenue Baptist Church, the Reverend Martin Luther King, Jr. Only twenty-seven years old, the well-educated King became a champion of the downtrodden and disfranchised. His oratorical skill, strategic savvy, mastery of biblical and constitutional conceptions of justice, and devotion to the nonviolent principles of India's Mohandas Gandhi all thrust him to the forefront of the black revolution that soon pulsed across the South and the rest of the nation.

★ Seeds of the Civil Rights Revolution

In 1946 President Harry Truman commissioned a report on blacks entitled "To Secure These Rights." Following the report's recommendations, Truman in 1948 ended segregation in federal civil service and the armed forces. Yet Congress stubbornly resisted passing civil rights legislation, and Truman's successor, Dwight Eisenhower, showed no real interest in the racial issue.

In the 1950s it was the Supreme Court that assumed civil rights leadership. Chief Justice Earl Warren, a former Republican governor of California, shocked traditionalists with his active judicial intervention in previously taboo social issues. Publicly snubbed and privately scorned by Ike, Warren courageously led the Court to address urgent issues that Congress and the president preferred to avoid.

Makers of America

The Great African American Migration

Among the groups most affected by the great social upheavals of World War II were African Americans. Predominantly a rural, southern people before 1940, African Americans were propelled by the war into the cities of the North and West, and by 1970 a majority lived outside the states of the Old Confederacy. The results of that massive demographic shift were momentous, for African Americans and for all of American society.

So many black southerners took to the roads during World War II that local officials lost track of the numbers. Black workers on the move crowded into boardinghouses, camped out in cars, and clustered in the juke joints of roadside America en route to their new lives.

Southern cotton fields and tobacco plantations had yielded but slender sustenance to African American farmers, most of whom struggled to make ends meet as tenants and sharecroppers. The Great Depression dealt yet another blow, for when New Deal farm programs paid growers to leave their land fallow, many landlords simply pocketed the money and evicted their tenants—white as well as black. As the Depression deepened, dispossessed former sharecroppers toiled as seasonal farmworkers or languished without jobs.

The spanking new munitions plants and bustling shipyards of the South offered little solace to African Americans. In 1940 and 1941 the labor-hungry war machine soaked up unemployed white workers but commonly denied jobs to blacks. Fed up with such injustices, many African Americans headed for shipyards, factories, and foundries on the Pacific Coast or north of the Mason-Dixon line, where their willing hands found work awaiting them.

Angered by continuing racism, black leaders cajoled President Roosevelt into issuing Executive Order 8802 in June 1941 declaring that "there shall be no discrimination in the employment of workers in defense industries or government because of race, creed, color, or national origin." Roosevelt's action was a tenuous, hesitant step, yet it was the first time since Reconstruction that the federal government had committed itself to ensuring justice for African Americans.

By war's end the great wartime exodus had scattered hundreds of thousands of African Americans to new regions and ways of life. In western and northern cities, blacks now competed for housing and jobs, and they also voted—many of them for the first time in their lives.

As early as 1945, NAACP leader Walter White concluded that the war "immeasurably magnified the Negro's awareness of the disparity between the American profession and practice of democracy." The wartime migration thus set the stage for the success of the civil rights movement. With their new political base outside the Old South, and with new support from the Democratic party, African Americans eventually forced an end to the hated segregationist practices that kept them from enjoying their full rights as citizens.

The Home Front Though often confronted by prejudice and discrimination, many African American migrants from the rural South found their first industrial jobs in wartime defense plants during World War II.

Brown v. Board of Education of Topeka, Kansas (1954) *Landmark Supreme Court decision that overturned* Plessy v. Ferguson *(1896) and abolished racial segregation in public schools. The Court reasoned that "separate" was inherently "unequal," rejecting the foundation of the Jim Crow system of racial segregation in the South. This decision was the first major step toward the legal end of racial discrimination and a major accomplishment for the civil rights movement.*

The unanimous decision of the Warren Court in *Brown v. Board of Education of Topeka, Kansas* in May 1954 was epochal. In a forceful opinion, the learned justices ruled that segregation in the public schools was "inherently unequal" and thus unconstitutional. The uncompromising decision reversed the Court's earlier declaration of 1896 in *Plessy* v. *Ferguson* (see p. 374) that "separate but equal" facilities were allowable under the Constitution. That doctrine was now dead. Desegregation, the justices insisted, must go ahead with "all deliberate speed."

The Border States generally made reasonable efforts to comply with this ruling, but in the Deep South diehards organized "massive resistance" against desegregation. More than a hundred southern congressmen and senators pledged their unyielding resistance to desegregation, and several states diverted funds to hastily created "private" schools where the integration order was more difficult to apply. Throughout the South, white citizens' councils, sometimes by the light of burning crosses, thwarted attempts to make integration a reality. Ten years after the Court's momentous ruling, fewer than 2 percent of the eligible blacks in the Deep South were sitting in classrooms with whites.

President Eisenhower remained reluctant to promote integration. He shied away from employing his vast popularity and the prestige of his office to educate white Americans about the need for racial justice. He complained that the Supreme Court's decision in *Brown* v. *Board of Education* had upset "the customs and convictions of at least two generations of Americans," and he steadfastly refused to issue a public statement endorsing the Court's conclusions.

But in September 1957 Ike was forced to act. Arkansas Governor Orval Faubus mobilized the National Guard to prevent nine black students from enrolling in Little Rock's Central High School. Confronted with a direct challenge to federal authority, Eisenhower sent troops to escort the children to their classes. In the same year Congress passed the first Civil Rights Act since Reconstruction, a mild measure that set up a Civil Rights Commission to investigate violations of civil rights. Blacks meanwhile continued to take the civil rights movement into their own hands. Martin Luther King, Jr., formed the Southern Christian Leadership Conference (SCLC) in 1957. The churches were the largest and best-organized black institutions that had been allowed to flourish in a segregated society, and the SCLC aimed to mobilize their vast power on behalf of black rights.

More spontaneous was the "sit-in" movement launched on February 1, 1960, by four black college freshmen in Greensboro, North Carolina. Without a detailed plan or institutional support, they demanded service at a whites-only Woolworth's lunch counter. The following day, eighty-five students joined in; by the end of the week, a thousand. The sit-in movement rolled swiftly across the South, swelling into a wave of wade-ins, lie-ins, and pray-ins to compel equal treatment in restaurants, transportation, employment, housing, and voter registration. In April 1960 southern black students formed the **Student Non-Violent Coordinating Committee (SNCC,** pronounced "snick"**)** to give more focus and force to these efforts. Young and impassioned, SNCC members would eventually lose patience with the tactics of the SCLC and the deliberate legalisms of the NAACP.

Student Non-Violent Coordinating Committee (SNCC) *Youth organization founded by southern black students in 1960 to promote civil rights. Drawing on its members' youthful energies, SNCC in its early years coordinated demonstrations, sit-ins, and voter registration drives.*

★ Eisenhower Republicanism at Home

Eisenhower had entered the White House in 1953 pledging his administration to a philosophy of "dynamic conservatism." While accepting basic New Deal reforms like Social Security and unemployment insurance, he was also determined to balance the federal budget and guard the Republic from what he called "creeping socialism." Eisenhower won southern support by endorsing the transfer of control over offshore oil fields from the federal government to the states. Ike also tried to curb the TVA by encouraging a private power company to build a generating plant to compete with the massive public utility.

Eisenhower responded to both domestic pressure and the Mexican government's worries that border crossings undercut the *Bracero* program of legally imported farmworkers (see p. 588). In a massive roundup dubbed **Operation Wetback** in reference to the migrants' watery route across the Rio Grande, as many as 1 million Mexicans were apprehended and returned to Mexico in 1954.

Operation Wetback (1954) *A government program to round up and deport as many as 1 million illegal Mexican migrant workers in the United States. The program was promoted in part by the Mexican government and reflected burgeoning concerns about non-European immigration to America.*

Meanwhile, in another of the rude and arbitrary reversals that have long afflicted the government's relations with Native Americans, Eisenhower sought to cancel the tribal preservation policies of the "Indian New Deal," in place since 1934 (see p. 561). He proposed to "terminate" the tribes as legal entities and to return to the assimilationist goals of the Dawes Severalty Act of 1887 (see p. 432). Most Indians resisted termination, and the policy was abandoned in 1961.

Eisenhower also backed a public works project that dwarfed anything the New Dealers had dreamed of. The **Federal Highway Act of 1956** authorized a $27 billion plan to build forty-two thousand miles of sleek, fast motorways. The president believed that such roads were essential to national defense, allowing U.S. troops to mobilize anywhere in the country in the event of a Soviet invasion. Beyond being a defense strategy, the construction of these modern, multilane roads created countless construction jobs, speeded the suburbanization of America, and exacerbated problems of air quality and energy consumption. It had disastrous consequences in many cities, as once-vibrant downtowns withered while shopping malls flourished in the far-flung suburbs.

Federal Highway Act of 1956 *Federal legislation signed by Dwight D. Eisenhower to construct thousands of miles of modern highways in the name of national defense. Officially called the National Interstate and Defense Highways Act, this bill dramatically increased the move to the suburbs, as white middle-class people could more easily commute to urban jobs.*

★ A "New Look" in Foreign Policy

The 1952 Republican platform called for a "new look" in foreign policy. It condemned the mere "containment" of communism as "negative, futile, and immoral." Incoming secretary of state John Foster Dulles promised not merely to stem the red tide but to "roll back" its gains and "liberate captive peoples." At the same time, the new administration promised to balance the budget by cutting military spending.

How were these two contradictory goals to be reached? Dulles answered with a **policy of boldness** in early 1954. Eisenhower would relegate the army and navy to the back seat and build up the Strategic Air Command's fleet of superbombers equipped with city-flattening nuclear bombs. These fearsome weapons would inflict "massive retaliation" on the Soviets or the Chinese in the event of hostilities. At the same time, Eisenhower sought a thaw in the Cold War through negotiations with the new Soviet leaders who came to power after Joseph Stalin's death in 1953.

In the end, the touted "new look" proved illusory. The new Soviet premier, burly Nikita Khrushchev, rudely rejected Ike's call in 1955 for "open skies" mutual inspection over both the Soviet Union and the United States. In 1956 the Hungarians rose up against their Soviet masters and felt badly betrayed when the United States turned a deaf ear to their desperate appeals for aid. The brutally crushed **Hungarian uprising** revealed the sober truth that America's mighty nuclear sledgehammer was too heavy a weapon to be used in such a relatively minor crisis. The strategic limitations of the "massive retaliation" doctrine were thus starkly exposed.

Southeast Asia provided further illustration of those limitations. In Vietnam and elsewhere, nationalist movements had sought for years to throw off the yoke of French colonial rule. The legendary Vietnamese leader, goateed Ho Chi Minh, had tried to appeal personally to Woodrow Wilson as early as 1919 to support self-determination for the peoples of Southeast Asia.

But Cold War events dampened the dreams of anticolonial Asian peoples. Their leaders—including Ho Chi Minh—became increasingly communist while the United States became increasingly anticommunist. By 1954 American taxpayers were financing nearly 80 percent of the costs of a bottomless French colonial war in Indochina. Despite this massive aid, French forces continued to crumble under pressure from Ho Chi Minh's nationalist guerilla forces, called the Viet Minh. In March 1954 a key French garrison was trapped hopelessly in the fortress of Dien Bien Phu. The new "policy of boldness" was now put to the test. Secretary Dulles, Vice President Nixon, and the chairman of the Joint Chiefs of Staff favored American intervention to bail out the beleaguered French. But Eisenhower held back.

The **Battle of Dien Bien Phu** proved a victory for the nationalists, and a multination conference at Geneva roughly halved Vietnam at the seventeenth parallel (see Map 36.2). The victorious Ho Chi Minh in the north consented to this arrangement on the assurance that Vietnam-wide elections would be held within two years. In the south a pro-Western

policy of boldness (1954) *Foreign-policy objective of Dwight Eisenhower's secretary of state John Foster Dulles, who believed in changing the containment strategy to one that more directly engaged the Soviet Union and attempted to roll back communist influence around the world. This policy led to a buildup of America's nuclear arsenal to threaten "massive retaliation" against communist enemies, expanding the Cold War's arms race.*

Hungarian uprising (1956) *Series of demonstrations in Hungary against the Soviet Union. Soviet Premier Nikita Khrushchev violently suppressed this pro-Western uprising, highlighting the limitations of America's power in Eastern Europe.*

Battle of Dien Bien Phu (1954) *Military engagement in French colonial Vietnam in which French forces were defeated by Vietnamese nationalists loyal to Ho Chi Minh. With this loss, the French ended their colonial involvement in Indochina, paving the way for America's entry.*

government under Ngo Dinh Diem was soon entrenched in Saigon. After Diem's regime and its American backers refused to hold the promised elections, communist guerillas heated up their campaign against Diem. The Americans had evidently backed a losing horse but could see no easy way to call off their bet.

★ Cold War Crises in the Middle East

Fears of Soviet penetration into the oil-rich Middle East further heightened Cold War tensions. The government of Iran, supposedly influenced by the Kremlin, began to resist the power of the gigantic Western companies that controlled Iranian petroleum. In response, the American Central Intelligence Agency (CIA) engineered a coup in 1953 that installed the youthful shah of Iran, Mohammad Reza Pahlavi, as dictator. Though successful in the short run in securing Iranian oil for the West, the American intervention left a bitter legacy of resentment among many Iranians. More than two decades later, they took their revenge on the shah and his American allies (see pp. 681–682).

The Suez crisis proved far messier than the swift strike in Iran. President Gamal Abdel Nasser of Egypt, an ardent Arab nationalist, had tentatively obtained American and British aid to build an immense dam on the Nile. But when Nasser began to flirt openly with the communist camp, Secretary of State Dulles dramatically withdrew the dam offer. Nasser promptly regained face by nationalizing the Suez Canal, owned chiefly by British and French stockholders.

Nasser's action placed a razor's edge at the jugular vein of Western Europe's oil supply. America's jittery British and French allies, deliberately keeping Washington in the dark, joined with Israel in an attack on Egypt late in October 1956. The invaders calculated

Suez crisis (1956) *International crisis launched when Egyptian president Gamal Abdel Nasser nationalized the Suez Canal, which had been owned mostly by French and British stockholders. The crisis led to a British and French attack on Egypt, which failed without aid from the United States. The Suez crisis marked an important turning point in the post-colonial Middle East and highlighted the rising importance of oil in world affairs.*

Egyptian Independence Leader Gamal Abdel Nasser, 1954 Shown here greeting exuberant supporters alongside the visiting Sudanese prime minister (left), Nasser became the first president under Egypt's new constitution in 1956. He was long a thorn in the flesh of American and European policymakers anxious to protect the precious oil resources of the Middle East. "Nasserism," his version of Pan-Arabism, won a great following in the Arab world during the 1950s and 1960s.

that the United States would supply them with oil while their Middle Eastern supplies were disrupted. But a furious President Eisenhower resolved to let them "boil in their own oil" and refused to release emergency supplies. The oil-less allies resentfully withdrew their troops.

The Suez crisis marked the last time that the United States could brandish its "oil weapon." As recently as 1940, the United States had produced two-thirds of the world's oil, but by 1948 America had become a net oil importer. The economic and strategic importance of the Middle East oil region began to grow dramatically.

The region's sandy sheikdoms increasingly resolved to reap for themselves the lion's share of the enormous oil wealth that Western companies pumped out of the scorching Middle Eastern deserts. In a portentous move, Saudi Arabia, Kuwait, Iraq, and Iran joined with Venezuela in 1960 to form the **Organization of Petroleum Exporting Countries (OPEC)**. In the next two decades, OPEC tightened its stranglehold on the Western economies.

Organization of Petroleum Exporting Countries (OPEC) *Cartel comprising Middle Eastern states and Venezuela first organized in 1960. OPEC aimed to control access to and prices of oil, wresting power from Western oil companies and investors. In the process, it gradually strengthened the hand of non-Western powers on the world stage.*

★ Round Two for Ike

The election of 1956 was a replay of the 1952 contest, with President Eisenhower pitted once more against Adlai Stevenson. Voters still liked Ike. Eisenhower piled up an enormous majority of 35,590,472 popular votes to Stevenson's 26,022,752; in the Electoral College the vote was an even more unbalanced 457 to 73. But Eisenhower failed to win for his party either house of Congress.

Ike nevertheless bestirred himself when it came to organized labor. Congressional investigations produced scandalous revelations of gangsterism and brass-knuckle tactics in many American unions, especially the Teamsters Union. The AFL-CIO, born of a merger of the two giants in 1955, expelled the Teamsters in 1957 for choosing leaders like mob-connected James R. "Jimmy" Hoffa. Later convicted of jury tampering, Hoffa served part of his sentence before disappearing without a trace—evidently the victim of gangsters he had crossed. To counter such corruption, Eisenhower persuaded Congress to pass the Landrum-Griffin Act in 1959. Designed to bring labor leaders to book for financial shenanigans and bullying tactics, it also expanded some of the anti-labor strictures of the earlier Taft-Hartley Act.

Soviet scientists astounded the world on October 4, 1957, by lofting into orbit around the globe a beep-beeping 184-pound "baby moon" (*Sputnik I*). A month later they launched 1,120-pound *Sputnik II* with a dog aboard. These amazing breakthroughs rattled American self-confidence. They cast doubts on America's vaunted scientific superiority and raised sobering military questions. If the Soviets could fire heavy objects into outer space, they certainly could reach America with intercontinental ballistic missiles (ICBMs).

"Rocket fever" swept the nation. Eisenhower established the National Aeronautics and Space Administration (NASA) and directed billions of dollars to missile development. After humiliating and well-advertised failures—notably the Vanguard missile, which blew up on national television just a few feet above the ground in 1957—in February 1958 the United States managed to put into orbit a grapefruit-sized satellite weighing 2.5 pounds. By the end of the decade, several satellites had been launched, and the United States had successfully tested its own ICBMs. The **Sputnik** scare also led to a critical comparison of the American educational system with that of the Soviet Union. In 1958 Congress passed the National Defense and Education Act (NDEA) to promote research and teaching in science, engineering, and foreign languages.

Sputnik (1957) *Soviet satellite first launched into earth orbit on October 4, 1957. This scientific achievement marked the first time human beings had put a man-made object into orbit and pushed the USSR noticeably ahead of the United States in the space race. A month later, the Soviet Union sent a larger satellite, Sputnik II, into space, prompting the United States to redouble its space exploration efforts and raising American fears of Soviet superiority.*

★ The Continuing Cold War

The fantastic race to create weapons of nuclear annihilation continued unabated. Worried scientists urged halting nuclear tests before the atmosphere became so polluted as to produce generations of mutants. The Soviets, after completing an intensive series of exceptionally "dirty" tests, proclaimed a suspension in March 1958 and urged the Western world to follow. Beginning in October 1958, Washington did halt both underground and

Contending Voices

The "Kitchen Debate"

To promote cultural exchange between the United States and the Soviet Union, both governments agreed to sponsor exhibits in each other's countries during the summer of 1959. On July 24, Vice President Richard Nixon (1913–1994) led Soviet Premier Nikita Khrushchev (1894–1971) on a tour of the American National Exhibition at Sokolniki Park in Moscow. As they explored the facilities, including a state-of-the-art kitchen in a model suburban home, the two leaders engaged in an impromptu debate that ranged from foreign policy to the relative merits of communism and capitalism to the significance of technological innovation for citizens. Nixon said (pointing to a washing machine):

"This is the newest model. This is the kind which is built in thousands of units for direct installation in the houses.... What we want to do is make easier the life of our housewives.... To us, diversity, the right to choose, the fact that we have 1,000 builders building 1,000 different houses, is the most important thing. We don't have one decision made at the top by one government official.... We have many different manufacturers and many different kinds of washing machines so that the housewives have a choice."

Khrushchev replied:

"Don't you have a machine that puts food into the mouth and pushes it down? Many things you've shown us are interesting but they are not needed in life. They have no useful purpose. They are merely gadgets.... You think the Russian people will be dumbfounded to see these things, but the fact is that newly built Russian houses have all this equipment right now. Moreover, all you have to do to get a house is to be born in the Soviet Union. You are entitled to housing. I was born in the Soviet Union. So I have a right to a house. In America, if you don't have a dollar, you have the right to choose between sleeping in a house or on the pavement."

> What does the exchange reveal about the premises of the ideological conflict between the United States and the Soviet Union during the Cold War?

---

atmospheric testing. But attempts to regularize suspensions by proper inspection sank on the reef of mutual mistrust.

The brusque Khrushchev, meanwhile, demanded in late 1958 that the Western powers remove their forces from West Berlin, and sought a face-to-face meeting with Eisenhower. Despite grave doubts about any tangible results, the president invited the Soviet leader to America in 1959. Khrushchev appeared in front of the U.N. General Assembly in New York before holding an encouraging meeting with Eisenhower at Camp David, the presidential retreat in Maryland's Catoctin Mountains.

Optimism evaporated when a follow-up Paris "summit conference," scheduled for May 1960, turned into an embarrassing fiasco. On the eve of the conference, the Soviets shot down an American U-2 spy plane deep in the heart of Russia. After bungling bureaucratic denials in Washington, "honest Ike" took the unprecedented step of assuming personal responsibility. Khrushchev stormed into Paris filing the air with invective, and the conference collapsed before it could get off the ground. The concord of Camp David was replaced with the grapes of wrath.

Meanwhile, the Cold War shook America's relations with its hemispheric neighbors. Latin Americans bitterly resented Uncle Sam's lavishing of billions of dollars on Europe while doling out only millions to its poor relations to the south. They also chafed at Washington's habit of intervening in Latin American affairs—as in a CIA-directed coup that ousted a leftist government in Guatemala in 1954. At the same time Washington continued to support—even decorate—bloody dictators who claimed to be combating communists.

One Latin American dictator, ironfisted Fulgencio Batista of Cuba, had encouraged huge investments of American capital, and Washington in turn had given him some support. But early in 1959 black-bearded Fidel Castro engineered a revolution that ousted Batista. Castro then denounced the Yankee imperialists and began to expropriate valuable American properties while pursuing a land-distribution program. Washington, finally losing patience, released Cuba from "imperialistic slavery" by cutting off the heavy U.S. imports of Cuban sugar. Castro retaliated with further wholesale confiscations of Yankee property and in effect made his left-wing dictatorship an economic and military satellite of Moscow. An exodus of anti-Castro Cubans headed for the United States, especially Florida. Nearly 1 million arrived between 1960 and 2000. Washington broke diplomatic relations with Castro's government early in 1961 and imposed a strict embargo on trade with Cuba.

★ Kennedy Challenges Nixon for the Presidency

Republicans approached the 1960 presidential campaign with Vice President Richard Nixon as their heir apparent. The "old" Nixon had been a no-holds-barred campaigner, especially in assailing Democrats and left-wingers. The "new" Nixon was represented as a mature, seasoned statesman. He had gained particular notice in a finger-pointing **kitchen debate** with Khrushchev in Moscow in 1959, where Nixon extolled the virtues of American consumerism over Soviet economic planning. The next year he handily won the Republican nomination.

On the Democratic side, John F. Kennedy, a youthful millionaire senator from Massachusetts, scored impressive victories in several primaries, overcoming the reluctance of many party bosses to nominate a Roman Catholic. Kennedy's closest rival, Texas Senator Lyndon B. Johnson, accepted second place on the ticket in a marriage of political convenience.

Senator Kennedy was the first Roman Catholic to be nominated by either party since Al Smith's ill-starred campaign in 1928. Smear artists revived the ancient charges about the Pope's controlling the White House. Kennedy rebutted the attacks and asked if some 40 million Catholic Americans were to be condemned to second-class citizenship from birth.

The Protestant Bible Belt South, ordinarily Democratic, had particular misgivings about the candidate's faith. "I fear Catholicism more than I fear communism," declaimed one Baptist minister in North Carolina. But if many southern Democrats stayed away from the polls because of Kennedy's Catholicism, northern Democrats in unusually large numbers supported Kennedy because of the bitter attacks on their Catholic faith.

Television may well have tipped the scales. The contestants crossed words in millions of living rooms. The debates reinforced the importance of image over substance in the television age. Many viewers found Kennedy's glamour and vitality far more appealing than Nixon's tired and pallid appearance.

Kennedy squeezed through with 303 electoral votes to 219,* but with a breathtakingly close popular margin of only 118,574 votes out of over 68 million cast (see Map 36.1). He was not only the first Roman Catholic but also, at forty-three, the youngest person to date to be elected president. Like Franklin Roosevelt, Kennedy ran well in the large industrial centers, where he had strong support from workers, Catholics, and African Americans. (During the campaign Kennedy had solicitously telephoned the pregnant Coretta King, whose husband, Martin Luther King, Jr., was then imprisoned in Georgia for a sit-in. Nixon declined to comment or communicate with Mrs. King, an early signal of the two parties' diverging racial strategies.)

President Eisenhower continued to enjoy extraordinary popularity to the final curtain. Despite Democratic gibes about "eight years of golfing and goofing," Eisenhower was widely admired and respected for his decency, goodwill, and moderation. The old soldier left office warning of the dangers of a burgeoning "**military-industrial complex**." Under his watch America had not only grown economically, but geographically as well: Alaska and Hawaii attained statehood in 1959.

★ A Cultural Renaissance

America's unprecedented global power in the heady post-World War II decades was matched by its new international ascendancy in the arts. Shedding the national inferiority complex that had vexed earlier generations, American creative genius exerted a powerful worldwide influence in painting, architecture, and literature.

New York became the art capital of the world after World War II. The tradition-free American environment seemed especially congenial to the experimental mood of much

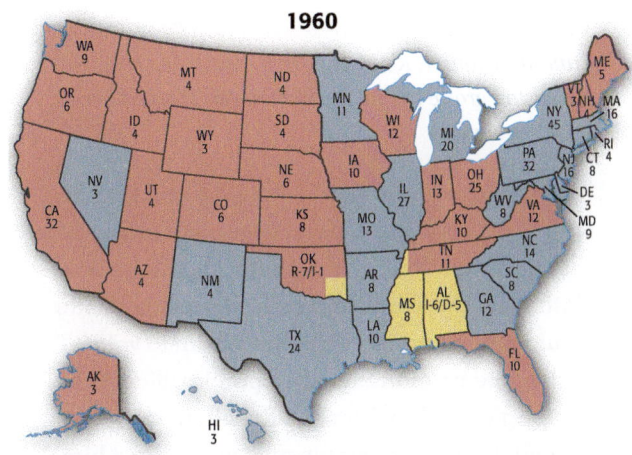

Map 36.1 Presidential Election of 1960 (with electoral vote by state) Kennedy owed his hairbreadth triumph to his victories in twenty-six of the forty largest cities—and to Lyndon Johnson's strenuous campaigning in the South, where Kennedy's Catholic religion may have been a hotter issue than his stand on civil rights.

kitchen debate (1959) *Televised exchange in 1959 between Soviet premier Nikita Khrushchev and American vice president Richard Nixon. Meeting at the American National Exhibition in Moscow, the two leaders sparred over the relative merits of capitalist consumer culture versus Soviet state planning. Nixon won applause for his staunch defense of American capitalism, helping lead him to the Republican nomination for president in 1960.*

military-industrialized complex *Term popularized by President Dwight Eisenhower in his 1961 Farewell Address, referring to the political and economic ties between arms manufacturers, elected officials, and the U.S. armed forces that created self-sustaining pressure for high military spending during the Cold War. Eisenhower also warned that this powerful combination left unchecked could "endanger our liberties or democratic process," favoring defense concerns over more peaceful goals that balanced security and liberty.*

---

*Six Democratic electors in Alabama, all eight unpledged Democratic electors in Mississippi, and one Republican elector in Oklahoma voted for Virginia Senator Harry F. Byrd, who ran as an independent.

Candidate John F. Kennedy (1917–1963), in a speech to a Houston group of Protestant ministers (September 12, 1960), declared:

"I believe in an America where the separation of church and state is absolute—where no Catholic prelate would tell the President, should he be a Catholic, how to act, and no Protestant minister would tell his parishioners for whom to vote ... and where no man is denied public office because his religion differs from the President who might appoint him or the people who might elect him."

abstract expressionism *An experimental style of mid-twentieth-century modern art exemplified by Jackson Pollock's spontaneous "action paintings," created by flinging paint on canvases stretched across the studio floor.*

International Style *Archetypal, post-World War II modernist architectural style, best known for its "curtainwall" designs of steel-and-glass corporate high-rises.*

Beat Generation *A small coterie of mid-twentieth-century bohemian writers and personalities, including Jack Kerouac, Allen Ginsberg, and Lawrence Ferlinghetti, who bemoaned bourgeois conformity and advocated free-form experimentation in life and literature.*

modern art. Jackson Pollock pioneered **abstract expressionism** in the 1940s and 1950s, dripping paint on huge flats stretched across his studio floor. Mark Rothko and his fellow "color field" painters also dispatched with representation, enveloping whole canvases with bold, shimmering swaths of color. "Pop" (short for *popular*) artists like Andy Warhol depicted mundane consumer items like soup cans and soda bottles, while Roy Lichtenstein parodied comic strips.

American architecture also reached new heights in the postwar era. Ultramodern skyscrapers conceived in the modernist or **International Style** arose in the nation's urban centers. High-rises like New York's United Nations headquarters (1952) and Seagram Building (1957) were essentially giant steel boxes wrapped in glass. Meanwhile, old master Frank Lloyd Wright continued to produce strikingly original designs like the round-walled Guggenheim Museum (1959) in New York. Louis Kahn employed plain geometric forms to make beautiful, simple buildings, like the serene Salk Institute (1965) in La Jolla, California. Chinese-born I.M. Pei designed numerous graceful buildings on college campuses as well as the dramatic National Gallery of Art (1978) in Washington.

Postwar America reaped its greatest cultural harvest in the field of literature. Searing realism characterized the earliest novels that portrayed soldierly life in World War II, like Norman Mailer's *The Naked and the Dead* (1948) and James Jones's *From Here to Eternity* (1951). But as time passed, realistic war writing fell from favor. Authors tended increasingly to write about the war in fantastic and even psychedelic prose. Joseph Heller's savagely satirical *Catch-22* (1961) dealt with the antics and anguish of American airmen in the wartime Mediterranean. The supercharged imagination of Kurt Vonnegut, Jr., produced works of puzzling complexity in inventive prose, including the darkly comic war tale *Slaughterhouse Five* (1969).

In the 1950s the broader culture as well as America's literary imagination became engaged as never before with psychological and particularly Freudian concepts, and postwar pens documented the internal effects of the nation's newly affluent, exuberantly consumerist society. One group of countercultural "Beat" writers rejected modern American life outright, seeking self-expression in stridently nonconformist lifestyles. Striving for liberation, these social drifters advocated marching to one's own "beat." Once "beaten down" by the relentless pressures of bourgeois existence, these bohemian hedonists also deemed themselves capable of "beatitude" or blessedness.

Among the close cohort of prominent Beat writers were Jack Kerouac (1922-1969), whose wild series of transcontinental road trips became the substance of his landmark novel *On the Road* (1957), a sort of pocket bible for social rebels in the late 1950s. Bearded and bespectacled Allen Ginsberg, the most eloquent spokesman of the **Beat Generation**, produced compelling poetry like "Howl" (1955), which proclaimed, "I saw the best minds of my generation destroyed by madness...." A public reading of Ginsberg's "Howl" in San Francisco launched a literary renaissance in that city centered around Lawrence Ferlinghetti's City Lights Bookstore. To literature, the Beats contributed a new style of free-form narration. Beyond the page their promotion of jazz, Eastern religious mysticism, sexual liberation, and extreme experience was eventually taken up by the 1960s "hippie" counterculture. But long after hippies had passed out of fashion, youngsters in America and elsewhere found inspiration in the writings of Kerouac, Ginsberg, and their fellow Beats.

A larger group of mainstream writers tackled the realities and dilemmas of postwar American society head-on. Pennsylvania-born John Updike celebrated the feats and failings of ordinary, small-town America in his four-part "Rabbit" series, beginning with *Rabbit, Run* (1960). Massachusetts-bred John Cheever, the "Chekhov of the exurbs," chronicled suburban manners and morals in novels like *The Wapshot Chronicle* (1957). Poets were often highly critical, even despairing, about the conformist character of mid-century American life. Descended from a long line of patrician New Englanders, Robert Lowell sought to apply the wisdom of the Puritan past to the perplexing present in allegorical poems like *For the Union Dead* (1964). Troubled Sylvia Plath crafted the moving

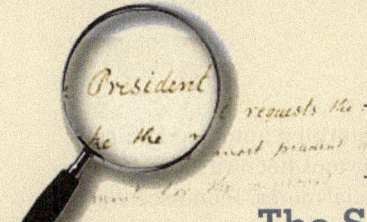

Examining the Evidence

The Shopping Mall as New Town Square, 1960

In this photograph Democratic presidential candidate John F. Kennedy is campaigning at the Bergen Mall in Paramus, New Jersey. Just one presidential contest earlier, a regional shopping center would have been a rare campaign stop. The Bergen Mall opened in 1957, a time when similar shopping centers were popping up in suburbanizing metropolitan areas all over the United States. Real estate developers watched Americans flee cities for suburbs, and they followed the money, locating shopping centers strategically at new highway intersections or along the busiest thoroughfares. As suburbanites increasingly found branches of their favorite department and chain stores closer to home during the 1950s and 1960s, they found it less and less necessary to go downtown. Shopping centers for their part went out of their way to sell themselves as modern-style downtowns worthy of being the public core of new suburban communities, even though legally they were privately owned space. They provided the full range of shops and services once found in city centers, including restaurants, post offices, Laundromats, banks, and even chapels. Shopping centers offered entertainment, from movie theaters and skating rinks to free open-air concerts, carnivals, and exhibitions. They made auditoriums available for community meetings. And they attracted public events such as Kennedy on the stump.

1. Look closely at this photograph. What kind of audience greeted candidate Kennedy at the Bergen Mall in 1960? How different might the crowd have looked in a more socially diverse urban center such as Manhattan or in nearby Newark, the largest city in New Jersey at the time?

2. What did it mean for sites of consumption, such as privately owned shopping centers, to take on the roles and responsibilities previously associated with urban streets, squares, and parks?

3. How might current struggles of downtown merchants against "big-box" chain stores such as Walmart be compared to this history of continuing changes in American public and consumer spaces?

verses of *Ariel* (published posthumously in 1966) and a disturbing autobiographical novel, *The Bell Jar* (1963), but her career was cut short when she took her own life in 1963. Playwrights were also acute observers of postwar American social mores. Tennessee Williams wrote a series of searing dramas about psychological misfits struggling to hold themselves together amid the disintegrating forces of modern life. Noteworthy were *A Streetcar Named Desire* (1947) and *Cat on a Hot Tin Roof* (1955), each delivering powerful critiques of the contemporary restrictions placed on women's lives. Arthur Miller brought to the stage searching probes of American values, notably *Death of a Salesman* (1949) and *The Crucible* (1953), which treated the Salem witch trials as a dark parable warning against the dangers of McCarthyism. Lorraine Hansberry offered an affecting portrait of African American struggles in *A Raisin in the Sun* (1959). Edward Albee exposed the rapacious underside of middle-class life in *Who's Afraid of Virginia Woolf?* (1962).

Underrepresented groups gained new prominence in midcentury literary circles. Ralph Ellison depicted the African American's often tortured quest for personal identity in *Invisible Man* (1952), a haunting novel narrated by a nameless black person who finds that none of his supposed supporters can see him as a real man. James Baldwin won plaudits as a novelist and essayist, particularly for his sensitive reflections on the racial question in *The Fire Next Time* (1963). Black nationalist LeRoi Jones, who changed his name to Imamu Amiri Baraka, crafted powerful plays such as *Dutchman* (1964).

The South boasted its own literary revival, led by veteran Mississippi author William Faulkner, a Nobel Prize winner in 1950. The **Southern Renaissance** writers brought a new critical appreciation to the region's burdens of history and racism. Tennesseean Robert Penn Warren immortalized Louisiana politico Huey Long in *All the King's Men* (1946). Southern renaissance writers like Georgian Flannery O'Connor perceptively tracked the changes reshaping the postwar South. Virginian William Styron confronted the harsh history of his home state in a controversial fictional representation of an 1831 slave rebellion, *The Confessions of Nat Turner* (1967).

Especially bountiful was the harvest of books by Jewish novelists. Bernard Malamud rendered a touching portrait of a family of New York Jewish storekeepers in *The Assistant* (1957). Philip Roth wrote comically about young New Jersey suburbanites in *Goodbye, Columbus* and penned an uproarious account of a sexually obsessed New Yorker in *Portnoy's Complaint* (1969).

★ Kennedy's "New Frontier" Spirit

Complacent and comfortable as the 1950s closed, Americans elected in 1960 a young, vigorous president who pledged "to get the country moving again." As John F. Kennedy announced in his stirring inaugural address on January 20, 1961, "the torch has been passed to a new generation of Americans." Speaking crisply with staccato finger jabs at the air, Kennedy personified the glamour and vitality of the new generation.

The youngest president ever elected assembled one of the youngest cabinets, including his brother, Robert F. Kennedy, as attorney general. Business whiz Robert S. McNamara left the presidency of the Ford Motor Company to take over the Defense Department. Along with other young advisers (many boasting Harvard degrees), these appointees made up an inner circle notable for its aura of brash confidence and self-conscious sophistication.

From the outset Kennedy inspired high expectations, especially among the young. His depiction of America's potential for greatness as a "**New Frontier**" quickened patriotic pulses. He brought a warm heart to the Cold War when he proposed the **Peace Corps**, an army of idealistic and mostly youthful volunteers bringing American know-how to underdeveloped countries. He summoned citizens to service with his clarion call to "ask not what your country can do for you but what you can do for your country."

But the soaring rhetoric did not quite match the political situation. Kennedy came into office with fragile Democratic majorities in Congress. Southern Democrats threatened to team up with Republicans and ax New Frontier proposals like medical assistance for the aged and increased federal aid to education. Kennedy forced an expansion of the conservative-dominated House Rules Committee, but despite this victory his key medical

---

Southern Renaissance *A literary outpouring among mid-twentieth-century southern writers, begun by William Faulkner and marked by a new critical appreciation of the region's burdens of history, racism, and conservatism.*

New Frontier (1961–1963) *President Kennedy's nickname for his domestic policy agenda. Buoyed by youthful optimism, the program included proposals for the Peace Corps and efforts to improve education and health care.*

Peace Corps *A federal agency created by President Kennedy in 1961 to promote voluntary service by Americans in foreign countries. The Peace Corps provides labor power to help developing countries improve their infrastructure, health care, educational systems, and other aspects of their societies. Part of Kennedy's New Frontier vision, the organization represented an effort by postwar liberals to promote American values and influence through productive exchanges across the world.*

and education bills stalled in Congress. In 1963 Congress even voted down an administration-endorsed bill slashing income and corporate tax rates to boost the economy.

That tax bill hinted at the Kennedy administration's complex relationship with big business. Kennedy intended his tax cutting to mollify businessmen wary of a big-government liberal in the White House. But he could also be a tough negotiator with corporate titans when he wanted to. When steel managers raised prices after a noninflationary wage agreement with labor in 1962, Kennedy called them onto the Oval Office carpet and unleashed his Irish temper. Overawed, they backed down.

Kennedy's New Frontier vision also extended to the "final frontier." Early in his term, the president promoted a multibillion-dollar project dedicated, as he put it, to "landing a man on the Moon and returning him safely to earth." Though he summoned stirring rhetoric about expanding human possibilities, the moon shot was really a calculated plan to restore America's international prestige, severely damaged by the Soviet *Sputnik* successes (see p. 637). $24 billion later, in July 1969, two NASA astronauts triumphantly planted their footprints—and the American flag—on the moon's dusty surface. As people around the globe huddled around televisions to watch the **Apollo** mission live, the world had never seemed so small and interconnected, nor the United States so dominant.

> *Richard Goodwin (b. 1931), a Kennedy aide and Peace Corps staffer, eloquently summed up the buoyantly optimistic mood of the early 1960s:*
>
> "For a moment, it seemed as if the entire country, the whole spinning globe, rested, malleable and receptive, in our beneficent hands."

Apollo (1961–1975) *Program of manned space flights run by America's National Aeronautics and Space Administration (NASA). The project's highest achievement was the landing of Apollo 11 on the moon on July 20, 1969.*

★ Foreign Flare-ups and "Flexible Response"

A few months after settling into the White House, in June 1961, the new president met Soviet Premier Nikita Khrushchev in Vienna. The tough-talking Soviet leader adopted a belligerent attitude, threatening to cut off Western access to Berlin. Though visibly shaken, the president refused to be bullied.

The Soviets backed off from their most bellicose threats, but their "puppet" East German regime suddenly began to construct the **Berlin Wall** in August 1961. A barbed-wire-and-concrete barrier, the "Wall of Shame" looked like a gigantic enclosure around a prison. The Wall stood for almost three decades as an ugly scar symbolizing the post–World War II division of Europe into two hostile camps.

Kennedy meanwhile turned his attention to Western Europe, now miraculously prospering after the Marshall Plan and the growth of the American-encouraged **European Economic Community (EEC)**, the free-trade area that later evolved into the European Union. Kennedy secured passage of the Trade Expansion Act in 1962, authorizing tariff cuts of up to 50 percent to promote trade with the EEC countries. This act led to the so-called Kennedy Round of tariff negotiations, concluded in 1967. These liberalized trade policies inaugurated a new era of such robustly invigorated international commerce that a new word was coined to describe it: *globalization*.

Special problems for U.S. foreign policy emerged from the worldwide decolonization of European overseas possessions after World War II. Cold War entanglements in these new nations threatened to escalate all too quickly into a nuclear confrontation between the United States and the USSR. Kennedy felt hamstrung by the knowledge that in a crisis he had the Devil's choice between humiliation and nuclear incineration. With Defense Secretary McNamara, he pushed an alternative strategy of "flexible response"—developing an array of military "options" that could be precisely matched to gravity of the crisis at hand. To this end, Kennedy increased spending on conventional military forces and bolstered the Special Forces (Green Berets) specializing in anti-guerilla fighting.

The doctrine of "flexible response" seemed sane enough, but it too contained lethal logic. It potentially lowered the level at which diplomacy would give way to shooting. It also provided a mechanism for a progressive, and possibly endless, stepping-up of the use of force. Vietnam soon presented a grisly proof of these pitfalls.

The corrupt, right-wing Ngo Dinh Diem government in Saigon, despite a deluge of American dollars, had ruled shakily since the partition of Vietnam in 1954 (see p. 635).

Berlin Wall *Fortified and guarded barrier between East and West Berlin erected on orders from Soviet premier Nikita Khrushchev in 1961 to stop the flow of people to the West. Until its destruction in 1989, the wall was a vivid symbol of the divide between the communist and capitalist worlds.*

European Economic Community (EEC) *Free-trade zone in Western Europe created by Treaty of Rome in 1957. Often referred to as the "Common Market," this collection of countries originally included France, West Germany, Italy, Belgium, the Netherlands, and Luxembourg. The body eventually expanded to become the European Union, which by 2005 included twenty-seven member states.*

Anti-Diem agitators threatened to topple the pro-American government from power. In a fateful decision late in 1961, Kennedy ordered a sharp increase in the number of "military advisers" (U.S. troops) in South Vietnam.

American forces allegedly entered Vietnam to foster political stability—to help protect Diem from the communists long enough to allow him to enact promised social reforms. But the Kennedy administration eventually despaired of the reactionary Diem and in November 1963 encouraged a successful coup against him. Ironically, the United States thus contributed to precisely the process of political disintegration that its original policy had meant to prevent. Kennedy still told the South Vietnamese that it was "their war," but he had made dangerously deep political commitments. By the time of his death, he had ordered more than fifteen thousand American men into the Asian slaughter pen. A graceful pullout was becoming increasingly difficult (see Map 36.2).

Bay of Pigs invasion (1961) *CIA plot in 1961 to overthrow Fidel Castro by training Cuban exiles to invade and supporting them with American airpower. The mission failed and became a public relations disaster early in John F. Kennedy's presidency.*

Cuban missile crisis (1962) *Standoff between John F. Kennedy and Soviet premier Nikita Khrushchev in October 1962 over Soviet plans to install nuclear weapons in Cuba. Although the crisis was ultimately settled in America's favor and represented a foreign-policy triumph for Kennedy, it brought the world's superpowers perilously close to the brink of nuclear confrontation.*

★ Cuban Confrontations

Although the United States regarded Latin America as its backyard, its southern neighbors feared and resented the powerful Colossus of the North. In 1961 Kennedy extended the hand of friendship with the Alliance for Progress (*Alianza para el Progreso*), hailed as a Marshall Plan for Latin America and intended to quiet communist agitation. But results were disappointing; there was little alliance and even less progress. American handouts had little positive impact on Latin America's immense social problems.

President Kennedy also struck below the border with brass knuckles. He had inherited from the Eisenhower administration a CIA-backed scheme to topple Fidel Castro from power by invading Cuba with anticommunist exiles. On April 17, 1961, some twelve hundred exiles landed at Cuba's Bay of Pigs. When the ill-starred **Bay of Pigs invasion** bogged down, Kennedy stood fast in his decision to keep hands off, and the bullet-riddled band of anti-Castroites surrendered.

The Bay of Pigs blunder, along with continuing American covert efforts to assassinate Castro and overthrow his government, naturally pushed the Cuban leader even further into the Soviet embrace. Wily Chairman Khrushchev lost little time taking full advantage of his Cuban comrade's location just ninety miles off Florida's coast. In October 1962 aerial photographs by American spy planes revealed that the Soviets were secretly and speedily installing nuclear-tipped missiles in Cuba.

Kennedy and Khrushchev now began a nerve-racking game of "nuclear chicken." The president, on October 22, 1962, ordered a naval "quarantine" of Cuba and demanded immediate removal of the threatening weaponry. He also served notice on Khrushchev that any attack on the United States from Cuba would trigger nuclear retaliation against the Russian heartland. For an anxious week, Americans waited while Soviet ships approached the patrol line established by the U.S. Navy off Cuba. The world teetered breathlessly on the brink of global atomization. In this tense eyeball-to-eyeball confrontation, Khrushchev finally flinched. On October 28 he agreed to a partially face-saving compromise, by which he would pull the missiles out of Cuba. The United States in return quietly agreed not to invade the island and to remove from Turkey some of its own missiles targeted at the Soviet Union.

Fallout from the **Cuban missile crisis** was considerable. A disgraced Khrushchev was ultimately hounded out of the Kremlin and became an "unperson." Kennedy, apparently sobered by the appalling risks he had just run, pushed harder for a nuclear test-ban treaty with the Soviet Union. After prolonged negotiations in Moscow, a pact prohibiting trial nuclear explosions in the atmosphere was signed in late 1963.

Failed Bay of Pigs Invasion, 1961 Cuban soldiers demonstrate a beach gun they used against a brigade of ex-Cubans who furtively invaded Cuba as agents of the United States. The debacle was one of several unsuccessful American attempts to overthrow Cuban leader Fidel Castro.

Map 36.2 Vietnam and Southeast Asia, 1954–1975 Le Ly Hayslip (b. 1949) was born in a peasant village in South Vietnam, just south of Da Nang. In her memoir, *When Heaven and Earth Changed Places*, she describes the trauma endured by ordinary Vietnamese as a result of America's fight against the Viet Cong: "In 1963—the year the Viet Cong came to my village—American warplanes bombed Man Quang. It was at noon, just when the children were getting out of school. My aunt Thu and her pregnant daughter-in-law were making lunch for her husband and four grandchildren when the air-raid signal blared. They all jumped under the wooden table and sheltered the pregnant woman with their bodies—even the little kids. A bomb fell in Aunt Thu's front yard.... Hot shrapnel tore through everyone except the pregnant woman. Aunt Thu and one of her grandchildren were killed. The passing fragment left only a weeping hole where her generous heart had been."

Most significant was Kennedy's speech at American University in Washington, D.C., in June 1963. The president urged Americans to abandon a view of the Soviet Union as a Devil-ridden land filled with fanatics and instead to deal with the world "as it is, not as it might have been had the history of the last eighteen years been different." Kennedy thus tried to lay the foundations for a realistic policy of peaceful coexistence with the Soviet Union. Here were the modest origins of the policy that later came to be known as "détente" (French for "relaxation of tension").

★ The Struggle for Civil Rights

Kennedy had campaigned with a strong appeal to black voters, but he proceeded gingerly to redeem his promises on civil rights. Political concerns stayed his hand. Elected by a wafer-thin margin, he needed southern legislators to pass his medical and educational bills, which he believed would eventually benefit black Americans. Bold moves for racial justice would have to wait.

But events soon scrambled these careful calculations. After the wave of sit-ins that surged across the South in 1960, groups of **Freedom Riders** fanned out to end segregation in facilities serving interstate bus passengers. A white mob torched a Freedom Ride bus near Anniston, Alabama in May 1961, and Attorney General Robert Kennedy's personal representative was beaten unconscious in another anti–Freedom Ride riot in Montgomery. When southern officials proved unwilling or unable to stem the violence, Washington dispatched federal marshals to protect the Freedom Riders.

Reluctantly but fatefully, the Kennedy administration had now joined hands with the civil rights movement. For the most part, the relationship between Martin Luther King, Jr., and the Kennedys was a fruitful one. Encouraged by Robert Kennedy, the Student Non-Violent Coordinating Committee and other civil rights groups inaugurated the **Voter Education Project** to register the South's historically disfranchised blacks.

Integrating southern universities was as challenging as registering African Americans to vote. Some desegregated painlessly, but the University of Mississippi ("Ole Miss") became a volcano. A twenty-nine-year-old air force veteran, James Meredith, encountered

Freedom Riders *Organized mixed-race groups who rode interstate buses deep into the South to draw attention to and protest racial segregation, beginning in 1961. This effort to challenge racism, which involved the participation of many northern young people as well as southern activists, proved a political and public relations success for the civil rights movement.*

Voter Education Project (1962–1968) *Effort by SNCC and other civil rights groups to register the South's historically disenfranchised black population. The project typified a common strategy of the civil rights movement, which sought to counter racial discrimination by empowering people at grassroots levels to exercise their civic rights through voting.*

Freedom Ride, 1961 Rampaging whites near Anniston, Alabama, burned this bus carrying an interracial group of Freedom Riders on May 14, 1961.

violent opposition when he attempted to register in October 1962. In the end President Kennedy was forced to send in four hundred federal marshals and three thousand troops to enroll Meredith in his first class—in colonial American history.

In the spring of 1963, Martin Luther King, Jr., launched a campaign against discrimination in Birmingham, Alabama, the most segregated big city in America. Previous attempts to crack the city's rigid racial barriers had produced more than fifty cross burnings and eighteen bomb attacks since 1957. King advised his organizers that "some of the people sitting here will not come back alive from this campaign." Events soon confirmed this grim prediction of violence. Watching developments on television screens, a horrified world saw peaceful civil rights marchers repeatedly repelled by police with attack dogs and electric cattle prods. High-pressure fire hoses shot water at demonstrators with enough force to knock bricks loose from buildings or strip bark from trees at a distance of one hundred feet. Little children were bowled down the street like tumbleweeds.

> *In his civil rights address of June 11, 1963, President John F. Kennedy (1917–1963) said:*
>
> "If an American, because his skin is dark, cannot eat lunch in a restaurant open to the public; if he cannot send his children to the best public school available; if he cannot vote for the public officials who represent him; if, in short, he cannot enjoy the full and free life which all of us want, then who among us would be content to have the color of his skin changed and stand in his place?"

Jolted by these vicious confrontations, President Kennedy delivered a memorable televised speech to the nation on June 11, 1963. Calling the situation a "moral crisis," and drawing on the same spiritual traditions as Martin Luther King, Jr., he declared that the principle at stake "is as old as the Scriptures and as clear as the American Constitution." He called for new civil rights legislation to protect black citizens. In August King led 200,000 black and white demonstrators in a peaceful **March on Washington** in support of the proposed legislation. In an electrifying speech from the Lincoln Memorial, King declared, "I have a dream that my four little children will one day live in a nation where they will not be judged by the color of their skin but by the content of their character."

Still the violence continued. On the very night of Kennedy's stirring television address a white gunman shot down Medgar Evers, a black Mississippi civil rights worker. In September 1963 an explosion blasted a Baptist church in Birmingham, killing four black girls who had just finished their Sunday school lesson called "The Love That Forgives."

March on Washington (1963) *Massive civil rights demonstration in August 1963 in support of Kennedy-backed legislation to secure legal protections for American blacks. One of the most visually impressive manifestations of the civil rights movement, the march was the occasion of Martin Luther King's famous "I Have a Dream" speech.*

★ The Killing of Kennedy

Violence haunted America in the mid-1960s, and it stalked onto center stage on November 22, 1963. While riding in an open limousine in downtown Dallas, Texas, President Kennedy was shot in the brain by a concealed rifleman and died within seconds. Vice President Johnson was promptly sworn in as president on a waiting airplane and flown back to Washington with Kennedy's body.

As a stunned nation grieved, the tragedy grew still more unbelievable. The alleged assassin, a furtive figure named Lee Harvey Oswald, was himself shot to death in front of the television cameras by a self-appointed avenger, Jack Ruby. So bizarre were the events surrounding the two murders that even an elaborate official investigation conducted by Chief Justice Warren could not quiet all doubts and theories about what had really happened.

For several days, the nation was steeped in sorrow. Not until then did many Americans realize how fully their young, vibrant president and his captivating wife had cast a spell over them. Chopped down in his prime after only slightly more than a thousand days in the White House, Kennedy was acclaimed more for the ideals he had enunciated and the spirit he had kindled than for his concrete achievements. In later years revelations about Kennedy's womanizing and allegations about his involvement with organized crime figures tarnished his reputation. But despite those accusations, his apparent vigor, charisma, and idealism made him an inspirational figure for a rising "baby boom" generation. Few could foresee that the decade following his death would explode into extraordinary ferment at home and abroad.

CHAPTER SUMMARY

American society grew ever more prosperous in the postwar era, as science, technology, and the Cold War fueled burgeoning new industries such as electronics and aviation. Women joined the movement into the increasingly white-collar work force and chafed at widespread restrictions they faced. A new consumer culture, centered around television, fostered an ethic of leisure and enjoyment, including more open expressions of sexuality in popular entertainment.

Enormously popular as the victorious Supreme Allied Commander in World War II, Dwight Eisenhower was nominated by enthusiastic Republicans and breezed to victory in the election of 1952. "Ike" was ideally suited to soothe an America badly shaken by the Cold War and Korea. Seeking stability in domestic affairs, Eisenhower reacted cautiously to the beginnings of the civil rights movement led by Martin Luther King, Jr., but sent troops to Little Rock to enforce court orders for desegregation. Eisenhower's domestic policies were moderately conservative, leaving most of the New Deal in place while spending vast sums on a new interstate highway system.

Despite John Foster Dulles's tough talk, Eisenhower's foreign policies were also generally cautious. He avoided direct military intervention in Vietnam, although aiding South Vietnamese leader Diem, and pressured Britain, France, and Israel to resolve the Suez crisis. Eisenhower also sought negotiations to thaw the frigid Cold War. Dealing with Nikita Khrushchev proved difficult, however, as *Sputnik*, the Berlin Crisis, the U-2 incident, and Fidel Castro's Cuban revolution all kept Cold War tensions high. In a tight election, Senator John Kennedy defeated Eisenhower's vice president, Richard Nixon. Kennedy called for the country to "get moving again" by more vigorously countering the Soviets.

America's power and affluence contributed to a postwar cultural renaissance. Painting and architecture undertook bold experiments in modernism. In literature, the Beat writers challenged conventional forms as well as conformist lifestyles. African American, southern, and Jewish writers all had a striking impact on American thought and writing.

Kennedy's vigorous New Frontier initiatives stirred a spirit of idealism, but many of his programs became bogged down in Congress. Cold War confrontations over Berlin and Russian missiles in Cuba created threats of nuclear war but were successfully defused. Countering communism's threat through the doctrine of "flexible response" led the administration into dangerous involvement in Vietnam and elsewhere.

Kennedy was slow to endorse the civil rights movement, but eventually King and other activists created a moral groundswell that led Kennedy to endorse racial justice and new civil rights legislation. While Kennedy's sudden death left most of his goals unfulfilled, his charisma and idealism had inspired a generation.

KEY TERMS

The Feminine Mystique (629)
rock 'n' roll (629)
Checkers Speech (630)
Montgomery bus boycott (632)
Brown v. Board of Education of Topeka, Kansas (634)
Student Non-Violent Coordinating Committee (SNCC) (634)
Operation Wetback (634)
Federal Highway Act of 1956 (635)
policy of boldness (635)
Hungarian uprising (635)
Battle of Dien Bien Phu (635)
Suez crisis (636)
Organization of Petroleum Exporting Countries (OPEC) (637)
Sputnik (637)
kitchen debate (639)
military-industrial complex (639)
abstract expressionism (640)
International Style (640)
Beat Generation (640)
Southern Renaissance (642)
New Frontier (642)
Peace Corps (642)
Apollo (643)
Berlin Wall (643)
European Economic Community (EEC) (643)
Bay of Pigs invasion (644)
Cuban missile crisis (644)
Freedom Riders (646)
Voter Education Project (646)
March on Washington (647)

PEOPLE TO KNOW

Dwight D. ("Ike") Eisenhower
Richard M. Nixon
Betty Friedan
Elvis Presley
Rosa Parks
Martin Luther King, Jr.
Earl Warren
John Foster Dulles
Nikita Khrushchev
Ho Chi Minh
Gamal Abdel Nasser
Fidel Castro
John F. Kennedy
Lyndon B. Johnson
Jackson Pollock
Andy Warhol
Jack Kerouac
Allen Ginsberg
Arthur Miller
Ralph Ellison
Robert F. Kennedy
Robert S. McNamara
Ngo Dinh Diem
James Meredith

MindTap is a fully online, highly personalized learning experience built upon Cengage Learning content. MindTap combines student learning tools—readings, multimedia, activities, and assessments—into a singular Learning Path that guides students through the course.

Chapter 37

The Stormy Sixties
1963–1973

There's a battle outside and it is ragin'
It'll soon shake your windows and rattle your walls
For the times they are a-changin'

BOB DYLAN, 1963

Chapter Outline

- Lyndon Baines Johnson and the "Great Society"
- From Civil Rights to Black Power
- The Vietnam Disaster
- The Election of Richard Nixon
- The Cultural Upheavals of the 1960s
- Nixon and the Vietnam War
- New Policies toward China and the Soviet Union
- Nixon's Domestic Policies
- Nixon's Re-election and Watergate
- Israelis, Arabs, and Oil
- Thinking Globally: The Global 1960s
- Varying Viewpoints: The Sixties: Constructive or Destructive?

Iconic historical decades rarely align perfectly with the actual calendar. What many Americans remember as the tumultuous "sixties" did not truly come to pass until after the shocking slaying of President John F. Kennedy, and its several upheavals in culture and politics extended well into the following decade. Between President Kennedy's assassination in 1963 and President Nixon's resignation in 1974, Americans experienced a sexual revolution, a civil rights revolt, the emergence of a "youth culture," a devastating war in Vietnam, a massive enlargement of the federal government, and the beginnings of a feminist uprising. The era's close left Americans exhausted, divided, and disillusioned—but also permanently transformed in myriad ways.

FOCUS QUESTIONS

1. What was Lyndon Johnson's distinctive style in the presidency, and what were the legislative goals of his "Great Society"?

2. How was the idealistic and nonviolent spirit of the civil rights movement transformed in the mid-1960s by white racial "backlash," black power, and urban rioting?

3. How did Lyndon Johnson and his advisers lead the United States deeper into the Vietnam quagmire, and why did that war create such deep divisions in American politics and society?

4. What were the roots of the cultural rebellion of the 1960s, and what were its short-term and long-term consequences?

5. What were Richard Nixon's greatest foreign and domestic policy achievements, and how was his presidency destroyed by the Watergate crimes?

650

CHRONOLOGY

1963	▪ Kennedy assassinated; Johnson assumes presidency	1969	▪ Astronauts land on moon ▪ Stonewall Inn riot in New York City
1964	▪ Twenty-fourth Amendment (abolishing poll tax in federal elections) ratified ▪ "Freedom Summer" voter registration in the South ▪ Gulf of Tonkin Resolution ▪ Johnson defeats Goldwater for presidency ▪ War on Poverty begins ▪ Civil Rights Act	1970	▪ Nixon orders invasion of Cambodia ▪ Kent State and Jackson State incidents ▪ Environmental Protection Agency (EPA) created ▪ Clean Air Act
		1971	▪ Pentagon Papers published ▪ Twenty-sixth Amendment (lowering voting age to eighteen) passed
1965	▪ Great Society legislation ▪ Voting Rights Act	1972	▪ Nixon visits China and Soviet Union; Shanghai Communiqué begins "normalization" of U.S.–Chinese relations ▪ ABM and SALT I treaties ratified ▪ Nixon defeats McGovern for presidency
1965–1968	▪ Race riots in U.S. cities		
1966	▪ France withdraws from NATO		
1967	▪ Six-Day War between Israel and Egypt	1973	▪ Treaty of Paris enacts cease-fire in Vietnam and U.S. withdrawal ▪ War Powers Act ▪ OPEC oil embargo ▪ Endangered Species Act ▪ Chilean president Salvador Allende killed in CIA-backed coup ▪ *Roe v. Wade*
1968	▪ North Vietnamese army launches Tet offensive in South Vietnam ▪ Worldwide protests ▪ Martin Luther King, Jr., and Robert Kennedy assassinated ▪ Prague Spring crushed by Soviet army ▪ Nixon defeats Humphrey and Wallace for presidency		
		1974	▪ OPEC ends embargo, increases oil prices

★ The LBJ Brand on the Presidency

With President Kennedy struck down, the torch passed to craggy-faced Lyndon Baines Johnson, a Texan who towered six feet three inches. The new president hailed from the populist hill country west of Austin, Texas, and had supported New Deal measures as a young Congressman. But Johnson had trimmed his sails to the right in order to win statewide elections in Texas, including an eighty-seven vote victory in the 1948 Senate race that earned him the nickname "Landslide Lyndon."

Entrenched in the Senate, Johnson became the powerful majority leader and a master wheeler-dealer. He could move political mountains or checkmate opponents as the occasion demanded, using what came to be known as the "Johnson treatment"—a flashing display of backslapping, flesh-pressing, and arm-twisting that overbore friend and foe alike. His ego and vanity were legendary.

As president, Johnson quickly shed the conservative coloration of his Senate years to reveal the latent liberal underneath. With Johnson's vigorous prodding, and after a lengthy conservative filibuster, Congress at last passed the landmark **Civil Rights Act of 1964**. The act banned racial discrimination in most private facilities open to the public, including theaters, hospitals, and restaurants. It strengthened the federal government's power to end segregation in schools and other public places. Title VII of the Act barred employers from discriminating based on race or national origin in hiring, and empowered the Equal Employment Opportunity Commission (EEOC, a body Kennedy had created in 1961) to enforce the law.

When conservatives tried to derail the legislation by adding a prohibition on sexual, as well as racial, discrimination, the tactic backfired. The bill's opponents cynically

Civil Rights Act of 1964 *Federal law that banned racial discrimination in public facilities and strengthened the federal government's power to fight segregation in schools. Title VII of the act prohibited employers from discriminating based on race in their hiring practices, and empowered the Equal Employment Opportunity Commission (EEOC) to regulate fair employment.*

calculated that liberals would not be able to support a bill that threatened to wipe out laws that singled out women for special protection because of their sex. But the act's Title VII passed with the sexual clause intact. It soon proved to be a powerful instrument of federally enforced gender equality, as well as racial equality. Johnson struck another blow for women and minorities in 1965 when he issued an executive order requiring all federal contractors to take **affirmative action** against discrimination.

Johnson rammed Kennedy's stalled tax bill through Congress and added proposals of his own for a billion-dollar "War on Poverty." Initial political impetus for the antipoverty campaign came from Michael Harrington's surprise bestseller *The Other America* (1962), which revealed that in affluent America 20 percent of the population—and over 40 percent of the black population—suffered in poverty. Johnson's War on Poverty became part of a far-reaching reform program that he dubbed the **Great Society**. Epitomizing the confidence of the era, the Great Society project entailed a sweeping array of measures encompassing New-Deal style social programs and major public investment in education and the arts.

affirmative action Program designed to redress historic racial and gender imbalances in jobs and education. The term grew from an executive order issued by Lyndon B. Johnson in 1965 mandating that projects paid for with federal funds take concerted action against discrimination based on race in their hiring practices. In the late 1960s, President Nixon's Philadelphia Plan changed the meaning of affirmative action to require attention to certain groups, rather than protect individuals against discrimination.

Great Society (1964–1968) President Lyndon Johnson's term for his domestic policy agenda. Billed as a successor to the New Deal, the Great Society aimed to extend the postwar prosperity to all people in American society by promoting civil rights and fighting poverty. Great Society programs included the War on Poverty, which expanded the Social Security system by creating Medicare and Medicaid to provide health care for the aged and the poor. Johnson also signed laws protecting consumers and empowering community organizations to combat poverty at grassroots levels.

★ Johnson Battles Goldwater in 1964

Johnson's nomination by the Democrats in 1964 was a foregone conclusion; he was chosen by acclamation in Atlantic City. The Republicans, convening in San Francisco, nominated box-jawed Senator Barry Goldwater of Arizona, a bronzed and bespectacled champion of rock-ribbed conservatism. The American stage was thus set for a historic clash of political principles.

Goldwater's forces had galloped out of the Southwest to ride roughshod over the moderate Republican "eastern establishment." Insisting that the GOP offer "a choice, not an echo," Goldwater attacked the federal income tax, the Social Security system, the Tennessee Valley Authority, civil rights legislation, the nuclear test-ban treaty, and, most loudly, the Great Society. His fiercely dedicated followers proclaimed, "In Your Heart You Know He's Right," which prompted the Democratic response, "In Your Guts You Know He's Nuts." Goldwater warmed right-wing hearts when he proclaimed that "extremism in the defense of liberty is no vice. And . . . moderation in the pursuit of justice is no virtue."

The senator owed his nomination to a burgeoning conservative movement that was gaining strength in the mushrooming middle-class suburbs of the Sunbelt. Led intellectually by vibrant writers like William F. Buckley and others on the *National Review* magazine, enthusiastic conservatives organized groups like Young Americans for Freedom. They were especially well received in the once-solidly Democratic South, where the civil rights movement met strong white opposition. Upon signing the Civil Rights Act of 1964 Lyndon Johnson had reputedly told an aide, "We have lost the South for a generation."

Democrats gleefully exploited the image of Goldwater as a trigger-happy cowboy who would "Barry us" in the rubble of World War III. Johnson cultivated the contrasting image of a resolute statesman by seizing upon the Tonkin Gulf episode early in August 1964. Unbeknownst to the American public or Congress, U.S. Navy ships had been cooperating with South Vietnamese gunboats in provocative raids along the coast of North Vietnam. Two of these American destroyers were allegedly fired upon by the North Vietnamese on August 2 and 4, although exactly what happened still remains unclear.

Johnson nevertheless promptly called the attacks "unprovoked" and ordered a "limited" retaliatory air raid. He loudly proclaimed that he sought "no wider war"—thus implying that the truculent Goldwater did. Johnson also used the incident to spur congressional passage of the all-purpose Tonkin Gulf Resolution. With only two dissenting votes in both chambers, the lawmakers virtually abdicated their war-declaring powers and handed the president a blank check to use further force in Southeast Asia.

The towering Texan rode to a spectacular victory in November 1964. A stampede of 43,129,566 Johnson votes trampled the Republican ticket with its 27,178,188 supporters. The tally in the Electoral College was 486 to 52. Goldwater carried only his native Arizona and five other states—all of them, tellingly, in the racially restless South. Johnson's record-breaking 61 percent of the popular vote swept lopsided Democratic majorities into both houses of Congress.

⭐ The Great Society Congress

Johnson's huge victory temporarily smashed the conservative congressional coalition of southern Democrats and northern Republicans. A wide-open legislative road stretched before the Great Society programs, as the president skillfully ringmastered his two-to-one Democratic majorities. Congress poured out a flood of legislation, comparable only to the output of the New Dealers in the Hundred Days Congress of 1933, as Johnson delivered at last on long-deferred Democratic promises of social reform.

Besides a greatly expanded War on Poverty, Johnson also prodded Congress into creating two new cabinet offices: the Department of Transportation and the Department of Housing and Urban Development (HUD), to which he named the nation's first black cabinet secretary, respected economist Robert C. Weaver. Other noteworthy laws established the National Endowments for the Arts and the Humanities, designed to lift the level of American cultural life.

Even more impressive were the Big Four legislative achievements that crowned LBJ's Great Society: aid to education, medical care for the elderly and indigent, immigration reform, and a new voting rights bill.

Johnson's federal program for education neatly avoided the thorny question of church and state by channeling educational aid to students, not schools, thus allowing funds to flow to hard-pressed parochial institutions. With a keen eye for the dramatic, LBJ signed the education bill in the humble one-room Texas schoolhouse he had attended as a boy.

Medicare for the elderly, accompanied by Medicaid for the poor, became a reality in 1965. Like the New Deal's Social Security program, Medicare and Medicaid created "entitlements." That is, they conferred rights on certain categories of Americans in perpetuity, without the need for repeated congressional approval. These programs were part of a spreading "rights revolution" that materially improved the lives of millions of Americans—but also eventually undermined the federal government's financial health.

Immigration reform was the third of Johnson's Big Four feats. The Immigration and Nationality Act of 1965 abolished at last the "national-origins" quota system that had been in place since 1921 (see p. 521). The act also doubled to 290,000 the number of immigrants allowed to enter annually, and provided for the admission of close relatives of U.S. citizens without limits. The "family unification" provision swelled immigration, and to the surprise of the act's sponsors, the sources of immigration shifted heavily from Europe to Latin America and Asia, dramatically changing the racial and ethnic composition of the American population.

Great Society programs came in for rancorous political attack in later years. Conservatives charged the billions spent for "social engineering" had simply been flushed down the waste pipe. Yet the poverty rate declined measurably in the ensuing decade. Medicare dramatically reduced poverty among America's elderly, and antipoverty programs like Project Head Start sharply improved the educational performance of underprivileged youth. Infant mortality rates also fell in minority communities as general health conditions improved.

⭐ Battling for Black Rights

With the last of his Big Four reforms, the Voting Rights Act of 1965, Johnson made heartening headway against one of the most persistent American evils, racial discrimination. The Civil Rights Act of 1964 had prohibited racial discrimination in public accommodations and employment and strengthened school desegregation. But the problem of voting rights remained. Throughout the South, only about 5 percent of eligible blacks were registered to vote. Ballot-denying devices like the poll tax, literacy tests, and barefaced intimidation still barred black people from the political process.

Beginning in 1964, opening up the polling booths became the chief goal of the black movement in the South. The Twenty-fourth Amendment, ratified in January 1964, abolished the poll tax in federal elections. (See the Appendix.) Singing "We Shall Overcome," blacks joined hands with white civil rights workers—many of them student volunteers from the North—in a massive voter-registration drive in Mississippi during the **Freedom Summer** of 1964.

Freedom Summer (1964) A voter registration drive in Mississippi spearheaded by a coalition of civil rights groups. The campaign drew the activism of thousands of black and white civil rights workers, many of whom were students from the North, and was marred by the abduction and murder of three such workers at the hands of white racists.

Mississippi Freedom Democratic party (1964) *Political party organized by civil rights activists to challenge Mississippi's delegation to the Democratic National Convention, who opposed the civil rights planks in the party's platform. Claiming a mandate to represent the true voice of Mississippi, where almost no black citizens could vote, the MFDP demanded to be seated at the convention but were denied by party bosses. The effort was both a setback to civil rights activism in the South and a motivation to continue to struggle for black voting rights.*

Voting Rights Act of 1965 *Legislation pushed through Congress by President Johnson that prohibited ballot-denying tactics, such as literacy tests and intimidation. The Voting Rights Act was a successor to the Civil Rights Act of 1964 and sought to make racial disenfranchisement explicitly illegal.*

Black Panther party *Organization of armed black militants formed in Oakland, California, in 1966 to protect black rights. The Panthers represented a growing dissatisfaction with the nonviolent wing of the civil rights movement and signaled a new direction to that movement after the legislative victories of 1964 and 1965.*

Black Power *Doctrine of militancy and separatism that rose in prominence after 1965. Black Power activists rejected Martin Luther King's pacifism and desire for integration. Rather, they promoted pride in African heritage and an often militant position in defense of their rights.*

But events soon blighted bright hopes. In late June 1964, one black and two white civil rights workers disappeared in Mississippi. Their badly beaten bodies were later found buried beneath an earthen dam. In August an integrated **Mississippi Freedom Democratic party** delegation was denied its seat at the national Democratic convention.

Early in 1965 Martin Luther King, Jr., resumed the voter-registration campaign in Selma, Alabama. State troopers with tear gas and whips assaulted King's peaceful demonstrators as they marched to Montgomery. A Boston Unitarian minister was killed, and a few days later a white Detroit woman was shotgunned to death by Klansmen on the highway near Selma.

As the nation recoiled in horror before these violent scenes, President Johnson, speaking in soft southern accents, delivered a compelling address on television. What happened in Selma, he insisted, concerned all Americans, "who must overcome the crippling legacy of bigotry and injustice." Then, in a stirring adaptation of the anthem of the civil rights movement, the president concluded: "And we shall overcome." Following words with deeds, Johnson speedily shepherded through Congress the landmark **Voting Rights Act of 1965**, signed into law on August 6. It outlawed literacy tests and sent federal voter registrars into several southern states.

The passage of the Voting Rights Act, exactly one hundred years after the conclusion of the Civil War, climaxed a century of awful abuse and robust resurgence for African Americans in the South. The act did not end discrimination and oppression overnight, but it placed an awesome lever for change in blacks' hands. Black southerners now had power and began to wield it without fear of reprisals. In the following decade, for the first time since emancipation, African Americans began to migrate *into* the South.

★ Black Power

The Voting Rights Act of 1965 marked the last major victory of the southern-focused, integrationist, nonviolent civil rights struggle—what one activist called the "classical phase" of the movement. From then on, racial conflict, especially in the urban North, took on new potency and ideological coloring after Jim Crow's final demise in the South. As if to symbolize this shift, just five days after President Johnson signed the voting law, a bloody riot erupted in Watts, a black ghetto in Los Angeles. The week-long violence left thirty-one blacks and three whites dead, more than a thousand people injured, and hundreds of buildings charred and gutted. The Watts explosion heralded a new phase of the black struggle—increasingly marked by militant confrontation, focusing on northern and western cities, led by radical and sometimes violent spokespersons, and often aiming not at interracial cooperation but at black separatism.

The pious Christian moderation of Martin Luther King, Jr., came under heavy fire from this second wave of younger black leaders. Embodying this new militancy was Malcolm X. Born Malcolm Little, he was at first inspired by the militant black nationalists in the Nation of Islam, founded by Elijah Muhammad. A brilliant and charismatic preacher, Malcolm X trumpeted black separatism and inveighed against the "blue-eyed white devils." Eventually, Malcolm distanced himself from Elijah Muhammad's separatist preachings and moved toward mainstream Islam. In early 1965 he was cut down by Nation of Islam gunmen while speaking to a large crowd in New York City.

The **Black Panther party** meanwhile openly brandished weapons in the streets of Oakland, California. Then in 1966 Trinidad-born Stokely Carmichael, a leader of the Student Non-Violent Coordinating Committee (SNCC), began to preach the doctrine of **Black Power**, which, Carmichael said, "will smash everything Western civilization has created." Some advocates of Black Power insisted that they simply intended the slogan to describe a broad-front effort to exercise the political and economic rights gained by the civil rights movement. But other African Americans, recollecting previous black nationalist movements such as that of Marcus Garvey earlier in the century (see p. 530), breathed a vibrant separatist meaning into the concept of Black Power. They emphasized African American distinctiveness, shed their "white" names for new African identities, and demanded black studies programs in colleges and universities.

Ironically, just as the civil rights movement had achieved its greatest legal and political triumphs, city-shaking riots erupted in the black ghettos of several American cities. A bloody outburst in Newark, New Jersey, in the summer of 1967, took twenty-five lives. Federal troops restored order in Detroit, Michigan, after forty-three people died in the streets. As in Los Angeles, black rioters torched their own neighborhoods, attacking police officers, and even firefighters, who had to battle both flames and mobs chanting, "Burn, baby, burn." These outbursts angered many white Americans, who threatened to retaliate with their own "backlash" against ghetto arsonists and killers. Inner-city anarchy baffled many northerners, who had considered racial problems a purely "southern" question. But black concerns had moved north—as had nearly half the nation's black people. Residential discrimination and deindustrialization all directly affected African Americans, who suffered unemployment at twice the rate of whites. Despair deepened when the magnetic and moderate voice of Martin Luther King, Jr., was forever silenced by a sniper's bullet in Memphis, Tennessee, on April 4, 1968. A martyr for justice, King had bled and died on the peculiarly American thorn of race. The killing of King cruelly robbed the American people of one of the most inspirational leaders in their history—at a time when they could least afford to lose him. This outrage triggered a nationwide outburst of violent riots that cost over forty lives.

Rioters noisily made news, but thousands of other blacks quietly made history. Their voter registration had shot upward, and by the late 1960s several hundred blacks held elected office in the Old South. Cleveland, Ohio, and Gary, Indiana, elected black mayors. By 1972 nearly half of southern black children sat in integrated classrooms. Actually, more schools in the South were integrated than in the North. About a third of black families had risen economically into the ranks of the middle class—though an equal proportion remained below the "poverty line." King left a shining legacy of racial progress, but he was cut down when the job was far from done.

★ Vietnam Vexations

While violence at home eclipsed Johnson's legislative triumphs, foreign flare-ups were threatening his political life. The United States was sinking deeper into the monsoon mud of Vietnam. After communist guerillas attacked an American air base in February 1965, Johnson ordered retaliatory air strikes and for the first time sent regular American troops. Before 1965 was ended, some 184,000 American soldiers were slogging through the jungles and rice paddies of South Vietnam searching for guerillas.

Johnson had now taken the first fateful steps down a slippery path. He and his advisers believed that a fine-tuned, step-by-step "escalation" of American force would drive the enemy to defeat with a minimum loss of life. But the enemy matched every increase in American firepower with more men and more wiliness in the art of guerrilla warfare.

Contending Voices

Differing Visions of Black Freedom

Dr. Martin Luther King, Jr. (1929–1968) and Malcolm X (1925–1965) not only differed in the goals they held out to their fellow African Americans—King urging racial integration and Malcolm X black separatism—but also in the means they advocated to achieve them. In his famous "I Have a Dream" speech during the interracial March on Washington on August 28, 1963, King spoke to a quarter of a million people assembled at the Lincoln Memorial:

"In the process of gaining our rightful place we must not be guilty of wrongful deeds. Let us not seek to satisfy our thirst for freedom by drinking from the cup of bitterness and hatred.... We must not allow our creative protest to degenerate into physical violence. Again and again we must rise to the majestic heights of meeting physical force with soul force."

About three months later, Malcolm X rejected King's "peaceful, turn-the-other-cheek revolution":

"Revolution is bloody, revolution is hostile, revolution knows no compromise, revolution overturns and destroys everything that gets in its way. And you, sitting around here like a knot on the wall, saying, 'I'm going to love these folks no matter how much they hate me,'... Whoever heard of a revolution where they lock arms..., singing 'We shall overcome?' You don't do that in a revolution. You don't do any singing, you're too busy swinging."

> Why did King see nonviolence as key to achieving movement goals? What might explain some African Americans' growing receptivity to militant and separatist appeals over the course of the 1960s?

The South Vietnamese themselves were meanwhile becoming spectators in their own war, as the fighting became increasingly Americanized. Corrupt and collapsible governments succeeded each other in Saigon with bewildering rapidity. Yet American officials continued to talk of defending a faithful democratic ally. Washington "hawks" also defended the action as a test of Uncle Sam's commitment and of the reliability of his numerous treaty pledges to resist communist encroachment. Persuaded by such panicky thinking, Johnson steadily raised the military stakes in Vietnam. By 1968 he had poured more than half a million troops into Southeast Asia, and the annual bill for the war was exceeding $30 billion. Still, the end was nowhere in sight.

America could not defeat the enemy in Vietnam, but it seemed to be defeating itself. World opinion grew increasingly hostile; the blasting of an underdeveloped country by a mighty superpower struck many critics as obscene. Several nations expelled American Peace Corps volunteers. President Charles de Gaulle withdrew France from NATO in 1966 and ordered all American troops out of the country.

Overcommitment in Southeast Asia also tied America's hands elsewhere. Attacked by Soviet-backed Egypt, Jordan, and Syria, a beleaguered Israel stunned the world with a military triumph in June 1967. When the smoke cleared after the **Six-Day War**, Israel expanded to control new territories in the Sinai Peninsula, the Golan Heights, the Gaza Strip, and the West Bank of the Jordan River, including Jerusalem. The Israelis eventually withdrew from the Sinai after signing a peace treaty with Egypt, but they refused to relinquish the other areas without a treaty and began moving Jewish settlers into the heavily Arab district of the West Bank. The Six-Day War markedly intensified the problems of the already volatile Middle East, leading to an intractable standoff between the Israelis and more than a million resentful Palestinians under their control.

Domestic discontent festered as the Vietnamese entanglement dragged on. Antiwar demonstrations had begun on a small scale with campus "teach-ins" in 1965. Gradually these protests mounted to tidal-wave proportions. As the long arm of the military draft dragged more and more young men off to the Southeast Asian slaughter pen, resistance stiffened. Thousands of draft registrants fled to Canada; others publicly burned their draft cards. Hundreds of thousands of chanting marchers filled the streets of New York, San Francisco, and other cities. Many Americans felt pangs of conscience at the ghastly spectacle of their countrymen burning peasant huts and blistering civilians with napalm.

Opposition in Congress to the Vietnam involvement centered in the influential Senate Committee on Foreign Relations, headed by Senator J. William Fulbright of Arkansas. A constant thorn in the side of the president, he staged a series of widely viewed televised hearings in 1966 and 1967, during which prominent personages aired their views, largely antiwar. Gradually the public came to feel that it had been lied to about the causes and "winnability" of the war. A yawning credibility gap opened between the government and the people. New flocks of antiwar "doves" were hatching daily.

By early 1968 the brutal and futile struggle had become the longest and most unpopular foreign war in the nation's history. The government had failed utterly to explain to the people what was supposed to be at stake in Vietnam. American casualties, killed and wounded, already exceeded 100,000. More bombs had been dropped on Vietnam than on all enemy territory in World War II.

The war was also ripping apart the fabric of American society and even threatening to shred the Constitution. In 1967 President Johnson ordered the CIA, in clear violation of its charter as a *foreign* intelligence agency, to spy on domestic antiwar activities. He also encouraged the FBI to turn its counterintelligence program against the peace movement, subverting leading "doves" with false accusations that they were communist sympathizers. These clandestine tactics made the FBI look like a totalitarian state's secret police rather than a guardian of American democracy.

As the war dragged on, evidence mounted that America had been entrapped in an Asian civil war, fighting against highly motivated rebels who were striving to overthrow an oppressive regime. Yet Johnson clung to his basic strategy of ratcheting up the pressure bit by bit. He stubbornly assured doubting Americans that he could see "the light at the end of the tunnel." But to growing numbers of Americans, it seemed that Johnson was bent on "saving" Vietnam by destroying it.

Six-Day War (1967) *Military conflict between Israel and its Arab neighbors, including Syria, Egypt, and Jordan. The war ended with an Israeli victory and territorial expansion into the Sinai Peninsula, the Golan Heights, the Gaza Strip, and the West Bank. The 1967 war was a humiliation for several Arab states, and the territorial disputes it created formed the basis for continued conflict in the region.*

The Mechanized War High technology and modern equipment, such as this helicopter, gave the Americans in Vietnam a huge military advantage. But unaccompanied by a clear political purpose and a national will to win, technological superiority was insufficient to achieve final victory.

★ Vietnam Topples Johnson

Hawkish illusions that the struggle was about to be won were shattered by a blistering communist offensive launched in late January 1968, during Tet, the Vietnamese New Year. At a time when the Viet Cong were supposedly licking their wounds, they suddenly and simultaneously mounted savage attacks on twenty-seven key South Vietnamese cities, including the capital, Saigon. Although eventually beaten off with heavy losses, they demonstrated anew that victory could not be gained by Johnson's strategy of gradual escalation. With an increasingly insistent voice, American public opinion demanded a speedy end to the war. But American military leaders responded to the Tet attacks with a request for 200,000 more troops. The size of the request staggered many policymakers.

Meanwhile, Senator Eugene J. McCarthy of Minnesota was sharply challenging the president from within his own party for the 1968 Democratic presidential nomination. McCarthy, a sometime poet and devout Catholic, gathered a small army of antiwar college students as campaign workers. Going "clean for Gene," with shaven faces and shortened locks, they helped him gain an impressive 41.4 percent of the Democratic vote in the New Hampshire primary on March 12, 1968. Although still second to Johnson's 49.6 percent, McCarthy's showing was devastating for the president. Johnson's star fell further four days later when Senator Robert F. Kennedy of New York, an outspoken dove on the war, threw his hat into the ring. The charismatic and handsome Kennedy, heir to his murdered brother's mantle of leadership, stirred a passionate response among workers, African Americans, Latinos, and young people.

These startling events abroad and at home were not lost on LBJ. In a bombshell address on March 31, 1968, he announced that he would freeze American troop levels and scale down the bombing. Then, Johnson startled his vast television audience by firmly declaring that he would not be a candidate for the presidency in 1968.

Johnson's "abdication" had the effect of preserving the military status quo. The United States could maintain the maximum *acceptable* level of military activity in Vietnam with one hand, while trying to negotiate a settlement with the other. North Vietnam shortly agreed to negotiations in Paris, but progress was glacially slow, as prolonged bickering developed over the very shape of the conference table.

The Presidential Sweepstakes of 1968

The summer of 1968 was one of the hottest political seasons in the nation's history. Johnson's heir apparent for the Democratic nomination was his loyal vice president, Hubert Humphrey. Senators McCarthy and Kennedy meanwhile dueled in several state primaries, with Kennedy's bandwagon gathering ever-increasing speed. But on June 5, 1968, on the night of his exciting victory in the California primary, Kennedy was shot to death by a young Arab immigrant.

Angry antiwar forces, deprived by an assassin's bullet of one of their candidates, streamed menacingly into Chicago for the Democratic convention in August 1968. Mayor Richard Daley responded by arranging for barbed-wire barricades around the convention hall, as well as thousands of police and National Guard reinforcements. Some militant demonstrators baited the officers in blue by calling them "pigs," shouting obscenities, and hurling cans of excrement at police lines. As people the world over watched on television, the exasperated "peace officers" broke into a "police riot," clubbing and manhandling innocent and guilty alike. Acrid tear gas fumes hung over the city even as Humphrey steamrollered to a first-ballot nomination. The Humphrey forces also blocked the dovish McCarthyites' attempt to secure an antiwar platform plank and hammered into place their own declaration that armed force would be relentlessly applied until the enemy showed more willingness to negotiate.

Scenting victory over the badly divided Democrats, the Republicans convened in plush Miami Beach, Florida, where former vice president Richard Nixon arose from his political grave to win the nomination. As a "hawk" on Vietnam and a right-leaning middle-of-the-roader on domestic policy, Nixon was acceptable to both the Goldwater

The Siege of Chicago, 1968 Antiwar protesters staged demonstrations in the streets of Chicago during the Democratic National Convention in August 1968. Some 2,500 members of the radical Youth International Party (known as the Yippies) planned a peaceful "festival of light" across the street from the convention hall, but instead found themselves drawn into a melee with the police and National Guardsmen. The confrontation in Chicago badly tarnished Democratic candidate Hubert Humphrey's presidential campaign. His Republican opponent, Richard Nixon, won the presidency with calls for an "honorable peace" in Vietnam and "law and order" at home.

conservatives and party moderates. He appealed to white southern voters and to the "law and order" element when he tapped as his running mate Maryland Governor Spiro T. Agnew, noted for his tough stands against dissidents and black militants. The Republican platform called for victory in Vietnam and a strong anticrime policy.

Adding color and confusion to the campaign was the third-party candidacy of the segregationist former Alabama governor George C. Wallace. Wallace jabbed repeatedly at "pointy-headed bureaucrats" and taunted hecklers as "bums" who needed a bath. He also called for prodding blacks back into their place. Wallace and his running mate, former air force general Curtis LeMay, also proposed smashing the North Vietnamese to smithereens by "bombing them back to the Stone Age."

Between the positions of the Republicans and the Democrats on Vietnam, there was little choice. Both candidates were committed to keeping on the war until the enemy would settle for an "honorable peace," which seemed to mean an "American victory." The millions of "doves" had no place to roost, and many refused to vote at all. Humphrey, scorched by the LBJ brand, went down to defeat as a loyal prisoner of his chief's policies.

Nixon, who had lost a cliffhanger to Kennedy in 1960, won one in 1968. He garnered 301 electoral votes with 43.4 percent of the popular tally (31,785,480), compared with 191 electoral votes and 42.7 percent of the popular votes (31,275,166) for Humphrey (see Map 37.1). Unlike most new presidents, Nixon faced congressional majorities of the opposing party in both houses. Wallace won an impressive 9,906,473 popular votes and 46 electoral votes, all from five states of the Deep South, four of which the Republican Goldwater had carried in 1964. Wallace remained a formidable force, for he had amassed the largest third-party popular vote in American history to that point and was the last third-party candidate to win any electoral votes. (Ross Perot in 1992 enjoyed a greater popular vote margin but won no states; see p. 704.) Wallace had also resoundingly demonstrated the continuing power of "populist" politics, which appealed to voters' fears and resentments rather than to the better angels of their nature. His candidacy foreshadowed a coarsening of American political life that would take deep root in the ensuing decades.

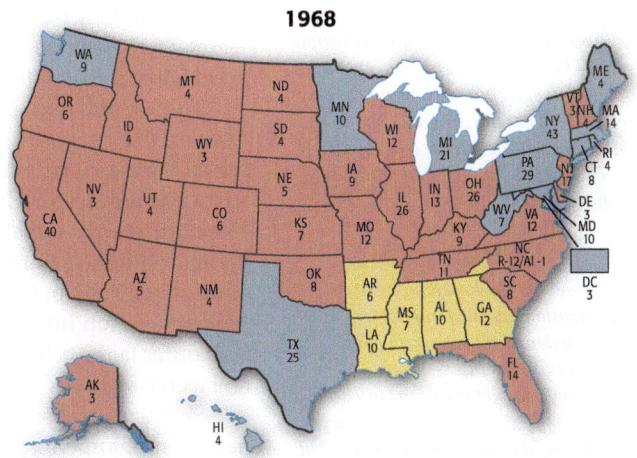

Map 37.1 Presidential Election of 1968 (with electoral vote by state) George Wallace won in five states and denied a clear majority to either of the two major-party candidates in twenty-five other states. A shift of some fifty thousand votes might have thrown the election into the House of Representatives, giving Wallace the strategic bargaining position that he sought.

Talented but tragedy-struck Lyndon Johnson returned to his Texas ranch in January 1969 and died there four years later. His party and his vice president Humphrey had been defeated, yet Johnson's legislative leadership for a time had been remarkable. No president since Lincoln had worked harder or done more for civil rights. None had shown more compassion for the poor, blacks, and the ill educated.

But by 1966 Johnson was already sinking into the Vietnam quicksand. His attempt to provide both guns and butter prevented him from delivering on either in sufficient quantity. The War on Poverty met resistance as stubborn as the Viet Cong and eventually went down to defeat. Johnson crucified himself on the cross of Vietnam. His decision to enlarge the conflict cost him his political future. By not escalating the fighting further he offended the "hawks," by refusing to back off altogether he antagonized the "doves." Like the Calvinists of colonial days, luckless Lyndon Johnson was damned if he did and damned if he did not.

★ The Cultural Upheaval of the 1960s

The struggles of the 1960s against racism, poverty, and the war in Vietnam had momentous cultural consequences. Everywhere in 1960s America, a newly negative attitude toward all kinds of authority began to take hold. Disillusioned by the discovery that American society was not free of racism, sexism, imperialism, and oppression, many young

Stonewall Rebellion (1969) *Uprising in support of equal rights for gay people sparked by an assault by off-duty police officers at a gay bar in New York. The rebellion led to a rise in activism and militancy within the gay community and furthered the sexual revolution of the late 1960s.*

Students for a Democratic Society (SDS) *A campus-based political organization founded in 1961 by Tom Hayden that became an iconic representation of the New Left. Originally geared toward the intellectual promise of "participatory democracy," SDS emerged at the forefront of the civil rights, antipoverty, and antiwar movements during the 1960s.*

people lost their traditional moral rudders. Neither families nor churches nor schools seemed to be able to define values and shape behavior with the certainty of shared purpose that many people believed had once existed.

The nation's mainstream Protestant denominations, which had dominated American religious life for centuries, lost their grip and many of their churchgoing parishioners. The liberal Protestant churches suffered the most. They increasingly ceded religious authority to conservative evangelicals while surrendering cultural authority to secular professionals and academic social scientists. Religious upheaval even churned the tradition-bound Roman Catholic Church, among the world's oldest and most conservative institutions. The Second Vatican Council, meeting from 1962 to 1965, passed reforms aimed at modernizing church liturgy and practices and encouraging more ecumenical interactions with other faiths. Clerics abandoned their Roman collars and the Latin Mass; folk songs replaced Gregorian chants; and meatless Fridays became ancient history.

Skepticism about authority had deep historical roots in American culture, and it had even bloomed in the supposedly complacent and conformist 1950s. "Beat" poets like Allen Ginsberg and iconoclastic novelists like Jack Kerouac had voiced dark disillusion with the materialistic pursuits of "establishment" arrogance of the Eisenhower era. In movies like *Rebel Without a Cause* (1955), the attractive young actor James Dean expressed the restless frustration of many young people.

The disaffection of the young crescendoed in the tumultuous 1960s, as the first baby boomers reached college age. One of the first organized protests against established authority broke out at the University of California at Berkeley in 1964, in the aptly named Free Speech Movement. Students objected to an administrative ban on the use of campus space for political debate, and accused the Cold War "megaversity" of promoting corporate interests rather than humane values.

But in only a few years, the clean-cut Berkeley activists and their sober-minded sit-ins would seem downright quaint. Fired by outrage against the war in Vietnam, some sons and daughters of the middle class became radical political rebels. Others turned to mind-bending drugs, tuned in to "acid rock," and dropped out of "straight" society. Others joined communes or "alternative" institutions. *Patriotism* became a dirty word. Beflowered women and long-haired men with earrings heralded the rise of a self-conscious "counterculture" stridently opposed to traditional American ways.

Social upheaval in the 1960s was hardly confined to the United States as youth-driven political and social conflict roiled nations around the world (see "Thinking Globally: The Global 1960s," p. 661). The newfound power of popular youth culture—especially the urgent rock 'n' roll of the Beatles, Janis Joplin, and Jimi Hendrix—proved global in its reach, helping to stitch together generational styles, norms, and touchstones across borders.

The 1960s also witnessed a "sexual revolution," though its novelty and scale are often exaggerated. Without doubt, the introduction of the birth-control pill in 1960 made unwanted pregnancies much easier to avoid and sexual appetites much easier to satisfy. The Mattachine Society, founded in Los Angeles in 1951, was a pioneering advocate for gay rights. A brutal attack on gay men by off-duty police officers at New York's Stonewall Inn in 1969 proved a turning point, when the victims fought back in what became known as the **Stonewall Rebellion**.

Launched in youthful idealism, many of the cultural "revolutions" of the 1960s sputtered out in violence and cynicism. **Students for a Democratic Society (SDS)**, once at the forefront of antipoverty and antiwar campaigns, had by decade's end spawned an underground terrorist group called the Weather

The Free Speech Movement, Berkeley, California, 1964 The Free Speech Movement on the campus of the University of California at Berkeley marked the first of the large-scale student mobilizations that rocked campuses across the country throughout the rest of the 1960s. Here a student schooled in passive resistance is dragged by police to a waiting bus.

Thinking Globally

The Global 1960s

Social upheaval in the 1960s was a global phenomenon. As young people born in the wake of World War II came of age around the world, they everywhere challenged established authority, customs, and institutions. Antiwar protests and demonstrations for social rights shook the political and cultural foundations of peoples on every inhabited continent.

Worldwide turmoil was propelled by worldwide forces. A massive "baby boom" swelled the demographic profile of nations on all continents. Western youth approached adulthood buoyed by postwar prosperity and major public investments in higher education. The leading edge of boomers entered college in the 1960s, just as the international equilibrium was increasingly challenged by Cold War tensions, threats of thermonuclear war, and rapid decolonization in Asia and Africa. Affluent, educated, and idealistic, conscious of their shared generational identity, and impatient with their elders, these young people formed the vanguard of political and social turmoil in one country after another.

Western Europe, long culturally aligned with the United States, paralleled the American experience most closely. Young people in the North Atlantic world adopted what one historian has called an "international language of dissent." Thinkers as disparate as Berlin-born philosopher Herbert Marcuse, American sociologist C. Wright Mills, and Martinique-born psychiatrist Frantz Fanon rejected the stark Cold War dichotomies between capitalist and communist states and inspired Western youth to ferociously condemn repressive and imperialistic tendencies in their own societies. On both sides of the Atlantic, the American war in Vietnam catalyzed protest.

Upheaval was hardly confined to the capitalist West. Peace, economic growth, and expanding education also emboldened a postwar generation in Soviet bloc countries to voice political dissent. A Soviet intelligence officer cabled Soviet premier Leonid Brezhnev in 1968 that "opposition" was one of the "harmful developments among our youth."

The global tumult swept up peoples in the "Third World" as well, even as Western radicals made folk heroes of revolutionaries like Cuba's Che Guevara and Congo's Patrice Lumumba. In China, Mao Zedong launched the "Cultural Revolution" in 1966 to purge all bourgeois vestiges from the emerging Chinese nation. Young and ideologically hypercharged Red Guards made war on the "Four Olds": old customs, old culture, old habits, and old ideas. Millions perished before Mao finally began to rein in the rampaging bullies in 1969.

The year 1968 became synonymous with unrest in many lands. Within the Soviet bloc, Western-inspired Czechoslovakian reformers launched the liberating "Prague Spring." For eight months political freedom blossomed, until ruthlessly cut down by Soviet tanks. In May, leftist French students, backed by massive workers' strikes, nearly toppled the government of President Charles de Gaulle.

By the early seventies, repression and exhaustion began to dissipate the global unrest. But despite backlash and disillusionment, the upheavals of the 1960s left a permanent mark on societies around the world. New "post-materialist" concerns about culture, identity, the environment, and human rights began to enter the political mainstream. A new skepticism about authority and a loosening of cultural mores transformed societies the world over as a lasting consequence of the global 1960s.

Paris, 1968 Protests ripped through the world in 1968. In Paris student battles with campus authorities and police triggered a massive nationwide labor strike and nearly brought down the French government.

661

Underground. Peaceful civil rights demonstrations had given way to blockbusting urban riots. What started as apparently innocent experiments with drugs like marijuana and LSD had fried many youthful brains and spawned a loathsome underworld of drug lords and addicts.

Strait-laced guardians of respectability denounced the self-indulgent romanticism of the "flower children" as the beginning of the end of modern civilization. Sympathetic observers hailed the "greening" of America—the replacement of materialism and imperialism by a new consciousness of human values. But the upheavals of the 1960s could be largely attributed to three *P*'s: the youthful population bulge, protest against racism and the Vietnam War, and the prosperity that seemed a permanent fixture of postwar America The counterculture may not have fully replaced traditional values by the end of the "sixties," but it had weakened their grip, perhaps permanently.

Vietnamization *Military strategy launched by Richard Nixon in 1969. The plan reduced the number of American combat troops in Vietnam and left more of the fighting to the South Vietnamese, who were supplied with American armor, tanks, and weaponry.*

Nixon Doctrine *President Nixon's plan for "peace with honor" in Vietnam. The doctrine stated that the United States would honor its existing defense commitments but, in the future, countries would have to fight their own wars.*

silent majority *Nixon administration's term to describe generally content, law-abiding, middle-class Americans who supported both the Vietnam War and America's institutions. As a political tool, the concept attempted to make a subtle distinction between believers in "traditional" values and the vocal minority of civil rights agitators, student protesters, counterculturalists, and other seeming disruptors of the social fabric.*

★ Nixon "Vietnamizes" the War

Inaugurated on January 20, 1969, Richard Nixon urged the American people, torn with dissension over Vietnam and race relations, to "stop shouting at one another." The new president seemed an unlikely conciliator of the clashing forces that appeared to be ripping apart American society. Solitary and suspicious by nature, Nixon could be brittle and testy in the face of opposition. He also harbored bitter resentments against the "liberal establishment." But Nixon brought one hugely valuable asset with him to the White House—his expertise in foreign affairs.

The first burning need was to quiet the public uproar over Vietnam. President Nixon's announced policy, called **Vietnamization**, was to withdraw the 540,000 U.S. troops in South Vietnam over an extended period. The South Vietnamese—with American money, weapons, training, and advice—could then gradually take over the burden of fighting their own war. This so-called **Nixon Doctrine** furthermore proclaimed that in the future, America's allies would have to fight their own wars without the support of large bodies of American ground troops.

Nixon sought to win the war by other means without the further spilling of American blood. But even this much involvement was distasteful to the American "doves," many of whom demanded a prompt, complete, and unconditional withdrawal. Antiwar protesters staged a massive national Vietnam moratorium in October 1969, as nearly 100,000 people jammed Boston Common and some 50,000 filed by the White House carrying lighted candles.

Undaunted, Nixon launched a counteroffensive by appealing to the "**silent majority**" who presumably supported the war and rejected the counterculture. Though ostensibly conciliatory, Nixon's appeal was in fact deeply divisive. His intentions soon became clear when he unleashed tough-talking Vice President Agnew to attack the "nattering nabobs of negativism" who demanded quick withdrawal from Vietnam. Nixon himself in 1970 sneered at the student antiwar demonstrators as "bums."

By January 1970 the Vietnam conflict had become grotesquely unpopular, even among troops in the field. Because draft policies largely exempted college students and those with high skills, the armed forces in Vietnam were mainly composed of the least privileged young Americans. African Americans were disproportionately represented in the army and accounted for a disproportionately high share of combat casualties. Black and white soldiers alike floundered through booby-trapped swamps and steaming jungles, often unable to distinguish friend from foe among the Vietnamese peasants. Morale plummeted, as drug abuse, mutiny, and sabotage dulled the army's fighting edge, and

---

A Marine Corps officer expressed the disillusion that beset many American troops in Vietnam:

"For years we disposed of the enemy dead like so much garbage. We stuck cigarettes in the mouths of corpses, put *Playboy* magazines in their hands, cut off their ears to wear around our necks. We incinerated them with napalm, atomized them with B-52 strikes, shoved them out the doors of helicopters above the South China Sea.... All we did was count, count bodies. Count dead human beings.... That was our fundamental military strategy. Body count. And the count kept going up."

rumors spread that soldiers were murdering ("fragging") their own officers with fragmentation grenades. Domestic disgust with the war further deepened amid revelations that American troops had slaughtered innocent women and children in the village of **My Lai** in 1968.

★ "Cambodianizing" the Vietnam War

For several years the North Vietnamese and Viet Cong had been using Cambodia, bordering South Vietnam on the west, as a springboard for troops, weapons, and supplies. Suddenly, on April 29, 1970, without consulting Congress, Nixon ordered American troops to invade officially neutral Cambodia.

Angry students nationwide responded to this newest escalation of the fighting with rock throwing, window smashing, and arson. At **Kent State University** in Ohio, jumpy members of the National Guard fired into a noisy student crowd, killing four and wounding many more. At historically black Jackson State College in Mississippi, the highway patrol killed two students.

Nixon withdrew the American troops from Cambodia after only two months. But in America the Cambodian invasion amplified the bitterness between "hawks" and "doves." Disillusionment with "whitey's war" increased ominously among African American troops. The Senate (though not the House) overwhelmingly repealed the Gulf of Tonkin blank check that Congress had given Johnson in 1964. American youths were only slightly mollified when the government reduced draft calls, introduced a draft lottery, and lowered the voting age to eighteen through approval of the Twenty-sixth Amendment in 1971 (see Appendix).

New combustibles fueled the fires of antiwar discontent in June 1971, when a former Pentagon official leaked to the *New York Times* the **Pentagon Papers**, a top-secret Pentagon study that documented the blunders and deceptions of the Kennedy and Johnson administrations, especially the provoking of the 1964 North Vietnamese attack in the Gulf of Tonkin.

My Lai *Vietnamese village that was the scene of a military assault on March 16, 1968, in which American soldiers under the command of 2nd Lieutenant William Calley murdered hundreds of unarmed Vietnamese civilians, mostly women and children. The atrocity produced outrage and reduced support for the war in America and around the world when details of the massacre and an attempted cover-up were revealed in November 1969.*

Kent State University *Scene of massacre of four college students by National Guardsmen on May 4, 1970, in Ohio. In response to Nixon's announcement that he had expanded the Vietnam War into Cambodia, college campuses across the country exploded in violence. On May 14 and 15, students at historically black Jackson State College in Mississippi were protesting the war as well as the Kent State shooting when highway patrolmen fired into a student dormitory, killing two students.*

Pentagon Papers *Secret U.S. government report detailing early planning and policy decisions regarding the Vietnam War under Presidents Kennedy and Johnson. Leaked to the New York Times in 1971, it revealed instances of governmental secrecy, lies, and incompetence in the prosecution of the war.*

The War at Home, Spring 1970 President Nixon's order to invade Cambodia sparked angry protests on American campuses. At Kent State University in Ohio, the nation watched in horror as four student demonstrators were shot by jittery National Guardsmen.

★ Nixon's Détente with Beijing (Peking) and Moscow

Even as the war in Vietnam ground on, Nixon pursued a dramatic Cold War diplomatic initiative in Beijing and Moscow. The two great communist powers, China and the Soviet Union, were clashing bitterly over their rival interpretations of Marxism. Nixon astutely perceived that the Chinese-Soviet tension afforded the United States an opportunity to play off one antagonist against the other, gaining new leverage on the world stage. Nixon's thinking was reinforced by his bespectacled and German-accented national security adviser, Dr. Henry A. Kissinger, who in 1969 had begun negotiating secretly with North Vietnamese officials in Paris while preparing the president's path to Beijing and Moscow.

Nixon, heretofore an uncompromising anticommunist, startled the nation by making an historic journey to China in February 1972. He capped the visit with the Shanghai Communiqué, in which the two nations agreed to "normalize" their relationship. Nixon next traveled to Moscow in May 1972 to play his "China card" in a game of high-stakes diplomacy in the Kremlin. The Soviets, hungry for American foodstuffs and alarmed over the possibility of intensified rivalry with an American-backed China, were ready to deal.

Nixon's visits ushered in an era of **détente**, or relaxed tension, with the two communist powers and led to several significant agreements in 1972, including an antiballistic missile (ABM) treaty and a series of arms-reduction agreements known as SALT (Strategic Arms Limitations Talks) aimed at freezing the numbers of long-range nuclear missiles for five years. The ABM and SALT accords constituted long-overdue first steps toward slowing the arms race, though both parties forged ahead with the development of "MIRVs" (multiple independently targeted reentry vehicles) equipped with large numbers of warheads, several to a rocket.

Nixon's détente diplomacy did, to some extent, de-ice the Cold War. Yet Nixon remained staunchly anticommunist when the occasion seemed to demand it. He strongly opposed the election of the outspoken Marxist Salvador Allende as president of Chile in 1970. His administration and the Central Intelligence Agency worked covertly to undermine the legitimately elected leftist president. When the Chilean army overthrew and killed Allende in 1973, many observers smelled a Yankee rat—an impression that deepened when Washington warmly embraced Allende's successor, military dictator General Augusto Pinochet.

détente *From the French for "reduced tension," the period of Cold War thawing when the United States and the Soviet Union negotiated reduced armament treaties under Presidents Nixon, Ford, and Carter. As a policy prescription, détente marked a departure from the policies of proportional response, mutually assured destruction, and containment that had defined the earlier years of the Cold War.*

★ Nixon on the Home Front

Nixon had lashed out during the campaign at the "permissiveness" and "judicial activism" of the Supreme Court, presided over by Chief Justice Earl Warren. The Warren Court's controversial decisions on sexual freedom, civil rights, criminal law, the practice of religion, and the structure of political representation had reflected its deep concern for the individual, no matter how lowly.

In *Griswold v. Connecticut* (1965), the Court struck down a state law that prohibited the use of contraceptives, even among married couples. The Court proclaimed (critics said "invented") a "right of privacy" that soon provided the basis for decisions protecting women's abortion rights. Controversial decisions in the cases of *Escobedo* (1964) and *Miranda* (1966) gave accused criminals the right to remain silent. The latter case gave rise to the **Miranda warning** that arresting officers must read to suspects. These several court rulings sought to prevent abusive police tactics, but they appeared to conservatives to coddle criminals and subvert law and order.

Conservatives also objected to the Court's views on religion. In two stunning decisions, *Engel* v. *Vitale* (1962) and *School District of Abington Township* v. *Schempp* (1963), the justices argued that the First Amendment's separation of church and state meant that public schools could not require prayer or Bible reading. From 1954 on, the Court came under relentless criticism, the bitterest since New Deal days. Fulfilling campaign promises, President Nixon undertook to change the Court's philosophical complexion.

Miranda warning *A statement of an arrested person's constitutional rights, which police officers must read during an arrest. The warning came out of the Supreme Court's decision in* Miranda v. Arizona *in 1966 that accused people have the right to remain silent, consult an attorney, and enjoy other protections. The Court declared that law enforcement officers must make sure suspects understand their constitutional rights, thus creating a safeguard against forced confessions and self-implication.*

He sought appointees who would strictly interpret the Constitution, cease "meddling" in social and political questions, and not coddle radicals or criminals. The Senate in 1969 speedily confirmed his nomination of white-maned Warren E. Burger of Minnesota to succeed the retiring Earl Warren as chief justice. Before the end of 1971 the Court counted four conservative Nixon appointments out of nine members.

Yet Nixon was to learn the ironic lesson that many presidents have learned about their Supreme Court appointees: once seated on the high bench, the justices are fully free to think and decide according to their own consciences, not according to the president's expectations. The Burger Court that Nixon shaped proved reluctant to dismantle the "liberal" rulings of the Warren Court; it even produced the most controversial judicial opinion of modern times, the momentous *Roe v. Wade* decision in 1973, which legalized abortion (see p. 679).

Surprisingly Nixon presided over significant expansion of the welfare programs that conservative Republicans routinely denounced. He approved increased funds for entitlements like Food Stamps, Medicaid, and Aid to Families with Dependent Children (AFDC), while adding a generous new program, Supplemental Security Income (SSI), to assist the indigent, blind, and disabled. Nixon also guaranteed automatic Social Security cost-of-living increases to protect the elderly against the ravages of inflation. Ironically, this "indexing" actually helped to fuel the inflationary fires.

Amid much controversy, Nixon in 1969 implemented his so-called **Philadelphia Plan** requiring construction unions to establish "goals and timetables" for the hiring of black apprentices. Soon extended to all federal contracts, the Philadelphia Plan required employers to meet hiring quotas or to establish "set-asides" for minority contractors. Nixon's policy went beyond earlier definitions of "affirmative action" designed to aid *individuals*, and instead conferred privileges on certain *groups*. While opening broad employment and educational opportunities for minorities and women, this approach opened a Pandora's box of protest from critics who assailed this "reverse discrimination" imposed by executive orders and unelected courts, not by democratically elected representatives.

Among Nixon's legacies was the creation in 1970 of the **Environmental Protection Agency (EPA)**, which climaxed two decades of mounting concern for the environment. Scientist and author Rachel Carson gave the environmental movement a huge boost in 1962 when she published *Silent Spring*, an enormously effective piece of latter-day muckraking that exposed the poisonous effects of pesticides. On April 22, 1970, millions of environmentalists around the world celebrated the first **Earth Day** to raise awareness and to encourage their leaders to act. In the wake of what became a yearly event, the U.S. Congress passed the Clean Air Act of 1970 and the Endangered Species Act of 1973. The EPA now stood on the frontline of the battle for ecological sanity and made notable progress in reducing automobile emissions and cleaning up befouled waterways and toxic waste sites.

The federal government also expanded its regulatory reach on behalf of workers and consumers. Late in 1970 Nixon signed the Occupational Safety and Health Administration (OSHA) into law, creating an agency dedicated to improving working conditions. The Consumer Product Safety Commission (CPSC) followed two years later, holding companies to account for selling dangerous products.

Appointing conservative Supreme Court justices, soft-pedaling civil rights, and opposing school busing to achieve racial balance were all parts of a GOP electoral approach that Nixon advisers called the "**southern strategy**." By deliberately seeking to convert disillusioned white southern Democrats to the Republican cause, Nixon set in motion a sweeping political realignment that eventually transformed the American party system.

★ The Nixon Landslide of 1972

Nearly four years had passed since Nixon had promised, as a presidential candidate, to end the war and "win" the peace. Yet in the spring of 1972 the fighting escalated anew to alarming levels when the North Vietnamese, heavily equipped with foreign

Philadelphia Plan (1969) *Program established by Richard Nixon to require construction trade unions to work toward hiring more black apprentices. The plan altered Lyndon Johnson's concept of "affirmative action" to focus on groups rather than individuals.*

Environmental Protection Agency (EPA) *A governmental organization signed into law by Richard Nixon in 1970 designed to regulate pollution, emissions, and other factors that negatively influence the natural environment. The creation of the EPA marked a newfound commitment by the federal government to actively combat environmental risks and was a significant triumph for the environmentalist movement.*

Earth Day (1970) *International day of celebration and awareness of global environmental issues launched by conservationists on April 22, 1970.*

southern strategy (1972) *Nixon reelection campaign strategy designed to appeal to conservative whites in the historically Democratic South. The president stressed law and order issues and remained noncommittal on civil rights. This strategy typified the regional split between the two parties as white southerners became increasingly attracted to the Republican party in the aftermath of the civil rights movement.*

tanks, burst through the demilitarized zone (DMZ) separating the two Vietnams. Nixon reacted promptly by launching massive bombing attacks on strategic centers in North Vietnam, including Hanoi, the capital. Either Moscow or Beijing, or both, could have responded explosively, but neither did, thanks to Nixon's shrewd diplomacy.

The continuing Vietnam conflict spurred the rise of South Dakota Senator George McGovern to the 1972 Democratic nomination. McGovern's promise to pull the remaining American troops out of Vietnam in ninety days earned him the backing of the large antiwar element in the Democratic party. But his appeal to racial minorities, feminists, leftists, and youth alienated the traditional working-class backbone of his party. Moreover, the discovery shortly after the convention that McGovern's running mate, Missouri Senator Thomas Eagleton, had undergone psychiatric care—including electroshock therapy—forced Eagleton's ouster from the ticket and virtually doomed the Democrats' hopes of recapturing the White House.

Nixon's campaign emphasized that he had wound down the "Democratic war" in Vietnam from some 540,000 troops to about 30,000. His candidacy received an added boost just twelve days before the election when the high-flying Dr. Kissinger announced that "peace is at hand" in Vietnam and that an agreement would be reached in a few days.

Nixon won the election in a landslide. His lopsided victory encompassed every state except Massachusetts and the nonstate District of Columbia (which was granted electoral votes by the Twenty-third Amendment in 1961 (see Appendix). He piled up 520 electoral votes to 17 and a popular majority of 47,169,911 votes to 29,170,383. McGovern had counted on a large vote from young people, but less than half the eighteen-to-twenty-one age group even bothered to register to vote. Dominated by conflict over both Vietnam and the counterculture, the 1972 presidential election proved to be the last election of the sixties era.

★ The Secret Bombing of Cambodia and the War Powers Act

The dove of peace, "at hand" in Vietnam just before the balloting, took flight after the election. Nixon launched a furious two-week bombing of North Vietnam that drove the North Vietnamese negotiators to agree to a cease fire in the Treaty of Paris on January 23, 1973, nearly three months after peace was prematurely proclaimed.

Nixon hailed the face-saving cease-fire agreement as "peace with honor," but the boast rang hollow. The United States was to withdraw its remaining 27,000 or so troops and could reclaim some 560 American prisoners of war. The North Vietnamese were allowed to keep some 145,000 troops in South Vietnam, where they still occupied about 30 percent of the country. This shaky "peace" was in reality little more than a thinly disguised American retreat.

The constitutionality of Nixon's continued aerial battering of Cambodia had meanwhile been coming under increasing fire. In July 1973 America was shocked to learn that the U.S. Air Force had already secretly conducted some thirty-five hundred bombing raids against North Vietnamese positions in Cambodia, beginning in March 1969 and continuing for some fourteen months prior to the open American incursion in May 1970. The most disturbing feature of these sky forays was that, while they were going on, American officials, including the president, had sworn that Cambodian neutrality was being respected. Countless Americans began to wonder what kind of representative government they had if they were fighting a war they knew nothing about.

Defiance followed secretiveness. After the Vietnam cease-fire in January 1973, Nixon brazenly continued large-scale bombing of communist forces in order to help the rightist Cambodian government, and he repeatedly vetoed congressional efforts to stop him. The years of bombing inflicted grisly wounds on Cambodia, blasting its people and revolutionizing its politics. The long-suffering Cambodians soon groaned under the sadistic heel of Pol Pot, a murderous tyrant who dispatched as many as 2 million of his people to their graves.

Congressional opposition to the expansion of presidential war-making powers by Johnson and Nixon led to the **War Powers Act** in November 1973. Passed over Nixon's veto, it required the president to report to Congress within forty-eight hours after committing troops to a foreign conflict. Such a limited authorization would have to end within sixty days unless Congress extended it for thirty more days.

The War Powers Act was but one manifestation of what came to be called the "New Isolationism," a mood of caution and restraint in the conduct of the nation's foreign affairs after the bloody and futile misadventure in Vietnam. Meanwhile, the draft ended in January 1973, although it was retained on a standby basis. The armed forces were to be all volunteers.

> The Washington Post *(July 19, 1973)* carried this news item:
>
> "American B-52 bombers dropped about 104,000 tons of explosives on Communist sanctuaries in neutralist Cambodia during a series of raids in 1969 and 1970.... The secret bombing was acknowledged by the Pentagon the Monday after a former Air Force major ... described how he falsified reports on Cambodian air operations and destroyed records on the bombing missions actually flown."

★ The Arab Oil Embargo and the Energy Crisis

The long-rumbling Middle East erupted anew in October 1973, when the rearmed Syrians and Egyptians unleashed surprise attacks on Israel. Kissinger, who had become secretary of state in September, hastily flew to Moscow to restrain the Soviets, who were arming the attackers. Believing that the Kremlin was poised to fly combat troops to the Suez area, Nixon placed America's nuclear forces on alert and ordered a gigantic airlift of nearly $2 billion in war materials to the Israelis. This assistance helped save the day, as the Israelis aggressively turned the tide and threatened Cairo itself until American diplomacy brought about an uneasy cease-fire in what became known as the Yom Kippur War.

America's policy of backing Israel against its oil-rich neighbors exacted a heavy penalty. Late in October 1973, the OPEC nations announced an embargo on oil shipments to the United States and several European allies supporting Israel. What was more, the oil-rich Arab states cut their oil production, further ratcheting pressure on the entire West, whose citizens suffered a long winter of lowered thermostats and speedometers. Lines at gas stations grew longer as tempers grew shorter. The shortage triggered a major economic recession not just in America, but also in France and Britain. In an increasingly globalized, interconnected world, all nations soon felt the crunch of the "energy crisis."

The five months of the Arab "blackmail" embargo in 1974 clearly signaled the end of an era—the era of cheap and abundant energy. American oil production peaked in 1970 and then began a long decline. Blissfully unaware of their dependence on foreign suppliers, Americans, like revelers on a binge, had more than tripled their oil consumption since the end of World War II. The number of automobiles increased 250 percent between 1949 and 1972, and Detroit's engineers gave nary a thought to building more fuel-efficient engines.

By 1974 America was oil-addicted and extremely vulnerable to any interruption in supplies. That stark fact deeply colored the diplomatic and economic history of the next three decades and beyond, as the Middle East loomed ever larger on the map of America's strategic interests. The United States finally began to initiate conservation measures such as a national speed limit of fifty-five miles per hour to conserve fuel. Detroit's automakers began their slow, grudging adjustment to the dawning age of energy dependency. But full reconciliation to that uncomfortable reality was a long time coming.

War Powers Act (1973) *Law passed by Congress limiting the president's ability to wage war without congressional approval. The act required the president to notify Congress within forty-eight hours of committing troops to a foreign conflict. An important consequence of the Vietnam War, this piece of legislation sought to reduce the president's unilateral authority in military matters.*

Varying Viewpoints

The Sixties: Constructive or Destructive?

The 1960s were convulsed by controversy, and they have remained controversial ever since. Conflicts raged in that turbulent decade between social classes, races, sexes, and generations. More than five decades later, conservative Republicans continue to campaign on a repudiation of the government activism that marked the sixties and a reaffirmation of the "traditional values" that sixties culture supposedly trashed. Liberal Democrats, for their part, continued to press for affirmative action for women and minorities, protection for the environment, an expanded welfare state, and sexual tolerance—all legacies of the stormy sixties.

Four issues dominate historical discussion of the 1960s: the civil rights struggle; the Great Society's "War on Poverty"; the Vietnam War and the antiwar movement; and the emergence of the "counterculture."

Although most scholars praise the civil rights achievements of the 1960s, they disagree over how to conceptualize the rise of Black Power and the militants' rejection of nonviolence. The Freedom Riders and Martin Luther King, Jr., find much more approval in most history books than do Malcolm X or the Black Panther party. But such scholars as William L. Van Deburg in *New Day in Babylon* (1992) and Peniel Joseph, *Waiting 'Til the Midnight Hour* (2006), argue that the "flank effect" of radical Black Power radicals like Stokely Carmichael actually enhanced the bargaining position of moderates such as Dr. King. Scholars of what Jacquelyn Hall has term the "long civil rights movement" meanwhile challenge the very notion of a sharp dividing line distinguishing the "classical" phase of the movement from a militant post-1965 phase.

Johnson's War on Poverty has found its liberal defenders in scholars like Allen Matusow (*The Unraveling of America*, 1984) and John Schwarz (*America's Hidden Success*, 1988). Schwarz demonstrates, for example, that Medicare and Social Security reforms virtually eliminated poverty among America's elderly. But conservative writers like Charles Murray (*Losing Ground*, 1984) and Lawrence Meade (*Beyond Entitlements*, 1986) argue that the War on Poverty did not simply fail to eradicate poverty among the so-called underclass; it actually deepened the dependency of the poor on the welfare state and even generated a multigenerational "cycle" of poverty.

The antiwar movement protesting America's policy in Vietnam initiated many young people into politics and "movement culture," with its sense of community and shared purpose. But scholars disagree over the movement's real effectiveness in checking the war. Writers such as John Lewis Gaddis (*Strategies of Containment*, 1982) explain America's eventual withdrawal from Vietnam essentially without reference to the protesters in the streets, while other like Adam Garfinkle (*Telltale Hearts*, 1995) argue that antiwar activism actually prolonged the war. By contrast, Todd Gitlin (*The Sixties: Years of Hope, Days of Rage*, 1987) and Tom Wells (*The War Within*, 1994) insist that mass protest was the force that finally ended the war.

Debate over the counterculture not only pits liberals against conservatives but also pits liberals against radicals. A liberal historian such as William O'Neill (*Coming Apart*, 1971) might sympathize with what he considers some of the worthy values pushed by student activists, but he also claims that much of the sixties "youth culture" degenerated into hedonism, arrogance, and social polarization. In contrast, historians such as Michael Kazin and Maurice Isserman argue that cultural radicalism and political radicalism were two sides of the same coin. Sara Evans shows in *Personal Politics* (1980) that "the personal *was* the political" for many women, and finds the roots of modern feminism in the sexism women activists encountered in the civil rights and antiwar movements.

Some scholars have begun to look at the origins of the conservative movement even during the liberal ascendency of the 1960s. Historians like Lisa McGirr (*Suburban Warriors*, 2001) and Rick Perlstein (*Before the Storm*, 2001) argue that Barry Goldwater's defeat in 1964 actually kick-started the conservatism that led to Ronald Reagan and both George Bushes. Rebecca Klatch shows in *A Generation Divided* (1999) how the New Right fed off the New Left, reshaping American politics in profound ways.

While critics may argue over the "good" versus the "bad" sixties, there is no denying the degree to which that tumultuous decade shaped the world in which we now live.

CHAPTER SUMMARY

Johnson succeeded the assassinated Kennedy and overwhelmingly defeated the militantly conservative Goldwater in the 1964 election. Johnson used his strong electoral mandate and huge congressional majorities to push through a mass of liberal Great Society legislation, including Medicare, Medicaid, federal aid to education, and immigration reform.

With Johnson's support, the civil rights movement won great legislative victories with the Civil Rights Act of 1964 and the Voting Rights Act of 1965. But Martin Luther King's nonviolent civil rights movement was increasingly overshadowed by more militant voices, as Northern ghettos erupted in violence amid calls for black power and black nationalism. A growing white backlash reduced sympathies for further integration and civil rights gains.

Faced with the possible collapse of corrupt and unpopular South Vietnamese governments, Johnson escalated military involvement Vietnam. As the number of troops and casualties grew without producing military success, dovish protests against the war gained strength. Political opposition forced Johnson not to seek reelection. Senators Eugene McCarthy and Robert Kennedy led antiwar challenges to Johnson's designated successor, Hubert Humphrey. Humphrey won the nomination, but deep Democratic divisions over the war allowed Nixon to win the White House. The third-party candidacy of George Wallace revealed the growth of an angry "populist" politics. The political upheavals of the 1960s also produced a youthful "counterculture" that revolted against authority and weakened all mainstream American institutions, including government and religion. The counterculture, which began in idealism, eventually faded amidst growing cynicism and economic anxiety in the 1970s.

Nixon's "Vietnamization" policy reduced American ground participation in the war, but his Cambodia invasion sparked massive domestic protest. Nixon's journeys to Communist Moscow and Beijing (Peking) established a new rapprochement with these powers, which Nixon and Kissinger used to advantage in continuing the Vietnam War. In domestic policy, Nixon appointed more conservative justices to the Supreme Court. He expanded social welfare programs and promoted environmental protection and workplace safety. On race relations he pursued a "southern strategy" that successfully moved southern white Democrats into the Republican party.

Nixon won a landslide victory in 1972 over the strongly antiwar Democratic nominee McGovern. After a fierce postelection bombing campaign, a cease fire agreement allowed the remaining U.S. troops to leave Vietnam. But revelations of the secret bombing of Cambodia led to congressional outrage and the War Powers Act. The Middle East war of 1973 and the Arab oil embargo created an energy and economic crisis. Americans gradually awoke to their costly and dangerous dependence on increasingly expensive Middle Eastern oil, and slowly began to take tentative steps toward conservation.

KEY TERMS

Civil Rights Act of 1964 (651)
affirmative action (652)
Great Society (652)
Freedom Summer (653)
Mississippi Freedom Democratic party (654)
Voting Rights Act of 1965 (654)
Black Panther party (654)
Black Power (654)
Six-Day War (656)
Stonewall Rebellion (660)
Students for a Democratic Society (SDS) (660)
Vietnamization (662)
Nixon Doctrine (662)
silent majority (662)
My Lai (663)
Kent State University (663)
Pentagon Papers (663)
détente (664)
Miranda warning (664)
Philadelphia Plan (665)
Environmental Protection Agency (EPA) (665)
Earth Day (665)
southern strategy (665)
War Powers Act (667)

PEOPLE TO KNOW

Malcolm X
Eugene McCarthy
George C. Wallace
Henry A Kissinger
Warren E. Burger
Rachel Carson
George McGovern

 MindTap is a fully online, highly personalized learning experience built upon Cengage Learning content. MindTap combines student learning tools—readings, multimedia, activities, and assessments—into a singular Learning Path that guides students through the course.

Chapter 38

Challenges to the Postwar Order
1973–1980

I must say to you that the state of the Union is not good.

GERALD FORD, 1975

Chapter Outline

- Watergate
- Economic Stagnation
- Nixon's Resignation and the Ford Presidency
- Feminism and Race in the 1970s
- Carter's Troubled Presidency
- The Energy Crisis and Inflation
- The Iranian Hostage Humiliation
- *Examining the Evidence:* The "Smoking Gun" Tape, June 23, 1972, 10:04–11:39 A.M.
- *Thinking Globally:* The Era of Globalization
- *Makers of America:* The Vietnamese
- *Makers of America:* The Feminists

"stagflation" Term referring to the simultaneous occurrence of low employment growth and high inflation in the national economy. The phenomenon characterized the economic troubles of the 1970s and posed both an intellectual challenge to economists and a policymaking challenge to government officials.

Americans in the 1970s struggled through a crisis of confidence in their leaders and institutions, as well as wrenching transformations in the nation's economy and politics. The engines of postwar economic growth and broadly shared prosperity sputtered to a near-halt, giving way to a bewildering mixture of stagnation and inflation that was soon dubbed **"stagflation."** Some of the major pillars of the postwar order began to crumble: Keynesian economic policies (see p. 566); an expanding welfare state; shared prosperity; and stable corporations matched by strong labor unions. Simultaneously, conflicts intensified about gender, religion, and America's role in the world. The patterns that emerged out of the crucible of these unsettling years persisted into the new century, including political polarization, a weakened federal government, the invigoration of free-market economic doctrines, rising inequality, and the re-assertion of traditionalist cultural values.

FOCUS QUESTIONS

1. How did the Watergate scandal lead to Nixon's resignation? How successful was Gerald Ford's "unelected presidency" in restoring trust in government after the disillusionment of Watergate and Vietnam?

2. How were the stagnating economy, the energy crisis, and Middle East foreign policy all closely linked in the 1970s? Why did both Republican and Democratic administrations have so little success in addressing these issues?

3. Why did the feminist movement make such dramatic gains in the 1970s, at a time when others like the civil rights movement stalled or prompted political backlash?

4. How did Jimmy Carter's presidential campaign and the turn toward "market economics" both reflect Americans' growing disillusionment with government in the 1970s?

5. How did the Iranian crisis intensify public disaffection with the Carter administration?

CHRONOLOGY

1972	■ Nixon defeats McGovern for presidency ■ Equal Rights Amendment passes Congress (not ratified by states) ■ Title IX of Education Amendments passed	1975	■ Helsinki accords ■ South Vietnam falls to communists
		1976	■ Carter defeats Ford for presidency
1973	■ Treaty of Paris enacts cease-fire in Vietnam and U.S. withdrawal ■ Agnew resigns; Ford appointed vice president ■ *Frontiero* v. *Richardson* ■ *Roe* v. *Wade*	1978	■ Camp David accords between Egypt and Israel ■ *United States* v. *Wheeler*
		1979	■ Iranian revolution and oil crisis ■ SALT II agreements signed (never ratified by Senate) ■ Soviet Union invades Afghanistan
1973–1974	■ Watergate hearings and investigations	1979–1981	■ Iranian hostage crisis
1974	■ Nixon resigns; Ford assumes presidency ■ *Milliken* v. *Bradley*	1980	■ United States boycotts Summer Olympics in Moscow

★ Watergate and the Unmaking of a President

Richard Nixon's electoral triumph in 1972 was almost immediately sullied—and eventually undone—by the **Watergate** scandal. On June 17, 1972, five men were arrested inside the Watergate office complex in Washington after attempting to plant electronic "bugs" in the Democratic party's headquarters. They were soon revealed to be working for the Republican Committee to Re-Elect the President—popularly known as CREEP. The Watergate break-in turned out to be just one in a series of Nixon administration "dirty tricks" that included forging documents to discredit Democrats, using the Internal Revenue Service to harass innocent citizens named on a White House "enemies list," burglarizing the office of the psychiatrist who had treated the leaker of the Pentagon Papers, and perverting the FBI and CIA to cover the tricksters' tracks.

The moral stench hanging over the White House worsened when Vice President Spiro Agnew was forced to resign in October 1973 for taking bribes from Maryland contractors. In the first use of the Twenty-fifth Amendment (see the Appendix), Nixon nominated and Congress confirmed Agnew's successor, a twelve-term congressman from Michigan, Gerald ("Jerry") Ford.

Amid a mood of growing national outrage, a select Senate committee conducted widely televised hearings about the Watergate affair in 1973–1974. Nixon indignantly denied any prior knowledge of the break-in and any involvement in the legal proceedings against the burglars. But when a former White House aide revealed that a secret taping system had recorded Nixon's Oval Office conversations, a Pandora's Box of incriminating evidence lay open.

Nixon at first agreed only to the publication of the "relevant" portions of the tapes, with many sections missing (including Nixon's frequent obscenities, which were excised with the phrase "expletive deleted"). But on July 24, 1974, the president suffered a disastrous setback when the Supreme Court unanimously ruled that "executive privilege" gave him no right to withhold evidence relevant to possible criminal activity. Skating on thin ice over hot water, Nixon reluctantly complied.

Watergate *Series of scandals that resulted in President Richard Nixon's resignation in August 1974 amid calls for his impeachment. The episode sprang from a failed burglary attempt at Democratic party headquarters in Washington's Watergate Hotel during the 1972 election.*

Nixon, the Law-and-Order Man

Examining the Evidence
The "Smoking Gun" Tape, June 23, 1972, 10:04–11:39 A.M.

The technological capability to record Oval Office conversations combined with Richard Nixon's obsession with documenting his presidency to give the public—and the Senate committee investigating his role in the break-in of the Democratic National Committee headquarters in the Watergate Office Tower—rare access to personal conversations between the president and his closest advisers. This tape, which undeniably exposed Nixon's central role in constructing a "cover-up" of the Watergate break-in, was made on Nixon's first day back in Washington after the botched burglary of June 17, 1972. In this conversation with White House Chief of Staff H. R. Haldeman, Nixon devised a plan to block a widening FBI investigation by instructing the director of the CIA to deflect any further FBI snooping on the grounds that it would endanger sensitive CIA operations. Nixon refused to turn over this and other tapes to Senate investigators until so ordered by the Supreme Court on July 24, 1974. Within four days of its release on August 5, Nixon was forced to resign. After eighteen months of protesting his innocence of the crime and his ignorance of any effort to obstruct justice, Nixon was finally undone by the evidence in this incriminating "smoking gun" tape. While tapes documented two straight years of Nixon's Oval Office conversations, other presidents, such as Franklin Roosevelt, John F. Kennedy, and Lyndon Baines Johnson, recorded important meetings and crisis deliberations. Since Watergate, however, it is unlikely that any president has permitted extensive tape recording, depriving historians of a unique insight into the inner workings of the White House.

1. Should taped White House discussions be part of the public record of a presidency? If so, who should have access to the records?
2. What else might historians learn about the president and the administration from a tape such as this one, besides the specific details of the Watergate cover-up?
3. Why did this conversation especially lead to near-unanimous calls for Nixon's impeachment or resignation from Republicans and Democrats alike?

Haldeman: . . . yesterday, they concluded it was not the White House, but are now convinced it is a CIA thing, so the CIA turn off would . . .

President: Well, not sure of their analysis, I'm not going to get that involved. I'm (unintelligible).

Haldeman: No, sir. We don't want you to.

President: You call them in.

President: Good. Good deal! Play it tough. That's the way they play it and that's the way we are going to play it.

Haldeman: O.K. We'll do it.

President: Yeah, when I saw that news summary item, I of course knew it was a bunch of crap, but I thought ah, well it's good to have them off on this wild hair [sic] thing because when they start bugging us, which they have, we'll know our little boys will not know how to handle it. I hope they will though. You never know. Maybe, you think about it. Good!

President: When you get in these people when you . . . get these people in, say: "Look, the problem is that this will open the whole, the whole Bay of Pigs thing, and the President just feels that" ah, without going into the details . . . don't, don't lie to them to the extent to say there is no involvement, but just say this is sort of a comedy of errors, bizarre, without getting into it, "the President believes that it is going to open the whole Bay of Pigs thing up again. And, ah because these people are plugging for, for keeps and that they should call the FBI in and say that we wish for the country, don't go any further into this case," period!

Source: Nixon Presidential Materials Project, National Archives and Records Administration

---

"smoking gun" tape *Recording made in the Oval Office in June 1972 that proved conclusively that Nixon knew about the Watergate break-in and endeavored to cover it up. The tape's release led to a complete breakdown in congressional support for Nixon after the Supreme Court ordered he hand the tape to investigators.*

Three subpoenaed tapes of conversations with his chief aide on June 23, 1972 proved fatal. One of them—the notorious **"smoking gun" tape** (see Examining the Evidence box above)—revealed the president giving orders, six days after the Watergate break-in, to use the CIA to hold back an inquiry by the FBI. Nixon's own tape-recorded words convicted him of having been an active party to the attempted cover-up. The House Judiciary Committee proceeded to draw up articles of impeachment, based on obstruction of justice, abuse of the powers of the presidential office, and contempt of Congress.

The public's wrath proved to be overwhelming. Republican leaders in Congress concluded that the guilty and unpredictable Nixon was a loose cannon on the deck of the ship of state. They frankly informed the president that his impeachment by the full House and removal by the Senate were foregone conclusions and that he would do best to resign.

Left with no better choice, Nixon choked back his tears and announced his resignation in a dramatic television appearance on August 8, 1974. Few presidents had flown so high, and none had sunk so low. In his Farewell Address, Nixon admitted having made some "judgments" that "were wrong." Unconvinced, countless Americans would change the song "Hail to the Chief" to "Jail to the Chief."

The nation had survived a wrenching constitutional crisis, confirming that the impeachment machinery forged by the Founding Fathers could work when public opinion overwhelmingly demanded that it be implemented. The principles that no person is above the law and that presidents must be held to strict accountability for their acts were strengthened. The United States of America, on the eve of its two-hundredth birthday as a republic, had eventually cleaned its own sullied house, giving an impressive demonstration of self-discipline and self-government to the rest of the world. But the toll exacted by Watergate on the public's faith in government proved steep indeed. Americans' disillusionment deepened as the economy fell into a prolonged slump.

Sources of Stagnation

Even as the 1960s lurched to a close, the fantastic quarter-century economic boom of the post-World War II era was already showing signs of petering out. Americans had doubled their average standard of living in the twenty-five years after World War II, But in the years after 1970 the median income of the average family stagnated and failed to decline only because of the addition of working wives' wages to family incomes. The rising baby-boomers now faced the depressing prospect of a living standard lower than that of their parents. As the postwar wave of robust economic growth crested in the early 1970s, the "can-do" American spirit gave way to an unaccustomed sense of limits.

What caused the sudden slump in productivity? Some observers cited the increasing presence in the work force of women and teenagers, who typically had fewer skills than male adult workers and were less likely to take the full-time long-term jobs where skills might be developed. Other commentators blamed declining investment in new machinery, the heavy costs of compliance with government-imposed safety and health regulations, and the general shift of the economy from manufacturing to services, where productivity gains were allegedly more difficult to achieve. Yet in the last analysis much mystery attended the productivity slowdown, and economists continued to wrestle inconclusively with the puzzle.

The Vietnam War also precipitated painful economic distortions. The disastrous conflict in Southeast Asia drained tax dollars from needed improvements in education, deflected scientific skill and manufacturing capacity from the civilian sector, and touched off a sickening spiral of inflation. Sharply rising oil prices in the 1970s also fed inflation, but its deepest roots lay in deficit spending in the 1960s—especially Lyndon Johnson's insistence on simultaneously fighting the war in Vietnam and funding Great Society programs at home, all without a tax increase to finance the added expenditures.

The effects of inflation were deeply felt. Prices increased astonishingly throughout the 1970s. The cost of living tripled in the dozen years after Richard Nixon's inauguration, in the longest and steepest inflationary cycle in American history.

Other weaknesses in the nation's economy were also laid bare by the abrupt reversal of America's financial fortunes in the 1970s. The competitive advantage of many American businesses had been so enormous after World War II that businesses had small incentive to modernize plants and seek more efficient methods of production. The defeated German and Japanese people had meanwhile clawed their way out of the ruins of war and built wholly new factories with the most up-to-date technology and management techniques. The sale of the first Japanese-made Toyota automobile in the United States

Thinking Globally

The Era of Globalization

Early in the twentieth century, Woodrow Wilson envisioned a world order organized around the principles of self-determination and free trade. But his dream perished in the turbulent aftermath of World War I. Two decades later President Franklin Roosevelt, who had served in Wilson's administration, was determined not to squander another opportunity for American international leadership at the conclusion of World War II. He championed a Wilsonian set of principles promoting national self-determination and global free trade—as famously outlined in the "Atlantic Charter" that he and British prime minister Winston Churchill announced in August 1941.

To a remarkable degree, the world order that the United States helped to construct at the end of World War II embodied those very principles. Washington midwifed an array of multilateral institutions to promote international trade and investment, support the rule of law, and nurture democracy. They included the World Bank, to fund postwar reconstruction; the International Monetary Fund (IMF), to stabilize world currencies; and the General Agreement on Tariffs and Trade (GATT), to lower barriers to international commerce. In the ensuing decades, 102 nations, accounting for 80 percent of world trade, signed GATT (succeeded by the World Trade Organization, or WTO, in the 1990s). The United States also took the lead in founding and funding the United Nations (U.N.), which worked to arbitrate international disputes, improve standards of living worldwide, and encourage decolonization, particularly in Asia and Africa.

Outside the Soviet bloc, these institutions nourished a golden era of economic growth that stretched through the 1960s. America boomed. Bolstered by international trade and investment, Europe and Japan also experienced a postwar quarter-century of dazzlingly rapid "catch-up" growth as their economies chased American levels of productivity and living standards.

But globalization bred new dilemmas as well as opportunities. It intensified international competition as well as cooperation. And it ensured that economic shocks could no longer be easily contained within national borders.

First Europe and Japan and then nations in the postcolonial "developing" world like South Korea and eventually China began to challenge American products in world markets—and to threaten American jobs at home. Meanwhile, the end of the Bretton Woods system of fixed exchange rates in 1973 and the growing ease with which capital could cross borders weakened governments' capacity to manage their own national economies. Alongside these international pressures emerged a worldwide political and intellectual shift to the right. In the late 1970s and early 1980s, free-market, anti-regulatory, labor-skeptical governments came to power not only in Ronald Reagan's America but also in countries such as Britain, Australia, and West Germany.

Great Hopes for World Peace with the United Nations, 1947 The achievements of the new international regime were dramatic. International trade doubled in the 1950s and again in the 1960s. By century's end, the volume of global commerce was ten times larger than in 1950. Increased trade fueled postwar recovery in Europe and Japan and set several underdeveloped countries—notably Taiwan, Singapore, South Korea, India, and China—on the path to modernization and prosperity.

The full effects of an economically liberalized world order were long muffled by the Cold War, since Eastern Europe and the Soviet Union were conspicuous nonparticipants in the emerging global economy. But the dissolution of the Soviet bloc in the early 1990s unleashed the full force of globalization. International trade, investment, and migration exploded. Global trade, already at record levels, nearly quadrupled between 1990 and 2012. The exponential growth of manufacturing in the developing world put still more pressure on workers and wages in the developed world. And as economies have globalized, so has inequality both within and between nations. Environmental degradation and exploitative labor practices have also accompanied worldwide industrial growth.

But such problems should not obscure the profound benefits of the global order forged in the wake of World War II. As goods, workers, and investment capital have flowed across borders, so have advances in medicine, nutrition, and standards of living. Since 1950 the average life expectancy worldwide has increased by twenty years, with the biggest gains in the developing world. Rising prosperity has also strengthened the middle classes in developing countries, with democracy often following in the footsteps of prosperity. The number of electoral democracies increased from 44 in 1950 to 118 in 2012. Recent studies confirm that states with open trade policies are three times more likely to protect civil liberties than those without such policies. On balance, the liberalized world order that the United States took the lead in building after World War II left an impressive legacy of international stability, global growth, and freedom from fear and want for millions of human beings—a lasting testament to Woodrow Wilson's vision and to Franklin Roosevelt's leadership. The challenge remains to bring to this new global order the same aspiration for economic equality that propelled Roosevelt's New Deal many decades ago.

in 1957 proved to be a harbinger of the dawning era of global economic competition (see "Thinking Globally: The Era of Globalization," above). By the 1970s Japanese efforts paid handsome rewards, as they came to dominate industries like steel, automobiles, and consumer electronics—fields in which the United States had once been unchallengeable.

The sickly economic performance of the 1970s hung over the decade like a pall. It frustrated both policymakers and citizens who keenly remembered the growth and optimism of the postwar years. The overachieving generation who had won the war had never met a problem they could not solve. Now a stalemated, unpopular war and a stagnant, unresponsive economy ended the liberal dream, vivid since New Deal days, that an affluent society could spend its way to social justice.

★ The First Unelected President

Gerald Rudolph Ford, the first man to be made president solely by a vote of Congress, entered the besmirched White House in August 1974 with serious handicaps. He was widely—and unfairly—suspected of being little more than a dim-witted former college football player. President Johnson had sneered that "Jerry" was so lacking in brainpower that he could not walk and chew gum at the same time. Worse, Ford had been selected, not elected, vice president, following Spiro Agnew's resignation in disgrace. The sour odor of illegitimacy hung about this president without precedent.

Then, out of a clear sky, Ford granted a complete pardon to Nixon for any crimes he may have committed as president, discovered or undiscovered. Democrats were outraged, and lingering suspicions about the pardon cast a dark shadow over Ford's prospects of being elected president in his own right in 1976.

Ford at first sought to enhance the so-called détente with the Soviet Union that Nixon had crafted. In July 1975 President Ford joined leaders from thirty-four other nations in Helsinki, Finland, to sign several sets of historic accords. One group of agreements officially wrote an end to World War II by finally legitimizing the Soviet-dictated boundaries of Poland and other Eastern European countries. In return, the Soviets signed a "third basket" of agreements, guaranteeing more liberal exchanges of people and information between East and West and protecting certain basic human rights. The Helsinki accords kindled small dissident movements in Eastern Europe and even in the USSR itself, but the Soviets soon poured ice water on these sputtering flames of freedom.

Western Europeans cheered the Helsinki conference as a milestone of détente. But in the United States critics increasingly charged that détente was proving to be a one-way street. American grain and technology flowed to the USSR, and little of comparable importance flowed back. Moscow also continued its human rights violations, including restrictions on Jewish emigration. Despite these difficulties, Ford at first clung stubbornly to détente. But the American public's fury over Moscow's double-dealing steadily grew. The thaw in the Cold War was threatening to prove chillingly brief.

★ Defeat in Vietnam

Early in 1975 the North Vietnamese gave full throttle to their long-expected drive southward. President Ford urged Congress to vote still more weapons for Vietnam. But his plea was in vain, and the South Vietnamese quickly and ingloriously collapsed.

The dam burst so rapidly that the remaining Americans had to be frantically evacuated by helicopter, the last of them on April 29, 1975. Also rescued were about 140,000 South Vietnamese, most of them so dangerously identified with the Americans that they feared a bloodbath by the victorious communists. Ford compassionately admitted these people to the United States, where they added further seasoning to the melting pot. Eventually some 500,000 arrived (see "Makers of America: The Vietnamese," p. 677).

The long, frustrating Vietnam War thus ended not with a bang but a whimper. In a technical sense the Americans had not lost the war; their client nation had. The United States had fought the North Vietnamese to a standstill and had then withdrawn its troops in 1973, leaving the South Vietnamese to fight their own war, with generous shipments of costly American weaponry. The estimated cost to America was $118 billion in current outlays, together with some 56,000 dead and 300,000 wounded. The people of the United States had in fact provided just about everything, except the will to win—and that could not be injected by outsiders.

Technicalities aside, America had lost more than a war. It had lost face in the eyes of foreigners, lost its own self-esteem, lost confidence in its political leadership and its military prowess, and lost much of the economic muscle that had made possible its global preeminence since World War II. Americans reluctantly came to realize that their power as well as their pride had been deeply wounded in Vietnam and that recovery would be slow and painful.

★ Feminist Victories and Defeats

As the army limped home from Vietnam, most of the protest movements of the 1960s, including the antiwar movement, had long since splintered and stalled. One major exception to this pattern stood out: the American feminist movement. Although they had their differences, feminists showed vitality and momentum by winning legislative and judicial victories and provoking an intense rethinking of gender roles. (On the roots of this movement, see "Makers of America: The Feminists," p. 678).

Equal Rights Amendment (ERA)
An amendment that declared full constitutional equality for women. Although it passed both houses of Congress in 1972, a concerted grassroots campaign by antifeminists led by Phyllis Schlafly persuaded enough state legislatures to vote against ratification. The amendment failed to become part of the Constitution.

Thousands of women marched in the Women's Stride for Equality on the fiftieth anniversary of woman suffrage in 1970. In 1972 Congress passed Title IX of the Education Amendments, prohibiting sex discrimination in any federally assisted educational program. This act created opportunities for girls' and women's athletics at schools and colleges, giving birth to a new "Title IX generation" that would reach maturity by century's end and help professionalize women's sports as well. The **Equal Rights Amendment (ERA)** to the Constitution won congressional approval in 1972. It declared, "Equality of rights under the law shall not be denied or abridged by the United States or by any State

Makers of America

The Vietnamese

At first glance, the towns of Westminster and Fountain Valley, California seem to resemble other California communities nearby. Tract homes line residential streets; shopping centers flank the busy thoroughfares. But these are no ordinary American suburbs. Instead, they make up "Little Saigons," vibrant outposts of Vietnamese culture in the contemporary United States.

Before South Vietnam fell in 1975, few Vietnamese ventured across the Pacific. Only in 1966 did U.S. immigration authorities even designate "Vietnamese" as a separate category of newcomers, and most early immigrants were the wives and children of U.S. servicemen. But as the communists closed in on Saigon, many Vietnamese, particularly those who had worked closely with American or South Vietnamese authorities, feared for their future. Gathering together as many of their extended-family members as they could assemble, thousands of Vietnamese fled for their lives. In a few hectic days in 1975, some 140,000 Vietnamese escaped before the approaching gunfire, a few dramatically clinging to the bottoms of departing helicopters. Another 60,000 refugees escaped at the same time over land and sea to Hong Kong and Thailand, where they waited nervously for permission to move on.

To accommodate the refugees, the U.S. government set up camps across the United States. Arrivals were crowded into army barracks affording little room and less privacy. These were boot camps not for military service but for assimilation into American society. A rigorous program trained the Vietnamese in English, forbade children from speaking their native language in the classroom, and even immersed them in American slang. Many resented this attempt to mold them, to strip them of their culture.

Vietnamese discontent boiled over when authorities prepared to release the refugees from camps and board them with families around the nation. The resettlement officials had decided to find a sponsor for each Vietnamese family—an American family that would provide food, shelter, and assistance for the refugees until they could fend for themselves. But the Vietnamese people cherish their traditional extended families—grandparents, uncles, aunts, and cousins living communally with parents and children. As soon as refugees could, they relocated from the rural districts where they had been scattered to established Vietnamese enclaves around San Francisco, Los Angeles, and Dallas.

Soon a second throng of Vietnamese immigrants pushed into these Little Saigons. Fleeing from the ravages of poverty and from the oppressive communist government, these stragglers had crammed themselves and their few possessions into little boats, hoping to reach Hong Kong or get picked up by friendly ships. Eventually, many of these "boat people" reached the United States. Usually less educated than the first arrivals and receiving far less resettlement aid from the U.S. government, they were, however, more willing to start at the bottom. Today these two groups total more than half a million people. Differing in experience and expectations, the Vietnamese share a new home in a strange land. Their uprooting is an immense, unreckoned consequence of America's longest war.

Preserving the Past A Vietnamese American boy learns classical calligraphy from his grandfather.

Makers of America

The Feminists

A well-to-do housewife and mother of seven, Elizabeth Cady Stanton (1815-1902) was an unlikely revolutionary. Yet this founding mother of American feminism devoted seven decades of her life to the fight for women's rights.

Young Elizabeth Cady drew her inspiration from the fight against slavery. When she and her new husband, abolitionist Henry Stanton, attended the World Anti-Slavery Convention in London, she was insulted that women were forced to sit in a screened-off balcony above the convention floor. Stanton went on to organize the Seneca Falls Convention in 1848. There she presented her Declaration of Sentiments, which proclaimed that "all men *and women* are created equal" and demanded women's rights to own property, enter the professions, and vote.

Early feminists encountered a mountain of hostility to their cause. Stanton failed in her struggle to include women in the Fourteenth Amendment to the U.S. Constitution, which granted equal citizenship to African Americans. She died before her dream of woman suffrage was realized in the Nineteenth Amendment (1920). Yet by imagining women's emancipation as an expansion of America's founding principles of citizenship, Stanton charted a path that other feminists would follow a century later.

Historians use the terms *first wave* and *second wave* to distinguish the women's movement of the nineteenth century from that of the late twentieth century. The woman most often credited with launching the "second wave" is Betty Friedan (1921-2006). Growing up in Peoria, Illinois, Friedan had seen her mother grow bitter over sacrificing a journalism career to raise her family. Friedan's best seller *The Feminine Mystique* (1963) exposed the quiet desperation of millions of housewives trapped in the "comfortable concentration camp" of the suburban home. In 1966 Friedan cofounded the National Organization for Women (NOW), the chief political and more moderate wing of second-wave feminism.

Just as first-wave feminism grew out of abolitionism, the second wave drew ideas, leaders, and tactics from the civil rights movement of the 1960s. Civil rights workers and feminists alike focused on equal rights. NOW campaigned vigorously for an Equal Rights Amendment, which fell just three states short of ratification in 1982.

Second-wave feminism also had an avowedly radical wing, supported by younger women eager to challenge almost every traditional male and female gender role and to take the feminist cause to the streets. Among these women was Robin Morgan (b. 1941), a civil rights activist who encountered in the movement the same sexism that plagued society at large. Women in the movement who protested against gender discrimination met ridicule, as in SNCC leader Stokely Carmichael's retort, "The only position for women in SNCC is prone." Morgan went on to found WITCH (Women's International Terrorist Conspiracy from Hell), made famous by its protest at the 1968 Miss America pageant in Atlantic City, New Jersey. There demonstrators threw symbols of women's oppression—bras, girdles, and dishcloths—into trash cans. (Contrary to news stories, they did not burn the bras.)

As the contrast between WITCH and NOW suggests, second-wave feminism was a remarkably diverse movement. Feminists disagreed over many issues—from pornography and marriage to how much to expect from government, capitalism, and men. Some feminists placed a priority on gender equality—for example, full female service in the military. Others defended a feminism of gender difference—such as maternity leave and other special protections for women in the workplace.

Still, beyond these differences feminists had much in common. Most advocated a woman's right to choose abortion and regarded the law as a key weapon against gender discrimination. By the early twenty-first century radical and moderate feminists alike could take pride in a host of achievements that had changed the landscape of gender relations beyond what most people could have imagined at midcentury. Yet, like Elizabeth Cady Stanton, second-wave feminists also shared the burden of understanding that the goals of genuine equality would take more than a lifetime to achieve.

Marching for Women's Rights, 1977 A multiethnic and multiracial group of women, accompanied by noted "second-wave" feminists Bella Abzug (in hat) and Betty Friedan (far right), helped to carry a torch from Seneca Falls, New York, birthplace of the feminist movement, to Houston, Texas, site of the National Women's Conference.

on account of sex." Twenty-eight of the necessary thirty-eight states quickly ratified the amendment, first proposed by suffragists in 1923. Hopes rose that the ERA might soon become the law of the land.

Even the Supreme Court seemed to be on the movement's side. In *Reed* v. *Reed* and *Frontiero* v. *Richardson* (1973), the Court challenged sex discrimination in legislation and employment. And in the landmark case of **Roe v. Wade** (1973), the Court struck down laws prohibiting abortion, arguing that a woman's decision to terminate a pregnancy was protected by the constitutional right of privacy.

But the feminist movement soon faced a formidable backlash. In 1972 President Nixon vetoed a proposal to set up nationwide public day care, saying it would weaken the American family. The Catholic Church and evangelical denominations organized a powerful grassroots movement to oppose the legalization of abortion.

For many feminists, the most bitter defeat was the death of the ERA. Antifeminists, led by conservative activist Phyllis Schlafly, argued that the ERA would remove traditional protections women enjoyed by forcing the law to see them as men's equals. They further believed the amendment would threaten the basic family structure of American society. Schlafly charged that the ERA's advocates were just "bitter women seeking a constitutional cure for their personal problems." Her STOP ERA movement proved stunningly successful. Grassroots antifeminist activists organized state-level efforts to block ratification. In 1979 Congress extended the deadline for ratification of the amendment. But the battle was lost. The ERA died in 1982, three states short of success.

Politics and policy made up only part of the story of second-wave feminism, however. The women's movement proved to be an undeniably transformative force in the 1970s. Women's labor force participation accelerated, as medicine, law, and higher education opened their doors to female career-seekers. Feminist enterprises proliferated, from battered women's shelters to women's support groups. Newly frank discussions of women's sexuality abounded. Perhaps most profoundly, ongoing transformations of the size and structure of American families—including the growing numbers of divorced, single-parent, and dual-income households—would ensure women's centrality to battles over lifestyle choices and family values for years to come.

Roe v. Wade (1973) Landmark Supreme Court decision that forbade states from barring abortion by citing a woman's constitutional right to privacy. Seen as a victory for feminism and civil liberties by some, the decision provoked a strong counterreaction by opponents to abortion, galvanizing the pro-life movement.

★ The Seventies in Black and White

Although the civil rights movement had fractured, race remained an explosive issue in the 1970s. The Supreme Court in *Milliken* v. *Bradley* blind-sided school integrationists when it ruled that desegregation plans could not require students to move across school-district lines. The decision effectively exempted suburban districts from shouldering any part of the burden of desegregating inner-city schools, thereby reinforcing "white flight" to the suburbs and forcing all the problems of desegregation into the least prosperous districts. Conflicts over desegregation thereafter often pitted the poorest, most disadvantaged elements of the white and black communities against one another.

Affirmative action programs also remained highly controversial. White workers who were denied advancement and white students who were refused college admission cried "reverse discrimination," charging that racial or ethnic background was now outweighing ability and achievement.

In 1978 the Supreme Court, in a five-to-four decision, upheld the claim of one white Californian, Allan Bakke, that his application to medical school had been turned down because of an admission policy that favored minority applicants. In a tortured decision, the Court ordered the University of California at Davis medical school to admit Bakke and declared that preference in admissions could not be based on ethnic or racial identity alone. Yet at the same time, the Court said that racial factors might be taken into account in a school's overall admissions policy for purposes of assembling a diverse student body. In an impassioned dissent, the Court's only black justice, Thurgood Marshall, warned that the denial of racial preferences might sweep away years of civil rights progress. But many conservatives cheered the decision as affirming the principle that justice is colorblind.

Inspired by the civil rights movement, Native Americans in the 1970s gained remarkable power through using the courts and well-planned acts of civil disobedience.

But while blacks had fought against segregation, Indians used the tactics of the civil rights movement to assert their status as separate semi-sovereign peoples. Indian activists captured the nation's attention by seizing the island of Alcatraz in San Francisco Bay in 1970 and the village of Wounded Knee, South Dakota, in 1972. In the case of *United States* v. *Wheeler* (1978), the Supreme Court declared that Indian tribes possessed a "unique and limited" sovereignty, subject to the will of Congress but not to individual states.

★ The Bicentennial Campaign and the Carter Victory

America's two-hundredth birthday, in 1976, fell during a presidential election year—a fitting coincidence for a proud democracy. President Gerald Ford energetically sought the Republican nomination in his own right and defeated challenger Ronald Reagan, former actor and governor of California. Reagan's pursuit of the GOP nomination was propelled by a swelling conservative movement that came to be known as the **"New Right."**

The New Right's cadre of activists and political organizers were mainly veterans of Barry Goldwater's failed 1964 presidential campaign. They spent the 1970s building a network of advocacy groups, political action committees, and think tanks. More populist in tone than previous generations of political conservatives, the New Right emphasized hot-button cultural issues—from the ERA and abortion to busing and school curricula—as well as a nationalist foreign-policy outlook. Though Reagan fell short at the Republican convention in 1976, he and the movement behind him grew substantially more powerful over the next four years.

The Democratic standard-bearer in 1976 was fifty-one-year-old James Earl Carter, Jr., a dark-horse candidate who galloped out of obscurity during the long primary-election season. A former Georgia governor who insisted on the humble "Jimmy" as his first name, this born-again Baptist touched many people with his down-home sincerity. Untainted by ties with a corrupt and cynical Washington, Carter ran against the memory of Nixon and Watergate as much as he ran against Ford. His most effective campaign pitch was his promise that "I'll never lie to you."

Carter squeezed out a narrow victory on election day, with 51 percent of the popular vote. The electoral count stood at 297 to 240. The winner swept every state except Virginia in his native South. Especially important were the votes of African Americans, 97 percent of whom cast their ballots for Carter. But in yet another sign of the changing political alignments in the South, Ford actually beat Carter among white southerners, garnering 53 percent of their votes to Carter's 46 percent.

Carter enjoyed hefty Democratic majorities in both houses of Congress. Hopes ran high that the stalemate of the Nixon-Ford years between a Republican White House and a Democratic Capitol Hill would now be ended. At first Carter enjoyed notable political success, as Congress granted his requests to create a new cabinet-level Department of Energy and to cut taxes.

But Carter's honeymoon did not last long. An inexperienced outsider, he had campaigned against the Washington "establishment" and never quite made the transition to being an insider himself. Carter repeatedly rubbed congressional fur the wrong way, and critics charged that he isolated himself in a shallow pool of fellow Georgians, whose ignorance of the ways of Washington compounded the problems of their greenhorn chief.

★ Carter's Humanitarian Diplomacy

As a committed Christian, President Carter displayed from the outset an overriding concern for "human rights" as the guiding principle of his foreign policy. In the African nations of Rhodesia (later Zimbabwe) and South Africa, Carter and his eloquent United Nations ambassador, Andrew Young, championed the oppressed black majority.

The president's most spectacular foreign-policy achievement came in September 1978 when he invited President Anwar Sadat of Egypt and Prime Minister Menachem Begin of Israel to the woodsy presidential retreat at Camp David, Maryland. Skillfully

---

"New Right" Term for a loose network of conservative political activists and organizations that emerged in the 1970s and 1980s. More populist in tone than previous generations of conservatives, the New Right emphasized hot-button cultural issues like abortion, busing, and prayer in school. They also espoused a nationalist foreign policy outlook that rejected détente and international treaties.

serving as go-between, Carter persuaded the two visitors to sign a preliminary accord (September 17, 1978) whereby Israel agreed to withdraw from territory conquered in the 1967 war and Egypt promised to respect Israel's borders. Both parties pledged themselves to sign a formal peace treaty within three months.

Carter achieved further diplomatic success by resuming full diplomatic relations with China in 1979. He also concluded two treaties turning over the Panama Canal to the Panamanians. Over the protests from conservatives, including Ronald Reagan, the United States agreed to give up complete control on December 31, 1999.

Despite these dramatic accomplishments, trouble stalked Carter's foreign policy. Overshadowing all international issues was the ominous reheating of the Cold War with the Soviet Union. Détente fell into disrepute as Cuba deployed thousands of troops, assisted by Soviet advisers, in Angola, Ethiopia, and elsewhere in Africa to support revolutionary factions. Arms-control negotiations with Moscow stalled in the face of this Soviet military meddling.

★ Economic and Energy Woes

Adding to Carter's mushrooming troubles was the failing health of the economy. A stinging recession during Ford's presidency had brought the inflation rate down slightly to just under 6 percent, but from the moment Carter took over, prices resumed their dizzying ascent, driving the inflation rate well above 13 percent by 1980. The soaring bill for imported oil plunged America's balance of payments deeply into the red.

The "oil shocks" of the 1970s taught Americans a painful but necessary lesson: that they could never again seriously consider a policy of economic isolation, as they had tried to do between the two world wars. For most of American history, foreign trade had accounted for no more than 10 percent of gross national product (GNP). But huge foreign-oil bills drove that figure upward in the 1970s. By century's end, some 27 percent of GNP depended on foreign trade. Unable to dominate international trade and finance as they once had, Americans would have to master foreign languages and study foreign cultures if they wanted to prosper in the rapidly globalizing economy.

Yawning deficits in the federal budget, reaching nearly $60 billion in 1980, further aggravated the U.S. economy's inflationary ailments. The elderly and other Americans living on fixed incomes suffered from the shrinking dollar. People with money to lend pushed interest rates ever higher. The "prime rate" (the rate of interest that banks charged their very best customers) vaulted to an unheard-of 20 percent in early 1980. The high cost of borrowing money shoved small businesses to the wall and strangled the construction industry.

Carter diagnosed America's economic disease as stemming primarily from the nation's costly dependence on foreign oil. Unfortunately, his legislative proposals in April 1977 for energy conservation ignited a blaze of indifference among the American people, who had already forgotten the long gasoline lines of 1973.

Events in Iran jolted Americans out of their complacency about energy supplies in 1979. The imperious Mohammad Reza Pahlavi, installed as shah of Iran with help from America's CIA in 1953, had long ruled his oil-rich land with a will of steel. His repressive regime was finally overthrown in January 1979 in a violent revolution spearheaded by Muslim fundamentalists who denounced the United States as the "Great Satan." The crippling upheavals soon spread to Iran's oil fields. As Iranian oil supplies stopped flowing, Americans once more found themselves waiting impatiently in long lines at gas stations or buying gasoline only on specified days.

President Jimmy Carter (b. 1924) delivered what became known as his "malaise" speech (although he never used the word) on television in 1979. In time cultural conservatives would take up his theme to support their call for a return to "traditional values":

"In a nation that was proud of hard work, strong families, close-knit communities, and our faith in God, too many of us now tend to worship self-indulgence and consumption. Human identity is no longer defined by what one does, but by what one owns. But we've discovered that owning things and consuming things does not satisfy our longing for meaning. We've learned that piling up material goods cannot fill the emptiness of lives which have no confidence or purpose.... The symptoms of this crisis of the American spirit are all around us."

Contending Voices

The Political Mobilization of Business

In August 1971, the corporate lawyer Lewis Powell (1907–1998)—soon to be appointed by President Nixon to the Supreme Court—wrote a confidential memo to the director of the U.S. Chamber of Commerce decrying what he described as a broad-based ideological assault on capitalist principles under way in American academia, media, and politics. Powell then presciently proposed that American businesses collectively marshal a long-range countermovement within those same institutions to reclaim public favor and power.

"No thoughtful person can question that the American economic system is under broad attack.... [T]he time has come—indeed, it is long overdue—for the wisdom, ingenuity and resources of American business to be marshalled against those who would destroy it.... [O]ne should not postpone more direct political action, while awaiting the gradual change in public opinion to be effected through education and information. Business must learn the lesson, long ago learned by labor and other self-interest groups. This is the lesson that political power is necessary; that such power must be assiduously cultivated; and that when necessary, it must be used aggressively and with determination—without embarrassment and without the reluctance which has been so characteristic of American business."

Seven years later, in 1978, United Auto Workers president Douglas Fraser (1916–2008) announced his resignation from a joint forum for business and labor leaders in a scathing open letter. He decried what he saw as a new aggressiveness and political hostility on the part of American business.

"I believe leaders of the business community, with few exceptions, have chosen to wage a one-sided class war today in this country—a war against working people, the unemployed,

---

As this second oil crisis deepened, President Carter sensed the rising temperature of popular discontent. In July 1979 he retreated to the presidential mountain hideaway of Camp David, where he remained largely out of public view for ten days. Like a royal potentate of old summoning the wise men of the realm for their counsel in a time of crisis, Carter called in more than one hundred leaders from all walks of life to give him their views. Meanwhile, the nation waited anxiously for the results of these extraordinary deliberations.

When Carter finally came down from the mountaintop on July 15, 1979, he stunned a perplexed nation with his **malaise speech**, chiding his fellow citizens for falling into a "moral and spiritual crisis" and for being too concerned with "material goods." A few days later, the president fired four of his cabinet secretaries and circled the wagons of his Georgia advisers more tightly around the White House. Critics began to wonder aloud whether Carter, the professed man of the people, was losing touch with the popular mood of the country.

★ The Turn Toward the Market

The energy crisis, stagflation, and Carter's political woes helped to nurture a powerful conservative challenge to the very foundations of the postwar American "social contract," which had featured a strong federal government, active economic regulation, expanded social provision, and a large measure of income equality. Now the emphasis shifted to the energy and promise of the free market, and the burdens and dangers of "big government."

An influential group of thinkers known as "neoconservatives," many of them former liberals appalled by what they regarded as the excesses of the 1960s, spearheaded this conservative revival. They championed free-market capitalism liberated from government restraints and sharply questioned the efficacy of the welfare programs spawned by Lyndon Johnson's Great Society. They called for the restoration of traditional values at home and took tough, harshly anti-Soviet positions in foreign policy.

Prominent among pro-market thinkers was the Nobel Prize–winning economist Milton Friedman, a long-standing critic of Keynesian economics and activist government. He achieved a new level of popular influence in 1979 with a best-selling book he co-wrote with his wife Rose called *Free to Choose*. The book and an accompanying public television documentary argued for the superiority of free markets in solving social problems and protecting individual liberty.

Conservative thinking complemented conservative action. Corporate political action committees mushroomed from 89 in 1974 to 1,024 in 1980, while the number of companies with registered lobbyists shot up from 175 in 1971 to nearly 2,500 in 1982. Concerted conservative opposition killed two labor law reform bills during Carter's presidency, as well as a minimum wage hike and the establishment of a Consumer Protection Agency. Critics also pinned the blame for stagflation on onerous government regulations, contributing to a sweeping deregulatory movement in areas as disparate as transportation, communications, and banking.

Significantly, President Carter also supported deregulation and the liberation of market forces. Younger congressional Democrats also began to move away from the New Deal–era positions of their elders. "We're not a bunch of little Hubert Humphreys," one of them declared in 1974, scornfully repudiating his party's 1968 presidential nominee and one of the most prominent liberals of the postwar era. Though spearheaded by a resurgent Republican right, the turn toward the market attracted bipartisan support—in America and elsewhere (see "Thinking Globally: The Era of Globalization" pp. 674–675).

The most politically explosive aspect of the new antigovernment politics centered on taxes. A "tax revolt" in California and other states in 1978 soon snowballed into a revolutionary new tax-cutting agenda for the conservative movement nationwide—one that rewrote the script of American politics in the following decade (see Chapter 39, pp. 689–690).

> the poor, the minorities, the very young and the very old, and even many in the middle class of our society. The leaders of industry, commerce and finance in the United States have broken and discarded the fragile, unwritten compact previously existing during a past period of growth and progress."

> How accurate were Powell's and Fraser's descriptions of the American scene in the 1970s? What underlying changes in the economy and society supported their assertions?

★ Foreign Affairs and the Iranian Imbroglio

Hopes for a less dangerous world rose slightly in June 1979, when President Carter met with Soviet leader Leonid Brezhnev in Vienna to sign the long-stalled **SALT II** (Strategic Arms Limitation Talks II) agreements, limiting the levels of lethal strategic weapons in the Soviet and American arsenals. But conservative critics of the president's defense policies, still regarding the Soviet Union as the Wicked Witch of the East, unsheathed their long knives to carve up the SALT treaty when it came to the Senate for debate in the summer of 1979.

Political earthquakes in the petroleum-rich Persian Gulf region finally buried all hopes of ratifying the SALT II treaty. On November 4, 1979, a mob of passionately

malaise speech *National address by Jimmy Carter in July 1979 in which he chided American materialism and urged a communal spirit in the face of economic hardships. Although Carter intended the speech to improve both public morale and his standing as a leader, it had the opposite effect and was widely perceived as a political disaster for the embattled president.*

SALT II *Strategic Arms Limitation Treaty agreement between Soviet leader Leonid Brezhnev and American president Jimmy Carter. Despite an accord to limit weapons between the two leaders, the agreement was ultimately scuttled in the U.S. Senate following the Soviet invasion of Afghanistan in 1979.*

An Apostle for Capitalism Milton Friedman receives the cash award that accompanied his Nobel Prize in economics in 1976. Friedman won the Nobel at just the point in the 1970s that the free-market outlook he espoused began to gain new prominence in the broader political culture.

anti-American Muslim militants stormed the United States embassy in Tehran, Iran and took all of its occupants hostage. The captors then demanded that American authorities ship the exiled shah from the United States back to Iran.

Americans agonized over both the fate of the hostages and the stability of the entire Persian Gulf region, so dangerously close to the Soviet Union. The Soviet army then aroused the West's worst fears on December 27, 1979, when it blitzed into the mountainous nation of Afghanistan, next door to Iran, and appeared to be poised for a thrust at the oil jugular of the gulf.

President Carter reacted vigorously to these alarming events. He slapped an embargo on the export of grain and high-technology machinery to the USSR, called for a boycott of the upcoming Olympic Games in Moscow, and requested that young people (including women) be made to register for a possible military draft. Proclaiming that the United States would "use any means necessary, including force," to protect the Persian Gulf against Soviet incursions, Carter grimly conceded that he had misjudged the Soviets. The SALT II treaty became a dead letter in the Senate. Meanwhile, the Soviet army met unexpectedly stiff resistance in Afghanistan and became bogged down in a nasty, decade-long guerrilla war that came to be called "Russia's Vietnam."

The Iranian hostage crisis was Carter's—and America's—bed of nails. The captured Americans languished in cruel captivity, while the nightly news broadcasts showed humiliating scenes of Iranian mobs burning the American flag and spitting on effigies of Uncle Sam.

Carter at first tried to apply economic sanctions and the pressure of world opinion against the Iranians. But the president's frustration grew as the political turmoil in Iran rumbled on endlessly. Carter at last ordered a daring rescue mission. A highly trained commando team penetrated deep into Iran's sandy interior, but when equipment failures prevented some members of the team from reaching their destination, the mission had to be scrapped. As the commandos withdrew in the dark desert night, two of their aircraft collided, killing eight of the would-be rescuers.

The disastrous failure of the rescue raid proved anguishing for Americans. The episode seemed to underscore the nation's helplessness and even incompetence in the face of a mortifying insult to the national honor. The stalemate with Iran dragged on throughout the rest of Carter's term, providing an embarrassing backdrop to the embattled president's struggle for reelection.

As the 1980 presidential race approached, a discontented and divided American public looked to close the book on a frustrating decade. What Americans could not fully know at the time was how much lasting change had already taken place in such a relatively brief period. The long postwar boom and broadly shared prosperity were gone for good, replaced in coming decades by more fitful and less equitable spurts of growth. An ascendant conservative movement criticized government activism and promoted free-market policies. Economic inequality and political polarization grew alike in the decades to come. Yet perhaps paradoxically, the dawning era of dampened economic growth, governmental paralysis, and widening income disparity also witnessed increasing tolerance and inclusion of racial and ethnic minorities, immigrants, gays and lesbians, and women, all of whose horizons broadened dramatically in the decades ahead.

Iranian hostage crisis *The 444 days, from November 1979 to January 1981, in which American embassy workers were held captive by Iranian revolutionaries. The hostage crisis began when revolutionaries stormed the American embassy, demanding that the United States return the shah to Iran for trial. After diplomatic efforts proved unable to gain the hostages' relief, a military rescue attempt by the Carter administration ended in failure and loss of American life. The crisis ended with the hostages' release the day Ronald Reagan became president, January 20, 1981.*

CHAPTER SUMMARY ★ ★ ★ ★ ★ ★ ★ ★ ★ ★ ★ ★ ★

Nixon's landslide 1972 election victory was negated as the widespread Watergate scandal erupted. Nixon fought efforts by prosecutors to obtain relevant evidence, but the revelation of his own involvement in the Watergate crimes and coverup finally compelled him to resign in 1974.

Unelected President Gerald Ford took office amidst an emerging "stagflation" that combined low economic growth with inflation, signaling the end of the long postwar era of prosperity and relative economic equality. Ford attempted to sustain Nixon's détente policy with the Soviet Union, but faced growing criticism that the Soviets had turned the policy entirely to their advantage. The Communist Vietnamese finally overran the South Vietnamese government in 1975, confirming Americans' sense of diminished world power and pride.

The major social movement to survive the sixties was feminism, which achieved widespread breakthroughs in employment, culture, and social organization, though failing to pass the Equal Rights Amendment. Race remained an explosive issue, as divisive issues of busing and affirmative action eroded the good will created by the civil rights movement. A growing New Right movement throughout the 1970s mobilized around cultural issues like abortion and affirmation action as well as a militantly anticommunist foreign policy,

Campaigning against Watergate and a corrupt Washington, outsider Jimmy Carter won a slender victory over Ford in 1976, but proved unable to work with Congress or improve the economy once he took office. His Camp David agreement brought peace between Egypt and Israel, but the Iranian revolution led to a new energy crisis that compounded already severe inflation and recession. Growing criticism of big government and federal regulation of the economy led to a major turn toward free-market solutions.

The Soviet invasion of Afghanistan and the holding of American hostages in Iran added to Carter's woes and a general American sense of frustration and helplessness. Economic weakness and foreign policy failures did not, however, prevent a growing tolerance and inclusion of minorities and immigrants within American society.

KEY TERMS

- "stagflation" (670)
- Watergate (671)
- "smoking gun" tape (672)
- Equal Rights Amendment (ERA) (676)
- *Roe v. Wade* (679)
- New Right (680)
- malaise speech (683)
- SALT II (683)
- Iranian hostage crisis (684)

PEOPLE TO KNOW

- Gerald ("Jerry") Ford
- Phyllis Schlafly
- James Earl ("Jimmy") Carter, Jr.
- Milton Friedman
- Robin Morgan
- Leonid Brezhnev

 MindTap is a fully online, highly personalized learning experience built upon Cengage Learning content. MindTap combines student learning tools—readings, multimedia, activities, and assessments—into a singular Learning Path that guides students through the course.

Chapter 39

The Resurgence of Conservatism
1980–1992

It will be my intention to curb the size and influence of the federal establishment and to demand recognition of the distinction between the powers granted to the federal government and those reserved to the states or to the people.

RONALD REAGAN, INAUGURAL ADDRESS, 1981

Chapter Outline

- Ronald Reagan and the New Right
- "Reaganomics" and Its Consequences
- Reagan Renews the Cold War
- The Iran-Contra Scandal
- Reagan's Economic Legacy
- The Religious Right and Conflict over Abortion
- George H.W. Bush
- The End of the Cold War
- The Persian Gulf War, 1991
- Bush's Battles at Home
- *Varying Viewpoints: Where Did Modern Conservatism Come From?*

"It's morning in America" was the slogan of Republican candidate Ronald Reagan in his 1984 presidential campaign. Certainly the 1980s were a new day for America's conservative right. Census figures confirmed that the average American was older than in the stormy sixties and much more likely to live in the South or West, the traditional bastions of conservatism, where many citizens harbored suspicions of federal power. The conservative cause drew added strength from the emergence of a "New Right" movement that focused on cultural issues like abortion, pornography, homosexuality, feminism, and affirmative action. Increasingly politicized evangelical Christian groups such as the Moral Majority became leading actors in New Right campaigns. Together, the culture-focused New Right and more traditional anti-government conservatives added up to a powerful political combination, devoted to changing the very character of American society.

FOCUS QUESTIONS

1. What social and cultural forces led to the dramatic rise of Ronald Reagan and the "New Right" in the early 1980s?
2. What were the essential elements of the "Reagan revolution" in economic and social policy, and what were Reaganism's short-term and long-term consequences?
3. How and why was the renewed Cold War of the early 1980s followed by the easing of tensions and the Reagan-Gorbachev agreements later in the decade? What caused the collapse of communism first in Eastern Europe and then in Soviet Union in 1989–1991?
4. How did the religious right transform American politics, and how were issues like abortion and affirmative action addressed by the public and the Supreme Court?
5. What were the causes and consequences of the Persian Gulf War? Why did President George H.W. Bush leave Saddam Hussein in power in Iraq?

CHRONOLOGY

1980	Reagan defeats Carter for presidency	1987	Stock market plunges 508 points Third Reagan-Gorbachev summit meeting in Washington, D.C.; INF treaty signed
1981	Iran releases American hostages "Reaganomics" spending and tax cuts passed Solidarity movement in Poland O'Connor appointed to Supreme Court (first woman justice)	1988	Fourth Reagan-Gorbachev summit meeting in Moscow Bush defeats Dukakis for presidency
1981–1991	United States aids anti-leftist forces in Central America	1989	Chinese government suppresses prodemocracy demonstrators in Tiananmen Square *Webster* v. *Reproductive Health Services* Eastern European countries oust communist governments Berlin Wall torn down
1982	Recession hits U.S. economy Israel invades Lebanon		
1983	Reagan announces SDI plan (Star Wars) U.S. marines killed in Beirut, Lebanon U.S. invasion of Grenada	1990	Iraq invades Kuwait East and West Germany unite Americans with Disabilities Act (ADA)
1984	Reagan defeats Mondale for presidency Soviet Union boycotts Summer Olympics in Los Angeles	1991	Persian Gulf War Thomas appointed to Supreme Court Gorbachev survives coup attempt and resigns as Soviet president Soviet Union dissolves
1985	Gorbachev comes to power in Soviet Union, announces *glasnost* and *perestroika* First Reagan-Gorbachev summit meeting in Geneva		
1986	Reagan administration backs Aquino in Philippines Iran-Contra affair revealed Second Reagan-Gorbachev summit meeting in Reykjavik, Iceland	1992	Twenty-seventh Amendment (prohibiting congressional pay raises from taking effect until an election seats a new session of Congress) ratified *Planned Parenthood* v. *Casey*

★ The Election of Ronald Reagan, 1980

Ronald Reagan was well suited to lead the gathering conservative crusade. Reared in a generation whose values were formed well before the upheavals of the 1960s, he naturally sided with the New Right on social issues. In economic and social matters alike, he denounced the activist government and failed "social engineering" of the 1960s. Just as his early political hero, Franklin Roosevelt, had championed the "forgotten man" against big business, Reagan championed the "common man" against big government. He condemned federal intervention in local affairs, favoritism for minorities, and the elitism of arrogant bureaucrats. He aimed especially to win over from the Democratic column working-class and lower-middle-class white voters by implying that the Democratic party had become the the party of big government and the exclusive tool of its minority constituents.

An actor-turned-politician, Reagan enjoyed enormous popularity with his crooked grin and aw-shucks manner. The son of an impoverished Irish-American father from a small Illinois town, Reagan got his start in the depressed 1930s as a radio sports announcer in Iowa. He became a B-grade Hollywood star in the 1940s and helped purge communists from the Screen Actors Guild as the organization's president in the 1950s. In 1954 he became a spokesman for General Electric and began preaching a conservative, antigovernment line. Reagan's growing skill at promoting the conservative cause inspired a group

> *In a speech to the National Association of Evangelicals on March 8, 1983, President Ronald Reagan (1911–2004) defined his stand on school prayer:*
>
> "The Declaration of Independence mentions the Supreme Being no less than four times. 'In God We Trust' is engraved on our coinage. The Supreme Court opens its proceedings with a religious invocation. And the Members of Congress open their sessions with a prayer. I just happen to believe the schoolchildren of the United States are entitled to the same privileges as Supreme Court Justices and Congressmen."

of wealthy California businessmen to help him launch his political career as governor of California from 1966 to 1974.

By 1980 the Republican party was ready to challenge the Democrats' hold on the White House. Bedeviled abroad and becalmed at home, Jimmy Carter's administration struck many Americans as bungling and befuddled. Carter's inability to control double-digit inflation was especially damaging.

Disaffection with Carter's apparent ineptitude ran deep even in his own Democratic party, in which an "ABC" (Anybody But Carter) movement gathered steam. The liberal wing of the party found its champion in Senator Edward Kennedy of Massachusetts, the last survivor of the assassin-plagued Kennedy brothers. He and Carter slugged it out in a series of bruising primary elections, while delighted Republicans decorously proceeded to name Reagan their presidential nominee. In the end Kennedy's candidacy fell victim to the country's conservative mood and to lingering suspicions about a 1969 automobile accident on Chappaquiddick Island, Massachusetts, in which a young woman assistant was drowned when Kennedy's car plunged off a bridge. A badly battered Carter, his party divided and in disarray, was left to do battle with Reagan.

The Republican candidate proved to be a formidable campaigner. Using his professional acting skills to great advantage, Reagan attacked the incumbent's fumbling performance in foreign policy and blasted the Democratic party's "big-government philosophy." Galloping inflation, sky-high interest rates, and a faltering economy put Carter on the defensive. He countered ineffectively that Reagan was a trigger-happy cold warrior who might push the country into nuclear war.

President Ronald Reagan Older than any man previously elected to the presidency, Reagan displayed youthful vigor both on the campaign trail and in office.

Carter's spotty record in office was no defense against Reagan's popular appeal. On election day Reagan rang up a spectacular victory, bagging more than 51 percent of the popular vote while 41 percent went to Carter. Reflecting a small but vocal protest against both candidates, nearly 7 percent of the electorate voted for liberal Republican congressman John Anderson, who ran as an independent. The electoral count stood at 489 for Reagan and 49 for Carter, making Carter the first elected president to be unseated by voters since Herbert Hoover in 1932. Equally startling, the Republicans gained control of the Senate for the first time in twenty-six years. Leading Democratic liberals, including George McGovern, had been targeted for defeat by well-heeled New Right groups. They went down like dead timber in the conservative windstorm that swept the country.

Carter showed dignity in defeat. An unusually intelligent, articulate, and well-meaning president, he had been hampered by his lack of managerial talent and badly buffeted by events beyond his control, such as the soaring price of oil, runaway inflation, and the galling insult of the hostages still held in Iran. Though unsuccessful in the White House, Carter earned much admiration in later years for his humanitarian and human rights activities. He received the Nobel Peace Prize in 2002.

★ The Reagan Revolution

Reagan's arrival in Washington was triumphal. The Iranians contributed to the festive mood by releasing the hostages on Reagan's Inauguration Day, January 20, 1981, after 444 days of captivity.

The new president, a hale and hearty sixty-nine-year-old devoted to fiscal fitness, sought nothing less than the dismantling of the welfare state and the reversal of the political evolution of the preceding half century. Years of New Deal–style tax-and-spend programs, Reagan jested, had created a federal government that reminded him of the definition of a baby as a creature who was all appetite at one end, with no sense of responsibility at the other.

On his conservative crusade for smaller government, less bureaucracy, and freer markets, Reagan found common cause with the new leader of America's oldest ally, Great Britain. Conservative Margaret Thatcher became Britain's first female Prime Minister in 1979. With a mandate to improve her nation's economy, which had suffered through the 1970s as the United States had, she embarked on a mission to reduce the power of labor unions and government involvement in business, two of Reagan's chief goals. The philosophic kinship between "Ronnie and Maggie," as the press dubbed the two heads of state, went beyond economics. Emboldened by each other, they strengthened the Anglo-American alliance through muscular foreign policy against a number of foes, especially the Soviet bloc. Their common refrain was that free markets made free peoples and that shrinking government meant keeping their nations safer from communism.

By the early 1980s, this antigovernment message found a receptive audience in the United States. In the two decades since 1960, federal spending had risen from about 18 percent of gross national product to nearly 23 percent. After four decades of advancing New Deal and Great Society programs, a strong countercurrent took hold. Californians staged a "tax revolt" in 1978 (known by its official ballot title of **Proposition 13**) that slashed property taxes and forced painful cuts in government services. The California "tax quake" jolted other state capitals and even rocked the pillars of Congress in Washington, D.C. Ronald Reagan had ridden this political shock wave to presidential victory in 1980 and proceeded to rattle the "welfare state" to its very foundations.

Reagan pursued his smaller-government policies with near-religious zeal and remarkable effectiveness. He proposed a new federal budget that necessitated cuts of some $35 billion, mostly in social programs like food stamps and federally funded job-training centers. Reagan worked naturally in harness with the Republican majority in the Senate, while in the Democratic House he enterprisingly wooed a group of mostly southern conservative Democrats (dubbed **boll weevils**), who abandoned their own party's leadership to follow the president. The new president's political hand was further strengthened after a failed assassination attempt in March 1981 brought an outpouring of sympathy and support.

Proposition 13 (1978) *A successful California state ballot initiative that capped the state's real estate tax at 1 percent of assessed value. The proposition radically reduced average property tax levels, decreasing revenue for the state government and signaling the political power of the "tax revolt," increasingly aligned with conservative politics.*

boll weevils *Term for conservative southern Democrats who voted increasingly for Republican issues during the Carter and Reagan administrations.*

★ The Battle of the Budget

Swept along on a tide of presidential popularity, Congress swallowed Reagan's budget proposals. The new president's triumph amazed political observers, especially defeated Democrats. He had descended on Washington like an avenging angel of conservatism, kicking up a blinding whirlwind of political change in pursuit of his Reaganomics agenda. His impressive performance demonstrated the power of the presidency with a skill not seen since Lyndon Johnson's day.

Reagan hardly rested to savor the sweetness of his victory. The second part of his economic program called for substantial reductions in marginal tax rates over a period of three years. Many Democrats, the president quipped, had "never met a tax they didn't hike." Thanks largely to Reagan's skill as a television performer and the continued defection of the "boll weevils" from the Democratic camp, the president again had his way. In late 1981 Congress approved a set of far-reaching tax reforms that lowered individual tax rates, reduced federal estate taxes, and created new tax-free savings plans for small investors. Reagan's "supply-side" economic advisers argued that a combination of budgetary discipline and tax reduction would stimulate new investment, boost productivity, foster dramatic economic growth, and eventually even boost tax revenues and reduce the deficit.

At first, **supply-side economics** seemed to be a beautiful theory mugged by a gang of brutal facts, as the economy slid into its deepest recession since the 1930s. Unemployment

supply-side economics *Economic theory that underlay Ronald Reagan's tax and spending cuts. Contrary to Keynesianism, supply-side theory declared that government policy should aim to increase the supply of goods and services, rather than the demand for them. It held that lower taxes and decreased regulation would increase productivity by providing increased incentives to work, thus increasing productivity and the tax base.*

reached nearly 11 percent in 1982, businesses folded, and several bank failures jolted the nation's entire financial system. The automobile industry, once the brightest jewel in America's industrial crown, reported losses in the hundreds of millions of dollars.

Ignoring the yawping pack of Democratic critics, President Reagan and his economic advisers serenely waited for their supply-side economic policies to produce the promised results. The supply-siders seemed to be vindicated when a healthy economic recovery finally got under way in 1983. Yet the economy of the 1980s was not uniformly sound. For the first time in the post-World War II era, income gaps widened between the richest and the poorest Americans. The poor got poorer and the very rich grew fabulously richer, while middle-class incomes largely stagnated. Symbolic of the new income stratification was the emergence of "yuppies," or young urban professionals. Sporting Rolex watches and BMW sports cars, they made a near-religion out of conspicuous consumption. Though numbering only about 1.5 million people, yuppies showcased the values of materialism and the pursuit of wealth that came to symbolize the high-rolling 1980s.

Some economists located the sources of the economic upturn neither in the president's budget cuts and tax reforms nor in the go-get-'em avarice of the yuppies. It was massive military expenditures, they argued, that constituted the real foundations of 1980s prosperity. Reagan cascaded nearly 2 trillion dollars onto the Pentagon in the 1980s, asserting the need to close the "window of vulnerability" in the armaments race with the Soviet Union. Ironically, this conservative president thereby plunged the government into a red-ink bath of deficit spending that made the New Deal look downright stingy. Federal budget deficits topped $100 billion in 1982, and the government's books were nearly $200 billion out of balance in every subsequent year of the 1980s.

★ Reagan Renews the Cold War

Hard as nails toward the Soviet Union in his campaign speeches, Reagan saw no reason to soften up after he checked in at the White House. He claimed that the Soviets were "prepared to commit any crime, to lie, to cheat" in pursuit of their goals of world conquest. He denounced the Soviet Union as "the focus of evil in the modern world."

Reagan believed in negotiating with the Soviets—but only from a position of overwhelming strength. Accordingly, his strategy for dealing with Moscow was simple: by enormously expanding U.S. military capabilities, he could threaten the Soviet leaders with a fantastically expensive new round of the arms race. Desperate to avoid economic ruin, Kremlin leaders would come to the bargaining table and sing Reagan's tune.

This strategy resembled a riverboat gambler's ploy. It wagered the enormous sum of Reagan's defense budgets on the hope that the other side would not call Washington's bluff and initiate a new cycle of arms competition. Reagan played his trump card in this risky game in March 1983 when he announced his intention to pursue a high-technology missile defense system called the **Strategic Defense Initiative (SDI)**, popularly known as Star Wars. The plan called for orbiting battle stations in space that could fire laser beams or other forms of concentrated energy to vaporize intercontinental missiles on liftoff. Most scientists considered this an impossible goal, but the deeper logic of SDI lay in its fit with Reagan's overall Soviet strategy. By pitching the arms contest onto a stratospheric plane of technology and astronomical expense, it would help force the Kremlin's hand.

Relations with the Soviets further nose-dived in late 1981 when the government of Poland, needled by a popular union movement called "Solidarity," clamped martial law on the troubled country. Reagan saw the heavy fist of the Kremlin inside this Polish iron glove, and he imposed economic sanctions on Poland and the USSR alike.

Dealing with the Soviet Union was additionally complicated by the inertia and ill health of the aging oligarchs in the Kremlin, three of whom died between late 1982 and early 1985. Relations grew even more tense when the Soviets, in September 1983, blasted from the skies a Korean airliner that had inexplicably violated Soviet airspace. Hundreds of civilians, including many Americans, plummeted to their deaths. By the end of 1983, all arms-control negotiations with the Soviets were broken off. The Cold War chill deepened further in 1984, when USSR and Soviet-bloc athletes boycotted the Olympic Games in Los Angeles.

Strategic Defense Initiative (SDI)
Reagan administration plan announced in 1983 to create a missile defense system over American territory to block a nuclear attack. Derided as "Star Wars" by critics, the plan typified Reagan's commitment to vigorous defense spending even as he sought to limit the size of government in domestic matters.

Map 39.1 The Middle East A combination of political instability and precious petroleum resources has made the region from Egypt to Afghanistan an "arc of crisis."

⭐ Troubles Abroad

The ever-volatile Middle Eastern pot continued to boil ominously. Israel badly strained its bonds of friendship with the United States by continuing to allow new settlements to be established in the occupied territory of the Jordan River's West Bank (see Map 39.1). Israel further raised the stakes in the Middle East in June 1982 when it invaded neighboring Lebanon, seeking to suppress once and for all the guerrilla bases from which Palestinian

691

fighters harassed beleaguered Israel. The Palestinians were bloodily subdued, but Lebanon, already pulverized by years of episodic civil war, was plunged into armed chaos.

President Reagan sent American troops to Lebanon in 1983 as part of an international peacekeeping force, but their presence did not bring peace. A suicidal bomber crashed an explosives-laden truck into a United States Marine Corps barracks on October 23, 1983, killing more than two hundred marines. President Reagan soon thereafter withdrew the remaining American troops, while miraculously suffering no political damage from this horrifying and humiliating attack. His mystified Democratic opponents began to call him the "Teflon president," to whom nothing hurtful could stick.

Central America, in the United States' own backyard, also rumbled menacingly. A leftist revolution had deposed the long-time dictator of Nicaragua in 1979. President Carter had tried to ignore the hotly anti-American rhetoric of the revolutionaries, known as **Sandinistas**, and to establish good diplomatic relations with them. But cold warrior Reagan took their rhetoric at face value and hurled back at them some hot language of his own.

Sandinistas *Leftwing anti-American revolutionaries in Nicaragua who launched a civil war in 1979.*

Reagan accused the Sandinistas of turning their country into a forward base for Soviet and Cuban military penetration of all of Central America. Brandishing photographs taken from high-flying spy planes, administration officials claimed that Nicaraguan leftists were shipping weapons to revolutionary forces in tiny El Salvador, torn by violence since a coup in 1979.

Reagan sent military "advisers" to prop up the pro-American government of El Salvador. He also provided covert aid, including the CIA-engineered mining of harbors, to the rebel **contras** opposing the anti-American Sandinista government of Nicaragua. Reagan flexed his military muscles elsewhere in the turbulent Caribbean. In a dramatic display of American might, in October 1983 he dispatched a heavy-firepower invasion force to the island of Grenada, where a military coup had killed the prime minister and brought Marxists to power. Swiftly overrunning the tiny island and ousting the insurgents, American troops vividly demonstrated Reagan's determination to assert the dominance of the United States in the Caribbean, just as Theodore Roosevelt had done (see Map 39.2).

contras *Anti-Sandinista fighters in the Nicaraguan civil war. The contras were secretly supplied with American military aid, paid for with money the United States clandestinely made selling arms to Iran.*

Map 39.2 Central America and the Caribbean This region, so important to the United States throughout its history, remained a hotbed of unrest through the last years of the Cold War and beyond.

★ Round Two for Reagan

A confident Ronald Reagan, bolstered by a buoyant economy at home and by the popularity of his defiant posture abroad, met little opposition in his bid for a second White House term in 1984. His Democratic opponent was former Vice President Walter Mondale, who made history by naming as his own vice-presidential running mate Congresswoman Geraldine Ferraro of New York. She was the first woman ever to appear on a major party presidential ticket. But even this dramatic gesture could not salvage Mondale's candidacy. On election day Reagan walked away with 525 electoral votes to Mondale's 13, winning everywhere except in Mondale's home state of Minnesota and the District of Columbia. Reagan also overwhelmed Mondale in the popular vote—52,609,797 to 36,450,613.

Shrinking the federal government and reducing taxes had been the main objectives of Reagan's first term; foreign-policy issues dominated his second term. The president soon found himself contending for the world's attention with a charismatic new Soviet leader, Mikhail Gorbachev, installed as chairman of the Soviet Communist party in March 1985. Gorbachev was personable, energetic, imaginative, and committed to radical reforms in the Soviet Union. He announced two policies with remarkable, even revolutionary, implications. **Glasnost**, or "openness," aimed to ventilate the secretive, repressive stuffiness of Soviet society by introducing free speech and a measure of political liberty. **Perestroika**, or "restructuring," was intended to revive the moribund Soviet economy by adopting many of the free-market practices of the capitalist West.

Both glasnost and perestroika required that the Soviet Union shrink the size of its enormous military machine and redirect its energies to the civilian economy. That requirement, in turn, necessitated an end to the Cold War. Gorbachev accordingly made warm overtures to the West, including an announcement in April 1985 that the Soviet Union would cease to deploy intermediate-range nuclear forces (INF) targeted on Western Europe, pending an agreement on their complete elimination. He pushed this goal when he met with Ronald Reagan at their first of four summit meetings, in Geneva in November 1985. A second summit meeting, in Reykjavik, Iceland in October 1986, broke down when a furious Reagan stormed out, convinced that Gorbachev had come to end plans for the beloved SDI. But at a third summit, in Washington, D.C. in December 1987, the two leaders at last signed the **Intermediate-Range Nuclear Forces (INF) Treaty**, banning all of these missiles from Europe. Reagan and Gorbachev capped their new friendship in May 1988 at a final summit in Moscow. There President Reagan, who had entered office condemning the "evil empire" of Soviet communism, warmly praised Gorbachev. Reagan, the consummate cold warrior, had been flexible and savvy enough to seize a historic opportunity to join with the Soviet chief to bring the Cold War to a kind of conclusion. For this, history would give both leaders high marks.

Glasnost Meaning "openness," a cornerstone along with perestroika of Soviet president Mikhail Gorbachev's reform movement in the USSR in the 1980s. These policies resulted in greater market liberalization, access to the West, and ultimately the end of communist rule.

Perestroika Meaning "restructuring," a cornerstone along with glasnost of Soviet president Mikhail Gorbachev's reform movement in the USSR in the 1980s. These policies resulted in greater market liberalization, access to the West, and ultimately the end of communist rule.

Intermediate-Range Nuclear Forces (INF) Treaty (1987) Arms limitation agreement settled by Ronald Reagan and Mikhail Gorbachev after several attempts. The treaty banned all intermediate-range nuclear missiles from Europe and marked a significant thaw in the Cold War.

★ The Iran-Contra Imbroglio

Two foreign-policy problems seemed insoluble to Reagan: the continuing captivity of a number of American hostages seized by Muslim extremist groups in bleeding, battered Lebanon; and the continuing grip on power of the left-wing Sandinista government in Nicaragua. The president repeatedly requested that Congress provide military aid to the contra rebels fighting against the Sandinista regime. Congress repeatedly refused, and the administration grew increasingly frustrated, even obsessed, in its search for a means to help the contras.

Unknown to the American public, some Washington officials saw a possible linkage between the two thorny problems of the Middle Eastern hostages and the Central American Sandinistas. In 1985 American diplomats secretly arranged arms sales to Iran, which was mired in a devastating war with neighboring Iraq. In return, the Iranians helped obtain the release of at least one American hostage held by Middle Eastern terrorists. Meanwhile, the money Iran paid for the American weapons was diverted to the contras in Nicaragua. These actions brazenly violated a congressional ban on military aid to the Nicaraguan rebels—not to mention Reagan's repeated vow that he would never negotiate with terrorists. Washington also continued to support Iraqi dictator Saddam Hussein, to whom it sold weapons he then used against Iran.

Secretly Supporting the Contras The Reagan administration went to great and illegal lengths to provide aid for the Nicaraguan "contras"—armed resistors to the leftwing Sandinista regime, which had ruled the country since 1979. Fittingly, one of these patrolling rebels wears a USA baseball cap.

News of these secret dealings broke in November 1986 and ignited a firestorm of controversy. President Reagan claimed he was innocent of wrongdoing and ignorant of his subordinates' activities. Although Reagan was never found to have lied outright, a congressional committee condemned the "secrecy, deception, and disdain for the law" displayed by administration officials and concluded that "if the president did not know what his national security advisers were doing, he should have."

The **Iran-Contra affair** cast a dark shadow over Reagan's foreign policy record. Critics pounced on the portrait of him as a lazy, inattentive chief executive as proof that the movie-star-turned politician was a mental lightweight. But despite these damaging revelations, Reagan remained among the most popular and beloved presidents in modern American history.

Iran-Contra affair *Major political scandal of Ronald Reagan's second term that was revealed in 1986. An illicit arrangement of selling "arms for hostages" with Iran and using money to support the contras in Nicaragua, the scandal deeply damaged Reagan's credibility.*

★ Reagan's Economic Legacy

Ronald Reagan had taken office vowing to invigorate the American economy by rolling back government regulations, lowering taxes, and balancing the budget. He did ease many regulatory rules, and he pushed major tax-reform bills through Congress in 1981 and 1986. But a balanced budget remained grotesquely out of reach. The combination of tax reduction and huge increases in military spending opened a vast "revenue hole" of $200 billion in annual deficits. In his eight years in office, President Reagan added nearly $2 trillion to the national debt—more than all his predecessors combined.

On March 4, 1987, President Ronald Reagan somewhat confusingly tried to explain his role (or lack of role) in the arms-for-hostages deal with Iran:

"A few months ago I told the American people I did not trade arms for hostages. My heart and my best intentions still tell me that is true, but the facts and the evidence tell me it is not."

The staggering deficits of the Reagan years assuredly constituted a great economic failure. And because foreign lenders, especially the Japanese, financed so much of the Reagan-era debt, the deficits virtually guaranteed that future generations of Americans would have to either work harder than their parents, lower their standard of living, or both, to pay their foreign creditors.

But if the deficits represented an economic failure, they also constituted, strangely enough, a kind of political triumph. The sky-high budget deficits actually served one of Reagan's paramount goals: slowing the growth of government and making new social spending practically and politically impossible for the foreseeable future. Ronald Reagan thus secured one of his dearest political objectives to a degree few presidents have managed to achieve. For better or worse, the consequences of "Reaganomics" would be large and durable.

> *Hollywood director Oliver Stone's (b. 1946) film* Wall Street *both romanticized and vilified the business culture of the 1980s. The character of Gordon Gekko, inspired by real-life corporate raider Ivan Boesky, captured the spirit of the times:*
>
> "Ladies and gentlemen, greed is good. Greed works, greed is right. . . . Greed for life, money, love, knowledge, has marked the upward surge of mankind—and greed, mark my words, will save the malfunctioning corporation called the U.S.A."

★ The Religious Right

Religion pervaded American politics in the 1980s. Especially conspicuous was a coalition of conservative evangelical Christians known as the religious right. In 1979 the Reverend Jerry Falwell, an evangelical minister and founder of Liberty University in Lynchburg, Virginia, launched a political advocacy group called the **Moral Majority**. Falwell preached with great success against sexual permissiveness, abortion, feminism, and the spread of gay rights. In its first two years, the Moral Majority registered between 2 million and 3 million voters. Using radio, direct-mail marketing, and cable TV, Falwell and other "televangelists" reached huge audiences in the 1980s, collected millions of dollars, and became aggressive political advocates of conservative causes.

In their movement zeal and morally charged political approach, members of the religious right resembled the left-wing protesters of the 1960s. In many ways the religious right of the 1980s was a reflection of, or an answer to, sixties radicalism. Feminists in the 1960s declared that "the personal is the political." The religious right did the same. What had in the past been personal matters—gender roles, homosexuality, and prayer—became the organizing ground for a powerful political movement. Like advocates of multiculturalism and affirmative action, the religious right practiced a form of "identity politics." But rather than defining themselves as Latino voters or gay voters, they declared themselves Christian or pro-life voters. The New Right also mimicked the New Left in some of its tactics. If the left had consciousness-raising sessions, the right had prayer meetings. Adherents articulated their positions in a language of rights, as in the "right-to-life" (or anti-abortion) movement. Protesters in the 1960s blocked entrances to draft offices; protesters in the 1980s blocked entrances to abortion clinics.

Several leaders of the religious right fell from grace in the latter part of the decade. One tearfully admitted to repeated trysts with prostitutes. Another went to prison following revelations of his own financial and sexual misconduct. But such scandals would not shake the faith of America's conservative Christians or diminish the new political clout of activist, evangelical religionists.

Moral Majority *Political action committee founded by evangelical Reverend Jerry Falwell in 1979 to promote traditional Christian values and oppose feminism, abortion, and gay rights. The group was a major linchpin in the resurgent religious right of the 1980s.*

★ Conservatism in the Courts

If the budget was Reagan's chief weapon in the war against the welfare state, the courts became his principal instrument in the "cultural wars" demanded by Christian conservatives. By the time he left office, Reagan had appointed a near-majority of all sitting federal judges. Equally important, he had named three conservative-minded justices to the U.S. Supreme Court. They included Sandra Day O'Connor, a brilliant, public-spirited Arizona judge. When she was sworn in on September 25, 1981, she became the first woman to ascend to the high bench in the Court's nearly two-hundred-year history.

Reaganism repudiated two great icons of the liberal political culture: affirmative action and abortion. The Court showed its newly conservative colors in 1984, when it decreed, in a case involving Memphis fire fighters, that union rules about job seniority could outweigh affirmative-action concerns in guiding promotion policies in the city's fire department. In two cases in 1989 (*Ward's Cove Packing v. Antonia* and *Martin v. Wilks*), the Court made it more difficult to prove that an employer practiced racial discrimination in hiring and made it easier for white males to argue that they were the victims of reverse discrimination. The contentious issue of abortion also reached the Court in 1989. In the case of *Roe v. Wade* in 1973, the Supreme Court had prohibited states from making laws that interfered with a woman's right to an abortion during the early months of pregnancy. For nearly two decades, that decision had been the bedrock principle on which "pro-choice" advocates built their case for abortion rights. It had also provoked bitter criticism from Roman Catholics and various "right-to-life" groups, who wanted a virtually absolute ban on all abortions. In *Webster v. Reproductive Health Services*, the Court in 1989 seriously compromised *Roe*'s protections by approving a Missouri law that imposed certain restrictions on abortion. In 1992's *Planned Parenthood v. Casey*, the Court held that states could restrict access to abortion so long as they did not place an "undue burden" on the woman. The *Webster* and *Casey* decisions galvanized right-to-life and pro-choice organizations alike. Bruising, divisive battles loomed as state legislatures across the land confronted abortions.

★ Referendum on Reaganism in 1988

Republicans lost control of the Senate in the off-year elections of November 1986. Hopes rose among Democrats that the "Reagan revolution" might be showing signs of political vulnerability at last. The newly Democratic majority in the Senate flexed its muscles in 1987 when it rejected Robert Bork, an ultraconservative nominee for the Supreme Court.

Democrats relished the prospect of making political hay out of both the Iran-Contra affair and disquieting signs of economic trouble. The "double mountain" of deficits—the federal budget deficit and international trade deficit—continued to grow ominously. Falling real estate prices caused hundreds of savings and loan (S&L) institutions to fail, especially in the Southwest. A massive federal rescue operation for the S&Ls cost well over $500 billion.

Meanwhile, a wave of mergers, acquisitions, and leveraged buyouts washed over Wall Street, leaving many brokers and traders mega-rich and many companies saddled with mega-debt. A cold spasm of fear struck the money markets on **Black Monday**, October 19, 1987, when the leading stock-market index plunged 508 points—the largest one-day decline in history to that point. This crash, said *Newsweek* magazine, heralded "the final collapse of the money culture . . . , the death knell of the 1980s." But as Mark Twain famously commented about his own obituary, this announcement proved premature.

Black Monday *October 19, 1987. Date of the largest single-day decline in the Dow Jones Industrial Average until September 2001. The downturn indicated instability in the booming business culture of the 1980s but did not lead to a serious economic recession.*

Hoping to cash in on these ethical and economic anxieties, a pack of Democrats—dubbed the "Seven Dwarfs" by derisive Republicans—chased after their party's 1988 presidential nomination. The handsome and charismatic Democratic front runner, former Colorado senator Gary Hart, was forced to drop out of the race after charges of sexual misconduct. African American candidate Jesse Jackson, a rousing speechmaker who hoped to forge a "rainbow coalition" of minorities and the disadvantaged, campaigned energetically. But the Democratic nomination in the end went to the coolly cerebral governor of Massachusetts, Michael Dukakis. Republicans nominated Reagan's vice president, George H.W. Bush, who ran largely on the Reagan record of tax cuts, strong defense policies, toughness on crime, opposition to abortion, and a long-running if hardly robust economic expansion. Dukakis made little headway exploiting the ethical and economic sore spots and came across to television viewers as almost supernaturally devoid of emotion. On election day the voters gave him just 41,016,429 votes to 47,946,422 for Bush. The Electoral College count was a lopsided 111 to 426.

★ George H.W. Bush and the End of the Cold War

George Herbert Walker Bush was born with a silver ladle in his mouth. His father had served as a U.S. senator from Connecticut, and young George had enjoyed a first-rate education at Yale. After service in World War II and success in the Texas oil business, he turned to public service. Bush served briefly as a congressman from Texas and then held various posts in several Republican administrations, including emissary to China, ambassador to the United Nations, director of the Central Intelligence Agency, and vice president. He capped this long political career when he was inaugurated president in January 1989, promising to work for "a kinder, gentler America."

In the first months of the Bush administration, the communist world commanded the planet's fascinated attention. Everywhere in the communist bloc it seemed, astoundingly, that the season of democracy had arrived.

In China hundreds of thousands of prodemocracy demonstrators thronged Beijing's Tiananmen Square in the spring of 1989. But in June of that year, China's aging and autocratic rulers brutally crushed the prodemocracy movement. Tanks rolled over the crowds, and machine-gunners killed hundreds of protesters. World opinion roundly condemned the bloody suppression of the prodemocracy demonstrators. President Bush joined in the criticism. Yet despite angry demands in Congress for punitive restrictions on trade with China, the president insisted on maintaining normal relations with Beijing.

In his state of the union address on January 31, 1990, President George H.W. Bush (b. 1924) declared:

"The events of the year just ended, the revolution of '89, have been a chain reaction, changes so striking that it marks the beginning of a new era in the world's affairs."

Just six months later, speaking at Stanford University, Soviet president Mikhail Gorbachev (b. 1931) said:

"The Cold War is now behind us. Let us not wrangle over who won it. It is in the common interest of our two countries and nations not to fight this trend toward cooperation, but rather to promote it."

Stunning changes also shook Eastern Europe. Long oppressed by puppet regimes propped up by Soviet guns, the region was revolutionized in just a few startling months in 1989. The Solidarity movement in Poland led the way when it toppled Poland's communist government in August. With dizzying speed, communist regimes collapsed in Hungary, Czechoslovakia, East Germany, and even hyper-repressive Romania. In December 1989, jubilant Germans danced atop the hated Berlin Wall, symbol of the division of Germany and all of Europe into two armed and hostile camps. The wall itself soon came down, heralding the imminent end of the forty-five-year-long Cold War. With the approval of the victorious Allied powers of World War II, the two Germanys, divided since 1945, were at last reunited in October 1990.

Most startling of all were the changes that rolled over the heartland of world communism, the Soviet Union itself. Mikhail Gorbachev's policies of glasnost and perestroika

Tiananmen Square, Beijing, China, June 1989 The Chinese communist state mobilized all its forces against students demonstrating for a more democratic China.

Contending Voices

Who Ended the Cold War?

In a roundtable discussion in 1995, former British prime minister Margaret Thatcher (1925–2013) and former Soviet leader Mikhail Gorbachev (b. 1931), among others, debated the question of how and why the Cold War came to an end. Margaret Thatcher suggested that SDI was the cause:

"There was one vital factor in the ending of the Cold War: Ronald Reagan's decision to go ahead with the Strategic Defense Initiative.... That was a completely different level of defense. It required enormous computer capability, which he knew at the time the Soviet Union could not match. And that was the end of the arms race as we had been pursuing it."

Mikhail Gorbachev disagreed:

"If you accept that reforms in the Soviet Union started under the pressure from the West, particularly as a result of the implementation of SDI, that would distort the real picture and offer the wrong lesson for the future.... [T]he first impulses for reform were in the Soviet Union itself, in our society which could no longer tolerate the lack of freedom, where no one could speak out or choose their own party or select their own creed.... This was the decisive factor, not SDI."

> Who should get the lion's share of the credit for ending the Cold War: U.S. president Ronald Reagan, or Soviet leader Mikhail Gorbachev? Was it U.S. strategy or internal developments within the Soviet Union that principally drove events?

---

had set in motion a groundswell that surged out of his control. Old-guard hard-liners, in a last-gasp effort to preserve the tottering communist system, attempted to dislodge Gorbachev with a military coup in August 1991. With the support of Boris Yeltsin, president of the Russian Republic (one of several republics that composed the Union of Soviet Socialist Republics), Gorbachev foiled the plotters. But his days were numbered. In December 1991 Gorbachev resigned as Soviet president, and the Soviet Union dissolved into fifteen sovereign republics, with Russia the most powerful state and Yeltsin the dominant leader (see Map 39.3).

The demise of the Soviet Union wrote a definitive finish to the Cold War era. More than four decades of nail-biting tension between the two nuclear superpowers, the Soviet Union and the United States, evaporated when the USSR dismantled itself. With the Soviet Union swept into the dustbin of history and communism apparently headed for extinction, Bush spoke hopefully of a "new world order," where democracy would reign and diplomacy would supersede weaponry. Some observers even saw in these developments the "end of history," in the sense that democracy, victorious in its two-century-long struggle against foes on the left and right, had no ideological battles left to fight.

But the disintegration of the Soviet Union posed rankling questions. Who would honor arms-control agreements with the United States? Which of the successor states of the former Soviet Union would take command of the formidable Soviet nuclear arsenal?

Throughout the former Soviet empire, waves of nationalistic fervor and long-suppressed ethnic hatred rolled across the vast land as communism's roots were wrenched out. A particularly nasty conflict erupted in 1991, when the Chechnyan minority tried to declare their independence from Russia, prompting President Yeltsin to send in Russian troops. Ethnic warfare flared in other disintegrating communist countries as well, notably in misery-drenched Yugoslavia, racked by vicious "ethnic cleansing" campaigns against various minorities.

The end of the Cold War proved a mixed blessing for the United States. For nearly half a century the containment of Soviet communism had been the paramount goal of U.S. foreign policy. Indeed the Cold War era had been the only lengthy period in American history when the United States had consistently pursued an internationalist foreign policy. With the Soviet threat now canceled, would the United States revert to its traditional isolationism? What principles would guide American diplomacy now that "anticommunism" had lost its relevance.

The Soviet-American rivalry, with its demands for high levels of military preparedness, had also deeply shaped and even invigorated the U.S. economy. Huge economic sectors such as aerospace were heavily sustained by military contracts. When the Pentagon in 1991 closed thirty-four military bases and canceled a $52 billion order for a navy attack plane, unemployment soared in southern California and other areas that had once been drenched with Pentagon dollars. The problems of weaning the U.S. economy from its decades of dependence on defense spending tempered the euphoria of Americans as they welcomed the Cold War's long-awaited finale.

Map 39.3 The End of the Cold War Changed the Map of Europe

⭐ The Persian Gulf War

Sadly, the end of the Cold War did not mean the end of all wars. President Bush flexed the United States' still-intimidating military muscles in tiny Panama in December 1989, when he sent airborne troops to capture dictator Manuel Noriega.

Still more ominous events in the summer of 1990 severely tested Bush's dream of a democratic and peaceful new world order. On August 2 Saddam Hussein, the brutal and ambitious ruler of Iraq, sent his armies to overrun Kuwait, a tiny, oil-rich sheikdom on Iraq's southern frontier. Saddam design was to seize Kuwait's oil, gain control of the world's economic jugular in the Persian Gulf, and perhaps totally extinguish the Arabs' enemy, Israel.

On August 2, 1990, Saddam's army roared into Kuwait. The speed and audacity of the invasion were stunning, but the world responded just as swiftly. The United Nations Security Council unanimously condemned the invasion on August 3 and demanded the immediate and unconditional withdrawal of Iraq's troops. In November the Security Council delivered an ultimatum to Saddam to leave Kuwait by January 15, 1991, or U.N. forces would "use all necessary means" to expel his troops.

In a logistical operation of astonishing complexity, the United States spearheaded a massive international military deployment on the sandy Arabian Peninsula. As the January 15 deadline approached, some 539,000 U.S. soldiers, sailors, and pilots swarmed into the Persian Gulf region. They were joined by nearly 270,000 troops from twenty-eight other countries in the coalition opposed to Iraq. When all diplomatic efforts to resolve the crisis failed, the U.S. Congress voted on January 12, 1991, to approve the use of force.

The United States and its U.N. allies unleashed a thirty-seven-day air attack that pummeled targets in occupied Kuwait and in Iraq itself. On February 23, 1991, the dreaded and long-awaited land war began. Dubbed **Operation Desert Storm**, it lasted only four days—the "hundred-hour war." With lightning speed the U.N. forces penetrated deep into

Operation Desert Storm (1991)
U.S.-led multicountry military engagement in January and February of 1991 that drove Saddam Hussein's Iraqi army out of neighboring Kuwait. In addition to presaging the longer and more protracted Iraq War of the 2000s, the 1991 war helped undo what some called the "Vietnam Syndrome," a feeling of military uncertainty that plagued many Americans.

Iraq, outflanking the occupying army in Kuwait. Allied casualties were amazingly light, whereas much of Iraq's remaining fighting force was quickly destroyed or captured. On February 27 Saddam accepted a cease-fire, and Kuwait was liberated.

Most Americans cheered the war's rapid and enormously successful conclusion. Many people echoed President Bush's sentiments when he declared, "By God, we've kicked the Vietnam Syndrome once and for all!" But when the smoke cleared, Saddam Hussein had survived to menace the world another day. America and its allies had agreed to the liberation of Kuwait, but Bush, fearing that a full assault on Baghdad would cost many lives and much public support, stopped well short of overthrowing the tyrant Saddam. The perpetually troubled Middle East knew scarcely less trouble after Desert Storm had ceased to thunder, and the United States, for better or worse, found itself more deeply ensnared in the region's web of mortal hatreds and intractable conflicts.

★ Bush on the Home Front

George H.W. Bush partly redeemed his pledge to work for a "kinder, gentler America" when he signed the **Americans with Disabilities Act (ADA)** in 1990, a landmark law prohibiting discrimination against the 43 million U.S. citizens with physical or mental disabilities. The president also signed a major water projects bill in 1992 that put the interests of the environment on a par with those of agriculture, especially in California's heavily irrigated Central Valley.

The new president continued to aggravate the explosive "social issues" that had so divided Americans throughout the 1980s, especially the nettlesome questions of affirmative action and abortion. Bush challenged the legality of college scholarships targeted for racial minorities, and repeatedly threatened to veto civil rights legislation that would make it easier for employees to prove discrimination in hiring and promotion. Most provocatively, in 1991 Bush nominated for the Supreme Court the conservative African American jurist Clarence Thomas, a stern critic of affirmative-action policies. Thomas's nomination was loudly opposed by labor, civil rights, and women's organizations. Reflecting irreconcilable divisions over affirmative action and abortion, the Senate Judiciary Committee concluded its hearings with a divided seven-to-seven vote and forwarded the matter to the full Senate without a recommendation. Then, just days before the Senate was scheduled to vote in early October 1991, a press leak revealed that Anita Hill, a University of Oklahoma law professor, had accused Thomas of sexual harassment. The Senate Judiciary Committee was forced to reopen its hearings.

For days a prurient American public sat glued to their television sets as Hill graphically detailed her charges of sexual improprieties and Thomas angrily responded. In the end, by a fifty-two to forty-eight vote, the Senate confirmed Thomas as the second African American ever to sit on the supreme bench (Thurgood Marshall was the first). While many hailed Hill as a heroine for focusing the nation's attention on issues of sexual harassment, Thomas maintained that her widely publicized, unproved allegations amounted to "a high-tech lynching for uppity blacks who in any way deign to think for themselves, to do for themselves." Many women, enraged by the all-male judiciary committee's behavior in the Thomas hearings, grew increasingly critical of the president's uncompromising stand on abortion. A "gender gap" opened between the two political parties, as pro-choice women grew increasingly cool toward the strong anti-abortion stand of the Republicans.

Still more damaging to President Bush's political health, the economy sputtered and stalled almost from the outset of his administration. By 1992 the unemployment rate exceeded 7 percent, while the federal budget deficit continued to mushroom cancerously, topping $250 billion in each of Bush's years as president. In a desperate attempt to stop the hemorrhage of red ink, Bush agreed in 1990 to a budget that included $133 billion in new taxes.

Bush's 1990 tax and budget package added up to a political catastrophe. In his 1988 presidential campaign, Bush had belligerently declared, "Read my lips—no new taxes." Now he had flagrantly broken that campaign promise. The budget deal deeply divided his own party. An ascendant congressional wing of hard-line conservatives, led by Georgia congressman Newt Gingrich, voted against their own president's hard-fought agreement. After Bush's debacle, a blanket opposition to tax increases of any kind became an entrenched part of mainstream Republican orthodoxy, setting the stage for irreconcilable political conflicts ahead.

Americans with Disabilities Act (ADA) (1990) *Landmark law signed by President George H.W. Bush that prohibited discrimination against people with physical or mental handicaps. It represented a legislative triumph for champions of equal protections to all.*

Varying Viewpoints

Where Did Modern Conservatism Come From?

Ronald Reagan's elections surprised many historians. Reflecting a liberal political outlook that is common among academic scholars, they were long accustomed to understanding American history as an inexorable, almost evolutionary, unfolding of liberal principles, including the quests for economic equality, social justice, and active government. Even the "New Left" revisionists of the 1960s who decried liberalism's deficiencies assumed that the deep currents of American history flowed leftward. Whether liberal or revisionist, most scholars writing in the first three post–World War II decades dismissed conservatism as an obsolete political creed and psychoanalyzed its adherents as fringe wackos—paranoid McCarthyites or racist demagogues who, in the words of liberal critic Lionel Trilling, trafficked only in "irritable mental gestures which seem to resemble ideas." Such an outlook is conspicuous in books such as Daniel Bell's *The Radical Right* (1963), and Richard Hofstadter's *The Paranoid Style in American Politics* (1965).

Yet what flowed out of the turbulent decade of the 1960s was not a strengthened liberalism but a revived conservatism. Ronald Reagan's huge political success, followed by continued conservative strength through the 1990s and 2000s, compelled a thorough reexamination of the tradition of American conservatism and the sources of its modern resurgence.

Historians such as Leo Ribuffo and Alan Brinkley have argued that characters from earlier eras once dismissed as irrational crackpots—including religious Fundamentalists and depression-era figures like Huey Long and Father Charles Coughlin—articulated values deeply rooted and widely shared in American culture. They offered a vision of free individuals, minimal government, and autonomous local communities that harked back to the "civic republicanism" in the era of young nationhood.

But modern conservatism, however deep its roots, is also a product of the recent past. Many students of the postwar right emphasize the theme of "backlash." They explain conservatism's rise as a populist reaction among working-class whites to the racial, cultural, and economic disruptions of the 1960s. Thomas and Mary Edsall's *Chain Reaction* (1991) and Ron Formisano's *Boston Against Busing* (1991) emphasize class tensions and economic insecurity as causes of battles over taxes and busing.

Other historians have challenged the "backlash" proponents' depiction of conservative politics in reactionary terms. Kim Phillips-Fein (*Invisible Hands*, 2006) outlined the role of conservative businessmen in promoting premarket ideology, while Rick Perlstein (*Before the Storm*, 2001) and Jonathan Schoenwald (*A Time for Choosing*, 2001) unearthed the deliberate conservative movement-making of the 1960s. Other scholars like Lisa McGirr, Thomas Sugrue, and Lizebeth Cohen have shown how the New Deal and Cold War ironically served to foster a suburban politics hostile to taxes and government redistributism.

Even as they trace the roots of the conservative revival to the early postwar years, scholars have come to see the 1970s as a "*Pivotal Decade*" (the title of Judith Stein's 2010 book). The work of Bruce Schulman, Jefferson Cowie, and Laura Colman shows how 1970s activists took advantage of disillusionment with government to mobilize new constituencies on behalf of conservatism. Their agenda combined antigovernment, free-market economic policies with an emphasis on hot-button "social issues" related to gender, reproductive policy, and cultural production. Scholars like Donald Critchlow and Darren Dochuk have shown that this latter cultural element of conservative mobilization had origins dating to the midcentury.

The flowering of scholarship on American conservatism has demonstrated, above all, that the forces that propelled Reagan to power in 1980 were neither aberrant not fleeting. Rather, they reflected outlooks deeply rooted in American culture and drew strength from core developments in the American state and economy in the twentieth century. American historians, like American citizens, are unlikely to ignore the conservative tradition again.

CHAPTER SUMMARY ★ ★ ★ ★ ★ ★ ★ ★ ★ ★ ★ ★ ★

Reagan led Republicans to sweeping victories in 1980 and 1984 over divided and demoralized Democrats. Riding a conservative national tide, Reagan pushed both his "supply-side" economic program of reduced social welfare programs, lower taxes, and massive military expenditures. These policies brought economic recovery and lower inflation, as well as high interest rates and dramatically bigger federal budget deficits.

Reagan revived the Cold War confrontation with the Soviet Union, and engaged the United States in assertive military support for anti-leftist forces in Latin America and elsewhere. The ratcheting up of military spending, along with the attempted reforms led by Mikhail Gorbachev, contributed to a series of successful arms limitation talks that reduced Cold War tensions in the mid-1980s. The Iran-Contra affair tarnished Reagan's international legacy, but his economic policies guaranteed success for his goal of curbing further growth in the welfare state.

Religious conservatives of the New Right assumed growing influence on American politics, borrowing many tactics from the sixties New Left. The Supreme Court under Reagan and his successor, George H.W. Bush, became increasingly conservative, as the Court partially overturned previous rulings on issues of abortion and affirmative action.

In foreign affairs, Bush promoted a "new world order" after the collapse of communism in Eastern Europe and the Soviet Union in 1989–1991. But Saddam Hussein's invasion of Kuwait brought war to the Middle East. With America as the only remaining superpower, Bush led an international coalition to victory in the Persian Gulf War, but the Middle East remained a dangerous tinderbox despite new efforts to resolve the Israel-Arab conflict. Bush supported the Americans with Disabilities Act, but also pushed conservative social issues and nominated the controversial Clarence Thomas to the Supreme Court. Economic recession and Bush's tax increase created a growing conservative opposition within the Republican party, led by Congressman Newt Gingrich.

KEY TERMS

- Proposition 13 (689)
- boll weevils (689)
- supply-side economics (689)
- Strategic Defense Initiative (SDI) (690)
- Sandinistas (692)
- contras (692)
- glasnost (693)
- perestroika (693)
- Intermediate-Range Nuclear Forces (INF) Treaty (693)
- Iran-Contra affair (694)
- Moral Majority (695)
- Black Monday (696)
- Operation Desert Storm (699)
- Americans with Disabilities Act (ADA) (700)

PEOPLE TO KNOW

- Ronald Reagan
- Margaret Thatcher
- Mikhail Gorbachev
- Saddam Hussein
- Jerry Falwell
- Sandra Day O'Connor
- George H.W. Bush
- Boris Yeltsin
- Manuel Noriega
- Clarence Thomas

MindTap is a fully online, highly personalized learning experience built upon Cengage Learning content. MindTap combines student learning tools—readings, multimedia, activities, and assessments—into a singular Learning Path that guides students through the course.

Chapter 40

America Confronts the Post–Cold War Era
1992–2000

As the Cold War gives way to the global village, our leadership is needed more than ever, because problems that start beyond our borders can quickly become problems within them.

WILLIAM J. CLINTON, 1995

Chapter Outline

- Bill Clinton in the White House
- Congressional Republicans Battle Clinton
- Clinton and the Prosperous '90s Economy
- Racial Gains and Tensions
- Globalization and U.S. Foreign Policy
- Clinton's Impeachment and Acquittal
- The Controversial 2000 Election
- Postmodern American Culture
- *Makers of America: The Latinos*

The collapse of the Soviet Union and the democratization of its client regimes in Eastern Europe ended the four-decade-old Cold War and left the United States the world's sole remaining superpower. Americans welcomed these changes but seemed unsure how to exercise their unprecedented economic and military might in this new international scenario. The culture wars that had started in the 1960s fed ferociously partisan political squabbles that distracted the nation from the urgent task of clearly defining its role in the age of globalization.

Amidst this deepening partisan polarization, a sustained ten-year economic expansion powerfully shaped American society and politics in the 1990s. The second half of the decade was a particularly giddy boom era, as an exuberant financial sector and ascendant information technology firms helped to propel the economy to near-full employment—and the federal budget to record surpluses. But the good times were not to last.

FOCUS QUESTIONS

1. How did President Bill Clinton attempt to navigate between traditional liberal Democratic values and his claim to be a centrist "new Democrat"?
2. What caused the growing polarization between the conservative Republican movement and the Clinton administration?
3. Why did issues of race and women's rights remain controversial in the 1990s, even as many blacks and women made substantial social and economic gains?
4. How did President Clinton survive the Lewinsky scandal and subsequent impeachment?
5. How did multiculturalism, postmodernism, and new media change and splinter American culture?

CHRONOLOGY

1992	Clinton defeats Bush and Perot for presidency	1999	Senate acquits Clinton on impeachment charges
1993	NAFTA signed		Kosovo crisis; NATO warfare with Serbia
1994	Republicans win majorities in both houses of Congress		Protest in Seattle against World Trade Organization
1996	Welfare Reform Bill becomes law	2000	United States normalizes trade relations with China
	Clinton defeats Dole for presidency		George W. Bush wins presidency in Electoral College; Albert Gore takes popular vote
1998	Clinton-Lewinsky scandal		
	Al Qaeda bombing of the U.S. embassies in Kenya and Tanzania		
	House of Representatives impeaches Clinton		

★ Bill Clinton: The First Baby-Boomer President

As the last decade of the twentieth century opened, a slumbering economy, a widening gender gap, and a rising anti-incumbent spirit spelled opportunity for Democrats, frozen out of the White House for all but four years since 1968. In a bruising round of primary elections, Governor William Jefferson ("Bill") Clinton of Arkansas weathered blistering accusations of womanizing and draft evasion to emerge as his party's standard-bearer, with another southern white male moderate, Tennessee Senator Albert Gore, as his vice presidential running mate.

Clinton claimed to be a "New Democrat," chastened by his party's long exile in the political wilderness. With other centrist Democrats, he had formed the **Democratic Leadership Council (DLC)** to point the party away from its traditional anti-business, dovish, champion-of-the-underdog orientation and toward pro-growth, strong defense, and anticrime policies. The DLC's ascendance as a business-friendly faction within the country's center-left party underscored the degree to which market-oriented thinking and policies had come to dominate American politics in the last decades of the twentieth century.

Trying to wring one more win out of the social issues that had underwritten two Reagan and one Bush presidential victories, the 1992 Republican convention emphasized "family values" as it nominated President George H.W. Bush and Vice President J. Danforth Quayle for a second term. But Bush's listless campaign could not keep pace with the super-energetic and phenomenally articulate Clinton. Bush claimed credit for ending the Cold War and trumpeted his leadership in the Persian Gulf War. But pocketbook problems as the economy dipped into recession swayed more voters than pride in past foreign policy.

At Clinton's campaign headquarters, a simple sign reminded staffers of his principal campaign theme: "It's the economy, stupid." Reflecting pervasive economic unease and the virulence of the throw-the-bums-out national mood, nearly 20 percent of voters cast their ballots for independent presidential candidate H. Ross Perot, a bantamweight, jug-eared Texas billionaire who harped incessantly on federal deficit problems and boasted of the fact that he had never held any public office.

With a record turnout of 100 million voters on election day, the final tally gave Clinton 44,909,889 popular votes and 370 votes in the Electoral College. He was the first baby boomer to ascend to the White House, a distinction reflecting the electoral profile of the population. Bush polled 39,104,545 popular votes and 168 electoral votes. Perot won no electoral votes but did gather 19,742,267 popular votes—the strongest showing for an independent or third-party candidate since Theodore Roosevelt ran on the Bull Moose ticket in 1912. Democrats also racked up clear majorities in both houses of Congress. The new Congress included thirty-nine African Americans, forty-eight women, and record numbers of Hispanics, Asian Americans, and Indians.

Democratic Leadership Council (DLC)
Nonprofit organization of centrist Democrats founded in the mid-1980s. The group attempted to push the Democratic party toward pro-growth, strong defense, and anti-crime policies. Among its most influential early members was Bill Clinton, whom it held up as an example of "third way" politics.

The Clintons Campaign, 1992 Bill and Hillary Clinton wave to a crowd of forty thousand in St. Louis on the last stop of the Clinton-Gore campaign's cross-country bus tour. The Arkansas governor was a famously tireless and effective campaigner, and he and his wife, an attorney and political force in her own right, would prove to be a powerful team in national politics for decades to come.

★ A False Start for Reform

Badly overestimating his electoral mandate for liberal reform, the young president made a series of costly blunders upon entering the White House. He stirred a hornet's nest of controversy by advocating an end to the ban on gays and lesbians in the armed forces. Confronted with fierce opposition, the president finally settled for a **"Don't Ask, Don't Tell"** policy that quietly accepted gay and lesbian soldiers and sailors without officially acknowledging their presence in the military. (Congress finally repealed the discriminatory policy in 2010.)

Even more damaging to Clinton's political standing was the fiasco of his attempt to reform the nation's health care system. In a dramatic but risky move, the president appointed his wife, Hillary Rodham Clinton, as the director of a task force charged with redesigning the medical-service industry. Their stupefyingly complicated plan was dead on arrival when presented to Congress in October 1993. The First Lady was doused with a torrent of abuse for her role in producing this legislative turkey, but she eventually rehabilitated herself sufficiently to win election as U.S. senator from New York in 2000—the first First Lady ever to hold elective office.

President Clinton had better luck with a deficit-reduction bill that passed Congress in 1993, which combined with an increasingly buoyant economy help shrink federal deficits. By 1998 Clinton's policies seemed to have caged the ravenous deficit monster, as Congress argued over the unfamiliar question of how to spend projected federal budget *surpluses*.

Clinton succeeded in getting through Congress a far-reaching anti-crime bill that provided for 100,000 new police officers, construction of more prisons, and a ban on some assault weapons (the ban expired in 2004). Several states also stiffened law enforcement practices, until America's incarceration rate became the highest in the world. The country's violent crime rate began to decline substantially after 1995—a striking nationwide trend that continued into the new century.

"Don't Ask, Don't Tell" From 1993 to 2010, the policy affecting homosexuals in the military. It emerged as a compromise between the standing prohibition against homosexuals in the armed forces and President Clinton's push to allow all citizens to serve regardless of sexual orientation. Military authorities were forbidden to ask about a service member's orientation, and gay service personnel could be discharged if they publicly revealed their homosexuality. At President Obama's urging, Congress repealed DADT in 2010, permitting gays to serve openly in uniform.

Bombing of Federal Building in Oklahoma City, 1995 A truck bomb killed 168 people in this federal office building in the worst act of terrorism in the United States until September 11, 2001. Convicted on eleven counts for the attack, antigovernment militant Timothy McVeigh became the first person executed by the federal government in nearly forty years in 2001.

Despite such legislative achievements, a sour antigovernment mood persisted. A huge explosion destroyed a federal office building in Oklahoma City in 1995, taking 168 lives, in retribution for a 1993 standoff in Waco, Texas, between federal agents and the Fundamentalist sect known as the Branch Davidians. That showdown had ended in the destruction of the sect's compound and the deaths of many Branch Davidians, including women and children. Events like the **Oklahoma City bombing** brought to light a secretive underground of paramilitary private "militias" composed of alienated citizens armed to the teeth and ultra-suspicious of all government.

Even many law-abiding citizens shared to some degree in the antigovernment attitudes that drove the militia members to murderous extremes. Thanks largely to the disillusioning agony of the Vietnam War and the naked cynicism of Richard Nixon in the Watergate scandal, the confidence in government that came naturally to the generation that had licked the Great Depression and won the Second World War was in short supply by century's end. Reflecting that pervasive disenchantment with politics and politicians, several states passed term-limit laws for elected officials, although the Supreme Court ruled in 1995 that the restrictions did not apply to federal officeholders.

★ The Politics of Distrust

Clinton's failed initiatives and widespread antigovernment sentiment afforded conservative Republicans a golden opportunity in 1994, and they seized it aggressively. Led by outspoken Georgia representative Newt Gingrich, Republicans offered voters a **Contract with America**

Oklahoma City bombing (1995)
Truck-bomb explosion that killed 168 people in a federal office building on April 19, 1995. The attack was perpetrated by right-wing and antigovernment militant Timothy McVeigh, who was later executed by the U.S. government for the crime.

Contract with America (1994)
Multipoint program offered by Republican candidates and sitting politicians in the 1994 midterm election. The platform proposed smaller government, congressional ethics reform, term limits, greater emphasis on personal responsibility, and a general repudiation of the Democratic party. This articulation of dissent was a significant blow to the Clinton administration and led to the Republican party's takeover of both houses of Congress for the first time in half a century.

that promised an all-out assault on budget deficits and radical reductions in welfare programs. Their campaign succeeded fabulously, as a conservative tornado roared across the land in the 1994 congressional elections. Republicans picked up eleven governorships, eight Senate seats, and fifty-three seats in the House (where Gingrich became Speaker), giving them control of both chambers of Congress for the first time in forty years. The 1994 midterms wiped out the remaining conservative congressional Democrats, concentrated in the South. Their replacement by newly empowered southern Republicans accelerated the ideological and geographical sorting of the two parties, which in turn only intensified the political combat in Washington.

In 1996 the new Congress achieved a major conservative victory when it compelled a reluctant Clinton to sign the Welfare Reform Bill, which made deep cuts in welfare grants and required able-bodied welfare recipients to find employment. Though liberal Democrats howled with pain at this law, Clinton's acceptance of welfare reform was part of his shrewd political strategy of accommodating the electorate's conservative mood by moving to the right.

Even as he signed the welfare-reform bill, Clinton denounced provisions that tightly restricted welfare benefits for both legal and illegal immigrants. These measures, like the Illegal Immigration Act of 1996 and a proposal to declare English the country's "official language," reflected a rising tide of anti-immigrant sentiment as the numbers of newcomers climbed to all-time highs, especially in the Southwest. Though anti-immigrant sentiment galvanized many voters, it also risked alienating the country's rapidly growing Latino population (see "Makers of America: The Latinos," p. 709).

Welfare reform marked a landmark legislative victory for the so-called "Republican Revolution" in Congress, but Republicans then proceeded to overplay their mandate for conservative retrenchment. Many Americans gradually came to feel that the Gingrich Republicans were bending the bow too far, especially when Speaker Gingrich advocated provocative ideas like sending the children of welfare families to orphanages. In a tense confrontation in 1995 between the Democratic president and the Republican Congress over proposed cuts to Medicare and education, the federal government was forced to shut down for nearly a month until a budget package was agreed upon. The shutdown bred a backlash against the GOP that helped President Clinton rebound from his political near-death experience.

Contending Voices

Welfare Reform Divides the Democrats

The 1996 Welfare Reform Bill, formally named the Personal Responsibility and Work Opportunity Act, badly split the president's fellow Democrats. Bill Clinton's (b. 1946) decision to sign it—after having vetoed two previous versions passed by the Republican-controlled Congress—occurred on the eve of a looming reelection campaign. His signing reflected his determination to be a "New Democrat" open both to market-based reform and scaled-back welfare programs.

Fellow New Democrats like Connecticut senator Joseph Lieberman (b. 1942) supported this approach. As Lieberman explained in an op-ed endorsing the Senate version of the bill:

"Welfare makes it feasible for a man to father a child without worrying about being a parent. It makes it possible for a young woman (too often a teen-age girl) to have a child, move away from home, get an apartment and survive—without working....

The Senate bill provides hope for poor Americans, and for taxpayers who want a Government that spends their money wisely and better reflects American values of work, family, and responsibility.... Most important, it would put an end to the policy of something for nothing, of penalizing work and marriage, and isolating the poor from the economic and cultural mainstream."

But leading liberal activists, among them the Clinton ally and Children's Defense Fund president Marian Wright Edelman (b. 1939), lambasted Clinton:

(continued)

★ Clinton Comes Back

As the 1996 election approached, the Republicans chose Kansas Senator Robert Dole as their presidential candidate. A decorated World War II veteran, Dole had a dry wit and deadpan manner that did not translate well on the campaign trail. In a bland contest, both parties fought for moderate "swing voters." One such swing constituency—middle class female suburbanites—introduced the term *soccer moms* into the national lexicon. Targeting soccer moms made excellent political sense because for the first time a majority of Americans now lived in the suburbs.

Welfare Reform Bill (1996)
Legislation that made deep cuts in welfare grants and required able-bodied welfare recipients to find employment. Part of Bill Clinton's campaign platform in 1992, the reforms were widely seen by liberals as an abandonment of key New Deal/Great Society provisions to care for the impoverished.

> *(continued)*
>
> "President Clinton's signature on pending 'welfare reform' legislation makes a mockery of his pledge not to hurt children. It will leave a moral blot on his presidency and on our nation that will never be forgotten.
>
> This legislation is the biggest betrayal of children and the poor since the Children's Defense Fund began. It takes no political courage to stand up to two-month-old babies or to play election year games of political chicken at preschoolers' expense."
>
> What explains the emergence of a pro-welfare-reform wing within the Democratic party during the prosperous 1990s? How did both sides invoke traditional American values in making their cases?

Buoyed by a healthy economy and by his artful trimming to the conservative wind, Clinton breezed to an easy victory, with 47,401,898 popular votes to Dole's 39,198,482. Dole's victory in eight southern states, however, underscored how the once safely-Democratic "solid South" had by century's end become Republican territory. The Reform party's egomaniacal leader, Ross Perot, ran a distant third, picking up less than half the votes he had garnered in 1992. Clinton won 379 electoral votes, Dole only 159. But Republicans retained control of Congress.

As Clinton began his second term—the first Democratic president since Franklin Delano Roosevelt to be reelected—the heady promises of far-reaching reform with which he had entered the White House four years earlier were no longer heard. Still facing Republican majorities in both houses of Congress, Clinton proposed only modest legislative goals, even though soaring tax revenues generated by the prosperous economy produced in 1998 a balanced federal budget for the first time in three decades.

★ Racial Progress and Perils

In his second term, Clinton cleverly managed to put Republicans on the defensive by claiming the political middle ground on contentious issues. He now warmly embraced the landmark Welfare Reform Bill of 1996 that he had initially been slow to endorse. Juggling the political hot potato of affirmative action, Clinton pledged to "mend it, not end it." When voters in California in 1996 approved Proposition 209, prohibiting affirmative-action preferences in government and higher education, the number of minority students in the state's public universities temporarily plummeted. A federal appeals court decision, *Hopwood v. Texas*, had a similar effect in Texas. Clinton criticized these broad assaults on affirmative action but stopped short of trying to reverse them, aware that public support for affirmative action, especially among white Americans, had diminished since the 1970s.

Beyond affirmative action, the racial divisions that still loomed large in American culture and politics became searingly apparent in Los Angeles in 1992. Like New York a century earlier, the southern California metropolis had become a magnet for minorities, especially immigrants from Asia and Latin America. When a mostly white Los Angeles jury exonerated white police officers who had been videotaped ferociously beating a black suspect, the minority neighborhoods in South Central Los Angeles erupted in rage. Arson and looting laid waste to entire city blocks, and scores of people were killed. In a sobering demonstration of the complexity of modern American racial rivalries, many black rioters vented their anger at the white police by attacking Asian shopkeepers.

> *In 1990 the African American intellectual Shelby Steele (b. 1946) declared in his provocative book,* The Content of Our Character,
>
> "What is needed now is a new spirit of pragmatism in racial matters where blacks are seen simply as American citizens who deserve complete fairness and in some cases developmental assistance, but in no case special entitlements based on color. We need deracinated social policies that attack poverty rather than black poverty and that instill those values that make for self-reliance."

The Los Angeles riots vividly testified to black skepticism about the American justice system. Just three years later, again in Los Angeles, the televised spectacle of former football star O.J. Simpson's trial for allegedly murdering his white former wife fed white disillusionment with the state of race relations. After months of testimony that seemed to point to Simpson's guilt, the jury acquitted him, presumably because certain Los Angeles police officers involved in the case had been shown to harbor racist sentiments. The reaction to the Simpson verdict revealed the yawning chasm that separated white and black America, as most whites believed Simpson guilty, while a major of African-Americans felt the not-guilty verdict was justified.

Makers of America

The Latinos

Today Mexican food is handed through fast-food drive-up windows in all fifty states and Spanish-language broadcasts fill the airwaves. Latinos send representatives to Congress and mayors to city hall, record hit songs, paint murals, and teach history. Latinos, among the fastest-growing segments of the U.S. population, include Puerto Ricans, frequent voyagers between their native island and northeastern cities; Cubans, many of them refugees from the communist dictatorship of Fidel Castro, concentrated in Miami and southern Florida; and Central Americans, fleeing the ravages of civil war in Nicaragua and El Salvador.

But the most populous group of Latinos derives from Mexico. The first significant numbers of Mexicans began heading for *El Norte* ("the North") around 1910, when the upheavals of the Mexican Revolution stirred and shuffled the Mexican population into more or less constant flux. Their northward passage was briefly interrupted during the Great Depression, when thousands of Mexican nationals were deported. But immigration resumed during World War II, and since then a steady flow of legal immigrants has passed through border checkpoints, joined by countless millions of their undocumented countrymen and countrywomen stealing across the frontier on moonless nights.

Many of these Mexicans came to work in the fields, following the ripening crops northward to Canada through the summer and autumn months. Others found work in the cities of the Southwest—El Paso, Los Angeles, Houston, and San Bernardino. Houses may have been shabby in the barrios, but these Mexican neighborhoods provided a sense of togetherness, a place to raise a family, and the chance to join a mutual aid society. Such societies, or *mutualistas*, sponsored baseball leagues, helped the sick and disabled, and defended their members against discrimination.

Mexican immigrants lived so close to the border that their native country acted like a powerful magnet, drawing them back time and time again. Mexicans frequently returned to see relatives, and relatively few became U.S. citizens. In addition, the Mexican government sometimes discouraged Mexicans from becoming citizens of their adopted country. In the 1910s and 1920s the Mexican consulate in Los Angeles launched a Mexicanization program among the immigrants. The consulate sponsored parades on *Cinco de Mayo* ("Fifth of May"), celebrating Mexico's defeat of a French army in 1862, and opened Spanish-language schools for children.

Since World War II, American-born generations have carried on the fight for political representation, economic opportunity, and cultural preservation. After years of struggle, the United Farm Workers Organizing Committee (UFWOC), headed by Cesar Chavez, succeeded in improving working conditions for mostly Chicano farm laborers. Flexing their political muscles, Latinos have since the 1980s helped elect their co-ethnics as mayors of Miami, Denver, San Antonio, and Los Angeles.

Fresh arrivals from Mexico and other Latin American nations daily swell Latino communities across America. By 2012, Latinos made up 17 percent of the total U.S. population, with an even greater proportion in California (38 percent), Arizona (30 percent), New Mexico (47 percent), and Texas (38 percent). As the United States moves through the twenty-first century, it is taking on a pronounced Spanish accent.

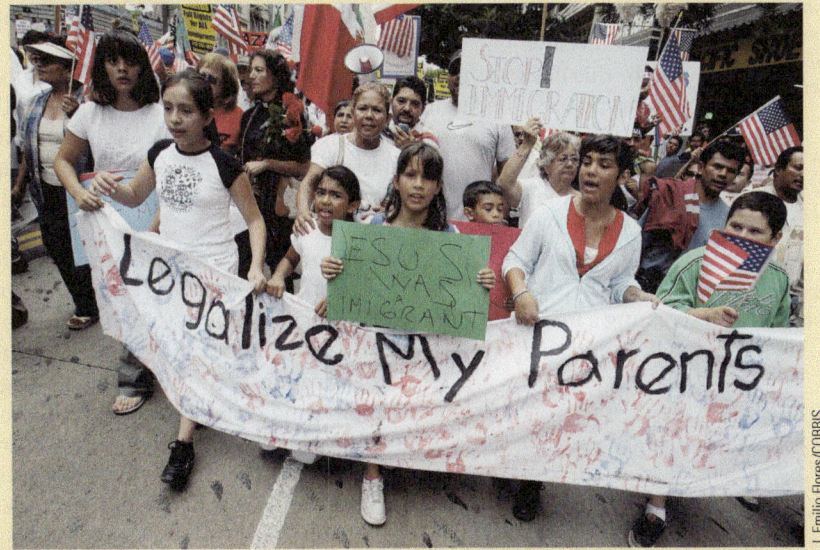

Demonstrating for Immigrant Rights, Los Angeles, 2007 Latinos march in downtown Los Angeles in support of legalizing undocumented parents who have children born in the United States. U.S. law gives the right of citizenship to anyone born on American soil ("jus soli"), but not necessarily to the parents of that child.

America's increasingly segmented residential landscapes reflected the stubborn racial divide. At the end of the twentieth century, minorities made up majorities within many American cities, while whites dominated the suburbs. In 2002, 52 percent of all blacks lived in central cities compared with only 21 percent of whites. Some of these urban white residents were well-to-do gentrifiers, whose restoration of decaying neighborhoods sent real estate values soaring and many minority residents packing to deepening concentrations of inner-city poverty.

Many successful black beneficiaries of the civil rights revolution of the 1950s and 1960s followed whites to the prosperous middle-class suburbs, while less affluent minorities began populating the first ring of post-World War II suburbs, now often badly deteriorated. Some cities like New York and San Francisco boomed with finance and technology economies, while others like Detroit and Cleveland struggle to replace once-prosperous industries.

African American gains in the wake of the civil rights victories of the 1950s and 1960s could be measured in other ways than shifting residential addresses. The number of black elected officials rose above the nine thousand mark in 2000, including more than three dozen members of Congress and the mayors of several large cities. By the turn of the new century, blacks had also dramatically advanced in higher education, although the political assault against affirmative action in California and elsewhere compounded obstacles to advancement for many young African Americans.

Racial divisions in the 1990s also manifested themselves politically in massive partisan disparities among black and white voters. African Americans proved themselves among Bill Clinton's most fiercely loyal supporters, giving him 83 percent of their vote in 1992 and 84 percent in 1996. As a politician, Clinton had an easy and authentic personal connection with the African American community. But far more significant was the electoral sorting of the two major parties, with racial minorities becoming ever larger and more consequential components of the Democratic base.

★ Globalization and Its Discontents

Clinton's major political advantage in his second term was the roaring economy, which by 2000 had sustained the longest period of growth in American history. The Federal Reserve's low-interest, easy-money policies and the explosive growth of new Internet ("dot-com") businesses helped fuel the boom. Unemployment crept down to 4 percent, sending employers scrambling madly for workers, while inflationary pressure remained remarkably low.

In this heady atmosphere, Clinton and congressional Republicans found common ground in pursuing fateful new efforts at financial deregulation. These included loosening federal regulation of "derivatives" trading as well as repealing the depression-era Glass-Steagall Act that had barred commercial banks from dealing in securities. Later, amidst the financial tumult of the 2000s, the deregulatory wave of the go-go nineties came in for heavy retrospective criticism.

Clinton encountered more controversy over trade policy. He had shown political courage by supporting the **North American Free Trade Agreement (NAFTA)** in 1993, creating a free-trade zone encompassing Mexico, Canada, and the United States. Clinton took another step in 1994 toward a global free-trade system when he vigorously promoted the creation of the **World Trade Organization (WTO)**. But simmering discontent over trade policy boiled over when Clinton hosted the meeting of the WTO in Seattle. The city's streets filled with protesters railing against what they viewed as the human and environmental costs of economic globalization.

Despite such protests, Clinton vigorously pursued trade-expansion initiatives through his presidency. As the emerging powerhouse of China loomed ever larger, Clinton soft-pedaled his earlier criticism of Beijing's human rights record and began seeking improved trade relations.

North American Free Trade Agreement (NAFTA) (1993) *Free-trade zone encompassing Mexico, Canada, and the United States. A symbol of the increased reality of a globalized marketplace, the treaty passed despite opposition from protectionists and labor leaders.*

World Trade Organization (WTO) (1995) *An international body to promote and supervise liberal trade among nations. The successor to the General Agreement on Tariffs and Trade, it marked a key world trade policy achievement of the Clinton administration.*

Speaking in Hanoi, Vietnam, in November 2000, Bill Clinton declared:

"Globalization is not something we can hold off or turn off. It is the economic equivalent of a force of nature—like wind or water."

His controversial China trade bill, passed by Congress in 2000, marked one more stride in the forward march of globalization.

Communications technology helped to accelerate the pace of globalization. The old industrial age was rapidly giving way to a new "information age" in which storing, organizing, and processing data were the most important industries of all. As the pace of the information age accelerated, the world shrank. Businesspeople could now instantaneously girdle the planet with transactions of prodigious scope and serpentine complexity.

But the very speed and efficiency of the new communications tools threatened to wipe out entire occupational categories, and even entire ways of life. Workers whose business was to mediate between product and client, like travel agents and bank tellers, were in danger of becoming casualties of the computer. White-collar jobs in financial services and engineering could now be "out-sourced" to countries such as Ireland and India. The related forces of the computer revolution and economic globalization defined the central opportunities and challenges for American workers as the new millennium dawned.

Protesting NAFTA, 1993 These members of the Teamsters Union feared that the adoption of the North American Free Trade Agreement would mean the replacement of high-paying American jobs with low-wage, nonunion Mexican labor. More than a decade later, the treaty still rankled. Policymakers disagreed about whether NAFTA had been damaging to American workers. In the 2008 election, the Republicans endorsed it, while the Democrats attacked it.

★ The Feminist Revolution

All Americans were caught up in the great economic changes of the late twentieth century, but no group was more profoundly affected than women. When that century opened, women made up about 20 percent of all workers. Over the next five decades they increased their presence in the labor force at a fairly steady rate, except for a temporary spurt during World War II. Then, beginning in the 1950s, women's entry into the workplace accelerated dramatically. By the 1990s nearly half of all workers were women, and the majority of working-age women held jobs outside the home.

Most astonishing was the upsurge in employment of mothers. In 1950, nearly 90 percent of mothers with children under the age of six did not work for pay. But half a century later, a majority of women with children as young as one year old were wage earners. Because most men did not take on tasks such as cooking, childcare, and housework, working women were expected to bring home the bacon and cook it, too.

The greater burdens of parenthood on women helped explain the persistence of occupational segregation and pay disparities through the 1990s. Women were far more likely than men to interrupt their careers to bear and raise children. Partly as a result, women continued to receive lower wages than men doing the same full-time work, and they tended to concentrate in lower paying occupations—the so-called the "pink-collar ghetto." And although they made up more than half the population, women in 2010 accounted for just 33 percent of lawyers and judges (up from 5 percent in 1970) and 32 percent of physicians (up from 10 percent in 1970).

Recognizing the new realities of the modern American household, Congress passed and President Clinton signed the Family and Medical Leave Act of 1993, which mandated job protection for working fathers as well as mothers who needed time off from work for family-related reasons. Over the course of the decade, some employers began providing paternity leave as well, but such leave was overwhelmingly unpaid. The concept of gender equality in family leave policies was more aspirational than real in most workplaces.

A New World for Women Revolutionary changes in the economy and in social values opened new career opportunities for women by the 1990s. In the decades after formerly all-male educational and professional institutions began opening their doors to women, myriad "firsts" in female leadership proliferated in areas ranging from law to business to government. In 1996, U.S. Marine Lieutenant General Carol Mutter became the first woman ever to receive a three-star rank in the U.S. armed forces. One year later, in 1997, Madeleine Albright became the first woman ever to serve as the U.S. secretary of state. Women athletes also came into their own in the wake of the feminist revolution. Venus and Serena Williams enthralled the tennis world as individual champions and as a doubles team beginning in the late 1990s.

Women's full-scale entrance into the work force inevitably affected family practices and structures, provoking passionate political conflicts over "family values." Indeed, the traditional nuclear family, once prized as the foundation of society and the nursery of the Republic, suffered heavy blows in the late twentieth century. By the 1990s one out of every two marriages ended in divorce. Births to unmarried women, once rare, became common. In the 1990s one out of four white babies, one out of three Latino babies, and two out of three African American babies were born to single mothers.

But if the *traditional* family was increasingly rare, the family itself remained a bedrock of American society at the close of the twentieth century. Children in households led by a single parent, stepparent, or grandparent, as well as children with gay or lesbian parents, encountered a degree of acceptance that would have been unimaginable a generation earlier. The family was not evaporating, but evolving into multiple, apparently viable forms.

⭐ Searching for a Post-Cold War Foreign Policy

The end of the Cold War dismantled the framework within which the United States had conducted foreign policy for nearly half a century. Throughout his presidency, Bill Clinton groped for a new formula to replace anticommunism as the basic premise of American diplomacy.

Absorbed by domestic issues, Clinton at first seemed uncertain and even amateurish in his conduct of foreign policy. He followed his predecessor's lead in dispatching American peacekeeping troops to Somalia, but quietly withdrew them after Somali rebels killed more than a dozen Americans in late 1993. Burned in Somalia, Washington stood on the sidelines in 1994 when catastrophic ethnic violence in the central African country of Rwanda resulted in the deaths of half a million people.

The Rwandan genocide painfully underscored a question dogging the sole remaining superpower in the post-Cold War era: What obligations did America have to intervene in military and humanitarian crises abroad? Events in the tormented Balkans in southeastern Europe provoked similar uncertainty. As vicious ethnic conflict raged through Bosnia, Washington dithered until finally committing American troops to a NATO peacekeeping contingent in 1995.

Yet NATO's presence in Bosnia failed to pacify the Balkans. When Serbian president Slobodan Milošević in 1999 unleashed a new round of "ethnic cleansing" in the region, this time against ethnic Albanians in the province of Kosovo, U.S.-led NATO forces launched an air war against Serbia. The bombing campaign eventually forced Milošević to accept a NATO peacekeeping force in Kosovo.

The Middle East remained a major focus of American diplomacy right up to the end of Clinton's tenure—and beyond. At a historic White House meeting in 1993, Israeli premier Yitzhak Rabin and Palestinian Liberation Organization (PLO) leader Yasir Arafat agreed in principle on Israeli withdrawal from the West Bank and Gaza Strip and self-rule for the Palestinians living there. But hopes flickered low two years later when Rabin fell to an assassin's bullet. Clinton and his second-term secretary of state, Madeleine Albright, spent the rest of the 1990s struggling in vain to broker the permanent settlement that continued to elude Israelis and Palestinians.

The Middle East served as the regional source for another thorny problem in the 1990s: the growth of radical, anti-American Islamic terrorism, organized most effectively in the transnational network known as Al Qaeda ("the base" in Arabic). The terrorist organization killed more than 230 people in simultaneous bombings of the American embassies in Kenya and Tanzania in 1998. Operatives bombed the USS *Cole* in Yemen two years later. Denouncing America's growing military presence in the Middle East, Al Qaeda leader Osama bin Laden declared war against all Americans and their Allies in a *fatwa* issued in 1998.

In his final years as president, Clinton stepped up his efforts to leave a legacy as an international peacemaker. He sought to reduce or end festering conflicts between Catholics and Protestants in Northern Ireland, between North and South Korea, and between India and Pakistan in South Asia. But despite these gestures, the guiding principles of American foreign policy in the post-Cold War era remained ill-defined and elusive.

⭐ Scandal and Impeachment

Scandal had dogged Bill Clinton from the beginning of his presidency. Critics brought charges of everything from philandering to illegal financial transactions. Allegations of corruption stemming from a real estate deal called **Whitewater** while he was governor of Arkansas triggered an investigation by a special prosecutor, but no indictment ever materialized. A mobilized conservative movement, with its own humming media infrastructure in print and talk radio, amplified each new whiff of scandal throughout the Clinton years.

All previous scandals were overshadowed by the revelation in January 1998 that Clinton had engaged in a sexual affair with a young White House intern, Monica Lewinsky, and then blatantly lied about it when he testified under oath in another woman's

Whitewater *A series of scandals during the Clinton administration that stemmed from a failed real estate investment from which the Clintons were alleged to have illicitly profited. The accusations prompted the appointment of a special federal prosecutor, though no indictments.*

civil suit accusing him of sexual harassment. Caught in his bold lie, the president made a humiliating confession, but his political opponents smelled blood in the water. In September 1998, the special prosecutor investigating Whitewater, who had broad powers to investigate *any* evidence of presidential malfeasance, presented a stinging report, including lurid sexual details, to the Republican-controlled House of Representatives. That report charged Clinton with eleven possible grounds for impeachment, all related to lying about the **Lewinsky affair**.

Lewinsky affair (1998–1999) *Political sex scandal that resulted in Bill Clinton's impeachment and trial by Congress. In 1998, Clinton gave sworn testimony in a sexual harassment case that he had never engaged in sexual activity with a White House intern named Monica Lewinsky. When prosecutors discovered evidence that the president had lied under oath about the affair, to which Clinton admitted, Republicans in Congress began impeachment proceedings. Although Clinton was ultimately not convicted by the Senate, the scandal put a lasting blemish on his presidential legacy.*

The House quickly cranked up the rusty machinery of impeachment. As an acrid partisan atmosphere enveloped the capital, House Republicans in December 1998 eventually passed two articles of impeachment against the president: perjury before a grand jury and obstruction of justice. Crying foul, the Democratic minority charged that, however deplorable Clinton's personal misconduct, sexual transgressions did not rise to the level of "high crimes and misdemeanors" prescribed in the Constitution (see Art. II, Sec. IV in the Appendix). The House Republican managers (prosecutors) of impeachment replied that perjury and obstruction were grave public issues and that nothing less than "the rule of law" was at stake.

As cries of "honor the Constitution" and "sexual McCarthyism" filled the air, the nation debated whether the president's peccadilloes amounted to high crimes or low follies. Most Americans apparently leaned toward the latter view. In the 1998 midterm elections, voters reduced the House Republicans' majority, causing fiery House Speaker Newt Gingrich to resign his post. Although Americans held a low opinion of Clinton's slipshod personal morals, most liked the president's political and economic policies and wanted him to stay in office.

In early 1999, for the first time in 130 years, the nation witnessed an impeachment proceeding in the U.S. Senate. Dusting off ancient precedents from Andrew Johnson's trial, the one hundred senators solemnly heard arguments and evidence in the case. With the facts widely known and the two parties' political positions firmly locked in, the trial's outcome was a foregone conclusion. On the key obstruction of justice charge, five northeastern Republicans joined all forty-five Democratic senators in voting not guilty. The fifty Republican votes for conviction fell far short of the constitutionally required two-thirds majority. The vote on the perjury charge was forty-five guilty, fifty-five not guilty.

★ Clinton's Legacy and the 2000 Election

Beyond the obvious stain of impeachment, Clinton's legacy was mixed. His sound economic policies encouraged growth and trade in a rapidly globalizing, post–Cold War world. Yet as a New Democrat and avowed centrist, Clinton did more to consolidate than to reverse the Reagan-Bush revolution against New Deal liberalism that had for half a century provided the compass for the Democratic party and the nation. Further, by setting such a low standard in his personal conduct, he replenished the sad reservoir of public cynicism about politics that Vietnam and Watergate had created a generation before.

Nonetheless, as the end of the Clinton term and the beginning of the new millennium approached, the Democrats stayed on their political course and nominated loyal vice president Albert Gore for president. Gore faced the tricky challenge of linking himself to Clinton-era peace and prosperity while at the same time distancing himself from his boss's personal foibles. He chose as his running mate Connecticut Senator Joseph Lieberman, an outspoken Clinton critic and the first Jew nominated to a major national ticket. Their Republican challenger, George W. Bush, won the nomination on the strength of his father's name and his years as governor of Texas. Bush surrounded himself with Washington insiders, including vice-presidential nominee Richard Cheney, and, in a clear jab at Clinton, promised to "restore dignity to the White House."

Rosy estimates that the federal budget would produce a surplus of some $2 trillion in the coming decade set the stage for the presidential contest. Echoing the Republican creed of smaller government, Bush argued for returning the budget surplus to "the people" through massive tax cuts and for promoting private sector programs, such as school vouchers and a reliance on "faith-based" institutions to help the poor. Gore proposed smaller tax cuts, targeted at middle-income and lower-income people, and strengthening Social Security. In an era of peace, foreign policy figured hardly at all in the campaign.

Pollsters predicted a close election, but none foresaw the epochal cliffhanger that the election became. On election day, the country split nearly evenly between the two candidates, and it was soon clear that Florida's electoral votes would determine the winner. Television news programs announced that Bush had won the Sunshine State, and Al Gore called the Texas governor to concede defeat. Yet just an hour later Gore's camp decided that Florida was too close to call and the vice president—in perhaps the most awkward phone call in modern politics—retracted his concession.

What ensued was a five-week political standoff over how to count the votes in Florida. Democrats argued that some ballots were confusing or misread by machines, and asked for recounts in several counties. Republicans claimed that such a recount would amount to "changing the rules in the middle of the game" and thus thwart the rule of law. After weeks of legal bickering, the Supreme Court finally intervened. By a five-to-four vote along partisan lines, the Court reasoned that, because neither Florida's legislature nor its courts had established a uniform standard for evaluating disputed ballots, the hand counts amounted to an unconstitutional breach of the Fourteenth Amendment's equal protection clause.

That ruling gave Bush the White House but cast a dark shadow of illegitimacy over his presidency. Bush officially won Florida by 537 votes out of 6 million cast, and he squeaked by in the Electoral College, 271 to 266 (see Map 40.1). The national popular vote went decisively to Gore, 50,999,897 to 50,456,002. For the first time since 1888, a candidate had won the White House with fewer popular votes than his opponent. Calls to abolish the Electoral College, however, were few and muted (see Art. V of the Constitution).

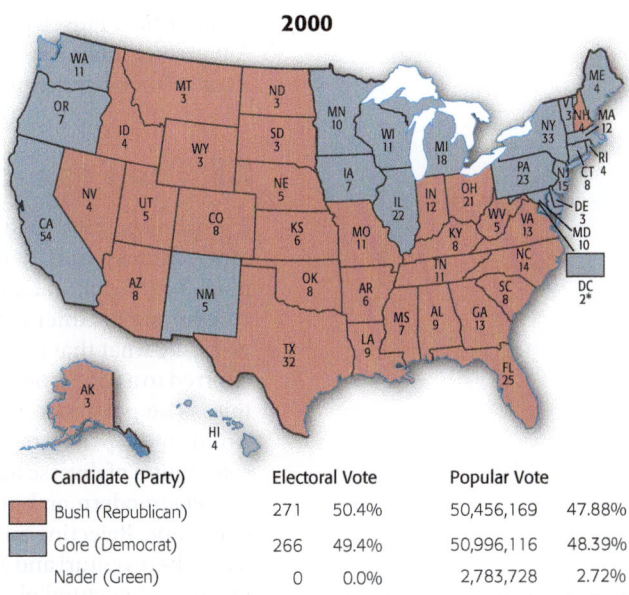

Map 40.1 Presidential Election of 2000 (with electoral vote by state) Although Democrat Albert Gore won the popular election for president by half a million votes, George W. Bush's contested 537-vote advantage in Florida gave him a slight lead in the Electoral College. The 2.7 million popular votes won by Green party candidate and consumer activist Ralph Nader almost surely deprived Gore of victory, casting Nader in the role of spoiler. Bush's failure to win the popular vote inspired critics to protest at his inauguration with placards reading "Hail to the Thief."

African Americans voted for Gore over Bush by a ratio of ten to one, signaling the deepening racial polarization of party politics at the turn of the new century. Many black Floridians also complained that election officials had unfairly disqualified their votes or even turned them away from the polls, as in the "Jim Crow" era.

★ E Pluribus Plures

America's culture proved no less fractious than the nation's politics as the century drew to a close. What united many key late-century developments in American intellectual life and artistic production became—ironically enough—diversity itself.

Controversial issues of color and culture also pervaded the realm of ideas in the late twentieth century. Echoing early-twentieth-century "cultural pluralists" like Horace Kallen and Randolph Bourne, many intellectuals after 1970 embraced the creed of "multiculturalism." The new mantra celebrated diversity for its own sake and stressed the need to preserve and promote, rather than squash, a variety of distinct ethnic and racial cultures in the United States.

The nation's classrooms became battlegrounds for the debate over America's commitment to pluralism. Multiculturalists attacked the traditional curriculum as "Eurocentric" and advocated greater focus on the achievements of African Americans, Asian Americans, Latinos, and Native Americans. In response, critics charged that too much stress on ethnic difference would come at the expense of national cohesion and an appreciation of common American values.

The Census Bureau further enlivened the debate when in 2000 it allowed respondents to identify themselves with more than one of the six standard categories (black, white, Latino, American Indian, Asian, and Native Hawaiian or Pacific Islander). Signifying a mounting revolution in attitudes toward race, nearly 7 million Americans chose to describe themselves as biracial or multiracial. By the early twenty-first century many Americans, including public figures like golfer Tiger Woods, actress Rosario Dawson, and Barack Obama, were proclaiming their mixed heritage with pride.

★ The Postmodern Mind

A growing comfort with multiplicity not only characterized Americans' attitudes toward race, ethnicity, and identity in the later twentieth century. This same outlook energized much of the cultural and intellectual output of the era. Commentators often described contemporary Americans as living in a "postmodern" age, though few could agree on precisely what that term meant. But whatever else it denoted, *postmodernism* generally referred to a condition of fragmented perspectives, multiple truths, and constructed identities. The postmodern mind rejected rational, totalizing descriptions of the self or the world, and replaced modernism's faith in certainty, objectivity, and unity with an eclectic celebration of diverse and overlapping outlooks.

Postmodern architecture made the most visible imprint on the American cultural landscape. Rejecting austere modernist functionalism and minimalism, postmodernists like Robert Venturi and Michael Graves revived decorative details and celebrated a playful mix of architectural elements. The flight from stark modernism took especially fanciful forms in Frank Gehry's use of luminous, undulating sheets of metallic skin in the widely hailed Guggenheim Museum (1997) in Bilbao, Spain, and the Walt Disney Concert Hall (2003) in Los Angeles.

Visual artists also felt the eclectic urge. Cindy Sherman, Jenny Holzer, and Kara Walker combined old and new media to confront, confound, and even offend the viewer. Jeff Koons and Shepard Fairey used industrial materials and pop culture to blur the hidebound distinction between highbrow and lowbrow cultures. These pastiches of disparate fragments came to symbolize postmodern art.

Architect Frank Gehry's Walt Disney Concert Hall, Los Angeles, California, Completed in 2003

Postmodern literature, like art, had deep roots in the second half of the twentieth century, as writers like Kurt Vonnegut and Thomas Pynchon pioneered the use of nonlinear narratives and other experimental forms. A new generation of writers working in the 1990s, including Jeffrey Eugenides and Michael Chabon, adapted these techniques for contemporary audiences. David Foster Wallace playfully lampooned North America's dystopian future in *Infinite Jest* (1996), complete with calendar years named after corporate sponsors.

Other major works of contemporary fiction complemented postmodernism's ethos of pluralism and cultural diversity. Toni Morrison wove a bewitching portrait of maternal affection amidst the horrors of slavery in *Beloved* (1987), and in 1993 became the first African American woman to win the Nobel Prize for literature. E. Annie Proulx's moving tale of homoerotic love between two cowboys in "Brokeback Mountain" (1997) reached a mass audience in 2005 in an award-winning motion picture.

Immigration also yielded a rich cultural harvest. Asian American authors flourished, among them playwright David Hwang, novelist Amy Tan, and novelist Jhumpa Lahiri, whose *Interpreter of Maladies* (1999) explored the sometimes painful relationship between immigrant Indian parents and their American-born children. Latino writers made their mark as well. Junot Diaz's Pulitzer Prize-winning *The Brief Wondrous Life of Oscar Wao* (2007) brilliantly bridged the worlds of the Dominican Republic and New Jersey in a dazzling concoction of street-smart Spanglish. On the stage, the AIDS epidemic inspired Tony Kushner's sensationally inventive *Angels in America* (1991) as well as Jonathan Larson's musical *Rent* (1996).

> *In her touching novel* The Joy Luck Club, *Amy Tan explored the complex dilemmas of growing up as a Chinese American:*
>
> "'A girl is like a young tree,' [my mother] said, 'You must stand tall and listen to your mother standing next to you. That is only way to grow strong and straight. But if you bend to listen to other people you will grow crooked and weak....' Over the years I learned to choose from the best opinions. Chinese people had Chinese opinions. American people had American opinions. And in almost every case, the American version was much better. It was only later that I discovered there was a serious flaw with the American version. There were too many choices, so it was easy to get confused and pick the wrong thing."

★ Niche Nation

When it came to popular arts—music, film, television—the postmodern cast of much late- and turn-of-the-century work was even more pronounced, and for good reason. Basic changes in communications technology and media markets simultaneously enabled artists to mix disparate elements in new ways while rendering commercial popular culture itself ever more microtargeted and niche-oriented. As crowning exemplars of the mix-and-mash approach to cultural production, hip-hop artists from Public Enemy to Jay-Z "sampled" beats from other sound recordings to create something simultaneously familiar and new.

From the rise of cable television, which smashed the dominance of the Big Three broadcast networks, to the coming of the Internet, with its endless capacity to forge specialized networks of the likeminded, late-twentieth-century communications technology fragmented the consuming public in such a way as to give new voices the potential to find sustaining audiences. An independent film movement transformed the world of American cinema in the late 1980s and 1990s, as iconoclasts like Quentin Tarantino, the Coen brothers, and Kathryn Bigelow found commercially viable strategies for pursuing unconventional cinematic visions. Tarantino's *Pulp Fiction* (1994) and David Lynch's *Mulholland Drive* (2001), notable for their nonlinear storylines, cinematic allusions, and dark comedic stylings, were prime examples of postmodern film. Beginning in the late 1990s, cable television entered a golden era, as high-quality dramas such as *The Sopranos* (1999–2007) and *The Wire* (2002–2008) enjoyed commercial and critical success.

In the niche logic of popular art in the postmodern age, audience fragmentation enabled more and fresher voices to be heard. But it also ensured that, compared to previous eras, fewer national experiences and cultural events were collectively shared by large numbers of citizens. In this way, popular culture matched ongoing developments in the society at large, as turn-of-the-century America became an ever more pluralist, hybridized, and boisterously diverse nation.

CHAPTER SUMMARY

The dynamic young "baby-boomer" Bill Clinton defeated President George H.W. Bush in 1992, and promoted an ambitious reform agenda within the context of his centrist New Democrat ideology, which broke the traditional Democratic affinity for labor and government social programs. Clinton's efforts to reform health care and promote gun control met strong resistance, but his economic policies helped to spark a decade-long expansion. Presenting an aggressively conservative agenda, Republicans gained control of Congress in 1994 for the first time in forty years. But overreaching by the Newt Gingrich-led Republicans enabled Clinton to revive and win a second term by defeating Kansas Senator Robert Dole in 1996.

In his second term, Clinton downplayed reform and successfully claimed the political middle ground. Racial issues, including affirmative action and criminal justice, caused continuing controversies as well as periodic outbursts of violence. While some African Americans made great social and economic gains, residential segregation sustained the strong link between poverty and race.

The booming economy encouraged bipartisan deregulation efforts, and enhanced Clinton's efforts to develop even more free trade agreements in line with the successful North American Free Trade Agreement (NAFTA). Women became nearly half of the work force, but continued to suffer low pay and less opportunities, partly because of family responsibilities. Family life adapted in striking ways to social economic change, even as the "traditional" family came under severe pressure.

Clinton recovered from early foreign policy stumbles in Africa with a successful intervention in the former Yugoslavia. But efforts at Middle East peace stalled. Clinton's affair with Monica Lewinsky led to his highly partisan impeachment in 1998 and acquittal in 1999. Clinton's vice president, Albert Gore, won a majority of the popular vote in the close election of 2000, but lost to Texas governor George W. Bush in the Electoral College by four votes after a Supreme Court ruling.

American culture grew more diverse and sometimes conflict-ridden in the late twentieth century. Multiculturalism, postmodernism, and the fragmentation of once-national media opened doors to fresh voices and minority perspectives, though the sense of shared cultural experience and ideas diminished.

KEY TERMS

- Democratic Leadership Council (DLC) (704)
- Don't Ask, Don't Tell (705)
- Oklahoma City bombing (706)
- Contract with America (706)
- Welfare Reform Bill (707)
- North American Free Trade Agreement (NAFTA) (710)
- World Trade Organization (WTO) (710)
- Whitewater (713)
- Lewinsky affair (714)

PEOPLE TO KNOW

- William Jefferson ("Bill") Clinton
- H. Ross Perot
- Hillary Rodham Clinton
- Newt Gingrich
- Robert Dole
- Monica Lewinsky

MindTap is a fully online, highly personalized learning experience built upon Cengage Learning content. MindTap combines student learning tools—readings, multimedia, activities, and assessments—into a singular Learning Path that guides students through the course.

Chapter 41

The American People Face a New Century
2001–2015

We remain a young nation. But in the words of Scripture,
the time has come to set aside childish things.

BARACK OBAMA, INAUGURAL, 2009

Chapter Outline

- George W. Bush and September 11, 2001
- The Iraq War
- George W. Bush's Troubled Second Term
- Barack Obama and the "Great Recession"
- Obama's Foreign and Domestic Policies
- The Politics of Inequality
- Obama's Reelection and Second-Term Stalemate
- Immigration and Civil Rights
- The American Prospect

weapons of mass destruction (WMD)
Refers to weapons—nuclear, biological, and chemical—that can kill large numbers of people and do great damage to the built and natural environment. The term was used to refer to nuclear weapons during the Cold War. The Bush administration's claim that Saddam Hussein had developed WMD provided the rationale for the United States' invasion of Iraq in 2003. These weapons were never found after the invasion.

In 2000 George W. Bush won a bitterly contested presidential election that left the nation more rancorously divided than ever, until the spectacular terrorist attacks on September 11, 2001, called forth, at least temporarily, a resurgent sense of national unity. Bush responded to the 9/11 attacks by invading the terrorist haven of Afghanistan. And then, controversially claiming that Iraq possessed **weapons of mass destruction (WMD)** and had ties to terrorists, Bush proceeded to invade Iraq as well. After the failure to find WMD and with over four thousand American battle deaths in the prolonged Iraq War, a war-weary country, nostalgic for the prosperity and peace of the 1990s, made history by electing the first African American president, Barack Obama, in 2008.

President Obama inherited a crushing economic crisis, soon dubbed "The Great Recession." Its scale was exceeded in modern times only by the Great Depression of the 1930s. Like Franklin Roosevelt in the depression era, Obama seized the occasion to pursue major reforms in health care and financial regulation. But unlike FDR, Obama triggered a powerful Republican backlash that erased the Democratic majority in the House of Representatives in the congressional elections of 2010. Obama's reelection two years later neither restored Democratic control to the House nor tempered the rancor of political divisions in the country, which threatened to turn the federal government into a useless laughing-stock. A standoff between the House and the president over the nation's debt ceiling led to an unprecedented downgrade in the government's credit rating in 2011, and a second standoff over funding the Patient Protection and Affordable Care Act shut down the government entirely for more than two weeks in 2013.

The paradox of rising economic inequality amidst expanding social inclusiveness continued to shape the new century as it had the closing decades of the previous one. A painfully slow economic recovery and stubbornly high unemployment in the years following the 2008 financial crisis highlighted growing gaps in income and wealth, even as the country remained intractably divided over appropriate remedies. At the same time, American society grew more diverse in the twenty-first century, as evidenced by the biracial president and the multiracial political coalition that twice elected him. No less dramatic was the extraordinarily rapid expansion of popular acceptance of gay and lesbian Americans.

CHRONOLOGY

2000	George W. Bush wins presidency in Electoral College; Albert Gore takes popular vote	2010	Patient Protection and Affordable Care Act passed Wall Street Reform and Consumer Protection Act passed "Don't Ask, Don't Tell" policy repealed Supreme Court decision in *Citizens United* v. *Federal Election Commission* Republicans retake control of the House
2001	Bush's $1.3 trillion tax cut passes Congress Congress passes No Child Left Behind Act Terrorists attack New York City and Washington, D.C., on September 11 U.S. invades Afghanistan Congress passes USA Patriot Act		
		2011	U.S. withdraws from Iraq U.S. begins troop withdrawal from Afghanistan U.S. forces kill Osama Bin Laden First debt-ceiling crisis between President Obama and the GOP-led House
2002	Bush labels Iraq, Iran, and North Korea "axis of evil" Congress authorizes use of force against Iraq U.N. Security Council demands that Iraq comply with weapons inspections Republicans regain Senate		
		2012	Supreme Court upholds the Affordable Care Act Obama defeats Romney to win reelection
2003	U.S. invades Iraq Second Bush tax cut Saddam Hussein captured in Iraq Supreme Court narrowly approves affirmative action	2013	Supreme Court repeals Section 4 of the Voting Rights Act Supreme Court rules the Defense of Marriage Act unconstitutional Second debt-ceiling crisis between President Obama and GOP-led House Budget dispute causes a 16-day federal government shutdown
2004	Gay marriage controversy erupts Iraqi interim government installed Bush defeats Kerry for presidency		
2005	Iraq elects permanent government but quickly descends into sectarian conflict	2014	U.S. begins air attacks against Islamic State in Iraq and Syria Republicans gain control of Senate in mid-term confessional elections
2006	Saddam Hussein executed Democrats retake control of Congress		
2007	U.S. troop surge in Iraq	2015	U.S. and Cuba resume diplomatic relations Congress authorizes Obama to negotiate Pacific Partnership free trade agreement *King* v. *Burwell* upholds Affordable Care Act *Obergefell* v. *Hodges* declares same-sex marriage a constitutional right
2008	Barack Obama elected 44th president of the United States		
2009	American Recovery and Reinvestment Act passed		

FOCUS QUESTIONS

1. What was the impact of the September 11 terrorist attacks on the United States? What were the accomplishments and failures of the post–9/11 wars in Afghanistan and Iraq?

2. How did George W. Bush's troubled second term and the "Great Recession" of 2008 contribute to the election of the upstart Barack Obama?

3. What were Obama's strongest efforts to respond to the "Great Recession," and how did his assertive policies provoke the angry Tea Party backlash?

4. What caused the dramatic rise in economic inequality in early twenty-first century America, and how did the widening income gap contribute to growing political and social polarization?

5. How did controversial issues of immigration, civil rights, and civil liberties contribute to political "gridlock" in Washington, and why were political leaders unable to find suitable room for compromise?

Bush Begins

As the son of the forty-first president, George W. Bush became the first presidential offspring since John Quincy Adams to reach the White House. Affecting the chummy manner of a self-made good ol' boy—though he held degrees from Yale and Harvard—Bush promised to bring to Washington the conciliatory skills he had honed as the Republican governor of Texas.

But as president, Bush soon proved to be more of a divider than a uniter, less a "compassionate conservative" than a crusading ideologue. Religious traditionalists cheered, but liberals jeered, when he withdrew American support from international health programs that sanctioned abortion and sharply limited government-sponsored research on embryonic stem cells. Bush pleased corporate chieftains but angered environmentalists by repudiating a major international effort to slow global warming, the **Kyoto Treaty** limiting greenhouse gas emissions.

The centerpiece of Bush's fiscal policy was a whopping $1.3 trillion tax cut, passed by Congress in 2001, followed by a second cut in 2003. Together with a softening economy, these measures turned the federal budget surpluses of the late 1990s into yawning deficits that reached nearly $460 billion by 2008.

Kyoto Treaty *International treaty to limit greenhouse gas emissions. It was negotiated and opened for signatories in 1997 and took effect in 2005. Although it was signed by 169 (of 192) countries, the Bush administration rejected the plan as too costly in 2001.*

Terrorism Comes to America

On September 11, 2001, the long era of America's impregnable national security violently ended. On a balmy late-summer morning, suicidal terrorists slammed two hijacked airliners, loaded with passengers and jet fuel, into the twin towers of New York City's World Trade Center. They flew a third plane into the military nerve-center of the Pentagon, near Washington, D.C., killing 189 people. Heroic passengers forced a fourth hijacked aircraft to crash in rural Pennsylvania, killing all 44 aboard but depriving the terrorists of a fourth weapon of mass destruction.

As the two giant New York skyscrapers thunderously collapsed, some three thousand innocent victims perished, including hundreds of New York's police and fire department rescue workers. A stunned nation blossomed with flags, as grieving and outraged Americans struggled to express their sorrow and solidarity in the face of catastrophic terrorism of **9/11**.

President Bush responded with a sober but stirring address to Congress nine days later. His solemn demeanor and the gravity of the situation helped to dissipate the cloud of illegitimacy that had shadowed his presidency since the disputed election of 2000. While emphasizing his respect for the Islamic religion and Muslim people, Bush identified the principal enemy as Osama bin Laden, head of a shadowy terrorist network **Al Qaeda**. Since 1998 bin Laden had taken refuge in landlocked Afghanistan, ruled by an Islamic fundamentalist party, the Taliban. Bin Laden drew on popular Muslim opposition to Washington's policies in the Middle East, including its military presence there and its unwavering support of Israel. He also benefited from broader, worldwide resentment of America's enormous economic, military, and cultural power. Ironically, America's most conspicuous strengths had made it a conspicuous target.

When the Taliban refused to hand over bin Laden, Bush ordered a massive military campaign against Afghanistan. Within three months, American and Afghan rebel forces had overthrown the Taliban but failed to find bin Laden, and Americans continued to live in fear of future attacks. Confronted with this unconventional, diffuse menace, antiterrorism experts called for new tactics of "asymmetrical warfare," employing not just traditional military muscle but also counterinsurgency tactics like innovative intelligence gathering and the training of local police forces.

The terrorists' blows diabolically coincided with the onset of a recession. The already gathering economic downdraft worsened as edgy Americans shunned air travel and the tourist industry withered. In the anxious atmosphere Congress in 2001 rammed through the **USA Patriot Act**, which permitted extensive telephone and e-mail surveillance and authorized the detention and deportation of immigrants suspected of terrorism. Just over

9/11 (2001) *Common shorthand for the terrorist attacks that occurred on September 11, 2001, in which nineteen militant Islamist men hijacked and crashed four commercial aircraft. Two planes hit the twin towers of the World Trade Center in New York City, causing them to collapse. One plane crashed into the Pentagon in Washington, D.C., and the fourth, overtaken by passengers, crashed into a field in rural Pennsylvania. Nearly three thousand people were killed in the worst case of domestic terrorism in American history.*

Al Qaeda *Arabic for "The Base," an international alliance of anti-Western Islamic Fundamentalist terrorist organizations founded in the late 1980s by veterans of the Afghan struggle against the Soviet Union. The group was headed by Osama bin Laden and has taken responsibility for numerous terrorist attacks, especially after the late 1990s. Al Qaeda organized the attacks of September 11, 2001, in the United States from its headquarters in Taliban-controlled Afghanistan. Since the U.S.-led invasion of Afghanistan in 2001 and the launch of the "global war on terror," the group has been weakened but still poses significant threats around the world.*

USA Patriot Act (2001) *Legislation passed shortly after the terrorist attacks of September 11, 2001 that granted broad surveillance and detention authority to the government.*

a year later, Congress created a new cabinet-level **Department of Homeland Security** to protect the nation's borders and ferret out potential attackers. The Justice Department meanwhile rounded up hundreds of immigrants and held them without *habeas corpus* (formal charges in an open court). As hundreds of Taliban fighters captured in Afghanistan languished in legal limbo and demoralizing isolation in the **Guantanamo Detention Camp** on the American military base at Guantanamo, Cuba, public-opinion polls showed Americans sharply divided on whether the terrorist threat fully warranted such drastic encroachments on America's venerable tradition of protecting civil liberties.

Catastrophic terrorism posed an unprecedented challenge to the United States. The events of that murderous September morning brought a long chapter in American history to a dramatic climax. All but unique among modern peoples, American for nearly two centuries had been spared from foreign attack on their homeland. That unusual degree of virtually cost-free national security had undergirded the values of openness and individual freedom that defined the distinctive character of American society. Now American security and American liberty alike were dangerously imperiled.

The Toll of Terror Grief overcame this exhausted firefighter during the search for survivors in the wreckage of New York City's World Trade Center.

Department of Homeland Security
Cabinet-level agency created in 2003 to unify and coordinate public safety and antiterrorism operations within the federal government.

Guantanamo Detention Camp
Controversial prison facility constructed after the U.S.-led invasion of Afghanistan in 2001. Located on territory occupied by the U.S. military, but not technically part of the United States, the facility serves as an extra-legal holding area for suspected terrorists.

★ Bush Takes the Offensive against Iraq

On only its second day in office, the Bush administration warned that it would not tolerate Iraq's continued defiance of United Nations weapons inspections, mandated after Iraq's defeat in the 1991 Persian Gulf War. Iraqi dictator Saddam Hussein, after playing hide and seek with the inspectors for years, expelled them from his country in 1998. President Clinton then declared, with congressional approval, that Saddam's removal ("regime change") was an official goal of U.S. policy. But no sustained military action against Iraq had followed. Now, in the context of the new terrorist threat, the Bush administration focused on Iraq with a vengeance.

In January 2002, mere months after the September 11 attacks, Bush claimed that Iraq, along with Iran and North Korea, constituted an "axis of evil" that gravely menaced American security. Iraqi tyrant Saddam Hussein, defeated but not destroyed by Bush's father in 1991, became the principal object of the new president's wrath. Unlike the elder Bush, who had carefully assembled a broad international coalition to fight the Persian Gulf War, his son was brashly determined to break with longstanding American traditions and wage a preemptive war against Iraq—and to go it alone if necessary. The younger Bush thus stood revealed as a daring risk-taker willing to embrace bold, dramatic policies, foreign as well as fiscal.

Itching for a fight, and egged on by hawkish Vice President Richard Cheney and other "neoconservative" advisers, Bush accused the Iraqi regime of developing weapons of mass destruction ("WMD") and supporting terrorist organizations like Al Qaeda. Most controversially, Bush also suggested that a liberated, democratic Iraq might provide a beacon of hope to the Islamic world and thereby begin to improve the political equation in the volatile Middle East. To skeptical observers, including America's European allies, Bush's ambition to create a democracy in long-suffering Iraq, burdened with centuries of internecine conflict, seemed naïvely utopian. Secretary of State Colin Powell warned about the long-term consequences of invading and occupying an unstable, religiously and culturally divided nation of 25 million people. "You break it, you own it," he told the president.

Congress nevertheless passed a resolution in October 2002 authorizing the president to employ armed force to defend against Iraqi threats to America's national security. But with United Nations inspectors unable to find weapons of mass destruction in Iraq, the U.N. Security Council declined to authorize the use of force against Saddam Hussein.

In this tense and confusing atmosphere, Bush, with Britain his only major ally, launched the long-anticipated invasion of Iraq on March 19, 2003. Saddam Hussein's vaunted military machine collapsed almost immediately. In less than a month Baghdad had fallen and Saddam had been driven from power. From the deck of a U.S. aircraft carrier off the California coast, speaking beneath a banner declaring "Mission Accomplished," Bush triumphantly announced on May 1, 2003, that "major combat operations in Iraq have ended."

> *In his 2002 state of the union address, President Bush declared:*
>
> "Iraq continues to flaunt its hostility toward America and to support terror. The Iraqi Regime has plotted to develop anthrax, and nerve gas, and nuclear weapons for over a decade.... This is a regime that has agreed to international inspections, then kicked out the inspectors. This is a regime that has something to hide from the civilized world.
>
> States like these, and their terrorist allies, constitute an axis of evil, arming to threaten the peace of the world. By seeking weapons of mass destruction, these regimes pose a grave and growing danger. They could provide these arms to terrorists, giving them the means to match their hatred. They could attack our allies or attempt to blackmail the United States. In any of these cases, the price of indifference would be catastrophic."

⭐ Owning Iraq

President Bush's words quickly came back to haunt him and America's forces in Iraq. Neoconservative pundits in Washington had predicted that American soldiers would be greeted as liberators and that Saddam's ouster would lead to flowering democracy across the Middle East. In reality, post-Saddam Iraq quickly devolved into a seething cauldron of violence.

The country's largest religious groups, Sunni and Shia Muslims, clashed violently, especially in the capital city of Baghdad. Both groups attacked American forces, especially after their decision to disband the Iraqi army. A locally grown insurgency quickly spread, and occupying Iraq became ever more perilous for American troops. Hatred for Americans only worsened with revelations in April 2004 that Iraqi prisoners in Baghdad's **Abu Ghraib prison** had been tortured and humiliated by their American captors. Amid this chaos, jihadist terrorists from around the region flooded into Iraq, often fueling the intra-Iraqi conflicts to further their own radical Islamic vision. Although Al Qaeda had had no link to Iraq under Saddam, as Bush had falsely alleged, the organization certainly moved in afterward. These three sources—Shia/Sunni violence, counter-occupation insurgency, and jihadist terrorism—fed a spiraling maelstrom of bloodshed. By the end of 2006, more Americans had died in Iraq than in the attacks of September 11.

In the summer of 2004, the American military ceded political power and limited sovereignty to an interim Iraqi government. A series of national elections led to a constitution, parliamentary representatives, and eventually a president. But the minority Sunnis, who had held power under Saddam Hussein, feared reprisals under a majority Shia government. Many Sunnis turned to bombings and political assassinations.

Abu Ghraib prison *A detention facility near Baghdad, Iraq. Under Saddam Hussein, the prison was the site of infamous torturing and execution of political dissidents. In 2004, during the U.S. occupation of Iraq, the prison became the focal point of a prisoner-abuse and torture scandal after photographs surfaced of American soldiers mistreating, torturing, and degrading Iraqi war prisoners and suspected terrorists. The scandal was one of several dark spots on the public image of the Iraq War and led to increased criticism of Secretary of Defense Donald Rumsfeld.*

⭐ Reelecting George W. Bush

Americans had rarely been as divided as they were in the first years of the twenty-first century. Civil libertarians worried that the government was trampling personal freedoms in the name of fighting terrorism. Revelations in 2002 about flagrant corporate fraud fed rampant popular disillusion with the business community. Cultural tensions brewed over the rights of gay and lesbian Americans when leaders in San Francisco and Massachusetts permitted same-sex couples to marry in 2004. Affirmative action continued to spark sharp debate, as the Supreme Court permitted some preferential treatment in admitting minority undergraduate and law students to the University of Michigan in 2003.

No Child Left Behind Act (2001)
An education bill created and signed by the George W. Bush administration. Designed to increase accountability standards for primary and secondary schools, the law authorized several federal programs to monitor those standards and increased choices for parents in selecting schools for their children. The program was highly controversial, in large part because it linked results on standardized tests to federal funding for schools and school districts.

Amid these divisions, George W. Bush positioned himself to run for reelection. He proclaimed that his tax cuts had spurred economic growth. Targeting what he called "the soft bigotry of low expectations," he championed the **No Child Left Behind Act** of 2001, which mandated sanctions against schools that failed to meet federal performance standards. He played to cultural conservatives by opposing stem cell research and called for a constitutional amendment to ban gay marriage. But most of all, he promoted himself as a stalwart leader in wartime, warning the country not to "change horses midstream."

After an intense round of primary elections, the embattled Democrats chose lanky and long-jawed Massachusetts Senator John Kerry to represent their ticket. A more old-fashioned liberal than Clinton, Kerry pushed progressive visions of government and counted on his Vietnam War record to counter charges that he would be weak in the face of terrorism. In spite of increased public misgivings about the war in Iraq, Bush nailed down a decisive victory in November 2004. He received the first popular vote majority in more than a decade, 60,639,281 to 57,355,978, and won the Electoral College, 286 to 252. This time his victory was clear, constitutional, and uncontested.

★ Bush's Bruising Second Term

Reelection, George W. Bush announced, gave him "political capital," which he intended to spend on an aggressive domestic agenda. The appointment of two new conservative Supreme Court justices (John G. Roberts and Samuel A. Alito, Jr.) upon the retirement of Sandra Day O'Connor and the death of Chief Justice William Rehnquist seemed to bode well for his ambitions. But Bush soon overplayed his hand. Attacking the core of New Deal liberalism, Bush proposed a radical program to privatize much of Social Security, providing incentives for younger Americans to fund their own retirements through personal accounts. A massive outcry led by the American Association of Retired Persons (AARP) and other liberal groups reminded Americans how much they loved Social Security, warts and all. Bush's proposal faded away within six months of his reelection. The same fate befell a proposed constitutional amendment to ban same-sex marriage, which had been a major issue in the 2004 campaign.

The president also took (faulty) aim at the contentious issue of immigration reform. Bush worked with a bipartisan group of legislators on a proposed law to establish a guest-worker program for undocumented workers and to create a path to citizenship, albeit after paying a fine. But nativist forces condemned the plan as "amnesty," businesses protested the burden of verifying the right to work, and immigrant rights advocates charged that the program would create "second class citizens." In the end the compromise bill pleased no one and died an ignominious political death.

Perhaps the most tragic and avoidable of Bush's missteps came in the botched response to the deadly **Hurricane Katrina**, which devastated New Orleans and much of the Gulf Coast in late August 2005, flooding 80 percent of the historic city and causing over 1,300 deaths and $150 billion in damages. The Federal Emergency Management Agency (FEMA) proved pathetically inept in New Orleans, and Bush came in for still more criticism. A consensus began to build that Bush was a genial personality but an impetuous, unreflective, and frequently feckless leader, a president in over his head.

Hurricane Katrina (2005) *The costliest and one of the deadliest hurricanes in the history of the United States, which killed over a thousand Americans. The storm ravaged the Gulf Coast, especially the city of New Orleans, in late August 2005. In New Orleans, high winds and rain caused the city's levees to break, leading to catastrophic flooding, particularly in the city's most impoverished wards. A tardy and feeble response by local and federal authorities exacerbated the damage and led to widespread criticism of the Federal Emergency Management Agency (FEMA).*

As charges of dictatorial power-grabbing and incompetence mounted during Bush's second term, Republicans fell victim in midterm elections of 2006 to the same anti-incumbency sentiment they had ridden to power twelve years before. Democrats regained control of both houses of Congress, and California Democrat Nancy Pelosi became the first woman to serve as Speaker of the House.

The biggest factor in the Democratic sweep was the perceived mishandling of the war in Iraq. By late 2005 polls revealed that a majority of Americans considered the war a mistake. Secretary of Defense Donald Rumsfeld, who had badly mismanaged events on the ground, resigned after the Republicans "thumping" in the 2006 midterm elections. In 2007 Bush launched a "surge" of twenty thousand additional American troops that brought a modest measure of stability to Iraq, but public opinion solidified even more strongly against the war.

★ The Presidential Election of 2008

With neither the sitting president nor vice president running, the 2008 election was truly "open" for the first time in eighty years. The Democratic race soon tightened into a fiercely fought contest between forty-six-year-old Illinois Senator Barack Obama and the pre-campaign favorite, former First Lady and New York Senator Hillary Rodham Clinton. Obama narrowly prevailed, surviving Clinton's attacks on his inexperience. Son of a black Kenyan father and a white mother from Kansas, Obama had a cosmopolitan background well suited to the age of globalization. He strengthened his national security credentials by picking Delaware Senator Joseph Biden as his running mate.

In keeping with the country's anti-Bush mood, Republicans nominated long-time Arizona Senator John McCain, a Vietnam War hero with a record of bipartisan reform. To galvanize the conservative base of his party, McCain chose telegenic Alaska Governor Sarah Palin as his running mate. But Palin's inexperience and weak grasp of issues made her at least as much a liability as an asset to the Republican ticket.

Armed with an unprecedented war chest of nearly $700 million, Obama seized the advantage in both the "air war" (television) and the "ground war" (door-to-door campaigning by his legions of volunteers). His poise and gravitas in televised debates favorably impressed many voters, and his campaign slogan "Yes we can" excited widespread hope and enthusiasm. Then, just six weeks before election day, a sudden economic maelstrom gave his campaign a buoyant boost.

The American housing price bubble, fed by the Federal Reserve System's easy-money policies and banks' lax lending practices, burst at last. By 2008 the collapse in real estate values was generating a tsunami of mortgage defaults. Bankers and other lenders watched in horror as countless homeowners defaulted and mortgage-backed securities sank precipitously. Aggressive "**deleveraging**" set in worldwide, as financial institutions from Tokyo to New York sold assets at ever-declining prices. Credit markets soon froze everywhere, and stocks fell into a deep swoon. The gravest financial hurricane since the Great Depression of the 1930s was gathering ever-increasing force.

deleveraging *The inverse of "leveraging," whereby businesses increase their financial power by borrowing money (debt) in addition to their own assets (equity). In times of uncertainty or credit tightening, the same businesses seek to improve their debt-to-equity ratios by shedding debt through the sale of assets purchased with borrowed money.*

The New First Family President-elect Barack Obama, wife Michelle, and daughters Sasha and Malia, on election night 2008 in Chicago's Grant Park.

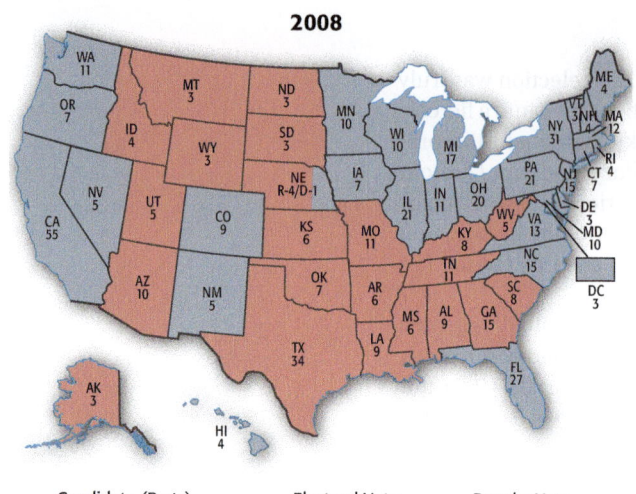

Map 41.1 Presidential Election of 2008 A record voter turnout, swelled by millions of young new voters, African Americans, and Latinos, gave Senator Barack Obama an Electoral College landslide and the Democratic party solid control of both houses of Congress. Obama redrew the electoral map by taking nine states won by George W. Bush in 2004.

In contrast to the infamous 1929 crash, it took days, not years, for a terrified Bush Administration to intervene on a gigantic scale. The federal government nationalized the country's two biggest mortgage companies, the Federal National Mortgage Association ("Fannie Mae") and the Federal Home Mortgage Corporation ("Freddie Mac"), and effectively took over the world's biggest insurance company, the American International Group (AIG). Treasury Secretary Henry Paulson next persuaded Congress to create the Troubled Assets Relief Program (TARP), authorizing a whopping $700 billion to buy "toxic" assets and inject cash directly into the nation's biggest banks and corporations.

Candidate Obama seized the political opportunity presented by the mounting economic crisis and declared that electing McCain would amount to a "third Bush term." Obama called for reviving the faltering economy with bold public investments and infrastructure repair, which McCain derided as "socialism."

Unsettled by the galloping economic calamity, voters delivered a historic victory to Barack Obama. He garnered 53 percent of the popular vote, prevailing even in such traditional Republican strongholds such as Virginia, Nevada, and Colorado, and won the Electoral College 365 to 173 (see Map 41.1). Democrats also enlarged their majorities in the House and the Senate. Obama's victory reflected important, long-term demographic developments reshaping American politics. He drew support from youth, educated professionals, and racial and ethnic minorities. Thanks to the increased preponderance of such voters in the population, what had once been a marginal coalition behind George McGovern's candidacy in 1968 had become a formidable political force by 2008.

Obama's election opened a new chapter in the long-vexed history of American race relations. It also confronted the nation's first African American president with the daunting challenge of governing a country even as it sank into the deepest economic stress since the 1930s. "Black Man Given Nation's Worst Job" jibed the satirical magazine, *The Onion*.

★ Obama in the White House

Inspired by Barack Obama's vision of "hope," a vast and exuberant crowd gathered in Washington, D.C., to celebrate his inauguration. Youthful energy was in the air, though in his inaugural address Obama struck a sober note by calling on Americans to "put away childish things" and embrace "a new era of responsibility."

Obama's solemn tone was fitting. Even as he spoke, home construction was grinding to a halt, mortgage foreclosures were soaring, and countless businesses were shutting their doors. Most alarmingly, the economy was shedding a sickening 700,000 jobs a month. The unemployment climbed above 10 percent—the highest level since the early 1980s and perhaps heralding a return to the catastrophic joblessness of the Great Depression of the 1930s.

Obama strongly counterpunched against the deepening crisis. In his first hundred days he pushed through a series of major initiatives that included a new round of help for troubled banks, tax and mortgage relief, and a huge "stimulus" bill—the **American Recovery and Reinvestment Act**—that contained nearly a trillion dollars of tax cuts as well as new spending for jobs, infrastructure projects, and relief to state and local governments. The government also shored up bankrupt automakers General Motors and Chrysler as well as threatened banks and insurance companies. The nonpartisan Congressional Budget Office later estimated that those measures saved up to 3 million jobs, helping substantially to arrest the economy's freefall.

American Recovery and Reinvestment Act (2009) *Among the earliest initiatives of the Obama administration to combat the Great Recession. It was based on the economic theories of John Maynard Keynes that called for increased government spending to offset decreased private spending in times of economic downturn. The act was controversial from the outset, passing with no Republican votes in the House and only three in the Senate, and helping to foster the "Tea Party" movement to curb government deficits, even while critics on the left argued that the act's $787 billion appropriation was not enough to turn the economy around.*

By the summer of 2009, the worst of the panic was over, and the economy began to expand once more. Economists tempered their comparisons with the Great Depression and gave the turmoil the less frightening label "Great Recession." But the economy had been badly wounded and continued to suffer. Hopes for a rapid recovery proved false, and the first steps toward growth were feeble and faltering. The unemployment rate stayed stuck above 9 percent. As millions of Americans lost jobs and homes, and many more succumbed to anxiety and fear, the effects of the Great Recession wormed their way deeply into the American psyche and would not be quickly dislodged. Psychology and economics intersected, as newly anxious consumers cut back on spending, further burdening an already sluggish recovery.

Even while pursuing economic recovery, President Obama sought to achieve the long-sought goal of health-care reform. When attempts to enlist Republican support bogged down, he had to rely on Democrats alone to pass a landmark health bill, the Patient Protection and Affordable Care Act in March 2010. The new health-care law (popularly known as "Obamacare") mandated all Americans to purchase health insurance starting in 2014, provided subsidies for those below certain income thresholds, and funded a major expansion of public Medicaid insurance for the poorest Americans

Scarcely pausing, Obama soon followed his health-care success with the 2010 Wall Street Reform and Consumer Protection Act. The act aimed to curb the risky, high-flying practices that had contributed to the debacle of 2008 with new controls on banks, investment houses, and stock markets, and with new truth-in-lending rules to protect consumers.

Patient Protection and Affordable Care Act (2010) *Also known as "Obamacare," the act extended health-care insurance to some 30 million Americans, marking a major step toward achieving the century-old goal of providing universal health-care coverage.*

Wall Street Reform and Consumer Protection Act (2010) *Also known as the Dodd-Frank Act, after its Democratic sponsors, Connecticut senator Christopher Dodd and Massachusetts representative Barney Frank. In an effort to avoid another financial crisis like the Great Recession, the act updated many federal regulations affecting the financial and banking systems and created some new agencies, such as the Bureau of Consumer Financial Protection.*

Back to Backlash

Yet, in a polarized political environment, Obama had unusual difficulty reaping the political rewards of these legislative achievements. Critics on the left condemned him as too timid in merely halting, not reversing, the economy's decline. Critics on the right excoriated him as a big-government spendthrift who fostered ballooning federal budget deficits (though Bush-era tax cuts and declining tax revenues from the recession contributed to the deficits).

The conjunction of expanding federal programs and mounting deficits tapped into a deep vein of American wariness of "big government." Starting with vehement attacks on the health-care bill in the summer of 2009, angry protesters accused the Obama administration of promoting "socialism" and "unconstitutional" controls over individual lives. Calling themselves the "Tea Party" after the American Revolutionary Patriots, these aggrieved citizens combined a knack for street-theater demonstrations with nonstop Internet and media fulminations against the president and his party.

Heartened by the Tea Party's mobilization, Republicans determined to fight the administration tooth and nail. The president did succeed in appointing two new Supreme Court justices, Sonia Sotomayor (the Court's first Hispanic) on 2009 and Elena Kagan in 2010, bringing the number of female justices to three. But other efforts fell victim to the fervent minority's opposition, as gridlock held Washington in an iron grip.

As the Great Recession continued to weigh on the land, Republicans gained six Senate seats and a whopping sixty-three House seats in the midterm elections of 2010. President Obama glumly acknowledged his party's "shellacking," but did achieve several notable goals in the "lame duck" congressional session in December 2010, including a repeal of the military's "Don't Ask, Don't Tell" policy toward gays.

But legislative productivity came to an end in the new Congress, as partisans closed their ranks ever tighter. The once-routine matter of raising the federal debt ceiling turned into a fiercely partisan game of fiscal "chicken" in the summer of 2011. As the deadline for raising the ceiling loomed, the stock market swooned and the credit rating of the United States was downgraded for the first time in history. Only a last-minute deal between Obama and House Speaker John Boehner averted the exhaustion of America's borrowing authority. Republicans looked to the upcoming 2012 election with increasing hope for victory, while the spectacle of protracted partisan bickering deeply disillusioned many Americans of both parties.

Tea Party *A grassroots conservative political movement mobilized in opposition to Barack Obama's fiscal, economic, and health care policies. Named after the Boston Tea Party of the Revolutionary era, Tea Party protestors first demonstrated in early 2009, and they grew steadily in visibility and power as a pressuring force within the Republican Party through the 2010 midterm elections and beyond.*

⭐ New Directions in Foreign Policy

Along with economic problems, Obama inherited America's wars in Iraq and Afghanistan, as well as a raft of other foreign policy headaches. Seeking to chart a more tempered and pragmatic course after the neoconservative ventures of the Bush years, Obama assembled a veteran foreign policy team headed by former First Lady Hillary Rodham Clinton as secretary of state.

The president sought to wind down the Iraq War while leaving behind a reasonably stable country. Shortly after taking office, Obama announced that American combat operations in Iraq would end in summer 2010 and that all American combat troops would be withdrawn by 2011. Despite continuing violence and the agonizingly slow birth of a viable Iraqi government, the deadline for ending American-led operations was met and all combat forces removed from the country in December 2010. All told, nearly five thousand Americans—and vastly greater numbers of Iraqis—had perished in the years of the invasion and occupation.

Afghanistan was a pricklier nettle to grasp. Obama had declared the Afghan war necessary to defeat Al Qaeda and prevent future terrorism. But Afghan *jihadi* (militant Islamic) fighters grew stronger against an Afghan government plagued by incompetence and corruption. More ominously, the Taliban and Al Qaeda found refuge across the border in unstable but nuclear-armed Pakistan, creating the danger of an expanded conflict there as well.

Pressed by some to bolster the American commitment, and by others to seek a way out of the increasingly costly conflict, Obama chose to do both. In December 2009 he declared that American troops would begin to withdraw by 2011—but that in order to achieve that goal an additional thirty thousand U.S. soldiers would be sent to combat the insurgency. Despite this deployment, little progress was made in securing the country from terrorists, even as casualties mounted. Meanwhile, American forces achieved a dramatic success in neighboring Pakistan in May 2011 when they concluded a ten-year manhunt by killing 9/11 mastermind Osama bin Laden.

Falling short of his goals in Afghanistan, Obama made good on his pledge to begin withdrawing troops in 2011. But even as American ground combat operations in Afghanistan ended in 2014, the Obama administration increasingly relied on a controversial policy of aerial attacks by unmanned remotely piloted aircraft, popularly called "drones." The intensity of U.S. drone attacks sparked national and international outcries about this revolutionary new kind of warfare.

Obama also came under increasing pressure to honor his promise to roll back Bush-era antiterrorism policies. His administration did ban water-boarding and other practices widely considered torture. But the president's efforts to shut down the controversial military detention center in Guantanamo Bay, Cuba, were thwarted by Congress.

⭐ The Politics of Inequality

Chronically high unemployment and stubbornly anemic economic growth after the 2008 financial meltdown helped sharpen a national debate over class, inequality, and the role of government in the economy. The financial sector provided a particularly rich target for many Americans' ire. Financiers' soaring incomes helped to drive the surge in the richest Americans' income share. The fall of 2011 saw the emergence of an eclectic protest movement that colorfully dramatized the issue of rising inequality. "**Occupy Wall Street**" began as a small demonstration by youthful radicals who pitched their tents in New York's financial district. Similar encampments soon sprang up in other cities and popularized the slogan "We are the 99 Percent"—a reference to the concentration of wealth and income among the highest earning 1 percent of Americans. Though the protesters gradually decamped, President Obama acknowledged their cause in January 2012 by describing the challenge to restore broadly shared prosperity as "the defining issue of our time."

Growing inequality had deep roots and assumed dramatic proportions as the new century opened. In American society, during the last two decades of the twentieth

Occupy Wall Street *Name of the original protest that launched the populist, anti-Wall Street "Occupy" movement in late 2010 and early 2011. Youthful radicals pitched tents and occupied Zuccotti Park in New York's financial district beginning in September 2010 to protest inequality and corporate political power. This demonstration inspired similar occupations in many other cities.*

century the rich had grown fabulously richer, middle-class incomes had stagnated, and the poor were left to make do with an ever-shrinking share of the economic pie. Between 1968 and 2012, the share of the nation's income that flowed to the top 20 percent of household swelled from 40 percent to 51 percent. And the top 1 percent so frequently targeted by the Occupy movement saw their share of national income rise from 8.4 percent in 1968 to a whopping 19.3 percent in 2012.

Widening inequality could be measured in other ways as well. In 1965, chief executives typically earned 20 times as much as the average worker in their corporations. In 2012 they earned 273 times as much. Some 46.5 million people remained mired in poverty in 2012, or 15 percent of all Americans—up from 11.3 percent in 1973.

These figures offered a depressing indictment of the inequities afflicting an affluent and allegedly egalitarian republic. A similar trend toward inequality was evident in many industrial societies, but it was most pronounced in the United States. In the new century, Americans were no longer the world's wealthiest people, as they had been in the quarter-century after World War II.

What caused the widening income gap? Some critics pointed to the tax and fiscal policies of the Reagan and both Bush (father and son) presidencies, which favored the wealthy. But deeper running historical currents probably played a more powerful role, as suggested by similar trends lines in other industrialized societies. Among the most conspicuous causes were intensifying global competition; the shrinkage in high-paying manufacturing jobs for semiskilled and unskilled workers; the greater economic rewards commanded by educated workers in high-tech industries; the rise of the financial sector as a percentage of national GDP; the decline of unions; the growth of part-time and temporary work; the rising tide of relatively low-skill immigrants; and the increasing tendency of educated men and women to marry one another and both work, creating households with very high incomes.

Educational opportunities also had a way of perpetuating inequality, starting with the underfunding of many schools in poor urban areas and the soaring cost of higher education. A 2004 study revealed that at the 146 most selective colleges, two-thirds of the students came from families with incomes in the top 25 percent, compared to 6 percent of the students from the bottom income quartile.

The very nature of the contemporary economy seemed to pose daunting obstacles to creating more equitably shared prosperity. When the twentieth century opened, United States Steel Corporation was the flagship business of America's industrial revolution. A generation later, General Motors became the characteristic American corporation, signaling the historic shift to a mass consumer economy. Following World War II, the rise of International Business Machines (IBM) symbolized the transformation to the fast-paced "information age." But in a sobering illustration of the dynamics of the new economy, the most iconic American company of the contemporary age—Apple—only employed 43,000 Americans in 2012. When General Motors occupied a similar status in the American economy half a century earlier, it employed over 600,000 Americans.

Contending Voices

Populist Politics in a Polarized Age

Two grassroots movements with starkly differing political agendas but a similarly populist character emerged in the wake of the ongoing economic turmoil that broke out in 2008. Conservative Tea Party activists in 2009 and 2010 erupted in full-throated wrath against Barack Obama's policies—as well as against the moderate congressional Republicans they accused of being enablers. In September 2011, a small protest in New York City's Zuccotti Park grew into a short-lived but broad movement known as Occupy Wall Street, which condemned the capitalist system in general and economic inequality in particular.

Nancy Ripley (ca. 1935–2011), a Florida Tea Party participant, explained her motivation in 2010:

"People dissent when they feel they're not being heard.... We are outraged over the disregard for [the] Constitution, the way it is being diminished to provide more government programs that promote dependence and thwart motivation."

Bennett Weiss (born ca. 1948), interviewed in Zuccotti Park in 2011, described the chief goal of the Occupy activists:

"Economic justice, that's why we're here.... [W]e have to level the economic playing field so that we don't have an extreme concentration of wealth. It's pretty damn simple."

> What might account for the emergence of such ideologically disparate movements in the context of a shared economic crisis? Why were some Americans motivated to target "big government" even while others called on government to step up and address economic inequality?

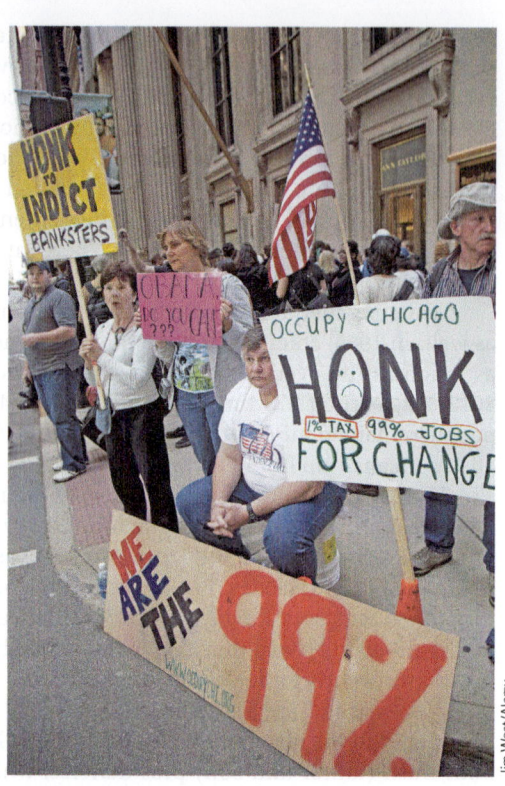

An Age of Discontent Dramatic protests from both the right and left sprang up during Barack Obama's first term as president. Tea Party rallies, such as this one in Washington, D.C. (left), expressed conservative resistance to the president's promise of "change." On the political left, meanwhile, the Occupy Wall Street protests in New York City against economic inequality spread like wildfire across the country, sparking satellite Occupy demonstrations like this one in Chicago (right).

★ Battling for the White House in 2012

To a striking degree, inequality—both economic and political—remained a central theme of the heated 2012 presidential race. Barack Obama sought reelection on the basis of his stewardship of the economy in crisis times, his signature health-care law (narrowly upheld in a Supreme Court decision that summer), and his winding down of two unpopular wars.

After a long, feisty primary season, the Republican party nominated former Massachusetts governor Mitt Romney and ultraconservative Wisconsin congressman Paul Ryan as their presidential and vice-presidential nominees. Romney, the first Mormon presidential candidate of a major party in American history, had a record as a moderate governor of liberal Massachusetts, but he secured the GOP's presidential nomination in 2012 by hewing to a much more conservative line, promising to repeal both the Affordable Care Act and the Wall Street Reform Act, cut domestic spending, and slash taxes.

The role of money in politics became a divisive issue in the race, thanks to a highly controversial 2010 Supreme Court decision, *Citizens United* v. *Federal Election Commission*. In a five-to-four ruling, the Court held that the First Amendment prohibited the government from limiting political expenditures made by corporations, unions, and advocacy groups. The decision helped to spur the proliferation of so-called "super-PACS," which, by avoiding any direct contributions to candidates and parties, could pour unlimited sums into the political arena. With the floodgates of political spending open as never before, the presidential race of 2012 proved to be the most expensive in American history, with both campaigns and their allies spending a combined total of over $2 billion.

On election day, Obama won a decisive victory over Romney, with 65,915,796 popular and 332 electoral votes to Romney's 60,933,500 and 206 votes. Obama prevailed in all of the states he had won in 2008 with the exception of Indiana and North Carolina. Democrats managed to retain control of the Senate but the House remained in GOP hands.

★ Second-Term Stalemate

Obama had expressed hope that a victory over Mitt Romney might "break the fever" of intractable opposition afflicting congressional Republicans. But with the partisan balance of power largely unchanged by the election and deep-seated ideological disagreements still defining the partisan divide, such a hope proved wishful thinking.

The first year of the president's second term was defined by legislative gridlock and a new period of white-knuckle budget brinksmanship with the John Boehner–led House. Spurred on by a still-potent Tea Party faction, House Republicans threatened once again to refuse to lift the debt ceiling without policy concessions from Obama. The stalemate led to a sixteen-day government closure in October 2013 before the GOP backed down and allowed for a vote temporarily raising the debt ceiling and funding the government.

These seemingly endless rounds of politically induced budget crises and governance-through-showdown raised alarming questions about the very capacity of the American political system to function in times of divided government and ideologically sorted parties. But they also rendered all the more unlikely any grand compromise to restore the country's long-term fiscal balance in the face of a rapidly aging population. Over 13 percent of Americans were over sixty-five in 2012, and projections were that one of every five people would be in the "sunset years" by 2050.

This greying of America brought fiscal strains, especially on the Social Security and Medicare systems. As the huge wave of post–World War II baby boomers entered retirement age, those programs' long-term "unfunded liability"—the difference between what the government had promised to pay to the elderly and the taxes it expected to take in over the next seventy-five years—reached $9.6 trillion. But the electoral power of older Americans, the Republicans' no-new-taxes orthodoxy, and the intractability of partisan warfare in government made addressing this imbalance ever more challenging.

★ Citizenship and Civil Rights

The vexed issue of immigration reform, especially with respect to the nation's 11 million "illegals," also continued to elude resolution during Obama's presidency. Obama and congressional Democrats in 2010 had pushed the DREAM Act (Development, Relief, and Education for Alien Minors Act), which would have created a path to citizenship for undocumented youths who either graduated from college or served in the U.S. armed forces, but

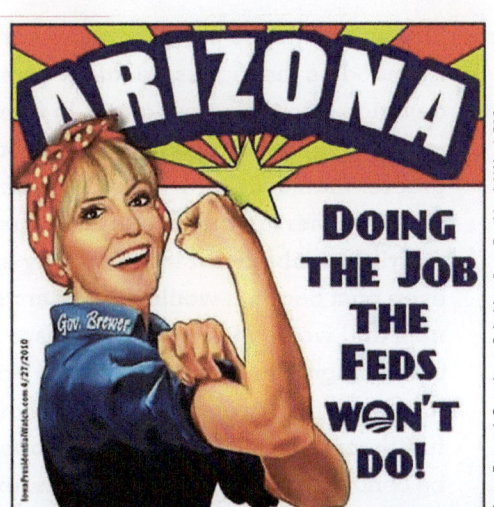

Immigration Confrontation When Arizona governor Jan Brewer signed a tough new bill in 2010 authorizing local police to crack down on illegal immigrants, the national debate over immigration policy grew still more bitterly divisive. Champions of the bill hailed Arizona for taking a stand in the void left by federal inaction. Critics denounced it as an invitation to the harassment of all Latinos—indeed, all people of color—regardless of their citizenship status.

it fell to a Republican filibuster in the Senate. Obama tried to make more comprehensive immigration reform a centerpiece of his second term. But though a bill offering undocumented immigrants a route to citizenship passed the Senate in the summer of 2013, the House refused to bring it to a vote.

House Republicans' opposition to the bill reflected deep anxieties felt by many Americans over the presence of millions of undocumented immigrants seeking jobs and benefiting from public services. The economic crisis had only exacerbated such anxiety. In 2010, legislators in Arizona, provoked by continuing immigrant flows over the state's long desert border with Mexico, passed a harsh anti-immigrant law requiring local police to detain people if there was "reasonable suspicion" that they were illegal. Critics complained that the law amounted to unfair "racial profiling" and that the state was unconstitutionally usurping federal responsibility for controlling immigration.

The Supreme Court waded further into politically charged waters in two landmark decisions in 2013. In *Shelby County* v. *Holder*, a narrow conservative majority declared unconstitutional Section 4 of the 1965 Voting Rights Act, which set a formula for determining which states—namely, those with a history of racial discrimination—were required to seek federal clearance for any changes to voting laws. The 2012 elections had occasioned controversy over state-level anti-voter-fraud laws featuring strict voter identification requirements and limited registration periods, which critics charged unfairly penalized minority, poor, and young voters. The Supreme Court's *Shelby* decision intensified the debate over voting rights in the twenty-first century.

Later the same year, a narrow *liberal* majority on the Court declared unconstitutional the 1996 Defense of Marriage Act, which had denied federal benefits to same-sex couples in states where gay marriage was legal. Though not explicitly declaring a blanket right to same-sex marriage in all states, the strongly worded decision provided a galvanizing spur to the legalization of gay marriage in more and more states.

Obama faced criticism in his second term for explosive revelations that his administration had approved sweeping National Security Administration (NSA) spying operations covering both domestic and international telephone and Internet communications. The revelations sparked anew impassioned debates over the tradeoff between security and civil liberties. They also served as a vivid reminder to Americans of the transformative impact of the Internet on their daily lives—and of the potential threats to privacy that the Internet enabled.

First created by the government for Cold War intelligence sharing, the Internet had spread like wildfire through American homes, schools, and offices starting in the mid-1990s. The percentage of households with Internet access skyrocketed from 18 percent in 1997 to about 75 percent in 2012. In rapidly increasing numbers, Americans turned to the Internet to communicate, shop, work, pay bills, and electronically bond with family, friends, and lovers. Fulfilling the promises of its early boosters, the Internet seemed to have a democratizing effect, spreading power and information among more and more people while upending the worlds of traditional media, business, and politics. But the growing centrality of the electronic online world to Americans' everyday lives also served to increase their vulnerability to potentially unwanted intrusions—from businesses, governments, and criminals alike.

★ Political Gridlock and Judicial Change

In the 2014 mid-term elections, Republicans cashed in on President Obama's declining job approval ratings, which sank to nearly 40 percent in some polls. Public frustration with an economic recovery that lit up the stock market

---

In Obergefell *v.* Hodges, *a five-to-four Supreme Court majority declared gay marriage a fundamental right under the Fourteenth Amendment. (See Appendix p. A-16.) As Justice Anthony Kennedy (b. 1936) wrote in the majority decision:*

"No union is more profound than marriage, for it embodies the highest ideals of love, fidelity, devotion, sacrifice, and family. In forming a marital union, two people become something greater than once they were. As some of the petitioners in these cases demonstrate, marriage embodies a love that may endure even past death. It would misunderstand these men and women to say they disrespect the idea of marriage. Their plea is that they do respect it, respect it so deeply that they seek to find its fulfillment for themselves. Their hope is not to be condemned to live in loneliness, excluded from one of civilization's oldest institutions. They ask for equal dignity in the eyes of the law. The Constitution grants them that right."

but failed to boost most household incomes fed discontent with the president's party, as did the stubborn unpopularity in some quarters of the Affordable Care Act, the signature achievement of Obama's first term. A rash of troubles abroad also plagued the president and his party alike. The unexpected emergence of the Islamic State of Iraq and Syria (ISIS), a ferocious jihadist movement, alarming in its brutality and in its territorial advance, cast doubts on the president's foreign policy skills, and further discredited his party's candidates.

As a result, in the 2014 midterm elections Republicans expanded their majority in the House and gained control of the Senate for the first time since 2006. Many observers attributed those results not to blossoming affection for Republicans, but to deep disillusionment with the Democratic administration.

With the Republicans in complete control of Congress, there seemed little chance of easing the stalemate with President Obama on the issues of immigration, gun control, and environmental policy. Republicans also remained sharply critical of Obama's Middle East policies, including his attempted agreement on nuclear weapons development with Iran, as well as his limited aerial responses aimed at weakening the Islamic State. Obama also sparked controversy when he met with Cuban President Raul Castro in April 2015 and announced that the two nations would work to restore normal diplomatic relations.

Obama did garner strong Republican support in 2015 for successful passage of the Trans-Pacific Partnership, a major free trade agreement among twelve Asia-Pacific nations, including the United States and China. Many Democrats voted against the deal, fearing a loss of U.S. jobs and the weakening of environmental protections.

With the president and Congress still largely at loggerheads, it was the Supreme Court that in 2015 decisively addressed two fiercely contested political issues. In *King v. Burwell*, the Court rejected a last-gasp legal challenge to federal subsidies for health insurance under the Affordable Care Act. Republicans still vowed to repeal and replace "Obamacare," but they would need to elect another president to do so. In *Obergefell v. Hodges*, the Court's majority declared that same-sex marriage was a fundamental right under the Constitution's Fourteenth Amendment, making it legal in all fifty states. The decision was a testimony to the power of the American commitment to the idea of equal rights for all, as well as to the lightning-speed transformation in public attitudes toward gay sexuality, marriage, and family, especially among younger citizens.

As a legion of candidates began to line up for the 2016 presidential elections, the two major parties were still sharply divided on issues of economics, immigration, and foreign policy. Whether new leadership or some fresh turn of events might make room for common ground to move the nation forward remained to be seen.

★ The American Prospect

Well beyond its two-hundredth birthday as the twenty-first century's second decade unspooled, the United States was both an old and a new nation. It boasted one of the longest uninterrupted traditions of democratic government of any country on earth. Indeed, it had pioneered the techniques of mass democracy and was, in that sense, the oldest modern polity. As one of the earliest countries to industrialize, America had also dwelt in the modern economic era longer than most nations. But the Republic was in many ways still youthful as well. Innovation, entrepreneurship, and risk-taking—all characteristics of youth—were honored national values.

America's twenty-first century had begun much like the twentieth, as society continued to be rejuvenated by fresh waves of immigrants, full of energy and ambition. The U.S. economy, despite the impact of the "Great Recession," remained an important engine of world economic growth. American inventions—especially computer and communications technologies—continued to transform the face of global society. Consumers from Berlin to Beijing seemed to worship the icons of American culture—downing soft drinks and donning blue jeans, watching Hollywood films and television series, listening to rock or country music, even adopting indigenous American sports like baseball and basketball. In the realm of consumerism, American products appeared to have Coca-Colonized the globe.

The history of American society also seemed to have increased global significance as the third millennium of the Christian era opened. Americans were a pluralistic people who had struggled for centuries to offer opportunity, tolerance, and justice to many different religious, ethnic, and racial groups. Their historical trials and triumphs could offer valuable lessons to the rapidly internationalizing planetary society that was emerging at the dawn of the twenty-first century.

Much history remained to be made as the country entered its third century of nationhood. The great social experiment of American democracy was far from completed as the United States faced its future. Astonishing breakthroughs in science and technology, especially in genetics, bioengineering, and communications, presented Americans with stunning opportunities as well as wrenching ethical choices. Global climate change made the responsible stewardship of a fragile planet more urgent than ever. Inequality and prejudice continued to challenge Americans to close the gap between their most hallowed values and the stark realities of society in the twenty-first-century United States. The terrorist attacks of September 11, 2001 violently heralded a new era of fear and anxiety. And the severe economic crisis that convulsed the nation and the world in 2008 demonstrated that free-market capitalism could still produce abundant misery as well as material abundance.

But men and women make history only within the framework bequeathed to them by earlier generations. For better or worse, they march forward along time's path bearing the burdens of the past. Knowing when they have come to a truly new turn in the road, when they can lay part of their burden down and when they cannot, or should not—all this constitutes the sort of wisdom that only historical understanding can engender. As Americans confront the unending challenges of the twenty-first-century world, they would do well to remember Woodrow Wilson's admonition of 1893, long before he became president. "Democratic Institutions are never done; they are like living tissue, always a-making. It is a strenuous thing, this of living the life of a free people."

CHAPTER SUMMARY ★★★★★★★★★★★★★★★★

George W. Bush took office after the close, bitter election of 2000, and began governing as a highly activist and often divisive conservative leader. His heavy defense expenditures and sharp tax cuts created huge federal budget deficits.

The September 11, 2001 terrorist attacks shocked and unified the nation, while propelling it out of its long centuries of relative safety from foreign attack on domestic soil. Bush responded by launching a "war on terror" that included a swift ouster of the Taliban in Afghanistan. He also launched a highly controversial war against Iraqi dictator Saddam Hussein, claiming that Iraq possessed weapons of mass destruction that threatened the United States. While Saddam was quickly overthrown, Iraq soon fell into chaos, featuring bloody factional religious conflicts and militant attacks on occupying American troops.

Bush won reelection in 2004 as a strong leader, but he suffered numerous failures and decreasing popularity in his second term. The administration's disastrous response to Hurricane Katrina and the continuing conflict in Iraq led to Democratic gains in 2006 midterm elections. In the 2008 campaign Democrats nominated youthful Senator Barack Obama, who defeated Republican Senator John McCain; Obama became the first black president in American history.

Obama's victory came partly because of a major financial crisis and economic collapse that began in fall 2008. The "Great Recession" cost millions of Americans their jobs and homes, and led to a stagnant economic environment that lingered for years. Obama responded vigorously to the crisis with a huge "stimulus" spending bill as well as reforms of health care and the financial system. But Obama's surge of federal activism prompted a fierce backlash by ultraconservative "Tea Party" citizens who attacked "big government" and the Democrats who supported it. Democrats suffered setbacks in the midterm elections of 2010.

Obama successfully wound down the Iraq War and brought American troops home, though the country remained unstable. Afghanistan proved more difficult to pacify, and even when ground troops left they were increasingly replaced by aerial "drone warfare" against terrorists. Al Qaeda leader Osama bin Laden was killed in neighboring Pakistan.

America's attention turned to issues of growing economic inequality in the early twenty-first century. A radical "Occupy Wall Street" movement attacked the wealthiest "1 percent." The movement faded, but the weak economic environment fostered growing debates about poverty and wealth, and especially the power of the immensely rich and growing financial sector.

Barack Obama won reelection against Republican Mitt Romney, a former Massachusetts governor and the first Mormon presidential candidate in American history. Obama attempted to expand his activist reforms in his second term, but conservative Republicans in control of the House blocked his efforts. The standoff between the president and Congress over the budget ceiling and other issues forced the government into "gridlock." Immigration reform remained a hotly contested issue in the country, but all attempts to find compromise legal solutions failed. Republicans made further gains in the midterm elections of 2014, and the partisan conflict between the president and Congress deepened. In 2015 the Supreme Court declared gay marriage a right under the Fourteenth Amendment.

American democracy remains a dynamic force in a new global and technological age. Issues of economic inequality, environmental degradation, and ethnic conflict demand urgent attention and engagement by American citizens. American culture and democracy can provide powerful resources for addressing the challenges of the nation's third century.

KEY TERMS

weapons of mass destruction (WMD) (719)
Kyoto Treaty (721)
9/11 (721)
Al Qaeda (721)
USA Patriot Act (721)
Department of Homeland Security (722)
Guantanamo Detention Camp (722)
Abu Ghraib prison (723)
No Child Left Behind Act (724)
Hurricane Katrina (724)
deleveraging (725)
American Recovery and Reinvestment Act (726)
Patient Protection and Affordable Care Act (727)
Wall Street Reform and Consumer Protection Act (727)
Tea Party (727)
Occupy Wall Street (729)

PEOPLE TO KNOW

John McCain
Sarah Palin
George W. Bush
Richard Cheney
Nancy Pelosi
Barack Obama
Joseph R. ("Joe") Biden

MindTap is a fully online, highly personalized learning experience built upon Cengage Learning content. MindTap combines student learning tools—readings, multimedia, activities, and assessments—into a singular Learning Path that guides students through the course.

DOCUMENTS

Declaration of Independence

In Congress, July 4, 1776

The Unanimous Declaration of the Thirteen United States of America

[Bracketed material in color has been inserted by the authors. For adoption background see pp. 105–106.]

When, in the course of human events, it becomes necessary for one people to dissolve the political bonds which have connected them with another, and to assume, among the powers of the earth, the separate and equal station to which the laws of nature and of nature's God entitle them, a decent respect to the opinions of mankind requires that they should declare the causes which impel them to the separation.

We hold these truths to be self-evident: That all men are created equal; that they are endowed by their Creator with certain unalienable rights; that among these are life, liberty, and the pursuit of happiness; that, to secure these rights, governments are instituted among men, deriving their just powers from the consent of the governed; that whenever any form of government becomes destructive of these ends, it is the right of the people to alter or to abolish it, and to institute new government, laying its foundation on such principles, and organizing its powers in such form, as to them shall seem most likely to effect their safety and happiness. Prudence, indeed, will dictate that governments long established should not be changed for light and transient causes; and accordingly all experience hath shown that mankind are more disposed to suffer, while evils are sufferable, than to right themselves by abolishing the forms to which they are accustomed. But when a long train of abuses and usurpations, pursuing invariably the same object, evinces a design to reduce them under absolute despotism, it is their right, it is their duty, to throw off such government, and to provide new guards for their future security. Such has been the patient sufferance of these colonies; and such is now the necessity which constrains them to alter their former systems of government. The history of the present King of Great Britain is a history of repeated injuries and usurpations, all having in direct object the establishment of an absolute tyranny over these states. To prove this, let facts be submitted to a candid world.

He has refused his assent to laws, the most wholesome and necessary for the public good. [See royal veto, p. 89.]

He has forbidden his governors to pass laws of immediate and pressing importance, unless suspended in their operation till his assent should be obtained; and, when so suspended, he has utterly neglected to attend to them.

He has refused to pass other laws for the accommodation of large districts of people [by establishing new countries], unless those people would relinquish the right of representation in the legislature, a right inestimable to them, and formidable to tyrants only.

He has called together legislative bodies at places unusual, uncomfortable, and distant from the depository of their public records, for the sole purpose of fatiguing them into compliance with his measures [e.g., removal of Massachusetts Assembly to Salem, 1774].

He has dissolved representative houses repeatedly, for opposing, with manly firmness, his invasions on the rights of the people [e.g., Virginia Assembly, 1765].

He has refused for a long time, after such dissolutions, to cause others to be elected; whereby the legislative powers, incapable of annihilation, have returned to the people at large for their exercise; the state remaining, in the mean time, exposed to all the dangers of invasions from without and convulsions within.

He has endeavored to prevent the population [populating] of these states; for that purpose obstructing the laws for naturalization of foreigners; refusing to pass others to encourage their migration hither, and raising the conditions of new appropriations of lands [e.g., Proclamation of 1763, p. 84].

He has obstructed the administration of justice, by refusing his assent to laws for establishing judiciary powers.

He has made judges dependent on his will alone, for the tenure of their offices, and the amount and payment of their salaries. [See Townshend Acts, p. 92.]

He has erected a multitude of new offices, and sent hither swarms of officers to harass our people and eat out their substance. [See enforcement of Navigation Laws, pp. 89, 90.]

He has kept among us, in times of peace, standing armies, without the consent of our legislatures. [See pp. 90, 92.]

He has affected to render the military independent of, and superior to, the civil power.

He has combined with others to subject us to a jurisdiction foreign to our constitution, and unacknowledged by our laws, giving his assent to their acts of pretended legislation:

> For quartering large bodies of armed troops among us [see Boston Massacre, pp. 92–93];
>
> For protecting them, by a mock trial, from punishment for any murders which they should commit on the inhabitants of these states [see 1774 "Intolerable Acts," p. 95];
>
> For cutting off our trade with all parts of the world [see Boston Port Act, p. 95];
>
> For imposing taxes on us without our consent [see Stamp Act, pp. 90–91];
>
> For depriving us, in many cases, of the benefits of trial by jury;
>
> For transporting us beyond seas, to be tried for pretended offenses;
>
> For abolishing the free system of English laws in a neighboring province [Quebec], establishing therein an arbitrary government, and enlarging its boundaries, so as to render it at once an example and fit instrument for introducing the same absolute rule into these colonies [Quebec Act, pp. 95–96];
>
> For taking away our charters, abolishing our most valuable laws, and altering fundamentally the forms of our governments [e.g., in Massachusetts, p. 95];
>
> For suspending our own legislatures, and declaring themselves invested with power to legislate for us in all cases whatsoever. [See Stamp Act repeal, pp. 91–92.]

He has abdicated government here, by declaring us out of his protection and waging war against us. [See George III's proclamation of colonies in rebellion, p. 103.]

He has plundered our seas, ravaged our coasts, burned our towns, and destroyed the lives of our people [e.g., the burning of Falmouth (Portland), p. 103].

He is at this time transporting large armies of foreign mercenaries [Hessians, p. 103] to complete the works of death, desolation, and tyranny already begun with circumstances of cruelty and perfidy scarcely paralleled in the most barbarous ages, and totally unworthy the head of a civilized nation.

He has constrained our fellow-citizens, taken captive on the high seas [by impressment], to bear arms against their country, to become the executioners of their friends and brethren, or to fall themselves by their hands.

He has excited domestic insurrection among us [i.e., among slaves], and has endeavored to bring on the inhabitants of our frontiers the merciless Indian savages, whose known rule of warfare is an undistinguished destruction of all ages, sexes, and conditions.

In every stage of these oppressions we have petitioned for redress in the most humble terms; our repeated petitions have been answered only by repeated injury [e.g., p. 103]. A prince, whose character is thus marked by every act which may define a tyrant, is unfit to be the ruler of a free people.

Nor have we been wanting in our attentions to our British brethren. We have warned them, from time to time, of attempts by their legislature to extend an unwarrantable jurisdiction over us. We have reminded them of the circumstances of our emigration and settlement here. We have appealed to their native justice and magnanimity; and we have conjured them, by the ties of our common kindred, to disavow these usurpations, which would inevitably interrupt our connections and correspondence. They, too, have been deaf to the voice of justice and of consanguinity [blood relationship]. We must, therefore, acquiesce in the necessity which denounces [announces] our separation, and hold them, as we hold the rest of mankind, enemies in war, in peace friends.

We, therefore, the representatives of the United States of America, in General Congress assembled, appealing to the Supreme Judge of the world for the rectitude of our intentions, do, in the name and by the authority of the good people of these colonies, solemnly publish and declare, That these United Colonies are, and of right ought to be, FREE AND INDEPENDENT STATES; that they are absolved from all allegiance to the British crown, and that all political connection between them and the state of Great Britain is, and ought to be, totally dissolved; and that, as free and independent states, they have full power to levy war, conclude peace, contract alliances, establish commerce, and do all other acts and things which independent states may of right do. And for the support of this declaration, with a firm reliance on the protection of Divine Providence, we mutually pledge to each other our lives, our fortunes, and our sacred honor.

[Signed by]

JOHN HANCOCK [President]
[and fifty-five others]

Constitution of the United States of America

[Boldface headings and bracketed explanatory matter and marginal comments (both in color) have been inserted for the reader's convenience. Passages that are no longer operative are printed in italic type.]

Article I. **PREAMBLE**

Section I. We the people of the United States, in order to form a more perfect union, establish justice, insure domestic tranquility, provide for the common defense, promote the general welfare, and secure the blessings of liberty to ourselves and our posterity, do ordain and establish this CONSTITUTION for the United States of America.

Section II. *Legislative Department*

Congress

Legislative power vested in a two-house Congress. All legislative powers herein granted shall be vested in a Congress of the United States, which shall consist of a Senate and a House of Representatives.

House of Representatives

1. The people elect representatives biennially. The House of Representatives shall be composed of members chosen every second year by the people of the several States, and the electors [voters] in each State shall have the qualifications requisite for electors of the most numerous branch of the State Legislature.

2. Who may be representatives. No person shall be a Representative who shall not have attained the age of twenty-five years, and been seven years a citizen of the United States, and who shall not, when elected, be an inhabitant of that State in which he shall be chosen.

See 1787 compromises, pp. 129–131.

3. Representation in the House based on population; census. Representatives and direct taxes[1] shall be apportioned among the several States which may be included within this Union, according to their respective numbers, *which shall be determined by adding to the whole number of free persons, including those bound to service for a term of years* [apprentices and indentured servants], *and excluding Indians not taxed, three-fifths of all other persons* [slaves].[2] The actual enumeration [census] shall be made within three years after the first meeting of the Congress of the United States, and within every subsequent term of ten years, in such manner as they shall by law direct. The number of Representatives shall not exceed one for every thirty thousand, but each State shall have at least one Representative; *and until such enumeration shall be made, the State of New Hampshire shall be entitled to choose three, Massachusetts eight, Rhode Island and Providence Plantations one, Connecticut five, New York six, New Jersey four, Pennsylvania eight, Delaware one, Maryland six, Virginia ten, North Carolina five, South Carolina five, and Georgia three.*

See 1787 compromises, pp. 129–131.

---

[1]Modified in 1913 by the Sixteenth Amendment re income taxes (see p. 497).

[2]The word *slave* appears nowhere in the original, unamended Constitution. The three-fifths rule ceased to be in force when the Thirteenth Amendment was adopted in 1865 (see p. 332 and amendments below).

4. Vacancies in the House are filled by election. When vacancies happen in the representation from any State, the Executive authority [governor] therefore shall issue writs of election [call a special election] to fill such vacancies.

See Johnson trial, pp. 360–361; Nixon trial preliminaries, pp. 671–673; and discussion of Clinton's impeachment, pp. 713–714.

5. The House selects its Speaker; has sole power to vote impeachment charges (i.e., indictments). The House of Representatives shall choose their Speaker and other officers; and shall have the sole power of impeachment.

Section III. Senate

1. Senators represent the states. The Senate of the United States shall be composed of two Senators from each State, *chosen by the legislature thereof,*[1] for six Years; and each Senator shall have one vote.

2. One-third of senators chosen every two years; vacancies. *Immediately after they shall be assembled in consequence of the first election, they shall be divided as equally as may be into three classes. The seats of the Senators of the first class shall be vacated at the expiration of the second year, of the second class at the expiration of the fourth year, and of the third class at the expiration of the sixth year,* so that one-third may be chosen every second year; *and if vacancies happen by resignation or otherwise, during the recess of the legislature of any State, the Executive* [governor] *thereof may make temporary appointments until the next meeting of the legislature, which shall then fill such vacancies.*[2]

3. Who may be senators. No person shall be a Senator who shall not have attained to the age of thirty years, and been nine years a citizen of the United States, and who shall not, when elected, be an inhabitant of that State for which he shall be chosen.

4. The vice president presides over the Senate. The Vice President of the United States shall be President of the Senate, but shall have no vote, unless they be equally divided [tied].

5. The Senate chooses its other officers. The Senate shall choose their other officers, and also a President *pro tempore*, in the absence of the Vice President, or when he shall exercise the office of the President of the United States.

See Johnson trial, pp. 360–361; and discussion of Clinton's impeachment, pp. 713–714.

6. The Senate has sole power to try impeachments. The Senate shall have the sole power to try all impeachments. When sitting for that purpose, they shall be on oath or affirmation. When the President of the United States is tried, the Chief Justice shall preside[3]: and no person shall be convicted without the concurrence of two-thirds of the members present.

7. Penalties for impeachment conviction. Judgment in cases of impeachment shall not extend further than to removal from office, and disqualification to hold and enjoy any office of honor, trust or profit under the United States: but the party convicted shall nevertheless be liable and subject to indictment, trial, judgment and punishment, according to law.

Section IV. Election and Meetings of Congress

1. Regulation of elections. The times, places and manner of holding elections for Senators and Representatives shall be prescribed in each State by the legislature thereof; but the Congress may at any time by law make or alter such regulations, except as to the places of choosing Senators.

2. Congress must meet once a year. The Congress shall assemble at least once in every year, and such meeting *shall be on the first Monday in December, unless they shall by law appoint a different day.*[4]

---

[1] Repealed in favor of popular election in 1913 by the Seventeenth Amendment.
[2] Changed in 1913 by the Seventeenth Amendment.
[3] The vice president, as next in line, would be an interested party.
[4] Changed in 1933 to January 3 by the Twentieth Amendment (see p. 565 and below).

Section V. Organization and Rules of the Houses

1. Each house may reject members; quorums. Each house shall be the judge of the elections, returns and qualifications of its own members, and a majority of each shall constitute a quorum to do business; but a smaller number may adjourn from day to day, and may be authorized to compel the attendance of absent members, in such manner, and under such penalties, as each house may provide.

See "Bully" Brooks case, pp. 300–301.

2. Each house makes its own rules. Each house may determine the rules of its proceedings, punish its members for disorderly behavior, and with the concurrence of two-thirds, expel a member.

3. Each house must keep and publish a record of its proceedings. Each house shall keep a journal of its proceedings, and from time to time publish the same, excepting such parts as may in their judgment require secrecy; and the yeas and nays of the members of either house on any question shall, at the desire of one-fifth of those present, be entered on the journal.

4. Both houses must agree on adjournment. Neither house, during the session of Congress, shall, without the consent of the other, adjourn for more than three days, nor to any other place than that in which the two houses shall be sitting.

Section VI. Privileges of and Prohibitions upon Congressmen

1. Congressional salaries; immunities. The Senators and Representatives shall receive a compensation for their services, to be ascertained by law and paid out of the treasury of the United States. They shall in all cases except treason, felony and breach of the peace, be privileged from arrest during their attendance at the session of their respective houses, and in going to and returning from the same; and for any speech or debate in either house, they shall not be questioned in any other place [i.e., they shall be immune from libel suits].

2. A congressman may not hold any other federal civil office. No Senator or Representative shall, during the time for which he was elected, be appointed to any civil office under the authority of the United States, which shall have been created, or the emoluments whereof shall have been increased, during such time; and no person holding any office under the United States shall be a member of either house during his continuance in office.

Section VII. Method of Making Laws

See 1787 compromises, p. 130.

1. Money bills must originate in the House. All bills for raising revenue shall originate in the House of Representatives; but the Senate may propose or concur with amendments as on other bills.

Nixon, more than any predecessors, "impounded" billions of dollars voted by Congress for specific purposes because he disapproved of them. The courts generally failed to sustain him, and his impeachment foes regarded wholesale impoundment as a violation of his oath to "faithfully execute" the laws.

2. The president's veto power; Congress may override. Every bill which shall have passed the House of Representatives and the Senate, shall, before it become a law, be presented to the President of the United States; if he approve he shall sign it, but if not he shall return it with his objections to that house in which it shall have originated, who shall enter the objections at large on their journal, and proceed to reconsider it. If after such reconsideration two-thirds of that house shall agree to pass the bill, it shall be sent, together with the objections, to the other house, by which it shall likewise be reconsidered, and, if approved by two-thirds of that house, it shall become a law. But in all such cases the votes of both houses shall be determined by yeas and nays, and the names of the persons voting for and against the bill shall be entered on the journal of each house respectively. If any bill shall not be returned by the President within ten days (Sundays excepted) after it shall have been presented to him, the same shall be a law, in like manner as if he had signed it, unless the Congress by their adjournment prevent its return, in which case it shall not be a law [this is the so-called pocket veto].

3. All measures requiring the agreement of both houses go to president for approval. Every order, resolution, or vote to which the concurrence of the Senate and House of Representatives may be necessary (except on a question of adjournment) shall be presented to the President of the United States; and before the same shall take effect, shall be approved by him, or being disapproved by him, shall be repassed by two-thirds of the Senate and House of Representatives, according to the rules and limitations prescribed in the case of a bill.

Section VIII. Powers Granted to Congress

Congress has certain enumerated powers:

1. It may lay and collect taxes. The Congress shall have power to lay and collect taxes, duties, imposts, and excises, to pay the debts and provide for the common defense and general welfare of the United States; but all duties, imposts and excises shall be uniform throughout the United States;

2. It may borrow money. To borrow money on the credit of the United States;

3. It may regulate foreign and interstate trade. To regulate commerce with foreign nations, and among the several States, and with the Indian tribes;

For 1798 naturalization, see p. 152.

4. It may pass naturalization and bankruptcy laws. To establish an uniform rule of naturalization, and uniform laws on the subject of bankruptcies throughout the United States;

5. It may coin money. To coin money, regulate the value thereof, and of foreign coin, and fix the standard of weights and measures;

6. It may punish counterfeiters. To provide for the punishment of counterfeiting the securities and current coin of the United States;

7. It may establish a postal service. To establish post offices and post roads;

8. It may issue patents and copyrights. To promote the progress of science and useful arts by securing for limited times to authors and inventors the exclusive right to their respective writings and discoveries;

9. It may establish inferior courts. To constitute tribunals inferior to the Supreme Court;

See Judiciary Act of 1789, p. 142.

10. It may punish crimes committed on the high seas. To define and punish piracies and felonies committed on the high seas [i.e., outside the three-mile limit] and offenses against the law of nations [international law];

11. It may declare war; authorize privateers. To declare war,[1] grant letters of marque and reprisal,[2] and make rules concerning captures on land and water;

12. It may maintain an army. To raise and support armies, but no appropriation of money to that use shall be for a longer term than two years;[3]

13. It may maintain a navy. To provide and maintain a navy;

14. It may regulate the army and navy. To make rules for the government and regulation of the land and naval forces;

15. It may call out the state militia. To provide for calling forth the militia to execute the laws of the Union, suppress insurrections, and repel invasions;

See Whiskey Rebellion, pp. 144–145.

16. It shares with the states control of militia. To provide for organizing, arming, and disciplining the militia, and for governing such part of them as may be employed in the service of the United States, reserving to the States respectively the appointment of the officers, and the authority of training the militia according to the discipline prescribed by Congress;

17. It makes laws for the District of Columbia and other federal areas. To exercise exclusive legislation in all cases whatsoever, over such district (not exceeding ten miles square) as may, by cession of particular States, and the acceptance of

---

[1] Note that presidents, though they can provoke war (see the case of Polk, p. 276) or wage it after it is declared, cannot declare it.

[2] Papers issued private citizens in wartime authorizing them to capture enemy ships.

[3] A reflection of fear of standing armies earlier expressed in the Declaration of Independence.

Congress, become the seat of government of the United States,[1] and to exercise like authority over all places purchased by the consent of the legislature of the State, in which the same shall be, for the erection of forts, magazines, arsenals, dock-yards, and other needful buildings;—and

Congress has certain implied powers:

This is the famous "elastic clause"; see p. 144.

18. It may make laws necessary for carrying out the enumerated powers. To make all laws which shall be necessary and proper for carrying into execution the foregoing powers, and all other powers vested by this Constitution in the government of the United States, or in any departure or officer thereof.

Section IX. Powers Denied to the Federal Government

See 1787 slave compromise, p. 130.

1. Congressional control of slave trade postponed until 1808. *The migration or importation of such persons as any of the States now existing shall think proper to admit shall not be prohibited by the Congress prior to the year 1808; but a tax or duty may be imposed on such importation, not exceeding $10 for each person.*

See Lincoln's unlawful suspension, p. 319.

2. The writ of habeas corpus[2] may be suspended only in cases of rebellion or invasion. The privilege of the writ of habeas corpus shall not be suspended, unless when in cases of rebellion or invasion the public safety may require it.

3. Attainders[3] and ex post facto laws[4] forbidden. No bill of attainder or ex post facto law shall be passed.

4. Direct taxes must be apportioned according to population. No capitation [head or poll tax] or other direct, tax shall be laid, unless in proportion to the census or enumeration herein before directed to be taken.[5]

5. Export taxes forbidden. No tax or duty shall be laid on articles exported from any State.

6. Congress must not discriminate among states in regulating commerce. No preference shall be given by any regulation of commerce or revenue to the ports of one State over those of another; nor shall vessels bound to, or from, one State, be obliged to enter, clear, or pay duties in another.

See Lincoln's unlawful infraction, p. 319.

7. Public money may not be spent without congressional appropriation; accounting. No money shall be drawn from the treasury, but in consequence of appropriations made by law; and a regular statement and account of the receipts and expenditures of all public money shall be published from time to time.

8. Titles of nobility prohibited; foreign gifts. No title of nobility shall be granted by the United States; and no person holding office of profit or trust under them, shall, without the consent of Congress, accept of any present, emolument, office, or title, of any kind whatever, from any king, prince, or foreign state.

Section X. Powers Denied to the States

Absolute prohibitions on the states:

On contracts, see Fletcher v. Peck, p. 183.

1. The states are forbidden to do certain things. No State shall enter into any treaty, alliance, or confederation; grant letters of marque and reprisal [i.e., authorize

---

[1] The District of Columbia, ten miles square, was established in 1791 with a cession from Virginia (see p. 143).

[2] A writ of habeas corpus is a document that enables a person under arrest to obtain an immediate examination in court to ascertain whether he or she is being legally held.

[3] A bill of attainder is a special legislative act condemning and punishing an individual without a judicial trial.

[4] An ex post facto law is one that fixes punishments for acts committed before the law was passed.

[5] Modified in 1913 by the Sixteenth Amendment (see p. 497 and amendments below).

privateers]; coin money; emit bills of credit [issue paper money]; make anything but gold and silver coin a [legal] tender in payment of debts; pass any bill of attainder,[1] ex post facto,[1] or law impairing the obligation of contracts, or grant any title of nobility.

Conditional prohibitions on the states:

Cf. Confederation chaos, p. 125.

2. The states may not levy duties without the consent of Congress. No State shall, without the consent of Congress, lay any imposts or duties on imports or exports, except what may be absolutely necessary for executing its inspection laws: and the net produce of all duties and imposts, laid by any State on imports or exports, shall be for the use of the treasury of the United States; and all such laws shall be subject to the revision and control of the Congress.

3. Certain other federal powers are forbidden the states except with the consent of Congress. No State shall, without the consent of Congress, lay any duty of tonnage [i.e., duty on ship tonnage], keep [nonmilitia] troops or ships of war in time of peace, enter into any agreement or compact with another State, or with a foreign power, or engage in war, unless actually invaded, or in such imminent danger as will not admit of delay.

Article II. Executive Department

Section I. President and Vice President

1. The president is the chief executive; term of office. The executive power shall be vested in a President of the United States of America. He shall hold his office during the term of four years,[2] and, together with the Vice President, chosen for the same term, be elected as follows:

See 1787 compromise, p. 130.

See 1876 Oregon case, p. 373.

2. The president is chosen by electors. Each State shall appoint, in such manner as the legislature thereof may direct, a number of electors, equal to the whole number of Senators and Representatives to which the State may be entitled in the Congress; but no Senator or Representative, or person holding an office of trust or profit under the United States, shall be appointed an elector.

A majority of the electoral votes needed to elect a president. *The electors shall meet in their respective States, and vote by ballot for two persons, of whom one at least shall not be an inhabitant of the same State with themselves. And they shall make a list of all the persons voted for, and of the number of votes for each; which list they shall sign and certify, and transmit sealed to the seat of government of the United States, directed to the President of the Senate. The President of the Senate shall, in the presence of the Senate and House of Representatives, open all the certificates, and the votes shall be counted. The person having the greatest number of votes shall be the President, if such number be a majority of the whole number of electors appointed; and if there be more than one who have such majority, and have an equal number of votes, then the House of Representatives shall immediately choose by ballot one of them for President; and if no person have a majority, then from the five highest on the list the said house shall in like manner choose the President. But in choosing the President the votes shall be taken by States, the representation from each State having one vote; a quorum for this purpose shall consist of a member or members from two-thirds of the States, and a majority of all the States shall be necessary to a choice. In every case, after the choice of the President, the person having the greatest number of votes of the electors shall be the Vice President. But if there should remain two or more who have equal votes, the Senate shall choose from them by ballot the Vice President.*[3]

See Burr-Jefferson disputed election of 1800, pp. 157–158.

See Jefferson as vice president in 1796, p. 150.

---

[1] For definitions see footnotes 3 and 4 on preceding page.
[2] No reference to reelection; for anti–third term Twenty-second Amendment, see below.
[3] Repealed in 1804 by the Twelfth Amendment (for text see below).

To provide for foreign-born people, like Alexander Hamilton, born in the British West Indies.

Modified by Twentieth and Twenty-fifth Amendments below.

3. Congress decides time of meeting of Electoral College. The Congress may determine the time of choosing the electors and the day on which they shall give their votes; which day shall be the same throughout the United States.

4. Who may be president. No person except a natural-born citizen, *or a citizen of the United States at the time of the adoption of this Constitution*, shall be eligible to the office of President; neither shall any person be eligible to that office who shall not have attained to the age of thirty-five years, and been fourteen years a resident within the United States [i.e., a legal resident].

5. Replacements for president. In case of the removal of the President from office or of his death, resignation, or inability to discharge the powers and duties of said office, the same shall devolve on the Vice President, and the Congress may by law provide for the case of removal, death, resignation, or inability, both of the President and Vice President, declaring what officer shall then act as President, and such officer shall act accordingly, until the disability be removed, or a President shall be elected.

6. The president's salary. The President shall, at stated times, receive for his services a compensation, which shall neither be increased or diminished during the period for which he shall have been elected, and he shall not receive within that period any other emolument from the United States, or any of them.

7. The president's oath of office. Before he enter on the execution of his office, he shall take the following oath or affirmation:—"I do solemnly swear (or affirm) that I will faithfully execute the office of the President of the United States, and will to the best of my ability preserve, protect and defend the Constitution of the United States."

Section II. Powers of the President

See cabinet evolution, p. 141.

1. The president has important military and civil powers. The President shall be commander in chief of the army and navy of the United States, and of the militia of the several States, when called into the actual service of the United States; he may require the opinion, in writing, of the principal officer in each of the executive departments, upon any subject relating to the duties of their respective offices, and he shall have power to grant reprieves and pardons for offenses against the United States, except in cases of impeachment.[1]

For president's removal power, see p. 360.

2. The president may negotiate treaties and nominate federal officials. He shall have power, by and with the advice and consent of the Senate, to make treaties, provided two-thirds of the Senators present concur; and he shall nominate, and by and with the advice and consent of the Senate, shall appoint ambassadors, other public ministers and consuls, judges of the Supreme Court, and all other officers of the United States, whose appointments are not herein otherwise provided for, and which shall be established by law: but the Congress may by law vest the appointment of such inferior officers, as they think proper, in the President alone, in the courts of law, or in the heads of departments.

3. The president may fill vacancies during Senate recess. The President shall have power to fill up all vacancies that may happen during the recess of the Senate, by granting commissions which shall expire at the end of their next session.

Section III. Other Powers and Duties of the President

For president's personal appearances, see p. 497.

Messages; extra sessions; receiving ambassadors; execution of the laws. He shall from time to time give to the Congress information of the state of the Union, and recommend to their consideration such measures as he shall judge necessary and expedient; he may, on extraordinary occasions, convene both houses, or either of

---

[1] To prevent the president's pardoning himself or his close associates, as was feared in the case of Richard Nixon. See pp. 671–673.

them, and in case of disagreement between them, with respect to the time of adjournment, he may adjourn them to such time as he shall think proper; he shall receive ambassadors and other public ministers; he shall take care that the laws be faithfully executed, and shall commission all the officers of the United States.

Section IV. Impeachment

See discussion of Presidents Johnson, pp. 360–361; Nixon, pp. 671–673; and Clinton, pp. 713–714.

Civil officers may be removed by impeachment. The President, Vice President and all civil officers[1] of the United States shall be removed from office on impeachment for, and on conviction of, treason, bribery, and other high crimes and misdemeanors.

Article III. *Judicial Department*

Section I. The Federal Courts

See Judiciary Act of 1789, p. 142.

The judicial power belongs to the federal courts. The judicial power of the United States shall be vested in one Supreme Court, and in such inferior courts as the Congress may from time to time ordain and establish. The judges, both of the Supreme and inferior courts, shall hold their offices during good behavior, and shall, at stated times, receive for their services a compensation which shall not be diminished[2] during their continuance in office.

Section II. Jurisdiction of Federal Courts

1. Kinds of cases that may be heard. The judicial power shall extend to all cases, in law and equity, arising under this Constitution, the laws of the United States, and treaties made, or which shall be made, under their authority;—to all cases affecting ambassadors, other public ministers and consuls;—to all cases of admiralty and maritime jurisdiction;—to controversies to which the United States shall be a party;—to controversies between two or more States;—*between a State and citizens of another State*[3];—between citizens of different States;—between citizens of the same State claiming lands under grants of different States, and between a State, or the citizens thereof, and foreign states, citizens or subjects.

2. Jurisdiction of the Supreme Court. In all cases affecting ambassadors, other public ministers and consuls, and those in which a State shall be a party, the Supreme Court shall have original jurisdiction.[4] In all the other cases before mentioned, the Supreme Court shall have appellate jurisdiction,[5] both as to law and fact, with such exceptions, and under such regulations, as the Congress shall make.

3. Trial for federal crime is by jury. The trial of all crimes, except in cases of impeachment, shall be by jury; and such trial shall be held in the State where the said crimes shall have been committed; but when not committed within any State, the trial shall be at such place or places as the Congress may by law have directed.

---

[1] i.e., all federal executive and judicial officers, but not members of Congress or military personnel.

[2] In 1978, in a case involving federal judges, the Supreme Court ruled that diminution of salaries by inflation was irrelevant.

[3] The Eleventh Amendment (see below) restricts this to suits by a state against citizens of another state.

[4] i.e., such cases must originate in the Supreme Court.

[5] i.e., it hears other cases only when they are appealed to it from a lower federal court or a state court.

Section III. Treason

See Burr trial, p. 164.

1. Treason defined. Treason against the United States shall consist only in levying war against them, or in adhering to their enemies, giving them aid and comfort. No person shall be convicted of treason unless on the testimony of two witnesses to the same overt act, or on confession in open court.

2. Congress fixes punishment for treason. The Congress shall have power to declare the punishment of treason, but no attainder of treason shall work corruption of blood, or forfeiture except during the life of the person attained.[1]

Article IV. Relations of the States to One Another

Section I. Credit to Acts, Records, and Court Proceedings

Each state must respect the public acts of the others. Full faith and credit shall be given in each State to the public acts, records, and judicial proceedings of every other State.[2] And the Congress may by general laws prescribe the manner in which such acts, records, and proceedings shall be proved [attested], and the effect thereof.

Section II. Duties of States to States

1. Citizenship in one state is valid in all. The citizens of each State shall be entitled to all privileges and immunities of citizens in the several States.

This stipulation is sometimes openly flouted. In 1978 Governor Jerry Brown of California, acting on humanitarian grounds, refused to surrender to South Dakota an American Indian, Dennis Banks, who was charged with murder in an armed uprising.

2. Fugitives from justice must be surrendered by the state to which they have fled. A person charged in any State with treason, felony, or other crime, who shall flee from justice, and be found in another State, shall on demand of the executive authority [governor] of the State from which he fled, be delivered up, to be removed to the State having jurisdiction of the crime.

Basis of fugitive-slave laws; see pp. 287–289.

3. Slaves and apprentices must be returned. *No person held to service or labor in one State, under the laws thereof, escaping into another, shall, in consequence of any law or regulation therein, be discharged from such service or labor, but shall be delivered up on claim of the party to whom such service or labor may be due.*[3]

Section III. New States and Territories

e.g., Maine (1820); see p. 181.

1. Congress may admit new states. New States may be admitted by the Congress into this Union; but no new State shall be formed or erected within the jurisdiction of any other State; nor any State be formed by the junction of two or more States, or parts of States, without the consent of the legislatures of the States concerned as well as of the Congress.[4]

2. Congress regulates federal territory and property. The Congress shall have power to dispose of and make all needful rules and regulations respecting the territory or other property belonging to the United States; and nothing in this Constitution shall be so construed as to prejudice any claims of the United States, or of any particular State.

Section IV. Protection to the States

See Cleveland and the Pullman strike, pp. 444–445.

United States guarantees to states representative government and protection against invasion and rebellion. The United States shall guarantee

---

[1] i.e., punishment only for the offender; none for his or her heirs.
[2] e.g., a marriage in one is valid in all.
[3] Invalidated in 1865 by the Thirteenth Amendment (for text see below).
[4] Loyal West Virginia was formed by Lincoln in 1862 from seceded Virginia. This act was of dubious constitutionality and was justified in part by the wartime powers of the president. See pp. 314–315.

to every State in this Union a republican form of government, and shall protect each of them against invasion; and on application of the legislature, or of the executive [governor] (when the legislature cannot be convened), against domestic violence.

Article V. *The Process of Amendment*

The Constitution may be amended in four ways. The Congress, whenever two-thirds of both houses shall deem it necessary, shall propose amendments to this Constitution, or, on the application of the legislature of two-thirds of the several States, shall call a convention for proposing amendments, which, in either case, shall be valid to all intents and purposes, as part of this Constitution, when ratified by the legislatures of three-fourths of the several States, or by conventions in three-fourths thereof, as the one or the other mode of ratification may be proposed by the Congress; provided *that no amendments which may be made prior to the year one thousand eight hundred and eight shall in any manner affect the first and fourth clauses in the ninth section of the first article;*[1] and that no State, without its consent, shall be deprived of its equal suffrage in the Senate.

Article VI. *General Provisions*

This pledge honored by Hamilton, pp. 142–143.

1. The debts of the Confederation are taken over. All debts contracted and engagements entered into, before the adoption of this Constitution, shall be as valid against the United States under this Constitution, as under the Confederation.

2. The Constitution, federal laws, and treaties are the supreme law of the land. This Constitution, and the laws of the United States which shall be made in pursuance thereof; and all treaties made, or which shall be made, under the authority of the United States, shall be the supreme law of the land; and the judges in every State shall be bound thereby, anything in the Constitution or laws of any State to the contrary notwithstanding.

3. Federal and state officers bound by oath to support the Constitution. The Senators and Representatives before mentioned, and the members of the several State legislatures, and all executive and judicial officers, both of the United States and of the several States, shall be bound by oath or affirmation to support this Constitution; but no religious test shall ever be required as a qualification to any office or public trust under the United States.

Article VII. *Ratification of the Constitution*

See 1787 irregularity, pp. 131–133.

The Constitution effective when ratified by conventions in nine states. The ratification of the conventions of nine States shall be sufficient for the establishment of this Constitution between the States so ratifying the same.

Done in Convention by the unanimous consent of the States present, the seventeenth day of September in the year of our Lord one thousand seven hundred and eighty-seven and of the Independence of the United States of America the twelfth. In witness whereof we have hereunto subscribed our names.

[Signed by]

G° WASHINGTON

Presidt and Deputy from Virginia

[and thirty-eight others]

---

[1]This clause, regarding slave trade and direct taxes, became inoperative in 1808.

AMENDMENTS TO THE CONSTITUTION

Amendment I. *Religious and Political Freedom*

For background of Bill of Rights, see pp. 141–142.

Congress must not interfere with freedom of religion, speech or press, assembly, and petition. Congress shall make no law respecting an establishment of religion,[1] or prohibiting the free exercise thereof; or abridging the freedom of speech, or of the press; or the right of the people peaceably to assemble, and to petition the government for a redress of grievances.

Amendment II. *Right to Bear Arms*

The people may bear arms. A well-regulated militia being necessary to the security of a free State, the right of the people to keep and bear arms [i.e., for military purposes] shall not be infringed.[2]

Amendment III. *Quartering of Troops*

See Declaration of Independence and British quartering above.

Soldiers may not be arbitrarily quartered on the people. No soldier shall, in time of peace, be quartered in any house without the consent of the owner, nor in time of war, but in a manner to be prescribed by law.

Amendment IV. *Searches and Seizures*

A reflection of colonial grievances against the crown.

Unreasonable searches are forbidden. The right of the people to be secure in their persons, houses, papers, and effects, against unreasonable searches and seizures, shall not be violated, and no [search] warrants shall issue but upon probable cause, supported by oath or affirmation, and particularly describing the place to be searched, and the persons or things to be seized.

Amendment V. *Right to Life, Liberty, and Property*

When witnesses refuse to answer questions in court, they routinely "take the Fifth Amendment."

The individual is guaranteed certain rights when on trial and the right to life, liberty, and property. No person shall be held to answer for a capital, or otherwise infamous crime, unless on a presentment [formal charge] or indictment of a grand jury, except in cases arising in the naval forces, or in the militia, when in actual service in time of war or public danger; nor shall any person be subject for the same offense to be twice put in jeopardy of life or limb; nor shall be compelled in any criminal case to be a witness against himself, nor be deprived of life, liberty, or property, without due process of law; nor shall private property be taken for public use [i.e., by eminent domain] without just compensation.

Amendment VI. *Protection in Criminal Trials*

See Declaration of Independence above.

An accused person has important rights. In all criminal prosecutions, the accused shall enjoy the right to a speedy and public trial, by an impartial jury of the State and district wherein the crime shall have been committed, which district shall

---

[1] In 1787 "an establishment of religion" referred to an "established church," or one supported by all taxpayers, whether members or not. But the courts have often acted under this article to keep religion, including prayers, out of the public schools.

[2] The courts long held that the right to bear arms was a limited right linked to the maintenance of militias. But in the case of *District of Columbia v. Heller* in 2008, the Supreme Court defined the right to bear arms as an individual right, not contingent on "participation in some corporate body." Yet the Court still left the door open to some kinds of gun-control legislation.

have been previously ascertained by law, and to be informed of the nature and cause of the accusation; to be confronted with the witnesses against him; to have compulsory process [subpoena] for obtaining witnesses in his favor, and to have the assistance of counsel for his defense.

Amendment VII. **Suits at Common Law**

The rules of common law are recognized. In suits at common law, where the value in controversy shall exceed twenty dollars, the right of trial by jury shall be preserved, and no fact tried by a jury shall be otherwise re-examined in any court of the United States, than according to the rules of the common law.

Amendment VIII. **Bail and Punishments**

Excessive fines and unusual punishments are forbidden. Excessive bail shall not be required, nor excessive fines imposed, nor cruel and unusual punishment inflicted.

Amendment IX. **Concerning Rights Not Enumerated**

The Ninth and Tenth Amendments were bulwarks of southern states' rights before the Civil War.

The people retain rights not here enumerated. The enumeration in the Constitution, of certain rights, shall not be construed to deny or disparage others retained by the people.

Amendment X. **Powers Reserved to the States and to the People**

A concession to states' rights, p. 143.

Powers not delegated to the federal government are reserved to the states and the people. The powers not delegated to the United States by the Constitution, nor prohibited by it to the States, are reserved to the States respectively, or to the people.

Amendment XI. **Suits Against a State**

The federal courts have no authority in suits by citizens against a state. The judicial power of the United States shall not be construed to extend to any suit in law or equity, commenced or prosecuted against one of the United States by citizens of another State, or by citizens or subjects of any foreign state. [Adopted 1798.]

Amendment XII. **Election of President and Vice President**

Forestalls repetition of 1800 electoral dispute, pp. 157–158.

See 1876 disputed election. pp. 371–372.

See 1824 election, pp. 190–192.

1. Changes in manner of electing president and vice president; procedure when no presidential candidate receives electoral majority. The electors shall meet in their respective States, and vote by ballot for President and Vice President, one of whom, at least, shall not be an inhabitant of the same state with themselves; they shall name in their ballots the person voted for as President, and in distinct ballots the person voted for as Vice President, and they shall make distinct lists of all persons voted for as President, and of all persons voted for as Vice President, and of the number of votes for each, which lists they shall sign and certify, and transmit sealed to the seat of government of the United States, directed to the President of the Senate;—the President of the Senate shall, in the presence of the Senate and House of Representatives, open all the certificates and the votes shall be counted;—the person having the greatest number of votes for President shall be the President, if such number be a majority of the whole number of electors appointed; and if no person have such majority, then from the persons having the highest numbers not exceeding three on the list of those voted for as President, the House of

Representatives shall choose immediately, by ballot, the President. But in choosing the President, the votes shall be taken by States, the representation from each State having one vote; a quorum for this purpose shall consist of a member or members from two-thirds of the States, and a majority of all the States shall be necessary to a choice. And if the House of Representatives shall not choose a President whenever the right of choice shall devolve upon them, before *the fourth day of March*[1] next following, then the Vice President shall act as President, as in the case of the death or other constitutional disability of the President.

2. Procedure when no vice presidential candidate receives electoral majority. The person having the greatest number of votes as Vice President, shall be the Vice President, if such number be a majority of the whole number of electors appointed; and if no person have a majority, then from the two highest numbers on the list the Senate shall choose the Vice President; a quorum for the purpose shall consist of two-thirds of the whole number of Senators, and a majority of the whole number shall be necessary to a choice. But no person constitutionally ineligible to the office of President shall be eligible to that of Vice President of the United States. [Adopted 1804.]

Amendment XIII. Slavery Prohibited

For background, see pp. 332–333.

Slavery forbidden. 1. Neither slavery[2] nor involuntary servitude, except as a punishment for crime whereof the party shall have been duly convicted, shall exist within the United States, or any place subject to their jurisdiction.

2. Congress shall have power to enforce this article by appropriate legislation. [Adopted 1865.]

Amendment XIV. Civil Rights for Ex-slaves,[3] etc.

For background, see pp. 354–355.

For corporations as "persons," see p. 395.

1. Ex-slaves made citizens; U.S. citizenship primary. All persons born or naturalized in the United States, and subject to the jurisdiction thereof, are citizens of the United States and of the State wherein they reside. No State shall make or enforce any law which shall abridge the privileges or immunities of citizens of the United States; nor shall any State deprive any person of life, liberty, or property, without due process of law; nor deny to any person within its jurisdiction the equal protection of the laws.

Abolishes three-fifths rule for slaves, Art. I., Sec. II, para. 3.

2. When a state denies citizens the vote, its representation shall be reduced. Representatives shall be apportioned among the several States according to their respective numbers, counting the whole number of persons in each State, excluding Indians not taxed. But when the right to vote at any election for the choice of Electors for President and Vice President of the United States, Representatives in Congress, the executive and judicial officers of a State, or the members of the legislature thereof, is denied to any of the male inhabitants of such State, being twenty-one years of age and citizens of the United States, or in any way abridged, except for participation in rebellion, or other crime, the basis of representation therein shall be reduced in the proportion which the number of such make citizens shall bear to the whole number of male citizens twenty-one years of age in such State.[4]

Leading ex-Confederates denied office. See p. 355.

3. Certain persons who have been in rebellion are ineligible for federal and state office. No person shall be a Senator or Representative in Congress, or Elector of President and Vice President, or hold any office, civil or military, under the

---

[1]Changed to January 20 by the Twentieth Amendment (for text see below).

[2]The only explicit mention of slavery in the Constitution.

[3]Occasionally an offender is prosecuted under the Thirteenth Amendment for keeping an employee or other person under conditions approximating slavery.

[4]The provisions concerning "male" inhabitants were modified by the Nineteenth Amendment, which enfranchised women. The legal voting age was changed from twenty-one to eighteen by the Twenty-sixth Amendment.

United States, or under any State, who, having previously taken an oath, as a member of Congress, or as an officer of the United States, or as a member of any State legislature, or as an executive or judicial officer of any State, to support the Constitution of the United States, shall have engaged in insurrection or rebellion against the same, or given aid or comfort to the enemies thereof. But Congress may, by a vote of two-thirds of each house, remove such disability.

The ex-Confederates were thus forced to repudiate their debts and pay pensions to their own veterans, plus taxes for the pensions of Union veterans, their conquerors.

4. Debts incurred in aid of rebellion are void. The validity of the public debt of the United States, authorizing by law, including debts incurred for payment of pensions and bounties for services in suppressing insurrection or rebellion, shall not be questioned. But neither the United States nor any State shall assume or pay any debt or obligation incurred in aid of insurrection or rebellion against the United States, or any claim for the loss or emancipation of any slave; but all such debts, obligations, and claims shall be held illegal and void.

5. Enforcement. The Congress shall have power to enforce, by appropriate legislation, the provisions of this article. [Adopted 1868.]

Amendment XV. *Suffrage for Blacks*

For background, see pp. 355–357.

Black males are made voters. 1. The right of the citizens of the United States to vote shall not be denied or abridged by the United States or by any State on account of race, color, or previous condition of servitude.

2. The Congress shall have power to enforce this article by appropriate legislation. [Adopted 1870.]

Amendment XVI. *Income Taxes*

For background, see p. 497.

Congress has power to lay and collect income taxes. The Congress shall have power to lay and collect taxes on incomes, from whatever source derived, without apportionment among the several States, and without regard to any census or enumeration. [Adopted 1913.]

Amendment XVII. *Direct Election of Senators*

Senators shall be elected by popular vote. 1. The Senate of the United States shall be composed of two Senators from each State, elected by the people thereof, for six years; and each Senator shall have one vote. The electors in each State shall have the qualifications requisite for electors of [voters for] the most numerous branch of the State legislatures.

2. When vacancies happen in the representation of any State in the Senate, the executive authority of such State shall issue writs of election to fill such vacancies: Provided, that the Legislature of any State may empower the executive thereof to make temporary appointments until the people fill the vacancies by election as the Legislature may direct.

3. This amendment shall not be so construed as to affect the election or term of any Senator chosen before it becomes valid as part of the Constitution. [Adopted 1913.]

Amendment XVIII. *National Prohibition*

For background, see pp. 522–524.

The sale or manufacture of intoxicating liquors is forbidden. 1. *After one year from the ratification of this article the manufacture, sale, or transportation of intoxicating liquors within, the importation thereof into, or the exportation thereof from the United States and all territory subject to the jurisdiction thereof, for beverage purposes, is hereby prohibited.*

2. *The Congress and the several States shall have concurrent power to enforce this article by appropriate legislation.*

3. *This article shall be inoperative unless it shall have been ratified as an amendment to the Constitution by the legislatures of the several States, as provided by the Constitution, within seven years from the date of the submission thereof to the States by the Congress.* [Adopted 1919; repealed 1933 by Twenty-first Amendment.]

Amendment XIX. Woman Suffrage

For background, see p. 507.

Women guaranteed the right to vote. 1. The right of citizens of the United States to vote shall not be denied or abridged by the United States or by any State on account of sex.

2. Congress shall have power to enforce this article by appropriate legislation. [Adopted 1920.]

Amendment XX. Presidential and Congressional Terms

Shortens lame duck periods by modifying Art. I, Sec. IV, para. 2.

1. Presidential, vice presidential, and congressional terms of office begin in January. The terms of the President and Vice President shall end at noon on the 20th day of January, and the terms of Senators and Representatives at noon on the 3d day of January, of the years in which such terms would have ended if this article had not been ratified; and the terms of their successors shall then begin.

2. New meeting date for Congress. The Congress shall assemble at least once in every year, and such meeting shall begin at noon on the 3d day of January, unless they shall by law appoint a different day.

3. Emergency presidential and vice presidential succession. If, at the time fixed for the beginning of the term of the President, the President-elect shall have died, the Vice President–elect shall become President. If a President shall not have been chosen before the time fixed for the beginning of his term, or if the President-elect shall have failed to qualify, then the Vice President–elect shall act as President until a President shall have qualified; and the Congress may by law provide for the case wherein neither a President-elect nor a Vice President–elect shall have qualified, declaring who shall then act as President, or the manner in which one who is to act shall be selected, and such persons shall act accordingly until a President or Vice President shall have qualified.

4. The Congress may by law provide for the case of the death of any of the persons from whom the House of Representatives may choose a President whenever the right of choice shall have devolved upon them, and for the case of the death of any of the persons from whom the Senate may choose a Vice President whenever the right of choice shall have devolved upon them.

5. Sections 1 and 2 shall take effect on the 15th day of October following the ratification of this article.

6. This article shall be inoperative unless it shall have been ratified as an amendment to the Constitution by the Legislatures of three-fourths of the several States within seven years from the date of its submission. [Adopted 1933.]

Amendment XXI. Prohibition Repealed

For background, see p. 559.

1. Eighteenth Amendment repealed. The eighteenth article of amendment to the Constitution of the United States is hereby repealed.

2. Local laws honored. The transportation or importation into any State, Territory, or Possession of the United States for delivery or use therein of intoxicating liquors, in violation of the laws thereof, is hereby prohibited.

3. This article shall be inoperative unless it shall have been ratified as an amendment to the Constitution by conventions in the several States, as provided in the Constitution, within seven years from the date of the submission thereof to the States by the Congress. [Adopted 1933.]

Amendment XXII. Anti–Third Term Amendment

Sometimes referred to as the anti–Franklin Roosevelt amendment.

1. Presidential term is limited. No person shall be elected to the office of President more than twice, and no person who has held the office of President, or acted as President, for more than two years of a term to which some other person was elected President shall be elected to the office of President more than once. But this article shall not apply to any person holding the office of President when this article was proposed by the Congress [i.e., Truman], and shall not prevent any person who may be holding the office of President, during the term within which this article becomes operative [i.e., Truman] from holding the office of President or acting as President during the remainder of such term.

2. This article shall be inoperative unless it shall have been ratified as an amendment to the Constitution by the legislatures of three-fourths of the several States within seven years from the date of its submission to the States by the Congress. [Adopted 1951.]

Amendment XXIII. District of Columbia Vote

Designed to give the District of Columbia three electoral votes and to quiet the century-old cry of "No taxation without representation." Yet the District of Columbia still has only one nonvoting member of Congress.

1. Presidential electors for the District of Columbia. The District, constituting the seat of government of the United States, shall appoint in such manner as the Congress shall direct:

A number of electors of President and Vice President equal to the whole number of Senators and Representatives in Congress to which the District would be entitled if it were a State, but in no event more than the least populous State; they shall be in addition to those appointed by the States, but they shall be considered for the purposes of the election of President and Vice President, to be electors appointed by a State; and they shall meet in the District and perform such duties as provided by the twelfth article of amendment.

2. Enforcement. The Congress shall have the power to enforce this article by appropriate legislation. [Adopted 1961.]

Amendment XXIV. Poll Tax

Designed to end discrimination against poor people, including southern blacks who were often denied the vote through inability to pay poll taxes. See pp. 653–654.

1. Payment of poll tax or other taxes not to be prerequisite for voting in federal elections. The right of citizens of the United States to vote in any primary or other election for President or Vice President, for electors for President or Vice President, or for Senator or Representative in Congress, shall not be denied or abridged by the United States or any State by reason of failure to pay any poll tax or other tax.

2. Enforcement. The Congress shall have the power to enforce this article by appropriate legislation. [Adopted 1964.]

Amendment XXV. Presidential Succession and Disability

1. Vice president to become president. In case of the removal of the President from office or of his death or resignation, the Vice President shall become President.[1]

Gerald Ford was the first "appointed president." See p. 671.

2. Successor to vice president provided. Whenever there is a vacancy in the office of the Vice President, the President shall nominate a Vice President who shall take office upon confirmation by a majority vote of both Houses of Congress.

---

[1] The original Constitution (Art. II, Sec. I, para. 5) was vague on this point, stipulating that "the powers and duties" of the president, but not necessarily the title, should "devolve" on the vice president. President Tyler, the first "accidental president," assumed not only the powers and duties but the title as well.

3. Vice president to serve for disabled president. Whenever the President transmits to the President pro tempore of the Senate and the Speaker of the House of Representatives his written declaration that he is unable to discharge the powers and duties of his office, and until he transmits to them a written declaration to the contrary, such powers and duties shall be discharged by the Vice President as Acting President.

4. Procedure for disqualifying or requalifying president. Whenever the Vice President and a majority of either the principal officers of the executive departments or of such other body as Congress may by law provide, transmit to the President pro tempore of the Senate and the Speaker of the House of Representatives their written declaration that the President is unable to discharge the powers and duties of his office, the Vice President shall immediately assume the powers and duties of the office as Acting President.

Thereafter, when the President transmits to the President pro tempore of the Senate and the Speaker of the House of Representatives his written declaration that no inability exists, he shall resume the powers and duties of his office unless the Vice President and a majority of either the principal officers of the executive department[s] or of such other body as Congress may by law provide, transmit within four days to the President pro tempore of the Senate and the Speaker of the House of Representatives their written declaration that the President is unable to discharge the powers and duties of his office. Thereupon Congress shall decide the issue, assembling within forty-eight hours for that purpose if not in session. If the Congress, within twenty-one days after receipt of the latter written declaration, or, if Congress is not in session, within twenty-one days after Congress is required to assemble, determines by two-thirds vote of both Houses that the President is unable to discharge the powers and duties of his office, the Vice President shall continue to discharge the same as Acting President; otherwise, the President shall resume the powers and duties of his office. [Adopted 1967.]

Amendment XXVI. Lowering Voting Age

A response to the current revolt of youth. See p. 663.

1. Ballot for eighteen-year-olds. The right of citizens of the United States, who are eighteen years of age or older, to vote shall not be denied or abridged by the United States or any state on account of age.

2. Enforcement. The Congress shall have the power to enforce this article by appropriate legislation. [Adopted 1971.]

Amendment XXVII. Restricting Congressional Pay Raises

Reflects anti-incumbent sentiment of early 1990s. First proposed by James Madison in 1789; took 203 years to be ratified.

Congress not allowed to increase its current pay. No law varying the compensation for the services of the Senators and Representatives shall take effect, until an election of Representatives shall have intervened. [Adopted 1992.]

INDEX

AARP (American Association of Retired Persons), 724
Abbott, Lyman: on cities, 404
ABC (Anybody but Carter) movement, 688
ABC-1 agreement, 584
ABC powers, 500
Abilene, Kansas, 435
ABM treaty, 664
Abolition and abolitionism, 252, 260; African Americans and, 263-265; Brown, John, and, 305; early, 135, 262-263; Emancipation Proclamation and, 331, 332; feminism and, 678; Fugitive Slave Law and, 287-288; Kansas-Nebraska Act and, 294; in North, 266; propaganda in, 263; radical, 263-265; runaway slaves and, 284; southern backlash and, 265-266; violence against, 265, 266; women and, 241, 250, 263. *See also* Antislavery movement
Abortion rights: Bush, George H.W., and, 700; Reagan and, 695; right-to-life movement and, 695; *Roe v. Wade* and, 665, 679; Supreme Court on, 665, 679, 696
Abraham Lincoln Brigade, 573
Absalom, Absalom! (Faulkner), 532
Abstract expressionism, 640
Abu Ghraib prison, 723
Abzug, Bella, 678
Acadia and Acadians, 79
Accommodation: by Indians, 40, 198; by Washington, Booker T., 416
Acheson, Dean, 614, 617, 630
Acid rock, 660
Acoma, Battle of (1599), 18-19
"Acres of Diamonds" (Conwell), 395
Activism. *See* specific presidents and movements
Act of Toleration (Maryland, 1649), 28
ADA. *See* Americans with Disabilities Act
Adams, Abigail, 111, 136, 175
Adams, Charles Francis, 318, 423
Adams, Henry, 173; on Grant, 366; writings of, 423
Adams, John, 87, 423; 1796 election and, 150; 1800 election and, 156, 157-158, 158 (map); avoidance of war by, 151, 152; Boston Massacre and, 93; on commerce, 67 (map); Constitutional Convention and, 129; death of, 167; on education, 71; Federalist party and, 150, 157; at First Continental Congress, 96; France and, 150-151; Hamilton and, 151, 157; independence and, 106; Jefferson and, 150; midnight judges and, 160-161; Treaty of Paris and, 114; XYZ Affair and, 150
Adams, John Quincy, 306, 423; 1824 election and, 190-192; 1828 election and, 192-193, 193 (map); *Amistad* slave rebellion and, 262; Gag Resolution and, 266; Ghent negotiations and, 175; on Missouri Compromise, 183; nationalism of, 183, 185, 192; presidency of, 192; as secretary of state, 183-184, 185-186, 192; translation of von Gentz's work by, 115
Adams, Samuel, 60; as antifederalist, 132, 133; committees of correspondence and, 94; Constitutional Convention and, 129; First Continental Congress and, 96; as rebellion leader, 94, 97
Adamson Act (1916), 498

Adams-Onís Treaty (1819), 185. *See also* Florida Purchase Treaty (1819)
Addams, Jane, 478; on ethnic diversity, 522; Hull House and, 410, 481; as pacifist, 479; on vote for women, 420
Adjusted Compensation Act (1924), 537
Adkins v. Children's Hospital, 536, 537
Admiralty courts, 90
Adult education, 415
Adultery, 56
Adventists, 235
Adventures of Huckleberry Finn, The (Twain), 422
Adventures of Tom Sawyer, The (Twain), 422
Advertising: in 1920s, 526, 528-530; in 1950s, 629, 630; on radio, 528
Affirmative action, 652; Bush, G.H.W., and, 700; in California, 708; Clinton and, 708; Nixon and, 652, 665; Reagan and, 695-696; reverse discrimination and, 665; Supreme Court and, 723
Affluence: in 1950s, 605, 628-630; colonial, 44; in suburbs, 407; after World War II, 620-621. *See also* Prosperity
Affluent Society, The (Galbraith), 630
Affordable Care Act (Obamacare, 2010), 727, 730, 733
Afghanistan: Bush, G.W., and, 721; fundamentalist terrorists in, 721; Soviet invasion of, 683, 684; Taliban in, 721
AFL. *See* American Federation of Labor
AFL-CIO, 637
AF of L. *See* American Federation of Labor
Africa: Belgium and, 470; cultural roots from, 261; Europeans and, 12-13; formation of, 5; freed blacks to, 262-263; imperialism in, 344, 470; Portugal and, 12-13; Seven Years' War in, 81; slavery and, 2, 12-13; after World War II, 674. *See also* African Americans; Slave trade
African Americans: in 1970s, 678-679; 1976 election and, 680; in 1990s, 708; 2000 election and, 715; abolitionism and, 263-265; American Revolution and, 98-99; Black Codes and, 182, 353-354; as Buffalo Soldiers, 430; Civil Rights Act (1964) and, 651-652; in Civil War, 323, 333; Colored Farmers' National Alliance and, 380, 444; in Congress, 358; as cowboys, 435; culture of, 63, 64-65, 252; discrimination against, 53, 135, 374; draft riots and, 320; education for, 238, 239, 416; equality for, 678; farming by, 379-380; Great Migration to North, 506-507, 633; as homesteaders, 436; Jim Crow and, 374, 381, 529, 631; Ku Klux Klan and, 359-360; labor unions and, 399, 400, 401; in Lincoln's funeral procession, 342; literature by, 423, 642; as Loyalists, 99, 107; lynchings of, 374, 381, 421; migration after World War II, 624; in military, 662; mortgage loans to, 624; music of, 65, 424, 530; panic of 1873 and, 370; Philadelphia Plan and, 665; after Reconstruction era, 373-374; rights of, 653-654; Roosevelt, F.D., and, 558, 591; segregation and, 365; sharecropping and tenant farming by, 353, 374; in South, 360, 361, 365, 374, 380-381, 397; in Spanish-American War, 457; as strikebreakers, 506; subjugation of, 479; in suburbs, 710; on Supreme Court, 700; talented tenth of, 416;

voting rights for, 344, 355, 356, 381, 646-647, 653; in War of 1812, 175; woman's suffrage movement and, 421; women and, 263, 284, 420, 421; in World War II, 589; after World War II, 604. *See also* Civil rights; Civil rights movement; Desegregation; Obama, Barack; Segregation; Slaves and slavery
African Diaspora, 29, 55 (map)
African Methodist Episcopal Church, 350
Africans: in Americas, 2; as Carolina labor, 29; slavery and, 2. *See also* African Americans; Slaves and slavery
Afrikaners (Boers), 443
Agassiz, Louis, 415
Age and aging: of population, 212, 731
Agencies, federal. *See* specific agencies
Age of Innocence, The (Wharton), 422
Age of Jackson, The (Schlesinger), 209
Age of Reason, The (Paine), 233
Age of Reform, The (Hofstadter), 383
Aggression: Japanese, 548, 581, 591; before World War II, 475, 574
Agnew, Spiro T., 662, 671, 675
Agribusiness, 439; after World War II, 621
Agricultural Adjustment Act (AAA): of 1933, 553; of 1938, 556, 560
Agricultural Adjustment Administration (AAA), 559-560
Agricultural Marketing Act (1929), 543-544
Agriculture, 385, 404; in Americas, 6-7, 8; as big business, 439-440; in Caribbean region, 14; cash crops in, 226; in Civil War, 318, 321; commercialization of, 118; Coolidge and, 540; decline in, 397; Dust Bowl and, 560-561, 560 (map); in England, 23; Jefferson and, 154; mechanization of, 226, 321, 439; Mexican labor in, 709; in New Deal, 556, 559-560; plantation, 66, 256; railroads and, 227, 389; settlements and, 8; in South, 51, 348, 396; in West, 226, 436-437; in World War II, 586; after World War II, 621. *See also* Farms and farming; Planters and plantations; specific crops
Aguinaldo, Emilio, 457, 462
AIDS (acquired immunodeficiency syndrome): literature about, 717
Aid to Families with Dependent Children (AFDC), 775
Airlift: in Berlin, 611
Airplanes and airlines: jets, 628; Lindbergh and, 527; in World War I, 527
Alabama: cotton in, 221; secession of, 308, 315 (map); slavery in, 260, 261
Alabama (ship), 318
Alamo: Battle of, 205, 207; mission at, 19
Alamogordo, New Mexico, atomic testing in, 599
Alaska: gold in, 449; land bridge to, 6; purchase of, 361; Russia and, 185, 361; statehood for, 639
Alaska Natives, 434
Albany: in American Revolution, 109; as port city, 45
Albany Congress (1754), 81
Albee, Edward, 642
Albright, Madeleine, 712, 713
Alcatraz, Indian seizure of, 680
Alcohol: corn distilled into, 226; during Great Depression, 559; prohibition of, 506, 522-524; temperance movement and, 240, 482. *See also* Eighteenth Amendment

Alcott, Bronson, 247
Alcott, Louisa May, 247
Aldrich, Nelson, 490
Aleutian Islands, 592, 593
Alexander I (Russia), 175
Algeciras, Spain, international conference at, 469
Alger, Horatio, 421
Algiers, 162
Algonquin Indians, 27
Alien Laws, 152
Alito, Samuel A., Jr., 724
Allegheny Mountains, 212
Allen, Ethan, 102
Allen brothers, 126
Allende, Salvador, 664
Alliance(s): Franco-American (1778), 110, 147, 148, 149; after World War II, 613. *See also* specific alliances
Alliance for Progress, 644
Allies (World War I), 500, 501, 503; Hitler stopped by, 593; at Paris Peace Conference, 512–513; U.S. mobilization and, 505–506; war debts and, 541–542
Allies (World War II), 585; Cold War and, 609; D-Day landing by, 594–595; end of war and, 599–602; Nuremberg war crimes trial and, 610; second front and, 593–594
All the King's Men (Warren), 642
Almshouses, 65
Al Qaeda, 713, 721; Iraq and, 722, 723; Obama and, 723; in Pakistan, 728
Altgeld, John Peter, 400, 445, 477
Amendments. *See* specific amendments
America(s): Africans in, 13; agriculture in, 6–7, 8; formation of, 5; land bridge to, 6, 7 (map); peopling of, 6–7; voyages to, 15 (map). *See also* Colonies and colonization; Exploration; New World; specific locations
America First Committee, 575
American Anti-Slavery Society, 262, 263
American Association of Retired Persons (AARP), 724
American Colonization Society, 263
American Dilemma, An (Myrdal), 631
American Diplomacy (Kennan), 516
American dream, 390
American Expeditionary Forces (AEF), 508, 509
American Federation of Labor (AFL), 400–401, 506
American Indians. *See* Native Americans; specific groups
American International Group (AIG), 726
Americanization, 47, 462; of immigrants, 479
American Legion, 537
American Liberty League, 564
American Missionary Association, 350
American Negro Slavery (Phillips), 267
American party, 302. *See also* Know-Nothing party
American Peace Society, 240
American plan, 520
American Political Tradition and the Men Who Made It, The (Hofstadter), 209
American Populism (McMath), 383
American Protective Association, 412
American Railway Union, 445
American Revolution (1775–1783), 344; African Americans in, 98–99; allies and enemies in, 97, 98; American strengths and weaknesses in, 97–98; armed forces in, 97; battles in, 97, 99, 101, 102–103, 104 (map), 108–109, 113 (map); British strengths and weaknesses in, 97–98; British surrender at Yorktown, 114; in Canada, 103–104, 104 (map); as colonial conflict, 147; diplomacy in, 109–110; events leading to, 88–97; finances in, 97, 98, 114; France and, 98, 109–110, 112, 114; French Revolution and, 115, 146, 147; globalization of, 110, 112; Hessian soldiers in, 97, 103, 105, 108; historians' viewpoints on, 116; impact of, 3, 120, 135, 136; independence and, 2; Loyalists in, 97, 103, 106–108; militiamen in, 97, 98; Native Americans in, 30–31, 97, 112; navy in, 108, 113–114; in North, 104 (map); Patriots in, 98, 105, 106, 121; privateering in, 113–114; roots of, 88; in South, 103, 112, 113 (map); Treaty of Paris after, 114–115; at Valley Forge, 98; in West, 112–113; women in, 111, 136
American Samoa, 453
"American Scholar, The" (Emerson), 247
American Slavery, American Freedom (Morgan), 47, 75
American Slavery As It Is (Weld), 263
Americans with Disabilities Act (ADA, 1990), 700
American System (1824), 178
American system of manufacturing, 390
American Temperance Society, 240
American Tobacco Company, 396
American Tragedy, An (Dreiser), 531
America's Hidden Success (Schwarz), 668
Amish, 220
Amistad (ship), slave rebellion on, 262
Amman, Jacob, 220
Amnesty, for ex-Confederates, 369
"Amos 'n' Andy," 528
Amputation, in Civil War, 320
Anabaptists, 220
Anarchy and anarchism, 127, 400, 412, 445
Anasazi peoples, 8
Ancient Order of Hibernians, 216
Anderson, Fred, 116
Anderson, Jourdon, 352
Anderson, Sherwood, 532
Andrews, Charles, 116
Andros, Edmund, 41
Angels in America (Kushner), 717
Anglican Church (Church of England): in colonies, 2, 32, 69; disestablishment of, 135; English Royalists and, 41; Loyalists and, 108; Puritans and, 36, 37
Anglo-American Convention (1818), 184, 273
Anglo-American relations: in early 1800s, 271, 273; Reagan-Thatcher and, 689
Anglos: in California, 279; in Southwest, 439; zoot-suit riots and, 589
Anglo-Saxons: Strong on superiority of, 452
Anglo-Spanish wars, 30
Angola: Cuba and, 681; slaves from, 53
Animals, 13, 14, 213
Annapolis, naval academy at, 248
Annapolis Convention (1786), 128
Anne (England), 73
Annexation: of Hawaii, 453–454, 457; of Philippines, 458; of Puerto Rico, 344, 458, 459–460; of Texas, 206, 269, 272, 273
Antarctica, 5
Antebellum era. *See* South
Anthony, Susan B., 238, 241, 357, 420
Anthracite coal mines, 482
Anti-abortion movement, 695
Anti-ballistic missile (ABM) treaty, 664
Anticlericalism, 233
Anticolonialism, 635
Anti-crime bill: Clinton and, 705
Antietam: Battle of (1862), 330–331
Antifederalists, 131–134, 132 (map), 141
Antifeminism, 679
Antiforeignism. *See* Anti-immigrant sentiment

Anti-immigrant sentiment, 218–219, 302, 344, 364, 375, 410–413
Anti-Imperialist League, 459
Antilynching crusade, 421
Anti-Masonic party, 201, 202
Anti-miscegenation laws: repeal of, 631
Antin, Mary, 408
Antinomianism, 38
Antipolygamy laws (1862 and 1882), 236
Anti-Saloon League, 482
Anti-Semitism: Holocaust and, 576. *See also* Jews and Judaism; Ku Klux Klan
Antislavery movement: Fugitive Slave Law and, 288–289; Kansas and, 298–300; Mennonites and, 53; Mexican War and, 276, 280–281; petitions to Congress, 266; Quakers and, 44, 135, 262; on race and slavery, 262; after Revolution, 135; in South, 252; Whigs and, 289; women in, 241, 250. *See also* Abolition and abolitionism
Anti-sweatshop law, 410
Antiterrorism policies, 728
Antitrust laws: farmers and, 540; Roosevelt, T., and, 483; Sherman Anti-Trust Act and, 396; Wilson on, 493. *See also* Corporations; Trust(s)
Antiwar movement: in Vietnam War, 656, 658, 661, 662; in World War I, 505
Anzio, 594
Apache Indians, 10 (map), 14, 429, 430
Apollo mission, 643
Appalachian region: formation of, 5, 6; Indians of, 32; mountain whites in, 62, 257–259; movement west of, 84; textile mills in, 397
Appeal to the Colored Citizens of the World (Walker), 263
Appeasement: before World War II, 574
Apple (corporation), 729
Appliances: in 1920s, 526; after World War II, 620
Appomattox Courthouse, Lee's surrender at, 341–342
Apprenticeships, 52
Arabic (ship), sinking of, 501
Arabs and Arab world: oil embargo and, 667; Suez crisis and, 636–637; Truman and, 613. *See also* Middle East; specific locations
Arafat, Yasir, 713
Arapaho Indians, 430
Araucanian people (Argentina), 442
Architecture: City Beautiful movement and, 424; colonial, 72; Gothic, 245; Greek Revival, 245; International Style of, 640; postmodern, 716; skyscrapers and, 406; Spanish, 279
Ardennes Forest, battle in, 598
Argentina: frontier in, 442; immigrants in, 215, 442; revolution in, 196
Argonne Forest, World War I in, 511
Ariel (Plath), 642
Aristocracy: French Revolution and, 147; planters in, 255–256, 261
Arizona, 427, 437; Latinos in, 709; Mexican migrants in, 499; Native Americans and, 430
Arkansas: Dust Bowl in, 560 (map), 561; secession by, 314, 315 (map)
Arkansas River region, 78
Arkies, 560, 561
Armada (Spain), 22–23
Armed forces: African Americans in, 323, 333, 430, 457; in Civil War, 316, 322, 323, 327, 333; desegregation of, 617, 619; in Hawaii, 454; Indian removal and, 198; Indian Wars and, 430, 431 (map); under Jefferson, 161–162; Lincoln and, 319; McCarthy, Joseph, and, 617; in Mexican War, 280; segregation of, 591; in Spanish-American War, 457; strikes and, 374, 380, 445; in War of 1812, 172;

women in, 322. *See also* Military; Soldiers; Wars and warfare; specific branches, battles, and wars
Armed Neutrality: in American Revolution, 112
Armistice: in Korean War, 630; in Spanish-American War, 458; in World War I, 511
Armitage, David, 116
Armour, Philip, 394, 435
Arms and armaments. *See* Weapons
Arms race. *See* Nuclear arms race
Armstrong, Louis, 530, 531, 532
Army. *See* Armed forces; Military
Army-McCarthy hearings, 617
Army of the Potomac, 327, 328, 333
Arnold, Benedict, 102, 103, 104 (map), 109, 112
Aroostook War (1842), 271
Arsenal of democracy, U.S. as, 579
Art(s): colonial, 72; modernism in, 531–532; naturalism in, 421, 423; New Deal and, 557; popular, 717; postmodern, 716–717; realism in, 421, 423–424; regionalism in, 421, 423; after World War II, 640. *See also* specific arts and artists; specific types
Arthur, Chester A., 376
Arthur, T.S., 240
Articles of Confederation (1777): amending, 125; Constitution vs., 130; powers of government under, 125; ratification of, 98, 124; taxes under, 125; trade under, 125; weaknesses of, 118
Artisans: African, 63; at Oneida Community, 244
"Aryans": in Nazi Germany, 600
Ashburton, Lord (Alexander Baring), 271
Asia and Asian Americans: Hawaiian labor from, 454; immigration and, 374, 469, 653; imperialism and, 470–471; isolationism from, 571; rivalries in, 469; Russia and, 442; trade routes to, 11, 12 (map); in West, 439; after World War II, 674. *See also* specific groups and locations
As I Lay Dying (Faulkner), 532
Assassinations. *See* specific individuals
Assembly lines, 221
Assimilation: of ethnic groups, 586; of Native Americans, 198, 432–434, 635
Assistant, The (Malamud), 642
Associated Press, 418
Association, The, 96
Assumption, of state debts, 142–143
Astor, John Jacob, 230
"Asymmetrical warfare," 721
Atchison, David, 298 (map)
Atchison, Topeka and Santa Fe Railroad, 388
Athletics. *See* Sports
Atlanta, in Civil War, 338, 340
Atlanta Constitution, 396, 397
Atlanta University, 416
Atlantic Charter (1941), 580, 674
Atlantic Monthly, 418, 421
Atlantic Ocean region: economy of, 13; slave trade in, 54, 55 (map)
Atmospheric testing: prohibition of, 644
Atomic bombs: justification of, 602; Soviet, 614; U.S. bombing of Japan, 599; in World War II, 599; Yalta conference and, 608. *See also* Nuclear weapons
Atomic Energy Commission, 614
Attu, in World War II, 592, 593
Attucks, Crispus, 93
Auctions: farm, 440; slave, 260
Audiotapes: of Nixon, 671, 672
Audubon Society, 486, 487
Auschwitz, 576
Austerlitz, Battle of, 164

Austin, Stephen, 205
Australia: formation of, 5; frontier in, 442; gold in, 449; immigrants to, 408
Australian ballot, 480
Austria: France and, 145; after World War II, 610
Austria-Hungary, World War I and, 500
Authoritarianism: in 1930s, 557. *See also* Dictators; Fascism
Autobiography (Franklin), 72, 245
Autobiography of Alice B. Toklas, The (Stein), 531
Automobiles and automobile industry: in 1920s, 526–527; in 2000s, 726; Ford and, 391, 474; growth of, 526–527; Model T and, 26, 391, 527; oil industry and, 393; social change and, 527
Aviation. *See* Airplanes
Awakening, The (Chopin), 423
Awful Disclosures (Monk), 218
Axis powers (World War II), 572. *See also* Italy; Japan; Nazi Germany
Ayers, Edward L., 383
Azores, 12
Aztecs, 6, 7, 8, 16, 17

Babbitt (Lewis), 532
Baby boom and boomers, 588; in 1960s, 661; in 1970s, 673; Clinton as, 704; Kennedy, John F., and, 647; retirement ages of, 731; after World War II, 624
Backcountry, 2, 73, 257
Bacon, Nathaniel, and Bacon's Rebellion, 51, 53, 59
Baer, George F., 482
Bahamas, 13
Bailey, James A., 424
Bailyn, Bernard, 47, 116
Baker, Anthony St. John, 177
Baker, Josephine, 631
Baker, Ray Stannard, 479
Bakke, Allan, 679
Balanced budget, 708
Balboa, Vasco Nuñez, 16
Baldwin, James, 642
Balkans: NATO and, 713
Ballinger, Richard, 490
Baltimore, Lord, 28
Baltimore, Maryland, 140, 174, 175, 289, 305, 306
Bancroft, George, 116, 248–249, 280
Bank(s) and banking: American System and, 178; Great Recession and, 553, 727; loan to federal government, 382; national system of, 321, 345; in New Deal, 555; panic of 1819 and, 179; panic of 1837 and, 203; western "wildcat," 180, 201, 202; Wilson and, 497. *See also* Economy; Federal Reserve entries
Bank notes: satiric political humor and (1837), 204. *See also* Currency
Bank of the United States: Hamilton vs. Jefferson on, 143–144; Jackson and, 199–200, 201; Jeffersonian Democrats and, 143–144; land speculation and, 179; *McCulloch v. Maryland* and, 182–183, 200; nationalism and, 178; revival of, 203–204; Tyler and, 271
Bankruptcy: laws in colonies, 89; in panic of 1873, 370; of railroads, 389
Bank War, 199–201
Baptists, 413, 350; black, 350; class and, 235; Fundamentalism and, 525; in Old Northwest, 182; revivalism and, 234; in Rhode Island, 39; slavery and, 235
Baraka, Imamu Amiri (Le Roi Jones), 642
Barbados: Carolina settlers from, 29; slave code (1661) in, 29
Barbary States, pirates and, 162, 178

Barbed wire, 435, 437
Barnard College, 239
Barnum, Phineas T., 424
Barter: Indian trade and, 27
Barton, Bruce, 526
Barton, Clara, 322
Baruch, Bernard, 506
Baseball: in late 1800s, 425; in 1920s, 526; franchise changes in 1950s, 629
Basketball, 425; in 1950s, 629
Bastille: storming of, 146
Bataan Death March, 591
Batista, Fulgencio, 572, 638
Battle of Britain, 576–578
Battles. *See* specific battles and wars
Bay Colony. *See* Massachusetts Bay Colony
Bay of Pigs invasion (Cuba), 644
Beale, Howard K., 362, 472
Beard, Charles, 137, 310, 383
Beard, Mary, 310, 383
Bear Flag Republic, 277
Beat Generation, 640, 660
Beatles, 629, 660
Beavers: trapping of, 78
Becker, Carl, 116, 137
Beecher family: Catharine, 224, 241, 263; Henry Ward, 263, 298, 419; Lyman, 263. *See also* Stowe, Harriet Beecher
Beer: German immigrants and, 217
Beer and Wine Revenue Act (1933), 553
Before the Storm (Perlstein), 668, 701
Begin, Menachem, 680–681
Beijing: Tiananmen Square protest in, 697. *See also* China
Belgium, 271, 470; in World War II, 575
Belknap, William, 369
Bell, Alexander Graham, 392
Bell, Daniel, 701
Bell, John, 306, 307 (map)
Bellamy, Edward, 419
Bellegrove Plantation (Louisiana), 264
Bell Jar, The (Plath), 642
Beloved (Morrison), 717
Benedict, Michael, 362
Benedict, Ruth, 558
Benevolent societies, 350
Ben Hur:... (Wallace), 421
Benson, Lee, 209
Benton, Thomas Hart, 275
Berger, Victor L., 490
Bering land bridge, 6, 7 (map)
Berkeley, California: Free Speech Movement in, 660
Berkeley, William, 51
Berlin, Germany: airlift in, 611; end of World War II and, 598; military occupation of, 610–611
Berlin, Ira, 267
Berlin Wall, 643, 697
Bernstein, Barton J., 568, 602
Bessemer-Kelly process, 393
Bethune, Mary McLeod, 558
Beveridge, Albert J., 458
Beyond Entitlements (Meade), 668
Bible: Darwinism and, 415; Fundamentalists and, 525; Luther on, 35; reading in school, 664
Bible Belt South, 525, 639
Bible Commonwealth: Massachusetts as, 38–39
Bible Communism, 244
Bicameral Congress, 129
Bicentennial, 680
Biddle, Nicholas, 200, 201
Biden, Joseph ("Joe"): 2008 election and, 725

Big business, 398; agriculture as, 439–440; cattle raising as, 435; conservation and, 487; muckrakers and, 478–479; New Deal and, 561; railroads as, 389; support for, 374. *See also* Business; Commerce; Corporations
Bigelow, Kathryn, 717
Big Five, 610
Big Four (Allies): at Paris Peace Conference, 512; after World War II, 610
Big Four (railroad backers), 387
Big Four legislative programs: of Johnson, L.B., 653
Big government, 590, 682; Carter and, 688; conservation and, 487; Obama and, 727; Reagan on, 687, 688
Big stick policy: of Roosevelt, T., 466, 466 (map), 467, 483, 489
Big Three (Allies): at Tehran, 594, 596; at Yalta, 608
Big Two (Allies): in World War II, 594
Billion-Dollar Congress, 379
Bill of rights: absence in Constitution, 132, 133; in state constitutions, 122
Bill of Rights (U.S.), 141–142
Billy the Kid, 442
Bin Laden, Osama, 713, 721, 723, 728
Biology: theology and, 525
Biracial Americans, 716
Birds: conservation of, 487
Birmingham, Alabama: church bombing in, 647; King in, 647
Birth control, 419, 420; movement for, 528; in Oneida Colony, 243; "pill" and, 660; Supreme Court ruling on, 664; as taboo topic, 224–225
Birth of a Nation (movie), 528
Birthrate: in Chesapeake region, 50; decline in, 420; in New England, 55; of New Immigrants, 410; population increase and, 50, 214
Bismarck, Otto von, 220, 344
Bison. *See* Buffalo
Bitter Cry of the Children, The (Spargo), 479
Black belt, 261
Black Codes, 182, 353–354
Black Culture and Black Consciousness (Levine), 267
Black Elk (Oglala Sioux), 432, 433
Blackface performance, 529
Blackfoot Indians, 14
Black Friday (September 24, 1868), 368
Black Hawk (Sauk chief), 199
Black Hawk War (1832), 199
Black Hills, gold in, 430
Black Legend, 19
Black list: of labor agitators, 398
Black Loyalists, exodus of, 99, 107
Black Methodists, 64–65
Black Monday (October 19, 1987), 698
Black Muslims. *See* Nation of Islam
Black Panther party, 654
Black Power movement, 654–655, 668
Blacks. *See* African Americans; Africans; Slaves and slavery
Black Star Line Steamship Company, 530
Black studies programs, 654
Black Tuesday, 544
Blackwell, Elizabeth, 241, 243, 322
Bladensburg, in War of 1812, 174
Blaine, James G., 371, 376–377, 378
Blake, Eubie, 532
Bleeding Kansas, 298 (map), 300
Bleeding Sumner, 300–301
Blessed Among Nations (Rauchway), 383
Blithedale Romance, The (Hawthorne), 243
Blockade: of Berlin, 611; in Mexican War, 280; by North (Union, Civil War), 314, 316, 317, 319, 321, 324, 328–329; in War of 1812, 173; in World War I, 501, 511
Blockade running, 316, 328–329
Bloomer, Amelia, 241, 242, 243
Blue-collar jobs, 409, 628–629
Blue laws: in Pennsylvania, 44
Blues music, 528
Boarding schools, for Indian children, 432
Boat people, from Vietnam, 677
Boats. *See* Ships and shipping
Boehner, John, 727, 731
Boeing Company, 628
Boers, 443, 453
Boer War, 467
Bohlen, Charles, 597
Boldness policy, of Dulles, 635
Boll weevils, southern Democrats as, 689
Bolshevik Revolution (1917), 519; U.S. and, 608
Bolsheviks: fears of, 519; in World War I, 508. *See also* Soviet Union
Bombs and bombings: atomic bombs and, 599, 602; of Cambodia, 666–667; Haymarket, 400; of Japan, 593; of Nazi Germany, 593; of Oklahoma City Federal Building, 706; of Vietnam, 656, 666
Bonds: for Civil War financing, 321
Bonneville, Lake, 6
Bonus Expeditionary Force (BEF, Bonus Army), 546, 548
Books: in late 1800s, 418; textbook reforms, 237. *See also* Literature
Boom-and-bust cycles: after World War I, 540
Boomers, in Oklahoma land rush, 437
Boomtowns, 434
Boone, Daniel, 84
Booth, John Wilkes, 342
Borah, William, 514
Border ruffians, 298
Borders. *See* Boundaries
Border States, 314–315, 330, 341 (map); Emancipation Proclamation and, 331, 332
Bork, Robert, 696
Borneo, 470
Bosnia, 713
Boss (political), 376, 378; immigrants and, 408–410; Tweed as, 358, 368, 369, 377, 408
Boston: in American Revolution, 103; British troops in, 41; committees of correspondence in, 94; Irish immigrants in, 215; population of, 61, 140; sewage system in, 214; tax protests in, 94
Boston Against Busing (Formisano), 701
Boston Associates, 224
Bostonians, The (James), 422
Boston Massacre (1770), 93
Boston Port Act (1774), 95
Boston Tea Party (1773), 94, 95
Boundaries: Britain and, 95, 115, 273; British Guiana-Venezuela dispute over, 453; of Louisiana Purchase, 165 (map); New Mexico-Texas dispute over, 284; of Oregon, 273, 275, 275 (map); of Poland, 675; of Texas, 205, 275; Treaty of Paris and, 115; of tribal territories, 62; Turner on, 449; U.S.-Canadian, 271
"Bounty brokers," 320
Bourbon monarchy, 147
Bourne, Randolph, 522, 715
Bowie, James, 205
Boxer Rebellion (China), 465
Boxing, 425, 526
Boycotts: colonial, 96; of Olympic Games, 684; of segregated buses, 632
Boyle, Caleb, 153
Bozeman Trail, 430

Bracero program, 588, 634
Braddock, Edward, 81
Bradford, William, 37, 49
Brain Trust, 552
Brandeis, Louis D.: on banking system, 497; on ethnic diversity, 522; on Supreme Court, 498; women's labor and, 481
Brandywine Creek, Battle of, 99, 109
Brant, Joseph (Mohawk chief), 112
Brazil: slaves in, 259
Breakers: slave drivers as, 261
Breckinridge, John C., 305, 306, 307 (map)
Breed's Hill, 102
Breen, T.H., 116
Bretton Woods Conference (1944), 609–610
Bretton Woods system, 674
Brewer, Jan, 731
Brezhnev, Leonid, 661, 683
Bricker, John W., 595, 617
Brief Wondrous Life of Oscar Wao, The (Diaz), 717
Brinkley, Alan, 568, 701
Britain: Battle of, 576–578. *See also* England (Britain)
British Broadcasting Corporation (BBC), 543
British East India Company, 94
British Empire, 2. *See also* England (Britain)
British Guiana, Venezuela and, 453
British West Indies, 28–29. *See also* West Indies
Broadcast television, 717
Brock, Isaac, 172
"Brokeback Mountain" (Proulx), 717
Brook Farm, 243
Brooklyn Bridge, 406
Brooklyn Dodgers, 631
Brooks, Preston S., 300–301
Brotherhood of Sleeping Car Porters, 589
Brown, John, 253, 285; at Harpers Ferry, 304–305; at Pottawatomie Creek, 300
Brown, Moses, 219
Brown, Robert, 116, 137
Brownson, Orestes, 218
Brown University, 71
Brown v. Board of Education of Topeka, Kansas, 634
Bruce, Blanche K., 358
Bryan, William Jennings: 1896 election and, 383, 445–448, 448 (map); 1900 election and, 465; 1908 election and, 488; 1912 election and, 492; Cross of Gold speech of, 441, 446; free silver and, 382; in Scopes trial, 525; on trusts, 477
Bryant, William Cullen, 246
B-29 bombers, 593
Buccaneers, 22
Buchanan, James, 300, 301, 302, 308, 378
Buck, Pearl S., 558
Buckley, William F., 652
Budget: balanced, 708; crises in, 731
Budget deficits: Bush, George H.W., and, 700; Bush, George W., and, 721; Carter and, 681; Cleveland and, 381; Clinton and, 705; Obama and, 727; Reagan and, 690, 694–695
Buena Vista, Battle of, 277–278, 277 (map)
Buenos Aires, 405
Buffalo (bison), 14, 213, 365, 389, 429, 431–432, 433
Buffalo, New York, 229
Buffalo Hunt, The (Remington), 429
Buffalo Soldiers, 430
Buffer colony: Georgia as, 32
Bulfinch, Charles, 177
Bulgaria, 501, 608
Bulge, Battle of the, 598
Bullion: from New World, 15

Bull moose Progressives, 492–493, 502
Bull Run (Manassas Junction): First Battle of (1861), 327; Second Battle of (1862), 329–330
Bunau-Varilla, Philippe, 467
Bundy, McGeorge, 602
Bunker Hill, Battle of, 102–103
Bureau of Corporations, 483
Bureaus of government. *See* specific bureaus
Burger, Warren E., as Chief Justice, 665
Burgoyne, John ("Gentleman Johnny"), 109
Burke, Edmund, 97
Burma (Myanmar): Britain and, 470; in World War II, 591
Burma Road, 591
Burnaby, Andrew, 83
Burned-Over District, 235
Burnham, Daniel, 424
Burnham, Thomas Mickell, 191
Burnside, A.E., 333
Burr, Aaron, 158, 158 (map), 163–164
Bus boycott, in Montgomery, 632
Bush, George Herbert Walker: 1988 election and, 696; 1992 election and, 704; Cold War and, 696–698; home front and, 700; Panama and, 699
Bush, George Walker: 2000 election and, 714–715, 715 (map); 2004 election and, 723–724; Afghanistan and, 721; Iraq and, 722–723; Kyoto Treaty and, 721; September 11, 2001, terrorist attacks and, 721
Bushman, Richard, 75
Business: in 1890s depression, 381; Carter and, 681; in Civil War, 321; Coolidge and, 540; foreign investment in, 391; Harding and, 537, 538, 539; Kennedy, John F., and, 643; in panic of 1873, 370; policy toward, 364; political mobilization of, 682; taxation and, 533; Wilson and, 497. *See also* Corporations; Trust(s)
Business class, 402
Business organization: forms of, 222, 390, 392; horizontal integration, 392; vertical integration, 392
Butler, Andrew, 300
Butler, Benjamin F., 360, 369
Butler, Elihu, 199
Butow, R.J.C., 602
Butternut region: 1864 election in, 341 (map); Civil War and, 314; Emancipation Proclamation and, 332
Butternuts, 182
Byrd, Harry E., 639n

Cabinet (furniture): 17th century, 46
Cabinet (presidential): establishment of, 141. *See also* specific presidents
Cable television, 717
Cabot, John (Giovanni Caboto), 15 (map), 18
Cabrillo, Juan Rodriquez, 19
Cadillac, Antoine, 79
Cahokia: Fort, 79, 113; settlement at, 8
Calhoun, John C., 256, 278, 288, 289; nullification and, 195; as secretary of war, 186; on slavery, 284–285; Whigs and, 202
California: acquisition of, 269, 275–276; agriculture as big business in, 439–440; Chinese immigrants in, 374, 375; cotton in, 286n; Dust Bowl migrants in, 560 (map), 561; as free state, 284, 287; Japanese immigrants in, 469–470, 587; Latinos in, 709; Mexican migrants in, 499; Mexican War and, 277, 281, 282; military spending in, 698; population of, 275, 622; progressive reforms in, 480; Proposition 13 in, 689; Proposition 209 in, 708; Reagan as governor of, 688; Spain and, 19; tax revolt in (1978), 683; University of, 660; water for, 700

California Bear Flag Republic, 277
California gold rush, 279, 284, 290
Californios, 279
Callender, James, 152, 159
Call of the Wild, The (London), 422, 487
Calvinism, 35, 58, 233
Cambodia, 470; Vietnam War and, 663, 666–667
Cambridge University, 71
Campaigns (political): of 1828, 192–193; of 1840, 206–207; of 1896, 445–447; whispering, 157. *See also* Elections
Camp David, Maryland: Eisenhower-Khrushchev meeting at, 638
Camp David Agreement (1978), 681
Camp meetings, 234
Canada: in American Revolution, 103–104, 104 (map); border with Maine, 271; British in, 60; *Caroline* incident and, 271; France and, 77–79; frontier in, 126, 442, 443; gold in Klondike of, 449; immigrants to, 408; Iroquois in, 31; as New France, 77–79; North-West Mounted Police in, 442, 443; Quebec Act and, 95, 96 (map), 103; rebellions in, 203, 271; runaway slaves to, 284; Treaty of Paris and, 83; War of 1812 and, 172–174, 177
Canadian Shield, 5, 6
Canals: across Isthmus of Panama, 466–468; Erie, 178, 227; in transportation revolution, 118. *See also* specific locations
Canal Zone, 468
Canary Islands, 12
Canning, George, 185, 186
Cape Breton Island, 79
Cape Colony, 443
Capital city: Philadelphia as, 109. *See also* District of Columbia; Washington, D.C.
Capital investment: money for, 391; for slaves, 256
Capitalism, 395; free-market, 209; growth of, 15; industrial, 402; New Deal and, 567, 568
Capitol (building): burning of, 174
Capone, Al ("Scarface"), 524
Capper-Volstead Act (1921), 540
Caravel, 12
Caribbean region: during Cold War, 692, 692 (map); colonies in, 28–29; slavery in, 21, 28, 29, 54; Spain and, 15; sugar industry in, 21, 28–29; U.S. and, 466 (map), 467, 468, 489, 498, 499 (map), 692; War of Jenkins's Ear in, 79. *See also* West Indies; specific locations
Carlisle Indian School, 432
Carmichael, Stokely, 654, 678
Carnegie, Andrew: public libraries and, 418; in steel industry, 379, 393; vertical integration and, 392
Carolina: Barbados settlers in, 29; colonization of, 29–32; Indians of, 29; separation of, 31; slaves in, 29. *See also* North Carolina; South Carolina
Caroline affair (1837), 271
Carpenter, (Mrs.) Herbert, 475
Carpentier, Georges, 526
Carpetbaggers, 358, 528
Carranza, Venustiano, 500
Cars. *See* Automobiles and automobile industry
Carson, Rachel, 486, 665
Carter, James Earl, Jr. ("Jimmy"): 1976 election and, 680; 1980 election and, 688; economy, energy, and, 681–682; foreign policy of, 680–681; human rights and, 680–681; Iran hostage crisis and, 683–684; "malaise speech" of, 681, 682; Nobel Peace Prize and, 688; Panama and, 681

Carthage, Illinois, 236, 237 (map)
Cartier, Jacques, 18
Cartwright, Peter, 234
Carver, George Washington, 416
Casablanca conference (1943), 594
Cascade Mountains, 5, 6
Cash-and-carry policy, 575
Cash-crop agriculture, 226
Cash registers, 392
Cass, Lewis, 283, 284
Cassatt, Mary, 424
Castro, Fidel, 638, 644, 709
Casualties: in Iraq War, 728; in Korean War, 630; in Persian Gulf War, 700; in Philippines insurgency, 462; in Spanish-American War, 457; in Vietnam War, 656, 676. *See also* specific battles and wars
Catawba Indians, 27
Catch-22 (Heller), 22
Cather, Willa, 531
Catherine the Great (1683–1727), 112
Catholic Church: abortion and, 679, 696; in colonies, 28, 32, 39; Democrats and, 371; French Huguenots and, 77; French Revolution and, 147; immigrants and, 217, 218, 220, 302, 407–408; in Ireland, 22; Kennedy, J.F., and, 639, 639 (map); in Maryland, 28; in New France, 77, 78; New Immigrants and, 407–408, 414; in New Mexico, 19; in Philippines, 458; of Polish immigrants, 523; Protestant Reformation and, 22, 35–36; reforms in 1960s, 660; in Rhode Island, 39; Smith, Alfred E., and, 542
Catlin, George, 78, 214, 433
Cat on a Hot Tin Roof (Williams), 642
Catt, Carrie Chapman, 420, 507
Cattle: long-horned, 435; in North America, 14; on Plains, 389, 435
Cattle drives, railroads and, 435
Cavalry, in Civil War, 316, 328
Cavour, Camillo di, 344
Cayuga Indians, 30, 112
Census: by 1669, 25; of 1790, 140; of 1890, 411; of 1900, 411; of 1980, 213 (map); of 2000, 715–716. *See also* Population
Central America: during Cold War, 692, 692 (map); filibustering in, 290; immigrants from, 709; Mayans in, 6; peopling of, 6, 7 (map); Reagan and, 692. *See also* Latin America; specific locations
Central Europe: Soviets and, 608
Central government. *See* Government (U.S.)
Central High School, Little Rock, 634
Central Intelligence Agency. *See* CIA
Central Pacific Railroad, 387, 388
Central Powers (World War I), 500
Century of Dishonor, A (Helen Hunt Jackson), 432
Chabon, Michael, 717
Chain Reaction (Edsall and Edsall), 701
Champlain, Lake: in American Revolution, 103, 109; in War of 1812, 172, 173
Champlain, Samuel de, 77
Chancellorsville, Virginia, battle at, 333
Chants Democratic (Wilentz), 209
Chappaquiddick, Kennedy, Edward, and, 688
Chapultepec, battle at, 280
Charities: depression of 1890s and, 381
Charles I (England), 29, 37, 39, 40
Charles II (England), 29, 39, 41, 43, 51
Charleston (Charles Town), 305; in American Revolution, 103, 112; after Civil War, 349; Loyalists in, 103, 108; population of, 61, 140; religious toleration in, 29; Vesey rebellion in, 195

Charters: colonial, 24, 28, 37, 39; of Connecticut, 39, 41; of Massachusetts, 37, 41; of Rhode Island, 39, 41; of United Nations, 610; of Virginia Company, 24, 28
Chase, Salmon, 339, 340
Château-Thierry, Battle of, 509
Chattanooga, Battle of, 337
Chattel: slaves as, 259
Chautauqua movement, 415
Chavez, Cesar, 709
Cheap-money supporters, 370
Checkers Speech (Nixon), 630
Checks and balances, 131, 135
Cheever, John, 640
Cheney, Richard, 714, 722
Cherokee Indians: accommodation by, 198; in Appalachian region, 32; in Civil War, 315; population of, 10; Trail of Tears and, 198, 199
Chesapeake affair, 164
Chesapeake region: agriculture in, 66; Civil War in, 329; colonies in, 25-28; cultural clashes in, 25-26; English colonies in, 25-26; environment of, 50; freemen in, 51; in Revolution, 114; slaves in, 27, 63; tobacco in, 27-28, 50-51, 63; War of 1812 and, 174
Chesnutt, Charles W., 423
Cheyenne, Wyoming, 435
Cheyenne Indians, 429, 430
Chiang Kai-shek. *See* Jiang Jieshi
Chicago, 292, 364, 405; Dearborn Street in (c. 1900), 365; Democratic National Convention (1968) in, 658; fire in (1871), 407; gang wars of 1920s in, 524; Haymarket Square episode in, 400; Hull House in, 410; immigrants in, 408; meatpacking industry in, 485; population of, 214; Pullman strike in, 445; race riot in (1919), 507; Republican convention in (1920), 515; Sanitary Fair in, 322; skyscrapers in, 406; stockyards in, 435; World's Columbian Exposition in, 424. *See also* Illinois
Chicago Tribune: 1948 election and, 620
Chickamauga, battle of, 337
Chickasaw Indians, 198, 315
Chief Joseph (Nez Perce), 430, 431 (map)
Chief Justice (Supreme Court). *See* specific individuals
Chiefs (Indian), 429
Childbearing: in New England, 55, 56
Child labor, 397, 399, 415, 420; abuses of, 479; Polish, 523; restrictions on, 410, 498, 536, 555, 558
Child-rearing: Spock on, 621-622; of whites by slaves, 261
Children: baby boom and, 624; in Chesapeake region, 50; in child-centered families, 225; in factories, 222; families of, 712; of freed slaves, 349, 351; health care for, 507; of immigrants, 408, 409; Native American, 432; in New England, 56; in Oneida Community, 244; of planters, 261; slave, 261
Children's Bureau, 481
Chile: Allende in, 664; revolution in, 196; U.S. demands on, 453
China: Boxer Rebellion in, 465; Carter and, 681; communism in, 614; economic development in, 674; Hong Kong and Macao returned to, 471; human rights record in, 710; Japan and, 463, 548, 581; Korean War and, 615; loans to, 498; Mao in, 661; Nine-Power Treaty and, 538; Nixon and, 664; Open Door policy toward, 463-465, 471, 489, 538; Polo, Marco, in, 11; as "Sick Man of East Asia," 538; Soviet Union and, 608; Tiananmen Square protest in, 697; U.S. investment in, 498; Wanghia Treaty and, 291; after World War II, 613-614

Chinatowns, 375
Chinese Exclusion Act (1882), 344, 375, 376, 631
Chinese immigrants, 407; in California, 374; as farm labor, 440; in Hawaii, 454; as railroad labor, 387, 388; segregation of, 470
Chippewa Indians, 429
Chivington, J.M., 430
Choctaw Indians, 10, 198, 315
Chopin, Kate, 423
Choris, Ludwig: *Dance of Native Californians...*, 279
Christianity: in 1950s, 629; clergy and, 66; conservatism and, 617; crusaders and, 11; Darwinism and, 415; evolution and, 524-525; Indians and, 16, 19, 40, 198, 432; liberal Protestants and, 413; in Maryland, 28; of slaves, 64-65, 261. *See also* Catholic Church; Missions and missionaries; Protestant Reformation; Religion(s); specific religions
Christian Science, 414
Chrysler: government support for, 726
Church(es): in 1920s, 528; attendance in (1850), 233; black, 350, 357; in colonies (1775), 69; Great Awakening and, 69-71, 232, 234-235; in Massachusetts Bay Colony, 37; parish, 57; in Pennsylvania, 43; urban challenges to, 413-415. *See also* Religion(s); specific groups
Church and state. *See* Separation of church and state
Churchill, Winston: at Atlantic Conference, 580; at Casablanca, 594; on lend-lease, 579 (map); at Tehran Conference, 594, 597; on United States, 606; in World War II, 576, 602; at Yalta conference, 608
Church of Christ: Fundamentalism in, 525
Church of Christ, Scientist (Christian Science), 414
Church of England. *See* Anglican Church
Church of Jesus Christ of Latter-Day Saints. *See* Mormons
CIA (Central Intelligence Agency): Chile and, 664; Cuba and, 644; Guatemala and, 638; Iran and, 636; Vietnam and, 656
Cigarettes, production of, 396
Cincinnati, 220, 226
CIO. *See* Committee for Industrial Organization; Congress of Industrial Organizations
Circuit riders, Methodist, 234
Circus, 424
Cities and towns: architecture in, 72; boomtowns, 434; cow towns, 435; department stores in, 406; economic inequality in, 230; education in, 415; families in, 419-420; growth of, 397, 405-406; immigrants in, 215, 408; minorities in, 710; movement from rural areas to, 364; Native American migration to, 589; in New England, 56-57; Polish immigrants in, 523; population of, 44, 61, 140, 214, 364, 404, 405, 406; progressivism in, 480; railroads and, 386-387, 389; religion and, 413-415; segregation in, 624; slums in, 214, 406-407; in South, 54, 348, 349; suburbs and, 622-624; in West, 439; World War II migration to, 589. *See also* Company town; Suburbs; Urbanization; specific locations
Citizenship: blacks and, 302; Chinese Americans and, 376; for Filipinos, 464; Fourteenth Amendment and, 345, 355; Mexican nationals and, 709; for Native Americans, 432; for Puerto Ricans, 459, 460
Citizen-soldiers, in Civil War, 323
Citizens United v. *Federal Election Commission*, 730
City Beautiful movement, 424

City manager system of government, 480
City planning, 424
Civic virtue, 105, 127, 136
Civil disobedience: by Native Americans, 679-680. *See also* Civil rights movement; Nonviolent resistance; specific groups
Civilian Conservation Corps (CCC), 553, 555
Civil liberties: in 21st century, 723; in Civil War, 319; McCarthyism and, 617; World War I and, 505
Civil rights: Fourteenth Amendment and, 345, 355; Kennedy, John F., and, 639, 639 (map); 646-647; Klan and, 520; of Puerto Ricans, 460; Roosevelt, Franklin D., on, 591; Truman and, 619; after World War II, 604, 631-632. *See also* Civil rights movement; specific groups
Civil Rights Act: of 1875, 373; of 1957, 634; of 1964, 651-652, 653
Civil Rights Cases (1883), 373
Civil rights movement: African American migration and, 633; higher education and, 416; under Johnson, L.B., 653-655; Montgomery bus boycott and, 632; Native Americans and, 680; as Second Reconstruction, 362. *See also* Desegregation; State(s); Voting and voting rights
Civil service, 498; reform of, 369, 371, 376, 377; segregation ended in, 632
Civil Service Commission, 376
Civil war(s): in England, 29, 40; in Kansas, 298 (map), 300
Civil War (U.S., 1861-1865), 252, 253, 315-317; African Americans in, 323, 333; battles and campaigns (1861-1862), 327-331, 330 (map), 333, 336, 336 (map); battles and campaigns (1863-1865), 330 (map), 333-334, 334 (map), 336-338, 336 (map), 338 (map), 340-341; Border States in, 314-315; Californios and, 279; casualties in, 323, 331, 333, 341, 343; compromise before, 309; diplomacy during, 317-319; draft in, 319-320; effects of, 343, 345; emancipation and, 316; Emancipation Proclamation and, 322, 330, 331, 332-333; events leading to, 296-306; financing of, 320-321, 434; Fort Sumter attack and, 313-314; historians on, 310, 345; leadership in, 319; Lee's surrender in, 341-342; limitations on liberties in, 319; main thrusts in (1861-1865), 330 (map); medical care in, 320, 322, 323; Mexican War and, 280, 281; monetary costs of, 343; nationalism and, 309; Native Americans in, 315; politics in, 338-340; secession of South and, 306-308, 308 (map), 309, 314, 315 (map); as Second American Revolution, 310; slavery and, 252, 253, 326; soldiers in, 316, 320, 322, 323, 327, 329; strategy in, 328, 339, 341; as total war, 328, 338; veterans of, 323, 368, 372; in West, 314, 336-337, 336 (map); women in, 285, 322. *See also* Confederate States of America; North (Union, Civil War)
Civil Works Administration (CWA), 556-557
Claflin, Tennessee, 419
Clark, George Rogers, 113, 115
Clark, William, 163
Class(es): colonial, 54, 59; in Gilded Age, 374, 395; machine age and, 397; "new rich," 394; Second Great Awakening and, 235; in South, 54; transfer of power among, 310. *See also* Elites; specific groups
Class conflict: in American Revolution, 105; in French Revolution, 147; in Gilded Age, 374; in Jacksonian era, 209; social mobility and, 64-65, 402
Clay, Henry, 270, 290, 379; 1824 election and, 190-191; 1832 election and, 201; 1844 election

and, 273, 274; 1848 election and, 283; American System and, 178; Bank War and, 200, 201; Compromise of 1850 and, 285, 288; Compromise Tariff of 1833 and, 195–196; Ghent negotiations and, 175; as Great Compromiser, 271, 274; Missouri Compromise and, 181; as secretary of state, 191; as Speaker of the House, 190–191; Whigs and, 202
Clayton, Thomas, 52
Clayton Anti-Trust Act (1914), 497
Clayton-Bulwer Treaty (1850), 290, 467
Clean Air Act (1970), 665
"Clear and present danger," 505
Clemenceau, Georges, 512
Clemens, Samuel Langhorne. *See* Twain, Mark
Clergy: colonial, 66; in Massachusetts Bay Colony, 38; old and new lights in, 70
Clerical work, 322
Clermont (ship), 227
Cleveland, Grover: 1884 election and, 377; 1888 election and, 378–379; 1892 election and, 380 (map), 381; 1896 election and, 446; civil service reform and, 378; depression of 1893 and, 381–382; gold crisis and, 382; Hawaiian annexation and, 454; on immigrants, 413; Pullman strike and, 445; tariff issue and, 382; Venezuelan boundary dispute and, 453
Climate: Americas and, 14; of New England, 55. *See also* Environment
Clinton, DeWitt, 227
Clinton, Hillary Rodham, 705; 2008 election and, 725; heath care reform and, 705; as secretary of state, 728; as U.S. senator, 705
Clinton, William Jefferson ("Bill"), 703, 704–715; 1992 election and, 704; 1996 election and, 707–708; affirmative action and, 708; balanced budget of, 700; economy and, 710 711; foreign policy of, 713; impeachment of, 713–714; legacy of, 714–715; as New Democrat, 704; race and, 708; trade and, 710
Clipper ships, 228
Clothing: Civil War and, 316, 321, 322, 323; of Klan, 359; manufacturing of, 221, 321; ready-to-wear, 406; reform in women's, 241–243
Coal and coal industry: Molly Maguires and, 216; strikes against, 482–483; unions in, 216. *See also* Mines and mining
Coalition: New Deal, 568
Coast Ranges, 5, 6
Cochran, Thomas, 345
Codes: in World War II, 581, 593
"Code talkers" (World War II), 589
Codfishing, in Newfoundland, 57
Cody, William F. ("Buffalo Bill"), 425, 432
Coen brothers, 717
Coeur d'Alene strike, 380
Cohan, George M., 505
Cohen, Lizebeth, 568, 701
Coins. *See* Currency
Coin's Financial School (Harvey), 444
Cold Harbor, battle at, 341
Cold War, 604, 606–618; Carter and, 681; containment doctrine in, 611–613; Eisenhower and, 635–638; end of, 605, 693, 696–698; foreign policy after, 713; global village after, 703; home front during, 616–617; Kennan and, 612; Korea and, 630; Latin America and, 638; McCarthyism during, 617; in Middle East, 636–637; nuclear testing and, 637–638; politics and, 617–618; Reagan and, 690; responsibility for, 625. *See also* Korean War
Cold Water Army, 240
Cole (ship), attack on, 713
Collective bargaining, 401

Collective security, 504
College of New Jersey. *See* Princeton University
College of William and Mary, 57, 69
Colleges. *See* Higher education; Universities and colleges
Collier's, 478, 479
Collinson, Peter, 27
Colman, Laura, 701
Cologne, bombing of, 593
Colombia, 467. *See also* New Granada
Colonialism: of Wilson, 516; World War I and, 512
Colonies and colonization: American culture and, 47; arts in, 72; in Asia, 470–471; in Carolinas, 29–32; in Chesapeake region, 25–28; churches in (1775), 69; committees of correspondence in, 94; culture in, 47; decolonization and, 643; diversity among, 2, 61–62, 62 (map); Dutch, 41–43; economy in, 68; English, 2–3, 21, 22, 24–25, 27–32, 60; families in, 50, 55–56, 123; French, 77–79; French Southeast Asian, 635; lifestyle in, 45, 50, 54, 56–59; literature in, 72; manufacturing in, 68; mercantilism and, 88–90; nationalism and, 344; in Newfoundland, 11, 22; newspapers in, 73; in North, 35–37, 39–40; plantation, 27, 28, 29–32; politics in, 73–74; populations of, 27, 44, 50, 61–62, 97; proprietary, 28, 29, 44, 73; Quakers in, 2, 38, 39, 43–45; religious denominations in, 28, 29, 32, 35–36, 37–39, 69; royal, 28, 37, 40, 41; after Seven Years' War (1763), 3, 83–84; similarities in, 2, 58, 74; slavery in, 27, 28, 32, 53, 63; smuggling in, 68, 89, 92; society in, 53–54, 58–59, 64–66; in South, 53–54; Spanish, 18–19, 21; Swedish, 42–43; taxation of, 3, 73, 90–91; thirteen original, 60; trade in, 67, 67 (map), 68; unity of, 3, 40–41; voting rights in, 38, 39, 41, 74; in West Indies, 28–29; women in, 50, 55–56, 58. *See also* Imperialism; specific locations
Colorado, 437; gold in, 434; woman suffrage in, 434
Colorado River region, 18
Color barrier, in baseball, 631
Colored Farmers' National Alliance, 380, 444
Colored National Labor Union, 399
Colt, Samuel, 221, 222
Columbia, South Carolina, 195, 338
Columbian Centinel (newspaper), 179
Columbian exchange, 13–14
Columbian Exposition. *See* World's Columbian Exposition
Columbia River region, 272, 273
Columbus, Christopher, 2, 4, 9, 13, 15 (map), 460
Comanche Indians, 429; as "code talkers," 589
Comanche Village, A (Catlin), 433
Combinations (business), 390, 394, 395
"Combine" (farm machine), 439
Coming Apart (O'Neill), 668
Commerce: under Articles of Confederation, 125; colonial, 89; after Revolution, 122; waterborne, 45. *See also* Interstate commerce; Trade
Commerce and Culture (Heyrmann), 75
Commerce and Labor Department, 483
Commerce Department, 483
Commerce-raiders (ships), 318
Commission form, of government, 480
Committee for Industrial Organization (CIO), 563
Committee on Public Information, 504–505
Committees of correspondence, 94, 105
Committee to Defend America by Aiding the Allies, 578

Common Sense (Paine), 91, 105
Common Sense Book of Baby and Child Care, The (Spock), 621–622
Commonwealth v. *Hunt*, 224
Communication(s): globalization and, 711; radio and film revolution in, 527–528; telegraph and, 222, 228, 229; telephone and, 392
Communism: Bush, George H.W., and, 697; in China, 614; immigrants and, 412; at Oneida Community, 244; red scare (1919–1920) and, 519–520, 537; threat of, after World War II, 609 (map); Truman Doctrine and, 612; Truman on, 619; World War II and, 585–586
Compact theory, 153
Company town: corporate, 398; New Amsterdam as, 42
Compass, 13
Competition: British, 121; business organization and, 393; global economic, 675; in international system, 470; railroads and, 390
Complex marriage, 243, 244
Compromise of 1820. *See* Missouri Compromise (1820)
Compromise of 1850, 252, 286–289, 292, 294; debates before, 285–286, 289; slavery after, 287 (map)
Compromise of 1877, 373
Compromise Tariff (1833), 195–196
Computers, 628
Comstock, Anthony, 419
Comstock Law, 419
Comstock Lode, 434
Concentration camps, in World War II, 598
Concept of Jacksonian Democracy, The (Benson), 209
Concord, battle of, 97, 101
Conestoga wagon, 226
Confederate congress, 315
Confederate States of America (Civil War South): advantages/disadvantages of, 315–317; black soldiers and, 333; Californios and, 279; Davis as president of, 308, 309, 319; debt of, 355; diplomatic mediation and, 330; draft by, 320; Emancipation Proclamation in, 332; finances of, 321; food shortages in, 316; foreign intervention and, 317–318; formation of, 308; Fort Sumter assault by, 313–314; Indians and, 315; railroads in, 316, 336; slaves in, 333; soldiers of, 323, 327; women in, 322, 324. *See also* Civil War (U.S., 1861–1865); South
Confessions of Nat Turner, The (Styron), 642
Confiscation, of Loyalist estates, 108, 122
Congo region: Belgium in, 470; Lumumba in, 661
Congregational Church: class and, 235; in New England, 38, 57, 69, 71, 108, 135; in Old Northwest, 182
Congress (U.S.): in 1946, 618; African Americans in, 358; under Articles of Confederation, 125; bicameral, 129; Billion-Dollar, 379; conservatives in (1990s), 706–707; in Constitution, 130; Crédit Mobilier scandal and, 369; declaring war, 130; elections of 1918 and, 511; ex-Confederates in, 354; in Great Depression, 554; Great Society legislation and, 653; Johnson, Andrew, and, 354–355, 360–361; Kennedy, J.F., and, 642–643; lend-lease and, 579; Obama and, 727, 732–733; Old Guard in, 515; readmittance of states and, 353; War of 1812 and, 169. *See also* Continental Congress entries; Elections; House of Representatives (U.S.); Senate (U.S.); specific individuals

Congressional Budget Office: on jobs saved during Great Recession, 726
Congressional Committee on the Conduct of the War, 338, 339
Congressional elections. *See* Elections
Congressional Medals of Honor, in Civil War, 333
Congressional Reconstruction, 354; Radical Reconstruction and, 355-359
Congress of Industrial Organizations (CIO), 563
Congress of Racial Equality (CORE), 589
Congress of the Socialist Party (France), 471
Congress of Vienna (1814-1815), 175
Conjure Women, The (Chesnutt), 423
Conkling, Roscoe ("Lord Roscoe"), 371, 376
Connecticut: Dutch in, 39; English grant to, 39, 41; Fundamental Orders in, 39; government of, 73; Hartford Convention and, 176; state constitution in, 39
Conquistadores, 14-15, 16, 17, 18, 433
Conscience Whigs, 272, 278, 284
Conscientious objectors: in World War I, 508
Conscription. *See* Draft (military)
Consensus view of historians, 137
Conservation, 555; of natural resources, 214; Roosevelt, T., and, 485-487; Taft and, 490. *See also* Environment
Conservatism: in 1960s, 652, 668; 1980 election and, 605; in 1980-1990s, 682-683, 686-700, 701; in 1990s, 706-707; affirmative action and, 652; Christian, 617; Constitution ratification and, 131, 134-135; in courts, 695-696; ERA and, 676; neoconservatism and, 682; origins of modern, 701; postrevolutionary, 131; Reagan and, 680, 687-695; of Supreme Court, 565; Whigs and, 202
Consolidation, 392, 394
Constitution ("Old Ironsides") (frigate), 172, 173
Constitution(s): Articles of Confederation as, 125; of colonies, 37, 39; Confederate, 319; Fundamental Orders as, 39; Lecompton, 300; of states, 121-122; of states, in Reconstruction, 356, 357
Constitution (U.S.), 334; antifederalist opposition to, 131-134, 132 (map); Articles of Confederation compared to, 130; Bill of Rights and, 141-142; compromises in, 128, 129-131; elastic clause of, 144; Electoral College in, 130, 131; executive in, 130; historians' viewpoints on, 137; House of Representatives in, 130; interstate commerce in, 395; judicial review and, 161; literal interpretation (strict construction) of, 143; loose constructionism and, 144, 178, 183; Marshall and, 183; presidency in, 130; ratification of, 131-135, 132 (map), 137; representation in, 130; Senate in, 130; signing of, 131, 133; slavery and, 130-131; three-fifths clause in, 130, 158. *See also* Bill of Rights; specific amendments
Constitutional Convention (1787): compromises at, 128, 129-131; conservatism at, 129, 131; delegates to, 128-129; Great Compromise of, 130
Constitutional conventions: in Massachusetts, 121; in Philadelphia, 128-131; in Reconstruction, 357, 358
Constitutional Union party, 306
Constraints school, 568
Consumer Product Safety Commission (CPSC), 665
Consumers and consumerism: in 1920s, 525-526; in 1950s, 629-630; department stores and, 406; installment buying and, 223; mass consumption economy and, 525-526; progressivism and, 481; Roosevelt, T. and, 485

Containment doctrine: in Cold War, 611-613
Continental Army: Society of the Cincinnati and, 135; von Steuben on, 114; Washington as commander of, 102
Continental Congress (First), 96, 98, 135
Continental Congress (Second): appeals to Britain, 101; call for new state constitutions, 121; Declaration of Independence and, 105-106; diplomacy and, 109; economic problems and, 101; power of, 105; Washington and, 102
Continental economy, 229
"Continental Sunday," 217
Contraception. *See* Birth control
Contraction policy, 370
Contracts: of indentured servant (1746), 52; labor, 350, 353, 546; Supreme Court and, 183; yellow-dog, 558
Contract with America (1994), 706-707
Contras, 693-694
Convention of 1800, 151
Conventions, nominating, 201, 515
Conversion: to Calvinism, 35; to Christianity by Spanish, 19; of Indians, 78; Puritans and, 35; revivalism and, 234
Convicts, 66
Conwell, Russell, 395
Coolidge, Calvin, 535; 1920 election and, 515; 1924 election and, 540, 541 (map); 1928 election and, 542; foreign policy of, 538; presidency of, 539-542; veterans' compensation and, 537; war debts and, 542
Cooper, James Fenimore, 177-178, 213, 246
Cooper, John Milton, Jr., 516
Cooperatives: farmers', 442, 444; producers', 400; for women, 420
Copley, John Singleton, 72, 90, 123
Copper, 391
Copperheads, 339-340
Coral Sea, Battle of the, 592
Corbett, "Gentleman Jim," 425
CORE (Congress of Racial Equality), 589
Corinth, Mississippi, 336
Corn (maize), 6, 8, 10, 14, 226, 439
Cornbury, Lord, 73
Cornell University, 417
Cornwallis, Charles, 107, 112, 114
Coronado, Francisco, 14, 18-19
Corporations: billion-dollar, 393; "dummy" homesteaders of, 436; as employers, 398; farmers and, 441; horizontal integration in, 392; incorporation laws and, 222; mining, 434; political contributions and, 376; rights of, 395; Roosevelt, T., and, 483-484; vertical integration in, 392. *See also* Antitrust movement; Business
Corps of Discovery, 163, 273
Corregidor: in World War II, 591
Corrupt bargain (1824), 190-192
Corruption: 1884 election and, 376-377; in Civil War, 321, 391; Crédit Mobilier, 368-369; of federal Indian agents, 430; under Grant, 366, 368-369; under Harding, 536, 539; Homestead Act and, 436; Iran-Contra affair and, 693-694; in labor, 637; Plunkitt on, 377; in railroads, 368, 389-390; in Reconstruction governments, 358; spoils system and, 194, 376, 377; Tweed Ring and, 368; in XYZ Affair, 150
Cortés, Hernán, 15, 16, 17
Cosmopolitan, 478, 479
Cost-of-living increases, 665
Cott, Nancy, 250
Cotton, John, 38
Cotton and cotton industry: boll weevil and, 440; in California, 286n; in Civil War,

316-317; in Great Depression, 559, 560; mechanization of, 219, 221; North and, 266; prices of, 440; slavery and, 119, 219, 259, 260; in South, 252, 254, 396; Texas and, 272. *See also* Textile industry
Cotton famine, 316-317
Cotton gin, 219, 221, 252, 254
Cotton Kingdom, 221, 226, 229, 255
Coughlin, Charles, 557, 701
Council of Economic Advisers, 618
Counterculture: in 1960s, 660-662; Beat writers in, 640
Counterinsurgency: in Afghanistan, 721
Countryman, Edward, 116
Coups: in Hawaii, 454; in Iran, 636; in Soviet Union, 698; in Vietnam, 644
Coureurs de bois, 78, 79
Court-packing plan (1937), of Roosevelt, F.D., 565-566
Courts: admiralty, 90; conservatism in, 695-696; federal, 142, 345. *See also* Supreme Court (U.S.)
Covenant: Atlantic Charter as, 580; of League of Nations, 512
Covenant doctrine, 37, 38
Covered wagons, 226, 273
Covert operations: by CIA, 664
Cowboys, 435, 442
Cowie, Jefferson, 701
Cowpens, battle of, 112
Cox, James M., 515
Coxey, Jacob S., and Coxey's Army, 445
Craft unions, 407
Crane, Stephen, 422
Crash (financial). *See also* Depressions; Great Depression; Panics
Craven, Avery, 310
Crawford, William H., 190, 191
Creation of the American Republic, The (Wood), 137
Credit: in 2008, 725; American, abroad, 127, 381; American System and, 178; in company towns, 398; for farmers, 374, 498; panic of 1837 and, 203; panic of 1873 and, 370
Credit cards, 629
Crédit Mobilier scandal, 368-369, 389
Creditors: England as, 89, 115; European, 468
Creek Indians, 10, 32, 84, 198, 315
Creel, George, 504-505
CREEP (Committee to Re-Elect the President), 671
Crèvecoeur, Michel-Guillaume Jean de, 61
Crime(s): anti-crime bill and, 705; in cities, 406; convicts and, 66; decline in violent, 705. *See also* Gangsters
"Crime Against Kansas, The" (Sumner), 300
Crimean War, 240
Crimes against humanity, 610
Criminals: rights of, 664
Criminal syndicalism laws, 519
Critchlow, Donald, 701
Crittenden, John Jordan, 309, 315
Crittenden amendments and Compromise, 309, 315
Croats, 407
Crockett, Davy, 205, 208
Croly, Herbert, 493
Cromwell, Oliver, 29
Cronon, William, 47
Crop-lien system, 374
Crops: cash, 439; colonial, 27-28, 66; in Columbian exchange, 13, 14; in southeast, 10; in Virginia, 27-28, 66; in West, 226. *See also* specific crops
Crosby, Alfred W., 47

Cross of Gold speech (Bryan), 441, 446
Crow Indians, 429
Crown Point, battle at, 102
Crucible, The (Miller), 642
Crusaders, 11
Crystal Palace, at World's Fair, 222
Cuba, 458; Bay of Pigs invasion of, 644; Castro in, 638; filibustering expeditions in, 290; Guantanamo Detention Camp in, 722; Guevara and, 661; Platt Amendment and, 460–461, 572; revolutionary movements and, 681; Spain and, 16, 290, 454; Spanish-American War in, 457; U.S. intervention in, 461, 468, 489
Cuban Americans, 709
Cuban missile crisis, 644
Cult of domesticity, 224, 225, 241, 629
Cult of Reason, 147
Cultural diversity: postmodern, 717
Cultural pluralism, 522, 715
Cultural Revolution (China), 661
Culture(s): in late 19th century, 425; in 1920s, 521–522; in 1960s, 639–642, 659–662; African American, 63, 64–65, 252, 261; American, 47, 733; Benedict's studies of, 558; in Chesapeake region, 25–26; Chinese immigrant, 375; colonial, 47; of immigrants, 216, 220; of Italian immigrants, 409; of *mestizos*, 16; Native American, 429, 432, 433; of New Immigrants, 408; slave, 63, 64–65, 252, 261; Spanish-Indian, 16
Cumberland River region, Civil War and, 336, 336 (map)
Cumberland Road, 180, 226–227
Currency: in American Revolution, 98, 114; after American Revolution, 143; coinage of silver dollars, 370; colonial shortage of, 89; deflation of, 370, 440; inelasticity of, 497; inflation of, 98, 114; panic of 1837 and, 203; printing of, 345; standard banknote, 321; "Wildcat," 180, 202; worldwide, 674. *See also* Bank notes; Coins; Economy; Greenbacks; Money
Curriculum: in colleges, 417–418
Cushing, Caleb, 291
Custer, George Armstrong, 430
Customs duties, 320, 321. *See also* Tariff(s)
Czechoslovakia: communist collapse in, 697; Nazi attack on, 574; Prague Spring in, 661; Soviets and, 612

Da Gama, Vasco, 13
Daguerre, Louis, and daguerreotype, 245
Dakotas: Native Americans in, 429. *See also* North Dakota; South Dakota
Dakota Sioux Indians, 432
Daley, Richard M., 658
Dallas, Texas: Kennedy, J.F., assassination in, 647
Dams: environment and, 486, 487; in Great Depression, 558, 559; on Tennessee River, 562
Dance: African ringshout, 63, 65; dance halls and, 419
Dance of Native Californians . . . (Choris), 279
"Dark-horse" candidates, 273, 289, 376
Darrow, Clarence, in Scopes trial, 525
Dartmouth, 71
Dartmouth College v. Woodward, 183
Darwin, Charles, 395, 415
Darwinism, 524–525; interpretation of, 452–453; Social Darwinism and, 395. *See also* Evolution
Daugherty, Harry M., 536, 537, 539
Daughters of Liberty, 92
Daughters of the American Revolution, 410

Davis, David Brion, 267
Davis, Jefferson, 256, 322; in Black Hawk War, 199; Lincoln's assassination and, 343; as president of the Confederate States, 308, 309, 330, 348; as secretary of war, 291
Davis, John W., 540, 541 (map)
Dawes, Charles, 542
Dawes Plan (1924), 542
Dawes-Severalty Act (1887), 432, 434, 561, 635
Dawson, Rosario, 716
Day care: Nixon veto of, 679
"Day of Doom" (Wigglesworth), 38
D-Day (June 6, 1944), 594–595
Dean, James, 660
Death of a Salesman (Miller), 642
Death rates. *See* Casualties; Mortality
Debates: of 1850, 285–286, 289; Lincoln-Douglas, 303, 304
De Bry, Theodore, 3
Debs, Eugene V.: 1908 election and, 488; 1912 election and, 493; 1920 election and, 515; Harding pardon of, 505; Pullman strike and, 445; World War I and, 505
Debt(s): assumption of state, 142–143; to British creditors after Revolution, 115; Confederate, 355; consumer, 526; of farmers, 440; imprisonment for, 222, 239; international, after World War I, 541–542; public, after Revolution, 127; in Revolution, 115; of sharecroppers, 374; of workers, 398. *See also* National debt
Debt ceiling, Obama and, 731
Debtor(s): panic of 1873 and, 370; prisons for, 179, 239
Decatur, Stephen, 151, 178
Declaration of Independence (U.S.), 335; equality in, 135; Jefferson and, 3, 106, 153; natural rights in, 3, 106; Second Continental Congress and, 105–106
Declaration of Sentiments, 243
Declaration of the Rights of Man (France, 1789), 146
Declaratory Act (1766), 92
Decolonization, 471, 643, 661, 674
Deep South, 63; cotton economy in, 259; slavery in, 260, 261. *See also* South (region)
Deere, John, 226
Defense of Marriage Act (1996), 732
Defense spending: after Cold War, 698; in World War II, 589; after World War II, 614. *See also* Military spending
Deficit. *See* Budget deficits
Deficit-reduction bill (1993), 705
Deflation, 370, 440
Deganawidah (Iroquois), 30
De Gaulle, Charles, 656, 661
Degler, Carl, 568
De Grasse, Admiral, 114
Deism, 233
De Lancey family, 43
Delany, Martin, 263
Delaware: as Border State, 314; as middle colony, 45; as proprietary colony, 73
Delaware River region, 42, 44, 45, 108
De La Warr, Lord, 25, 45
"Deliveraging," 725
Demagogues, in Great Depression, 557
Demilitarized zone (DMZ): in Vietnam, 666
Democracy: Civil War and, 343; imperialism and, 471; Jacksonian, 179, 208, 209; mass, 119, 196, 209; Massachusetts Bay Colony and, 38; in middle colonies, 45; nationalism and, 344; in North Carolina, 31; in politics, 207–208, 479; slavery and, 253; Truman on, 619

Democracy in America (Tocqueville), 196–197
Democratic Leadership Council (DLC), 704
Democratic National Convention: of 1848, 283; of 1852, 289; of 1860, 305–306; of 1964, 654; of 1968, 658
Democratic party: 1844 election and, 273–274; 1860 election and, 305–306, 307 (map); 1900 election and, 451; Civil War and, 320, 339; Clinton and, 704; Copperheads in, 339–340; Douglas and, 304; Emancipation Proclamation and, 332; in Gilded Age, 371; Irish and, 217; Jacksonian, 179, 208, 209; Kansas-Nebraska Act and, 294; racial minorities in, 710; sectionalism and, 294, 300; in South, 357; war faction in, 339, 340, 351. *See also* Elections; specific leaders
Democratic Promise: The Populist Moment in America (Goodwyn), 383
Democratic-Republican party: as Democrats, 202; Federalists vs., 150, 153–154; French Revolution and, 147; internal improvements and, 154; under Jackson, 192; Jay's Treaty and, 149; under Jefferson, 145, 153; Neutrality Proclamation and, 148; pro-French view of, 154; Sedition Act and, 152; Virginia and Kentucky Resolutions and, 153; War of 1812 and, 169. *See also* Elections
Demography: baby boom and, 624; Columbian exchange and, 13–14; westward shift of U.S. center, 212–213, 213 (map). *See also* Census
Demonstrators. *See* Protest(s)
Dempsey, Jack, 526
Denmark: Nazis in, 575; Virgin Islands purchased from, 498
Denver, 439
Departments of government. *See* specific departments
Department stores: female clerks in, 420; growth of, 406
Deportation: of alien radicals, 519; of aliens, 152
Deposit, right of, 162
Depressions: of 1837, 203; of 1870s, 370, 374, 390; of 1893, 381–382, 392, 444; farm (1920s), 540. *See also* Great Depression; Panics; Recession
Deregulation: Carter and, 683; criticism of, 710
Derivatives: federal regulation of, 710
Desegregation: in 1970s, 679; of armed forces, 617, 619; schools and, 634, 679; after World War II, 631–632. *See also* Civil rights movement; Integration
Deseret, 237 (map)
"Desert Fox" (Rommel), 593
Desertion, in Civil War, 327, 332, 338
Desert Storm, 699–700
Des Moines: naming of, 78
De Soto, Hernando, 14
Destruction of the Indies, The (Las Casas), 17
Détente policy, 646, 664, 675, 676, 681
Detroit: automobile industry in, 526; founding of, 79; Pontiac's uprising and, 84; race riots in, 589, 655; state election in, 191; in War of 1812, 172, 173
Developing world, 674
Dewey, George, 456–457, 524
Dewey, John, 522
Dewey, Thomas E.: 1940 election and, 578–579; 1944 election and, 595–596; 1948 election and, 618–619
Dey of Algiers, 127
Dial, The, 241
Días, Bartholomeu, 13
Diaz, Junot, 717
Dickinson, Emily, 247–248

Dickinson, John, 91
Dictators: in Iran, 636; Stalin as, 572. *See also* specific individuals
Diem, Ngo Dinh, 636, 644
Dien Bien Phu, Battle of, 635
Diet: of Civil War soldiers, 323; colonial, 74; of Native Americans, 10
Dime novels, 421
Diner's Club, 629
Dingley Tariff Bill (1897), 449
Diphtheria, 66
Diplomacy. *See* Foreign policy; specific presidents
Diplomatic mediation, 330
Direct election: of representatives, 131; of senators, 379, 480
"Direct tax" clause, 382
"Dirty tricks": by Nixon, 671
Disarmament, after World War I, 538
Discourse of the Plantation of Virginia, A (Percy), 24
Discrimination: ADA and, 700; against Asian students, 469–470; ban on, 633, 651, 653; against Chinese, 375; Civil Rights Act (1964) and, 654–655; decline after World War II, 631; economic, against South, 396; against Filipinos, 464; gender (sex), 678; in housing, 624; against Irish, 216; reverse, 665, 696; in World War II, 591. *See also* Affirmative action; Race and racism; specific groups
Disease: in Chesapeake region, 25; of Civil War soldiers, 323; colonial, 25, 26–27, 40, 50; in Columbian exchange, 14; in Hawaii, 454; immigration and, 215; in Mexican War, 280; Native Americans and, 2, 14, 19, 25, 26–27, 40, 279, 429; in Spanish-American War, 458; in Virginia, 25, 50. *See also* Medicine; specific diseases
Disestablishment, of Anglican Church, 135
Disfranchisement: of blacks, 360, 374, 381; of ex-Confederates, 353, 357
Disney Concert Hall, Los Angeles, 716
Disneyland, 629
Dissent: in New Amsterdam, 42
District of Columbia: abolition of slavery in, 284; electoral votes in, 666; location of, 143; slave trade abolished in, 287. *See also* Washington, D.C.
Diversity: in 2000s, 719; in Charleston, 29; colonial, 2, 61–62, 62 (map); in Congress (1992), 704; cultural, 717; of feminist movement, 678; of immigrants, 215; in middle colonies, 2, 45, 62; in Pennsylvania, 44, 61, 62; religious, 44, 61, 235, 414; in two-party system, 208
Division of labor, 229
Divorce: increase in, 419; in New England, 56; revolution, 420
Divorce Bill, 203
Dix, Dorothea, 240, 322
Dixie. *See* South (region)
Dixiecrats, in 1948, 619
DNA: testing, 157, 159
Dochuk, Darren, 701
Doctors. *See* Medicine; Physicians
Dodge City, 435
Doheny, Edward L., 539
Dole, Robert, 707–708
Dollar: gold standard and, 555
Dollar diplomacy, 489, 499
Domestic feminism, 225
Domesticity: cult of, 224, 225, 241
Domestic policy. *See* Home front; specific presidents
Domestic service: black women in, 420. *See also* Servants

Dominican Republic, 14, 468; U.S. troops in, 489, 498
Dominion of New England, 41
Donnelly, Ignatius, 444
"Don't Ask, Don't Tell" (DADT) policy, 705
Dos Passos, John, 508
Dot-com businesses, 710
Doughboys, 507–508
Douglas, Stephen A., 302, 303, 355; 1860 election and, 305–306, 307 (map); Compromise of 1850 and, 285, 288; death of, 339; Kansas-Nebraska Act and, 292–294, 293 (map), 301; Lincoln debates with, 303, 304; popular sovereignty and, 292, 300, 304; on slavery, 293
Douglass, Frederick, 360; as abolitionist, 265; Civil War and, 333; violence against, 265
"Doves" (Vietnam War), 656, 659, 662
Dow, Neal S., 240
Draft (military): in Civil War, 319–320, 345; in Vietnam War, 656, 663; in World War II, 576
Drake, Francis, 22
Drama: in 1920s, 532; after World War II, 642
DREAM Act (Development, Relief and Education for Alien Minors Act), 731–732
Dred Scott v. *Stanford*, 252, 296, 302, 304
Dreiser, Theodore, 406, 478, 531
Dress reform, 241–243
Drinking and drunkenness. *See* Alcohol; Temperance movement
Drive-ins: cafés as, 623
Drone attacks, 728
Drought: in Great Plains, 436, 437, 440; in Texas (1887), 378
Drug culture, 660
Drugs: "miracle," 599; safety of, 485
Dry farming, 437
"Dry" laws, 52, 482
Dual-income families, 679
DuBois, Ellen, 250
Du Bois, W.E.B., 362, 416
Duels: Burr-Hamilton, 163–164
Due process clause, 395
Dukakis, Michael, 696
Duke, James Buchanan, 396
Duke University, 396
Dulles, John Foster, 635, 636
Dumbbell tenement, 406
Dunbar, Paul Laurence, 423
Dunkirk, evacuation of, 575
Dunmore, Lord, 99
Dunn, Richard S., 47
Dunne, Finley Peter, 457
Dunning, William A., 362
Duquesne, Fort, 80, 81
Dust Bowl, 437, 560–561, 560 (map)
Dutch: colonies of, 41–43; England, Sweden, and, 42–43; as immigrants, 62. *See also* Holland
Dutch East India Company, 42
Dutch East Indies (Indonesia): in World War II, 581, 591
Dutchman (Baraka), 642
Dutch Reformed Church, 35, 42
Dutch Republic, 42. *See also* Holland
Dutch West India Company, 42
Duties. *See* Sugar Act; Tariff(s); Taxation
Dysentery, 50, 323, 458

Eagleton, Thomas, 666
Eakins, Thomas, 423
Earth: as ecological system, 486
Earth Day, 486, 665
East (region): revivalism and, 235; western commerce and, 178

East Asia: Japanese aggression in, 548, 581, 591; naval treaties and, 538; U.S. and, 291. *See also* Asia; specific locations
Eastern Europe: collapse of communism in, 697–698; global economy and, 675; immigrants from, 391, 407–408; Soviets and, 608, 610; after World War II, 608. *See also* specific locations
Eastern Orthodox church, 408
East Germany, 610, 611 (map); Berlin Wall and, 643; communist collapse in, 697. *See also* Germany; West Germany
East Indies, 42. *See also* Dutch East Indies (Indonesia); specific locations
East Jersey: in Dominion of New England, 41; Quakers and, 44. *See also* New Jersey
East St. Louis, Illinois: Cahokia and, 8; race riot in, 507
Ecological imperialism, 213
Ecological science, 486
Ecology. *See* Environment entries
Economic Interpretation of the Constitution of the United States, An (Beard), 137
Economy: in 1920s, 525–526, 532–533; in 1950s, 604, 628–630; in 1970s, 673–675; in 2008, 726–727; of Atlantic region, 13; boom in (1950–1970), 620–624; Bush, George H.W., and, 700; in Carolina, 29; Carter and, 681–682, 688; in Civil War, 310, 316, 321; after Civil War, 348; Clinton and, 708, 710–711; colonial, 68; continental, 229; controls after World War I, 537; Coolidge and, 540; Embargo Act (1807) and, 165–166; in Europe after World War II, 612–613; German postwar, 610; Gilded Age and, 385; global, 673–675; in Great Depression, 552, 553–557; Great Recession and, 727; growth of, 385, 733; Hoover and, 544–545; immigrants and, 218–219; after industrialization, 474; inequality in, 230; in Japan, 617; Keynes and, 566; mass consumer, 525–526; mercantilism and, 88–90; New World bullion and, 15; one-crop, 256; politics and (1920–1932), 535–549; in postrevolutionary America, 122; railroads and, 227, 389; Reagan and, 689–690, 694–695; in Revolution, 97, 98, 114; service-based, 628; slavery and, 260; in South, 256, 260, 316, 396, 416; stagflation in, 670; transportation revolution and, 118; Vietnam War and, 673, 676; War of 1812 and, 174; Wilson and, 497; women and, 224; in World War I, 505–507; World War II and, 575, 601; after World War II, 609–610, 618. *See also* Depressions; Inflation; Panics; Recession; Tariff(s); specific presidents
Ecosystems, 13
Eddy, Mary Baker, 414
Edict of Nantes, 77
Edison, Thomas Alva, 392, 424
Edo Bay, U.S. warships in, 291
Edsall, Thomas and Mary, 701
Education: adult, 415; for African Americans, 416; blacks in, 238, 239; Bush, George W., and, 724; Catholic Church and, 218; coeducation, 239; compulsory, 415; Dewey and, 524; for freedmen, 285, 350, 351; immigrants and, 216, 218, 409; inequality and, 729; Johnson, L.B., and, 653; levels of (1870–2010), 417; in middle colonies, 72; in New England, 56–57, 71; progressive, 524; public, 256, 359, 415, 416; for Puerto Ricans, 460; reforms in, 236–237, 415, 417–418; sciences and, 637; slaves and, 262; in South, 72, 236, 237; for women, 136, 238, 239; after World War II, 621. *See also* Higher education; Schools; Universities and colleges

Education Amendments (1972), 676
Education of Henry Adams, The (Adams), 423
Edwards, Jonathan, 70
EEC. *See* European Economic Community
Egypt, 317; Camp David Agreement and, 680–681; Six-Day War and, 656; Suez Canal crisis and, 636–637; Yom Kippur War and, 667
Eighteenth Amendment, 421, 482, 506, 522
Eight-hour workday, 398, 498
Einstein, Albert, 599, 614
Eisenhower, Dwight D. ("Ike"), 627; 1948 election and, 619; 1952 election, 630; 1956 election and, 637; civil rights and, 632, 634; Cold War and, 635–638; D-Day and, 594; highways and, 635; Khrushchev and, 638; labor and, 637; "military-industrial complex" warning by, 693; "new look" in foreign policy of, 635–636; social issues and, 634–635; Suez crisis and, 637; in World War II, 589–590, 594, 602
El Alamein, 593
Elastic clause, of Constitution, 144
Elba, Napoleon on, 173
Elbe River, 598
Elderly. *See* Age and aging; Social Security
"Elect," 35, 57
Elected officials. *See* Officeholders
Elections: of 1796, 150; of 1798–1799, 152; of 1800, 118, 130, 156, 157–158, 158 (map); of 1804, 164, 166; of 1808, 166; of 1812, 172; of 1816, 179; of 1820, 182; of 1824, 130, 189, 190–192; of 1828, 189, 192–193, 193 (map), 196; of 1832, 201; of 1836, 202; of 1840, 189, 206–207, 270; of 1844, 272, 273–274; of 1848, 283–284; of 1852, 289; of 1856, 294; of 1858, 303, 304; of 1860, 296, 305–306, 307 (map); of 1862, 332; of 1864, 340, 341 (map); of 1866, 355; of 1868, 367–368; of 1872, 369, 420; of 1874, 370; of 1876, 371–372, 373, 373 (map); of 1878, 370; of 1880, 376, 444; of 1884, 376–377; of 1888, 378–379; of 1890, 379; of 1892, 379–380, 380 (map), 444; of 1894, 382; of 1896, 382, 383, 441, 445–448, 448 (map); of 1900, 465; of 1904, 487; of 1908, 488; of 1912, 491, 492–493; of 1916, 502, 502 (map); of 1918, 511; of 1920, 515, 527, 536; of 1924, 540, 541 (map); of 1928, 542; of 1932, 547, 550, 552; of 1936, 563–565; of 1940, 578–579; of 1944, 595–596; of 1946, 618; of 1948, 618–619; of 1952, 630; of 1956, 637; of 1960, 638–639, 639 (map); of 1964, 652; of 1968, 657, 658–659, 659 (map); of 1972, 665–666; of 1976, 675, 680; of 1980, 605, 684, 687–688; of 1984, 693; of 1986, 696; of 1988, 696; of 1992, 704; of 1996, 707–708; of 2000, 714–715, 715 (map); of 2004, 723–724; of 2006, 724; of 2008, 725–726, 726 (map); of 2014, 732–733; of 2016, 733; of senators, 131, 379
Electoral College, 130, 131, 140, 273, 302, 355. *See also* Elections
Electoral commission (1877), 373
Electoral Count Act (1877), 373
Electric dynamo, 392
Electricity, 406; New Deal programs and, 561; TVA and, 562; after World War II, 621
Electric lightbulb, 392, 393
Electric railways, 392
Electric trolleys, 406
Electronic media, 732
Electronics, 628
Elementary schools, 56, 72, 415
Eliot, Charles W., 418
Eliot, T.S., 531, 532
Elites: southern, 381
Elizabeth I (England), 22, 23

Elkins, Stanley, 267
Elkins Act (1903), 483
Ellington, Duke, 530
Ellis Island, 409
Ellison, Ralph, 642
El Salvador: immigrants from, 709; U.S. intervention in, 692
Emancipation, 265, 343; freedmen's responses to, 349–350; Lincoln and, 316, 328; in North, 135
Emancipation Proclamation (1863), 322, 330, 331, 332–333
Embar
Embargo: on Arab oil, 667; on Cuban trade, 638; on Japan in World War II, 581; Jefferson's, 165–166; on Soviet trade, 684
Embargo Act (1807), 165–166
Emergency Banking Relief Act (1933), 553, 555
Emergency Quota Act (1921), 521
Emerson, Ralph Waldo, 211, 232, 258 (map); on Brown, John, 305; conservation and, 486; on Fugitive Slave Law, 286, 287 (map), 294; on individualism, 212–213; on Lexington and Concord battles, 97; lyceums and, 238, 247; on Mexico, 252, 281; on Quakers, 43; on reform, 232; transcendentalism of, 246–247; Unitarianism and, 233; on westward movement, 212
Emissions: reducing, 665
Empires: North American wars for, 80–83, 80 (map), 148 (map); of United States, 365, 451, 459, 462, 470, 471. *See also* specific empires
Employers, 401; ten-hour day and, 222
Employment: in suburbs, 623; white-collar vs. blue-collar, 628–629; of women, 224, 322, 397, 588, 629; in World War II, 588. *See also* Labor; Unemployment; Workers
Employment Act (1946), 618
Enclosures: in England, 23
Encomienda system, 15
Endangered Species Act (1973), 486, 665
"Enemies list": of Nixon, 670
Energy and energy crisis: Carter and, 681–682; after World War II, 621. *See also* Oil and oil industry
Energy Department, 680
Engel v. *Vitale,* 664
Engines: cotton gin as, 219; internal combustion, 393. *See also* Steam power
England (Britain): ABC-1 agreement with, 584; abolition and, 263; Anglo-American Convention and, 184; army of, 89, 92–93, 97; boundary settlement with U.S. (1818), 184 (map); *Caroline* affair and, 271; centers of influence in U.S. after 1783, 148–149, 148 (map); Central America and, 290; Chesapeake colonies of, 25–26; China and, 291; Civil War (U.S.) and, 317–318, 328, 330–331, 332, 337; colonies of, 2–3, 21, 22, 24–25, 27–32, 60; cotton trade and, 255; D-Day and, 594; debt after World War I and, 542; Dutch colonies and, 42–43; economy in, 545; Elizabeth I and, 22, 23; before empire, 22–24; exploration by, 15 (map), 18; France and, 3, 79, 164; in French and Indian War, 81–83; Ghent, Treaty of, and, 175, 177; Great Rapprochement with, 453; immigrants from, 23, 407; imperialism of, 22–24, 470; impressment by, 149, 164; Indians and, 24–25; Industrial Revolution in, 219; Ireland and, 22; Laird rams crisis and, 318, 337; lend-lease and, 578; Lexington and Concord and, 97; literature in, 23; Maine-Canada boundary dispute and, 271; mercantilism and, 89–90; migration from (ca. 1630–1642), 37; at Munich Conference, 574; naval disarmament and, 538; New World exploration by, 15 (map), 18; New York colony and, 43; North American wars of, 148 (map); Nova Scotia to, 79; Oregon and, 184, 268, 272–273, 275; Panama Canal and, 467; panic of 1837 and, 203; Paris, Treaty of (1783) and, 115; political union with Scotland, 76; postrevolutionary relations with, 126; Protestantism and, 22; Reagan and, 689; Seven Years' War and, 81, 87; slave trade and, 54, 259; Spanish America and, 79; Texas and, 271, 272; thirteen original colonies and, 60; trade with, 68; *Trent* affair and, 318; Venezuela/British Guiana boundary dispute and, 453; Versailles Treaty and, 513; War of 1812 and, 169, 172–175; War of Jenkins's Ear and, 79; women workers in World War II, 588; in World War I, 500; in World War II, 475, 575–578. *See also* American Revolution; Colonies and colonization
English Civil War, 29, 40
English language: as "official language," 707
Enigma codes, in World War II, 593
Enlightenment, 146
Entertainment: colonial, 74. *See also* Movies and movie industry; specific types
Entitlement programs, 653
Enumerated products: shipping of, 89
Environmental Protection Agency (EPA), 486, 665
Environment and environmentalism: Chesapeake and, 50; Earth Day and, 486, 665; Kyoto Treaty and, 721; New England and, 55, 58; protectors of, 486; Roosevelt, T., and, 485–487; West and, 213, 436–437, 439; westward movement and, 213–214. *See also* Conservation
Epidemics: influenza pandemic (1918–1919) and, 511; in Mexico, 17. *See also* Disease; specific conditions
Episcopalians, 135, 235, 413
Equal Employment Opportunity Commission (EEOC), 651
Equality: after American Revolution, 135–136; Civil Rights Act (1964) and, 652; Du Bois on, 416; for gays, 660; gender, 136; social, 197; Tocqueville on, 196–197; Washington, Booker T., and, 416. *See also* specific groups
Equal rights: after World War II, 631–632. *See also* Civil rights; Civil rights movement
Equal Rights Amendment (ERA): in 1923, 528; in 1972, 676–679
ERA. *See* Equal Rights Amendment
Era of Good Feelings: Monroe in, 118, 179; second, 287
Erie Canal, 178, 227
Erie Railroad, 390
Erosion, in Dust Bowl (1930s), 560–561, 560 (map)
Esch-Cummins Transportation Act (1920), 537
Escobedo case, 664
Espionage Act (1917), 505
"Establishment": in 1960s, 660; Carter and, 680
Estancias (ranches), 442
Estlin, Mary A., on Frederick Douglass, 265
Ethiopia, 470; Cuba and, 681; Italian attack on, 572, 573
Ethnic cleansing, 713
Ethnic groups: in 1790, 215–217, 220; assimilation in World War II, 586; communities of, 521–522; in former Yugoslavia, 698, 713; in middle colonies, 45; in Pennsylvania, 44. *See also* Race and racism; specific groups

Ethnocultural School of historians, 310
Eugenides, Jeffrey, 717
Eurasia: formation of, 5; land bridge from, 6, 7 (map)
Eurocentrism: Americanization and, 47
Europe: Africa and, 12–13; Armed Neutrality and, 112; Civil War (U.S.) and, 313, 317–319, 320; democracy and, 185; depression of 1890s and, 381; immigrants from, 215, 407–408; isolationism from, 571; after Napoleon, 185; nation-states in, 344; Native American contact and, 433; price revolution in, 15; Seven Years' War in, 81; tariffs and, 538; World War I and, 500–504; World War II and, 593–595, 596–598, 596 (map); after World War II, 612–613, 674. *See also* specific wars and locations
European Economic Community (EEC), 643
European Union (EU), 643
Evangelicalism: in 1960s, 660; abortion and, 263, 679; Anti-Masons and, 201; in Bible Belt, 525; in Great Awakening, 70, 234; New Right and, 695; in Second Great Awakening, 261
Evans, Hiram Wesley, 520
Evans, Sara, 668
Everett, Edward, 245
Everglades: Seminoles in, 199
Evers, Medgar, 647
Everybody's magazine, 478
Evolution: Darwinism and, 415; Fundamentalists on, 524–525
Exchange rates, fixed, 674
Excise taxes, 143, 144, 160, 320, 369
Executive branch: in Great Depression, 558; in state constitutions, 122
Executive Office, 566
Executive Orders: No. 8802, 633; No. 9066, 586; No. 9981, 617
Expansion and expansionism: in 1840s, 215, 269, 273; American, 84; Democrats and, 273; Mexican War and, 278, 280, 290; Native Americans and western, 112; of New England, 56; of New France, 78–79; of South, 32, 290; U.S. overseas, 365, 452–453, 455 (map), 472; War of 1812 and, 171. *See also* Exploration; Imperialism; Westward movement; specific locations
Ex parte Milligan, 357
Exploration: by Columbus, 9, 13, 15 (map); English, 15 (map), 18; French, 15 (map), 18, 77–79; of Louisiana Purchase, 163, 165 (map); by Norse, 11; Portuguese, 12–13; Spanish, 13, 14–15. *See also* Space exploration
Exports: from Carolina, 29; colonial, 67, 89; of cotton, 255; growth of, 385; of tobacco, 50–51
Extraterritoriality, 291

Fabian socialism, 419
Factories: children in, 222; in Civil War, 316; Embargo Act and, 166; reforms of, 222, 224, 481; spread of, 178, 221; women in, 224, 225, 588; working conditions in, 222, 398, 482–483. *See also* Manufacturing
Factory girls, 224
Factory system, 118, 219, 221
Fair competition codes (NRA), 558
Fair Deal, 620
Fair Employment Practices Commission (FEPC), 589, 591
Fairey, Shepard, 716
Fair Labor Standards Act (1938), 556, 563
Faith-based social-welfare initiatives, 714
Fall, Albert B., 536, 539

Fallen Timbers, Battle of, 149
"Fall of the House of Usher, The" (Poe), 248
Falmouth (Portland), Maine, burning of, 103, 105
Falwell, Jerry, 695
Families: in 1950s, 629; in American Revolution, 98; in Chesapeake region, 50; child-centered, 225; of Chinese immigrants, 375; in cities, 419–420; in Civil War, 315; colonial, 50, 55–56, 123; feminism and, 711–712; of freedmen, 349; on homesteads, 435, 436; of Irish immigrants, 217; Iroquois, 30; of Italian immigrants, 409; "modern," 225; in New England, 55–56; pioneer, 212; single-parent, 679, 712; size of, 224–225, 397, 420; slave, 63, 256, 259, 260, 261; slaveowning, 257; in South, 397; in tenements, 406; women in, 225. *See also* Marriage
Family and Medical Leave Act (1993), 711
Family unification program, 653
Family values, in 1990s, 704, 712
Famine, in Ireland, 215, 217
Fannie Mae. *See* Federal National Mortgage Association
Fanon, Frantz, 661
FAO (Food and Agricultural Organization), 610
Far East: Yalta conference on, 608
Farewell Address: of Nixon, 673; of Washington, 149, 163
Farewell to Arms, A (Hemingway), 531
Farm bloc, 540
Farmers' Alliance, 379, 380–381, 444
Farms and farming: African Americans and, 379–380; cash crops and, 226, 439; in Central Valley (California), 439–440; during Civil War, 321; cooperatives and, 442; credit for, 374; debt of, 440; dry, 437; Dust Bowl and, 560–561, 560 (map); Embargo Act and, 165; in England, 23; Erie Canal and, 227; Grange and, 441–443; Greenback movement of, 443–444; grievances of, 440–441; Homestead Act and, 435–436; Hoover and, 543–544; immigrants and, 217, 407; interest rates for, 498; Japanese Americans in, 587; labor unions and, 399; in Maryland, 28; mechanization of, 226, 439; migrant labor for, 439, 440, 464; Native American, 433; New Deal and, 559–560; in Old Northwest, 182, 227; People's party and, 364, 383; protest in, 390; railroads and, 227, 389, 390, 441; sharecropping in, 353, 374, 396; in South, 54, 256, 257, 379–380; subsistence, 257; tariffs and, 379, 544; tenant, 23, 374, 440; in West, 435–437; in world economy, 440, 441. *See also* Agriculture
Farragut, David G., 336, 340
Fascism: Rome-Berlin Axis and, 572. *See also* Italy; Nazi Germany; Spain
Fast-food production, 629
Fathers. *See* Families; Men
Fatwa: bin Laden and, 713
Faubus, Orval, 634
Faulkner, William, 532, 642
FDR. *See* Roosevelt, Franklin Delano
Federal Art Project, 557
Federal budget. *See* Balanced budget; Budget deficits
Federal courts, 142, 345. *See also* Courts; Supreme Court (U.S.)
Federal Deposit Insurance Corporation (1933), 553, 555
Federal Emergency Management Agency (FEMA), 724
Federal Emergency Relief Act (1933), 553, 555
Federal Emergency Relief Administration (FERA, 1933), 553, 555

Federal Farm Board, 543
Federal Farm Loan Act (1916), 498
Federal government. *See* Government (U.S.)
Federal Highway Act (1956), 635
Federal Home Mortgage Corporation ("Freddie Mac"), 726
Federal Housing Administration (FHA), 556
Federal Housing Authority (FHA), 624
Federalist, The (Madison, Jay and Hamilton): Constitution and, 134; No. 10, 134, 135
Federalist party: Adams, John and, 150, 157; Alien and Sedition Acts and, 152; clash with antifederalists, 131–134, 132 (map); decline of, 158, 179; vs. Democratic-Republicans, 150, 153–154; Embargo Act and, 166; French Revolution and, 147; Hamiltonian wing of, 145, 153, 157; Hartford Convention and, 176; Judiciary Act and, 160–161; Marshall, John, and, 134; Neutrality Proclamation and, 148; patronage and, 160; Virginia and Kentucky resolutions and, 153; war faction of, 151; War of 1812 and, 169; XYZ Affair and, 150. *See also* Elections
Federal National Mortgage Association ("Fannie Mae"), 726
Federal Reserve Act (1913), 497
Federal Reserve Board, 497
Federal Reserve Notes, 497
Federal Reserve System, 321; economic policies of, 710; independent treasury and, 203–204
Federal Securities Act (1933), 553, 561
Federal spending. *See* Spending
Federal Trade Commission Act (1914), 497
Feminine Mystique, The (Friedan), 629, 678
Feminism: in 1960s, 629; in 1970s, 676–679; before Civil War, 678; domestic, 225; ERA (1972) and, 676; first-wave, 678; Gilman and, 420; literature and, 420, 422, 423; pacifism of, 507; progressivism and, 478; revolution by, 711–712; second-wave, 604, 678, 679; woman suffrage and, 419–420, 507. *See also* Women
Ferdinand of Aragon, 13
Ferlinghetti, Lawrence, 640
Ferraro, Geraldine, 693
Fertility rate, 214, 224
Fetterman, William J., 430
Fiction, 299
Field, Cyrus, 228, 394
Field hospitals, in Civil War, 323
Fifteenth Amendment, 356, 357, 360
Fifth Amendment, 302
"Fifty-four forty or fight," 275
Fifty-niners, 321, 434
Filibuster, in Senate, 732
Filibustering expeditions, 290
Filipinos and Filipino Americans, 457, 458, 462–463, 464
Fillmore, Millard, 286, 288, 291, 302
Films. *See* Movies and movie industry
Finance(s): in 1970s, 673–674; in 2008, 725; in American Revolution, 97, 98, 114; in Civil War, 320–321; in War of 1812, 174; Wilson's reforms and, 497; in World War I, 501. *See also* Economy; Spending
Financial panics. *See* Panics
Financial reforms, 270
Financial sector: corruption in, 368
Financier, The (Dreiser), 478
Finland: in World War II, 575
Finney, Charles Grandison, 234–235, 263
Firearms. *See* Weapons
Fire-bombing: of Japanese cities, 598, 602
"Fire-eaters," 283, 285, 286, 294; 1860 election and, 306

Fire Next Time, The (Baldwin), 642
Fireside chats, 555
First Amendment, 505, 664
First Anglo-Powhatan War (1614), 25
First Battle of Bull Run (1861), 327
First Continental Congress. *See* Continental Congress (First)
First Great Awakening, 69–71
First Lady. *See* specific individuals
1st Virginia Regiment, 253
First-wave feminism, 678
First World War. *See* World War I
Fischer, David Hackett, 47
Fishing: in New England, 57, 67
Fisk, "Jubilee Jim," 368
Fiske, John, 137
Fitzgerald, F. Scott, 531, 532
Fiume, in Versailles Treaty, 512
Five Civilized Tribes, 198, 199, 315
Five-Power Naval Treaty (1922), 538
Flappers, 530, 531
Fletcher v. *Peck,* 183
Flexible response doctrine, 643–644
Flophouses, 406–407
Florida, 430; 2000 election and, 715; acquisition of, 185; Compromise of 1877 and, 372, 373; Cubans in, 638; Jackson in, 184; Ponce de León in, 14; secession of, 308, 315 (map); Seminole Indians in, 184, 199; slavery in, 260; Spain and, 30, 32, 79, 84, 127
Florida Purchase Treaty (1819), 185
Flower children, 662
Flu: in 1918–1919, 511
Foch, Ferdinand, 509
Folger, Bathsheba, 46
Folklore: cowboys in, 435; mining frontier and, 434
Folk music, 245
Folkways: colonial, 74
Following the Color Line (Baker), 479
Foner, Eric, 310, 345, 362
Food: colonial, 74; in Columbian exchange, 13–14; shortages in Civil War, 316, 323; in World War I, 506
Food Administration: in World War I, 506
Food and Agricultural Organization (FAO), 610
Food Stamps (entitlement program), 665
Football, 425, 629
Foraker Act (1900), 459
Forbes, Charles R., 539
Force Acts (1870 and 1871), 360
Forced Founders (Holton), 116
Ford, Gerald ("Jerry"), 670; 1976 election and, 675, 680; assumption of presidency, 675–676; as vice president, 671, 675; Vietnam War and, 676
Ford, Henry, 391
Fordism, 526
Ford Motor Company: Model T Ford and, 474, 526–527; River Rouge plant of, 526
Fordney-McCumber Tariff Law (1922), 538
Ford's Theater, Lincoln's assassination at, 342
Foreclosures: in Great Recession, 726; in panic of 1819, 179
Foreigners. *See* Immigrants and immigration
Foreign policy: after Civil War, 451; after Cold War, 713; containment as, 611–612; dollar diplomacy in, 489; Hamilton vs. Jefferson on, 145; isolationism in, 163, 541–542; nationalism in, 183–185; of progressive-era presidents, 474; of Wilson, 498, 499–505. *See also* Imperialism; Manifest Destiny; Monroe Doctrine; specific issues and presidents
Foreign Relations of the United States, 597
Forest Reserve Act (1891), 485

Forests, 389, 485, 487, 490
Forest Service, 487
"Forgotten man": Roosevelt, F.D., on, 552, 565, 567
Formisano, Ron, 701
Formosa (Taiwan), 344, 470; economic development in, 674
Fort(s): in American Revolution, 113; French, 79, 80; in French and Indian War, 80, 81. *See also* specific forts
Fort Henry and Fort Donelson, Battle of, 336
For the Union Dead (Robert Lowell), 640
Fort Laramie, Treaty of (1851), 429
"Fortress America," 578
Fortress Europe, 594
Fort Sumter, attack on, 313–314
Forty-Eighters, 220
Forty-niners, 284
Foster, Stephen C., 245
Four-Power Treaty, 538
Fourteen Points (Wilson), 504, 511, 513
Fourteenth Amendment, 345, 355, 356, 360; birthright citizenship in, 376; corporation as person in, 395; equal protection clause of, 374; *male* inserted in, 357; Supreme Court on, 373; women and, 357, 678
Fourth party system, 448
Fox-Genovese, Elizabeth, 267
Fox Indians, 199
Fragging, 663
France: American Revolution and, 98, 109–110, 112, 114; Canada and, 77–79; Civil War and, 330–331, 337; D-Day and, 594–595; debt after World War I and, 542; England and, 3, 79, 164; exploration by, 15 (map), 18, 77–79; Four-Power Treaty and, 538; Huguenots in, 77; imperialism of, 470; Indochina and, 470; Jay's Treaty and, 150; Louisiana and, 32, 79, 162; Mexico and, 318–319; Mississippi River exploration by, 79; at Munich Conference, 574; Native Americans and, 77, 79; NATO and, 656; Neutrality Proclamation and, 148; New World and, 15 (map), 77–79; North American wars of, 80–83, 80 (map); Ohio River region and, 77, 79; postrevolutionary relations with, 127; after Seven Years' War, 81, 84; slave emancipation and, 146; Southeast Asian colonial rule by, 635; Spain and, 79; Texas and, 78, 271, 272; Treaty of Paris (1783) and, 114–115; Versailles Treaty and, 512; West Indies and, 68, 149, 150–151; in World War I, 500, 509, 509 (map), 511; in World War II, 575–576, 580, 594–595; XYZ affair and, 150. *See also* French Revolution; New France
Franciscans, in California, 19, 279
Franco, Francisco, 572, 573
Franco-American alliance (1778), 110, 147, 148, 149
Franklin, Benjamin: *Autobiography* of, 72, 245; at Constitutional Convention, 129, 130; Deism and, 233; education and, 73; electricity experiments by, 72; as envoy to France, 98, 109, 110, 114; as federalist, 132; Great Awakening and, 70; on Indian life, 27; "Join or Die" cartoon by, 81; library and, 72–73; on mercantilist system, 89; as Patriot, 106; in Philadelphia, 45; *Poor Richard's Almanack* by, 72; portrait of, 110; travel by, 110; Treaty of Paris and, 114
"Franklin chest," 46
Fraser, Douglas, 682
Fraternal societies, 350
Frazier-Lemke Farm Bankruptcy Act (1934), 556, 561

Freake, Elizabeth and Mary, 56
Freddie Mac. *See* Federal Home Mortgage Corporation
Fredericksburg, Virginia, Battle of, 333, 337
Frederick the Great (Prussia), 81
Free blacks: citizenship and, 302; in Civil War, 333; in Reconstruction, 358; in South, 259; War of 1812 and, 175. *See also* African Americans
Freedman's Savings and Trust Company, 370
Freedmen: Black Codes and, 353–354; at constitutional conventions, 357, 358; education for, 350; land for, 350, 354; letter to old master, 352; responses to freedom, 349–350; rights for, 345, 353, 355, 361; schools of, 350, 351; Union League and, 357; voting and, 355, 356, 357, 371
Freedmen's Bureau, 345, 350, 354, 362
Freedom(s): former slaves and, 349–350; of press, 73; of speech, 152, 266. *See also* specific rights and freedoms
Freedom dues, for indentured servants, 51
Freedom Riders, 646
Freedom Summer (1964), 653
Free enterprise, Jefferson and, 397
"Free incorporation" laws, 222
Free love, 243, 419
Freeman, Elizabeth "Mumbet," 136
Free market: in 1970s, 674; Friedman, Milton, and, 683; Reagan and Thatcher on, 689
Free-market capitalism, 209, 734
Freemen: in Chesapeake region, 51; in Massachusetts Bay Colony, 38
Freeport Doctrine, 304
Freeport question, 304
Free silver, 381, 382, 444, 446, 447. *See also* Silver
Free Soil, Free Labor, Free Men (Foner), 310
Free-soilers, 266, 294, 298–300, 302
Free Soil party, 265, 283–284, 289
Free speech: clear and present danger and, 505; criminal syndicalism laws and, 519; Sedition Act and, 152; slavery controversy and, 266
Free Speech Movement, 660
Free states, 284, 287, 292, 293 (map)
Free to Choose (Friedman and Friedman), 682
Free trade: in Atlantic Charter, 674
Frémont, John C., 277, 301, 303, 304
French and Indian War (1754–1763): colonies after, 3, 83–84; in North America, 80–83, 80 (map); Washington in, 80, 81. *See also* Seven Years' War
French Empire, 77
French Revolution (1793–1802), 344; American Revolution and, 115, 146, 147; Austria and, 145; Bastille and, 146; as class conflict, 147; impact of, 145, 147; Reign of Terror in, 147
French West Indies, 68, 149. *See also* West Indies
Freud, Sigmund, and Freudianism, 530, 640
Friedan, Betty, 629, 678
Friedman, Milton, 682, 683
Friedman, Rose, 682
From Here to Eternity (Jones), 640
From Puritan to Yankee (Bushman), 75
Frontier, 427; in American Revolution, 112–113; boundaries of, 449; "closing" of, 437, 449; colonial, 62, 84; conservation movement and, 487; federal government and, 364; global, 442–443; movement to, 212–213; as safety valve, 437–439; Scots-Irish on, 62
Frontiero v. *Richardson,* 679
"Frontier thesis" (Turner), 437, 442; historians on, 449

Fronts. *See* World War I; World War II
Frost, Robert, 532
Frostbelt, 622
Fuels: after World War II, 621
Fugitive-slave law (1793), 285
Fugitive Slave Law (1850), 286, 287-289, 287 (map), 289, 290, 294, 297
Fugitive slaves. *See* Runaway slaves
Führer. *See* Hitler, Adolf
Fuller, Margaret, 241, 243
Fulton, Robert, 227
Functionalism, 716
Fundamentalism, 525; evolutionary theory and, 524-525; Islamic, 721; Modernists vs., 528
Fundamental Orders, 39
Funding at par, 142
Fur trade: American, 213; British-Indian, 126, 272; French, 78

Gabriel (slave), 262
Gaddis, John Lewis, 625, 668
Gadsden, James, 291
Gadsden Purchase, 291, 292 (map)
Gag Resolution, 266
Gaine, Hugh, 107
Galbraith, John Kenneth, 630
Gallatin, Albert, 160
Galveston, Texas, reforms in, 480
Gandhi, Mohandas (Mahatma), 247, 632
Gang-labor slavery, 54, 63
Gangsters: in 1920s, 524; in labor unions, 637
Gans, Herbert, 623
Garfield, James A., 376
Garfinkle, Adam, 668
Garment industry, 221, 420
Garrison, William Lloyd, 263, 265, 266, 289
Garvey, Marcus, 530, 654
Gasoline engine, 527
Gates, Horatio, 109
Gauges, railroad, 228
Gay marriage. *See* Same-sex marriage
Gay rights activists, 660
Gays and lesbians: in 1960s, 660; Bush, George W., and, 724; in military, 705; as parents, 712; rights of, 723
Gaza Strip, 656
Gehry, Frank, 716
Gender and gender issues: equality and, 652, 678, 711; family leave policies and, 711; imperialism and, 472; separate spheres and, 481; slavery and, 267; women as workers and homemakers, 629; women's roles and, 481; after World War II, 604, 621. *See also* Men; Women
Gender equality, 136
Gender gap: between political parties, 700
General Agreement on Tariffs and Trade (GATT), 610, 674
General amnesty act (1872), 369
General Court (Massachusetts Bay Colony), 38
General Motors: government support for, 726; sit-down strike at, 563, 564; status of, 729
Generation Divided, A (Klatch), 668
Genêt, Edmond, 148
Genocide: in Rwanda, 713; in World War II, 576, 598
Genovese, Eugene, 267, 310
Gentlemen's Agreement (1907-1908), 470, 587
Geography: American Revolution and, 98; of North America, 5-6
Geology: of North America, 5-6
George II (England), 32
George III (England), 93, 97, 103, 106, 108, 112, 114
George, Henry, 385, 419; on wealth, 385

Georgia: in American Revolution, 112; as buffer colony, 32; in Civil War, 337-338, 338 (map); colonization of, 32; Constitution and, 131; secession of, 308, 315 (map); slavery in, 32, 63, 131, 260, 261; War of Jenkins's Ear in, 79
Georgian style architecture, 72
German Samoa, 453
German soldiers: as Hessians, 97, 103, 105, 108
Germantown, Pennsylvania, battle at, 109
Germany: China and, 463; education models from, 415, 417; England and, 453; immigrants from, 61-62, 118, 215, 216-217, 220, 302, 407; imperialism of, 344, 470; partition of, 610-611, 611 (map); reparations and, 541, 542; reuniting of, 697; Samoan Islands and, 453; in Seven Years' War, 81; unification of, 344; and United States in Great Depression, 600; in World War I, 500-503, 505, 508; after World War I, 511; before World War II, 475; after World War II, 610-611; Yalta conference and, 608. *See also* Nazi Germany
Geronimo (Apache), 430
Gestapo, 600
Gettysburg, Battle of, 334, 334 (map), 337
Gettysburg Address, 252, 334-336
Ghent, Treaty of (1814), 175, 177
Ghost Dance religious movement, 432
Ghost towns, 434
Gibbons, James (Cardinal), 414
GI Bill, 409, 618, 619
Gibson, Charles Dana, 397
Gibson Girl, 397
Gilbert, Humphrey, 22
Gilbert Islands, in World War II, 593
Gilded Age: class and, 374, 395; political parties in, 371; politics in, 371, 382; progressive historians and, 383; in South, 362
Gilded Age, The (Warner and Twain), 383, 422
Giles, W.B., 166
Gilman, Charlotte Perkins, 420
Ginés de Sepulveda, Juan, 14
Gingrich, Newt, 700, 706-707, 714
Ginsberg, Allen, 640
Ginzberg, Lori, 250
Gipson, Lawrence, 116
Gitlin, Todd, 668
Glaciers, 6
Gladden, Washington, 410
Glasnost, 693, 697-698
Glass-Steagall Banking Reform Act (1933), 553, 555, 710
Glidden, Joseph F., 437
Global economy: Columbus and, 13
Globalization, 710-711; in 1960s, 643; of American Revolution, 110; Carter, trade, and, 681; era of, 674-675; industrial competition and, 673-675
Global village, 703
Glorious Revolution (England, 1688-1689), 41
Gloucester (warship), 460
Godey's Lady's Book, 238
Godkin, Edwin L., 419
Goebbels, Joseph, 576
Goering, Hermann, 602
Goethals, George Washington, 468
Golan Heights, 656
Gold: from Africa, 12; Aztec, 17; in Bank of America, 199; in Black Hills, 430; depression of 1890s and, 381; discoveries of, 434, 449; mining, 434; panic of 1873 and, 370; Pikes Peak and, 434, 437; reserves in Treasury, 381, 382; Roosevelt, F.D., and, 553, 555; vs. silver, 370, 379, 381, 382; Spain and, 14

"Gold Bugs," 446
Golden spike, 387, 388
Gold market: Fisk-Gould scandal and, 368
Gold rush, in California, 279, 284, 290
Gold standard, 382, 446, 555
Gold Standard Act (1900), 449
Goldwater, Barry, 652, 668
Goliad, 205
Gompers, Samuel, 400, 497, 506
Goodbye, Columbus (Roth), 642
Good Earth, The (Buck), 558
Good Neighbor policy, 571-572
Goodwin, Richard, 643
Goodwyn, Lawrence, 383
Goodyear, Charles, 222
G.O.P. (Grand Old Party). *See* Republican Party
Gorbachev, Mikhail: Cold War and, 625, 697, 698; end of Soviet Union and, 698; glasnost and perestroika of, 693, 697-698
Gordon, Linda, 568
Gore, Albert, 704, 714-715; 2000 election and, 714, 715, 715 (map)
Gorgas, William C., 460, 468
Gospel of wealth, 395, 413
Gotcher, Mrs. E., 484
Gothic architecture, 245
Gould, Jay, 368, 390, 394, 398, 400
Government: Articles of Confederation and, 125; Cherokee, 198; of colonies, 28, 37, 38, 73-74; Confederate, 315, 319; Hamilton and, 129; in Kansas, 298-300; of Massachusetts Bay Colony, 37, 38; nationalism and, 171, 344; of New France, 77; of Pennsylvania, 44; of Plymouth Colony, 36; progressivism in cities and states and, 480; radical regimes, 358-359; ten-percent, 353; in Virginia, 28; women in, 712. *See also* Government (U.S.)
Government (U.S.): and business, 446; check on slavery, 252; Civil War and power of, 344, 345; closure in 2013, 731; depression of 1890s and, 381; growth during World War II, 590; immigrants and, 408; income from tariffs, 143; intervention by, 590; prohibition and, 522-524; Reagan and, 689; Roosevelt, F.D., and, 475; shutdown of (1990s), 707; stock speculation in 1920s and, 533; and welfare of people, 476. *See also* specific issues
Government girls, 322
Governors: colonial, 73-74
Gower, George, 23
Gradualism, Washington, Booker T., and, 416
Graduated income tax, 379
Grady, Henry W., 396, 397
Graft. *See* Corruption
Graham, Billy, 629
Grain: during Civil War, 318; colonial, 67; harvesting, 226; panic of 1837 and, 203; world market for, 439, 440
Grand Alliance, in World War II. *See* Allies (World War II)
Grand Army of the Republic (GAR), 371, 372, 378
Grand Canyon, 437
Grand Central Terminal (New York), 424
Grand Coulee Dam, 558, 559
Grandfather clause, 381
Grandparents, in New England, 56
Grand Teton: naming of, 78
Grange, 390, 441-443
Granger Laws, 443
Grant, Ulysses S., 366; 1868 election and, 367-368; 1872 election and, 369; 1876 election and, 371; cabinet of, 368, 369; in Civil War, 317, 328, 336, 337, 340-341; corruption

under, 366, 368–369; in Mexican War, 280; panic of 1873 and, 370; on unconditional surrender, 336
Grapes of Wrath, The (Steinbeck), 560, 561
Graves, Michael, 716
Gray, Robert, 273
Great American Desert, 436, 437
Great Awakening: First, 69–71; Second, 232, 234–235, 237
Great Basin, 6
Great Britain. *See* England (Britain)
"Great Compression, The," 604
Great Compromise, 130
Great Depression (1929–1941), 402, 475; 1929 crash and, 544–545; agriculture in, 556, 559–560; demagogues during, 557; Dust Bowl in, 560–561, 560 (map); economic impact of (1929–1940), 553–557, 558–563; economy in, 552, 553–557; in Germany and United States, 600; Hoover and, 544–548; radicalism of New Deal in, 568; unemployment in, 556–557, 558–559; World War II and, 590. *See also* New Deal; specific acts
Great English Migration (1630s), 37
Great Gatsby, The (Fitzgerald), 531
Great Ice Age, 6
Great Lakes region: British in, 172, 173, 177; Erie Canal and, 178, 227; formation of, 6; French in, 78; Native Americans in, 27, 62; shipping system in, 391, 392; in War of 1812, 172, 173, 175
Great Migration: of blacks to North, 506, 633
Great Northern Railroad, 388
Great Plains: Dust Bowl in, 560–561, 560 (map); homesteads in, 436; horses in, 14, 26; Native Americans in, 428–434; Shelterbelt project in, 486; Sioux Indians in, 10 (map). *See also* Plains Indians; West
Great powers: naval race in late 1800s, 453
Great railroad strike, 374
Great Rapprochement, 453
Great Recession: of 2008, 605, 718, 727, 733
Great Salt Lake, 6, 237 (map)
Great Sioux Reservation (Dakotas), 429, 430
Great Society, 604, 652; funding of, 673
Great Train Robbery, The (movie), 528
Great White Fleet, 470–471
Greece: immigrants from, 407; Truman Doctrine and, 612
Greek Revival architecture, 245
Greeley, Horace, 316, 332, 369
Greenback Labor party, 370, 443–444, 477
Greenback movement, 441
Greenbacks: in Civil War, 320–321; panic of 1873 and, 370. *See also* Currency; Paper money
Green Berets, 643
Greene, Jack, 75
Greene, Nathanael, 112
Greenhouse gases, 721
Greenville, Treaty of (1795), 149
Greer (destroyer): Nazi attack on, 580
Grenada, U.S. invasion of, 692
Grenville, George, 90, 91
Griffin, James, 52
Griffith, D.W., 528
Grimké, Angelina and Sarah, 241
Griswold v. Connecticut, 664
Gross national product (GNP): federal spending and, 689; foreign trade and, 681; after World War II, 590, 618
Guadalcanal Island, 592–593
Guadalupe Hidalgo, Treaty of (1848), 237 (map), 278, 282
Guam, 344, 458; in World War II, 591, 593

Guantanamo: Detention Camp at, 722; naval base at, 461
Guatemala, CIA-directed coup in, 638
Guerrière (ship), 173
Guerrilla warfare: by Filipinos, 462; in Palestine, 691; against Russia in Afghanistan, 684; by Seminoles, 199; in Vietnam War, 655
Guevara, Che, 661
Guggenheim Museum: in Bilbao, Spain, 716; in New York, 640
Guiteau, Charles J., 376
Gulf of Mexico region: geography of, 6
Gulf War. *See* Persian Gulf War
Gullah language, 63
Gunboats, 336
Guthrie, Oklahoma, 437
Gutman, Herbert, 402

Habeas corpus, writ of, 319
Hahn, Steven, 362
Haiti: dollar diplomacy in, 489; on Hispaniola, 14; slave revolt in, 265; U.S. intervention in, 498, 572
Hakluyt, Richard, 24
Haldeman, H.R., 672
Hale, John P., 289
Half-Breeds, 371
Half-Way Covenant, 57
Hall, Basil, on cotton belt, 256
Hall, Jacquelyn, 668
Halsey, Harlan P., 421
Hamilton, Alexander, 139; Adams, John, and, 151, 157; Annapolis Convention and, 128; Bank of the United States and, 143–144; Burr and, 163–164; at Constitutional Convention, 128, 129; death of, 164; as Federalist, 134; financial plan of, 142–143; French Revolution and, 147; Jefferson and, 142, 143–144, 145, 154; loose construction theory of, 144, 178; portrait of, 145; on Quebec Act, 96 (map); trade and, 143; as treasury secretary, 141, 142–144; Zenger and, 73
Hampton Institute, 416
Hancock, John, 89, 97, 129
Hancock, Winfield Scott, 376
Handsome Lake (Iroquois), 31
Handy, W.C., 530
Hanna, Marcus Alonzo (Mark), 445–446, 447, 465
Hansberry, Lorraine, 642
Harding, Warren G., 535, 536–539; 1920 election and, 515, 527, 536; cabinet of, 536; corruption under, 536, 539; Debs pardoned by, 505; foreign policy of, 538; on normalcy, 474, 518; Supreme Court and, 536–537
Hard-money advocates, 370, 446
Harlem Renaissance, 530
Harmar, Josiah, 149
Harper's (Harper's New Monthly Magazine), 418
Harpers Ferry, Brown, John at, 304–305
Harper's Weekly, 369
Harrington, Michael, 652
Harrison, Benjamin, 378–379, 380 (map), 454
Harrison, William Henry, 270, 378; 1836 election and, 202; 1840 election and, 206–207; on Tecumseh, 168; Tippecanoe battle and, 167, 206; War of 1812 and, 173, 176
Hart, Gary, 696
Harte, Bret, 423, 434
Hartford, 39
Harvard University, 18, 56–57, 74, 239, 416, 418
Harvester trust, 394
Harvey, William Hope, 444
Haselbock, Joe, 484

Hatch Act (1939), 556, 566
Haussmann, Georges-Eugène, 424
Havana, 455
Hawaii: annexation of, 453–454, 457; European diseases in, 454; Filipino laborers in, 464; immigrant workers in, 454; Japanese migration to, 587; Pearl Harbor attack in, 475, 581–582; statehood for, 639
Hawaiian Sugar Planters Association, 464
"Hawks" (Vietnam War), 656, 658–659
Hawley, Willis, 543
Hawley-Smoot Tariff (1930), 543, 544, 552
Hawthorne, Nathaniel, 56, 243, 248
Hay, John, 461–462, 463, 465
Hay-Bunau-Varilla Treaty (1902), 467
Hayden, Tom, 660
Hayes, Rutherford B.: 1876 election and, 372, 373, 373 (map); railroad strike and, 374
Haymarket Square episode, 400, 445
Hayne, Robert, 195
Hay-Pauncefote Treaty (1901), 290, 467
Hayslip, Le Ly, 645 (map)
Haywood, William D. ("Big Bill"), 505
H-bomb. *See* Hydrogen bomb
Headright system, 51
Head Start, 653
Health and health care: in Chesapeake region, 50; Clinton, Hillary, and, 705; maternal and infant, 507; in New England, 55, 58; Obama and, 727, 730. *See also* Disease; Medical care; Medicine
Hearst, William Randolph, 418, 452, 499
Hebrew schools, 408
Heller, Joseph, 640
"Hello girls," 397
Helper, Hinton R., 297
Helsinki accords (1975), 676
Hemings, Madison, 159
Hemings, Sally, Jefferson and, 157, 159
Hemingway, Ernest, 531
Hendrix, Jimi, 660
Henretta, James, 402
Henry VII (England), 15 (map)
Henry VIII (England), 22, 36
Henry, Patrick: as antifederalist, 132, 134, 135; Constitutional Convention and, 129; First Continental Congress and, 96
Henry Street Settlement, 410
Hepburn Act (1906), 483
Heresy: Hutchinson and, 38–39
Hermitage (Nashville, Tennessee), 193
Hessians, in American Revolution, 97, 103, 105, 108
Hetch Hetchy Valley, flooding of, 487
Hewitt, Nancy, 250
Heyrmann, Christine, 75
Hiawatha (Iroquois), 11, 30
Hicks, John D., 383
"High crimes and misdemeanors," 361
Higher education: blacks in, 238, 239, 416, 710; support for, 237–238, 344; for women, 238, 239, 416. *See also* Universities and colleges
High Federalists, 150
High schools, 415
High-tech industries, 628
Highways. *See* Roads and highways
Hill, Anita, 700
Hill, James J., 388, 483
Hillbillies, 257, 397
"Hindrances to Revivals" (Finney), 235
Hine, Lewis, photography of, 399, 523
Hip-hop, 717
Hirohito (Japan), 599
Hiroshima, atomic bombing of, 599, 602
Hispanics: in Southwest, 439. *See also* Latinos

Hispaniola: Columbus in, 14; *encomienda* system in, 15. *See also* Dominican Republic; Haiti
Hiss, Alger, 616
History and historians: on American Revolution, 116; on antebellum reformers, 250; on causes of Civil War, 310; on colonial society, 75; consensus view of, 137; on Constitution, 137; on distinctiveness of America, 47; on Europeanization of America, 47; imperial school of, 116; on Jacksonian democracy, 209; Nationalist school of, 137; on nature of slavery, 267; on New Deal, 568; progressive school of, 116, 137; revisionist and postrevisionist, 625; social movements and, 116; of technology, 223; transatlantic view of, 116; on U.S. imperialism, 472; Whig view of history, 116
History of the United States During the Administrations of Jefferson and Madison (Adams), 423
History of the United States of America (Bancroft), 116
Hitler, Adolf, 557, 600, 601; aggression by, 475, 574; Holocaust and, 576; last days of, 596–597; Lebensraum (living space) and, 576; lend-lease and, 580; militarization by, 574; Rome-Berlin Axis and, 572; Roosevelt, F.D., compared with, 600; Spanish Civil War and, 573; suicide of, 598; in World War II, 593
Hitler-Stalin pact (1939), 574–575, 580
Hoar, George F., 458
Hoban, James, 177
Hoboes (tramps), 381
Ho Chi Minh, 471, 635
Hoffa, James R. ("Jimmy"), 637
Hofstadter, Richard, 209, 383, 472, 701
Holding companies, 497
Holidays: colonial celebration of, 74
Holland: in American Revolution, 110; Separatists in, 36; Texas and, 271. *See also* Dutch
Holloway, Houston H., 350
Holocaust (World War II), 598; refugees from, 576
Holt, Michael, 310
Holton, Woody, 116
Holy Land: crusaders in, 11
Holzer, Jenny, 716
Home front: Bush, George H.W., and, 664–665; in Cold War, 616–617; Nixon and, 664–665; in World War I, 508; in World War II, 589–590
Home guards, in Confederacy, 333
Homeland Security Department, 722
Home Loan Bank Bill, 547
Home Owners' Loan Corporation (HOLC, 1933), 553
Home Owners' Refinancing Act (1933), 553
Homer, Winslow, 238, 423
Home rule: for American colonists, 81
Homestead Act: of 1860, 303; of 1862, 321, 344, 354, 435–436
Homesteading, 435–436
Homestead Strike, 379–380
Homosexuals. *See* Gays and lesbians
Honduras, 489
Hong Kong, 291, 471, 591
Hooker, Joseph ("Fighting Joe"), 333–334
Hooker, Thomas, 39
Hoover, Herbert, 535; 1928 election and, 542–543; 1932 election and, 552; as commerce secretary, 536, 537; economy and, 544–545; as Food Administration head, 506; Great Depression and, 544–548; on New Deal, 565; political cartoon about, 547; on poverty, 535

Hoovervilles, 545, 546
Hopkins, Harry L., 555, 556, 557
Hopwood v. *Texas*, 708
Horizontal integration, 392
Horses: in Great Plains, 14, 26, 429, 433; in North America, 14, 26; transportation and, 68
Horseshoe Bend, Battle of, 175
Hospitals: field (Civil War), 323
Hostage crisis (Iran, 1979), 683–684, 688
Hostages, in Lebanon, 693
Households: in market economy, 224; slave, 261; women's roles in, 711
House of Burgesses (Virginia): committees of correspondence and, 94; formation of, 28
House of Mirth, The (Wharton), 422
House of Representatives (U.S.): Clay as Speaker of, 190; in Constitution, 130; direct election to, 131; Gag Resolution in, 266; impeachment in, 360; presidential elections and, 158, 190, 191; war hawks in, 169. *See also* Congress (U.S.); Senate (U.S.)
House Un-American Activities Committee (HUAC), 616
Housing: colonial, 28; discrimination in, 624; Iroquois, 30, 31; in New Deal, 556, 562; of pioneers, 212; on plantations, 256, 264; price bubble in, 725; slums and, 406–407, 477–478; sod, 436; in suburbs, 622–624; after World War II, 620
Housing Act (1949), 620
Housing and Urban Development Department (HUD), 653
Houston, Sam, 205, 206, 206 (map), 308 (map)
Hovenden, Thomas, 305
Howard, Oliver O., 350
Howard University, 350, 416
Howe, Daniel Walker, 209
Howe, Elias, 221, 223
Howe, William, 108, 109
Howells, William Dean, 421, 530
"Howl" (Ginsberg), 640
How the Other Half Lives (Riis), 477–478
HUD. *See* Housing and Urban Development Department
Hudson, Henry, 42
Hudson Bay: England and, 79; native peoples of, 21
Hudson River region, 42, 43, 45, 108, 112
Hudson River school, 245
Hudson's Bay Company, 272
Huerta, Victoriano, 499–500
Hughes, Charles Evans, 502; 1916 election and, 502, 502 (map); as secretary of state, 536, 538
Hughes, Langston, 532
Huguenots, 35, 62, 77
Hull, Cordell, 576
Hull House, 410, 481
Hulsart, C.B., 249
Hulton, Ann, 94
Human rights: in Atlantic Charter, 580; China and, 710; Helsinki accords and, 676; slavery and, 259
Human sacrifices: Aztec, 7
Humphrey, Hubert H., 658, 659, 659 (map), 683
Hundred Days (New Deal), 553–555; legislation passed in, 553, 558, 561; liquor industry and, 559
Hungary: communist collapse in, 697; uprising of 1956 in, 635; after World War II, 610
Hunting: colonial, 74; by Plains Indians, 433
Huntington, Collis P., 387
Huron Indians, 77
Hurricane Katrina, 724
Hurston, Zora Neale, 532

Hussein, Saddam, 693, 699
Hutchinson, Anne, 38–39
Hutchinson, Thomas, tea tax and, 94
Hwang, David, 717
Hydroelectric power, 561, 562
Hydrogen bomb, 614. *See also* Atomic bombs; Nuclear weapons

IBM (International Business Machines), 628, 729
Ice Age, 6
Ickes, Harold L., 558
Idaho, 434, 437
Idealism: diplomacy and, 110; of Wilson, 496, 503–504, 512–513, 516
Identity: ethnic, 521–522; family, of slaves, 261; multicultural, 62
Identity politics, of religious right, 695
"I Have a Dream" speech (King), 647
Illegal immigration, 375, 709, 732
Illinois, 314, 443; in American Revolution, 113; factory inspection in, 481; Native Americans in, 199. *See also* Chicago
Illinois River region, 78
Illiteracy: in 1860, 237; of blacks (1900), 416; of slaves, 262. *See also* Literacy tests
Immigrants and immigration: in 1775, 61–62, 62 (map); in 1830–1900, 215; in 1920s, 520–522; Alien Laws and, 152; after American Revolution, 118; annual, 522; antiforeignism and, 218–219, 302, 344, 364, 410–413; Bush, George W., and, 724; to Chesapeake region, 50, 51; in cities, 215; in Civil War, 316, 317, 323; culture of, 216, 220, 375, 408, 409; education for, 216, 218, 415; Filipino, 463, 464; Japanese, 587; jobs for female, 420; Johnson, L.B., and, 653; labor of, 216, 217, 224, 391, 398, 412; Latino, 709; literature and, 218, 717; as Loyalists, 107; Mexican, 634; New, 407–408, 409–413, 521; to New England, 57, 62; Obama and, 731–732; Old, 407; Polish, 523; political machines and, 408–410; population of, 61–62, 215, 217, 256, 407, 408; Puerto Rican, 460; quota system and, 344; radicalism and, 397; railroads and, 216, 374, 389; reasons for, 215, 408; reforms of, 522, 731–732; repatriation of, 409; restrictions on, 344, 376, 407, 412–413; social change and, 474; as soldiers in Civil War, 323; South and, 256; terrorism by, 721–722; Vietnamese, 677; after World War I, 474–475. *See also* Illegal immigration; specific groups and locations
Immigration Act: of 1924, 521; of 1929, 521
Impeachment: of Clinton, 713–714; of Johnson, Andrew, 360–361; Nixon and, 673; Tyler and, 271
Impending Crisis of the South, The (Helper), 297
Imperialism: in 1920s, 541; American, 344, 352–353, 458–459, 462, 470, 471, 472; Asia and, 463–465, 470–471; debate over, 458, 459; ecological, 213; economic, 472; English, 22–24; global, 470–471; Japanese, 489; at Paris Peace Conference, 471, 512–513; in Philippines, 365, 458, 459, 462; Russian, 489; scramble for Africa and, 470; and westernization, 470; Wilson and, 498
Imperialism: The Highest Stage of Capitalism (Lenin), 472
Imperial school of historians, 116
Imports: nonimportation agreements and, 91, 92, 93
Impressment, 149, 164; in Civil War, 333
Inauguration. *See* specific presidents

Incas, 6, 8, 15
Income: after World War II, 620, 673. *See also* Wages
Income gap. *See* Wealth gap
Income taxes, 320; graduated, 379; Sixteenth Amendment and, 497
Incorporation laws, 222
Indentured servants: in Chesapeake, 28, 51; contract of (1746), 52; in Maryland, 28, 51; in Virginia, 51
Independence: in Egypt, 636; of Mexico, 205; of Netherlands, 41; of Philippines, 471, 498, 571; of Vietnam, 471. *See also* American Revolution
Independence Hall (Philadelphia), 128
Independent Treasury Bill (1840), 204
Independent treasury system, 203; Polk and, 275; Whig party and, 270
India, 317; economic development in, 674; exploration of, 13; outsourcing of jobs to, 711; Pakistan and, 713. *See also* Gandhi, Mohandas
Indiana, 149, 167, 220, 314
Indian Affairs, Bureau of, 199
"Indian New Deal," 561, 635
Indian policy: forced assimilation, 432-434; removal as, 198, 199; reservation system and, 25, 365, 429-430, 431, 432
Indian Removal Act (1830), 199
Indian Reorganization Act (1934), 434, 556, 561
Indians: naming of, 13. *See also* Native Americans; specific groups
Indian Territory, 427; in Civil War, 315; Indian removal to, 198, 199, 429-430
Indian wars (1860-1890), 430, 431 (map), 433
Indies: Columbus and, 13; use of term, 13. *See also* Dutch East Indies; West Indies; specific locations
Indigenous peoples: in Americas, 26, 62; in Russia, 442. *See also* Native Americans; specific groups
Indigo: slaves and, 2
Individualism: Indian tribal organization and, 434; industrial society and, 364; of pioneers, 212-213; Tocqueville on, 197
Indochina: France and, 470, 635. *See also* Cambodia; Laos; Vietnam
Indonesia (Dutch East Indies): in World War II, 581, 591
Industrial capitalism, 402
Industrialization: economic development after, 474; higher education and, 418; historians on, 345, 402; imperialism and, 470; inventions and, 221; South and, 365, 396-397; spread of, 221, 364. *See also* Industry
Industrial Revolution, 324, 470; impact of, 397-398, 402; spread of, 219, 221, 364-365, 385
Industrial Workers of the World (IWW, Wobblies), 505, 506
Industry: in 1920s, 526-527, 537; American system of manufacturing and, 391; during Civil War, 316, 317, 321, 344; Federal Trade Commission and, 497; global competition and, 673-675; in Great Depression, 558-559; high-tech, 628; in middle colonies, 45; tariffs and, 378, 379; women workers in, 224, 225, 322, 397, 420; World War I and, 501; in World War II, 586, 589; after World War II, 621. *See also* Computers; Industrialization; Manufacturing; specific industries
Inequality: 2012 election and, 730; Civil War and racial, 345; economic, 230, 728; politics of, 728-729. *See also* Income gap; specific groups
Infantile paralysis (polio), 551

Infant mortality, 653
Infinite Jest (Wallace), 717
Inflation: in 1970s, 673; in American Revolution, 98, 114; under Carter, 681; during Civil War, 321; under Clinton, 710; free silver and, 444, 446; in Germany, 542; in New Deal, 555; panic of 1873 and, 370; in Revolution, 98, 114. *See also* Economy
Influence of Sea Power upon History, 1660-1783, The (Mahan), 453
Influenza pandemic (1918-1919), 511
Information age, 729
INF Treaty. *See* Intermediate-Range Nuclear Forces Treaty
Inheritance: primogeniture and, 23
Inhuman Bondage (Davis), 267
Initiative, 379, 479
Injunctions: against strikers, 398, 445
Inner cities: migration from, 624; race riots in, 655
Inner-ring suburbs, 623
Innovations: in transportation, 229, 391. *See also* Inventions
Inoculation: for smallpox, 66
Insanity, reforms in treatment of, 239-240
Installment buying, 223
Institutes of the Christian Religion (Calvin), 35
Instruments (musical): African, 65
Insular Cases (1901), 460
Insurance: health-care, 727; life, 479; old-age, 620; unemployment, 555; for veterans, 537
Insurrectos, 454
Integration (racial): Eisenhower and, 634; of schools, 634, 655. *See also* Civil rights movement; Desegregation; State(s)
Intellectual thought: in 1920s, 530-532; Enlightenment and, 146; "Gospel of Wealth" and, 395; pragmatism and, 418; Social Darwinism and, 395. *See also* Art(s); Literature; Philosophy; specific works and writers
Inter-American Conference for the Maintenance of Peace (1936), 572
Interchangeable parts, 221, 391
Interest rates: in 1970s, 680; in late 19th century, 440
Interlocking directorates, 392, 497
Intermarriage: European-Indian (Spanish America), 16, 17; by Filipino Americans, 464
Intermediate-Range Nuclear Forces (INF) Treaty (1987), 693
Internal combustion engine, 393
Internal improvements, 154, 178, 202, 229
Internal slave trade, 259, 260
International Bank for Reconstruction and Development. *See* World Bank
International Monetary Fund (IMF), 609, 674
International organizations. *See* specific organizations
International Style: of architecture, 640
International trade. *See* Trade
Internet: dot-com businesses and, 710; privacy and, 732
Internment camps, in World War II, 586
Interpreter of Maladies (Lahiri), 717
Interstate commerce, 128, 390, 395, 483; Federal Trade Commission and, 497; Supreme Court on, 558
Interstate Commerce Act (1887), 390-391, 396
Interstate Commerce Commission (ICC), 391, 483, 537
Interstate highways. *See* Roads and highways
Intervention: in Caribbean, 466 (map), 468, 498; in Cuba, 290, 572; governmental, 590; in Haiti, 498, 572; in Latin America, 541,

571-572, 638, 692; in Mexico, 499-500, 541; in World War II, 575. *See also* specific locations
Intolerable Acts (1774), 95
Inventions: cotton gin, 219, 221; by Edison, 392; employment for women and, 392, 397; by Franklin, 72; for mass textile production, 221; mechanical reaper, 222, 226; patents for, 221, 223; sewing machines, 221, 223; steel plow, 226; telegraph, 222, 228, 229. *See also* specific inventions and inventors
Investment(s): foreign, 498; foreign, in U.S., 385, 391; Great Depression and, 561; Great Recession and, 727; international, 675; in Latin America, 499; in Puerto Rico, 458; slaves as, 259. *See also* Capital investment
Invisible Hands (Phillips-Fein), 701
Invisible Man (Ellison), 642
Iran: CIA coup in, 636; hostage crisis in, 683-684, 688; oil from, 681; in OPEC, 637; revolution in (1979), 681; Soviet Union and, 611
Iran-Contra affair, 693-694
Iraq: Bush, George W., and, 722-723; in OPEC, 637; in Persian Gulf War, 699-700; Saddam Hussein in, 699; after World War I, 512. *See also* Iraq War
Iraq War (2003-2011), 605, 722-723; Obama and, 728; weapons of mass destruction and, 719, 722
Ireland: England and, 22; outsourcing of jobs to, 711. *See also* Irish immigrants; Northern Ireland
Irish Americans: 1884 election and, 377; Chinese immigrants and, 374; free blacks and, 216; labor unions and, 216; in New York draft riots, 320; population of, 215, 217; railroad labor of, 216, 386, 388. *See also* Irish immigrants
Irish immigrants, 62, 118, 215-216, 217, 259, 302, 407; as wage labor in South, 259, 264. *See also* Irish Americans
Iron and iron industry, 316; in Midwest, 271, 391
Ironclad oaths, 398
Ironclads (ships), 329
Iron curtain, 610
Iron Heel, The (London), 422
Iroquois Confederacy: in American Revolution, 30-31, 112; military alliance of, 11, 30-31; Sixth Nation of, 32
Iroquois Indians: in Appalachian region, 32; British and, 81, 84; empire of, 11, 30-31, 30 (map); French and, 77
Irreconcilables, 514 537
"Irrepressible conflict" speech (Seward), 306
Irrigation, 8, 236, 437, 485-487
Irving, Washington, 177-178, 246
Isaac, Rhys, 75
Isabella of Castile, 13
ISIS. *See* Islamic State of Iraq and Syria (ISIS)
Islam. *See* Arabs and Arab world; Muslims
Islamic Fundamentalists, 721
Islamic State of Iraq and Syria (ISIS), 733
Islamic terrorism, 713
Island-hopping: in World War II, 593
Isolationism: end of, 604; "new," 667; public opinion polls on, 577; Roosevelt, F.D., and, 571; Washington and, 163; after World War I, 474, 537-538, 541-542; before World War II, 475, 548, 572-573, 574, 578
Israel: in 1980s, 691-692; Camp David Agreement and, 680-681; Clinton and, 713; PLO and, 713; Six-Day War and, 656; Truman and, 613; Yom Kippur War (1973) and, 667

Issei, 587
Isserman, Maurice, 668
Italian Americans: in suburbs, 409; in World War II, 409
Italy, 344, 470; Ethiopia attacked by, 572, 573; immigrants from, 215, 227, 407, 409; imperialism of, 344; New Orleans lynching and, 453; rebellions in, 185; in Rome-Berlin Axis, 572; unification of, 344, 409; Versailles Treaty and, 512; in World War I, 500; after World War I, 512; in World War II, 594. *See also* Mussolini, Benito; World War II
Iwo Jima, in World War II, 598
IWW. *See* Industrial Workers of the World

Jackson, Andrew, 256, 270; 1824 election and, 190, 191; 1828 election and, 192-193, 193 (map); 1832 election and, 201; Bank War and, 199-201; cabinet of, 201; Florida invasion by, 184; inauguration of, 193, 227-228; on law, 189; Lone Star Republic and, 206; Native Americans and, 198-199; Nullification Crisis and, 195-196; on privilege, 208; spoils system and, 194; Tariff of Abominations and, 195; in War of 1812, 174-175, 176
Jackson, Helen Hunt, 432
Jackson, Jesse, 696
Jackson, Kenneth, 568
Jackson, Thomas J. ("Stonewall"), 316, 327, 333, 334
Jacksonian democracy, 179, 208, 209
Jackson State College: shootings at, 663
Jamaica: Black Loyalists in, 99; as British colony, 28, 60
James I (England): Separatists and, 36; Virginia and, 24, 28
James II (England, Duke of York), 41, 43, 45
James, Henry, 421, 422, 423, 530
James, William, 410, 418, 422, 459
Jameson, J. Franklin, 116
Jamestown: discipline in, 26; settlement at, 21, 24-25; slaves in, 53
Japan, 344; atomic bombings of, 599; China and, 463, 465, 548, 581; economic competition from, 673-674; Great White Fleet in, 471; imperialism and, 470-471, 489; Korea and, 344, 468, 470; Manchuria and, 548; military aggression by, 548; military occupation of, 613; modernization of, 344; naval disarmament and, 538; *Panay* incident and, 574; Pearl Harbor attack by, 475, 581-582; Perry in, 291; Russian war with, 468, 469; Versailles Treaty and, 572; in World War I, 500; after World War I, 512; before World War II, 475; World War II and, 581, 591-593, 598-599; after World War II, 674; Yalta conference and, 608. *See also* Japanese Americans
Japanese Americans, 587; relocation centers for, 586, 587; segregation of, 469-470; in World War II, 586
Japanese immigrants: in California, 469; in Hawaii, 454
Jarvis, John Wesley, 199
Jay, John: as chief justice, 142; as federalist, 134, 153; as secretary for foreign affairs, 127; Treaty of Paris and, 114, 115. *See also* Jay's Treaty
Jay's Treaty, 149, 150
Jazz, 63, 530, 531
Jazz age, 524, 527
Jazz Singer, The (movie), 528, 529
Jefferson, Thomas, 156; 1796 election and, 150; 1800 election and, 118, 156, 157-158, 158 (map); 1804 election and, 164; Adams, John, and, 150; on agriculture and manufacturing, 154; as architect, 245; Bank of the United States and, 143-144; Congress and, 160; on constitutional change, 120; Constitutional Convention and, 128, 129; death of, 167; Declaration of Independence and, 3, 106, 153; Deism and, 233; on demigods, 128; on despotism, 147; on education, 236; Embargo Act and, 165-166; Hamilton and, 142, 143-144, 145, 154; Hemings, Sally, and, 157, 159; inauguration of, 158, 160; on Jackson, 194; Louisiana Purchase and, 118, 162-163, 165 (map); military and, 161-162; on Missouri Compromise, 181, 181 (map), 183; patronage and, 160; portraits of, 153; as president, 158, 160-166, 177; on rebellion, 129; as secretary of state, 141; slavery and, 66, 154, 252, 254; strict construction theory of, 143; on town meetings, 57; University of Virginia and, 153, 238; viewpoints of, 154; Virginia and Kentucky resolutions and, 153; Washington and, 143
Jeffersonian Republicans. *See* Democratic-Republican party
Jenkins, Robert, 79
Jeremiah, 57
Jerusalem, 656
Jesuits, 78
Jet planes, 628
Jews and Judaism: colonial, 29, 39; Hitler and, 574, 600; Holocaust and, 576, 598; as immigrants, 62, 220, 407, 408, 420; literature after World War II, 642; in Maryland, 28; Nazi Germany and, 600; in Rhode Island, 39; in Russia, 408; in Soviet Union, 676; on Supreme Court, 498; as vice presidential candidate, 714. *See also* Israel
Jiang Jieshi (Chiang Kai-shek), 608, 614
Jihadi fighters: in Afghanistan, 728
Jihadist terrorism, in Iraq, 723
Jim Crow laws, 374, 381, 529, 631, 654
Jingoism, 462
Jobs: in cities, 406; of Irish immigrants, 216; New Deal creation of, 555-557; outsourcing of, 711; for women, 322, 420. *See also* Employment; Labor; Workers
"Johnny Reb" (Civil War), 323
Johns Hopkins University, 417
Johnson, Andrew, 257, 350-351; 1864 election and, 340; Congress and, 354-355; Fourteenth Amendment and, 355; Freedmen's Bureau and, 350; impeachment of, 360-361; pardons by, 348; Reconstruction plan of, 353; white supremacy of, 350
Johnson, Hiram W., 480
Johnson, Lyndon Baines, 604; 1960 election and, 639; 1964 election and, 652; 1968 election and, 657; assumption of presidency by, 647; cabinet of, 653; civil rights movement and, 653-655; Great Society of, 652, 653; presidency of, 651-657; Vietnam War and, 655-657; War on Poverty of, 652
Johnson, Samuel, 61
Johnson, Walter, 267
Johnson Debt Default Act (1934), 573
Joint Chiefs of Staff, 613, 615
Joint-stock companies, 23, 24
Jolson, Al, 528, 529
Jones, Jacqueline, 267
Jones, James, 640
Jones, John Paul, 113
Jones, Le Roi (Imamu Amiri Baraka), 642
Jones Act (1916), 498
Joplin, Janis, 660

Joseph, Chief (Nez Perce), 430, 431 (map)
Josephson, Matthew, 402
Journalism. *See* Magazines; Newspapers; Press; Yellow journalism
Joy Luck Club, The (Tan), 717
Juárez, Benito, 318
Judaism. *See* Jews and Judaism
Judicial branch: in state constitutions, 122. *See also* Courts; Supreme Court (U.S.)
Judicial nationalism, 182-183
Judiciary Act: of 1789, 142, 161; of 1801, 160-161
Jungle, The (Sinclair), 485
Jury: racial discrimination and, 373
Justice Department: antitrust prosecutions by, 396
Juvenile delinquency, reforms and, 480

Kagan, Elena, 727
Kahn, Louis, 640
Kaiser: Wilhelm II (Germany) as, 500, 511
Kallen, Horace, 522, 715
Kamikaze suicide pilots, 599
Kanagawa, Treaty of (1854), 291
Kansas: in 1854, 292, 293 (map); black migration to, 349; Bleeding Kansas, 298 (map), 300; proslavery vs. antislavery factions in, 294, 296, 298-300
Kansas City, stockyards in, 435
Kansas-Nebraska Act (1854), 252, 292-294, 304
Kansas Pacific Railroad, 390, 431, 432
Kaskaskia: Fort, 79, 113
Katrina, Hurricane, 724
Katz, Michael, 402
Katznelson, Ida, 568
Kazin, Michael, 668
KDKA radio station, 527
Kearney, Denis, 374
Kearney, Stephen W., 277
Kearny (destroyer), attack on, 580
Keelboats, 227
Kelley, Florence, 410, 481
Kelley, Oliver H., 441-442
Kellogg, Frank B., 538
Kellogg-Briand Pact (1928), 538
Kelly, "Honest John," 217
Kelly, Ned, 442
Kelly, William, 392
Kennan, George F., 516, 612
Kennedy, Anthony, 732
Kennedy, Edward, 688
Kennedy, John F. ("Jack"): 1960 election and, 638-639, 639 (map); assassination of, 647; cabinet of, 642; campaigning by, 641; civil rights and, 639, 639 (map), 646-647; Cuban missile crisis and, 644; foreign policy under, 643-646; inauguration of, 642; New Frontier of, 642-643; Vietnam War and, 643-644
Kennedy, Robert F. ("Bobby"): 1968 election and, 657, 658; assassination of, 658; civil rights and, 646
Kennedy Round, 643
Kent State University, shootings at, 663
Kentucky: as Border State, 314; landscape in, 213; as state, 140
Kentucky and Virginia resolution (1798). *See* Virginia and Kentucky resolutions
Kenya, embassy bombing in, 713
Kerosene, 393
Kerouac, Jack, 640, 660
Kerry, John F., 2004 election and, 724
Kessler-Harris, Alice, 568
Key, Francis Scott, 174
Keynes, John Maynard, 566
Keynesianism, 566, 670

Khrushchev, Nikita S.: Cuban missile crisis and, 644; Eisenhower and, 638; Kennedy and, 643; Nixon's kitchen debate with, 638
Kickbacks: to rail shippers, 390
Kindergarten, 216, 415
King, Coretta Scott, 632, 639
King, Martin Luther, Jr.: arrest of, 632; assassination of, 655; in Birmingham, 647; goals of, 655; "I Have a Dream" speech of, 647; influences on, 247; Kennedys and, 639, 646; SCLC and, 634; voter registration and, 654
King Cotton, 219, 256, 317
King George's War (1744-1748), 79
King Philip's War, 40
King's Mountain, battle of, 112
King v. Burwell, 733
King William's War (1689-1697), 79
Kiowa Indians, 429
Kipling, Rudyard, 459
Kiska (island), in World War II, 592, 593
Kissinger, Henry A., 516, 664, 666
Kitchen debate (1959), 639
Kitty Hawk, Wright brothers at, 527
Klan. *See* Ku Klux Klan
Klatch, Rebecca, 668
Knickerbocker Group, 245
Knickerbocker's History of New York (Irving), 246
Knights of Labor, 399-400, 563
Knock, Thomas J., 516
Know-Nothing party, 218, 294, 302
Knox, Henry, as secretary of war, 141
Knox, Philander C., 489
Koehler, Robert, 401
Köhler Codes of Nuremberg, 18
Kolko, Gabriel and Joyce, 625
Koons, Jeff, 716
Korea: Eisenhower in, 630; Japan and, 344, 468, 470. *See also* Korean War; North Korea; South Korea
Korean Americans: segregation of, 469
Korean War, 614-616, 615 (map), 621; end of, 630
Korematsu v. United States, 586
Kosovo, 713
Kramer, Paul, 472
Kremlin. *See* Soviet Union
Krimmel, John Lewis, 197
Kristallnacht, 576
Ku Klux Klan (KKK): in 1920s, 520, 521, 528; comeback of, 475; in Old Northwest, 182; during Reconstruction, 359-360
Kupperman, Karen, 47
Kurile Islands, 608
Kushner, Tony, 717
Kuwait: Iraq and, 699-700; in OPEC, 637
Kyoto Treaty, 721

Labor: in 1920s, 537; African, 53, 63; Chinese immigrants as, 375, 387, 388, 440; for cotton industry, 119, 219; Eisenhower and, 637; factory system and, 222, 224; Filipino, 464; of freedmen, 350; in Great Depression, 558-559; in Hawaii, 454; immigrant, 216, 217, 398; industrial, 222, 224; of Irish immigrants, 216, 217, 259, 264, 386, 388; of Italian immigrants, 409; in Maryland, 28; Mexican, 440, 709; migrant farm, 440, 444; in New Deal, 562-564; of pioneers, 226; slave, 53, 63, 252, 254, 259, 260; slave vs. free, 265-266, 284; southern, 259, 396, 397; Square Deal for, 482-483; for sugar industry, 21, 28, 29; in tobacco industry, 27, 28; for transcontinental railroad, 386, 387, 388; in World War I, 506-507; in World War II, 588. *See also* Child labor; Labor unions; Servants; Slaves and slavery; Workers; Work force
Labor contracts, freedmen and, 350, 353
Labor Day, 401
Labor Department, 483; Children's Bureau in, 481; Women's Bureau in, 481
Labor movement, 413; early efforts at organization, 224; weakness of, 374. *See also* Labor unions; Strikes
Labor unions: in 1920s, 537; in 1950s, 604, 629; in 1970s, 670; African Americans and, 399; Civil War and, 398; Clayton Anti-trust Act and, 497; decline of, 729; Eisenhower and, 637; ethnic rivalries and, 522; Hoover and, 543; immigrants and, 216, 412; injunctions used against, 398, 445; of Irish miners, 216; laws against, 222; National Labor Union and, 399; New Deal and, 558-559, 563; Sherman Anti-Trust Act and, 396; Taft-Hartley Act and, 618; yellow-dog contracts and, 546. *See also* Strikes; specific unions and industries
Lafayette, Marquis de (Gilbert du Motier), 98, 146
LaFeber, Walter, 472
La Follette, Robert M. ("Fighting Bob"), 480; 1912 election and, 491; 1924 election and, 540, 541 (map)
La Follette Seamen's Act (1915), 498
Lahiri, Jhumpa, 717
Laird rams (Confederate warships) crisis, 318, 337
Laissez-faire philosophy, 378, 395, 477
Lake Erie, Battle of, 173
Lakes. *See* specific lakes
Lakota (Sioux) Indians, 26
Lame-duck period, 158, 308
Lancaster Turnpike, 226
Land: in California, 439; of Californios, 279; in Carolina, 29; in Chesapeake, 27, 28; in colonies, 23, 26, 27, 28, 32, 43, 44; for cotton, 255, 256; Dawes Act and Indian, 432, 434; Dust Bowl and, 560-561, 560 (map); Erie Canal and, 227; for freedmen, 350, 354; grants to railroads, 386, 387 (map), 388, 389, 436; Homestead Act and, 321, 344, 435-436; homesteads from public lands, 303; in Maryland, 28; Mexican Cession, 278, 279, 280; in middle colonies, 44, 45; Native American, 25, 167, 432, 434, 437; in New England, 43; in Old Northwest, 125, 126 (map), 182; pioneers' use of, 213, 436, 437; speculation in, 179; states' claims and, 124; for sugar cultivation, 28-29; tobacco damage to, 27, 32, 50; for transcontinental railroad, 291-292, 292 (map), 386, 387 (map), 388; western cessions to U.S. (1782-1802), 124 (map). *See also* Public lands
Land Act (1820), 180
Land bridge: to Americas, 6, 7 (map)
Land-grant colleges, 344, 417
Landon, Alfred M., 563-564, 577
Landrum-Griffin Act (1959), 637
Lane Theological Seminary, 263
Language(s): Gullah as, 63
L'Anse aux Meadows, 11
Laos, 470
Larson, Jonathan, 717
La Salle, Robert, 19, 78, 79
Las Casas, Bartolomé de, 14, 15, 17
Last Moments of John Brown (Hovenden), 305
Last of the Mohicans, The (Cooper), 246
Latin America: Alliance for Progress and, 644; Cold War and, 638; democracy in, 185; Good Neighbor policy and, 571-572; immigrants from, 653; Iran-Contra affair and, 693-694; Mexican War and, 280; Monroe Doctrine and, 186, 187; Roosevelt Corollary and, 478; slavery in, 54; U.S. intervention in, 498-500, 499 (map), 692. *See also* Central America; Cuba; South America; Spanish America; specific locations
Latinos, 709. *See also* Hispanics; Immigrants and immigration
Latrobe, Benjamin Henry, 177
Laud, William, 37
Law(s): bankruptcy, 89; fundamental, in state constitutions, 122; in Massachusetts Bay Colony, 38. *See also* Tariff(s); specific laws
"Law and order": Nixon on, 659, 671
Law enforcement: Clinton and, 705; Irish immigrants as police and, 216. *See also* Crime(s); Police
Lawrence, Kansas, proslavery attack on, 300
Lawyers: colonial, 66
Lazarus, Emma, 413
League of Nations: Covenant of, 512; Italian takeover of Ethiopia and, 572; mandates of, 512; Paris Peace Conference and, 513; United Nations and, 610; U.S. and, 537; Wells, H.G., on, 512; Wilson and, 504, 512, 514, 516; World Court and, 541
League of Women Voters, 551
Leapfrogging strategy: in World War II Pacific region, 593
"Learning by doing" philosophy, 524
Lease, Mary Elizabeth, 444
Leatherstocking Tales (Cooper), 246
Leather trust, 394
Leaves of Grass (Whitman), 247
Lebanon: American hostages in, 693; Israeli invasion of, 691-692; U.S. Marines in, 692
Lebensraum (living space): Hitler on, 576
Lecompton Constitution, 300
Lee, Mother Ann, 243
Lee, Richard Henry, 105, 106, 132
Lee, Robert E.: in Civil War, 316, 328, 329-330, 333-334, 337, 340, 341; at Harpers Ferry, 305; in Mexican War, 280; surrender of, 341-342
Leffler, Melvyn, 625
Leftist school of historians, 402
Left wing (political), 519
Legal Tender Act, 370
"Legend of Sleepy Hollow, The" (Irving), 246
Legislation: colonial taxation and, 73, 90; environmental, 486; for Great Society, 653; of Hundred Days Congress (1933), 553; later New Deal (1933-1939), 556. *See also* Law(s); specific types
Legislatures: colonial, 73; in Kansas, 298; state, 122, 359. *See also* Congress (U.S.)
Leisler's Rebellion, 59
Leisure: in 1950s, 629; colonial, 74; in late 19th century, 424-425; of southern planters, 256. *See also* Entertainment
LeMay, Curtis, 659
Lend-lease, 578, 579-580, 579 (map), 608
Lend-Lease Bill (1941), 579
Lenin, Vladimir I., 472
Lennon, John, 629
Leopold (Belgium), 470
Lesbians. *See* Gays and lesbians
Leuchtenburg, William, 568
Levine, Lawrence, 267
Levitt, William, 624
Levittown, 624
Levittowners, The (Gans), 623
Lewinsky, Monica, and Lewinsky affair (1998-1999), 713-714
Lewis, John L., 563
Lewis, Meriwether, 163

Lewis and Clark expedition. *See* Corps of Discovery
Lexington, battle of, 97, 101
Leyte Island, battle at, 598
Libel, 73
Liberalism: of German immigrants, 216; New Left and, 701; after World War I, 519-520
Liberal Protestants, 413
Liberal Republican party, 369
Liberator, The, 263, 265
Liberia, 470; freed blacks in, 263
Liberties. *See* Civil liberties; Freedom(s)
Liberty party, 265; 1844 election and, 274
Libraries: colonial, 72-73; private subscription, 73, 238; public, 73, 393, 418
Library of Congress, 418
Lichtenstein, Roy, 640
Lieberman, Joseph, 714
Life expectancy: in 1920s, 524; in Chesapeake, 50; in New England, 55; worldwide, since 1950, 675
Life insurance companies, 479
Lifestyle: in 1920s, 528-530; in 1950s, 628-629; American, 60; automobile and, 527; of Civil War soldiers, 323; after Civil War, 397; colonial, 45, 50, 54, 56-59; of consumer culture, 629-630; of Iroquois, 30; under Jim Crow, 631; in middle colonies, 45; in New England, 56-58; of pioneers, 212-213; of Plains Indians, 433; on plantations, 54, 256; progressive reforms and, 479; of slaves, 63, 64, 260-261; in South, 54, 256, 257, 374; suburban, 622-624, 623; urban, 406, 419-420; in Virginia, 50; after World War II, 604-605, 620-621, 673. *See also* Culture(s); Society; specific groups
Lighting: lightbulb and, 392, 393. *See also* Electricity
Lightning: Franklin and, 72
Liliuokalani (Hawaii), 454
Lily, The, 242
Lima, Peru: university in, 18
Limerick, Patricia Nelson, 449
Limited liability, 222
Limited war, 615-616
Lincoln, Abraham, 366; 1860 election and, 296, 305-306, 307 (map); 1864 election and, 340, 341 (map); abolitionism and, 266; assassination of, 342-343, 353; background of, 303-304; in Black Hawk War, 199; Border States and, 314-315; on Brown, John, 304; in Civil War, 314, 317, 327, 328, 330, 333, 334, 336; colonization of freed blacks and, 263; on Crittenden amendments, 309; Emancipation Proclamation of, 316, 330, 331, 332-333; Fort Sumter and, 313-314; funeral procession for, 342; Gettysburg Address of, 252, 334-336; on government, 312; *House Divided* speech of, 296; in Illinois legislature, 304; inauguration of, 312, 313, 347; Kansas-Nebraska Act and, 304; leadership by, 319; Mexican War and, 276; in Old Northwest, 182; political efforts against, 338-339; on race, 303; on Reconstruction, 347, 353; in Republican party, 294; on saving the Union, 253, 296, 316, 326; on secession, 313; on slavery proponents, 254, 260; Stowe, Harriet Beecher, and, 297; *Trent* affair and, 318
Lincoln-Douglas debates, 303, 304
Lindbergh, Charles A., 527, 578
Lindsay, Vachel, 447
Link, Arthur S., 516
Linotype machine, 418
Liquor. *See* Alcohol

Literacy: freedmen and, 350; in New England, 56. *See also* Illiteracy
Literacy tests: for immigrants, 412-413; for voting, 360, 374, 381
Literary Digest, 577
Literature, 365; in 1920s, 530-532; antislavery, 297; black dialect and folklore in, 423; colonial, 72; in England, 23; feminist, 420, 422, 423; immigrant, 218, 717; individualism in, 213; national, 177-178, 245-246; naturalism in, 421, 422-423; post-Civil War, 421-423; postmodern, 717; realism in, 421-422; reform, 418-419; regionalism in, 421, 423; transcendentalist, 246-248; *Uncle Tom's Cabin,* 297, 298, 299, 300; western, 434; by women, 247, 297, 422, 423; after World War II, 640-642; WPA and, 557. *See also* Novels; specific works and authors
Little Bighorn, Battle of the, 430
Little Rock, Arkansas, school integration in, 634
"Little Saigons," 677
Little Turtle (Miami chief), 149
Little Women (Alcott), 247
Litwack, Leon, 362
Livestock, 58
Living standards. *See* Lifestyle
Livingston, Robert R., 162
Livingston family, 43
Lloyd, Henry Demarest, 477
Lloyd George, David, 512
Loans: to Allies (World War I), 541, 542; by Morgan, J.P., to U.S.government, 382
Lochner v. *New York,* 482
Locke, John, 246
Lockouts, 398
Lodge, Henry Cabot, 413, 452, 512; Versailles Treaty and, 514
Lomax, Alan, 510
London: population of, 405; World's Fair in, 222
London, Jack, 422, 423, 487
London Economic Conference (1933), 571
Lonely Crowd, The (Riesman), 630
Lone Star Republic, 206, 271-272
Long, Huey P. ("Kingfish"), 557, 600, 642, 701
Long, John D., 456
Long Drive, 435
Longhouse, 30, 31
Longhouse religion, 31
Long Island, Battle of (1776), 108
"Long Telegram" (Kennan), 612
Looking Backward (Bellamy), 419
Lookout Mountain (Tennessee), 337
Loose construction theory, 144, 178, 183
Lords Proprietors, 29
Los Angeles: Latinos in, 709; racism in, 708; suburbia and, 623
Losing Ground (Murray), 668
"Lost Cause," 343, 348, 354
Lotteries: colonial, 74
Louis XVI (France, 1754-1793), 145
Louisbourg, capture and return of, 79, 82
Louisiana, 358; Civil War in, 336; Compromise of 1877 and, 372, 373; France and, 32, 79, 162; secession of, 308, 315 (map); slavery in, 260, 261; Spain and, 84, 162
Louisiana Purchase: Jefferson and, 118, 162-163, 165 (map); Lewis and Clark exploration of, 163, 165 (map); slavery and, 252
L'Ouverture, Toussaint, 162, 304
Lovejoy, Elijah P., 266
Lowell, James Russell, 276, 309
Lowell, Massachusetts, textile mills in, 222, 224
Lowell, Robert, 640

Loyalists (Spain), 573
Loyalists (U.S.): black, 99, 107; confiscation of property of, 108, 122; departure of, 121; in postrevolutionary America, 115; in Revolutionary period, 3, 94, 97, 103, 106-108; Treaty of Paris and, 115. *See also* American Revolution; Tories
"Loyal opposition," 145
Loyalty program, of Truman, 616
"Luck of Roaring Camp, The" (Harte), 423
Lumber: colonial, 57, 68; farmers and, 389; timber and, 68
Lumumba, Patrice, 661
Lusitania (passenger liner), 501
Luther, Martin, 35
Lutherans, 371
Luzon, Philippines, 598
Lyceums, 238, 247
Lynch, David, 717
Lynchings: of African Americans, 374, 381, 631; crusade against, 421; of Italians, in New Orleans, 453
Lyon, Mary, 152, 238
Lyrics of Lowly Life (Dunbar), 423

Macao, 291, 471
MacArthur, Douglas: Bonus Army and, 546-548; Korean War and, 615; Truman and, 616; World War II and, 591, 598, 602, 613
Macdonough, Thomas, 173
Machine politics. *See* Political machines; Tammany Hall
Machinery: in 1920s, 526-527; laborsaving, 321; for mining, 434
Macon's Bill No.2 (1810), 167
Macy's, 406
Madeira, 12
"Mademoiselle from Armentières" (song), 509, 510
Madison, James: 1808 election and, 166; 1812 election and, 172; Bill of Rights and, 141, 142; at Constitutional Convention, 129, 133; embargoes and, 167; on extensive republic, 137; as federalist, 134, 137; inauguration of, 166, 221; internal improvements and, 178; as secretary of state, 161; on slavery, 136; Virginia and Kentucky resolutions and, 153; War of 1812 and, 169
Magazines: growth of, 238; social reform, 418-419. *See also* Press
Magee, John, 301
Maggie: A Girl of the Streets (Crane), 422
Mahan, Alfred Thayer, 453, 462
Mail: under Articles of Confederation, 125; Pony Express and, 228-229
Mailer, Norman, 640
Maine: in American Revolution, 103; boundary dispute in, 271; separation from Massachusetts, 181; settlements in, 39-40
Maine (ship), 454-455, 456
Maine Law (1851), 240
Mainland colonies. *See* England (Britain); specific locations
Main Street (Lewis), 532
Maize. *See* Corn
Makin Island: in World War II, 593
"Malaise speech" (Carter), 681, 682
Malamud, Bernard, 642
Malaria, 323, 458; Africans and, 29; in Chesapeake, 50; in Columbian exchange, 14
Malaya: in World War II 591, 591
Malay Peninsula, 470
Malcolm X, 654, 655
Malden, Fort, in War of 1812, 173
Male, use of term in Constitution, 357

Mali, 12
Malinche (Doña Marina), 15, 17, 18
Malone, Dumas, 159
Malthus, Thomas, 395
Mamout, Yarrow, 64
Manassas Junction. *See* Bull Run
Manchuria: Japan and, 344, 548; Russo-Japanese War and, 468; Taft and, 489; in World War II, 608; after World War II, 615
Mandan Indians, 429
Mandates (League of Nations): Pacific islands as Japanese, 512
Manhattan Island, 42, 108
Manhattan Project, 599
Manifest Destiny, 275; 1844 election and, 273-274; Mexican War and, 278, 280, 290; of Russians and South Africans, 442; use of term, 269, 273
Manila: battle at, 457, 458; in World War II, 591, 598
Manioc: in Columbian exchange, 14
Manitoba, exploration of, 78
Mann, Horace, 236
Man Nobody Knows, The (Barton), 526
Manufacturing: in 1920s, 526-527; in Civil War, 321; colonial, 68; cotton, 219, 221; Embargo Act and, 166; factory system in, 178, 221; global economy and, 675; growth of, 391; interchangeable parts in, 221; mechanization and, 221, 391-392; nationalism and, 178; panic of 1857 and, 303; in postrevolutionary era, 122; South and, 256; War of 1812 and, 176; of weapons, 221. *See also* Factories; Industrialization; Industry; Production; Tariff(s)
Manumission, 267
Mao Zedong (Mao Tse-tung), 614, 661
Maps, of New World, 9
Marble Faun, The (Hawthorne), 248
Marbury, William, 161
Marbury v. *Madison*, 161
March on Washington: in 1941, 589; in 1963, 647
Marcuse, Herbert, 661
Marcy, William, 194
Mariana Islands, 593, 598
Marina (Doña). *See* Malinche
Marine Corps: bombing of barracks in Lebanon, 692; Brown, John, and, 305; in Cuba, 468; in Dominican Republic, 498; establishment of, 150; in Mexican War, 280; in Nicaragua, 489; in World War I, 507. *See also* Armed forces; Military
Market(s): for farm produce, 439, 440, 441; international, 379, 398, 452
Market economy, 257; in 1970s, 682-683; gender roles in, 241; growth of, 118; Whigs and, 202
Market revolution, 229-230
Market Revolution, The: Jacksonian America 1815-1846 (Sellers), 209
Marne, Second Battle of, 509
Marriage: changes in, 224; complex, 243, 244; of freedmen, 349; interracial, 135; in late 19th century, 420; in New England, 55, 56; polygamy and, 236, 437; same-sex, 724, 732, 733; slaves and, 261; southern planters and, 261; working women and, 397. *See also* Families; Intermarriage
Marshall, George C., 602, 612, 617
Marshall, John: Burr's trial and, 164; as Chief Justice, 161, 182-183; as federalist, 134; judicial doctrine under, 161, 182-183; XYZ affair and, 150
Marshall, Thurgood, 679, 700
Marshall Field's, 406

Marshall Islands: in World War II, 593
Marshall Plan, 612-613
Martial law: in Maryland, 314
Martin v. *Wilks*, 66
Mary II (England), 41
Maryland: Articles of Confederation and, 124; as Border State, 314; Catholicism in, 28; Civil War in, 329-331; Constitution and, 133; early settlements in, 25 (map); population of, 50, 61; as proprietary colony, 28, 73; religious toleration in, 28; tobacco and, 27-28, 66; western land claims and, 124
Mason-Dixon Line, 284, 633
Masonic order, 201
Massachusetts: Boston Massacre in, 93; charter of, 37, 41; committees of correspondence in, 94; Constitution and, 133; dissension in, 38-39; government in, 37, 38; Hartford Convention and, 176; Intolerable Acts and, 95; Maine and, 181; population of, 61; as royal colony, 37, 41; School Law of 1647 in, 57; Shays's Rebellion and, 127; state constitution in, 121-122
Massachusetts Bay Colony, 37-39, 40, 40 (map), 41
Massasoit (Wampanoag Indians), 40
Mass consumer economy, 525-526
Mass democracy, 119, 196, 209
"Massive retaliation" doctrine, 635
Mass media: movies and, 528. *See also* specific forms
Mass production, 391
Mass transit, 406
Materialism: in 1980s, 690
Mathematics: Aztec, 7
Mather, Cotton, 66
Matrilineal cultures, 11
Mattachine Society, 660
Matusow, Allen, 668
Maximilian (Austria), in Mexico, 318-319
Mayan language, 15
Mayans, 6
May Day strikes (1886), 400
Mayflower (ship), 36, 37
Mayflower Compact, 36-37
Mayors: black, 655
McAdoo, William, 492
McAuliffe, A.C., 598
McCain, John, 2008 election and, 725, 726, 726 (map)
McCarran Internal Security Bill (1950), 617
McCarthy, Eugene, 657, 658
McCarthy, Joseph, and McCarthyism, 617
McCarthy, Margaret, 216
McCartney, Paul, 629
McClellan, George B.: 1864 election and, 340, 341 (map); in Civil War, 327-328, 330, 333
McClure's, 478
McCormick, Cyrus, 226
McCormick reaper, 222, 226, 318
McCulloch v. *Maryland*, 182-183, 200
McDonald, Forrest, 137
McDonald's, 629
McGirr, Lisa, 668, 701
McGovern, George, 666, 688
McGuffey, William H., 237
McGuffey's Readers, 237
McHenry, Fort, 174
McKay, Claude, 532
McKay, Donald, 228
McKinley, William, 448, 457; 1896 election and, 445-448, 448 (map); 1900 election and, 465; assassination of, 465; Cuba and, 455-456; imperialism and, 458, 459, 462; Philippines and, 458, 459; tariffs and, 449

McKinley Tariff (1890), 379, 382, 445, 449, 454
McLaughlin, James, 432
McMath, Robert C., 383
McNamara, Robert S., 642
McNary-Haugen Bill, 540
McPherson, James, 345
McVeigh, Timothy, 706
Mead, Margaret, 558
Meade, George G., 334, 340
Meade, Lawrence, 668
Measles, 25
Meat Inspection Act (1906), 485
Meatpacking industry, 394; food safety and, 485
Mechanical reapers, 222, 226, 318, 321
Mechanization: of agriculture, 226, 321, 439; in Civil War, 321; of cotton industry, 219, 221; industrial growth and, 219, 391-392; in textile industry, 219; after World War II, 621
Media: online, 732. *See also* Mass media; specific forms
Medicaid, 653, 665
Medical schools, 66
Medicare, 653, 707
Medicine: in Civil War, 320, 322, 323; colonial, 66; patent medicine, 479; women in, 241. *See also* Drugs
Mediterranean region: pirates and trade in, 178
Meetinghouses: in New England, 56; of Quakers, 43
Megalopolis, 406
Meiji Japan, 587
Mellon, Andrew W., 526, 533, 536
Melting pot: in colonies, 32
Melville, Herman, 213, 248, 249
Men: immigrant, 409; pioneer, 212; voting rights for, 41, 357. *See also* immigrants and immigration
Mencken, H.L., 531, 557
Mennonites, 53, 220
Mentally ill, treatment of, 239-240
Mercantilism, 88-90, 470
Merchants: in crop-lien system, 374; in middle colonies, 65. *See also* Commerce; Trade
Meredith, James, 646-647
Merit system, 378
Merrimack (ship), battle with *Monitor*, 329
Mesabi iron ore, 271, 391
Mesabi Range, 392
Mesoamerica. *See* America(s); Mexico; specific locations
Mestizos, 16, 17
Metacom (Wampanoag), 40
Methodists: black, 64-65; class and, 235; in Old Northwest, 182; revivalism and, 234; slavery and, 235
Metropolitan areas. *See* Cities and towns; Urban areas; specific locations
Metropolitan Opera House, 424
Metternich, Klemens von, 187, 344
Mettler, Suzanne, 568
Meuse-Argonne offensive, 511
Mexican Cession, 278, 279, 280, 281, 282, 286
Mexicans and Mexican Americans: *Bracero* program and, 588, 634; in California, 275, 279; as migrant farm labor, 440; migration to U.S., 634; zoot-suit riots and, 589. *See also* Hispanics; Latinos
Mexican War, 276-278; Californios and, 279; casualties of, 280; expansionism attempts after, 290-291; major campaigns of, 277 (map); slavery controversy after, 252, 280-281; transportation and, 290, 291; Treaty of Guadalupe and, 237 (map), 278; viewpoints on, 280

Mexico: Aztecs in, 6, 7, 8, 16, 17; California and, 269, 275–276, 279; European conquest of, 15, 17–18; Gadsden Purchase and, 291; independence of, 205; maize in, 6–7, 8; Maximilian as emperor of, 318–319; population of, 709; revolution in, 196; Roosevelt, F.D., and, 572; silver from, 14; slave emancipation by, 205; Spanish in, 14, 16, 17; Texas and, 205–206, 206 (map), 269, 271, 272, 275–276; U.S. intervention in, 499–500, 541; Zimmermann note and, 503
Mexico City, 278; cathedrals of, 17; university in, 18
Miami Confederacy, 148–149
Michigan, 294
Michilimackinac, Fort, 172
Middle class: in developing countries, 675; suburbanites in, 623; women in, 397, 410; workers and, 398; after World War II, 620–621
Middle colonies: agriculture in, 67; diversity in, 2, 45, 62; education in, 72; government of, 45; land in, 44, 45; settlements in, 43 (map); social structure in, 65. *See also* specific locations
Middle East: Arab oil embargo and, 667; Clinton and, 713; Cold War and, 636–637; Iran-Contra affair and, 693–694; Obama and, 733; oil from, 621; Six-Day War in, 656; after World War II, 613, 691 (map); written culture of, 4; Yom Kippur War (1973) and, 667. *See also* Arabs and Arab world; Iraq War; specific countries
Middlemen: Muslim, 11; northern, 256
Middle passage, 53, 54
Midnight judges, 160–161
Midway, Battle of, 591–592
Midwest: colleges in, 416; German immigrants in, 216, 220; Grange in, 442; Republicans in, 294, 371
Midwifery, 56
Migrant farm workers, 439, 440, 464
Migration: across Bering land bridge, 6, 7 (map); African American, 349, 506–507, 633, 654; from cities, 226; to cities, 140, 214; colonial, 58; Great English Migration, 37; Mexican, 499, 634; Native American, 26, 27, 589; to Old Northwest, 182; to suburbs, 622–624; to West, 437, 439; during World War II, 588–589. *See also* Immigrants and immigration; Westward movement
Military: African Americans in, 662; in Civil War, 316, 322, 323, 327; Cold War end and, 698; desegregation of, 617, 619; homosexuals in, 705; under Jefferson, 161–162; Kennedy, John F., and, 643; NSC-68 and, 614; in Pennsylvania, 44; spending on, 590, 614; women in, 322, 508, 712; in World War II, 602. *See also* Armed forces; Militia; Wars and warfare; specific battles and wars; specific branches
Military academy: at West Point, 280
Military districts, in South, 356, 356 (map)
Military draft. *See* Draft (military)
"Military-industrial complex": Eisenhower warning about, 693
Military occupation. *See* Occupation (military)
Military Reconstruction, 356–357, 356 (map), 367
Military spending, 590; in 1950s, 628; under Reagan, 690; in Vietnam, 656. *See also* Defense spending
Military tribunals: Supreme Court on, 357
Militia: in American Revolution, 97, 98; black, 357; in Civil War, 253, 314, 326; colonial, 97, 98;

Mormon, 236; private paramilitary, 706; Whiskey Rebellion and, 144
Millennium: politics and, 714
Miller, Arthur, 642
Miller, William, and Millerites (Adventists), 235
Milliken v. *Bradley*, 679
Millionaires: Civil War and, 321, 391; opposing views of, 395; railroads and, 389; Social Darwinists on, 395
Millionaires' Club: Senate as, 480
Mills: in South, 396–397
Mills, C. Wright, 662
Milošević, Slobodan, 713
Milwaukee: German immigrants in, 220
Mines and mining: railroads and, 389, 434; Square Deal for labor and, 482; strikes in, 380; in West, 284, 434. *See also* Coal and coal industry; Gold; Silver
Minimalism, 716
Minimum wage, 555; Truman and, 620; for women, 537, 565
Minnesota, 271
Minorities: affirmative action and, 665; in American Revolution, 98–99; in Europe, 408; as Loyalists, 99, 107; populations in cities and suburbs, 710; scholarships for, 700; in World War II, 586; after World War II, 604. *See also* Race and racism; specific groups
Minstrel shows, 245, 424
"Miracle" drugs, 599
Miranda case and warning, 664
MIRVs (multiple independently targeted reentry vehicles), 664
Miss America pageant, protest at, 678
Missiles: Cuban missile crisis and, 644; INF Treaty and, 693; SDI system and, 690. *See also* Nuclear weapons
Missionary Ridge (Tennessee), 337
Mission Indians, 279
Missions and missionaries: to Africa, 263; in California, 19, 279; in China, 291, 463; French Catholic, 78; Great Awakening and, 71, 234; in Hawaii, 453–454; for Indians, 19, 71, 78, 198; in Oregon, 273; in Philippines, 458; in Texas, 19. *See also* Religion(s); specific groups
Mississippi: cotton in, 221; French in, 79; integration in, 646–647; secession of, 308, 315 (map); slavery in, 260, 261
Mississippian culture, 8
Mississippi Freedom Democratic party, 654
Mississippi River region: in Civil War, 336, 336 (map), 337; exploration of, 19, 78, 79, 163; geography of, 6; slavery in, 260; Spanish control of, 126–127; steamboats on, 227; War of 1812 in, 174–175
Missouri: border ruffians from, 298; as Border State, 314; slavery in, 180–181, 181 (map), 252
Missouri (ship), Japanese surrender on, 599
Missouri Compromise (1820), 252; repeal of, 292, 293, 293 (map), 294, 296, 302; slavery and, 181, 181 (map), 183
Missouri River region, 6, 78
Mobile, Alabama, 340
Mobility: social, 64–65, 230, 402
Mobilization, for World War I, 505–506
Moby Dick (Melville), 248, 249
Moctezuma, 17
Model T Ford, 391, 474, 526–527
Modernism, 531; in architecture, 640; in literature, 531–532
Modernists, vs. Fundamentalists in religion, 528
Mohawk Indians, 30, 112

Molasses Act (1733), 68
Molly Maguires, 216
Monarchs and monarchies: after Napoleon, 185; in Spain, 13. *See also* specific rulers and locations
Mondale, Walter, 693
Monetary policy, 364, 367; in 1870s, 370; gold vs. silver in, 370
Money: in 1920s, 533; rag, 321; from wildcat banks, 180, 202. *See also* Bank(s) and banking; Currency; Greenbacks; Paper money
Money power, 393
Money supply, 381
Monitor (ship), battle with *Merrimack*, 329
Monk, Maria, 218
Monkey Trial, 525
Monmouth, New Jersey, battle in, 112
Monopoly, 364, 396; curbing of, 479; in oil industry, 394; railroads as, 390; Roosevelt, T., and, 483; Wilson and, 497. *See also* Trust(s)
Monroe, James, 171; 1816 election and, 179; 1820 election and, 182; cabinet of, 185, 186; in Era of Good Feelings, 118, 179; foreign policy under, 183–187; Jackson and, 184; Louisiana Purchase and, 162; presidency of, 179, 182, 183–187
Monroe, Marilyn, 630
Monroe Doctrine (1823), 272, 276, 313; appraisal of, 187; British Guiana-Venezuela dispute and, 453; French violation of, 318–319; principles of, 118, 186; Roosevelt Corollary to, 468, 498
Montana, 434, 437
Montcalm, Marquis de, 83
Montgomery, Alabama: bus boycott in, 632; King in, 632, 654
Montgomery, Bernard, 593
Montgomery, David, 402
Montgomery, Richard, 103
Monticello, 154, 245
Montréal: in American Revolution, 103; in French and Indian War, 82, 83; in War of 1812, 172
Mont-Saint Michel and Chartres (Adams), 423
Moody, Dwight Lyman, 413, 414
Moon landing, 643
Moonshiners, 144
Moore's Creek Bridge, battle of (1776), 103
Moors, 13, 16
Morality: in 1920s, 531; of Civil War soldiers, 323; new (late 19th century), 419
Moral Majority, 695
Morgan, Edmund S., 47, 75, 116
Morgan, Jennifer, 267
Morgan, J.P., and Company, 501
Morgan, J. Pierpont (J.P.), 413; Carnegie and, 393; competition and, 392; loan to U.S., 382; Northern Securities and, 483
Morgan, Philip D., 267
Morgan, Robin, 678
Mormons, 119, 235–236, 237 (map), 427, 437
"Morning in America" (Reagan), 686
Morocco: in World War II, 594
Morrill Land-Grant College Act (1862), 344, 354, 417
Morrill Tariff Act (1861), 320
Morris, Roger, 122
Morrison, Toni, 717
Morse, Samuel F.B., 222, 229
Mortality: immigrant, 215; infant, 653; slave, 53, 54
Mortgages: to African Americans, 624; on farms, 440, 556, 561; federal help for, 556
Morton, "Jelly Roll," 530

Morton, Sterling, 575
Motherhood, republican, 123, 136
Mothers: single, 712; in work force, 711
Mott, Lucretia, 241
Mound Builders, 8
Mountains: formation of North American, 5
Mountain whites, in South, 257–259, 314, 315, 320; resistance to secession, 308 (map)
Mount Holyoke Seminary (College), 238
Mount Vernon, Virginia, 103
Movies and movie industry, 392; growth of, 528; postmodern, 717; "talkies" in, 528; in World War I, 505
Muckrakers, 478–479
Mugwumps, 377
Muhammed, Elijah, 654
Muir, John, 486, 487
Mulattoes, 93, 260
Mulberry Street (New York City), 407
Muller v. Oregon, 481, 484, 536–537
"Mulligan letters": of Blaine, 377
Multiculturalism, 62, 522
Multiracial society: in Puerto Rico, 460; in United States, 716
Munich Conference (1938), 574
Munitions. *See* Weapons
Münster, Sebastian, 9
Murals: of Federal Art Project, 557
"Murders in the Rue Morgue, The" (Poe), 248
Murray, Charles, 668
Muscle Shoals, 561
Music: in 1880s and 1890s, 424; in 1920s, 530; in 1950s, 629–630; acid rock, 660; African American, 65; blues, 424, 528; folk, 245; jazz, 63, 424, 530; military marching-band, 462; ragtime, 424; spirituals, 65, 261, 424; World War I songs and, 505, 509, 510
Muskets, mass production of, 221
Muslims: expulsion of Moors from Spain and, 13, 16; as trade middlemen, 11. *See also* Islamic entries
Mussolini, Benito, 572, 573, 575; Allied invasion of Italy and, 594; Spanish Civil War and, 573
Mutter, Carol, 712
Mutual aid societies, 350
Mutualistas (mutual aid societies), 709
Myanmar, 470
My Lai massacre, 663
Myrdal, Gunnar, 631

NAACP (National Association for the Advancement of Colored People), 362, 416, 589
Nader, Ralph, 715 (map)
NAFTA. *See* North American Free Trade Agreement
Nagasaki, atomic bombing of, 599, 602
Nahuatl language, 15
Naismith, James, 425
Naked and the Dead, The (Mailer), 640
Napalm, 656
Napoleon Bonaparte (France): Britain and, 164; Convention of 1800 and, 151; exile of, 173; Louisiana and, 162; U.S. relations with, 167; War of 1812 and, 173; at Waterloo, 147, 177
Napoleon III (France), 318, 319
Napoleonic Wars (1803–1815), 175
Narragansett Indians, 40
Narrative of the Life of Frederick Douglass, 265
NASA (National Aeronautics and Space Administration), 643
Nash, Gary, 116
Nassau, in Civil War, 328
Nasser, Gamal Abdel, 636

Nast, Thomas, political cartoons by, 368, 369
Natchez, Mississippi, 127
Nation (journal), 418–419
Nation, Carrie, 421
National Aeronautics and Space Administration. *See* NASA
National American Woman Suffrage Association, 420, 421
National Association for the Advancement of Colored People. *See* NAACP
National Association of Colored Women, 421
National Banking Act, 321, 497
National Banking System, 321, 345
National Child Labor Committee, 399
National Consumers League, 410, 481
National debt, 355; in 1920s, 533; Reagan and, 694
National Defense and Education Act (NDEA), 637
National Endowments for the Arts and the Humanities, 653
National Gallery of Art: design of, 640
National Grange of the Patrons of Husbandry. *See* Grange
National Guard: at Democratic National Convention (1968), 658; at Kent State, 663; at Little Rock's Central High School, 634
National Housing Act (1934), 556
National Industrial Recovery Act (1933), 553
National Intelligencer (newspaper), 179
Nationalism: Adams, John Quincy, and, 183, 185, 192; American System and, 178; Civil War and, 309, 344; in England, 23; in foreign policy, 183–185, 186, 187; in former Soviet Union, 698; imperialism and, 470, 471; judicial, 182–183; Monroe Doctrine and, 186, 187; in South, 309; in Southeast Asia, 635; War of 1812 and, 118, 171, 177–178; western settlement and, 213–214; before World War II, 571. *See also* New Nationalism
Nationalist China, 613–614
Nationalist School of historians, 137, 310
National Labor Relations (Wagner) Act (1935), 556, 563, 565
National Labor Relations Board, 563
National Labor Union, 399
National Organization for Women (NOW), 678
National Origins Act (1924), 344
National origins of immigrants: quotas based on, 653
National parks, 214, 437
National Recovery Administration (NRA), 553, 558
National Republicans: 1828 election and, 192; 1832 election and, 201
National Road, 226–227
National Security Act (1947), 613
National Security Administration (NSA): domestic and international spying operations of, 732
National Security Council (NSC), 613; NSC-68 of, 614–615
National War Labor Board (NWLB), 588
National Woman's party, 528
National Woman Suffrage Association, 507
National Women's Conference, 678
National Youth Administration: Office of Minority Affairs in, 558
Nation of Islam, 530, 654
Nation-states: nationalism and, 344; in North America, 8
Nation Under Our Feet, A: . . . (Hahn), 362
Native Americans: in 1970s, 679–680; in American Revolution, 30–31, 97, 112; assimilation of, 198, 432–434; Bacon's Rebellion and, 51; boarding schools for, 432;

British and, 24–25; buffalo and, 14, 365, 429, 431–432; in California, 275, 279; Christianity and, 16, 19, 40, 198; in Civil War, 315; colonists and, 32, 39, 40; Dawes Act and, 432; disease and, 2, 14, 19, 25, 26–27, 40, 279, 429; Dutch and, 42; education for, 198, 432, 434; Eisenhower and, 635; European marriages with, 16, 17; France and, 77, 79; in French and Indian War, 3, 81; after French and Indian War, 84; fur trade and, 30; Ghost Dance religious movement of, 432; horses and, 26, 429; Jackson and, 198–199; Louisiana Purchase and, 163; migration from reservations, 589; mission Indians and, 279; missions for, 19, 71, 78, 198; in New England, 39, 40, 58; New World of, 26–27; Pennsylvania and, 44; Plains Indians, 26, 364–365; population of, 11, 14, 428; Puritans and, 39, 40; railroad construction and, 386; removal of, 198, 199, 200 (map); reservations for, 25, 31, 365, 429–430, 431, 432; resistance by, 198; Sand Creek massacre against, 430; as slaveowners, 198; Spain and, 15, 127; at time of European contact, 8, 10–11, 10 (map); trade and, 27; treaties with, 25, 40, 149, 429; tribal sovereignty and, 149, 680; in Virginia, 24–25; War of 1812 and, 175, 176; wars with, 148–149, 430, 431 (map); in West, 439; as West Indian labor, 29; in World War II, 589; Wounded Knee Massacre and, 432. *See also* specific groups
Nativism, 218, 344, 407, 410–413. *See also* Anti-immigrant sentiment
NATO (North Atlantic Treaty Organization), 613; Balkan region and, 713; French withdrawal from, 656
Nat Turner's rebellion, 262, 265
Naturalism, 421, 422–423
Naturalization law (1802), 160
Natural resources: in Alaska, 361; conservation of, 214, 485–487; development of, 555; management of, 487; regulation of, 364; transport of, 391. *See also* Raw materials
Natural selection, 415
Nature: Darwin on, 415; Native Americans and, 11. *See also* Conservation; Environment
Nauvoo, Illinois, 237 (map)
Navajo Indians, 10 (map); as "code talkers," 589
Naval Academy (Annapolis), 248, 280
Naval stations (bases): in Cuba, 572; in World War II, 578
Naval stores: colonial, 68
Navigation: Portuguese, 13
Navigation Laws: of 1650, 89; enforcement of, 41, 90; postrevolution, 126
Navy: in American Revolution, 113–114; British, 83, 89, 108, 149, 173–174, 259, 318; of Chile, 453; Five-Power Naval Treaty (1922) and, 538; Japanese, 468; Spanish Armada and, 22–23. *See also* Submarines
Navy (U.S.): African Americans in, 333; in American Revolution, 108; in Civil War, 318, 328–329, 333, 336; Great White Fleet of, 470–471; Guantánamo base of, 461; Hawaii and, 454; imperialism and, 453; under Jefferson, 162; in Mexican War, 280; pirates in North Africa and, 162, 178; in Spanish-American War, 456–457; in War of 1812, 172, 173–174; in World War I, 507; in World War II, 580, 593, 599. *See also* specific battles and wars
Navy Department, creation of, 150
Nazi Germany: Holocaust and, 576, 598; Italy invaded by, 594; Soviet Union and, 574–575, 580, 608; surrender of, 594. *See also* Germany; Hitler, Adolf; World War II

Nazi-Soviet (Hitler-Stalin) pact (1939), 574–575, 580
NDEA (National Defense and Education Act), 637
Nebraska, 292; in 1854, 293 (map); organization of, 292; Stevenson, Robert Louis, on, 438
Necessity, Fort, 80
"Negro March on Washington" (1941), 589
"Negro spirituals," 65, 261, 424
Neighborhoods, 406
Neoconservatism, 682, 722, 723
Neonationalist school of historians, 310
Netherlands: independence of, 41; New Netherland and, 41–43; World War II in, 575. *See also* Dutch; Holland
Networks: television, 717
Neutrality: in 1930s, 538, 542, 573; in 1940, 578; lend-lease and, 578, 579–580; World War I and, 500; before World War II, 573, 574–575, 576–578, 581. *See also* Isolationism
Neutrality Acts: of 1935, 1936, 1937, 573, 575; of 1939, 574, 575
Neutrality Proclamation (1973), 147–148
Nevada, 434
Nevins, Allan, 310
New Amsterdam, 42, 43
Newark, race riots in, 655
New Day in Babylon (Van Deburg), 668
New Deal, 475, 552; agriculture and, 556, 559–560; banking and, 555; conservation and, 555; critics of, 566–567; end of, 566; historians on, 568; housing in, 556; Hundred Days in, 553–555; for Indians, 561; job creation and, 555–557; labor and, 562–564; major measures (early, 1933), 553; major measures (later, 1933–1939), 556; political coalition in, 568; radicalism of, 568; Social Security and, 562, 565; women during, 557–558. *See also* Great Depression; Roosevelt, Franklin Delano
New Democrat, Clinton as, 704
New England: Andros in, 41; Dominion of, 41; education in, 56–57, 71; Embargo Act and, 165; environment of, 55, 58; expansion of, 39–40, 40 (map); factories in, 221; families in, 55–56; farmers in, 57; fishing in, 57, 67; Great Migration to, 37; Hartford Convention and, 176; historians from, 249; Indians of, 39, 40, 58; lifestyle in, 56–58; Louisbourg capture by, 79; Loyalists in, 108; lumber in, 57; marriage in, 55, 56; Patriots in, 117; Pilgrims in, 36–37, 40; Puritans in, 2, 35–36, 37–39, 56, 57; republicanism in, 105; secession and, 163, 166; social structure in, 65–66; southern cotton and, 266; town meetings in, 57, 74; War of 1812 and, 169, 173, 176; witch trials in, 57; women's property rights in, 56. *See also* specific locations
New England Confederation (1643–1684), 40–41
New England Emigrant Aid Company, 298
Newfoundland: England and, 22; fishing in, 57; Norse in, 11
New France (Canada), 77–79. *See also* Canada
New Freedom, 492, 493, 495
New Guinea, 470, 593, 598
New Hampshire: Constitution and, 133; as royal colony, 40
New Harmony, Indiana, 242, 243
New Haven, 39
New Immigrants, 407–408, 409–413, 415; in 1920s, 521
"New Isolationism," 667
New Jersey: American Revolution in, 108; Constitution and, 129; East and West Jersey and, 44; Loyalists in, 108; as middle colony, 45

New Jersey Plan, 129
Newlands Act (1902), 485
New Left, 660, 668, 695, 701; school of historians, 472, 701
New light clergy, 70
"New look," in foreign policy, 635–636
New Mexico, 284, 291, 427, 437; Chaco Canyon in, 8; Coronado in, 19; Latinos in, 709; Mexican migrants in, 499; Native Americans in, 430; slavery in, 287; Texas and, 284
New morality (late 19th century), 419
New Nationalism, 490, 493
"New Negro," 532
New Netherland, 41–43
New Orleans, Louisiana, 453; Battle of, 174–175; in Civil War, 336; French in, 79, 162; Hurricane Katrina in, 724; population of, 214; Spanish in, 84
New Panama Canal Company, 467
New Right, 668, 680, 688
New Scotland. *See* Nova Scotia
New South, 358, 396, 397
New Spain, 279
Newspapers: antislavery, 263; colonial, 73; Federalist, 134; foreign-language, 408; Hearst and, 418; Jefferson on, 154; Linotype and, 418; Pulitzer and, 418; after Revolution, 145; Sedition Act and, 152; yellow journalism and, 418
New Sweden, 42, 43
New Western historians, 449
"New woman," 397
New World: bullion from, 15; Columbus and, 9, 13, 15 (map); European diseases in, 14, 19, 25, 26–27, 40; France and, 15 (map), 77–79; indirect discoverers of, 11; maps of, 9; of Native Americans, 26–27; Old World flora and fauna in, 13, 14; Portugal and, 12–13; Spain and, 13, 14–15. *See also* America(s); specific locations
"New world order," 698
New York (city), 407; almshouses in, 65; in American Revolution, 108, 112; Central Park in, 424; draft riots in, 320; Henry Street Settlement in, 410; immigrants in, 215, 408, 409; Leisler's Rebellion in, 59; Loyalists in, 108; New Amsterdam as, 42, 43; population of, 61, 140, 214, 405; as port city, 45; postwar arts in, 640; Puerto Ricans in, 459, 460; Tammany Hall in, 216, 377; Tweed Ring in, 358, 368; water supply in, 215
New York (colony): in Dominion of New England, 41; Dutch and, 42, 43; as middle colony, 45; New Netherland as, 42, 43
New York (state): in 1800 election, 157–158, 158 (map); in American Revolution, 108, 109, 112; Burned-Over District in, 235; Constitution and, 133, 134; Erie Canal and, 178, 227; Irish in, 215; Iroquois in, 30, 31; Oneida Community in, 242, 243, 244; secession and, 163; in War of 1812, 169, 173, 175
New York Evening Post, 444
New York slave revolt (1712), 63
New York Sun, 477
New York Times, 368
New York Tribune, 332, 369
New York World, 418
Nez Perce Indians, 430, 431 (map)
Nguyen Sinh Cung (Ho Chi Minh), 471
Niagara, in War of 1812, 172
Nicaragua: British-U.S. interests in, 290; filibustering expedition to, 290; immigrants from, 709; Panama Canal and, 467; Sandinistas in, 692; U.S. troops in, 489, 541

Niebuhr, Reinhold, 617
Nightclubs, 419
Nimitz, Chester W., 591, 593, 602
9/11. *See* September 11, 2001, terrorist attacks
Nine-Power Treaty (1922), 465, 538
Nineteenth Amendment, 474, 507, 508, 537
Ninth Amendment, 142
Nissei, 587
Nixon, Richard M.: 1952 election and, 630; 1960 election and, 638–639, 639 (map); 1968 election and, 658–659, 659 (map); 1972 election and, 665–666; Arab oil embargo and, 667; Cambodia and, 663; China and, 664; day care veto by, 679; domestic policy of, 664–665; Khrushchev and, 638; pardon of, 675; Philadelphia Plan of, 652; as red-hunter, 616–617; resignation of, 672; Supreme Court and, 665, 671; Vietnam War and, 662–663; Watergate and, 671–673
Nixon Doctrine, 662
Nobel Peace Prize: to Addams, Jane, 410; to Carter, 688; to Roosevelt, T., 469
Nobel Prize for Literature: to Buck, 558; to Hemingway, 531; to Steinbeck, 557
Noche triste, 17
No Child Left Behind Act (2004), 724
Nominating conventions, 201
Nonaggression treaty: Nazi-Soviet, 574–575
Nonimportation agreements, 91, 92, 93
Non-Intercourse Act (1809), 166, 167
Nonintervention policy: toward Latin America, 186; Morton on, 575
Nonslaveowners, in South, 257
Nonviolent resistance, 632, 654
Norfolk, Virginia, in Revolution, 103, 105
Noriega, Manuel, 699
Normalcy, 474, 518
Normal schools, 415
Normandy landing, 594–595, 597
Norris, Frank, 422
Norris–La Guardia Anti-Injunction Act (1932), 546
Norse, in North America, 11
North (region): abolitionism and, 266; African American migration to, 506–507, 588, 633; American Revolution in, 104 (map); antislavery literature in, 297; Black Codes and, 354; Brown, John, and, 305; colonies in, 180; Compromise of 1850 and, 287, 288; Democrats in, 371, 552; *Dred Scott* decision and, 302; economic stake in South, 266; economy in, 622; emancipation in, 135; free blacks in, 259; Fugitive Slave Law and, 287–289, 294; immigrants in, 216, 220, 256; Kansas-Nebraska Act and, 292–293, 294; Missouri Compromise and, 181, 181 (map); Ostend Manifesto and, 290; panic of 1857 in, 303; railroads in, 228; slavery and, 63; Southern resentment of, 256; wage slaves in, 222, 265–266. *See also* North (Union, Civil War)
North (Union, Civil War): advantages/disadvantages of, 315–317; draft by, 319–320; economic boom in, 321; Emancipation Proclamation and, 332; financing of war by, 320–321; immigrants in, 316, 317; Indians and, 315; southern sympathizers in, 339–340; war aims of, 316. *See also* Civil War (U.S., 1861–1865)
North, Lord, 93, 97, 114
North Africa: disputes in, 469; pirates of, 127, 162, 178; World War II in, 593, 594, 596 (map)
North America: before 1754, 85 (map); after 1763, 85 (map); British dominance in, 60;

continent of, 5; corn in, 6–7, 8, 10, 14; early civilizations in, 8, 10–11, 10 (map); English in, 60; formation of, 5–6; land bridge to, 6, 7 (map); Norse exploration of, 11; Spanish frontier in, 16
North American Free Trade Agreement (NAFTA), 710, 711
North American Indians. *See* Native Americans
North American Review (magazine), 178, 238
North Atlantic Treaty Organization. *See* NATO
North Carolina: American Revolution in, 103; Civil War in, 338; Constitution and, 133, 134; creation of, 31; population of, 61; Roanoke Island in, 3, 22; secession by, 314, 315 (map); universities in, 237. *See also* Carolina
North Dakota, 437. *See also* Dakotas
Northeast (region): Erie Canal and, 178, 227; Industrial Revolution in, 221; Irish immigrants in, 215, 217; Republicans in, 371
Northern Ireland: Catholic-Protestant conflict in, 713. *See also* Ireland
Northern Pacific Railroad, 388, 436
Northern Securities Company, 483
North Korea, 614, 615, 713. *See also* Korea; Korean War
North Vietnam, 657; bombings of, 666; Nixon and, 664. *See also* Vietnam War
North-West Mounted Police (Mounties), 442, 443
Northwest Ordinance (1787), 124, 125
Norway: Nazis in, 575
"No taxation without representation," 90–91
Nova Scotia, 79, 99, 107
Novels, 297; in 1930s, 558; adventure, 248; dime, 421; New World, 246. *See also* Literature
Noyes, John Humphrey, 244
Noyes, Pierrepont, 244
NRA. *See* National Recovery Administration
NSA. *See* National Security Administration
NSC. *See* National Security Council
Nuclear arms race: Nixon and, 664; Reagan and, 690
Nuclear family, 712
Nuclear weapons, 604; Cuban missile crisis and, 644; détente policy and, 664; "flexible response" and, 643; in former Soviet Union, 698; H-bomb and, 614; "massive retaliation" policy and, 635; Soviet, 614; testing of, 637–638; U.N. monitoring of, 610. *See also* Atomic bombs
Nueces River region, 275, 276
Nullification, 343; Alien and Sedition Acts and, 153; of colonial legislation, 89; Tariff of Abominations and, 195; during War of 1812, 176
Nullification Crisis (1832), 195–196, 265
Nuremberg Laws, 600
Nuremberg war crimes trial (1946), 610
Nurseries, 420
Nursing: in Civil War, 322, 323; women in, 224; in World War I, 508
Nye, Gerald, 573

Oakley, Annie, 425
Oath of allegiance: in Lincoln's Reconstruction plan, 353; in Wade-Davis Bill, 353
Obama, Barack, 719; 2008 election and, 725; 2012 election and, 730; biracial heritage of, 716; family of, 725; foreign policy of, 728; gays in military and, 705; second term of, 731
"Obamacare," 727, 730, 733
Obergefell v. *Hodges*, 732
Oberlin College, 235, 238, 239

Occupation (military): of Germany, 610, 611, 611 (map); of Japan, 613; of South, 349, 356, 356 (map)
Occupational Safety and Health Administration (OSHA). *See* OSHA
Occupations (jobs). *See* Jobs
"Occupy Wall Street," 728, 730
O'Connor, Flannery, 642
O'Connor, Sandra Day, 695, 724
Octopus, The (Norris), 422
Officeholders: blacks as, 358, 710; ex-Confederates as, 354, 355
Office of Minority Affairs, in National Youth Administration, 558
Office of Price Administration (OPA), 588
Office of Scientific Research and Development, 590
Officers: in Civil War, 280, 316, 317; in Mexican War, 280
Of Plymouth Plantation (Bradford), 37
Ogallala, Nebraska, 435
Ogden, Utah, transcontinental railroad in, 387
Oglala Sioux Indians, 432
Oglethorpe, James, 32
Ohio, 140, 149, 220, 314
"Ohio gang": Harding and, 536
"Ohio Idea," 367, 368
Ohio River region: in American Revolution, 113; French and Indian War in, 80–83, 80 (map); French-British conflict over, 79–80; French in, 77, 79; geography of, 6; Miami Confederacy in, 148–149; Mound Builders of, 8; roads and canals in, 178, 180
Ohio State University, 417
Oil and oil industry: Arab oil embargo and, 667; Carter and, 681–682; CIA in Iran and, 636; Eisenhower and, 634; Iran and, 611; Israel and, 613; Middle East and, 636; in Pennsylvania, 321; Rockefeller in, 392, 393–394; Teapot Dome scandal and, 539; in World War II, 581; after World War II, 581. *See also* Energy and energy crisis
Oil shocks, 681
Okies, 560, 561
Okinawa, 470, 598
Oklahoma, 427; Dust Bowl in, 560 (map), 561; land rush in, 437; Native Americans in, 198, 199, 315
Oklahoma City bombing, 706
Old-age insurance, 620
Older Americans. *See* Age and aging
Old Guard (Republican party), 490, 491, 515, 536–537; Roosevelt, F.D., and, 554
Old Immigrants, 407
Old light clergy, 70
Old Northwest (region), 263, 332; Black Codes in, 182; farming in, 182, 227; land cessions of 1782–1802, 124 (map); Land Ordinance of 1785 in, 125, 126 (map); slavery banned in, 125, 252
Old South. *See* South
Old World: flora and fauna from, 13, 14
Oligarchy: of money, 397; Mormon, 236; in South, 255–256
Oliver, Joseph "King," 530, 531
Olmsted, Frederick Law, 220, 424
Olney, Richard, 391, 445, 453
Olympic Games: boycott of (1980), 684; boycott of (1984), 690
Oñate, Juan de (Don), 18
One-crop economy, 256, 440
101st Airborne Division, 598
Oneida Community, 242, 243, 244
Oneida Indians, 30, 112
O'Neill, Eugene, 532

O'Neill, William, 668
Onondaga Indians, 30, 112
On the Duty of Civil Disobedience (Thoreau), 246, 247
On the Road (Kerouac), 640
OPEC (Organization of Petroleum Exporting Countries), 637, 667
Open Door note, 463
Open Door policy, toward China, 463–465, 471, 489, 538
"Open skies" inspection program, 635
Operation Desert Storm, 699–700
Operation Dixie, 618
Operation Wetback, 634
Oppenheimer, J. Robert, 614
Order of the Star-Spangled Banner, 218
Orders in Council, 164, 167
Oregon (state): progressive reform in, 480, 484
Oregon Country: acquisition of, 273; boundary dispute in, 273, 275, 275 (map); British claims in, 184, 269
Oregon Trail, 273
Organization of Petroleum Exporting Countries (OPEC), 637, 667
Organized crime, 524. *See also* Crime(s); Gangsters
Organized labor. *See* Labor; Labor unions
Original sin, Calvin on, 35
"Origins and Principles of the American Revolution, Compared with the French" (von Gentz), 115
Oriskany, battle at, 109
Orlando, Vittorio, 512
Orr, James Lawrence, 354
Osbourne, Frances, 438
Osceola (Seminole leader), 199
OSHA (Occupational Safety and Health Administration), 665
Ostend Manifesto, 290
O'Sullivan, John L., 269
Oswald, Lee Harvey, 647
Other America, The (Harrington), 652
Other People's Money and How the Bankers Use It (Brandeis), 497
Ottawa Indians, 84
Our Country: Its Possible Future and Its Present Crisis (Strong), 452
"Outcasts of Poker Flat, The" (Harte), 423
Outsourcing, 711
Overland Monthly, 418
Overland trails. *See* Trail(s)
OVERLORD, in World War II, 597
"Over There" (song), 505
Owen, Robert, and Owenites, 242, 243

Pacific Northwest: British claims in, 269, 272, 273; Lewis and Clark in, 273
Pacific Ocean region, 291; Balboa and, 16; Japanese migration to, 587; travel to, 290, 291; after World War I, 512; World War II in, 581–582, 591–592, 592 (map)
Pacific Railroad Act, 354
Pacifism: of Addams, Jane, 410, 479; of progressive-era feminists, 507
Padrone system, 409
Page, William, 249
Pahlavi, Mohammad Reza (Shah), 626, 681
Paine, Albert Bigelow, 422
Paine, Thomas, 101; *Age of Reason, The,* by, 233; *Common Sense* by, 91, 105; Constitutional Convention and, 129; France and, 146; republicanism and, 105
Painting: colonial, 72; Hudson River school, 245; national, 178; WPA and, 557. *See also* Art(s)

Index

Pakistan: India and, 713; Taliban and Al Qaeda in, 728
Palestine: Israel and, 613, 656, 691-692, 713. *See also* Middle East
Palestine Liberation Organization (PLO), 713
Palin, Sarah, 725
Palmer, A. Mitchell, 519
Palmer, John, 182
Panama: Balboa in, 16; Noriega captured in, 699; U.S. intervention in, 572
Panama Canal, 498; building of, 466-468; return to Panamanians, 681
Panama Canal Zone, 468
Pan-Arabism: Nasser and, 636
Panay gunboat, Japanese bombing of, 574
Pandemic: influenza (1918-1919), 511
Panics: of 1819, 179; of 1837, 203-204; of 1857, 303; of 1873, 370, 374; of 1893, 381-382, 401, 444; of 1907, 488
Paper money: in Civil War, 320-321; colonial issuing of, 89; Continentals as, 98; exchanged for gold, 370, 381, 449; of private banks, 199; after Revolution, 139
Paranoid Style in American Politics, The (Hofstadter), 701
Pardons: Alien and Sedition Acts and, 160; in Haymarket episode, 400; by Johnson, Andrew, 348, 353; of Nixon, 675
Paris, 424; 1968 protests in, 661; liberation of (1944), 595; summit conference in (1960), 638
Paris, Treaties of: of 1763, 82, 83, 84; of 1783, 114-115; of 1898, 458-459
Paris Peace Conference (1919), 512-513; Ho Chi Minh at, 471
Parity prices, 559
Parkman, Francis, 249
Parks, Rosa, 632
Parliament (England): Declaratory Act (1766) and, 92; Intolerable Acts (1774) and, 95; Navigation Law (1650) and, 89; Puritans and, 37; rights over colonies, 89, 92; Stamp Act (1765) and, 90, 91-92; Sugar Act (1764) and, 90; Townshend Acts (1767) and, 92, 93; virtual representation by, 91
Parochial schools, 408, 415
Participatory democracy, 660
Partitions: of Germany (1945), 610, 611, 611 (map)
Parton, James, 159
Patent(s), 221, 223, 391-392
Patent medicines, 479
Patent Office, 221
Paternalism, 267
Patient Protection and Affordable Care Act (Obamacare, 2010), 727, 730, 733
Patriot Act (2001), 721
Patriotism: in 1960s, 660; in Civil War, 323; English, 23; in World War I, 505; in World War II, 586
Patriots, 98, 105, 106, 121. *See also* American Revolution
Patronage: in 1870s, 371, 373, 377; Adams, John Quincy, and, 192; Federalist, 160; Jefferson and, 160
Patrons of Husbandry. *See* Grange
Patroonships, 42
Patterns of Culture (Benedict), 558
Patterson, James, 568
Patton, Gorge S. ("Blood 'n' Guts"), 594
Paul, Alice, 507, 528
Paulson, Henry, 726
Paupers, 66
Pawnee Indians, 429
Payne-Aldrich Bill (1909), 490

Peace Corps, 642, 656
Peace crusade: in antebellum era, 240. *See also* Pacifism
Peace Democrats, 339, 340
Peaceful coexistence policy, 646
Peacekeeping: in Bosnia, 713; in Somalia, 713
Peace movement: in Vietnam War, 656
Peale, Charles Willson, 64, 72, 110, 245
Peanuts: uses of, 416
Pearl Harbor: Japanese attack on, 475, 581-582; U.S. interests in, 454
Peculiar institution, slavery as, 180, 181, 192, 252, 262, 310, 343
Pei, I.M., 640
Pelosi, Nancy, 724
Pendleton Act (1883), 376
Penicillin, 599
Peniel, Joseph, 668
Peninsula Campaign (Civil War), 328
Penn, William, 44
Pennsylvania: Amish in, 220; Civil War in, 334, 334 (map); Constitution and, 133; Delaware and, 45; diversity in, 44, 61, 62; German immigrants in, 61-62, 220; Irish immigrants in, 216; Loyalists in, 108; as middle colony, 45; petroleum industry in, 321; population of, 61; as proprietary colony, 44, 73; Quakers in, 2, 43-45; religious toleration in, 44; Scots-Irish in, 44, 62; terrorist plane crash in, 721; western land claims and, 124; Whiskey Rebellion in, 144
Pennsylvania Dutch, 61-62
Pensacola, Florida, 184
Pensions: military, 378, 379
Pentagon: after Cold War, 698; terrorist plane crash and, 721
Pentagon Papers, 663, 671
People(s): of Americas, 6-7. *See also* specific groups
People in Revolution, A (Countryman), 116
People's party: origin of, 379, 444. *See also* Populists
People's Republic of China. *See* China
Pequot Indians, 40
Pequot War, 40
Percy, George, 24
Perestroika, 693, 697-698
Perkins, Frances, 558
Perkins, Maria, on internal slave trade, 260
Perlstein, Rick, 668, 701
Perot, H. Ross, 704, 708
Perry, Matthew C., 291, 587
Perry, Oliver Hazard, 172-173
Pershing, John J ("Black Jack"): Villa and, 500; World War I and, 511
Persian Gulf region: Iran hostage crisis in, 683-684, 688
Persian Gulf War, 699-700
Personal liberty laws, 288-289
Personal Politics (Evans), 668
Peru: Incas in, 6, 8, 15; revolution in, 196; silver from, 14, 15; Spanish in, 14, 16
Pesticides, 665
Pet banks, 201, 203
Petition(s): antislavery, 266; right of, 266
Petroleum. *See* Oil and oil industry
Pharmaceuticals. *See* Drugs
Philadelphia, 405; almshouses in, 65; in American Revolution, 109, 112; Bank of the United States in, 144; Constitutional Convention in, 128-131; elections in, 197; First Continental Congress in, 96; Franklin in, 45; Independence Hall in, 128; libraries in, 73; population of, 44, 61, 140, 214; as port city, 45; religious violence in, 218; Second Continental Congress in, 101

Philadelphia (frigate), 151
Philadelphia Plan (Nixon, 1969), 652, 665
Philanthropy, 365, 393, 416; higher education and, 417
Philip II (Spain), 22
Philippines: annexation of, 458, 459, 462, 464, 471; anti-American insurgency in, 462; anti-imperialists and, 459; Dewey in, 456-457; independence for, 498, 571; Jones Act and, 498; MacArthur and, 591, 598; McKinley and, 458, 459, 462; Seven Years' War in, 81; Spanish-American War in, 365; United States and, 344, 472; in World War II, 591
Phillips, David G., 479
Phillips, Ulrich Bonnell, 267
Phillips, Wendell, 263, 331
Phillips-Fein, Kim, 701
"Philosophic Cock, A" (Federalist print), 159
Philosophy: transcendentalism, 246-248
Phonographs, 392, 434, 530
Phony war (World War II), 575
Photography: of Hine, 399; invention of, 245
Physicians: colonial, 66; women as, 241, 322
Pickett, George, 334
Pickett's charge, 334, 334 (map)
Picture brides, Japanese women as, 587
Piedmont region, textile mills in, 397
Pierce, Franklin: 1852 election and, 289; Cuba and, 290; Kansas-Nebraska Bill and, 301
Pietists, 220
Pike, Zebulon M., 163
Pikes Peak, 434, 437
Pilgrims: at Plymouth, 36-37, 40
Pill, the: in 1960s, 660
Pillow, Fort, massacre of black soldiers at, 333
Pinchot, Cornelia, 486
Pinchot, Gifford, 485, 486, 487, 490
Pinckney's Treaty (1795), 149, 162
"Pink-collar ghetto," 711
Pinkerton's Detective Agency, 328, 379-380
Pinochet, Augusto, 664
Pioneers: during Civil War, 321; farming by, 226, 436; international, 442-443; from North to Kansas, 298; in Oregon, 273; railroads and, 389; westward movement and, 84, 212-213, 436, 439
Pirates: of North Africa, 127, 162, 178
Pitt, William, 81, 82-83
Pittsburgh, 80, 392
"Pivotal Decade" (Stein), 701
Pizarro, Francisco, 15, 16
Plains Indians: buffalo and, 365, 429; in Civil War, 315; culture of, 429, 433; European invasion and, 433; horses and, 429; lifestyle of, 433; reservations for, 429-430, 431, 432; warfare with, 430, 431 (map); westward expansion and, 364-365, 428-434
Plains of Abraham, 82-83, 84
Planned economy: Roosevelt, F.D., and, 567
Planned parenthood, Willard and, 421
Planned Parenthood v. *Casey*, 696
Planters and plantations: as aristocracy, 255-256, 353; in Carolina, 29; during Civil War, 333; after Civil War, 348, 350, 362, 396; colonial, 27, 28, 29-32; Cotton Kingdom and, 255; financial instability of, 256; in Hawaii, 454; headright system and, 51; intermarriage of, 261; layout of, 264; northern banks and, 266; plantation agriculture and, 256; slavery and, 2, 12, 13, 29, 63, 64, 252, 259-261; in South, 54, 255-256; in sugar industry, 12, 29; women and, 64, 256
Plants: in Columbian exchange, 13, 14
Platforms (political), 201
Plath, Sylvia, 640-642

Platt Amendment (1901), 460–461, 572
Platte River region, 78
Plattsburgh, battle near, 173
Playboy (magazine), 630
Playwrights: after World War II, 642. *See also* Drama
Pledge of Allegiance: "under God" in, 617
Plenty Coups (Indian spokesman), 434
Plessy v. Ferguson, 374
Plows, 226, 436
Plow-under program, 559–560
Plunkitt, George Washington, 377
Pluralism: cultural, 522, 715; postmodern, 717
Plutocracy, 324, 382, 395
Plymouth Colony: Indians and, 40; Pilgrims at, 36–37, 40
Plymouth Plantation, 36, 37
Pocahontas, 24–25, 26, 27
Pocket vetoes, 353
Poe, Edgar Allan, 248
Poets and poetry: in 1920s, 531–532; African American, 423; Beats and, 640, 660; colonial, 72; of Knickerbocker Group, 246; post–World War II, 640–641; transcendentalist, 247–248. *See also* Literature; specific writers
Point Four program: of Truman, 620
Poland: boundaries of, 675; Hitler and, 575; immigrants from, 227, 407; Solidarity movement in, 690, 697; Soviet Union and, 608; after World War II, 610. *See also* Polish Americans
Police: in Haymarket Square, 400; increase in 1990s, 705; Irish immigrants as, 216
Polio, Roosevelt, F.D., and, 551
Polish Americans, 523
Political cartoons: anti-Cleveland, 378; on Big Stick policies, 467; Brooks caning Sumner, 301; on Bryan, 446; about Hoover, 547; on immigration, 412; "Join or Die" (Franklin), 81; by Nast, Thomas, 368, 369; on robber barons, 394
Political machines, 193, 194, 377, 408, 480; immigrants and, 408–410
Political parties: Civil War and, 310; emergence of, 119, 144–145; evolution of major, 189; in Gilded Age, 371; sectionalism in, 290; two-party system and, 145, 189, 194, 208. *See also* specific parties
Political science, 119
Politics: abolitionists and, 265; business and, 682; Civil War and, 338–340; Cold War and, 617–618; colonial, 73–74; democracy in, 207–208, 479; economy and, 535–549; fourth party system and, 448; freedmen and, 357–358; in Gilded Age, 371, 382; Grangers in, 442–443; of inequality, 728–729; Irish immigrants in, 216, 217; minorities in, 710; populist, 207–208; presidential, 447; progressivism and, 479–480
Polk, James K., 283; 1844 election and, 273, 274; California and, 275, 276, 277, 281; Cuba and, 290; Mexican War and, 275–276, 277, 278; Oregon and, 275; tariff and, 274; Texas and, 272, 274, 275, 276
Pollock, Jackson, 640
Polls: public opinion, 577
Poll tax, 374, 381
Polo, Marco, 11
Polygamy, 236, 437
Ponce de León, Juan, 14
Pontiac's uprising, 84
Pony Express, 228–229
Pools (railroad), 390
Poor people: attitudes toward, 395; imprisonment for debt and, 239. *See also* Poverty

Poor Richard's Almanack (Franklin), 72
Poor whites, 257
"Pop" art, 640
Pope, Joseph, 46
Popé's Rebellion, 19
Popular consent, 253
Popular culture, 716; postmodern, 717. *See also* Music
Popular sovereignty, 283, 288, 302, 304, 309, 344; in Kansas, 292, 300
Population: in 1790 census, 140; in 1860, 214; in 1870 census, 366, 404; 1950–2013, 622 (map); baby boom and, 624; of Cahokia, 8; in Chesapeake region, 50; of Chinese ancestry, 375; in cities, 44, 61, 214, 364, 404, 405, 406; during Civil War, 316; colonial, 27, 44, 50, 61–62, 97; Columbian exchange and, 13–14; of England, 23, 61, 97; of farmers, 441; of free blacks, 259; immigrants in, 61–62, 215, 217, 256, 407, 408; Native American, 11, 14, 434; of New France, 77; of Philadelphia, 44, 61; of Puerto Rico, 460; representation by, 130; of runaway slaves, 285; of rural areas, 61; shift to cities, 140; slave, 27, 29, 53, 54, 252, 259, 260; of Virginia, 27, 50, 61; westward movement of, 140, 212–213, 213 (map); white, 256–259. *See also* Census
Populist Revolt, The (Hicks), 383
Populists, 382, 395, 445; 1892 election and, 379, 380, 380 (map); 1896 election and, 441; African American vote and, 380–381; farmers as, 364, 444; historians on, 383; platform of, 379, 444; progressivism and, 477; racism and, 381, 444; as reformers, 383. *See also* People's party
Populist Vision, The (Postel), 383
Port Hudson, battle at, 336
Portnoy's Complaint (Roth), 642
Portrait of a Lady, The (James), 422
Port Royal, Nova Scotia, 79
Portsmouth, New Hampshire, Russo-Japanese peace conference at, 468
Portugal: Africa and, 12–13; imperialism of, 470; New World exploration by, 12–13, 15 (map); Treaty of Tordesillas and, 14
Postal system: colonial, 125. *See also* Mail
Postel, Charles, 383
Postindustrial economy, 628
Postmodernism, 716–717
Postrevisionist historians, 625
Potato crop, in Ireland, 215, 217
Potsdam conference (1945), 599
Pottawatomie Creek, murders at, 300
Potter, David M., 310
Pound, Ezra, 531–532
Poverty: in 2012, 729; in cities, 477–478; Hoover on, 535; Johnson, Lyndon B., and, 652; in Puerto Rico, 460. *See also* Poor people
Poverty line, 460, 655
Powderly, Terence V., 400
Powell, Colin, 722
Powell, John Wesley, 437
Powell, Lewis, 682
Power (political): of Bank of the United States, 143; Civil War and federal, 344, 345; industry and, 365; in South, 373
Powhatan, 24, 25, 26
Pragmatism, 418
Pragmatism (James), 418
Prague Spring: in Czechoslovakia, 661
Pratt, Julius, 472
Praying towns, 40, 62
Predestination, 35
Pregnancy: in Chesapeake region, 50; in New England, 55, 56

Presbyterians and Presbyterianism, 35, 69, 71, 108, 182, 235
Prescott, William Hickling, 249
Preservationists, 486, 487. *See also* Conservation
Presidency: constitutional powers of, 130; election to, 130, 131; in Gilded Age, 382; Jackson and, 200; power of, 130, 200; Roosevelt, T., and, 489, 578–579; two-term tradition in, 149, 371; "Virginia dynasty" and, 176, 179, 190. *See also* specific individuals
Presidential elections. *See* Elections
Presidential Reconstruction, 353
Presley, Elvis, 629, 630
Press: freedom of, 73. *See also* Journalism; Newspapers
Press gangs, 164
Price(s): inflation and, 321
Price discrimination, 497
Price revolution: in Europe, 15
Primary schools, 71, 236
Prime rate, 681
Primogeniture, 23
Princeton, New Jersey, in American Revolution, 108
Princeton University, 71
Príncipe, 12
Principles of Psychology (James), 418
Printing presses, 13
Prisons: Clinton and, 705; debtors', 179, 239; reform in, 239
Privacy rights, 664, 732
Privateers, in American Revolution, 113–114
Pro-choice advocates, 696
Proclamation of 1763, 84
Producers' cooperatives, 400
Production: assembly-line, 221; cotton, 219, 221; factory system of, 118, 219, 221; farm, 439; tobacco, 50–51. *See also* Mass production
Productivity: in 1970s, 673
Professional schools, 417
Professions: clergy, 66; lawyers, 66; physicians, 66, 241; women in, 224, 241, 322, 410
Profiteers: in American Revolution, 99; in Civil War, 321
Progress and Poverty (George), 419
Progressive education, 524
Progressive historians, 116, 137, 310, 383
Progressive party: 1912 election and, 492–493; 1916 election and, 502; 1924 election and, 540, 541 (map); 1948 election and, 619
Progressivism, 474, 476, 477–482; Bull Moose, 492–493; in cities and states, 480; muckrakers and, 478–479; New Deal reforms and, 554–555; political, 479–480; prohibition and, 522–524; roots of, 477–478; social gospel and, 410, 478; women and, 480–482
Prohibition, 421, 506, 522–524; repeal of, 559
Project Head Start, 653
Promised Land, The (Antin), 408
Promise of American Life, The (Croly), 493
Promise of the New South (Ayers), 383
Promontory Point, Utah, transcontinental railroad at, 388
Propaganda: abolitionist, 263; in World War I, 504–505, 506, 511; in World War II, 586
Property: for Irish immigrants, 216; slaves as, 302; as voting requirement, 41; women's rights to, 241, 243, 359, 420
Prophet, the. *See* Tenskwatawa
Proposition 13 (California), 689
Proposition 209 (California), 708
Proprietary colonies, 28, 29, 44, 73
Proprietors: in New England, 56; in Pennsylvania, 44

Proslavery arguments, 262, 265-266
Prosperity: in 1900, 465; in 1920s, 525-526; in 2000s, 728-729; before Civil War, 254, 286; global, 675; of Sunbelt, 622; after World War II, 620-621. *See also* Affluence; Great Depression
Prostitution, 375, 387; reforms of, 480
Protective tariffs, 178, 320, 321, 441
Protest(s): in 1950s, 632; in 1960s, 660-662; colonial, 53, 90; of farmers, 390; against trade policy, 710; against Vietnam War, 656, 658, 661, 662. *See also* Revolts and rebellions; Revolution(s); specific movements
Protestant ethic, 38
Protestantism: in 1960s, 660; Anti-Masons and, 201; Catholicism of immigrants and, 28, 302; in England, 22; in Ireland, 22; liberal, 413; in Maryland, 28; revivalism and, 69-71, 119, 233-235
Protestant Reformation, 22, 35-36
Proulx, E. Annie, 717
Psychology. *See* Freud, Sigmund
Public facilities, segregation of, 365, 374, 381
Public health programs, 524
Public lands: Ballinger-Pinchot quarrel over, 490; for higher education, 417; homesteads from, 303, 344, 435-436. *See also* Land
Public opinion: polling in 1930s, 577
Public schools: German immigrants and, 216; growth of, 415; in Old Northwest, 125; secondary, 71, 237; South and, 236, 256, 359, 416; tax-supported schools and, 236, 415. *See also* Education; Schools
Public utilities: regulation of, 480
Public Utility Holding Company Act (1935), 556, 561
Public works: Coxey and, 445; in South, 359
Public Works Administration (PWA), 553, 558
Pueblo Indians: abuse of, 18-19; agriculture of, 8; at Battle of Acoma, 18-19
Puerto Ricans, 459, 709; immigration of, 459; U.S. citizenship for, 459, 460. *See also* Hispanics; Latinos
Puerto Rico: government of, 459; multiracial population of, 460; Spanish-American War in, 458; U.S. acquisition of, 344, 458, 459-460, 471, 472
Pugilism, 425
Pujo, Arsene, 497
Pulitzer, Joseph, 418, 452
Pullman, George, 389
Pullman Palace Car Company, 445
Pullman Palace Cars, 228
Pullman strike, 445, 446
Pump priming, 546, 555, 566
Punishment: of slaves, 261
Pure Food and Drug Act (1906), 485
Puritans and Puritanism: Congregational Church and, 38; conversion by, 35; in England, 23; government and, 37; Great English Migration (1630s) and, 37; Half-Way Covenant and, 57; Hutchinson, Anne, and, 38-39; Indians and, 39, 40; jeremiad and, 57; New England society and, 2, 35-36, 37-39, 56, 57; non-Separatist, 37; Republicans and, 371; women's property rights and, 56
Putney Association, 244
Pynchon, Thomas, 717

Quakers: antislavery sentiment of, 44, 135, 262; Emerson on, 43; in Massachusetts Bay Colony, 38; in Pennsylvania, 2, 43-45; in Rhode Island, 39
"Quarantine Speech" (F.D. Roosevelt), 570, 574
Quarles, Benjamin, 250
Quartering Act: of 1765, 90, 92; of 1774, 95
Quayle, J. Danforth, 704
Québec: before and after 1774, 96 (map); in American Revolution, 103, 104 (map); Battle of, 83; France and, 21, 77; in French and Indian War, 82-83; Indians in, 77
Quebec Act (1774), 95, 96 (map), 103
Queen Anne's War (1702-1713), 79
Quetzalcoatl (god), 17
Quotas: on immigrants, 474, 521, 522, 653

Rabbit, Run (Updike), 640
Rabin, Yitzhak, 713
Race and racism: in 1790, 216; in 1970s, 679-680; on 2000 census, 715-716; 2000 election and, 715; in Black Codes, 353-354; Clinton and, 708; Executive Order 8802 against, 633; free blacks and, 259; imperialism and, 472; labor unions and, 399, 618; minority populations and, 710; in Philippines, 462; Populist party and, 380-381, 444; against Puerto Ricans, 460; segregation and, 365, 374, 381; slavery and, 63, 257, 262; in South, 257, 262, 361, 365, 381; in suburbs, 623; Supreme Court on, 696; voting rights and, 732; of Wilson, 498; after World War II, 631-632. *See also* African Americans; Civil rights; Civil rights movement; Ku Klux Klan
Race riots: in 1960s, 655; in Chicago (1919), 507; in Detroit, 589; in East St. Louis, 507; between Irish and blacks, 216; in Los Angeles, 708; during Reconstruction, 356; in Watts, 654; during World War I, 506-507; after World War I, 474-475
Racial code of conduct, southern, 374
Racketeers, 524
Radcliffe College, 239
Radical abolitionism, 263-265
Radicalism, 397; of New Deal, 568; after World War I, 474, 519
Radical Reconstruction, 355-359
Radical Republicans, 353, 355, 356, 362, 373; during Civil War, 339; Johnson, Andrew and, 360-361
Radical Right, The (Bell), 701
Radical Whigs, 88
Radio: 1928 election and, 543; government ownership of, 543; as revolution, 527-528
Ragged music, 424
"Rag money," 321
Railroad(s): in 1920s, 537; buffalo and, 365, 431-432; in Canada, 442; Chinese workers on, 387, 388; in Civil War, 316, 336; consolidation of, 537; corruption and, 368, 389-390; farming and, 389, 390, 436, 441; gauges of, 228; growth of, 227-228, 386-389; immigration and, 216, 389; Irish workers on, 216, 386, 388; iron and, 392; land grants to, 386, 387 (map), 388, 389, 436; magnates in, 388; Manchurian, 489; overbuilding by, 388-389; Plains Indians and, 364-365, 431; ranching and, 435; rate-setting systems of, 390, 396; in receivership, 381; refrigerator cars and, 392, 440; regulation of, 390-391, 442, 483; revolution in, 228 (map), 389; in Russia, 442; in South, 291-292, 316, 336, 348; speculation in, 389, 390; steel rail and, 389; strikes against, 374, 400, 445; time zones and, 389; transcontinental, 291-292, 354, 373, 386-387, 388; in transportation revolution, 118; in West, 291-292, 292 (map), 386, 387 (map), 389, 436; in World War I, 506; in World War II, 588
Railway Labor Board, 537

"Rainbow coalition," 696
Raisin in the Sun, A (Hansberry), 642
Raleigh, Walter, 21, 22
Ramona (Helen Hunt Jackson), 432
Ranching, in West, 435
Ranchos, 279
Randall, James G., 310
Randolph, A. Philip, 589
Randolph, John, 191
Rankin, Jeannette, 503
Rate setting (railroads), 390, 396
Ratification: of Articles of Confederation, 98, 124; of Constitution (U.S.), 131-135, 132 (map), 137; of ERA (1972), 676-679; of Versailles Treaty, 513-514
Rationalism, religion and, 233
Rational use philosophy, 486
Rauchway, Eric, 383
Rauschenbusch, Walter, 410
"Raven, The" (Poe), 248
Raw materials, 389; in New World, 13, 89; in South, 396. *See also* Natural resources
Reagan, Ronald, 686; 1976 election and, 680; 1980 election and, 605, 687-688; 1984 election and, 693; affirmative action and, 695-696; as California governor, 688; Cold War and, 625, 690; conservatism and, 680, 687-695; economy under, 689-690, 694-695; foreign policy of, 689, 693; inauguration of, 688; Iran-Contra affair and, 693-694; Lebanon and, 692; Nicaragua and, 692; Panama Canal and, 681; postrevisionists on, 625; referendum on (1986), 696; on school prayer, 688
Reaganomics, 689-690, 695
"Reagan revolution," 688-689
Real estate: collapse of values, 725
Realism: in arts, 421, 423-424; in literature, 421-422, 640
Reapers, mechanical, 222, 226, 318, 321
Rearmament: after World War I, 572; after World War II, 613
Rebates: railroad, 390
Rebellions. *See* Revolts and rebellion
Rebel Without a Cause (movie), 660
"Rebel yell," 316
Recall, 479-480
Recession: in 1914, 501; of 1920-1921, 525; in 1980s, 689-690; in 2000s, 719, 721, 727; Ford, Gerald, and, 681
Reclamation, 485
Reclamation, Bureau of, 487
Reconcentration camps: in Cuba, 454; in Philippines, 462
Reconquista (Spain), 16
Reconstruction: in Asia after World War II, 613-614
Reconstruction (U.S.), 253, 347; Black Codes during, 353-354; Congressional, 354; constitutional amendments in era of, 332, 344, 355, 356, 357; end of, 373; freedmen during, 349-350, 351; Johnson, Andrew, and, 351; Ku Klux Klan during, 359-360; legacy of, 361; Lincoln's plan for, 353; Military, 356-357, 356 (map); presidential, 353; radical, 355-359; scalawags and carpetbaggers in, 358; scholarship on, 362; Second, 362, 374; white resistance to, 359-360
Reconstruction Act (1867), 356, 356 (map)
Reconstruction Finance Corporation (RFC), 546
Recovery, New Deal programs and, 554
Recreation. *See* Leisure
Red army: in World War II, 593
Red Badge of Courage, The (Crane), 422

Redcoats, 89, 92–93, 97. *See also* Armed forces; Regulars
Redeemers, 357, 359, 373
Redemption Day (1879), 370
Red Guards (China), 661
Red scare: 1919–1920, 519–520, 537; after World War II, 616–617. *See also* McCarthy, Joseph, and McCarthyism
Reed, Thomas B. ("Czar"), 379, 449
Reed, Walter, 460
Reed v. Reed, 679
Referendum, 379, 479
Reform(s): age of, 239–240; in Catholic Church, 660; in cities and states, 480; civil service, 368, 371, 376, 377, 378; under Clinton, 707–708; in education, 236–237, 417–418; of factories, 222, 224, 481; financial, 270; of health care, 653; historians on antebellum reformers, 250; of immigration policy, 522, 724; imprisonment for debt and, 222, 239; Indian policy and, 432–434; literature, 419; muckrakers and, 478–479; New Deal, 553–557; Populists and, 383; progressive, 474, 476, 477–482; during Reconstruction, 359; religion and, 22, 35–36, 232, 410; Roosevelt, Eleanor, and, 551; settlement houses and, 410; in Soviet Union, 698; temperance, 240, 421; transcendentalism and, 246–248; utopian movement and, 119; by Wilson, 493; women and, 239, 410. *See also* specific issues and reformers
Reformation: Protestant, 22, 35–36
Reform Bill (Britain): of 1832, 196; of 1867, 343, 344
Refrigeration, in railroad cars, 392, 440
Refugees: in Civil War, 350; from Dust Bowl, 561; from Holocaust, 576; Vietnamese, 677; in World War II, 598
Regionalism: in arts, 421, 423; Civil War and, 310, 345; economic specialization and, 229; in literature, 421, 423; Second Great Awakening and, 235. *See also* Sectionalism
Regulars (British soldiers), 81
Regulation: of corporations, 483; of factories, 222, 224; of natural resources, 364; under Nixon, 665; of private enterprise, 364; of public utilities, 480; of railroads, 390–391, 483; Reagan and, 694; of trusts, 395–396; Wilson and, 493; of workplace, 482
Rehnquist, William, 724
Reign of Terror (French Revolution), 147
Relief efforts: in Great Depression, 475, 554–557
Religion(s): in 1950s, 629; in 1960s, 660; in British and Spanish Empires, 35–38; colonial, 28, 29, 32, 35–36, 37–39, 69; diversity in, 44, 61, 235, 414; evolution and, 415, 524–525; feminization of, 235; Great Awakening and, 69–71, 232, 234–235; of immigrants, 217, 218, 220, 407–408, 414; in Maryland, 28; in New France, 77; in Old Northwest, 182; in Pennsylvania, 44; political candidates and, 542, 543; political parties and, 371; reform and, 22, 35–36, 232; revival of, 69–71, 119, 233–235; slave, 64–65, 261, 265; social gospel and, 410, 478; Supreme Court on, 664; wars of, 16. *See also* specific groups
Religious orders. *See* specific orders
Religious right, 695
Religious Society of Friends. *See* Quakers
Religious toleration: in New England, 39; in Pennsylvania, 44; in plantation colonies, 28, 29, 32
Relocation centers, for Japanese Americans, 586, 587

Remington, Frederic, 429, 454
Removal policy, for Native Americans, 198, 199, 200 (map), 429–430
Renaissance: exploration and, 13
Rent (Larson), 717
Reorganization Act (1939), 556, 566
Reparations (German): after World War I, 541, 542
Repatriation, of New Immigrants, 409
Representation: in colonial legislatures, 73; equal, 130; freedmen and southern, 354, 355; by population, 130; taxation without, 90–91; virtual, 91
Representative government: in Pennsylvania, 44; in Virginia, 28
Republicanism: anarchy and, 127; civic virtue and, 105, 127; defined, 88; extensive republic and, 137; Paine and, 105; ratification and, 137
Republican motherhood, 123, 136
Republican party: 1860 election and, 305–306, 307 (map); in 1920s, 535; abolitionist backing of, 265; Civil War veterans in, 371; Contract with America (1994) and, 706; *Dred Scott* decision and, 302; Eisenhower and, 634–635; ex-Confederates in Congress and, 354; in Gilded Age, 371; Half-Breed faction of, 371; hard-money policy of, 346, 370; Lincoln in, 294, 296, 304; Old Guard of, 490, 491, 515, 536–537; origin of, 294; Ostend Manifesto and, 291; presidency and, 447–448; protective tariffs and, 320; radical faction in, 339, 353, 355, 356, 362; Reconstruction and, 353, 355–359, 361; in South, 259; Stalwart faction of, 371, 376; as Union party, 340, 351, 367; Wilson and, 511–512. *See also* Elections; specific leaders
Republican Revolution: in Congress, 707
Republicans (early 1800s). *See* Democratic-Republican party; National Republicans
Republic Steel Company, massacre at, 563
Research and development (R and D): after World War II, 621
Reservations (Indian), 25, 31, 365, 429–430, 431, 432
Resettlement: of Vietnamese immigrants, 677
Resettlement Administration (1935), 556
Resources. *See* Natural resources
Responsorial style, of slave preaching, 261
Restoration (England), 29
Resumption Act (1875), 370
Reuben James (destroyer), attack on, 580
Revels, Hiram, 358
Revenues: Hamilton's financial structure and, 143
Revere, Paul: Boston Massacre engraving by, 93; portrait of, 90
Reverse discrimination, 665, 696
Revisionist historians, 472, 625, 701
Revivals and revivalism, religious, 69–71, 119, 233–235, 257
Revolts and rebellions: *Amistad*, 262; Bacon's Rebellion, 51, 53, 59; Boxer, 465; in Canada, 203; in Europe (1820s), 185; by Filipinos against U.S., 462; by Gabriel, 262; Leisler's Rebellion, 59; Lone Star, 205–206; New York slave revolt (1712), 63; by Panama, 467; Popé's, 19; Shays's Rebellion, 127; South Carolina slave revolt (1739), 63; against Spain, 454; by Toussaint L'Ouverture, 162; by Turner, Nat, 262, 265; by Vesey, Denmark, 195, 262; Whiskey Rebellion, 144
Revolution(s): of 1800, 158, 160; of 1848, 282; Bolshevik (1917), 519; in Cuba (1959), 638; in Iran (1979), 681; market, 229–230; in Mexico,

196; in Texas (1836), 205–206, 206 (map); in transportation, 118, 229. *See also* American Revolution
Rhineland: Hitler in, 574; post-World War I, 512
Rhode Island: in American Revolution, 112; charter of, 39, 41; Constitution and, 133, 134; government of, 73; religious toleration in, 39
Rhodes, Cecil, 470
Rhodes, James Ford, 310
Rhodesia (Zimbabwe), 680
Ribuffo, Leo, 701
Ricardo, David, 395
Rice and rice industry: in Carolina, 29; slaves and, 2, 64
Richmond, Virginia: as capital of Confederacy, 314; in Civil War, 327, 328, 342
Rickover, H.G., 455
Rider, Alexander, 234
Riesman, David, 630
Rights: colonial, 74; for freedmen, 353; to privacy, 664; of slaves, 261; in Virginia, 24. *See also* African Americans; Bill of Rights; Civil rights; Women's rights; specific rights and freedoms
Right-to-life movement, 695, 696
Right wing (political): New Right and, 695
Riis, Jacob A., 477–478
Ringshout dance, 63, 65
Rio Grande River region, 276, 277, 277 (map), 429, 634; *conquistadores* in, 18; Pueblo Indians in, 8; as Texas boundary, 275
Riots: at Democratic National Convention (1968), 658; draft (New York City), 320; zoot-suit, 589. *See also* Race riots
"Rip Van Winkle" (Irving), 246
Rise of American Civilization, The (Beard and Beard), 383
Rise of Silas Lapham, The (Howells), 421
Rivers: in middle colonies, 45. *See also* specific river regions
Roads and highways: in 1920s, 527; American System and, 178; colonial, 68; construction of, 180; Federal Highway Act (1956) and, 635; National Road, 226–227; westward movement and, 180; after World War II, 621
Roanoke Island, English colonization of, 3, 22
Roaring Twenties, 518–533
Robber barons, 383, 394, 402
Robert Gould Shaw Memorial, 424
Roberts, Grace, 463
Roberts, John G., 724
Roberts, Oral, 629
Roberts, Owen J., 565
Robeson, Paul, 631
Robin Moor (merchant ship), 580
Robinson, Jackie, 631
Roca, Julio (Argentina), 442
Rochambeau, Comte de, 112, 114
Rockefeller, John D., 319, 413, 417; horizontal integration and, 392; in oil industry, 393–394; wealth of, 395
Rockefeller Foundation, 524
Rock 'n' roll music, 629
Rocky Mountains, 5, 6, 78, 213
Roe v. Wade, 665, 679
Rohm, Ernst, 600
Rolfe, John, 25, 27
Roman Catholic Church. *See* Catholic Church
Romania, 608, 697
Rome: in World War II, 594
Rome-Berlin Axis, 572
Rommel, Erwin, 593
Romney, Mitt: 2012 election and, 730
Roosevelt, Eleanor, 551–552, 557–558

Roosevelt, Franklin Delano, 550, 600; 1932 election and, 547, 550, 552; 1936 election and, 563-565; 1940 election and, 578-579; 1944 election and, 595-596; Brain Trust of, 552; on civil rights, 591; critics of, 566-568; death of, 598; Executive Order 8802 and, 633; fireside chats of, 555; foreign policy of, 571-578, 579-582; globalization and, 674, 675; Hitler compared with, 600; labor and, 563; lend-lease and, 578, 579-580; New Deal of, 475, 552; Supreme Court and, 565-566; at Tehran Conference, 594, 597; two-term tradition and, 149; World War II and, 576, 584, 602; at Yalta Conference, 608. *See also* Great Depression; New Deal; World War II

Roosevelt, Theodore ("Teddy"): 1900 election and, 465; 1904 election and, 487; 1908 election and, 488; 1912 election and, 491, 492-493; 1916 election and, 502; on American Revolution, 90; as assistant naval secretary, 456; assumption of presidency, 465; big stick policy of, 483, 489; conservation and, 485-487; corporations and, 483; Cuba and, 455-456; foreign policy of, 466, 466-468 (map), 470-471, 474; Gentlemen's Agreement and, 470, 587; imperialism of, 452, 472; as New York governor, 465; Nobel Peace Prize to, 469; Panama Canal and, 466-468; on patronage system, 377; Philippines and, 456; as president, 466; reform and, 474, 479; as Rough Rider, 457; Russo-Japanese War and, 468; Square Deal of, 476, 482-483; Taft and, 488, 490, 491; as vice president, 465; World War I and, 501

Roosevelt, Theodore, Jr., 537
Roosevelt Corollary, to Monroe Doctrine, 468, 498, 571
Root, Elihu, 462
Root-Takahira agreement (1908), 471
Rosenberg, Julius and Ethel, 616
"Rosie the Riveter" (character), 588
Roth, Philip, 642
Rothko, Mark, 640
Rouge River plant: of Ford, 526
Roughing It (Twain), 228, 422
Rough Riders, 457
Royal African Company, 53
Royal Air Force, 576-578
Royal colonies: government in, 73; Massachusetts as, 37, 41; New Hampshire as, 40; Virginia as, 28
Royalists: in England, 41
Royal Navy. *See* Navy, British
Ruby, Jack, 647
Ruhr Valley, French in, 542
Rumsfeld, Donald, 723, 724
Runaway slaves, 256, 262, 284-285, 287-289, 333
Rural areas: movement to cities from, 364; population in, 61, 140; in South, 365, 396
Rush-Bagot agreement (1817), 177
Russia, 469; Alaska and, 185, 361; in Armed Neutrality, 112; China and, 463, 471; frontier in, 442; imperialism of, 489; Jewish people and, 408; Oregon claims of, 272; after Soviet Union, 698; in World War I, 500. *See also* Bolshevik entries; Soviet Union
Russian Republic, after Soviet Union, 698
Russo-Japanese War (1904), 468
Rutgers, 71
Ruth, George H. ("Babe"), 526
Rwanda, ethnic genocide in, 713
Ryan, Mary, 250

Saar Valley, after World War I, 512
Sabotage: in World War I, 500-501, 506
SAC. *See* Strategic Air Command

Sacajawea, 163
Sacco, Nicola, 520
Sacrifices: by Aztecs, 7
Sadat, Anwar, 680-681
Saddam Hussein, 693, 699, 723
Safety-valve theory, 437-439
Sage, Russell, 394
Sahara Desert region, 12
Saigon, 657. *See also* Vietnam; Vietnam War
Sailors: protections for, 498
St. Augustine, Florida: Spain and, 18
St. Bartholomew's Day (1572), 77
St. Clair, Arthur, 149
Saint-Gaudens, Augustus, 424
St. Lawrence River region: England in, 79; France and, 18, 79; geography of, 6
St. Leger, Barry, 109
St. Louis (ship), Jewish refugees on, 576
"St. Louis Blues," 530
St. Louis Post-Dispatch, 418
St. Marks, 184
St. Mihiel, battle at, 509 (map), 511
St. Valentine's Day massacre (1929), 524
"Saints," Puritans as, 35, 36, 38
Saipan, 598
Sakhalin Island, 468, 608
Salem witch trials, 57
Salk Institute, 640
Saloons, 482, 524
SALT (Strategic Arms Limitation Talks): SALT II (1979), 683
Salutary neglect, as British policy, 41
Salvation Army, 414
Sambo stereotype, 267
Same-sex marriage, 724, 732, 733
Samoa, 344; U.S.-German conflict over, 453
San Antonio: Alamo in, 19, 205, 207
Sand Creek, Colorado, massacre at, 430
San Diego: missions in, 19
Sandinistas, 692, 693-694
San Francisco, 439; beat writers in, 640; Chinese immigrants in, 374, 375; segregation of Asian students in, 469-470
San Francisco Bay region, 279
San Francisco Examiner, 418
Sanger, Margaret, 528
Sanitation: in cities, 214-215, 406; colonial, 74; in meatpacking industry, 485
San Jacinto, Battle of, 205
San Joaquin River region, 6, 561
Santa Anna, Antonio López de, 205, 206 (map), 277, 278
Santa Fe, New Mexico: founding of, 19; Mexican War in, 277; Spanish settlement at, 21
Santa Fe Trail, 277
Santiago, Cuba, Spanish-American War in, 457
Santo Domingo, 162
São Tomé, 12
Saratoga, Battle of, 99, 109, 110
Sargent, John Singer, 423-424
Saskatchewan, exploration of, 78
Satellite (space). *See* Space exploration
Saudi Arabia, 637
Sauk Indians, 199
Savannah (steamer), 228
Savannah, Georgia: in Civil War, 338; religious toleration in, 32
Savannah Indians, 29
Savings and loan (S&L) institutions: failures of, 696
Scabs, 224, 398
Scalawags, 358
Scandals. *See* Corruption
Scarlet Letter, The (Hawthorne), 56, 248
Schechter case, 558

Schenck v. *United States*, 505
Schlafly, Phyllis, 676, 679
Schlesinger, Arthur M., Jr., 209
Schoenwald, Jonathan, 701
School District of Abington Township v. *Schempp*, 664
School Law of 1647 (Massachusetts), 57
School prayer, 664, 688
Schools: desegregation and, 634; elementary, 415; freedmen, 350, 351; Hebrew, 408; high schools, 415; integration of, 655; medical, 66; in middle colonies, 72; for Native Americans, 432; in New England, 56-57, 71; parochial, 408, 415; segregation of, 365, 469-470; in South, 72; teacher-training (normal), 415. *See also* Education; Higher education; Public schools; Universities and colleges
Schulman, Bruce, 701
Schurz, Carl, 216
Schwarz, John, 668
Science: in Cold War, 637; Darwinism and, 415; Franklin and, 72; higher education and, 417, 418; political, 119; World War II and, 590. *See also* Technology
Science and Health with Key to the Scriptures (Eddy), 414
Sciences, 734
Scientific Management, 526
SCLC. *See* Southern Christian Leadership Conference
Scopes, John T., and Scopes Trial, 525
Scotland: immigrants from, 62; political union with England, 76
Scots-Irish, 44, 62, 62 (map)
Scott, Dred, 302
Scott, Winfield, 278, 289
Scribner's Monthly, 418
Sculpture, 424
SDI. *See* Strategic Defense Initiative
SDS. *See* Students for a Democratic Society (SDS)
Sea dogs (England), 22
Seagram Building, 640
Sea otters, 213
Seaports: Irish immigrants in, 217; in New England, 45. *See* Seaports; specific locations
Seattle, Washington: general strike in, 519
SEC. *See* Securities and Exchange Commission
Secession, 313, 319, 343, 345, 348; Compromise of 1850 and, 285, 289; Garrison and, 265, 266; New England and, 163, 166; of South, 306-308, 309, 314, 315 (map); Southern opposition to, 308 (map)
Second Agricultural Adjustment Act (1934), 556, 560
Second American Revolution, Civil War as, 310
Second Anglo-Powhatan War (1644), 25
Secondary schools: public, 71, 237
Second Battle of Bull Run (1862), 329-330
Second Continental Congress. *See* Continental Congress (Second)
Second front, in World War II, 593-594, 597, 608
Second Great Awakening, 232, 234-235, 237, 261, 263, 297
Second Vatican Council, 660
Second War for American Independence, War of 1812 as, 176-177
Second-wave feminism, 604, 678, 679
Second World War. *See* World War II
Secota (de Bry engraving of town), 3
Secret societies, 201
Sectionalism, 282; in 1860 election, 305-306; Civil War and, 310, 345; Constitution and, 130; political parties and, 290; in Revolution,

130; slavery in territories and, 180, 284; *Uncle Tom's Cabin* and, 297; War of 1812 and, 169, 176; after War of 1812, 179
Secularization program, in Mexico, 279
Securities: in Great Depression, 561
Securities and Exchange Commission (SEC), 556, 561
Security Council (U.N.), 610
Sedgwick, Susan Anne Livingston Ridley, 136
Sedition Act: of 1798, 152; of 1918, 505
Segregation: in 1920s, 529; in 1950s, 631–632; of armed forces, 591; of Asians, 469–470, 587; in cities, 406, 624; Civil Rights Act (1964) and, 651; Jim Crow laws and, 374, 381, 529, 631; in South, 365, 374, 631; Wilson and, 498; after World War II, 631–632. *See also* African Americans; Civil rights movement; Race and racism
Selective breeding program (Oneida Community), 244
Selective Service System, 613
Self-determination, 471; in Atlantic Charter, 674; popular sovereignty and, 283; South and, 309; for Southeast Asia, 635; Wilson and, 504, 512
"Self-Reliance" (Emerson), 213
Self-rule: in English colonies, 2
Sellers, Charles, 209
Selma, Alabama, civil rights movement in, 654
Seminole Indians, 184, 198, 199, 315
Senate (U.S.): African Americans in, 358; in Constitution, 130; election to, 131, 379; impeachment in, 360; as Millionaires' Club, 480; Sumner-Brooks clash in, 300–301; Versailles Treaty and, 514. *See also* Congress(U.S.); House of Representatives (U.S.)
Seneca Falls Convention, for women's rights, 241, 243, 507, 678
Seneca Indians, 30, 112
Senegal: slaves from, 53
Senior citizens. *See* Elderly
Sensationalism, in newspapers, 418
"Separate but equal" facilities, 634; Supreme Court on, 374
Separate spheres, 481
Separation of church and state: educational aid and, 653; Johnson, L.B., and, 653; Kennedy, J.F., on, 639; in Massachusetts Bay Colony, 38; and school prayer and Bible reading, 664; in Virginia, 135
Separatism: Du Bois and, 416
Separatists, 36, 37. *See also* Pilgrims
Sepsis, in Civil War, 323
September 11, 2001, terrorist attacks, 601, 721–722
Sequoia National Park, 437
Sequoyah (Cherokee), 198
Serbia, 500
Serra, Junipero, 19, 279
Servants: Irish immigrants as, 217. *See also* Indentured servants; Slaves and slavery
Service-based economy, 628
Servicemen's Readjustment Act (GI Bill, 1944), 618
Set-asides, by employers, 665
Settlement(s): agriculture and, 8; in Middle Colonies, 43 (map); Norse, 11. *See also* Exploration; specific locations
Settlement houses, 410, 479, 480–481
Settlers. *See* Pioneers
Seven Days' Battles, 328, 331
Seventeenth Amendment, 480
Seventh of March speech (Webster), 286
Seven Years' War (1756–1763): colonies after, 3, 83–84; England after, 87; worldwide involvement in, 81. *See also* French and Indian War
Sewage systems, 214–215
Sewall, Samuel, 63
Seward, William H.: 1856 election and, 301; 1860 election and, 306; "higher law" speech of, 286; purchase of Alaska and, 361; as secretary of state, 314, 318–319
Seward's Folly, 361
Sewing machines, 221, 223, 321, 322
Sex and sexuality: in 1920s, 528–530; in 1950s, 630; feminism and, 679; new morality and, 419; Oneida Community and, 244. *See also* Gays and lesbians; Gender and gender issues
Sexual harassment: Clinton, Bill, and, 714; Thomas, Clarence, and, 700
Sexually transmitted diseases, 14
Sexual revolution: in 1960s, 660
Seymour, Horatio, 368
Shafter, William R., 457
Shah of Iran, 636, 681
Shakers, 243
Shakespeare, William, 23
"Shame of the Cities, The" (Steffens), 478
Shandong Peninsula, in Treaty of Versailles, 512
Shanghai Communiqué, 664
Sharecroppers, 353, 374, 396, 444
"Share Our Wealth" program, 557
Shaw, Robert Gould, 424
Shawnee Indians, 167–168
Shawnee Mission, proslavery supporters in, 298
Shays, Daniel, 127, 129, 131
Shays's Rebellion (1786), 127
Sheen, Fulton J., 629
Sheffield, Lord, 126
Shelby County v. *Holder*, 732
Shelterbelt project, 486
Shenandoah Valley, Civil War in, 340
Sheppard-Towner Maternity Act (1921), 507
Sheridan, Philip, 340, 431
Sherman, Cindy, 716
Sherman, William Tecumseh, 337–338, 340, 348
Sherman Anti-Trust Act (1890), 396, 497
Sherman Silver Purchase Act (1890), 381; repeal of, 382
Sherman's march, 337–338, 338 (map) 339
Sherwin, Martin J., 602
Shia Muslims, in Iraq, 723
Shiloh, Battle of, 336
Ships and shipping: in American Revolution, 113–114; caravels and, 12; in Civil War, 318, 328–329, 336; clipper ships, 228; on Erie Canal, 178, 227; French seizure of, 164; on Great Lakes, 391, 392; gunboats, 336; ironclads, 329; iron tramp steamers, 228; after Revolution, 122; shipbuilding and, 67, 68; transoceanic steamships, 215; in World War I, 501; in World War II, 580, 593. *See also* Navy (U.S.); specific types
Shopping malls: highways and, 635; as town square, 641
Siberia: land bridge from, 6
Sicily: in World War II, 594
Sierra Club, 486, 487
Sierra Leone, 262
Sierra Nevada Mountains: formation of, 5, 6; gold in, 284; transcontinental railroad in, 387
"Significance of the Frontier in American History, The" (Turner), 437, 449
Silent majority, 662
Silent Spring (Carson), 486, 665
Silver: from Americas, 14, 15; in Bank of the United States, 199; coinage of, 370, 379, 381, 444; discoveries of, 434; free silver, 381, 382, 444, 446, 447; government purchases of, 379; mining of, 434; as Populist issue, 444, 447; from Spanish New World, 14. *See also* Currency
Silver, Timothy, 47
Simpson, O.J., 708
Sinclair, Harry F., 539
Sinclair, Upton, 485
Singapore: economic development in, 674
Singer, Isaac, 221, 223
Single-parent families, 679, 712
Single-tax plan, 419
Sioux Commission, 430
Sioux Indians, 429, 430; in Great Plains, 10 (map), 26; horses and, 14, 26. *See also* Lakota (Sioux) Indians
Sister Carrie (Dreiser), 406, 423
Sit-down strikes, 563, 564
"Sit-in" movement, 634, 646, 660
Sitkoff, Harvard, 568
Sitting Bull, 430
Six-Day War, 656
Sixteenth Amendment, 382, 497
Sixties: evaluation of, 668. *See also* specific issues
Sixties, The: Years of Hope, Days of Rage (Gitlin), 668
69th New York State Militia, 329
Sketch Book, The (Irving), 246
Skilled workers, 399, 400, 401
Sklar, Kathryn, 250
Skyscrapers, 406
Slater, Samuel, 219, 222
Slaughterhouse Five (Vonnegut), 640
Slave and Citizen (Tannenbaum), 267
Slave auction, 260
Slave-catchers, 288, 289
Slave codes: in Barbados, 29; in Virginia (1705), 53, 63
Slaveholders (slaveowners): in Civil War, 315; Confederate draft and, 320; free blacks as, 53; Native Americans as, 198, 315; population of, 255, 256–257; religion, slaves, and, 265
"Slave power," 272, 343
Slavery (Elkins), 267
Slaves and slavery: abolition of, 345; African, 2, 12–13; American-born, 63, 64; in American Revolution, 99; after American Revolution, 135–136; biological reproduction and increase in, 252, 259, 260; in Brazil, 259; in Chesapeake, 27, 63; Civil War and, 252, 253, 310, 317, 331, 333, 343, 345; after Civil War, 349; colonial, 27, 28, 32, 53, 63; comparison of U.S. and world, 259; after Compromise of 1850, 287 (map); cotton production and, 119, 219, 252, 254; criticism of, 63, 262; culture of, 63, 64–65, 252, 261; distribution of (1820 and 1860), 258 (map); *Dred Scott* decision and, 252, 302, 304; effects on slaves, 262; effects on whites, 262; Emancipation Proclamation and, 316, 330, 331, 332; families of, 63, 256, 259, 260, 261; gang-labor, 54, 63; gender differences in, 267; in Georgia, 32, 63, 131; German immigrants and, 216; global attempts to abolish, 263; government checks on, 252; historians' conceptions of, 267; housing for, 264; indentured servants and, 28, 51; Jefferson and, 66, 154, 252, 254; in Kansas and Nebraska, 298, 300; as labor, 53, 63, 252, 254, 259, 260, 265–266; legal status of (Revolution-Civil War), 130; life of,

63, 64, 260–261; as "mammy," 261; marriage of, 261; in Maryland, 28, 63; master-slave relationship in, 265, 267, 349; Mexican War and, 280–281; Missouri Compromise and, 181, 181 (map), 183, 252; in New England, 57; in North Carolina, 32; Northwest Ordinance and, 125; paternalism and, 267; as peculiar institution, 180, 181, 192, 252; on plantations, 2, 12, 13, 29, 63, 64, 256, 259–261; popular sovereignty and, 283; in population, 27, 29, 53, 54, 252, 259, 260; proslavery arguments, 262, 265–266; in Puerto Rico, 460; Quakers and, 44; religion and, 64–65, 261, 265; revolts and rebellions by, 63, 262; runaway, 256, 262, 284–285, 287–289, 333; in southern society, 62, 63, 257; in territories, 257, 266, 269, 282, 287, 292–293; in Texas, 205, 206, 272; in Thirteenth Amendment, 332; three-fifths clause and, 130, 158; Toussaint L'Ouverture rebellion and, 162; *Uncle Tom's Cabin* and, 297, 298, 299, 300; in Virginia, 27, 63; as wealth, 256, 259; in West Indies, 28, 29, 53, 55 (map), 259; "white slave" traffic and, 479; women as, 64, 260, 267. *See also* African Americans; Africans; Freedmen; Slave trade
Slave states, 284, 292, 293 (map)
Slave trade, 262; abolition in District of Columbia, 287; African, 2, 12–13, 53, 54, 55 (map); in Atlantic region, 54, 55 (map); colonial, 53, 54, 55 (map); Constitution and, 131; efforts to stop, 54; internal, 259, 260; prohibition of, 252, 259
Slavocracy, 280, 294, 324
Slidell, John, 276
Slovaks, 407
Slumlords, 562
Slums, 214, 406–407, 413, 477–478, 562; urban reforms and, 480
Smallpox: in Columbian exchange, 14; inoculation for, 66; in Mexico, 17; Native Americans and, 25, 84
Smith, Alfred E."Al," 542, 543
Smith, Gerald L.K., 557
Smith, John, 24–25
Smith, Jonathan, 134
Smith, Joseph, 235–236, 237 (map)
Smith, Josiah, Jr., 99
Smith Act (1940), 616
Smith-Connally Anti-Strike Act (1943), 588
"Smoking gun" tape, of Nixon, 672
Smuggling: colonial, 68, 89, 92; of slaves, 259
SNCC. *See* Student Nonviolent Coordinating Committee
"Soccer moms," 707
Social classes. *See* Class(es)
Social Darwinists, 395
Social engineering, 653
Social gospel movement, 410, 478
Socialism, 397; Berger and, 490; Christian, 410; Debs and, 445, 488, 493, 515; Eisenhower on, 634; Fabian, 419; immigrants and, 412; progressive movement and, 478; red scare and, 520; Roosevelt, F.D., and, 551, 567; utopian, 419; World War I and, 505
Social mobility: class tensions and, 64–65, 402; myths of, 230
Social Security: Bush, George W., and, 724; under Nixon, 665
Social Security Act (1935), 562, 565, 600
Social welfare: faith-based, 714. *See also* Medicare; Social Security; Welfare programs; specific programs
Social welfare agency: Freedmen's Bureau as, 345

Social work (profession), 410, 420
Society: in 1920s, 528–530; in 1950s, 628–630; in 1960s, 659–662; in 2000s, 719; American, 47; colonial, 53–54, 58–59, 64–66; English, 37; global, 734; industrial, 364–365; inequalities in, 728–729; Native American, 8; Quaker, 43; radio and, 527–528; in South, 53–54, 66, 255–256. *See also* Great Society; Lifestyle
Society of Friends. *See* Quakers
Society of the Cincinnati, 135
Soil: tobacco damage to, 27, 32, 50. *See also* Dust Bowl
Soil Conservation and Domestic Allotment Act (1936), 556, 560
Soil Conservation Service, 486
Soldiers: in American Revolution, 97, 98–99; British, 89, 92–93, 97; in Civil War, 316, 320, 322, 323, 329; colonial militia as, 97, 98; in Spanish-American War, 458; women as, 322; in World War I, 507–508; yellow fever experiments on, 460. *See also* Armed forces; Military; specific battles and wars
Solidarity movement (Poland), 690, 697
Solid South, 708. *See also* Democratic party; Republican party; South
Solomon Islands: in World War II, 592–593
Somalia, peacekeeping troops in, 713
Sone, Monica, 586
Songs: in World War I, 505, 509, 510. *See also* Music
Sons of Liberty, 92, 95
Sooners, Oklahoma land rush and, 437
Sopranos, The (television program), 717
Sotomayor, Sonia, 727
Soul by Soul (Johnson), 267
Souls of Black Folk, The (Du Bois), 416
Sound and the Fury, The (Faulkner), 532
Sousa, John Philip, 462
South (region): 1860 election and, 305–306; abolitionism in, 265; African American migration from, 506–507; African Americans in, 360, 361, 365, 380–381, 654; agriculture in, 348, 396; American Revolution in, 103, 112, 113 (map), 114; antislavery literature in, 297; antislavery sentiment in, 252, 265; backlash against abolitionism in, 265–268; Bible Belt in, 525; Black Codes in, 353–354; on Brown, John, 305; Carolina colonies and, 29–32; Chesapeake colonies in, 25–28; after Civil War, 324, 348, 349; Compromise of 1850 and, 286, 288; cotton in, 252, 255, 256, 440; Democratic party in, 371; *Dred Scott* decision and, 302; economy in, 256, 260, 416; education in, 72, 236, 237, 256, 416; expansionism of, 290; Farmers' Alliance in, 444; free blacks in, 259; Fugitive Slave Law and, 287, 289; Grange in, 442; immigrants in, 256, 259; industrialization and, 365, 396–397; integration in, 634; Jim Crow in, 374, 381, 529, 631; Kansas-Nebraska Act and, 292–293, 294; Ku Klux Klan in, 359–360; lifestyle in, 54; Lincoln's assassination and, 343; literature and, 423, 642; "Lost Cause" of, 343, 348, 354; military districts in, 356–357, 356 (map); Missouri Compromise and, 181, 181 (map); nonslaveowners in, 257; northern economic stake in, 266; officeholders from, 354, 355, 358; opposition to secession in, 308 (map); panic of 1857 in, 303; plantation system in, 54, 255–256; Populists in, 380–381, 444; proslavery arguments in, 262, 265–266; prosperity of, 622; race riots in, 356; railroads in, 354, 373, 390; Reconstruction and, 356–357, 356 (map), 357–359, 361, 373; Redeemers in, 357, 359, 373; resentment of

the North, 256, 309; on role of freedmen, 354; runaway slaves and, 284–285; secession of, 306–308, 309, 314, 315 (map); sectional balance and, 284, 287; segregation in, 631–632; slavery in, 62, 63, 255, 256, 258 (map), 259–262; slavery in territories and, 257, 266, 269, 282, 287; society in, 53–54, 66; Spanish-American War and, 462; Tallmadge amendment and, 180; Tariff of Abominations and, 195; textile industry in, 396–397; transcontinental railroad and, 291–292; unionization in, 618; white majority in, 256–259; in World War II, 589. *See also* Civil War (U.S., 1861–1865); Confederate States of America; Sunbelt; specific colonies and states
South Africa, 442, 443, 449; Carter and, 680; England and, 453
South America: immigrants to, 408; peopling of, 6, 7 (map). *See also* Latin America; specific locations
South Carolina, 358; American Revolution in, 103, 112; in Civil War, 338; Compromise of 1877 and, 372, 373; Constitution and, 131, 133; creation of, 31; Fort Sumter attack and, 313–314; Nullification Crisis and, 195–196; secession of, 306–308, 315 (map); slave revolt in, 63, 262; slavery in, 53, 63, 131, 260, 261; Spain and, 79; Tariff of Abomination and, 195
South Dakota, 430, 437
Southeast (region): crops in, 10; Indian removal from, 199
Southeast Asia: 1954–1975, 645 (map); Eisenhower and, 635. *See also* Vietnam; Vietnam War; specific regions
Southern Christian Leadership Conference (SCLC), 634
Southern Europe, immigrants from, 391, 407–408
Southern Pacific Railroad, 292 (map), 388, 480
Southern Renaissance writers, 642
Southern strategy (Nixon), 665
South Korea, 614, 615, 713; economic competition by, 674; Soviet downing of airliner, 690. *See also* Korea; Korean War
South Vietnam, 644, 662; immigrants from, 677; Nixon and, 662. *See also* Vietnam War
Southwest (region), 427; Anasazi peoples of, 8; corn in, 8; cotton in, 119; Hispanics in, 10 (map), 16, 430; Mexican immigrants in, 279; Mexican War in, 277, 277 (map), 281; peoples of, 8; slavery in, 252; travel to, 291. *See also* West
Sovereignty: of Indian tribes, 149; state, 121, 122. *See also* Popular sovereignty
Soviet Union: in Afghanistan, 683, 684; atomic bomb of, 614; Carter and, 681; China and, 608, 664; Cold War and, 625; collapse of, 605, 675, 698; Cuba and, 638; détente and, 645, 675; Eastern Europe and, 608, 610; Egypt and, 636; global economy and, 675; Iran and, 611; Korea and, 614; lend-lease to, 580; Middle East and, 636; Nazi invasion of, 580; Nazi-Soviet nonaggression pact and, 574–575, 580; nuclear weapons testing by, 637–638; postwar fears of, 609 (map); Reagan, Gorbachev, and, 693; Reagan and, 690; red scare after World War II and, 616–617; space exploration by, 637; Spanish Civil War and, 573; sphere of influence after World War II, 608; as superpower, 608–609; women workers in World War II, 588; in World War II, 593, 594, 599; Yalta conference and, 608. *See also* Bolshevik entries; Cold War; Russia

Soviet Union (former), 698
Space exploration: moon landing and, 643; Soviet, 637
Spain, 344; in American Revolution, 110; California and, 19, 279; Caribbean region and, 15; colonies of, 18–19, 21; Columbus and, 13; *conquistadores* and, 14–15, 16, 17, 18; conversion of Indians to Christianity by, 19; Cuba and, 16, 290, 454, 458; exploration by, 13, 14–15; Florida and, 30, 32, 79, 84, 127; France and, 79; Gulf of Mexico and, 79; immigrants from, 215; Louisiana and, 84, 162; *Maine* (ship) and, 455; Mexico and, 14, 16, 17; New World and, 13, 14–15, 15 (map); Oregon and, 185, 272; Pinckney's Treaty and, 149, 162; postrevolutionary relations with, 126–127; Puerto Rico and, 458, 460, 461; rebellions in, 185; after Seven Years' War, 84; Texas and, 19, 185, 204–205; trans-Appalachian area and, 114, 115; Treaty of Paris (1783) and, 114, 115; Treaty of Tordesillas and, 14; unification of, 13; War of Jenkins's Ear and, 79. *See also* Spanish America
Spanish America: British trade in, 79; spread of, 18–19. *See also* Latin America
Spanish-American War, 365, 456, 461–462; in Cuba, 457; in Philippines, 456–457; Rough Riders in, 457; Treaty of Paris (1898) and, 459; U.S. as world power after, 474; yellow journalism and, 455, 456
Spanish Armada, 22–23
Spanish Civil War (1936–1939), 573
Spanish Empire: in New World, 22
Spanish Netherlands. *See* Holland
Spargo, John, 479
SPARs (U.S. Coast Guard Women's Reserve), 588
Speakeasies, 524
Speaker of the House. *See* specific individuals
"Special creation" doctrine, 415
Special Forces (Green Berets), 643
Specie Circular (1836), 202
Specie payments, 434
Spectator sports, 425
Speculation: in 1920s, 532–533; in American Revolution, 114; depression of 1890s and, 381; in land, 179; panic of 1819 and, 179; panic of 1837 and, 203; in plantation system, 256; stock, 389
Speech, freedom of. *See* Free speech
Spencer, Herbert, 395
Spending: political, 730; in World War II, 590. *See also* Military spending
Spheres of influence: European, in China, 463; Soviet, 608
Spies and spying: in Civil War, 285, 322, 333; by NSA, 732; Rosenberg, Julius and Ethel, and, 616; U-2 incident and, 638
Spinsters, 241
Spirit of St. Louis (plane), 527
Spirituals, 65, 261, 424
Spock, Benjamin, 621–622
Spoils system, 194, 376, 377
Sports: in late 1800s, 425; in 1920s, 526; 1950s commercialization of, 629; colonial, 74; women in, 712
Spot resolutions, 276
Sputnik I and *II*, 637, 643
Spy, The (Cooper), 246
Squanto (Wampanoag), 40
Square Deal, 482–483
Squatters, in North Carolina, 31
Stagecoaches, 226, 228
Stagflation, 670, 683

Stalin, Joseph: death of, 635; as dictator, 572; Hitler-Stalin pact (1939), 574–575; at Potsdam conference, 599; at Tehran Conference, 594, 597; World War II and, 599; at Yalta conference, 608. *See also* Soviet Union
Stalingrad, battle at, 593
Stalwart faction, of Republican party, 371, 376
Stamp Act (1765), 90, 91–92
Stamp Act Congress (1765), 91
Stampp, Kenneth, 267, 362
Standardization: of time zones, 389
Standard of living. *See* Lifestyle
Standard Oil Company, 392, 394, 398; Tarbell's on, 478
Stanford, Leland, 387
Stanford (Leland Stanford Junior) University, 387, 417, 424
Stanton, Edwin M., 319, 342, 360
Stanton, Elizabeth Cady, 241, 243, 357, 420, 678
Stanton, Henry, 678
"Star Spangled Banner, The," 174
"Starving time," in Jamestown, 25
State (nation): church separation from, 38, 135
State(s): Alaska as, 639; Border States, 314–315; constitutions of, 121–122; federal assumption of debts and, 142–143; free, 284, 287, 292, 293 (map); Hawaii as, 639; immigrants and, 408; progressivism in, 480; prohibition in, 421; ratification of Constitution by, 131–135, 132 (map), 137; readmittance to Union, 353, 356; slave, 284, 292, 293 (map); sovereignty of, 121, 122; term-limit laws in, 706; western, 437; woman's suffrage in, 420. *See also* specific states
State Department: McCarthyism and, 617
States' rights, 270, 356; Calhoun and, 195; in Civil War, 318; *Gibbons v. Ogden* and, 183; Jefferson and, 143; Virginia and Kentucky resolutions and, 153
Statue of Liberty, 409, 413
Steam power: steamboats, 180, 227, 229; transoceanic steamships, 215
Steel industry, 392–393; Bessemer-Kelly process in, 393; Carnegie in, 379, 392, 393; labor in, 391; Morgan and, 393; "Pittsburgh plus" pricing system in, 396; railroads and, 389; in South, 396; strikes in, 379–380, 506, 537, 563
Steel plow, 226
Steffens, Lincoln, 478
Stein, Gertrude, 531
Stein, Judith, 701
Steinbeck, John, 557, 560, 561
Stem cell research, 721, 724
Stenographers, 397
Stephens, Alexander, 354
Stevens, Thaddeus, 354, 355, 360, 361
Stevenson, Adlai E.: 1952 election and, 630; 1956 election and, 637
Stevenson, Robert Louis, 438
Stewart, James Brewer, 250
Stimson, Henry L., 548
Stimson Doctrine, 548
Stock(s): index of prices (1926), 544; speculation in, 389, 390; trusts and, 392
Stockholders, in Lancaster Turnpike, 226
Stock market: in 1920s, 532–533; 1929 collapse of, 544–545; Black Monday (October 19, 1987) and, 696; Great Recession and, 732–733; manipulation in, 368; New Deal legislation and, 561
Stock ticker, 392
Stock watering, 390

Stone, Lucy, 241, 243
Stone, Oliver, 695
Stonewall Rebellion, 660
Stoughton, William, 34
Stowe, Harriet Beecher, 224, 240, 263; *Uncle Tom's Cabin*, 260, 263, 297, 298, 299, 300
Strange Interlude (O'Neill), 532
Strategic Air Command (SAC), 628, 635
Strategic Arms Limitation Talks. *See* SALT
Strategic Arms Reduction Treaty. *See* START
Strategic Defense Initiative (SDI, Star Wars), 690, 698
Strategies of Containment (Gaddis), 668
Streetcar Named Desire, A (Williams), 642
Strict construction theory, 143
Strike, The (Koehler), 401
Strikebreakers, 224, 398, 412
Strikes, 398; in 1830s and 1840s, 224; before 1835, 222; in 1881–1900, 401; in coal industry, 482–483; for eight-hour day, 400; in Great Depression, 563; Homestead, 379–380; in mining industry, 380; in Paris (1968), 661; Pullman, 445, 446; against railroads, 374, 400, 445; Seattle general strike, 519; in steel industry, 379–380, 506, 537; as unpatriotic, 398; World War I and, 506; during World War II, 588
Strong, Josiah, 452
Stuart, Gilbert, 245
Stuart, "Jeb," 328
Student Nonviolent Coordinating Committee (SNCC), 634, 646, 654
Students for a Democratic Society (SDS), 660–661
Stuyvesant, Peter, 42, 43
Styron, William, 642
Submarines: in World War I, 501, 502; in World War II, 578, 580, 581, 593, 598
Sub-Saharan Africa: Europeans and, 12
Subsidies: to farmers, 559–560
Subsistence farming, 257
Substitutes, in Civil War, 319, 320
Suburban Warriors (McGirr), 668
Suburbs: African Americans in, 710; Federal Housing Act (1956) and, 635; immigrants in, 409; shopping malls in, 635, 641; transportation from, 406; wealthy in, 407; whites in, 679; after World War II, 605, 622–624. *See also* Cities and towns
Subversives: after World War II, 617
Subways, 406
Sudetenland, Hitler and, 574
Suez Canal, 398; in World War II, 593
Suez crisis (1956), 636–637
Suffrage: black, 356, 381; universal male, 119, 358; woman, 357, 420–421, 434, 474, 475, 507. *See also* Voting and voting rights; Woman suffrage
Suffragists, 420
Sugar Act (1764), 90
Sugar and Slaves (Dunn), 47
Sugar and sugar industry: in Caribbean region, 21, 28–29; in Columbian exchange, 14; in Cuba, 454; in Hawaii, 454; plantations and, 12, 29, 264; slaves for, 21, 28, 29, 264; sugar trust and, 394
Sugrue, Thomas, 601
Sullivan, John L., 425
Sullivan, Louis, 406
Summit conferences: in Paris (1960), 638
Sumner, Charles, 283, 300–301, 355
Sumner, William Graham, 395
Sun Also Rises, The (Hemingway), 531
Sunbelt, 589, 621–622, 622 (map)
Sun Dance, 432

Sunday, Billy, 519, 524
Sunni Muslims, in Iraq, 723
"Super-PACS," 730
Superpowers, 608–609
Supplemental Security Income (SSI), 665
Supply-side economics, 689–690
Supreme Court (U.S.): on 2000 election, 715; on abortion rights, 665, 679, 695; on affirmative action, 695–696, 723; *Amistad* slave rebellion and, 262; on birthright citizenship, 376; Bush, George W., and, 724; civil rights and, 632–634; *Civil Rights Cases* (1883) and, 373; *Dred Scott* case and, 252, 296, 302, 304; on executive power, 558; under Grant, 370; Harding and, 536–537; on income tax, 382; *Insular Cases* of, 460; judicial review and, 161; justices added to, 370; Marshall on, 161, 182–183; on military tribunals, 357; Native Americans and, 198; Nixon and, 665; Obama and, 727; organization of, 142; railroad regulation and, 390, 443; Reagan and, 695; Roosevelt, F.D., and, 565–566; Sedition Act and, 152; on separate but equal facilities, 374; on ten-hour workday, 482; Thomas, Clarence, on, 700; women on, 695; women workers and, 481. *See also* specific justices and cases
Surgery, 320. *See also* Medicine
Surplus: agricultural, 540
Survival of the fittest, 395
Susquehanna River region, 45
Sussex pledge, 501–502, 503
Swartwout, Samuel, 194
Sweatshops: legislation for, 410; working conditions in, 481
Sweden: Dutch colonies and, 42–43; immigrants from, 62
Sweet potatoes, 14
Swift, Gustavus F., 394, 435
Switzerland: immigrants from, 62
Symonds, James, 46
Symphony orchestras, 424
Synagogues, 408
Syndicalism: criminal syndicalism laws and, 519
Syphilis: in Columbian exchange, 14
Syria: Israel and, 667; after World War I, 512

Taensa Indians, 78
Taft, Robert A.: 1940 election and, 578; lend-lease and, 579
Taft, William Howard: 1908 election and, 488; 1912 election and, 491; cabinet of, 489; conservation and, 490; dollar diplomacy of, 489; foreign policy of, 474, 489; as governor of Philippines, 463; presidency of, 489–490; reform and, 474; Roosevelt, T., and, 488, 490, 491; trusts and, 483, 490
Taft-Hartley Act (1947), 618, 619, 637
Taino Indians, 14, 460, 461
Taiwan. *See* Formosa (Taiwan)
Taliban: in Afghanistan, 721; in Pakistan, 728
"Talkies": in 1920s, 528
Talleyrand, Charles Maurice de, 150, 151
Tallmadge amendment, 180
Tammany Hall, 216, 377
Tampico Incident (1914), 500
Tan, Amy, 717
Taney, Roger B., 302
Tanks, in World War II, 594
Tannenbaum, Frank, 267
Tanzania, embassy bombing in, 713
Tappan, Arthur, 263
Tappan, Lewis, 263, 266
Tarantino, Quentin, 717

Tarawa: in World War II, 593
Tarbell, Ida M., 478
Tariff(s), 364, 369; of 1816, 178, 221; of 1832, 195, 271; of 1842, 271; of 1857, 303; of Abominations (1828), 195; after American Revolution, 143; Cleveland and, 378; colonial, 143; Compromise Tariff of 1833, 195–196; Dingley (1897), 449; Fordney-McCumber (1922), 538; Hamilton and, 143; Hawley-Smoot (1930), 543, 544, 552; Kennedy Round and, 643; McKinley (1890), 379, 382, 445, 454; Morrill (1861), 320; Payne-Aldrich (1909), 490; protective, 178, 320, 321, 441; Underwood (1913), 497; Walker (1846), 274; Wilson-Gorman (1894), 382; after World War I, 542. *See also* Trade
Taverns: colonial, 68
Taxation: in 1920s, 526, 533; under Articles of Confederation, 125; Bush, George H.W., and, 700; in California, 689; in Civil War, 320, 321, 345; of colonies, 3, 73, 90–91; conservatives on, 683; for education, 415; by England, 3, 73, 90–91; of farmers, 440–441; Reagan and, 69, 694; representation and, 90–91; in South, 321, 359. *See also* Excise taxes; Income taxes; Tariff(s)
Tax revolt (1978), 683, 689
Taylor, Zachary: 1848 election and, 283, 284; Compromise of 1850 and, 286; in Mexican War, 276, 277–278
Tea, taxes on, 92, 93, 94, 95
Teachers: training of, 415; women as, 224, 350
"Teach-ins," 656
Teamsters Union, 637; NAFTA and, 711
Tea Party, 727, 731
Teapot Dome scandal, 539
Technology: communications, 222, 527–528; historians of, 223; nationalism and, 344. *See also* Innovations; Inventions; specific inventions
Tecumseh (Shawnee), 167–168
Teenagers: education for, 415; in Mexican War, 280. *See also* Young people
Tehran Conference (1943), 594, 597
Telegraph, 222, 228, 229, 278, 398
Telephone, 392, 406
Telephone operators, 392, 397, 420
Televangelists, 695
Television, 629; in 1950s, 629, 630; 1952 election and, 630; 1960 election and, 639; cable, 717
Teller Amendment (1898), 456, 460
Telltale Hearts (Garfinkle), 668
Temperance movement, 240, 421, 482
Temperance pledge, 240
10 percent Reconstruction plan, 353
Tenant farming, 374, 440, 444
Tender Buttons (Stein), 531
Tenements, 406–407; dumbbell, 406; living conditions in, 478
Ten-hour day, 222
Ten-hour workday, 482, 484
Tennessee: Civil War in, 336, 337; Johnson, Andrew, in, 351; secession by, 314, 315 (map); as state, 140
Tennessee Coal and Iron Company, 483
Tennessee River region: Civil War and, 336, 336 (map); Muscle Shoals Bill and, 561
Tennessee Valley Authority (TVA, 1933), 486, 553, 555, 562, 634
Ten Nights in a Barroom and What I Saw There (Arthur), 240
Tenochtitlán, 17
Tenskwatawa ("the Prophet"), 167
Tenth Amendment, 142

Tenure of Office Act (1867), 360
"Termination program": for Native Americans, 635
Term-limit laws, 706
Terre Haute, naming of, 78
Territories: Northwest Ordinance and, 124, 125; popular sovereignty in, 283, 292; slavery in, 257, 266, 269, 282, 287, 292, 302
Terrorism: Islamic, 713; by Klan, 359–360; Oklahoma City bombing and, 706; September 11, 2001, attacks and, 605, 721–722. *See also* Violence
Test oaths, 43
Tet offensive, 657
Texas, 282, 291; annexation of, 206, 269, 272, 273, 274; British interests in, 271, 272; cattle ranching in, 435; France and, 78; German immigrants in, 220; Latinos in, 709; as Lone Star Republic, 206, 271–272; Mexican migrants in, 499; Mexico and, 205–206, 206 (map), 269, 271, 275, 278; New Mexico conflict with, 284, 286; secession of, 308, 308 (map), 315 (map); slavery in, 205, 206, 287; Spain and, 19, 185, 204–205
Texas (ship), 457
Texas A&M, 417
Texas and Pacific Railroad, 373, 390
Texas Revolution (1836), 205–206, 206 (map)
Textbooks, 178, 237, 415
Textile industry: British and, 91, 219, 316–317; children in, 222, 399; mechanization of, 219; in South, 396–397; southern cotton and, 221, 255, 266, 316; women in, 225. *See also* Cotton and cotton industry
Thames, Battle of the, 168, 173, 206
"Thanatopsis" (Bryant), 246
Thanksgiving Day, 37, 40, 74
Thatcher, Margaret, 689, 698
Theater. *See* Drama
Theology: biology and, 525
Theory of the Leisure Class, The (Veblen), 477
Thermonuclear weapons, 614
Thernstrom, Stephan, 402
Third parties, 380; in 1832, 201; in 1872, 369; in 1968, 659; in 1992, 704; in 1996, 708. *See also* specific parties
Third party system, 448
Thirteenth Amendment, 332, 344, 353
This Side of Paradise (Fitzgerald), 531
Thomas, Clarence, 700
Thompson's Skirt Factory, 225
Thoreau, Henry David, 242, 246, 247, 486
Three-fifths clause, 130, 158
Three Lives (Stein), 531
"Three Rs": in New Deal, 554
Thurmond, J. Strom, 619
Tiananmen Square protest, 697
"Ticket splitting," 371
Ticonderoga, Fort, battle at, 102
Tidewater region, 6
Tierra del Fuego, 21
Tilden, Samuel J., 368, 372, 373, 373 (map)
Till, Emmett, 631
Timber, 68
Timbuktu, 12
Time: regimentation of, 397; standardization of, 389
Time for Choosing, A (Schoenwald), 701
Time zones, 389
Tippecanoe, Battle of, 167, 206
Titan, The (Dreiser), 478
Title VII, of Civil Rights Act (1964), 651
Title IX, of Education Amendments, 676
Tobacco and tobacco industry: blacks and, 2, 27, 63; in Chesapeake region, 27–28, 50–51,

63; Maryland and, 28, 66; production of, 50-51; soil damage from, 27, 32, 50; in South, 27-28, 66, 396; trust, 394; Virginia and, 27-28, 66
Tocqueville, Alexis de: on democracy in U.S. and Europe, 196-197; on religion, 233; on women's rights, 241
Tokyo: firebombing of, 598
Tompkins, Sally, 322
Tongs, 375
Tonkin Gulf Resolution, 652, 663
Topeka, Kansas, free-soilers in, 300
Tordesillas, Treaty of, 14
Tories (American Revolution), 106. *See also* Loyalists (U.S.)
Torture: Obama and, 728
"To Secure These Rights" (report), 632
Total war, Civil War as, 328, 338
Town meetings, 57, 74
Towns. *See* Cities and towns
Townsend, Francis E., 557
Townshend, Charles ("Champagne Charley"), 92
Townshend Acts (1767), 92, 93
Trade: under Articles of Confederation, 125; British in Spanish America, 79; with China, 291; Clinton and, 710-711; colonial, 67, 67 (map), 68; with Cuba, 454; Embargo Act and, 165-166; fur, 78, 213; Hamilton and, 143; international, 398, 673-675; Kennedy, John F., and, 643; Native Americans and, 27; New World bullion and, 89; oil and, 681; postrevolution, 122, 143; restraint of, 395; triangular, 67. *See also* Commerce; Economy; Slave trade; Tariff(s); specific products
Trade associations, 537
Trade embargo. *See* Embargo Act (1807)
Trade Expansion Act (1962), 643
Trade routes: in 1492, 11, 12 (map)
Trade unions, 224
Trading posts: in Africa, 12; French, 79; for fur trade, 78; Russian in North America, 185
Trafalgar, Battle of, 164
Trail(s): Bozeman, 430; Oregon, 273; Santa Fe, 273
Trail of Tears, 198, 199
Trans-Allegheny area: as nation's breadbasket, 226
Trans-Appalachian area, 114, 115, 140, 167
Transatlantic telegraph, 228, 398
Transatlantic view of history, 116
Transcendentalism, 243, 246-248
Transcontinental railroads, 291-292, 293 (map), 435; construction of, 344, 354, 373, 386-387, 388; travel on, 438
Transistors, 628
Trans-Mississippi West, 164, 428, 438, 439
Trans-Pacific Partnership, 733
Transportation: American System and, 178; to California gold fields, 290; in cities, 406; in Civil War, 316; after Civil War, 348; colonial, 68; innovations in, 391; to Pacific Coast, 291; revolution in, 118, 229; roads in, 178, 180; in South, 54; steamboats in, 180, 227, 229; in West, 180. *See also* Automobiles and automobile industry; Railroad(s); specific forms
Transportation Department, 653
Trans-Siberian Railroad, 442
Travel. *See also* Transportation
Treason: Burr and, 164; Civil War and, 340
"Treason of the Senate, The" (Phillips), 479
Treasury Department: in Civil War, 320-321, 322; Fisk-Gould scandal and, 368; gold reserve and, 381, 382, 555; greenbacks and, 320-321, 370; specie payments by, 434; surplus of, 378
Treaties: with Hawaii, 454; on Maine boundary, 271; with Native Americans, 25, 40, 149, 429; by Texas, 271. *See also* specific treaties
Treaty ports, in China, 291
Trench warfare: in World War I, 502, 508
Trent affair, 318
Trenton, Battle of, 99, 108
Triangle Shirtwaist Company, fire at, 481, 482
Triangular trade, 67
Tribes (Native American), 429, 432, 561, 635; Dawes Act and tribal organization, 434; sovereignty of, 680. *See also* Native Americans
Trickle-down philosophy, of Hanna, 446
Trilling, Lionel, 701
Tripartite Pact (1935), 572
Tripolitan War, 162
Trist, Nicholas P., 278
Trolleys, electric, 406
Troops. *See* Armed forces; Military; Soldiers; specific battles and wars
Troy (New York) Female Seminary, 238
Truman, Harry S.: 1944 election and, 596; 1948 election and, 618-619; assumption of presidency, 607; China and, 614; civil rights and, 619, 632; Cold War policy of, 612; on communism and democracy, 619; Fair Deal of, 620; Korean War and, 615; loyalty program of, 616; MacArthur and, 616; Point Four program of, 620; at Potsdam, 599; red hunt and, 617
Truman Doctrine, 612
Trumbull, John, 72, 103, 145, 245
Trust(s), 448; attacks on, 395-396, 477; Fourteenth Amendment and, 395; in oil industry, 394; Rockefeller and, 392; Taft and, 483, 490; use of term, 392; Wilson and, 497. *See also* Antitrust movement; Corporations; specific corporations and trusts
Trustbusting, 483, 490
Trustees: of League of Nations, 512
Trusteeship Council (U.N.), 610
Truth, Sojourner, 263
Truth-in-lending rules, 727
Truth in Securities Act (1933), 561
Tubman, Harriet, 284, 285, 304
Tunisia: in World War II, 593
Turkey: Truman Doctrine and, 612; in World War I, 500
Turner, Frederick Jackson, 209; frontier thesis of, 437, 439, 442, 449; on West, 427
Turner, Nat, 262, 265, 304
Turnpikes, 118, 226. *See also* Roads and highways
Tuscarora Indians, 30, 32, 112
Tuscarora War, 32
Tuskegee Institute, 416
TVA. *See* Tennessee Valley Authority
Twain, Mark, 228, 421-422, 423, 424; as anti-imperialist, 459; Gilded Age and, 371, 383
Tweed, William Marcy ("Boss"), 358, 368, 369, 377, 408
Tweed Ring, 368
Twelfth Amendment, 150, 158, 190
Twentieth Amendment, 308, 565
Twenty-fifth Amendment, 671
Twenty-first Amendment, 559
Twenty-fourth Amendment, 653
Twenty-second Amendment, 149
Twenty-sixth Amendment, 663
Twenty-third Amendment, 666
Two-income households, 729
Two-party system, 145, 189, 194, 208
Tydings-McDuffie Act (1934), 571
Tyler, John: 1840 election and, 206, 270; Bank of United States and, 271; cabinet of, 271; Texas and, 272, 274; Whig party and, 270, 271
Typewriters, 392, 397
Typhoid, 50, 323, 458

U-boats. *See* Submarines
Uncle Tom's Cabin (Stowe), 240, 260, 297, 298, 299, 300, 317
Unconditional surrender: in Civil War, 336; in World War II, 594, 599, 602
Underground Railroad, 284, 288
Underwood Tariff (1913), 497, 538
Undocumented immigrants, 709, 732
Unemployment: in 1980s, 689-690; Bush, George H.W., and, 700; in California, 698; under Clinton, 710; in depression of 1837, 203; in depression of 1890s, 381; in England, 24; in Great Depression, 556-557, 558-559, 562, 566; in panic of 1873, 370; in World War II, 590. *See also* Employment; Great Recession
Unemployment insurance, 555, 562
Unemployment Relief Act (1933), 553
UNESCO (United Nations Educational, Scientific, and Cultural Organization), 610
UNIA. *See* United Negro Improvement Association
Unification: of Italy, 344, 409; Korea and, 614
Union (Civil War North). *See* Civil War (U.S., 1861-1865); North (Union, Civil War)
Union (political): Civil War and, 253, 314-315, 326; Jackson and, 195; supremacy of, 253
Unionists, 308 (map), 314; mountain whites as, 257-259, 308 (map); in South Carolina, 195
Union League, 357
Union of Soviet Socialist Republics. *See* Soviet Union
Union Pacific Railroad, 390; scandal and, 368-369; transcontinental railroad and, 293 (map), 386-387, 388
Union party, 340, 351, 367
Unions. *See* Labor unions
Unitarians, 233, 235
United Auto Workers, 682
United Farm Workers Organizing Committee (UFWOC), 709
United Mine Workers, 563
United Nations (U.N.), 610; achievements of, 674; headquarters of, 640; Iraq and, 699, 723; Korean War and, 615; League of Nations and, 516; Persian Gulf crisis and, 699-700
United Negro Improvement Association (UNIA), 530
United States: in 20th century, 474; boundary settlement with Britain (1818), 184 (map); expansion (1857-1917), 455 (map); and Germany in Great Depression, 600; imperialism and, 344, 352-353, 458-459, 462, 470, 471, 472; as superpower, 608-610; as unified country, 344; as world power, 461-462, 472. *See also* specific issues
United States Housing Authority (USHA), 556, 562
U.S. Sanitary Commission, 322; Sanitary Fair of, 322
United States Steel Corporation, 393, 563, 729
United States v. *Wheeler*, 60
United States v. *Windsor*, 483
U.S. v. *Wong Kim Ark*, 376
Universal suffrage: male, 119, 344

A56   Index

Universities and colleges: 1960s protests in, 660; for African Americans, 263, 416; Berkeley Free Speech Movement and, 660; black studies programs in, 654; colonial, 71–72; curriculum in, 417–418; family incomes of students, 729; GIs in, 618, 619; government cooperation with, 590; Jackson State College shootings and, 663; Kent State University shootings and, 663; land-grant, 344, 417; new light-founded, 71; philanthropy for, 417; Second Great Awakening and, 237; in Spanish colonies, 18; "teach-ins" in, 656; women in, 416. *See also* specific locations
University of California, 417; Free Speech Movement and, 660
University of Chicago, 417
University of Michigan: affirmative action in, 723
University of Pennsylvania, 72
University of Virginia, 153, 238, 245
Unraveling of America, The (Matusow), 668
Unskilled workers, 375, 391, 398, 401; in labor unions, 399, 400, 563; wages for, 230
Updike, John, 640
Upper South: internal slave trade and, 259. *See also* South (region)
Urban areas. *See* Cities and towns; Metropolitan areas; Suburbs
Urban Crucible, An (Nash), 116
Urbanization, 214, 392, 408. *See also* Cities and towns
USA Patriot Act (2001), 721
USSR. *See* Soviet Union
Utah, 284, 437; Mormons in, 236, 237 (map), 427; slavery in, 287; woman suffrage in, 434
Utopian communities: dress reform and, 242; in wilderness, 243–244
Utrecht, Peace of (1713), 79
U-2 spy plane incident, 638

Vallandigham, Clement L., 339–340
Valley Forge, Pennsylvania, 98, 109
Van Buren, Martin, 379; 1836 election and, 202; 1840 election and, 206–207; 1844 election and, 273; 1848 election and, 283, 284; labor movement and, 222; panic of 1837 and, 203–204
Van Cortlandt, Catherine, 107
Van Deburg, William L., 668
Vanderbilt family: "Commodore" Cornelius, 389, 390; William H., 390
Van Dyck, Henry, 530
Vanzetti, Bartolomeo, 520
Varieties of Religious Experience (James), 418
Vassar College, 416
Vaudeville, 424
Veblen, Thorstein, 477
V-E (Victory in Europe) Day (1945), 598
Venereal disease, in World War I, 509
Venezuela: British Guiana boundary dispute with, 453; in OPEC, 637; revolution in, 196
Venturi, Robert, 716
Veracruz, Mexico, 278, 500
Vermont, 126, 140
Verrazano, Giovanni da, 15 (map), 18
Versailles Treaty (1919), 512–513; collapse of, 515; Nazis and, 572; U.S. rejection of, 513–514
Vertical integration, 392
Vesey, Denmark, 195, 262
Veterans: in Bonus Army, 546–547; of Civil War, 323, 368, 372; pensions for, 378, 379; after World War I, 537
Veterans Administration (VA), 618, 624
Veterans Bureau, 537, 539
Vetoes: by Cleveland, 378; by Grant, 370; by Jackson, 200; by Johnson, Andrew, 354, 360; by Lincoln, 353; by Tyler, 271

Vice president. *See* specific individuals
Vicksburg, Mississippi, siege of, 336, 337
Victory gardens, 506
Viet Cong, 645, 657
Viet Minh, 635
Vietnam, 470; 1954–1975, 645 (map); nationalism in, 635–636; partition of, 643; self-determination and, 471. *See also* Vietnam War
Vietnamese Americans, 677
Vietnamization, 662
Vietnam War, 604, 625; Cambodia and, 663; economic effects of, 673, 676; historians on, 625; Johnson, L.B., and, 655–657; Kennedy, John F., and, 643–644; Nixon and, 662–663, 665–666; protests against, 656, 658, 661, 662; Tonkin Gulf Resolution and, 652; U.S. defeat in, 676
Vigilantes: African Americans and, 631
Villa, Francisco ("Pancho"), 500
Villages. *See* Cities and towns; specific locations
Vincennes: Fort, 79, 113
Vinland, 11
Violence: against abolitionists, 265, 266; against Chinese immigrants, 374; by Ku Klux Klan, 359–360; labor, 364, 400; Protestant vs. Catholic, 28. *See also* Lynchings; Terrorism
Virginia: in American Revolution, 99; Bacon's Rebellion in, 51, 53, 59; capital of, 143; church and state separation in, 135; Civil War in, 333, 340, 341; committees of correspondence in, 94; Constitution and, 129, 133, 134; disease in, 25, 50; early settlements in, 25–26, 25 (map); "first families" of, 207; Jamestown settlement in, 21, 24–25, 26, 53; lifestyle in, 50; Loyalists in, 107; population of, 27, 50, 61; representative government in, 28; Roanoke colony and, 3, 22; secession by, 314, 315 (map); slavery in, 27, 53, 259, 260, 262, 265; tobacco and, 27–28, 66
Virginia (ship), 329
Virginia and Kentucky resolutions (1798), 153
Virginia City, Nevada, 434
Virginia Company, 24, 25, 28, 36
"Virginia dynasty," 176, 179, 190
Virginia Plan, 129
Virginia Statute for Religious Freedom (1786), 135, 153
Virgin Islands, purchase from Denmark, 498
Virtual representation, theory of, 91
Visual artists: postmodernist, 716
V-J (Victory in Japan) Day (1945), 599
Volstead Act (1919), 522
Voltaire, 76
Volunteers: in Civil War, 314, 315, 319, 320, 333
Von Gentz, Friedrich, 115
Von Moltke, Helmuth, 323
Vonnegut, Kurt, Jr., 640, 717
Von Steuben, Baron, 98, 109, 114
Voter Education Project, 646
Voter-registration laws, in South, 374
Voting and voting rights: African American, 344, 355, 357, 365, 374, 381, 646–647, 653; age for, 663; Australian ballot and, 480; colonial, 38, 39, 41, 74; freedmen and, 355, 356, 357; German immigrants and, 216; Irish and, 217; in Kansas, 298, 300; literacy tests for, 360, 374, 381; political machines and, 410; voter turnout and, 196, 371, 448; for women, 357, 420–421, 434, 474, 480, 507. *See also* Elections
Voting Rights Act (1965), 653, 654; Section 4 of, 732

Voyages of discovery: English, 15 (map); to New World, 15 (map); Portuguese, 12–13, 15 (map)
Voyageurs, 78

Wabash, St.Louis & Pacific Railroad Company v. Illinois, 390, 443
Wabash Railroad, 400
WACs (Women's Army Corps), 588
Wade-Davis Bill, 353
Wages: in 1920s, 537; factory system and, 222; in Great Depression, 558; industrialization and, 397–398; minimum, 555; in southern textile mills, 397; for unskilled workers, 230; for women, 397. *See also* Income
Wages and Hours Bill (1938), 556, 563
Wage slaves, 222
Wagner, Robert F., 563
Wagner Act (1935), 556, 563
Wagons, 226
Waiting 'Til the Midnight Hour (Joseph), 668
Wake Island: in World War II, 591
Wald, Lillian, 410, 478
Walden: Or Life in the Woods (Thoreau), 247
Walker, David, 263
Walker, Kara, 716
Walker, Mary Richardson, 436
Walker, Robert J., 274
Walker, William, 290
Walker Tariff (1846), 274
Walking city, 406
Walkouts, labor, 562–563
Wallace, David Foster, 717
Wallace, George C., 659, 659 (map)
Wallace, Henry A., 595, 612, 619
Wallace, Lewis, 421
Wall Street: in 1920s, 532–533; bombing on (1920), 519; Populists and, 383, 444
Wall Street (movie), 695
Wall Street Reform and Consumer Protection Act (2010), 727, 730
Walt Disney Concert Hall, Los Angeles, 716
Wampanoag Indians, 40
Wanghia, Treaty of (1844), 291
Wapshot Chronicle, The (Cheever), 640
War College (Washington), 462
War crimes: Japanese, 602; Nuremberg trial (1946) and, 610
Ward, Aaron Montgomery, 439
War debts: Allied (World War I), 541, 542
War Democrats, 339, 340, 351
War Department: black volunteers and, 333
Ward's Cove Packing v. *Antonia*, 696
War hawks, 167, 168, 169
Warhol, Andy, 640
War Industries Board, 506, 537
Warner, Charles Dudley, 383, 422
War News from Mexico (Woodville), 278
War of 1812 (1812–1814), 171–178; battles of, 173, 174–175, 174 (map); in Canada, 172–174, 177; effects of, 171; finances and, 174; Madison and, 169; nationalism and, 118, 171, 177–178; Native Americans and, 175, 176; as Second War for American Independence, 176–177; Treaty of Ghent and, 175, 177; war hawks and, 169
War of attrition, in Civil War, 341
War of Independence. *See* American Revolution
War of Jenkins's Ear, 79
War of the Austrian Succession (1740–1748), 79
War on Poverty, 652, 659, 668
War on terror, 721
War Powers Act (1973), 667
War Production Board (WPB), 586

War Refugee Board, 576
Warren, Earl, and Warren Court, 632–634; civil rights and, 632–634; individual rights and, 664; Kennedy assassination and, 647
Warren, Mercy Otis, 175
Warren, Robert Penn, 642
Wars and warfare: "asymmetrical warfare," 721; French North American, 80–83, 80 (map); Kellogg-Briand Pact outlawing, 538; for North American empires, 80–83, 80 (map), 148 (map); peace crusade against, 240; religious, 16; total war, Civil War as, 328. See also Armed forces; Guerrilla warfare; Military; specific battles and wars
War Within, The (Wells), 668
Washakie (Shoshone Indian), 427
Washington (state), 273, 437
Washington, Booker T., 262, 416
Washington, D.C.: burning of, 174, 177; as capital, 143, 160; Coxey's Army in, 445; women workers in (Civil War), 322. See also District of Columbia; March on Washington
Washington, George: American Revolution and, 98, 102, 108, 109, 112, 114; Bank of the United States and, 143, 144; cabinet of, 141; as commander of Continental Army, 102; at Constitutional Convention, 128–129, 133; contributions of, 149; Electoral College and, 140; Farewell address by, 149, 163; as federalist, 132, 134; First Continental Congress and, 96; in French and Indian War, 80, 81, 83; inaugural of, 140; Jay's Treaty and, 149; Jefferson and, 143; Neutrality Proclamation of, 147–148; in Ohio River region, 80; pastimes of, 74; portraits of, 103, 245; on proclamation of 1763, 84; Revolution and, 98, 102, 108, 109, 112, 114; Second Continental Congress and, 102; second term of, 145; smallpox and, 66; Whiskey Rebellion and, 144
Washington Disarmament Conference (1921–1922), 538
Washington Naval Treaty, 572
Waste Land, The (Eliot), 532
Water: in cities, 214–215, 406; in West, 436–437, 700
Water-boarding, 728
Water cure, 462
Watergate scandal, 671–673
Waterloo, Battle of, 147, 177
Waterways: in South, 54. See also Canals; specific locations
Watson, Thomas Edward ("Tom"), 380–381
Watts, Los Angeles, race riot in, 654
WAVES (Women Accepted for Volunteer Emergency Service), 588
"Waving the bloody shirt," 368, 376, 377
Wayne, "Mad" Anthony, 149
Wealth Against Commonwealth (Lloyd), 477
Wealth and wealthy: in 1920s, 532–533; Civil War draft and, 319, 320; in colonies, 44; in cotton and, 255; critiques of, 477; industry and, 365, 393, 394, 397; in North (Civil War), 316, 320; of planters, 348; in post-Civil War South, 324, 348; from railroads, 389; rich/poor gulf in, 230, 256, 397; slaves as, 256, 259; Social Darwinism and, 395; after World War II, 620–621
Wealth gap, 230, 256, 397, 624; in 1980s, 690; in 2000s, 729. See Income gap
Weapons: in 1920s, 538; in American Revolution, 98; in Civil War, 316; Fourteen Points and, 504; in Iran-Contra affair, 693, 694; lend-lease program and, 578, 579–580, 579 (map); manufacturing of, 221; of mass destruction (WMD), 719, 722; Sharps rifles, 298; World War II production of, 586. See also Atomic bombs; Nuclear weapons; SALT; specific types
Weary Blues, The (Hughes), 530
Weather Underground (U.S.), 660–662
Weaver, James B., 388, 440; 1880 election and, 440; 1892 election and, 379, 380, 380 (map), 444
Weaver, Robert C., 653
Weber, David J., 449
Webster, Daniel: Bank War and, 200; Compromise of 1850 and, 286, 288, 289; *Dartmouth* case and, 183; on Hamilton, 142; on secession, 282; as secretary of state, 270, 271; Union and, 266, 290; Whigs and, 202
Webster, Noah, 237
Webster v. Reproductive Health Services, 696
Weld, Theodore Dwight, 263
Welfare programs: Clinton reforms of, 707–708; expansion of, 604; Nixon and, 665; Social Security and, 562. See also Great Society
Welfare Reform Bill (1996), 707, 708
Welfare state: in 1970s, 670; progressives and, 481; Reagan and, 689
Wells, H.G., 512
Wells, Ida B., 421
Wells, Tom, 668
Welsh immigrants, 62
"We Shall Overcome" (song), 653
Wesley, John, 32
West (region): African Americans in, 284; American Revolution in, 112–113; Chinese immigrants in, 374, 375; cities in, 439; Civil War in, 314, 336–337, 336 (map); education in, 237; farming in, 179, 435–437; formation of, 6; growth of, 118, 180; historians' view of, 449; homesteading in, 435–436; land in, 124, 180; literature on, 423; mining in, 284, 434; Native Americans in, 364–365, 428–434, 439; prosperity of, 622; railroads and, 291–292, 292 (map), 386, 387 (map), 389, 436; ranching in, 435; road building in, 180; routes to (before Civil War), 180; slavery and, 252; transportation and communication in, 180, 228; water in, 436–437. See also Southwest; Sunbelt; Trail(s); Westward movement
West, Benjamin, 72
West Africa, 12
West Africa Squadron (Royal Navy), 259
West Bank, 656, 691, 713
West Coast (U.S.): Japanese immigrants on, 587
Western Europe: in 1960s, 661; immigrants from, 407; after World War II, 612–613. See also specific locations
Western front, in World War I, 509
Westernization: imperialism and, 470
West Florida: Jackson and, 184; Spanish claims in, 127, 184. See also Florida
West Germany, 610, 611 (map). See also East Germany; Germany
West Indies: American-French hostilities in, 150–151; Britain and, 28–29; colonial trade and, 68; colonies in, 28–29; France and, 68, 149, 150–151; Seven Years' War in, 81; slavery in, 28, 29, 53, 55 (map), 259, 263; Spain and, 15
West Jersey: in Dominion of New England, 41; Quakers and, 44. See also New Jersey
West Point, 112, 280
West Virginia, in Civil War, 314
West Virginia (battleship), destruction of, 582
Westward movement, 437; from 1790–2010, 213 (map); in Civil War, 321; physical environment and, 213–214; Plains Indians and, 364–365, 428; reasons for, 212; west of Appalachians, 84, 212–213, 213 (map). See also Migration; West (region)
"Wet" cities, 482
Weyler y Nicolau, Valeriano ("Butcher"), 454, 462
Whaling, 67, 249
Wharton, Edith, 422, 423, 530
What Hath God Wrought:... (Howe), 209
What Social Classes Owe to Each Other (Sumner), 395
Wheat, 66, 437, 439
Wheatley, Phillis, 72
Wheeler, Burton, 579, 581
Wheeler, Joseph ("Fighting Joe"), 462
When Heaven and Earth Changed Places (Le Ly Hayslip), 645 (map)
Whig party (England), 88
Whig party (U.S.): 1836 election and, 202; 1840 election and, 206–207; 1844 election and, 273–274; 1848 election and, 283–284; 1852 election and, 289; 1856 election and, 302; Conscience Whigs in, 272, 278; demise of, 289–290; Democrats compared to, 208; Lincoln in, 276; origin of, 202; panic of 1837 and, 203; Tyler and, 270, 271. See also Patriots
Whig view of history, 116
Whirling Thunder, 199
Whiskey: distilling, 62; excise tax on, 143, 144
Whiskey Rebellion, 144
Whiskey Ring, 369
Whispering campaigns, 157
Whistler, James, 423
White, John, 3, 58
White, Richard, 47, 449
White, Walter, 633
White, William Allen, 492
White citizens' councils, 634
White-collar workers, 321, 402, 420, 628–629
Whitefield, George, 70, 263
White flight: to suburbs, 624, 679
White House: burning of, 174; portrait of, 177
Whiteman, Paul, 530
Whites: in antebellum South, 256–259; black soldiers and, 333; effects of slavery on, 262; freedmen and, 349, 357, 358; jazz and, 530; Native Americans and, 429; poor, 257; proslavery arguments and, 262, 265–266; slave women and, 260; in South, 358, 359–360, 374, 397; in suburbs, 623; "white slavery" and, 479
"Whites only" regulations, 631, 632
White supremacy: black abolitionists and, 263–265; black political power and, 358; Johnson, Andrew, and, 350; in South, 360
Whitewater affair, 714
Whitman, Walt, 247
Whitney, Eli, 219, 221, 252, 254
Whittier, John Greenleaf, 298
WHO (World Health Organization), 610
Who's Afraid of Virginia Woolf? (Albee), 642
Wigglesworth, Michael, 38
Wilberforce, William, 263
Wilberforce University, 263
Wildcat banks, 180, 201, 202
Wilderness: environmentalists and, 486; nationalism and, 213–214; Roosevelt, T., and, 486, 487; utopias in, 243–244
Wilderness Campaign, 341
"Wild West" shows, 425
Wilentz, Sean, 209
Wiley, Harvey W., 479
Wilhelm II (Kaiser, Germany), 453, 500
Wilkinson, James, 164

Willamette River region, 6, 273
Willard, Emma, 238
Willard, Frances E., 421, 482
William III (England), 41
Williams, Roger, 39
Williams, Tennessee, 642
Williams, Venus and Serena, 712
Williams, William Appleman, 472
Willkie, Wendell L., 1940 election and, 578-579
Will to Believe, The (James), 418
Wilmot, David, 280
Wilmot Proviso, 280-281, 282, 283
Wilson, Woodrow: 1912 election and, 492-493; 1916 election and, 502, 502 (map); 1918 elections and, 511-512; death of, 515; education of, 417; foreign policy of, 498, 499-505; Fourteen Points of, 504; globalization and, 674, 675; idealism of, 496, 503-504; New Freedom of, 492, 493, 495; progressivism under, 495; reform and, 474; segregation under, 498; Versailles Treaty and, 513; World War I and, 503-506
Wilson-Gorman Tariff (1894), 382, 449
Winesburg, Ohio (Anderson), 532
Wings of the Dove, The (James), 422
Winthrop, John, 37, 38, 39
Wire, The (television program), 717
Wisconsin, 294; German immigrants in, 216, 220; Native Americans in, 199; progressive reforms in, 480
WITCH (Women's International Terrorist Conspiracy from Hell), 678
Witch hunts: in Salem, Massachusetts, 57
Wobblies. *See* Industrial Workers of the World
Wolfe, James, 82-83
"Wolf packs," in World War II, 593
Woman's Christian Temperance Union (WCTU), 421, 482
Woman's Rights Convention (Seneca Falls), 241, 243
Woman suffrage: Addams on, 420; African American women and, 421; movement for, 420-421; Nineteenth Amendment and, 474; progressives and, 480; in western states, 420, 434; during World War I, 507, 508
Women: in 1920s, 528-530; in abolitionist movement, 241, 250, 263, 284; affirmative action and, 665; African American, 263, 284, 357, 421; American Revolution and, 111, 136; after American Revolution, 136; automobiles and, 527; Chinese immigrant, 375; in cities, 420; in Civil War, 285, 322, 323, 324; colonial, 50, 55-56, 58; cult of domesticity and, 224, 225, 241; dress reform and, 241-243; education for, 136, 238, 239; employment of, 629; equality for, 652; in factories, 224, 225; feminist revolution and, 711-712; Gibson Girl image for, 397; in industry, 322, 397; labor unions and, 399, 400, 401; literary contributions of, 297, 422, 423; in market economy, 241; in military, 508; minimum wage for, 537, 565; on mining frontier, 434; Native American, 11, 434; New Deal and, 557-558; new woman and, 397; as painter, 424; pioneer, 212, 436; on plantations, 64, 256; in Populist movement, 444; progressivism and, 480-482; in Quaker society, 241; in reform movements, 239, 419-420; religion and, 235; republican motherhood and, 123; rights of, 240-241; Roosevelt, Franklin D., and rights for, 591; Salem witch trials and, 57; settlement house movement and, 410; slave, 64, 260, 267; as soldiers, 322; on Supreme Court, 695; in textile mills, 397; Thomas, Clarence, hearings, and, 700; transcendentalism and, 247-248;
voting and, 357, 419-420, 434, 474, 480, 507; "white slave" traffic and, 479; in work force, 322, 397, 419, 420; in World War I, 508; in World War II, 588, 589; after World War II, 621
Women and Economics (Gilman), 420
Women's Army Corps. *See* WACs
Women's Bureau, 481
Women's club movement, 481, 487; African American, 421
Women's rights: after American Revolution, 136; march for (1977), 678; to property, 359, 420; Truth, Sojourner, and, 263
Women's rights movement: Civil War and, 322; feminists and, 678; Reconstruction-era Amendments and, 357. *See also* Feminism
Women's Trade Union League, 481, 551
Wood, Gordon, 137
Wood, Leonard, 457, 460
Woodhull, Victoria, 419
Woodhull and Claflin's Weekly, 419
Woods, Tiger, 716
Woodville, Richard Caton: *War News from Mexico* by, 278
Woodward, C. Vann, 383
Wool and wool industry: English trade and, 23; nonimportation agreements and, 91
Woolworth's, lunch counter sit-ins at, 634
Worcester, Samuel Austin, 199
Workday, 379; eight-hour, 399, 400, 498; limits on, 558; in mines, 483; ten-hour, 222, 482
Workers: during Civil War, 321, 323; Clayton Act and, 497; colonial, 66-68; factory, 222; farm, 440, 444, 464; Filipinos as, 464; immigrant, 216, 217; industrialization and, 397-398; railroad, 374; skilled, 399; unskilled, 230, 375, 391, 398, 399; women as, 322, 397, 419, 420, 481, 588; in World War I, 506-507. *See also* Labor; Labor unions
Work force: in 1950s, 628-629; in 1970s, 673; children in, 222, 397; education of, 621; families in, 397, 420; immigrants in, 224; women in, 322, 397, 419, 420, 528, 588, 589, 629, 679, 711, 712
Working class: imprisonment for debt and, 239; industrialization and, 398, 402
Working conditions: in factory system, 222; in sweatshops, 481; for women, 397; in workplace, 481
Workingmen's Compensation Act (1916), 498
Workplace: safeguards in, 481
Works Progress Administration (WPA, 1935), 556, 557
World Anti-Slavery Convention, 678
World Bank, 609, 674
World Court, 541
World power: United States as, 461-462, 472
World's Columbian Exposition, 424
World's Fair (London), 222
World Trade Center, terrorist attack on, 721
World Trade Organization (WTO), 674, 710
World War I (1914-1918), 503-511; airplanes in, 527; casualties in, 323, 511; civil liberties and, 505; economic controls after, 537; economy in, 505-507; in Europe, 596 (map); events leading to, 500-501; in France, 509 (map); home front in, 508; propaganda in, 504-505; soldiers in, 507-508; submarine warfare during, 501; U.S. entry into, 474, 503; U.S. neutrality and, 501; women during, 507, 508; workers in, 506-507
World War II (1939-1945), 584-602; African Americans and, 506-507, 589; appeasement before, 574; Asian reconstruction after, 613-614; atomic bombs in, 599; casualties in, 599, 601; comparative costs of, 601;
concentration camps in, 598; D-Day in, 594-595; draft in, 576; in Europe, 593-595, 596-598, 596 (map); European economy after, 612-613; home front in, 589-590; internal migration during, 588-589; isolationism before, 475; Japanese Americans in, 586; lend-lease and, 578, 579-580; lifestyle after, 604-605; Native Americans during, 589; in North Africa, 593, 596 (map); opening of, 574-575; in Pacific Ocean region, 581-582, 591-593, 592 (map); Pearl Harbor attack in, 475, 581-582; racism during, 591; second front in, 593-594; U.S. economy after, 612-613, 618; U.S. economy during, 589-590; wartime conferences during, 580, 594, 597, 599. *See also* specific countries
Worster, Donald, 449
Wounded Knee, South Dakota: Battle of, 432; Indian seizure of, 680
WPA. *See* Works Progress Administration
Wright, Orville and Wilbur, 527
Writers. *See* Literature; specific works and authors
Writ of habeas corpus, 319
Wyoming, 437; woman suffrage in, 420, 434
Wyoming Stock-Growers Association, 435

XYZ affair, 150

Yalta conference (1945), 608
Yamasee Indians, 32
Yankees: in New England, 211; in Old Northwest, 182
Yellow-dog contracts, 398, 546, 558
Yellow fever, 458, 460; in Columbian exchange, 14
Yellow journalism (yellow press), 418, 472; Hearst, Pulitzer, and, 418, 452, 454; *Maine* explosion and, 455, 456
Yellow peril, 469
Yellowstone National Park, 214, 437
Yeltsin, Boris, 698
Yemen, 713
Yiddish theater, 408
Yippies, 658
Yom Kippur War (1973), 667
York, Duke of. *See* James II (England, Duke of York)
Yorktown, Virginia: Battle of, 114; British surrender at, 114
Yosemite National Park, 437, 487
Yosemite Valley, 487
Young, Andrew, 680
Young, Brigham, 236
Young Men's Christian Association (YMCA), 414
Young people: in 1960s, 659-660, 661; antislavery literature and, 297; urban lifestyle and, 406. *See also* Teenagers
Young Women's Christian Association (YWCA), 414
Youth culture: protests in 1960s and, 660
Youth International Party (Yippies), 658
Yugoslavia: ethnic violence in, 698; Fiume, Italy, and, 512. *See also* Bosnia
Yuppies, 690

Zenger, John Peter, and Zenger trial, 73
Zimbabwe (Rhodesia), 680
Zimmermann, Arthur, 503
Zimmermann note, 503
Zones: in postwar Germany, 610, 611 (map)
Zoot suits, 589
Zouaves, 320
Zulus, 443